D0780837

THE NEW RAND McNALLY COLLEGE WORLD ATLAS

THE NEW RAND McNALLY COLLEGE WORLD ATLAS

Revised Edition

RAND McNALLY & COMPANY
Chicago / New York / San Francisco

Contents

Thematic Maps of the World

Environment Maps of the World

Metropolitan Maps of the World

Historical Maps of the World

Second 1985 printing

Library of Congress Catalog Card Number: 83-60218
Printed in the United States of America by Rand McNally & Company
SBN: 528-83187-9

Flags of the World 93

Reference Maps of the World

Europe

Asia

Africa

Australia / New Zealand

South America

North America

Historical Maps of the United States

Travel Maps of the United States

Tables, Charts, and Facts

Reference Map Index

Thematic Maps of the World

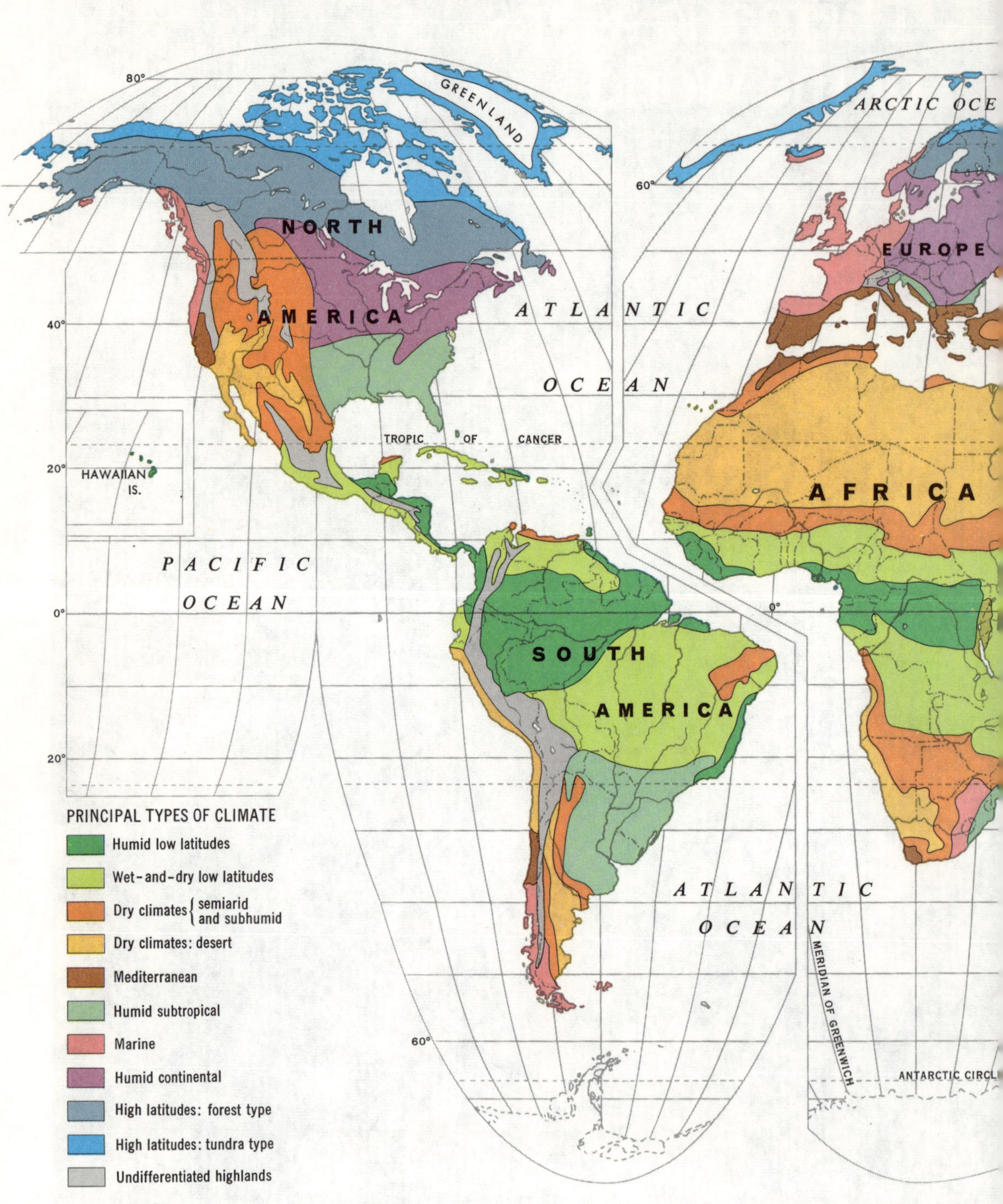
80°
GREENLAND
ARCTIC OCE
60°
NORTH
AMERICA
EUROPE
ATLANTIC
OCEAN
40°
TROPIC OF CANCER
20°
HAWAIIAN IS.
AFRICA
PACIFIC
OCEAN
0°
SOUTH
AMERICA
20°
ATLANTIC
OCEAN
MERIDIAN OF GREENWICH
60°
ANTARCTIC CIRCL
PRINCIPAL TYPES OF CLIMATE
Humid low latitudes
Wet-and-dry low latitudes
Dry climates { semiarid and subhumid
Dry climates: desert
Mediterranean
Humid subtropical
Marine
Humid continental
High latitudes: forest type
High latitudes: tundra type
Undifferentiated highlands

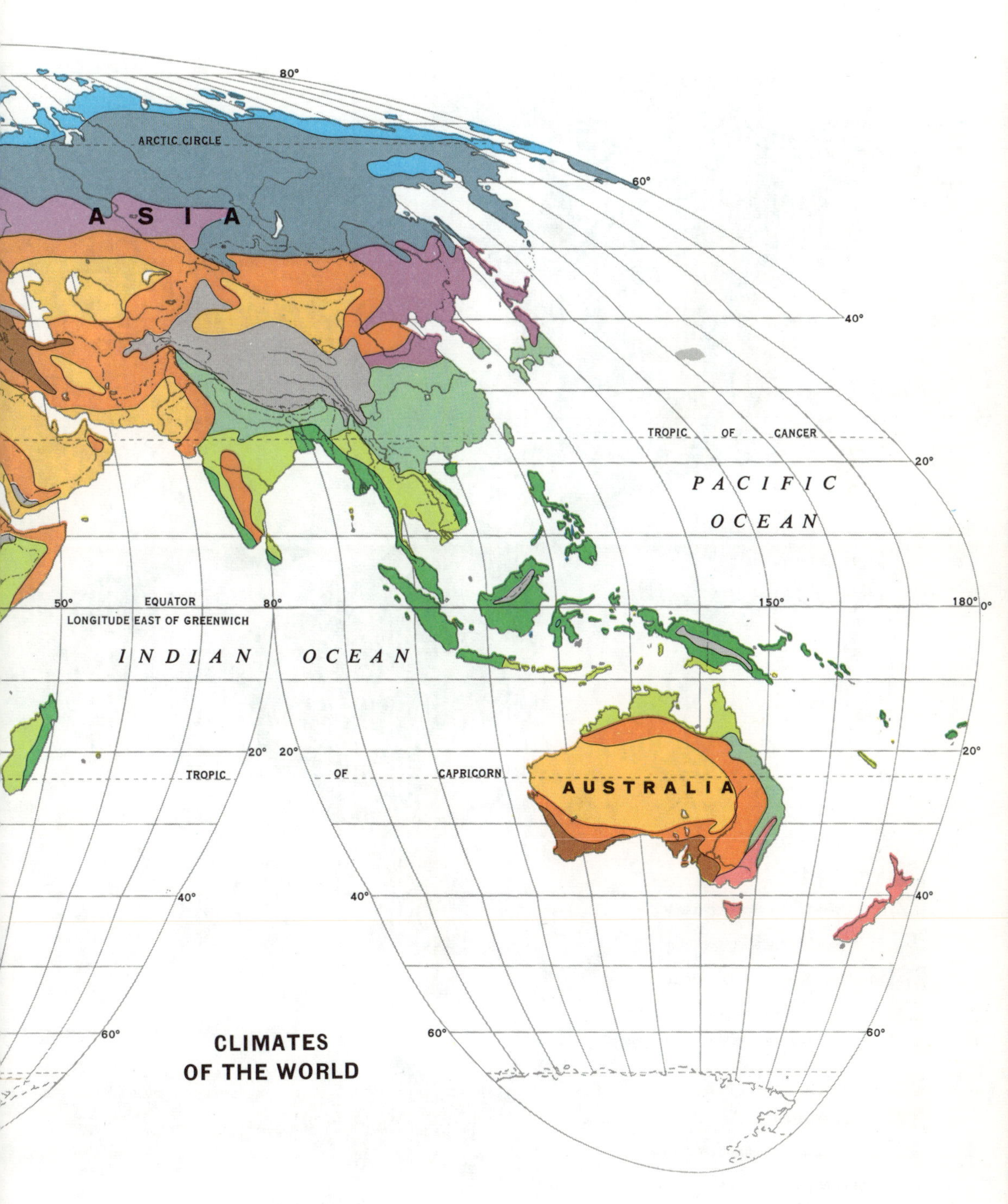
80°
ARCTIC CIRCLE
60°
A S I A
40°
TROPIC OF CANCER
20°
PACIFIC
OCEAN
50°
EQUATOR
80°
150°
180°
0°
LONGITUDE EAST OF GREENWICH
INDIAN OCEAN
20°
20°
TROPIC
OF
CAPRICORN
AUSTRALIA
20°
40°
40°
40°
60°
60°
60°
CLIMATES
OF THE WORLD

ARCTIC OCE
TUNDRA
NORTH AMERICA
TAIGA
PRAIRIE
EUROPE
ATLANTIC OCEAN
TROPIC OF CANCER
SAHARA
HAWAIIAN IS.
AFRICA
PACIFIC OCEAN
LLANOS
SELVAS
SOUTH AMERICA
CAMPOS
GRAN CHACO
ATACAMA
KALAHARI
NAMIB
VELD
PAMPAS
ATLANTIC OCEAN
MERIDIAN OF GREENWICH
ANTARCTIC CIRCLE
80°
60°
40°
20°
0°
120°
100°
KINDS OF VEGETATION
Needle-leaved forest
Broad-leaved forest mainly evergreen
Broad-leaved forest mainly deciduous
Mixed needle-leaved and broad-leaved forest
Shrub woodland (Mediterranean vegetation)
Grass with scattered trees or shrubs in regions of seasonal rainfall
Grassland
Desert grass, shrub
Tundra and high-mountain vegetation
Little or no vegetation

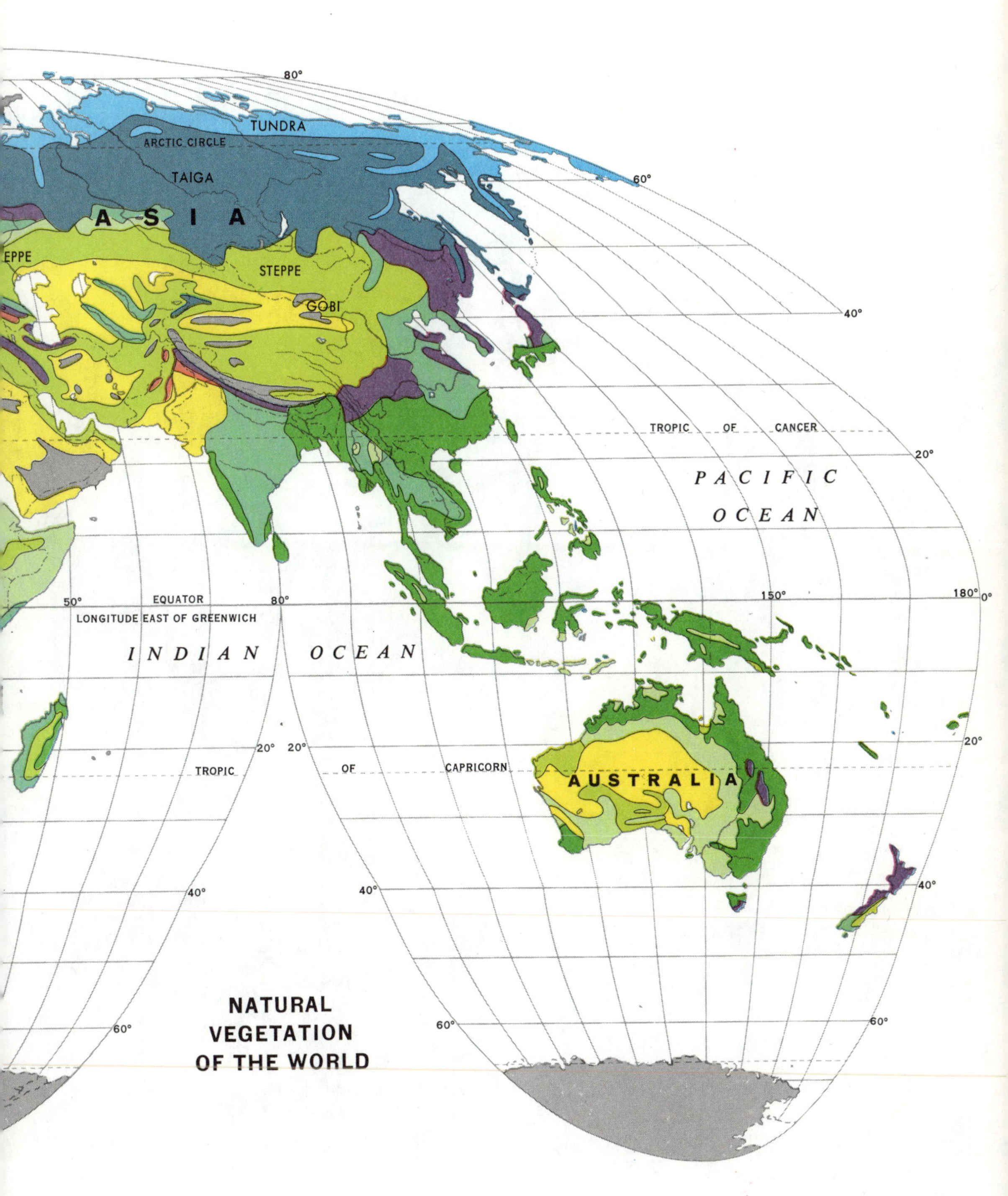
80°
TUNDRA
ARCTIC CIRCLE
TAIGA
60°
A S I A
EPPE
STEPPE
GOBI
40°
TROPIC OF CANCER
20°
PACIFIC
OCEAN
50°
EQUATOR
80°
150°
180°
0°
LONGITUDE EAST OF GREENWICH
INDIAN OCEAN
20°
20°
TROPIC OF CAPRICORN
AUSTRALIA
20°
40°
40°
40°
NATURAL
VEGETATION
OF THE WORLD
60°
60°
60°

180°
150°
120°
90°
60°
30°
0°
60°
30°
0°
30°
60°
180°
150°
120°
90°
60°
30°
0°

LAND USE
OF THE WORLD
30°
60°
90°
120°
150°
180°
0°
Manufacturing and commerce
Commercial farming and stock raising; Intensive subsistence farming, stock raising
Stock raising, extensive
Tropical subsistence agriculture
Nomadic herding
Forestry
Forestry, fishing, collecting, and hunting.
Nomadic herding, Hunting, fishing, collecting, forestry
Important fishing grounds
Little or no economic activity
Copyright © by Rand McNally & Co.

180°
150°
120°
90°
60°
30°
60°
30°
0°
30°
60°
60°
30°
90°
180°
150°
120°
TUNDRA SOILS Dwarf shrub- and moss-covere
soils of cold climates.
PODZOLIC SOILS Forested soils of humid, middle-latitude climates; includes many areas of bog soils.
CHERNOZEMIC SOILS Grass-covered soils of subhumid, semiarid middle-latitude climates; includes some soils of wet-dry tropical savannas such as black and dark gray clays.

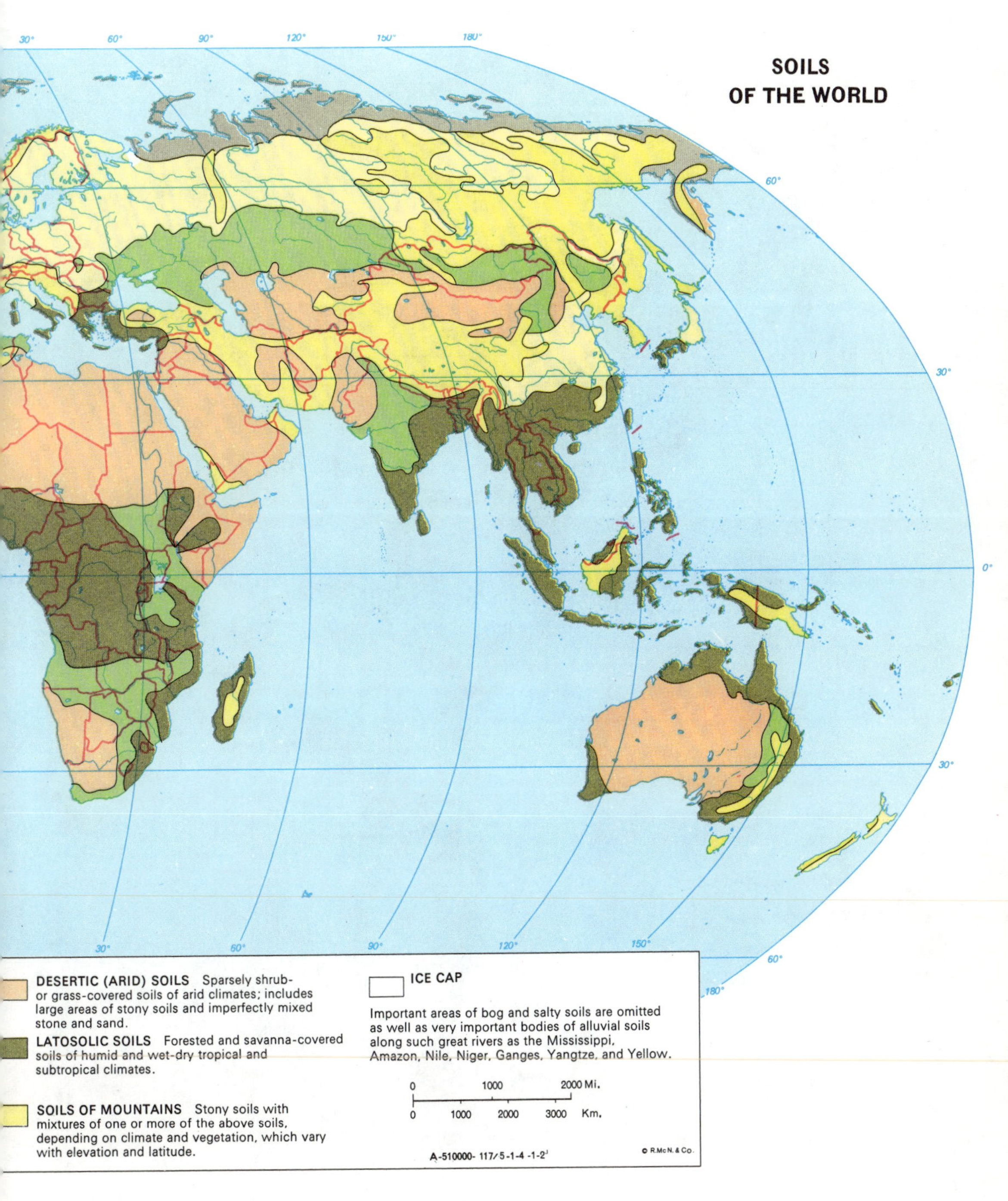
SOILS
OF THE WORLD
DESERTIC (ARID) SOILS Sparsely shrub- or grass-covered soils of arid climates; includes large areas of stony soils and imperfectly mixed stone and sand.
LATOSOLIC SOILS Forested and savanna-covered soils of humid and wet-dry tropical and subtropical climates.
SOILS OF MOUNTAINS Stony soils with mixtures of one or more of the above soils, depending on climate and vegetation, which vary with elevation and latitude.
ICE CAP
Important areas of bog and salty soils are omitted as well as very important bodies of alluvial soils along such great rivers as the Mississippi, Amazon, Nile, Niger, Ganges, Yangtze, and Yellow.
0 1000 2000 Mi.
0 1000 2000 3000 Km.
A-510000- 117/5-1-4 -1-2
© R.McN. & Co.

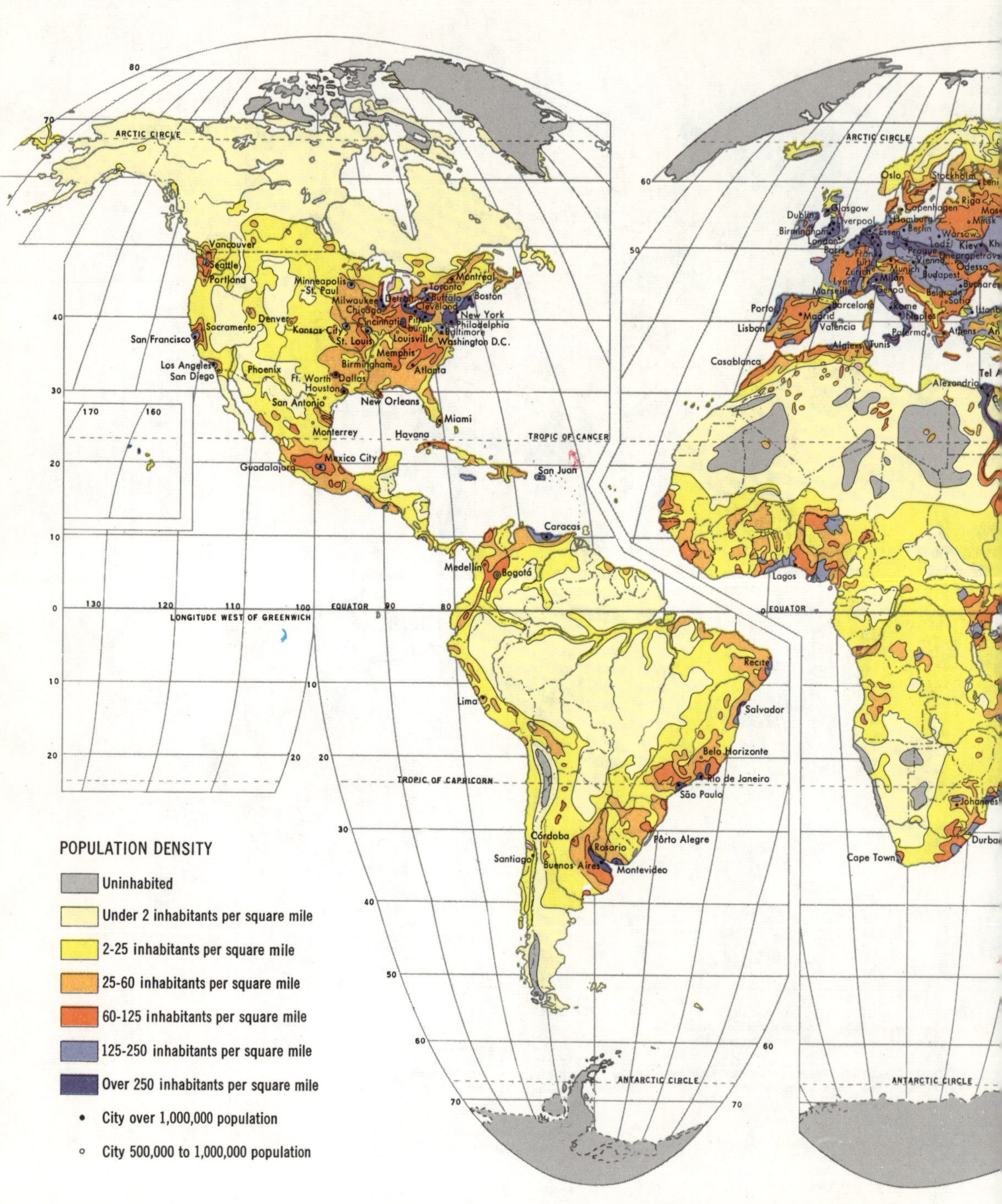
ARCTIC CIRCLE
TROPIC OF CANCER
EQUATOR
TROPIC OF CAPRICORN
ANTARCTIC CIRCLE
LONGITUDE WEST OF GREENWICH
Vancouver
Seattle
Portland
San Francisco
Sacramento
Los Angeles
San Diego
Phoenix
Denver
Minneapolis-St. Paul
Milwaukee
Chicago
Detroit
Toronto
Montreal
Buffalo
Cleveland
Boston
New York
Philadelphia
Baltimore
Washington D.C.
Pittsburgh
Cincinnati
Kansas City
St. Louis
Louisville
Memphis
Birmingham
Atlanta
Ft. Worth
Dallas
Houston
San Antonio
New Orleans
Miami
Havana
Monterrey
Mexico City
Guadalajara
San Juan
Caracas
Medellín
Bogotá
Lima
Recife
Salvador
Belo Horizonte
Rio de Janeiro
São Paulo
Pôrto Alegre
Córdoba
Rosario
Santiago
Buenos Aires
Montevideo
Dublin
Glasgow
Liverpool
Birmingham
London
Paris
Essen
Hamburg
Berlin
Copenhagen
Oslo
Stockholm
Riga
Minsk
Warsaw
Lodz
Kiev
Prague
Vienna
Munich
Zurich
Lyon
Milan
Genoa
Marseille
Budapest
Belgrade
Sofia
Odessa
Bucharest
Porto
Lisbon
Madrid
Barcelona
Valencia
Rome
Naples
Palermo
Athens
Algiers
Tunis
Casablanca
Alexandria
Lagos
Cape Town
POPULATION DENSITY
Uninhabited
Under 2 inhabitants per square mile
2-25 inhabitants per square mile
25-60 inhabitants per square mile
60-125 inhabitants per square mile
125-250 inhabitants per square mile
Over 250 inhabitants per square mile
City over 1,000,000 population
City 500,000 to 1,000,000 population

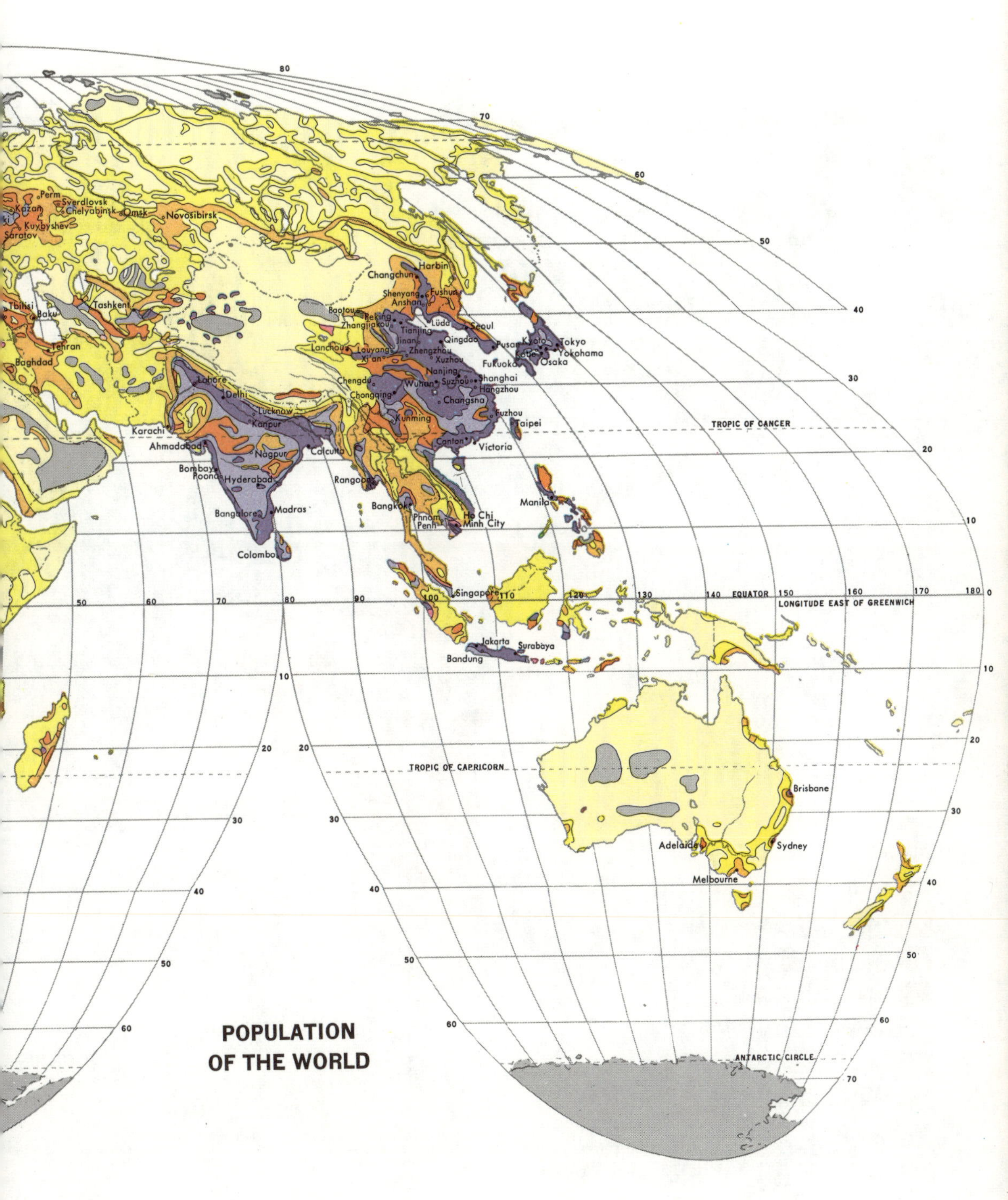

POPULATION
OF THE WORLD

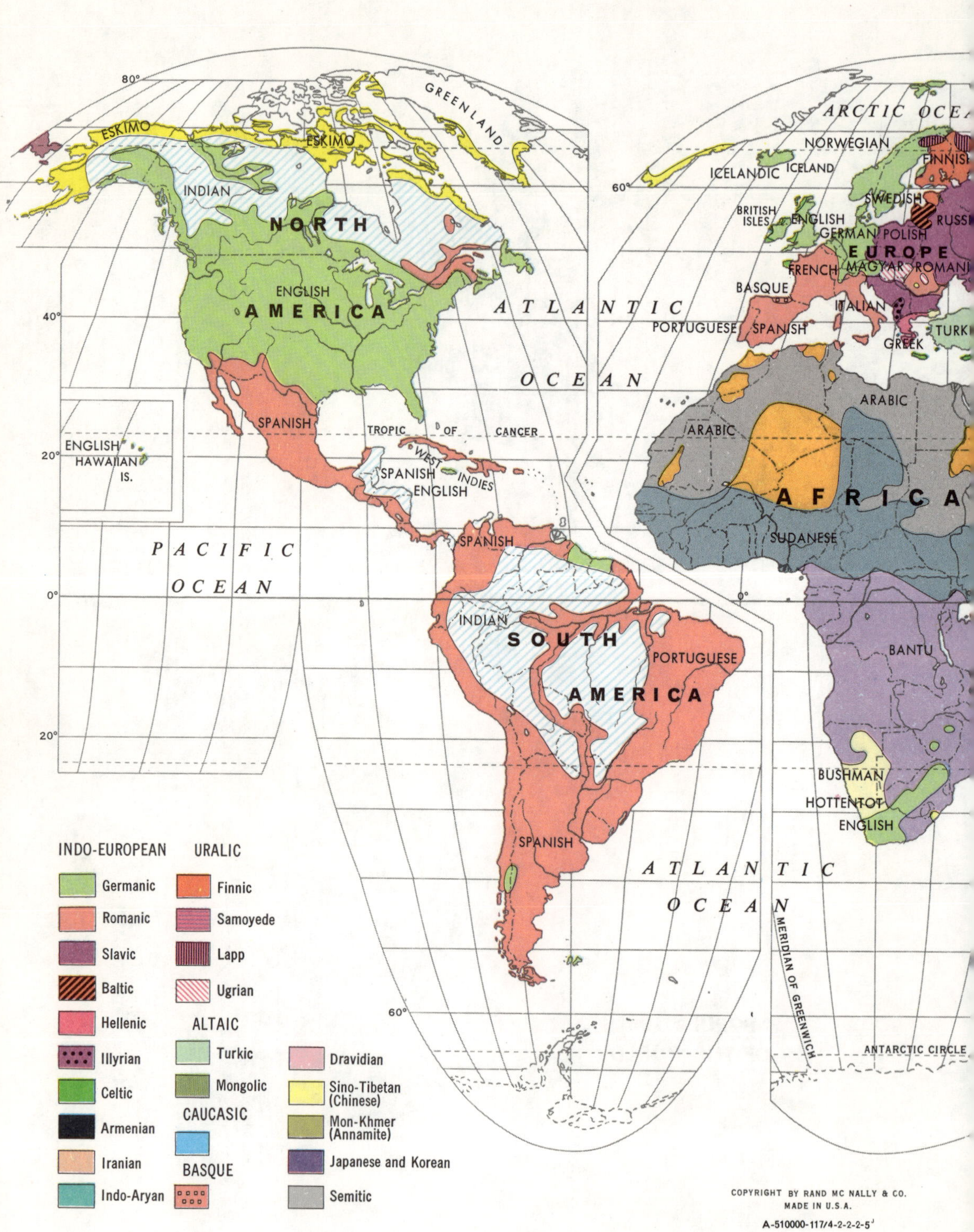

A-510000-117/4-2-2-2-5

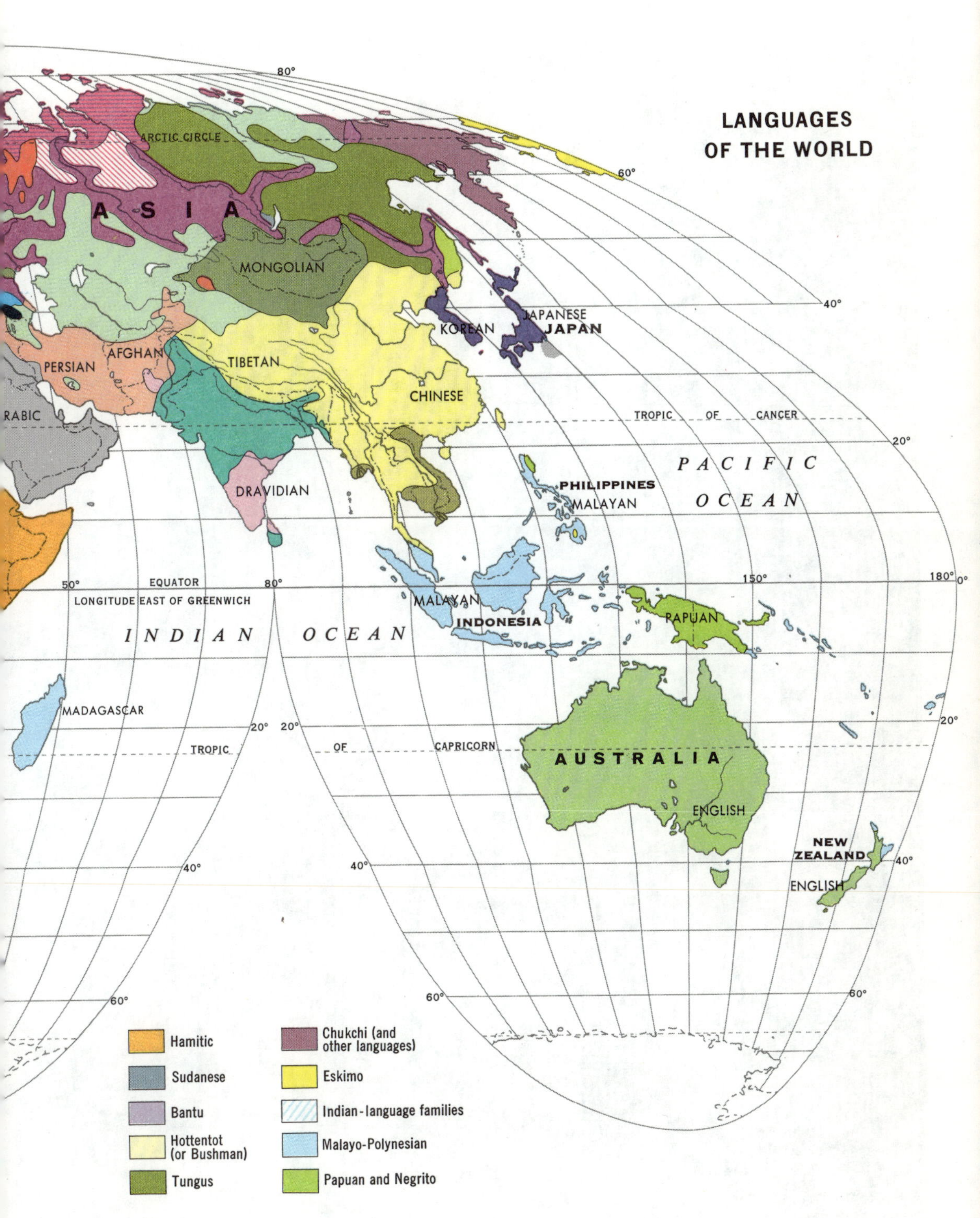
LANGUAGES OF THE WORLD
ASIA
ARCTIC CIRCLE
MONGOLIAN
KOREAN
JAPANESE
JAPAN
AFGHAN
PERSIAN
TIBETAN
CHINESE
RABIC
TROPIC OF CANCER
PACIFIC OCEAN
DRAVIDIAN
PHILIPPINES
MALAYAN
EQUATOR
LONGITUDE EAST OF GREENWICH
INDIAN OCEAN
MALAYAN
INDONESIA
PAPUAN
MADAGASCAR
TROPIC OF CAPRICORN
AUSTRALIA
ENGLISH
NEW ZEALAND
ENGLISH
80°
60°
40°
20°
0°
50°
150°
180°
Hamitic
Sudanese
Bantu
Hottentot (or Bushman)
Tungus
Chukchi (and other languages)
Eskimo
Indian-language families
Malayo-Polynesian
Papuan and Negrito

Environment Maps of the World

Introduction

The environment maps show the natural environment and how it has been modified by humans. Ten major environments are depicted, and these categories are identified and described in the legend below.

Classification is based upon the appearance and the general activity of an area. In mapping any distribution, however, it is necessary to limit the number of categories. Therefore, some gradations of meaning exist within each category. For example, "Grassland, grazing land" identifies the lush pampas of Argentina and the savannas of Africa as well as the steppes of the Soviet Union. Furthermore, certain enclaves that are not cropland may fall within the boundaries of cropland areas. Tracts such as these are included as part of the dominant environment surrounding them. Finally, boundaries on these maps, as on all maps, are never absolute but mark the center of transitional zones between categories.

The actual shapes of large metropolitan areas are shown. A red dot indicates concentrated urban development where a shape would be indistinguishable at the map scale. Black dots are used to locate places important as locational reference points.

From these maps, comprehensive observations may be made about major world environments. For example, the maps show that the world's urban areas are limited in extent, and relatively small portions of the earth's surface are made up of cropland. Vast areas show the limited influence of humanity upon the environment.

Environment Map Legend

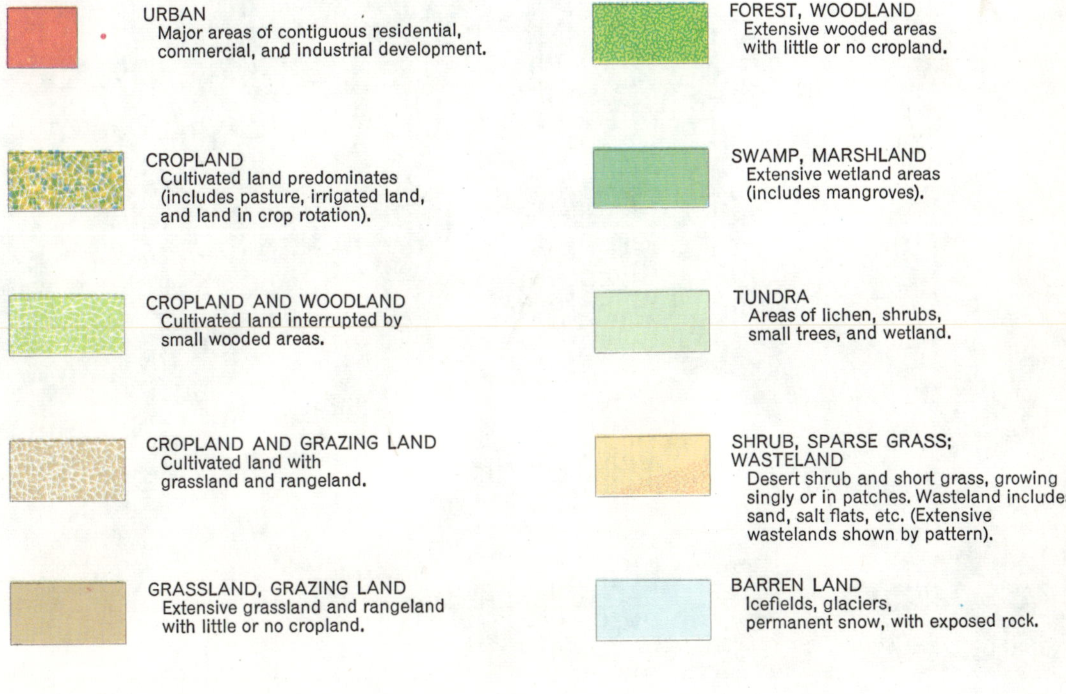
URBAN
Major areas of contiguous residential, commercial, and industrial development.
CROPLAND
Cultivated land predominates (includes pasture, irrigated land, and land in crop rotation).
CROPLAND AND WOODLAND
Cultivated land interrupted by small wooded areas.
CROPLAND AND GRAZING LAND
Cultivated land with grassland and rangeland.
GRASSLAND, GRAZING LAND
Extensive grassland and rangeland with little or no cropland.
FOREST, WOODLAND
Extensive wooded areas with little or no cropland.
SWAMP, MARSHLAND
Extensive wetland areas (includes mangroves).
TUNDRA
Areas of lichen, shrubs, small trees, and wetland.
SHRUB, SPARSE GRASS; WASTELAND
Desert shrub and short grass, growing singly or in patches. Wasteland includes sand, salt flats, etc. (Extensive wastelands shown by pattern).
BARREN LAND
Icefields, glaciers, permanent snow, with exposed rock.

OASIS
Important small areas of cultivation within grassland or wasteland.

• Selected cities as points of reference.

Urban
Cropland
Cropland & Woodland
Cropland & Grazing Land
Grassland, Grazing Land
Forest, Woodland
Swamp, Marshland
Tundra
Shrub, Sparse Grass, Wasteland (pattern)
Barren Land
Oasis
20°
10°
0°
10°
20°
30°
60°
50°
40°
ATLANTIC
OCEAN
North Sea
Baltic Sea
Gulf of Bothnia
Bay of Biscay
Adriatic Sea
Tyrrhenian Sea
Aegean Sea
Mediterranean Sea
Reykjavik
Narvik
Ume
Trondheim
Bergen
Oslo
Helsinki
Tallinn
Stockholm
Göteborg
Riga
Copenhagen
Glasgow
Belfast
MANCHESTER
Dublin
LONDON
Amsterdam
Hamburg
Elbe
BERLIN
Kaliningrad
Minsk
Antwerp
Essen
Leipzig
Oder
Warsaw
Frankfurt
Brest
PARIS
Seine
Loire
Strasbourg
Prague
Kraków
L'vov
Rhine
Munich
Danube
VIENNA
Zürich
Tisza
BUDAPEST
La Coruña
Bordeaux
Garonne
Lyon
Rhône
MILAN
Zagreb
Sava
Venice
Bilbao
Douro
PYRENEES
Ebro
Genoa
Belgrade
Bucharest
Danube
Lisbon
MADRID
Marseille
Sofia
BARCELONA
CORSICA
ROME
Tirane
Sevilla
SARDINIA
Naples
ISLAS BALEARES
Tanger
Algiers
Oran
Palermo
Athens
Casablanca
ATLAS MOUNTAINS
Tunis
SICILY
MALTA
CRETE
Longitude West of Greenwich
0°
Longitude East of Greenwich
10°
20°
Conic Projection
0 50 100 200 300 400 500 Miles
0 100 200 400 600 800 Kilometers

White Sea
Archangelsk
Nar'yan-Mar
Pechora
Ob'
Irtysh
Omsk
Novosibirsk
SVERDLOVSK
Perm'
Kirov
Vologda
Volga
Gorki
Kazan'
Kama
Ufa
Magnitogorsk
MOSCOW
Tula
Kuybyshev
Orsk
Karaganda
Balkhash
Saratov
Ural
Kzyl-Orda
Syr-Dar'ya
Aral'skoye More (Aral Sea)
PESKI KYZYLKUM
Kiev
Khar'kov
Don
VOLGOGRAD
CASPIAN DEPRESSION
Astrakhan'
Dnepropetrovsk
Donetsk
MANYCH DEPRESSION
Amu Dar'ya
PESKI KARAKUMY
Odessa
Krasnodar
Caspian Sea
Ashkhabad
Black Sea
BAKU
TBILISI
ISTANBUL
Ankara
ELBURZ MTS.
TEHRAN
DASHT-E-KAVIR
Tigris
Euphrates
Baghdad
Abadan
Nicosia
CYPRUS
Beirut
COPYRIGHT BY RAND McNALLY & COMPANY MADE IN U.S.A.

Urban
Cropland
Cropland & Woodland
Cropland & Grazing Land
Grassland, Grazing Land
Forest, Woodland
Swamp, Marshland
Tundra
Shrub, Sparse Grass, Wasteland (pattern)
Barren Land
Oasis
ATLANTIC OCEAN
North Sea
SPITSBERGEN
Gulf of Bothnia
Stockholm
Baltic Sea
Murmansk
Barents Sea
NOVAYA ZEMLYA
Kara Sea
Kara
Arkhangelsk
LENINGRAD
Sukhona
Ob
BERLIN
MUNICH
Warsaw
BUDAPEST
Dnepr
MOSCOW
Kiev
Don
Kazan'
Danube
SVERDLOVSK
Volga
Ural
Novosibirsk
ISTANBUL
Black Sea
VOLGOGRAD
Orsk
Irtysh
Karaganda
Mediterranean Sea
CAUCASUS MTS.
Caspian Sea
Aral Sea
Syr-Dar'ya
Ozero Balkhash
BAKU
Beirut
CAIRO
SYRIAN DESERT
Baghdad
Tigris
TEHRAN
Ashkhabad
Tashkent
TIEN SHAN
TAKLA MAKAN
DASHT-E KAVIR
HINDU KUSH
Kabul
Euphrates
ZAGROS MTS.
AN NAFŪD
Red Sea
Lambert Azimuthal Equal-Area Projection

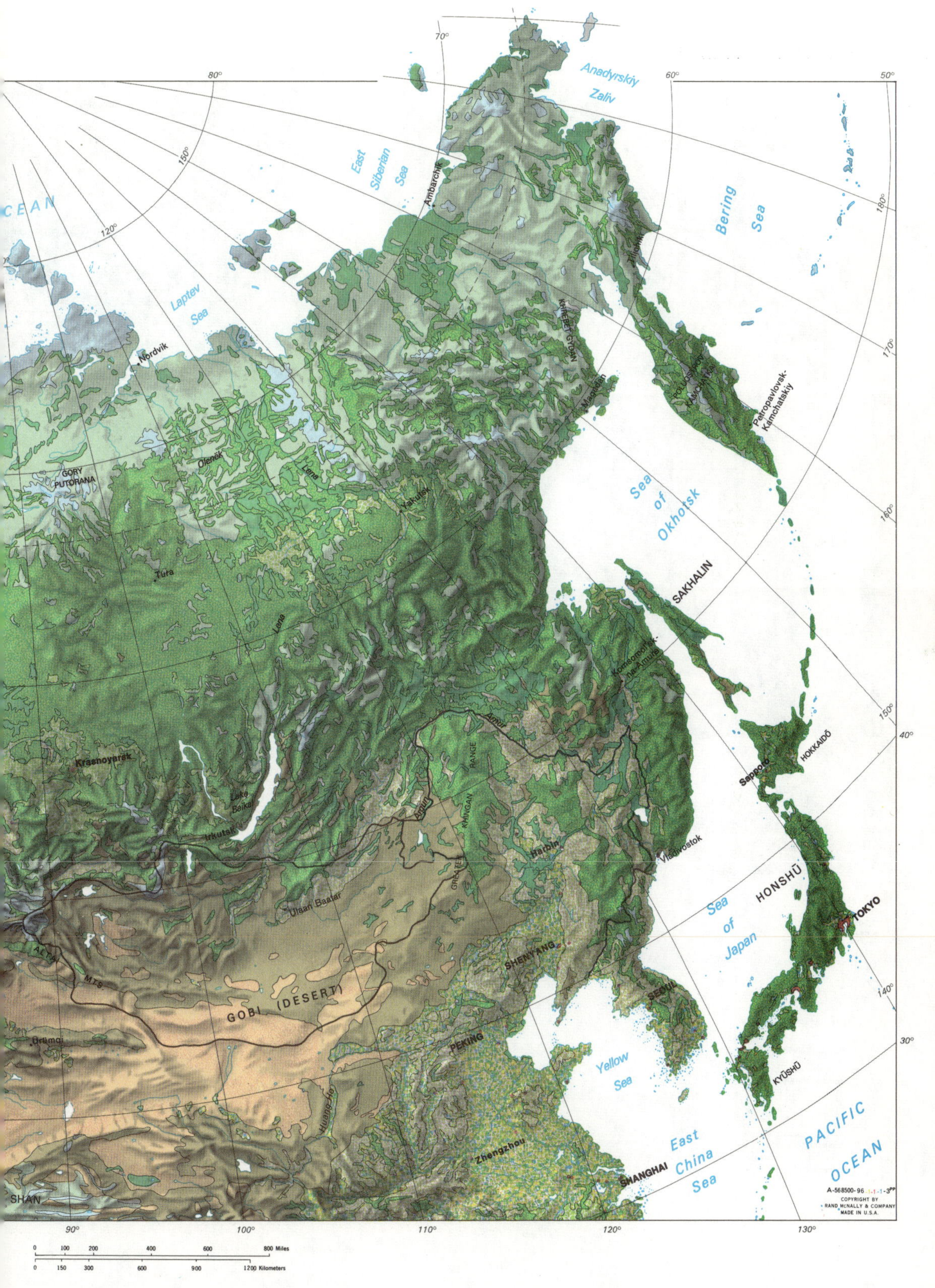

0 100 200 400 600 800 Miles

0 150 300 600 900 1200 Kilometers

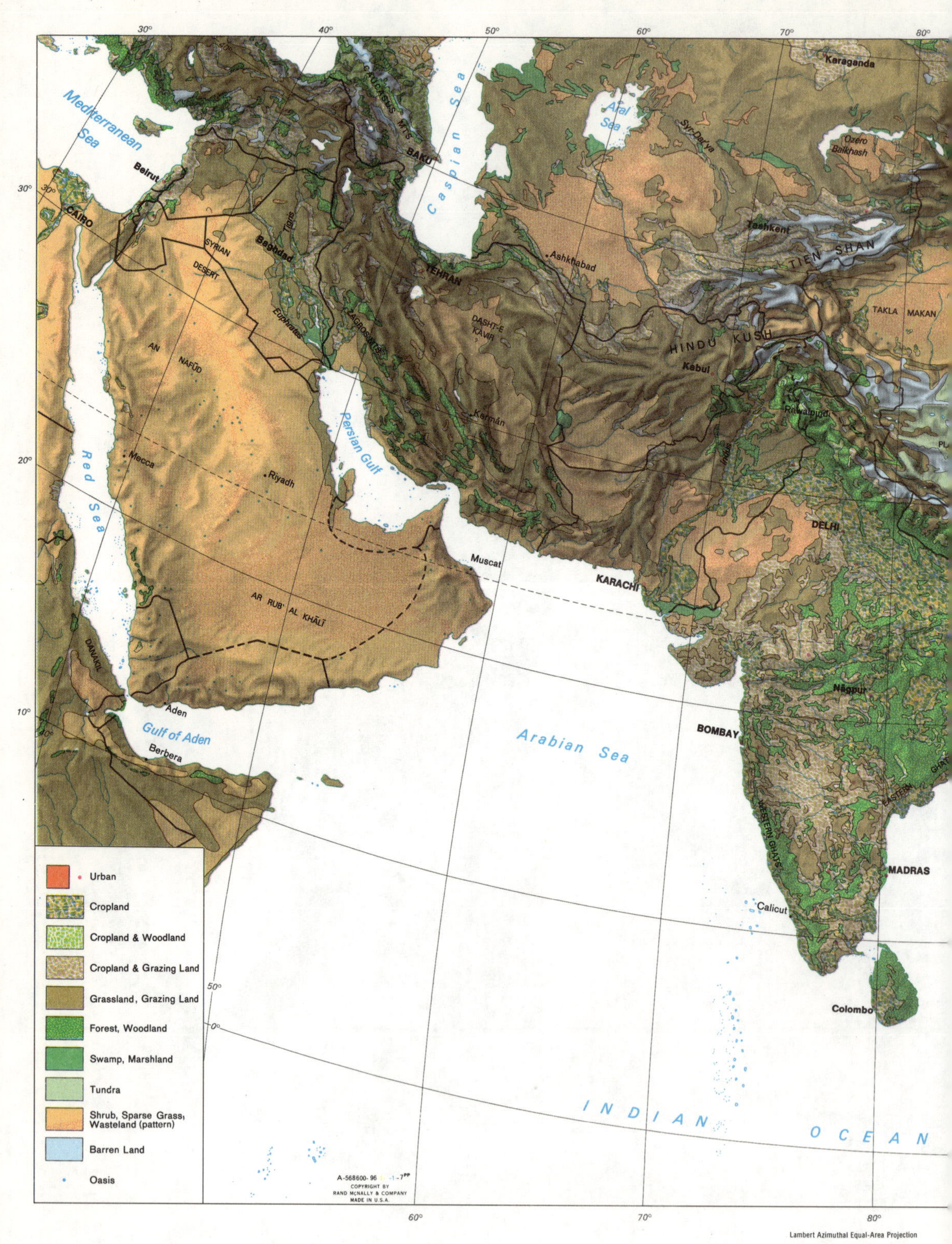
Mediterranean Sea
Beirut
CAIRO
Red Sea
Mecca
Riyadh
SYRIAN DESERT
Baghdad
AN NAFŪD
Tigris
Euphrates
CAUCASUS MTS.
BAKU
Caspian Sea
TEHRAN
ZAGROS MTS.
DASHT-E KAVIR
Kermān
Persian Gulf
Muscat
AR RUB' AL KHĀLĪ
DANAKIL
Aden
Gulf of Aden
Berbera
Aral Sea
Syr-Dar'ya
Ashkhabad
Tashkent
TIEN SHAN
Karaganda
Ozero Balkhash
TAKLA MAKAN
HINDU KUSH
Kabul
Rawalpindi
Indus
DELHI
KARACHI
Arabian Sea
BOMBAY
Nāgpur
WESTERN GHATS
EASTERN GHATS
MADRAS
Calicut
Colombo
INDIAN OCEAN
Urban
Cropland
Cropland & Woodland
Cropland & Grazing Land
Grassland, Grazing Land
Forest, Woodland
Swamp, Marshland
Tundra
Shrub, Sparse Grass, Wasteland (pattern)
Barren Land
Oasis
30°
40°
50°
60°
70°
80°
20°
10°
0°
Lambert Azimuthal Equal-Area Projection

Harbin
Vladivostok
Ulaan Baatar
GREATER KHINGAN RA.
ALTAI MTS.
GOBI (DESERT)
Ürümqi
SHENYANG
Sea of Japan
HONSHŪ
TOKYO
SEOUL
PEKING
Yellow Sea
KYŪSHŪ
Huang He
PACIFIC OCEAN
East China Sea
Zhengzhou
SHANGHAI
SHAN
WUHAN
TIBET
CHONGQING
Mekong
T'aipei
Tropic of Cancer
HIMALAYAS
Brahmaputra
Kunming
CANTON
Philippine Sea
Hanoi
HAINAN DAO
CALCUTTA
Mandalay
Salween
MANILA
Mekong
Sea
Bay of Bengal
Rangoon
Cebu
China
BANGKOK
MINDANAO
HO CHI MINH CITY
South
Andaman Sea
Kota Kinabalu
Celebes Sea
Manado
Medan
Kuching
SINGAPORE
BORNEO
CELEBES
SUMATRA
Equator
Ujung Pandang
Java Sea
JAKARTA
JAVA
90°
100°
120°
140°
130°
40°
30°
20°
10°
0°
0 100 200 400 600 800 Miles
0 150 300 600 900 1200 Kilometers

Lambert Azimuthal Equal-Area Projection

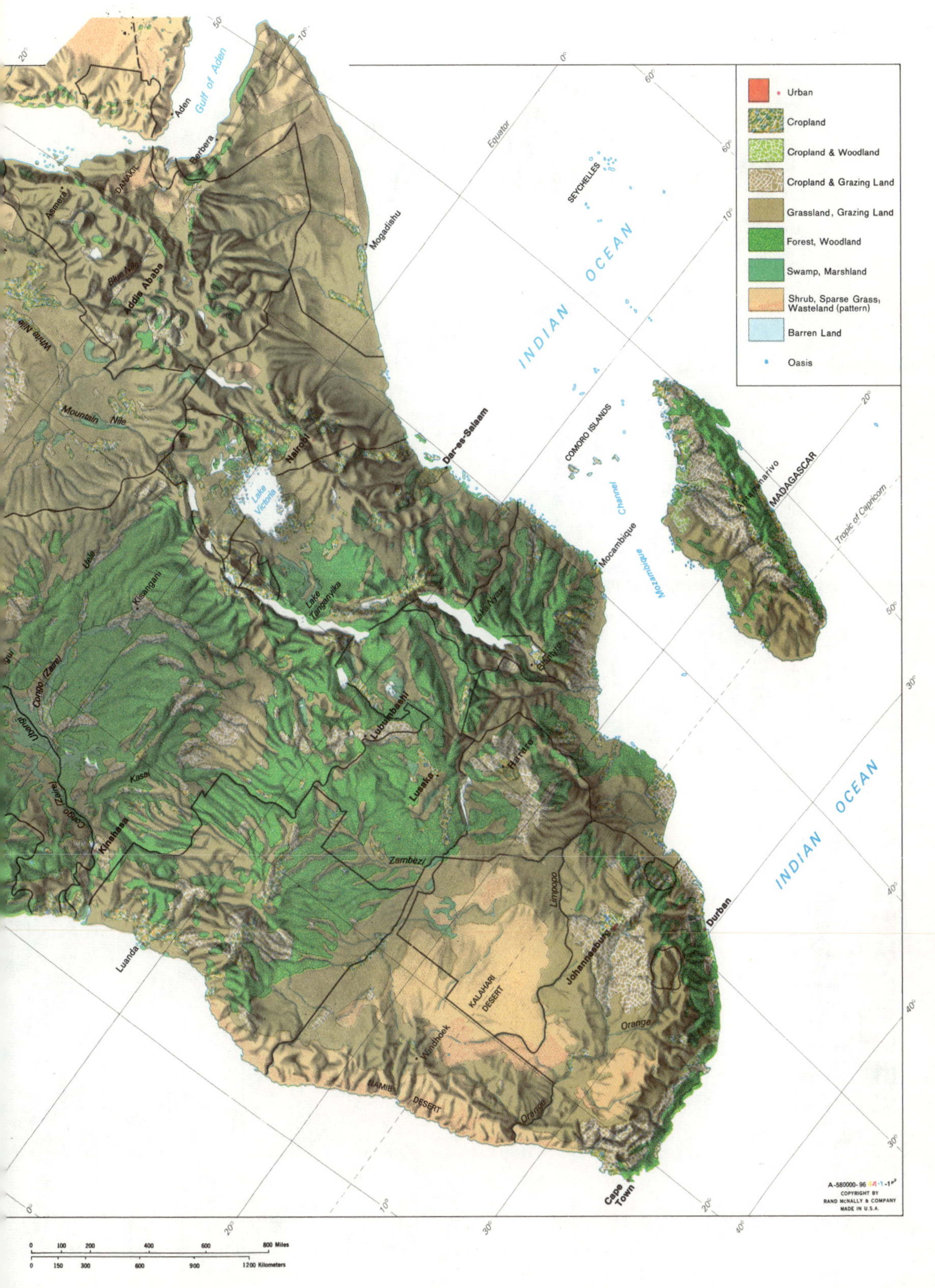
Urban
Cropland
Cropland & Woodland
Cropland & Grazing Land
Grassland, Grazing Land
Forest, Woodland
Swamp, Marshland
Shrub, Sparse Grass, Wasteland (pattern)
Barren Land
Oasis
Gulf of Aden
Aden
Berbera
DANAKIL
Asmera
Mogadishu
Blue Nile
Addis Ababa
White Nile
Mountain Nile
Nairobi
Dar-es-Salaam
Lake Victoria
Lake Tanganyika
Lake Nyasa
Kisangani
Uele
Congo (Zaire)
Ubangi
Kasai
Kinshasa
Lubumbashi
Lusaka
Harare
Zambezi
Luanda
Limpopo
KALAHARI DESERT
Windhoek
NAMIB DESERT
Orange
Johannesburg
Durban
Cape Town
Mocambique
Mozambique Channel
COMORO ISLANDS
SEYCHELLES
MADAGASCAR
Antananarivo
Tropic of Capricorn
Equator
INDIAN OCEAN
0 100 200 400 600 800 Miles
0 150 300 600 900 1200 Kilometers

BORNEO
CELEBES
SERAM
SUMATRA
Palembang
Banjarmasin
Java Sea
Ujung Pandang
JAKARTA
Surabaya
JAVA
SUMBA
TIMOR
Arafura Sea
Timor Sea
Darwin
Daly
Gulf of Carpentaria
INDIAN OCEAN
KIMBERLEY PLATEAU
Victoria
Broome
Fitzroy
Mount Isa
GREAT SANDY DESERT
Alice Springs
GIBSON DESERT
SIMPSON DESERT
Tropic of Capricorn
Carnarvon
GREAT VICTORIA DESERT
Lake Eyre
Kalgoorlie
NULLARBOR PLAIN
Lake Gairdner
FLINDERS RANGES
Broken Hill
DARLING RA.
Perth
Great Australian Bight
Murray
Adelaide
INDIAN OCEAN
Urban
Cropland
Cropland & Woodland
Cropland & Grazing Land
Grassland, Grazing Land
Forest, Woodland
Swamp, Marshland
Shrub, Sparse Grass, Wasteland (pattern)
Barren Land
Lambert Azimuthal Equal-Area Projection

150°
160°
170°
180°
Equator
KIRIBATI
0°
10°
20°
30°
40°
W GUINEA
NEW BRITAIN
SOLOMON ISLANDS
oresby
PACIFIC
OCEAN
Coral Sea
Cairns
Townsville
VANUATU
(NEW HEBRIDES)
SAMOA ISLANDS
Pago Pago
FIJI ISLANDS
Suva
NEW CALEDONIA
ÎLES LOYAUTÉ
Nouméa
Rockhampton
RANGE
TONGA ISLANDS
Brisbane
SYDNEY
Canberra
GREAT DIVIDING RANGE
MELBOURNE
Tasman Sea
PACIFIC
OCEAN
Auckland
NORTH ISLAND
TASMANIA
Hobart
Wellington
SOUTHERN ALPS
Christchurch
SOUTH ISLAND
Dunedin
STEWART ISLAND
A-590200-96
COPYRIGHT BY RAND McNALLY & COMPANY MADE IN U.S.A.
150°
160°
170°
180°
170°
160°
0 100 200 400 600 800 Miles
0 150 300 600 900 1200 Kilometers

Lambert Azimuthal Equal-Area Projection

Tropic of Capricorn
SÃO PAULO
RIO DE JANEIRO
Paraná
Asunción
GRAN
ANDES
San Miguel de Tucumán
Porto Alegre
Córdoba
PACIFIC
OCEAN
SANTIAGO
BUENOS AIRES
Montevideo
ATLANTIC
OCEAN
PAMPAS
Bahía Blanca
Puerto Montt
PATAGONIA
FALKLAND ISLANDS
Punta Arenas
TIERRA DEL FUEGO
SOUTH GEORGIA
Drake Passage
ANTARCTIC PENINSULA
Urban
Cropland
Cropland & Woodland
Cropland & Grazing Land
Grassland, Grazing Land
Forest, Woodland
Swamp, Marshland
Shrub, Sparse Grass, Wasteland (pattern)
Barren Land
COPYRIGHT BY RAND McNALLY & COMPANY
MADE IN U.S.A.
0 100 200 400 600 800 Miles
0 150 300 600 900 1200 Kilometers

Lambert Azimuthal Equal-Area Projection

ATLANTIC OCEAN
PACIFIC OCEAN
Gulf of Mexico
Caribbean Sea
Golfo de California
Tropic of Cancer
St. John's
Halifax
St Lawrence
MONTREAL
TORONTO
Lake Ontario
Lake Erie
Lake Huron
Lake Superior
Lake Michigan
DETROIT
CHICAGO
BOSTON
NEW YORK
PHILADELPHIA
WASHINGTON
Pittsburgh
Cincinnati
APPALACHIAN MOUNTAINS
Ohio
Nashville
Atlanta
Jacksonville
Miami
Nassau
BAHAMA ISLANDS
Havana
CUBA
JAMAICA
Kingston
Port au-Prince
HISPANIOLA
San Juan
PUERTO RICO
TRINIDAD
CARACAS
Maracaibo
Panamá
San José
Managua
San Salvador
Mérida
Minneapolis
Mississippi
Missouri
Kansas City
ST. LOUIS
Omaha
Rapid City
Denver
ROCKY MOUNTAINS
Dallas
Houston
New Orleans
Río Grande
Monterrey
SIERRA MADRE ORIENTAL
SIERRA MADRE OCCIDENTAL
SIERRA MADRE DEL SUR
MEXICO CITY
Guadalajara
Chihuahua
Mazatlán
La Paz
Albuquerque
Phoenix
Colorado
NEVADA
Lake City
LOS ANGELES
Urban
Cropland
Cropland & Woodland
Cropland & Grazing Land
Grassland, Grazing Land
Forest, Woodland
Swamp, Marshland
Tundra
Shrub, Sparse Grass, Wasteland (pattern)
Barren Land
0 100 200 400 600 800 Miles
0 150 300 600 900 1200 Kilometers
A-520000- 96
COPYRIGHT BY RAND McNALLY & COMPANY MADE IN U.S.A.

PACIFIC OCEAN
Vancouver
Seattle
Spokane
CASCADE RANGE
Portland
Columbia
Calgary
Regina
Lake Winnipeg
ROCKY MOUNTAINS
Bismarck
Billings
Boise
Medford
Rapid City
Missouri
Casper
Great Salt Lake
Salt Lake City
Reno
GREAT BASIN
SAN FRANCISCO
SIERRA NEVADA
Denver
Fresno
Las Vegas
Wichita
LOS ANGELES
Albuquerque
Amarillo
Colorado
Phoenix
San Diego
Red
El Paso
Odessa
PACIFIC OCEAN
Hermosillo
Gulf of California
Rio Grande
San Antonio
Chihuahua
SIERRA MADRE OCCIDENTAL
SIERRA MADRE ORIENTAL
Torreón
Monterrey
Rio Grande
50°
45°
40°
35°
30°
25°
125°
120°
115°
110°
105°
100°
D-520500-96
COPYRIGHT BY RAND McNALLY & COMPANY MADE IN U.S.A.

Moosonee
James Bay
Gulf of St. Lawrence
St. Lawrence
Quebec
Thunder Bay
Lake Superior
Sudbury
MONTREAL
Bangor
Halifax
Duluth
Lake Huron
Lake Michigan
Lake Ontario
TORONTO
BOSTON
Buffalo
Milwaukee
DETROIT
Lake Erie
NEW YORK
CHICAGO
Cleveland
Pittsburgh
PHILADELPHIA
WASHINGTON
Indianapolis
Cincinnati
Kansas City
Missouri
Mississippi
ST. LOUIS
Ohio
Norfolk
Roanoke
APPALACHIAN MOUNTAINS
OZARK PLATEAU
Nashville
Charlotte
Memphis
Arkansas
Little Rock
ATLANTIC OCEAN
Atlanta
Birmingham
Charleston
Red
Jacksonville
Tallahassee
New Orleans
Tampa
Gulf of Mexico
Miami
Nassau
Urban
Cropland
Cropland & Woodland
Cropland & Grazing Land
Grassland, Grazing Land
Forest, Woodland
Swamp, Marshland
Shrub, Sparse Grass, Wasteland (pattern)
Barren Land
Polyconic Projection
0 50 100 200 300 400 Miles
0 75 150 300 450 600 Kilometers

Metropolitan Maps of the World

Metropolitan Map Legend

Inhabited Localities

The symbol represents the number of inhabitants within the locality

- • 0—10,000
- ○ 10,000—25,000
- ⊙ 25,000—100,000
- ▣ 100,000—250,000
- ▣ 250,000—1,000,000
- ■ >1,000,000

The size of type indicates the relative economic and political importance of the locality

Écommoy
Trouville
Lisieux
St.-Denis
PARIS

Hollywood ■ Section of a City,
Westminster Neighborhood
Northland Center ■ Major Shopping Center

Urban Area (area of continuous industrial, commercial, and residential development)

Major Industrial Area

Wooded Area

Political Boundaries

International (First-order political unit)

Demarcated, Undemarcated, and Administrative

Demarcation Line

Internal

State, Province, etc. (Second-order political unit)

County, Oblast, etc. (Third-order political unit)

Okrug, Kreis, etc. (Fourth-order political unit)

City or Municipality (may appear in combination with another boundary symbol)

Capitals of Political Units

BUDAPEST Independent Nation

Recife State, Province, etc.

White Plains County, Oblast, etc.

Iserlohn Okrug, Kreis, etc.

Transportation

Road

PASSAIC EXPWY. (I-80) Primary

BERLINER RING Secondary

Tertiary

Railway

CANADIAN NATIONAL Primary

Secondary

Rapid Transit

Airport

LONDON (HEATHROW) AIRPORT

Rail or Air Terminal

■ SÜD BAHNHOF

REICHS-BRÜCKE Bridge

GREAT ST. BERNARD TUNNEL Tunnel

Houston Ship Channel Shipping Channel

Canal du Midi Navigable Canal

TO MALMÖ Ferry

Hydrographic Features

Shoreline

Undefined or Fluctuating Shoreline

Amur River, Stream

Intermittent Stream

SALTO ANGEL Rapids, Falls

Canal du Midi Navigable Canal

Irrigation or Drainage Canal

Los Angeles Aqueduct Aqueduct

Pier, Breakwater

GREAT BARRIER REEF Reef

L. Victoria Lake, Reservoir

Intermittent Lake

The Everglades Swamp

Miscellaneous Cultural Features

PARQUE NACIONAL LANÍN ▲ National or State Park or Monument

FORT DIX ■ Military Installation

GREENWOOD CEMETERY Cemetery

▲ SORBONNE Point of Interest (Battlefield, museum, temple, university, etc.)

STEPHANSDOM Church, Monastery

UXMAL Ruins

WINDSOR CASTLE Castle

Lighthouse

ASWĀN DAM Dam <> Lock

Crib Water Intake Crib

Quarry or Surface Mine

Subsurface Mine

Topographic Features

Mt. Kenya 5199 △ Elevation Above Sea Level

Elevations are given in meters

⋆ Rock

A N D E S KUNLUNSHANMAI Mountain Range, Plateau, Valley, etc.

BAFFIN ISLAND Island

POLUOSTROV KAMČATKA CABO DE HORNOS Peninsula, Cape, Point, etc.

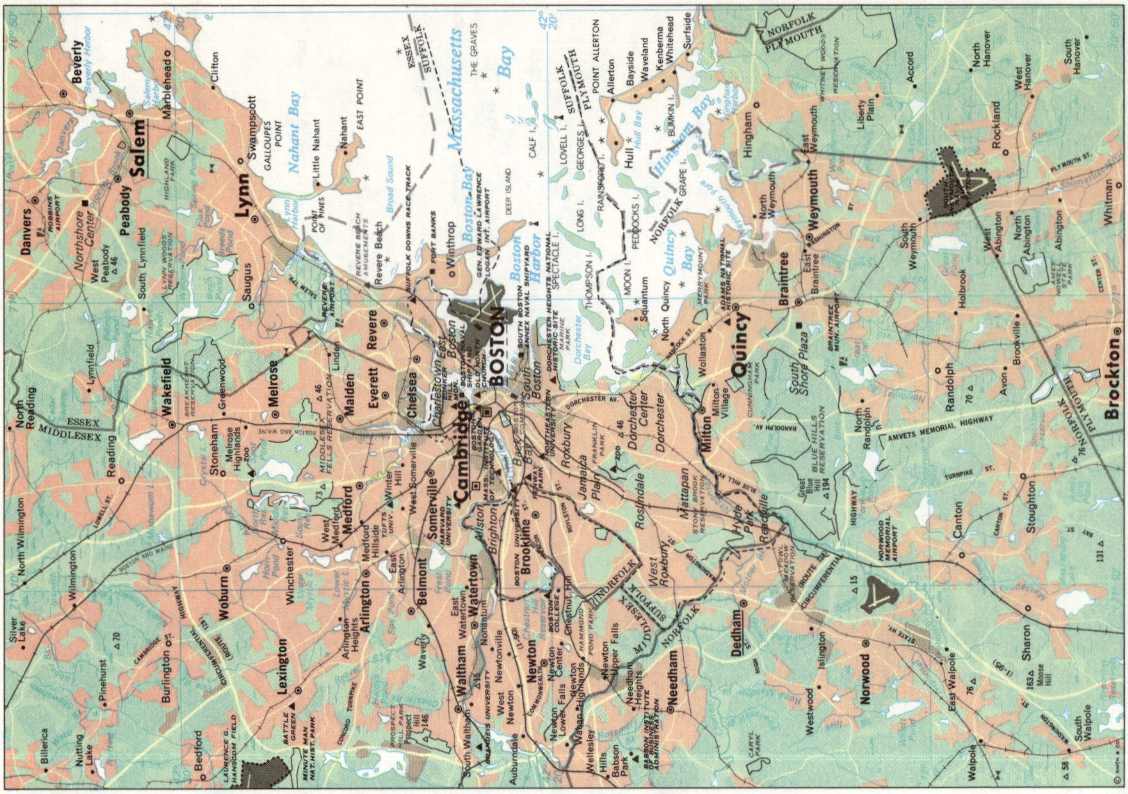

0 5 10 Miles

0 5 10 Kilometers

NEW YORK
Newark
Jersey City
Elizabeth
Paterson
Passaic
Hackensack
Yonkers
Mount Vernon
New Rochelle
Hempstead
Long Beach
Brooklyn
STATEN ISLAND
LONG ISLAND
Long Island Sound
ATLANTIC OCEAN
0 5 10 Miles
0 5 10 Kilometers
Copyright by Rand McNally & Co.
Made in U.S.A.

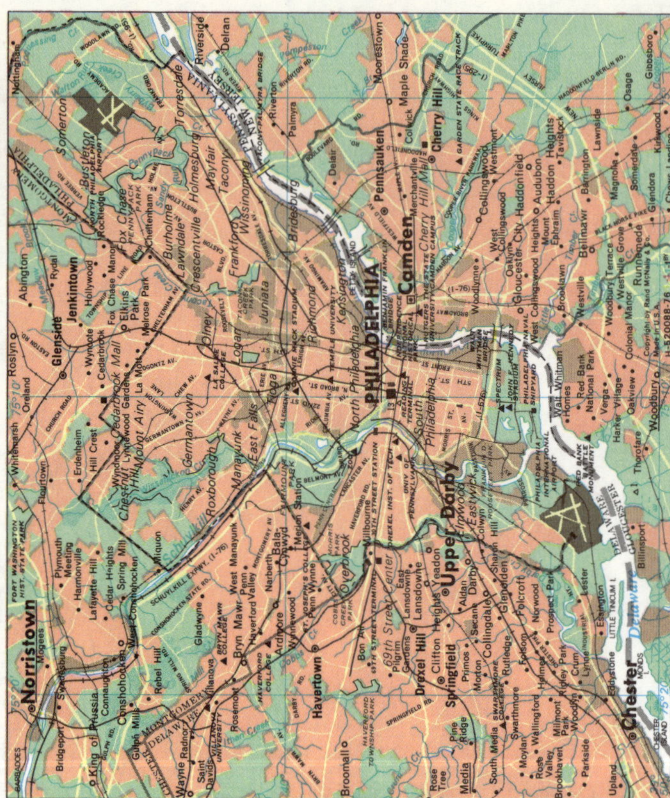

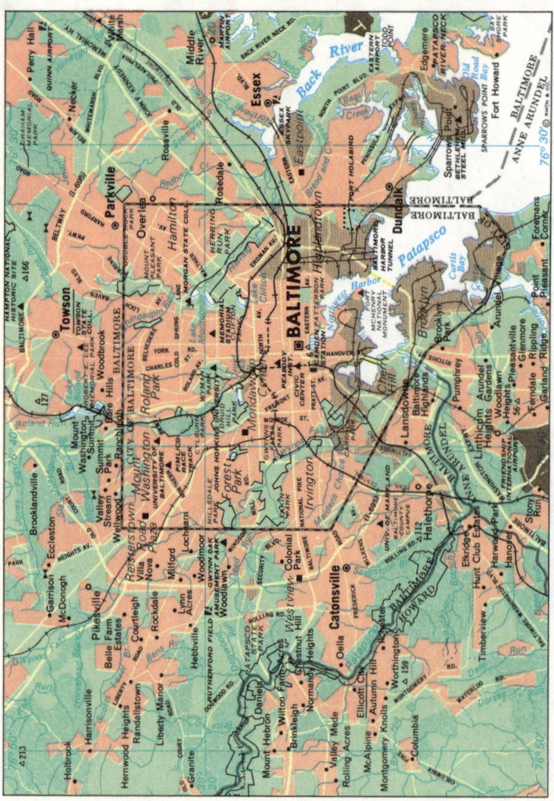

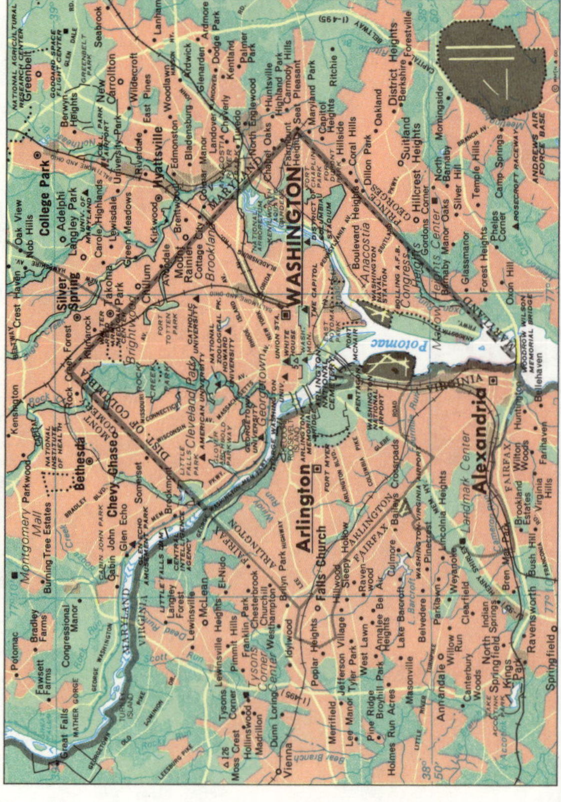

0 5 10 Miles
0 5 10 Kilometers

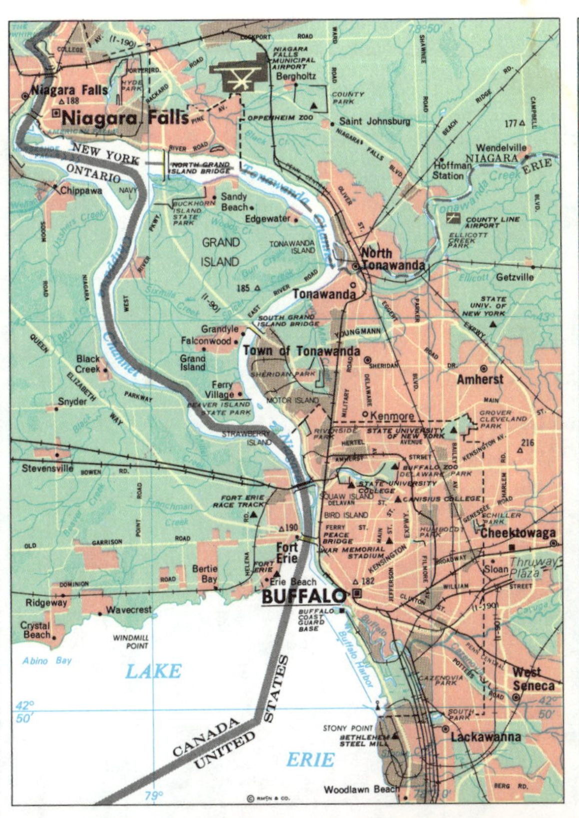

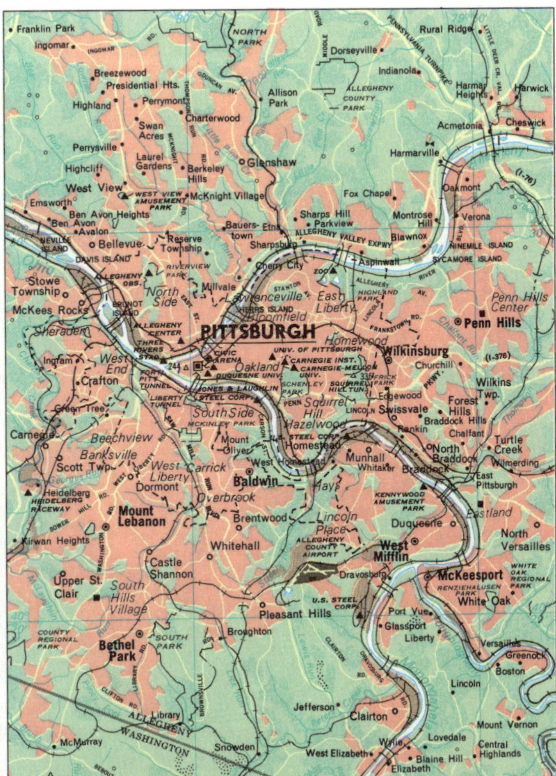

Niagara Falls
Niagara Falls
NEW YORK
ONTARIO
Chippawa
Bergholtz
Saint Johnsburg
Wendelville
NIAGARA
Hoffman Station
Sandy Beach
Edgewater
GRAND ISLAND
North Tonawanda
Tonawanda
Getzville
Grandyle
Falconwood
Town of Tonawanda
Grand Island
Black Creek
Snyder
Ferry Village
Amherst
Kenmore
Stevensville
Cheektowaga
Fort Erie
Sloan
Bertie Bay
Erie Beach
BUFFALO
Ridgeway
Wavecrest
Crystal Beach
Abino Bay
LAKE
ERIE
CANADA
UNITED STATES
West Seneca
Lackawanna
Woodlawn Beach

Franklin Park
Ingomar
Rural Ridge
Dorseyville
Indianola
Breezewood
Presidential Hts.
Highland
Perrymont
Charterwood
Allison Park
Harwick
Acmetonia
Cheswick
Perrysville
Swan Acres
Laurel Gardens
Berkeley Hills
Glenshaw
Harmarville
Highcliff
West View
McKnight Village
Fox Chapel
Oakmont
Emsworth
Ben Avon Heights
Ben Avon
Avalon
Bellevue
Reserve Township
Sharps Hill
Parkview
Montrose Hill
Verona
Blawnox
Sharpsburg
Aspinwall
Stowe Township
McKees Rocks
North Side
Millvale
Lawrenceville
East Liberty
Penn Hills
Sheraden
PITTSBURGH
Homewood
Wilkinsburg
Churchill
Ingram
West End
Crafton
Oakland
Squirrel Hill
Edgewood
Swissvale
Wilkins Twp.
Forest Hills
Braddock Hills
Green Tree
South Side
Hazelwood
Rankin
Chalfant
Turtle Creek
Carnegie
Beechview
Banksville
Scott Twp.
Mount Oliver
Homestead
Munhall
Whitaker
Braddock
North Braddock
Wilmerding
East Pittsburgh
Heidelberg
West Liberty
Dormont
Carrick
Baldwin
Hays
Overbrook
Mount Lebanon
Brentwood
Eastland
Kirwan Heights
Lincoln Place
Duquesne
North Versailles
Whitehall
West Mifflin
Castle Shannon
Upper St. Clair
South Hills Village
Dravosburg
McKeesport
White Oak
Pleasant Hills
Port Vue
Glassport
Liberty
Broughton
Bethel Park
Versailles
Greenock
Boston
Lincoln
Jefferson
Clairton
Mount Vernon
Library
Snowden
McMurray
Lovedale
West Elizabeth
Wylie
Blaine Hill
Elizabeth
Central Highlands
Frank

Wolverine Lake
Walled Lake
Wing Lake Shores
Bloomfield Village
Birmingham
Oakland Mall
Fraser
Macomb Mall
Lake
Franklin
Beverly Hills
Bingham Farms
Clawson
Madison Heights
Warren
Roseville
St. Clair Shores
Berkley
Royal Oak
Lathrup Village
Universal Mall
Farmington Hills
Huntington Woods
Center Line
St. Clair
Novi
Farmington
Southfield
Oak Park
Pleasant Ridge
Ferndale
Hazel Park
East Detroit
Royal Oak Township
MACOMB
WAYNE
OAKLAND
Clarenceville
Northland
Eastland
Grosse Pointe Woods
Northville
Redford Township
Livonia Mall
Redford
Harper Woods
Grosse Pointe Shores
Highland Park
Grosse Pointe Farms
Livonia
Brightmoor
Hamtramck
Grosse Pointe
Grosse Pointe Park
Plymouth
Strathmoor
Wonderland Center
UNITED STATES
CANADA
MICHIGAN
ONTARIO
Westland Center
Dearborn Heights
DETROIT
Riverside
Westland
Garden City
Fairlane Town
Windsor
Tecumseh
St. Clair Beach
Dearborn
Inkster
Devonshire Plaza
Wayne
Melvindale
River Rouge
Sheldon
Allen Park
Lincoln Park
Ecorse
La Salle
Romulus
Taylor
Copyright by Rand McNally & Co.
Made in U.S.A.
H-520089-76

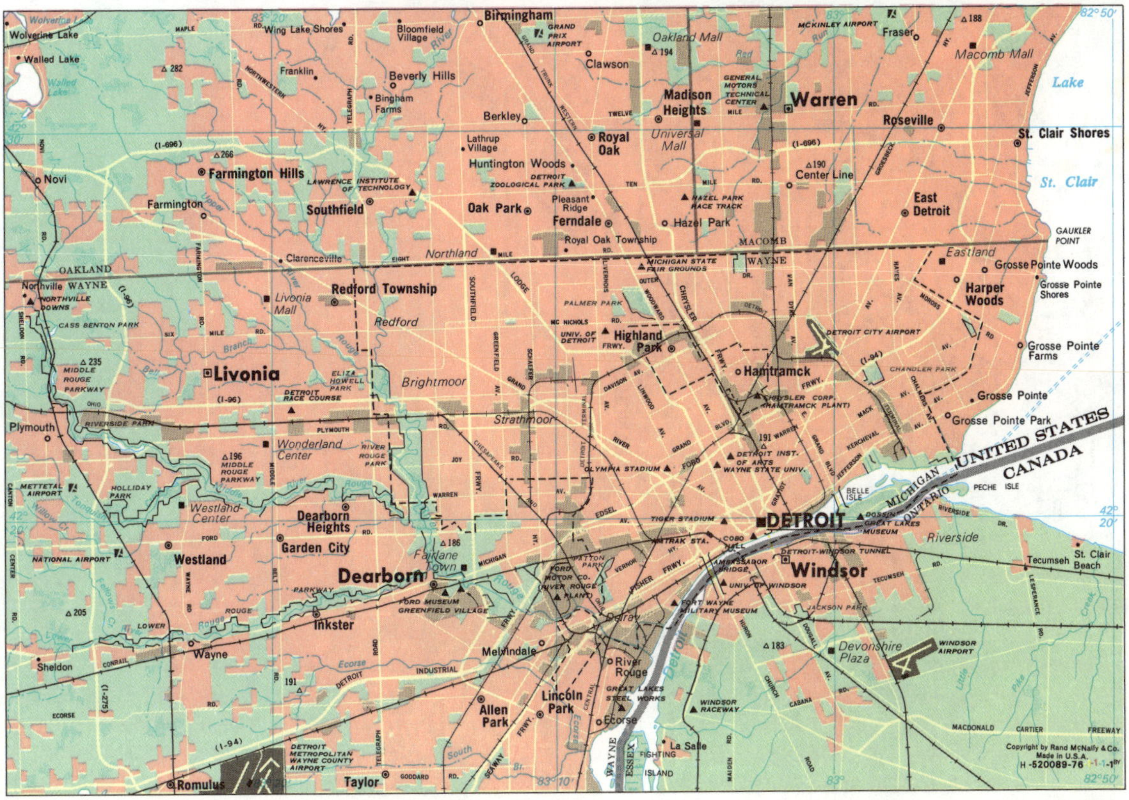

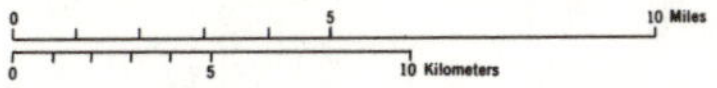

0
5
10 Miles
0
5
10 Kilometers

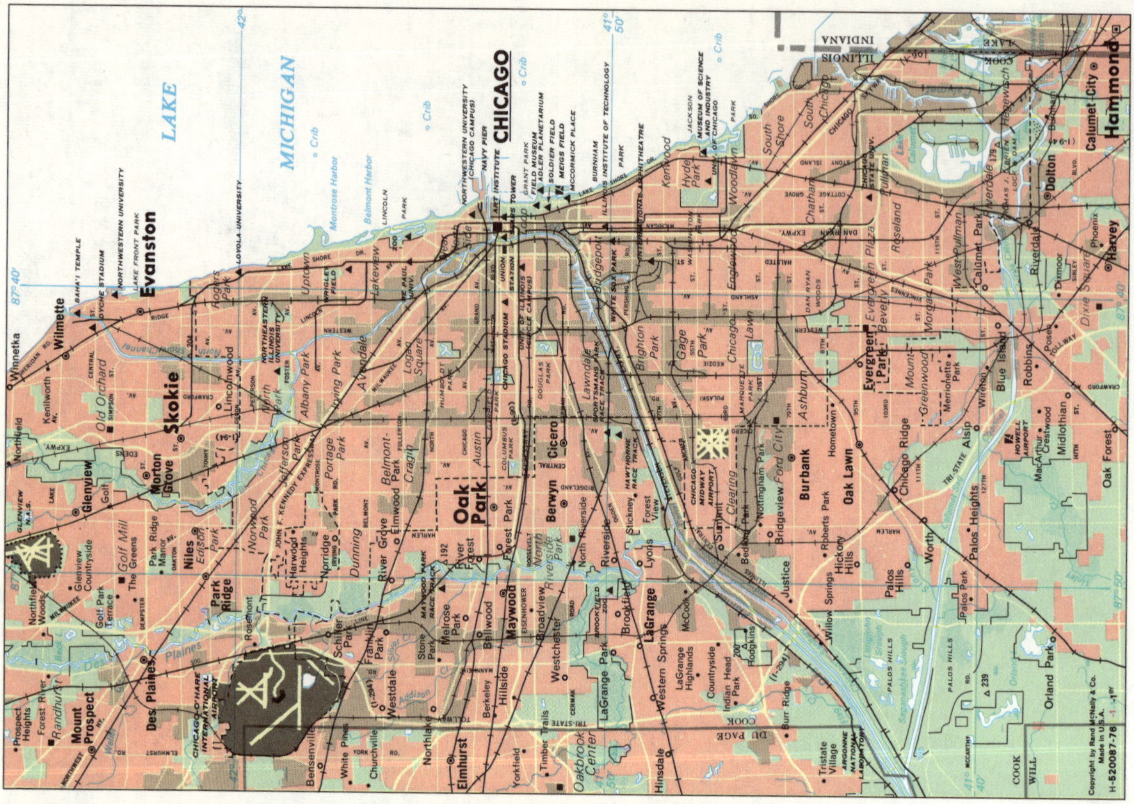

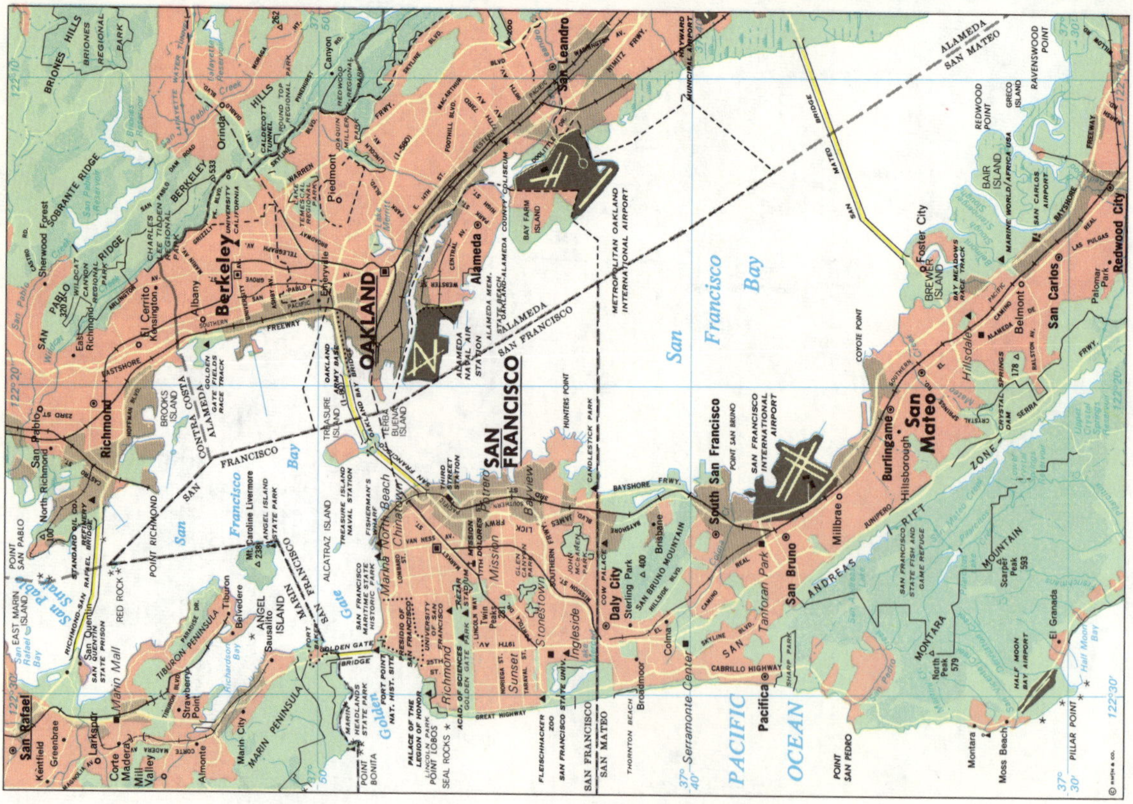

0 5 10 Miles

0 5 10 Kilometers

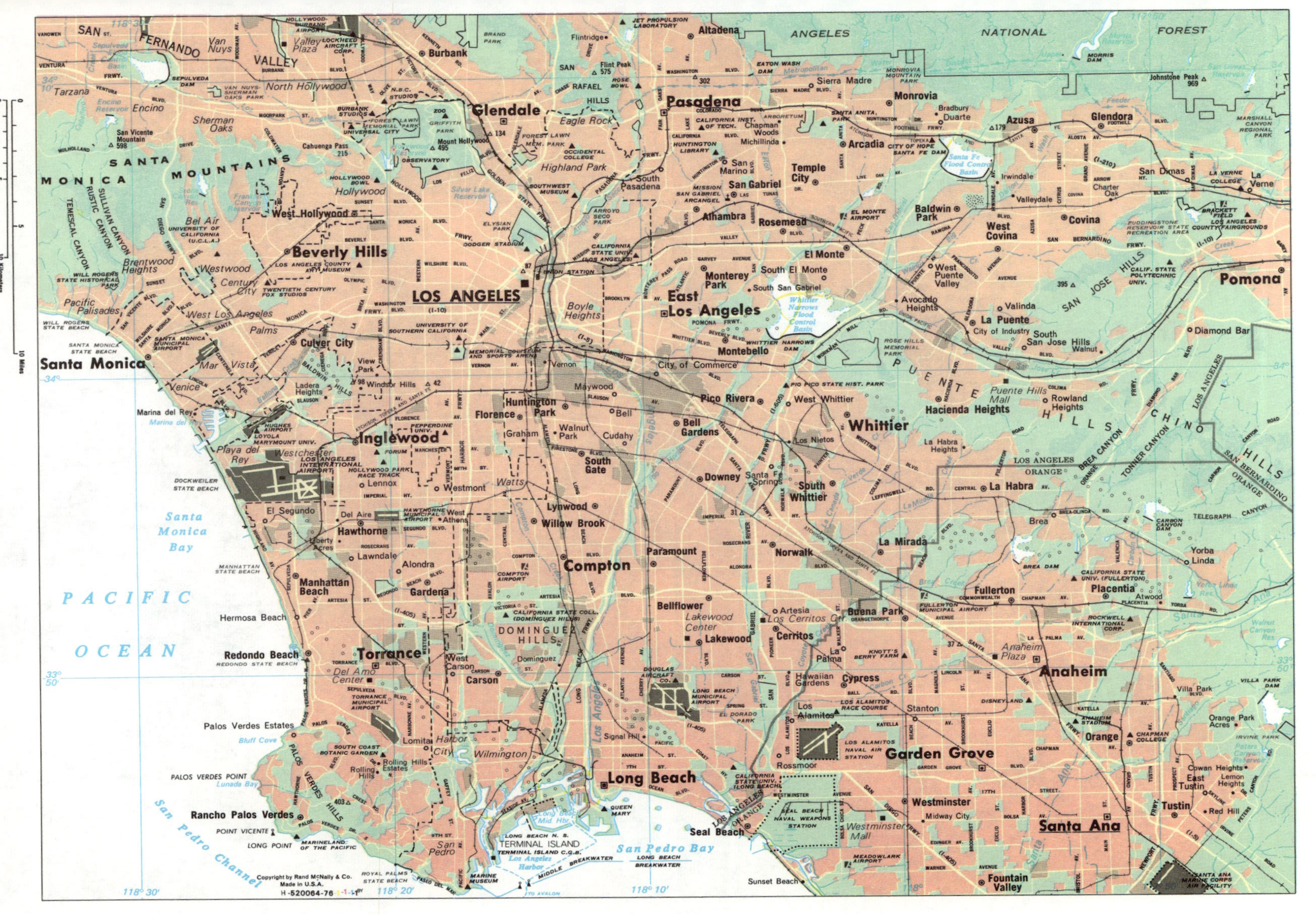

ANGELES NATIONAL FOREST
SANTA MONICA MOUNTAINS
SAN FERNANDO VALLEY
SAN RAFAEL HILLS
SAN JOSE HILLS
PUENTE HILLS
CHINO HILLS
DOMINGUEZ HILLS
PALOS VERDES HILLS
PACIFIC OCEAN
Santa Monica Bay
San Pedro Bay
San Pedro Channel
LOS ANGELES
East Los Angeles
Pasadena
Glendale
Burbank
Beverly Hills
West Hollywood
Hollywood
Santa Monica
Culver City
Inglewood
Hawthorne
Torrance
Redondo Beach
Hermosa Beach
Manhattan Beach
El Segundo
Gardena
Compton
Lynwood
Long Beach
Seal Beach
Lakewood
Bellflower
Paramount
Downey
Norwalk
Whittier
Pico Rivera
Montebello
Monterey Park
Alhambra
San Gabriel
Temple City
El Monte
Arcadia
Monrovia
Sierra Madre
Altadena
Azusa
Glendora
Covina
West Covina
Baldwin Park
La Puente
San Dimas
La Verne
Pomona
Diamond Bar
Hacienda Heights
La Habra
Brea
Fullerton
Placentia
Yorba Linda
Anaheim
Orange
Santa Ana
Tustin
Garden Grove
Westminster
Fountain Valley
Cypress
Buena Park
La Mirada
Cerritos
Los Alamitos
Stanton
Carson
Wilmington
San Pedro
Rancho Palos Verdes
Palos Verdes Estates
Marina del Rey
Venice
Encino
Tarzana
Sherman Oaks
Van Nuys
North Hollywood
Pacific Palisades
0 5 10 Miles
0 5 10 Kilometers
Copyright by Rand McNally & Co.
Made in U.S.A.
H-520084-76

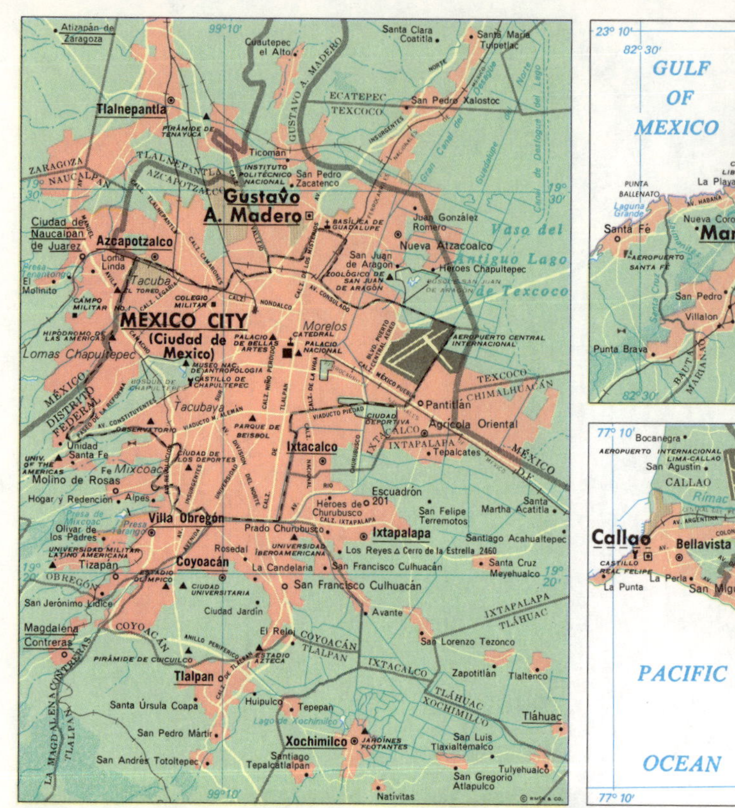

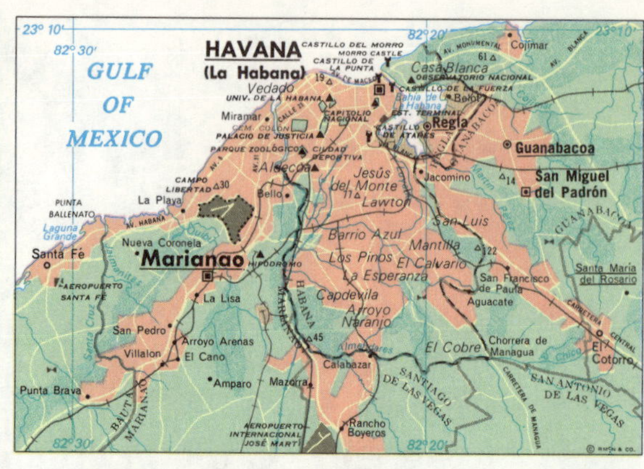

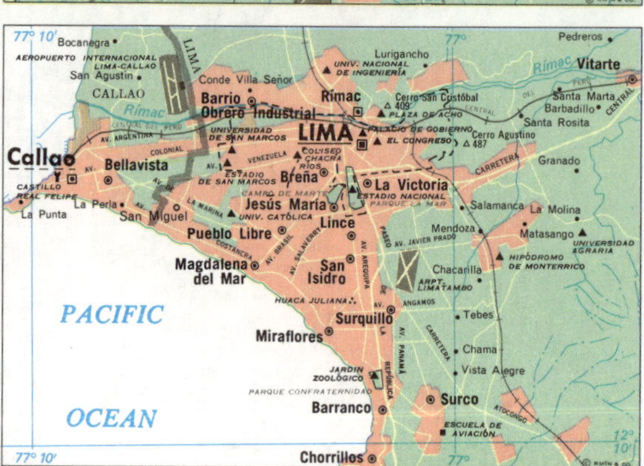

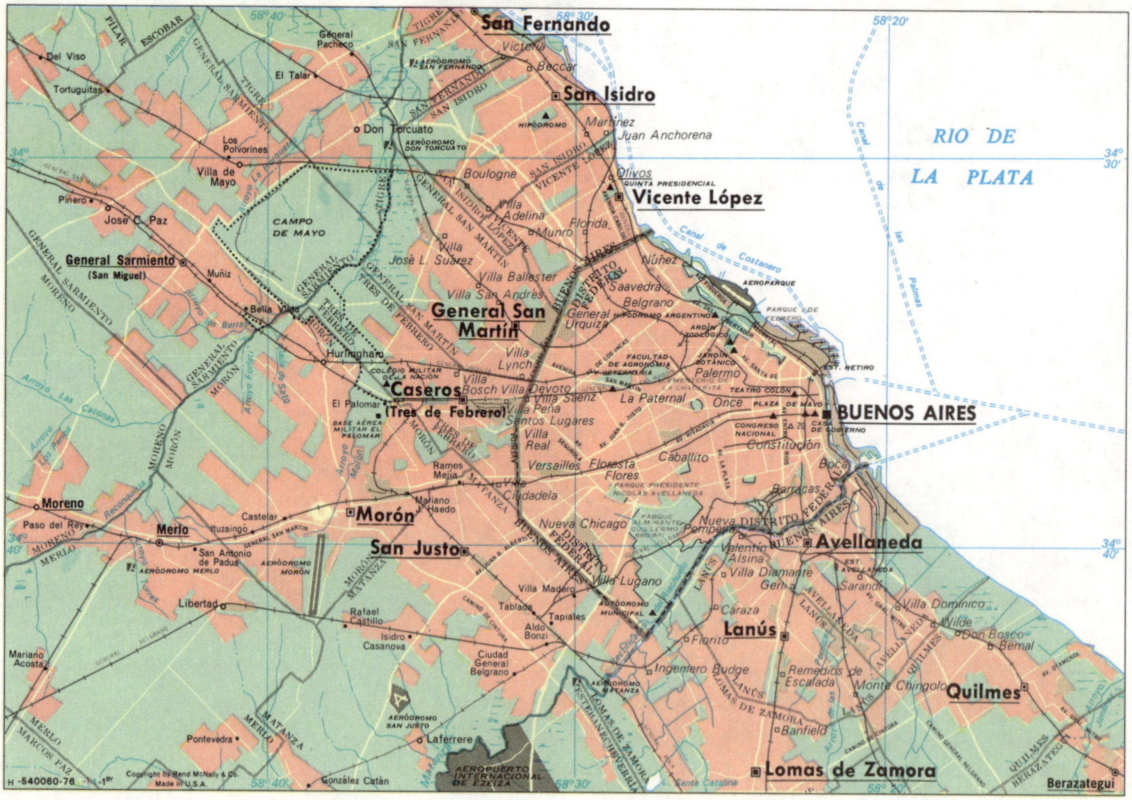

RIO DE LA PLATA
BUENOS AIRES
San Fernando
Victoria
Beccar
San Isidro
Martínez
Juan Anchorena
Olivos
Vicente López
Florida
Munro
Villa Adelina
Boulogne
Don Torcuato
Del Viso
Tortuguitas
El Talar
General Pacheco
Los Polvorines
Villa de Mayo
Pinero
José C. Paz
General Sarmiento (San Miguel)
Muñiz
Bella Vista
Campo de Mayo
José L. Suárez
Villa Ballester
Villa San Andrés
General San Martín
Hurlingham
Caseros (Tres de Febrero)
El Palomar
Villa Devoto
Villa Lynch
Núñez
Saavedra
Belgrano
General Urquiza
Aeroparque
Palermo
La Paternal
Once
Villa Pueyrredón
Santos Lugares
Villa Real
Versailles
Floresta
Flores
Caballito
Constitución
Boca
Barracas
Nueva Pompeya
Nueva Chicago
Ciudadela
Ramos Mejía
Mariano Haedo
Morón
Castelar
Ituzaingó
Merlo
Moreno
Paso del Rey
San Antonio de Padua
San Justo
Libertad
Rafael Castillo
Isidro Casanova
Villa Madero
Tablada
Tapiales
Aldo Bonzi
Villa Lugano
Valentín Alsina
Villa Diamante
Avellaneda
Sarandí
Villa Domínico
Wilde
Don Bosco
Bernal
Quilmes
Berazategui
Lanús
Caraza
Florito
Ingeniero Budge
Remedios de Escalada
Monte Chingolo
Banfield
Lomas de Zamora
Ciudad General Belgrano
Laferrere
González Catán
Pontevedra
Mariano Acosta
Aeropuerto Internacional de Ezeiza
Aeródromo San Justo
Aeródromo Merlo
Aeródromo Morón
58°40′
58°30′
58°20′
34°30′
34°40′

0 5 10 Miles
0 5 10 Kilometers

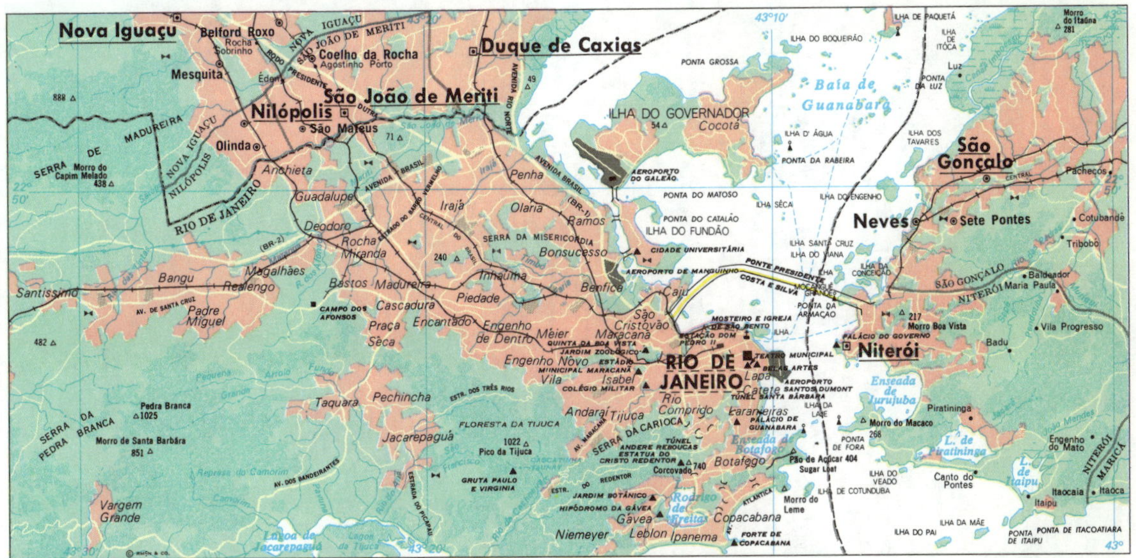

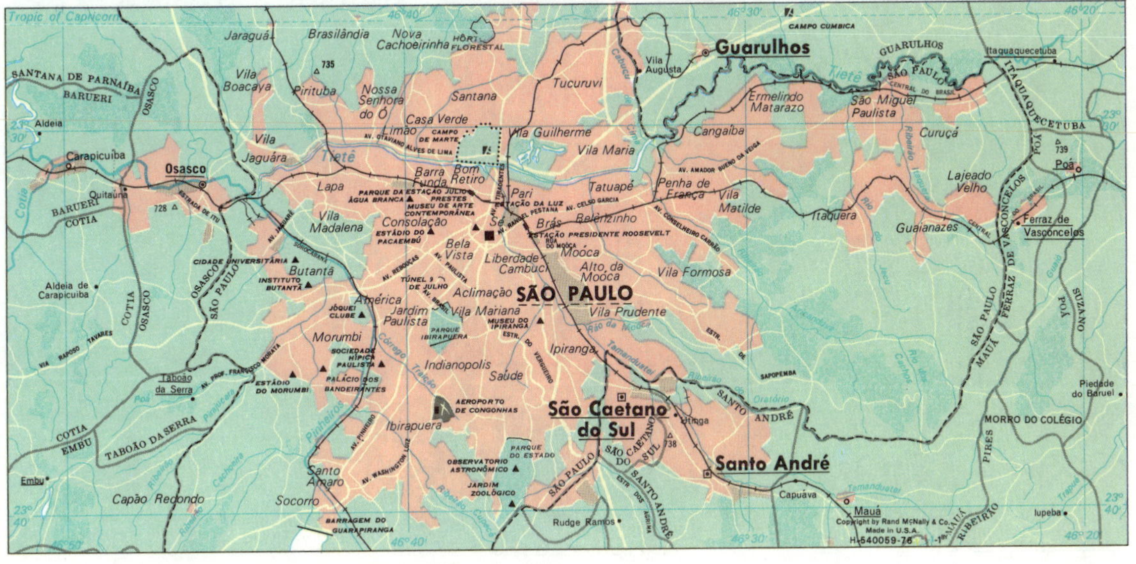

0 5 10 Miles

0 5 10 Kilometers

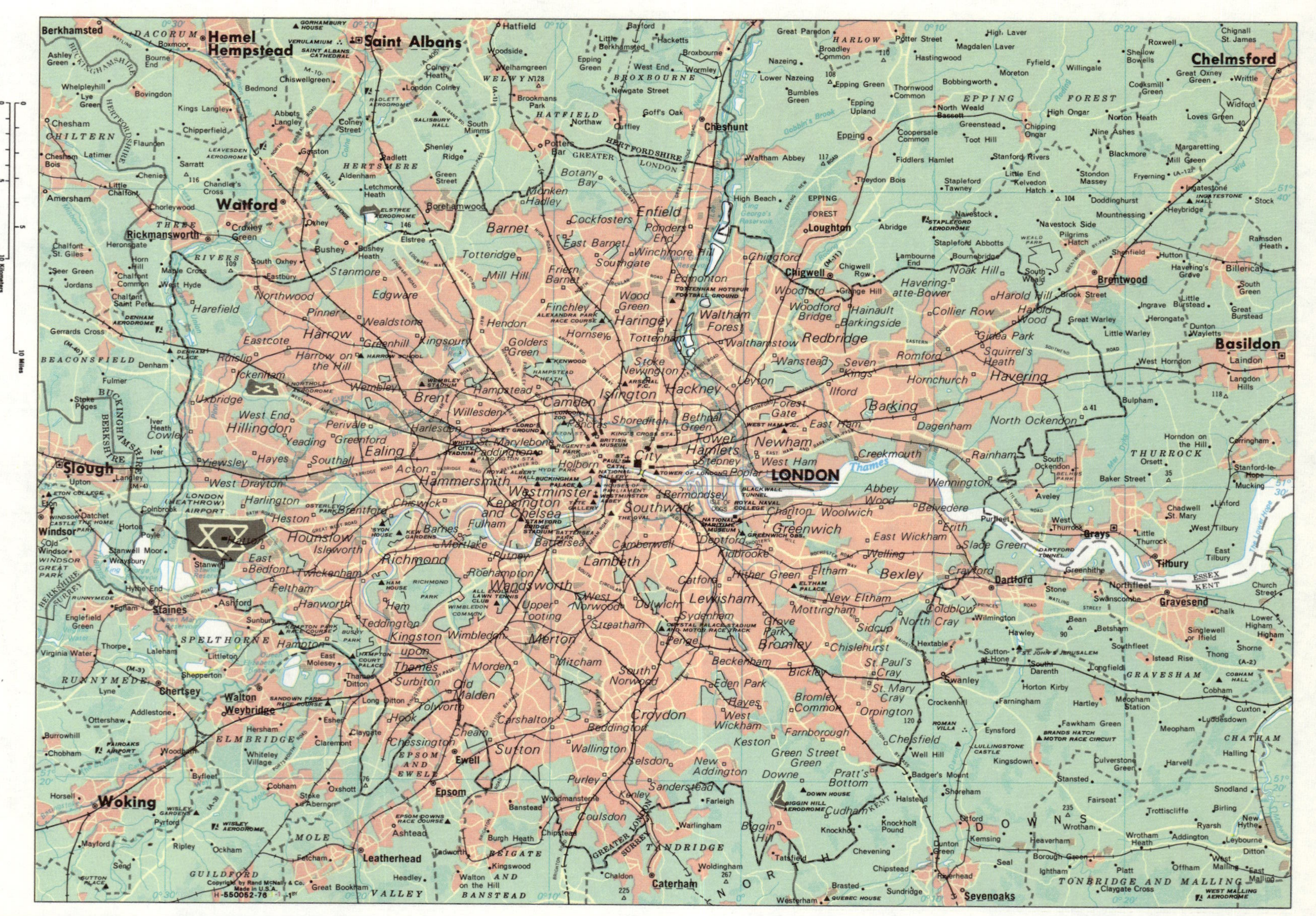
Chelmsford
Basildon
Brentwood
Romford
Havering
LONDON
Thames
Dartford
Gravesend
Tilbury
Grays
Watford
Saint Albans
Hemel Hempstead
Rickmansworth
Slough
Windsor
Staines
Chertsey
Woking
Leatherhead
Epsom
Sutton
Croydon
Bromley
Caterham
Sevenoaks
Orpington
Bexley
Barking
Ilford
Loughton
Chigwell
Cheshunt
Enfield
Barnet
Harrow
Richmond
Kingston upon Thames
Wimbledon
Westminster
Hertfordshire
Buckinghamshire
Berkshire
Surrey
Kent
Essex
Greater London
0 5 10 Miles
0 5 10 Kilometers
Copyright by Rand McNally & Co. Made in U.S.A. H-550052-76

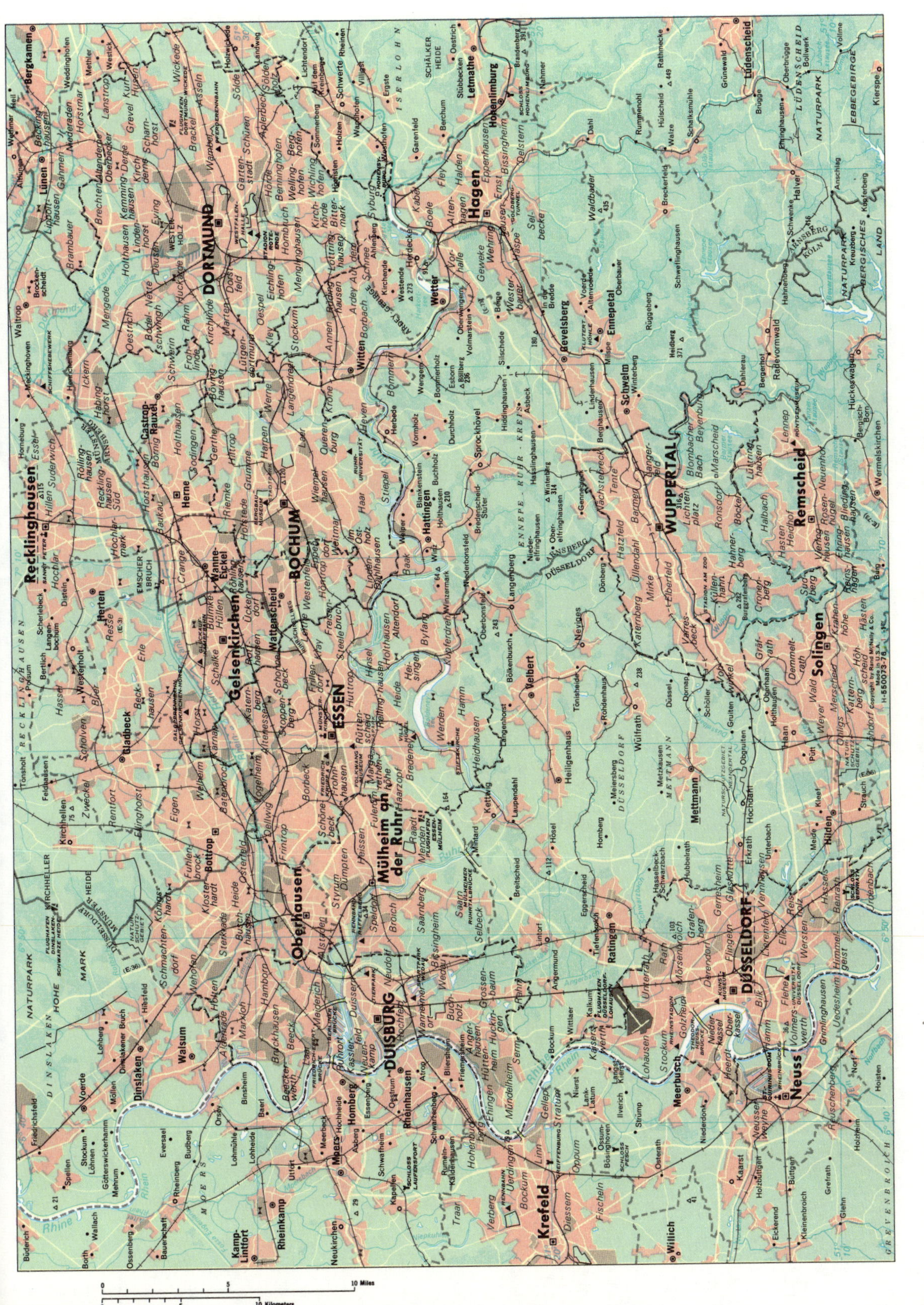
Recklinghausen
Dortmund
Bochum
Gelsenkirchen
Essen
Oberhausen
Mülheim an der Ruhr
Duisburg
Bottrop
Gladbeck
Herne
Castrop-Rauxel
Lünen
Bergkamen
Hagen
Witten
Wetter
Hattingen
Velbert
Wuppertal
Remscheid
Solingen
Düsseldorf
Neuss
Krefeld
Moers
Rheinhausen
Dinslaken
Walsum
Voerde
Kamp-Lintfort
Rheinkamp
Ratingen
Mettmann
Hilden
Schwelm
Ennepetal
Gevelsberg
Lüdenscheid
Hohenlimburg
Letmathe
Willich
Meerbusch
Herten
Wattenscheid
Wanne-Eickel
Rhine
Ruhr
10 Miles
10 Kilometers

Liverpool Bay
Formby
Crosby
Bootle
LIVERPOOL
Birkenhead
Wallasey
Ormskirk
Skelmersdale
Saint Helens
Huyton
Widnes
Runcorn
Mersey
Ellesmere Port
Speke
Halewood
Prescot
Kirkby
Maghull
Frodsham
Neston
WIRRAL
CHESHIRE
CLWYD
ENGLAND
WALES
Dee
Bolton
Bury
Rochdale
Oldham
Salford
MANCHESTER
Ashton-under-Lyne
Stockport
Stretford
Sale
Altrincham
Wilmslow
Didsbury
Wythenshawe
Heywood
Middleton
Royton
Denton
Hyde
Cheadle
Hazel Grove
Bramhall
Marple
Eccles
Swinton
Farnworth
Irlam
Urmston
Chorlton-cum-Hardy
Withington
Droylsden
Failsworth
Dukinfield
Stalybridge
GREATER MANCHESTER
TRAFFORD
MACCLESFIELD
PEAK DISTRICT NATIONAL PARK
PARIS
Saint-Denis
Versailles
Saint-Germain-en-Laye
Poissy
Sarcelles
Nanterre
Puteaux
Suresnes
Rueil-Malmaison
Saint-Cloud
Boulogne-Billancourt
Issy-les-Moulineaux
Montrouge
Vincennes
Montreuil
Bobigny
Aubervilliers
Saint-Ouen
Clichy
Levallois-Perret
Neuilly-sur-Seine
Courbevoie
Colombes
Asnières
Gennevilliers
Argenteuil
Sartrouville
Maisons-Laffitte
Épinay-sur-Seine
Drancy
Le Blanc-Mesnil
Aulnay-sous-Bois
Livry-Gargan
Bondy
Pantin
Chelles
Champigny-sur-Marne
Saint-Maur-des-Fossés
Créteil
Maisons-Alfort
Ivry-sur-Seine
Villejuif
Vitry-sur-Seine
Choisy-le-Roi
Orly
Antony
Sceaux
Clamart
Meudon
Sèvres
Palaiseau
Massy
Villeneuve-Saint-Georges
Seine
Marne
Copyright by Rand McNally & Co.
0 5 10 Miles
0 5 10 Kilometers

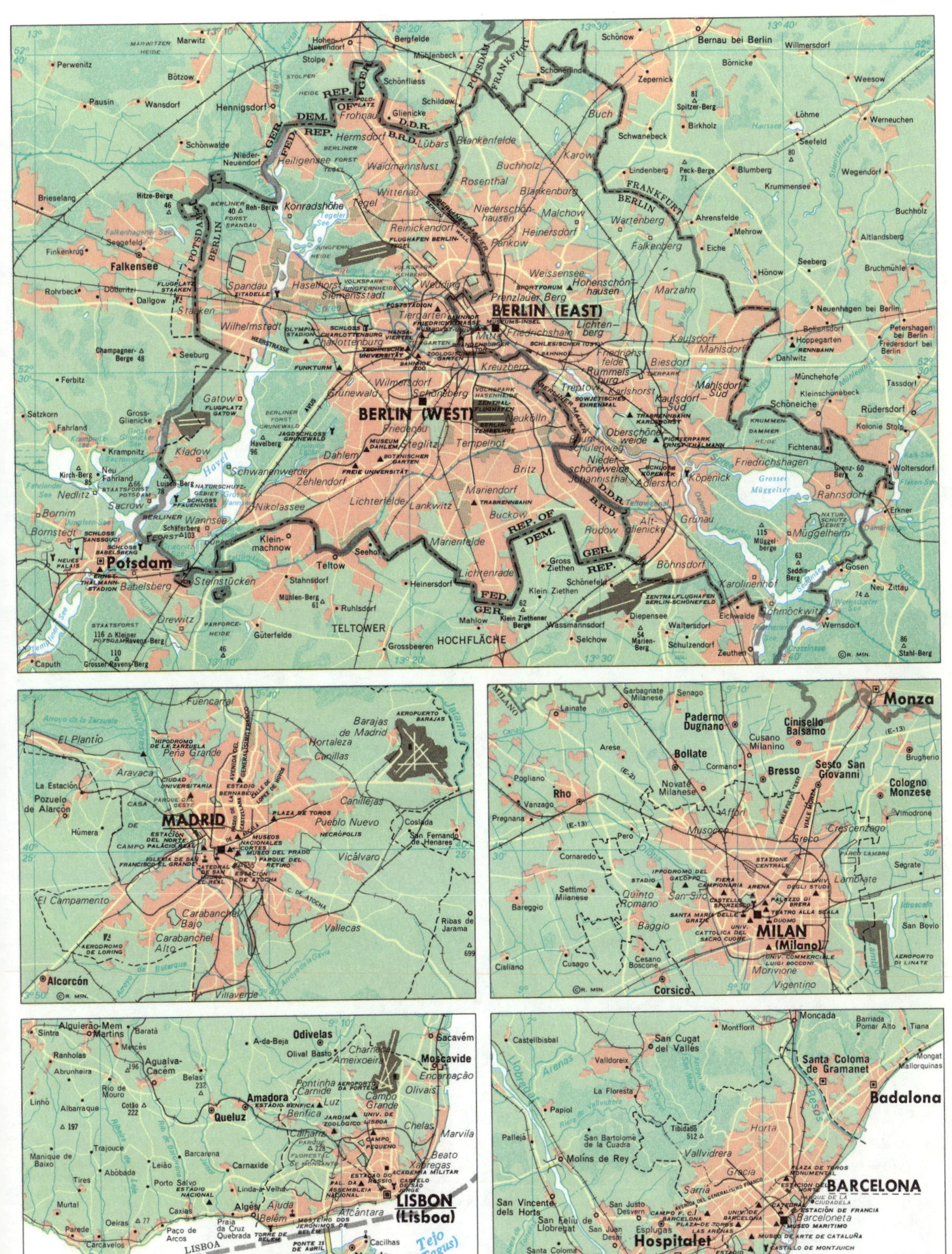

0 5 10 Miles

0 5 10 Kilometers

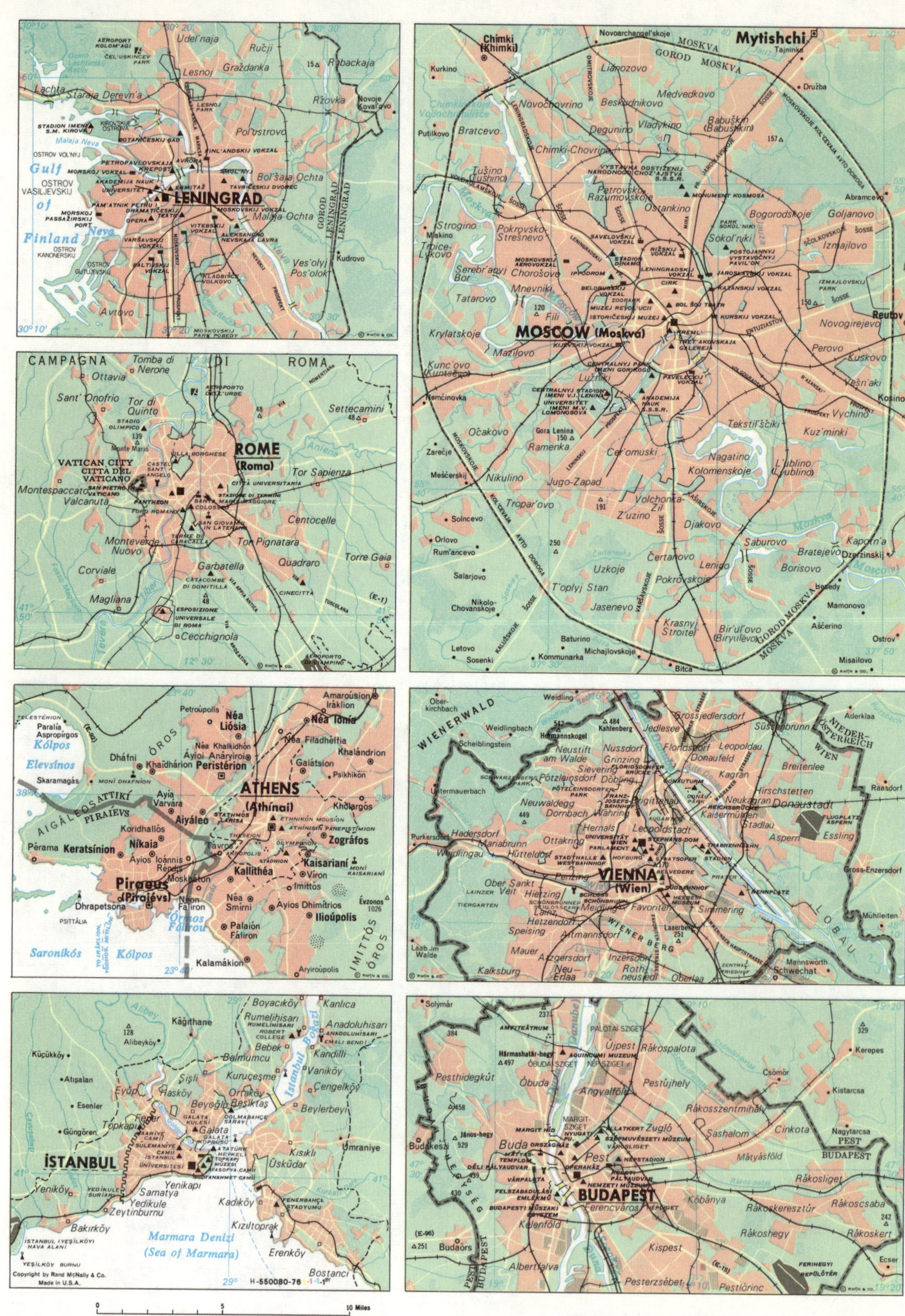
LENINGRAD
Gulf of Finland
Udel'naja
Lesnoj
Graždanka
Ručji
Rybackaja
Lachta
Staraja Derevn'a
Ržovka
Novoje Koval'ovo
Pol'ustrovo
Bol'šaja Ochta
Malaja Ochta
Ves'olyj Pos'olok
Kudrovo
Avtovo
Neva
GOROD LENINGRAD
MOSCOW (Moskva)
Mytishchi
Chimki (Khimki)
Novoarchangel'skoje
GOROD MOSKVA
Lianozovo
Medvedkovo
Novochovrino
Beskudnikovo
Degunino
Vladykino
Babuškin (Babushkin)
Bratcevo
Kurkino
Putilkovo
Chimki-Chovrino
Tušino (Tushino)
Petrovsko-Razumovskoje
Ostankino
Strogino
Pokrovsko-Strešnevo
Bogorodskoje
Goljanovo
Sokol'niki
Izmajlovo
Abramcevo
Tatarovo
Mnevniki
Fili
Krylatskoje
Mazilovo
Novogirejevo
Reutov
Perovo
Kuskovo
Kunc'ovo (Kuntsevo)
Nemčinovka
Očakovo
Ramenka
Čer'omuški
Tekstil'ščiki
Kuz'minki
Vychino
Kosino
Nagatino
Kolomenskoje
L'ublino (Lyublino)
Jugo-Zapad
Nikulino
Tropar'ovo
Volchonka-Zil
Z'uzino
Djakovo
Saburovo
Bratejevo
Kapotn'a
Dzerzhinskij
Uzkoje
Čertanovo
Lenino
Borisovo
T'oplyj Stan
Jasenevo
Krasnyj Stroitel
Bir'ul'ovo (Biryulëvo)
Mamonovo
Ostrov
Solncevo
Orlovo
Rum'ancevo
Salarjovo
Nikolo-Chovanskoje
Letovo
Sosenki
Kommunarka
Baturino
Michajlovskoje
Bitca
Misailovo
ROME (Roma)
CAMPAGNA DI ROMA
Tomba di Nerone
Ottavia
Sant' Onofrio
Tor di Quinto
Settecamini
VATICAN CITY CITTÀ DEL VATICANO
Montespaccato
Valcanuta
Tor Sapienza
Centocelle
Monteverde Nuovo
Tor Pignatara
Torre Gaia
Corviale
Quadraro
Garbatella
Magliana
Cecchignola
Tevere
ATHENS (Athínai)
Petroúpolis
Néa Liósia
Néa Ionía
Amaroúsion
Iráklion
Néa Filadhélfia
Khalándrion
Galátsion
Psikhikón
Peristérion
Dháfni
Khaïdhárion
Kólpos Elevsínos
Skaramagás
Aiyáleo
Kholargós
Zográfos
Nikaia
Keratsínion
Pérama
Kallithéa
Kaisarianí
Víron
Piraeus (Piraiévs)
Néa Smírni
Ilioúpolis
Palaión Fáliron
Kalamákion
Aryiroúpolis
Saronikós Kólpos
Imittós Óros
VIENNA (Wien)
WIENERWALD
NIEDER-ÖSTERREICH
WIEN
Kahlenberg
Jedlesee
Grossjedlersdorf
Süssenbrunn
Floridsdorf
Leopoldau
Donaufeld
Kagran
Breitenlee
Neustift am Walde
Nussdorf
Grinzing
Sievering
Döbling
Pötzleinsdorf
Neuwaldegg
Dornbach
Hirschstetten
Donaustadt
Kaisermühlen
Stadlau
Aspern
Essling
Raasdorf
Hadersdorf
Mariabrunn
Hütteldorf
Ottakring
Hernals
Leopoldstadt
Penzing
Ober Sankt Veit
Hietzing
Meidling
Favoriten
Simmering
Speising
Atzgersdorf
Mauer
Kalksburg
Inzersdorf
Rothneusiedl
Oberlaa
Schwechat
Mannswörth
LOBAU
Gross-Enzersdorf
Mühlleiten
ISTANBUL
Boyacıköy
Kanlıca
Rumelihisarı
Anadoluhisarı
Kâğıthane
Alibeyköy
Küçükköy
Bebek
Kandilli
Balmumcu
Vaniköy
Kuruçeşme
Çengelköy
Şişli
Ortaköy
Beşiktaş
Beylerbeyi
Hasköy
Eyüp
Beyoğlu
Galata
Topkapı
Kısıklı
Ümraniye
Üsküdar
Yeniköy
Samatya
Yenikapı
Yedikule
Zeytinburnu
Kadıköy
Bakırköy
Kızıltoprak
Erenköy
Bostancı
Marmara Denizi (Sea of Marmara)
İstanbul Boğazı
BUDAPEST
Solymár
Újpest
Rákospalota
Óbuda
Pesthidegkút
Angyalföld
Pestújhely
Rákosszentmihály
Zugló
Sashalom
Cinkota
Buda
Pest
Budakeszi
Mátyásföld
Rákosliget
Kőbánya
Ferencváros
Rákoskeresztúr
Rákoscsaba
Kelenföld
Rákoshegy
Rákoskert
Budaörs
Kispest
Albertfalva
Pesterzsébet
Pestlőrinc
Kerepes
Csömör
Kistarcsa
Nagytarcsa
Ecser
Copyright by Rand McNally & Co.
Made in U.S.A.
10 Miles
10 Kilometers

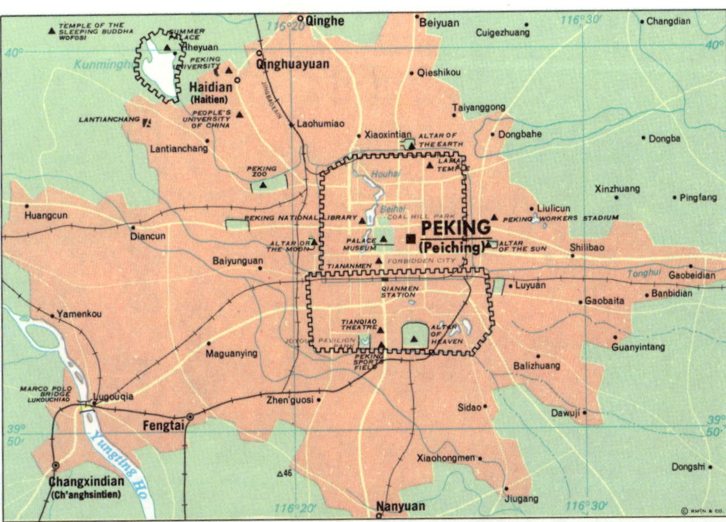

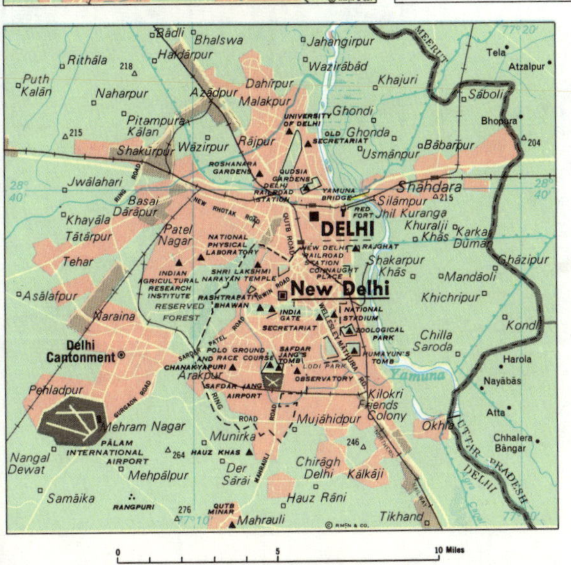

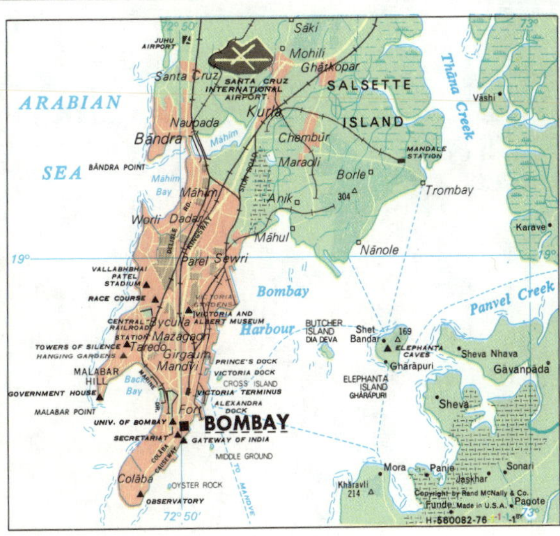

0 5 10 Miles

0 5 10 Kilometers

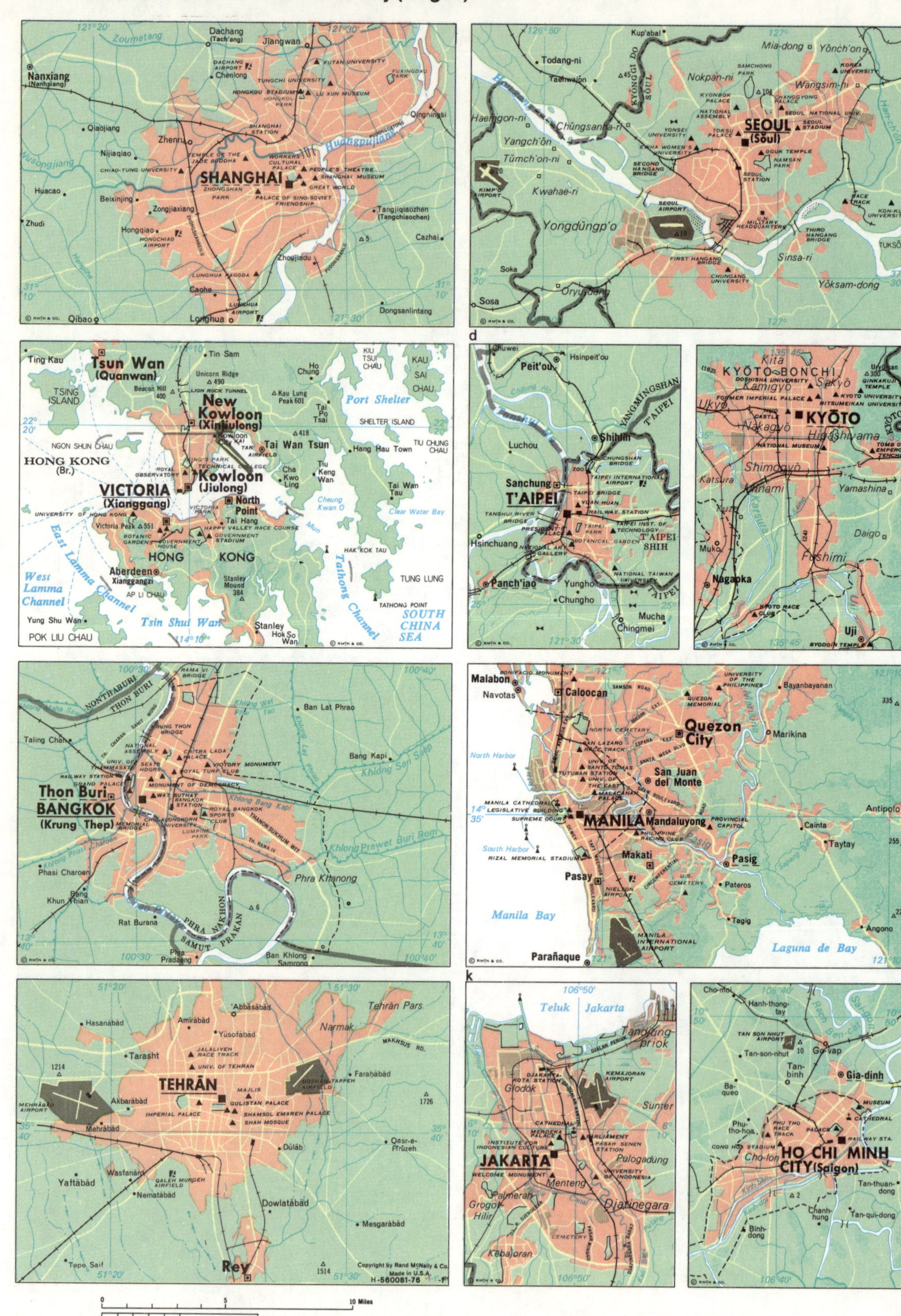

0 5 10 Miles

0 5 10 Kilometers

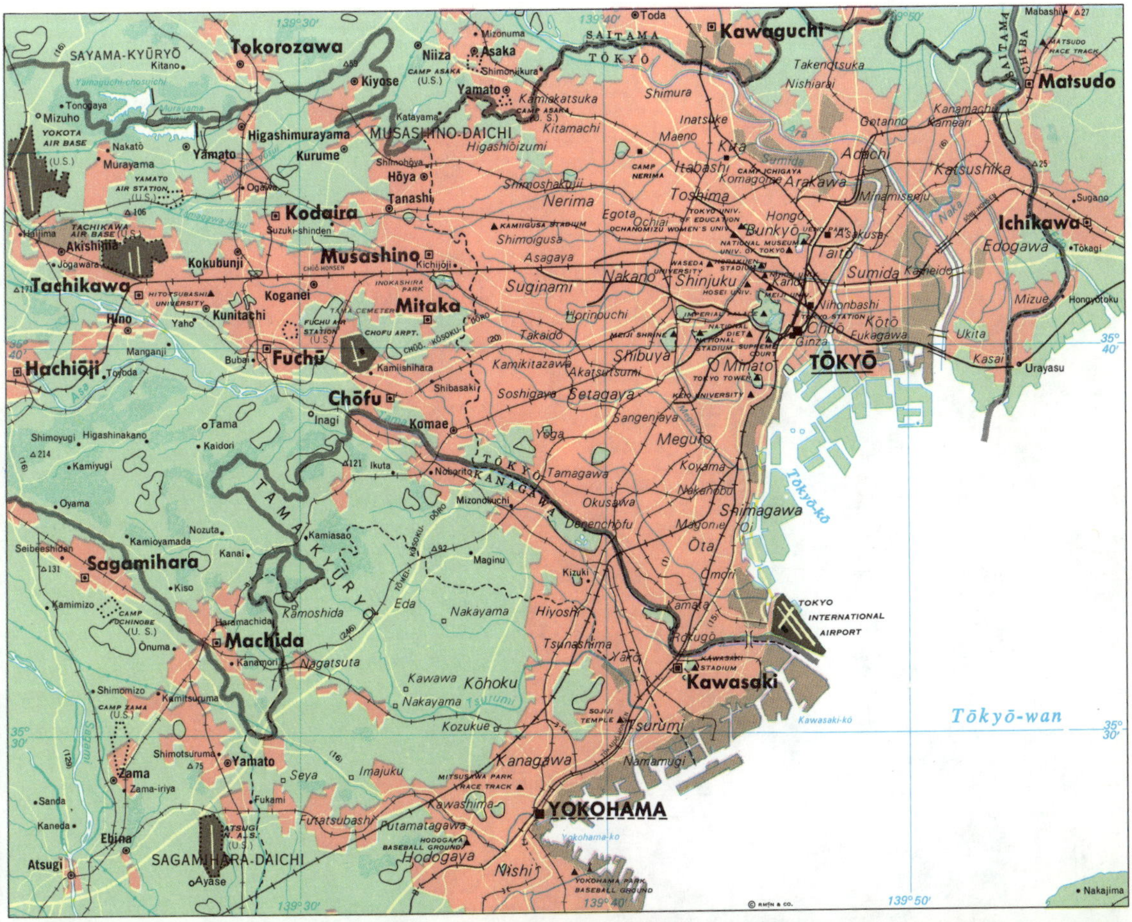

SAYAMA-KYŪRYŌ
Kitano
Tokorozawa
Niiza
Asaka
Mizonuma
Toda
Kawaguchi
SAITAMA
TŌKYŌ
CHIBA
Matsudo
Mabashi
Takenotsuka
Nishiarai
Shimura
Kiyose
CAMP ASAKA (U.S.)
Shimoniikura
Yamato
Kamiakatsuka
Kitamachi
Tonogaya
Mizuho
YOKOTA AIR BASE (U.S.)
Nakato
Murayama
Higashimurayama
Yamato
Kurume
MUSASHINO-DAICHI
Higashiōizumi
Inatsuke
Maeno
Kita
Gotanno
Kanamachi
Kameari
Adachi
Katsushika
YAMATO AIR STATION (U.S.)
Ogawa
Shimohōya
Hōya
CAMP NERIMA
Itabashi
CAMP ICHIGAYA
Komagome
Arakawa
Minamisenju
Tanashi
Shimoshakujii
Nerima
Toshima
Ichikawa
Sugano
Kodaira
Suzuki-shinden
KAMIIGUSA STADIUM
Shimoigusa
Egota
Ochiai
TOKYO UNIV. OF EDUCATION
OCHANOMIZU WOMEN'S UNIV.
Hongō
Bunkyō
Asakusa
Edogawa
Tōkagi
TACHIKAWA AIR BASE (U.S.)
Haijima
Akishima
Jogawara
Kokubunji
Musashino
Kichijōji
CHŪŌ HONSEN
Asagaya
NATIONAL MUSEUM
UNIV. OF TOKYO
Taitō
Sumida
Kameido
Tachikawa
HITOTSUBASHI UNIVERSITY
Koganei
INOKASHIRA PARK
Suginami
Nakano
WASEDA UNIVERSITY
Shinjuku
HOSEI UNIV.
Mizue
Hon-gyōtoku
Kunitachi
Mitaka
Hino
Yaho
FUCHU AIR STATION (U.S.)
CHOFU ARPT.
Horinouchi
IMPERIAL PALACE
Nihonbashi
TOKYO STATION
Kōtō
Fukagawa
Ukita
Chūō
Ginza
Manganji
Bubai
Fuchū
Takaidō
MEIJI SHRINE
NATIONAL DIET
NATIONAL STADIUM
SUPREME COURT
Kasai
Urayasu
Hachiōji
Toyoda
Kamiishihara
Kamikitazawa
Akatsutsumi
Shibuya
Minato
TŌKYŌ
TOKYO TOWER
Shibasaki
Chōfu
Soshigaya
Setagaya
KEIO UNIVERSITY
Shimoyugi
Higashinakano
Tama
Inagi
Komae
Sangenjaya
Meguro
Kaidori
Yoga
Kamiyugi
Ikuta
Noborito
KANAGAWA
Tamagawa
Koyama
Oyama
Mizonokuchi
Okusawa
Nakanobu
Tōkyō-kō
TAMA-KYŪRYŌ
Nozuta
Kamiasao
Denenchōfu
Shinagawa
Magome
Ōi
Kamioyamada
Seibeeshinden
Kanai
Maginu
Ōta
Sagamihara
Kizuki
Omori
Kiso
Eda
Kamata
TOKYO INTERNATIONAL AIRPORT
Kamimizo
CAMP FUCHINOBE (U.S.)
Haramachida
Kamoshida
Nakayama
Hiyoshi
Rokugō
Ōnuma
Machida
Kanamori
Nagatsuta
Tsunashima
Yako
KAWASAKI STADIUM
Kawasaki
Kawawa
Kōhoku
Shimomizo
Kamitsuruma
Nakayama
CAMP ZAMA (U.S.)
Kozukue
SOJIJI TEMPLE
Tsurumi
Kawasaki-kō
Tōkyō-wan
Shimotsuruma
Yamato
Kanagawa
Namamugi
Zama
Zama-iriya
Seya
Imajuku
MITSUSAWA PARK RACE TRACK
Sanda
Fukami
Kaneda
Kawashima
YOKOHAMA
Futatsubashi
Putamatagawa
Ebina
ATSUGI N.A.S. (U.S.)
Yokohama-kō
Atsugi
SAGAMIHARA-DAICHI
HODOGAYA BASEBALL GROUND
Hodogaya
Ayase
Nishi
YOKOHAMA PARK BASEBALL GROUND
Nakajima
© R.McN. & CO.

MEIJINO-MORI-MINO-KOKUTEI-KŌEN
Fukui
Syukunoshō
Takatsuki
Shōdai
Uyama
Nagao
Tonda
Yamaguchi
Najiō
Kawanishi
Minō
Ikeda
Nose
Arino
Tsukumono
Hanchō
Ibaraki
Hirakata
Tsuda
Maitani
Kamishinden
Katano
Arima
Funasaka
Takarazuka
CAMP SENZO
OSAKA INTERNATIONAL AIRPORT
Toyonaka
Yamada
Kōri
Kisabe
Taishaku-zan 586
Shikami-yama 550
SETO-NAIKAI-KOKURITSU-KŌEN
CAMP ITAMI
Senriyama
KANSAI UNIVERSITY
Settsu
Neyagawa
Kisaichi
Hyōgo
Tanigami
Rokkō-zan 932
Itami
KWANSEI GAKUIN UNIVERSITY
Hattori
Suita
ROKKŌ-SANCHI
Hirota
Shijōnawate
Iwazono
Higashiyodogawa
Kadoma
Kitatawara
KONGŌ-IKOMA-KOKUTEI-KŌEN
Obu
Obu-tōge 365
Maya-san 699
KOBE UNIVERSITY
Okamoto
Nishinomiya
SAN'YŌ HONSEN
ŌSAKA-HEIYA
Asahi
Moriguchi
Ashiya
Futatabi-yama 468
Nada
KOSHIEN STADIUM
Naruo
Jūsō
Yodo
Miyakojima
Daitō
Amagasaki
Umeda
Kita
Jōtō
Kōnoike
Fukiai
Higashinada
Nishiyodogawa
Fukushima
OSAKA UNIVERSITY
IKOMA TUNNEL
Shirakawa-tōge 190
Ikuta
KŌBE
Konohana
ŌSAKA
Higashi
OSAKA CASTLE
Ishikiri
Ikoma
Ikoma-yama 642
Nishi
Minami
Higashinari
Kōbe-kō
Shinsai-bashi
Nagata
Minato
Naniwa
Ikuno
Moto-machi
Higashiōsaka
Suma
Tennōji
Kizuri
IKOMA-SANCHI
OSAKA
NARA
WADA-MISAKI
SUMA BEACH
Ōsaka-kō
Taishō
Abeno
Kyūhōji
Yamamoto
Nishinari
Higashisumiyoshi
Heguri
Ōsaka-Wan
Kyūhōji
Yao
Sumiyoshi
Onchi
Tainaka
Sango
Yamato
YAO AIRPORT
Kashiwara
Ōji
Matsubara
Fujiidera
Sakai

0 5 10 Miles
0 5 10 Kilometers

H-590056-76

0 5 10 Miles
0 5 10 Kilometers

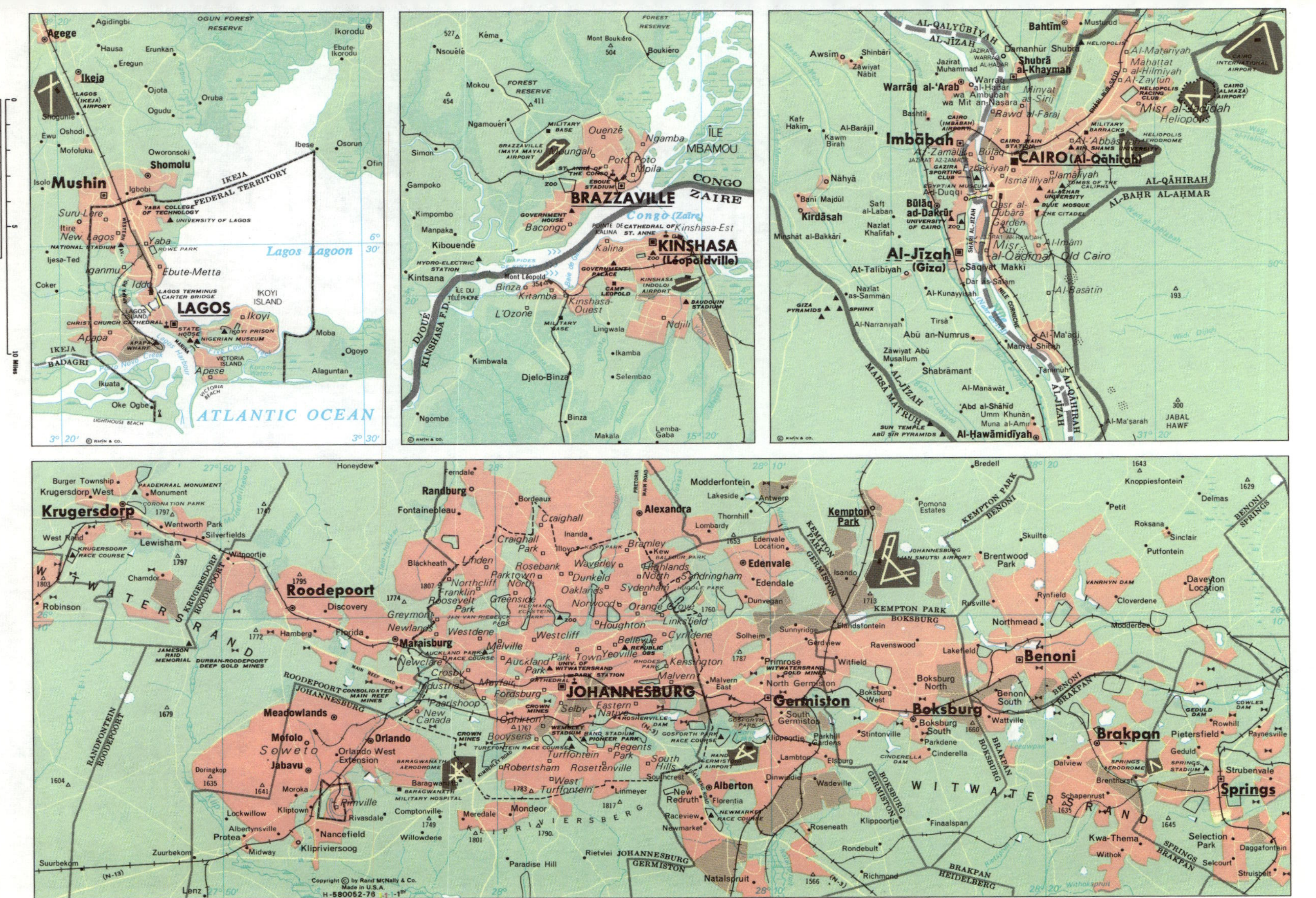
LAGOS
Lagos Lagoon
ATLANTIC OCEAN
IKOYI ISLAND
IKEJA FEDERAL TERRITORY
Mushin
Ikeja
Shomolu
Agege
BRAZZAVILLE
KINSHASA (Léopoldville)
Congo (Zaïre)
CONGO
ZAIRE
ÎLE MBAMOU
CAIRO (Al-Qāhirah)
Al-Jīzah (Giza)
Imbābah
Old Cairo
Heliopolis
Shubrā al-Khaymah
Būlāq ad-Dakrūr
Kirdāsah
Krugersdorp
Roodepoort
Randburg
Alexandra
Kempton Park
Edenvale
JOHANNESBURG
Germiston
Boksburg
Benoni
Brakpan
Springs
Alberton
Meadowlands
Orlando
Soweto
Jabavu
Maraisburg
Florida
WITWATERSRAND
KLIPRIVIERSBERG
Copyright © by Rand McNally & Co.
Made in U.S.A.
0 5 10 Miles
0 5 10 Kilometers

Historical Maps of the World

THE ANCIENT WORLD
In the 7th Century B.C.
MILES 0 50 100 200 300 400
Greeks
Phoenicians
Assyrian Empire
Etruscans
Greek Colonies
Achaean
Corinthian
Dorian
Euboean
Ionian
Parent locations in red
Phoenician Colonies
Other cities
A-454064-29-1-1-1
Copyright by Rand McNally & Company, Made in U.S.A.
NEAR EASTERN KINGDOMS
612-550 B.C.
Babylonian
Egyptian
Lydian
Median
Atlantic Ocean
IBERIA
(SPAIN)
Mediterranean Sea
AFRICA
LIBYA
ARABIA
ARMENIA
MEDIA
ASSYRIAN EMPIRE
Pontus Euxinus (Black Sea)
Caspian Sea
Carthage
Rome
Athens
Corinth
Sparta
Byzantium
Babylon
Nineveh
Tyre
Jerusalem

CLASSICAL GREECE
and
ATHENIAN EMPIRE
About 450 B.C.
MILES 0 50 100
Athenian Empire about 450 B.C.
Allied States
Subjects of Athens
PAEONIA
MACEDON
THRACE
EPIRUS
THESSALY
CHALCIDICE
DOLOPIANS
AETOLIA
ACARNANIA
ACHAEA
ELIS
ARCADIA
MESSENIA
LACONIA
BOEOTIA
ATTICA
EUBOEA
TROAS
HELLESPONTINE PHRYGIA
BITHYNIA
MYSIA
AEOLIS
LYDIA
IONIA
CARIA
PHRYGIA
PISIDIA
LYCIA
PAMPHYLIA
CRETE
CYPRUS
RHODES
Aegean Sea
Thracian Sea
Ionian Sea
Myrtoan Sea
Cretan Sea
Mediterranean Sea
Lycian Sea
Pontus Euxinus (Black Sea)
Propontis
Hellespont
Pella
Amphipolis
Philippi
Abdera
Maronea
Mesambria
Perinthus
Selymbria
Byzantium
Calchedon (Chalcedon)
Astacus
Heraclea Pontica
Cius
Ancore
Dascylium
Cyzicus
Parium
Lampsacus
Abydus
Sestus
Cardia
Aenus
Sigeum
Ilium
Assus
Adramyttium
Mytilene
Pergamum
Cyme
Phocaea
Magnesia
Sardes
Smyrna
Clazomenae
Erythrae
Chios
Teos
Colophon
Ephesus
Samos
Priene
Miletus
Tralles
Alabanda
Mylasa
Halicarnassus
Caunus
Cos
Cnidus
Ialysus
Camirus
Rhodes
Lindus
Telmessus
Xanthus
Phaselis
Celaenae
Ipsus
Stagira
Acanthus
Olynthus
Potidaea
Mende
Scione
Torone
Dium
Myrina
Methone
Pydna
Larissa
Pherae
Pagasae
Pharsalus
Cynoscephalae
Lamia
Thermopylae
Histiaea
Chalcis
Eretria
Delphi
Amphissa
Naupactus
Thermum
Orchomenos
Chaeronea
Thebes
Leuctra
Plataea
Tanagra
Delium
Decelea
Marathon
Eleusis
Athens
Piraeus
Megara
Corinth
Sicyon
Patrae
Elis
Pisa
Olympia
Mantinea
Nemea
Cleonae
Argos
Mycenae
Tiryns
Epidaurus
Troezen
Aegina
Tegea
Megalopolis
Messene
Pylos
Methone
Corone
Asine
Sparta
Amyclae
Corcyra
Dodona
Ambracia
Cydonia
Rhithymna
Cnossus
Gortyna
Lato
Praesus
Hierapytna
Priansus
Lissus
Carpasia
Aphrodisium
Lapethus
Cerynia
Salamis
Soli
Idalium
Golgi
Arsinoe
Tamassus
Citium
Paphos
Palaeapaphos
Amathus
Curium
A-451461-29-1-1-1
Copyright by Rand McNally & Company, Made in U.S.A.

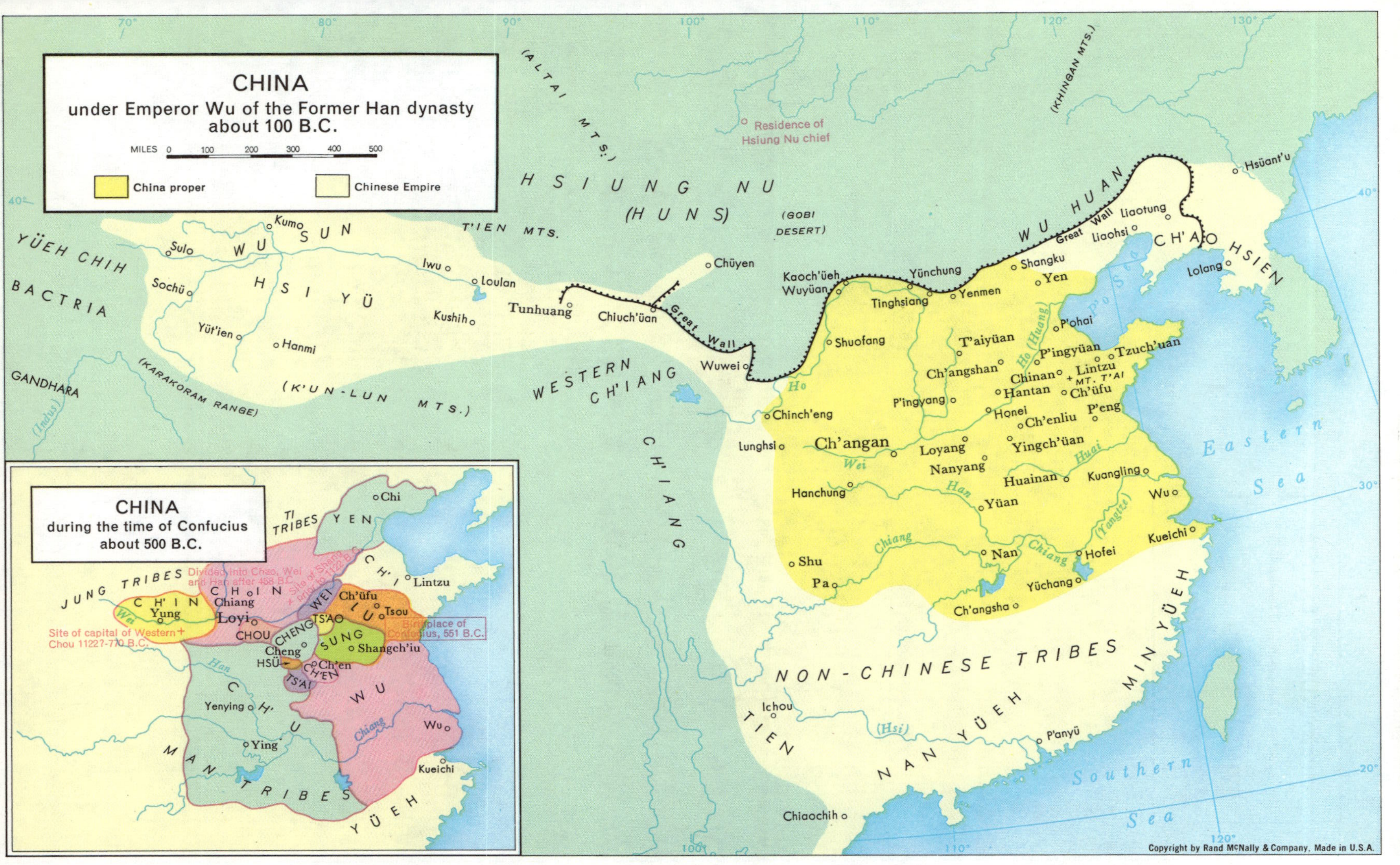
CHINA
under Emperor Wu of the Former Han dynasty
about 100 B.C.
MILES 0 100 200 300 400 500
China proper
Chinese Empire
CHINA
during the time of Confucius
about 500 B.C.
(ALTAI MTS.)
(KHINGAN MTS.)
Residence of Hsiung Nu chief
HSIUNG NU
(HUNS)
(GOBI DESERT)
WU HUAN
Great Wall
Hsüant'u
Liaotung
Liaohsi
CH'AO HSIEN
Lolang
WU SUN
Kumo
T'IEN MTS.
YÜEH CHIH
Sulo
BACTRIA
Sochü
HSI YÜ
Iwu
Loulan
Chüyen
Kaoch'üeh
Wuyüan
Yünchung
Shangku
Yen
Yenmen
Tinghsiang
Tunhuang
Chiuch'üan
Kushih
Yüt'ien
Hanmi
GANDHARA
(Indus)
(KARAKORAM RANGE)
(K'UN-LUN MTS.)
WESTERN CH'IANG
Wuwei
Shuofang
T'aiyüan
P'ohai
Ho (Huang)
P'ingyüan
Tzuch'uan
Ch'angshan
Chinan
Lintzu
MT. T'AI
Hantan
Ch'üfu
P'ingyang
Ho
Chinch'eng
Honei
Ch'enliu
P'eng
Lunghsi
Ch'angan
Wei
Loyang
Yingch'üan
Huai
Eastern Sea
Nanyang
Hanchung
Han
Huainan
Kuangling
Wu
Yüan
(Yangtze)
CH'IANG
Kueichi
Chiang
Shu
Nan
Hofei
Pa
Yüchang
Ch'angsha
MIN YÜEH
NON-CHINESE TRIBES
Ichou
TIEN
(Hsi)
NAN YÜEH
P'anyü
Southern Sea
Chiaochih
Chi
TI TRIBES
YEN
CH'I
Lintzu
JUNG TRIBES
Divided into Chao, Wei and Han after 453 B.C.
CHIN
Chiang
CH'IN
Yung
Wei
Loyi
WEI
Ch'üfu
LU
Tsou
TSAO
Birthplace of Confucius, 551 B.C.
Site of capital of Western Chou 1122?-770 B.C.
CHOU
CHENG
Cheng
SUNG
Shangch'iu
HSÜ
Ch'en
CH'EN
TS'AI
Han
CH'U
Yenying
WU
Chiang
Wu
Ying
MAN TRIBES
Kueichi
YÜEH
Copyright by Rand McNally & Company. Made in U.S.A.

ALEXANDER'S EMPIRE
MILES 0 50 100 200 300 400
Allied Territory
Independent States
Subject Territory
Route of Alexander
Borysthenes
Olbia
Don
Lake Maeotis
Phanagoria
Danube
THRACE
MACEDON
Black Sea
CAUCASUS MOUNTAI
Phasis
Sinope
Amphipolis
Abdera
Pella
Thessalonica
Pydna
CORCYRA
EPIRUS
THESSALY
Calchedon
Byzantium
Lysimachia
LEMNOS
Heraclea
Nicomedia
BITHYNIA
PAPHLAGONIA
Amasia
Trapezus
Pergamum
Cyzicus
LESBOS
Delphi
Thebes
Aegean Sea
CHIOS
Smyrna
Sardes
Ancyra
Gordium
CAPPADOCIA
PELOPONNESUS
Megalopolis
Athens
Corinth
Ipsus
PHRYGIA
Halys
ARMENIA
Ephesus
Magnesia
Miletus
Sparta
Halicarnassus
CARIA
Iconium
PISIDIA
LYCAONIA
TAURUS MTS.
Mediterranean Sea
RHODES
LYCIA
Perge
CILICIA
Tarsus
Issus
Zeugma
CRETE
Gortyn
COELE-SYRIA
Antioch
Nisibis
Gaugamela
Arbela
MESOPOTAMIA
ASSYRIA
ZAGRUS
CYPRUS
Salamis
Paphos
Citium
Apamea
Ptolemais
Cyrene
Barca
CYRENAICA
Byblos
SYRIA
Palmyra
Dura
Tigris
Damascus
Sidon
Tyre
PHOENICIA
Euphrates
Ctesipho
Seleucia
Samaria
Jerusalem
PALESTINE
Babylon
BABYLON
Naucratis
Alexandria
Gaza
Pelusium
Memphis
Route of Alexander
Arsinoe
Oasis of Siwah
EGYPT
Oxyrhynchus
Nile
SINAI
LIBYA
Myos Hormos
ARABIA
Ptolemais
Red Sea
Thebes
Syene
Berenice
10°
20°
30°
40°
50°

HELLENISTIC WORLD
3rd Century B.C.
ANTIGONID KDM.
Pella
EPIRUS
AETOLIAN LEAGUE
Athens
Sparta
ACHAIAN LEAGUE
CRETE
CYPRUS
Black Sea
BITHYNIA
PONTUS
Pergamum
Independent about 230 B.C.
Mediterranean Sea
Cyrene
Alexandria
PTOLEMAIC KINGDOM
LIBYA
Antioch
SELEUCID KINGDOM
Babylon
Red Sea
ARABIA
Persian Gulf
Caspian Sea
Aral Sea
PARTHIA
Independent about 260 B.C.
BACTRIA
Independent about 225 B.C.
Arabian Sea
Aral Sea
Jaxartes
Oxus
Caspian Sea
Alexandria Eschate
Maracanda
SOGDIANA
MARGIANA
Sarnius
Zariaspa (Bactra)
BACTRIA
GANDHARA
HINDU KUSH RANGE
Route of Alexander
Nicaea
Taxila
Bucephala
Sagala
Hydaspes
Hydraotes
Hyphasis
HYRCANIA
Hecatompylus
Ragae
Ecbatana
PARTHIA
ARIA
Alexandria Ariorum (Mod. Herat)
ARACHOSIA
Alexandria Arachoton (Mod. Kandahar)
SIANA
DRANGIANA
Alexandria Opiana
Indus
INDIA
Pasargadae
Persepolis
CARMANIA
PERSIA
GEDROSIA
Patala
Persian Gulf
Arabian Sea

ROMAN REPUBLIC
In the Time of Caesar and Cicero
MILES 0 50 100 200 300 400
Roman Provinces
Parthian Empire
Client Kingdoms and Dependencies
Battlefields
Atlantic Ocean
North Sea
BRITANNIA
English Channel
NERVII
BELGAE
TREVERI
Lutetia
Sequana (Seine)
GAUL
VENETI
Liger
Alesia
Rhenus (Rhine)
GERMA
CELTAE
AEDUI
SEQUANI
HELVETII
Garumna
ARVERNI
Rhodanus
AQUITANI
PYRENEES
TRANSALPINE GAUL
Narbo
Massilia
Aquae Sextiae
ALPS
Vercellae
Verona
Trebia
CISALPINE GAUL
Mutina
Rubicon
Lucca
Sarsina
L. Trasimene
APENNINES
ILLYRICUM
Adriatic Sea
Amiternum
ITALY
Corfinium
Rome
Tusculum
Ostia
Arpinum
Formiae
Suessa
Capua
Cannae
Rudiae
Neapolis
Beneventum
Brund
Tarentu
Heraclea
Dyrrh
Durius
Iberus
Numantia
(Ebro)
HITHER SPAIN
Tagus
(Guadiana)
Anas
FARTHER SPAIN
Saguntum
Italica
Gades
Munda
Strait of Gibraltar
New Carthage
BALEARIC ISLANDS
CORSICA
SARDINIA
Tyrrhenian Sea
Mylae
Messana
Ionia Sea
Lilybaeum
SICILY
Agrigentum
Gela
Syracuse
Mediterranean
MAURETANIA
ATLAS MTS.
Cirta
Utica
Carthage
Zama
Thapsus
AFRICA
NUMIDIA
50°
40°
30°
20°
10°
0°

SARMATIA
Borysthenes (Dnieper)
Tanais (Don)
Rha (Volga)
Daix (Ural)
Lake Maeotis (Sea of Azov)
Pontus Euxinus (Black Sea)
(Danube)
CAUCASUS
Caspian Sea
Cyrus
THRACE
Byzantium
Philippi
Propontis
Nicomedia
BITHYNIA
Amasia
PONTUS
ARMENIA
Artaxata
Lake Thospitis
Lake Matianus
Tigranocerta
GALATIA
CAPPADOCIA
Pergamum
ASIA
Cynoscephalae
Pharsalus
Aegean Sea
Ephesus
Magnesia
Athens
Corinth
Megalopolis
Sparta
DELOS
LYCAONIA
TAURUS MTS.
COMMAGENE
Tarsus
CILICIA
Carrhae
PARTHIAN EMPIRE
Ecbatana
Euphrates
Tigris
Antioch
SYRIA
Ctesiphon
Seleucia
Babylon
Susa
RHODES
CYPRUS
CRETE
Damascus
JUDAEA
Jerusalem
Gaza
Cyrene
Alexandria
Pelusium
KINGDOM OF THE PTOLEMIES
Nile
ARABIA
Persian Gulf
Red Sea
30°
40°
50°
60°
20°

Atlantic Ocean
North Sea
Bay of Biscay
Mediterranean
Tyrrhenian Sea
SCOTIA
PICTS
SCANDIA
DIOCESE OF BRITAIN
DIOCESE OF GAUL
DIOCESE OF SPAIN
DIOCESE OF ITALY
DIOCESE OF ROME
DIOCESE OF AFRICA
VISIGOTHS
OSTROGO
ANGLO-SAXONS
FRANKS
BURGUNDIANS
HUNS
VANDALS
York
Chester
Lincoln
Caerleon
St. Albans
Colchester
London
Tournay
Cologne
Cambray
Soissons
Rouen
Reims
Treves
Mainz
Paris
Metz
Chalons
Orleans
Tours
Poitiers
Autun
Bordeaux
Lyon
Milan
Pavia
Salzburg
Aquileia
Genoa
Bologna
Ravenna
Pisa
Ancona
Spoleto
Rome
Naples
Toulouse
Arles
Narbonne
Pamplona
Saragossa
Braga
Lisbon
Toledo
Merida
Seville
Cadiz
Valencia
Cartagena
Tarragona
Tortosa
Barcelona
Ceuta
CORSICA
SARDINIA
BALEARIC ISLANDS
Palermo
Syracuse
Hippo Regius
Carthage
Tripoli
ALPS
PYRENEES
Rhine
Elbe
Weser
Oder
Danube
Seine
Loire
Garonne
Rhone
Duero
Ebro
Tagus
Guadiana
Guadalquivir
547
367-550
C. 450
C. 500
C. 449
358
486
507
451
452
443
415
412-507
409-429
568
489
410
455
429
10°
0°
50°
Routes of the Barbarians
Huns
Visigoths
Vandals
Franks
Lombards
Ostrogoths
Burgundians
Anglo-Saxons
375 —date people passed through region
200-375—stop in region
507 —final occupation of region

ROMAN EMPIRE ABOUT 400 A.D.
and The Barbarian Invasions
MILES 0 50 100 200 300 400 500
Prefecture of Gaul
Prefecture of Illyricum
Prefecture of Italy
Prefecture of the East
SLAVS
Dnieper
Don
Volga
Vistula
HUNS
100-372
150 A.D.
375
200-375
CARPATHIANS
Dniester
Bug
OSTROGOTHS
340-481
CHAZARS
CAUCASUS
Caspian Sea
Chersōn
Black Sea
Danube
DIOCESE OF DACIA
Naissus
DIOCESE OF THRACE
Odessus
Nicopolis
Philippopolis
Adrianople
Constantinople
DIOCESE OF MACEDONIA
Dyrrhachium
376-395
Thessalonica
Propontis
Heraclea
Nicomedia
Nicaea
Trebizond
ARMENIA
DIOCESE OF PONTUS
Caesarea
SASSANIAN OR NEW PERSIAN EMPIRE
Tigris
Euphrates
Dura
Edessa
Aegean Sea
LESBOS
CHIOS
ANDROS
SAMOS
Pergamum
Smyrna
Ephesus
Antiochia
DIOCESE OF ASIA
Athens
Corinth
Antioch
Apamea
Emesa
Damascus
DIOCESE OF THE EAST
RHODES
CYPRUS
CRETE
Sea
Tyre
Caesarea
Jerusalem
Alexandria
Cyrene
Berenice
DIOCESE OF EGYPT
Memphis
Nile
Red Sea
20°
30°
40°
50°
A-450008-29-1-1-1-1

A-469015-29-1-1-1[BY]

Uighur Capital
Orkhon
UIGHURS (EASTERN TURKS)
(GOBI DESERT)
KHITANS
Capital
P'O HAI
Liaotung
SILLA
Hanchow
Capital
Capital from 794
Heian
Nara
Capital from 710-784
JAPAN
Huang
Great Wall
Tunhuang
LUNG YU
T'UYÜHUNS
Shan
KUANNEI
T'aiyüan
HO TUNG
HOPEI
Huang
Yün
Weichow
HO NAN
Grand Canal
Loyang
TUCHI
Pien
Sung
Yangchow
Eastern Sea
CHINGCHI
Ch'angan
Soochow
SHANNAN HSI
SHANNAN TUNG
HUAINAN
Hsüan
Yüeh
Hangchow
Chiangling
T
Yangtze
CHINA
Ch'engtu
CHIENNAN
CH'IENCHUNG
CHIANGNAN HSI
CHIANGNAN TUNG
Ch'üanchow
UPA
Tali
NAN CHAO (T'AI)
Hsi
LINGNAN
Kwangchow
Southern Sea
Halin
PYU
ANNAM
Chiaochow
(HAINAN)
UPPER (LAND) CHENLA
CHAMPA
Amaravati
kshetra
MONS
Thaton
Mekong
DVARAVATI
LOWER (MARITIME) CHENLA
KAUTHARA
Virapura
PANDURANGA
TAMBRALINGA
LANGKASUKA
KEDAH
(SUMATRA)
(BORNEO)
Malayu
BANKA
SRIVIJAYA
Srivijaya
The Srivijayan Empire, perhaps under a Sailendran ruler, probably included more of Sumatra and Java and even portions of the Malay peninsula and Borneo by the end of the 8th Century
(JAVA)
SAILENDRAS
TARUMA
Borobodur
Built 772?
MATARAM
100°
110°
120°
130°
140°
30°
20°
10°
0°
10°

EUROPE AND
THE CRUSADER STATES
About 1140
MILES 0 50 100 200 300 400
THE CRUSADES
First Crusade
A...Bohemond
B...Godfrey
C...Raymond of Toulouse
D...Robert of Normandy
Second Crusade
E...Conrad III
F...Louis VII
Third Crusade
G...English Fleet
H...Frederick Barbarossa
J Philip
K...Richard
Fourth Crusade
First Crusade of Louis IX
Second Crusade of Louis IX
KINGDOM OF NORWAY
Bergen
Oslo
KINGDOM OF SWEDEN
KINGDOM OF DENMARK
Roskilde
Lund
Calma
SCOTLAND
Berwick
IRELAND
Armagh
Dublin
Waterford
Wexford
KINGDOM OF ENGLAND
Newcastle
York
Lincoln
Chester
London
Winchester
Southampton
Canterbury
North Sea
Atlantic Ocean
English Channel
Bay of Biscay
Calais
Bruges
Ghent
Hamburg
Oldenburg
Lübeck
Bremen
Brunswick
Magdeburg
Danz
Gneseno
Posen
Cologne
GERMAN-ROMAN OR HOLY ROMAN EMPIRE
Bouillon
Trier
Mainz
Nuremberg
Prague
Metz
Regensburg
Strassburg
Augsburg
Vienna
Basel
Salzburg
ALPS
Milan
Pavia
Venice
Turin
Genoa
Ravenna
Florence
Pisa
Rome
Zara
Spalato
Ragusa
Adriatic
KINGDOM OF FRANCE
Rouen
Reims
Paris
Rennes
Orleans
Troyes
Tours
Vezelay
Poitiers
Limoges
Clermont
Lyon
Angouleme
Bordeaux
Vienne
Toulouse
Narbonne
Aigues-Mortes
Avignon
Arles
Marseille
KDM. OF LEON
Leon
Oporto
PORTUGAL
Lisbon
Burgos
Pamplona
KDM OF NAVARRE
PYRENEES
KINGDOM OF CASTILE
Valladolid
Salamanca
Saragossa
Toledo
KDM. OF ARAGON
Lerida
Barcelona
DOMINIONS OF THE ALMORAVIDES
Cordova
Seville
Cadiz
Granada
Murcia
Valencia
Almeria
Cartagena
Tangier
BALEARIC ISLANDS
CORSICA
SARDINIA
Tyrrhenian Sea
Mediterranean
Naples
Amalfi
Bari
Brindisi
NORMAN KDM. OF SICILY
Messina
Reggio
Palermo
SICILY
Syracuse
Tunis
DOMINIONS OF THE ALMOHAD (UNITARIAN) MOHAMMEDANS
A-450023-29-1-1-1-1

CHARLEMAGNE'S EMPIRE 814
Showing Division by Treaty of Verdun 843
West Frankish Kingdom of Charles the Bald
East Frankish Kingdom of Louis the German
Central Kingdom of Lothaire
States of the Church
ENGLAND
WALES
London
Dublin
Chester
Thetford
Winchester
Canterbury
Crediton
North Sea
English Channel
FRISIA
Utrecht
Bremen
Verden
SAXONY
WILTZI
Elbe
Detmold
Corvey
Paderborn
THURINGIA
Cologne
Heristal
Aachen
Fulda
St. Riquier
Quierzy
Rouen
Soissons
Reims
AUSTRASIA
Trier
Mainz
Ingleheim
Worms
Thionville
Metz
Verdun
St. Denis
Paris
NORDGAU
Ratisbon
WENDS
MARCH OF BRITTANY
NEUSTRIA
Seine
Rennes
Orleans
Nantes
Tours
ALAMANNIA
Strassburg
Augsburg
Passau
BAVARIA
Salzburg
Langres
Auxerre
Luxeuil
Basel
St. Gall
CARINTHIA
AVARS
Loire
Chasseneuil
Bourges
Autun
Poitiers
ALPS
Atlantic Ocean
AQUITAINE
Saintes
Limoges
Clermont
Perigueux
Geneva
Lyon
Vienne
LOMBARDY
Milan
Pavia
Venice
Aquileia
MARCH OF FRIULI
CARNIOLA
Drave
Danube
Save
SERBS
Bordeaux
BURGUNDY
Genoa
Bologna
Ravenna
Roncesvalles
Toulouse
Nimes
Arles
Marseille
Florence
Pisa
Arno
Adriatic Sea
Pamplona
PYRENEES
SPANISH MARCH
Narbonne
STATES OF THE CHURCH
Spoleto
DUCHY OF SPOLETO
CALIPHATE OF CORDOVA
Saragossa
Ebro
Barcelona
Mediterranean Sea
CORSICA
Rome
DUCHY OF BENEVENTO
LITHUANIA
CUMANS OR POLOVZIANS
Dniester
Dnieper
CHAZARS
Caspian Sea
CAUCASUS
Cherson
Black Sea
Danube
KDM. OF BULGARIA
Varna
Trebizond
Constantinople
Nicomedia
Nicaea
Adrianople
Thessalonica
Angora
SELJUK KINGDOM OF ICONIUM
Dorylaeum
BYZANTINE EMPIRE
Aegean Sea
COUNTY OF EDESSA
Edessa
Mosul
Tigris
Heraclea
ARMENIA
Iconium
Smyrna
Thebes
Athens
Aleppo
PRIN. OF ANTIOCH
Antioch
Euphrates
CALIPHATE OF BAGDAD
Bagdad
Hamah
Homs
Tripoli
CO. OF TRIPOLI
Nicosia
Famagusta
CYPRUS
Limasol
RHODES
SULTANATE OF DAMASCUS
Damascus
Beirut
Tyre
Candia
CRETE
KINGDOM OF JERUSALEM
Acre
Tiberias
Jaffa
Jerusalem
Ascalon
Kerak
Damietta
Alexandria
Mansurah
CALIPHATE OF CAIRO
Cairo
Nile
Red Sea

THE AGE OF DISCOVERY
Spanish discoveries
Colombo Portuguese discoveries
Dutch Explorers
English Explorers
French Explorers
Italian Explorers
Russian Explorers
Portuguese Explorers
Spanish Explorers
Return voyages usually not shown
Pacific Ocean
Atlantic Ocean
Equator
Gulf of Mexico
Caribbean Sea
Hudson Bay
Baffin Bay
BAFFIN I.
GREENLAND
ICELAND
FAEROES IS.
Bristol
St. Malo
PORTUGAL
SPAIN
Lisbon
Sanlúcar
Palos
AZORES IS. (1431)
MADEIRA IS. (1330-1418)
CANARY IS. (1341)
CAPE VERDE IS. (1456)
C. BOJADOR
Rounded by Gil Eanes 1434
CAPE VERDE
Discovered by Dinis Dias 1445
Tombouctou
São Jorge da Mina
Vivaldi fate unknown 1291
Cíbola
Culiacán
Tenochtitlán
GUATEMALA
Hochelaga
Stadacona
S. SALVADOR
CUBA
ESPAÑOLA
BORINQUÉN (PUERTO RICO)
Panamá
Darien
Santa Marta
Coro
Guayaquil
Quito
Tumbes
Cajamarca
Lima
Cuzco
Santiago
Asunción
VERA CRUZ (Later Brazil)
Strait of Magellan
Bay of San Julian
TIERRA DEL FUEGO
Bay of San Julián (Magellan wintered 1520)
Rio de la Plata (Discovered by Vespucci 1501)
Marcos 1539
Ulloa 1539
Cortés 1519
Vespucci
Magellan 1521
(Route Suggested by George Emra Nunn 1934)
Miño & Gonzalez 1522
Columbus IV
Balboa 1509-1513
Pizzaro 1530
Aguirre 1561
Orellana 1541
Pizzaro 1532-1533
Valdivia 1540-1541
Gamboa 1579-1580
Cabeza de Vaca 1540
Rio de la Plata
Vespucci 1501
Magellan Expedition 1519
Vespucci 1498 (Conjectural)
Columbus I 1492
Vespucci 1497
Columbus II 1493
Columbus IV 1502
Columbus III 1498
Vespucci 1499
Vespucci 1501
Cabral 1500
da Gama
El Cano 1519
Cão 1482
Dei 1469
Velho 1431
Corte-Real 1500
Corte-Real 1501
El Cano 1522
Cabral 1500
Vasco da Gama 1497
Hudson 1610
Cabot
Frobisher 1576
Davis Str.
Davis 1587
Cartier 1535
Hudson 1609
John Cabot 1497
Baffin 1616
Frobisher 1576
Sebastian Cabot 1508
Cartier 1534
Projection courtesy of American Geographical Society

Atlassov 1697
Kolyma R.
Nizhne
Okhotsk
Yakutsk
Poyarkov
Lena
Amur
JAPAN
LADRONES (MARIANAS IS.)
GUAM
Magellan 1521
Equator
RYU KYU IS.
NOVAYA ZEMLYA
Enisei
L. Baikal (Discovered 1643)
Peking
Pires 1517
Mota 1542
FORMOSA
Perhaps visited by Europeans before Magellan. Spanish conquest began under Miguel Lopez de Legaspi, 1565.
Vilalobos 1542
Ob
CHINA (Ming Empire)
LUZON
Canton
Macau
Alvares
PHILIPPINE IS.
MINDANAO
NEW GUINEA (PAPUA)
After Magellan's death his expedition wandered aimlessly for months.
GILOLO
TERNATE
TIDORE
MOLUCCAS
BANDA IS.
Archangel
Chancellor
Jenkinson
Goes 1602-1607
TIBET
Brahmaputra
1513
Serrão 1512
Moscow
Volga
SIAM
Mandalay
Pegu
BORNEO
Mota
Alvares 1513
Abreu 1511
Conterini
Conterini 1474
Astrakhan
Jenkinson
Bokhara
Delhi
Ganges
Goes
Agra
Conti
AUSTRALIA (Undiscovered)
Derbend
Caspian Sea
INDIA (Mogul Empire after 1526)
Malacca
Conti
JAVA
Kaffa
Tiflis
Black Sea
Tabriz
PERSIA
Indus
SUMATRA
Damão
Diu
Bassein
Chaul
Ispahan
Baghdad
Basra
Ormuz
Conti
Mailapur
Goa
Vijayanagar
Sequeira 1509
Damascus
Jerusalem
Persian Gulf
Muscat
Cananor
Calicut
CEYLON
Mediterranean Sea
Alexandria
Cairo
Cochin
Colombo
Red Sea
Covilha
Cabral
Vasco da Gama 1498
Aden
Indian Ocean
ABYSSINIA
Covilha 1491?
El Cano commanding Victoria (Magellan) Expedition
Malindi
Mombasa
Kilwa
Covilha ?
Zaire and Mani Congo discovered by Diogo Cão 1482-1483
Mozambique
MADAGASCAR Discovered by Diogo Dias (Cabral Expedition 1500)
Sofala
CAPE CROSS Discovered by Diogo Cão 1485
Discovered by B. Dias 1488
Diogo Dias 1500
B. Dias 1487

EUROPE IN 1721
After the treaty of Utrecht, 1713, and Associated Treaties
Miles 0 50 100 200 300
Boundary of Holy Roman Empire
× × Dutch Barrier Forts
20°
10°
0°
50°
40°
SHETLAND ISLANDS
ORKNEY ISLANDS
HEBRIDES
Bergen
Stavanger
SCOTLAND
Aberdeen
KINGDOM OF GREAT BRITAIN
Edinburgh
Glasgow
Belfast
IRELAND
Dublin
Cork
York
Liverpool
Nottingham
WALES
ENGLAND
Norwich
Cambridge
Oxford
Bristol
Thames
London
Plymouth
Portsmouth
Dunkirk
BEACHY HEAD
North Sea
Atlantic Ocean
English Channel
LA HOGUE
THE UNITED NETHERLANDS
Amsterdam
The Hague
Utrecht
Ryswick
Antwerp
Neerwinden
Aachen
Oudenarde
Lille
Ramillies
Fontenoy
Malplaquet
AUSTRIAN NETHERLANDS
(1714)
Rouen
Reims
Paris
Seine
Brest
St. Malo
Lorient
Nancy
LORRAINE
Strassburg
Orléans
Loire
Nantes
Tours
Besançon
Basel
FRANCE
Bay of Biscay
Rochefort
Limoges
Angoulême
Lyon
Geneva
SAVOY
Turin
Bordeaux
Garonne
Rhone
CAPE FINISTERRE
Bayonne
Toulouse
Montpellier
Avignon
(To the Pope)
Marseille
Toulon
PYRENEES
Oporto
Burgos
Valladolid
Ebro
Duero
CATALONIA
Saragossa
Barcelona
PORTUGAL
Madrid
SPAIN
Tagus
Alcantara
Toledo
(To Bourbons, 1713)
Valencia
Lisbon
Guadiana
BALEARIC ISLANDS
MINORCA
(To Great Britain 1713)
MAJORCA
SARDINIA
(To Hapsburgs 17
(To Savoy 1720)
CORS
(To Ge
CAPE ST. VINCENT
Guadalquivir
Seville
Granada
Cartagena
Cadiz
CAPE TRAFALGAR
Gibraltar
(To Great Britain 1713)
Algiers
Medit

A-450035-29-1-2-1-1[BY]

EASTERN AND SOUTHERN ASIA
About 1775
MILES 0 500 1,000 2,000
China proper
Rest of Chinese Empire
Chinese territory to northern waters of Amur and Sakhalin
Dutch territory
British territory
Omsk
Tomsk
RUSSIAN OUTP
KAZAKHS
Kobdo
OIRAT MONGOLS
Tarbugatai
TIEN SHAN PEI LU
Ili (Kulja)
Urumtsi
Hami
BOKHARA
Bokhara
Kokand
KOKAND
Kashgar
TIEN SHAN NAN LU
Yarkand
UIGHURS
Khotan
KASHMIR
LADAKH
Leh
Kabul
Peshawar
Kandahar
AFGHAN EMPIRE
PUNJAB
Lahore
SIKHS
NGARI
TIBET
Multan
MOGUL EMPIRE
BALUCHISTAN
Indus
WEI
TSANG
Lhasa
RAJPUT STATES
Panipat
Delhi
NEPAL
SIND
Ajmir
Jodhpur
Jaipur
Agra
Ganges
Lucknow
OUDH
Allahabad
BHUTAN
Gwalior
Patna
BIHAR
Benares
BENGAL
ASSAM
GUJARAT
Ahmadabad
MARATHA EMPIRE
Narbada
Broach
Baroda
Murshidabad
Dacca
Chandernagore (Fr. from 1676)
Plassey
Surat
Burhanpur
Calcutta (Br. from 1690)
Chittagong
Arabian Sea
Bombay (Br. from 1660)
Bassein
Godavari
Poona
THE NIZAM
(Taken by Burma 178
Hyderabad
NORTHERN SARKARS
(Fr. 1753-1760) (Br. from 1766)
Bay of Bengal
GOA (Port. from 1510)
Masulipatam
MYSORE
CARNATIC
Seringapatam
Arcot
Pulicat (Br. from 1766)
Madras (Br. from 1639)
Calicut
Pondichéry (Fr. from 1673)
ANDAMAN ISLANDS (Br. 1792)
Trichinopoly
Negapatam
Cochin
Tanjore
TRAVANCORE
CEYLON (Dutch from Port. 1660) (Br. from Dutch 1796)
Kandy
Colombo
MOGUL EMPIRE
Under Aurangzeb 1690
MILES 0 500 1,000
Kabul
Lahore
Panipat
Delhi
Agra
RAJPUTS
Patna
Dacca
Surat
MARATHAS
GOLCONDA
GOA (Port.)
BIJAPUR
Madras (Br.)
Pondichéry (Fr.)

Irkutsk
BURIAT MONGOLS
Kiakhta
Nerchinsk
Amur
Tsitsihar
MANCHURIA
Kirin
Urga
MANCHUS
OUTER MONGOLIA
KHALKHA MONGOLS
FORTY NINE MONGOL BANNERS OF INNER MONGOLIA
TORGUT MONGOLS
CHAHAR MONGOLS
Jehol
Shengching (Mukden)
Kalgan
Peking
Great Wall
Paoting
CHIHLI
Taiyüan
SHANSI
KANSU
Huang
Tsinan
SHANTUNG
Grand Canal
KIANGSU
Lanchow
SHENSI
Sian
Kaifeng
HONAN
ANWEI
Chiangning
Anking
Hangchow
HUPEH
Wuchang
CHEKIANG
Chengtu
SZECHWAN
Yangtze
Salween
Changshao
HUNAN
Nanchang
KIANGSI
FUKIEN
Foochow
Kweiyang
KWEICHOW
Kweilin
Yünnan
YUNNAN
KWANGSI
KWANGTUNG
Kwangchow (Canton)
Macao
(Port. trading post from 1557)
Bhamo
TONGKING
Hanoi
Luang Prabang
Thanh Hoa
(Tongking, Annam and Cochin-China formed Vietnam Empire 1802)
Chiengsen
Chiengmai
Vientiane
(Laos states of Luang Prabang and Vientiane, under Siamese Suzerainty from 1778)
SIAM
Sukhotai
Martaban
Lopburi
Ayuthia
(Destroyed by Burmese in 1767)
ANNAM
Hué
Mekong
Tavoy
Bangkok
Siemreap
CAMBODIA
Phnom Penh
Mergui
COCHIN-CHINA
Saigon
(Taken by Annam 1776)
Ligor
Patani
KEDAH
PERAK
PAHANG
Penang
SELANGOR
(Dutch 1641-1795, 1818-1824)
(Br. 1795-1818, since 1824)
Malacca
JOHORE
RIAU ARCH
(Center of Bugis power)
SUMATRA
MINANGKABAU
Siak
Padang
Jambi
Palembang
BANGKA
BILLITON
BORNEO
BRUNEI
Succadana
Banjermassin
CELEBES
Macassar
Menado
MOLUCCAS
HALMAHERA
CERAM
Amboina
KOREA
Seoul
YEZO
JAPAN
HONSHU
Yedo
Kyoto
Osaka
Sakai
SHIKOKU
KYUSHU
Nagasaki
(Dutch trading post of Deshima from 1641)
LIUCHIU
Pacific Ocean
Zelandia Castel
(Dutch, 1624-1662)
FORMOSA
China Sea
Manila
PHILIPPINE ISLANDS
(Spain)
A-469036-29-1-1-1
Copyright by Rand McNally & Company, Made in U.S.A.

BRITISH NORTH AMERICA
UNITED STATES OF AMERICA
Disputed by Spain, Russia, and England
Nootka Sound
Claimed by Spain, but unoccupied
INTENDANCY OF NUEVA CALIFORNIA
San Francisco 1776
Monterey 1770
San Luis Obispo 1772
Santa Barbara
Los Angeles 1781
San Diego 1769
WESTERN INTERIOR PROVINCES
San Juan
INTENDANCY OF NUEVO MEXICO
Santa Fé 1609
PRESIDENCY
El Paso
INTENDANCY del Norte
OF SONORA (AUDIENCIA)
Chihuahua
INTENDANCY OF DURANGO
OF GUADALAJARA
VICEROYALTY OF NEW SPAIN
INTENDANCY OF VIEJA CALIFORNIA
La Paz 1535
Culiacán 1531
INTENDANCY OF GUADALAJARE
INTENDANCY OF ZACATECAS
EASTERN INTERIOR PROVINCES
San Antonio 1718
Laredo 1755
Saltillo
INTENDANCY OF SAN LUIS POTOSI
AUDIENCIA OF MEXICO
Queretaro 1550
Mexico City 1325
INTENDANCY OF VALLADOLID
INTENDANCY OF VERA CRUZ
Vera Cruz 1519
INTENDANCY OF OAXACA
CHIAPAS
St. Louis 1764
CAPTAINCY-GENERAL OF LOUISIANA
Disputed with U.S. 1783-1795
WEST FLORIDA
EAST FLORIDA
Pensacola 1698
New Orleans 1718
St. Augustine 1565
Gulf of Mexico
Habana
CAPTAINCY-GENERAL OF CUBA
Santiago 1514
INTENDANCY OF YUCATAN
Belice
CAPTAINCY-GENERAL (AUDIENCIA) OF GUATEMALA
Guatemala
San Salvador 1525
León 1525
Granada 1524
San José 1738
Cartago 1564
JAMAICA Br. 1655
Port au Prince 1749
Santo Domingo 1496
CAPTAINCY-GENERAL OF SANTO DOMINGO
Ceded to France 1795
PUERTO RICO
San Juan 1511
Caribbean Sea
Gulf of Maracaibo
Portobelo 1584
Panama 1519
Cartagena 1533
Santa Marta 1525
La Guaira 1588
Caracas 1567
CAPTAINCY-GENERAL OF CARACAS
TRINIDAD
Ceded to Great Britain, 1802
VICEROYALTY OF NEW GRANADA
AUDIENCIA OF SANTA FÉ
Bogotá
Established 1717, Restored 1740
Magdalena
Orinoco
Quito
PRESIDENCY (AUDIENCIA) OF QUITO
Guayaquil
GALAPAGOS IS.
Claimed by Spain, but unoccupied
Yapurá
Putumayo
Negro
Barcelos 1658
CAPTAINCY OF
Amazon
Stabroek (Georgetown)
Approx. 1740
Dutch in 1790
DUTCH GUIANA
Paramaribo 1640
Cayenne 1664
FRENCH GUIANA
CAPTAINCY OF
Belem 1616
São Luis
Atlantic Ocean
Tropic of Cancer
Pacific

LATIN AMERICA ABOUT 1790
MILES 0 250 500 1,000
European Colonies
Spain
Great Britain
Netherlands
Portugal
France
Seat of Government
1535 Lima Dates indicate year of founding
VICEROYALTY OF BRAZIL
Definitively established 1714
CAPTAINCY OF PERNAMBUCO
CAPTAINCY OF SERGIPE
CAPTAINCY OF BAÍA
CAPTAINCY OF ESPIRITO SANTO
CAPTAINCY OF MINAS GERAIS
CAPTAINCY OF RIO DE JANEIRO
CAPTAINCY OF SÃO PAULO
CAPTAINCY OF SANTA CATARINA
CAPTAINCY OF RIO GRANDE DO SUL
CAPTAINCY OF GOIAZ
CAPTAINCY OF MATO GROSSO
Recife (Pernambuco) c. 1561
Salvador (Baía) 1549
Tijuco (Diamantina)
Ouro Preto 1698
Rio de Janeiro 1567
Santos 1536
São Paulo 1554
Santa Anna (Goiaz) 1736
Villa Bella (Mato Grosso) 1752
Porto Alegre 1743
Rio Grande 1737
Principe da Beira 1760
Madeira
VICEROYALTY OF LA PLATA
(Established 1776)
PRESIDENCY (AUDIENCIA) OF CHARCAS
PARAGUAY
Abandoned Jesuit Missions
BANDA ORIENTAL
AUDIENCIA OF BUENOS AIRES
Chuquisaca 1538
La Paz 1548
Potosí 1545
Asunción 1537
Salta
Tucumán 1585
Santa Fé 1573
Córdoba 1573
Buenos Aires 1580
Colonia 1680
Montevideo 1724
Mendoza 1561
Rio de la Plata
Paraná
Uruguay
Pilcomayo
VICEROYALTY OF PERU
Established 1542
PRESIDENCY (AUDIENCIA) OF CUZCO
LIMA
Lima 1535
Callao 1537
Cuzco
Trujillo 1535
Ucayali
L. Titicaca
CAPTAINCY-GENERAL (AUDIENCIA) OF CHILE
Loosely joined to Peru
La Serena 1544
Santiago 1541
Valparaíso 1544
Concepción 1550
Valdivia 1552
PATAGONIA
CHILOE I.
TIERRA DEL FUEGO
CAPE HORN
Drake Passage
MALVINAS (FALKLAND ISLANDS)
Tropic of Capricorn
Ocean

EUROPEAN INVASIONS OF RUSSIA
MILES 0 50 100 200 300 400
1815 Boundaries
1920 Boundaries
States colored as of 1920
INVASIONS OF RUSSIA
INVASION ROUTES
Swedish invasions by Charles XII 1700-1709
Napoleon's invasion and retreat from Moscow 1812
Crimean War—Allied invasion of Evpatoriia and battle of Sevastopol
WORLD WAR I
British, French, and U.S. intervention in Russia
Deepest penetrations: (1) German 1918; (2) Polish 1920; and (3) Allied
WORLD WAR II
German advance to Dec. 1941
German advance in 1942
Russian front Dec. 1943
Eastern front Dec. 1944
CRIMEAN WAR
Allied assaults on Russian Coastal areas
Barents Sea
Norwegian Sea
(British, French, American 1918-1919)
Petsamo
Murmansk
NORWAY
SWEDEN
FINLAND
Gulf of Bothnia
White Sea
Arkhangelsk
Onega
Shenkursk
N. Dvina
Pechora
Ob
URAL MTS.
ALAND IS.
Helsinki
Vyborg
Lake Ladoga
Lake Onega
Leningrad was never captured by the Germans
Kronstadt
St. Petersburg (Leningrad)
Narva
Reval
DAGO
OSEL
GOTLAND
Parnau
ESTONIA
Tikhvin
Novgorod
Lake Ilmen
Pskov
Viatka (Kirov)
Perm (Molotov)
Kama
Volga
LATVIA
Riga
Dvinsk
LITHUANIA
Königsberg
EAST PRUSSIA
Kovno
Vilno
Grodno
Polotsk
Vitebsk
Velikie-Luki
Tver (Kalinin)
Borodino
Moscow
Viazma
Smolensk
Nizhni Novgorod (Gorki)
Kazan
Ufa
Minsk
Mogilev
Tula
Oka
RUSSIA
Samara (Kuibyshev)
Orenburg (Chkalov)
Penza
Orel
GERMANY
Berlin
Thorn
Warsaw
Kalisz
Brest
POLAND
Pripet
Vistula
Niemen
Berezina
Desna
Prague
CZECHOSLOVAKIA
Krakow
CARPATHIAN
Lvov
Tarnopol
Chernigov
Baturin
Zhitomir
Kiev
UKRAINE
Kharkov
Poltava
Kursk
Voronezh
Don
Saratov
Uralsk
Ural
Vienna
AUSTRIA
Danube
GALICIA
Budapest
HUNGARY
Theiss
BESSARABIA
MOLDAVIA
Jassy
Dniester
S. Bug
Dnieper
Ekaterinoslav (Dnepropetrovsk)
Donets
Tsaritsyn (Stalingrad)
Gurev
Astrakhan
TRANSYLVANIA
Nikolaev
Odessa
Kherson
Taganrog
Rostov
1855
Sea of Azov
Kinburn
RUMANIA
WALLACHIA
Galati
Bucharest
Evpatoriia
Kerch
Ekaterinodar (Krasnodar)
Stavropol
Kuban
Kuma
Sevastopol
Novorossiisk
1854
Belgrade
YUGOSLAVIA
Drave
Save
Morava
BULGARIA
Varna
Burgas
BALKAN MTS.
Sofia
Maritsa
Black Sea
(British 1918-1919)
(French 1918-19)
Grozny
CAUCASUS
Caspian Sea
ALBANIA
Vardar
Salonika
GREECE
Constantinople
Bosporus
Sinope
Batum
Tiflis
Kura
Baku
Krasnovodsk
Sea of Marmora
Sakarya
Angora
ARMENIA
Aras
Lenkoran
Aegean Sea
Dardanelles
TURKEY
Kizil Irmak
Smyrna
Konia
Menderes
TAURUS MTS.
Euphrates
Tigris
Tabriz
PERSIA
(British) (1918-19)
Teheran
Mosul
IRAQ
SYRIA
Aleppo
RHODES
1700-1702
1705
1707-1709
(British) (1918-19)
Allies
Germans 1918
Polish 1920
Russian front Dec. 1943
Eastern front Dec. 1944
German advance to Dec. 1941
German advance in 1941
German advance 1942
70°
60°
50°
40°
10°
0°
20°
30°
50°
A-470196-29-1-1-1-1

EXPANSION OF RUSSIA IN ASIA
MILES 0 100 200 400 600 800
Russia 1533
Russia 1598
Acquired to 1689
Greatest extent of Empire
Spheres of influence
Transiberian Railroad 1914
1595 Dates indicate establishment or conquest of cities.
1873 Dates indicate annexation of areas.
A-470295-29-1-1-1
Copyright by Rand McNally & Company, Made in U.S.A.

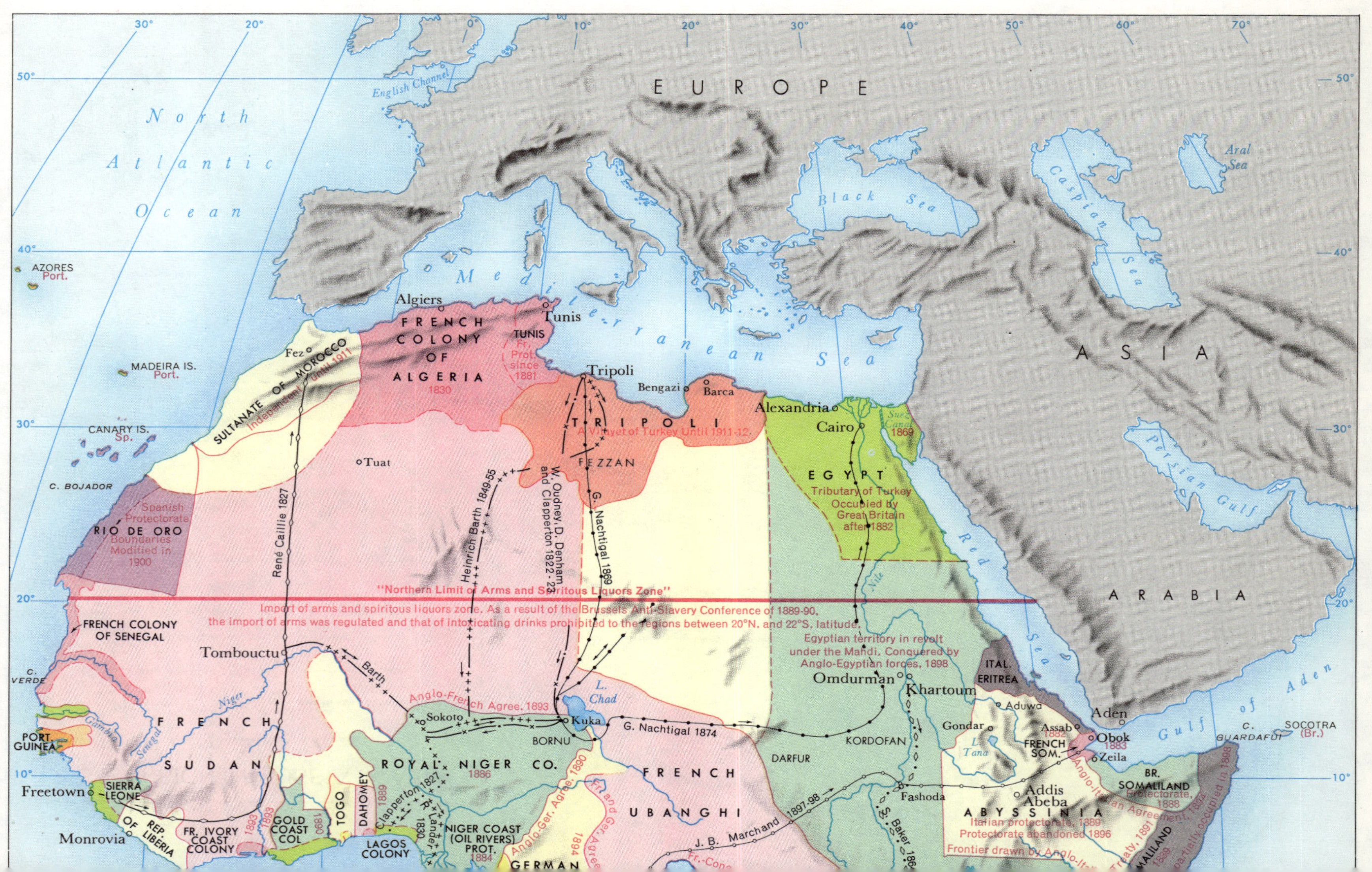

EUROPE
ASIA
ARABIA
Caspian Sea
Aral Sea
Black Sea
Mediterranean Sea
Red Sea
Persian Gulf
Gulf of Aden
North Atlantic Ocean
English Channel
AZORES Port.
MADEIRA IS. Port.
CANARY IS. Sp.
C. BOJADOR
C. VERDE
SOCOTRA (Br.)
C. GUARDAFUI
Suez Canal 1869
Alexandria
Cairo
EGYPT
Tributary of Turkey Occupied by Great Britain after 1882
Nile
Omdurman
Khartoum
Egyptian territory in revolt under the Mahdi. Conquered by Anglo-Egyptian forces, 1898
KORDOFAN
DARFUR
Fashoda
S. Baker 186
ITAL. ERITREA
Aduwo
Assab 1882
Aden
Obok 1883
FRENCH SOM.
Zeila
BR. SOMALILAND Protectorate, 1888
Gondar
L. Tana
Addis Abeba
ABYSSINIA
Italian protectorate, 1889 Protectorate abandoned 1896
Frontier drawn by Anglo-It
Anglo-Italian Agreement, 1894
Treaty, 1891
Partially occupied in 1889
Tripoli
Bengazi
Barca
TRIPOLI
A Vilayet of Turkey Until 1911-12
FEZZAN
G. Nachtigal 1869
G. Nachtigal 1874
W. Oudney, D. Denham and Clapperton 1822-23
Heinrich Barth 1849-55
Tunis
TUNIS Fr. Prot. since 1881
Algiers
FRENCH COLONY OF ALGERIA 1830
Tuat
Fez
SULTANATE OF MOROCCO Independent until 1911
René Caillie 1827
RIO DE ORO Spanish Protectorate Boundaries Modified in 1900
"Northern Limit of Arms and Spiritous Liquors Zone"
Import of arms and spiritous liquors zone. As a result of the Brussels Anti-Slavery Conference of 1889-90, the import of arms was regulated and that of intoxicating drinks prohibited to the regions between 20°N. and 22°S. latitude.
L. Chad
Kuka
BORNU
FRENCH UBANGHI
J. B. Marchand 1897-98
Fr. and Ger. Agree 1894
Anglo-Ger. Agree. 1890
GERMAN
Fr.-Cong
Anglo-French Agree. 1893
ROYAL NIGER CO. 1886
Sokoto
Clapperton 1827
Lander 1830
NIGER COAST (OIL RIVERS) PROT. 1884
Barth
LAGOS COLONY
DAHOMEY 1889
TOGO
GOLD COAST COL 1890
Tombouctu
Niger
FRENCH SUDAN
FR. IVORY COAST COLONY 1893
REP. OF LIBERIA
Monrovia
SIERRA LEONE
Freetown
PORT. GUINEA
Gambia
Senegal
FRENCH COLONY OF SENEGAL

THE PARTITION OF AFRICA
MILES 0 500 1,000
CONTROL OF TERRITORY
Great Britain 1885
Great Britain 1898
France 1885
France 1898
Turkey
Congo Free State 1885
Congo Free State (Belgium) 1898
Germany 1885
Germany 1898
Spain 1885
Spain 1898
Portugal 1885
Portugal 1898
Italy
South Atlantic Ocean
Indian Ocean
Mozambique Channel
CORISCO BAY
Rio Muni, Sp.
ANNOBAN
Sp.
COLONY OF FRENCH CONGO
1885
Brazzaville
Leopoldville
CABINDA
Port.
Boma
CONGO FREE STATE
Under Sovereignty of Leopold II of Belgium after 1885
1874-77
Anglo-Ger. Tr. 1890
L. Tanganyika
L. Mweru
L. Bangweolu
Ujiji
Stanley I 1871-72
Stanley II
Burton-Speke 1856
Anglo-German Treaty
1886
Anglo Ger. Treaty, 1890
GERMAN EAST AFRICA
PEMBA
ZANZIBAR
British Prot., 1890
Leased from Zanzibar 1888
Purchased 1890
Luanda
PORTUGUESE WEST AFRICA
ANGOLA
1885
1894
1891
Livingstone II 1854
Ivens and Capelo 1877-80
Benguela
Serpa-Pinto
Mossamedes
Capelo and Ivens 1884-85
1877-79
Anglo-Port. Agree. 1891
Anglo-Port. Boy. 1905
BRITISH CENTRAL AFRICA PROTECTORATE
1891
1894
Livingstone III 1860
L. Nyassa
Rovuma
Livingstone IV
PORT. EAST AFRICA
Mozambique
Livingstone III
Quelimane
Victoria Falls
Zambezi
Livingstone II 1856
C. FRIO
German-Port. Tr. 1886
GERMAN SOUTHWEST AFRICA
Anglo-Ger. Agree. 1890
BRITISH SOUTH AFRICA CO.
Chartered, 1889
Conquered Matabeleland, 1893
Anglo-Portuguese Frontier
"Southern Limit of Arms and Spirituous Liquors Zone"
WALFISH BAY
Br. 1878
BECHUANALAND PROTECTORATE
1885-
SOUTH AFRICAN REP (TRANSVAAL)
Pretoria
Limpopo
Lourenco Marques
SWAZILAND
Johannesburg
BECHUANALAND
British Colony
1885
Vaal
Lüderitz Bay
(Angra Pequena)
ORANGE FREE STATE
Serpa-Pinto
COLONY OF NATAL
Durban
Orange
Bloemfontein
Livingstone I 1849 & II 1854
BASUTOLAND
CAPE COLONY
Capetown
Br. 1806
C. OF GOOD HOPE
MADAGASCAR
French Conquest Completed 1896
Tamatave
Antananarive
A-480041-29-1-1-1-1
Copyright by Rand McNally & Company, Made in U.S.A.

THE WORLD ABOUT 1900
Showing the colonial empires,
showing also the more recent Arctic explorations
EQUATORIAL SCALE 1:131,472,000 2,075 STATUTE MILES TO ONE INCH
U.S. territory
British territory
French territory
German territory
Russian territory
Turkish territory
Italian territory
Belgian territory
Netherlands territory
Portuguese territory
Spanish territory
Japanese territory
(Robert Peary reached North Pole April 16 1909)
CAPE COLUMBIA
GRANT LAND
ELLESMERE
ISLAND
Kane Bay
Peary 1892-1895
Arctic Ocean
PRINCE PATRICK I.
Banks Strait
MELVILLE I.
DEVON I.
BANKS I.
Baffin Bay
GREENLAND
(To Denmark)
WRANGEL I.
VICTORIA
ISLAND
BOOTHIA PENINSULA
BAFFIN ISLAND
JAN MAYEN
(Nor.)
Peary 1886
Nordenskiöld 1883
DISKO I.
Nansen 1888
Nordenskiöld
Russian America until 1867
Ft. Yukon
KLONDIKE
Dawson
Ft. Selkirk
ALASKA
Nome City
St. Michaels
ST. LAWRENCE I.
(U.S.)
DOMINION OF CANADA
Hudson Bay
LABRADOR
(To Newfoundland)
Reykjavik
CAPE FAREWELL
FAEROES
(Denmark)
SHETLAND
ORKNEY IS.
SCOTLAND
Glasgow
IRELAND
Dublin
Bering Sea
Skagway
Juneau
Sitka
ALEUTIAN IS.
(U.S. 1867)
G. W. DeLong in Jeannette 1879
NEWFOUNDLAND
Vancouver
Seattle
Quebec
Montreal
Ottawa
Halifax
Chicago
Boston
New York
Washington
Pacific Ocean
Atlantic Ocean
Salt Lake City
San Francisco
UNITED STATES
Los Angeles
New Orleans
PORTUGAL
Lisbon
Gibraltar
AZORES
(Port.)
BERMUDA IS.
(Br.)
MADEIRA IS.
(Port.)
MIDWAY IS.
(U.S. after 1867)
Gulf of Mexico
MEXICO
BAHAMA IS. (Br.)
CANARY IS.
(Sp.)
RIO DE ORO
(Sp.)
HAWAIIAN IS.
(U.S. after 1898)
CUBA
(Sp. To 1898)
HAITI
PUERTO RICO (U.S. 1898)
DANISH WEST INDIES
GUADELOUPE (Fr.)
MARTINIQUE (Fr.)
BARBADOS (Br.)
TRINIDAD (Br.)
Verá Cruz
Mexico City
JAMAICA
BR.
GUAT.
HOND.
SALVADOR
NIC.
C. R.
Caribbean Sea
CAPE VERDE IS.
(Port.)
CLIPPERTON I.
(Fr.)
Caracas
VENEZUELA
PORT. GUINEA
SIERRA LEONE
LIBERIA
GOLD CO.
REP. OF COLOMBIA
Bogotá
BR. DU. FR.
GUIANA
CHRISTMAS I.
(Br. 1888)
Quito
ECUADOR
Belem
UNITED STATES OF BRAZIL
Recife
ASCENSION
(Br.)
MARQUESAS IS.
(Fr.)
PERU
BOLIVIA
Callao
Lima
São Salvador
SAMOA IS.
(Ger. 1899)
(U.S. 1899)
SOCIETY IS.
(Fr. 1880)
TUAMOTU IS.
(Fr. 1881)
Mollendo
La Paz
Arica
ST. HELENA
(Br.)
TONGA OR FRIENDLY IS.
(Br. 1899)
São Paulo
Rio de Janeiro
Antofagasta
PARAGUAY
Asuncion
Santos
EASTER I. (Chile)
Valparaiso
Santiago
Montevideo
URUGUAY
Buenos Aires
TRISTAN DA CUNHA
(Br.)
JUAN FERNANDEZ IS.
(Chile)
CHILE
ARGENTINA
FALKLAND IS.
(Br.)
TIERRA DEL FUEGO
CAPE HORN
160° 140° 120° 100° 80° 60° 40° 20°
80° 60° 40° 20° 0° 20° 40° 60°

Arctic Ocean
Fridtjof Nansen in Fram 1893-1896
SPITSBERGEN (Norway 1920)
FRANZ JOSEF LAND OR FRIDTJOF NANSEN LAND (Russia 1928)
NORTHERN LAND (NICHOLAS II)
Duke of Abruzzi in Stella Polare 1900
Duke of Abruzzi 1900
Beron Adolf Erik Nordenskiöld in Vega 1878-1879
NEW SIBERIAN ISLANDS
DE LONG IS.
DeLong 1879-1881
WRANGEL I.
De Long Strait
BEAR I. (Nor.)
Barents Sea
NOVAYA ZEMLYA
Kara Sea
TAIMYR PENINSULA
Nansen 1893-1896
Hammerfest
NORTH CAPE
Vardö
LOFOTEN
KDM. OF SWEDEN AND NORWAY
GR. DUCHY OF FINLAND
Russian Tsar Grand Duke since 1809
Archangel
RUSSIAN EMPIRE
Yakutsk
Christiania
Stockholm
St. Petersburg
Tobolsk
Tomsk
Krasnoyarsk
Moscow
Ufa
Kurgan
Omsk
Trans-Siberian Railway
Samara
Irkutsk
Lake Baikal
Chita
Blagoveshchensk
SAKHALIN (Russia 1875)
Petropavlovsk
Sea of Okhotsk
Hamburg
GER. EMP.
Berlin
Warsaw
Vienna
AUS. HUNG.
Budapest
Odessa
SERB.
RUM.
BUL.
Black Sea
ITALY
Rome
Naples
Constantinople
Aral Sea
Lake Balkhash
Caspian Sea
MONGOLIA
MANCHURIA
Urga
Khabarovsk
KURILE IS.
Harbin
Vladivostok
Moukden
KULJA (Russia 1871-1881)
EMPIRE OF CHINA
SINKIANG
Kashgar
Peking
Port Arthur (Russia 1898)
Weihaiwei (Br. 1898)
KOREA
EMPIRE OF JAPAN
Tokyo
Yokohama
TURKISH EMPIRE
GREECE
Merv (1885)
Teheran
Kabul
AFG.
TIBET
Lhasa
Ching, Manchu Dynasty since 1644
Tsing Tao (Ger. 1897)
Shanghai
Pacific Ocean
TUNIS
MALTA (Br.)
CRETE (Gr. 1898)
CYPRUS (Br. 1878)
Bagdad
PERSIA
BALUCH. (Br. 1876)
Delhi
NEPAL
BHUTAN
CHINA PROPER
RYUKYU IS. (Jap. 1879)
OGASAWARA IS. (BONIN IS.) (Jap. 1878)
TRIPOLI (Turk.)
Alexandria
EGYPT
ARABIA
BRITISH INDIAN EMPIRE
also many semiautonomous Indian states
BURMA
Macao (Port.)
Hong Kong (Br.)
FORMOSA (Jap. since 1895)
MARCUS I. (Jap. 1899)
OMAN
Muscat
Mecca
Calcutta
Mandalay
Kwangchawwan (Fr. 1898)
KURIA MURIA IS. (Br.)
GOA (Port.)
Bombay
INDIA
Rangoon
FR. INDO-CHINA
SIAM
Bangkok
MARIANAS (Ger. 1899)
WAKE I. (U.S. 1898)
SUDAN
ERIT.
ADEN
ABYSSINIA
SOCOTRA (Br. 1886)
Mahé (Fr.)
Madras
Pondichéry
ANDAMAN IS. (Br.)
PHILIPPINE IS. (U.S. 1899)
GUAM (U.S. 1898)
CAROLINES (Ger. 1899)
MARSHALL IS. (Ger. 1899)
Lake Chad
KAMERUN
FR. SOM.
BR. SOM.
IT. SOM.
LACCADIVE IS. (Br.)
CEYLON
MALDIVE IS. (Br.)
NICOBAR IS. (Br.)
STRAITS SETTLEMENTS
SARAWAK (Br. 1888)
N. BORNEO (1888)
PELEW IS. (Ger. 1899)
GILBERT IS. (Br. 1899)
CONGO FREE STATE
Ruled by Leopold II of Belgium
E. AFR.
Singapore
SUMATRA
BORNEO
MOLUCCA
NEW GUINEA
(Neth. 1901)
(Ger. 1884)
(Br. 1884)
NEW MECKLENBURG
BISMARCK IS. (Ger. 1884)
ELLICE IS. (Br. 1892)
GER. E. AFR.
ZANZIBAR (Br. 1890)
SEYCHELLES (Br.)
CELEBES
(Port.) TIMOR (Neth.)
NEW POMERANIA
SOLOMON IS. Div. between Br. and Ger. 1899
Loanda
ANGOLA
RHODESIA
COMORO IS. (Fr.)
JAVA
Indian Ocean
COCOS IS (Br. 1876)
Darwin
NORTHERN TERRITORY
NEW HEBRIDES
FIJI IS. (Br. 1874)
Mozambique
PORT. E. AFR.
MADAGASCAR (Fr. 1896)
MAURITIUS (Br.)
REUNION (Fr.)
GER. S.W. AFR.
BECHUANA-LAND
TRANS-VAAL
Lourenço Marques
COMMONWEALTH OF AUSTRALIA
(including Tasmania formed in 1901)
WESTERN AUSTRALIA
QUEENSLAND
NEW CALEDONIA (Fr.)
LOYALTY IS. (Fr. 1864)
ORANGE FREE STATE
CAPE COLONY
NATAL
Capetown
Brisbane
SOUTH AUSTRALIA
Perth
NEW SOUTH WALES
Sydney
Adelaide
VICTORIA
Melbourne
Ocean
TASMANIA
Wellington
NEW ZEALAND
Organized as a Dominion in 1907
20° 40° 60° 80° 100° 120° 140° 160°
80° 60° 40° 20° 0° 20° 40° 60°
A-410041-29-1-1-1-1

BALKAN PENINSULA TO 1914
Including Austria-Hungary, 1867
MILES 0 25 50 100 150
Austro-Hungarian Empire, 1867
Limit of Ottoman Empire, 1815
Boundary established by Congress of Berlin, 1878
Boundary established by Treaty of San Stefano, 1878
States colored as of 1914
GERMANY
RUSSIA
AUSTRIAN EMPIRE
KINGDOM OF HUNGARY
CARPATHIANS
GALICIA
RUTHENIA
BUKOVINA
TRANSYLVANIA
BANAT
CROATIA-SLAVONIA
BOSNIA-HERZEGOVINA
Occupied 1878, Annexed 1908
To Serbia 1833
DALMATIA
DINARIC ALPS
SERBIA
1804
Independent 1878
To Serbia 1833
To Serbia 1878
SANDJAK OF NOVI PAZAR
MONTENEGRO
To Montenegro 1878
To Montenegro 1913
ALBANIA
Independent 1912-13
MACEDONIA
To Serbia 1912-13
To Greece 1913
To Bulgaria 1913
BULGARIA
Independent 1908
BALKAN MTS.
SHIPKA PASS
EASTERN RUMELIA
United to Bulgaria 1885
RHODOPE MTS.
RUMANIA
Independent 1878
WALLACHIA
United with Moldavia 1856
MOLDAVIA
BESSARABIA
To Russia 1812
To Moldavia 1856
Returned to Russia 1878
DOBRUDJA
To Rumania 1878
Ceded to Rumania 1913
TURKEY
ANATOLIA
GREECE
Independent 1830
To Greece 1881
PINDUS MTS.
EUBOEA
MOREA
IONIAN ISLANDS
Br. Protectorate 1815-1863
To Greece 1863
Islands to Greece 1913
DODECANESE ISLANDS
To Italy 1912
CRETE
Autonomous 1898
United to Greece 1908-1913
ITALY
Adriatic Sea
Ionian Sea
Aegean Sea
Black Sea
Sea of Marmora
Straits of Otranto
Bosporus
Dardanelles
GALLIPOLI
Danube
Vistula
Theiss
Drava
Sava
Bosna
Neretva
Morava
Drin
Vardar
Struma
Mesta
Maritsa
Tundzha
Kamchia
Iskar
Iantra
Aluta
Oltul
Maros (Muresul)
Sereth (Siretul)
Prut
Dniester
Southern Bug
Gediz
Menderes
Lake Balaton
Lake Ohrid
IRON GATE
Krakow
Tarnow
Przemysl
Lemberg (Lvov)
Tarnopol
Prešov
Stanislav
Kamenets-Podolsk
Czernowitz
Balta
Vienna
Bratislava (Pressburg)
Gyor
Budapest
Debrecen
Graz
Maribor (Marburg)
Grosswardein (Oradea Mare)
Klausenberg (Cluj)
Szegedin
Arad
Zagreb (Agram)
Mohacs
Subotica
Temesvar
Hermannstadt (Sibiu)
Osijek (Esseg)
Novi Sad
Jassy
Kishinev
Bender
Odessa
Akkerman
Galati
Braila
Sulina
Banja Luka
Belgrade
Orsova
Ploesti
Bucharest
Požarevac
Craiova
Užice
Kragujevac
Zaječar
Sarajevo
Vidin
Turtukai
Silistria
Giurgevo
Ruschuk
Constantsa
Kuchuk-Kainardji
Split
Niš
Sistova
Plevna
Shumla
Varna
Mostar
Metković
Novi Pazar
Pirot
Caribrod
Tyrnovo
Dubrovnik (Ragusa)
Independent 1878
Peć
Priština
Vranje
Sofia
Slivno
Burgas
Cattaro
Cetinje
Kustendil
Samokov
Philippopolis (Plovdiv)
Prizren
Kumanovo
Scutari
Skoplje (Uskub)
Veles
Adrianople (Edirne)
Midia
Durazzo
Debar
Petrich
Strumitsa
Tirana
Ohrid
Serres
Kavalla
Constantinople
Unkiar-Skellesi
Bari
Brindisi
Taranto
Bitolj (Monastir)
Dedeagatch
Enos
THASOS
Berat
Salonika
SAMOTHRAKI
Valona
Kastoria
MT. ATHOS
IMBROS
Brusa
LIMNOS
Kalabaka
Larisa
Balikesir
CORFU
Jannina
Volos
MYTILENE
Akhisar
Preveza
LEVKAS
KEPHALONIA
Mesolonghi
CHIOS
Smyrna
Patrai
Athens
SAMOS
ZANTE
Nauplia
NICARIA
NAXOS
Kalamata
Navarino
KOS
Monemvasia
CERIGO
RHODES
KARPATHOS
Canea
Candia
16°
20°
24°
28°
48°
44°
40°
36°

EUROPE IN 1914
MILES 0 50 100 200 300 400
European Allied States of World War I
Central States of World War I
Neutral states
ICELAND (Danish)
THE FAEROES
SHETLAND ISLANDS (To Gr. Britain)
ORKNEY IS.
SCOTLAND
GREAT BRITAIN
IRELAND
WALES
ENGLAND
NORWAY
SWEDEN
FINLAND
DENMARK
THE NETHERLANDS
BEL.
LUX.
GERMAN EMPIRE
EAST PRUSSIA
FRANCE
SWITZ.
AUSTRIA-HUNGARY
BOHEMIA
MORAVIA
GALICIA
RUTHENIA
TRANSYLVANIA
BOSNIA
DALMATIA
TRENTINO
ITALY
SPAIN
PORTUGAL
AND.
RUSSIA
BALTIC PROVINCES
POLAND
BESSARABIA
CRIMEA
RUMANIA
DOBRUJA
BULGARIA
SERBIA
MONTE.
ALBANIA
GREECE
OTTOMAN EMPIRE
ASIA MINOR
KURDISTAN
ARMENIA
SYRIA
PALESTINE
GEORGIA
DAGHESTAN
AZERBAIJAN
TURKESTAN
SIBERIA
URAL MOUNTAINS
PERSIA
ARABIA
EGYPT
TRIPOLITANIA
Italian since 1912
TUNIS (French)
ALGERIA (French)
ATLAS MTS.
MOROCCO (French)
SPANISH AREA
RIO DE ORO (Spanish)
Gibraltar (Brit.)
MALTA (Br.)
CORSICA
SARDINIA
SICILY
BALEARIC IS.
MINORCA
MAJORCA
CRETE
RHODES
CYPRUS
DODECANESE IS.
Italian since 1912
Annexed by Gr. Br. 1914
Occupied by Britain 1882
British Protectorate 1914
IONIAN ISLANDS
SAMOS
ANDROS
NAXOS
GOTLAND
OLAND
ALAND IS.
BORNHOLM (To Denmark)
Sphere of Russian influence since 1907
Neutral Zone
British sphere of influence since 1907
Atlantic Ocean
Arctic Ocean
North Sea
Baltic Sea
Gulf of Bothnia
Gulf of Finland
Skagerrak
Bay of Biscay
Mediterranean Sea
Tyrrhenian Sea
Adriatic Sea
Ionian Sea
Aegean Sea
Black Sea
Sea of Azov
Caspian Sea
Aral Sea
Persian Gulf
Red Sea
L. Ladoga
L. Onega
Kola
Archangel
Helsingfors
Viborg
Kronstadt
St. Petersburg (Petrograd)
Novgorod
Vologda
Nizhni Novgorod
Kazan
Ufa
Samara
Orenburg
Moscow
Borodino
Smolensk
Tula
Penza
Riga
Memel
Königsberg
Vilna
Vitebsk
Grodno
Minsk
Mogilev
Briansk
Orel
Tambov
Saratov
Kursk
Voronezh
Tsaritsyn
Astrakhan
Brest Litovsk
Pinsk
Warsaw
Lodz
Lublin
Zhitomir
Kiev
Chernigov
Kharkov
Poltava
Ekaterinoslav
Taganrog
Rostov
Kherson
Odessa
Ekaterinodar
Vladikavkaz
Petrovsk
Derbent
Baku
Tiflis
Batum
Kars
Erivan
Lenkoran
Krasnovodsk
Bergen
Christiania
Stavanger
Uppsala
Stockholm
Copenhagen
Aberdeen
Edinburgh
Glasgow
Dublin
Liverpool
Hull
Manchester
Birmingham
London
Portsmouth
Plymouth
Amsterdam
Rotterdam
Antwerp
Brussels
Hamburg
Bremen
Berlin
Danzig
Tannenburg
Leipzig
Dresden
Cologne
Frankfurt
Mainz
Strassburg
Munich
Prague
Vienna
Bratislava
Budapest
Krakow
Lvov
Graz
Trieste
Ljubljana
Fiume
Temesvar
Hermannstadt
Jassy
Galatz
Bucharest
Constantsa
Belgrade
Sarajevo
Ragusa
Nish
Sofia
Philippopolis
Adrianople
Dede-Agach
Burgas
Skoplje
Salonika
Durazzo
Valona
Yannina
Athens
Sparta
Constantinople
Brusa
Smyrna
Angora
Konia
Adalia
Sinope
Sivas
Erzerum
Mosul
Bagdad
Basra
Aleppo
Damascus
Beirut
Nicosia
Haifa
Jaffa
Jerusalem
Port Said
Alexandria
Cairo
Tabriz
Resht
Teheran
Kermanshah
Yezd
Mohammerah
Candia
Brest
Versailles
Paris
Orléans
Bordeaux
Lyon
Geneva
Zurich
Grenoble
Marseille
Nice
Milan
Venice
Genoa
Bologna
Florence
Rome
Naples
Bari
Ajaccio
Cagliari
Palermo
Messina
Syracuse
Ferrol
Bilbao
Lisbon
Madrid
Barcelona
Valencia
Cordova
Tangier
Oran
Algiers
Bizerta
Tunis
Tripoli
Benghazi
Seine
Loire
Oise
Garonne
Rhone
Weser
Oder
Vistula
Danube
Drava
Sava
Tisa
Po
Duero
Tagus
Ebro
Guadiana
Guadalquivir
Dvina
Western Dvina
Volga
Kama
Ural
Don
Dnieper
Dniester
Bug
Pripet
Pechora
Ob
Syr Daria
Amu Daria
Tigris
Euphrates
Nile
Suez
APENNINES
ALPS
PYRENEES
CAUCASUS
A-450041-29-2-2-2-1
Copyright by Rand McNally & Company, Made in U.S.A.

A-450043-29-1-1-2-2BY

EUROPE 1922-40
MILES 0 50 100 200 300
Principal status quo powers
Principal Revisionist powers
1914 Boundaries
1922 Boundaries
UNION OF SOVIET SOCIALIST REPUBLICS
URAL MOUNTAINS
ASIA
TURKESTAN
PERSIA
UKRAINE
TURKEY
ASIA MINOR
KURDISTAN
SYRIA
IRAQ
Independent since 1932
ARABIA
TRANSJORDAN
Br. Mandate
PALESTINE
Br. Mandate
KUWAIT
ALEXANDRETTA
Annexed by Turkey 1939
CYPRUS (Br.)
REPUBLIC OF GEORGIA
REPUBLIC OF ARMENIA
REPUBLIC OF AZERBAIJAN
DAGHESTAN
KOLA PENINSULA
MURMAN COAST
Ceded to USSR 1940
Annexed by USSR 1940
To Bulgaria 1940
Bdry. of Armenia as arbitrated by President Wilson
Line of the treaty of Sevres
Bdry. between Syria and Turkey as Estab'd by Agree. Aug. 1921
Bdry. line between Fr. and Br. Mandate Terr's. as Estab'd. by Agree. Dec. 23, 1920
Black Sea
Caspian Sea
Aral Sea
Sea of Azov
White Sea
Persian Gulf
Red Sea
Dead Sea
L. Urmia
Lake Onega
Lake Ladoga
Ocean
Pechenga
Murmansk
Archangel
Kronstadt
Leningrad (Petrograd)
Vologda
Novgorod
Pskov
Yaroslavl
Kalinin (Tver)
Moscow
Gorkii (Nizhni Novgorod)
Kazan
Kirov
Molotov
Sverdlovsk
Cheliabinsk
Magnitogorsk
Kustanai
Akmolinsk
Ufa
Kuibyshev
Chkalov
Orsk
Uralsk
Saratov
Penza
Tambov
Vitebsk
Smolensk
Borisov
Minsk
Mogilev
Briansk
Orel
Tula
Riazan
Kursk
Voronezh
Chernigov
Kiev
Zhitomir
Kharkov
Poltava
Kirovograd (Elizavetgrad)
Dnepropetrovsk (Ekaterinoslav)
Taganrog
Rostov
Stalingrad
Astrakhan
Kishinev
Odessa
Cherson
Voroshilovsk (Stavropol)
Krasnodar (Ekaterinodar)
Novorossiisk (Anapa)
Sevastopol
Grozni
Petrovsk
Ordzhonikidze (Vladikavkaz)
Derbent
Sukhumi
Poti
Batum
Tiflis
Baku
Kars
Erivan
Lenkoran
Krasnovodsk
Tabriz
Teheran
Galatz
Constantsa
Varna
Burgas
Sinope
Samsun
Trebizond
Skutari
Eregli
Brusa
Ankara (Angora)
Tokat
Konia
Aidin
Adana
Adalia
Makri
Aleppo
Mosul
Latakia
Homs
Nikosia
Limasol
Beirut
Damascus
Bagdad
Acre
Jaffa
Amman
Jerusalem
Alexandria
Port Said
Cairo
Kuwait
RHODES
Ob
Pechora
Irtish
Ishim
Tobol
Kama
Belaia
Volga
Ural
Dvina
Vychegda
Oka
Don
Dnieper
Pripet
Bug
Dniester
Kuban
Terek
Kura
Kizil Irmak
Tigris
Euphrates
Nile
Bosporus

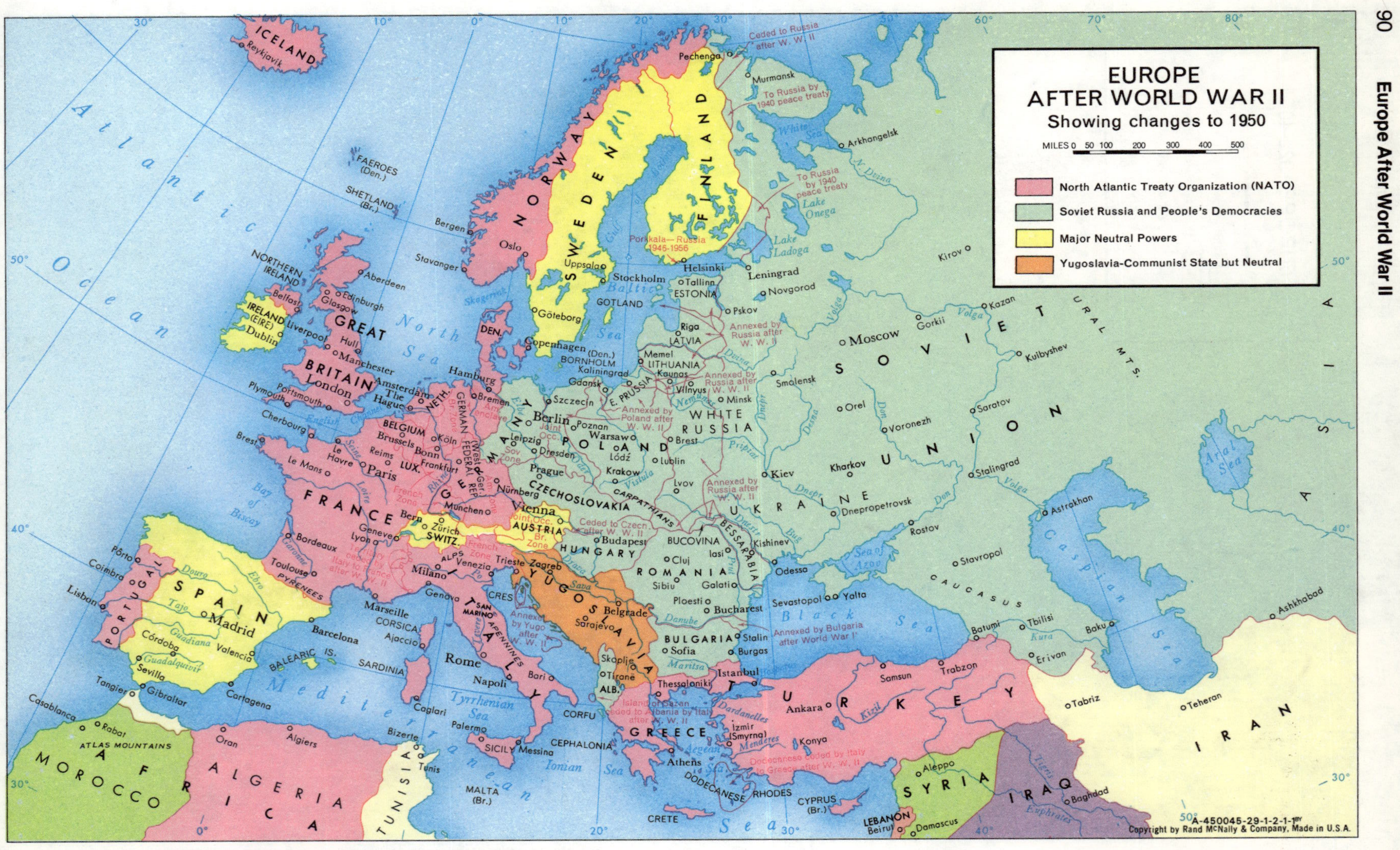

EUROPE
AFTER WORLD WAR II
Showing changes to 1950
MILES 0 50 100 200 300 400 500
North Atlantic Treaty Organization (NATO)
Soviet Russia and People's Democracies
Major Neutral Powers
Yugoslavia-Communist State but Neutral
A-450045-29-1-2-1-1RY
Copyright by Rand McNally & Company, Made in U.S.A.
ICELAND
Reykjavik
FAEROES (Den.)
SHETLANDS (Br.)
NORTHERN IRELAND
IRELAND (EIRE)
Dublin
Belfast
GREAT BRITAIN
London
Edinburgh
Glasgow
Aberdeen
Liverpool
Manchester
Hull
Portsmouth
Plymouth
NORWAY
Oslo
Bergen
Stavanger
SWEDEN
Stockholm
Uppsala
Göteborg
FINLAND
Helsinki
Pechenga
Porkkala—Russia 1945-1956
DEN.
Copenhagen
BORNHOLM (Den.)
GOTLAND
North Sea
Baltic Sea
Atlantic Ocean
Bay of Biscay
FRANCE
Paris
Le Havre
Cherbourg
Brest
Le Mans
Reims
Bordeaux
Toulouse
Lyon
Marseille
CORSICA
Ajaccio
BELGIUM
Brussels
LUX.
NETH.
Amsterdam
The Hague
GERMAN FEDERAL REP. (West Ger.)
GERMANY
Hamburg
Bremen
Köln
Bonn
Frankfurt
München
Nürnberg
Leipzig
Dresden
Berlin
SWITZ.
Bern
Zürich
Genève
AUSTRIA
Vienna
ITALY
Rome
Milano
Genova
Venezia
Trieste
Napoli
Bari
Palermo
Messina
SICILY
SARDINIA
Cagliari
SAN MARINO
APENNINES
ALPS
CRES
Tyrrhenian Sea
Ionian Sea
Mediterranean Sea
MALTA (Br.)
SPAIN
Madrid
Barcelona
Valencia
Cartagena
Córdoba
Sevilla
Gibraltar
BALEARIC IS.
PYRENEES
PORTUGAL
Lisbon
Pôrto
Coimbra
Tangier
MOROCCO
Rabat
Casablanca
ATLAS MOUNTAINS
AFRICA
ALGERIA
Algiers
Oran
TUNISIA
Tunis
Bizerte
POLAND
Warsaw
Gdańsk
Szczecin
Poznań
Łódź
Kraków
Lublin
E. PRUSSIA
CZECHOSLOVAKIA
Prague
HUNGARY
Budapest
YUGOSLAVIA
Belgrade
Zagreb
Sarajevo
Skoplje
ALB.
Tirane
ROMANIA
Bucharest
Cluj
Iasi
Galati
Ploesti
Sibiu
BUCOVINA
BESSARABIA
BULGARIA
Sofia
Stalin
Burgas
GREECE
Athens
Thessaloniki
CORFU
CEPHALONIA
CRETE
RHODES
DODECANESE
TURKEY
Istanbul
Ankara
Izmir (Smyrna)
Konya
Samsun
Trabzon
CYPRUS (Br.)
SYRIA
Aleppo
Damascus
LEBANON
Beirut
IRAQ
Baghdad
IRAN
Teheran
Tabriz
SOVIET UNION
Moscow
Leningrad
Novgorod
Pskov
Smolensk
Murmansk
Arkhangelsk
Kirov
Kazan
Gorkii
Kuibyshev
Saratov
Stalingrad
Astrakhan
Orel
Voronezh
Kharkov
Kiev
Dnepropetrovsk
Rostov
Odessa
Kishinev
Sevastopol
Yalta
Stavropol
Batumi
Tbilisi
Erivan
Baku
Ashkhabad
WHITE RUSSIA
Minsk
Brest
UKRAINE
Lvov
ESTONIA
Tallinn
LATVIA
Riga
LITHUANIA
Kaunas
Vilnyus
Memel
Kaliningrad
URAL MTS.
CAUCASUS
CARPATHIANS
ASIA
Caspian Sea
Black Sea
Aral Sea
White Sea
Lake Ladoga
Lake Onega
Sea of Azov
Ceded to Russia after W. W. II
To Russia by 1940 peace treaty
Annexed by Russia after W. W. II
Annexed by Poland after W. W. II
Ceded to Czech. after W. W. II
Annexed by Yugo after W. W. II
Annexed by Bulgaria after World War I
Dodecanese ceded by Italy to Greece after W. W. II

ASIA
After World War II
Showing changes to 1950
MILES 0 100 200 400 600
Korea divided in 1950 by the 38° parallel into the Democratic People's Republic (N. Korea) and the Republic of Korea (S. Korea)
Boundaries of 1950
A-469045-29-1-1-1
Copyright by Rand McNally & Company, Made in U.S.A.

Flags of the World

AFGHANISTAN
ALBANIA
ALGERIA
ANDORRA
ANGOLA
ANTIGUA
ARGENTINA
AUSTRALIA
AUSTRIA
BAHAMAS
BANGLADESH
BARBADOS
BELGIUM
BELIZE
BENIN
BHUTAN
BOLIVIA
BOTSWANA
BRAZIL
BRUNEI
BULGARIA
BURMA
BURUNDI
BYELORUSSIAN SOVIET SOCIALIST REPUBLIC
CAMBODIA (Kampuchea)
CAMEROON
CANADA
CAPE VERDE
CENTRAL AFRICAN REPUBLIC
CHAD
CHILE
CHINA
COLOMBIA
COMOROS
CONGO

COSTA RICA
CUBA
CYPRUS
CZECHOSLOVAKIA
DENMARK
DJIBOUTI
DOMINICA
DOMINICAN REPUBLIC
ECUADOR
EGYPT
EL SALVADOR
EQUATORIAL GUINEA
ETHIOPIA
FIJI
FINLAND
FRANCE
GABON
THE GAMBIA
GERMANY (EAST)
GERMANY (WEST)
GHANA
GREAT BRITAIN
GREECE
GRENADA
GUATEMALA
GUINEA
GUINEA-BISSAU
GUYANA
HAITI
HONDURAS
HUNGARY
ICELAND
INDIA
INDONESIA
IRAN

IRAQ IRELAND ISRAEL ITALY IVORY COAST

JAMAICA JAPAN JORDAN KENYA KIRIBATI

KOREA (NORTH) KOREA (SOUTH) KUWAIT LAOS LEBANON

LESOTHO LIBERIA LIBYA LIECHTENSTEIN LUXEMBOURG

MADAGASCAR MALAWI MALAYSIA MALDIVES MALI

MALTA MAURITANIA MAURITIUS MEXICO MONACO

MONGOLIAN PEOPLE'S REPUBLIC MOROCCO MOZAMBIQUE NAURU NEPAL

NETHERLANDS

NEW ZEALAND

NICARAGUA

NIGER

NIGERIA

NORWAY

OMAN

PAKISTAN

PANAMA

PAPUA-NEW GUINEA

PARAGUAY (obverse)

PERU

PHILIPPINES

POLAND

PORTUGAL

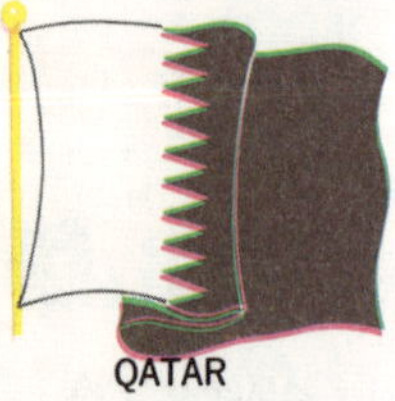

QATAR

ROMANIA

RWANDA

SAINT LUCIA

ST. VINCENT

SAN MARINO

SAO TOME AND PRINCIPE

SAUDI ARABIA

SENEGAL

SEYCHELLES

SIERRA LEONE

SINGAPORE

SOLOMON ISLANDS

SOMALIA

SOUTH AFRICA

SPAIN

SRI LANKA

SUDAN

SURINAME

SWAZILAND

SWEDEN
SWITZERLAND
SYRIA
TANZANIA
THAILAND
TOGO
TRINIDAD AND TOBAGO
TUNISIA
TURKEY
TUVALU
UGANDA
UKRAINIAN SOVIET SOCIALIST REPUBLIC
UNION OF SOVIET SOCIALIST REPUBLICS
UNITED ARAB EMIRATES
UNITED STATES
BURKINA FASO (Upper Volta)
URUGUAY
VANUATU
VATICAN CITY
VENEZUELA
VIETNAM
WESTERN SAMOA
YEMEN
PEOPLE'S DEMOCRATIC REPUBLIC OF YEMEN
YUGOSLAVIA
ZAIRE
ZAMBIA
ZIMBABWE
UNITED NATIONS
ORGANIZATION OF AFRICAN UNITY
ORGANIZATION OF AMERICAN STATES
COUNCIL OF EUROPE
RED CROSS
RED CRESCENT (Most Muslim countries)
RED MOGEN DAVID (Israel)

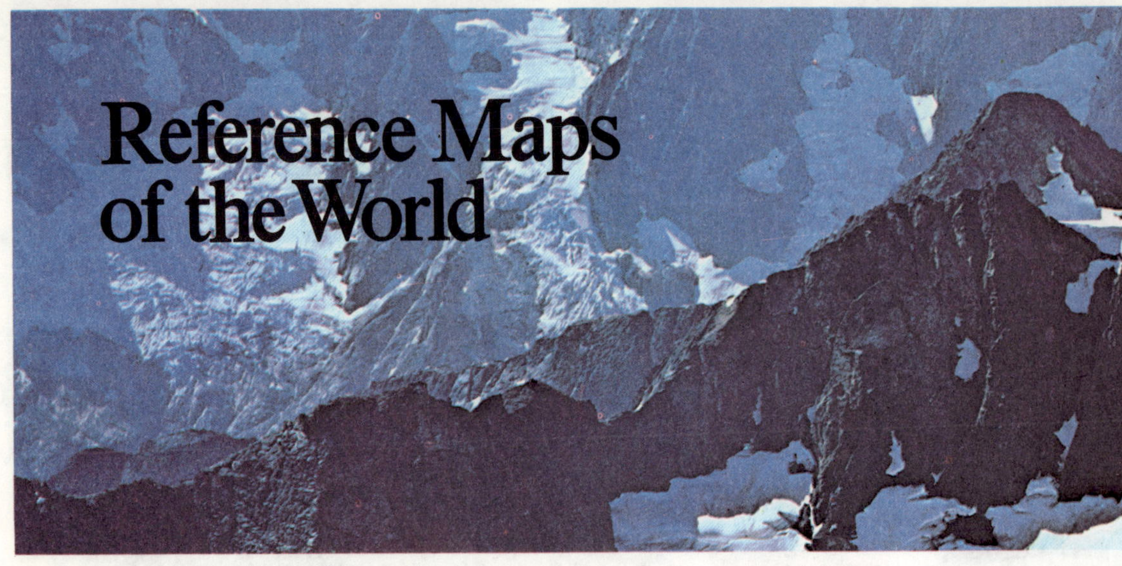

Reference Maps of the World

Reference Map Legend

CULTURAL FEATURES

Political Boundaries

International

Secondary (State, province, etc.)

County

Populated Places

Cities, towns, and villages

Symbol size represents population of the place

Chicago
Gary
Racine
Glenview
Edgewood

Type size represents relative importance of the place

Corporate area of large U.S. and Canadian cities and urban area of other foreign cities

Major Urban Area

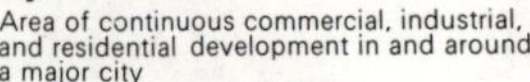

Area of continuous commercial, industrial, and residential development in and around a major city

Community within a city

Capital of major political unit

Capital of secondary political unit

Capital of U.S. state or Canadian province

County Seat

Military Installation

Scientific Station

Miscellaneous

National Park

National Monument

Provincial Park

Indian Reservation

Point of Interest

Ruins

Buildings

Race Track

Railroad

Tunnel

Underground or Subway

Dam

Bridge

Dike

LAND FEATURES

Passes =

Point of Elevation above sea level + 8,520 FT.

WATER FEATURES

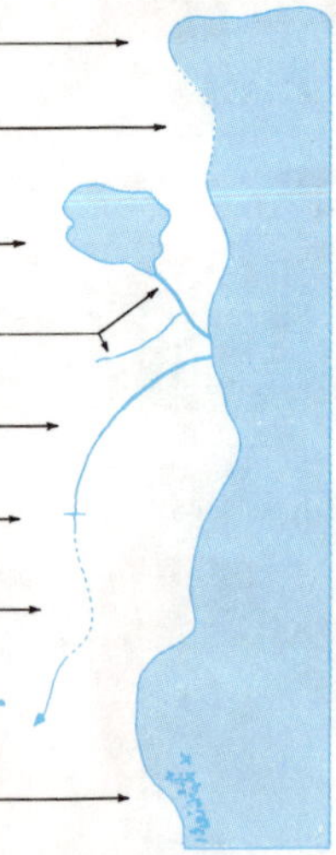

Coastlines and Shorelines

Indefinite or Unsurveyed Coastlines and Shorelines

Lakes and Reservoirs

Canals

Rivers and Streams

Falls and Rapids

Intermittent or Unsurveyed Rivers and Streams

Directional Flow Arrow

Rocks, Shoals and Reefs

TYPE STYLES USED TO NAME FEATURES

ASIA	Continent
DENMARK CANADA	Country, State, or Province
BÉARN	Region, Province, or Historical Region
CROCKETT	County
PANTELLERIA (ITALY)	Country of which unit is a dependency in parentheses
SRI LANKA (CEYLON)	Former or alternate name
Rome (Roma)	Local or alternate city name
Naval Air Station	Military Installation
MESA VERDE SAN XAVIER	National Park or Monument, Provincial Park, Indian Res.,
UINTA DESERT	Major Terrain Features
MT. MORIAH	Individual Mountain
STROMBOLI NUNIVAK	Island or Coastal Feature
Ocean Lake River Canal	Hydrographic Features

Note: Size of type varies according to importance and available space. Letters for names of major features are spread across the extent of the feature.

POLAR MAP of the WORLD
Air Distances 700 Shown in Statute Miles
Projection: Polar Azimuthal Equidistant
Scales: Along meridians, One inch = 1872 statute miles
Along parallels, as shown by diagram
Statute Miles
Equator
Pole
INDIAN OCEAN
PACIFIC OCEAN
ATLANTIC OCEAN
ARCTIC OCEAN
NORTH POLE
TROPIC OF CAPRICORN
TROPIC OF CANCER
EQUATOR
ARCTIC CIRCLE
INTERNATIONAL DATE LINE
SUNDAY
SATURDAY
AUSTRALIA
TASMANIA
Perth
Albany
Broome
Adelaide
Alice Springs
Darwin
Melbourne
Hobart
Canberra
Sydney
Brisbane
Townsville
INDONESIA
EAST INDIES
JAVA
SUMATRA
BORNEO
CELEBES
PHILIPPINES
Manila
NEW GUINEA
PAPUA NEW GUINEA
Port Moresby
BISMARCK ARCH.
CAROLINE ISLANDS
SOLOMON IS.
NEW CALEDONIA
Noumea
VANUATU
FIJI
Suva
KIRIBATI
MARSHALL IS.
WAKE I.
GUAM
MARIANA IS.
MIDWAY I.
ALEUTIAN IS.
PHOENIX IS.
WESTERN SAMOA
Apia
Pago Pago
HAWAIIAN ISLANDS
Honolulu
COCOS IS.
CHAGOS ARCHIPELAGO
KERGUELEN I.
SRI LANKA
Colombo
ANDAMAN IS.
INDIA
Madras
Hyderabad
Bombay
Calcutta
Delhi
Karachi
Lahore
PAKISTAN
AFGHANISTAN
Kabul
IRAN
Tehran
BURMA
Rangoon
THAILAND
Bangkok
LAOS
VIETNAM
Hanoi
Ho Chi Minh City
KAMP.
MALAYSIA
Singapore
Jakarta
HONG KONG
Canton
TAIWAN
CHINA
Lhasa
Shanghai
Nanjing
Peking
Chongqing
MONGOLIA
Ulan Bator
KOREA
Seoul
JAPAN
Tokyo
Osaka
Kobe
Yokohama
Hakodate
Okinawa
Vladivostok
Khabarovsk
Nikolaevsk
Yakutsk
Okhotsk
Petropavlovsk
Chita
Irkutsk
Novosibirsk
Omsk
Tashkent
Igarka
Salekhard
ASIA
SOVIET UNION
EUROPE
Moscow
Leningrad
Helsinki
Stockholm
Arkhangelsk
Murmansk
Kiev
Warsaw
Berlin
Vienna
Rome
Paris
London
Liverpool
Glasgow
Madrid
Lisbon
Gibraltar
Athens
Istanbul
Ankara
TURKEY
Tbilisi
Astrakhan
Volgograd
Baghdad
IRAQ
SYRIA
SUEZ CANAL
Cairo
Alexandria
EGYPT
SAUDI ARABIA
Riyadh
Mecca
Aden
U.A.E.
QATAR
SOCOTRA
SOMALIA
ETHIOPIA
Addis Ababa
KENYA
Nairobi
TANZANIA
Dar es Salaam
Mocambique
MOZAMBIQUE
Beira
MADAGASCAR
Antananarivo
Diego Suarez
Durban
Port Elizabeth
Johannesburg
SOUTH AFRICA
Cape Town
NAMIBIA
ANGOLA
Luanda
ZAMBIA
BOTSWANA
ZIMBABWE
ZAIRE
SUDAN
Khartoum
AFRICA
CENTRAL AFRICAN REP.
CHAD
Ndjamena
CONGO
Kinshasa
CAMEROON
GABON
NIGERIA
NIGER
LIBYA
Tripoli
Tobruk
Bengasi
ALGERIA
Algiers
Tunis
MOROCCO
Rabat
MALI
MAURITANIA
WESTERN SAHARA
Dakar
GUINEA-BISSAU
Freetown
Monrovia
IVORY COAST
Accra
Lagos
ASCENSION I.
CANARY IS.
MADEIRA IS.
AZORES
CAPE VERDE
ICELAND
Reykjavik
IRELAND
UNITED KINGDOM
FRANCE
SPAIN
GREENLAND
Thule
Godthåb
Julianehåb
NORTH AMERICA
CANADA
ALASKA
Nome
Barrow
Fairbanks
Anchorage
Juneau
Sitka
Edmonton
Vancouver
Seattle
Portland
Goose Bay
NEWFOUNDLAND
St. John's
Montreal
Ottawa
Toronto
Boston
New York
Philadelphia
Washington
Norfolk
Detroit
Chicago
Cleveland
Denver
Salt Lake City
San Francisco
Los Angeles
San Diego
El Paso
Dallas
Houston
New Orleans
Miami
UNITED STATES
BERMUDA IS.
Brownsville
MEXICO
Mexico City
Mérida
Havana
CUBA
BAHAMAS
WEST INDIES
JAMAICA
HAITI
DOM. REP.
PUERTO RICO
VIRGIN IS.
LEEWARD IS.
WINDWARD IS.
TRINIDAD AND TOBAGO
BELIZE
HOND.
GUATEMALA
EL SALVADOR
NIC.
COSTA RICA
PANAMA
PANAMA CANAL
CENTRAL AMERICA
Barranquilla
Caracas
VENEZUELA
GUYANA
SURINAME
FR. GUIANA
COLOMBIA
Bogotá
ECUADOR
Quito
ARCHIPIELAGO DE COLON (GALAPAGOS IS.)
PERU
Lima
BOLIVIA
La Paz
BRAZIL
Manaus
Belem
Teresina
Recife
Natal
Salvador
Brasilia
Rio de Janeiro
São Paulo
Porto Alegre
PARAGUAY
Asunción
URUGUAY
Montevideo
Buenos Aires
Rosario
ARGENTINA
Bahía Blanca
Arica
CHILE
Valparaiso
Santiago
Punta Arenas
CAPE HORN
FALKLAND IS. (ISLAS MALVINAS)
SOUTH GEORGIA
SOUTH AMERICA
ANTARCTICA
SOUTH POLE
ROSS ICE SHELF
Ross Sea
Weddell Sea
Amundsen Sea
Bellingshausen Sea
QUEEN MAUD LAND
MTS. FRIDTJOF NANSEN
MT. MARKHAM 14272
MT. EREBUS 12280
MT. SIPLE 10171
MT. SIDLEY 13717
VINSON MASSIF 16864
ANTARCTIC PENINSULA
LARSEN ICE SHELF
SOUTH ORKNEY IS.
PETER I ISLAND
ADELAIDE I.
CHARCOT I.
ALEXANDER I.
THURSTON I.
GETZ ICE SHELF
RONNE ICE SHELF
FILCHNER ICE SHELF
DAWSON LAMBTON GLACIER
COATS LAND
PRINCESS MARTHA COAST
QUEEN MAUD LAND
C. NORVEGIA
HUMBOLDT MOUNTAINS
ENDERBY LAND
AMERY ICE SHELF
AMERICAN HIGHLAND
DENMAN GLACIER
SHACKLETON ICE SHELF
WEST ICE SHELF
C. BOOTHBY
C. DARNLEY
WILKES LAND
SOUTH MAGNETIC POLE
VICTORIA LAND
C. ADARE
MT. SABINE 12201
C. COLBECK
FORD RANGE
BYRD LAND
Antarctic Circle
Longitude East of Greenwich
Statute Miles
PROJECTION
The Azimuthal Equidistant Polar Projection used for this map is true to scale along the meridians. It does, however, create an exaggeration in scale along the parallels which increases toward the map borders. This accounts for the distorted shape of Australia and other areas along corresponding parallels.
9100-22
Copyright by McNALLY & COMPANY
Made in U. S. A.

Graphic Linear Scale
Scale on the Equator 1:133,000,000
Statute Miles
Miller Cylindrical Projection

Longitude West of Greenwich

Longitude East of Greenwich

Arctic Ocean
Barents Sea
Denmark Strait
Norwegian Sea
Atlantic Ocean
North Sea
Bay of Biscay
Mediterranean Sea
Tyrrhenian Sea
Ionian Sea
Black Sea
GREENLAND (DEN.)
ICELAND
JAN MAYEN (NOR.)
FAEROE IS. (DEN.)
SHETLAND ISLANDS (BR.)
ORKNEY ISLANDS
HEBRIDES
Arctic Circle
NORWAY
SWEDEN
FINLAND
DENMARK
UNITED KINGDOM
IRELAND
NETH.
BELGIUM
LUX.
FED. REP. OF GER.
GER. DEM. REP.
POLAND
CZECHOSLOVAKIA
AUSTRIA
SWITZERLAND
LIECH.
HUNGARY
ROMANIA
YUGOSLAVIA
BULGARIA
ALB.
GREECE
TURKEY
FRANCE
ANDORRA
SPAIN
PORTUGAL
ITALY
SAN MARINO
CORSICA
SARDINIA
SICILY
MALTA
CRETE
BALEARIC ISLANDS
UNION OF SOVIET SOCIALIST REPUBLICS
R.S.F.S.R.
MOROCCO
ALGERIA
TUNISIA
LIBYA
EGYPT
SAHARA
ATLAS MOUNTAINS
Reykjavík
Oslo
Stockholm
Helsinki
Copenhagen (København)
Leningrad
Moscow (Moskva)
London
Dublin
Paris
Amsterdam
Brussels
Berlin
Warsaw (Warszawa)
Prague (Praha)
Vienna
Budapest
Bucharest
Belgrade
Sofia
Athens
İstanbul
Rome (Roma)
Madrid
Lisbon (Lisboa)
Bern
Kiev
Minsk
Vilnius
Riga
Tallinn
Algiers (El Djazaïr)
Tunis
Tripoli (Tarābulus)
Rabat
Valletta
Longitude West of Greenwich
Longitude East of Greenwich
B-550000-23 COSMO SERIES EUROPE WESTERN
Copyright by RAND McNALLY & COMPANY
Made in U. S. A.
Conic Projection
Statute Miles 100 0 100 200 300
Kilometers 100 0 100 200 300 400

Same Scale as Main Map
SHETLAND ISLANDS (SCOTLAND)
Lerwick
SCOTLAND
UNITED KINGDOM
NORTHERN IRELAND
IRELAND (EIRE)
WALES
ENGLAND
FRANCE
CHANNEL ISLANDS (BR.)
Atlantic Ocean
North Sea
Irish Sea
English Channel
London
Edinburgh
Glasgow
Belfast
Dublin
Cardiff
Birmingham
Manchester
Liverpool
Leeds
Sheffield
Bristol
Newcastle-on-Tyne
Aberdeen
Dundee
Cork
Limerick
Galway
Londonderry
Plymouth
Southampton
Portsmouth
Norwich
Cambridge
Oxford
Nottingham
Leicester
Hull
York
Inverness
Longitude West of Greenwich
Longitude East of Greenwich
H-553600-21
COSMO SERIES BRITISH ISLES
Copyright by RAND McNALLY & COMPANY
Made in U. S. A.
Statute Miles
Kilometers
Conic Projection

North Sea
UNITED KINGDOM
NETHERLANDS
FEDERAL REPUBLIC OF GERMANY
(WEST GERMANY)
BELGIUM
LUXEMBOURG
FRANCE
SWITZ.
ITALY
SPAIN
ANDORRA
MONACO
English Channel
Bay of Biscay
Mediterranean Sea
Gulf of Lions
CHANNEL ISLANDS (BR.)
BRITTANY
NORMANDY
MAINE
ANJOU
TOURAINE
CHAMPAGNE
LORRAINE
BURGUNDY
MASSIF CENTRAL
DAUPHINÉ
PROVENCE
GASCONY
PYRENEES
ALPS
JURA MTS.
London
Paris
Brussels (Bruxelles)
Amsterdam
The Hague ('s Gravenhage)
Rotterdam
Antwerp (Antwerpen)
Luxembourg
Bonn
Cologne
Lyon
Marseille
Bordeaux
Toulouse
Nantes
Rouen
Le Havre
Lille
Reims
Strasbourg
Nice
Geneva (Genève)
Bern
Basel
Bilbao
H-550900-21 -5 -11
COSMO SERIES FRANCE
Copyright by RAND McNALLY & COMPANY
Made in U. S. A.
Longitude East of Greenwich
Longitude West of Greenwich
Conic Projection
Statute Miles 25 0 25 50 75
Kilometers 25 0 25 50 100

COSMO SERIES GERMANY
Copyright by
RAND McNALLY & COMPANY
Made in U. S. A.
North Sea
DENMARK
NETHERLANDS
BELGIUM
LUXEMBOURG
FEDERAL
REPUBLIC OF
GERMANY
(WEST GERMANY)
GERMAN
DEMOCRATIC
REPUBLIC
(EAST GERMANY)
POLAND
CZECHOSLOVAKIA
AUSTRIA
SWITZERLAND
LIECHTENSTEIN
FRANCE
ITALY
YUGOSLAVIA
Adriatic Sea
Gulf of Genoa
Gulf of Venice
Kiel Bay
Hamburg
Bremen
Hannover
Berlin (West)
Berlin (East)
Leipzig
Dresden
Magdeburg
Rostock
Cologne (Köln)
Bonn
Düsseldorf
Dortmund
Essen
Frankfurt
Stuttgart
Munich (München)
Nürnberg (Nuremberg)
Amsterdam
The Hague ('s Gravenhage)
Rotterdam
Brussels (Bruxelles)
Antwerp
Liège
Luxembourg
Prague (Praha)
Vienna (Wien)
Linz
Graz
Salzburg
Innsbruck
Zürich
Bern
Basel
Geneva (Genève)
Lausanne
Milan (Milano)
Turin (Torino)
Genoa (Genova)
Venice (Venezia)
Bologna
Trieste
Ljubljana
Zagreb
Strasbourg
Nancy
Dijon
Lyon
Grenoble
Poznań
Szczecin (Stettin)
Statute Miles 25 0 25 50 75
Kilometers 25 0 25 50 100
Conic Projection
Longitude East of Greenwich

POLAND
CZECHOSLOVAKIA
SOVIET UNION
HUNGARY
AUSTRIA
ROMANIA
GERMAN DEMOCRATIC REPUBLIC (EAST GERMANY)
FEDERAL REPUBLIC OF GERMANY (WEST GERMANY)
DENMARK
SWEDEN
Baltic Sea
Warsaw (Warszawa)
Prague (Praha)
Berlin
Vienna (Wien)
Budapest
Kraków
Łódź
Wrocław (Breslau)
Poznań
Gdańsk (Danzig)
Kaliningrad (Königsberg)
Katowice
Bratislava
Conic Projection
Statute Miles
Kilometers
Copyright by RAND McNALLY & COMPANY Made in U. S. A.

SPAIN
PORTUGAL
FRANCE
ANDORRA
BALEARIC ISLANDS
MALLORCA
MENORCA
IBIZA
FORMENTERA
CANARY ISLANDS (SPAIN)
MADEIRA (PORTUGAL)
Bay of Biscay
Gulf of Lions
Atlantic Ocean
Mediterranean Sea
Madrid
Lisbon (Lisboa)
Barcelona
Valencia
Zaragoza
Sevilla
Málaga
Granada
Córdoba
Murcia
Cartagena
Valladolid
Bilbao
Santander
La Coruña
Gijón
Porto
Palma
Las Palmas
Funchal
Longitude West of Greenwich
Longitude East of Greenwich
Statute Miles 25 0 25 50 75
Kilometers 25 0 25 50 100
Conic Projection

SWITZERLAND
AUSTRIA
LIECHTENSTEIN
YUGOSLAVIA
ITALY
ALPS
APENNINE
TUNISIA
AFRICA
ALGERIA
MONACO
SAN MARINO
CORSICA (FR.)
SARDINIA (IT.)
SICILY
LIPARI IS.
Ligurian Sea
Tyrrhenian Sea
Adriatic Sea
Mediterranean Sea
Gulf of Venice
Gulf of Genoa
Gulf of Taranto
Gulf of Manfredonia
Bern
Zug
Luzern
Schwyz
Glarus
Vaduz
Innsbruck
Landeck
Imst
Murau
Spittal
Villach
Lienz
Davos
Chur
St. Moritz
Brig
Sion
Montreux
Fribourg
Interlaken
Locarno
Lugano
Bellinzona
Sondrio
Tirano
Merano
Bolzano
Bressanone
Trento
Rovereto
Riva
Belluno
Feltre
Tolmezzo
Udine
Cividale del Friuli
Gorizia
Monfalcone
Trieste
Pordenone
Conegliano
Treviso
Vittorio Veneto
Bassano del Grappa
Vicenza
Padova (Padua)
Venice (Venezia)
Mestre
Chioggia
Verona
Brescia
Bergamo
Lecco
Como
Varese
Milan (Milano)
Novara
Vercelli
Biella
Turin (Torino)
Asti
Alessandria
Pavia
Piacenza
Cremona
Mantova (Mantua)
Parma
Reggio nell' Emilia
Modena
Bologna
Ferrara
Rovigo
Adria
Ravenna
Imola
Faenza
Forlì
Cesena
Rimini
Riccione
Pesaro
Fano
Urbino
Senigallia
Ancona
Macerata
Fermo
Genoa (Genova)
Savona
La Spezia
Sanremo
Imperia
Ventimiglia
Nice
Cuneo
Carrara
Massa
Viareggio
Lucca
Pistoia
Prato
Pisa
Livorno (Leghorn)
Florence (Firenze)
Empoli
Siena
Arezzo
Cortona
Perugia
Assisi
Foligno
Spoleto
Terni
Orvieto
Viterbo
Grosseto
Piombino
Elba
Civitavecchia
Rieti
L'Aquila
Teramo
Pescara
Chieti
Vasto
Termoli
Vatican City
Rome (Roma)
Tivoli
Frascati
Velletri
Anzio
Latina
Frosinone
Cassino
Gaeta
Capua
Caserta
Benevento
Avellino
Naples (Napoli)
Pozzuoli
Ischia
Capri
Sorrento
Amalfi
Salerno
Foggia
Campobasso
Barletta
Trani
Bisceglie
Molfetta
Bari
Monopoli
Ostuni
Brindisi
Lecce
Otranto
Taranto
Matera
Potenza
Cosenza
Catanzaro
Crotone
Reggio di Calabria
Messina
Palermo
Trapani
Marsala
Agrigento
Caltanissetta
Enna
Catania
Siracusa
Ragusa
Cefalù
Bagheria
Ajaccio
Bastia
Corte
Bonifacio
Sassari
Olbia
Alghero
Nuoro
Oristano
Cagliari
Iglesias
Carbonia
Tunis
Bizerte
Kelibia
Pantelleria
Ustica
Rijeka (Fiume)
Pula
Zadar
Split
Šibenik
Dubrovnik
Mostar
Rome
Ostia Antica
Fiumicino
Frascati
Albano Laziale
Velletri
Aprilia
Latina
Anzio
Nettuno
Bracciano
Cerveteri
Monterotondo
Guidonia
Tivoli
Palestrina
Longitude East of Greenwich
Conic Projection
Statute Miles
Kilometers
H-551800-21
COSMO SERIES ITALY
RAND McNALLY & COMPANY
Made in U. S. A.

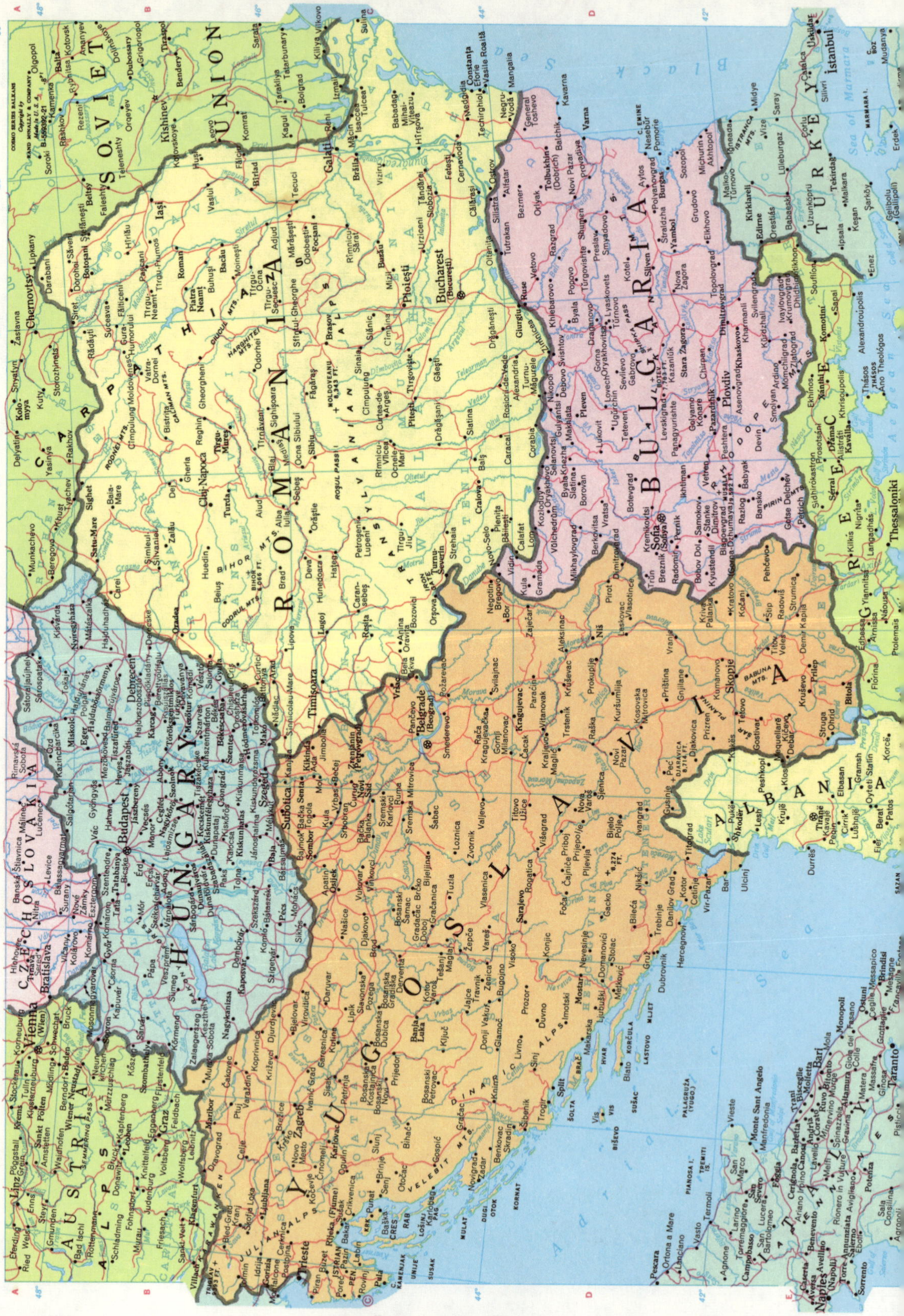

Statute Miles 25 0 25 50 75

Kilometers 25 0 25 50 100

Conic Projection

Longitude West of Greenwich
ICELAND
Reykjavík
Akureyri
Ísafjörður
Vatnajökull (Glacier)
Langjökull (Glacier)
Hofsjökull (Glacier)
North Atlantic Ocean
Same Scale as Main Map
Longitude East of Greenwich
Arctic Ocean
Barents Sea
North Cape
Hammerfest
Vardø
Kirkenes
Tromsø
Narvik
Lofoten
Vesterålen
Bodø
Kebnekaise 6,926 FT.
Kiruna
Gällivare
Luleå
Umeå
Oulu
Kemi
Tornio
Rovaniemi
Murmansk
Kola Peninsula
Arctic Circle
White Sea
Arkhangelsk
Belomorsk
Kem
Onega
Lake Onega
Petrozavodsk
Lake Ladoga
Leningrad
Sestroretsk
Kronshtadt
Pushkin
Gatchina
Vyborg
Helsinki
Turku (Åbo)
Tampere
Lahti
Kotka
Vaasa
Pori
Kuopio
Joensuu
Åland
Gulf of Bothnia
Gulf of Finland
Tallinn
Estonia
Latvia
Riga
Gulf of Riga
Hiiumaa
Saaremaa
Liepāja
Ventspils
Klaipėda (Memel)
Lithuania
Kaliningrad (Königsberg)
Gdańsk (Danzig)
Gdynia
Szczecin (Stettin)
Bydgoszcz
Poznań
Toruń
POLAND
Berlin
Hamburg
Bremen
Hannover
Lübeck
Kiel
Rostock
FED. REP. OF GER. (W. GER.)
GER. DEM. REP. (E. GER.)
DENMARK
Copenhagen (København)
Ålborg
Århus
Odense
Bornholm
Malmö
Lund
Helsingborg
Göteborg
Stockholm
Uppsala
Västerås
Örebro
Norrköping
Linköping
Jönköping
Karlskrona
Kalmar
Öland
Gotland
Visby
Gävle
Sundsvall
Härnösand
Östersund
Trondheim
Kristiansund
Molde
Ålesund
Bergen
Stavanger
Kristiansand
Oslo
Drammen
Larvik
Skagerrak
Kattegat
Norwegian Sea
Baltic Sea
NORWAY
SWEDEN
FINLAND
LAPLAND
SOVIET UNION
Jotunheimen
Dovrefjell
Hardangervidda
Conic Projection
Statute Miles 50 0 50 100 150
Kilometers 50 0 50 100 200
Cosmo Series Scandinavia
Copyright by Rand McNally & Company
Made in U. S. A.
H-559600-21
© RMcN&Co.

FINLAND
SWEDEN
SOVIET UNION
POLAND
CZECH.
HUNG.
ROMANIA
BULGARIA
YUGOSLAVIA
GREECE
TURKEY
Black Sea
Sea of Azov
Baltic Sea
Gulf of Bothnia
Gulf of Finland
Gulf of Riga
Aegean Sea
Lake Ladoga
Lake Onega
DONETS BASIN
KRYM (CRIMEA)
The annexation of Lithuania, Latvia and Estonia in 1940 by the Soviet Union has never been officially recognized by the United States Government.
Moscow (Moskva)
Leningrad
Helsinki
Stockholm
Tallinn
Riga
Vilnius
Minsk
Kiev
Kharkov
Odessa
Warsaw (Warszawa)
Bucharest (Bucureşti)
Sofia (Sofiya)
Istanbul
Gorki (Gor'kiy)
Volgograd (Stalingrad)
Rostov
Voroshilovgrad (Lugansk)
Donetsk
Dnepropetrovsk
Zaporozhye
Sevastopol
Simferopol
Kerch
Krasnodar
Saratov
Voronezh
Kursk
Orel
Tula
Kalinin
Smolensk
Vitebsk
Gomel
Kishinev
Kaliningrad (Königsberg)
Gdańsk (Danzig)
Longitude East of Greenwich
Statute Miles
Kilometers
Conic Projection
B-579400-21 COSMO W. SOVIET UNION
RAND McNALLY & COMPANY
Made in U. S. A.
©RMcN&Co.

Lambert Azimuthal Equal Area Projection
Statute Miles 100 0 100 200 300 400 500
Kilometers 100 0 100 300 500 700

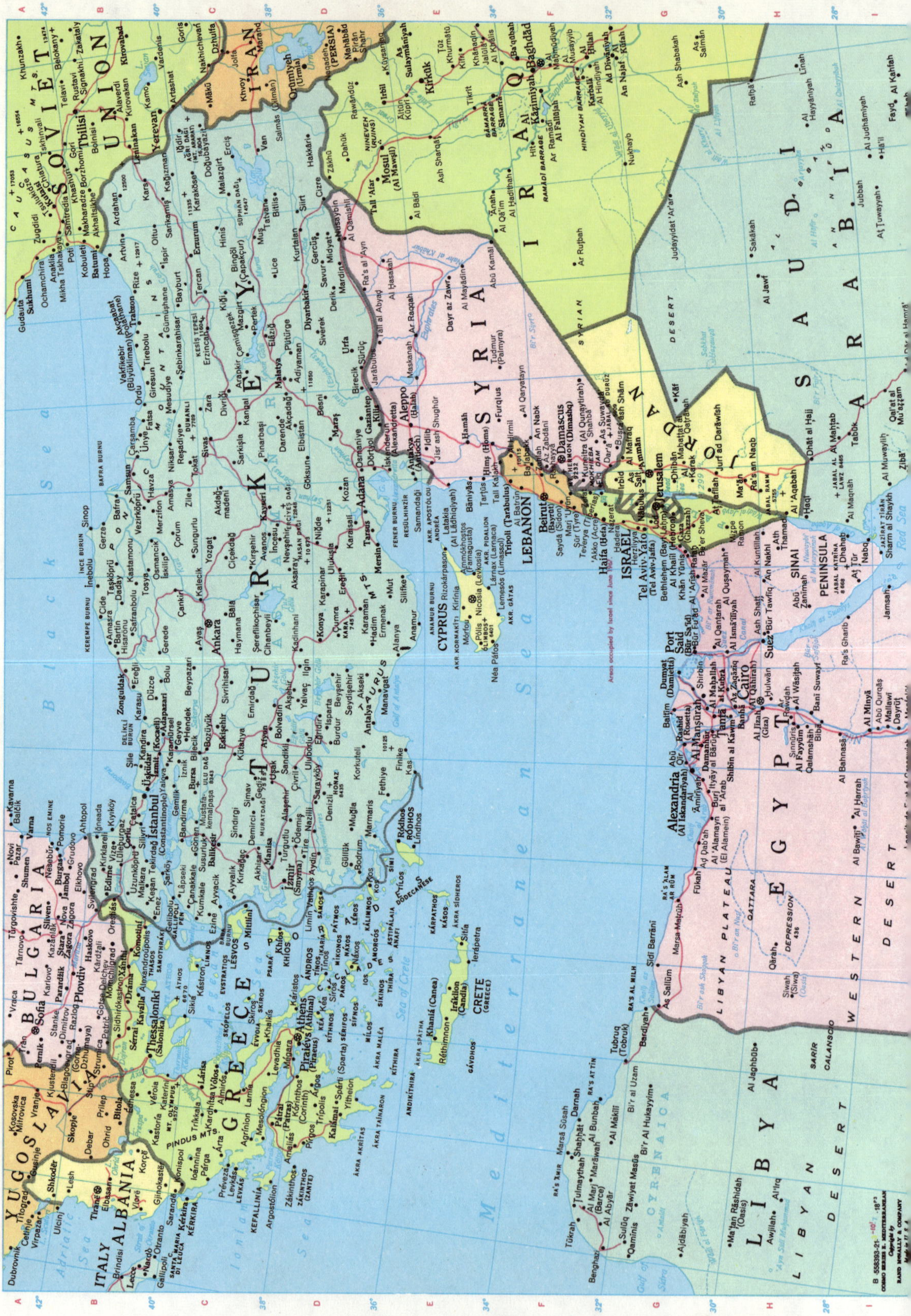

For Eastern Iraq, see map of Iran and Afghanistan.

Statute Miles 50 0 50 100 150

Kilometers 50 0 50 100 200

Lambert Conformal Conic Projection

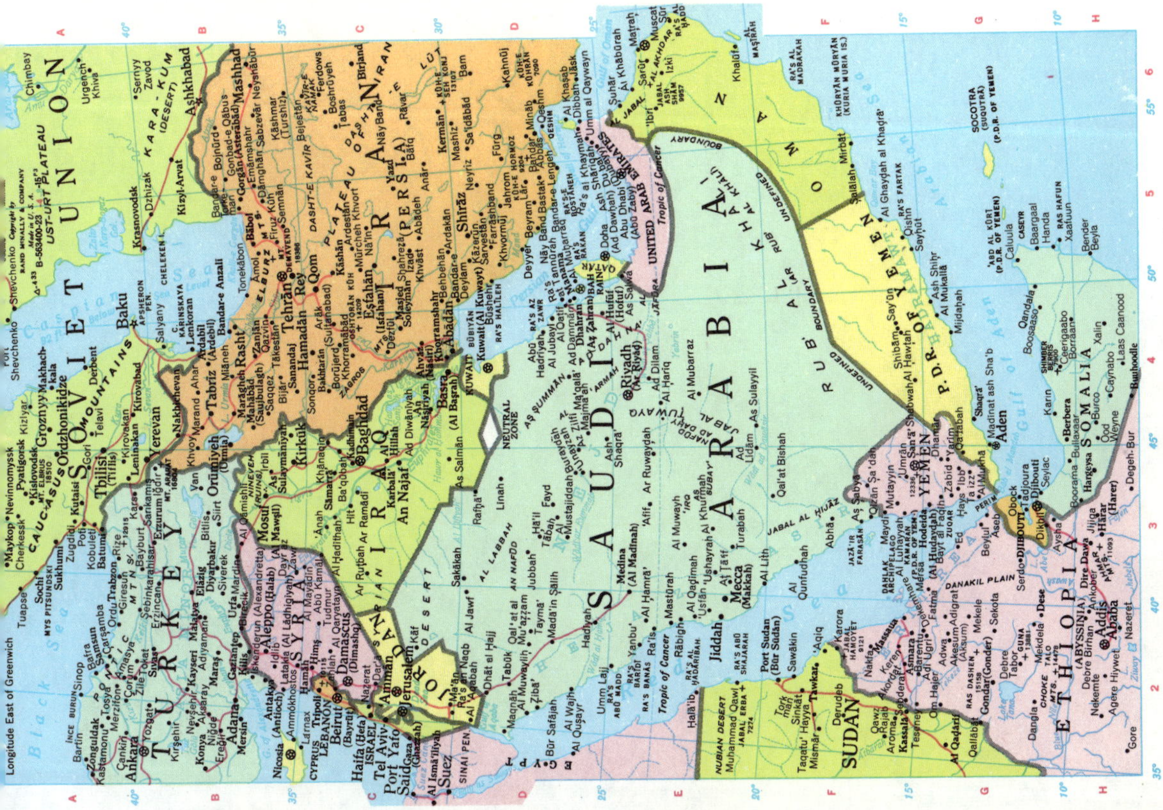

Lambert Conformal Conic Projection

Statute Miles 100 0 100 200 300

Kilometers 100 0 100 200 300 400

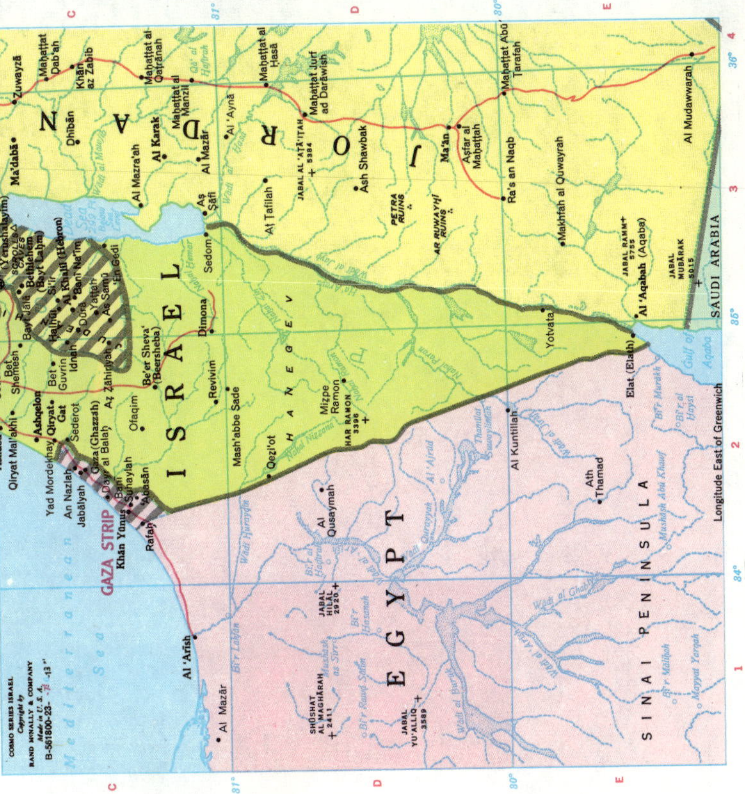

Lambert Conformal Conic Projection

Statute Miles 5 0 5 10 20 30 40 50

Kilometers 5 0 5 10 20 30 40 50 60

Statute Miles 100 0 100 300 500 700 900

Kilometers 100 0 100 300 700 1100

Lambert Azimuthal Equal Area Projection

SOVIET UNION
MONGOLIA
CHINA
NORTH KOREA
SOUTH KOREA
JAPAN
TAIWAN (FORMOSA)
INDIA
BURMA
LAOS
VIETNAM
THAILAND
BHUTAN
BANGLADESH
GOBI DESERT
PLATEAU OF MONGOLIA
INNER MONGOLIA (NEI MONGGOL)
HIMALAYAS
KUNLUN MOUNTAINS
TIBET (XIZANG)
XINJIANG UYGUR
DZUNGARIA
HOKKAIDO
HONSHŪ
SHIKOKU
KYŪSHŪ
SAKHALIN (SOV. UN.)
Sea of Japan
Yellow Sea
East China Sea
South China Sea
Pacific Ocean
Tropic of Cancer
Peking (Beijing)
Shanghai
Tianjin
Canton (Guangzhou)
Chongqing
Wuhan
Nanjing
Harbin
Shenyang
Seoul
Pyongyang
Tōkyō
Ōsaka
Taipei
Hanoi
Ulan Bator (Ulaanbaatar)
Victoria
Hong Kong (BR.)
Longitude East of Greenwich
Polyconic Projection
Statute Miles 100 0 100 200 300
Kilometers 100 0 100 200 300 400
B-560793-21
COSMO SERIES E. ASIA
Copyright by RAND McNALLY & COMPANY
Made in U. S. A.

SOVIET UNION
CHINA
KOREA
NORTH KOREA
SOUTH KOREA
JAPAN
HOKKAIDŌ
HONSHŪ
SHIKOKU
KYŪSHŪ
SAKHALIN (SOV. UN.)
SIKHOTE ALIN MOUNTAINS
Sea of Japan
East China Sea
Pacific Ocean
Sea of Okhotsk
NANSEI IS.
CHEJU ISLAND
TSU'SHIMA ISLANDS
OKI ISLANDS
GOTŌ ISLANDS
TOK ISLANDS (TAKE ISLANDS)
ULLŬNG I.
Harbin
Changchun
Jilin
Qiqihar
Mudanjiang
Jiamusi
Khabarovsk
Komsomolsk-na-Amure
Vladivostok
Nakhodka
Blagoveshchensk
Pyŏngyang
Seoul (Sŏul)
Inchŏn
Taejŏn
Taegu
Pusan
Kwangju
Chŏngjin
Hamhŭng
Wŏnsan
Kaesŏng
Tōkyō
Yokohama
Kawasaki
Nagoya
Kyōto
Ōsaka
Kōbe
Hiroshima
Kitakyūshū
Fukuoka
Nagasaki
Kumamoto
Kagoshima
Sapporo
Hakodate
Sendai
Niigata
Kanazawa
Shizuoka
Hamamatsu
Okayama
Wakayama
Yuzhno-Sakhalinsk
Statute Miles 50 0 50 100 150
Kilometers 50 0 50 100 200
Lambert Conformal Conic Projection
Longitude East of Greenwich
B-561900-21
COSMO SERIES JAPAN, KOREA
Copyright by RAND McNALLY & COMPANY
Made in U. S. A.
Statute Miles 0 10 20 30 40 50 100
© RM&Co

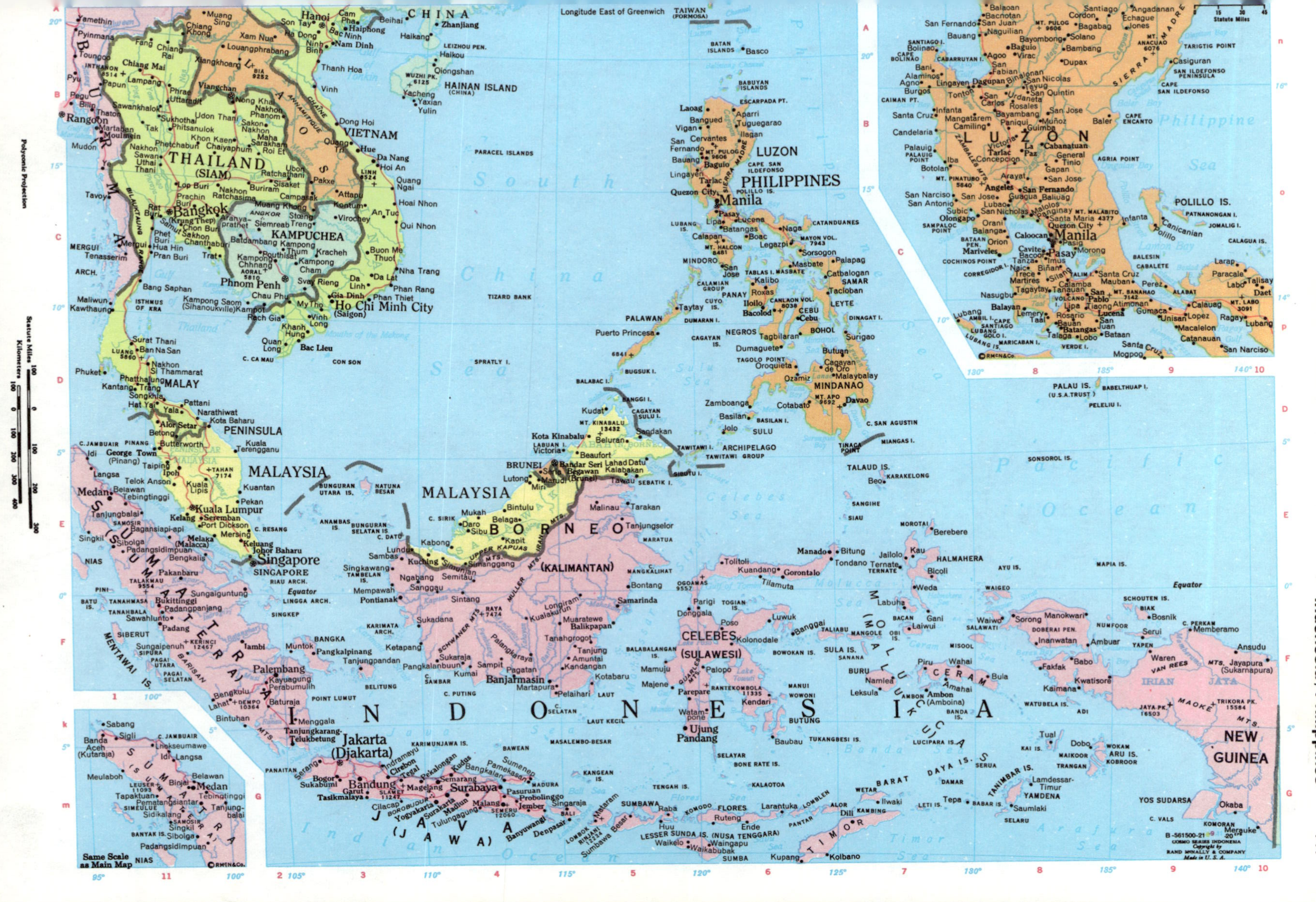
CHINA
Hanoi
HAINAN ISLAND (CHINA)
VIETNAM
Hue
Da Nang
THAILAND (SIAM)
Bangkok
KAMPUCHEA
Phnom Penh
Ho Chi Minh City (Saigon)
Rangoon
MALAY PENINSULA
MALAYSIA
Kuala Lumpur
Singapore
SINGAPORE
South China Sea
PARACEL ISLANDS
SPRATLY I.
TAIWAN (FORMOSA)
LUZON
PHILIPPINES
Manila
Quezon City
MINDORO
PANAY
NEGROS
CEBU
BOHOL
LEYTE
SAMAR
MINDANAO
Davao
Zamboanga
PALAWAN
Puerto Princesa
SULU ARCHIPELAGO
Celebes Sea
Pacific Ocean
BRUNEI
Kota Kinabalu
BORNEO (KALIMANTAN)
Banjarmasin
Samarinda
Pontianak
CELEBES (SULAWESI)
Ujung Pandang
Manado
HALMAHERA
Ternate
MOLUCCAS (MALUKU)
CERAM
Ambon (Amboina)
SUMATERA (SUMATRA)
Medan
Padang
Palembang
MENTAWAI IS.
INDONESIA
Jakarta (Djakarta)
Bandung
Semarang
Surabaya
JAWA (JAVA)
BALI
LESSER SUNDA IS. (NUSA TENGGARA)
FLORES
SUMBAWA
SUMBA
TIMOR
Kupang
IRIAN JAYA
Jayapura (Sukarnapura)
NEW GUINEA
Indian Ocean
Java Sea
Banda Sea
Arafura Sea
Timor Sea
Equator
Longitude East of Greenwich
POLILLO IS.
Philippine Sea
Same Scale as Main Map
Polyconic Projection
Statute Miles
Kilometers

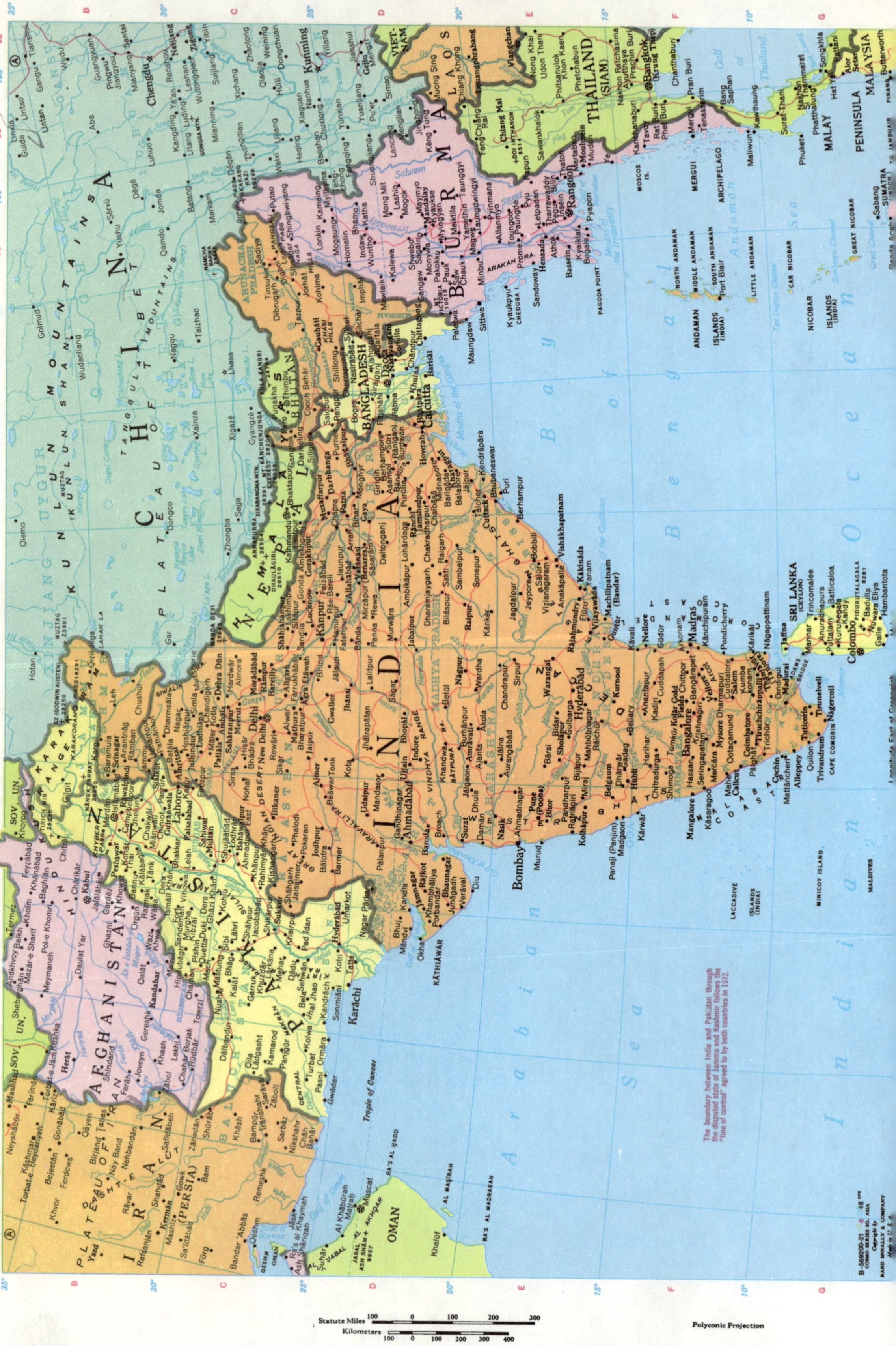

The boundary between India and Pakistan through the disputed state of Jammu and Kashmir follows the "line of control" agreed to by both countries in 1972.

Statute Miles 100 0 100 200 300

Kilometers 100 0 100 200 300 400

Polyconic Projection

Sinusoidal Projection

Statute Miles 100 0 100 300 500 700 900

Kilometers 100 0 100 300 500 700 900 1100 1300

AZORES (PORT.)
Same Scale as Main Map
CORVO
FLORES
GRACIOSA
SÃO JORGE
FAIAL
TERCEIRA
Horta
PICO
Angra do Heroísmo
SÃO MIGUEL
Ponta Delgada
SANTA MARIA
Atlantic Ocean
MADEIRA
PORTO SANTO
Funchal
MADEIRA ISLANDS (PORT.)
CANARY ISLANDS (SP.)
LANZAROTE
Arrecife
FUERTEVENTURA
Santa Cruz de la Palma
LA PALMA
TENERIFE
Santa Cruz de Tenerife
GOMERA
HIERRO
GRAN CANARIA
Las Palmas de Gran Canaria
CAPE JUBY
Tarfaya
Western Sahara has been occupied by Morocco
Mediterranean Sea
SPAIN
PORTUGAL
Lisbon (Lisboa)
Évora
Beja
CABO DE SÃO VICENTE
Faro
Sevilla
Córdoba
Granada
Cádiz
Málaga
Almería
Murcia
Cartagena
Albacete
Ciudad Real
Alicante
Gibraltar (U.K.)
Tanger (Tangier)
Ceuta (SP.)
Tétouan
Melilla (SP.)
Larache
Ksar el Kebir
Chechaouene
Ouezzane
Kenitra
Rabat
Salé
Fès
Taza
Meknès
Casablanca
Azemmour
Mohammedia
El Jadida
Settat
Berrechid
Khenifra
Azrou
Sidi Bennour
Safi
Youssoufia
Kasba Tadla
MOROCCO
Marrakech
Essaouira
Tamanar
JBEL TOUBKAL 13,661 FT.
CAP RHIR
Agadir
Taroudant
HAUT ATLAS
ANTI ATLAS
Zagora
Sidi Ifni
Tiznit
Foum el Hassane
Goulimime
Boudenib
Ksar es Souk
Guercif
Oujda
Figuig
Béchar
Béni Abbès
Tabelbala
Tindouf
HAMADA DU DRA
El Aaiún
CABO BOJADOR
Semara
WESTERN SAHARA
Bir Mogrein
Ain Ben Tili
Dakhla
PUNTA DURNFORD
Tropic of Cancer
ERG IGUIDI
Chenachane
ERG CHECH
Algiers (El Djazair)
Dellys
Cherchell
Ténès
Miliana
Blida
Médéa
Tizi Ouzou
Béjaïa (Bougie)
Djidjelli
Collo
Skikda (Philippeville)
Annaba (Bône)
Guelma
Constantine
Sétif
Batna
Aïn Beïda
Tébessa
Khenchela
Barika
M'Sila
Bou Saâda
Biskra
Tolga
Ech Cheliff
Mostaganem
Oran (Wahran)
Ghazaouet
Beni Saf
Mascara
Sidi bel Abbès
Tlemcen
Tiaret
Ksar el Boukhari
Djelfa
Laghouat
Aflou
El Kreider
Méchéria
Aïn Sefra
El Bayadh
HAUTS PLATEAUX
ATLAS SAHARIEN
El Meghaier
Touggourt
El Oued
Ghardaïa
Ouargla
El Goléa
GRAND ERG OCCIDENTAL
GRAND ERG ORIENTAL
Fort Mac Mahon
Timimoun
PLATEAU DU TADEMAÏT
ALGERIA
Adrar
Aoulef
Reggane
In Salah
PLAINE DU TIDIKELT
Bordj Omar Idriss
Illizi
Bordj Amguid
TASSILI N'AJJER
Djanet
Ouallene
TANEZROUFT
AHAGGAR
TAHAT 9,541 FT.
DJEBEL SERKOUT 7,566 FT.
Tamanrasset
TASSILI DU AHAGGAR
SAHARA
Sardinia (IT.)
Sicily
Palermo
Messina
Catania
MTE. ETNA 10,868 FT.
PANTELLERIA (IT.)
Bizerte
Tunis
Carthage
C. BON
Béja
El Kef
Nabeul
Zaghouan
Sousse
Monastir
Kairouan
El Mahdia
TUNISIA
Sfax
ÎLES KERKENNA
Gafsa
Gabès
Tozeur
Médenine
ÎLE DE DJERBA
ISOLE PELAGIE (IT.)
MALTA
Valletta
Tripoli (Tarabulus)
Zuwarah
Tajura
Al Khums
Misratah
Az Zawiyah
Gharyan
Nalut
Jadu
Mizdah
Qasr Bani Walid
Remada
TRIPOLITANIA
Darj
Ghudamis
AL HAMMADAH AL HAMRA
Al Qaryah ash Sharqiyah
LIBYA
AL JUFRA
Hun
Sawknah
OASES
HAMMADAT TINGHERT
FEZZAN
Brach
Sabhah
Awbari
Sardalas
Ghat
Marzuq
Zawilah
IDEHAN MARZUQ (DUNES)
El Qatrun
PLATEAU DE MANGUENI
PIC TOUSIDE 10,712 FT.
TIBESTI
Zouar
CAP BLANC
Nouadhibou
Fdérik
Choum
ADRAR
Atar
Chinguetti
MAKTEÏR
OUARANE
EL DJOUF
Taoudenni
MAURITANIA
Nouamghar
Nouakchott
Tidjikdja
Tichit
Moudjéria
Boutilimit
Tamchakett
Kiffa
Aleg
Boghé
Kaédi
Mederdra
Saint-Louis
Podor
Dagana
Matam
Oualâta
Néma
Timbédra
Mbout
Sélibaby
Nioro du Sahel
Nara
MALI
Tessalit
ADRAR DES IFORAS
Tin Zaouten
In Guezzam
Araouane
AZAOUAD
Kidal
VALLÉE DU TILEMSI
Bamba
Bourem
Gao
Ansongo
Ménaka
Goundam
Niafounké
Tombouctou (Timbuktu)
Hombori
Douentza
Mopti
Bandiagara
Djenné
Sokolo
Ké Macina
Ségou
San
Koutiala
Koulikoro
Bamako
Kita
Kayes
Bafoulabé
Banamba
Bougouni
Sikasso
Louga
Linguère
Rufisque
Thiès
Touba
Dakar
Diourbel
Kaolack
SENEGAL
Bakel
Banjul
GAMBIA
Georgetown
Tambacounda
Kolda
Bignona
Ziguinchor
Kédougou
GUINEA-BISSAU
Bissau
Bolama
Boké
Boffa
Gaoual
FOUTA DJALLON
Labé
Mamou
Dabola
Kindia
Conakry
Forécariah
Faranah
Kouroussa
Kankan
Siguiri
Dinguiraye
GUINEA
Port Loko
Freetown
Waterloo
Makeni
SIERRA LEONE
Moyamba
Bo
Kenema
Bonthe
Pujehun
Kailahun
PIC. DE TIBÉ 4,934 FT.
Beyla
Nzérékoré
NIMBA MTS.
LIBERIA
Gbanga
Robertsport
Monrovia
Careysburg
Marshall
Buchanan
River Cess
Greenville
Harper
CAPE PALMAS
Grand Cess
Tabou
Sassandra
IVORY COAST
Odienné
Boundiali
Korhogo
Mankono
Séguéla
Katiola
Bouaké
Man
Daloa
Gagnoa
Soubré
Divo
Agboville
Abidjan
Grand-Lahou
Grand-Bassam
Yamoussoukro
Dabakala
Bondoukou
Bouna
BURKINA FASO
Ouagadougou
Koudougou
Dédougou
Ouahigouya
Djibo
Dori
Kaya
Bobo Dioulasso
Houndé
Léo
Banfora
Gaoua
Tenkodogo
Fada Ngourma
Diapaga
Matiakoali
SUDAN
GHANA
Navrongo
Wa
Gambaga
Bole
Yendi
Tamale
Salaga
Wenchi
Sunyani
Kintampo
Mampong
ASHANTI
Kumasi
Obuasi
Koforidua
Dunkwa
Kade
Accra
Oda
Winneba
Saltpond
Cape Coast
Sekondi-Takoradi
Axim
C. THREE POINTS
Tarkwa
Aboisso
Bengourou
Enchi
TOGO
Sansanné-Mango
Sokodé
Blitta
Atakpamé
Lomé
BENIN
Natitingou
Djougou
Parakou
Kandi
Savé
Savalou
Abomey
Allada
Ouidah
Cotonou
Porto-Novo
Pobé
Kpandu
Keta
Ada
Bight of Benin
Gulf of Guinea
NIGER
Tillabéry
Niamey
Say
Dosso
Gaya
Tahoua
Madaoua
Birni-Nkoni
Dogondoutchi
Maradi
Zinder
Tessaoua
Gouré
Nguigmi
Agadez
In-Gall
AÏR
MONTS BAGZANE 6,234 FT.
MASSIF DE TARAZIT
Iferouane
TÉNÉRÉ
KAOUAR
Bilma
Agadem
BODÉLÉ
NIGERIA
Sokoto
Birnin Kebbi
Kaura Namoda
Gusau
Katsina
Kano
Gumel
Nguru
Hadejia
Zaria
Kaduna
Kontagora
Zungeru
Minna
Bida
Jebba
Ilorin
Kishi
Shaki
Oyo
Iwo
Ogbomosho
Oshogbo
Ilesha
Ife
Ibadan
Abeokuta
Ijebu Ode
Lagos
Benin City
Sapele
Agbor
Onitsha
Owerri
Warri
Forcados
Aba
Port Harcourt
Bonny
NIGER DELTA
Calabar
Enugu
Makurdi
Ibi
Lokoja
Idah
Ubiaja
Jos
Bukuru
Bauchi
Kafanchan
Pankshin
Gombe
Potiskum
Damaturu
Maiduguri
Dikwa
Geidam
Yola
Numan
Lau
Wawa
Yelwa
Koko
Baro
Ikeyin
Gaya
CHAD
Mao
Moussoro
Massakory
Ndjamena
Bongor
Lai
Moundou
Léré
Mora
Maroua
Garoua
MANDARA MTS.
CAMEROON
Kontcha
Ngaoundéré
Tibati
Banyo
Gashaka
GOTEL MTS.
Bamenda
Foumban
Dschang
Bafang
Nkongsamba
Bafia
MT. CAMEROON 13,354 FT.
Victoria
Buea
Douala
Edea
Yaoundé
Eséka
Mbalmayo
Akonolinga
Nanga Eboko
Doumé
Bétaré Oya
Batouri
Bertoua
Yokadouma
Lomié
Ebolowa
Kribi
Campo
Ambam
CENTRAL AFRICAN REP.
Bocaranga
Meiganga
Baboua
Bouar
Berbérati
Nola
Bayanga
BIOKO
Malabo
EQUATORIAL GUINEA
Bata
RÍO MUNI
EQUATORIAL GUINEA
ISLA DE CORISCO
Oyem
Evinayong
Mitzic
Makokou
Booué
MTS. DE CRISTAL
Libreville
PRÍNCIPE
SÃO TOMÉ AND PRINCIPE
SÃO TOMÉ
São Tomé
Equator
Lambaréné
Ndjolé
GABON
C. LOPEZ
Port-Gentil
Omboué
Sindara
Lastoursville
Moanda
Franceville
Sette Cama
Tchibanga
Mayumba
ANNOBÓN I. (EQUAT. GUI.)
Makoua
Fort Rousset
CONGO
Gamboma
Djambala
Ouesso
Pangala
Sibiti
Mayama
Brazzaville
Kinshasa (Léopoldville)
Pointe-Noire
ZAIRE
CAPE VERDE
Same Scale as Main Map
SANTO ANTÃO
SÃO VICENTE
SÃO NICOLAU
SAL
BOA VISTA
SÃO TIAGO
FOGO
MAIO
Praia
B-589700-22
COSMO SERIES N.W. AFRICA
Copyright by RAND McNALLY & COMPANY
Made in U. S. A.
Longitude West of Greenwich
Longitude East of Greenwich
Statute Miles 100 0 100 200 300
Kilometers 100 0 100 200 300 400
Sinusoidal Projection

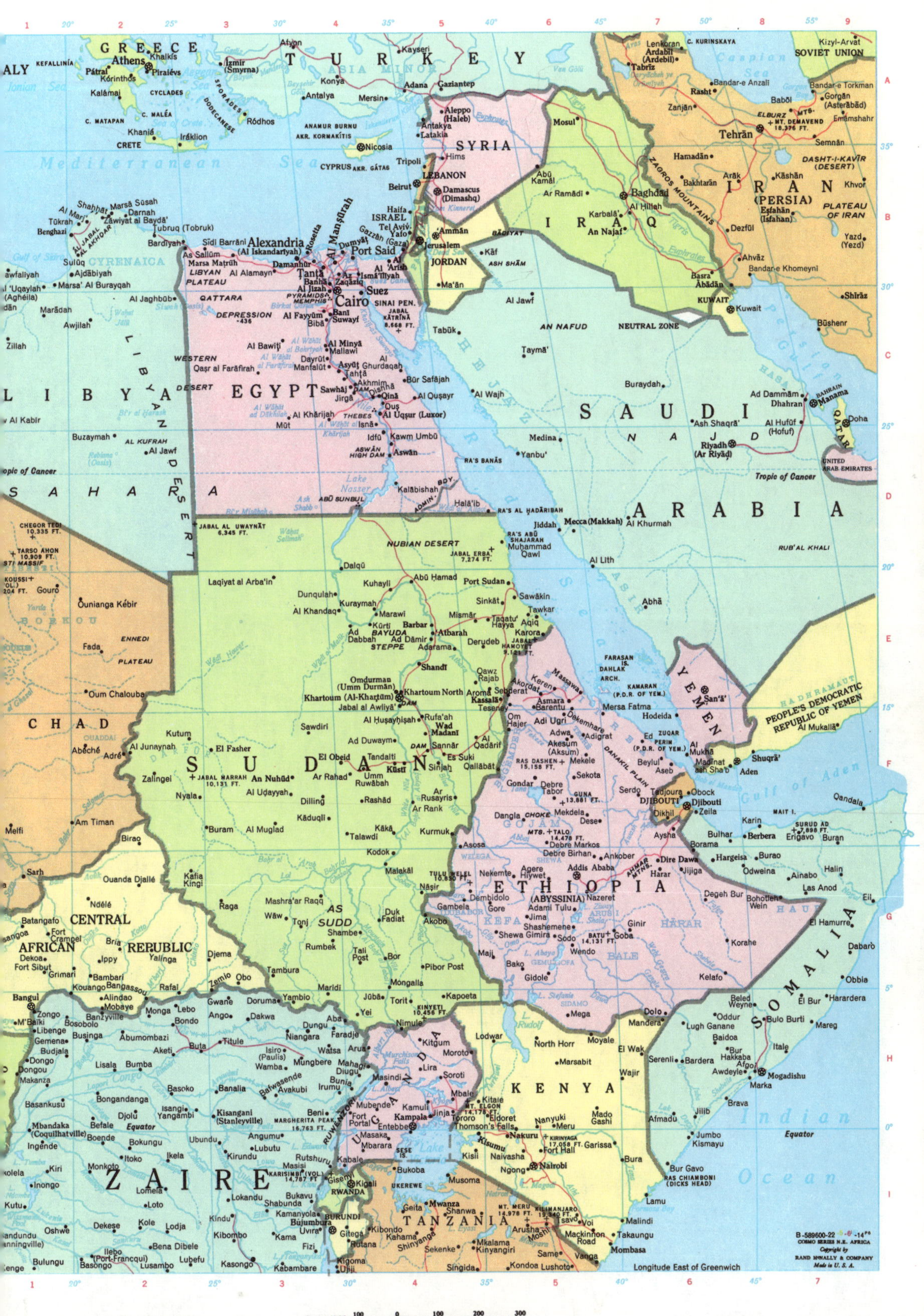

Sinusoidal Projection

Statute Miles 100 0 100 200 300

Kilometers 100 0 100 200 300 400

Statute Miles 100 0 100 200 300

Kilometers 100 0 100 200 300 400

Sinusoidal Projection

Lambert Azimuthal Equal Area Projection

Statute Miles 100 0 100 200 300

Kilometers 100 0 100 200 300 400

NORTH ISLAND
SOUTH ISLAND
NEW ZEALAND
Auckland
Wellington
Christchurch
Dunedin
Hamilton
Napier
Hastings
Rotorua
Invercargill
Nelson
QUEENSLAND
NEW SOUTH WALES
VICTORIA
SOUTH AUSTRALIA
AUSTRALIAN CAPITAL TERRITORY
GREAT ARTESIAN BASIN
Brisbane
Sydney
Newcastle
Canberra
Melbourne
Adelaide
Broken Hill
Rockhampton
Toowoomba
Tropic of Capricorn
GREAT BARRIER REEF
Tasman Sea
Indian Ocean
Great Australian Bight
Statute Miles
Kilometers
Lambert Conformal Conic Projection

Sinusoidal Projection

Statute Miles 100 0 100 300 500 700

Kilometers 100 0 100 300 500 700 900 1100

Longitude West of Greenwich

H -549200-21-4-5[BY]
COSMO SERIES SO. ARG. & CHILE
Copyright by
RAND McNALLY & COMPANY
Made in U. S. A.

Same Scale as Main Map

©RMcN&Co.

Statute Miles 50 0 50 100 150

Kilometers 50 0 50 100 150 200

Oblique Conic Conformal Projection

Longitude West of Greenwich
BRAZIL
PERU
BOLIVIA
PARAGUAY
CHILE
ARGENTINA
URUGUAY
Pacific Ocean
AMAZONAS
ACRE
RONDÔNIA
PARÁ
MATO GROSSO
MADRE DE DIOS
CUSCO
PUNO
AREQUIPA
MOQUEGUA
TACNA
PANDO
EL BENI
LA PAZ
COCHABAMBA
SANTA CRUZ
ORURO
POTOSÍ
CHUQUISACA
TARIJA
BOQUERÓN
OLIMPO
CHACO
PRESIDENTE HAYES
CONCEPCIÓN
AMAMBAY
SAN PEDRO
CANINDEYÚ
ALTO PARANÁ
CAAGUAZÚ
CAAZAPÁ
ITAPÚA
MISIONES
ÑEEMBUCÚ
PARAGUARÍ
GUAIRÁ
CORDILLERA
CENTRAL
JUJUY
SALTA
FORMOSA
TUCUMÁN
SANTIAGO DEL ESTERO
CATAMARCA
LA RIOJA
SAN JUAN
CÓRDOBA
SANTA FE
CORRIENTES
ENTRE RÍOS
MISIONES
RIO GRANDE DO SUL
ANTOFAGASTA
ATACAMA
TARAPACÁ
DESIERTO DE ATACAMA
ANDES
CORDILLERA OCCIDENTAL
CORDILLERA CENTRAL
CORDILLERA ORIENTAL
SERRA DOS PACAÁS NOVOS
SERRA DOS PARECIS
SERRA DOS APIACÁS
SERRA DO TOMBADOR
SERRA FORMOSA
SERRA DA CHAPADA
CORDILHEIRA DO NORTE
SIERRA DE CALALASTE
SIERRA DE FAMATINA
GRAN CHACO
Tropic of Capricorn
NEVADO ILLAMPU 23012
NEVADO SAJAMA 21391
VOL. MISTI +19101
CO. NUEVO MUNDO +19751
CERRO DE TOCORPURI 22,162
CERRO LEJÍA 18,996
VOLCÁN LLULLAILLACO 22057
OJOS DEL SALADO 22,590
CERRO DEL POTRO 19,127
PISSIS 22,546
PTA. FALSA CHIPANA
PTA. ANGAMOS
PTA. TETAS
PTA. SAN PEDRO
PTA. MORRO
La Paz
Sucre
Cochabamba
Oruro
Potosí
Santa Cruz
Trinidad
Tarija
Cobija
Asunción
Salta
San Salvador de Jujuy
San Miguel de Tucumán
Santiago del Estero
Catamarca
La Rioja
Córdoba
Santa Fe
Corrientes
Resistencia
Formosa
Posadas
Antofagasta
Iquique
Arica
Tacna
Arequipa
Puno
Rio Branco
Cuiabá
Corumbá
Concepción
Villarrica
Encarnación
Pilar
Paraná
Concordia
Salto
Coquimbo
La Serena
Copiapó
Rafaela
Oblique Conic Conformal Projection
Statute Miles 50 0 50 100 150
Kilometers 50 0 50 100 150 200

Statute Miles 50 0 50 100 150
Kilometers 50 0 50 100 150 200

Oblique Conic Conformal Projection

COLOMBIA
ECUADOR
PERU
BRAZIL
BOLIVIA
CHILE
VENEZUELA
AMAZONAS
ACRE
PANDO
LORETO
UCAYALI
HUÁNUCO
PASCO
JUNÍN
SAN MARTÍN
LA LIBERTAD
CAJAMARCA
MADRE DE DIOS
APURÍMAC
PUNO
AREQUIPA
MOQUEGUA
TACNA
TARAPACÁ
LA PAZ
BENI
COCHABAMBA
POTOSÍ
CAQUETÁ
PUTUMAYO
NARIÑO
GUAVIARE
VAUPÉS
GUAINÍA
NAPO
PASTAZA
MORONA-SANTIAGO
ESMERALDAS
Quito
Guayaquil
Cuenca
Lima
Callao
Iquitos
Trujillo
Chiclayo
Piura
Chimbote
Arequipa
Cuzco
Huancayo
Pucallpa
Ica
Tacna
Arica
Puno
Juliaca
La Paz
Oruro
Cochabamba
Sucre
Potosí
Leticia
Pasto
Ibarra
Ambato
Riobamba
Machala
Loja
Tumbes
Moyobamba
Tarapoto
Yurimaguas
Huánuco
Cerro de Pasco
La Oroya
Ayacucho
Abancay
Mollendo
Ilo
Pisco
Nazca
Puerto Maldonado
Equator
Pacific Ocean
CORDILLERA OCCIDENTAL
CORD. BLANCA
NEV. HUASCARÁN 22205
Amazon
Marañón
Ucayali
Huallaga
Putumayo
Napo
L. Titicaca
PACHACAMAC
MACHU PICCHU
CHAN-CHAN
ISLA PUNÁ
PUNTA GALERA
CABO PASADO
GALÁPAGOS (ECUADOR)
ARCHIPIÉLAGO DE COLÓN
I. DARWIN
I. WOLF
I. PINTA
I. MARCHENA
I. GENOVESA
I. SAN SALVADOR (JAMES)
I. BALTRA
I. STA. CRUZ (INDEFATIGABLE)
I. SAN CRISTÓBAL (CHATHAM)
I. STA. FÉ
I. ESPAÑOLA (HOOD)
I. STA. MARÍA
I. FERNANDINA
I. ISABELA
Puerto Baquerizo Moreno
Villamil
El Progreso
Same Scale as Main Map
Longitude West of Greenwich
B-549400-21
COSMO SERIES PERU, ECUADOR
Copyright by RAND McNALLY & COMPANY
Made in U. S. A.
Oblique Conic Conformal Projection
Statute Miles
Kilometers

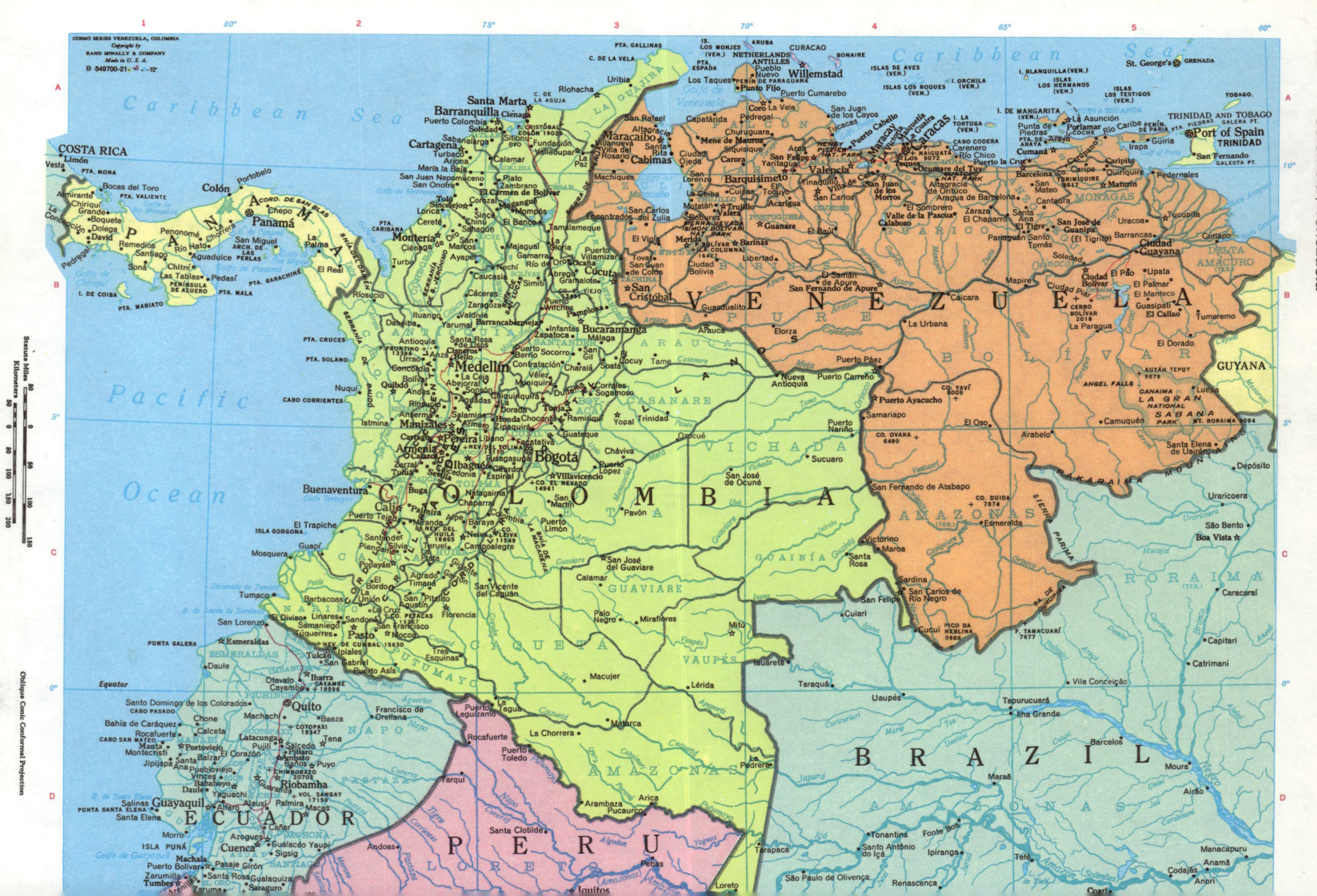
Caribbean Sea
Pacific Ocean
VENEZUELA
COLOMBIA
PANAMA
ECUADOR
PERU
BRAZIL
GUYANA
COSTA RICA
TRINIDAD AND TOBAGO
NETHERLANDS ANTILLES
Caracas
Bogotá
Quito
Panamá
Port of Spain
Willemstad
Medellín
Cali
Barranquilla
Cartagena
Maracaibo
Valencia
Barquisimeto
Guayaquil
Cúcuta
Bucaramanga
Equator
Statute Miles
Kilometers
Oblique Conic Conformal Projection

SOVIET UNION
ASIA
NORTH POLE
Arctic Ocean
GREENLAND (DENMARK)
ICELAND
Reykjavík
ELLESMERE
BAFFIN ISLAND
VICTORIA ISLAND
BANKS ISLAND
ALASKA
BROOKS RANGE
ALASKA RANGE
MT. MCKINLEY
Beaufort Sea
Baffin Bay
Davis Strait
Hudson Bay
CANADA
ROCKY MOUNTAINS
MACKENZIE MTS.
NEWFOUNDLAND
UNITED STATES
MEXICO
SIERRA MADRE OCCIDENTAL
SIERRA MADRE ORIENTAL
Pacific Ocean
Atlantic Ocean
Gulf of Mexico
Caribbean Sea
Tropic of Cancer
WEST INDIES
CUBA
BAHAMAS
JAMAICA
HAITI
DOM. REP.
PUERTO RICO (U.S.A.)
GREATER ANTILLES
CENTRAL AMERICA
BELIZE
GUATEMALA
HONDURAS
EL SALVADOR
NICARAGUA
COSTA RICA
PANAMA
SOUTH AMERICA
VENEZUELA
COLOMBIA
ANDES MTS.
BERMUDA IS. (BR.)
Anchorage
Fairbanks
Juneau
Whitehorse
Yellowknife
Edmonton
Calgary
Vancouver
Victoria
Regina
Winnipeg
Toronto
Ottawa
Montréal
Québec
Halifax
St. John's
Seattle
Portland
San Francisco
Los Angeles
San Diego
Las Vegas
Phoenix
Salt Lake City
Denver
Albuquerque
El Paso
Dallas
Houston
San Antonio
Oklahoma City
Kansas City
Omaha
Minneapolis
St. Paul
Chicago
Milwaukee
Detroit
St. Louis
Memphis
Nashville
Atlanta
New Orleans
Miami
Tampa
Jacksonville
Cleveland
Pittsburgh
Cincinnati
Washington, D.C.
Baltimore
Philadelphia
New York
Boston
Buffalo
Tijuana
Ciudad Juárez
Chihuahua
Monterrey
Guadalajara
Mexico City
Puebla
Veracruz
Mérida
Acapulco de Juárez
Havana
Kingston
Port-au-Prince
Santo Domingo
San Juan
Guatemala
San Salvador
Tegucigalpa
Managua
San José
Panama
Bogotá
Medellín
Barranquilla
Cartagena
Maracaibo
Longitude West of Greenwich
SOVIET UNION
ALASKA
Bering Sea
ALEUTIAN ISLANDS
Pacific Ocean
Same Scale as Main Map
© RMcN&Co.
Lambert Azimuthal Equal Area Projection
Statute Miles 100 0 100 200 300 400 500 600 700 800
Kilometers 100 0 100 200 400 600 800 1000

Statute Miles 50 25 0 50 100 150 200 250

Kilometers 50 0 100 200 300

Oblique Conic Conformal Projection

Oblique Conic Conformal Projection

Statute Miles 25 0 25 75 125

Kilometers 25 0 25 75 125 175

Same Scale as Main Map

Statute Miles 100 0 100 200 300

Kilometers 100 0 100 200 300 400

Lambert Conformal Conic Projection

Edmonton
Calgary
Red Deer
ALBERTA
Vancouver
Victoria
Prince George
Prince Rupert
Kamloops
Kelowna
Penticton
Vernon
Nanaimo
Port Alberni
Powell River
Dawson Creek
Bellingham
Port Angeles
QUEEN CHARLOTTE ISLANDS
VANCOUVER ISLAND
WASHINGTON
IDAHO
MONTANA
Longitude West of Greenwich
Oblique Cylindrical Projection
Statute Miles
Kilometers

COSMO SERIES ALBERTA
Copyright by RAND McNALLY & COMPANY
Made in U.S.A.
H 520201-2
Longitude West of Greenwich
Fort McMurray
Waterways
Anzac
Notikewin
Manning
Dixonville
Peace River
Grimshaw
Fairview
Berwyn
Nampa
Marie-Reine
Dawson Creek
Pouce-Coupe
Spirit River
Rycroft
Eaglesham
Girouxville
Falher
Donnelly
McLennan
Atikameg
Wabasca
Desmarais
PELICAN MTN.
Conklin
High Prairie
Grouard Mission
Lesser Slave Lake
Enilda
Joussard
Driftpile
Faust
Kinuso
Canyon Creek
Slave Lake
Spurfield
Smith
Hondo
Calling Lake
Wandering River
Imperial Mills
Sexsmith
Clairmont
Grande Prairie
Beaverlodge
Wembley
Hythe
Demmitt
Tupper
Valleyview
SWAN HILLS
Swan Hills
Iosegun Lake (Fox Creek)
Chisholm Mills
Flatbush
Fawcett
Jarvie
Athabasca
Colinton
Plamondon
Lac la Biche
Venice
Hylo
Rich Lake
Cold Lake
Grand Centre
Bonnyville
Fort Kent
Glendon
St. Paul
Elk Point
Lindbergh
Heinsburg
Fort Assiniboine
Windfall
Whitecourt
Blue Ridge
Barrhead
Westlock
Grande Cache
WILLMORE WILDERNESS PROVINCIAL PARK
Edson
Obed
Marlboro
Hinton
Entrance
Robb
Coalspur
Mercoal
Luscar
Cadomin
Foothills
Mountain Park
Jasper
JASPER NATIONAL PARK
MT. ROBSON 12972
YELLOWHEAD PASS
Edmonton
St. Albert
Stony Plain
Spruce Grove
Fort Saskatchewan
Sherwood Park
Devon
Leduc
Calmar
Thorsby
Drayton Valley
Lodgepole
Camrose
Wetaskiwin
Ponoka
Vegreville
Vermilion
Lloydminster
Wainwright
Viking
Kinsella
Rimbey
Nordegg
Rocky Mountain House
Sylvan Lake
Red Deer
Lacombe
Innisfail
Stettler
Castor
Coronation
Consort
Olds
Sundre
Didsbury
Three Hills
Trochu
Drumheller
Hanna
Oyen
Banff
Canmore
BANFF NATIONAL PARK
Lake Louise
Calgary
Cochrane
Airdrie
Okotoks
High River
Black Diamond
Turner Valley
Nanton
Claresholm
Vulcan
Brooks
Bassano
Medicine Hat
Redcliff
Fort Macleod
Lethbridge
Taber
Coaldale
Pincher Creek
Blairmore
Coleman
Cardston
Magrath
Raymond
Milk River
Coutts
Sweetgrass
Sunburst
WATERTON LAKES NAT. PARK
WATERTON-GLACIER INTERNATIONAL PEACE PARK
GLACIER NATIONAL PARK
ROCKY MOUNTAINS
BRITISH COLUMBIA
IDAHO
MONTANA
CANADA
U.S.
SASKATCHEWAN
Statute Miles
N. W. TER.
Ft. Smith
Ft. Fitzgerald
WOOD BUFFALO NAT. PARK
CARIBOU MTS.
Ft. Chipewyan
Ft. Vermilion
La Crête
Meander River
Paddle Prairie
Ft. McKay
Ft. McMurray
Peace River
Grande Prairie
Smith
Athabasca
AREA SHOWN ON MAIN MAP
Edmonton
Edson
Jasper
Nordegg
Red Deer
Banff
Calgary
Medicine Hat
Lethbridge
Trail
WASH.
IDA.
MONTANA
Statute Miles 10 0 10 20 30 40 50 60 70
Kilometers 10 0 10 20 40 60 80 100
Oblique Cylindrical Projection

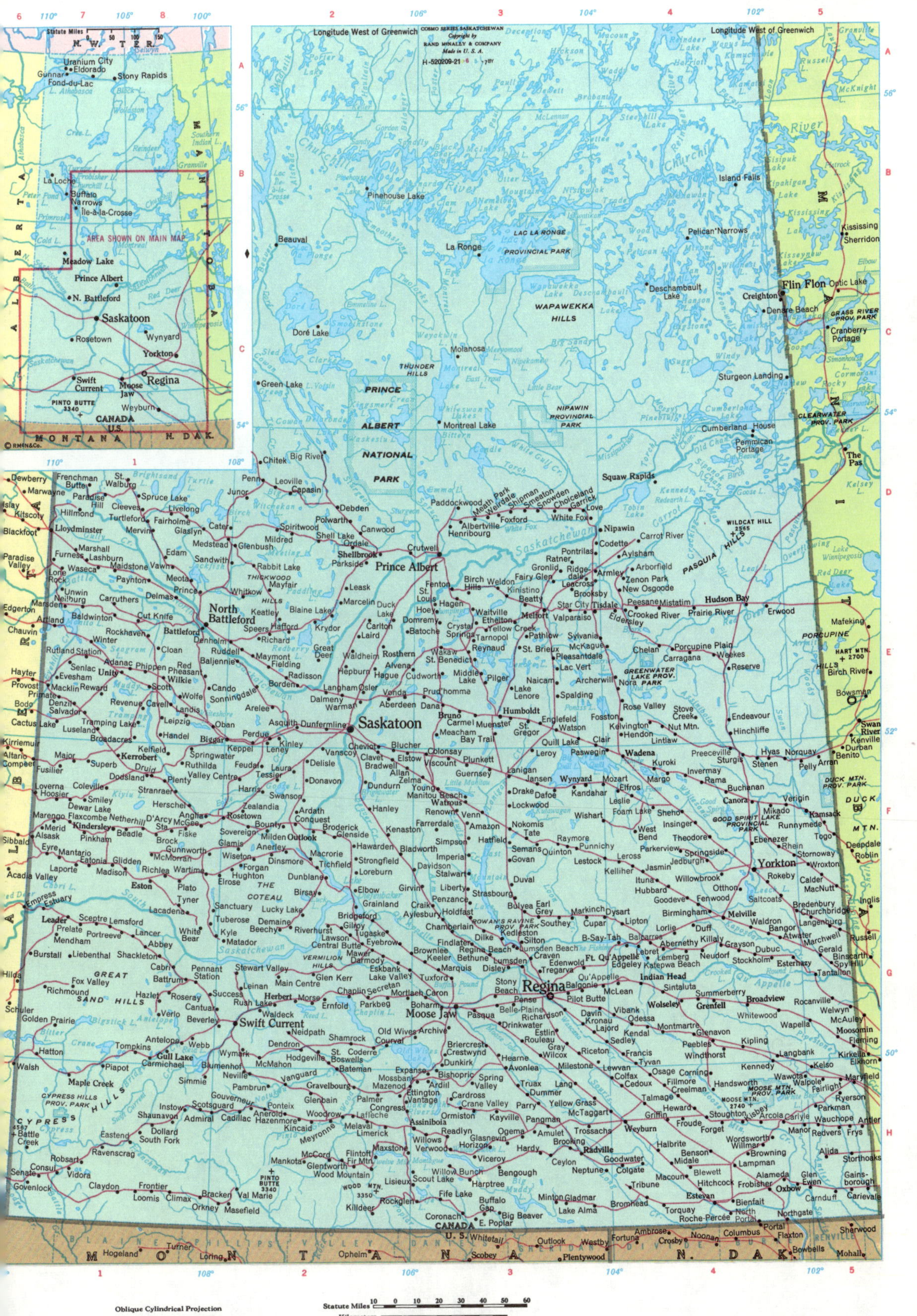

Oblique Cylindrical Projection

Statute Miles 10 0 10 20 30 40 50 60

Kilometers 10 0 10 20 40 60 80

Longitude West of Greenwich
H-520203-21- 7 BY
COSMO SERIES MANITOBA
Copyright by
RAND McNALLY & COMPANY
Made in U. S. A.
Hudson Bay
Port Nelson
York Factory
Thibaudeau
Weir River
Amery
Gillam
Lynn Lake
South Indian Lake
Southern Indian Lake
Churchill
Nelson
Split Lake
Ilford
Shamattawa
Nelson House
Thompson
Pikwitonei
Thicket Portage
Kississing
Sherridon
Snow Lake
Flin Flon
Herb Lake
Wabowden
Oxford House
Oxford Lake
Gods Lake
GRASS RIVER PROVINCIAL PARK
Cranberry Portage
Cross Lake
Sturgeon Landing
Cormorant
ROSS I.
CLEARWATER PROV. PARK
The Pas
Norway House
Island Lake
Moose Lake
LIMESTONE PT.
BIG MOSSY POINT
O N T A R I O
Grand Rapids
Easterville
LONG PT.
Lake Winnipeg
Barrows
PORCUPINE
Mafeking
HART MTN. +2700
HILLS
Birch River
Pelican Rapids
BIRCH I.
REINDEER ISLAND
BERENS I.
Berens River
Bowsman
Swan River
Duck Bay
Minitonas
Kenville
Durban
Benito
Arran
Pelly
Camperville
Skownan
DUCK MTN. PROV. PARK
DUCK MOUNTAIN
Pine River
Winnipegosis
Fork River
Kamsack
Ethelbert
BALDY MTN. 2727
Gypsumville
St. Martin Station
Anama Bay
Jackhead Harbour
Matheson Island
Little Bullhead
Loon Straits
Togo
Deepdale
Roblin
Sifton
Rorketon
Magnet
Steep Rock
Spearhill
PEONAN PT.
Moosehorn
Ashern
Hodgson
Fisher Branch
BLACK I.
Hecla
HECLA I.
Manigotagan
Bissett
Grandview
Gilbert Plains
Dauphin
Ochre River
Ste. Rose-du-Lac
Makinak
Laurier
Alonsa
McCreary
RIDING MOUNTAIN NATIONAL PARK
Inglis
Russell
Riverton
Arborg
Mulvihill
Eriksdale
Poplarfield
Chatfield
ELK I.
Victoria Beach
Gimli
Pine Falls
Lake Manitoba
Lundar
Oak Point
Inwood
St. Laurent
Winnipeg Beach
Teulon
Dunnottar
Great Falls
Grand Beach
Pointe-du-Bois
Lac-du-Bonnet
Scanterbury
Selkirk
Stonewall
Beausejour
WHITESHELL PROV. PARK
Whitemouth
Rennie
Minaki
Reddit
McIntosh
Vermilion Bay
Dryden
Wabigoon
Keewatin
Kenora
Hawk Lake
Eagle River
Ingolf
Portage-la-Prairie
Gladstone
Neepawa
Minnedosa
Rivers
Brandon
Carberry
Winnipeg
Oakville
Starbuck
Souris
Virden
Melita
Boissevain
Killarney
Morden
Winkler
Altona
Emerson
St. Pierre-Jolys
Steinbach
Ste. Anne-des-Chênes
Sprague
Middlebro
Piney
Vita
Sandilands
Woodridge
East Braintree
Indian Bay
AULNEAU PENINSULA
Lake of the Woods
Rainy Lake
Mine Centre
INTERNATIONAL PEACE GARDEN
TURTLE MTN.
Bottineau
Rolla
Dunseith
Mohall
Westhope
Sherwood
Hansboro
Rocklake
Calvin
Walhalla
Cavalier
Pembina
St. Vincent
Hamilton
Lancaster
Warroad
Roseau
Roosevelt
CANADA
U. S.
N. D A K. M I N N.
S A S K A T C H E W A N
O N T A R I O
N.W. TER.
Caribou
Churchill
C. CHURCHILL
Brochet
C. TATNAM
AREA SHOWN ON MAIN MAP
Statute Miles
Kilometers
Oblique Cylindrical Projection

Oblique Cylindrical Projection
Statute Miles 5 0 5 10 20 30 40 50
Kilometers 5 0 5 15 25 35 45 55 65 75
Toronto
Ottawa
Hamilton
London
Kitchener
Windsor
Detroit
Buffalo
Rochester
Kingston
MANITOULIN ISLAND
ALGONQUIN PROVINCIAL PARK
NEW YORK
MICHIGAN
QUEBEC
CANADA
U.S.
H-320206-21
COSMO SERIES ONTARIO
Copyright by RAND McNALLY & COMPANY
Made in U. S. A.

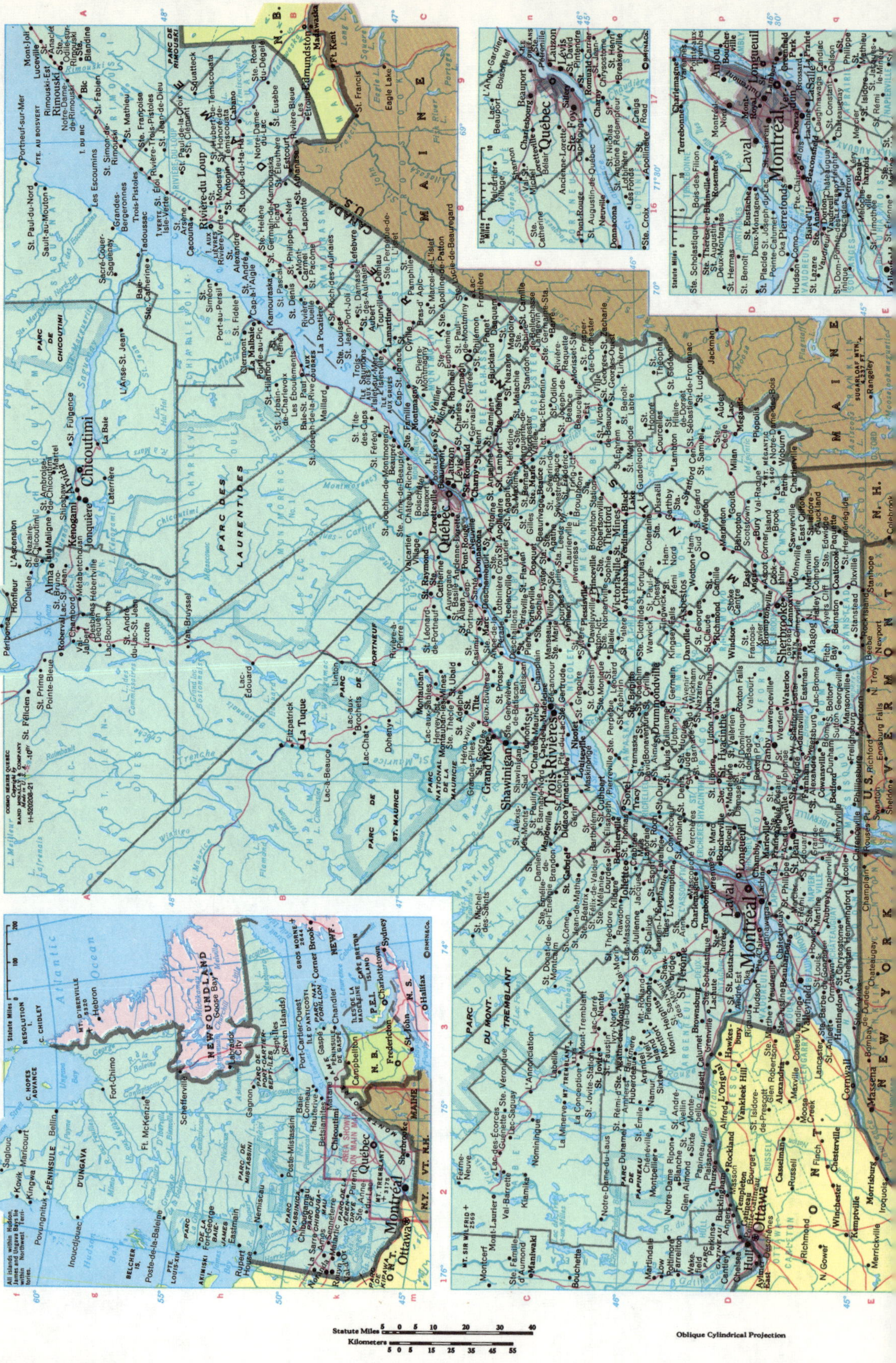

Statute Miles 5 0 5 10 20 30 40

Kilometers 5 0 5 15 25 35 45 55

Oblique Cylindrical Projection

QUEBEC
NEW BRUNSWICK
PRINCE EDWARD ISLAND
NOVA SCOTIA
CAPE BRETON ISLAND
ÎLES DE LA MADELEINE
MAINE
U.S.A.
CANADA
Gulf of St. Lawrence
Atlantic Ocean
Bay of Fundy
Cabot Strait
SABLE I.
Saint John
Fredericton
Moncton
Charlottetown
Halifax
Dartmouth
Sydney
Summerside
Truro
Yarmouth
Bathurst
Campbellton
Edmundston
Woodstock
Amherst
Antigonish
Lunenburg
Liverpool
Longitude West of Greenwich
H-520212-21
COSMO SERIES MARITIME PROV
Copyright by RAND McNALLY & COMPANY
Made in U. S. A.
Oblique Cylindrical Projection
Statute Miles
Kilometers

Statute Miles 5 0 5 10 20 30 40 50 60

Kilometers 5 0 5 10 20 30 40 50 60 70 80

Lambert Conformal Conic Projection

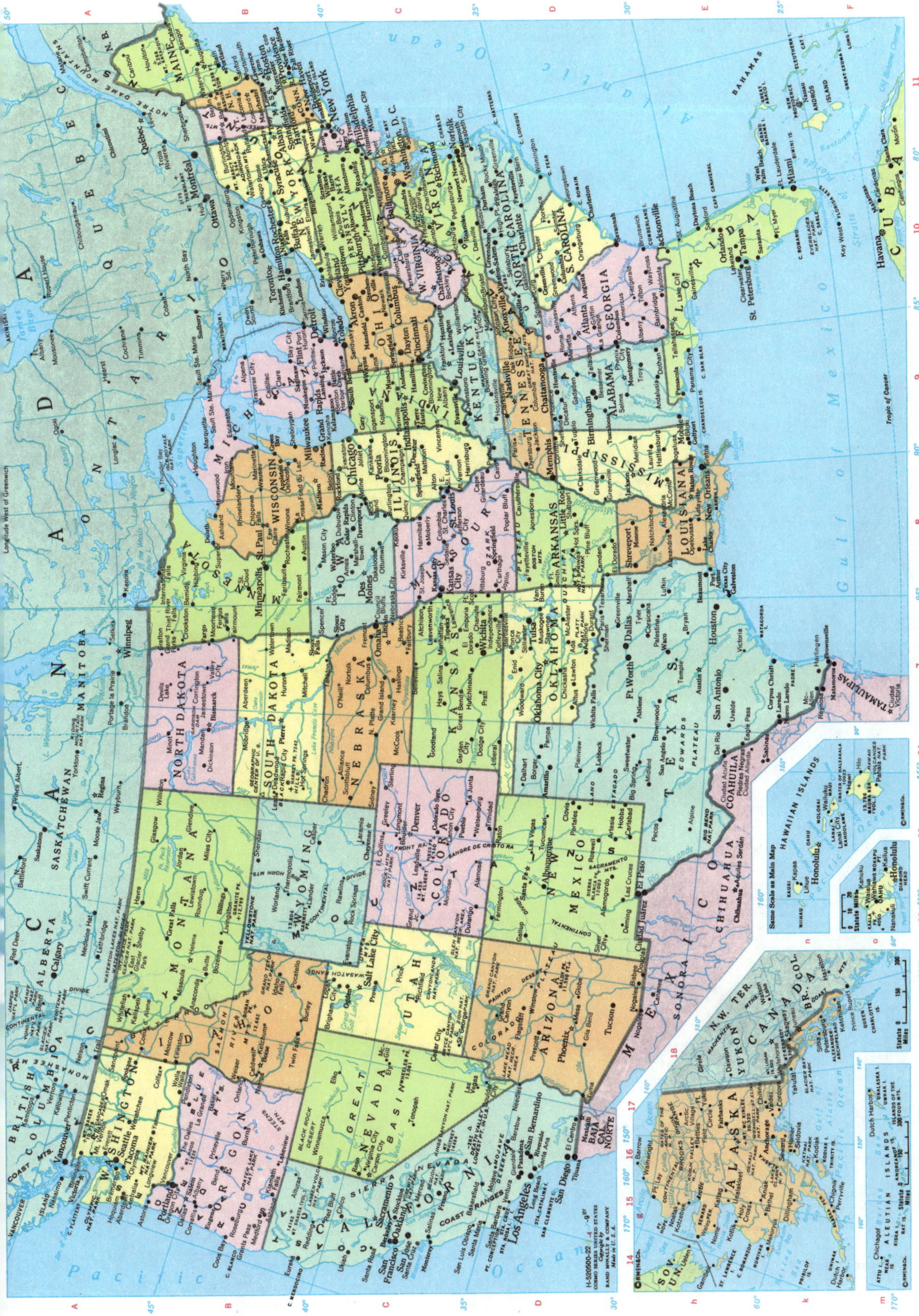

Lambert Conformal Conic Projection

Statute Miles 100 0 100 200 300

Kilometers 100 0 100 200 300 400

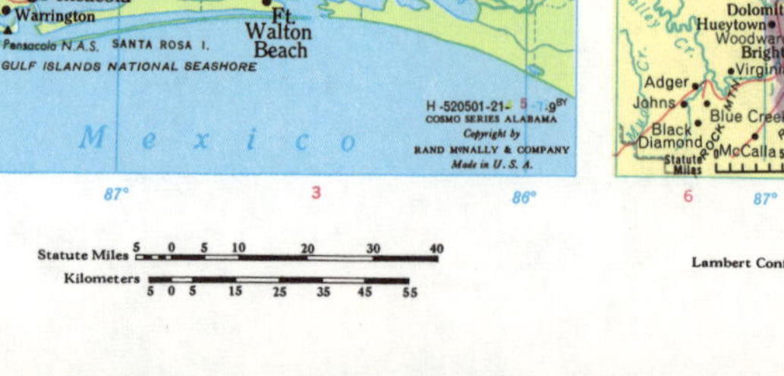

Lambert Conformal Conic Projection

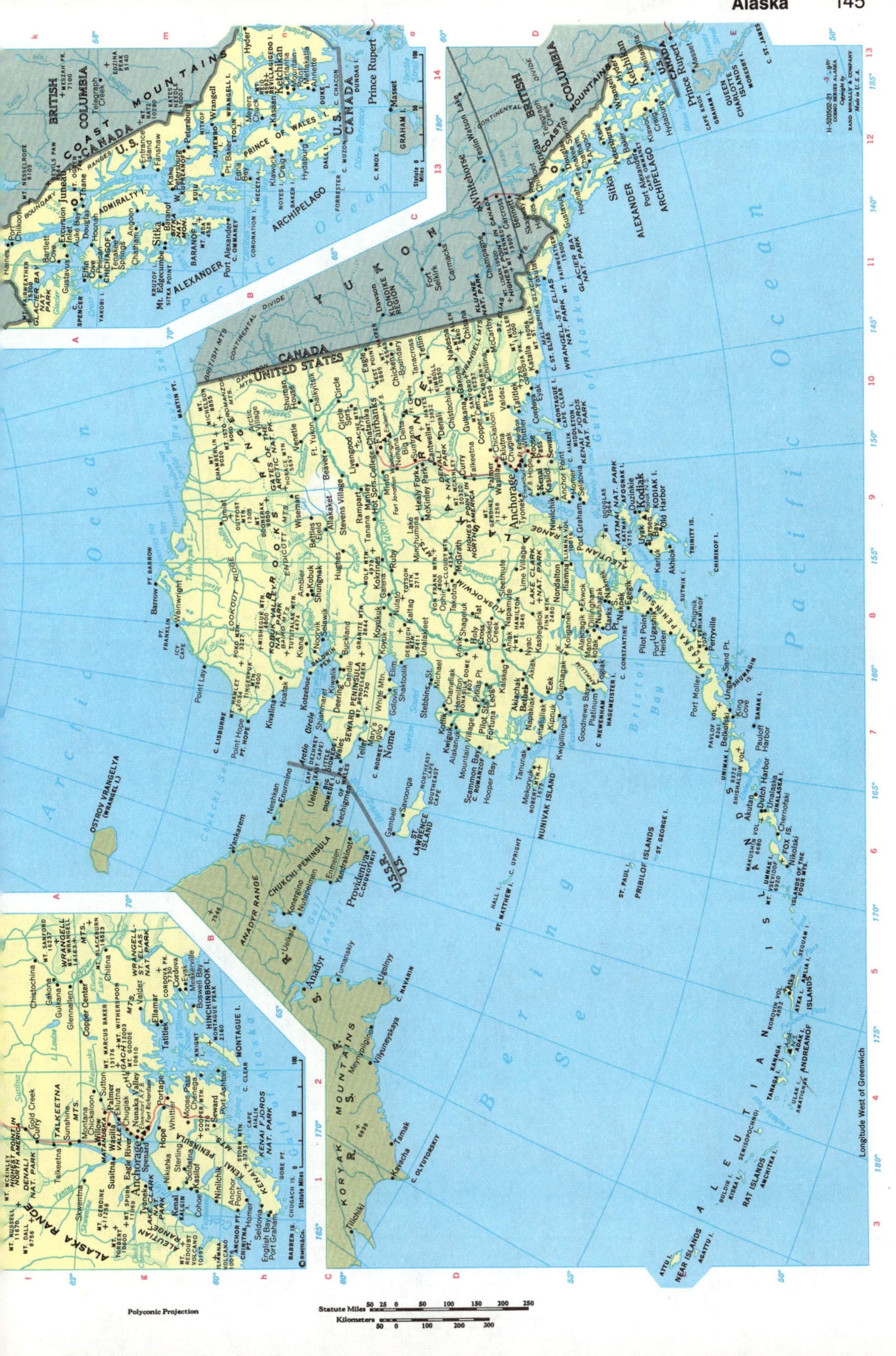
Polyconic Projection
Statute Miles 50 25 0 50 100 150 200 250
Kilometers 50 0 100 200 300
Longitude West of Greenwich

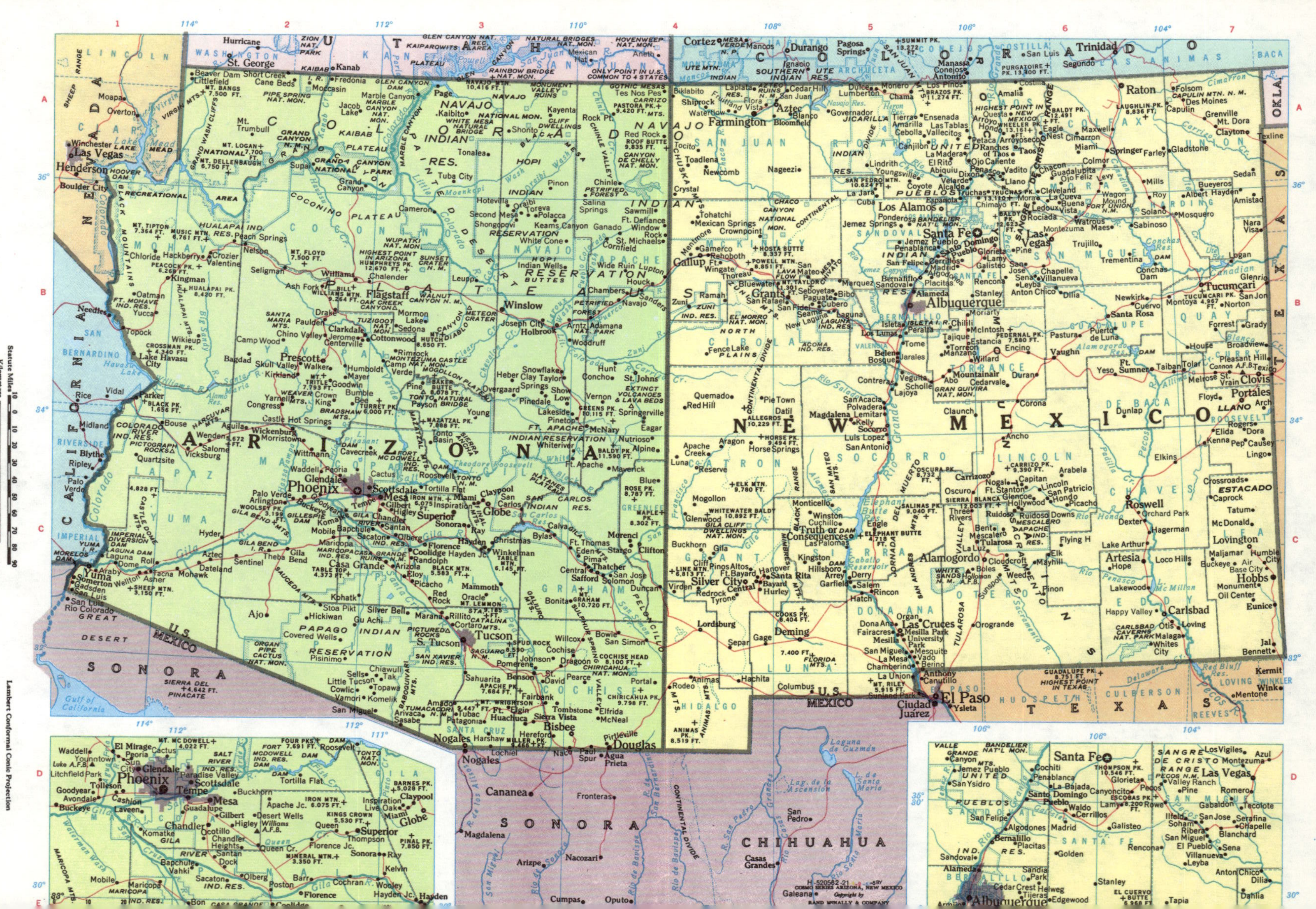
ARIZONA
NEW MEXICO
Phoenix
Tucson
Flagstaff
Albuquerque
Santa Fe
El Paso
Las Vegas
SONORA
CHIHUAHUA
Statute Miles 10 0 10 20 30 40 50 60 70 80 90
Kilometers 10 0 10 20 40 60 80 100 120
Lambert Conformal Conic Projection

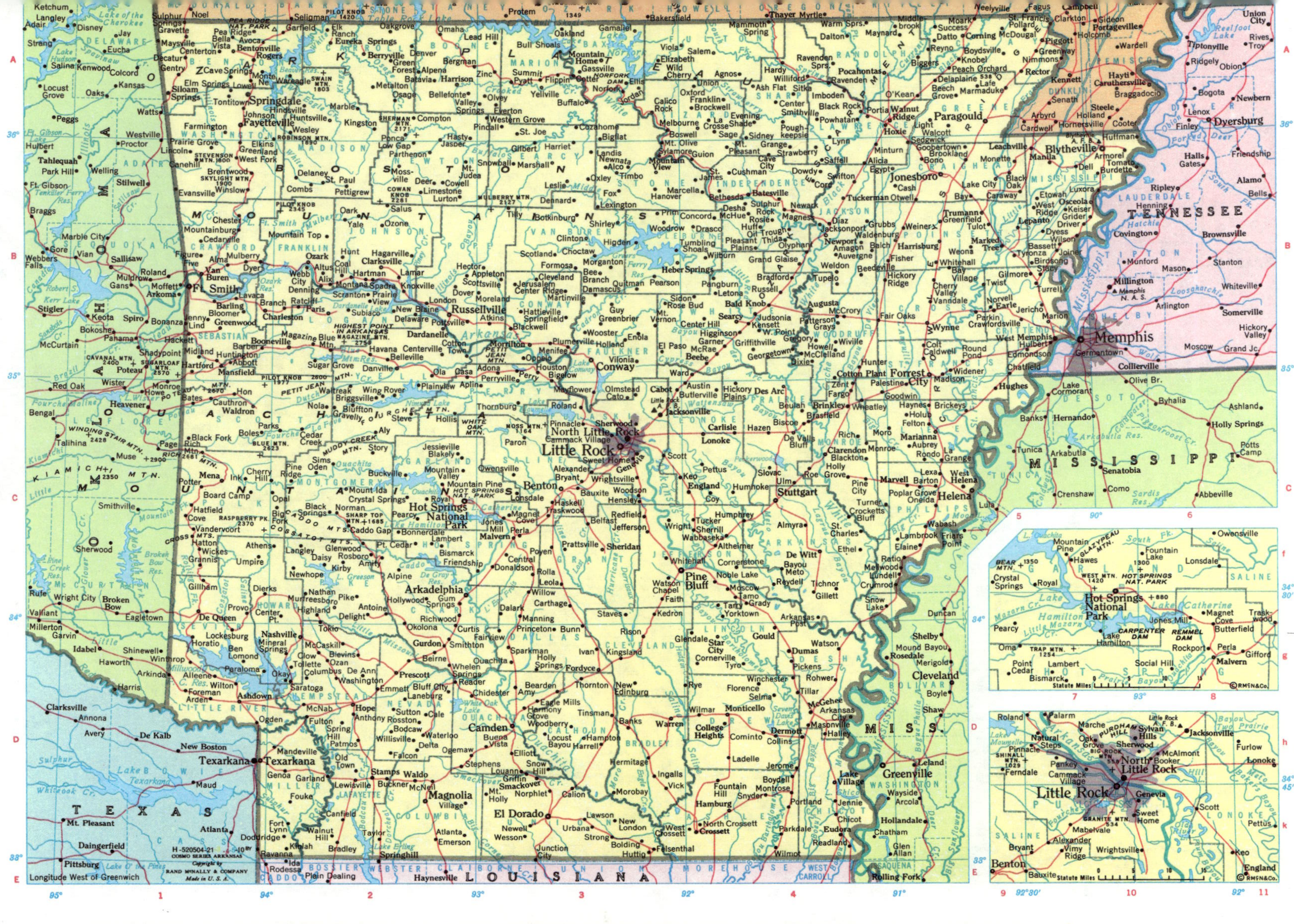

Lambert Conformal Conic Projection

Statute Miles 5 0 5 10 20 30 40

Kilometers 5 0 5 15 25 35 45 55

H-520505-21
COSMO SERIES CALIFORNIA

Longitude West of Greenwich

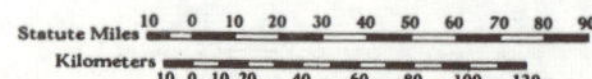

Lambert Conformal Conic Projection

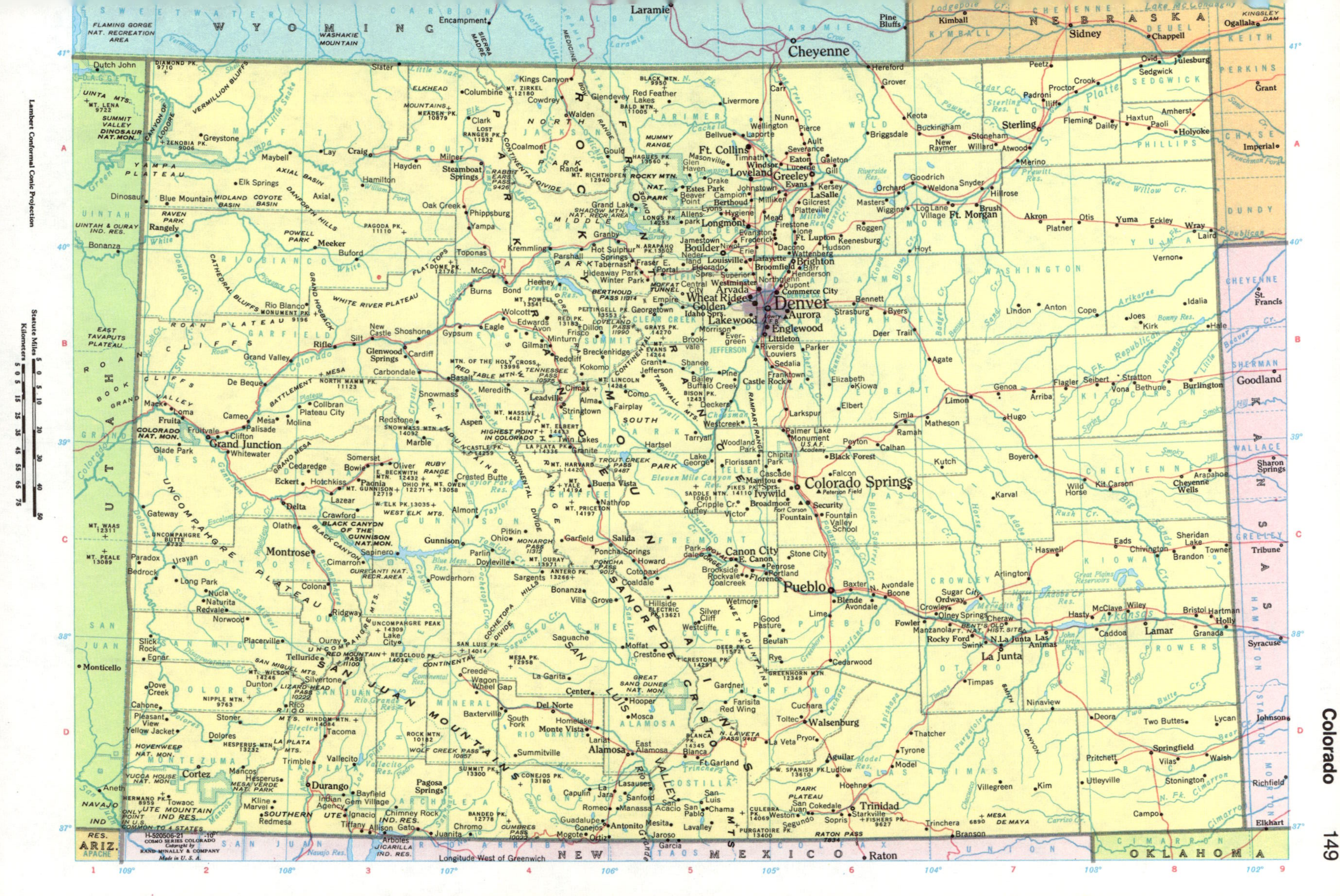
WYOMING
NEBRASKA
KANSAS
OKLAHOMA
NEW MEXICO
UTAH
ARIZ.
Denver
Colorado Springs
Pueblo
Ft. Collins
Greeley
Boulder
Grand Junction
Durango
Trinidad
Cheyenne
Laramie
Sidney
Goodland
Raton
SAN JUAN MOUNTAINS
SANGRE DE CRISTO MTS.
SAN LUIS VALLEY
CONTINENTAL DIVIDE
Lambert Conformal Conic Projection
Statute Miles
5 0 5 10 20 30 40 50
Kilometers
5 0 5 15 25 35 45 55 65 75
Longitude West of Greenwich

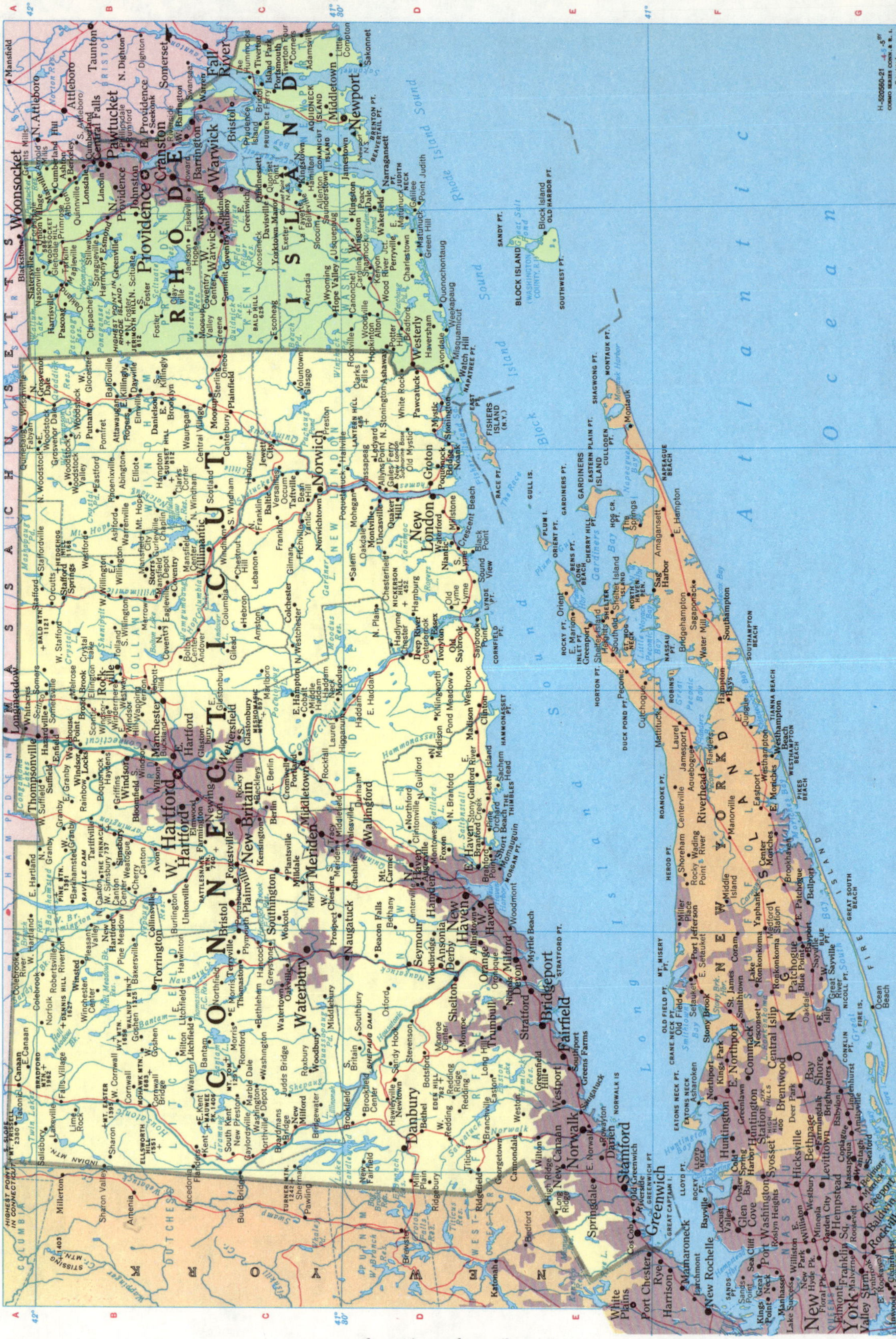

Statute Miles 5 0 5 10 15

Kilometers 5 0 5 10 15 20

Lambert Conformal Conic Projection

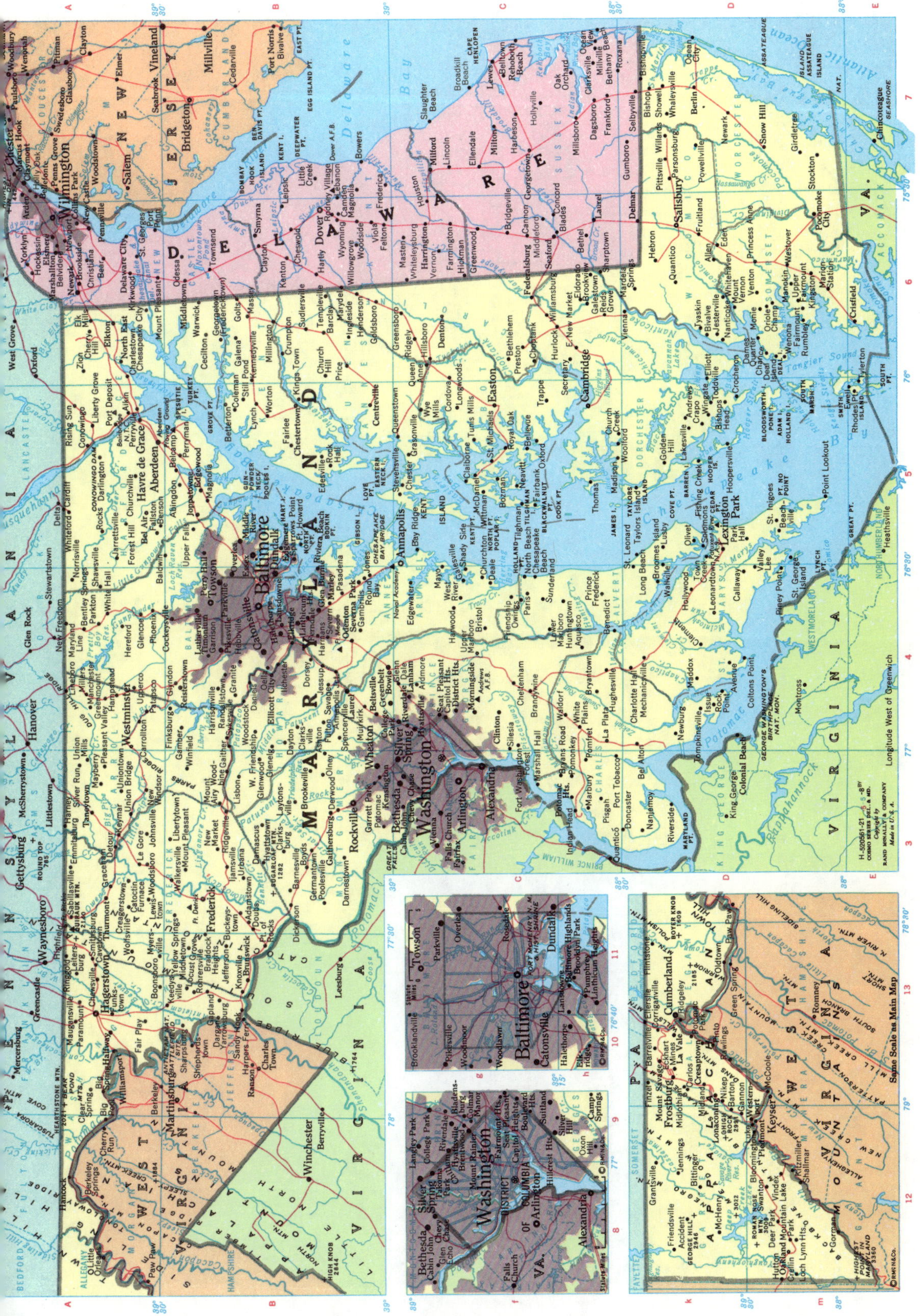

Lambert Conformal Conic Projection

Statute Miles 5 0 5 10 15 20

Kilometers 5 0 5 10 15 20 25 30

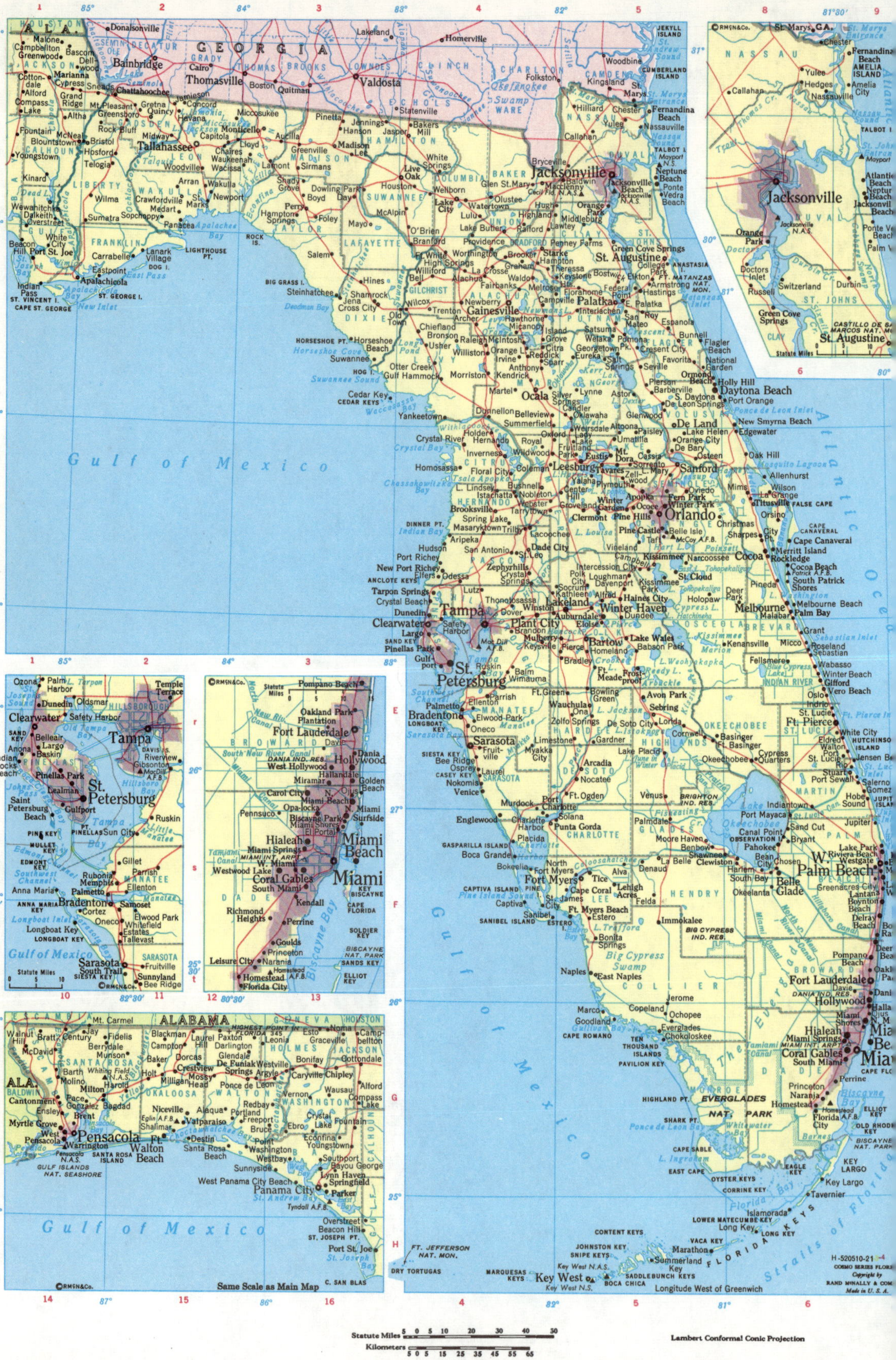

Same Scale as Main Map

Statute Miles 5 0 5 10 20 30 40 50

Kilometers 5 0 5 15 25 35 45 55 65

Lambert Conformal Conic Projection

Longitude West of Greenwich

H-520510-21 -4

COSMO SERIES FLORIDA

Copyright by RAND McNALLY & COMPANY

Made in U. S. A.

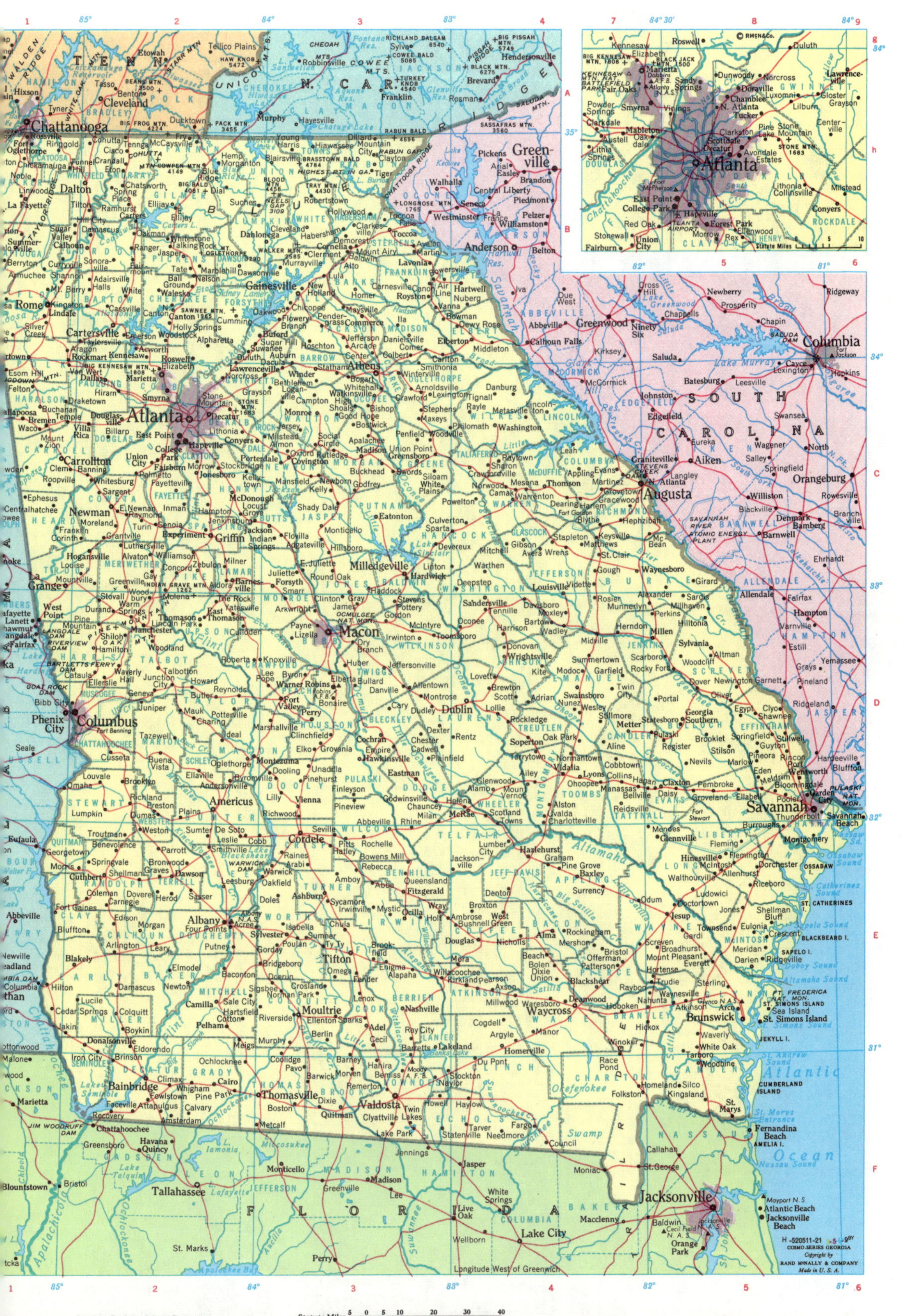

TENN.
N. CAR.
SOUTH CAROLINA
FLORIDA
Atlanta
Chattanooga
Greenville
Anderson
Columbia
Augusta
Athens
Macon
Columbus
Phenix City
Albany
Savannah
Valdosta
Tallahassee
Jacksonville
Brunswick
Waycross
Dublin
Milledgeville
Rome
Dalton
Gainesville
Atlantic Ocean
Longitude West of Greenwich
Lambert Conformal Conic Projection
Statute Miles
Kilometers
H-520511-21
COSMO SERIES GEORGIA
Copyright by RAND McNALLY & COMPANY
Made in U. S. A.

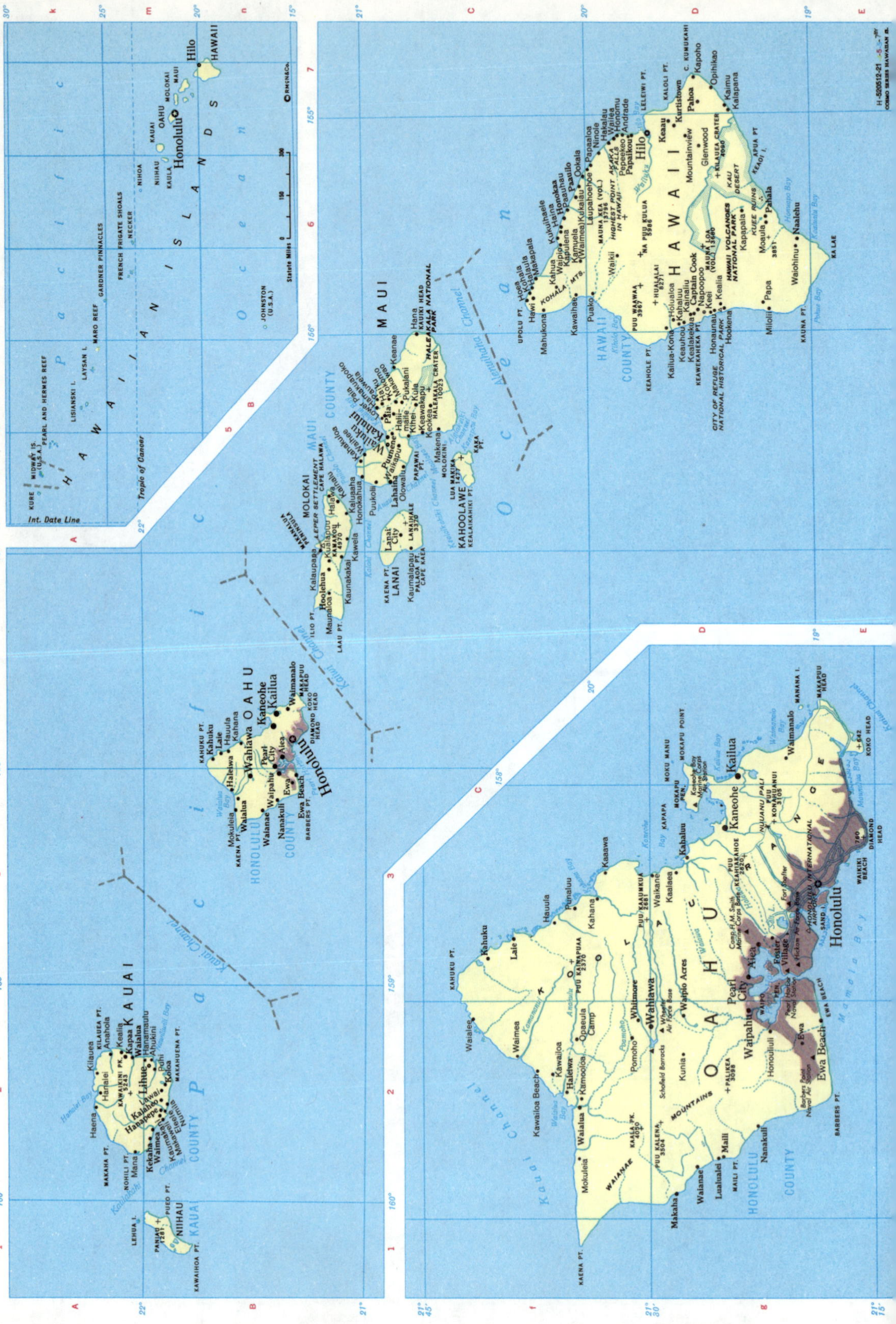

Statute Miles 5 0 5 10 20 30 40 50

Kilometers 5 0 5 10 20 30 40 50 60

Lambert Conformal Conic Projection

BRITISH COLUMBIA
ALBERTA
CANADA
UNITED STATES
Longitude West of Greenwich
COSMO SERIES IDAHO
Copyright by RAND McNALLY & COMPANY
Made in U.S.A.
GLACIER NATIONAL PARK
BLACKFEET INDIAN RESERVATION
ROCKY MOUNTAINS
BITTERROOT RANGE
CLEARWATER MOUNTAINS
SALMON RIVER MOUNTAINS
SAWTOOTH
LOST RIVER RANGE
LEMHI RANGE
BEAVERHEAD RANGE
BIG BELT MOUNTAINS
MONTANA
WYOMING
NEVADA
UTAH
OREGON
WASHINGTON
YELLOWSTONE NATIONAL PARK
GRAND TETON NAT. PARK
CRATERS OF THE MOON NAT. MON.
HELLS CANYON
SEVEN DEVILS MTS.
Spokane
Coeur d'Alene
Sandpoint
Bonners Ferry
Kalispell
Whitefish
Missoula
Helena
Great Falls
Butte
Anaconda
Bozeman
Livingston
Hamilton
Moscow
Pullman
Lewiston
Grangeville
Salmon
Challis
McCall
Ontario
Payette
Caldwell
Nampa
Boise
Mountain Home
Twin Falls
Burley
Pocatello
Blackfoot
Idaho Falls
Rexburg
St. Anthony
Ketchum
Sun Valley
Hailey
Gooding
Jerome
Rupert
American Falls
Soda Springs
Montpelier
Preston
Dillon
Stanley
Lambert Conformal Conic Projection
Statute Miles
Kilometers

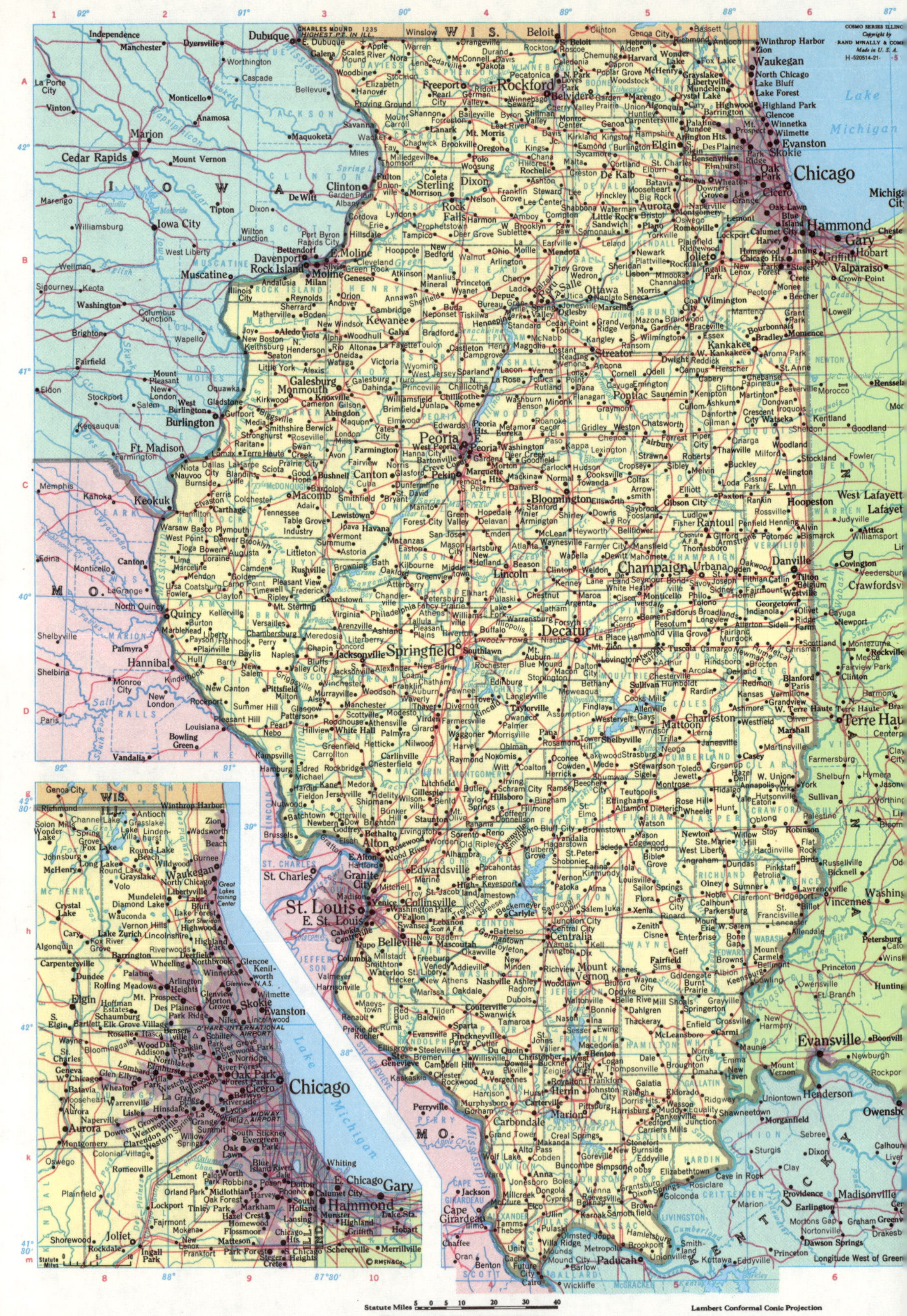
Chicago
Rockford
Peoria
Springfield
Decatur
Champaign
Bloomington
St. Louis
Lake Michigan
Waukegan
Evanston
Hammond
Gary
Joliet
Aurora
Elgin
Kankakee
Danville
Quincy
Galesburg
Moline
Rock Island
Davenport
Dubuque
Cedar Rapids
Iowa City
Burlington
Keokuk
Hannibal
Terre Haute
Evansville
Paducah
Cairo
Carbondale
Belleville
East St. Louis
Alton
Jacksonville
Mattoon
Charleston
Kewanee
Ottawa
La Salle
Pekin
Macomb
Effingham
Centralia
Mt. Vernon
Marion
Vincennes
IOWA
MO.
WIS.
IND.
KENTUCKY
Statute Miles
Kilometers
Lambert Conformal Conic Projection

Chicago
Lake Michigan
M I C H I G A N
Hammond
Gary
East Chicago
Michigan City
South Bend
Mishawaka
Elkhart
Goshen
La Porte
Valparaiso
Fort Wayne
Kokomo
Logansport
Peru
Wabash
Huntington
Marion
Lafayette
W. Lafayette
Frankfort
Crawfordsville
Danville
Terre Haute
Anderson
Muncie
Elwood
New Castle
Richmond
Connersville
Indianapolis
Speedway
Beech Grove
Shelbyville
Franklin
Martinsville
Bloomington
Columbus
Seymour
Bedford
Vincennes
Washington
Jasper
Evansville
New Albany
Jeffersonville
Louisville
Madison
Lawrenceburg
Cincinnati
Covington
Hamilton
Henderson
Owensboro
Kankakee
Joliet
Danville
Van Wert
K E N T U C K Y
O H I O
Highest point in Indiana 1257
Weedpatch Hill 1058
H-520515-21
COSMO SERIES INDIANA
Copyright by RAND McNALLY & COMPANY
Made in U. S. A.
Longitude West of Greenwich
Lambert Conformal Conic Projection
Statute Miles 5 0 5 10 15 20 25 30
Kilometers 5 0 5 15 25 35

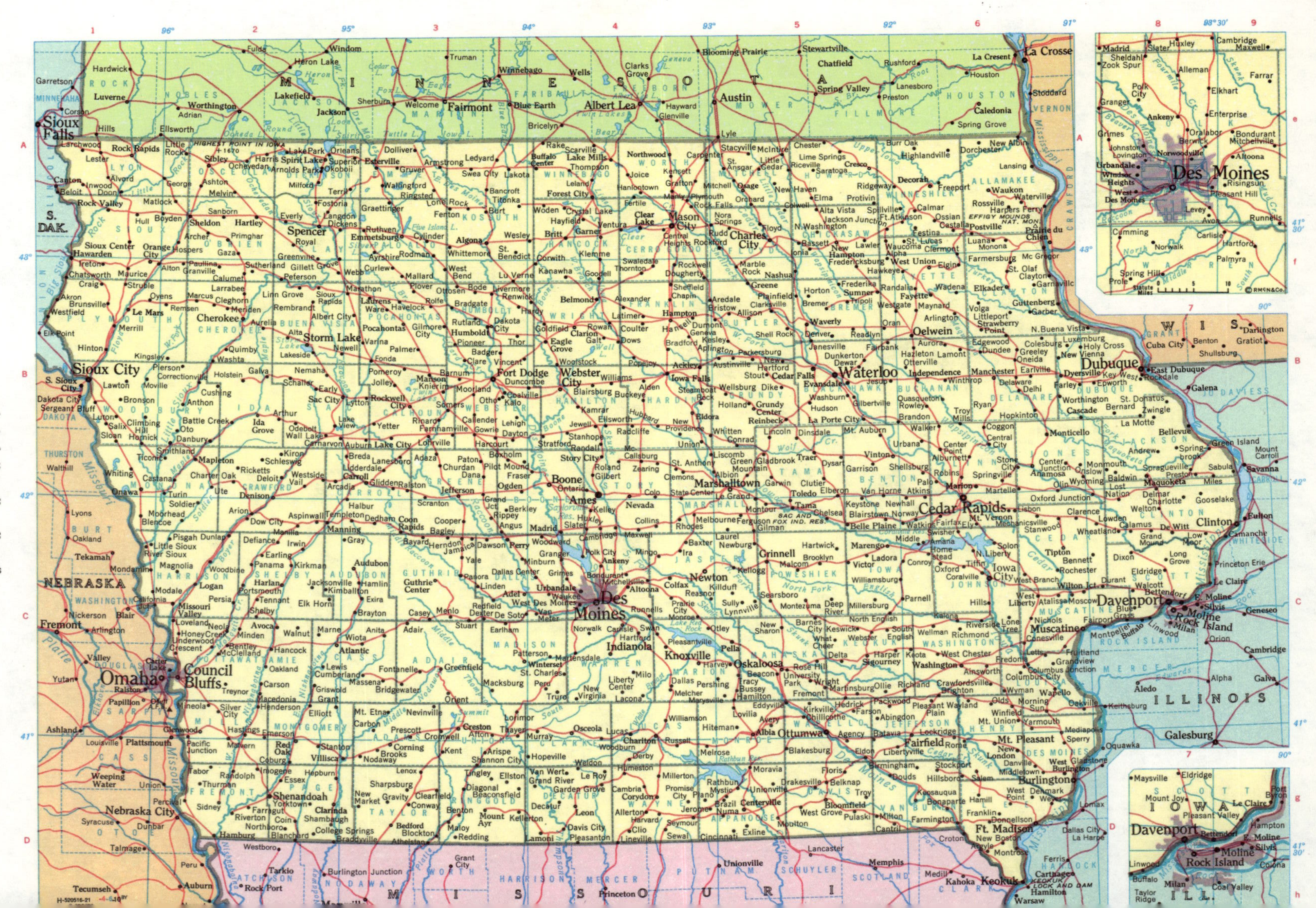
MINNESOTA
IOWA
ILLINOIS
MISSOURI
NEBRASKA
S. DAK.
WIS.
Des Moines
Council Bluffs
Omaha
Sioux City
Sioux Falls
Fort Dodge
Mason City
Waterloo
Cedar Rapids
Iowa City
Davenport
Dubuque
Burlington
Ottumwa
Clinton
Keokuk
La Crosse
Albert Lea
Austin
Statute Miles 5 0 5 10 20 30 40
Kilometers 5 0 5 15 25 35 45 55
Lambert Conformal Conic Projection

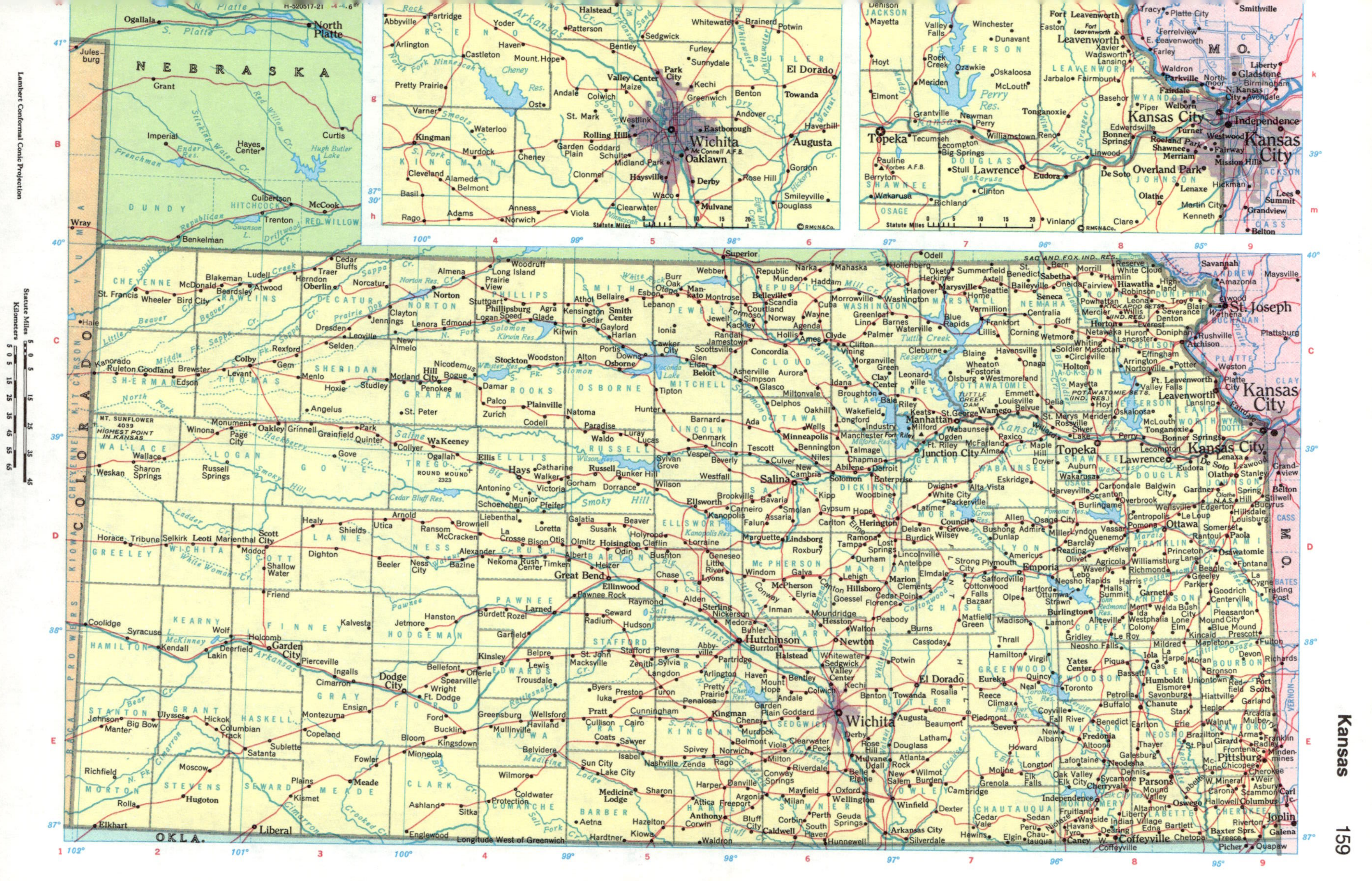
NEBRASKA
COLORADO
OKLA.
M O.
Wichita
Topeka
Kansas City
Lambert Conformal Conic Projection
Statute Miles 5 0 5 15 25 35 45
Kilometers 5 0 5 15 25 35 45 55 65

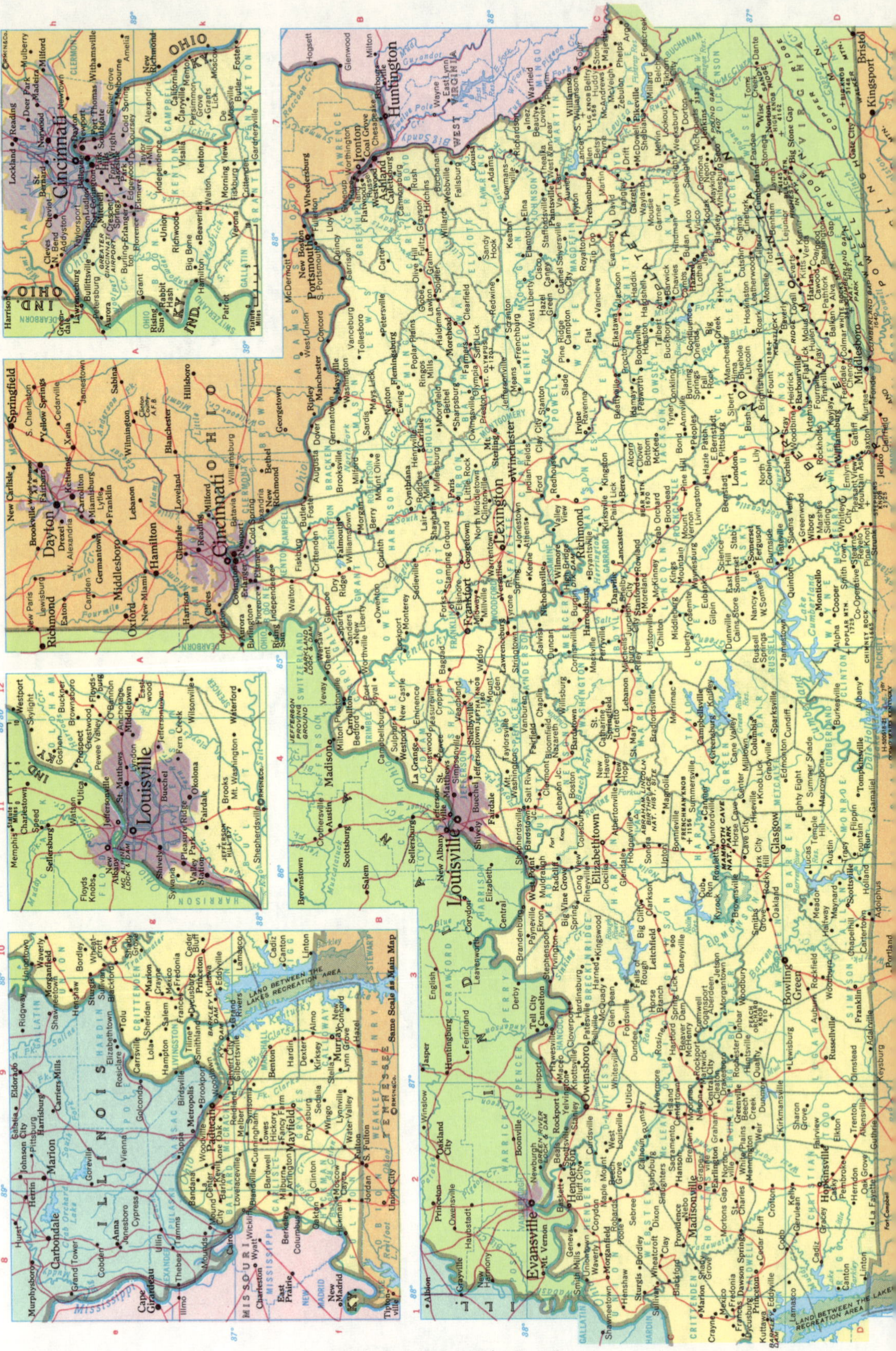

Statute Miles 5 0 5 10 20 30 40

Kilometers 5 0 5 10 20 30 40 50 60

Lambert Conformal Conic Projection

Lambert Conformal Conic Projection

Statute Miles 5 0 5 10 20 30 40

Kilometers 5 0 5 15 25 35 45 55

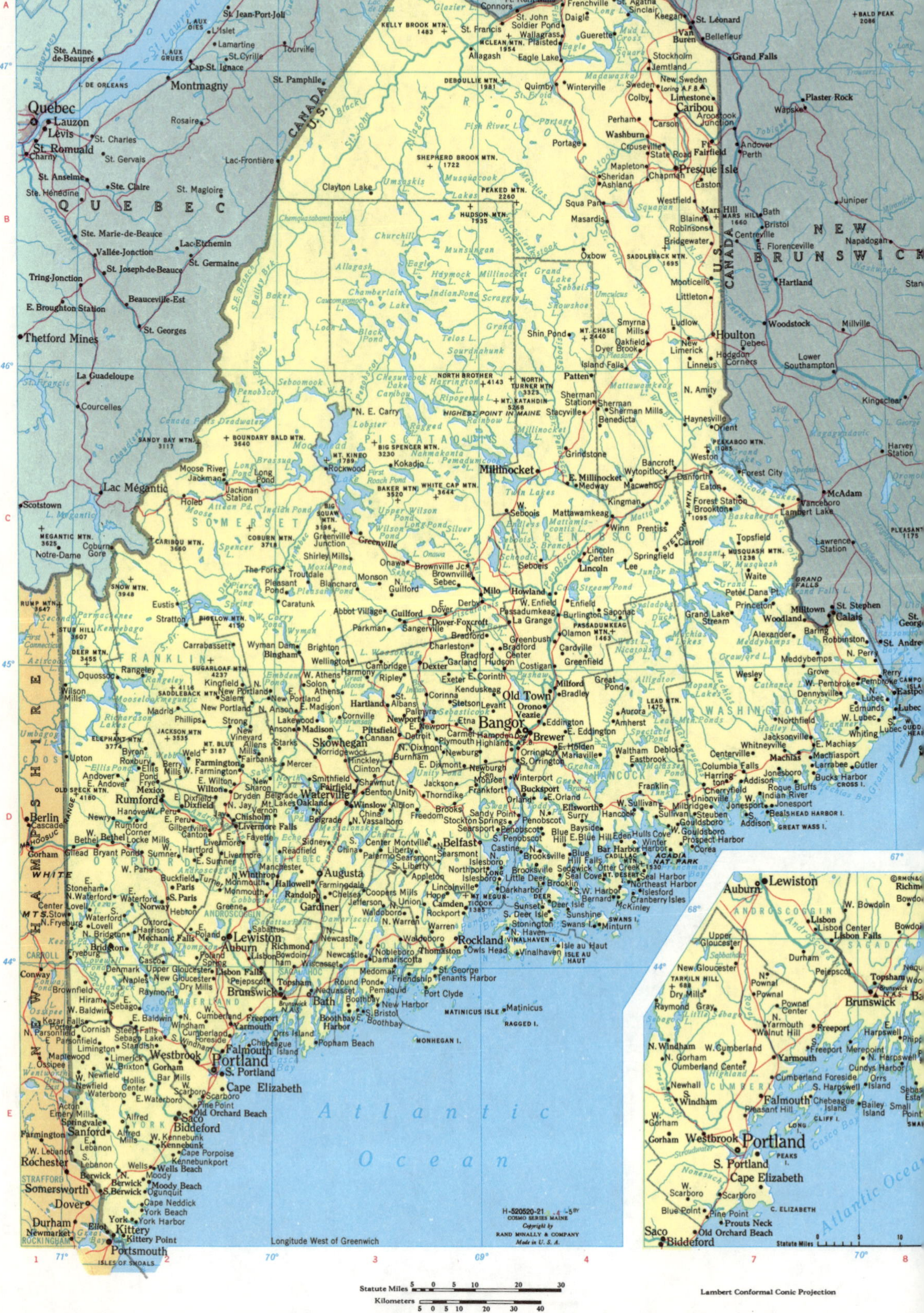

LAURENTIDES PROVINCIAL PARK
QUEBEC
NEW BRUNSWICK
CANADA
U.S.
Quebec
Lévis
Lauzon
Montmagny
Rivière Bleue
Edmundston
Madawaska
Ft. Kent
Van Buren
Caribou
Presque Isle
Houlton
Patten
Millinocket
Mt. Katahdin 5268 Highest Point in Maine
Lac Mégantic
Thetford Mines
Jackman
Greenville
Moosehead L.
Chesuncook Lake
Chamberlain L.
Allagash
Eagle Lake
Woodstock
McAdam
Calais
St. Stephen
Eastport
Lubec
Machias
Bangor
Brewer
Old Town
Orono
Dover-Foxcroft
Lincoln
Skowhegan
Waterville
Farmington
Rumford
Rangeley
Augusta
Gardiner
Lewiston
Auburn
Brunswick
Bath
Rockland
Camden
Belfast
Bucksport
Ellsworth
Bar Harbor
Acadia Nat. Park
Portland
S. Portland
Cape Elizabeth
Westbrook
Saco
Biddeford
Sanford
Kittery
Portsmouth
Dover
Somersworth
Rochester
Berlin
Conway
NEW HAMPSHIRE
SOMERSET
FRANKLIN
OXFORD
PISCATAQUIS
PENOBSCOT
AROOSTOOK
WASHINGTON
HANCOCK
YORK
Atlantic Ocean
Monhegan I.
Matinicus Isle
Vinalhaven
Isle au Haut
Longitude West of Greenwich
H-520520-21 COSMO SERIES MAINE
Copyright by RAND McNALLY & COMPANY Made in U. S. A.
Statute Miles 5 0 5 10 20 30
Kilometers 5 0 5 10 20 30 40
Lambert Conformal Conic Projection

VERMONT
NEW HAMPSHIRE
N. Y.
CONN.
R. I.
Atlantic Ocean
Massachusetts Bay
Cape Cod Bay
Nantucket Sound
Pittsfield
Springfield
Worcester
Lowell
Lawrence
Cambridge
Boston
Providence
Brockton
Fall River
New Bedford
Newport
Gloucester
CAPE COD
NANTUCKET ISLAND
MARTHAS VINEYARD
Longitude West of Greenwich
Lambert Conformal Conic Projection
Statute Miles 5 0 5 10 15 20
Kilometers 5 0 5 10 15 20 25
Copyright by RAND McNALLY & COMPANY
Made in U. S. A.

Statute Miles 5 0 5 10 20 30 40 50

Kilometers 5 0 5 15 25 35 45 55 65 75

Lambert Conformal Conic Projection

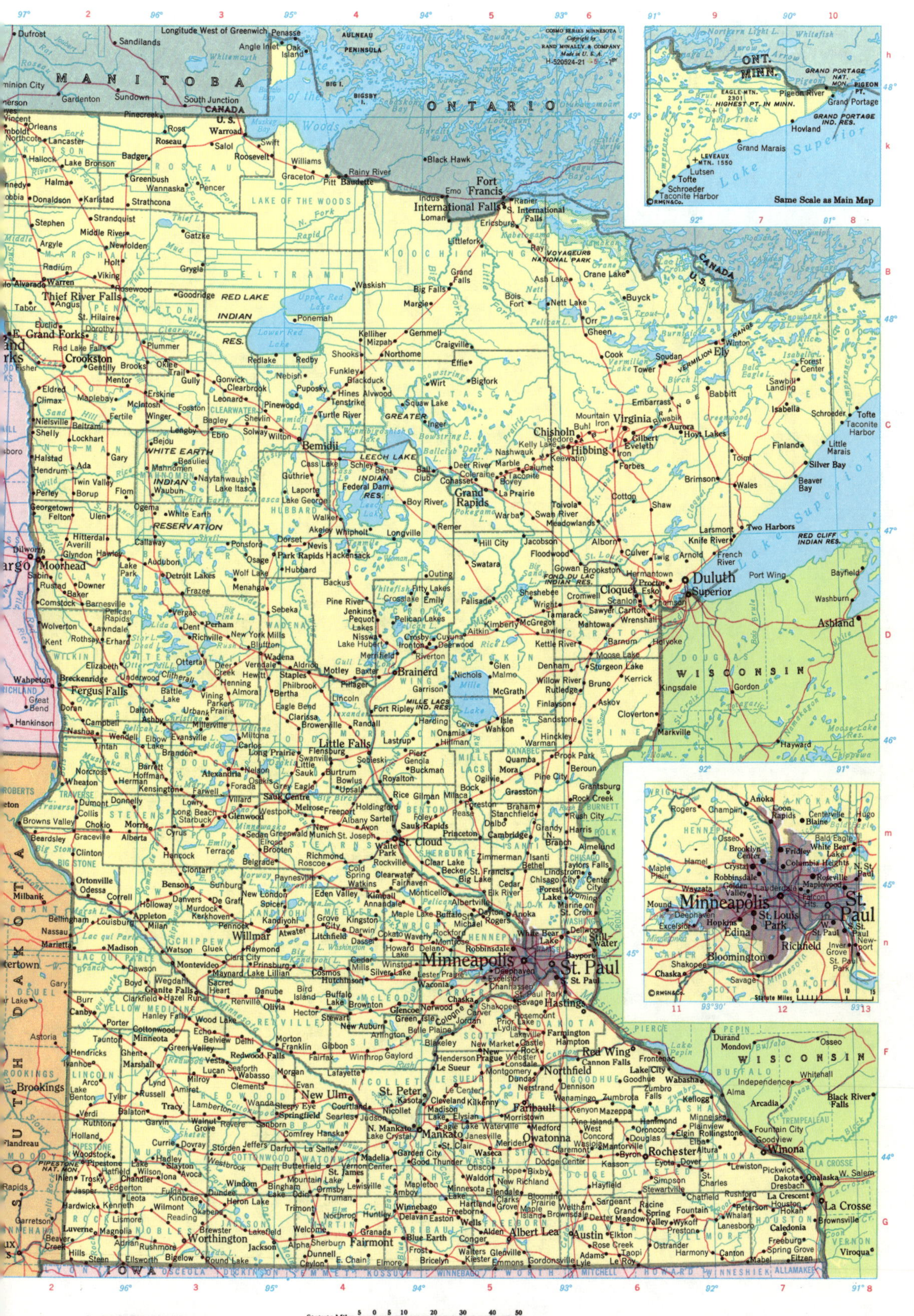
COSMO SERIES MINNESOTA
Copyright by
RAND McNALLY & COMPANY
Made in U.S.A.
H-520524-21
MANITOBA
ONTARIO
ONT.
MINN.
CANADA
U.S.
WISCONSIN
IOWA
SOUTH DAKOTA
NORTH DAKOTA
LAKE OF THE WOODS
RED LAKE
Lake Superior
Longitude West of Greenwich
Same Scale as Main Map
EAGLE MTN. 2301 HIGHEST PT. IN MINN.
LEVEAUX MTN. 1550
GRAND PORTAGE IND. RES.
GRAND PORTAGE NAT. MON.
VOYAGEURS NATIONAL PARK
RED LAKE INDIAN RES.
LEECH LAKE INDIAN RES.
WHITE EARTH INDIAN RESERVATION
FOND DU LAC INDIAN RES.
MILLE LACS IND. RES.
RED CLIFF INDIAN RES.
International Falls
Fort Frances
Bemidji
Thief River Falls
Grand Forks
Crookston
Fargo
Moorhead
Fergus Falls
Grand Rapids
Hibbing
Virginia
Ely
Duluth
Superior
Two Harbors
Grand Marais
Brainerd
St. Cloud
Little Falls
Alexandria
Willmar
Minneapolis
St. Paul
Stillwater
Hastings
Red Wing
Winona
La Crosse
Rochester
Austin
Albert Lea
Owatonna
Faribault
Northfield
Mankato
New Ulm
St. Peter
Fairmont
Worthington
Marshall
Pipestone
Brookings
Ortonville
Wahpeton
Breckenridge
Detroit Lakes
Wadena
Cloquet
Ashland
Anoka
Bloomington
Edina
Richfield
St. Louis Park
Hopkins
Fridley
Roseville
Lambert Conformal Conic Projection
Statute Miles 5 0 5 10 20 30 40 50
Kilometers 5 0 5 15 25 35 45 55 65

Statute Miles 5 0 5 10 20 30 40

Kilometers 5 0 5 15 25 35 45 55

Lambert Conformal Conic Projection

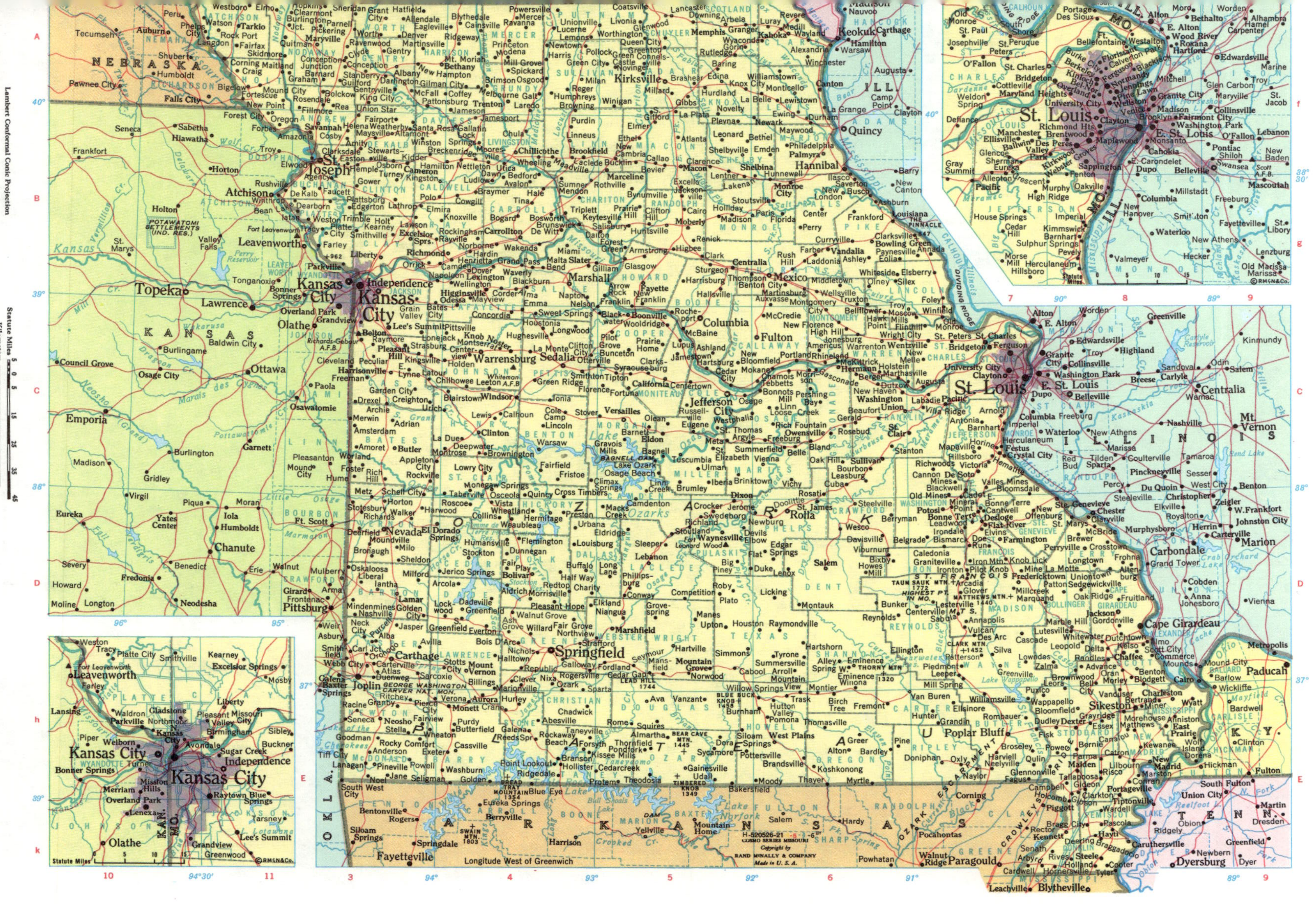
NEBRASKA
KANSAS
ILLINOIS
KENTUCKY
TENNESSEE
ARKANSAS
OKLA.
St. Louis
Kansas City
Jefferson City
Springfield
Columbia
St. Joseph
Topeka
Hannibal
Cape Girardeau
Joplin
Quincy
Paducah
Lambert Conformal Conic Projection
Statute Miles
Kilometers
Longitude West of Greenwich

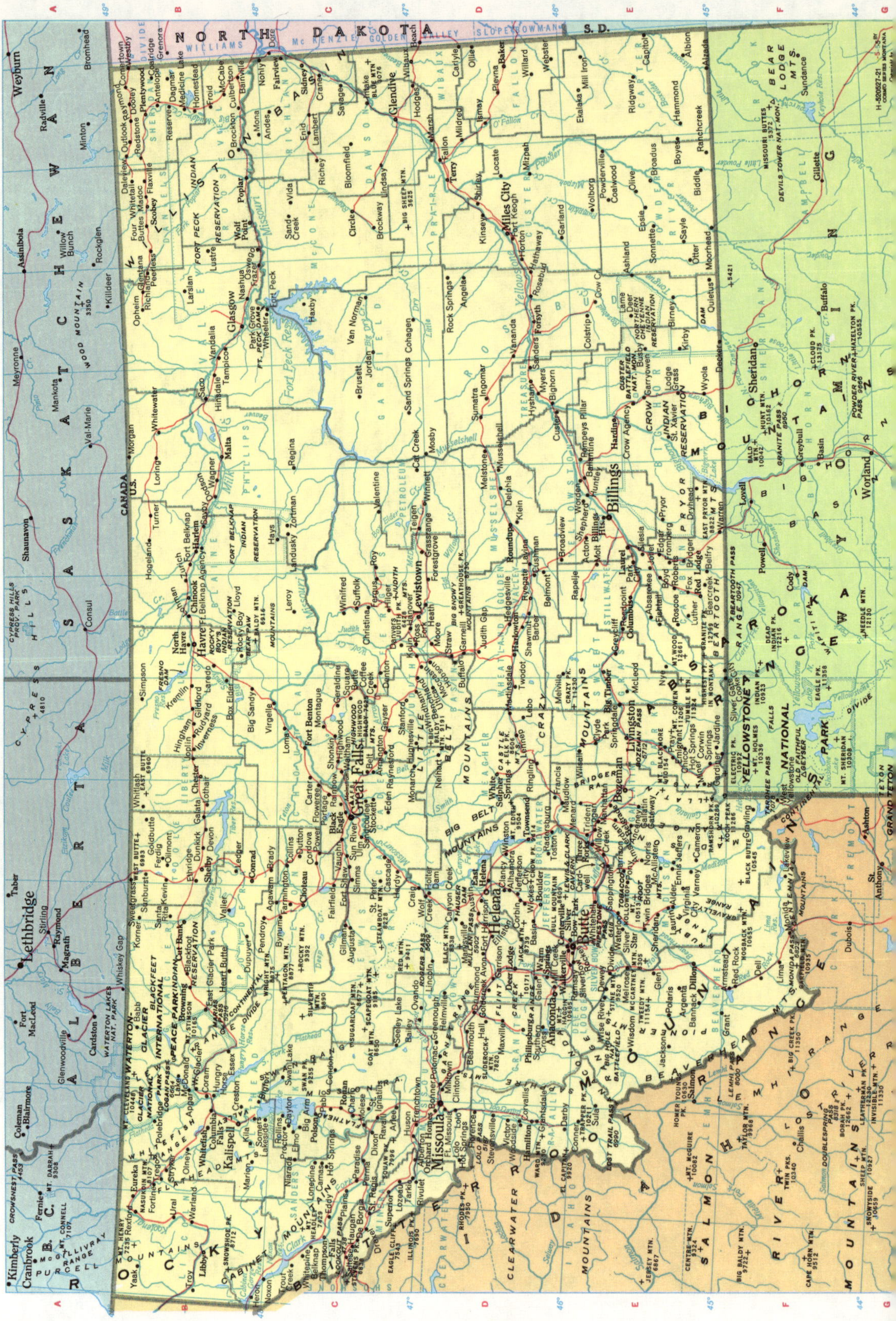

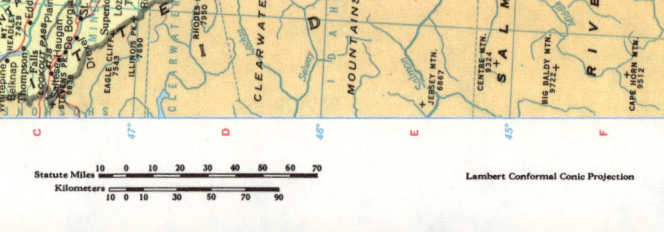

Statute Miles 10 0 10 20 30 40 50 60 70

Kilometers 10 0 10 30 50 70 90

Lambert Conformal Conic Projection

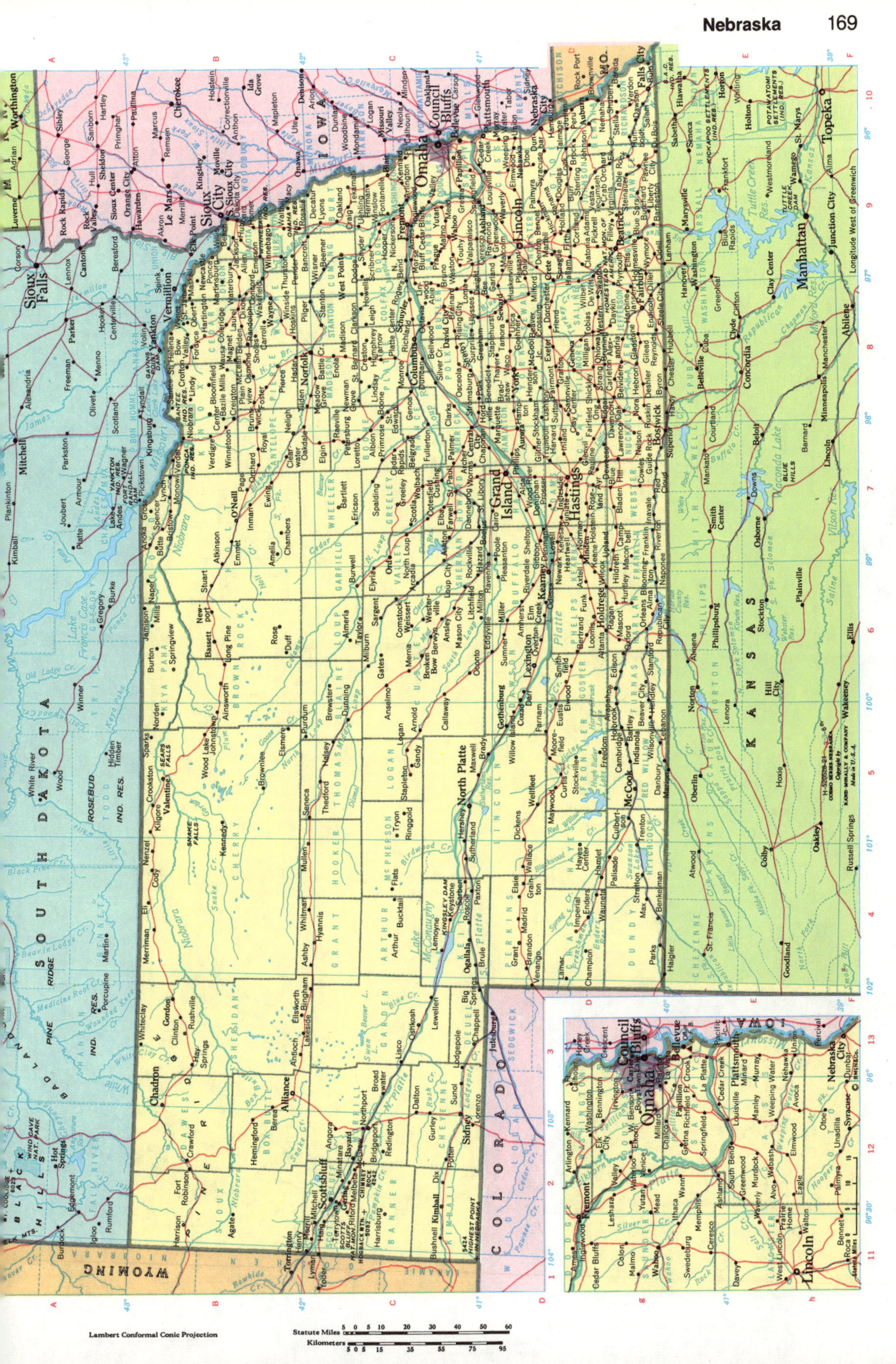
SOUTH DAKOTA
IOWA
KANSAS
COLORADO
WYOMING
MO.
Omaha
Lincoln
Grand Island
Hastings
Kearney
North Platte
Scottsbluff
Council Bluffs
Sioux City
Sioux Falls
Topeka
Manhattan
Lambert Conformal Conic Projection
Statute Miles
Kilometers

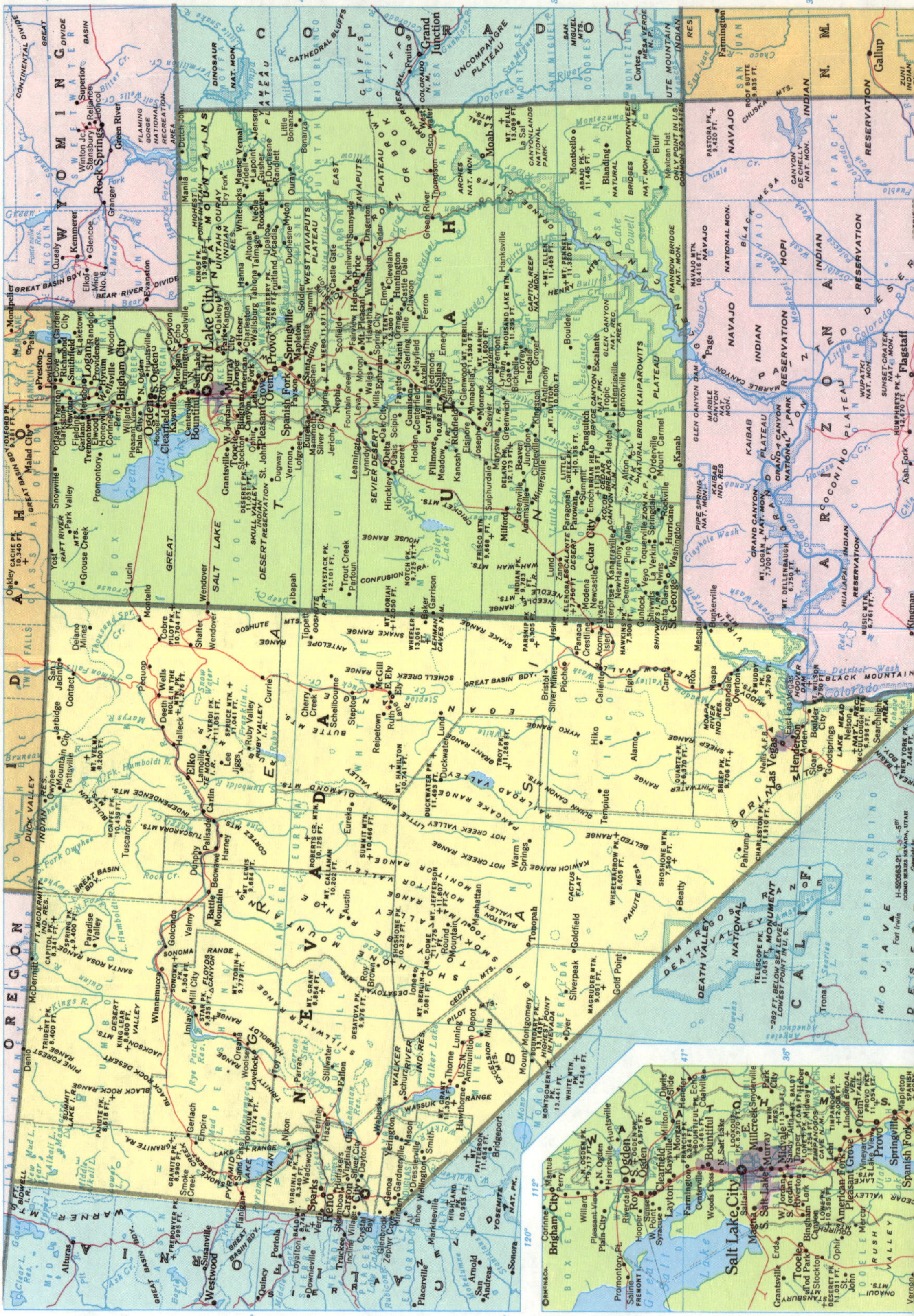

Statute Miles 5 0 5 10 20 30 40 50 60 70 80

Kilometers 5 0 10 20 40 60 80 100 120

Lambert Conformal Conic Projection

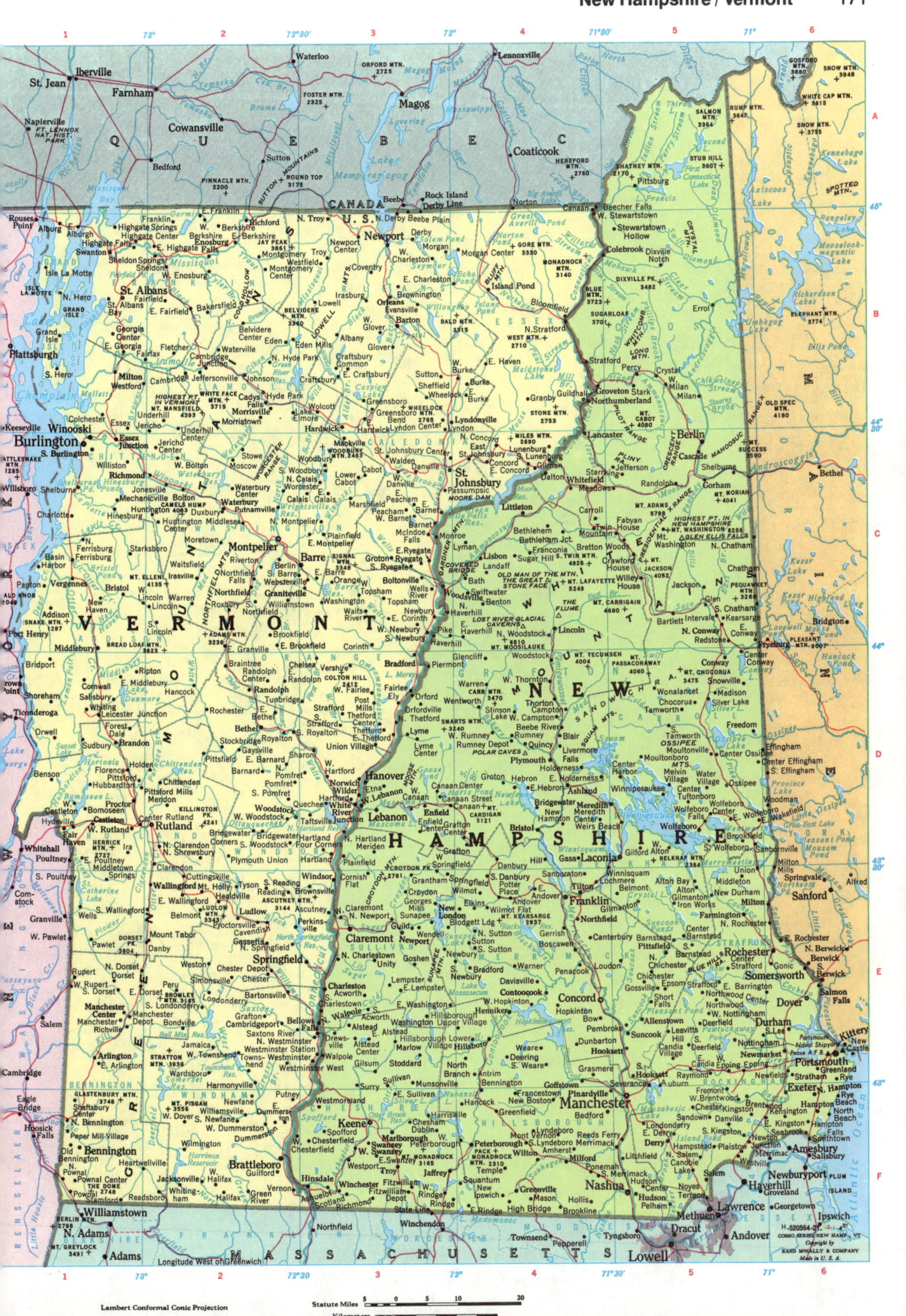
QUEBEC
CANADA
U. S.
VERMONT
NEW HAMPSHIRE
MASSACHUSETTS
MAINE
NEW YORK
Burlington
Montpelier
Barre
Rutland
St. Albans
St. Johnsbury
Newport
Bennington
Brattleboro
Springfield
Concord
Manchester
Nashua
Portsmouth
Keene
Laconia
Lebanon
Hanover
Claremont
Dover
Rochester
Berlin
Lowell
Lawrence
Haverhill
Sherbrooke
Magog
Coaticook
St. Jean
Iberville
Farnham
Cowansville
Plattsburgh
Lake Champlain
Lake Memphremagog
Lake Winnipesaukee
Connecticut R.
Merrimack R.
Atlantic Ocean
HIGHEST PT. IN VERMONT MT. MANSFIELD 4393
HIGHEST PT. IN NEW HAMPSHIRE MT. WASHINGTON 6288
Longitude West of Greenwich
H-520564-21 COSMO SERIES NEW HAMP.-VT
Copyright by RAND McNALLY & COMPANY
Made in U. S. A.
Lambert Conformal Conic Projection
Statute Miles 5 0 5 10 20
Kilometers 5 0 5 10 15 20 25

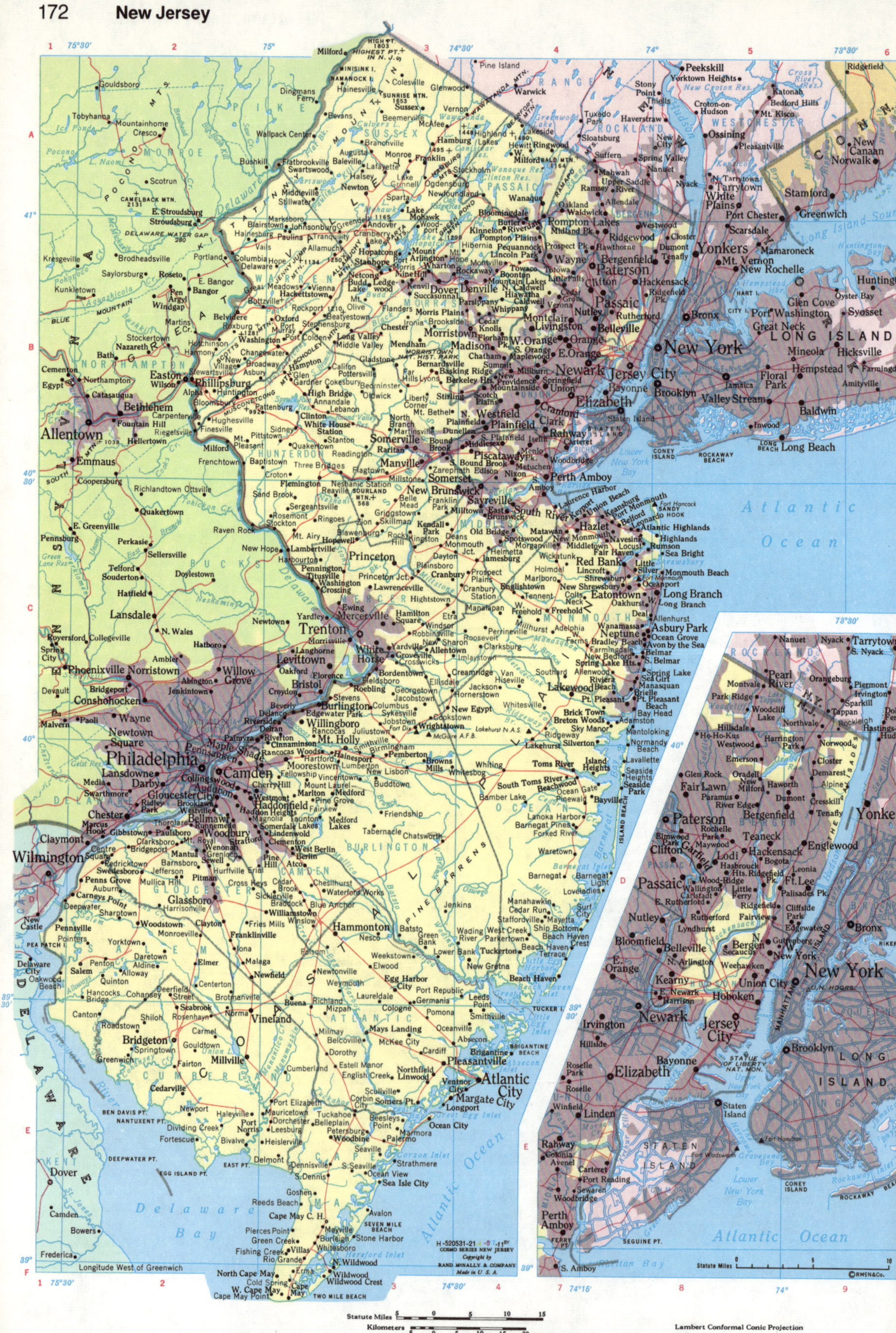
Atlantic Ocean
Delaware Bay
New York
Jersey City
Newark
Elizabeth
Paterson
Trenton
Camden
Philadelphia
Atlantic City
Allentown
Wilmington
LONG ISLAND
STATEN ISLAND
PINE BARRENS
H-520531-21 COSMO SERIES NEW JERSEY Copyright by RAND MCNALLY & COMPANY Made in U. S. A.
Longitude West of Greenwich
Statute Miles
Kilometers
Lambert Conformal Conic Projection

Lambert Conformal Conic Projection

Statute Miles 5 0 5 10 20 30 40

Kilometers 5 0 5 15 25 35 45 55

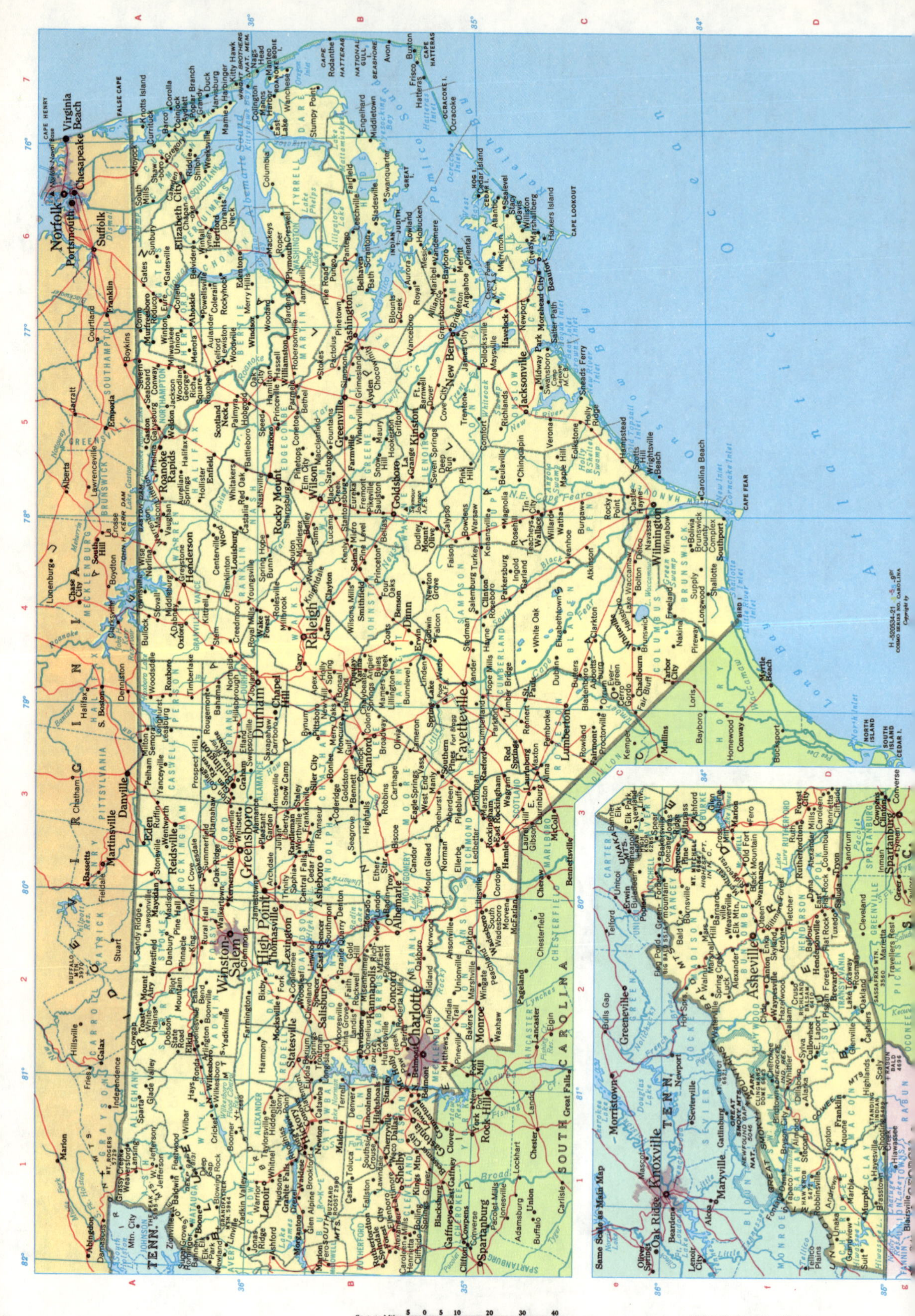
Same Scale as Main Map
Statute Miles 5 0 5 10 20 30 40
Kilometers 5 0 5 15 25 35 45 55
Lambert Conformal Conic Projection

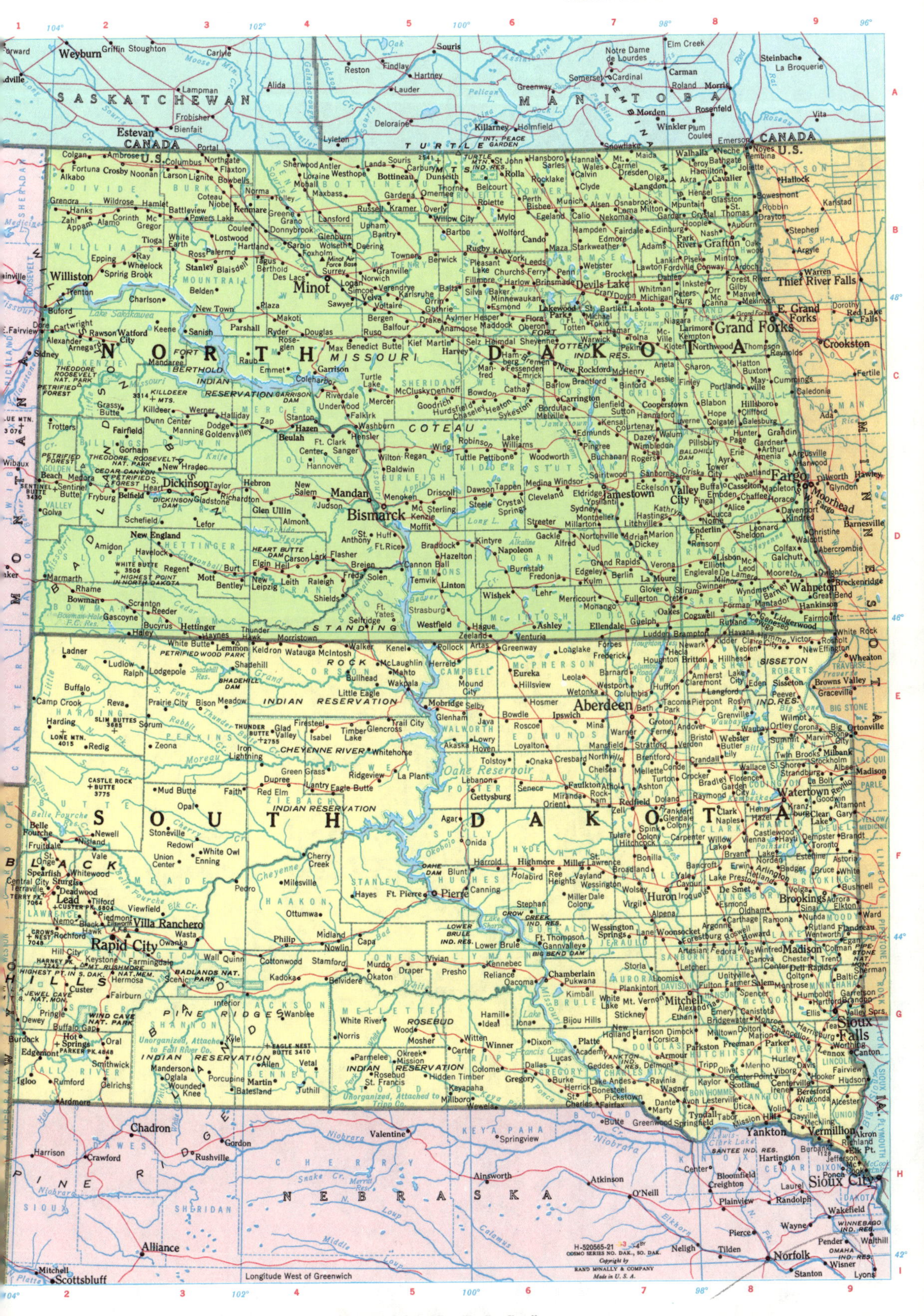
SASKATCHEWAN
MANITOBA
CANADA
U.S.
NORTH DAKOTA
SOUTH DAKOTA
NEBRASKA
MONTANA
MINNESOTA
IOWA
Bismarck
Fargo
Grand Forks
Minot
Williston
Dickinson
Jamestown
Devils Lake
Mandan
Valley City
Pierre
Sioux Falls
Rapid City
Aberdeen
Watertown
Brookings
Mitchell
Huron
Yankton
Vermillion
Sioux City
Moorhead
Thief River Falls
Norfolk
Scottsbluff
Alliance
Chadron
Valentine
Lake Sakakawea
Oahe Reservoir
STANDING ROCK INDIAN RESERVATION
CHEYENNE RIVER INDIAN RESERVATION
PINE RIDGE INDIAN RESERVATION
ROSEBUD INDIAN RESERVATION
FORT BERTHOLD INDIAN RESERVATION
BLACK HILLS
HARNEY PK. 7242 HIGHEST PT. IN S. DAK.
WHITE BUTTE 3506 HIGHEST POINT IN NORTH DAKOTA
BADLANDS NAT. PARK
WIND CAVE NAT. PARK
THEODORE ROOSEVELT NAT. PARK
Longitude West of Greenwich
H-520565-21
COSMO SERIES NO. DAK., SO. DAK.
Copyright by RAND McNALLY & COMPANY
Made in U. S. A.
Lambert Conformal Conic Projection
Statute Miles 5 0 5 10 20 30 40 50 60
Kilometers 5 0 5 15 25 35 45 55 65 75

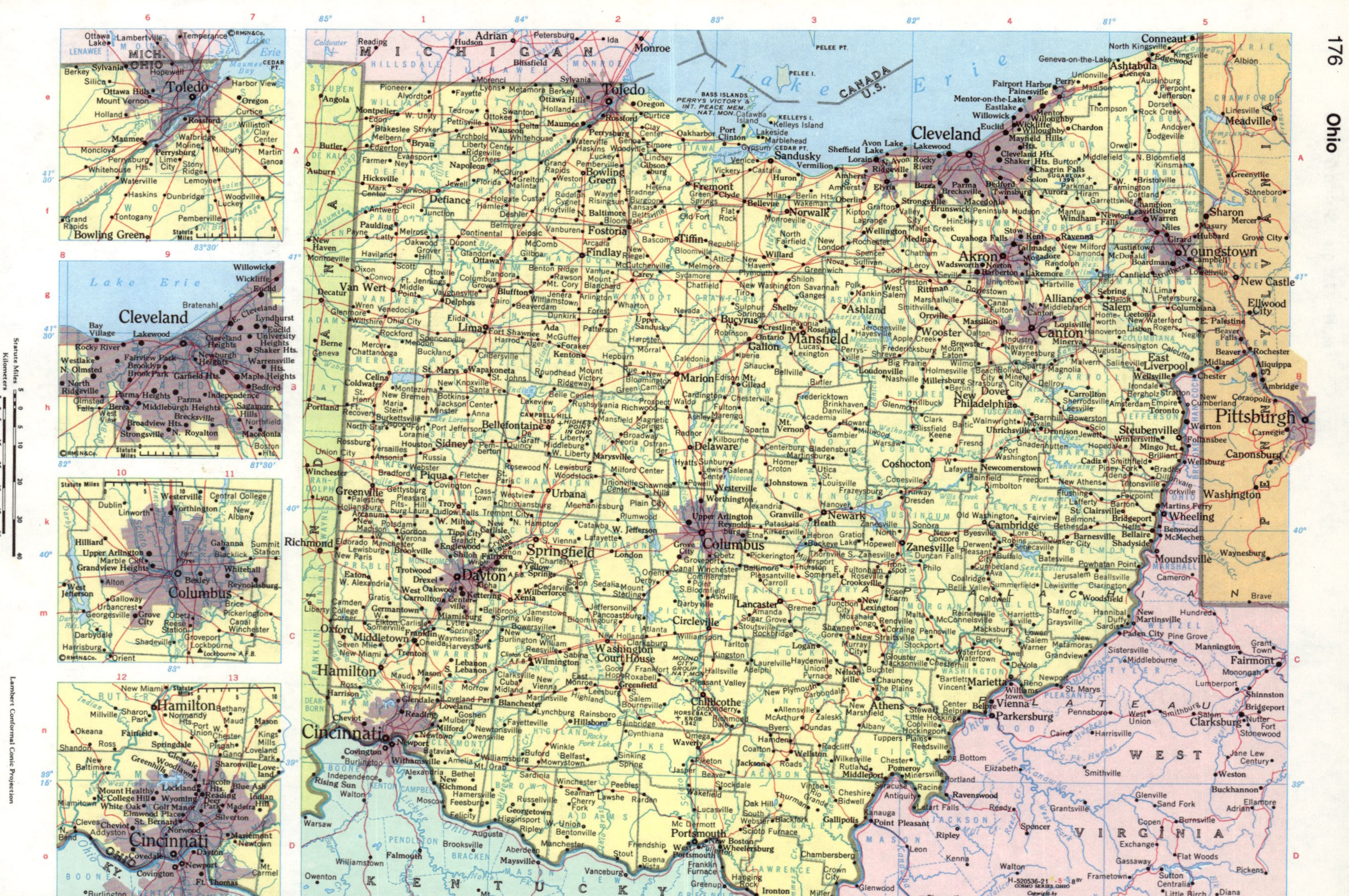
MICHIGAN
Lake Erie
CANADA
U.S.
PELEE PT.
PELEE I.
KELLEYS I.
BASS ISLANDS
PERRYS VICTORY & INT. PEACE MEM. NAT. MON.
INDIANA
PENNSYLVANIA
WEST VIRGINIA
KENTUCKY
Toledo
Cleveland
Akron
Canton
Youngstown
Pittsburgh
Sandusky
Lorain
Elyria
Mansfield
Marion
Lima
Findlay
Fostoria
Tiffin
Fremont
Bowling Green
Defiance
Van Wert
Columbus
Newark
Zanesville
Lancaster
Circleville
Chillicothe
Springfield
Dayton
Middletown
Hamilton
Cincinnati
Portsmouth
Athens
Marietta
Parkersburg
Steubenville
Wheeling
Cambridge
Coshocton
Wooster
Delaware
Sidney
Piqua
Urbana
Bellefontaine
Washington Court House
Wilmington
Xenia
Greenville
Ashtabula
Conneaut
Painesville
Norwalk
Ashland
Bucyrus
Alliance
Salem
Massillon
New Philadelphia
Dover
East Liverpool
Ironton
Gallipolis
Richmond
Monroe
Adrian
Meadville
Sharon
New Castle
Washington
Canonsburg
Moundsville
Fairmont
Clarksburg
Maysville
Lake Erie
Statute Miles
5 0 5 10 20 30 40
Kilometers
5 0 5 15 25 35 45 55
Lambert Conformal Conic Projection
©RMN&Co.
Copyright by RAND McNALLY & COMPANY

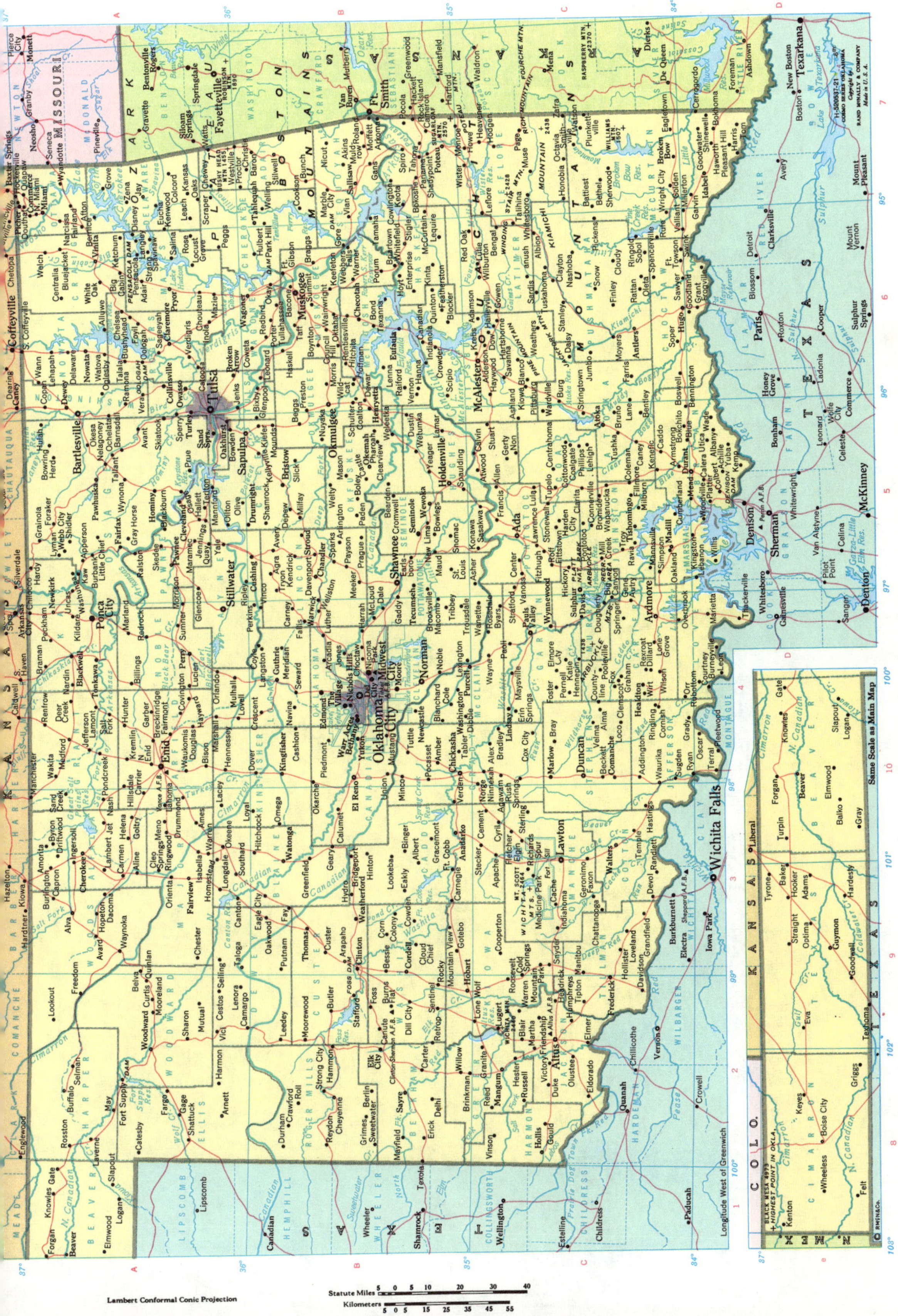
MISSOURI
ARKANSAS
KANSAS
TEXAS
COLO.
Oklahoma City
Tulsa
Lawton
Norman
Muskogee
Enid
Stillwater
Bartlesville
Ponca City
Shawnee
Ardmore
Wichita Falls
Ft. Smith
Fayetteville
Texarkana
Sherman
Denison
Paris
Denton
McKinney
Longitude West of Greenwich
Same Scale as Main Map
Lambert Conformal Conic Projection
Statute Miles 5 0 5 10 20 30 40
Kilometers 5 0 5 15 25 35 45 55

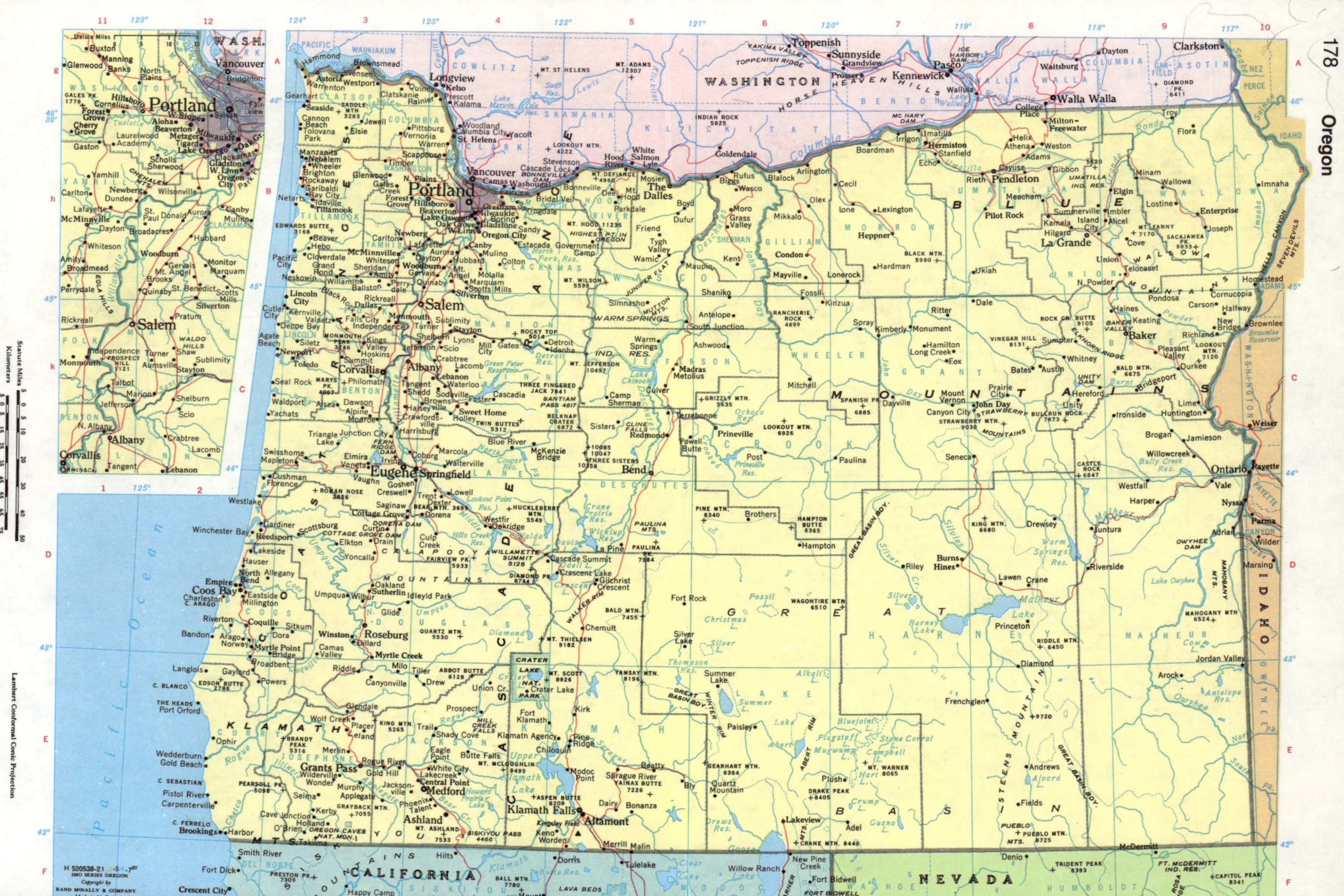

WASHINGTON
IDAHO
NEVADA
CALIFORNIA
Pacific Ocean
Portland
Salem
Eugene
Springfield
Medford
Klamath Falls
Bend
Pendleton
La Grande
Baker
Ontario
Coos Bay
Roseburg
Grants Pass
Ashland
The Dalles
Corvallis
Albany
Astoria
Walla Walla
Vancouver
Statute Miles 5 0 5 10 20 30 40 50
Kilometers 5 0 5 15 25 35 45 55 65 75
Lambert Conformal Conic Projection

Lambert Conformal Conic Projection
Statute Miles
Kilometers

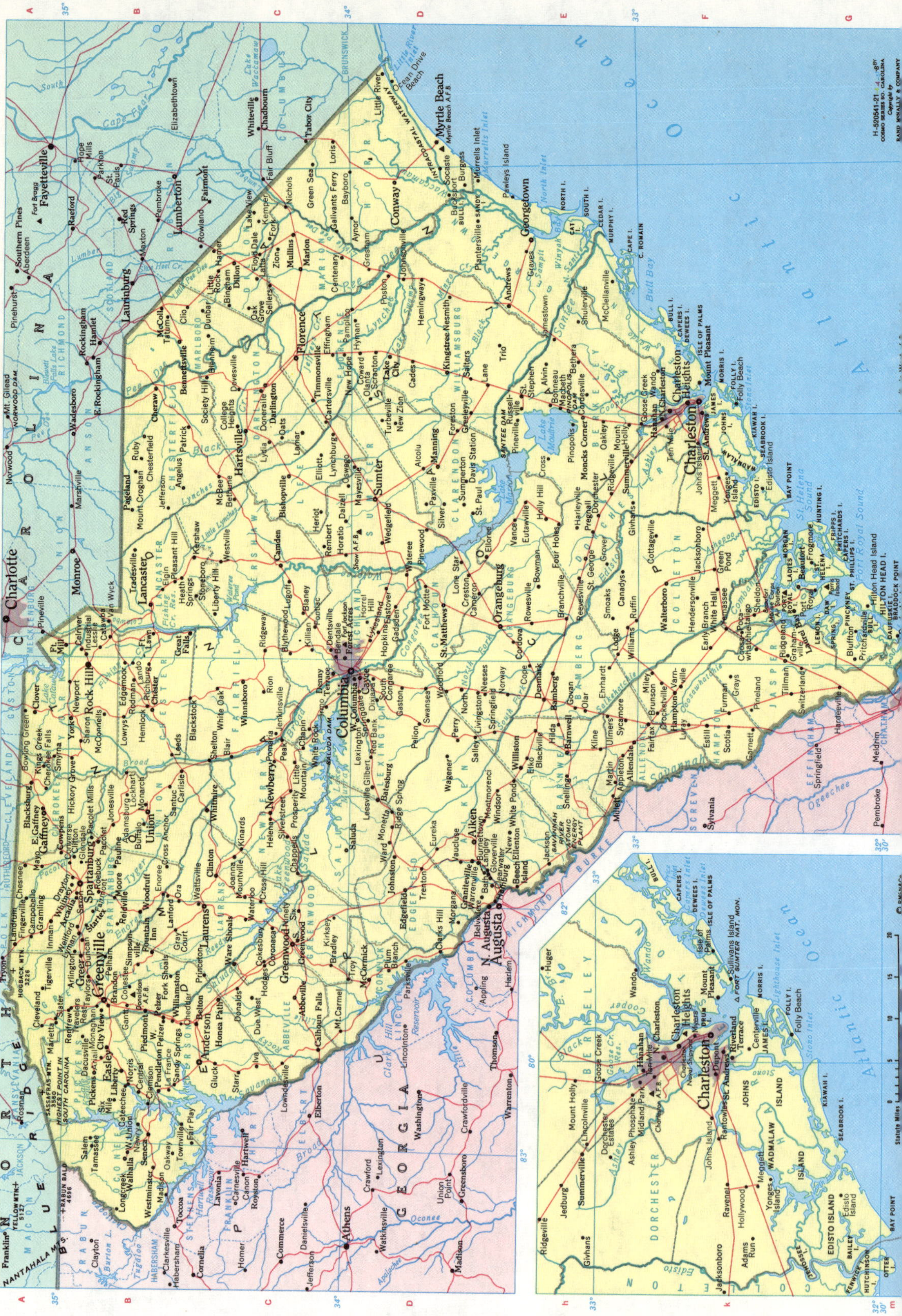

Statute Miles 5 0 5 10 20 30

Kilometers 5 0 5 15 25 35 45

Lambert Conformal Conic Projection

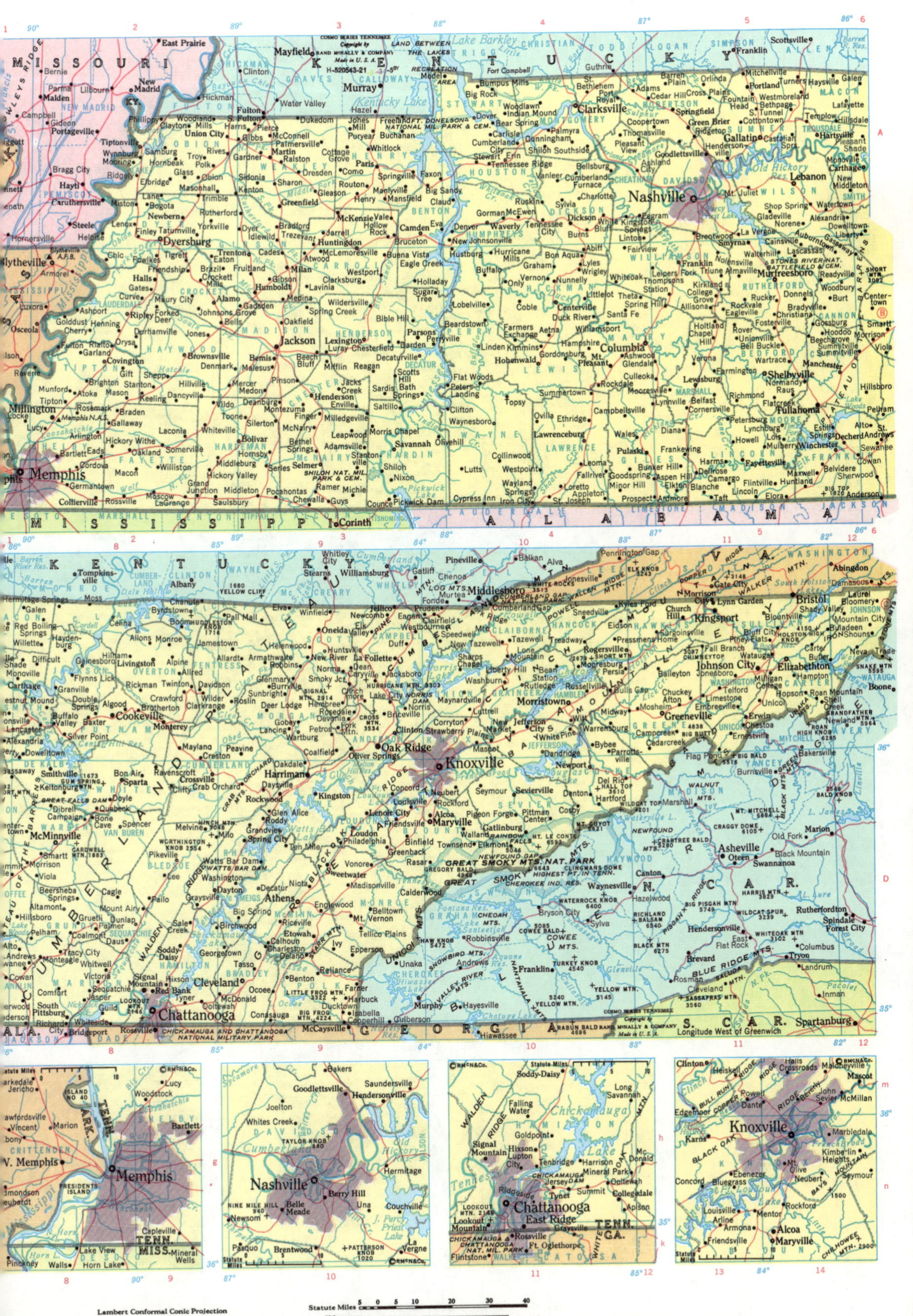
MISSOURI
KENTUCKY
MISSISSIPPI
ALABAMA
GEORGIA
N. CAR.
S. CAR.
VA.
Nashville
Memphis
Knoxville
Chattanooga
Jackson
Clarksville
Murfreesboro
Columbia
Kingsport
Johnson City
Bristol
Oak Ridge
Asheville
GREAT SMOKY MTS. NAT. PARK
SHILOH NAT. MIL. PARK & CEM.
CHICKAMAUGA AND CHATTANOOGA NATIONAL MILITARY PARK
STONES RIVER NAT. BATTLEFIELD & CEM.
Kentucky Lake
Lake Barkley
Longitude West of Greenwich
Lambert Conformal Conic Projection
Statute Miles
Kilometers

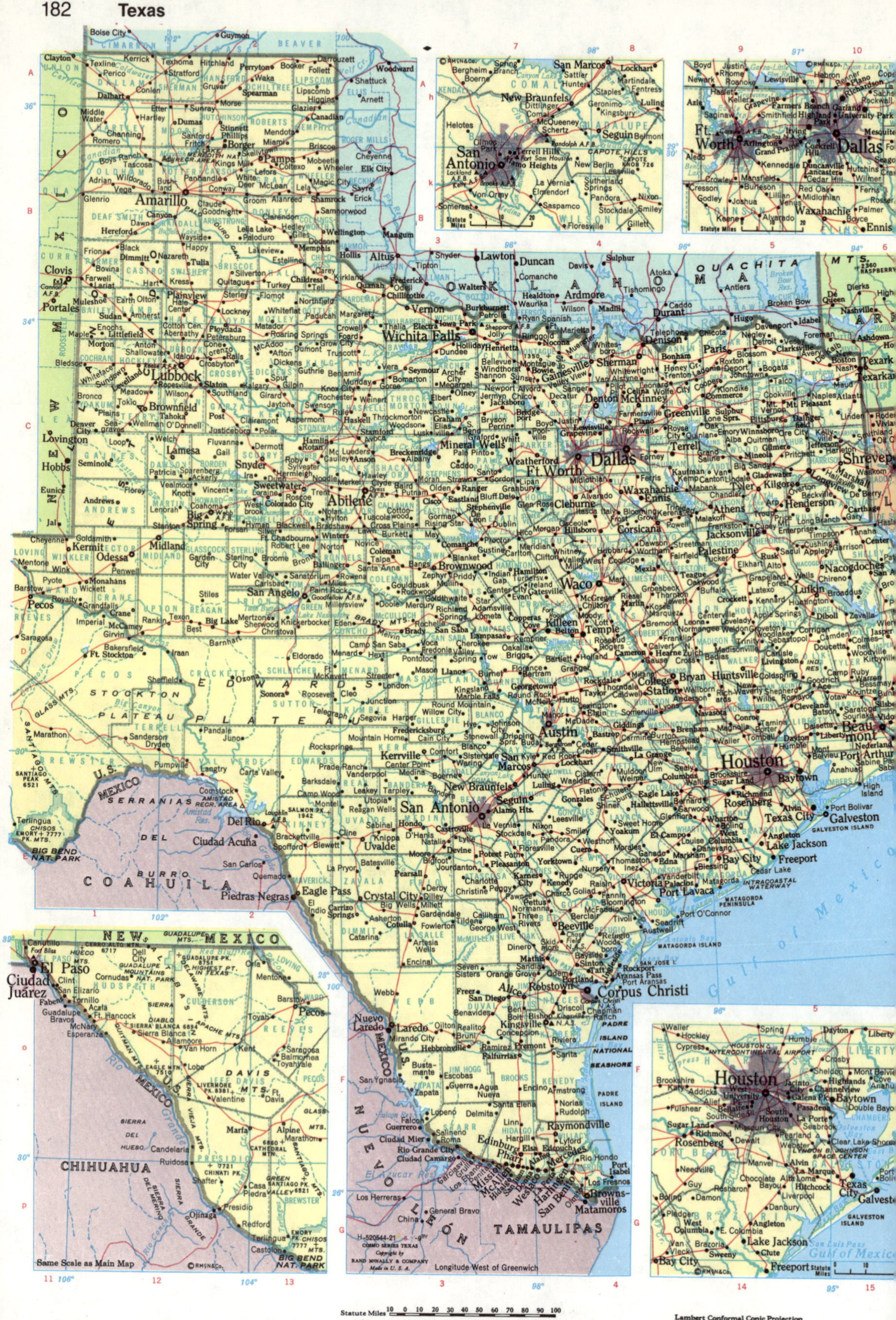
Amarillo
Lubbock
Abilene
Wichita Falls
Dallas
Ft. Worth
Waco
Austin
San Antonio
Houston
Galveston
Corpus Christi
Beaumont
El Paso
Ciudad Juárez
Laredo
Nuevo Laredo
Brownsville
Matamoros
Odessa
Midland
San Angelo
Tyler
Shreveport
Oklahoma City
Gulf of Mexico
EDWARDS PLATEAU
STOCKTON PLATEAU
COAHUILA
CHIHUAHUA
NUEVO LEÓN
TAMAULIPAS
NEW MEXICO
OKLAHOMA
OUACHITA MTS.
BIG BEND NAT. PARK
PADRE ISLAND NATIONAL SEASHORE
GALVESTON ISLAND
MATAGORDA ISLAND
Same Scale as Main Map
H-520644-21
COSMO SERIES TEXAS
Copyright by
RAND McNALLY & COMPANY
Made in U. S. A.
Longitude West of Greenwich
Statute Miles 10 0 10 20 30 40 50 60 70 80 90 100
Kilometers 10 0 10 20 40 60 80 100 120 140
Lambert Conformal Conic Projection

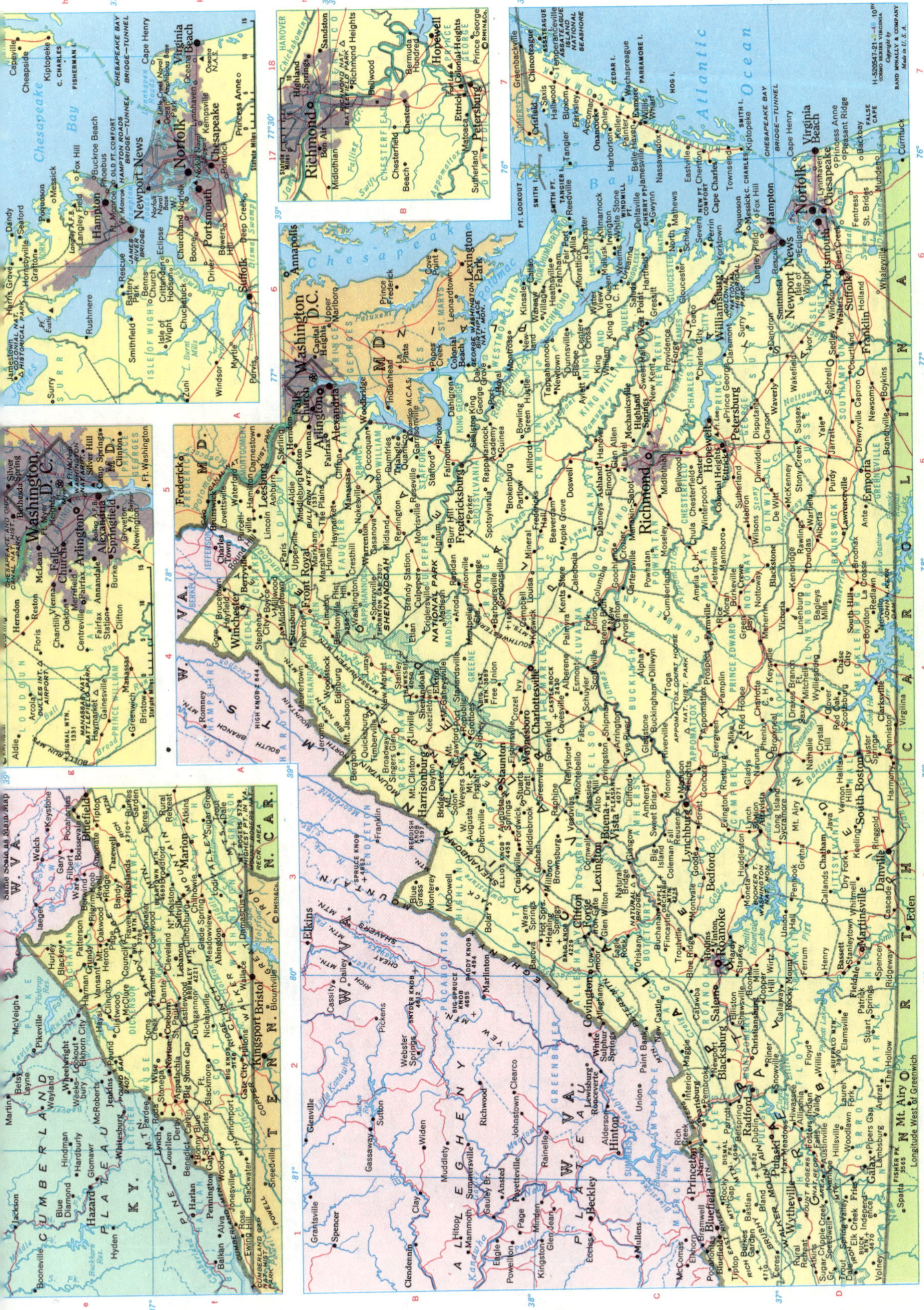

Lambert Conformal Conic Projection

Statute Miles 5 0 5 10 20 30 40

Kilometers 5 0 5 15 25 35 45 55

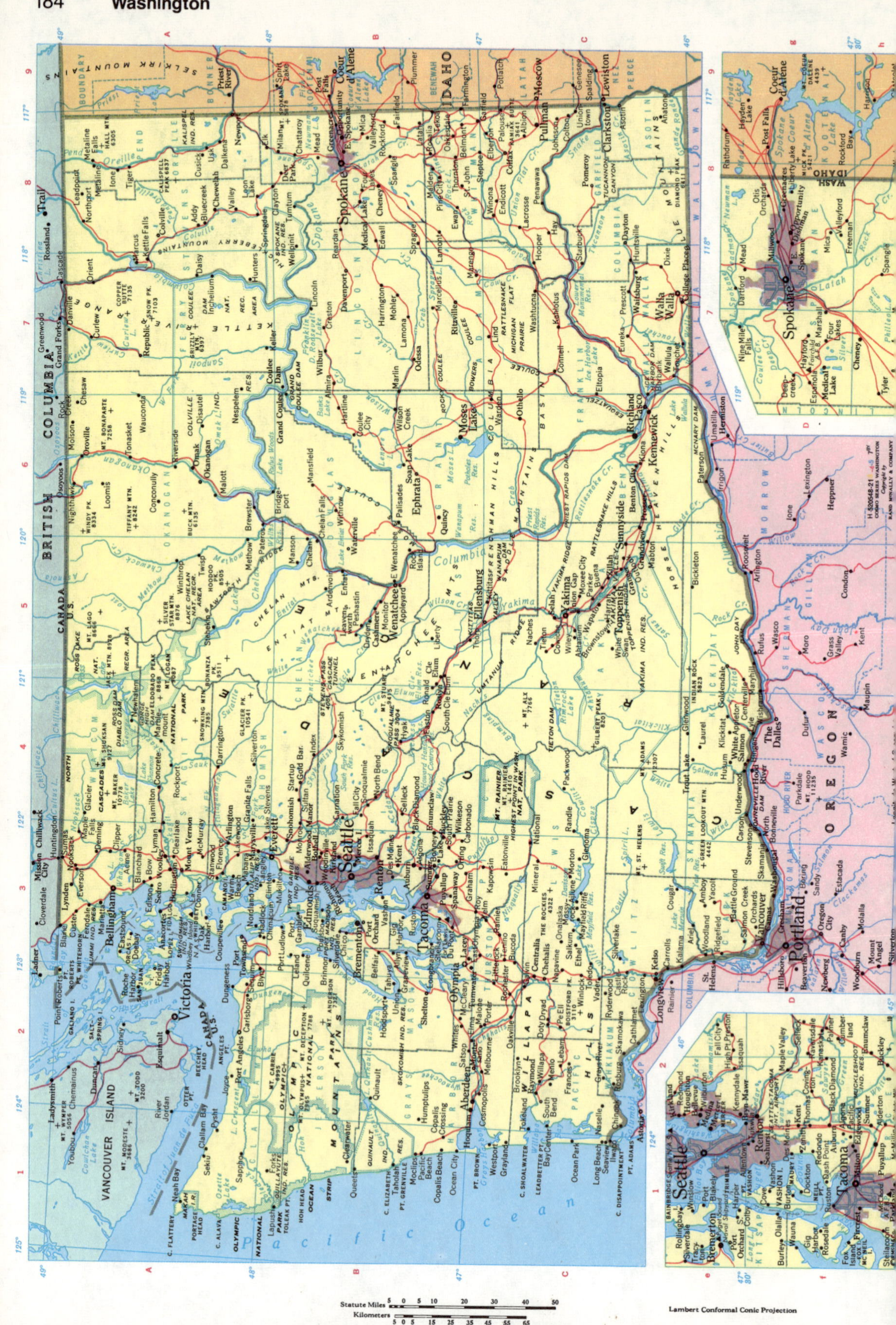
BRITISH COLUMBIA
CANADA
U.S.
IDAHO
OREGON
VANCOUVER ISLAND
Pacific Ocean
Seattle
Tacoma
Spokane
Olympia
Everett
Bellingham
Bremerton
Yakima
Wenatchee
Ellensburg
Walla Walla
Richland
Kennewick
Pasco
Vancouver
Portland
Victoria
Aberdeen
Longview
Moses Lake
Pullman
Lewiston
Clarkston
Coeur d'Alene
MT. RAINIER
MT. ST. HELENS
Columbia
Statute Miles
Kilometers
Lambert Conformal Conic Projection

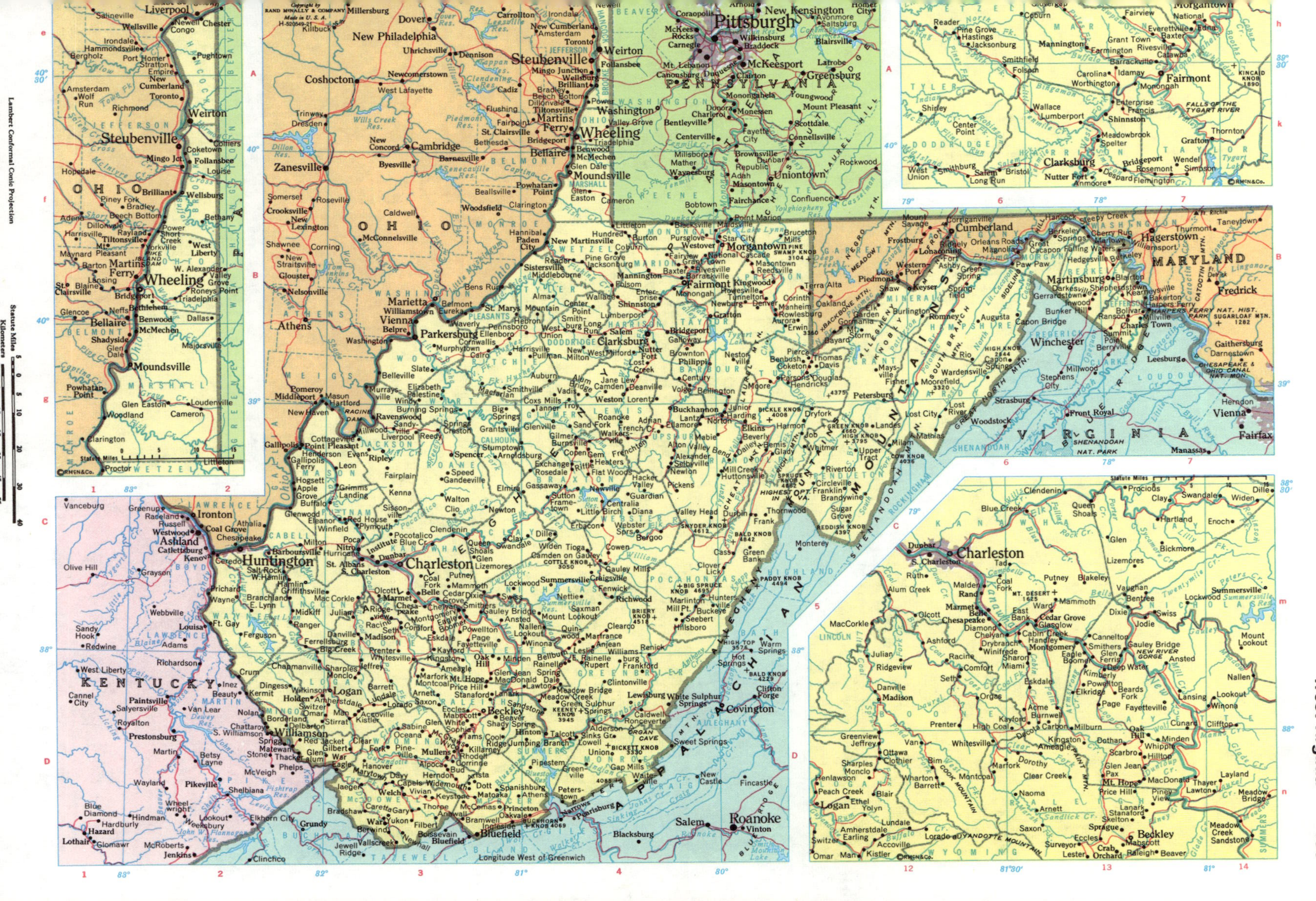
Lambert Conformal Conic Projection
Statute Miles 5 0 5 10 20 30 40
Kilometers 5 0 5 15 25 35 45 55
WEST VIRGINIA
MARYLAND
VIRGINIA
PENNSYLVANIA
OHIO
KENTUCKY
Charleston
Huntington
Wheeling
Parkersburg
Morgantown
Clarksburg
Fairmont
Pittsburgh
Steubenville
Weirton
Beckley
Bluefield
Cumberland
Hagerstown
Winchester
Roanoke
Martinsburg
Longitude West of Greenwich

Longitude West of Greenwich

Statute Miles 5 0 5 10 20 30 40

Kilometers 5 0 5 15 25 35 45 55

Lambert Conformal Conic Projection

H-520550-21
COSMO SERIES WISCONSIN

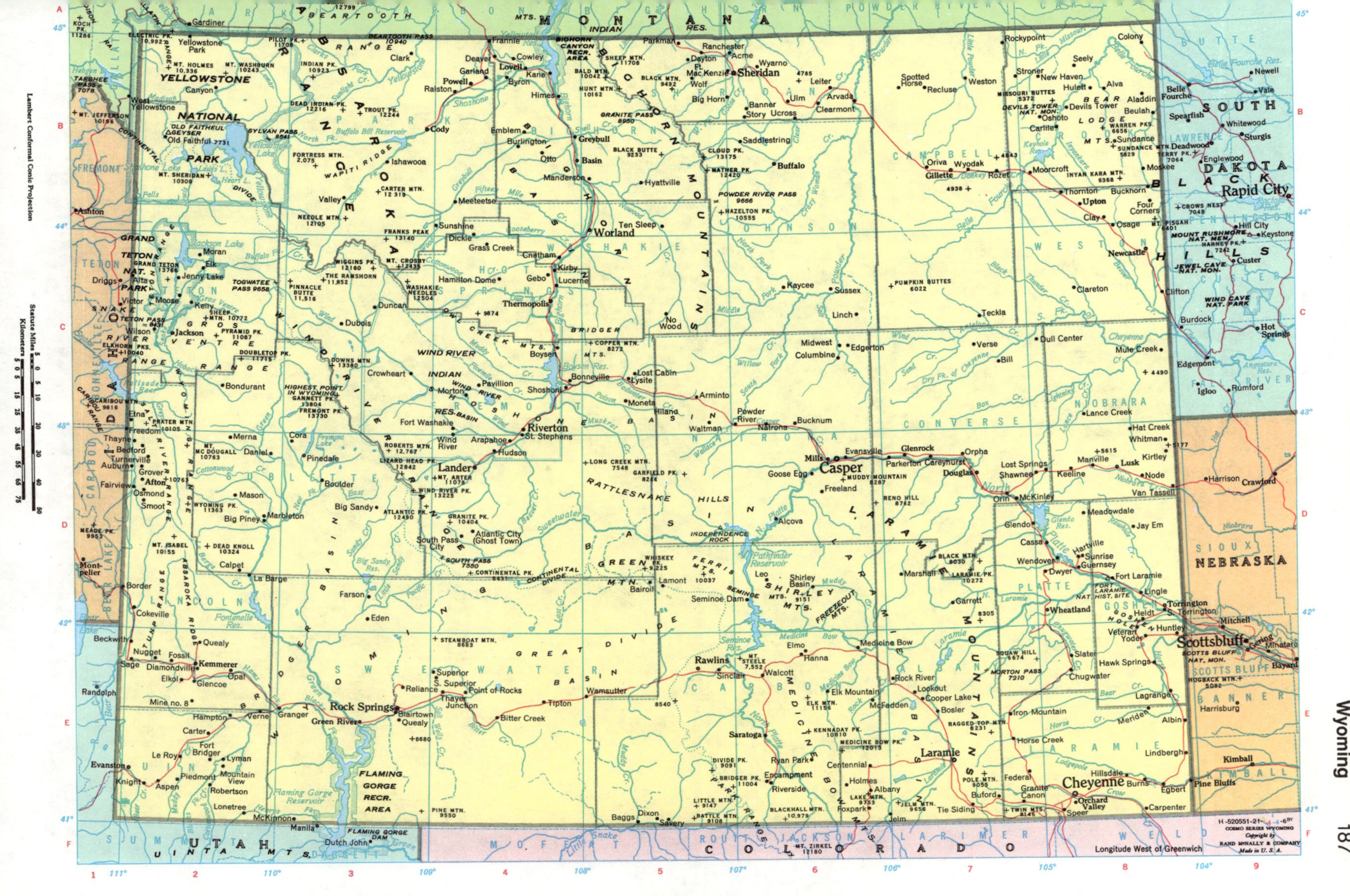
MONTANA
SOUTH DAKOTA
NEBRASKA
COLORADO
UTAH
IDAHO
Cheyenne
Casper
Laramie
Rock Springs
Sheridan
Rawlins
Riverton
Lander
Gillette
Cody
Worland
Evanston
Rapid City
Scottsbluff
YELLOWSTONE NATIONAL PARK
GRAND TETON NAT. PARK
BIGHORN MOUNTAINS
LARAMIE MOUNTAINS
WIND RIVER RANGE
GREAT DIVIDE BASIN
FLAMING GORGE RECR. AREA
DEVILS TOWER NAT. MON.
Longitude West of Greenwich
Lambert Conformal Conic Projection
Statute Miles
5 0 5 10 20 30 40 50
Kilometers
5 0 5 15 25 35 45 55 65 75

Historical Maps of the United States

Introduction

The search for adventure, wealth, and freedom has inspired those coming to America since the discovery of the New World. This vast land offered settlers abundant natural resources and the opportunity to experiment with social, religious, and political ideals. Freed from traditional constraints, Americans created an economy and industry that outstripped the combined production of European countries.

But along with its progress, the nation has also had its problems. Minority groups have long struggled for equality. As far back as the early 1800's, some people felt commercial development meant neglecting the consequences of uncontrolled growth. And World War II's legacy of America's continued expansion left the country somewhat unprepared for future problems. The energy crisis and worldwide inflation and instability now challenge the United States on several fronts.

Yet Americans are a confident and energetic people. Perhaps the experience of taming a continent, creating a vast industry, and absorbing millions of immigrants may be adequate preparation for meeting today's problems. History has shown that this nation is never more resourceful than when faced with a challenge.

The maps that follow chronicle the remarkable development of the United States from a colony to a great nation. Covering eight historical periods from 1700 to 1970, the maps illustrate the country's foundation and expansion westward, its richly varied population, and its three major conflicts—the Revolutionary and Civil wars and World War II. Text accompanying the maps provides detailed information about each period.

The American Colonies, 1700 *page 190*

The fabulous wealth discovered by Spain in Central and South America touched off a race among nations to share in the riches of the New World. By the early 1600's, Spain, France, and Great Britain had each made their claim for territory.

Dreams of finding easy treasure faded, and France and England realized the commercial and military value of these lands. With the exception of several settlements, few people immigrated to the French regions. But America fired the imagination of the British.

The early British settlers of Jamestown and similar camps struggled against disease and starvation, and many died. Slowly, however, the settlements began to prosper as more immigrants arrived, bringing their varied religious, social, and political beliefs.

Provincetown, Plymouth, Philadelphia, and the Chesapeake settlements became thriving commercial centers by the late 1600's. Boston and New York prospered as port cities, and coastal towns benefited from a growing fishing industry. The climate and farmlands of Maryland, Virginia, and the Carolinas proved ideal for cash crops such as tobacco and cotton. As the transplanted European population increased, native American Indians were forced out of coastal areas and pushed west.

By 1700, the colonies were loosely organized into eleven provinces. The population, with its unusual social, political, and religious makeup, was already markedly different from any society in Europe.

Independence, 1775–1783 *page 191*

The Revolutionary War instilled in the American people a sense of their nation's special destiny. The war arose from conflicts between a fiercely independent colonial population and a British government determined to tighten its control over King George's colonies. Colonial resistance became armed rebellion, and the war began in 1775.

At Lexington, Concord, and Bunker Hill, the British unexpectedly suffered heavy losses in defeating the Yankee militia. By July 1776, Britain was mounting a full-scale military effort to end the rebellion. Though well equipped and trained, the British had to fight an angry population in wilderness terrain. The Americans, outnumbered and poorly equipped, were fighting for their own land.

The British sought to isolate New England and defeated George Washington's Continental Army at Long Island and New York. But by the end of 1776, Continental troops had captured Princeton and Trenton. The American victory at Saratoga in October 1777 dealt a final blow to Britain's northern strategy.

From 1778 onward, Britain concentrated on the South and the coast, but British commander Cornwallis could not secure the countryside. In October 1781 at Yorktown, Cornwallis surrendered his entire command.

The peace treaty of 1783 recognized American independence and more than doubled the size of the former territory. The Americans believed their nation was destined to lead the world toward liberty.

MAP LEGEND

- Settled area: each dot represents 500 rural population.
- ● More than 5,000 people
- ○ Less than 5,000 people
- *Huron* Indian Tribe
- (1634) Founding Date

SCALE

miles 0 50 100 150

kilometers 0 50 100 150 200

Québec
Dec. 1775
Montgomery Aug.–Dec. 1775
Montréal
Nov. 1775
Arnold Sept.–Dec. 1775
MASS.
(District of Maine)
St. Leger July 1777
Lake Champlain
Fort Ticonderoga
May 1775
Burgoyne June 1777
Falmouth
NEW HAMPSHIRE
Fort Stanwix
Aug. 1777
Saratoga
Oct. 1777
Manchester
Fort Oswego
July 1777
Fort Niagara
Oriskany
Aug. 1777
Fort Herkimer
Stark
Bennington
Aug. 1777
Fort Pontchartrain
Geneseo
Loyalists & Brant
Herkimer & Arnold
Gates
Albany
Lexington & Concord
April 1775
Howe to Halifax Mar. 1776
Bunker Hill
June 1775
Cherry Valley
Nov. 1778
Loyalists & Brant
Johnson & Indians
Boston
Mar. 1776
Newtown
Aug. 1779
NEW YORK
MASS.
Providence
CONN.
R.I.
Fort Sandusky
Loyalist & Indian raid
Wyoming Valley
July 1778
Sullivan
New Haven
Washington
White Plains
Oct. 1776
Fort Lee
Nov. 1776
New York
Sept. 1776
Long Island Aug. 1776
Fort Pitt
Easton
PENNSYLVANIA
Princeton
Jan. 1777
Cornwallis
Howe from Halifax July 1776
Monmouth June 1778
Trenton Dec. 1776
Clark to Fort Vincennes Feb. 1778
Germantown
Oct. 1777
Valley Forge
Brandywine
Sept. 1777
Philadelphia Nov. 1777
Washington
Wilmington
Forts Mercer & Mifflin
Nov. 1777
MD.
Baltimore
NEW JERSEY
Proclamation Line 1763
VIRGINIA
DEL.
APPALACHIAN MOUNTAINS
Washington & Rochambeau (Fr.) Aug.–Sept. 1781
Boonesborough
Howe from New York July–Aug. 1777
Graves from New York
Charlottesville
Tarleton June 1781
Lafayette June–Sept. 1781
Richmond
Petersburg
Yorktown
Aug.–Oct. 1781
Norfolk
Off the Chesapeake Capes
Sept. 1781
Cornwallis May 1781
De Grasse (Fr.) from West Indies Sept. 1779
Guilford Courthouse
Mar. 1781
Salem
Frontier Settlers
Cornwallis Jan. 1781
Cornwallis April 1781
N.C.
Ferguson
King's Mountain
Oct. 1780
Charlotte
Cowpens
Jan. 1781
Morgan Dec. 1780
Cornwallis Aug. 1780
S.C.
Moore's Creek Bridge
Feb. 1776
Tarleton Jan. 1781
Winnsboro
Gates
Fort Ninety Six
June 1781
Greene Mar. 1781
Camden
Aug. 1780
Wilmington
Ft. Augusta
Feb. 1779
Rawdon
Eutaw Springs
Sept. 1781
Georgetown
Asche Feb. 1779
Briar Creek
Feb. 1779
Clinton & Cornwallis from New York Jan. 1780
Campbell from New York Dec. 1778
Charles Town
May 1780
May 1779
Oct. 1779
Prevost
Lincoln
Campbell Feb. 1779
GEORGIA
Savannah
Dec. 1778
Oct. 1779
D'Estaing (Fr.) from West Indies Sept. 1779
Prevost Jan. 1779
Copyright © by Rand McNally & Co. Made in U.S.A. All rights reserved.
MAP LEGEND
American Colonies
Indian Reserve
British Occupied City
American Occupied City
British Held Fort
American Held Fort
British Victory
American Victory
British Forces
American Forces
SCALE
miles 0 50 100 150
kilometers 0 50 100 150 200

The rallying cry of "Manifest Destiny!" reflected the American belief that Providence had granted the United States exclusive right to settle North America. An expanding population, European immigrants, commercial development, and a growing transportation system all played a part in the first great westward migration.

In 1803, Thomas Jefferson made the bold step of purchasing the Louisiana Territory from France. In 1819, Spain ceded the remainder of Florida to the Republic. Soon roads, railroads, and canal and river systems carried settlers into the Mississippi Valley and parts of Texas and opened the lands to eastern markets.

As the Louisiana Territory became densely settled, pioneers pushed beyond the formal borders of the country. Wagon trains headed west over the Oregon, Santa Fe, Frémont, and California trails. Mexico, attempting to stop the flow of settlers into its lands, was soon at war with America, losing Texas in 1836 and its southwestern territories in 1848. The Gadsden Purchase of 1853 completed America's southernmost border. American claim to the Oregon Territory was jointly held with Great Britain, and in 1848 the land was divided at the forty-ninth parallel. Settlers poured into these territories, and native American Indians were forced off their lands.

In a little over half a century, America had fulfilled its Manifest Destiny. Only the deepening conflict over slavery seemed to dim the nation's brilliant future.

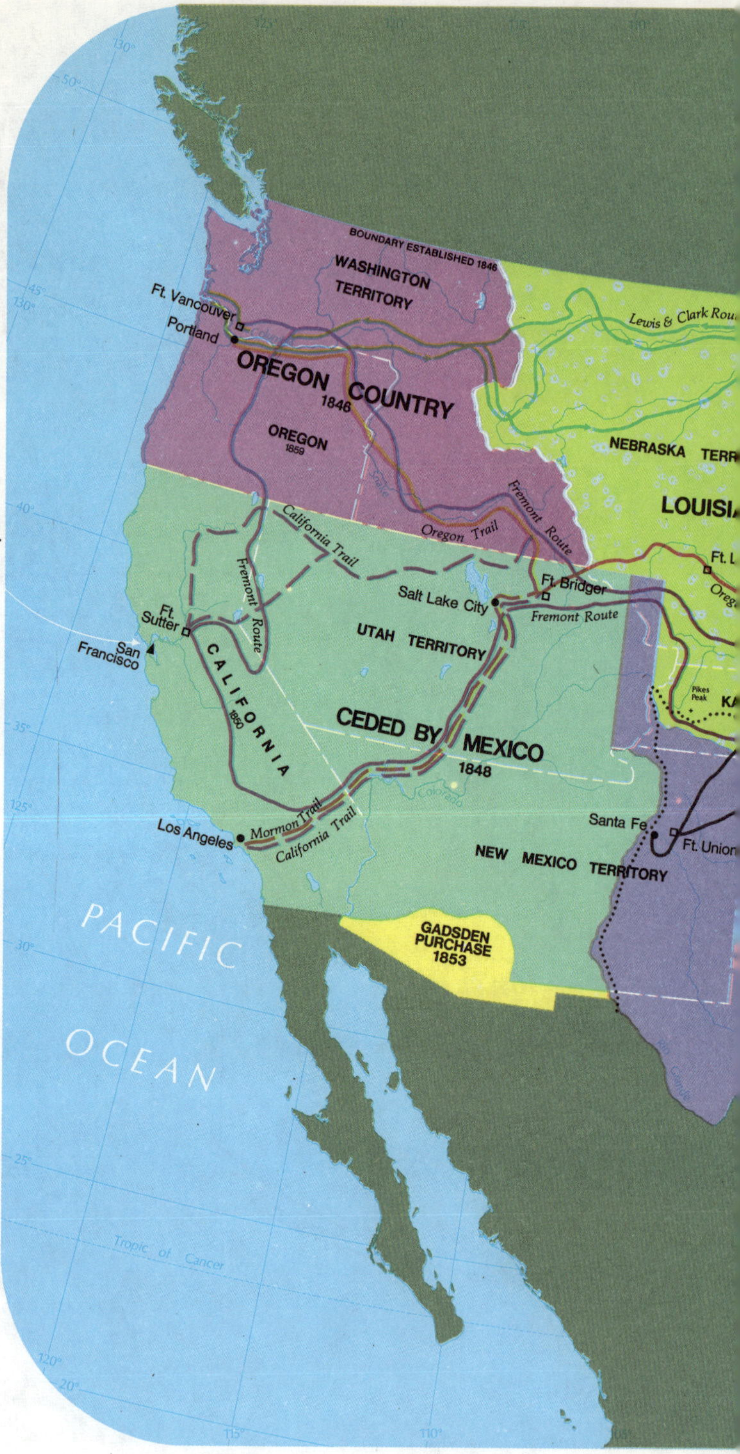

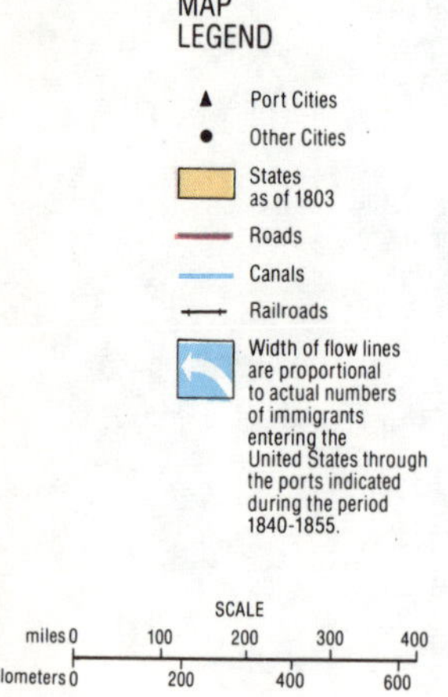

TITLE ESTABLISHED 1818
MINNESOTA 1858
(Unorganized)
PURCHASE 1803
WISCONSIN 1848
MICHIGAN 1837
NORTHWEST TERRITORY
IOWA 1846
Mormon Trail
Ft. Kearney
TERRITORY
Independence
ILLINOIS 1818
INDIANA 1816
OHIO 1803
MISSOURI 1821
INDIAN TERRITORY (Unorganized)
ARKANSAS 1836
TEXAS
NEXED 1845
LOUISIANA 1812
MISSISSIPPI TERRITORY
MISSISSIPPI 1817
ALABAMA 1818
GEORGIA
ANNEXED 1810
ANNEXED 1813
CEDED BY SPAIN 1819
FLORIDA 1845
Seminole War 1842
KENTUCKY
TENNESSEE
VIRGINIA
NORTH CAROLINA
SOUTH CAROLINA
PENNSYLVANIA
NEW YORK
NEW JERSEY
MARYLAND
DEL.
CONN.
R.I.
MASS.
VT.
N.H.
MAINE 1820
BY TREATY 1842
Calais
Portland
Boston
New York
Philadelphia
Baltimore
Washington
Norfolk
Oswego
Albany
Buffalo
Pittsburgh
Cleveland
Detroit
Chicago
Milwaukee
Indianapolis
Cincinnati
Louisville
Lexington
St. Louis
Nashville
Memphis
Atlanta
Charleston
Savannah
St. Augustine
Mobile
New Orleans
Galveston
San Antonio
The Alamo
LAKE SUPERIOR
LAKE MICHIGAN
LAKE HURON
LAKE ONTARIO
LAKE ERIE
Mississippi
Missouri
Ohio
Arkansas
Platte
ATLANTIC OCEAN
GULF OF MEXICO
Tropic of Cancer
Copyright © by Rand McNally & Co.
Made in U.S.A. All rights reserved.

MICHIGAN
LAKE MICHIGAN
LAKE ERIE
IOWA
ILLINOIS
INDIANA
PENNSYLVANIA
NEW YORK
N.J.
Chicago
Cleveland
New York
Pittsburgh
Wheeling
Gettysburg
Philadelphia
Springfield
Baltimore
Harpers Ferry
Washington D.C.
DEL.
MARYLAND
VIRGINIA
Fredericksburg
Richmond
Appomattox
Petersburg
Norfolk
Boonville
June 1861
St. Louis
Missouri
Mississippi
Cincinnati
Ohio
WEST VIRGINIA
(Entered Union 1863)
MISSOURI
Louisville
Buell
KENTUCKY
Bragg
Perryville
Oct. 1862
Paducah
Fort Henry
Feb. 1862
Fort Donelson
Feb. 1862
Nashville
Dec. 1864
Hood
Thomas
Franklin
ARKANSAS
Grant
Shiloh
Apr. 1862
Memphis
TENNESSEE
Murfreesboro
Knoxville
Tennessee
NORTH CAROLINA
Durham Station
Apr. 1865
Raleigh
Pulaski
Chattanooga
Nov. 1863
Chickamauga
Sept. 1863
Johnston
Pine Bluff
Oct. 1863
New Bern
SOUTH CAROLINA
Sherman
Columbia
Savannah
Atlanta
July-Sept. 1864
MISSISSIPPI
ALABAMA
GEORGIA
Charleston
Fort Sumter
Apr. 1861
LA.
Vicksburg
May-July 1863
Union Blockade of Southern Ports
Savannah
Port Hudson
July 1863
Baton Rouge
Farragut
Mobile
Mobile Bay
Aug. 1864
Pensacola
New Orleans
Apr. 1862
Jacksonville
St. Augustine
ATLANTIC OCEAN
Union Blockade of Gulf Ports
GULF OF MEXICO
FLORIDA
miles 0 50 100
kilometers 0 50 100 150
90°
85°
80°

By the 1860 presidential election, compromise on the issue of slavery could no longer hold the nation together. While the North vehemently denounced slavery, the South passionately defended its way of life. After Abraham Lincoln was elected, the South seceded from the Union and chose Jefferson Davis to head a new government in Richmond. By April 1861, the United States and the Confederacy were at war.

The Battle of Bull Run in July was a decisive Confederate victory. In early 1862, the Union army, under George Brinton McClellen and Ulysses S. Grant, took the offensive, winning at Fort Henry, Fort Donelson, and Shiloh. McClellen's subsequent move against Richmond was stopped by Confederate forces under Robert E. Lee. The Confederacy launched an invasion of the North, reaching Antietam before being pushed back into Virginia. Attempting a second invasion in July 1863, Lee was defeated at Gettysburg. Grant captured Vicksburg and, joining William Tecumseh Sherman, commander of the Tennessee troops, drove the Confederate troops back into Georgia.

In May 1864, Grant and George Meade, commander of the Army of the Potomac, marched toward Richmond. Sherman marched to the sea, capturing Atlanta, Savannah, and Columbia before turning north to Raleigh. On April 9, 1865, Lee surrendered to Grant at Appomattox.

Slavery had been abolished, and the South's economy lay in ruins. But the conflict had awakened the industrial might of the North. If one way of life had been lost, another was rising to take its place.

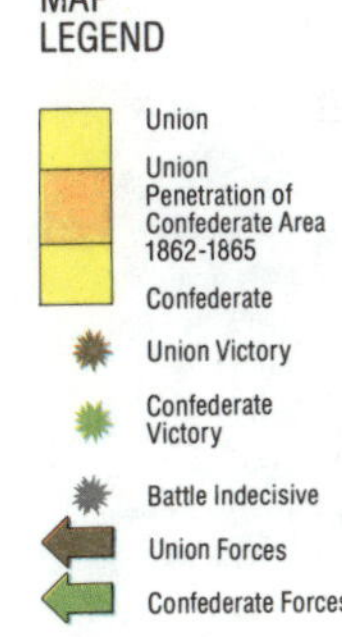

The final settlement of the West involved the greatest movement of people in the nation's history. In just thirty years, the "Great American Desert" was transformed into a mineral and agricultural empire.

The railroad boom opened the plains and mountain-desert regions to settlement. Between 1869 and 1884, four transcontinental railways were built; along with the overland stage, they linked the industrial East to the West. In a few years, the railroads were carrying cattle, grain, mail, payrolls, supplies and settlers into western territories.

The first settlers were miners. In the 1860's and 1870's, gold and silver strikes brought prospectors swarming into American Indian lands. War broke out with tribes in the North and the Southwest. Although the Indians won isolated battles, they could not prevail against the army's superior weapons. By 1887, the Indians and the buffalo were gone from the open range.

Ranchers and farmers followed in the miners' wake. From the mid-1860's to the late 1880's, a vast cattle empire dominated Texas, Wyoming, and Montana. But sheepherders soon challenged the ranchers, and farmers began fencing off grazing land and planting crops in the semiarid soil. In the end, windmills and barbed wire tamed the West as effectively as railroads and the Colt revolver.

By 1890, an almost continuous line of settlements stretched from the Midwest to the Pacific, and population in the territories had soared. The "frontier" had all but disappeared. Only the great waves of immigration in the early 1900's would compare with the extensive migration of this era.

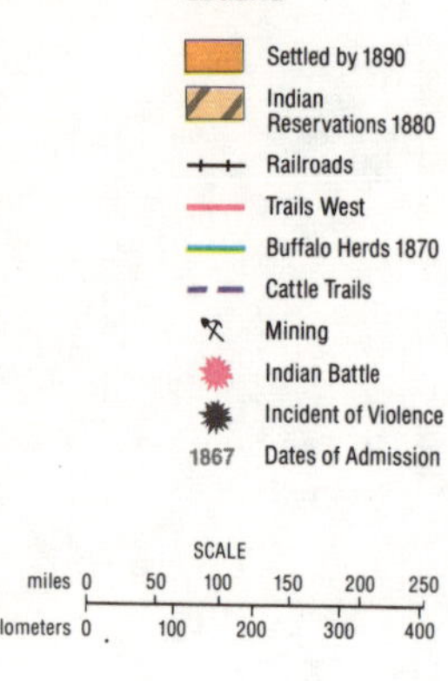

LAKE SUPERIOR
LAKE MICHIGAN
LAKE HURON
LAKE ERIE
NORTH DAKOTA
(Part of Dakota Territory until 1889)
SOUTH DAKOTA
(Part of Dakota Territory until 1889)
Bismarck
Northern Pacific
MINNESOTA
St. Paul
Minneapolis
Great Northern
End of James-Younger Gang
Northfield September 7, 1876
Younger Brothers Captured
Madelia September 11, 1876
WISCONSIN
MICHIGAN
Chicago
Cleveland
OHIO
IOWA
Des Moines
WYOMING TERRITORY
(1890)
Laramie
Cheyenne
Ogallala
NEBRASKA
(1867)
Union Pacific
Omaha
James-Younger
First Train Robbery
July 21, 1873
Pony Express
Overland Stage
Denver
Leadville
COLORADO
(1876)
St. Joseph
Jesse James
First Bank Robbery
February 14, 1866
ILLINOIS
INDIANA
Cincinnati
W.V.
St. Louis
James Brothers
Train Robbery
Oct. 3, 1879
KENTUCKY
VA.
Salina
Abilene
Sedalia
KANSAS
(1861)
MISSOURI
Wichita
Dodge City
Coffeyville
Butterfield Overland Mail
Illinois Central
TENNESSEE
N.C.
S.C.
Chattanooga
INDIAN TERRITORY
(OKLAHOMA 1907)
CHEYENNE
CHEROKEE
CREEK
ARRAPAHOE
CHICKASAW
CHOCTAW
APACHE
ARKANSAS
Judge Parkers
Federal Court
GEORGIA
Santa Fe
Ft. Smith
Adobe Walls 1874
NEW MEXICO TERRITORY
(1912)
Billy the Kid Killed
July 14, 1881
Lincoln County War
1875-1881
FORT STANTON
Western Trail
Dallas
Fort Worth
ALABAMA
LOUISIANA
MISSISSIPPI
Mobile
FLORIDA
Lake Pontchartrain
New Orleans
El Paso
Pecos Trail
Overland Mail
Butterfield
Chisholm Trail
Sedalia Trail
TEXAS
Lower Emigrant Trail
Southern Pacific
Judge Roy Bean
Houston
San Antonio
Rio Grande
Copyright © by Rand McNally & Co.
Made in U.S.A. All rights reserved.

For the first one hundred years of its history, the United States opened its doors to all nationalities. Millions journeyed to the American shores.

European immigrants arriving before and two decades after the Civil War came primarily from Ireland, England, Scandinavia, and Germany. The Irish tended to remain in the East. Others went to Oregon, then later to the northern plains states and Texas and California. Many were skilled farmers and artisans, blending into American life.

By the early 1900's, conditions in Europe led over eight million people to journey across the Atlantic. Most crowded into the cities' poorer sections, creating ethnic communities insulated from the language and customs of their new country. Yet these people answered the demand for labor and built the industrial might of the nation.

On the West Coast, the large number of Chinese and Japanese alarmed American workers. In 1882, the first in a series of immigration laws was passed, restricting the entry of Asians. Mexicans and Latin Americans often encountered the same resistance and hostility.

The South lacked heavy industry and available land, so immigrants favored the North and West. Also, restrictive immigration laws made it difficult for the foreign-born to settle in the South.

This constant stream of newcomers created a rich culture. Immigrants and their descendants have contributed immeasurably to the country's industry, science, and arts.

MAP
LEGEND

Immigrants

Foreign born whites and children of foreign or mixed parentage; by counties.

Source: U.S. Decennial Census, 1910

- Less Than 10%
- 10% To 25%
- 25% To 50%
- 50% To 75%
- 75% & Over

MONTANA 94,713 Total Foreign born population in 1910

SCALE

miles 0 100 200 300 400

kilometers 0 200 400 600

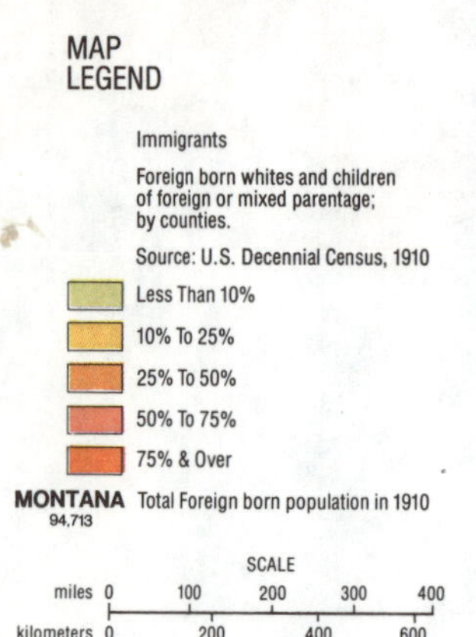

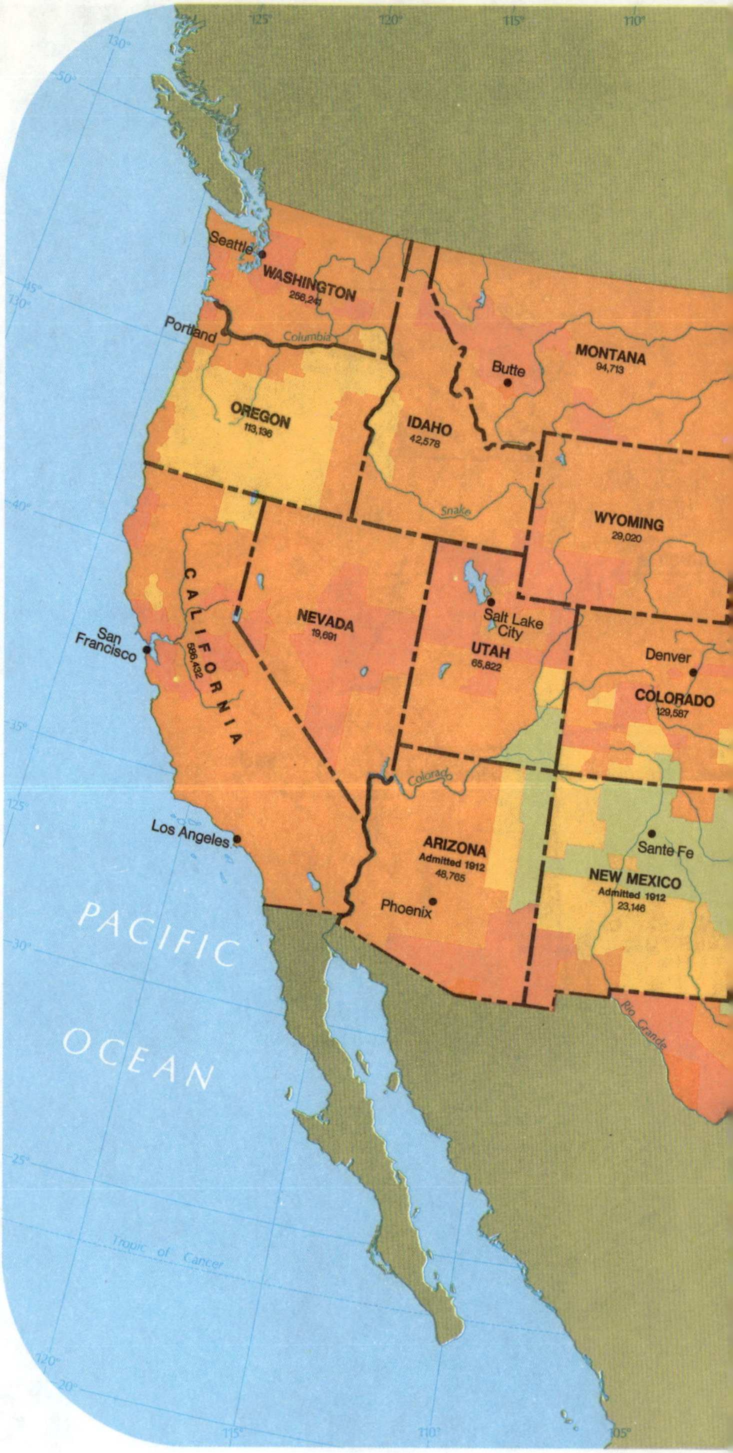

MINNESOTA
543,595
Minneapolis
WISCONSIN
512,865
Milwaukee
MICHIGAN
597,550
Detroit
LAKE SUPERIOR
LAKE MICHIGAN
LAKE HURON
LAKE ONTARIO
LAKE ERIE
IOWA
273,765
EBRASKA
176,662
KANSAS
135,450
Kansas City
MISSOURI
229,779
St. Louis
ILLINOIS
1,205,314
Chicago
INDIANA
159,663
OHIO
598,374
Cleveland
Cincinnati
NEW YORK
2,748,011
Buffalo
PENNSYLVANIA
1,442,374
Pittsburgh
Philadelphia
Newark
N.J.
New York
MAINE
110,562
VT.
49,921
N.H.
96,667
MASS.
1,059,245
Boston
CONN.
329,574
R.I.
179,141
Baltimore
MARYLAND
DEL.
17,492
Washington
D. C.
24,902
WEST VIRGINIA
57,218
VIRGINIA
27,057
KENTUCKY
40,162
Ohio
Missouri
TENNESSEE
18,607
Nashville
NORTH CAROLINA
6,092
SOUTH CAROLINA
6,179
Atlanta
GEORGIA
15,477
ALABAMA
19,286
MISSISSIPPI
9,770
Mississippi
ARKANSAS
17,046
OKLAHOMA
40,442
TEXAS
241,938
San Antonio
LOUISIANA
52,766
New Orleans
FLORIDA
40,633
Jacksonville
GULF OF MEXICO
ATLANTIC OCEAN
Tropic of Cancer

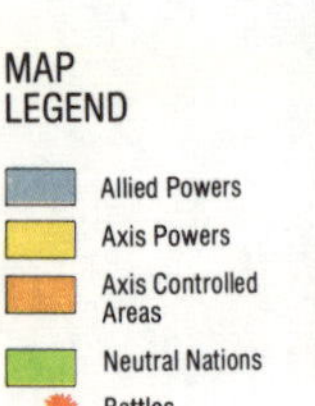

The United States entered World War II almost totally unprepared to fight on the two fronts of Europe and the Pacific. Yet its industrial capacity became a decisive factor in the Allied victory and eventually thrust America into a position of world leadership. Early in the war, however, the Axis powers seemed invincible.

By 1942, Germany had swept through most of Europe, isolated Great Britain, and launched an invasion of Russia. In North Africa, Rommel, commander of the German forces, threatened the vital Suez Canal. Russian leader Stalin desperately called for help to relieve his troops, but the Allies were not prepared to invade. Instead, in November 1942, Eisenhower, U.S. general and Allied Supreme Commander in North Africa, led an attack on Morocco and Algeria and by the next year had driven the Axis powers out of North Africa. Bolstered by American materiel, Soviet troops regained the offensive in the 1942–43 winter war and began forcing the Germans toward Berlin. The Allies landed at Normandy and southern France in June 1944. Caught between advancing Russian and Allied troops, Germany surrendered on May 7, 1945.

In the early months of the Pacific war, Japan had overrun Manchuria, Southeast Asia, Singapore, and Indonesia and had gained control of the seas. But by 1942, Allied forces had defeated the Japanese at the Coral Sea, Midway, and the Solomon Islands and in 1944 destroyed the remaining fleet at Leyte Gulf. MacArthur, commander of the U.S. forces in the Far East, liberated the Philippines in October of that year and with Nimitz, commander of the U.S. Pacific Fleet, launched an attack on Japan. Capturing one island after another, American forces were soon poised to invade the Japanese mainland. Instead, in early August 1945, the first atomic bombs were exploded over Hiroshima and Nagasaki. Japan surrendered on August 14.

The war profoundly changed the world. The United States and Russia now faced each other as rival superpowers over a divided Europe, and the power of the atom bomb haunted the world. It was hoped that the newly chartered United Nations would provide a forum for all nations to seek peaceful solutions to world problems and to begin building a lasting peace throughout the world.

Whenever opportunity has diminished in one region, Americans have moved to where jobs or land is more plentiful. Most recently, people have migrated to the West and South in search of opportunity.

Until the late 1950's, the industrial belt stretching from the Northeast to St. Louis continued to attract business and labor. Southern blacks and Appalachian whites migrated to the cities, while inner-city whites moved to the suburbs. By the late 1950's and early 1960's, many light industries were also leaving the inner city for the suburbs and the Sun Belt of the West and South. In addition, the aerospace and electronics industries drew a large work force to Florida, Texas, and California. Though the suburbs continued their growth, the inner-city areas of most northern cities began to lose population.

Changing American life-styles also contributed to the exodus to warmer climates. The ecology movement of the 1960's encouraged people to escape to less developed sections in the Southwest and Pacific states. More people looked to the Sun Belt as a place to retire.

By 1970, the search for a better life had created new communities and industrial areas in the South and West. Life-styles were changing, and there was a shift from heavy industry and manufacturing to light industry and service-oriented businesses. Cities in the industrial northern regions struggled to regain their vitality. As the shift in population continues, it remains to be seen what type of society will emerge from this latest American migration.

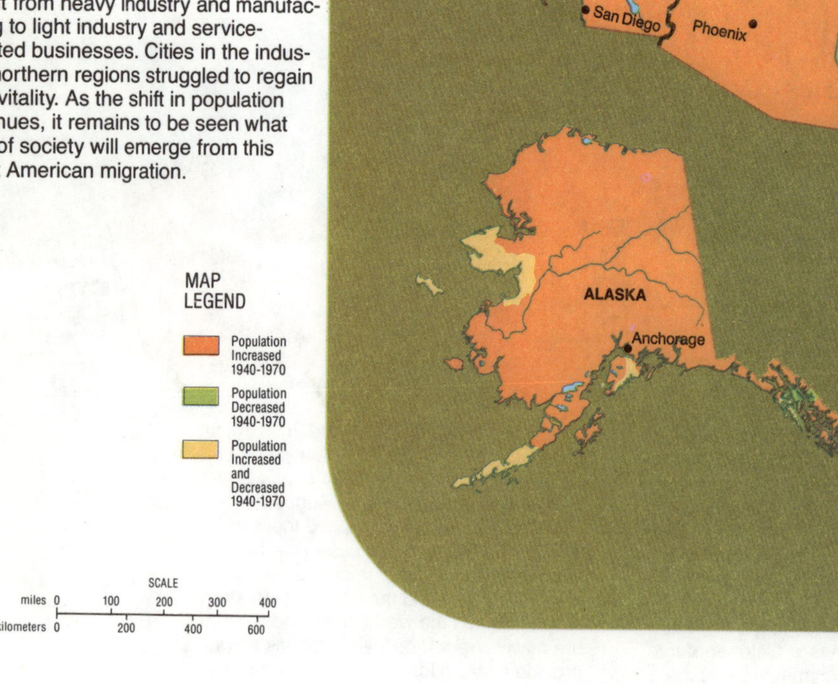

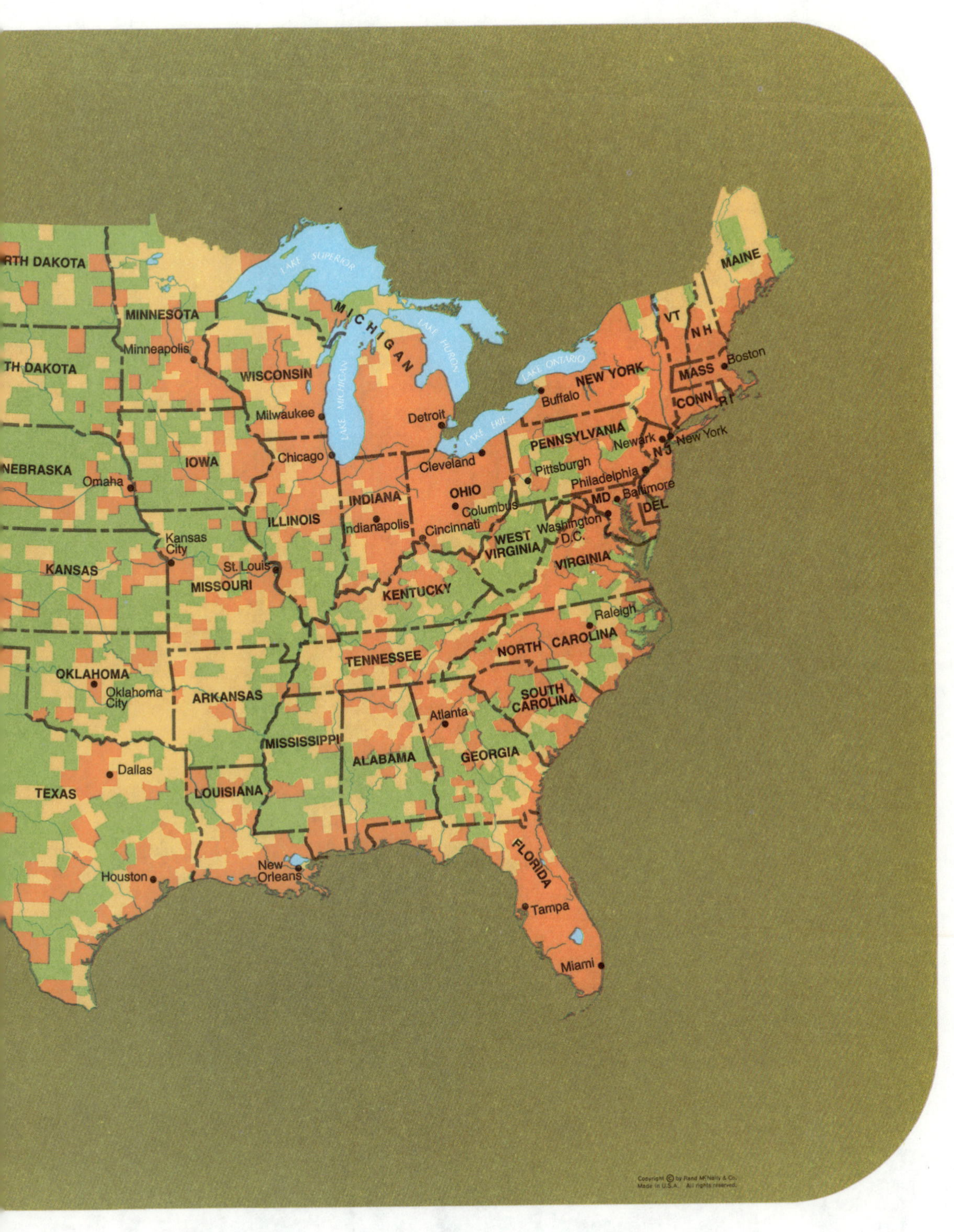
RTH DAKOTA
TH DAKOTA
NEBRASKA
KANSAS
OKLAHOMA
TEXAS
MINNESOTA
IOWA
MISSOURI
ARKANSAS
LOUISIANA
WISCONSIN
ILLINOIS
MICHIGAN
INDIANA
OHIO
KENTUCKY
TENNESSEE
MISSISSIPPI
ALABAMA
GEORGIA
FLORIDA
SOUTH CAROLINA
NORTH CAROLINA
VIRGINIA
WEST VIRGINIA
PENNSYLVANIA
NEW YORK
MD
DEL
NJ
CONN
RI
MASS
VT
NH
MAINE
LAKE SUPERIOR
LAKE MICHIGAN
LAKE HURON
LAKE ERIE
LAKE ONTARIO
Minneapolis
Omaha
Kansas City
Oklahoma City
Dallas
Houston
Milwaukee
Chicago
St. Louis
New Orleans
Detroit
Indianapolis
Cleveland
Columbus
Cincinnati
Pittsburgh
Buffalo
Philadelphia
Newark
New York
Baltimore
Washington D.C.
Raleigh
Atlanta
Tampa
Miami
Boston

Travel Maps
of the United States

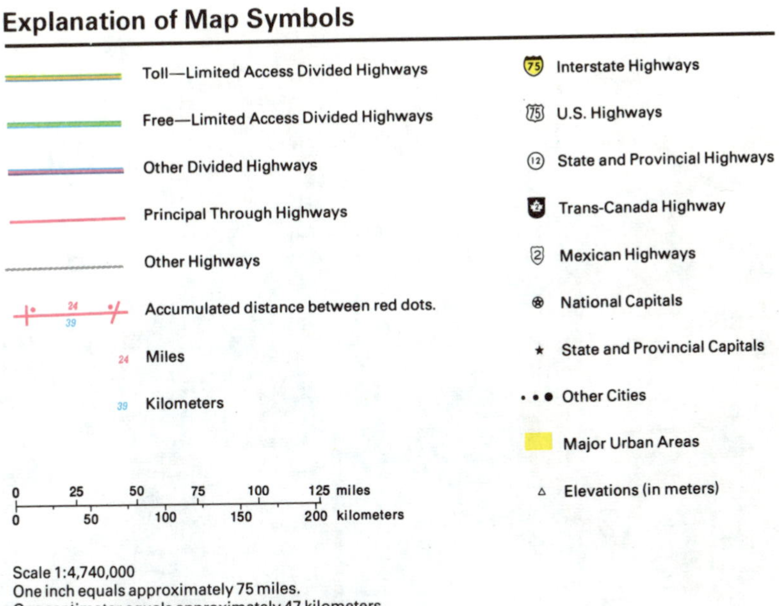

ALBERS CONICAL EQUAL AREA PROJECTION

Hawaii

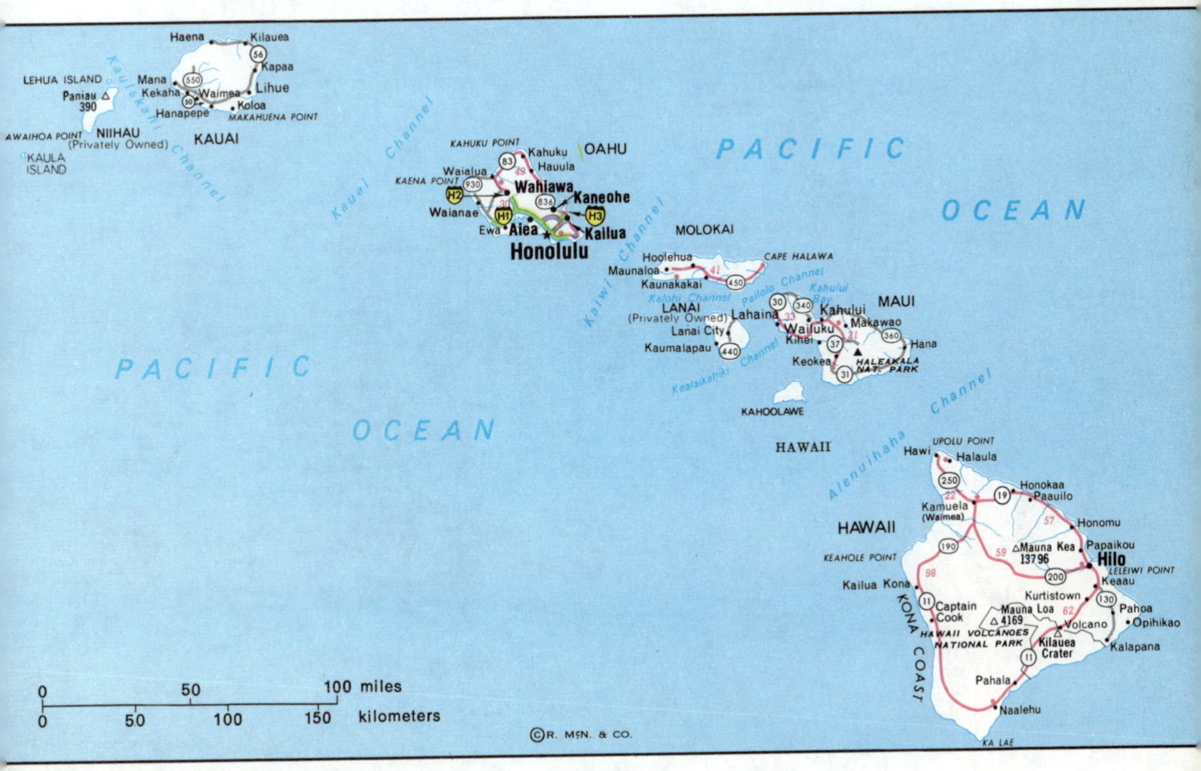

PACIFIC OCEAN
Haena
Kilauea
Kapaa
LEHUA ISLAND
Mana
Kekaha
Waimea
Lihue
Paniau 390
Hanapepe
Koloa
MAKAHUENA POINT
Kaulakahi Channel
KAWAIHOA POINT
NIIHAU (Privately Owned)
KAUAI
KAULA ISLAND
Kauai Channel
KAHUKU POINT
Kahuku
OAHU
Hauula
Waialua
KAENA POINT
Wahiawa
Kaneohe
Waianae
Ewa
Aiea
Kailua
Honolulu
Kaiwi Channel
MOLOKAI
Hoolehua
CAPE HALAWA
Maunaloa
Kaunakakai
Kalohi Channel
Pailolo Channel
Kahului Bay
LANAI (Privately Owned)
Lanai City
Kaumalapau
Lahaina
Kahului
Wailuku
Makawao
MAUI
Kihei
Hana
Keokea
HALEAKALA NAT. PARK
Kealaikahiki Channel
KAHOOLAWE
Alenuihaha Channel
HAWAII
UPOLU POINT
Hawi
Halaula
Honokaa
Paauilo
Kamuela (Waimea)
Honomu
Mauna Kea 13796
Papaikou
Hilo
LELEIWI POINT
Keaau
KEAHOLE POINT
Kailua Kona
Kurtistown
Captain Cook
Mauna Loa 4169
Pahoa
Opihikao
Volcano
HAWAII VOLCANOES NATIONAL PARK
Kilauea Crater
Kalapana
KONA COAST
Pahala
Naalehu
KA LAE

0 50 100 miles
0 50 100 150 kilometers

CANADA
UNITED STATES
ONTARIO
MICHIGAN
QUEBEC
INDIANA
OHIO
PENNSYLVANIA
NEW YORK
W. VIRGINIA
MARYLAND
Wawa
Chapleau
Foleyet
Kirkland Lake
Virginiatown
Noranda
Rouyn
Malartic
Val-d'Or
Bourlamaque
Matachewan
Englehart
Gogama
New Liskeard
Haileybury
Cobalt
Témiscaming
Whitefish Point
GRAND ISLAND
Grand Marais
PICTURED ROCKS NATIONAL LAKESHORE
Munising
Sault Ste. Marie
Newberry
Rexton
Manistique
Gladstone
Escanaba
Bruce Mines
Thessalon
Iron Bridge
Blind River
Spanish
Webbwood
Espanola
Algoma Mills
Levack
Chelmsford
Sudbury
Lively
Naughton
Coniston
Verner
Sturgeon Falls
North Bay
Mattawa
Saint Ignace
Mackinac Island
Mackinaw City
Cheboygan
DRUMMOND ISLAND
MANITOULIN ISLAND
Little Current
Manitowaning
South Baymouth
Byng Inlet
South River
Sundridge
Rogers City
Petoskey
Charlevoix
Gaylord
Alpena
Georgian Bay
Parry Sound
Huntsville
Bracebridge
Gravenhurst
Traverse City
Frankfort
Manistee
Cadillac
Grayling
Roscommon
Harrisville
Oscoda
Tawas City
LAKE HURON
BRUCE PENINSULA
Wiarton
Owen Sound
Meaford
Collingwood
Midland
Orillia
Barrie
Lindsay
Peterborough
Southampton
Port Elgin
Kincardine
Walkerton
Hanover
Mount Forest
Goderich
Clinton
Seaforth
Mitchell
Stratford
Kitchener
Waterloo
Guelph
Elora
Brampton
Aurora
Newmarket
Oshawa
Whitby
Cobourg
Brighton
Trenton
Bowmanville
Port Hope
TORONTO
Scarborough
Etobicoke
Mississauga
Oakville
Burlington
Hamilton
Cambridge
Dundas
Brantford
St. Catharines
Niagara Falls
Welland
Lake Ontario
Muskegon
Grand Rapids
Holland
Big Rapids
Mount Pleasant
Midland
Saginaw
Bay City
Bad Axe
Port Sanilac
Flint
Owosso
Lansing
East Lansing
Lapeer
Port Huron
Sarnia
London
Woodstock
St. Thomas
Kalamazoo
Battle Creek
Jackson
Ann Arbor
Pontiac
Royal Oak
Warren
Livonia
Dearborn
DETROIT
Windsor
Chatham
Leamington
Ypsilanti
Adrian
Monroe
Toledo
LAKE ERIE
POINT PELEE NAT. PARK
KELLEYS ISLAND
BUFFALO
Lackawanna
Cheektowaga
Tonawanda
Lockport
Batavia
Rochester
Dunkirk
Fredonia
Jamestown
Olean
Salamanca
Hornell
Corning
Erie
Ashtabula
Painesville
Mentor
Euclid
CLEVELAND
Lakewood
Shaker Heights
Parma
Lorain
Elyria
Sandusky
Akron
Youngstown
Warren
Canton
Massillon
Wooster
Mansfield
Sharon
New Castle
Meadville
Oil City
Franklin
Titusville
Bradford
Warren
South Bend
Elkhart
Goshen
Kendallville
Fort Wayne
Defiance
Bowling Green
Findlay
Tiffin
Fremont
Fostoria
Lima
Marion
Huntington
Wabash
Peru
Marion
Muncie
Anderson
New Castle
INDIANAPOLIS
Richmond
Dayton
Kettering
Springfield
Piqua
Sidney
Bellefontaine
Delaware
Columbus
Newark
Zanesville
Coshocton
Mount Vernon
Lancaster
Chillicothe
Circleville
Washington Court House
Middletown
Hamilton
CINCINNATI
Covington
Newport
Athens
Marietta
Parkersburg
Wheeling
Moundsville
Steubenville
Weirton
PITTSBURGH
McKeesport
Monessen
Washington
Butler
Kittanning
Indiana
Johnstown
Altoona
State College
Lewistown
Greensburg
Uniontown
Morgantown
Fairmont
Clarksburg
Cumberland
Hagerstown
Chambersburg
Gettysburg
Martinsburg
Winchester
WASHINGTON
Arlington
Alexandria
Front Royal
Harrisonburg
Portsmouth
Huntington
Ashland
Charleston
Gallipolis
Point Pleasant
Maysville
Frankfort
Lexington
Georgetown
Paris
Jeffersonville
Madison
Carrollton
Columbus
Franklin
Shelbyville
Clearfield
Williamsport
Erie

Québec
Ste.-Foy
Lauzon
Levis
Montmagny
La Tuque
Shawinigan
Trois-Rivières
Victoriaville
Thetford Mines
Drummondville
Sherbrooke
Granby
MONTREAL
Laval
Ottawa
Hull
Cornwall
Kingston
Watertown
Ogdensburg
Massena
Plattsburgh
Burlington
Montpelier
Barre
Rutland
Saranac Lake
ADIRONDACK MOUNTAINS
Glens Falls
Saratoga Springs
Utica
Rome
Syracuse
Schenectady
Amsterdam
Albany
Troy
Oneonta
CATSKILL MOUNTAINS
Binghamton
Kingston
Poughkeepsie
Newburgh
Middletown
Scranton
Wilkes-Barre
Hazleton
Allentown
Bethlehem
Easton
Reading
Pottsville
Paterson
Newark
NEW YORK
Jersey City
Elizabeth
Yonkers
White Plains
Stamford
Norwalk
Bridgeport
New Haven
Danbury
Waterbury
Meriden
Hartford
New Britain
Bristol
Springfield
Holyoke
Pittsfield
Worcester
Fitchburg
Lowell
Lawrence
Haverhill
BOSTON
Cambridge
Lynn
Salem
Quincy
Brockton
Providence
Pawtucket
Cranston
Warwick
Newport
Fall River
New Bedford
Norwich
New London
Westerly
Manchester
Nashua
Concord
Keene
Portsmouth
Dover
Rochester
Laconia
Portland
Saco
Biddeford
Lewiston
Brunswick
Bath
Augusta
Waterville
Bangor
Orono
Presque Isle
Caribou
Edmundston
Fredericton
Calais
Trenton
Levittown
Norristown
PHILADELPHIA
Camden
Chester
Wilmington
Vineland
Atlantic City
Cape May
Dover
BALTIMORE
Salisbury
Ocean City
CAPE COD NATIONAL SEASHORE
FIRE ISLAND NATIONAL SEASHORE
ACADIA NATIONAL PARK
MARTHA'S VINEYARD
NANTUCKET ISLAND
BLOCK ISLAND
WHITE MTS.
GREEN MTS.
CANADA
UNITED STATES
©RAND McNALLY & CO.

Richmond
Norfolk
Virginia Beach
Chesapeake
Portsmouth
Newport News
Hampton
Petersburg
Fredericksburg
Charlottesville
Lynchburg
Roanoke
Danville
Raleigh
Durham
Chapel Hill
Winston-Salem
Greensboro
High Point
Charlotte
Fayetteville
Wilmington
Myrtle Beach
Charleston
Columbia
Greenville
Spartanburg
Augusta
Savannah
Macon
ATLANTA
Columbus
Montgomery
Huntsville
Chattanooga
Knoxville
Nashville
Asheville
Lexington
Louisville
Evansville
Owensboro
Bowling Green
Huntington
Charleston
Salisbury
KENTUCKY
TENNESSEE
VIRGINIA
NORTH CAROLINA
SOUTH CAROLINA
GEORGIA
ALABAMA
MARYLAND
A P P A L A C H I

GEORGIA
FLORIDA
ALABAMA
Jacksonville
Tallahassee
Pensacola
Panama City
Gainesville
Ocala
Orlando
Daytona Beach
St. Augustine
Tampa
St. Petersburg
Clearwater
Lakeland
Sarasota
Bradenton
Fort Myers
Naples
West Palm Beach
Fort Lauderdale
Hollywood
MIAMI
Miami Beach
Coral Gables
Hialeah
Key West
Key Largo
Melbourne
Vero Beach
Fort Pierce
Titusville
Cocoa
Merritt Island
Sanford
Kissimmee
Valdosta
Thomasville
Waycross
Brunswick
Dothan
Moultrie
Okeechobee
Homestead
Florida City
Nassau
NEW PROVIDENCE
ANDROS ISLAND
GRAND BAHAMA
BIMINI ISLANDS
BERRY ISLANDS
GREAT ABACO
LITTLE ABACO ISLAND
Freeport
West End
Marsh Harbour
GREAT SALE CAY
MOORS ISLAND
Andros Town
Nicolls Town
Mastic Point
Cherokee Sound
WALT DISNEY WORLD
FLORIDA KEYS
DRY TORTUGAS
FORT JEFFERSON NAT. MON.
CAPE SABLE
CAPE ROMANO
CAPE CANAVERAL
CAPE SAN BLAS
CAPE SAINT GEORGE
LIGHTHOUSE POINT
EVERGLADES NATIONAL PARK
BISCAYNE NATIONAL PARK
BIG CYPRESS IND. RES.
MICCOSUKEE STATE IND. RES.
BRIGHTON INDIAN RESERVATION
CASTILLO DE SAN MARCOS NATIONAL MONUMENT
FORT MATANZAS NATIONAL MONUMENT
FORT FREDERICA NATIONAL MONUMENT
CUMBERLAND ISLAND NATIONAL SEASHORE
GULF ISLANDS NATIONAL SEASHORE
©RAND McNALLY & CO.

Amarillo
Oklahoma City
El Reno
Pampa
Shamrock
Sayre
Clinton
Weatherford
Elk City
Cheyenne
Norman
Shawnee
Seminole
Okmulgee
Henryetta
Checotah
Eufaula
McAlester
Hereford
Canyon
Dimmitt
Tulia
Clovis
Muleshoe
Plainview
Floydada
Littlefield
Lubbock
Levelland
Brownfield
Lamesa
Hobbs
Andrews
Seminole
Snyder
Sweetwater
Abilene
Big Spring
Midland
Odessa
Monahans
Crane
Kermit
Fort Stockton
Pecos
San Angelo
Ozona
Sonora
Junction
Kerrville
Fredericksburg
Austin
San Marcos
New Braunfels
San Antonio
Seguin
Del Rio
Ciudad Acuña
Uvalde
Eagle Pass
Piedras Negras
Crystal City
Carrizo Springs
Cotulla
Pearsall
Laredo
Nuevo Laredo
Zapata
Rio Grande City
McAllen
Edinburg
Reynosa
Harlingen
Brownsville
Matamoros
Kingsville
Alice
Corpus Christi
Robstown
Beeville
Victoria
Port Lavaca
Bay City
HOUSTON
Rosenberg
Bryan
College Station
Huntsville
Waco
Temple
Killeen
Belton
Georgetown
Taylor
Brownwood
Coleman
Brady
Lampasas
DALLAS
Fort Worth
Arlington
Grand Prairie
Irving
Garland
Mesquite
Richardson
Denton
McKinney
Sherman
Denison
Gainesville
Wichita Falls
Vernon
Quanah
Childress
Lawton
Duncan
Ardmore
Altus
Chickasha
Durant
Paris
Greenville
Terrell
Corsicana
Athens
Palestine
Jacksonville
Ennis
Waxahachie
Cleburne
Stephenville
Weatherford
Mineral Wells
Breckenridge
Cisco
Eastland
Ranger
Monterrey
Guadalupe
Monclova
Sabinas
Nueva Rosita
Sabinas Hidalgo
Villa Frontera
Cerralvo
LLANO ESTACADO
EDWARDS PLATEAU
STOCKTON PLATEAU
BALCONES ESCARPMENT
SERRANÍAS DEL BURRO
SIERRA MADRE ORIENTAL
UNITED STATES
MEXICO
NEW MEXICO
TEXAS
OKLAHOMA
COAHUILA
NUEVO LEON
TAMAULIPAS
PADRE ISLAND NATIONAL SEASHORE
MATAGORDA PENINSULA
AMISTAD NAT'L REC. AREA

GULF OF MEXICO

SOUTH DAKOTA
NEBRASKA
WYOMING
COLORADO
KANSAS
OKLAHOMA
TEXAS
NEW MEXICO
IOWA
SAND HILLS
BLUE HILLS UPLAND
LLANO ESTACADO
AGATE FOSSIL BEDS NATIONAL MONUMENT
SCOTTS BLUFF NAT'L MON.
ROSEBUD INDIAN RESERVATION
YANKTON IND. RES.
SANTEE INDIAN RESERVATION
WINNEBAGO INDIAN RESERVATION
OMAHA INDIAN RESERVATION
POTAWATOMIE INDIAN RESERVATION
OSAGE INDIAN RESERVATION
LAKE MEREDITH NAT'L RECR. AREA
Sioux Falls
Sioux City
Omaha
Lincoln
Council Bluffs
Bellevue
Norfolk
Columbus
Fremont
Grand Island
Kearney
Hastings
North Platte
Scottsbluff
McCook
Sterling
Valentine
Chadron
Alliance
Ogallala
Sidney
Beatrice
Topeka
Lawrence
Manhattan
Junction City
Salina
Hays
Great Bend
Hutchinson
Wichita
Dodge City
Garden City
Liberal
Emporia
Newton
El Dorado
Chanute
Winfield
Arkansas City
Independence
Coffeyville
Ottawa
Tulsa
Oklahoma City
Enid
Ponca City
Bartlesville
Stillwater
Norman
Lawton
Ardmore
Muskogee
Shawnee
Chickasha
Duncan
Altus
El Reno
McAlester
Amarillo
Lubbock
Plainview
Pampa
Borger
Dalhart
Hereford
Wichita Falls
Vernon
Clovis
Denison
Sherman
Gainesville
Paris
La Junta
Lamar
Dumas
RAND McNALLY & CO.

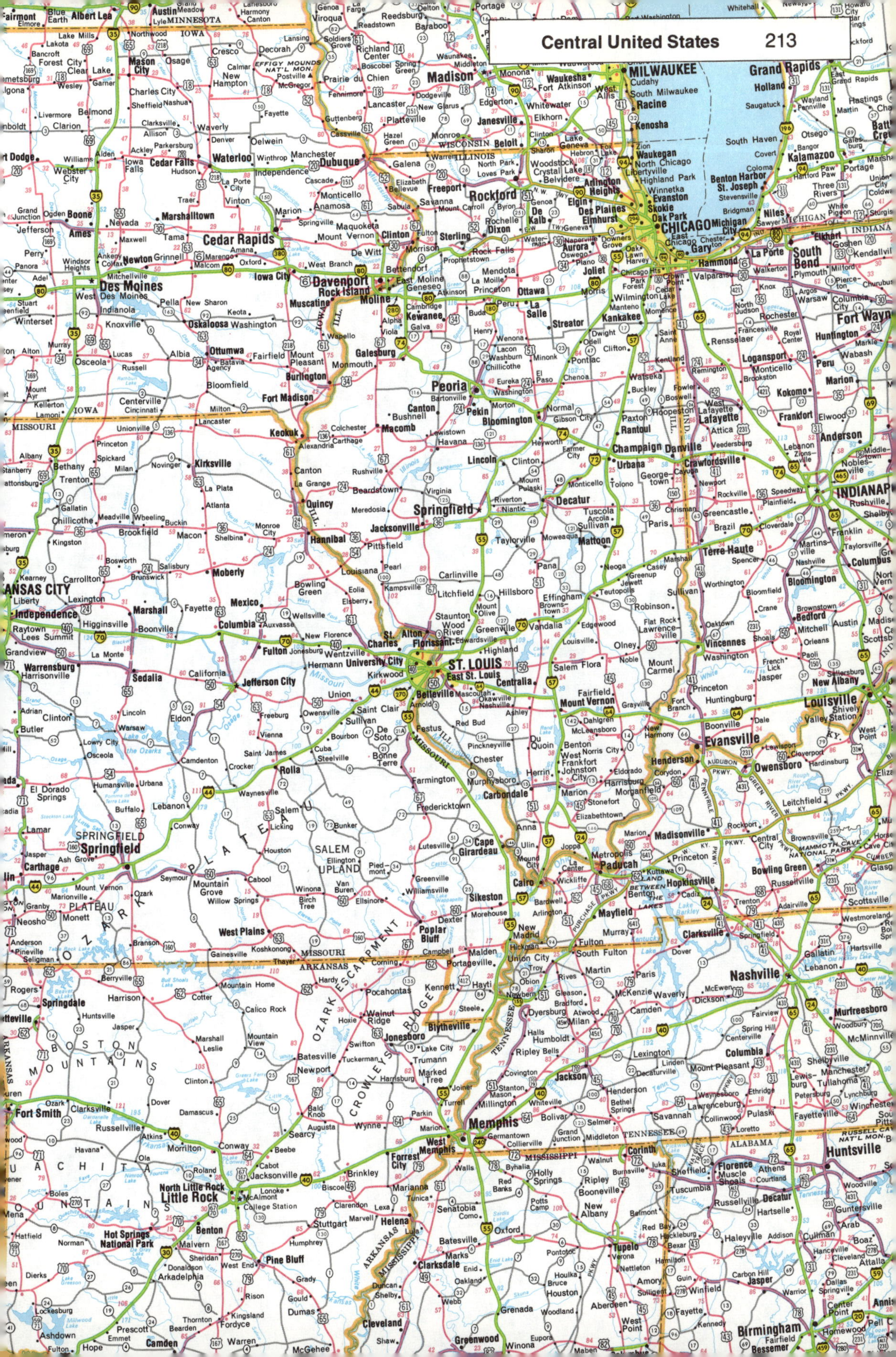

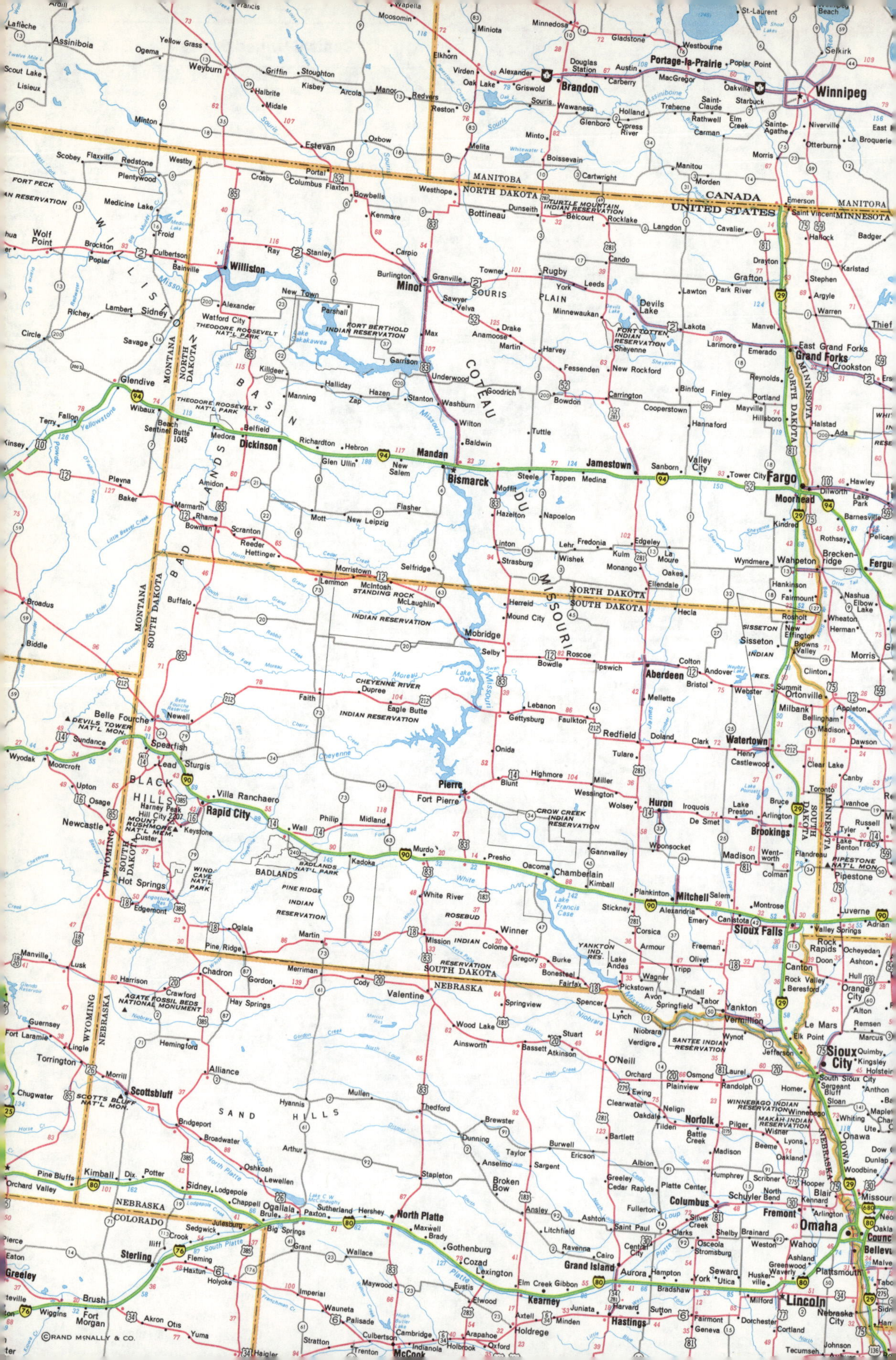

MANITOBA
NORTH DAKOTA
CANADA
UNITED STATES
MINNESOTA
MONTANA
SOUTH DAKOTA
NEBRASKA
WYOMING
COLORADO
IOWA
Winnipeg
Brandon
Portage-la-Prairie
Selkirk
Minnedosa
Virden
Souris
Boissevain
Morden
Emerson
Steinbach
Assiniboia
Weyburn
Estevan
Williston
Minot
Bismarck
Mandan
Dickinson
Jamestown
Fargo
Moorhead
Grand Forks
Devils Lake
Valley City
Wahpeton
Breckenridge
Rugby
Glendive
Sidney
Wolf Point
Culbertson
FORT PECK INDIAN RESERVATION
FORT BERTHOLD INDIAN RESERVATION
TURTLE MOUNTAIN INDIAN RESERVATION
FORT TOTTEN INDIAN RESERVATION
THEODORE ROOSEVELT NAT'L PARK
STANDING ROCK INDIAN RESERVATION
CHEYENNE RIVER INDIAN RESERVATION
SISSETON INDIAN RES.
CROW CREEK INDIAN RESERVATION
PINE RIDGE INDIAN RESERVATION
ROSEBUD INDIAN RESERVATION
YANKTON IND. RES.
SANTEE INDIAN RESERVATION
WINNEBAGO INDIAN RESERVATION
OMAHA INDIAN RESERVATION
PIPESTONE NAT'L MON.
DEVILS TOWER NAT'L MON.
MOUNT RUSHMORE NAT'L MEM.
WIND CAVE NAT'L PARK
BADLANDS NAT'L PARK
AGATE FOSSIL BEDS NATIONAL MONUMENT
SCOTTS BLUFF NAT'L MON.
WILLISTON BASIN
COTEAU DU MISSOURI
SOURIS PLAIN
BAD LANDS
BLACK HILLS
BADLANDS
SAND HILLS
Lake Sakakawea
Lake Oahe
Lake Francis Case
Missouri
Yellowstone
Lemmon
Mobridge
Aberdeen
Watertown
Brookings
Pierre
Fort Pierre
Huron
Mitchell
Sioux Falls
Yankton
Vermillion
Chamberlain
Rapid City
Spearfish
Sturgis
Belle Fourche
Hot Springs
Custer
Wall
Murdo
Winner
Valentine
Chadron
Alliance
Scottsbluff
Sidney
Ogallala
North Platte
Kearney
Grand Island
Hastings
Lincoln
Omaha
Fremont
Columbus
Norfolk
Sioux City
McCook
Holdrege
Lexington
Sterling
Greeley
Fort Morgan
Brush
Torrington
Newcastle
Sundance
Broadus
Baker
Bowman
Hettinger
©RAND McNALLY & CO.

CANADA
UNITED STATES
ONTARIO
MINNESOTA
MICHIGAN
WISCONSIN
IOWA
ILLINOIS
MISSOURI
LAKE SUPERIOR
LAKE MICHIGAN
ISLE ROYALE
ISLE ROYALE NATIONAL PARK
PUKASKWA NATIONAL PARK
VOYAGEURS NAT'L PARK
GRAND PORTAGE NAT'L MON.
APOSTLE ISLANDS NATIONAL LAKESHORE
PICTURED ROCKS NATIONAL LAKESHORE
SLEEPING BEAR DUNES NATIONAL LAKESHORE
EFFIGY MOUNDS NAT'L MON.
RED LAKE INDIAN RESERVATION
LEECH LAKE INDIAN RESERVATION
BAD RIVER INDIAN RESERVATION
LAC COURTE OREILLES INDIAN RES.
MESABI RANGE
HURON MOUNTAINS
KEWEENAW PENINSULA
DOOR PENINSULA
SUPERIOR UPLAND
Kenora
Dryden
Fort Frances
International Falls
Thunder Bay
Nipigon
Marathon
Duluth
Superior
Virginia
Hibbing
Ely
Grand Rapids
Brainerd
St. Cloud
MINNEAPOLIS
St. Paul
Rochester
Mankato
Albert Lea
Winona
La Crosse
Eau Claire
Wausau
Green Bay
Appleton
Oshkosh
Madison
MILWAUKEE
Racine
Kenosha
Sheboygan
Manitowoc
Marquette
Escanaba
Ironwood
Hancock
Houghton
Traverse City
Muskegon
Grand Rapids
Kalamazoo
South Bend
Gary
Hammond
CHICAGO
Waukegan
Evanston
Joliet
Aurora
Elgin
Rockford
Peoria
Bloomington
Davenport
Rock Island
Moline
Dubuque
Cedar Rapids
Iowa City
Waterloo
Cedar Falls
Des Moines
Ames
Fort Dodge
Mason City
Burlington
Fort Madison
Keokuk
Galesburg
Kewanee
Ottawa
Kankakee
Lafayette

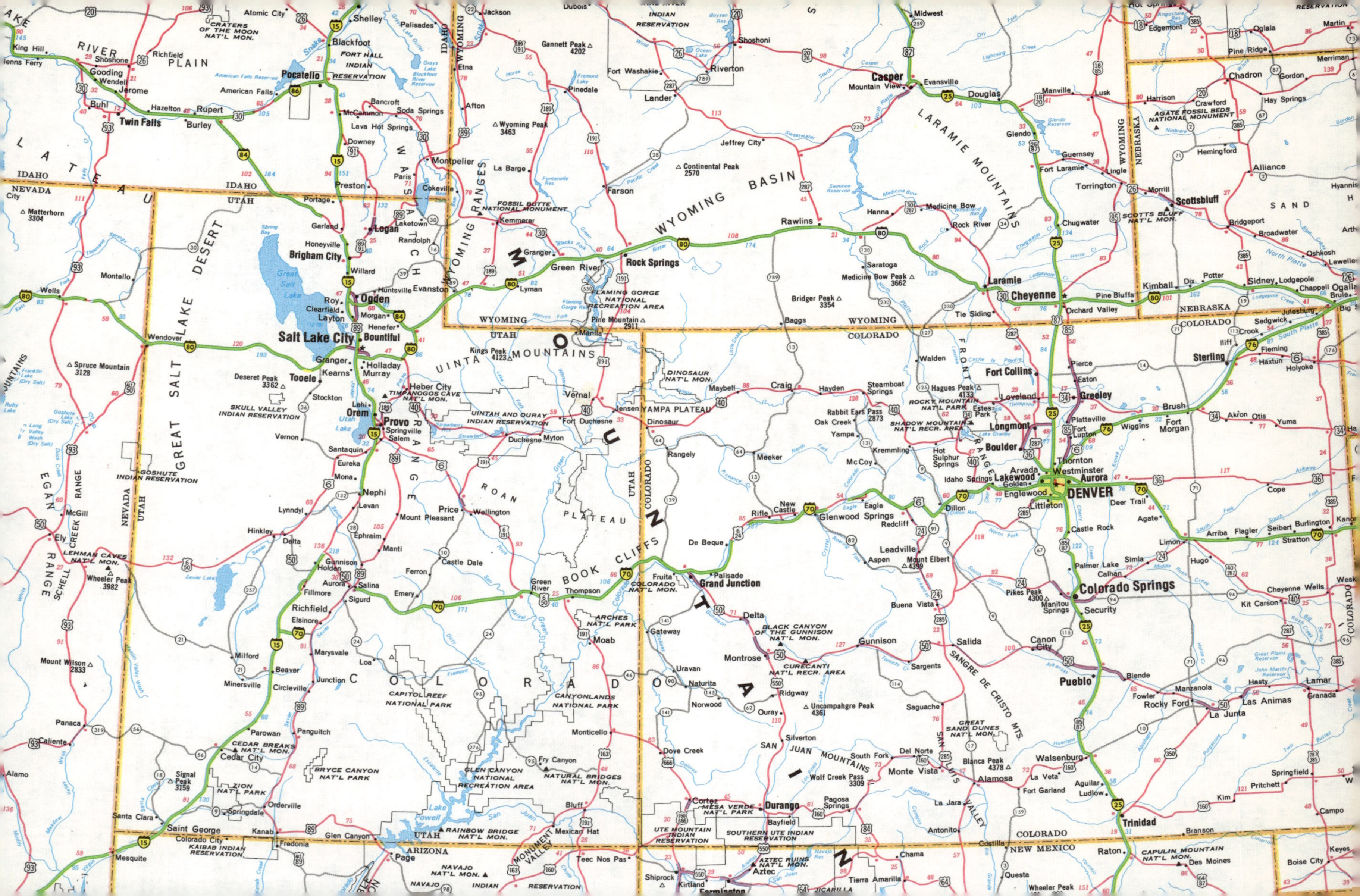

WYOMING
COLORADO
UTAH
NEBRASKA
IDAHO
NEVADA
ARIZONA
NEW MEXICO
DENVER
Salt Lake City
Colorado Springs
Pueblo
Cheyenne
Casper
Grand Junction
Provo
Ogden
Laramie
Rock Springs
Twin Falls
Pocatello
Boulder
Fort Collins
Greeley
Durango
Trinidad
Scottsbluff
GREAT SALT LAKE DESERT
WYOMING BASIN
LARAMIE MOUNTAINS
UINTA MOUNTAINS
SANGRE DE CRISTO MTS.
BOOK CLIFFS
ROAN PLATEAU
SAN JUAN MOUNTAINS

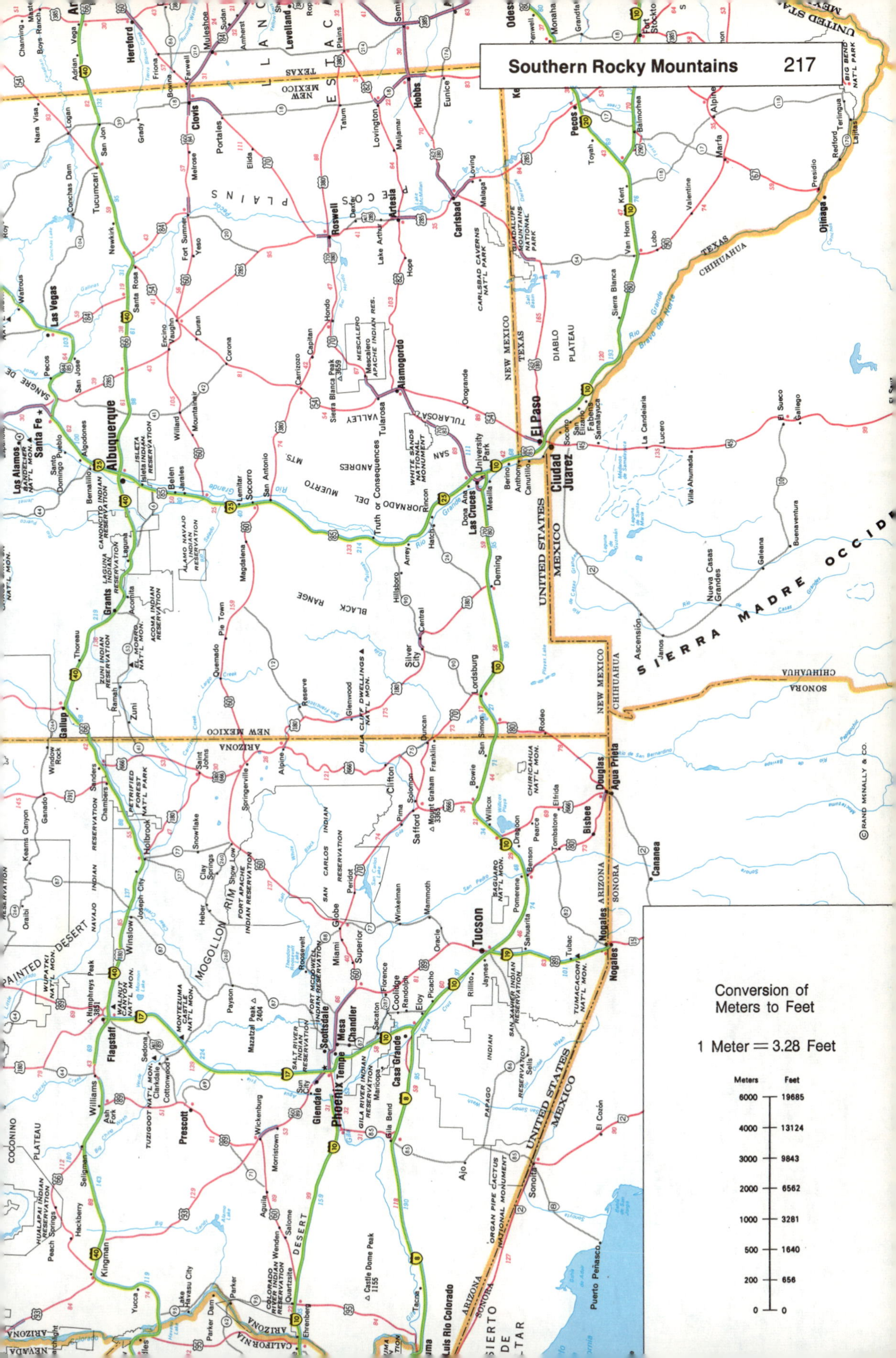
Conversion of Meters to Feet
1 Meter = 3.28 Feet
Meters Feet
6000 19685
4000 13124
3000 9843
2000 6562
1000 3281
500 1640
200 656
0 0
©RAND McNALLY & CO.
NEW MEXICO
TEXAS
ARIZONA
UNITED STATES
MEXICO
CHIHUAHUA
SONORA
SIERRA MADRE OCCIDENTAL
Albuquerque
Santa Fe
El Paso
Ciudad Juarez
Tucson
Phoenix
Flagstaff
Las Cruces
Roswell
Alamogordo
Carlsbad
Gallup
Nogales
Douglas
Agua Prieta
Kingman
Prescott
Clovis
Hobbs
Pecos
Las Vegas
Socorro
Deming
Lordsburg
Silver City
Grants
Tucumcari
Santa Rosa
Artesia
Bisbee
Cananea
Ojinaga
Presidio
Alpine
Marfa
Van Horn
Sierra Blanca
Yucca
Williams
Winslow
Holbrook
Globe
Safford
Casa Grande
Gila Bend
Ajo
Sonoita
Puerto Peñasco
Luis Rio Colorado
CARLSBAD CAVERNS NAT'L PARK
GUADALUPE MOUNTAINS NATIONAL PARK
WHITE SANDS NATIONAL MONUMENT
PETRIFIED FOREST NAT'L PARK
ORGAN PIPE CACTUS NATIONAL MONUMENT
SAGUARO NAT'L MON.
CHIRICAHUA NAT'L MON.
GILA CLIFF DWELLINGS NAT'L MON.
MOGOLLON RIM
DIABLO PLATEAU
COCONINO PLATEAU
PAINTED DESERT
BLACK RANGE
TULAROSA VALLEY
JORNADO DEL MUERTO
SAN ANDRES MTS.
BIG BEND NAT'L PARK

WASHINGTON
OREGON
IDAHO
CALIFORNIA
NEVADA
UTAH
WYOMING
Saint Helens
Minnehaha
Vancouver
PORTLAND
Milwaukie
Oregon City
Carson
Goldendale
Hood River
The Dalles
Wasco
Umatilla
Hermiston
Weston
Pendleton
Elgin
Enterprise
Garibaldi
Tillamook
Beaverton
Newberg
McMinnville
Woodburn
Mount Hood 3426
Tygh Valley
Maupin
Grass Valley
Heppner
UMATILLA INDIAN RESERVATION
Pilot Rock
Ukiah
DESCHUTES-UMATILLA PLATEAU
La Grande
North Powder
Rock Creek Butte 2775
Baker
BLUE MOUNTAINS
Lincoln City
Dallas
Salem
WARM SPRINGS INDIAN RESERVATION
Warm Springs
Mount Jefferson 3199
Madras
Spray
Long Creek
Newport
Toledo
Albany
Corvallis
Mill City
Detroit
Jefferson
Lebanon
Halsey
Waldport
Monroe
Sweet Home
Santiam Pass 1468
Sisters
Three Sisters 3074
Redmond
Prineville
OCHOCO MTS.
Mitchell
JOHN DAY FOSSIL BEDS NATIONAL MONUMENT
John Day
Prairie City
Strawberry Mountain 2755
Junction City
McKenzie Bridge
Eugene
Springfield
Florence
Creswell
Lowell
Cottage Grove
Bend
Seneca
Reedsport
Gardiner
Oakridge
OREGON DUNES NATIONAL RECREATION AREA
North Bend
Coos Bay
La Pine
Oakland
Crescent
Chemult
Bandon
Roseburg
Mount Thielsen 2799
Myrtle Creek
Langlois
Riddle
Canyonville
CRATER LAKE NAT'L PARK
Mount Scott 2721
Port Orford
Fort Klamath
Chiloquin
Paisley
Gold Beach
Grants Pass
Rogue River
Medford
Kerby
Ashland
OREGON CAVES NAT'L MON.
Klamath Falls
Bly
Brookings
O'Brien
Altamont
Merrill
Lakeview
Adel
Drake Peak 2562
New Pine Creek
Smith River
Crescent City
Tulelake
Mount Bidwell 2527
LAVA BEDS NAT'L MON.
Happy Camp
Yreka
Klamath
Orick
Weed
Mount Shasta 4317
Mount Shasta
Alturas
Canby
Cedarville
Orleans
HOOPA VALLEY INDIAN RESERVATION
Hoopa
Dunsmuir
Adin
Eagle Peak 3015
McKinleyville
Arcata
Eureka
Salyer
Bieber
Fall River Mills
Burney
Lewiston
Fortuna
Project City
Shasta
Redding
Anderson
Rio Dell
LASSEN VOLCANIC NAT'L PARK
Lassen Peak 3187
Susanville
Miranda
Chester
Westwood
Greenville
Garberville
Red Bluff
Gerber
Corning
Quincy
Leggett
Paradise
Portola
Laytonville
Orland
Chico
Oroville
Willows
Fort Bragg
Willits
Princeton
Mendocino
Redwood Valley
Maxwell
Ukiah
Talmage
Lucerne
Yuba City
Marysville
Tahoe City
Truckee
Grangeville
Riggins
Sacajawea Peak 2997
New Meadows
McCall
SALMON RIVER MOUNTAINS
Midvale
Huntington
Weiser
Payette
Ontario
Vale
Nyssa
Lowman
Idaho City
Caldwell
Marsing
Nampa
Boise
Mountain Home
SNAKE RIVER PLAIN
King Hill
Glenns Ferry
Bruneau
Jordan Valley
Burns
Crane
GREAT SANDY DESERT
HARNEY BASIN
COLUMBIA PLATEAU
DUCK VALLEY INDIAN RESERVATION
Owyhee
Mountain City
McDermitt
Granite Peak 2966
Duffer Peak 2864
Matterhorn 3304
BLACK ROCK DESERT
WARNER MOUNTAINS
Winnemucca
Golconda
Imlay
Battle Mountain
Beowawe
Carlin
Elko
Wells
Montello
Granite Peak 2760
Mount Tobin 2979
Ruby Dome 3471
RUBY MOUNTAINS
Spruce Mountain 3128
PYRAMID LAKE INDIAN RESERVATION
Lovelock
Nixon
Sparks
Reno
Fernley
Fallon
Carson City
Austin
Eureka
SHOSHONE MOUNTAINS
Mount Hamilton 3275
Ely
McGill
EGAN RANGE
LEHMAN CAVES NAT'L MON.
GOSHUTE INDIAN RESERVATION
Wendover
GREAT SALT LAKE DESERT
Salmon
Baker
Gibbonsville
BEAVERHEAD MOUNTAINS
LEMHI RANGE
Leadore
Diamond Peak 3718
Challis
Clayton
SAWTOOTH NATIONAL RECREATION AREA
Diamond Peak 3718
Borah Peak 3859
LOST RIVER RANGE
Sun Valley
Ketchum
Hailey
Moore
Arco
Butte City
Atomic City
CRATERS OF THE MOON NAT'L MON.
Richfield
Shoshone
Gooding
Wendell
Jerome
Buhl
Twin Falls
Hazelton
Rupert
Burley
American Falls
Pocatello
FORT HALL INDIAN RESERVATION
Blackfoot
Shelley
Idaho Falls
Ucon
Rigby
Rirle
Rexburg
Saint Anthony
Ashton
Dubois
Spencer
Lima
Dillon
Wisdom
Twin Bridges
Virginia City
Ennis
MADISON RANGE
Bozeman
Belgrade
Livingston
West Yellowstone
Mount Holmes 3150
Island Park
Grand Teton 4196
Victor
Palisades
Bancroft
Soda Springs
McCammon
Lava Hot Springs
Downey
Preston
Paris
Montpelier
Cokeville
Logan
Laketown
Randolph
Evanston
Garland
Honeyville
Brigham City
Willard
Huntsville
Ogden
Roy
Clearfield
Layton
Morgan
Henefer
Bountiful
Salt Lake City
Granger
Kearns
Holladay
Murray
Tooele
Stockton
Deseret Peak 3362
SKULL VALLEY INDIAN RESERVATION
Lehi
Orem
Provo
Springville
Salem
Heber City
TIMPANOGOS CAVE NAT'L MON.
Vernon
Santaquin
Eureka
Mona
Nephi
Levan
Lynndyl
Hinkley
Delta
Ephraim
Manti
Mount
Gunnison
Holden
Aurora
Salina
WASATCH RANGE
Portage
Great Salt Lake
Utah Lake

SAN FRANCISCO
Oakland
San Jose
Stockton
Modesto
Fresno
Bakersfield
Visalia
Salinas
Monterey
Santa Cruz
San Luis Obispo
Santa Barbara
Ventura
Oxnard
LOS ANGELES
Pasadena
Long Beach
Anaheim
Santa Ana
Riverside
San Bernardino
Palm Springs
SAN DIEGO
Tijuana
Mexicali
Calexico
El Centro
Yuma
Las Vegas
North Las Vegas
Henderson
Boulder City
Barstow
Needles
Kingman
Flagstaff
Prescott
Tempe
Saint George
Cedar City
YOSEMITE NATIONAL PARK
KINGS CANYON NATIONAL PARK
SEQUOIA NATIONAL PARK
DEATH VALLEY NATIONAL MONUMENT
JOSHUA TREE NAT'L MON.
GRAND CANYON
ZION NAT'L PARK
BRYCE CANYON NAT'L PARK
LAKE MEAD NATIONAL RECREATIONAL AREA
CHANNEL ISLANDS NATIONAL PARK
SIERRA NEVADA
SAN JOAQUIN VALLEY
COAST RANGES
MOJAVE DESERT
SONORA DESERT
BIG BASIN
DEATH VALLEY
IMPERIAL VALLEY
DESIERTO DE ALTAR
CALIFORNIA
NEVADA
ARIZONA
SONORA
BAJA CALIFORNIA NORTE
MEXICO
U.S.
CHANNEL ISLANDS
©RAND McNALLY & CO.

ALBERTA
SASKATCHEWAN
CANADA
UNITED STATES
MONTANA
WYOMING
IDAHO
Big Valley
Huxley
Craigmyle
Hanna
Munson
Drumheller
Youngstown
Chinook
Cereal
Oyen
Sibbald
Alsask
Flaxcombe
Kindersley
Brock
Dundurn
Young
Watrous
Dafoe
Kandahar
Craik
Holdfast
Southey
Chamberlain
Bethune
Silton
Craven
Tuxford
Pilot Butte
McLean
Regina
Moose Jaw
Caron
Mortlach
Herbert
Morse
Swift Current
Kyle
Cabri
Empress
Bindloss
Wardlow
Carseland
Bassano
Brooks
Tilley
Irricana
Stavely
Claresholm
Granum
Fort Macleod
Lethbridge
Coaldale
Taber
Burdett
Vauxhall
Redcliff
Medicine Hat
Irvine
Walsh
Maple Creek
Piapot
Gull Lake
Wilcox
Francis
Ardill
Yellow Grass
Weyburn
Ogema
Assiniboia
Lafleche
Meyronne
Ponteix
Aneroid
Cadillac
Admiral
Shaunavon
Eastend
Ravenscrag
Scout Lake
Lisieux
Minton
Val-Marie
Masefield
Morgan
Foremost
Magrath
Stirling
Warner
Cardston
Coutts
Sunburst
Kevin
Shelby
Cut Bank
Browning
East Glacier Park
Coram
Joplin
Chester
Rudyard
Gildford
Havre
North Havre
Chinook
Harlem
Dodson
Malta
Saco
Hinsdale
Glasgow
Nashua
Wolf Point
Poplar
Brockton
Culbertson
Bainville
Froid
Medicine Lake
Plentywood
Redstone
Flaxville
Scobey
Opheim
Westby
Loring
Big Sandy
Box Elder
Fort Belknap Indian Reservation
Rocky Boys Indian Reservation
Fort Peck Indian Reservation
Blackfeet Indian Reservation
Flathead Indian Reservation
Baldy Mountain 2108
Fort Peck
Fort Peck Lake
Frazer
Lambert
Sidney
Richey
Savage
Circle
Glendive
Wibaux
Jordan
Conrad
Brady
Dutton
Choteau
Fort Benton
Fairfield
Great Falls
Black Eagle
Ulm
Sandcoulee
Belt
Geyser
Stanford
Hobson
Lewistown
Grassrange
Winnett
Moore
Neihart
Big Baldy Mountain 2797
Judith Gap
Cascade
Wolf Creek
Red Mountain 2868
Lincoln
Arlee
Bonner
Drummond
Avon
Helena
East Helena
White Sulphur Springs
Martinsdale
Harlowton
Roundup
Klein
Melstone
Musselshell
Ingomar
Rosebud
Forsyth
Miles City
Kinsey
Terry
Fallon
Plevna
Baker
Deer Lodge
Philipsburg
Anaconda
Butte
Basin
Boulder
Crow Peak 2869
Townsend
Mount Edith 2897
Lavina
Ryegate
Wilsall
Clyde Park
Big Timber
Livingston
Bozeman
Belgrade
Manhattan
Three Forks
Whitehall
Bull Mountain 2624
Billings
Laurel
Columbus
Huntley
Ballantine
Worden
Custer
Hardin
Crow Agency
Custer Battlefield Nat'l Mon.
Crow Indian Reservation
Northern Cheyenne Indian Reservation
Busby
Ashland
Broadus
Biddle
Lodge Grass
Bighorn Canyon Nat'l Recr. Area
Park City
Joliet
Fromberg
Bridger
Roberts
Red Lodge
Granite Peak 3901
Wisdom
Twin Bridges
Virginia City
Ennis
Dillon
Sliderock Mountain 2384
Victor
Hamilton
Swan Peak 2821
Rocky Mountain 2863
Little Belt Mountains
Big Belt Mountains
Madison Range
Absaroka Range
Beaverhead Mountains
Lemhi Range
Lost River Range
Lewis Range
Bighorn Mountains
Big Horn Basin
Laramie Mountains
Gardiner
Yellowstone National Park
Mount Holmes 3150
West Yellowstone
Lima
Leadore
Salmon
Baker
Trout Peak 3732
Pahaska
Cody
Powell
Lovell
Cowley
Ranchester
Dayton
Sheridan
Clearmont
Buffalo
Greybull
Cloud Peak 4016
Manderson
Worland
Ten Sleep
Meeteetse
Carter Mountain 3724
Mount Sheridan 3142
Island Park
Spencer
Dubois
Ashton
Saint Anthony
Rexburg
Rigby
Ririe
Ucon
Idaho Falls
Shelley
Blackfoot
Fort Hall Indian Reservation
Pocatello
American Falls
Rupert
Burley
Hazelton
McCammon
Bancroft
Soda Springs
Lava Hot Springs
Downey
Preston
Montpelier
Paris
Cokeville
Diamond Peak 3718
Borah Peak 3859
Moore
Arco
Butte City
Atomic City
Craters of the Moon Nat'l Mon.
Richfield
Grand Teton Nat'l Park
Grand Teton 4196
Victor
Elk
Jackson
Palisades
Etna
Afton
Wyoming Peak 3463
La Barge
Pinedale
Gannett Peak 4202
Dubois
Hamilton Dome
Thermopolis
Wind River Indian Reservation
Shoshoni
Riverton
Fort Washakie
Lander
Jeffrey City
Continental Peak 2570
Farson
Casper
Mountain View
Evansville
Douglas
Glendo
Midwest
Kaycee
Pumpkin Buttes 1836
Gillette
Wyodak
Moorcroft
Rawlins
Hanna
Medicine Bow
Rock River
Fossil Butte National Monument
Missouri
Yellowstone
Idaho

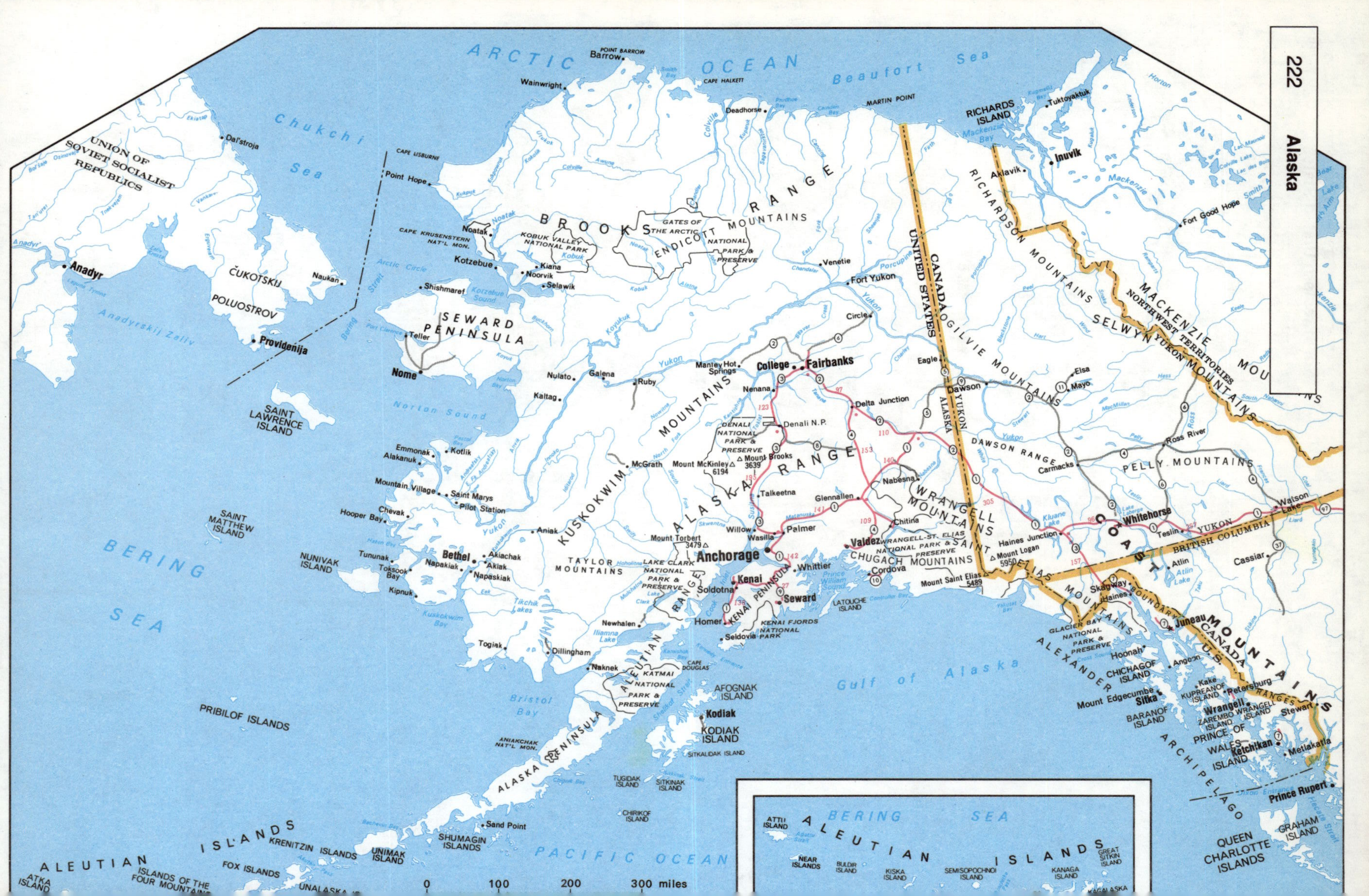

ARCTIC OCEAN
Beaufort Sea
Chukchi Sea
BERING SEA
Gulf of Alaska
PACIFIC OCEAN
Bristol Bay
Norton Sound
Kotzebue Sound
Anadyrskij Zaliv
Cook Inlet
CANADA
UNITED STATES
ALASKA
YUKON
BRITISH COLUMBIA
NORTHWEST TERRITORIES
UNION OF SOVIET SOCIALIST REPUBLICS
ČUKOTSKIJ POLUOSTROV
BROOKS RANGE
ENDICOTT MOUNTAINS
GATES OF THE ARCTIC NATIONAL PARK & PRESERVE
KOBUK VALLEY NATIONAL PARK
CAPE KRUSENSTERN NAT'L MON.
SEWARD PENINSULA
KUSKOKWIM MOUNTAINS
ALASKA RANGE
DENALI NATIONAL PARK & PRESERVE
WRANGELL MOUNTAINS
WRANGELL-ST. ELIAS NATIONAL PARK & PRESERVE
CHUGACH MOUNTAINS
SAINT ELIAS MOUNTAINS
COAST MOUNTAINS
KENAI PENINSULA
KENAI FJORDS NATIONAL PARK
LAKE CLARK NATIONAL PARK & PRESERVE
KATMAI NATIONAL PARK & PRESERVE
ANIAKCHAK NAT'L MON.
ALASKA PENINSULA
ALEUTIAN RANGE
TAYLOR MOUNTAINS
GLACIER BAY NATIONAL PARK & PRESERVE
ALEXANDER ARCHIPELAGO
RICHARDSON MOUNTAINS
MACKENZIE MOUNTAINS
SELWYN MOUNTAINS
OGILVIE MOUNTAINS
DAWSON RANGE
PELLY MOUNTAINS
ALEUTIAN ISLANDS
FOX ISLANDS
ISLANDS OF THE FOUR MOUNTAINS
KRENITZIN ISLANDS
PRIBILOF ISLANDS
SAINT LAWRENCE ISLAND
SAINT MATTHEW ISLAND
NUNIVAK ISLAND
KODIAK ISLAND
AFOGNAK ISLAND
SITKALIDAK ISLAND
UNIMAK ISLAND
SHUMAGIN ISLANDS
CHICHAGOF ISLAND
BARANOF ISLAND
PRINCE OF WALES ISLAND
QUEEN CHARLOTTE ISLANDS
GRAHAM ISLAND
RICHARDS ISLAND
ATKA ISLAND
ATTU ISLAND
NEAR ISLANDS
KISKA ISLAND
KANAGA ISLAND
Anchorage
Fairbanks
College
Juneau
Nome
Kotzebue
Barrow
Wainwright
Point Hope
Deadhorse
Bethel
Dillingham
Kodiak
Kenai
Seward
Valdez
Cordova
Sitka
Ketchikan
Wrangell
Petersburg
Skagway
Haines
Haines Junction
Whitehorse
Dawson
Inuvik
Aklavik
Tuktoyaktuk
Fort Good Hope
Eagle
Circle
Fort Yukon
Venetie
Delta Junction
Nenana
Talkeetna
Palmer
Wasilla
Willow
Whittier
Glennallen
Chitina
Nabesna
Homer
Soldotna
Seldovia
McGrath
Galena
Ruby
Nulato
Kaltag
Aniak
Naknek
Togiak
Teller
Shishmaref
Noatak
Kiana
Noorvik
Selawik
Providenija
Anadyr
Naukan
Dal'stroja
Mount McKinley 6194
Mount Brooks 3639
Mount Torbert 3479
Mount Logan 5950
Mount Saint Elias 5489
Prince Rupert
0 100 200 300 miles

United States Mileage Chart

83-7501 ©Rand McNally & Co.	Atlanta, Ga.	Boston, Mass.	Cheyenne, Wyo.	Chicago, Ill.	Cincinnati, Ohio	Cleveland, Ohio	Dallas, Texas	Denver, Colo.	Des Moines, Iowa	Detroit, Mich.	Houston, Texas	Indianapolis, Ind.	Kansas City, Mo.	Los Angeles, Calif.	Louisville, Ky.	Memphis, Tenn.	Milwaukee, Wis.	Minneapolis, Minn.	New Orleans, La.	New York, N.Y.	Omaha, Nebr.	Philadelphia, Pa.	Pittsburgh, Pa.	Portland, Oreg.	St. Louis, Mo.	Salt Lake City, Utah	San Francisco, Calif.	Seattle, Wash.	Toledo, Ohio	Tulsa, Okla.	Washington, D.C.	Wichita, Kans.
Albuquerque, N. Mex.	1381	2172	517	1281	1372	1560	638	417	977	1525	834	1266	782	807	1301	1010	1319	1190	1134	1979	858	1899	1619	1371	1038	604	1115	1440	1469	645	1824	593
Amarillo, Texas	1097	1897	511	1043	1096	1285	358	423	742	1269	596	991	547	1091	1019	726	1084	975	850	1704	643	1624	1344	1655	756	888	1399	1724	1210	361	1549	350
Atlanta, Ga.		1037	1442	674	440	672	795	1398	870	699	789	493	798	2182	382	371	761	1068	479	841	986	741	687	2601	541	1878	2496	2618	640	772	608	903
Austin, Texas	919	1911	994	1110	1083	1327	193	906	877	1315	164	1037	682	1374	982	615	1184	1129	517	1715	837	1615	1367	2069	823	1302	1748	2138	1256	450	1482	548
Baltimore, Md.	645	392	1608	668	497	343	1356	1621	981	503	1412	563	1048	2636	598	904	755	1073	1115	196	1113	96	218	2751	798	2044	2796	2681	444	1194	37	1244
Birmingham, Ala.	150	1165	1347	642	465	709	645	1286	787	724	639	475	697	2032	364	246	728	1006	342	969	898	869	741	2505	465	1781	2366	2535	665	647	736	778
Bismarck, N. Dak.	1495	1794	572	831	1118	1166	1141	671	670	1097	1384	1012	777	1617	1123	1228	758	427	1583	1633	581	1569	1283	1265	979	916	1604	1195	1063	958	1502	776
Boise, Idaho	2174	2639	732	1683	1906	2011	1582	811	1359	1942	1778	1800	1382	849	1893	1832	1692	1405	2078	2478	1227	2410	2122	432	1633	340	658	501	1908	1486	2343	1312
Boston, Mass.	1037		1907	963	840	628	1748	1949	1280	695	1804	906	1391	2979	941	1296	1050	1368	1507	206	1412	296	561	3046	1141	2343	3095	2976	739	1537	429	1587
Buffalo, N. Y.	859	446	1466	522	431	187	1346	1508	839	253	1460	481	966	2554	532	899	609	927	1217	372	971	353	216	2605	716	1902	2654	2535	298	1112	356	1162
Charleston, S. Car.	289	929	1722	877	603	730	1072	1678	1150	842	1054	696	1078	2459	591	660	964	1282	720	733	1266	633	666	2881	821	2158	2785	2890	783	1061	500	1192
Cheyenne, Wyo.	1442	1907		954	1174	1279	869	100	627	1211	1107	1068	650	1137	1161	1101	987	788	1361	1746	495	1678	1390	1159	901	436	1188	1228	1176	765	1611	583
Chicago, Ill.	674	963	954		287	335	917	996	327	266	1067	181	499	2054	292	530	87	405	912	802	459	738	452	2083	289	1390	2142	2013	232	683	671	696
Cincinnati, Ohio	440	840	1174	287		244	920	1164	571	259	1029	106	591	2179	101	468	374	692	786	647	693	567	287	2333	340	1610	2362	2300	200	736	481	787
Cleveland, Ohio	672	628	1279	335	244		1159	1321	652	170	1273	294	779	2367	345	712	422	740	1030	473	784	413	129	2418	529	1715	2467	2348	111	925	346	975
Columbus, Ohio	533	735	1235	308	108	139	1028	1229	618	192	1137	171	656	2244	209	576	395	713	894	542	750	462	182	2391	406	1671	2423	2321	133	802	387	852
Dallas, Texas	795	1748	869	917	920	1159		781	684	1143	243	865	489	1387	819	452	991	936	496	1552	644	1452	1204	2009	630	1242	1753	2078	1084	257	1319	365
Denver, Colo.	1398	1949	100	996	1164	1321	781		669	1253	1019	1058	600	1059	1120	1040	1029	841	1273	1771	537	1691	1411	1238	857	504	1235	1307	1218	681	1616	509
Des Moines, Iowa	870	1280	627	327	571	652	684	669		584	905	465	195	1727	566	599	361	252	978	1119	132	1051	763	1786	333	1063	1815	1749	255	443	984	392
Detroit, Mich.	699	695	1211	266	259	170	1143	1253	584		1265	278	743	2311	360	713	353	671	1045	637	716	573	287	2349	513	1647	2399	2279	59	909	506	940
Duluth, Minn.	1139	1428	918	465	752	800	1086	994	402	707	1307	646	597	2016	757	943	392	153	1331	1267	510	1203	917	1705	662	1315	2044	1635	697	845	1136	794
El Paso, Texas	1415	2316	754	1430	1515	1704	620	654	1126	1674	748	1410	931	790	1438	1072	1468	1339	1098	2123	1007	2043	1763	1635	1175	868	1164	1704	1618	780	1939	742
Flagstaff, Ariz.	1704	2495	757	1604	1695	1883	961	657	1300	1848	1157	1589	1105	484	1624	1333	1642	1481	1457	2302	1171	2222	1942	1241	1361	511	792	1347	1792	968	2147	916
Fort Wayne, Ind.	593	825	1093	156	153	197	983	1135	466	160	1105	118	586	2175	216	553	243	561	901	662	598	585	297	2239	353	1529	2281	2169	101	749	518	783
Fort Worth, Texas	826	1779	845	941	951	1183	31	757	708	1167	262	889	513	1356	850	483	1015	960	527	1583	655	1483	1235	1978	654	1211	1722	2047	1108	279	1350	359
Harrisburg, Pa.	700	373	1579	639	468	314	1383	1592	952	474	1439	534	1019	2607	569	931	726	1044	1142	180	1084	102	189	2722	769	2015	2767	2652	415	1165	107	1215
Helena, Mont.	2030	2388	685	1425	1712	1760	1554	781	1161	1691	1792	1606	1251	1190	1717	1702	1352	1020	2033	2227	1050	2163	1877	658	1493	477	1098	588	1657	1416	2096	1234
Houston, Texas	789	1804	1107	1067	1029	1273	243	1019	905	1265		987	710	1538	928	561	1142	1157	356	1608	865	1508	1313	2205	779	1438	1912	2274	1206	478	1375	608
Indianapolis, Ind.	493	906	1068	181	106	294	865	1058	465	278	987		485	2073	111	435	268	586	796	713	587	633	353	2227	235	1504	2256	2194	219	631	558	681
Jackson, Miss.	391	1406	1257	742	655	899	404	1169	809	914	406	646	644	1791	554	212	824	1036	178	1210	845	1110	939	2401	495	1646	2157	2470	855	527	977	708
Jacksonville, Fla.	306	1155	1748	980	746	915	990	1704	1176	1003	889	799	1104	2377	688	674	1067	1374	555	959	1292	859	851	2907	847	2184	2743	2924	944	1075	726	1206
Kansas City, Mo.	798	1391	650	499	591	779	489	600	195	743	710	485		1589	520	451	537	447	806	1198	201	1118	838	1809	257	1086	1835	1839	687	248	1043	197
Knoxville, Tenn.	193	911	1372	527	253	485	837	1328	800	512	893	346	728	2202	241	385	614	932	596	715	916	615	511	2531	471	1808	2510	2540	453	786	482	871
Las Vegas, Nev.	1964	2725	855	1772	1941	2097	1221	777	1445	2029	1417	1835	1365	282	1884	1593	1805	1607	1717	2548	1313	2468	2188	981	1621	433	564	1152	1994	1228	2393	1176
Lexington, Ky.	362	896	1233	352	78	317	861	1192	636	337	970	171	592	2180	72	409	439	757	727	703	758	623	343	2392	335	1669	2421	2365	278	731	514	782
Little Rock, Ark.	509	1434	1035	640	606	850	314	947	561	838	427	560	389	1687	505	138	715	813	418	1238	590	1138	890	2179	352	1438	1995	2228	779	271	1005	453
Los Angeles, Calif.	2182	2979	1137	2054	2179	2367	1387	1059	1727	2311	1538	2073	1589		2108	1817	2087	1889	1883	2786	1595	2706	2426	959	1845	715	379	1131	2276	1452	2631	1400
Louisville, Ky.	382	941	1161	292	101	345	819	1120	566	360	928	111	520	2108		367	379	697	685	748	687	668	388	2320	263	1597	2349	2305	301	659	582	710
Mackinaw City, Mich.	935	°916	1291	387	495	439	1281	1341	673	284	1427	460	864	2392	562	880	368	508	1247	906	805	842	556	2128	651	1691	2443	2058	328	1047	775	1061
Madison, Wis.	812	1103	912	140	427	475	968	954	286	406	1137	321	483	2012	432	622	77	272	1006	942	418	878	592	1950	358	1348	2100	1880	372	727	811	676
Memphis, Tenn.	371	1296	1101	530	468	712	452	1040	599	713	561	435	451	1817	367		612	826	390	1100	652	1000	752	2259	285	1535	2125	2290	654	401	867	532
Miami, Fla.	655	1504	2097	1329	1095	1264	1300	2037	1525	1352	1190	1148	1448	2687	1037	997	1416	1723	856	1308	1641	1208	1200	3256	1196	2532	3053	3273	1293	1398	1075	1529
Milwaukee, Wis.	761	1050	987	87	374	422	991	1029	361	353	1142	268	537	2087	379	612		332	994	889	493	825	539	2010	363	1423	2175	1940	319	757	758	734
Minneapolis, Minn.	1068	1368	788	405	692	740	936	841	252	671	1157	586	447	1889	697	826	332		1214	1207	357	1143	857	1678	552	1186	1940	1608	637	695	1076	644
Mobile, Ala.	335	1372	1443	851	706	950	590	1355	954	965	478	716	812	1977	605	363	933	1173	144	1176	1013	1076	982	2587	632	1832	2343	2651	906	713	943	893
Montreal, Que.	1181	318	1773	828	805	561	1705	1815	1146	562	1827	840	1305	2873	906	1273	915	1163	1591	378	1278	449	583	2755	1075	2209	2961	2685	621	1471	579	1502
Nashville, Tenn.	242	1088	1200	446	269	513	660	1156	628	528	769	279	556	2025	168	208	532	826	517	892	744	792	553	2359	299	1636	2333	2376	469	609	659	699
New Orleans, La.	479	1507	1361	912	786	1030	496	1273	978	1045	356	796	806	1883	685	390	994	1214		1311	1007	1211	1070	2505	673	1738	2249	2574	986	647	1078	816
New York, N. Y.	841	206	1746	802	647	473	1552	1771	1119	637	1608	713	1198	2786	748	1100	889	1207	1311		1251	100	368	2885	948	2182	2934	2815	578	1344	233	1394
Norfolk, Va.	540	558	1764	831	604	508	1329	1758	1141	666	1328	700	1162	2694	642	877	918	1236	1019	362	1273	263	384	2914	905	2200	2952	2844	607	1278	188	1352
Oklahoma City, Okla.	839	1641	697	787	840	1029	206	609	544	1013	449	735	349	1349	763	468	861	796	668	1448	455	1368	1088	1841	500	1100	1657	1910	954	105	1293	159
Omaha, Nebr.	986	1412	495	459	693	784	644	537	132	716	865	587	201	1595	687	652	493	357	1007	1251		1183	895	1654	449	931	1683	1638	681	387	1116	298
Orlando, Fla.	435	1294	1876	1109	875	1054	1078	1815	1305	1134	968	928	1226	2465	817	775	1196	1503	634	1098	1421	998	990	3034	976	2310	2831	3053	1075	1176	865	1307
Philadelphia, Pa.	741	296	1678	738	567	413	1452	1691	1051	573	1508	633	1118	2706	668	1000	825	1143	1211	100	1183		288	2821	868	2114	2866	2751	514	1264	133	1314
Phoenix, Ariz.	1793	2604	892	1713	1804	1992	998	792	1409	1957	1149	1698	1214	389	1733	1442	1751	1616	1494	2411	1290	2331	2051	1266	1470	648	763	1437	1901	1077	2256	1025
Pierre, S. Dak.	1361	1726	434	763	1050	1098	943	518	492	1029	1186	944	592	1524	1055	1043	690	394	1394	1565	391	1501	1215	1353	824	823	1575	1283	995	760	1434	578
Pittsburgh, Pa.	687	561	1390	452	287	129	1204	1411	763	287	1313	353	838	2426	388	752	539	857	1070	368	895	288		2535	588	1826	2578	2465	228	984	221	1034
Portland, Me.	1139	106	1986	1042	942	707	1850	2028	1359	775	1906	1001	1486	3074	1043	1398	1129	1447	1609	308	1491	398	663	3125	1236	2422	3174	3055	818	1632	531	1682
Portland, Ore.	2601	3046	1159	2083	2333	2418	2009	1238	1786	2349	2205	2227	1809	959	2320	2259	2010	1678	2505	2885	1654	2821	2535		2060	767	636	172	2315	1913	2754	1739
Raleigh, N. Car.	372	685	1695	784	534	561	1166	1661	1092	683	1160	631	1061	2545	541	728	871	1189	851	489	1214	389	445	2854	804	2131	2853	2797	624	635	256	1215
Rapid City, S. Dak.	1487	1859	295	896	1177	1231	1050	394	618	1162	1288	1071	708	1363	1182	1159	840	565	1507	1698	507	1634	1348	1204	950	662	1414	1134	1128	873	1567	691
Reno, Nev.	2374	2866	959	1913	2133	2238	1668	1011	1586	2170	1864	2027	1609	469	2120	2003	1946	1711	2164	2705	1454	2637	2349	538	1860	523	229	710	2135	1640	2570	1471
Richmond, Va.	510	535	1674	748	514	425	1266	1668	1058	583	1298	610	1072	2631	552	814	835	1153	989	339	1190	239	301	2831	815	2110	2862	2761	524	1211	106	1262
St. Louis, Mo.	541	1141	901	289	340	529	630	857	333	513	779	235	257	1845	263	285	363	552	673	948	449	868	588	2060		1337	2089	2081	454	396	793	447
Salt Lake City, Utah	1878	2343	436	1390	1610	1715	1242	504	1063	1647	1438	1504	1086	715	1597	1535	1423	1186	1738	2182	931	2114	1826	767	1337		752	836	1612	1172	2047	1003
San Antonio, Texas	983	1988	1027	1187	1160	1404	270	939	954	1392	197	1114	759	1363	1059	692	1261	1206	550	1792	914	1692	1444	2086	900	1319	1737	2155	1333	527	1559	625
San Diego, Calif.	2126	2955	1186	2064	2155	2343	1331	1108	1760	2308	1482	2049	1565	125	2084	1783	2102	1938	1827	2762	1641	2682	2402	1084	1821	764	504	1256	2252	1428	2607	1376
San Francisco, Calif.	2496	3095	1188	2142	2362	2467	1753	1235	1815	2399	1912	2256	1835	379	2349	2125	2175	1940	2249	2934	1683	2866	2578	636	2089	752		808	2364	1760	2799	1695
Seattle, Wash.	2618	2976	1228	2013	2300	2348	2078	1307	1749	2279	2274	2194	1839	1131	2305	2290	1940	1608	2574	2815	1638	2751	2465	172	2081	836	808		2245	1982	2684	1808
Spokane, Wash.	2340	2698	995	1735	2022	2070	1864	1089	1471	2001	2102	1916	1561	1205	2027	2012	1662	1330	2343	2537	1360	2473	2187	348	1803	712	882	278	1967	1726	2406	1544
Springfield, Ill.	592	1099	888	189	299	473	728	865	291	433	879	193	310	1899	275	370	263	480	758	906	412	826	546	2047	100	1324	2076	2039	377	494	751	507
Springfield, Mo.	652	1353	820	499	552	741	419	759	342	725	629	447	170	1636	475	281	573	594	636	1160	371	1080	800	1978	212	1254	1944	2009	666	185	1005	251
Toledo, Ohio	640	739	1176	232	200	111	1084	1218	255	59	1206	219	687	2276	301	654	319	637	986	578	681	514	228	2315	454	1612	2364	2245		850	447	884
Topeka, Kans.	863	1456	595	562	656	844	480	535	549	806	701	550	65	1531	585	508	598	508	863	1263	165	1183	903	1751	322	1028	1770	1802	750	223	1108	139
Tulsa, Okla.	772	1537	765	683	736	925	257	681	443	909	478	631	248	1452	659	401	757	695	647	1344	387	1264	984	1913	396	1172	1760	1982	850		1189	182
Washington, D. C.	608	429	1611	671	481	346	1319	1616	984	506	1375	558	1043	2631	582	867	758	1076	1078	233	1116	133	221	2754	793	2047	2799	2684	447	1189		1239
Wichita, Kans.	903	1587	583	696	787	975	365	509	392	940	608	681	197	1400	710	532	734	644	816	1394	298	1314	1034	1739	447	1003	1695	1808	884	182	1239	

Tables, Charts, and Facts

Gazetteer of the World

Note: In this Gazetteer, population figures for countries are recent estimates based on UN statistics except where otherwise stated. Populations of cities and towns are also the latest estimates or census figures. Adult literacy rates are generally for 1975, average life expectancies for 1978 and per capita GNPs (in US$) for 1979.

AFGHANISTAN, a landlocked republic in south-eastern Asia. The land is mostly mountainous: major ranges include the Hindu Kush and the Pamirs. The north is arid. Rainfall generally averages 300 mm (12 in). Temperatures vary from 49°C (120°F) in the south in summer to −26°C (−15°F) in winter in the mountains. Some 79 per cent of the workforce are farmers, mainly in the subsistence sector. Only 10 per cent of the land is cultivable, mostly in irrigated valleys. Many people are nomads: sheep are the most numerous animals. Natural gas is exported, but mining and manufacturing are small-scale. Afghanistan, once part of the Persian Empire, was conquered by Alexander the Great in 331 BC. Islam was introduced in the 8th century. Modern Afghanistan was founded in 1747 by an Afghan chief, Ahmad Shah. His dynasty continued until 1973 when a republic was declared. In 1979 Soviet troops invaded Afghanistan and a long war began against Muslim rebel forces opposed to the pro-Soviet government.

Area: 647,497 km^2 (250,014 sq mi); **Population:** 16,024,000; **Capital:** Kabul (pop 749,000); **Other cities:** Kandahar (209,000), Herat (157,000); **Highest point:** 7620 m (25,000 ft) in the Hindu Kush; **Official languages:** Pushtu, Dari (Persian); **Religion:** Islam; **Adult literacy rate:** 12 per cent; **Average life expectancy at birth:** 42 years; **Unit of currency:** Afghani; **Main exports:** cotton, natural gas, fruit, karakul skins; **Per capital GNP:** US$170.

ALBANIA, the smallest European communist nation, borders the Adriatic Sea. The climate on the dry coast is Mediterranean in type. The land is mostly mountainous. Farmland covers 17 per cent of Albania, with fertile basins in the wetter uplands where the rainfall averages 1800 mm (71 in). Maquis and oak and pine forest cover 44 per cent of the land and pasture another 25 per cent. Farming is collectivized and 62 per cent of the workforce is employed on farms. But mining and manufacturing are the leading industries. Ottoman Turks introduced Islam in the 15th century. Albania became independent in 1912 and a kingdom in 1928. After World War II a communist republic was set up In 1961 Albania broke with the USSR and became allied to China, which helped it to industrialize. Albania officially became an 'atheist state' in 1967. The special relationship with China ended in 1977, since when Albania has followed an independent course.

Area: 28,748 km^2 (11,100 sq mi); **Population:** 2,873,000; **Capital:** Tiranë (pop 198,000); **Other cities:** Shkodër (62,500), Durres (61,000); **Highest point:** Mt Korah, 2762 m (9063 ft); **Official language:** Albanian; **Religion:** formerly mainly Islam (all mosques and churches were closed in 1967); **Average life expectancy at birth:** 69 years; **Unit of currency:** Lek; **Main exports:** metal ores and metals (including chrome, copper, nickel), oil, bitumen, tobacco, fruit, vegetables; **Per capita GNP:** US$840.

ALGERIA, a large republic bordering the Mediterranean Sea in North Africa. The Sahara, which covers 85 per cent of the nation, yields oil and natural gas and oil accounts for 90 per cent of the exports. Between 1960 and 1980 the urban population increased from 30 per cent to 61 per cent. Of the workforce, agriculture now employs only 30 per cent, industry 25 per cent and services 45 per cent. Most people live in the northern Atlas mountain region and the fertile coastal plains. Barley, fruit, grapes, olives, vegetables and wheat are grown. Livestock are raised in the uplands. Islam and the Arabic language were introduced in the 7th century, but Berber languages survived in some areas. France ruled Algeria from 1848, but the Arab FLN (National Liberation Front) spear-headed a guerrilla war from 1954. In 1962 Algeria became independent: most of the 1 million French settlers left. Algeria became a one-party state, ruled by the FLN. An army junta took power in 1965, but the 1976 Constitution restored elections.

Area: 2,381,741 km^2 (919,646 sq mi); **Population:** 20,042,000; **Capital:** Algiers (pop 1,503,700); **Other cities:** Oran (485,000), Constantine (350,000), Annaba (313,000); **Highest point:** Mt Tahat, 2918 m (9573 ft); **Official language:** Arabic; **Religion:** Islam; **Adult literacy rate:** 37 per cent; **Average life expectancy at birth:** 56 years; **Unit of currency:** Dinar; **Main exports:** oil and oil products, natural gas, wine, fruit, vegetables; **Per capita GNP:** US$1580.

ANDORRA, a tiny, mountainous co-principality in the Pyrenees between France and Spain, Sovereignty is technically exercised by the 'co-princes', the Spanish Bishop of Urgel and the French President, but an elected, 28-member General Council effectively rules the state. Tourism is the main industry: over 6 million people visited Andorra in 1978. Tobacco is the chief cash crop.

Area: 453 km^2 (175 sq mi); **Population:** 32,700 (1980); **Capital:** Andorra la Vella (pop 12,000); **Official language:** Catalan; **Units of currency:** French franc, Spanish peseta.

ANGOLA, a republic in west-central Africa, including the small enclave of Cabinda. Behind the narrow coastal plain are plateaux. The altitude affects the climate which is generally warmest and wettest in the north. Savanna covers much of the country, with forests in the south and north-east. Most people speak Bantu languages. The main groups are the Ovimbundu, the Mbundu and the Kongo. Tribalism has divided the nationalist movement in Angola. About 60 per cent of the people are farmers, mostly at subsistence level. The main food crops are cassava and maize. Mining is becoming increasingly important. The Portuguese explored Angola's coasts in the 1480s and later engaged in the slave trade there. In 1961 nationalists began a war against the Portuguese. Angola achieved independence in 1975. In the power struggle at the time of independence, the socialist MPLA, supported by the Mbundu and by *mestiços*, emerged triumphant. But the southern Ovimbundu UNITA continued to resist into the 1980s, with assistance from South Africa.

Area: 1,246,700 km^2 (481,380 sq mi); **Population:** 7,414,000; **Capital:** Luanda (pop 481,000); **Other towns:** Huambo (62,000), Lobito (59,000); **Highest point:** Mt Moco, 2620 m (8596 ft); **Official language:** Portuguese; **Religion:** traditional religions, Christianity; **Adult literacy rate:** 20 per cent; **Average life expectancy at birth:** 41 years; **Unit of currency:** Kwanza; **Main exports:** oil, coffee, diamonds, iron ore, cotton, fish meal, sisal; **Per capita GNP:** US$440.

ANGUILLA, a low-lying coral island, about 110 km (68 mi) north-west of St Kitts, in the Leeward Islands. Its main products are lobsters and salt, but light industry and tourism have been developing recently. Anguilla has superb beaches and temperatures range between 24°C and 29°C (75°–84°F) all the year round. Anguilla became part of St Kitts-Nevis-Anguilla, a British Associated State, in 1967. But the Anguillans objected to rule from St Kitts and Britain appointed a Commissioner to handle the island's affairs. In 1976 Anguilla was granted a separate Constitution and formal separation from St Kitts-Nevis was achieved in 1980.

Area: 90 km^2 (35 sq mi); **Population:** 6500 (1977); **Status:** British colony.

ANTIGUA, including the smaller and also low-lying islands of Barbuda and the uninhabited Redonda in the Leeward Islands, became an independent nation in the Commonwealth in 1981. The British monarch is its Head of State. Antigua exports cotton and rum, but tourism is the most important industry in this dry, sunny country. Discovered by Christopher Columbus in 1493, Antigua was named after a church in Seville, Spain. British settlers colonized the islands in 1632 and they were declared a British possession in 1667. Antigua became a British Associated State in 1967. Most Antiguans are descendants of African slaves, but some are of European or Middle Eastern origin.

Area: 442 km^2 (171 sq mi); **Population:** 77,000; **Capital:** St John's (23,500).

ARGENTINA, South America's second largest nation after Brazil, extends north-south through more than 32° of latitude. As a result the climate varies considerably. There are four main regions. The tropical, largely forested north is comparatively little developed. The west is arid, except around 'oases' where such towns as Mendoza and Tucumán have grown up, rising in the far west to the Andes Mountains. Here, on the border with Chile is Mt Aconcagua, the highest mountain in the western hemisphere. Southern Argentina, called Patagonia, consists of sparsely populated, wind-swept and semi-arid plateaux. In the far south is half of the barren and cold archipelago, Tierra del Fuego, whose southern tip is only about 960 km (600 mi) from Antarctica. The fourth and most densely populated region is the central *pampas* (or plains) which cover nearly 25 per cent of the country. The soils of the pampas are fertile and the climate is mild, with an average annual temperature range of 9°–23°C (48°–73°F) and an average annual rainfall of 510–760 mm (20–30 in). The *pampas* lie to the north-west and south of Buenos Aires, the elegant capital city. About 90 per cent of the population is of European descent, another 8 per cent being *mestizos* of mixed white and Indian origin, and 2 per cent pure Indians. Argentina is one of the world's leading food producers. Dairy products, hides, maize, meat, oats, vegetable oils, wheat and wool are major products. About 11 per cent of the country is cultivated and pastureland

Argentinian cowboys who work on the pampas (grasslands) are called gauchos. Pasture covers more than two-fifths of Argentina and supports vast herds of cattle and sheep.

covers another 41 per cent. In 1979 Argentina had 60 million cattle and 35 million sheep. In recent years, mining (for coal and oil) and manufacturing have become important. In the late 1970s, they accounted for 45 per cent of the GDP (manufacturing making up 37 per cent), while agriculture contributed only 13 per cent. The other 42 per cent came from service industries. The cities are growing quickly. The proportion of people in urban areas increased from 74 per cent in 1960 to 82 per cent in 1980. The Spanish explorer Juan de Solás was the first European to see the Rio de la Plata estuary, into which the Paraguay and Uruguay rivers flow, in 1516. The first permanent Spanish settlers arrived in 1535 and the city of Buenos Aires was founded one year later, although it was not permanently settled until 1580. Spanish rule continued until Buenos Aires declared itself independent in May 1810, followed by the provinces in 1816. Civil disorder ensued until a federal Constitution was adopted in 1853. In recent years Argentina has been disturbed by political and economic turmoil. Between 1946 and 1981, the Republic of Argentina had 14 presidents, seven of whom were deposed. Kidnappings, political murders, high unemployment and inflation (averaging 120 per cent per year between 1970 and 1978) have created instability, aggravating the problems.

Area: 2,766,889 km^2 (1,068,360 sq mi); **Population:** 27,796,000; **Capital:** Buenos Aires (pop with suburbs, 9,677,000); **Other cities:** Rosario (798,000), Córdoba (798,000), La Plata (408,000); **Highest point:** Mt Aconcagua, 6960 m (22,835 ft); **Official language:** Spanish; **Religion:** mainly Roman Catholicism, **Adult literacy rate:** 94 per cent; **Average life expectancy at birth:** 71 years; **Unit of currency:** Peso; **Main exports:** vegetable products, food, drink and tobacco, animals and animal products, textiles and leather, machinery and transport equipment; **Per capita GNP:** US$2280.

AUSTRALIA, the world's sixth largest country, has a low average population density of 2 people per sq km (5 per sq mi), because large tracts are desert or semi-desert. Some 89 per cent of the population is urban (1980), with more than 50 per cent of the people concentrated in the four largest cities. The western part of Australia is a vast plateau, averaging 300 m (984 ft) above sea level, although occasional mountain ranges rise above this level. The central plains extend from the Gulf of Carpentaria in the north to the Great Australian Bight in the south. These plains include the Great Artesian Basin, comprising western Queensland, the south-east of the Northern Territory, the north-east of South Australia and the northern part of New South Wales. Here artesian wells tap ground water that originally fell as rain on the Great Dividing Range in the east, and which has seeped through aquifers beneath the plains. The Lake Eyre basin in the south-west of the Great Artesian Basin, is usually dry and covered by salt. It is an internal drainage basin. The highest peak in the Great Dividing Range, an uplifted block of land, is Mt Kosciusko, in that part of the Range called the Australian Alps. The Range continues in the island state of Tasmania in the south-east, which is separated from the mainland by the shallow Bass Strait. In the north-east is the Great Barrier Reef, the world's longest reef, 2027 km (1260 mi) long. Australia's chief rivers are the Murray, 2575 km (1600 mi) long, and its tributaries, including the Darling, 2740 km (1703 mi) long, in the south-east. The climate varies according to the latitude. The north is tropical with summer monsoon rains. In the south, winters are cooler and rains are

Sydney is Australia's largest conurbation and chief seaport. This view shows the expressway leading to Harbour Bridge.

brought by the prevailing westerlies. However, about two-thirds of Australia is too dry for farming. The tropical region in the north contains tropical forest and savanna and tropical crops, such as sugar-cane, flourish in Queensland. Deserts cover most of Western Australia, the southern part of Northern Territory, much of South Australia and the eastern parts of New South Wales. The mid-latitude grasslands are west of the Great Dividing Range in south-central Queensland and central New South Wales. The coastlands of New South Wales and south-eastern Victoria form a warm temperate zone, where eucalypt forests grow. The south-western part of Western Australia and parts of South Australia and western Victoria have a Mediterranean climate, with much scrub woodland vegetation. The cool temperate climate of Tasmania supports forests of beech and eucalypts. Australia has a wide range of animals, including kangaroos, koalas, platypuses and wallabies. Birds include the flightless emu and cassowary and the lyre bird. The first people in Australia were probably the Tasmanian Aborigines who were driven into Tasmania by the Australian Aborigines who arrived from Asia about 16,000 years ago. The Tasmanian Aborigines became extinct in 1876 and contact with Europeans caused the Australian Aborigines to decline in numbers. Today there are about 100,000 Australian Aborigines, but many are of mixed ancestry. Most Australians are of British origin, although the proportion of citizens of British origin has decreased to about 80 per cent. This is because many recent settlers have come from other parts of Europe. In 1978 industry accounted for 32 per cent of the GDP (manufacturing alone made up 19 per cent), agriculture for 5 per cent and services for 63 per cent. Australia has vast mineral reserves and is a major world producer of bauxite, iron ore and lead. Other metal ores, coal and oil are also mined, together with thorium and uranium. The Eastern Highlands contain many minerals, but the most spectacular finds since 1950 have been in Western Australia. The main product of the country is wool; Australia had 136 million sheep in 1980. New South Wales is the chief wool state, followed by Western Australia. There are also 26 million cattle and beef and dairy products are of great importance. Queensland is the chief cattle state. Only about 2 per cent of the land is cultivated, but yields are high and crops are varied because of the wide climatic range. But despite its importance, only 6 per cent of the workforce is employed in agriculture. Manufacturing industries are mostly in the towns and cities. The main steel centres are Newcastle, Wollongong and Whyalla. Dutch navigators landed in northern and eastern Australia in the early 17th century and in 1642 the Dutch explorer Abel Tasman discovered Tasmania without ever sighting the mainland. But the Dutch were not attracted by the arid coasts and their hostile inhabitants, the Aborigines. In 1770, however, the British Captain James Cook explored the fertile eastern coast and, in 1788, a British convict settlement was established on the present site of Sydney. In 1793 the first free settlers arrived. Gold rushes in the 1850s and 1890s accelerated immigration. In 1901 the Australian states united to form the Commonwealth of Australia and Parliament was moved to Canberra in Australian Capital Territory in 1927. Since 1945 immigrants to Australia have included people from central Europe, Greece, Italy, the Netherlands, Poland, Turkey and Yugoslavia, as well as Britons. In recent years, Australia's ties with Britain have been weakened by Britain's membership of the EEC and also by a new orientation of Australian foreign policy towards south-eastern Asia and the United States. But Australia, now one of the world's most prosperous nations, remains a member of the Commonwealth and the British monarch, represented by a Governor-General, is Head of State.

Area: 7,686,849 km^2 (2,968,071 sq mi); **Population:** 15,066,000; **Capital:** Canberra (pop 241,000); **Other cities:** Sydney (3,193,000), Melbourne (2,740,000), Brisbane (1,015,000), Adelaide (933,000), Perth (884,000), Newcastle (380,000), Wollongong (224,000), Hobart (168,000), Gold Coast (143,000), Geelong (141,000); **Highest point:** Mt Kosciusko, 2228 m (7310 ft), in the Australian Alps; **Official language:** English; **Religion:** mainly Anglicanism and Roman Catholicism; **Adult literacy rate:** 100 per cent; **Average life expectancy at birth:** 73 years; **Unit of currency:** Dollar; **Main exports:** metals and metal ores; cereals, meat, coal and coke, textiles, sugar and honey, iron and steel, **Per capita GNP:** US$9100.

AUSTRIA, a federal republic in central Europe. The Alps cover about 75 per cent of the land and tourism is a major industry, especially winter sports. The Danube river valley in the north is the chief farming region. Livestock are also important: the uplands contain much summer pasture. Forests occupy about 40 per cent of the land. Industry

STATES AND TERRITORIES OF AUSTRALIA

State or territory	Area (sq km)	Area (sq mi)	Population (1979)	Capital
Australian Capital Territory	2,432	939	227,200	Canberra
New South Wales	801,428	309,450	5,111,600	Sydney
Northern Territory	1,347,519	520,308	117,700	Darwin
Queensland	1,727,522	667,036	2,213,900	Brisbane
South Australia	984,377	380,091	1,297,200	Adelaide
Tasmania	68,322	26,385	420,100	Hobart
Victoria	227,618	87,889	3,874,500	Melbourne
Western Australia	2,527,621	975,973	1,257,000	Perth

accounted for 42 per cent of the GDP in 1978 (agriculture supplied 5 per cent). Iron ore and lignite are mined, forming the basis of the iron and steel industry. Vienna is the main manufacturing and cultural centre; 54 per cent of the people lived in urban areas in 1980. Austria, part of the Holy Roman Empire, became a possession of the Hapsburg family in 1282. From 1438 this family supplied all but one of the Holy Roman Emperors. After the Empire ended (1806), the Hapsburg ruler became Emperor of Austria. From 1867 Austria became part of the dual monarchy of Austria-Hungary, which collapsed in 1918 ending Hapsburg power. In 1938 Germany annexed Austria. In 1945 Austria was partitioned between the Allies, but it became a neutral federal republic in 1955.

Area: 83,849 km^2 (32,376 sq mi); **Population:** 7,526,000; **Capital:** Vienna (pop 1,615,000); **Other cities:** Graz (248,000), Linz (203,000), Salzburg (129,000), Innsbruck (115,000); **Highest point:** Gross Glockner, 3797 m (12,457 ft); **Official language:** German; **Religion:** Roman Catholicism (88 per cent); **Adult literacy rate:** 99 per cent; **Average life expectancy at birth:** 72 years; **Unit of currency:** Schilling; **Main exports:** iron and steel, machinery, timber and wood products, chemicals, textiles and craft items; **Per capita GNP:** US$8620.

BAHAMAS, a group of 14 large and about 700 small islands with a mild climate, to the south-east of Florida. Tourism is the main industry and 1.8 million tourists, many from the USA, visited the islands in 1979. Christopher Columbus discovered the islands in 1492: the island of San Salvador was probably his first landing place. The Bahamas became a British colony in 1717. Full independence within the Commonwealth was achieved in 1973. About 85 per cent of the people are descendants of African Negroes (former slaves).

Area: 13,935 km^2 (5381 sq mi); **Population:** 257,000; **Capital:** Nassau (pop 130,000); **Official language:** English; **Unit of currency:** Bahamian dollar; **Per capita GNP:** US$2780.

BAHRAIN, a densely populated island nation in the Persian Gulf. The capital Manama is on the largest island, also called Bahrain. This hot, arid country is an important oil producer and revenue from oil sales has been used to provide free education, health and other services. The Arabs occupied Bahrain in the 7th century. British influence began in the early 19th century and, in 1861, it became a British protectorate. It became a fully independent sheikhdom in 1971.

Area: 622 km^2 (240 sq mi); **Population:** 467,000; **Capital:** Manama (pop 114,000); **Official language:** Arabic; **Unit of currency:** Dinar; **Per capita GNP:** US$5640.

BANGLADESH, a densely populated country in Asia, is one of the world's poorest. It has a tropical monsoon climate, with hot, dry winters and hot, wet summers. It is mostly flat, largely occupying the fertile deltas of the Ganges, Brahmaputra and other rivers. The rivers are the main transport arteries but they often flood causing disease and starvation. Coastal floods are also caused when cyclones in the Bay of Bengal drive the sea inland. About 71 per cent of the mainly Muslim Bengali population is engaged in agriculture, which accounts for 57 per cent of the GDP (13 per cent comes from industry). In 1980 only 11 per cent of the population was urban. Formerly part of British India, Bangladesh became the province of East Pakistan in 1947. A bitter, 9-month war between East and West Pakistan in 1971 ended with the secession of East Pakistan which became the People's Republic of Bangladesh.

Area: 143,998 km^2 (55,601 sq mi); **Population:** 94,472,000; **Capital:** Dacca (pop 2,000,000); **Other cities:** Khulna (437,000), Chittagong (417,000); **Highest point:** Mt Keokradong, 1230 m (4035 ft); **Official language:** Bengali; **Religion:** Islam (80 per cent), Hinduism (10 per cent), Buddhism, Christianity; **Adult literacy rate:** 26 per cent; **Average life expectancy at birth:** 47 years; **Unit of currency:** Taka; **Main exports:** jute, hides and skins, leather, tea; **Per capita GNP:** US$100.

BARBADOS, the most easterly island in the West Indies. It is mostly flat, with a mild climate: annual temperatures average 25°–28°C (77°–82°F). More than 90 per cent of the people are descendants of African slaves, the rest being white or of mixed origin. Sugar and sugar products (molasses and rum) are the main products but tourism is now the chief industry; there were 371,000 visitors in 1979. British colonization dates back to 1628. Full independence within the Commonwealth was achieved in 1966.

Area: 431 km^2 (166 sq mi); **Population:** 257,000; **Capital:** Bridgetown (pop with suburbs 88,000); **Official language:** English; **Unit of currency:** Dollar; **Per capita GNP:** US$2400.

BELGIUM, a densely populated, prosperous industrial nation in western Europe. Two-thirds of the land is flat, but the largely forested Ardennes rise in the south-east. The navigable Meuse and Scheldt rivers drain the fertile central plains. Antwerp, near the mouth of the Scheldt, is the main port. The 66-km (41-mi) coastline contains several resorts and fishing ports. The climate is mild and average temperatures in Brussels range between 3°C (37°F) and 17°C (63°F). The rainfall averages 720 mm (28 in) on the coast and 1200 mm (47 in) in the Ardennes. Three languages are spoken: Flemish (a Dutch dialect) in the north; French by the Walloons in the south; and German by a small group in the south-east. Conflict between Flemish- and French-speakers has led to rioting and complaints about discrimination. The population is highly urbanized: 72 per cent lived in urban areas in 1980. The lowlands are intensely cultivated. Most farms are small and only 3 per cent of the workforce is engaged solely in agriculture (which accounts for 2 per cent of the GDP): many farmers have jobs in industry, which employs 43 per cent of the workforce and contributes 37 per cent of the GDP. The main crops are cereals, notably wheat, flax, potatoes and sugar beet. There are 2.9 million cattle and 5 million pigs. Coal is mined in the north-eastern Campine (Kempen) region, which has become a major industrial area. The older industrial areas are in the south, in the Sambre-Meuse valley. This zone is based on coalfields which extend from Mons to Liège, but extraction of the coal has become expensive and the region has declined in consequence. Antwerp is a major industrial centre, some industries being based on imported oil, as is Brussels whose varied industries produce luxury goods and many other items. Textiles are important, particularly in Flanders; the main centre is Ghent. Belgium was divided into small counties in the Middle Ages. It came under the Austrian Hapsburgs in 1477 and the Spanish Hapsburgs in 1506. After a spell of independence (1598–1621), it came successively under Spain, Austria, France and the Netherlands. It declared its independence from the Netherlands in 1830. Germany occupied Belgium in both World Wars. After World War II, Belgium recovered quickly through economic co-operation with the Netherlands and Luxembourg in the Benelux customs union. It joined the European Coal and Steel Community in 1953 and was a founder-member of the EEC in 1957. Brussels is headquarters of the EEC Commission and Council of Ministers. The Kingdom of Belgium is a constitutional, representative and hereditary monarchy, with an elected Senate and Chamber of Deputies.

Area: 30,513 km^2 (11,782 sq mi); **Population:** 9,941,000; **Capital:** Brussels (pop 1,009,000); **Other cities:** Ghent (242,000), Charleroi (222,000), Liège (220,000), Antwerp (194,000), Bruges (118,000), Namur (101,000); **Highest point:** Botrange Mt, 694 m (2277 ft); **Official languages:** Dutch, French, German; **Religions:** Roman Catholicism, Protestantism; **Adult literacy rate:** 99 per cent; **Average life expectancy at birth:** 72 years; **Unit of currency:** Belgian franc; **Main exports:** engineering products, textiles, chemicals, glass, food, diamonds; **Per capita GNP:** US$10,890.

BELIZE, which faces the Caribbean Sea in Central America, is flat in the north, with uplands in the south. Forests flourish and sugar-cane is the chief cash crop in this hot, wet nation. More than 50 per cent of the people are Creoles; most of the others are of Mayan Indian, black Carib or European descent. Britain's contacts with Belize date back to the early 17th century. Belize was first declared a British colony in 1862, although neighbouring Guatemala has claimed it since 1821. The continuing dispute with Guatemala delayed full independence for Belize until 1981.

Area: 22,965 km^2 (8867 sq mi); **Population:** 135,000; **Capital:** Belmopan (pop 4000); **Official language:** English; **Unit of currency:** Dollar; **Per capita GNP:** US$1030.

BENIN, a People's Republic on the Gulf of Guinea in West Africa. Behind the sandy coast are low plateaux, with the highest land in the north-west. The formerly forested south has an equatorial climate but winters are dry in the tropical northern savanna. The black African population is divided into 50 groups, the largest being the Fon, Adja, Bariba and Yoruba. Agriculture employs 46 per cent of the workforce and accounts for 31 per cent of the GDP (13 per cent comes from industry). The chief food crops are maize and millet and the chief cash crop is palm kernels and oil. Oil was discovered offshore in the late 1970s. Benin (known as Dahomey until 1975) was ruled by France from the 1890s to 1960. Between 1960 and 1972 there were 6 coups. In 1977 there was an unsuccessful attempt by mercenaries to overthrow the government.

This market is in La Paz, Bolivia's seat of government. La Paz stands in a valley in the Andes range and is the world's highest large city.

Area: 112,622 km^2 (43,486 sq mi); **Population:** 3,734,000; **Capital:** Porto Novo (pop 104,000); **Other cities:** Cotonou (178,000); **Official language:** French; **Religions:** traditional religions (65 per cent), Christianity (17 per cent), Islam (15 per cent); **Adult literacy rate:** 11 per cent; **Average life expectancy at birth:** 46 years; **Unit of currency:** Franc CFA; **Main exports:** palm kernels and oil, cotton, groundnuts; **Per capita GNP:** US$250.

BERMUDA, a British island colony in the North Atlantic, about 920 km (572 miles) from Cape Hatteras in the USA. Of the 150 islands, 20 are uninhabited. The climate is mild: annual temperatures average 21°C (70°F). About 60 per cent of the people are black. Tourism accounts for 41 per cent of the GDP: many of the 600,000 tourists come from the USA. Farming and fishing are important locally. Bermuda was named after its discoverer, the Spaniard Juan Bermúdez, in 1503. Britain took the islands in 1684 and internal self-government was granted in 1968.

Area: 53 km^2 (20 sq mi); **Population:** 62,000; **Capital:** Hamilton (pop 3000); **Per capita GNP:** US$9260 (1978).

BHUTAN, a mountainous landlocked kingdom between China and India. Most people, who are of Tibetan or Hindu Nepalese origin, live in fertile valleys where the climate is warm and wet. Agriculture, mostly at subsistence level, employed 93 per cent of the workforce in 1978; only 4 per cent lived in towns. Some rice, fruit and timber are exported.

American Indians hunt fish in the Xingu River in the Amazon basin of Brazil. Economic development is now threatening the survival of the Indians.

Most manufactures and fuels must be imported. Contact with the West began in 1774. The present ruling dynasty was founded in 1907, but an elected National Assembly can now dismiss the king. India assumed responsibility for Bhutan's foreign affairs in 1949.

Area: 47,000 km^2 (18,148 sq mi); **Population:** 1,352,000; **Capital:** Thimphu; **Official language:** Dzongkha; **Religion:** Buddhism; **Adult literacy rate:** 5 per cent; **Average life expectancy at birth:** 41 years; **Unit of currency:** Ngultrum; **Per capita GNP:** US$80.

BOLIVIA, a landlocked republic in South America. The Andes mountains in the south-west contain a central plateau, the Altiplano, where most Bolivians live. It has a cool climate, contrasting with the hot Amazon rain forests in the north-east. Lake Titicaca, the world's highest navigable lake, is on the border with Peru. More than 50 per cent of the people are American Indians, a third are *mestizos* and the rest of European origin. Agriculture employs 51 per cent of the people, but mining is the most valuable industry. Bolivia is the world's 2nd largest tin producer and antimony, copper, lead, oil and natural gas, silver and wolfram are also mined. Spain ruled Bolivia from 1532 to 1825 when Simón Bolívar's army liberated the country (then Upper Peru). Oil discoveries have recently offered hope for Bolivia, South America's poorest nation.

Area: 1,098,581 km^2 (424,188 sq mi); **Population:** 5,897,000; **Capital:** La Paz (seat of government, pop 655,000), Sucre (legal capital, 63,000); **Other cities:** Santa Cruz (256,000), Cochabamba (204,000); **Highest point:** Mt Tocopuri, 6755 m (22,162 ft); **Official language:** Spanish; **Religion:** Roman Catholicism; **Adult literacy rate:** 63 per cent; **Average life expectancy at birth:** 52 years; **Unit of currency:** Peso; **Main exports:** tin, oil, natural gas, cotton; **Per capita GNP:** US$550.

BOTSWANA, a thinly populated, landlocked republic in southern Africa. Most of the country is a plateau between 600 and 1200 m (1969–3937 ft) high. Average temperatures range between 27°C (81°F) and 32°C (90°F). The rainfall is less than 250 mm (10 in) in the south-west, but 760 mm (30 in) in the north. The Kalahari, a semi-desert, covers 84 per cent of the country and only a few nomadic Bushmen live there. Most people belong to the Bantu-speaking Tswana group, including the Bamangwato and Bangwaketse. They live mostly in the east around the Botswanan section of the Cape Town-Bulawayo railway. Minerals now dominate the economy: diamonds and copper-nickel matte made up 57 per cent of the exports in 1978. Most people work in agriculture. Arable land covers only 2 per cent of the country, but cattle farming is important – there were 3.3 million cattle in 1979. Botswana (formerly called Bechuanaland) became a British protectorate in 1885. It became fully independent within the Commonwealth in 1966.

Area: 600,372 km^2 (231,818 sq mi); **Population:** 820,000; **Capital:** Gaborone (pop 54,000); **Official language:** English; **Religions:** Christianity, traditional beliefs; **Adult literacy rate:** 20 per cent; **Average life expectancy at birth:** 46 years; **Unit of currency:** Pula; **Main exports:** diamonds, meat and meat products, copper, nickel; **Per capita GNP:** US$720.

BRAZIL, the world's 5th largest nation, occupies nearly half of South America. In the north, the equatorial Amazon basin covers more than 5.3 million km^2 (2 million sq mi). It contains the world's largest rain forest (*selvas*), which are now being reduced as economic development proceeds. The Amazon river, 6437 km (4000 mi) long, is the world's second longest, with a greater volume than any other. It is navigable into Peru. South of the *selvas* is a huge tropical grassland, plateau region, the *campos*. This region is still little developed despite the inauguration in its heart of the new capital of Brasilia in 1960. The north-east around Recife and Salvador has a forested coastal plain, but the inland plateaux are dry: long droughts cause much hardship to an already impoverished population. The central coastal region is the most densely populated and includes the great industrial cities of São Paulo and Rio de Janeiro. Inland are fertile plateaux and pleasant, mineral-rich highlands. The plateaux near São Paulo are Brazil's main coffee-producing region. The southern region around Porto Alegre has a temperate climate: pastoral farming is important. About 75 per cent of Brazil's population is of Portuguese or other

European origin. There are many people of mixed European/Indian/Negro descent, perhaps 200,000 pure Indians and some blacks: colour prejudice is almost absent. The population is increasing quickly (2.9 per cent per year in 1970–78). There is also a rapid shift of population from rural to urban areas. The urban population increased from 46 per cent in 1960 to 65 per cent in 1980 and slums now surround many cities. Agriculture still provides work for two-fifths of the people, although its contribution to the GDP is only 11 per cent. Brazil leads the world in producing bananas and coffee, and it is among the top world producers of beef, veal, cocoa; cotton, maize, sugar-cane, soya beans and tobacco. Industry accounts for 37 per cent of the GDP. Brazil is the leading producer in Latin America of cars, merchant ships, steel and cement. It has huge reserves of minerals, many of which are unexploited. Such minerals as asbestos, chrome ore, industrial diamonds, iron ore, quartz crystal and manganese are exported. In 1500 the Portuguese explorer Pedro Alvares Cabral claimed Brazil for Portugal. At that time an estimated 1.3 million Indians lived in the country. However, many were killed by Europeans and others died (and are still dying in the *selvas*) of European diseases to which they lack resistance. African slaves were introduced to work European estates. Brazil declared itself an independent empire in 1822 but it became a republic in 1889, one year after slavery was abolished. Since 1964 Brazil has been ruled by military regimes which have sought to modernize the economy, although in doing so they have been accused of infringing civil liberties.

Area: 8,511,965 km² (3,286,668 sq mi); **Population:** 133,882,000; **Capital:** Brasilia (pop 979,000); **Other cities:** São Paulo (8,408,000), Rio de Janeiro (5,395,000), Belo Horizonte (1,857,000), Salvador (1,446,000), Recife (1,184,000), Fortaleza (1,256,000), Pôrto Alegre (1,184,000), Nova Iguacu (1,130,000); **Highest point:** Pico da Bandeira, 2890 m (9482 ft); **Official language:** Portuguese; **Religion:** Roman Catholicism (91 per cent); **Adult literacy rate:** 76 per cent; **Average life expectancy at birth:** 62 years; **Unit of currency:** Cruzeiro; **Main exports:** coffee, machinery, soya beans, vehicles, cocoa; **Per capita GNP:** US$1690.

BRUNEI, a small Sultanate in north-western Borneo. Behind the narrow coastal plain, the interior is rugged and forested. The climate is tropical. Some 68 per cent of the people are of Malay origin and 25 per cent are Chinese. Oil is the main product. Natural gas, rubber and timber are also exported. Brunei ruled all of Borneo and nearby islands in the early 16th century, after which it declined. It was a British protectorate between 1888 and 1971 and became independent in 1983.

Area: 5765 km² (2226 sq mi); **Population:** 248,000; **Capital:** Bandar Seri Begawan (pop 58,000); **Official language:** Malay; **Unit of currency:** Brunei dollar; **Per capita GNP:** US$10,680.

BURKINA FASO. *See* **UPPER VOLTA**

BULGARIA, a Communist People's Republic facing the Black Sea in south-eastern Europe. The climate is transitional between Mediterranean and continental, the latter prevailing in the north and in the mountains. The mountains include the Balkans in the north and the higher Rhodope Mts in the south. The capital Sofia is in a fertile mountain basin. The River Danube plain is in the north, but the central plains are the main farming region, producing fruit, mulberry leaves, attar of rose, sugar beet, tobacco and wine. Agriculture accounted for 18 per cent of the GDP in 1978 (employing 40 per cent of the workforce). 64 per cent of the GDP came from industry: lignite, copper, iron ore and oil are mined and manufactures include cement, iron and steel goods and textiles. COMECON countries account for 80 per cent of Bulgaria's trade. Tourism is increasing. The Turks ruled Bulgaria from 1396. Bulgaria became an independent principality in 1878, East Rumelia (southern Bulgaria) being added in 1885. Bulgaria became an independent kingdom in 1908. After World War II, in which Bulgaria was allied with Germany, a Soviet-type republic was established.

Area: 110,912 km² (42,826 sq mi); **Population:** 8,999,000; **Capital:** Sofia (pop 1,032,000); **Other cities:** Plovdiv (333,000), Varna (279,000); **Highest point:** Musalla Mt, 2925 m (9596 ft); **Official language:** Bulgarian; **Religion:** Eastern Orthodox Church (27 per cent), Islam (7 per cent); **Average life expectancy at birth:** 72 years; **Unit of currency:** Lev; **Main exports:** machinery, metals and metal ores, food, tobacco, textiles; **Per capita GNP:** US$3690.

BURMA, a Socialist Republic in south-eastern Asia. The north, east and west are mountainous, but the southern valleys of the Irrawaddy and Sittang rivers are fertile. The Irrawaddy delta is one of the world's great rice-growing areas. The climate is tropical. The average temperature in the delta is 27°C (81°F) and the average annual rainfall is 2500 mm (98 in). Central Burma is much drier. Two-thirds of the people are Tibeto-Burmese and there are many small groups of isolated hill peoples. In 1978 agriculture employed 53 per cent of the workforce and accounted for 46 per cent of the GDP. Forests cover half the country and teak is a major product. Many minerals, including oil and natural gas, are mined. Manufacturing is mostly small-scale and concentrated in urban areas where 27 per cent of the people live. Britain took Burma between 1823 and 1855, making it a province of India. It became independent in 1948. Revolts by communists and hill tribesmen led to the setting up of military regimes in 1958 and again in 1962. The Union of Burma is now a one-party state.

Area: 676,552 km² (261,232 sq mi); **Population:** 35,211,000; **Capital:** Rangoon (pop 3,662,000); **Other cities:** Mandalay (417,000); **Highest point:** 5881 m (19,295 ft); **Official language:** Burmese; **Religion:** Buddhism; **Adult literacy rate:** 67 per cent; **Average life expectancy at birth:** 53 years; **Unit of currency:** Kyat; **Main exports:** teak, oil cake, jute, rubber, minerals; **Per capita GNP:** US$160.

BURUNDI, a small, densely populated, landlocked republic in east-central Africa. Part of Lake Tanganyika is in the Rift Valley in the west, with highlands and high plateaux in the east. The altitude moderates the equatorial climate. The highlands are grassy, but woodlands flourish on the warmer plateaux. There are a few pygmies, but the main ethnic groups are the Bantu-speaking Hutu (85 per cent) and the Hamitic Tutsi (13 per cent). Agriculture employs 85 per cent of the people, accounting for 56 per cent of the GDP. The pastoralist Tutsi entered the area from the north in the 17th century. They founded a feudal society under their *mwami* (king), making the Hutu serfs. Germany occupied Burundi and Rwanda (then Ruanda-Urundi) in 1890, but Belgium took the area in World War I. Burundi became an independent monarchy in 1962, but a republic was set up in 1966. Hutu attempts to overthrow the Tutsi government have all failed, leading to the deaths of thousands of Hutu.

Area: 27,834 km^2 (10,747 sq mi): **Population:** 4,293,000; **Capital:** Bujumbura (pop 157,000); **Official languages:** French, Kirundi; **Religions:** Roman Catholicism (60 per cent), Protestantism (7 per cent), traditional beliefs; **Adult literacy rate:** 25 per cent; **Average life expectancy at birth:** 45 years; **Unit of currency:** Burundi franc; **Main exports:** coffee (about 90 per cent); **Per capita GNP:** US$180.

CAMEROON, a republic in west-central Africa, bordering the Gulf of Guinea. Behind narrow coastal plains are plateaux that slope down in the north to the Lake Chad basin. The main uplands are on the western border: the highest peak is the volcanic Mt Cameroon on the coast. The equatorial south is forested; the tropical centre contains wooded savanna; the drier north has open grassland. Most people are black, speaking one of about 200 Bantu or Sudanic languages. Agriculture employs 82 per cent of the people. Mining (for bauxite and oil) is becoming important, but manufacturing is on a small scale. Portuguese explorers reached the coast in 1472. Germany made Cameroon a colony in 1884 but, after World War I, it was partitioned between Britain and France. French Cameroon became independent in 1960 and was joined in a federal republic in 1961 by part of British Cameroon – the other part joined Nigeria. A unitary state was established in 1972.

Area: 475,442 km^2 (183,579 sq mi); **Population:** 8,804,000; **Capital:** Yaoundé (pop 314,000); **Other cities:** Douala (458,000); **Highest point:** Mt Cameroon, 4070 m (13,353 ft); **Official languages:** English, French; **Religions:** Christianity (52 per cent), Islam (18 per cent), traditional beliefs; **Adult literacy rate:** 19 per cent; **Average life expectancy at birth:** 46 years; **Unit of currency:** Franc CFA; **Main exports:** coffee, cocoa, timber; **Per capita GNP:** US$560.

CANADA, the world's 2nd largest nation after the USSR, but it has only 2.5 persons per sq km (6 per sq mi). There are 7 main regions. The *Appalachian region* in the north-east is an extension of the Appalachian region in the USA. The *St Lawrence and Lower Great Lakes* region is Canada's most densely populated. The *Canadian Shield* is a vast region of ancient rocks, mineral deposits, and innumerable lakes and rivers. The *Hudson Bay* Lowland is a plain between the Canadian Shield and Hudson Bay. The *Western Interior Plains* are between the Canadian Shield and the *Western Mountains*, which include the Canadian Rockies and the Coast Range. In the far north are the bleak *Arctic Islands*. Canada has extremely cold winters, especially north of the Arctic Circle. Southern Canada has warm, moist summers. Rainfall varies from 2500 mm (98 in) per year in parts of the west to 300-500 mm (12–20 in) on the central prairies to 760 mm (30 in) in the south-east. Forests cover 35 per cent of Canada. There are also vast grasslands and tundra regions. The origins of the people are as follows: British (45 per cent), French (29 per cent), German (6 per cent), Italian (3 per cent) and Ukrainian (3 per cent). Most of the rest come from other parts of Europe. American Indians and Eskimos number 289,000 and 17,500 respectively. Canada has two official languages, English and French. Quebec is the main French-speaking province. In a referendum there in 1980, 40.5 per cent

The Niagara Falls are on the border between Canada and the United States between Lake Erie and Lake Ontario. The Falls are one of North America's finest natural wonders. Goat Island divides the Falls into the 56-metre (184-ft) high American Falls and the 54-metre (177-ft) high Canadian Falls. Much hydroelectricity is generated at the Falls.

COUNTRIES OF THE WORLD

PROVINCES AND TERRITORIES OF CANADA

Province or territory	Area (sq km)	Area (sq mi)	Population (1980)	Capital
Alberta	661,187	255,300	2,009,000	Edmonton
British Columbia	948,599	366,276	2,567,000	Victoria
Manitoba	650,089	251,014	1,030,000	Winnipeg
New Brunswick	73,437	28,356	701,000	Fredericton
Newfoundland	404,518	156,194	574,000	St John's
Northwest Territory	3,379,693	1,304,978	43,000	Yellowknife
Nova Scotia	55,491	21,426	847,000	Halifax
Ontario	1,068,586	412,606	8,500,000	Toronto
Prince Edward Is.	5,657	2,184	123,000	Charlottetown
Quebec	1,540,685	594,894	6,299,000	Quebec
Saskatchewan	651,902	251,795	957,100	Regina
Yukon Territory	536,326	207,088	22,000	Whitehorse

of the people voted for and 59.5 per cent against 'separatism'. Canada is a prosperous country. Only 7.2 per cent of the land is cultivated, but Canada is one of the world's leading producers of barley, fruits, oats, wheat, rye and timber. Livestock ranching and dairy farming are also important. But agriculture contributes only 4 per cent of the GDP as opposed to 31 per cent from industry. Canada is among the top six world producers of asbestos, copper, gold, iron ore, lead, molybdenum, natural gas, nickel, potash, silver, uranium and zinc. But more important than mining is manufacturing. The chief industrial area is the St Lawrence and Lower Great Lakes region. Much traffic is carried along the St Lawrence Seaway, the world's longest artificial seaway at 304 km (189 mi). Canada's first people, the Indians, entered North America from Asia around 20,000 years ago. The Eskimos were later arrivals. Vikings sailed down Canada's coasts in about AD 1000, but the first definite European landfall was made in 1497. Quebec was founded by Samuel de Champlain in 1604, but intense rivalry soon developed between the French and British. Between 1689 and 1763, the British conquered the French settlements. In 1867 the Dominion of Canada, comprising Quebec, Ontario, Nova Scotia and New Brunswick, was established. Canada is now a federation of 10 self-governing provinces and 2 territories. The federal parliament consists of a Senate and a House of Commons.

Area: 9,976,139 km^2 (3,852,019 sq mi); **Population:** 24,620,000; **Capital:** Ottawa (pop with suburbs 693,000); **Other cities:** Toronto (2,803,000), Montreal (2,802,000), Vancouver (1,166,000), Winnipeg (578,000), Edmonton (554,000), Quebec (542,000), Hamilton (529,000), Calgary (470,000); **Highest point:** Mt Logan, 6050 m (19,849 ft); **Official languages:** English, French; **Religions:** Roman Catholicism (46 per cent), Protestantism (42 per cent); **Adult literacy rate:** 98 per cent; **Average life expectancy at birth:** 74 years; **Unit of currency:** Dollar; **Main exports:** motor cars and vehicle parts, newsprint and wood pulp, oil and natural gas, wheat, industrial machinery, iron ore; **Per capita GNP:** US$9650.

CAPE VERDE, an island republic about 500 km (311 mi) west of Senegal in West Africa. The 10 large islands and 5 islets are of volcanic origin. The climate is tropical, but the rainfall is very unreliable. Most people are of mixed Portuguese and African origin; 28 per cent are classed as 'pure' Africans. Most people are subsistence farmers, but severe droughts in the 1970s forced many people to emigrate and the government has had to provide work for destitute farmers. Portugal claimed the islands in 1460. From 1836 to 1879, Cape Verde was ruled with Portuguese Guinea (now Guinea-Bissau) and close ties between the two territories continued. In 1963–74, Cape Verdeans fought alongside Guineans against the Portuguese in Portuguese Guinea. Independence for Cape Verde was achieved in 1975.

Area: 4033 km^2 (1557 sq mi); **Population:** 324,000; **Capital:** Praia (pop 21,000); **Highest point:** Pico do Cano, 2829 m (9281 ft); **Official language:** Portuguese; **Religions:** Roman Catholicism (97 per cent), Protestantism (3 per cent), a few animists; **Adult literacy rate:** 28 per cent; **Average life expectancy at birth:** 50 years; **Unit of currency:** Escudo; **Main exports:** fish and lobsters, salt, sugar, bananas; **Per capita GNP:** US$270.

CAYMAN ISLANDS, a British island group in the West Indies. These tropical islands export turtle shells, turtle meat and fish, but tourism is more important. The people are of European, African or mixed origin. Columbus discovered in the islands in 1503. Britons settled there in the 17th century.

Area: 259 km^2 (100 sq mi); **Population:** 11,000; **Capital:** George Town (pop 4000).

CENTRAL AFRICAN REPUBLIC, a landlocked nation, consists largely of plateaux between 600 and 900 m (1969–2953 ft). Temperatures average 26°C (79°F) all the year. The south has an average annual rainfall of 2030 mm (80 in); the far north gets 510 mm (20 in). The south is forested, but wooded savanna covers most of the land. Wildlife is abundant. Most people speak Sudanese languages. Agriculture employs 89 per cent of the workforce, contributing 36 per cent of the GDP. Diamonds are mined and large uranium deposits have been found, but manufacturing is on a small scale. The country became part of French Equatorial Africa in the 1880s. It became independent in 1960. From 1965 it was ruled by Jean-Bédel Bokassa who, in 1977, made himself 'emperor'. The country was then named the Central African Empire. Bokassa was overthrown in 1979 and the nation again became a republic.

Area: 622,984 km^2 (240,549 sq mi); **Population:** 2,086,000; **Capital:** Bangui (pop 302,000); **Official language:** French; **Religions:** Roman Catholicism (46 per cent), Protestantism (36 per cent), traditional beliefs; **Adult literacy rate:** 8 per cent (1973); **Average life expectancy at birth:** 46 years; **Unit of currency:** Franc CFA; **Main exports:** coffee, diamonds, timber, cotton; **Per capita GNP:** US$290.

CHAD, a landlocked nation in north-central Africa. Lake Chad, the remains of an inland sea, is in the west. Southern Chad is savanna-covered, but sandy deserts and bare rocky uplands, notably the high Tibesti massif, are in the north. About 100 languages are spoken in Chad. In the south, where most of the population lives, most people are Negroid. Muslim Arabs and Berbers live in the north. Cultural divisions have caused much civil conflict and periodic war since the mid-1960s. In 1980 Libyan troops intervened in Chad but they were replaced in 1981 by an OAU force. Agriculture employs 86 per cent of the workers in this poor nation. Cotton is the chief crop. Chad became a French colony in 1897 and an independent republic in 1960.

Area: 1,284,000 km^2 (495,782 sq mi); **Population:** 4,714,000; **Capital:** N'Djamena (pop 242,000); **Highest point:** Emi Koussi, 3415 m (11,204 ft); **Official language:** French; **Religions:** Islam (45 per cent), Christianity (5 per cent); traditional beliefs (50 per cent); **Adult literacy rate:** 15 per cent; **Average life expectancy at birth:** 43 years; **Unit of currency:** Franc CFA; **Main exports:** cotton (66 per cent), meat and cattle, fish; **Per capita GNP:** US$110.

CHILE, a narrow country stretching through 38° of latitude in South America. Its greatest width is about 400 km (249 miles). From west to east, there are generally three regions; coastal uplands, central lowland basins and valleys, and the high Andes. In the glaciated south, the coastal uplands are islands, the central lowlands becoming arms of the sea. Chile's climate changes north-south. The north is hot and arid, including the rainless Atacama Desert with its large mineral reserves. Central Chile, where most Chileans live, has hot summers and mild moist winters. The forested south with its beautiful fiords is cool: heavy rain falls in all seasons. Cape Horn, South America's stormy tip, is in the far south. People of mixed European and Indian origin make up 68 per cent of the population, Europeans 30 per cent, and Araucanian Indians 2 per cent. Agriculture provides work for 20 per cent of the people, accounting for 18 per cent of the GDP. Farmland covers 15 per cent of Chile, pasture 27 per cent and forests 29 per cent. The main farm products are barley, fruit, maize, wheat and wine. Industry accounts for 29 per cent of the GDP (with 20 per cent from manufacturing). Minerals include copper, which makes up 48 per cent of the exports, iron ore, nitrates and oil. Manufacturing industries are powered mainly by hydro-electricity. Chile was a Spanish colony for about 300 years before becoming independent in 1818. It gained its mineral-rich northern provinces in a war with Peru and Bolivia in 1879–83. In 1970 a Marxist government led by Salvador Allende was elected to office, but it was overthrown in 1973 by the armed forces. The military government of General Augusto Pinochet revived the flagging economy, but was accused of violating civil liberties.

Area: 756,945 km^2 (292,274 sq mi); **Population:** 11,478,000; **Capital:** Santiago (pop with suburbs 3,692,000); **Other cities:** Valparaiso (611,000), Concepción (513,000); **Highest point:** Ojos de Salado, 6885 m (22,590 ft); **Official language:** Spanish; **Religion:** Roman Catholicism (90 per cent); **Adult literacy rate:** 88 per cent; **Average life expectancy at birth:** 67 years; **Unit of currency:** Peso; **Main exports:** copper, paper and wood pulp, timber, iron ore, nitrates; **Per capita GNP:** US$1690.

CHINA, the world's 3rd largest country, contains about 20 per cent of the world's population. The land is extremely varied. In the north-east is the basin of the Hwang Ho, one of the world's longest rivers at 4345 km (2700 mi) long. It cuts through a loess plateau which has coloured its waters yellow. The lower course of the Hwang Ho crosses the North China Plain. To the north lie the central plain and eastern highlands of Manchuria. To the south, beyond the Tsin Ling Mountains lies the Yangtze Kiang basin of Central China. The Yangtze is Asia's longest river, 5470 km (3400 mi) in length. China's third important river basin is that of the Si Kiang in the south-east, south of the South China Highlands. Outer or Western China contains the high and vast Tibetan plateau which rises in the south to the Himalayan range, crowned by Mt Everest. In the far west are other ranges including the lofty Pamirs and Tien Shan. North-eastern China contains some large deserts, including the vast Tarim and Dzungaria basins. The Gobi desert straddles the frontier between Inner Mongolia (in China) and Mongolia. The climate varies from north to south. North-eastern China has bitterly cold winters and warm summers. The average annual rainfall is between 635 and 760 mm (25–30 in). Central China has milder winters and more rainfall – about 1000–1500 mm (39–59 in) per year, while south-eastern China has a subtropical monsoon climate and many places get more than 2030 mm (80 in) of rain per year. The north-eastern deserts have less than 100 mm (4 in). About 94 per cent of the population are Han, or true, Chinese. But there are also large national minorities, including Manchus, Mongols, Tibetans and Uighurs, who maintain their own cultures. The population is densest in the fertile river basins and along the coasts of eastern China. Some 25 per cent of the population lives in urban areas. The rural population has been encouraged to live in communes, which are groups of villages where up to 20,000 people work together, share the produce and get wages that are geared to production. Some 62 per cent of the workforce is engaged in agriculture. China leads the world in millet, rice and tobacco production. It is among the top three

COUNTRIES OF THE WORLD

Left and below: A vase of the Chinese Ch'ing dynasty (1644–1911) and a ginger jar of the Ming dynasty (1368–1644). Right: A jade Han-dynasty monster (206 BC–AD 220).

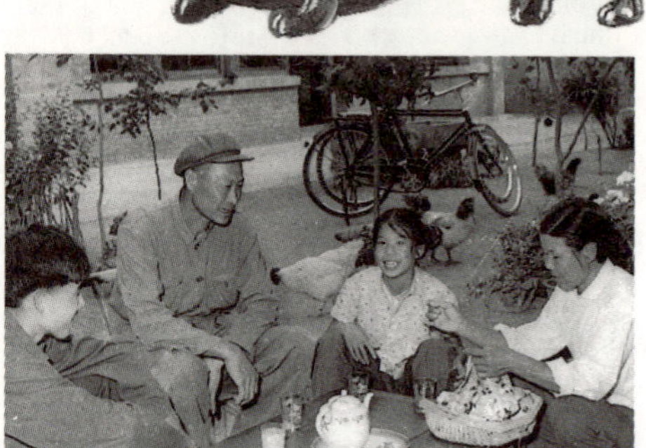

The family remains the most important social unit in China, despite Communist rule. China is a poor country in world terms, a consequence of its mainly peasant farming economy. But it has great resources and considerable economic potential.

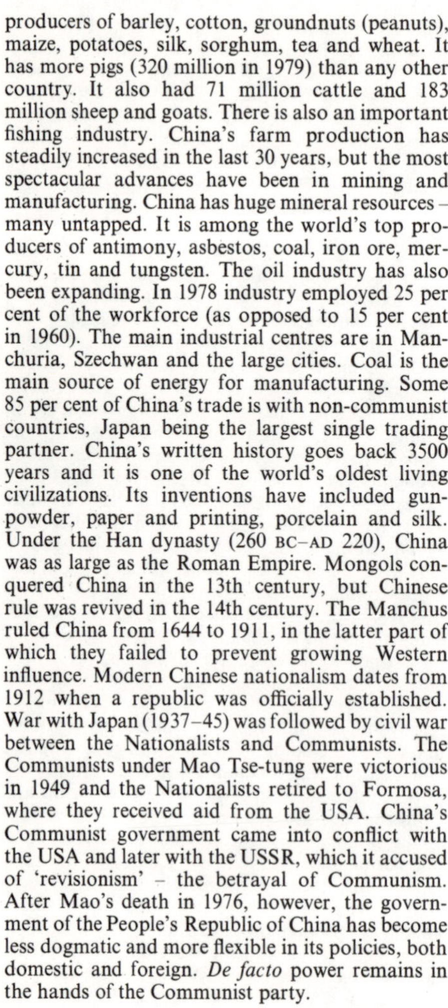

producers of barley, cotton, groundnuts (peanuts), maize, potatoes, silk, sorghum, tea and wheat. It has more pigs (320 million in 1979) than any other country. It also had 71 million cattle and 183 million sheep and goats. There is also an important fishing industry. China's farm production has steadily increased in the last 30 years, but the most spectacular advances have been in mining and manufacturing. China has huge mineral resources – many untapped. It is among the world's top producers of antimony, asbestos, coal, iron ore, mercury, tin and tungsten. The oil industry has also been expanding. In 1978 industry employed 25 per cent of the workforce (as opposed to 15 per cent in 1960). The main industrial centres are in Manchuria, Szechwan and the large cities. Coal is the main source of energy for manufacturing. Some 85 per cent of China's trade is with non-communist countries, Japan being the largest single trading partner. China's written history goes back 3500 years and it is one of the world's oldest living civilizations. Its inventions have included gunpowder, paper and printing, porcelain and silk. Under the Han dynasty (260 BC–AD 220), China was as large as the Roman Empire. Mongols conquered China in the 13th century, but Chinese rule was revived in the 14th century. The Manchus ruled China from 1644 to 1911, in the latter part of which they failed to prevent growing Western influence. Modern Chinese nationalism dates from 1912 when a republic was officially established. War with Japan (1937–45) was followed by civil war between the Nationalists and Communists. The Communists under Mao Tse-tung were victorious in 1949 and the Nationalists retired to Formosa, where they received aid from the USA. China's Communist government came into conflict with the USA and later with the USSR, which it accused of 'revisionism' – the betrayal of Communism. After Mao's death in 1976, however, the government of the People's Republic of China has become less dogmatic and more flexible in its policies, both domestic and foreign. *De facto* power remains in the hands of the Communist party.

Area: 9,596,961 km^2 (3,705,610 sq km); **Population:** 1,012,358,000; **Capital:** Peking (or Beijing, pop 8,706,000); **Other cities:** Shanghai (11,320,000), Tientsin (7,390,000), Chungking (6,200,000), Canton (5,000,000), Shenyang (4,400,000), Lüta (4,200,000), Wuhan (3,500,000), Nanking (2,400,000), Harbin (2,100,000); **Highest point:** Mt Everest, 8848 m (29,028 ft); **Official language:** Chinese; **Religions:** Confucianism, Taoism, Buddhism, Islam, Christianity; **Average life expectancy at birth:** 70 years; **Unit of currency:** Renminbi or Yuan; **Main exports:** industrial products (including petroleum, chemicals, machinery, equipment), agricultural products; **Per capita GNP:** US$230 (1978).

CHRISTMAS ISLAND, an Australian territory in the Indian Ocean populated by Chinese, Malays and Europeans. The only industry is phosphate mining. It came under the Governor of the Straits Settlement in 1889 and was incorporated with Singapore in 1900. Australia took over in 1958.

Area: 135 km^2 (52 sq mi); **Population:** 3200; **Status:** Australian external territory.

COCOS (KEELING) ISLANDS, an Australian territory in the Indian Ocean comprising 27 coral islands that export copra. Britain annexed them in 1857 and they came under the Governor of the Straits Settlement in 1886. They were placed under Australian rule in 1955.

Area: 14 km^2 ($5\frac{1}{2}$ sq mi); **Population:** 500; **Status:** Australian external territory.

COLOMBIA, a republic in north-eastern South America, contains three ranges of the Andes whose high, fertile valleys contain most of the people. In eastern Colombia, *llanos* grasslands merge into the forests of the upper Amazon and Orinoco basins. The coastal lowlands are hot and wet, with average temperatures of 26°–28°C (79°–82°F) and about 2540 mm (100 in) of rain. The highlands are cooler and less rainy. The *llanos* have dry winters but wet summers. More than two-thirds of the people are of mixed Indian and European origin; most others are of pure Indian, European or Negroid descent. Agriculture accounts for 31 per cent of the GDP. The chief export, coffee, is grown in the highlands. Industry accounts for 27 per cent of the GDP and 70 per cent of the people now live in urban areas. Spaniards opened up the region in the early 16th century. Spanish rule was overthrown in 1819. Greater Colombia then included Venezuela, Ecuador and parts of Panama. Venezuela and Ecuador soon split off and Panama broke away in 1903. A civil war in 1948–53 led to a military seizure of power but, after 1957, democracy was restored.

Area: 1,138,914 km^2 (439,761 sq mi); **Population:** 27,966,000; **Capital:** Bogotá (pop 3,831,000); **Other cities:** Medellin (1,442,000), Cali (1,255,000); **Highest point:** Pico Cristobal Colón, 5775 m (18,947 ft); **Official language:** Spanish; **Religion:** Roman Catholicism; **Adult literacy rate:** 81 per cent; **Average life expectancy at birth:** 62 years; **Unit of currency:** Peso; **Main exports:** coffee, emeralds, meat, sugar, petroleum, fuel oils, hides and skins; **Per capita GNP:** US$1010.

COMOROS, an island Federal and Islamic Republic at the northern end of the Mozambique Channel. Geographically, there are 4 islands: Njazidja, Nzwani, Mahoré (or Mayotte) and Mwali. The republic contains three of them, but Mayotte is a French territory. The islands are mountainous: Mt Kartala, 2361 m (7746 ft), is an active volcano. The population is mixed, including elements from Africa, Asia and Europe. These tropical islands have few resources and most people are subsistence farmers. They came under French protection in 1886–1909 and became a colony in 1912. In 1946 they became a French overseas department. The people voted for independence in 1974, except in Mayotte where a majority opposed it. In 1975 the Chamber of Deputies voted for immediate independence, which France recognized on January 1, 1976. But Mayotte (a French colony since 1843) became a *collectivité particuliére*, a status part-way between a French Overseas Territory and an Overseas Department.

Area: 2171 km^2 (838 sq mi); **Population:** 448,000; **Capital:** Moroni; **Official languages:** Arabic, French; **Religions:** mainly Islam, Roman Catholicism (4 per cent); **Average life expectancy at birth:** 42; **Unit of currency:** Franc CFA; **Main exports:** vanilla, vegetable oils, cloves, copra, coffee, cocoa; **Per capita GNP:** US$210.

CONGO, a People's Republic in equatorial Africa. Behind a narrow coastal plain is an upland region; the north is a swampy plain drained by the Congo (Zaire) and Oubangui rivers. High temperatures and heavy rainfall, except on the coast, have encouraged the growth of rain forests and woodland savanna. Most people speak Bantu languages (including Kongo, Téké, Mbochi), but 12,000 pygmies live in central Congo. Less than 2 per cent of Congo is cultivated, but agriculture employs 35 per cent of the workforce, accounting for 13 per cent of the GDP. Industry accounts for 33 per cent; oil extraction and processing industries are especially important. 37 per cent of the population lives in urban areas. Discovered in 1482, Congo later became a slave trade centre. French rule was established in the 1880s; Congo later became part of French Equatorial Africa. Full independence was achieved in 1960. Military governments have ruled the country since 1968.

Area: 342,000 km^2 (132,054 sq mi); **Population:** 1,613,000; **Capital:** Brazzaville (pop 301,000); **Other towns:** Pointe-Noire (147,000); **Official language:** French; **Religions:** traditional beliefs (50 per cent); Christianity (48 per cent), Islam (2 per cent); **Adult literacy rate:** 50 per cent; **Average life expectancy at birth:** 46 years; **Unit of currency:** Franc CFA; **Main exports:** oil, timber, potash, fertilizers, coffee, cocoa; **Per capita GNP:** US$630.

COOK ISLANDS, a self-governing territory of New Zealand in the South Pacific. Of the 15 islands, 9 are atolls and 6 volcanic. Most people are Polynesians. Exports include fruits and copra. The islands became a British protectorate in 1888 and part of New Zealand in 1901.

Area: 234 km^2 (90 sq mi); **Population:** 18,000; **Capital:** Avarua; **Official language:** English.

COSTA RICA, a Central American republic with coastlines on the Caribbean Sea and the Pacific Ocean. Inland it is mountainous with volcanic peaks. Fertile plateaux lie between the mountains. About 70 per cent of the people live in the largest of these, the Central Plateau. The tropical climate is modified by the relief. More than 80 per cent of the population is of European origin. There are 1200 Indians and a few thousand blacks, but most non-whites are of mixed European and Indian origin. Agriculture employs 29 per cent of the people, accounting for 22 per cent of the GDP; industry accounts for 27 per cent and services 51 per cent. The main cash crop is coffee. Costa Rica is one of the more prosperous nations of Central America. Spain ruled the country from around 1530 to 1821. Dictatorships and revolutions marred its early years of independence, but it has enjoyed democracy since 1919.

Area: 50,700 km^2 (19,576 sq miles); **Population:** 2,329,000; **Capital:** San José (pop 250,000); **Highest point:** Chirripo, 3820 m (12,861 ft); **Official language:** Spanish; **Religion:** Roman Catholicism; **Adult literacy rate:** 90 per cent; **Average life expectancy at birth:** 70 years; **Unit of currency:** Colón; **Main exports:** manufactures, coffee, bananas; **Per capita GNP:** US$1810.

CUBA, the largest nation in the West Indies. Small islands, reefs and mangrove swamps skirt much of the coast. More than half of the land is flat and fertile. Forested mountain ranges occupy about 25 per cent of the land, the rest being gently undulating country. The climate is tropical, with average temperatures of 22°–28°C (72°–82°F). The rainfall averages 1270 mm (50 in) per year. About 75 per cent of the people are descendants of Spaniards, the rest being blacks or mulattos. Some 65 per cent of the population lives in urban areas. Agriculture employs 25 per cent of the workforce, industry 31 per cent and service industries 44 per cent. About 34 per cent of Cuba is cultivated, most being government-owned. Sugar and its by-products, molasses and rum, are the main products. Minerals, tobacco, bananas and fish are also exported. Columbus discovered Cuba in 1492 and Spain ruled it between 1511 and 1898 (except when Britain occupied it in 1762–63). US influence was strong in the 20th century until Communist guerrillas led by Dr Fidel Castro seized power in 1959. Cuba became an ally of the USSR and, in the late 1970s and early 1980s, Cuban troops aided left-wing regimes in Africa.

Area: 114,524 km² (44,220 sq mi); **Population:** 10,346,000; **Capital:** Havana (pop 1,735,000); **Official language:** Spanish; **Religions:** Roman Catholicism, Protestantism; **Adult literacy rate:** 96 per cent; **Average life expectancy at birth:** 72 years; **Unit of currency:** Peso; **Main exports:** sugar (80 per cent); **Per capita GNP:** US$1410.

CYPRUS, an island republic in the north-eastern Mediterranean Sea. There are fertile coastal plains and a broad central plain (the Mesaoria). The Kyrenia and Karpass mountains are in the north and the Troödos mountains in the south. The climate is typically Mediterranean. Greek Cypriots form 80 per cent of the population, Turkish Cypriots 18 per cent and Armenian, Maronite and other minorities also live there. Communal conflict characterizes social life; most people feel themselves to be Greeks or Turks rather than Cypriots. About 60 per cent of the land is cultivated; one-third of the work-force is employed in farming. Agriculture supplies about half of the exports and minerals (notably copper) about 30 per cent. Britain rented Cyprus from the Ottoman Empire in 1878 but it annexed it in 1914 and proclaimed it a colony in 1927. A fierce guerrilla war preceded independence in 1960. The independence Constitution, providing for power-sharing between the communities, proved unworkable. In 1974 Turkish forces occupied the north. The island was partitioned, the northern 40 per cent being proclaimed the 'Turkish Cypriot Federated State'.

Area: 9251 km² (3572 sq mi); **Population:** 665,000; **Capital:** Nicosia (pop 121,000); **Other cities:** Limassol (102,000); **Highest point:** Mt Olympus, 1951 m (6401 ft); **Official languages:** Greek, Turkish; **Religions:** Eastern Orthodox Christianity, Islam; **Average life expectancy at birth:** 71 years; **Unit of currency:** Pound; **Main exports:** fruit and vegetables, manufactures (including wine), minerals; **Per capita GNP:** US$2940.

CZECHOSLOVAKIA, a landlocked Communist republic in eastern Europe. The saucer-shaped Bohemian plateau, bounded by mountains, is in the east. It is drained by the upper Elbe (the Vltava) on which Prague stands. Moravia, in the centre, is largely lowland, with rivers draining to the Danube. Slovakia, in the east, is mainly upland, with some plains in the south. The climate is continental. Average temperatures range between −7°C and 20°C (20°–68°F). The rainfall is between 500 and 1000 mm (20–39 in) per year. The people include the Czechs (65 per cent of the population), in Bohemia and Moravia, the Slovaks (30 per cent) and various minorities. Industry, which is nationalized, accounts for 72 per cent of the GDP: 63 per cent of the population lives in urban areas. The country is rich in coal and lignite and has many metal ores, although metals are imported. Farmland covers 55 per cent of the country. Crops include barley, hops, rye, sugar beet and wheat. The republic was created in 1918. Germany occupied Czechoslovakia in 1939. After World War II, in 1948, the Communists gained control. Demands for more freedom in 1968 led to an invasion by Soviet troops.

Area: 127,869 km² (49,373 sq mi); **Population:** 15,556,000; **Capital:** Prague (pop 1,189,000); **Other cities:** Brno (369,000); Bratislava (368,000); **Highest point:** 2655 m (8737 ft); **Official languages:** Czech, Slovak; **Religions:** Roman Catholicism, Protestantism; **Average life expectancy at birth:** 70 years; **Unit of currency:** Koruna; **Main exports:** machinery, industrial consumer goods, raw materials and fuels; **Per capita GNP:** US$5290.

DENMARK, the smallest but most densely populated nation in northern Europe. It consists of the low-lying Jutland peninsula and about 500 islands, the largest of which, Sjaelland, contains Copenhagen. Moraine covers much of the land, but two-thirds is fertile farmland or pasture. Animal products (bacon, butter, cheese, eggs) are particularly important as is sea fishing. But only 8 per cent of the workforce is engaged in agriculture, forestry and fishing. The leading sector of the economy is manufacturing. Products include superb silverware, furniture, processed food, chemicals, engineering goods, machinery and ships. Denmark formed a union with Norway and Sweden in the late 14th century. Sweden became independent in 1523 and Denmark ceded Norway to Sweden in 1814. Neutral in World War I, Denmark was occupied by Germany in World War II. After the war, it helped to set up the Nordic Council. It joined the EEC in 1973. The Faeroe Islands and Greenland are parts of Denmark.

Area: 43,069 km² (16,630 sq mi), not including Greenland; **Population:** 5,175,000; **Capital:** Copenhagen (pop 654,000); **Other cities:** Aarhus (245,000), Odense (169,000), Aalborg (154,000); **Highest point:** 173 m (568 ft); **Official language:** Danish; **Religion:** Lutheran Church; **Adult literacy rate:** 99 per cent; **Average life expectancy at birth:** 74 years; **Unit of currency:** Krone; **Main exports:** machinery and equipment, live animals and meat, dairy products and eggs, metals and metal manufactures; **Per capita GNP:** US$11,900.

DJIBOUTI, a small republic on the Red Sea in north-eastern Africa. The land is mostly hot desert. The people include the Somali-speaking Issas (40 per cent), the nomadic Afars (or Danakils, 33 per cent), both of whom are Muslims, and some

Europeans, Arabs and other foreigners. Stock raising is the main occupation. It became a French colony in 1881, called French Somaliland. In 1967 it was renamed the Territory of the Afars and Issas. It became independent as Djibouti in 1977.

Area: 22,000 km^2 (8495 sq mi); **Population:** 371,000; **Capital:** Djibouti (pop 150,000); **Official language:** French; **Main exports:** hides and skins, cattle; **Per capita GNP:** US$420.

DOMINICA, a volcanic island in the Windward Islands in the eastern Caribbean Sea. Its wet tropical climate supports dense forests. Most people are blacks or of mixed origin. There is a small Carib community, mostly of mixed origin. Agriculture and tourism are the main industries. Columbus discovered Dominica in 1493. It became a British colony in 1805 and a British Associated State in 1967. The Commonwealth of Dominica became an independent republic in 1978.

Area: 751 km^2 (290 sq mi); **Population:** 82,000; **Capital:** Roseau (pop 17,000); **Main exports:** bananas, citrus fruits; **Per capita GNP:** US$410.

DOMINICAN REPUBLIC, a nation occupying the eastern half of Hispaniola, an island in the West Indies. The land is mountainous and the climate tropical, with average temperatures of more than 20°C (68°F) and an average annual rainfall of 1000 mm (39 in). Rain forests are widespread, but the valleys are fertile. More than 70 per cent of the population is of mixed black and white descent, 15 per cent are white and 10 per cent are black. Agriculture employs 57 per cent of the workforce, contributing 21 per cent of the GDP (1978). Sugar is the chief export. Industry accounts for 35 per cent of the GDP: some bauxite, nickel, gold and silver are mined and there is some light industry. Tourism is increasingly important. Columbus discovered Hispaniola in 1492. Spain lost the area to France in 1795 but ruled it again in 1809–21. From 1822 to 1844 Haitians occupied the area. The Dominican Republic was founded in 1844, but its history has been marred by violence. From 1930–61 the country was a dictatorship. Elections were held in 1962, but a military coup in 1963 led to civil war in 1965 when US forces intervened. Since then the country has had elected governments.

Area: 48,734 km^2 (18,817 sq mi); **Population:** 5,776,000; **Capital:** Santo Domingo (pop 818,000); **Highest point:** Pico Duarte, 3124 m (10,249 ft); **Official language:** Spanish; **Religion:** Roman Catholicism; **Adult literacy rate:** 67 per cent; **Average life expectancy at birth:** 60 years; **Unit of currency:** Peso; **Main exports:** sugar, coffee; **Per capita GNP:** US$990.

ECUADOR, a republic on the Equator in north-western South America. It includes the 15 Galápagos Islands, about 970 km (603 mi) to the west. The Pacific coastlands have an average annual temperature of 27°C (81°F). The Andes ranges are much cooler; Quito at 2850 m (9350 ft) has an average temperature of 13°C (55°F). The hot Amazon basin occupies eastern Ecuador. The annual rainfall varies between 1020 and 1520 mm (40–60 in). More than half the people are Indians. There are also people of European, African and mixed descent. Agriculture employs 46 per cent of the people, contributing 21 per cent of the GDP. Industry accounts for 35 per cent, oil being the leading product. The Incas ruled the area from about 1470 until Spaniards conquered it in 1533. Independence was achieved in 1822 and Ecuador became a separate republic in 1830. Weak governments, armed rebellions and military coups have marred much of Ecuador's recent history. In 1979, however, elections were held and civilian rule was restored.

Area: 283,561 km^2 (109,489 sq mi); not including land disputed with Peru; **Population:** 8,893,000; **Capital:** Quito (pop 560,000); **Other cities:** Guayaquil (823,000); **Highest point:** Mt Chimborazo, 6272 m (20,577 ft); **Official language:** Spanish; **Religion:** Roman Catholicism; **Adult literacy rate:** 74 per cent; **Average life expectancy at birth:** 60 years; **Unit of currency:** Sucre; **Main exports:** oil, bananas, cocoa, coffee; **Per capita GNP:** US$1050.

EGYPT, an Arab Republic in north-eastern Africa. The fertile, irrigated Nile valley contains 99 per cent of the population, although it covers less than 4 per cent of the country. The Nile flows about 1200 km (746 mi) through Egypt. Near the Mediterranean Sea it divides into two branches, the Dumyat (Damietta) and Rashid (Rosetta), which enclose the triangular delta. The rest of Egypt is desert. The western (Libyan) desert contains several large oases and depressions, notably the Qattara depression, which is 133 m (436 ft) below sea level. The eastern, or Arabian, desert rises to highlands that border the Red Sea. But the highest peak, Jabal Katrinah, is in the Sinai peninsula, east of the Suez Canal. This international waterway, opened in 1869, is 173 km (107 mi) long, linking the Mediterranean and Red seas. Average temperatures in Egypt vary between 27°C and 32°C (81°–90°F) in summer and 13°–21°C (55°–70°F) in winter. The average annual rainfall is about 200 mm (8 in) in the far north and barely 25 mm (1 in) in the south. Most Egyptians are Arabs, but there are Berber, Nubian and Sudanese minorities. Egypt is a poor country, although it is the 2nd most industrialized in Africa. About 45 per cent of the population lives in urban areas and industry contributes 30 per cent of the GDP. Energy comes mainly from hydro-electric stations, especially at the Aswan High Dam. Manufactures include cement, chemicals, plastics, steel, sugar and textiles. Some phosphates, iron ore and oil are mined. Agriculture accounts for 29 per cent of the GDP, employing 51 per cent of the workforce. The chief export is cotton, but most farmers are peasants (*fellahin*) who practise subsistence farming. Tourism is important: over 1 million foreigners visited Egypt in 1979. Ancient Egypt's pyramids and other monuments are special attractions. Ancient Egypt's history is divided into 30 dynasties. The first began in 3100 BC, when Upper and Lower Egypt were united. It reached its peak under King Thutmose III (1490–36 BC). From 525 BC Egypt was mostly under foreign rule. In 30 BC it became part of the Roman empire and, in AD 395, it was the centre of

COUNTRIES OF THE WORLD

The pyramids of Egypt testify to the glories of one of the world's most important early civilizations. Today more than a million people visit Egypt every year to see the pyramids and other magnificent remains of ancient Egypt. The money they spend is a major source of foreign exchange. The camel of North Africa and South-West Asia is a leading work animal and a means of transport across the burning hot, arid wastes that fully justifies the animal's popular name, 'the ship of the desert'.

the Coptic Christian Church. Arabs occupied Egypt in 639–642, introducing Islam and Arabic. In 1517 Egypt became part of the Ottoman empire, but it came under French rule in 1798–1801. In 1881 Britain occupied Egypt and made it a protectorate in 1914. In 1922 Egypt gained a degree of independence, becoming a monarchy. In 1948–49 Egypt fought alongside other Arabs against the creation of the state of Israel. Egypt became a republic in 1953 and, in 1956, nationalized the Suez Canal. Anglo-French and Israeli forces invaded Egypt, but they withdrew under UN and US pressure. Short Egyptian-Israeli wars occurred in 1967 and 1973. President Anwar as-Sadat initiated peace talks with Israel in 1977 and a Peace Treaty (opposed by most Arab nations) was signed in 1979. Sadat was assassinated in 1981.

Area: 1,001,449 km^2 (386,683 sq mi); **Population:** 43,611,000; **Capital:** Cairo (pop 5,715,000); **Other cities:** Alexandria (2,259,000), Giza (854,000); **Highest point:** Jabal Katrinah, 2637 m (8652 ft); **Official language:** Arabic; **Religions:** Islam (91 per cent), Coptic Christianity; **Adult literacy rate:** 44 per cent; **Average life expectancy at birth:** 54 years; **Unit of currency:** Egyptian pound; **Main exports:** cotton and cotton textiles, rice, fruit, vegetables; **Per capita GNP:** US$460.

EL SALVADOR, a densely populated republic in Central America, with a 270 km (168 mi) long coastline on the Pacific Ocean. The country is mountainous and the altitude modifies the tropical climate. San Salvador has an average temperature range of 24°–26°C (75°–79°F) and about 1800 mm (71 in) of rain per year. About 90 per cent of the population is of mixed European and Indian descent. Agriculture employs 52 per cent of the workforce, accounting for 29 per cent of the GDP; the main crops being.coffee and cotton. Industry (mostly manufacturing) contributes 21 per cent of the GDP. Spain conquered the area in 1526. Independence from Spain was achieved in 1821 and El Salvador became an independent republic in 1841. The country has suffered from political instability. A military coup occurred in 1979 and a bitter war began between the US-backed government and left-wing guerrillas.

Area: 21,041 km^2 (8124 sq mi); **Population:** 4,820,000; **Capital:** San Salvador (pop 682,000); **Highest point:** Mt Santa Ana, 2385 m (7825 ft); **Official language:** Spanish; **Religion:** Roman Catholicism; **Adult literacy rate:** 62 per cent; **Average life expectancy at birth:** 63 years; **Unit of currency:** Colón; **Main exports:** coffee, cotton; **Per capita GNP:** US$670.

EQUATORIAL GUINEA, a republic in west-central Africa, comprises Río Muni on the mainland and the islands of Bioko (formerly Fernando Póo) and Pagalu. The islands are volcanic; Río Muni contains hills and plateaux. The climate is equatorial. The Bantu Fang form the majority in Río Muni. Fang, Bubi (the original inhabitants) and Fernandinos (descendants of liberated slaves) live on the islands. Most people are farmers: coffee is the main crop. Spain took the territory in the 1840s. Independence was achieved in 1968. The first President Francisco Macías Nguema ruled with much brutality until he was deposed in 1979.

Area: 28,051 km^2 (10,831 sq mi); **Population:** 378,000; **Capital:** Malabo (pop 37,000); **Highest point:** Pico de Santa Isabel, 3007 m (9865 ft); **Official language:** Spanish; **Religions:** Roman Catholicism (88 per cent), traditional religions (8 per cent); **Average life expectancy at birth:** 43 years; **Unit of currency:** Ekuele; **Main exports:** cocoa, coffee, timber; **Per capita GNP:** US$330 (1976).

ETHIOPIA, a republic in north-eastern Africa. The highlands are divided into two blocks by the deep Rift Valley. Lowlands occur in the east near the Red Sea coast. The main river, the Blue Nile, flows from Lake Tana in the north. The lowlands are hot and arid, contrasting with the cooler, moister uplands. About 100 languages are spoken: most belong to the Cushitic, Semitic or Nilotic families. Cushites include the nomadic Galla, the largest single ethnic group. The Amhara, who form the ruling class, speak a Semitic language while Nilotic languages are spoken by Negroid people in the east. Agriculture employs 81 per cent of the population. It accounts for 54 per cent of the GDP. Coffee makes up about 75 per cent of the exports.

Finland is a tranquil, beautiful land of forests and lakes. The lakes occupy ice-scoured rock basins or depressions dammed by moraine deposited during the Pleistocene Ice Age. Forestry is a major industry. Paper, pulp and other timber products account for 40 per cent of Finland's export earnings. But heavy industry has increased greatly in recent years and, in consequence, the proportion of Finns who live in urban areas increased from 38 per cent in 1960 to 62 per cent in 1980.

Ethiopia is the home of an ancient monarchy which embraced Christianity in the 4th century AD. It never became a colony, although it was occupied by Italy in 1935–41. The monarchy was abolished in 1974 and the country was ruled by a left-wing military group. Aided by the USSR, government forces fought against secessionist forces in Eritrea in the east and against Somali-speaking people in the Ogaden in the south-east.

Area: 1,221,900 km² (471,804 sq mi); **Population:** 34,244,000; **Capital:** Addis Ababa (pop 1,104,000); **Other cities:** Asmara (353,000); **Highest point:** Ras Dashan, 4620 m (15,157 ft); **Official language:** Amharic; **Religions:** Orthodox (Coptic) Christianity (46 per cent), Islam (34 per cent), traditional beliefs (14 per cent); **Adult literacy rate:** 10 per cent; **Average life expectancy at birth:** 39 years; **Unit of currency:** Ethiopian dollar; **Main exports:** coffee, hides and skins, pulses; **Per capita GNP:** US$130.

FALKLAND ISLANDS, a British colony in the South Atlantic, about 480 km (298 mi) east of the Strait of Magellan. There are 200 islands but only two are sizeable. Sheep farming is the main occupation. France founded a settlement in 1764 followed by Britain in 1765. Spain took over in 1770. From the early 19th century, independent Argentina claimed the islands which became a British Crown Colony in 1832. In 1982 Argentine forces occupied the islands and Britain sent a task force to recover the territory.

Area: 12,173 km² (4700 sq mi); **Population:** 1776 (1979).

FIJI, a nation in the south-central Pacific. Two mountainous, volcanic islands, Viti Levu and Vanua Levu, make up 87 per cent of the total area, although there are 320 other small islands. About 48 per cent of the people are Indians (mainly Hindus); 44 per cent are Melanesians; there are also Europeans, Chinese and other Pacific islanders. Agriculture is the main activity and tourism is important. Discovered in 1643, the islands became a British colony in 1874 and an independent nation within the Commonwealth in 1970.

Area: 18,274 km² (7056 sq mi); **Population:** 656,000; **Capital:** Suva (pop 64,000); **Main exports:** sugar, coconut oil; **Per capita GNP:** US$1690.

FINLAND, a republic in north-eastern Europe. It contains 55,000 or so lakes that fill hollows created during the Ice Age; water covers 9 per cent of the country. Much of Lapland in the north is within the Arctic Circle. Winters are long and severe, but the short summers are warm. Forests cover more than four-fifths of the country and timber has been the mainstay of the economy. About 62 per cent of the people live in urban areas and industry contributes 35 per cent of the GDP, as opposed to 8 per cent from agriculture, which is mostly confined to the far south. In the past Sweden and Russia have struggled for control of the Baltic Sea region. Russia occupied Finland in 1809 but Finland declared itself independent in 1917, becoming a republic in 1919. In 1939 the USSR declared war on Finland and Finland lost one-third of its territory. It allied itself to Germany but lost more land to the USSR after World War II. Finland signed peace treaties with the USSR in 1948, 1955 and 1970.

Area: 337,009 km² (130,127 sq mi); **Population:** 4,829,000; **Capital:** Helsinki (pop with suburbs, 893,000); **Other cities:** Tampere (243,000), Turku (240,000); **Highest point:** 1328 m (4357 ft); **Official languages:** Finnish, Swedish; **Religion:** Lutheran National Church (90 per cent); **Adult literacy rate:** 100 per cent; **Average life expectancy at birth:** 72 years; **Unit of currency:** Markka; **Main exports:** paper and paperboard, machinery and transport equipment, wood and wood pulp; **Per capita GNP:** US$8260.

FRANCE, the 2nd largest nation in Europe after the USSR. Mountain ranges (the French Alps which contain France's highest peak, Mont Blanc, and the lower Jura Mts) form the south-eastern border. The Vosges Mts are in the north-east, overlooking the Rhine rift valley and the scenic Massif Central, which rises to 1886 m (6188 ft), is in south-central France. This latter region contains the headwaters of the Dordogne, Garonne,

Top left: France contains many magnificent medieval churches, including the 12th-13th-century cathedral at Chartres. Top right: Vineyards are a common sight in France, which leads the world in producing top-quality wine. Above: Superb châteaux adorn many rural areas in France.

Loire and Seine rivers. The north-west peninsula, including Brittany, is lower but also scenic, with a superb indented coastline. The Paris basin is a saucer-shaped depression enclosed by rings of hills with outward facing scarps. The Aquitaine basin in the south-west is a low plain, partly fringed by coastal sand dunes. It extends to the high Pyrenees along the border with Spain. The Rhône-Saône valley, in the south-east between the Massif Central and the south-eastern mountains, ends in the marshy Camargue. The climate varies from the moist, temperate north to the Mediterranean coastlands, with their hot, dry summers and mild, moist winters. The climate also changes from west to east. The west has a maritime temperate climate moderated by the North Atlantic Drift, but to the east it becomes increasingly continental, with colder winters especially in upland regions. Rain falls all the year round except for the Mediterranean region. Several minority languages are spoken: Breton, a Celtic tongue, in Brittany; Basque in the western Pyrenees; Catalan in the eastern Pyrenees; Provençal in the south-east; and German in the north-east. Foreign-born people, including Portuguese, Algerians, Spaniards and Italians, make up about 6½ per cent of the population. Some 78 per cent of the population lives in urban areas; industry and services accounted for 37 per cent and 51 per cent of the GDP respectively in 1978. The chief mineral resource is iron ore, notably in Lorraine. Some coal, oil and natural gas are mined, but France imports much coal from West Germany. Energy also comes from hydro-electric stations and the River Rance tidal power station in Brittany. There is a wide range of manufacturing industries. Paris is known especially for its luxury and fashion products; Lyons is known for textiles; Marseilles and Bordeaux are major industrial ports; and Lille, on the north-western coalfield, is centre of a large industrial region. Farming is also important. In 1978 it contributed 5 per cent of the GDP (as against 10 per cent in 1960), employing 9 per cent of the workforce (22 per cent in 1960). Despite this trend away from the land, the proportion of farm workers in France is three times that in West Germany and the UK. The leading farming regions are the Paris basin, the Loire valley, the Aquitaine basin and the Rhône-Saône valley. Arable land covers 32 per cent of the country, pasture 24 per cent, vineyards 2 per cent, and forests 26 per cent. Agricultural yields per hectare tend to be low, because a high proportion of the farms are small and unmechanized, but France is a leading producer of wheat, barley, oats, flax and sugar beet. Livestock, including dairy cattle, are extremely important; in 1979 there were 23.5 million cattle, 11.5 million sheep and 11.7 million pigs. France is famous for its quality wines and cheeses, which are associated with particular regions. The fishing industry employs 28,000 fishermen. The tourist industry, a major source of foreign earnings, employs about half a million people. West Germany is France's leading trading partner; the EEC as a whole accounts for more than half of France's trade. The Romans conquered France (then called Gaul) in the 50s BC and imposed on it a common language and government. Roman rule declined because of attacks by Germanic tribes. In AD 486 the Frankish realm (as France was called) became independent under a Christian king, Clovis. Charlemagne, who became king in 768, extended the Frankish realm and, in 800, he was crowned Emperor of the West by the Pope. In 843, however, his empire was divided into three, with France coming under Charles the Bald. France contracted in size and, after the Norman invasion of Britain

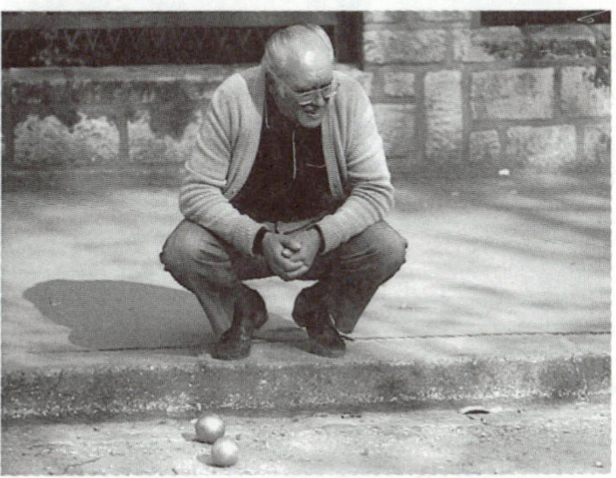

Boules, *or bowls, is a popular game in France. It can be played on any piece of land and does not require carefully prepared lawns.*

in 1066, large areas came under English rule. Following the French victory by Joan of Arc at Orléans in 1429, English rule in France was finally ended in 1453. A powerful monarchy was established, but in 1792 the 1st Republic was set up, a consequence of the French Revolution of 1789. In 1799 Napoleon Bonaparte took power. After a period of brilliant military exploits, which took him as far as Moscow, he was finally defeated in 1815. The monarchy was restored until 1848 when the short-lived 2nd Republic was established by a revolution. In 1852 Napoleon's nephew Napoleon III became monarch. The 3rd Republic began in 1875. In the 20th century France suffered greatly during World Wars I and II. In 1946 a new Constitution established the 4th Republic. But economic recovery was delayed by costly colonial wars and political instability, although France sponsored the successful European Coal and Steel Community (founded in 1952) and was a founder member of the EEC in 1957. In 1958 Charles de Gaulle was elected President. He introduced a new Constitution, extending the President's powers and establishing the 5th Republic. Under stable right-wing governments, France made rapid economic progress. In 1981 the French socialist leader François Mitterrand was elected President and his Socialist Party gained majorities in parliament, which consists of two houses: the 305-member Senate and the 491-member National Assembly.

Area: 547,026 km² (211,219 sq mi); **Population:** 54,414,000; **Capital:** Paris (pop with suburbs, 8,550,000); **Other cities:** Lyons (1,171,000), Marseilles (1,071,000), Lille (936,000), Bordeaux (612,000), Toulouse (510,000), Nantes (454,000), Nice (438,000); **Highest point:** Mt Blanc, 4810 m (15,781 ft); **Official language:** French; **Religions:** Roman Catholicism, Islam (about 2 million people in 1978); Protestantism (about 750,000 people); **Adult literacy rate:** 99 per cent; **Average life expectancy at birth:** 73 years; **Unit of currency:** Franc; **Main exports:** cars, chemical products, iron and steel, textiles and leather goods, electrical equipment, wine, cereals; **Per capita GNP:** US$9940.

FRENCH GUIANA, a French Overseas Department on the Atlantic Ocean in north-eastern South America. Most of the land is low-lying with uplands in the south. Average temperatures are between 29°C and 32°C (84°–90°F) all the year round. Cayenne has an average annual rainfall of 3560 mm (140 in); parts of the interior are even rainier. Dense forest covers 88 per cent of the land. Most people are Creoles; pure Indians make up 11 per cent of the population. Cultivated land covers only 6000 ha. Bananas, maize, manioc and rice are the main crops. Shrimp fishing is important, but the main prospect is the bauxite deposits that have been discovered recently. The territory came under French control by the mid-17th century. The French set up convict settlements – Devil's Island was the best known. These were all closed by 1945 and Guiana became a department of France in 1946.

Area: 91,000 km² (35,137 sq mi); **Population:** 76,000; **Capital:** Cayenne (pop 36,000); **Per capita GNP:** US$2580.

FRENCH POLYNESIA, a French Overseas Territory in the eastern Pacific Ocean. There are about 130 tropical islands scattered across 4 million km² (1.5 million sq mi). The island groups are: the *Windward Islands*, including Tahiti and Moorea, capital Papeete; the *Leeward Islands* which, with the Windward Is, are often called the Society Islands, main town Uturoa; the *Tuamotu Archipelago*, comprising 78 atolls; the *Gambier Islands*, chief town Rikitea; the *Austral* (*Tubuai*) *Islands*, chief town Mataura; and the *Marquesas Islands*. Tourism is the main industry and copra the leading product. The islands have been French protectorates since 1843. They were given the status of an Overseas Territory in 1958.

Area 4000 km² (1544 sq mi); **Population:** 166,000; **Capital:** Papeete; **Per capita GNP:** US$6350.

GABON, a republic on the equator in west-central Africa. Behind the coastal plain are plateaux and mountains. Most of Gabon is in the River Ogooué drainage basin. Average annual temperatures are between 26°C and 28°C (79°–82°F). The average annual rainfall varies from 1500 mm (59 in) in the south-west to 4000 mm (157 in) in the north-west. Rain forests cover 75 per cent of the land. About 40 languages are spoken: the Bantu-speaking Fang form the largest ethnic group; a few pygmies form the smallest. About 70 per cent of the population is engaged in agriculture, the chief cash crops being cocoa, coffee, palm oil and bananas. But the main wealth of Gabon, which has the 2nd highest per capita GNP in Africa, comes from oil and natural gas, manganese and uranium. France established a settlement on the coast in 1843 and founded Libreville for free slaves in 1849. Gabon became a French colony in the 1880s and an independent republic in 1980. Many people visit Gabon to see the Nobel prize winner Dr Schweitzer's mission hospital at Lambaréné, which was founded in 1910.

Area: 267,667 km² (103,352 sq mi); **Population:** 667,000; **Capital:** Libreville (pop 251,000); **Highest point:** Mt Iboundji, 1580 m (5184 ft); **Official language:** French; **Religions:** Roman Catholicism (60 per cent), Protestantism and local Christian sects (29 per cent), traditional beliefs (10 per cent), Islam (1 per cent); **Adult literacy rate:** 30 per cent; **Unit of currency:** Franc CFA; **Main exports:** oil, manganese, uranium and thorium, timber; **Per capita GNP:** US$3280.

GAMBIA, in West Africa, is the smallest nation in mainland Africa. It is a narrow strip of land bordering the Gambia River, being entirely enclosed by Senegal except along its short Atlantic coast. The climate is tropical, with an average annual temperature of 27°C (81°F) and an average annual rainfall of 750–1140 mm (30–45 in). Wooded savanna covers much of the land. The largest of the 5 main ethnic groups are the Mandingo and the Fulbe (or Fulani). About 85 per cent of the population is engaged in agriculture, which accounts for 60 per cent of the GDP. The only major cash crop is groundnuts; they usually make up over 90 per cent of the exports. Tourism is expanding rapidly. Gambia became a British colony in 1888. Full independence was achieved in 1965 and Gambia became a republic in 1970. Attempts to merge Gambia and Senegal failed until 1981 when Senegalese troops helped to put down a coup in Gambia. Following the coup, Gambia and Senegal set up a confederation called Senegambia, which came into effect in 1982, although both countries retained their sovereignty.

Area: 11,295 km² (4361 sq mi); **Population:** 642,000; **Capital:** Banjul (pop 39,000); **Official language:** English; **Religions:** Islam (80 per cent), Christianity, traditional beliefs; **Adult literacy rate:** 35 per cent; **Average life expectancy at birth:** 41 years; **Unit of currency:** Dalasi; **Main exports:** groundnuts, groundnut products; **Per capita GNP:** US$260.

GERMANY, EAST, officially the German Democratic Republic. The Baltic sea coast is fringed by sand bars and lagoons. The north is part of the North European Plain, which is largely covered by moraine, including hills of boulder clay, between which there are many lakes and marshes, and vast areas of glacial sands, many of which are heathlands. Soil fertility is generally low. The south, which is more fertile, contains low plateaux and mountains, including the Harz Mountains and the Thüringer Wald in the south-west and the Erzgebirge in the south-east. The main rivers are the Elbe which flows into West Germany, and the Oder-Neisse rivers which form the frontier with Poland. Most river valleys run from south-east to north-west. They are wide and shallow, having been formed by melt waters from receding glaciers at the end of the Ice Age. The climate is continental, with an average annual range of −1°C (30°F) in winter to 19°C (66°F) in summer. Rainfall varies between 530 and 640 mm (21–25 in). About 77 per cent of the population lives in urban areas, industry and services accounting for 69 per cent and 21 per cent of the GDP respectively in 1978. East Germany is the world's top producer of lignite and has large deposits of potash. It also mines copper, iron ore, nickel, tin and uranium, but many metals are imported. Before World War II, East Germany's economy was primarily agricultural. After 1945 the USSR encouraged the setting up of manufacturing industries and East Germany is now one of the world's top 10 industrial powers. Most factories are government-owned. About one-third of the output comes from engineering industries. Consumer goods, precision and optical goods, chemicals, textiles and plastics are all important. The main industrial centres are the Dresden, Erfurt, Gera, Halle, Karl-Marx-Stadt and Leipzig districts in the south and the area around Berlin. Agriculture accounted for 10 per cent of the GDP in 1978, employing 10 per cent of the workforce. Arable land covers 44 per cent of the area, pasture 11 per cent and forests 27 per cent. The north contains large state and collective farms (once privately owned), but the most fertile land is in the centre and south. Barley, oats, potatoes, rye, sugar beet and wheat are leading crops. In 1979 there were 5.6 million cattle, 12.1 million pigs and 2 million

Leipzig, East Germany's second largest city, is a major industrial, commercial and cultural centre. It is about 150 km (93 miles) south-south-west of Berlin. Leipzig is also known for its industrial fairs, and its old buildings and cultural life have recently been attracting many tourists.

Above: The Brandenburg Gate stands in East Berlin, just behind the wall that separates the capital of Communist East Germany from West Berlin. Above right: The Rhine valley in West Germany is a vital artery of trade. Much of the valley is adorned by castles and pretty villages.

sheep. In 1945 Germany was partitioned and East Germany, including East Berlin, corresponds to the former Soviet Occupation Zone. After World War II, the country's population was swollen by German-speaking refugees from Poland and Czechoslovakia. Discontent with the Soviet-controlled Communist government, which led to riots in East Berlin in 1953, caused many refugees and East Germans to migrate to West Germany. By 1961, after nearly 3 million people had emigrated, the government built the Berlin Wall. In 1972 tensions were eased when a treaty was signed establishing diplomatic relations between West and East Germany. This led to the admission of both Germanies to the UN in 1973. Effective power in East Germany is vested in the Socialist Unity Party.

Area: 108,178 km^2 (41,770 sq mi); **Population:** 16,748,000; **Capital:** East Berlin (pop 1,134,000); **Other cities:** Leipzig (564,000), Dresden (515,000), Karl-Marx-Stadt (315,000), Magdeburg (284,000); **Highest point:** Brocken, 1142 m (3747 ft); **Official language:** German; **Religion:** Protestantism, Roman Catholicism; **Average life expectancy at birth:** 72 years; **Unit of currency:** Mark; **Main exports:** engineering goods, precision instruments, optical equipment, chemicals; **Per capita GNP:** US$6430.

GERMANY, WEST, officially the Federal Republic of Germany. The coasts on the Baltic and North seas are fringed by sandy islands and dunes. The northern plains, drained by the Elbe, Weser and Ems rivers, are largely covered by moraine deposited during the Ice Age. Generally infertile, the natural vegetation is moorland and heath, as on the Lüneburg Heath, but large areas have been cleared for farming. Central Germany contains hills, plateaux and low block mountains. The northern foothills are a fertile loess belt, but the leading region is the industrial Ruhr valley, with its rich coalfield. South-western Germany, the chief farm region, includes *horsts* (block mountains) that border the Rhine rift valley, which extends more than 300 km (186 mi) from Basle to Bingen. The horsts include the Black Forest and the Odenwald. The south-east is an upland zone which includes the scenic Bavarian Alps in the far south, where the highest peak, the Zugspitze, is situated. The Danube, which rises in the Black Forest, is Europe's 2nd longest river after the Volga in the USSR. It drains much of the south-east. Average annual temperatures range from 0°C to 16°C (32°–61°F) in the north. The centre and south have slightly warmer summers (the Rhine rift valley is the warmest place) and colder winters; for instance, Munich in the south-east has average annual temperatures between −2°C and 18°C (28°–64°F). Rainfall varies between 510 and 1020 mm (20–40 in) per year. West Germany's population was reduced by about 7 million in World War II but it now has half as many people again as it had in 1939. This was not the consequence of natural population increase (which averaged 0.1 per cent per year in 1970–78) but rather of immigration. After World War II millions of refugees from East Germany and eastern Europe flooded in; nearly 25 per cent of West Germans today are former refugees. Also in recent years, many immigrants, or 'guest workers', from Turkey, Yugoslavia, Italy and other places have found jobs in the country: there were 1.9 million such workers in West Germany in 1979. West Germany is a highly industrialized nation, having achieved an 'economic miracle' since 1945. In 1978 industry accounted for 48 per cent of the GDP, agriculture 3 per cent, and services 49 per cent. In 1980 85 per cent of the people lived in urban areas. The largest city, West Berlin, is an enclave in East Germany. Hamburg and Bremen are the chief seaports, but the river port of Duisburg, at the confluence of the Ruhr and Rhine, has a greater annual tonnage of shipping than Hamburg. The ships ply to Rotterdam in the Netherlands which handles a substantial part of German trade. West Germany is the world's 8th largest coal-producer (the main coalfields being the Ruhr, Aachen and Saar), the 3rd largest producer of lignite and it also produces some iron ore, potash, salt, metal ores and oil. Lignite is used in the chemical industry, as is imported petroleum which has enabled industrial development in such cities as Munich and Nuremberg, far from any coalfield. Chemical and iron and steel industries underpin the economy. Other major industries include electrical engineering, machinery, textiles and vehicles. Agriculture employed only 4 per cent of the workforce in 1978 (as opposed to 14 per cent in 1960). But farming remains important, although food is imported. Arable land covers 29.3 per cent of the country, pasture 19.3 per cent, and orchards and vineyards 0.9 per cent. The main crops in the north are potatoes and rye. In the central uplands and south-west, crops include fruits, grapes (for wine), hops, tobacco, sugar beet and wheat. The south-east is mainly pastoral. In 1979 there were 15 million cattle: dairy products are especially important. The EEC accounts for nearly half of the external trade. Between the 4th and 6th centuries AD, German tribes conquered the western provinces of the Roman Empire. The Frankish ruler Charlemagne, who became Emperor of the West in 800, united German tribes into a *Reich* (empire) but it divided into a loose federation of principalities in the 9th century. In the 12th century, German territory was extended to Prussia but, by the 15th century, the country was again disunited. Martin Luther launched the Reformation in 1517, splitting Germany along religious lines. In 1618 religious conflict sparked off the 30 Years' War which ravaged Germany. At the end of the war, however, the combined electorate of Brandenburg and the Duchy of Prussia emerged as a strong Protestant state: its ruler Frederick took the title 'King of Prussia' in 1701. Prussia became a major European state and its troops played a major part in the defeat of Napoleon at Waterloo in 1815. In the following Congress of Vienna, Prussian territory was extended. German nationalism developed and in the 1860s Prince Otto von Bismarck placed Prussia at the head of the movement for German unity. Following victory in the Franco-Prussian War (1870–71), a 2nd Reich was set up with the Prussian king becoming *Kaiser* (emperor). After World War I, a republic was established. Adolf Hitler became Chancellor in 1933 inaugurating the 3rd Reich. In 1945 Germany was divided into 4 military zones, governed by the Americans, British, French and Russians. Berlin was also partitioned into 4 zones. By 1948 the American, British and French zones had amalgamated. But the Russians kept control of their zone and East Berlin. In 1949 West Germany became a federal republic and East Germany a people's democracy. A treaty between the two Germanies (1972) lessened tension and paved the way for their entry into the UN.

Area: 248,577 km² (95,981 sq mi); **Population:** 61,392,000; **Capital:** Bonn (pop 286,000); **Other cities:** West Berlin (1,902,000); Hamburg (1,653,000), Munich (1,300,000), Cologne (976,000), Essen (653,000), Frankfurt am Main (628,000), Dortmund (610,000), Düsseldorf (595,000), Stuttgart (582,000), Duisburg (559,000), Bremen (556,000), Hanover (536,000); **Highest point:** Zugspitze, 2968 m (9738 ft); **Official language:** German; **Religions:** Protestantism (49 per cent), Roman Catholicism (45 per cent); **Adult literacy rate:** 99 per cent; **Average life expectancy at birth:** 72 years; **Unit of currency:** Mark; **Main exports:** finished and semi-finished manufactures, chemicals, coke, consumer products; **Per capita GNP:** US$11,730.

GHANA, a republic in West Africa. It is mostly low-lying and contains the man-made Lake Volta, area, 8482 km² (3275 sq mi). The most fertile region is in the hilly south-west. The only highlands are in the south-east. The average annual temperature is 26°C (79°F) in the south and 28°C (82°F) in the north. The south-west has more than 2000 mm (79 in) of rain per year, the south-east has 730 mm (29 in), and the north 1080 mm (43 in). The people are Negroid: about 100 languages and dialects are spoken. Agriculture employs 54 per cent of the workforce, contributing 38 per cent of the GDP. The main crop and export is cocoa. Bauxite, diamonds, gold and manganese are mined, but manufacturing is small-scale. Portuguese mariners reached Ghana in 1471. The coast became a British colony in 1875 but the Ashanti prevented colonization of the interior until 1901. Independence was achieved in 1957 and Ghana became a republic in 1960. From 1966 to 1979 military and civilian regimes alternated. A new Constitution in 1979 led to the election of a civilian government, but this was overthrown in December 1981.

Area: 238,537 km² (92,105 sq mi); **Population:** 12,413,000; **Capital:** Accra (pop with suburbs, 738,000); **Highest point:** Mt Afadjato, 885 m (2904 ft); **Official language:** English; **Religions:** Christianity, traditional beliefs, Islam; **Adult literacy rate:** 30 per cent; **Average life expectancy at birth:** 48 years; **Unit of currency:** Cedi; **Main exports:** cocoa, timber, gold; **Per capita GNP:** US$400.

GIBRALTAR, a British fortress occupying a rocky peninsula in southern Spain. The climate is Mediterranean in type. Most people are of British, Genoese, Portuguese, Maltese or Spanish descent. English and Spanish are spoken. There is no agriculture or mining. Most people work in the ship repair depot, the NATO bases or in tourism. Gibraltar became a British colony in 1713. Spain has demanded its return but nearly all Gibraltarians voted in 1967 to retain the British connection.

Area: 6½ km² (2½ sq mi); **Population:** 31,000; **GNP per capita:** US$4320.

GREECE, a republic in south-eastern Europe. It contains the southern part of the mountainous and deeply indented Balkan peninsula and many islands. The southern Peloponnesus is linked to the north by the narrow Isthmus of Corinth. The 6.4 km (4 mi) long Corinth Canal cuts through the Isthmus, connecting the Gulf of Corinth to the Saronic Gulf. The northern part of the peninsula contains the Pindus Mts and Greece's highest peak, Mt Olympus. It also includes the Plain of Thessaly, the largest lowland apart from the coastal plains of Macedonia and Thrace in the north-east. Islands make up 20 per cent of the area of Greece. The Cyclades are 220 islands east of the Peloponnesus in the Aegean Sea. The South Sporades (or Dodecanese), including Rhodes, are Aegean islands nearer to Turkey than Greece. The North Sporades are north-east of Euboea. The Ionian Islands, including Corfu, lie off the west coast. In the south, the largest island, Crete, covers 8331 km^2 (3217 sq mi). The climate is Mediterranean, with hot, arid summers and mild, moist winters, but winters are severe in the mountains. Until recently most Greeks lived in tiny farming communities. But today 62 per cent of the population lives in urban areas, as opposed to 43 per cent in 1960. Industry now accounts for 31 per cent of the GDP compared with 17 per cent from agriculture. Mining is not important but Greece has many processing industries and manufactures are now the leading exports. Only one-third of the land is cultivable. Citrus fruits, grapes, olives, tobacco and wheat are major crops. In 1979 there were 8 million sheep, 4 million goats and nearly 1 million cattle. In 1978 5 million tourists visited Greece, providing much foreign exchange. The merchant navy, one of the world's largest, is another money-earner. Thousands of Greeks emigrate every year, finding work especially in Australia, West Germany and the US. Crete was the centre of the first Greek civilization (the Minoan) between about 3000 and 1400 BC. On the mainland, the Mycenean period (1580–1100 BC) ended when Dorians invaded the peninsula from the north. In about 750 BC the Greeks began to colonize the Mediterranean and trade brought wealth to Greece. Athens reached its peak in 461–431 BC but, in 338 BC, Macedonia became the dominant power. In 334–331 BC Alexander the Great conquered South-west Asia. In 146 BC Greece became a Roman province and, in AD 365, it became part of the East Roman (Byzantine) Empire, which collapsed when the Turks took Constantinople (Istanbul) in 1453. The Greeks rebelled against Turkey in the 1820s and became an independent monarchy in 1830. After World War II, when Greece was occupied by Germany, a civil war raged between communist and nationalist forces until 1949. From 1967 Greece was a military dictatorship. This regime collapsed in 1974 when it failed to stop the Turkish invasion of northern Cyprus. Democracy was restored and Greece became a republic. Greece joined the EEC in 1981.

Area: 131,944 km^2 (50,947 sq mi); **Population:** 9,665,000; **Capital:** Athens (pop with suburbs, 2,540,000); **Other cities:** Salonika (346,000); **Highest point:** Mt Olympus, 2917 m (9570 ft); **Official language:** Greek; **Religion:** Eastern Orthodox Christianity (98 per cent). **Adult literacy rate:** 88 per cent (1972 est); **Average life expectancy at birth:** 73 years, **Unit of currency:** Drachma; **Main exports:** manufactured goods, food and live animals, raw materials, beverages and tobacco, chemicals; **Per capita GNP:** US$3890.

GREENLAND, a self-governing Danish county. It is the world's largest island and contains the world's 2nd largest ice sheet: only 341,700 km^2 (131,938 sq mi), or 16 per cent of the land, is ice-free. The main industry is fishing. Vikings founded a colony in Greenland in about AD 960 but it disappeared about 500 years later. Greenland became a Danish colony in 1721 and a Danish county in 1953. A 21-member parliament was elected in 1979.

Area: 2,175,600 km^2 (840,050 sq mi); **Population:** 50,000; **Capital:** Godthaab (pop 9000); **Per capita GNP:** US$7990.

GRENADA, a West Indian nation, the southernmost in the Windward Islands. The land is mountainous and largely forested. Temperatures remain around 27°C (81°F) throughout the year. Descendants of African slaves form the largest ethnic group. Most of the rest are of mixed black and European descent. The main exports are cocoa, nutmegs and bananas. Tourism is becoming important. Columbus discovered the island in 1498. In 1674–1763 it was a French colony. Thereafter, except for a period of French rule in 1779–83, it was ruled by Britain. It became a British Associated State in 1967 and a fully independent monarchy in the Commonwealth in 1974.

The skyline of Athens, capital of Greece, is dominated by the Acropolis, a rocky hill on which the ruins of the Parthenon and other ancient temples testify to 'the glory that was Greece'.

Greenland is thinly populated and ice sheets cover more than four-fifths of its area. Fishing is the leading industry and tiny fishing villages are scattered along its fiord-strewn coasts.

Area: 344 km^2 (133 sq mi); **Population:** 113,000; **Capital:** St George's (pop 30,000); **Official language:** English; **Per capita GNP:** US$630.

GUADELOUPE, a French Overseas Department in the Lesser Antilles. There are two main islands, Basse-Terre (or Guadeloupe) and Grande-Terre, and five small ones. Mt Soufriére, a volcano on Basse-Terre, is 1467 m (4813 ft) high. Temperatures exceed 24°C (75°F) for most of the time and the rainfall is more than 2000 mm (79 in) per year. Most people are of mixed African, Asian and French descent. Bananas and sugar are the main crops. Columbus discovered the islands in 1493. France colonized them in 1635 but had to fight off British attacks and put down a slave revolt in 1703. Slavery was abolished in 1848. Guadeloupe became a French Overseas Department in 1946.

Area: 1779 km^2 (687 sq mi); **Population:** 332,000; **Capital:** Basse-Terre (pop 15,000); **Per capita GNP:** US$3260.

GUAM, an 'unincorporated territory' of the United States in the Marianas Archipelago in the North Pacific Ocean. There are volcanic mountains in the south of the island and coral reefs in the north. The climate is tropical and crops include bananas, cassava, citrus fruits, coconuts, maize, sugar-cane, sweet potatoes and taro. Fishing is important and tourism is developing. Many people are Chamorros, of mixed Indonesian and Spanish descent. Spain ceded Guam to the US in 1898. The island was occupied by Japan in 1941–44. Full US citizenship for Guam's people was conferred in 1950.

Area: 549 km^2 (212 sq mi); **Population:** 99,000; **Capital:** Agaña; **Per capita GNP:** US$7830.

GUATEMALA, a Central American republic. Coastal lowlands face the Pacific Ocean in the south-west; a central highland region with 27 volcanoes, some active, is in the earthquake-prone centre; a low forested plain covers the north; and there is a short Caribbean coastline. The altitude modifies the climate. The capital, at about 1500 m (4291 ft), has average temperatures between 16°C and 20°C (61°–68°F) and 1320 mm (52 in) of rain per year. The lowlands are hotter and generally wetter. More than 50 per cent of the people are Indians; most of the rest are mixed European and Indian origin. In 1978 57 per cent of the people were farmers, mainly in the highlands. Coffee is the main crop. Mining is becoming important, especially for nickel. Spain conquered the area in the 1520s. Guatemala became independent in 1821 but attempts to form a Central American Federation failed and Guatemala became an independent republic in 1839. Dictatorships and violence have marred its modern history. In the 1970s Guatemala came into conflict with Britain over its claims on Belize, which was a British territory until 1981.

Area: 108,889 km^2 (42,045 sq mi); **Population:** 7,436,000; **Capital:** Guatemala City (pop 1,500,000); **Highest point:** Tajumulco, 4220 m (13,845 ft); **Official language:** Spanish; **Religion:** Roman Catholicism; **Adult literacy rate:** 47 per cent; **Average life expectancy at birth:** 57 years; **Unit of currency:** Quetzal; **Main exports:** coffee, cotton, bananas, beef; **Per capita GNP:** US$1020.

GUINEA, a West African republic. Behind the Atlantic coastal plain is the Fouta Djallon plateau, where the Gambia, Niger and Senegal rivers rise. The north-east contains the Upper Niger plains, while the south-east is mountainous, rising to Mt Nimba on the border. Guinea has a tropical monsoon climate and savanna covers most areas. Most people are Negroes and a large number of tribal languages are spoken. In 1978 82 per cent of the population was engaged in agriculture, which accounted for 32 per cent of the GDP. Industry accounted for 41 per cent of the GDP in 1978. The leading industry is bauxite mining: Guinea is the world's 2nd largest producer. France annexed part of Guinea in 1849 and gradually extended its rule. In 1958 the people of Guinea voted for independence. France withdrew its personnel and equipment rapidly and chaos was prevented only with Ghanaian and Soviet aid. Guinea adopted socialist policies and a one-party system of government. Despite attempted coups, Guinea's first president, Sékou Touré, survived into the 1980s. But most people remain poor.

Area: 245,957 km^2 (94,970 sq mi); **Population:** 5,741,000; **Capital:** Conakry (pop 526,000); **Highest point:** Mt Nimba, 1752 m (5748 ft); **Official language:** French; **Religions:** Islam (70 per cent), traditional beliefs, Christianity; **Adult literacy rate:** 10 per cent (1970); **Average life expectancy at birth:** 43 years; **Unit of currency:** Syli; **Main exports:** bauxite and aluminium, palm kernels, pineapples, coffee; **Per capita GNP:** US$270.

GUINEA-BISSAU, a West African republic. The land is mostly low-lying, with a broad coastal plain and flat offshore islands. It has a tropical monsoon climate. Most people are Negroes belonging to various tribal groups. There is a small mestiço (mulatto) community of Guinean and Cape Verdean descent. It has played an important part in the government. Most people are subsistence farmers, although arable land covers only 12 per cent of the country. The main food crop is rice; the main cash crop is groundnuts. There is no mining and little manufacturing. Portuguese explorers first sighted the coast in 1446. In 1836–79 Portugal ruled the country jointly with the Cape Verde Islands, establishing close ties that were to continue. A long guerrilla war began in 1963, led by Guineans and Cape Verdeans. Guinea-Bissau became independent in 1974, followed by Cape Verde in 1975, although no fighting had occurred on the islands. Guinea-Bissau became a one-party socialist state. A military coup in 1980 caused a deterioration in relations with Cape Verde, with which Guinea-Bissau had hoped to amalgamate.

Area: 36,125 km^2 (13,949 sq mi); **Population:** 817,000; **Capital:** Bissau (pop 109,000); **Official language:** Portuguese; **Religions:** Islam, traditional beliefs, Christianity; **Adult literacy rate:** 25 per cent; **Average life expectancy at birth:** 39

years; **Unit of currency:** Escudo; **Main exports:** groundnuts, fish; **Per capita GNP:** US$170.

GUYANA, a republic in north-eastern South America. Behind the flat, cultivated coastal zone, which is about 48 km (30 mi) wide, the land rises to a hilly upland and then to the Guiana Highlands in the east and south. Forest covers 83 per cent of the land with grassland in the highest mountain areas. The main river is the Essequibo. The climate is tropical and the rainfall varies between 2290 mm (90 in) on the coast to 1470 mm (58 in) inland. Most people live in the coastal zone: 51 per cent are of Asian origin; 33 per cent are descendants of African slaves; about 10 per cent are of mixed origin; and 5 per cent are Indians who live mostly in the forested interior. Antagonism between the two main groups has been reflected in political life. Bauxite is the main resource and diamonds and gold are also mined. The chief cash crop is sugar and the main food crop is rice. The Dutch and British struggled for ascendancy in the 17th and 18th centuries. The territory was finally ceded to Britain in 1814. Independence was achieved in 1966. The 1980 Constitution provided for a 53-member National Assembly.

Area: 214,969 km² (83,005 sq mi); **Population:** 887,000; **Capital:** Georgetown (pop with suburbs, 183,000); **Highest point:** Mt Roraima, 2810 m (9219 ft); **Official language:** English; **Religions:** Christianity (over 50 per cent), Hinduism (33 per cent), Islam (10 per cent); **Unit of currency:** Guyanese dollar; **Main exports:** bauxite and alumina, sugar and byproducts, rice, timber; **Per capita GNP:** US$570.

HAITI, a republic in the western part of the West Indian island of Hispaniola. The interior consists of wooded mountains: the Massif du Nord, the Massif de la Selle (in the south-east), and the Massif de la Hotte (in the south-west), Most people live on the fertile plains which make up about one-fifth of the country. About 95 per cent of the population is of black African descent. The mulattoes who form 5 per cent make up a social elite. Most people are subsistence farmers. The chief cash crops are coffee and sugar. Haiti is the poorest nation in Latin America. Columbus discovered Hispaniola in 1492 and Spain became established in the east (now the Dominican Republic), while France took the west in 1697. Independence was proclaimed in 1804 after a successful slave revolt in the 1790s. Haiti had a disturbed history in 1843–1915 when 16 of its 20 rulers were either deposed or assassinated. The US occupied Haiti from 1915 to 1934. In 1957 François Duvalier became president, assuming dictatorial powers and maintaining his authority through voodoo and his *Tontons macoutes* (police). He died in 1971 and was succeeded by his son, Jean-Claude Duvalier.

Area: 27,750 km² (10,715 sq mi); **Population:** 5,220,000; **Capital:** Port-au-Prince (pop 507,000); **Highest point:** Pic La Selle, 2680 m (8793 ft); **Official language:** French; **Religions:** Roman Catholicism, Protestantism; **Adult literacy rate:** 23 per cent; **Average life expectancy at birth:** 51 years; **Unit of currency:** Gourde; **Main exports:** coffee, manufactures; **Per capita GNP:** US$260.

HONDURAS, a wedge-shaped Central American republic. It has a 720 km (447 mi) coastline on the Caribbean Sea and an outlet to the Pacific Ocean through the Gulf of Fonseca. Behind the hot and humid Caribbean coastal plain, there are mountains and high plateaux with a healthy climate. Most Hondurans are of mixed European and Indian origin. About 8 per cent are pure Indians and 2 per cent are Negroes. Honduras is Central America's poorest nation. In 1978 64 per cent of the people were engaged in agriculture, which accounted for 32 per cent of the GDP. Bananas and coffee are the main cash crops. Forests cover 45 per cent of the country and timber is exported. Some lead, zinc and silver are also exported and there are many, mostly small, manufacturing and processing industries. Spain ruled Honduras between 1525 and 1821. It became part of a Central American Federation but it withdrew in 1838. Independent Honduras suffered from autocratic rulers, internal violence and disputes with neighbouring countries. In recent years, military regimes have alternated with elected civilian governments.

Area: 112,088 km² (43,280 sq mi); **Population:** 3,941,000; **Capital:** Tegucigalpa (pop 445,000); **Highest point:** Cerros de Celaque, 2865 m (9400 ft); **Official language:** Spanish; **Religion:** Roman Catholicism; **Adult literacy rate:** 57 per cent; **Average life expectancy at birth:** 57 years; **Unit of currency:** Lempira; **Main exports:** bananas, coffee, meat, timber; **Per capita GNP:** US$530.

HONG KONG, a British colony on the south-eastern coast of China, consisting of 236 islands and an area on the mainland. Most of the land is rocky and hilly. The climate is tropical with heavy monsoon rains in May–September. Most people are Chinese; some are refugees from Communist China. There is little farmland in this densely populated colony (90 per cent of the population lives in urban areas) and much food is imported although every possible piece of land is farmed. Fishing is also important (many people live on boats), but the economy is based on manufacturing and entrepôt trade. A great variety of light manufactures are exported to Western nations, bringing much wealth to Hong Kong. Hong Kong Island was ceded to Britain in 1842. Kowloon peninsula and Stonecutters Island were added in 1860 and the New Territories, comprising numerous islands and an area on the mainland, were obtained from China in 1898.

Area: 1045 km² (403 sq mi); **Population:** 4,957,000; **Capital:** Victoria (pop 767,000); **Adult literacy rate:** 90 per cent; **Average life expectancy at birth:** 72 years; **Unit of currency:** Hong Kong dollar; **Main exports:** a wide range of light manufactures; **Per capita GNP:** US$4000.

HUNGARY, a landlocked People's Republic in eastern Europe. It is mostly low-lying and drained by the Danube and the Tisza, its tributary. The

COUNTRIES OF THE WORLD

Iceland is dotted with volcanoes, geysers and hot springs, barren lava fields, ice caps and valley glaciers. There are more than 100 volcanoes, including clusters of craters like those in the picture, and about one out of every four volcanoes has erupted in historic times. The reason for all this volcanic activity is that Iceland straddles the northern part of the mid-Atlantic ridge, along which new coastal rock is being formed. This addition of this rock is slowly widening the Atlantic Ocean and Iceland itself.

fertile, hilly Little Alföld is in the north-west. It is separated from the Great Alföld, or Hungarian Plain (56 per cent of the country), by a limestone ridge, the Bakony Forest. Low mountains north-east of Budapest are renowned for their wine. Winters are cold and summers hot. The rainfall averages 635 mm (25 in) on the plains, and 790 mm (31 in) on the uplands. Hungarians, or Magyars, are of Finno-Ugric and Turkic descent, mixed with local peoples. In 1980 64 per cent of the population lived in urban areas. Industry, which has developed rapidly in the last 30 years, accounted for 59 per cent of the GDP in 1978. Bauxite, coal and some other minerals are produced, but many raw materials must be imported. More than 50 per cent of the factories, all of which are nationalized, are in or around Budapest. Farming employs 18 per cent of the workforce and accounts for 15 per cent of the GDP. Arable land, orchards and vine-yards cover 53 per cent of the land, pasture 14 per cent and forests 17 per cent. Maize and wheat are the main crops. There are about 2 million cattle, 2.8 million sheep, 8 million pigs and 63 million poultry. Hungary and Austria jointly controlled the Austro-Hungarian Empire from 1867 until it broke up in 1918. In World War II Hungary supported Germany but when it tried to negotiate a separate armistice, it was invaded by German troops. Soviet forces occupied Hungary in 1945 and a communist government was in power by 1948. In 1956 Russian troops put down an anti-Stalinist uprising. Since then, anti-Soviet feeling has been suppressed.

Area: 93,030 km^2 (35,921 sq mi); **Population:** 10,850,000; **Capital:** Budapest (pop 2,093,000); **Highest point:** Mt Kékes, 1015 m (3330 ft); **Official language:** Magyar (Hungarian); **Religions:** Roman Catholicism (50 per cent), Protestantism; **Adult literacy rate:** 98 per cent; **Average life expectancy at birth:** 70 years; **Unit of currency:** Forint; **Main exports:** transport equipment, electrical goods, bauxite and aluminium, food, pharmaceuticals, wine; **Per capita GNP**: US$3850.

ICELAND, an island republic in the North Atlantic Ocean. Large snowfields, glaciers, volcanoes, hot springs (which are used to heat homes in Reykjavik) and a deeply indented coastline are features of this rugged island. The warm North Atlantic Drift keeps the southern coats ice-free in winter. Summers are cool. Less than 1 per cent of the land is cultivated; the main crops are hay, potatoes and turnips. Iceland has about 57,000 cattle and 797,000 sheep, but fishing is the main industry. Norewegian Vikings colonized Iceland in AD 874. In 1262 it was united with Norway and, in 1380, it came under Denmark. Independence was achieved in 1918 although it stayed under the nominal rule of the Danish monarch. It became a republic in 1944. Between 1958 and 1976 it was involved in various fishing disputes. In 1963 it acquired a new volcanic island, Surtsey, which appeared from the sea near Iceland.

Area: 103,000 km^2 (39,771 sq mi); **Population:** 234,000; **Capital:** Reykjavik (pop 84,000); **Highest point:** Oraefajökull, 2119 m (6952 ft); **Official language:** Icelandic; **Religion:** Evangelical Lutheran; **Unit of currency:** Krona; **Main exports:** fish and whale products; **Per capita GNP:** US$10,490.

INDIA, the world's 7th largest nation, but the 2nd largest in terms of population. The Himalayan mountains in the north include India's highest peak, Nanda Devi. In the north-west Kashmir contains parts of the Karakoram and Hindu Kush ranges. The Indus, Ganges and Brahmaputra rivers rise in the Himalayas and reach the sea via broad alluvial plains. The fertile northern plains of India are densely populated. To the south, the Vindhya range borders the Deccan, a huge, triangular-shaped plateau. It is bounded by two other ranges: the Western Ghats and the lower Eastern Ghats. The main rivers, the Cauvery, Krishna and Godavari, flow from west to east into the Bay of Bengal. The climate and vegetation vary greatly. The highest mountains have an Arctic climate; the Thar desert borders Pakistan; Cherrapunji in the north-east holds the world rainfall record for one year – 26,461 mm (1041.7 in) were recorded in 1860–61; and the Deccan lies in the tropics. Most of India has three seasons: winter in October-February when it is cool and dry; the hot season in March–June when temperatures reach 49°C (120°F) in the northern plains; and the rainy season, June–September, when monsoon winds are drawn into

The river Ganges which drains the northern alluvial plains of India is regarded as sacred by Hindus, who make up just over four-fifths of India's population. Pilgrims visit the holy city of Varanasi on the Ganges to bathe in the water, regarding this as a form of spiritual cleansing. Religion plays a vital part in Indian life, as shown by the Hindu prohibition on the slaughter of cattle. Non-violence, as advocated by Mahatma Gandhi in the struggle for independence, and respect for life, are basic Hindu principles.

eastern India from the south-west. Hundreds of languages are spoken in India, but the government recognizes only 15 national languages: Assamese, Bengali, Gujerati, Hindi, Kannada, Kashmiri, Malayalam, Marathi, Oriya, Punjabi, Sanskrit, Sindhi, Tamil, Telegu and Urdu. India is a mainly poor agricultural nation; only 22½ per cent of the population lived in urban areas in 1980. In 1978 agriculture employed 74 per cent of the workforce and accounted for 40 per cent of the GDP (industry for 26 per cent and services 34 per cent). India is the world's top producer of groundnuts, hemp (fibre), sugar-cane and tea; the 2nd leading producer of millet, rice and sorghum; the 3rd largest producer of coconuts, copra and tobacco; and the 4th producer of cotton and wheat. It has more cattle (182 million) than any other nation, but Hinduism forbids their slaughter. India has various minerals, including bauxite, coal, iron ore and manganese. Manufacturing has expanded greatly since 1947; the chief products are textiles, but there is also much heavy industry. Most Indians are descendants of the original Dravidians and the Aryans who invaded India in about 1500 BC. India gave birth to several religions, including Hinduism, Buddhism, Jainism and Sikhism. The Muslim Mughal Empire was founded in 1526, but it declined in the 17th century. The British East India Company became the dominant European trading group in India in 1757 and, in 1858, Britain took over the rule of India. Independence was achieved in 1947 when British India was partitioned into the mainly Hindu India and the Muslim Pakistan. A war in Kashmir ended in 1949 with its partition. India became a republic in 1950. It has been ruled by the Congress party which has controlled the bicameral parliament except in 1977–80.

Area: 3,287,590 km² (1,269,415 sq mi); **Population:** 698,632,000; **Capital:** Delhi (pop 3,647,000); **Other cities:** Calcutta (7,031,000); Bombay (5,971,000), Madras (3,170,000), Hyderabad (1,796,000), Ahmadabad (or Ahmedabad, 1,742,000), Bangalore (1,654,000), Kanpur (1,275,000), Pune (1,135,000); **Highest point:** Nanda Devi, 7817 m (25,646 ft); **Official languages:** Hindi, English; **Religions:** Hinduism (82.7 per cent), Islam (11.2 per cent), Christianity (2.6 per cent), Sikhism (1.9 per cent), Buddhism (0.7 per cent), Jainism (0.5 per cent); **Adult literacy rate:** 36 per cent; **Average life expectancy at birth:** 51 years: **Unit of currency:** Rupee; **Main exports:** textiles, jute, tea; **Per capita GNP:** US$190.

INDONESIA, an island republic in South-East Asia. The largest regions are Kalimantan (part of Borneo), Sumatra, West Irian (part of New Guinea), Sulawesi (Celebes) and Java, the most densely populated island. There are many mountain ranges and more active volcanoes than in any other country: 77 have erupted in recent times. The climate is equatorial, hot and wet all the year round. Rain forests cover large areas. Most people are of Malay origin, mixed with Melanesians and Australasians, and at least 70 languages are spoken. In 1980 20 per cent of the population lived in urban areas. Agriculture employs 60 per cent of the workforce, accounting for 31 per cent of the GDP (33 per cent came from industry and 36 per cent from services). Rice is the main food. Coffee, copra, palm oil and kernels, rubber, tea and tobacco are major cash crops. Forestry is important. Indonesia is the leading oil producer in the Far East. Manufacturing is important, including shipbuilding, textiles, cement and chemicals. Indonesian princes adopted Islam in the 16th century as a political weapon against the Portuguese traders. It gradually replaced Hinduism. Dutch influence began in the late 16th century and the territory became Dutch in 1799. The Republic of Indonesia was formed in 1949. In 1957 army officers revolted because of communist influence in the government: a civil war continued until 1961. The formation of Malaysia in 1963 led to fighting between the two nations in 1964. A communist attempt to overthrow the government failed in 1965. Military leaders seized power in 1966, outlawing the Communist Party and ending confrontation with Malaysia. East (formerly Portuguese) Timor was incorporated into Indonesia in 1976.

Area: 2,027,087 km² (782,705 sq mi); **Population:** 146,527,000; **Capital:** Djakarta (pop 6,506,000); **Other cities:** Surabaya (1,762,000), Bandung (1,265,000), Semarang (916,000); **Highest point:** Djaja Peak (Mt Carstensz), 5030 m (16,503 ft); **Official language:** Bahasa Indonesian; **Religions:**

Islam (80 per cent), Christianity, Hinduism, Buddhism; **Adult literacy rate:** 62 per cent; **Average life expectancy at birth:** 47 years; **Unit of currency:** Rupiah; **Main exports:** oil (73 per cent), coffee, rubber, palm products, tin, tea, tobacco; **Per capita GNP:** US$380.

IRAN, a republic in south-western Asia. Around a barren plateau, which contains the Dasht e Kavir (Great Salt Desert) and the Dasht e Lut (Great Sand Desert), are mountains: the highest are the northern Elburz Mts; the Zagros Mts in the west and south; and several ranges in the east. The only fertile areas are near the Caspian Sea and in mountain foothills. The central plateau is arid and hot, but the Zagros Mts can be bitterly cold. Rainfall in the Caspian Sea region is about 2000 mm (79 in) per year; the south-east is arid. About 90 per cent of the people are Shia Muslims. Ethnically, two-thirds of the people are Persian in type and one-fourth are Turki. There are some Arabs and Sunni Muslim Kurds live in the north. In 1980 50 per cent of the population lived in urban areas. Industry, mainly oil and gas production, accounted for 54 per cent of the GDP in 1978, as opposed to 9 per cent from agriculture, although 40 per cent of the people were farmers. Cereals, fruit, cotton and tobacco are grown. Income from oil has been used to develop heavy industries and improve social services. Ancient Persia was a powerful empire between 550 and 330 BC. The country was Islamized in AD 641. Later it was invaded by Turks and Mongols. In the 19th century Britain and France competed for influence. In 1925 the Pahlavi family took power. In 1979 the Shah, Mohammad Reza Pahlavi, left Iran after much rioting. A religious leader, Ayatollah Khomeini, exiled since 1964, returned and Iran became an Islamic Republic. War broke out between Iran and Iraq in 1980.

Area: 1,648,000 km^2 (636,331 sq mi); **Population:** 40,288,000; **Capital:** Tehran (pop 4,496,000); **Other cities:** Esfahan (672,000), Mashhad (670,000), Tabriz (599,000); **Highest point:** Mt Damavand, 5604 m (18,386 ft); **Official language:** Persian (Farsi); **Religion:** Islam; **Adult literacy rate:** 50 per cent; **Average life expectancy at birth:** 52 years; **Unit of currency:** Rial; **Main exports:** oil, natural gas, cotton; **Per capita GNP:** US$2160 (1977).

IRAQ, a republic in south-western Asia. It contains Mesopotamia, the valleys of the Tigris and Euphrates rivers where the ancient civilizations of Babylonia and Assyria arose. There are swamps in the south where the two rivers join, deserts in the west and mountains in the north-east. Summers are hot and winters cool. The rainfall is generally 250 mm (10 in), but more falls on the uplands. More than half of the people are Shia Muslims. In 1978 72 per cent of the people lived in urban areas, as compared with 43 per cent in 1960. Oil production dominates the economy. The main crops are dates, cereals, pulses and cotton. In 1979 Iran had 11.6 million sheep, 3.6 million goats and 2.7 million cattle. Manufacturing is expanding but, in 1980, the Israelis destroyed a nuclear reactor near Baghdad in a lightning raid. Iraq was Islamized in AD 637 and, in 1638, it became part of the Ottoman Empire. British forces occupied Iraq in World War I and stayed until it became an independent monarchy in 1932. Since the 1950s oil production has provided income for developing social services. In 1958, however, the monarchy was overthrown and the army established a republic. Fighting with the Sunni Muslim Kurds in the north broke out in the 1960s. The Kurds wanted a Kurdish state, joining Kurdish territory in Iran, Turkey and the USSR, but they failed. A peace agreement was signed in 1974. War between Iraq and Iran broke out in 1980.

Area: 434,924 km^2 (167,934 sq mi); **Population:** 13,977,000; **Capital:** Baghdad (pop 3,206,000); **Other cities:** Basrah (334,000), Mosul (293,000); **Official language:** Arabic; **Religion:** Islam; **Average life expectancy at birth:** 55 years; **Unit of currency:** Iraqui dinar; **Main exports:** oil, iron ore, copper; **Per capita GNP:** US$2410.

IRELAND, REPUBLIC OF, occupies 80 per cent of the island of Ireland. It contains 26 counties, divided into 4 provinces: Connacht, Leinster, Munster and Ulster. But the 6 north-eastern counties of Ulster constitute Northern Ireland, which is part of the United Kingdom. Central Ireland is a moraine-covered lowland, containing areas of peat bog and some rich farmland. A broken rim of uplands surrounds the plain. The highest peak, Carrantuohill, is in scenic County Kerry in the south-west. The River Shannon, 386 km (240 mi) long, is the longest river in the British Isles. Along its course are several lakes, including Lough Ree and Lough Derg. Ireland has mild, wet winters and cool, wet summers. The average annual temperature range is around 5°–15°C (41°–59°F). The uplands have an average annual rainfall of 1020 to 1520 mm (40–60 in) and the lowlands about 760 mm (30 in). Most people are of Celtic or mixed Celtic and English descent. About 20 per cent speak Irish, but English is used in daily life. In 1980 58 per cent of the population lived in urban areas. In 1978 20 per cent were employed in agriculture, 37 per cent in industry and 43 per cent in services. But farming forms the basis of the economy. Arable land and pasture cover two-thirds of the land. Major crops are barley, hay, oats, potatoes, sugar beet and wheat. In 1979 there were 7.1 million cattle, 3.4 million sheep and 1.1 million pigs. There are many processing industries. The only large-scale manufacturing industries are in Dublin and Cork: most of the minerals and raw materials needed are imported. Fishing employs about 9000 men. Tourism is important: nearly 10 million people visited Ireland in 1979. Celts from France and Spain settled in Ireland in the early 4th century BC. Christianity was introduced by St Patrick in AD 432. Vikings arrived in about 795, but most of them were driven out in the 11th century. The Normans invaded Ireland in the 12th century and the island came under English rule. Much of Ireland's subsequent history was concerned with a struggle against English rule and, from the 1530s, the preservation of Roman Catholicism. In 1801 the Act of Union created the

Top left: Iran is an Islamic nation as exemplified by this mosque at Isfahan. Top right: Rural Ireland has great charm. Above: The Dome of the Rock in Jerusalem contains a rock on which Abraham supposedly prepared to sacrifice Isaac.

United Kingdom of Great Britain and Ireland. A potato famine in the 1840s, caused by a blight, led to the deaths of more than a million Irish people; another million emigrated. In 1916 there was an uprising in Dublin (the Easter Rebellion) which was put down. In 1919–21 the Irish fought for independence, finally achieving dominion status as the Irish Free State. Northern Ireland remained part of the UK. Ireland became a republic in 1949 and it joined the EEC in 1973. The unification of Ireland remains a central political issue.

Area: 70,283 km^2 (27,138 sq mi); **Population:** 3,366,000; **Capital:** Dublin (pop 545,000); **Other cities:** Cork (139,000), Limerick (61,000); **Highest point:** Carrantuohill, 1042 m (3419 ft); **Official languages:** Irish, English; **Religion:** mainly Roman Catholicism; **Adult literacy rate:** 98 per cent; **Average life expectancy at birth:** 73 years; **Unit of currency:** Pound; **Main exports:** dairy products, meat and meat products, beer, whiskey; **Per capita GNP:** US$4230.

ISRAEL, a Middle Eastern republic created in 1948. The Galilee highlands containing Mt Meron are in the north. To the east is an extension of the East African Rift Valley, enclosing the Sea of Galilee (Lake Tiberias), the River Jordan and, in the south, the Dead Sea whose shoreline is 393 m (1289 ft) below sea level, the world's lowest point on land. South of the Galilee Highlands are fertile plains and hilly regions. The Negev in the far south is desert. The coast has a Mediterranean climate; the rainfall decreases inland and to the south. More than 80 per cent of the people are Jews: the rest are Arabs. In 1980 89 per cent of the population lived in urban areas. In 1978 agriculture accounted for 7 per cent of the GDP, industry 37 per cent and services 57 per cent. Israel makes most industrial products and diamond finishing is the most valuable industry. Farming is efficient because of extensive irrigation and co-operative and collective farming methods. Cereals, citrus fruits, cotton, olives, tobacco and vegetables are important. About 1.1 million tourists visited Israel in 1979. Israel did not exist as a state for about 2500 years before 1948. Some Jews have always lived in Palestine, but most Israelis are descendants of settlers since the 1880s or recent immigrants. Britain ruled Palestine from 1917 but withdrew in 1948 when Israelis fought against their Arab neighbours, holding most of Palestine. In short Arab-Israeli wars in 1956, 1967 and 1973, Israel gained Arab territory. But in 1979 Israel and Egypt signed a peace treaty which led to a gradual return of the Sinai to Egypt.

Area: 20,770 km^2 (8020 sq mi); **Population:** 4,093,000; **Capital:** Jerusalem (pop 398,000); **Other cities:** Tel-Aviv/Jaffa (336,000), Haifa (229,000); **Highest point:** Mt Meron, 1208 m (3963 ft); **Official languages:** Hebrew, Arabic; **Religions:** Judaism, Islam; **Adult literacy rate:** 88 per cent; **Average life expectancy at birth:** 72 years; **Unit of currency:** Shekel; **Main exports:** cut diamonds, chemical and oil products, beverages and tobacco, citrus fruits; **Per capita GNP:** US$4170.

COUNTRIES OF THE WORLD

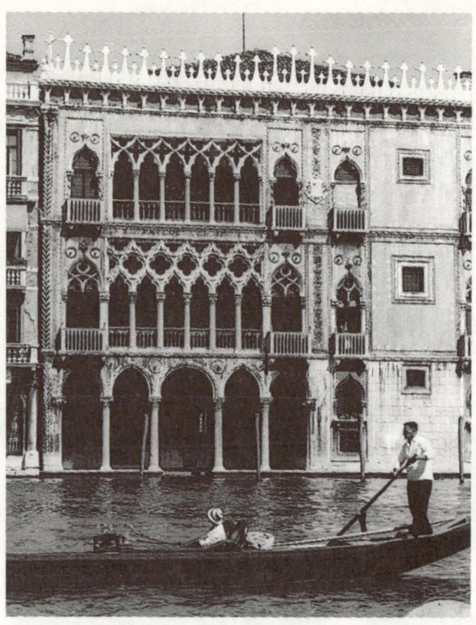

Many of Italy's cities are museums of history and architecture. Left: The Forum at Rome recalls the days when the city was the capital of the western world. Above: Superb medieval buildings in Venice can be viewed from gondolas. Right: Exquisite churches, palaces and magnificent art galleries are among the many attractions of Florence.

ITALY, a republic in southern Europe. It consists largely of a 1220 km (758 mi) long peninsula projecting like a boot between the Adriatic Sea to the east and the Ligurian and Tyrrhenian seas to the west. The scenic Alps, Italy's highest region, form a broad arc in the north. They overlook the North Italian plain which consists mainly of the River Po drainage basin. This is Italy's most densely populated region. The Po is Italy's longest river – it is about 650 km (404 mi) long. The Apennine Mts occupy much of peninsular Italy. Their highest point is Monte Corno, 2914 m (9560 ft) high, north-east of Rome. Within the Apennines are many fertile valleys and basins, and there are some rich coastal plains. Most rivers are short. The most important are the Arno on which Florence stands and the Tiber which flows through Rome. In the south-west are a series of volcanoes: Vesuvius, 1277 m (4190 ft) is near the port of Naples; Stromboli and Vulcano in the Lipari Islands; and Etna, Europe's highest volcano, reaches 3363 m (11,033 ft) in Sicily. Sicily is the largest of Italy's 70 or so islands, covering 25,708 km² (9926 sq mi). Southern Italy is subject to earthquakes: it lies near a subduction zone in the Earth's crust. Italy's second largest island is Sardinia to the west. This rugged island covers 24,090 km² (9302 sq mi). Southern Italy has hot, dry summers and mild winters. Winter rainfall is highest in the mountains and it increases northwards. Winters are colder in the more continental North Italian plain, where temperatures in January average between 1°C and 3°C (34°–37°F). The Alps are cold and snowy. In 1980 69 per cent of the population lived in urban areas. In 1978 industry accounted for 42 per cent of the GDP, agriculture for 7 per cent and services for 51 per cent. Oil and natural gas are extracted in the North Italian plain and in Sicily, but oil and coal have to be imported. Hydro-electric projects are numerous and 32 per cent of Italy's total electricity supply came from hydro-electric plants in 1977. Generally, Italy lacks minerals and metal ores are major imports. Leading industrial products include textiles, especially silk, engineering goods, including transport equipment and motor vehicles (Alfa-Romeo, Fiat and Maserati are internationally known names), office and household equipment, chemicals and iron and steel. There are also many craft industries. The chief industrial region is the triangular area formed by Turin, Milan and Genoa. Farmland covers about two-thirds of the land, but agriculture now employs only 13 per cent of the workforce, as opposed to 31 per cent in 1960. Forests cover 21 per cent of the land, but timber is imported. Major crops include barley, citrus and other fruits, grapes (for wine-making), maize, olives, sugar beet, tobacco, vegetables and wheat. In 1979 there were 8.6 million cattle, 9.8 million pigs and 10 million sheep and goats. Italy is a major milk producer and its cheeses, such as Gorgonzola, are famous. In the 1970s Italy's main trading partners were West Germany, France, the United States and the UK. Adverse trade balances were partly covered by income from the huge tourist industry: Italy received 48.7 million foreign visitors in 1979. Tourist attractions include sunny beaches, historic sites, like the Forum in Rome and the lost city of Pompeii, the Vatican City State, and magnificent medieval cities, such as Florence and Venice, with their superb art galleries and churches. The most prosperous parts of Italy are in the north; this is reflected in the migration of poor farmers from the south to the north or abroad. The Roman empire developed around 500 BC and lasted until the 5th century AD. In the Middle Ages, Italy was divided into small rival states, although these made an enormous contribution to the Renaissance in

the 14th–16th centuries. After a long struggle for unity which began in 1848, Italy became a united kingdom in 1861 under King Victor Emmanuel II of Sardinia, although the Papal territories were not added until 1870. Italy entered World War I on the side of the Allies. In 1922 Benito Mussolini and his Fascist party took power. In 1935 Italian forces invaded Ethiopia and Italy entered World War II in 1940 on Germany's side. Italy surrendered in 1943 and declared war on Germany. In 1946 the monarchy was abolished and Italy became a republic. It was a founder member of NATO in 1949 and of the EEC in 1958. The economy expanded rapidly and attempts were made through the EEC to increase job opportunities for people in the relatively impoverished south. However, a succession of weak coalition governments, unemployment, high inflation (averaging 14 per cent per year in 1970–78), strikes and terrorist violence and assassinations have marred progress in recent years. Italy has a bicameral parliament, with an elected, 600-member Chamber of Deputies and a Senate elected on a regional basis. Members of both houses serve 5-year terms.

Area: 301,225 km² (116,310 sq mi); **Population:** 58,085,000; **Capital:** Rome (pop 3,700,000); **Other cities:** Milan (4,000,000), Naples (1,250,000), Turin (1,000,000), Genoa (850,000), Palermo (694,000), Bologna (487,000), Florence (465,000); **Highest point:** Mt Rosa, 4634 m (15,203 ft); **Official language:** Italian; **Religion:** Roman Catholicism; **Adult literacy rate:** 98 per cent; **Average life expectancy at birth:** 73 years; **Unit of currency:** Lira; **Main exports:** machinery, motor vehicles, iron and steel, textiles, footwear, plastics, fruit and vegetables; **Per capita GNP:** US$5240.

IVORY COAST, a republic in West Africa with a 550 km (342 mi) coastline on the Gulf of Guinea. Behind the broad coastal lowlands are high plains between 150 and 450 m (492–1476 ft). The main highlands are in the north-west: the highest peak, Mt Nimba, is on the Ivory Coast-Liberia-Guinea border. The south has an equatorial climate. The north is often scorched by the north-easterly Harmattan, a wind from the Sahara that may raise temperatures to 38°C (100°F). There is some forest in the south but savanna is the main type of vegetation. About 60 languages and dialects are spoken by the Negroid peoples. Ivory Coast is prosperous by African standards, but prosperity is confined mostly to the south-east. In 1978 agriculture employed 81 per cent of the workforce and accounted for 21 per cent of the GDP: 23 per cent came from industry and 56 per cent from services. Ivory Coast leads the world in cocoa production and is the 4th largest coffee producer. There is some mining, but the processing and consumer goods industries in Abidjan make a larger contribution to the economy. Ivory Coast became a French colony in 1893, although French influence dates back to the 17th century. Independence was achieved in 1960, since when Ivory Coast has pursued private enterprise economic policies, proving to be one of the most stable nations in Africa.

Area: 322,463 km² (124,510 sq mi); **Population:** 9,564,000; **Capital:** Abidjan (pop 686,000); **Highest point:** Mt Nimba, 1752 m (5748 ft); **Official language:** French; **Religions:** traditional beliefs (56 per cent), Islam (24 per cent), Roman Catholicism (20 per cent); **Adult literacy rate:** 20 per cent; **Average life expectancy at birth:** 46 years; **Unit of currency:** Franc CFA; **Main exports:** coffee, cocoa, timber, petroleum products; **Per capita GNP:** US$1060.

JAMAICA, a West Indian island nation. The land is mainly mountainous, with spectacular scenery. The coast has a tropical climate, with average temperatures of 27°–30°C (81°–86°F), although there are pleasant ocean breezes. The altitude lowers temperatures inland. The Blue Mountains have an average annual rainfall of 5000 mm (197 in). The coasts are drier: Kingston has about 760 mm (30 in) per year. More than 75 per cent of the people are black, 14 per cent are of mixed black and white origin, and there are minorities of Asians, Afro-Asians and whites. In 1980 50 per cent of the population lived in urban areas where manufacturing is growing. Jamaica is the world's 3rd largest producer of bauxite, the main export. Agriculture employs 28 per cent of the people: bananas and sugar are the main products. Tourism is a major industry and more than 500,000 visitors went to Jamaica in 1978. Discovered by Columbus in 1494, Jamaica was ruled by Spain until 1655 when the English captured it. Full independence in the Commonwealth was achieved in 1962. The Head of State is the British monarch who is represented by a Governor-General.

Area: 10,991 km² (4244 sq mi); **Population:** 2,297,000; **Capital:** Kingston (pop 635,000); **Highest point:** Blue Mt Peak, 2256 m (7402 ft); **Official language:** English; **Religion:** Christianity, (Rastafarian minority); **Adult literacy rate:** 86 per cent; **Average life expectancy at birth:** 70 years; **Unit of currency:** Dollar; **Main exports:** alumina and bauxite, sugar; **Per capita GNP:** US$1240.

COUNTRIES OF THE WORLD

Left: Express trains reflect Japan's outstanding technological progress in recent times, while the volcano Mount Fuji reminds us that Japan lies on a particularly unstable part of the Earth's crust. Religion plays a major part in life in Japan and Mount Fuji is a sacred mountain. Above: The Kinkakuji Temple is in Tokyo. Shintoism and Buddhism are Japan's chief religions. Right: This mosque is in Nairobi, capital of Kenya.

JAPAN, an island nation in the Far East that is separated from the Asian mainland by the Sea of Japan. There are 4 large islands (Honshu, Hokkaido, Kyushu and Shikoku) and about 3000 small ones, including the Ryukyu island chain that stretches towards Taiwan. The islands are largely mountainous, the most rugged region being the Japanese Alps on Honshu, including the highest peak Fujiyama, a dormant volcano south-west of Tokyo which last erupted in 1707. Japan contains more than 160 volcanoes; 54 are active. Earthquakes are common; about 1500 occur every year, but most cause little damage. The world's most destructive earthquake occurred in the Kwanto plain in 1923 when 575,000 buildings in Tokyo and Yokohama were destroyed and 143,000 lives were lost. Volcanic and seismic activity are caused because Japan lies above a subduction zone where the Pacific plate is being forced beneath the Eurasian plate. Earthquakes originating offshore trigger off tsunamis, destructive waves that strike the coasts with great force. Along the deeply indented coasts are some small coastal plains that are alluvial deltas formed by the short rivers that cascade from the mountains. The longest river, the Shinano on Honshu, is only 480 km (298 mi) long. Japan has a monsoon climate, with plentiful rain. The heaviest rains fall in June–July and September–October and typhoons are common. Temperatures are affected by the warm Kuro Siwa ocean current which comes from the south and the cold Oyashio current that chills the coasts of western Hokkaido and northern Honshu. Average January temperatures are −6°C (21°F) in Hokkaido and 7°C (45°F) in southern Kyushu. Average July temperatures are 20°C (68°F) in the north and 28°C (82°F) in the south. Most people are Mongoloid descendants of people who came from mainland Asia and Pacific islands. But one of the earliest peoples is Caucasoid. These are the bushy-haired Ainu, 15,000 of whom live in Hokkaido. Japan is Asia's most prosperous and industrialized nation. In 1980 78 per cent of the population lived in urban areas, compared with 62 per cent in 1960. In 1978 industry employed 39 per cent of the workforce, services 48 per cent and agriculture 13 per cent. Contributions to the GDP were industry 40 per cent, services 55 per cent and agriculture 5 per cent. Some minerals, including coal and copper, are mined, but the amounts are generally too small for the needs of manufacturers. Hence, many materials, including iron ore and oil, must be imported. Japan has a wide range of light and heavy industry. It is the world's 3rd largest producer of electrical energy, after the US and the USSR. In 1977 hydroelectricity made up 14 per cent of the total and nuclear power 6 per cent. Japan leads the world in producing many items, including motor cycles, merchant ships and television sets. Only the US makes more motor vehicles and Hong Kong more radios. Japan's main industrial regions are in the coastal lowlands between Tokyo and northern Kyushu. Most of Japan is too mountainous for farming; forests cover nearly 70 per cent of the land. Arable land makes up less than 15 per cent of Japan, but yields are high and farming intensive. Rice is the chief food and is grown on nearly 50 per cent of the farmland. Other major crops are barley, fruits, soya beans and wheat. Cattle number about 4.1 million and pigs 9.5 million: goats and sheep are unimportant because of the lack of pasture. About 50 per cent of Japan's protein comes from its large fishing and whaling industry. Seaweed is also harvested for food. But food is imported: it made up 13 per cent of the imports in 1979. According to tradition, Japan's monarchy dates back to 660 BC. Buddhism was introduced in AD 552. Emperors ruled Japan until a new warrior class, the *shoguns* ('great generals'), emerged in the 12th century. In 1192 the first shogun took power, ruling in the name of the emperor. Shogun rule continued until Emperor Meiji regained power in 1868. European contacts began when Portuguese navigators reached Japan in 1542. But in 1637 Japan expelled all Europeans, except for the Dutch, from Japan and outlawed Christianity. Isolationism continued until, in 1854, the American Commander Perry, with a fleet of warships, forced Japan to

agree a treaty with the US. This was followed by treaties with other western powers. Japan's imperialist ambitions began in the 1880s. In 1894–95 it fought a war with China and in 1904–05 it defeated Russia in a dispute over Russia's claims on Korea. In 1931 it occupied Manchuria and, in 1937, started a war with China. In 1941 Japan attacked US bases at Pearl Harbor, but defeat in World War II came when the US dropped atomic bombs on Hiroshima and Nagasaki in 1945. The US occupied Japan until 1952. In the 1960s and 1970s Japan became one of the world's great industrial powers. The 1947 Constitution made Japan a constitutional monarchy. The Emperor is Head of State. Power is vested in the Diet, which consists of an elected 511-member House of Representatives and a 252-member House of Chancellors.

Area: 372,313 km^2 (143,759 sq mi); **Population:** 120,055,000; **Capital:** Tokyo (pop 11,695,000); **Other cities:** Yokohama (2,786,000), Osaka (2,682,000), Nagoya (2,079,000), Kyoto (1,468,000), Sapporo (1,397,000), Kobe (1,372,000), Kitakyushu (1,068,000), Kawasaki (1,050,000); **Highest point:** Fujiyama, 3776 m (12,388 ft); **Official language:** Japanese; **Religions:** mainly Shintoism and Buddhism; **Adult literacy rate:** 99 per cent; **Average life expectancy at birth:** 76 years; **Unit of currency:** Yen; **Main exports:** chemicals, electronic goods, machinery and transport equipment, optical equipment, ships, textiles; **Per capita GNP:** US$8800.

JORDAN, a kingdom in south-western Asia. The fertile western uplands (the West Bank, occupied by Israel) overlook the rift valley which contains the River Jordan and the Dead Sea whose shoreline is 393 m (1289 ft) below sea level, the world's lowest point on land. The valley continues south to the Gulf of Aqabah, Jordan's only outlet to the sea. The east consists mainly of barren uplands: the highest point is Jebel Ram, 1754 m (5755 ft) high in the south. About 87 per cent of Jordan is desert. Some highland regions are cooler and have an average annual rainfall of 520 mm (20 in). Most people are Arabs and 56 per cent lived in urban areas in 1980. In 1978 agriculture employed 27 per cent of the population, industry 39 per cent and services 34 per cent; they contributed 11 per cent, 29 per cent and 60 per cent respectively to the GDP. Fruit and vegetables are grown and there are about 1.25 million sheep and goats. The main export is phosphates. British forces occupied what is now Israel and Jordan in World War I. Transjordan became a separate country in 1923 and full independence was achieved in 1946. In 1948 Jordan was involved in the Arab-Israeli war and, in 1949, it adopted its present name, the Hashemite Kingdom of Jordan. In 1967 Israel occupied the West Bank, Jordan's most fertile region. In 1970–71 civil war broke out when Jordan tried to expel militant refugees belonging to the Palestinian Liberation Organization. In 1975, however, King Hussein gave up his claim to the West Bank and passed responsibility for it to the PLO.

Area: 97,740 km^2 (37,740 sq mi); **Population:** 3,403,000; **Capital:** Amman (pop 750,000); **Official language:** Arabic; **Religion:** Islam; **Adult literacy rate:** 70 per cent; **Average life expectancy at birth:** 56 years; **Unit of currency:** Jordanian dinar; **Main exports:** phosphates, fruit and vegetables; **Per capita GNP:** US$1180.

KAMPUCHEA, officially Democratic Kampuchea, is a South-East Asian nation formerly called Cambodia and, briefly, the Khmer Republic. Much of the land is low-lying, in the drainage basin of the lower Mekong River; hills surround the plain. Kampuchea has a tropical monsoon climate and dense forests cover nearly 50 per cent of the land. Khmers make up 90 per cent of the population. There are Chinese and Vietnamese minorities. The economy is based on agriculture. Rice occupied much of the cultivated land (15 per cent of the total), but reliable data has not been available since the capital Phnom Penh fell to communist forces (the Khmer Rouge) in 1975. In 1978 Vietnamese forces invaded the country but resistance was reported to be continuing into the 1980s. The impressive Khmer empire flourished in the area between 800 and 1450. The country was a French colony in 1863–1954. In the 1970s the country became involved in the Vietnamese War when North Vietnamese took supplies for South Vietnamese guerrillas through Kampuchea.

Area: 181,035 km^2 (69,902, sq mi); **Population:** 8,559,000 (1978 est); **Capital:** Phnom Penh (formerly 2.5 million); **Official language:** Khmer; **Religion:** Buddhism; **Unit of currency:** Riel; **Main exports:** rice, rubber; in the 1970s the economy came to a virtual standstill.

KENYA, an East African republic. Behind the narrow coastal plain is a large grassy or savanna-covered plateau broken by volcanic mountains, including the highest peak, Mt Kenya. The East African Rift Valley in Kenya contains lakes Nakuru, Naivasha and Turkana. Part of Lake Victoria is in the south-east. The altitude moderates the equatorial climate, but only 15 per cent of Kenya has a reliable 760 mm (30 in) of rain per year. There are about 40 language groups: the largest are the Kikuyu and Luo. In 1978 agriculture employed 79 per cent of the workforce, industry 8 per cent and services 13 per cent: their contributions to the GDP were 41 per cent, 19 per cent and 40 per cent respectively. The chief cash crops are coffee and tea. In 1979 there were 10.5 million cattle, 4 million sheep and 4.5 million goats. Mining

COUNTRIES OF THE WORLD

Beirut, capital of Lebanon, is the country's chief seaport and educational centre. It was devastated by fighting in summer 1982 between Israeli forces and the Palestinian Liberation Movement.

is not important but manufacturing is growing rapidly. In 1979 350,000 tourists visited Kenya enjoying the wildlife, scenery and beaches. Kenya's coast became a British protectorate in 1895 and Kenya was declared a British colony in 1920. Independence was achieved in 1963 and republican status was adopted in 1964. Since then Kenya has enjoyed stable government.

Area: 582,646 km² (224,973 sq mi); **Population:** 16,922,000; **Capital:** Nairobi (pop 700,000); **Other cities:** Mombasa (340,000); **Highest point:** Mt Kenya, 5199 m (17,057 ft); **Official languages:** English, Swahili; **Religions:** traditional beliefs, Islam, Christianity (25 per cent); **Adult literacy rate:** 40 per cent; **Average life expectancy at birth:** 53 years; **Unit of currency:** Kenya shilling; **Main exports:** coffee, petroleum products, tea, cement, hides, meat; **Per capita GNP:** US$380.

KIRIBATI, an island republic in the Central Pacific. It includes Ocean (Banaba) Island, the 16 Gilbert Islands, 8 of the 11 Line Islands (the rest are uninhabited US dependencies), and the 8 Phoenix Islands. The climate is hot and generally wet. Most people are Micronesians. Copra is the only export. The Gilbert and Ellice Islands became a British protectorate in 1892. Banaba was added in 1900, the Line Islands in 1919, and the Phoenix Islands in 1937. The Ellice Islands became a separate country, Tuvalu, in 1975. Kiribati (pronounced *Kiribas*) became fully independent in 1979.

Area: 684 km² (264 sq mi); **Population:** 60,000; **Capital:** Tarawa; **Per capita GNP:** US$670.

KOREA, NORTH, officially the Democratic People's Republic of Korea. The northern part of a peninsula, North Korea is mostly mountainous, the population being concentrated in coastal plains in the east. The average annual temperature range is between −7°C (19°F) and 21°C (70°F) and the annual rainfall is between 580 and 1140 mm (23–45 in). The people are Mongoloid. Only 16 per cent of the land is cultivable, but in 1978 agriculture employed 49 per cent of the workforce, industry 32 per cent and services 19 per cent. Rice is the main crop in irrigated areas: maize, millet and wheat grow in drier places. There are many minerals – coal, copper, iron ore, lead, manganese, nickel, tungsten and zinc. There are many light and heavy industries. Korea was partitioned in 1945. The USSR occupied the north above latitude 38°N; the US controlled the south. The occupying powers withdrew in 1949. War between North and South (aided by other powers) raged between 1950–53, the cease-fire line being the present border. Talks on reunification in 1980 failed. See **Korea, South** for earlier history.

Area: 120,538 km² (46,543 sq mi); **Population:** 18,908,000; **Capital:** Pyongyang (pop 1,500,000); **Highest point:** Paektu-San, 2744 m (9003 ft); **Official language:** Korean; **Religion:** Buddhism; **Average life expectancy at birth:** 63 years; **Unit of currency:** Won; **Main exports:** iron ore, pig iron, other metal ores; **Per capital GNP:** US$1130.

KOREA, SOUTH, a republic in the Far East. The land is mostly mountainous with many islands in the west. Average annual temperatures vary from −3°C (27°F) to 24°C (75°F), although winters are warmer in the far south. Winters are dry. The average annual rainfall is between 1140 and 1400 mm (45–55 in). Forests cover 70 per cent of the land. Since partition, industry has overtaken agriculture in importance in South Korea. It accounted for 36 per cent of the GDP in 1978 (as opposed to 19 per cent in 1960). Agriculture accounted for 24 per cent (40 per cent in 1960) and services 40 per cent. Tungsten is the chief mineral; small deposits of many other minerals occur. The chief manufactures are light consumer goods, but chemical and heavy industries are growing. The chief crops are rice and other grains and tobacco. Livestock raising and fishing are also important. Korea became a united kingdom in the 7th century AD. It was occupied by Mongols between the 13th and 14th centuries and it was conquered by China in 1627. It became isolated until Japan forced it to open some ports to trade in 1876. In 1895 Japan defeated China in Korea and in 1905 it prevented Russia from taking it. Korea became a Japanese colony in 1910. In 1945 it was divided between the USSR and the US but their forces withdrew in 1949. In the Korean War (1950–53) the UN supported the South and Communist China the North. In the 1960s and 1970s the army has played an important part in the government of South Korea and attempts at reunification have failed.

Area: 98,484 km^2 (38,027 sq mi); **Population:** 39,546,000; **Capital:** Seoul (pop 8,367,000); **Other cities:** Pusan (3,160,000), Taegu (1,607,000), Inchon (1,084,000); **Highest point:** Halla-San, 1950 m (6398 ft); **Official language:** Korean; **Religions:** Buddhism, Confucianism, Christianity; **Adult literacy rate:** 93 per cent; **Average life expectancy at birth:** 63 years; **Unit of currency:** Won; **Main exports:** textiles, manufactures, chemicals; **Per capita GNP:** US$1500.

KUWAIT, a small Emirate at the head of the Persian Gulf. This low-lying, desert nation has erratic rainfall between 10 mm (0.4 in) per year and 380 mm (15 in). The average summer temperature is 24°C (75°F) but it occasionally soars to 52°C (126°F). Winters are cooler. Most people are Arabs. Kuwait has the world's highest per capita GNP, because of its oil production, which began in 1946. It is now one of the world's 10 top producers and revenue from oil sales finances one of the world's most elaborate welfare states. In 1899 Kuwait accepted British protection for certain rights. Kuwait became independent in 1914, but Britain remained responsible for Kuwait's foreign policy until 1961, when Kuwait became fully independent.

Area: 17,818 km^2 (6880 sq mi); **Population:** 1,516,000; **Capital:** Kuwait (pop 400,000); **Official language:** Arabic; **Religion:** Islam; **Adult literacy rate:** 60 per cent; **Average life expectancy at birth:** 69 years; **Unit of currency:** Kuwait dinar; **Main export:** oil; **Per capita GNP:** US$17,270.

LAOS, a poor, landlocked People's Democratic Republic in South-East Asia. Forested mountains and plateaux cover much of the country: most people live in the Mekong River plains. Laos has a tropical monsoon climate, with most rain in May–September. The average annual rainfall is 1020–2030 mm (40–80 in) in the north and 3800 mm (150 in) in southern uplands. The Lao-Lum (or Valley Lao, a Thai people, make up 56 per cent of the population; the Lao-Theung, consisting of many groups of animist tribes in the uplands, make up 34 per cent; and the Lao-Soung, including the Meo and Yao who are shifting agriculturalists, make up 9 per cent. Among the minorities, the Chinese and Vietnamese are important in business. In 1978 75 per cent of the people were employed in agriculture, which accounted for 60 per cent of the GDP, as opposed to 14 per cent from industry and 26 per cent from services. Rice is the main food crop; timber and coffee are the main exports. Tin is the only important mineral. A united kingdom was established in what is now Laos and northern Thailand in the 14th century. But Thailand and Laos were often in conflict. Laos became a French protectorate in 1893. Full independence as a kingdom was achieved in 1954. From 1953 there was a long struggle between the Royal Lao government and the pro-communist Pathet Lao (the Lao Patriotic Front's armed force). A coalition government was established in 1973, but the Pathet Lao took over in 1975. The King abdicated.

Area: 236,800 km^2 (91,434 sq mi); **Population:** 3,611,000 **Capital:** Vientiane (pop 90,000); **Highest point:** Phu Bia, 2820 m (9252 ft); **Official language:** Lao; **Religions:** Buddhism, animism; **Average life expectancy at birth:** 42 years; **Unit of currency:** Kip; **Main exports:** timber, coffee; **Per capita GNP:** US$90 (1978).

LEBANON, a Middle Eastern republic. Behind the narrow coastal plain are the western Lebanon Mts, an interior plateau containing the fertile Bekaa valley, and the Anti-Lebanon Mts in the east. The climate is Mediterranean in type. Most people are Arabs but only 60 per cent of the population is Muslim: the rest are Christians. Lebanon has long been a financial and commercial centre and, in normal times, it has a major tourist industry. Hence, services are the leading sector of the economy, followed by industry and agriculture. Consumer goods are manufactured and cereals and fruit are the main farm products; 38 per cent of the land is cultivated. Lebanon was the centre of the ancient Phoenician empire. It came under the Romans in 64 BC and under Ottoman rule from 1517. France became involved from the 1860s in order to protect the Maronite (Christian) community which was under attack from the Druses, a sect founded in the 11th century AD. France ruled Lebanon from 1918 to 1946 when it became a fully independent republic. Lebanon was involved in the Arab-Israeli War in 1948; in 1969 and 1973 Lebanese forces clashed with Palestinian refugees; and in 1975–76 civil war broke out between Muslim and Christian forces. In 1978 Israel invaded southern Lebanon to destroy Palestinian bases but largely withdrew when a UN force arrived. There was more fighting in 1982. Lebanon's Constitution is carefully designed to balance Muslim and Christian representation.

Area: 10,400 km^2 (4016 sq mi); **Population:** 3,325,000; **Capital:** Beirut (pop 702,000); **Highest point:** Qurnet es Sauda, 3083 m (10,115 ft); **Official language:** Arabic; **Religions:** Islam, Christianity; **Average life expectancy at birth:** 65 years; **Unit of currency:** Lebanese pound; **Main exports:** jewellery, precious metals/stones, textiles; **Per capita GNP:** US$1070 (1974).

LESOTHO, a landlocked kingdom enclosed by South Africa. It was formerly called Basutoland. Mostly mountainous, it includes the high Drakensberg range, but most people live in the western lowlands and the southern Orange River valley. The climate is continental, with warm, moist summers and cold, dry winters. The people, called Basotho, speak Sesotho and English. In 1978 agriculture employed 87 per cent of the people. It accounted for 36 per cent of the GDP, with 15 per cent from industry and 49 per cent from services. Arable land covers 12 per cent of the land and pasture 82 per cent. The chief food crops are cereals and vegetables. The main exports are wool, mohair and alluvial diamonds. In 1979 there were 1.3 million sheep, 730,000 goats and 550,000 cattle. Tourism is increasing, mainly from South Africa. The nation was founded in the 1820s by Moshoeshoe I who united refugees from tribal wars in South Africa. The country became a British protectorate in 1884 and an independent kingdom in 1966, although it remained heavily dependent economically on South Africa. In the early 1980s a clandestine Lesotho Liberation Movement carried out a number of bombings in Maseru and other places.

Area: 30,355 km^2 (11,721 sq mi); **Population:** 1,406,000; **Capital:** Maseru (pop 60,000); **Highest point:** Thabana Ntlenyana, 3482 m (11,424 ft); **Official languages:** English, Sesotho; **Religion:** Christianity (80 per cent); **Adult literacy rate:** 55 per cent; **Average life expectancy at birth:** 50 years; **Unit of currency:** Loti; **Main exports:** wool, mohair, diamonds; **Per capita GNP:** US$340.

LIBERIA, a republic in West Africa. Behind the coastal plain, with its mangrove swamps and savanna country, are forested plateaux and grassy highlands. Average annual temperatures are between 21°C (70°F) and 26°C (79°F). The average rainfall on the coast is about 2540–4060 mm (100–160 in) per year; inland areas have 1780 mm (70 in). There are 16 main language groups. The 50,000 or so Americo-Liberians, descendants of freed slaves, have been important in ruling Liberia. In 1978 71 per cent of the workforce was employed in agriculture, which accounted for 35 per cent of the GDP. Industry accounted for 28 per cent and services for 37 per cent. Since 1973 iron ore has been the main product, having overtaken rubber. The main food crops are cassava and rice. Liberia has a large merchant navy: many foreign ships register in Liberia because of the low fees. In 1822 the American Colonization Society founded Monrovia for freed slaves. In 1847 Liberia became an independent republic, with a Constitution much like that of the US, but US influence remained strong. In 1980 there was a military coup led by Master-Sergeant Samuel Doe who led a military junta.

Area: 111,369 km^2 (43,002 sq mi); **Population:** 1,992,000; **Capital:** Monrovia (pop 220,000); **Highest point:** Mt Nimba, 1752 m (5748 ft); **Official language:** English; **Religion:** mainly Christianity; **Adult literacy rate:** 30 per cent; **Average life expectancy at birth:** 48 years; **Unit of currency:** Liberian dollar; **Main exports:** iron ore and concentrates, timber, rubber; **Per capita GNP:** US$490.

LIBYA, officially the Socialist People's Libyan Arab Jamahiriyah. (*Jamahiriyah* means 'state of the masses'.) About 95 per cent of Libya is desert or semidesert. The land rises towards the south. Most people live in the north-eastern and north-western coastal plains. Average annual temperatures on the coast range between 12°C–27°C (54°F–81°F). The world's highest shade temperature, 57.7°C (136.4°F) was recorded in 1922 at Al'Aziziyah, south of Tripoli. The rainfall averages 200–610 mm (8–24 in) per year in the north-east and 330 mm (13 in) in the north-west. Most people are of Arab or Berber origin. Industry, mainly oil production, dominates the economy, providing 71 per cent of the GDP in 1978, compared with 2 per cent from agriculture and 27 per cent from services. The main food crops are cereals, dates, olives and vegetables. There were 4.8 million sheep and 2.1 million goats in 1979. The Turks controlled Libya from 1551 to 1911, when Italy occupied Tripoli. Italy lost Libya in World War II. Libya was divided between Britain and France until it became an independent kingdom in 1951. Col Mu'ammar Gaddafi led a military coup in 1969, deposing the king and setting up a republic. In 1977 Libya became a Jamahiriyah, which was a form of direct democracy. With its great wealth, Libya has become involved in the affairs of many other countries. For example, it has opposed Egypt's peace initiative with Israel and it intervened in the Chad civil war between 1980 and 1981.

Area: 1,759,540 km^2 (679,399 sq mi); **Population:** 3,224,000; **Capital:** Tripoli (pop 837,000); **Other cities:** Benghazi (372,000); **Highest point:** Mt Bette, 2286 m (7500 ft); **Official language:** Arabic; **Religion:** Islam; **Adult literacy rate:** 50 per cent; **Average life expectancy at birth:** 55 years; **Unit of currency:** Libyan dinar; **Main export:** oil; **Per capita GNP:** US$8210 (the highest in Africa).

LIECHTENSTEIN, a small principality between Austria and Switzerland, with which it has close links. For example, it uses Swiss currency and is united with Switzerland in a customs union. The Rhine and Ill river plains are in the north, with mountains in the south. Most people are Roman Catholic. Farming, including the cultivation of cereals, fruits and vines and cattle rearing, was the most valuable activity, when light industry overtook it. The sale of postage stamps and tourism are also important. Liechtenstein was founded in 1719. It was part of the German Confederation from 1815, but it has been independent since 1866 and neutral since 1868. It is a constitutional monarchy with a unicameral parliament of 15 elected members.

Area: 157 km^2 (61 sq mi); **Population:** 26,000; **Capital:** Vaduz (pop 5000); **Official language:** German; **Per capita GNP:** US$8000 (1974).

LUXEMBOURG, a Grand Duchy between Belgium, France and West Germany. The north is part of the Ardennes plateau, with fertile lowlands in the south. The climate is mild and moist. Most people are Roman Catholics. Iron ore is the chief resource and there are large iron and steel works. About 52 per cent of the land is farmed: barley, oats, potatoes, sugar beet and wheat are major crops. Luxembourg became a Grand Duchy in 1354. The Spanish and then the Austrian Hapsburgs ruled it from 1482 to 1795, when France annexed it. In 1815 it became part of the Netherlands. In 1830 much of the Grand Duchy went to Belgium, but in 1839 the remaining eastern part (modern Luxembourg) achieved autonomy, although it was ruled by Dutch kings until 1890 when it broke away from the Netherlands. Germany occupied the country in World Wars I and II. In 1944 Belgium, the Netherlands and Luxembourg formed the Benelux Customs Union. Luxembourg was a founder member of NATO in 1949 and of the EEC in 1957. It is a constitutional monarchy with an elected Chamber of Deputies.

Area: 2586 km^2 (999 sq mi); **Population:** 360,000; **Capital:** Luxembourg (pop 80,000); **Official languages:** French, Luxemburgish; **Unit of currency:** Franc; **Per capita GNP:** US$12,280.

MACAO, or Macau, a small Portuguese territory on the south-eastern coast of China. It is densely populated. Most people are Chinese: less than 3 per cent are Portuguese. Little land is available for farming. There is a small fishing industry and manufacturing is important, especially textiles. Transit trade with China and tourism are other sources of income. Macao has been Portuguese since 1557. It became the chief European trading centre in China, but it declined after the British established Hong Kong in 1842.

Area: 16 km^2 (6 sq mi); **Population:** 330,000; **Capital:** Macao (pop 157,000); **Unit of currency:** Pataca; **Per capita GNP:** US$1750.

MADAGASCAR, an island republic separated from the African mainland by the 400 km (249 mi) wide Mozambique Channel. It was called the Malagasy Republic in 1960–75. A plateau 900–1500 m (2953–4921 ft) high covers about 66 per cent of the country; volcanic peaks, such as the Massif du Tsaratanana, rise above it. The coastal plain in the east is narrow, with broader lowlands in the west. The forested east coast is hot and humid. The grassy and savanna-covered plateau is cool, with an average annual temperature range of 14°–21°C (57°–70°F): the rainfall is between 1010 and 2030 mm (40–80 in) per year. The north-west is wet but the south-western lowlands are semi-desert. The people are of Indonesian and African origin: the largest of the main 18 groups is the Merina. In 1978 agriculture employed 86 per cent of the workforce, contributing 38 per cent of the GDP; industry accounted for 19 per cent and services 43 per cent. Only 5 per cent of the land is arable, 60 per cent is pasture and 21 per cent forest. Rice is the main food and coffee, cloves and vanilla are the main cash crops. There is little mining but there are many small processing industries and oil refining is important. Portuguese mariners discovered the island in 1500. France made it a protectorate in 1885. By 1896 the French had annexed the entire island and abolished the Merina monarchy. Independence was achieved in 1960. From 1972 the army has played a major part in government.

Area: 587,041 km^2 (226,670 sq mi); **Population:** 9,167,000; **Capital:** Antananarivo (pop 400,000); **Highest point:** Massif du Tsaratanana, 2876 m (9436 ft); **Official languages:** French, Malagasy; **Religions:** traditional beliefs (57 per cent), Christianity (40 per cent), Islam (3 per cent); **Adult literacy rate:** 50 per cent; **Average life expectancy at birth:** 46 years; **Unit of currency:** Franc Malgache; **Main exports:** coffee, cloves, vanilla; **Per capita GNP:** US$290.

MALAWI, a landlocked republic in southern Africa. It includes part of Lake Malawi (Nyasa) in the East African Rift Valley. The River Shire flows from the lake into the Zambezi in Mozambique. There are scenic highlands west of Lake Malawi, but the highest peak Mt Mlanje is east of the River Shire. An inland drainage basin around Lake Chilwa is in the south-east. The lowlands are hot and humid. The rainfall averages 760–1020 mm (30–40 in) per year. The highlands are wetter and cool. The people speak a number of Bantu languages. Agriculture employed 43 per cent of the workforce in 1978, accounting for 43 per cent of the GDP; industry contributed 19 per cent and services 38 per cent. Maize is the chief food crop. Tobacco accounted for 49 per cent of the exports and tea for 24 per cent in 1977. Arable land covers 19 per cent of the country, pasture 16 per cent, forests 20 per cent and water 21 per cent. The territory became the British Central African Protectorate in 1891: it was renamed Nyasaland in 1907. It became independent as Malawi in 1964 and adopted republican status in 1966. A one-party state, it has enjoyed stable government under its president-for-life, Dr Hastings Kamuzu Banda.

Area: 118,484 km^2 (45,749 sq mi); **Population:** 6,376,000; **Capital:** Lilongwe (pop 103,000); **Other cities:** Blantyre-Limbe (229,000); **Highest point:** Mt Mlanje, 3000 m (9843 ft); **Official languages:** English, Chichewa; **Religions:** traditional beliefs, Christianity (20 per cent); **Adult literacy rate:** 25 per cent; **Average life expectancy at birth:** 46 years; **Unit of currency:** Kwacha; **Main exports:** tobacco, tea, sugar, groundnuts; **Per capita GNP:** US$200.

MALAYSIA, a South-East Asian monarchy. It contains the southern Malay peninsula and Sabah and Sarawak in northern Borneo. Forested mountains cover large areas. The most important lowlands are in the Malay peninsula. The climate is tropical, with average annual temperatures of 21°–32°C (70°–90°F) and the average rainfall is about 2500 mm (98 in). The Malay peninsula contains 84 per cent of the population. In the country as a whole, 47 per cent are Malays, 34 per cent are Chinese, 9 per cent are Indians and Pakistanis, 5 per cent are Dayaks, 5 per cent belong to other tribes in Borneo, and 2 per cent belong to other groups. In 1978 agriculture employed 50 per cent of the workforce, but industry accounted for 32 per cent of the GDP, as opposed to 25 per cent from agriculture and 43 per cent from services. Tin is the main mineral. Some oil is also produced and manufacturing is increasing. The main cash crops are rubber and palm oil; rice is the main food crop. Timber is also important. Portuguese traders reached Malacca in 1509 but the Dutch took over in 1641. The British East India Company became established in Penang in 1786 and, in 1826, Penang, Malacca and Singapore became the British Straits Settlement. Britain took over its government in 1867. In 1888 North Borneo (Sabah) and Sarawak became British protectorates. Malaysia was created in 1963 when Malaya, Singapore, Sabah and Sarawak joined in a federation, although this led to fighting with Indonesia. However, Singapore seconded from the federation in 1965. Malaysia's Constitution provides that the 9 Rulers of the Malay states elect one of their number every 5 years to be *Yang di-Pertuan Agong* (Supreme Head of the Federation).

COUNTRIES OF THE WORLD

Area: 329,749 km^2 (127,324 sq mi); **Population:** 14,777,000; **Capital:** Kuala Lumpur (pop 770,000); **Highest point:** Mt Kinabalu, 4102 m (13,458 ft); **Official language:** Malay; **Religions:** mainly Islam, also Buddhism, Hinduism, Christianity; **Adult literacy rate:** 60 per cent; **Average life expectancy at birth:** 67 years; **Unit of currency:** Malaysian dollar; **Main exports:** rubber, tin, timber, palm oil; **Per capita GNP:** US$1320.

MALDIVES, an island republic about 650 km (404 mi) south-west of Sri Lanka. It includes about 2000 coral islands. Fishing is the main industry. Coconuts, millet and fruits are grown. The Maldives came under British protection in 1887. Full independence was achieved in 1965. The Maldives became a republic in 1968.

Area: 298 km^2 (115 sq mi); **Population:** 167,000; **Capital:** Malé (pop 30,000); **Official language:** Divehi; **Religion:** Islam; **Unit of currency:** Rupee; **Per capita GNP:** US$200.

MALI, a landlocked republic in north-western Africa. Plains cover most of Mali, with uplands in the north-east and south. The River Niger flows in a broad arc through southern Mali. Two-fifths of the river's total length of 4000 km (2486 mi) is in Mali. Average annual temperatures are 24°–35°C (75°–95°F). Bamako has about 1120 mm (44 in) of rain per year: the north is desert. There are people of Arab and Berber origin, such as Tuaregs, and some of mixed Caucasoid/Negroid origin, such as the Fulbe (Fulani). But more than 80 per cent of the population is Negroid. Agriculture employed 88 per cent of the workforce in 1978, accounting for 37 per cent of the GDP, as opposed to industry 18 per cent and services 45 per cent. Cultivated land covers only 8 per cent of this poor country. The chief cash crop is cotton. In 1979 Mali had 4.5 million cattle, 6.1 million sheep and 5.8 million goats. Mali was part of several medieval empires: Ancient Ghana, Mali and Songhai. In 1880 France made the area (then called French Sudan) a protectorate. Full independence was achieved in 1960. The army ruled from 1968 but elections were held in 1979. Mali is a one-party state.

Area: 1,240,000 km^2 (478,793 sq mi); **Population:** 6,966,000; **Capital:** Bamako (pop 404,000); **Official language:** French; **Religions:** Islam (65 per cent), traditional beliefs (30 per cent), Christianity (5 per cent); **Adult literacy rate:** 10 per cent; **Average life expectancy at birth:** 42 years; **Unit of currency:** Mali franc; **Main exports:** cotton and cotton products, groundnuts, live animals; **Per capita GNP:** US$140.

MALTA, a Mediterranean island republic, south of Sicily. It includes Malta, 246 km^2 (95 sq mi), Gozo, 67 km^2 (26 sq mi), Comino, 3 km^2 (1 sq mi) and two islets. The climate is Mediterranean in type. Most people are of Arab, Italian and English descent. Cultivable land covers 39 per cent of the country but only 6 per cent of the workforce is engaged in agriculture and fishing, as opposed to 28 per cent in manufacturing. In 1979 Malta received 618,000 tourists. Malta was held by the Phoenicians, Greeks, Carthaginians, Romans, Byzantines and Arabs until 1091 when it was joined to Sicily. From 1530 it was ruled by the Knights of St John. Napoleon's forces took it in 1798 but Britain aided the Maltese to drive out the French. In 1814 Malta became a British colony. It became fully independent in 1964 and a republic in 1974.

Area: 316 km^2 (122 sq mi); **Population:** 340,000; **Capital:** Valletta (pop 14,000); **Official languages:** Maltese, English; **Religion:** Roman Catholicism; **Unit of currency:** Maltese pound; **Main exports:** manufactures, machinery and transport equipment, food; **Per capita GNP:** US$2640.

MARTINIQUE, a French Overseas Department in the Lesser Antilles, between Dominica and St Lucia. It is a mountainous, volcanic island, with a warm, humid climate. The people are of African, Asian and French origin. The main activity is farming, but light manufacturing is developing. Discovered by Columbus in 1493, the island has been French for most of the time since 1635. It became a French Overseas Department in 1946.

Area: 1102 km^2 (426 sq mi); **Population:** 326,000; **Capital:** Fort-de-France (pop 99,000); **Highest point:** Mt Pelée, 1463 m (4800 ft); **Exports:** sugar, bananas, rum; **Per capita GNP:** US$4680.

MAURITANIA, an Islamic Republic in north-western Africa. Low plateaux cover most of the country which lies largely in the Sahara. But the fertile River Senegal plains are in the south-west. Average annual temperatures are between 25°C and 32°C (77°–90°F) and there are large diurnal variations in the Sahara. The average rainfall is 660 mm (26 inches) per year in the savanna-covered south. The north has little rainfall. About 80 per cent of the population is of Arab and Berber origin. The others are Negroid. Agriculture, particularly livestock rearing, employed 86 per cent of the workforce in 1978, accounting for 26 per cent of the GDP, as opposed to industry and services 37 per cent each. In 1979 Mauritania had 8.4 million sheep and goats and 1.6 million cattle. Sea fishing is important but the chief resource is iron ore: Mauritania is Africa's 3rd largest producer. Copper is also mined. France ruled Mauritania from 1903 to 1960. In 1976 Mauritania acquired one-third of neighbouring Western (formerly Spanish) Sahara. After prolonged resistance by Saharan guerrillas and an internal military coup in 1978, Mauritania withdrew from Western Sahara in 1979.

Area: 1,030,700 km^2 (397,977 sq mi); **Population:** 1,721,000; **Capital:** Nouakchott (pop 135,000); **Official language:** Arabic, French; **Religion:** Islam; **Adult literacy rate:** 17 per cent; **Average life expectancy at birth:** 42 years; **Unit of currency:** Ouguiya; **Main exports:** iron ore, fish, copper; **Per capita GNP:** US$320.

MAURITIUS, an island nation east of Madagascar in the Indian Ocean. It includes the mountainous, volcanic island of Mauritius and Rodrigues, 104 km^2 (40 sq mi) in area, which is about 560 km (348 mi) to the east. The climate is warm and humid, but it is modified by the altitude. The people are of Asian Hindu descent (53 per cent), Asian Muslim descent (17 per cent), and European, mixed and African descent (28 per cent). Sugar and its by-products form the basis of the economy. Tourism is increasing: foreign visitors numbered 128,000 in 1979. Britain captured Mauritius from France in 1810. It achieved independence in the Commonwealth in 1968 as a constitutional monarchy: the British monarch, represented by a Governor-General, is Head of State.

Area: 2045 km^2 (790 sq mi); **Population:** 973,000; **Capital:** Port Louis (pop 146,000); **Official language:** English; **Religions:** Hinduism, Christianity, Islam, Buddhism; **Unit of currency:** Rupee; **Main exports:** sugar, clothing; **Per capita GNP:** US$1040.

MEXICO, a republic in North America. It is largely mountainous, with high plateaux and volcanic peaks. The lowlands are in the Yucatán peninsula and along the Pacific and Gulf of Mexico coasts. The chief mountain ranges are the Sierra Madre Occidental and the Sierra Madre Oriental which enclose the central plateaux. These are dotted with lakes and volcanoes: one, Citlaltépetl, is Mexico's highest peak. The 760 km (472 mile) long peninsula, Lower or Baja California, is mostly separated from the rest of Mexico by the Gulf of California. It is a rugged, arid region. Mexico straddles the Tropic of Cancer, but there are 3 main climatic regions determined by the altitude: the tropical *tierra caliente*, below 1000 m (3281 ft); the mild *tierra templada*, between 1000 and 2500 m (3281–8202 ft), in which Mexico City is situated; and the *tierra fria* above 2500 m (8202 ft) with its cold winters. Rainfall in central Mexico averages 400–800 mm (16–31 in), but the north-west is arid. People of mixed European and Indian origin form 55 per cent of the population; Indians 29 per cent and Europeans 15 per cent. In 1978 agriculture employed 39 per cent of the people, industry 26 per cent and services 35 per cent. Contributions to the GDP were agriculture 11 per cent, industry 37 per cent and services 52 per cent. Crops vary according to the altitude. They include coffee, cotton, maize, sisal and sugar. In 1979 Mexico had 29.9 million cattle, 7.8 million sheep, 8.1 million goats and 12.6 million pigs. Mining is important. Mexico is a major oil producer. Coal, copper, gold, iron ore, lead, manganese, mercury, silver, zinc and other minerals are mined. Manufacturing includes light and heavy industry: textiles and steel are leading manufactures. Aztec and other Indian ruins are tourist attractions: 3.7 million tourists visited Mexico in 1978. Spain ruled Mexico from 1521 to 1821. The country became a republic in 1824. Instability, wars and dictatorships marred Mexico's progress. From 1917, however, Mexico has made social and economic progress. Membership of the Latin American Free Trade Association since 1961 has helped to reduce Mexico's dependency on the United States.

Area: 1,972,547 km^2 (761,646 sq mi); **Population:** 74,539,000; **Capital:** Mexico City (pop 9,618,000); **Other cities:** Guadalajara (1,725,000), Monterrey (1,132,000); **Highest point:** Citlaltépetl, 5760 m (18,898 ft); **Official language:** Spanish; **Religion:** mainly Roman Catholicism; **Adult literacy rate:** 76 per cent; **Average life expectancy at birth:** 65 years; **Unit of currency:** Peso; **Main exports:** manufactures, oil, coffee, sugar, cotton; **Per capita GNP:** US$1590.

MONACO, a tiny principality on the Mediterranean Sea in south-eastern France. There are 4 districts: Monaco-Ville, the capital; la Condamine, a resort area; Monte-Carlo, a luxury resort with a famous casino; and Fontvieille. French currency is used. From 1297 Monaco belonged to the Genoese Grimaldi family. It became fully independent in 1861 and joined a customs union with France in 1865. In 1963 it ceased to be a tax haven for French citizens. Monaco is a constitutional monarchy with an elected National Council and Communal Council.

Area: 190 ha (467 acres); **Population:** 25,000; **Capital:** Monaco; **Official language:** French.

Below: An Aztec mask. The Aztecs ruled Mexico from the 13th to the early 16th centuries, but they were crushed by Spanish conquistadores. Below right: Acapulco, a major resort on the Pacific coast of Mexico, attracts many foreign tourists.

COUNTRIES OF THE WORLD

MONGOLIA, a landlocked People's Republic in northern Asia. A featureless plateau covers much of Mongolia, with mountains in the west and the Gobi desert, which covers one-third of the country, in the south. The main rivers are the Selenga, which flows into Lake Baykal, and the Kerulen, a tributary of the Amur River. The climate is severe. Temperatures average about 15°C (59°F) in July, but they plummet to −34°C (−29°F) in January. The average annual rainfall ranges from 500 mm (20 in) in the north to 130 mm (5 in) in the Gobi desert. The land is thinly populated. In 1978 agriculture employed 56 per cent of the people, industry 21 per cent and services 23 per cent. Most people were formerly nomadic herdsmen and in 1979 there were 14 million sheep, 4.7 million goats, 2.5 million cattle and 2 million horses. But all farmland is now organized in large state or collective farms: these farms own 80 per cent of the animals. Some oil, coal and other minerals are produced, but manufacturing is small-scale. The Mongol Empire became important in the 13th century under Genghis Khan. Mongolia became a Chinese province in 1691 but it became an independent Buddhist kingdom in 1912. In 1924 the communist Mongolian People's Republic was set up and religion was suppressed in the 1930s. Mongolia has been a member of COMECON since 1962.

Area: 1,565,000 km² (604,283 sq mi); **Population:** 1,772,000; **Capital:** Ulan Bator (pop 400,000); **Official language:** Mongol; **Religion:** formerly Tibetan Buddhist Lamaism; **Average life expectancy at birth:** 63 years; **Unit of currency:** Tugrik; **Main exports:** cattle and horses, wool and hair, grains, hides, furs; **Per capita GNP:** US$780.

Mongolia's economy was traditionally based on nomadic herding and most people lived in tents called ger *or* yurts. *These portable homes were made of felt which was stretched over a wooden frame. In recent years, an increasing number of Mongolians have adopted a more settled life.*

MONTSERRAT, a British colony in the Leeward Islands of the West Indies. It is volcanic and largely mountainous: earthquakes are common. Agriculture is the main industry: hot peppers, tomatoes and manufactures are exported. In 1979 14,400 tourists visited Montserrat. Columbus discovered the island in 1493. Irish settlers colonized it in 1632. It came under the British Crown in 1783.

Area: 98 km² (38 sq mi); **Population:** 12,000; **Chief town:** Plymouth (pop 3000); **Per capita GNP:** US$920 (1978).

MOROCCO, a monarchy in north-eastern Africa. The folded Atlas ranges cover much of the country: the highest point is Djebel Toubkal in the High Atlas range. The Anti-Atlas in the south is an uplifted rim of the African plateau. The fertile Rharb-Sebou lowlands and the Moulouya valley are in the north. Low plateaux border the narrow coastal plain in central Morocco. Tangier has an average annual temperature range of 11°–29°C (52°–84°F), but the south is cooler because of the cold Canaries current offshore. The average annual rainfall is about 760 mm (30 in) in some uplands, but the south and east merge into the Sahara. Most people are Arabs. About 30 per cent are Berbers and there is a small European minority. In 1978 agriculture employed 53 per cent of the workforce, but contributed only 14 per cent to the GDP, as opposed to 36 per cent from industry. Barley, citrus fruits, grapes and wheat are important crops. There are 13 million sheep, 3.6 million cattle and 5.6 million goats. Forestry and fishing are also important, but the main resource is phosphates. Iron ore, lead, manganese, oil, zinc and other minerals are mined. France ruled most of Morocco from 1912, although Spain held the north. Morocco became an independent kingdom in 1956, but Spain retained garrisons at Ceuta and Melilla. In 1976 Morocco and Mauritania partitioned the barren but phosphate-rich Western (formerly Spanish) Sahara. But guerrilla forces resisted the Moroccan and Mauritanian troops. In 1979 Mauritania withdrew and Morocco took the entire territory. The war continued into the 1980s.

Area: 446,550 km² (172,423 sq mi), not including Western Sahara; **Population:** 21,280,000; **Capital:** Rabat (pop 368,000); **Other cities:** Casablanca (1,506,000), Marrakesh (333,000), Fès (325,000); **Highest point:** Mt Toubkal, 4165 m (13,665 ft); **Official language:** Arabic; **Religion:** Islam; **Adult literacy rate:** 28 per cent; **Average life expectancy at birth:** 55 years; **Unit of currency:** Dirham; **Main exports:** phosphates, citrus fruits, fish; **Per capita GNP:** US$740.

MOZAMBIQUE, a People's Republic in south-eastern Africa. Coastal plains cover 44 per cent of the land, plateaux and hills 43 per cent and uplands 13 per cent. The main rivers are the Rovuma, Zambezi and Limpopo. Lake Nyasa (Malawi) is shared with Malawi and Tanzania. There is also a man-made lake behind the Cabora Bassa Dam on the Zambezi. The centre and north have a tropical climate. The far south is subtropical. The rainfall is generally low: Maputo has 760 mm (30 in) per year. There are 12 major Bantu-speaking tribes and more than 30 minor ones. Agriculture employed 67 per cent of the people in this poor nation in 1978, accounting for 45 per cent of the GDP; industry contributed 16 per cent. Arable land covers 4 per cent of the land and pasture 56 per cent. Leading crops are cashew nuts, copra, cotton,

This Berber family lives north of the Atlas mountains in Morocco. Berbers were the original inhabitants of north-western Africa, but they rapidly embraced Islam during the Arab conquest of North Africa between the 7th and the 12th centuries, although they retained their own language. Today some Berbers are nomadic herdsmen; others are sedentary farmers or skilled craftsmen. About three out of every ten Moroccans are Berbers.

groundnuts, maize, rice, sisal, sugar-cane and tobacco. Disease-carrying tsetse flies restrict livestock-rearing. Some coal is mined and the towns contain some industries. Portugal became established in Mozambique in the early 16th century. A guerrilla war (1964–74) preceded independence in 1975. The Constitution of 1978 vests power in the sole political party, FRELIMO, and declares socialism to be the national objective.

Area: 783,030 km² (302,346 sq mi); **Population:** 10,987,000; **Capital:** Maputo (pop 355,000); **Official language:** Portuguese; **Religions:** mainly traditional beliefs, Christianity (21 per cent), Islam (12 per cent); **Adult literacy rate:** 15 per cent (1975); **Average life expectancy at birth:** 46 years; **Unit of currency:** Metical; **Main exports:** cashew nuts, textiles, tea, cotton, sugar; **Per capita GNP:** US$250.

NAMIBIA, a South African-ruled country whose status is disputed. It is called South West Africa by South Africa. Behind the coastal plain (the Namib desert) is the central plateau. The Kalahari, a semi-desert, is in the east. The north is tropical and the south sub-tropical. More than 66 per cent of Namibia has less than 400 mm (16 in) of rain per year. The Namib is almost rainless: the northern interior is the wettest place. The people include Europeans (12 per cent), people of mixed origin (6 per cent), Khoisan and related peoples, including Nama (Hottentots) and Bushmen (16 per cent) and Bantu-speaking people who make up the rest of the population. Mining contributes 33 per cent of the GDP. Diamonds, lead, tin, zinc and uranium are exported. Agriculture contributes 13 per cent: the main activity is pastoralism. Fishing contributes 3 per cent and manufacturing 7 per cent. Britain annexed Walvis Bay in 1878 and later transferred it to South Africa. Germany took the rest of the country in 1884. South Africa occupied it in World War I. In 1920 the League of Nations mandated South Africa to rule the country. But in 1946 it refused to accept the trusteeship status that replaced the old mandate. The UN and South Africa have since been in dispute, despite many attempts to achieve a settlement. A guerrilla war, begun in 1966, continued into the 1980s.

Area: 824,292 km² (318,278 sq mi); **Population:** 1,066,000; **Capital:** Windhoek (pop 76,000); **Highest point:** 2483 m (8146 ft); **Official languages:** Afrikaans, English; **Religions:** Christianity, traditional beliefs (17 per cent), **Adult literacy rate:** 12 per cent (1971); **Unit of currency:** Rand; **Main exports:** diamonds and other minerals, fish products, livestock, karakul pelts; **Per capita GNP:** US$1220.

NAURU, an island republic close to the equator in the western Pacific Ocean. A raised atoll, it contains rich phosphate deposits on which the economy is based. 50 per cent of the people are Polynesians, 27 per cent are other Pacific islanders, 16 per cent are Chinese and 7 per cent are Europeans. Discovered in 1798, Nauru was annexed by Germany in 1888. Australia occupied it in 1914 and the League of Nations mandated Britain to rule it in 1920. Full independence, with a special relationship with the Commonwealth, was achieved in 1968.

Area: 21 km² (8 sq mi); **Population:** 7250; **Capital:** Nauru; **Main export:** phosphates.

NEPAL, a landlocked monarchy between China and India. It includes some of the world's highest peaks in the Himalayas, including Mt Everest on the Chinese border. Two-thirds of Nepal is mountainous. There are temperate valleys and warm plains near the Indian border. The people are of Tibetan or Indian descent, including the warlike Gurkhas. In 1978 93 per cent of the people worked in agriculture, which accounted for 62 per cent of the GDP. Hydro-electricity and manufacturing are developing. The monarchs were figureheads between 1846 and 1951, but their power was restored in 1951. The monarch assumed absolute power in 1960, but a National Parliament was elected in 1981.

Area: 140,797 km² (54,365 sq mi); **Population:** 14,932,000; **Capital:** Katmandu (pop 195,000); **Highest point:** Mt Everest, 8848 m (29,028 ft); **Official language:** Nepáli; **Religion:** Hinduism (90 per cent); **Adult literacy rate:** 19 per cent; **Life expectancy at birth:** 43 years; **Unit of currency:** Rupee; **Main exports:** grains, timber, cattle, hides, resins, medicinal herbs; **Per capita GNP:** US$130.

NETHERLANDS, a prosperous monarchy, is one of the Low Countries. It is at the western edge of the North European Plain. About 40 per cent of the country is below sea-level at high tide: the sea is held back by dykes which enclose polders (reclaimed areas). The most recent polders are in

COUNTRIES OF THE WORLD

Amsterdam, capital of the Netherlands, is built around a network of concentric and radial canals. The city contains about 400 bridges.

The Maoris of New Zealand are a Polynesian people known for their skill in wood, stone and bone carving. Images of human figures are called tikis.

the IJsselmeer (Zuider Zee) and the Delta region in the south-west. Polders make up more than 25 per cent of the land. The centre of the country consists of the flood plains of the Rhine and Maas (Meuse) rivers, and their branches (the IJssel, Lek and Waal). The Schelde river enters the sea in the south-west. The coastal region contains many islands, deep estuaries, marshes, sand dunes and polders. The highest land is in the south-east (Limburg). The annual temperature range is 2°–20°C (36°–68°F) and the average annual rainfall is about 760 mm (30 in). With about 350 people per sq km (908 per sq mi), the Netherlands is one of the world's most densely populated nations: 76 per cent lived in urban areas in 1980. In 1978 agriculture employed 6 per cent of the workforce, industry 45 per cent and services 49 per cent; they accounted for 4 per cent, 34 per cent and 62 per cent respectively of the GDP. Nearly 70 per cent of the land is farmed. Most farms are small but the yields are among the world's highest. Livestock are important: in 1980 there were 5.2 million cattle, 10.1 million pigs and 81.2 million poultry. Butter, cheese and eggs are major products. Leading crops include flowers and bulbs, potatoes, sugar beet and wheat. There is little mining apart from the extraction of natural gas and oil: in 1979 the Netherlands was the world's 4th largest natural gas producer and Western Europe's 5th oil producer. The chief manufacturing region is the Randstadt, a ring of cities around the polders of the west-centre: Rotterdam with its port Europoort, The Hague, Haarlem, Amsterdam and Utrecht. Eindhoven is another industrial centre. Petroleum products, ships, radio and television sets, textiles, and china and earthenware goods are major products. The country has been largely independent since the late 16th century. In the 17th century it built up a large overseas empire. France invaded the Netherlands in 1795 but it became a constitutional monarchy in 1815. In 1830 Belgium broke away followed by Luxembourg in 1890. Neutral in World War I, the Netherlands was occupied by Germany in 1940. After the war its economy thrived within the Benelux Customs Union. It joined NATO in 1949, the European Coal and Steel Community in 1953, and the EEC in 1957. Its last 2 monarchs, Queen Wilhelmina and Queen Juliana, both abdicated in favour of their daughters. Queen Beatrix became Head of State in 1980. Parliament consists of a First, or Upper, Chamber with 75 members elected by the provincial legislatures, and a Second Chamber of 150 directly elected deputies.

Area: 40,844 km² (15,771 sq mi); **Population:** 14,324,000; **Capital:** Amsterdam (pop with suburbs, 1,015,000); **Other cities:** Rotterdam (1,018,000), The Hague (675,000), Utrecht (482,000), Eindhoven (369,000); **Highest point:** 332 m (1056 ft); **Official language:** Dutch; **Religions:** Roman Catholicism, Protestantism; **Adult literacy rate:** 99 per cent; **Average life expectancy at birth:** 74 years; **Unit of currency:** Florin (Guilder); **Main exports:** chemicals, petroleum products, machinery and engineering products, food, textiles; **Per capital GNP:** US$10,240.

NETHERLANDS ANTILLES, two groups of Dutch islands in the Caribbean Sea. Curaçao, Aruba and Bonaire are near the Venezuelan coast. St Maarten, St Eustatius and Saba are in the northern Leeward Islands, east of Puerto Rico. The refining of oil from Venezuela is the main industry. The islands became Dutch in the 17th century and were called Curaçao until 1949. They achieved full autonomy in internal affairs in 1954.

Sheep graze on Braemar Station at the foot of the Southern Alps on South Island, New Zealand. Lamb and wool are among the chief products.

Area: 961 km² (371 sq mi); **Population:** 273,000; **Capital:** Willemstad on Curaçao (pop 155,000); **Per capita GNP:** US$3540.

NEW CALEDONIA, a French Overseas Territory in the south-western Pacific, including New Caledonia and various small island dependencies, such as the Loyalty Islands. This tropical, mountainous country has a mainly Melanesian and European population. It possesses large reserves of nickel, chrome ore, iron ore and manganese, together with deposits of many other minerals. Only 6 per cent of the land is cultivable. Coffee, coconuts and meat are the main products. New Caledonia was discovered by Captain James Cook in 1774. It became a French colony in 1853 and an Overseas Territory in 1958.

Area: 19,058 km² (7359 sq mi); **Population:** 171,000; **Capital:** Nouméa (pop 74,000); **Per capita GNP:** US$5620.

NEW ZEALAND, a member nation of the Commonwealth in the south-western Pacific Ocean. It contains North Island, 114,681 km² (44,281 sq mi), South Island, 150,452 km² (58,093 sq mi), Stewart Island, 1735 km² (670 sq mi), the Chatham Islands, 963 km² (372 sq mi) and some smaller islands. North Island, where most people live, contains fertile plains, a volcanic central plateau, and fold mountain ranges in the east. Active volcanoes include Ngauruhoe, 2291 m (7516 ft), Ruapehu, 2796 m (9173 ft) and Tongariro, 1968 m (6457 ft). Lake Taupo in the centre is in a crater of an extinct volcano. North of the lake, hot springs are utilized to produce electricity. The eastern fold mountains continue in South Island as the Southern Alps, which reach their highest point in Mt Cook. Glaciers flow down high valleys and the south-western coast is glaciated with scenic fiords. Important lowlands include the Canterbury Plains in the east and the Otago plateau in the south-east. New Zealand has a cool, temperate climate. The average annual temperature range at Dunedin is 6°–14°C (43°–57°F), while at Auckland it is 11°–19°C (52°–66°F). Heavy rain falls in the Southern Alps but the Canterbury plains get only about 600 mm (24 in). North Island has between 1000–2000 mm (39–79 in) per year. About 91 per cent of the population is of European, mostly British, origin; 8 per cent are Maoris and 1 per cent other Pacific peoples. In 1978 agriculture employed 10 per cent of the workforce, accounting for 10 per cent of the GDP; industry employed 35 per cent and contributed 31 per cent of the GDP. Farming is efficient and yields high. In 1979 there were 8.5 million cattle and 78 million sheep. Wool, beef, lamb, mutton and dairy products are the leading exports. Arable farming is less important than pastoralism, but cereals, fruits, tobacco and vegetables are all important. New Zealand has a few minerals, including some coal and ironsands. Nearly 70 per cent of the electricity, however, is generated by hydro-electric stations. Most older manufacturing industries process farm products, but New Zealand now has a variety of light and heavy industry. Tourism is growing: there were 339,000 tourists in 1979–80. Maoris probably settled in New Zealand in the 14th century. The Dutch navigator Abel Tasman reached New Zealand in 1642 but his discovery was kept a secret. Captain James Cook rediscovered it in 1769. Wars between early British settlers and the Maoris occurred between 1845 and 1870, reducing the Maori population to 42,000: they numbered 270,000 in 1976. New Zealand became an independent dominion in 1907. Its parliament consists of a House of Representatives which, in 1978, had 92 members elected for 3-year terms. The British monarch, represented by a Governor-General, is Head of State.

Area: 268,676 km² (103,742 sq mi); **Population:** 3,400,000; **Capital:** Wellington (pop 350,000); **Other cities:** Auckland (806,000), Christchurch (327,000), Hamilton (158,000), Dunedin (120,000); **Highest point:** Mt Cook, 3764 m (12,349 ft); **Official language:** English; **Religion:** Christianity; **Adult literacy rate:** 99 per cent; **Average life expectancy at birth:** 73 years; **Unit of currency:** New Zealand dollar; **Main exports:** meat, wool, dairy products, hides, aluminium; **Per capita GNP:** US$5940.

NICARAGUA, a Central American republic. Forested plains border the Caribbean Sea. In the centre is a highland region with some active volcanoes. It is broadest and highest in the north. The Pacific coastlands contain two huge lakes, Managua and Nicaragua. The country has a hot and humid climate. About 80 per cent of the people are of mixed white and Indian origin, 10 per cent are blacks and 4 per cent are pure Indians. Agriculture employed 44 per cent of the workforce in 1978, contributing 23 per cent of the GDP (26 per cent came from industry). Coffee, cotton and meat are major products. Gold, silver and copper are mined and manufacturing is expanding rapidly. Spain conquered Nicaragua in the early 16th century. Independence was achieved in 1821, but the country came under Mexico in 1822 and in 1823–38 it was part of the Central American Federation. A new Constitution was adopted in 1974, providing for a bicameral parliament. But in 1979 the left-wing Sandinist National Liberation Front overthrew the government. A Junta of National Reconstruction was formed to rule the country.

Area: 130,000 km² (50,196 sq mi); **Population:** 2,851,000; **Capital:** Managua (pop 553,000); **Highest point:** Cordillera Isabella, 2438 m (7999 ft); **Official language:** Spanish; **Religion:** Roman Catholicism; **Adult literacy rate:** 57 per cent; **Average life expectancy at birth:** 55 years; **Unit of currency:** Córdoba; **Main exports:** coffee, cotton, meat, chemical products; **Per capita GNP:** US$660.

NIGER, a poor landlocked republic in north-central Africa. The highest peaks are in the Aïr massif in the north; plateaux and plains cover most of Niger. The only river is the Niger in the south-west. The north is mostly in the hot Sahara, although there is some pasture in the Aïr massif. The far south has about 560 mm (22 in) of rain per year. Nomadic Tuaregs live in the Sahara, but most of the people are black Africans who live in the south. In 1978 agriculture employed 91 per cent of the workforce, accounting for 43 per cent of the GDP. Live animals, animal products, groundnuts and vegetables are important products. Niger also has large uranium deposits. France occupied Niger in 1897–1900. Full independence was achieved in 1960. In 1974 a military group seized power and a Supreme Military Council was appointed to rule the country.

Area: 1,267,000 km² (489,218 sq mi); **Population:** 5,600,000; **Capital:** Niamey (pop 225,000); **Official language:** French; **Religions:** Islam (85 per cent), traditional beliefs (14.5 per cent), Christianity; **Adult literacy rate:** 8 per cent; **Average life expectancy at birth:** 42 years; **Unit of currency:** Franc CFA; **Main exports:** uranium concentrates, live animals, vegetables, groundnuts; **Per capita GNP:** US$240.

NIGERIA, a Federal Republic in West Africa. Most of the country is drained by the Niger and Benue rivers. North of these rivers are the high plains of Hausaland and higher plateaux. The land descends to the Sokoto plains in the north-west and the Lake Chad internal drainage basin in the north-east. South and west of the Niger River are hilly uplands bordered by a broad coastal plain which extends to the huge, swampy Niger delta. In the south-east the land rises to mountains on the Cameroon border. The climate is equatorial. Temperatures average 27°C (81°F) throughout the year. In the south Lagos has an average annual rainfall of 1780 mm (70 in) while the north has 250–1000 mm (10–39 in). Forest is the typical vegetation in the south with savanna in the north and semi-desert in the Chad basin. About 250

languages and dialects are spoken in Nigeria, Africa's most populous nation. The largest groups are the Muslim Hausa and Fulani in the north, the Ibo in the south-east and the Yoruba in the south-west. Agriculture employed 56 per cent of the population in 1978 but accounted for only 34 per cent of the GDP, as opposed to 43 per cent from industry. Tropical crops remain important, but oil has dominated the economy in recent years, accounting for more than 90 per cent of the exports. Revenue from oil sales is being used to diversify the economy and to improve the infrastructure, including the building of a new federal capital at Abuja in central Nigeria, which is due to be completed in the mid-1980s. Southern Nigeria was a centre of the slave trade from the 15th century. Britain abolished the slave trade in 1807 and, in 1861, annexed Lagos to stop the slave trade there. Between 1885 and 1903 Britain extended its control over Nigeria. Full independence was achieved in 1960 and Nigeria became a republic in 1963. From 1966–79 military regimes ruled Nigeria. In 1967–70 a civil war occurred when the people of the south-east tried to secede and set up a new nation, Biafra. Nigeria has sought to reduce tensions caused by cultural diversity by extending powers to the states, which number 19. Civilian rule was restored in 1979 under a Constitution that provides for a federal parliament consisting of a 96-member Senate and a 449-member House of Representatives, and an elected Governor and a State House of Assembly for each of the states.

Area: 923,768 km² (356,688 sq mi); **Population:** 88,847,000; **Capital:** Lagos (pop 1,061,000), but Abuja is scheduled to become capital in the mid-1980s; **Other cities:** Ibadan (847,000), Ogbomosho (432,000), Kano (399,000), Oshogbo (282,000), Ilorin (282,000); **Highest point:** about 2130 m (6988 ft) on Cameroon border; **Official language:** English; **Religions:** Islam, Christianity, traditional beliefs; **Average life expectancy at birth:** 48 years; **Unit of currency:** Naira; **Main exports:** oil, cocoa, palm kernels, tin, rubber; **Per capita GNP:** US$670.

NIUE ISLAND, a self-governing territory of New Zealand in the Cook Is in the South Pacific. These coral islands export copra and fruit. Britain annexed the island in 1899; New Zealand took over in 1901. It has been self-governing since 1974.

Opposite: Most people in northern Nigeria, including the Hausa and Fulani, are Muslims and mosques are common sights. Christianity and traditional religions are more important in southern Nigeria. Above: Norway's many fiords provide shelter for small fishing villages.

Area: 259 km² (100 sq mi); **Population:** 3954 (1976); **Chief town:** Alofi.

NORFOLK ISLAND, an Australian territory in the south-western Pacific. The climate of this volcanic island is pleasant: tourism is important. The island was an Australian penal colony in the 19th century. Most of the islanders are descendants of the *Bounty* mutineers.

Area: 36 km² (14 sq mi); **Population:** 2180 (1979); **Chief town:** Kingstown.

NORWAY, a monarchy in the western part of the mountainous Scandinavian peninsula. The Kjölen mountains form much of the border with Sweden. In the south there is an extensive region of high plateaux and mountains, including the highest peak, Galdhöppigen. The only large lowlands are in the south-east. The climate is mild, especially in winter, when the western coasts are warmed by the North Atlantic Drift. Even at North Cape, Norway's and Europe's most northerly point, the sea never freezes. Norway is thinly populated. In 1978 agriculture, forestry and fishing employed 8 per cent of the workforce and contributed 5 per cent of the GDP as opposed to 36 per cent from industry. Only 2 per cent of the land is cultivated and food must be imported. Coniferous forests cover 26 per cent of the land and the pulp and paper industry is important. Fishing is an important activity for people who live in the fiords or on the 50,000 or so islands. Bergen is the chief fishing port. Norway has rich oil reserves in the North Sea: it is Western Europe's 2nd largest oil producer. Iron ore, copper, lead and zinc are also mined and a high proportion of Norway's exports come from the electro-metallurgical, electro-chemical and paper industries. Hydro-electric power stations provide electricity for most purposes. Norway's large merchant shipping fleet is another major source of income. Between 1380 and 1814 Norway was united with Denmark under Danish rule. After a brief period of independence, Norway entered into a union with Sweden. This union was dissolved in 1905 and the Norwegians elected their own monarch, Haakon VII. After World War II, when it was occupied by Germany, Norway has made much economic progress and it now enjoys one of the world's highest standards of living. It rejected EEC membership in 1971. Norway is a constitutional monarchy with an elected *Storting* (parliament).

Area: 324,219 km² (125,188 sq mi); **Population:** 4,138,000; **Capital:** Oslo (pop 455,000); **Other cities:** Bergen (209,000), Trondheim (135,000); **Highest point:** Galdhöppigen, 2472 m (8110 ft); **Official language:** Norwegian; **Religion:** Evangelical Lutheran Church; **Adult literacy rate:** 99 per cent; **Average life expectancy at birth:** 75 years; **Unit of currency:** Krone; **Main exports:** machinery and transport equipment, metals and metal products, oil, animal products, paper; **Per capita GNP:** US$10,710.

OMAN, a Sultanate in the south-eastern corner of the Arabian peninsula. Behind the fertile northern coast (the Batinah north-west of Muscat) is a barren upland that merges into an arid interior plateau. The only other fertile region is in the far south (Dhufar). Temperatures at Muscat vary between 21°C and 43°C (70°–109°F). The average annual rainfall is only 10 mm (0.4 inches). Arabs make up 90 per cent of the population. There are also some Indians, Iranians, Negroes and Pakistanis. Most people are farmers or fishermen, but the oil industry dominates the economy. Oil production began in 1967 and it is now the leading export, although dates, dried fish, limes and other fruits, tobacco and vegetables are also exported. Muscat was a major Indian Ocean trading centre from early times. Portugal controlled it in 1508–1648. The present royal family was founded in 1741. Britain established a special relationship with the area in 1891. Oman is now an independent, absolute monarchy, but it retains ties with Britain, which helped to suppress left-wing guerrilla activity in the south in 1964–75.

Area: 212,457 km² (82,035 sq mi); **Population:** 950,000; **Capital:** Muscat (pop 7000); **Highest point:** Jabal Akhdar, 3047 m (9997 ft); **Official language:** Arabic; **Religion:** Islam; **Adult literacy rate:** 20 per cent; **Unit of currency:** Rial Omani; **Main exports:** oil, dates, limes, tobacco, frankincense; **Per capita GNP:** US$2970.

PACIFIC ISLANDS, TRUST TERRITORY OF, Micronesian islands governed by the United States since 1946. It includes the Mariana Is (excluding Guam), the Caroline Is and the Marshall Is. Tourism, fishing and farming are the main activities. From the late 1970s the US established Constitutions and set up local governments with the aim of creating a new status, either full independence or a continuing free association.

Area: 1779 km² (687 sq mi); **Population:** 149,000; **Capital:** Saipan; **Official language:** English; **Per capita GNP:** US$1340.

COUNTRIES OF THE WORLD

PAKISTAN, an Islamic Republic in southern Asia. The land is mountainous in the north where the Hindu Kush and Himalayas rise. Central and southern Pakistan contain fertile plains drained and irrigated by the River Indus and its tributaries (the Beas, Chenab, Jhelum, Ravi and Sutlej). The south-west includes the arid Baluchistan plateau and the Thar desert is in the south-east. Winters are cold in the mountainous north and cold north-easterly winds chill the northern plains in November–February. For example, the average January temperature in Lahore is 12°C (54°F) as compared with 18°C (64°F) in Karachi. In the hot season, March–May, the average temperature in Karachi rises to 29°C (84°F) but the northern plains are even hotter. It is cooler in the monsoon season, June–October, but the rainfall brought by the south-westerly winds is generally low. Karachi has an average annual rainfall of only 130 mm (5 in) although the north-east has 630–760 mm (25–30 in). Modern Pakistanis are descendants of the many peoples who have invaded the area. Several languages are spoken, including Urdu, Punjabi, Sindhi, Pashto and Baluchi. In 1980 72 per cent of the population of this extremely poor country lived in rural areas. Agriculture is the main activity, accounting for 32 per cent of the GDP as opposed to 24 per cent from industry in 1978. Leading crops are rice, winter wheat, cotton, maize and sugar-cane. Hydro-electricity is important and Pakistan has large reserves of natural gas. Textiles, cement, sugar and fertilizers are leading manufactures. The Indus valley was the home of early civilizations dating back to 2500 BC. Islam was introduced in the 8th century AD. From 1526 the area came under the Mughal Empire, but this began to decline in the 17th century. By the 19th century, Britain was the dominant power and Pakistan became part of British India. At independence in 1947, however, the predominantly Muslim Pakistan broke away from India, although fighting for the disputed province of Kashmir continued until 1949. Newly-independent Pakistan consisted of two parts: West Pakistan, now Pakistan itself, and East Pakistan which became Bangladesh after a civil war in 1971. Pakistan withdrew from the Commonwealth in 1972, and armed forces took over the government in 1977.

Area: 803,943 km² (310,421 sq mi); **Population:** 85,558,000; **Capital:** Islamabad (pop 235,000); **Other cities:** Karachi (3,499,000), Lahore (2,165,000), Faisalbad (822,000), Rawalpindi (615,000); **Official language:** Urdu; **Religions:** Islam (88 per cent), Hinduism (11 per cent), Christianity, Buddhism; **Adult literacy rate:** 21 per cent; **Average life expectancy at birth:** 52 years; **Unit of currency:** Rupee; **Main exports:** cotton and cotton goods, rice, carpets and rugs, leather; **Per capita GNP:** US$270.

PANAMA, a narrow Central American republic linking North and South America. Behind the Pacific and Caribbean coastal plains the interior is mountainous, the highest peak being Mt Chiriqui in the west. Panama's greatest width is only about 190 km (118 mi). It is at its narrowest at the point where the 81.6 km (50.7 mi) long Panama Canal is situated. The United States governed the Panama Canal Zone, a strip of land along the Canal, until 1979 when it reverted to Panama, although the US retained control over the Canal itself until 1999. Panama has a tropical climate, with an average annual rainfall of 3300 mm (130 in) on the Caribbean coast and 1500 mm (59 in) on the Pacific coast. More than 75 per cent of the people are of mixed white and Indian descent and in 1980 54 per cent of the population lived in urban areas. Only 18.5

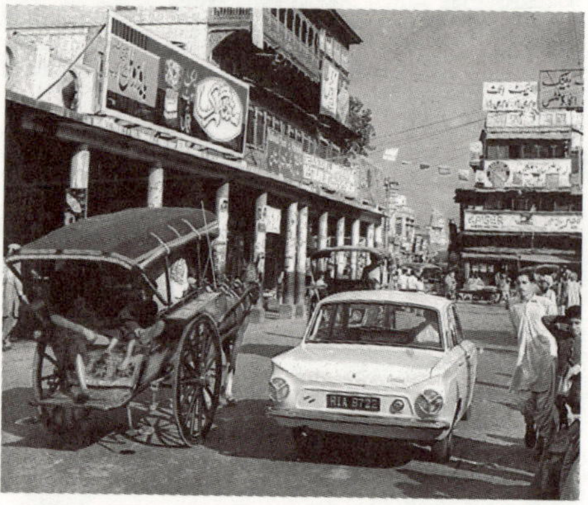

per cent of the land is cultivated, although agriculture employed 35 per cent of the workforce in 1978, compared with 18 per cent in industry and 47 per cent in services. Bananas, rice and sugar-cane are major crops and there are copper reserves. But Panama's chief resource is the Canal. Panama became independent from Spain in 1819 as part of Colombia. It became a separate nation in 1914.

Area: 75,650 km² (29,210 sq mi); **Population:** 2,012,000; **Capital:** Panamá (pop 467,000); **Highest point:** Mt Chiriqui, 3374 m (11,070 ft); **Official language:** Spanish; **Religions:** Roman Catholicism (95 per cent); **Adult literacy rate:** 78 per cent; **Average life expectancy at birth:** 70 years; **Unit of currency:** Balboa; **Main exports:** petroleum products, bananas, sugar, shrimps; **Per capita GNP:** US$1350.

PAPUA NEW GUINEA, a nation in the south-western Pacific Ocean. It consists of the eastern part of New Guinea, the Bismarck Archipelago, including Manus Is, New Britain and New Ireland; Bougainville and Buka in the northern Solomon Is; the D'Entrecasteaux Is; the Louisiade Archipelago and the Trobriand Is; and about 600 smaller islands. New Guinea contains forested mountain ranges and broad, swampy river valleys. There are 40 active volcanoes in the north: this volcanic zone extends eastwards through the islands. The climate is hot and humid, but the uplands are cooler, Port Moresby has an average annual rainfall of 1200 mm (47 in). About 700 languages are spoken by the various tribal groups, a few of which have never come into contact with Western civilization. Tribal warfare still occurs. Agriculture employed 82 per cent of the people in 1978, accounting for 33 per cent of the GDP as opposed to 26 per cent from industry. The main resource, copper, is mined on Bougainville. Coffee, cocoa, copra, timber and fish are other major products. The Dutch took western New Guinea in 1828. Germany took the north-east in 1884 and Britain took the south-east, transferring it to Australia in 1906. Australia occupied German New Guinea in 1914 and ruled it with the south-east, called Papua. The combined territory was named Papua New Guinea in 1971 and it achieved full independence as a monarchy in the Commonwealth in 1975.

Opposite: Rawalpindi is Pakistan's fourth largest city. It is a commercial and industrial centre. Above left: Asunción, Paraguay's capital, was founded on the Paraguay River by Spanish pioneers in 1537. Above: Inca ruins in the Peruvian Andes. The Incas were conquered by Spanish conquistadores in the early 16th century.

Area: 461,691 km² (178,270 sq mi); **Population:** 3,221,000; **Capital:** Port Moresby (pop 122,000); **Highest point:** Mt Wilhelm, 4694 m (15,400 ft); **Official language:** English; **Religions:** Protestantism (61 per cent), Roman Catholicism (31 per cent), tribal beliefs; **Adult literacy rate:** 32 per cent; **Average life expectancy at birth:** 50 years; **Unit of currency:** Kina; **Main exports:** copper ore and concentrates, coffee, cocoa, copra; **Per capita GNP:** US$650.

PARAGUAY, a landlocked republic in South America. Its main river, the Paraguay, divides it into the Chaco, a thinly populated, flat region of marsh and scrubland in the west, and a fertile plain and hills, rising to the Parana plateau, in the east. The climate is subtropical. About 75 per cent of the people are of mixed Indian and white descent, 21 per cent are of European origin, and 3 per cent are pure Indians. Agriculture employed 50 per cent of the workforce in 1978 and accounted for 32 per cent of the GDP, as compared with 24 per cent from industry. Cotton and soya beans are major crops. Forestry is also important: the bark of the quebracho tree is used to make tannin. Yerba maté, the plant from which a green tea is made, grows wild. In 1979 Paraguay had 5.2 million cattle. Mining is unimportant and most manufacturing is involved in processing farm products. Paraguay declared its independence in 1811. Wars against its neighbours in 1865–70 and in 1932–35 have marred its progress. A military coup in 1954 brought Gen Alfredo Stroessner to power. He introduced the 1967 Constitution which provides for a bicameral parliament (a Senate and Chamber of Deputies).

Area: 406,752 km² (157,056 sq mi); **Population:** 3,254,000; **Capital:** Asunción (pop 463,000); **Official language:** Spanish; **Religion:** mainly Roman Catholicism; **Adult literacy rate:** 81 per cent; **Average life expectancy at birth:** 63 years; **Unit of currency:** Guarani; **Main exports:** cotton, soya beans, timber; **Per capita GNP:** US$1060.

PERU, a republic in western South America. Behind the narrow, arid coastal plain are high Andean ranges. These mountains, which reach their highest peak at Mt Huascarán, contain the headwaters of the Amazon River, notably the Maranon and Ucayali. Lake Titicaca, the world's highest navigable lake, straddles the border with Bolivia. It has a total area of 8290 km² (3201 sq mi). Eastern Peru is in the low Amazon basin. The climate is tropical, but the highlands are cooler. People of mixed Indian and white origin and a roughly equal number of pure Indians make up the bulk of the population. There are also some people of European and Negroid origin. In 1978 39 per cent of the people worked in agriculture, which accounted for 21 per cent of the GDP (23 per cent came from industry). Sugar, cotton, coffee and wool are important: in 1979 there were 14.5 million sheep and 4.2 million cattle. Fishing is usually a major industry but catches in the late 1970s were reduced because of overfishing and abnormal conditions. Peru produces oil and a variety of minerals, which provide its main wealth. These include copper, lead, zinc, silver and iron ore. Manufacturing industries are mostly based in Lima. Spain conquered the Incas in 1531–33 and ruled Peru until it declared its independence in 1821. Military governments have governed for long periods, but democratic rule was restored in 1980. The 1980 Constitution provided for a bicameral parliament, with a Senate and a Chamber of Deputies.

Area: 1,285,216 km² (496,252 sq mi); **Population:** 18,786,000; **Capital:** Lima (pop 3,158,000); **Other cities:** Arequipa (305,000); **Highest point:** Mt Huascarán, 6768 m (22,205 ft); **Official languages:** Spanish, Quechua; **Religion:** Roman Catholicism; **Adult literacy rate:** 72 per cent; **Average life expectancy at birth:** 56 years; **Unit of currency:** Gold sol; **Main exports:** minerals and metals, fish and fish-meal, oil; **Per capita GNP:** US$730.

PHILIPPINES, a South-East Asian republic consisting of more than 7000 islands. The largest, Luzon, 104,682 km² (40,420 sq mi), and Mindanao, 94,625 km² (36,537 sq mi), together make up two-thirds of the land area. The large islands are volcanic and mountainous, but many islands are small coral outcrops. The country has a tropical monsoon climate. The plains are hot and humid: the uplands are cooler. Manila has an average annual rainfall of 2080 mm (82 in). Most Filipinos are of Malay-Polynesian origin. There are also some people of Pygmy, European and mixed descent. The Philippines is Asia's only predominantly Christian country. Agriculture employed 48 per cent of the workforce in 1978, but it accounted for only 27 per cent of the GDP, as opposed to industry 35 per cent and services 38 per cent. Rice and maize are the main food crops. Coconut products and sugar-cane are major cash crops. Copper is the leading mineral. Textiles, footwear, chemicals, beverages and food are leading manufactures. Nearly a million tourists visited the country in 1979. Spain ruled the Philippines from 1565 to 1898, when the archipelago was ceded to the United States. Independence was achieved in 1946. Communist guerrillas and political rivalries caused instability and martial law was declared in 1972.

Area: 300,000 km² (115,837 sq mi); **Population:** 50,697,000; **Capital:** Manila (pop 1,626,000); **Other cities:** Quezon City (1,166,000), Davao (611,000); **Highest point:** Mt Apo, 2954 m (9692 ft); **Official language:** Philipino; **Religions:** Roman Catholicism (85 per cent), Islam (4 per cent); **Adult literacy rate:** 87 per cent; **Average life expectancy at birth:** 60 years; **Unit of currency:** Peso; **Main exports:** coconut oil, copper concentrates, timber; **Per capita GNP:** US$600.

PITCAIRN ISLAND, a British possession in the South Pacific Ocean (latitude 25°05′S, 130°05′W). Fruit and vegetables are grown, but postage stamps are the island's main source of revenue. Discovered in 1767, it received its first inhabitants, 9 *Bounty* mutineers and 18 Tahitians, in 1790. In 1856 the entire population (then 194) moved to Norfolk Island, but 43 returned in 1859–64. Britain took responsibility for the island in 1898.

Area: 5 km² (2 sq mi); **Population:** 63 (1981).

POLAND, a People's Republic in eastern Europe. Behind the lagoon-fringed Baltic coast is a broad plain, the northern part of which is mostly covered by infertile glacial deposits and forest. The central lowlands, in which Warsaw, Poznan and Łódź are situated, are more fertile. A low plateau in the south rises to the Sudeten Mts in the south-west and the Carpathians in the south-east. The plateau contains much fertile land and the major industrial region built around the Upper Silesian coalfield, major industrial centres being Katowice, Krakow and Wroclaw. The south is drained by the Oder and Vistula river systems. The climate becomes more continental from west to east, where the average annual temperature range is −5°–18°C (23°–64°F). Summers become warmer from north to south. Warsaw has an average annual rainfall of 560 mm (22 in): the south is wetter. In 1978 33 per cent of the population was employed in agriculture and 39 per cent in industry, as compared with 48 per cent and 29 per cent respectively in 1960. Farmland covers 60 per cent of Poland: unusually for a Communist country, 75 per cent is privately owned. Cereals, potatoes and sugar beet are major crops. In 1979 Poland had 13 million cattle, 21 million pigs, 85 million poultry and 4.2 million sheep. Poland is the world's 4th largest coal producer and it has large reserves of copper, lignite, lead, nickel, salt, sulphur and zinc. But much iron ore for the large steel industry is imported. With its massive, government-owned light and heavy industries, Poland is now one of the world's 15 top industrial nations. Poland's frontiers have changed several times in the last 200 years. In the late 18th century it disappeared from the map. Nominal independence was restored in 1807, but it was partitioned between Austria, Prussia and Russia in 1815. Poland was proclaimed an independent republic in 1918 but, in 1939, it was divided between Germany and the USSR. It again became independent in 1945, losing land to the USSR but gaining some from Germany. A Communist government was set up, but its attempts to nationalize farmland and discourage religious worship have failed. Dissatisfaction with the pro-Soviet government was expressed in strikes and riots in 1970, 1976 and again in 1980, when a strike committee demanded the right to form independent trade unions. A national confederation of unions (Solidarity) was formed, but its leaders were arrested in December 1981 when a military government took power.

Area: 312,677 km² (120,732 sq mi); **Population:** 36,300,000; **Capital:** Warsaw (pop 1,572,000); **Other cities:** Łódź (832,000), Krakow (705,000), Wroclaw (608,000), Poznan (544,000); **Highest point:** Rysy Peak in the High Tatra, 2503 m (8212 ft); **Official language:** Polish; **Religion:** Roman Catholicism (93 per cent); **Adult literacy rate:** 98 per cent; **Average life expectancy at birth:** 71 years: **Unit of currency:** Zloty; **Main exports:** coal, lignite, coke, iron and steel goods, ships, transport equipment, textiles, food; **Per capita GNP:** US$3830.

PORTUGAL, a republic in the Iberian peninsula. Much of the land is an extension of the Spanish meseta: there are plateaux and continuations of the central Sierras of Spain. Lowlands border the coast. Portugal has hot, dry summers and mild, moist winters, but the rainfall decreases and temperatures increase from north to south. Lisbon has an average annual temperature range of 10°–21°C (50°–70°F) and 760 mm (30 in) of rain per year. Portugal has a lower per capita GNP than any other country in Western Europe. In 1978 agriculture, forestry and fishing employed 27 per cent of the workforce. It accounted for 13 per cent of the GDP, as opposed to 46 per cent from industry and 41 per cent from services. Cereals are the main crops. About 12 per cent of the land is devoted to vineyards and olive groves. Forests cover one-third of Portugal, which leads the world in cork production. About 37,000 people worked in fishing in 1979: sardines and cod form the bulk of the catch. Portugal produces some minerals, including coal, copper and some iron ore. Manufacturing, including iron and steel, chemicals and textiles, has increased rapidly in recent years. About 3 million tourists visited Portugal in 1977. Portugal's modern frontiers were established in the 13th century and Spain recognized Portugal as an independent kingdom in 1385. In the 15th century Portugal initiated the Age of Exploration and built up a large overseas empire. Portuguese power began to decline in the 16th century. Brazil was lost in 1822. In 1910 the monarchy was abolished and a republic proclaimed. Between the 1930s and early 1970s Portugal had an autocratic government. A coup in 1974 led to the restoration of democracy and to independence to Angola, Cape Verde, Guinea-Bissau and Mozambique in Africa.

Below left: Gdansk, formerly Danzig, is a Baltic seaport and industrial centre in Poland. Strikes and riots in the city in the 1970s and 1980s were linked with a workers' movement to establish free trade unions in Communist Poland. Below: The Madeira Islands are a volcanic archipelago in the Atlantic Ocean west of Morocco. These Portuguese islands produce wine and attract many tourists.

Area: 92,082 km² (35,555 sq mi); **Population:** 10,390,000; **Capital:** Lisbon (pop with suburbs, 1,034,000); **Other cities:** Porto (693,000); **Highest point:** Malhao, 1991 m (6532 ft); **Official language:** Portuguese; **Religion:** Roman Catholicism; **Adult literacy rate:** 70 per cent; **Average life expectancy at birth:** 69 years; **Unit of currency:** Escudo; **Main exports:** timber and wood products, textiles, machinery, wine, chemicals, sardines; **Per capita GNP:** US$2160.

PUERTO RICO, a United States self-governing Commonwealth in the Caribbean Sea. The land is mostly rugged and scenic. The climate is tropical. Most people are of African and European descent. Over-population has caused substantial emigration to the US. Sugar cane is the chief product, but light industry and tourism are important. Columbus discovered the island in 1493 and it became a Spanish possession. It was ceded to the US in 1898. It has most of the powers of an American state, but its citizens cannot vote in US elections.

Area: 8897 km² (3435 sq mi); **Population:** 3,666,000; **Capital:** San Juan (pop 433,000); **Official languages:** Spanish, English; **Main exports:** sugar, rum, tobacco; **Per capita GNP:** US$2970.

QATAR, an Arab Emirate occupying a peninsula in the Persian Gulf. This hot, arid and mostly desert nation has little agriculture, although fruits and vegetables are grown. Oil, which was discovered in the 1930s, dominates the economy. Much oil revenue has been used to finance an elaborate welfare state. Qatar signed a treaty of friendship with Britain in 1916, but it became fully independent in 1971 when Britain withdrew from the Gulf.

Area: 11,000 km² (4247 sq mi); **Population:** 294,000; **Capital:** Doha (pop 130,000); **Official language:** Arabic; **Religion:** Islam; **Unit of currency:** Qatar Riyal; **Main export:** oil; **Per capita GNP:** US$16,590.

RÉUNION, a French Overseas Department about 780 km (485 mi) east of Madagascar. It contains 9 dormant and 1 active volcanoes. The island has a tropical climate and sugar cane is the chief product. The people are descendants of African slaves, French settlers, Malays, Indians and other South-East Asians. France annexed Réunion in the 1640s. It became an Overseas Department in 1946.

Area: 2510 km² (969 sq mi); **Population:** 546,000; **Capital:** St Denis (pop 104,000); **Highest point:** 3069 m (10,069 ft); **Religion:** Roman Catholicism; **Main exports:** sugar, molasses and rum; **Per capita GNP:** US$4180.

COUNTRIES OF THE WORLD

Attractive villages are a feature of the Romanian countryside. In 1980, 52 per cent of the population of Romania lived in rural areas, as compared with 66 per cent in 1960. Although the rural population has declined, it is still substantially greater than in most eastern European countries. Industry is currently expanding and so the population drift from the countryside to the cities will probably continue.

ROMANIA, a Socialist Republic on the Black Sea. Transylvania forms the heart of Romania. It includes a central plateau surrounded by the Bihor Mts to the west, the Carpathians to the east and the Transylvanian Alps to the south, where the country's highest peak is situated. In the far west are fertile plains. Other plains lie in the east and south. They are drained by the River Danube and its tributaries. A limestone plateau (Dobrogea) borders the Black Sea coast. The climate is continental. The average rainfall varies from 400 mm (16 in) in the east to 1400 mm (55 in) in the mountains. The people are descendants of several peoples, including the Romanized Dacian tribes of the Danube valley and Slavs. The Romanian language is based on Latin and contains many Slav words. In 1978 agriculture employed 50 per cent of the workforce, industry 31 per cent and services 19 per cent. Farmland covers 63 per cent of the country; most is government-owned. Cereals, potatoes, oilseeds and sugar beet are major crops and, in 1979, Romania had 6.5 million cattle, 10.9 million pigs and 15.8 million sheep. There are rich mineral resources, including oil and natural gas, coal, lignite, copper, chromite, gold, iron ore, manganese and zinc. The manufacturing sector has expanded greatly since the 1960s. In 1861 Moldavia and Walachia united to form the monarchy of Romania, which gradually extended its frontiers. In World War II it supported Germany at first but joined the Allies in 1944. In 1947 King Michael abdicated and a Communist government took control. In the 1970s, however, Romania pursued foreign policies that were increasingly independent of the USSR.

Area: 237,500 km² (91,704 sq mi); **Population:** 22,653,000; **Capital:** Bucharest (pop with suburbs, 1,960,000); **Highest point:** Moldoreanu, 2543 m (8343 ft); **Official language:** Romanian; **Religion:** Romanian Orthodox Church (80 per cent); **Adult literacy rate:** 98 per cent; **Average life expectancy at birth:** 70 years; **Unit of currency:** Leu; **Main exports:** machinery, ores and metals, oil and natural gas, food, chemicals; **Per capita GNP:** US$1900.

RWANDA, a small, poor, landlocked republic in east-central Africa. The East African Rift Valley in the west contains part of Lake Kivu. It is bordered by highlands that descend in a series of plateaux to the River Kagera in the east. The equatorial climate is modified by the altitude. Bantu-speaking Hutu form 90 per cent of the population. There are also Nilo-Hamitic Tutsi and Pygmy, European and Asian minorities. Agriculture employed 91 per cent of the workforce in 1978, accounting for 46 per cent of the GDP (22 per cent came from industry and 32 per cent from services). The main cash crop is coffee. Cassiterite is mined and there are various small-scale manufacturing industries. Rwanda and Burundi were once part of German East Africa, but Belgium occupied them in 1916 and ruled them as Ruanda-Urundi. A Hutu peasants' revolt in 1959 caused the deaths of many Tutsi, who formed the ruling class. The Tutsi monarchy was abolished and Rwanda became an independent republic controlled by the Hutu in 1962. Communal conflict caused instability in the 1960s and 1970s.

Area: 26,338 km² (10,170 sq mi); **Population:** 5,067,000; **Capital:** Kigali (pop 118,000); **Highest point:** 4507 m (14,787 ft); **Official languages:** Kinyarwanda, French; **Religions:** traditional beliefs (about 50 per cent), Christianity; **Adult literacy rate:** 23 per cent; **Average life expectancy at birth:** 46 years; **Unit of currency:** Rwanda franc; **Main exports:** coffee, tin, tea; **Per capita GNP:** US$210.

ST HELENA, a British island territory in the South Atlantic, about 1930 km (1199 mi) west of Angola. It is a mountainous, volcanic island. There is some farming and fishing, but no mining or industry. St Helena became a British colony in 1833. In 1922 the volcanic island of Ascension, 1130 km (702 mi) to the north-west, was made a dependency of St Helena, as were the 4 islands of Tristan da Cunha in 1938. Ascension Island covers 88 km² (34 sq mi) and has a population of 991 (1979). Tristan da Cunha has an area of 98 km² (38 sq miles) and 320 people (1979).

Area: 122 km² (47 sq mi); **Population:** 5200 (1979); **Chief town:** Jamestown (pop 1500).

ST KITTS-NEVIS, a British Associated State in the Leeward Is in the West Indies. The islands are of volcanic origin and export sugar and molasses. From 1623 they came under alternate French and British rule, but they were ceded to Britain in 1783. In 1967 St Kitts (or Christopher)-Nevis-

Left: Castries is the capital of St Lucia, a beautiful island in the West Indies. Although small, Castries is becoming a tourist centre.

Anguilla became an Associated State in the Commonwealth. Britain appointed a Commissioner to handle Anguilla's affairs, and it was formally separated from St Kitts-Nevis in 1980. St Kitts-Nevis gained full independence in 1983.

Area: 262 km² (101 sq mi); **Population:** 51,000; **Chief town:** Basseterre (pop 14,700); **Per capita GNP:** US$780.

ST LUCIA, a picturesque island nation in the Windward Is in the West Indies. Volcanic in origin, it has a tropical climate and bananas, cocoa, coconut oil and copra, and textiles are exported. Tourism is developing; there were 107,000 visitors in 1978. The island was contested between Britain and France from 1605, but it was ceded to Britain in 1814. Self-government was achieved in 1967 and full independence within the Commonwealth was gained in 1979.

Area: 616 km² (238 sq mi); **Population:** 130,000; **Capital:** Castries (pop 45,000).

ST PIERRE AND MIQUELON, a French Overseas Department consisting of 8 islands off the southern coast of Newfoundland, Canada. These rocky islands have a temperate, moist climate. The people are descendants of French immigrants, who have maintained their French culture. Fishing and fish processing are the main activities. The islands have been French almost continuously since 1660.

Area: 242 km² (93 sq mi); **Population:** 6000; **Capital:** St Pierre.

ST VINCENT AND THE GRENADINES, a West Indian nation in the Windward Is, consisting of the island of St Vincent, 345 km² (133 sq mi), and the small islands that make up the Northern Grenadines. St Vincent is a volcanic island with a tropical climate. Most people are blacks or of mixed origin. Farming is the main activity, but tourism is expanding. France and Britain alternately held St Vincent until it finally became British in 1805. It became a British Associated State in 1969 and a fully independent member of the Commonwealth in 1979.

Area: 388 km² (150 sq mi); **Population:** 113,000; **Capital:** Kingstown (pop 23,000); **Main export:** bananas; **Per capita GNP:** US$490.

SAMOA, AMERICAN, a group of 8 islands in the South Pacific, about 1050 km (652 mi) north-east of Fiji. The largest island, Tutuila, contains the capital Pago Pago. This mountainous island has heavy rainfall: the climate throughout is tropical. Most people are Polynesians. The chief exports are fish products, copra and handicrafts. The first recorded European landfall was in 1722. In 1899 a treaty between the US, Britain and Germany assigned the eastern Samoan islands to the US and the western islands (now Western Samoa) to Germany. A popularly elected Samoan Governor was inaugurated in 1978.

Area: 197 km² (76 sq mi); **Population:** 35,000; **Capital:** Pago Pago; **Per capita GNP:** US$8030.

SAMOA, WESTERN, a Pacific island nation about 720 km (447 mi) north-east of Fiji. The largest islands are Savai'i, 1714 km² (662 sq mi), and Upolu, 1118 km² (432 sq mi), where the capital Apia is situated. There are also two small islands, Manono and Apolima, and several uninhabited islets. The islands are volcanic in origin and have a tropical climate. The people are Polynesians and Christianity is the main religion. The chief products are bananas, cocoa and coconuts. Germany ruled the islands before World War I and New Zealand was in control in 1920–61. Western Samoa became a fully independent monarchy on January 1, 1962. HH Malietoa Tanumafili II became Head of State in 1963 and Western Samoa became a member of the Commonwealth in 1970.

Area: 2842 km² (1097 sq mi); **Population:** 164,000; **Capital:** Apia (pop 32,000).

SAN MARINO, Europe's smallest independent republic. It is landlocked and situated in central Italy, south of Rimini. Its capital is on the slopes of Mt Titano, a 743 m (2438 ft) high spur of the Apennines. Most people are farmers, but tourism is the main industry. Building stone, textiles and wine are exported. Founded in the 4th century AD, San Marino joined a customs union with Italy in 1862.

Area: 61 km² (24 sq mi); **Population:** 21,000; **Capital:** San Marino (pop 4000).

SÃO TOMÉ AND PRINCIPE, an island republic in the Gulf of Guinea. It includes the volcanic island of São Tomé, 854 km² (330 sq mi) in area, Principe to the north, and some smaller islands. The people are descendants of slaves from the mainland and Europeans. Agriculture is the main activity. Portuguese mariners discovered the then uninhabited islands in 1471. From 1522 they were governed as a province of Portugal until full independence was achieved in 1975.

Area: 964 km² (372 sq mi); **Population:** 110,000; **Capital:** São Tomé (pop 17,000); **Highest point:**

2024 m (6640 ft); **Official language:** Portuguese; **Religion:** Roman Catholicism; **Unit of currency:** Dobra; **Main exports:** cocoa, copra, palm kernels; **Per capita GNP:** US$450.

SAUDI ARABIA, a kingdom occupying much of the Arabian peninsula. Behind the narrow, Red Sea coastal plain is a highland zone, including the Hejaz in the north and the Asir highlands in the south. East of these highlands are plateaux that slope gently towards the Persian Gulf coastal plain. The plateaux, which cover 90 per cent of the country, include the Nafud Desert in the north and the Rub'al-Khali (the 'Empty Quarter') in the south. The lowlands are hot, but the altitude modifies temperatures. The rainfall varies between 380 mm (15 in) in the Asir highlands to 80 mm (3 in) at Riyadh: virtually no rain falls in the Rub'al-Khali. Most Saudis are Muslim Arabs and Mecca, the birthplace of the Prophet Muhammad, and Medina are the two holiest places of Islam. In 1978 agriculture employed 62 per cent of the workforce, but it accounted for only 1 per cent of the GDP, while industry accounted for 76 per cent (of which only 5 per cent came from manufacturing). The economy is dominated by oil which was discovered in 1938. In 1980 only the USSR and US produced more oil than Saudi Arabia. The country was under the nominal rule of the Ottoman Turks in 1517–1916, when they were driven out. In 1927 the Sultan of Nejd, Abd Al-Aziz Ibn Saud, founded modern Saudi Arabia and became its king. The king now rules with a cabinet, but remains the focus of power. In recent years revenue from oil has been used to develop welfare services, industries, transport facilities and water conservation and land reclamation projects.

Area: 2,149,690 km² (830,045 sq mi); **Population:** 9,418,000; **Capital:** Riyadh (pop 669,000); **Other cities:** Jidda (561,000); Mecca (367,000), Medina (198,000); **Highest point:** around 3048 m (10,000 ft) in the Asir range; **Official language:** Arabic; **Religion:** Islam; **Average life expectancy at birth:** 53 years; **Unit of currency:** Riyal; **Main export:** oil; **Per capita GNP:** US$7370.

SENEGAL, a West African republic. It is mostly low-lying and covered by savanna. There is a low plateau in the south-east. Senegal is drained by the Senegal, Saloum, Gambia and Casamance rivers. The climate on the coast is pleasant but the interior is hot. The rainfall increases from the arid north to the south. Dakar has an average annual rainfall of 580 mm (23 in) while the far south-west has 1630 mm (64 in). Most people are Negroid. Agriculture employed 77 per cent of the workforce in 1978 but accounted for only 26 per cent of the GDP as opposed to 25 per cent from industry. Groundnuts and groundnut products dominate the economy. There were 2.8 million cattle and 2.9 million sheep and goats in 1979. Dakar is West Africa's most industrialized city. Tourism is growing: there were 198,000 tourists in 1979. French contacts date back to the early 17th century, but France did not colonize all of Senegal until 1887. In 1959 Senegal became part of the Federation of Mali, but it became a separate, fully independent republic in 1960. In 1981 Senegalese troops helped to put down an uprising in Gambia, which is an enclave within Senegal. Soon afterwards Senegal and Gambia set up a confederation called Senegambia. This came into being in February 1982, although both nations retained their sovereignty.

Area: 196,192 km² (75,754 sq mi); **Population:** 5,967,000; **Capital:** Dakar (pop 800,000); **Official language:** French; **Religions:** Islam (90 per cent), traditional beliefs (5 per cent), Christianity (5 per cent); **Adult literacy rate:** 10 per cent; **Average life expectancy at birth:** 42 years; **Unit of currency:** Franc CFA; **Main exports:** groundnuts and groundnut products, fish, phosphate of lime; **Per capita GNP:** US$430.

SEYCHELLES, an Indian Ocean island republic north-east of Madagascar. There are about 90 islands. The rugged Mahé, or Granitic, islands make up 80 per cent of the area: the rest are flat coral islands. The largest island, Mahé, 144 km² (56 sq mi), contains the capital Victoria. The climate is tropical. Most people are Creoles, of mixed French and African origin. There are also some Chinese, Europeans and Indians. Tourism and agriculture are the main activities. French settlers arrived in the 1770s. Britain ruled the islands from 1810 until independence in the Commonwealth was achieved in 1976. A successful coup took place in 1977, but a mercenary invasion in 1981 was defeated.

Area: 280 km² (108 sq mi); **Population:** 70,000; **Capital:** Victoria (pop 23,000); **Official languages:** English, French; **Religion:** Roman Catholicism (90 per cent); **Unit of currency:** Rupee; **Main exports:** copra, cinnamon, fish; **Per capita GNP:** US$1400.

SIERRA LEONE, a West African republic. Behind the broad coastal plain are interior plateaux and mountains. The climate is tropical. Freetown has an average annual rainfall of 3360 mm (132 in): the wettest months are July–September. Most people are black Africans: there are 18 main groups. A Creole minority is composed of descendants of freed slaves brought to Freetown 200 years ago. In 1978 agriculture employed 67 per cent of the workforce and accounted for 39 per cent of the GDP, as compared with industry 22 per cent. Rice is the main food crop and coffee, cocoa and palm kernels are the chief cash crops. But diamonds and bauxite made up 67 per cent of the exports in 1978. Forestry and fishing are expanding, as is manufacturing, and tourism is being developed. In 1787 Britain founded Freetown as a settlement for freed slaves. In 1808 the Sierra Leone peninsula was made a colony and the interior was declared a protectorate in 1898. Full independence was achieved in 1961. Sierra Leone became a republic in 1971: it is now a one-party state with an elected House of Representatives.

Area: 71,740 km² (27,700 sq mi); **Population:** 3,643,000; **Capital:** Freetown (pop 274,000); **Highest point:** 1948 m (6391 ft); **Official language:** English: **Religions:** mainly traditional beliefs,

Islam (20 per cent), Christianity; **Adult literacy rate:** 15 per cent; **Average life expectancy at birth:** 46 years; **Unit of currency:** Leone; **Main exports:** diamonds, coffee, cocoa, bauxite; **Per capita GNP:** US$250.

SINGAPORE, a prosperous island republic off the southern tip of the Malay peninsula. A causeway links Singapore Island to the mainland. There are also many islets that make up 8 per cent of the country. The climate is hot and humid. Temperatures stay around 25°–27°C (77°–81°F) throughout the year and the average annual rainfall is 2440 mm (96 in). The main groups of people are Chinese (76 per cent), Malays (15 per cent) and Indians (7 per cent). Agriculture employed only 2 per cent of the people in 1978 and accounted for 2 per cent of the GDP. Industry contributed 35 per cent and services 63 per cent. Manufacturing is extremely important. The many products include ships, petrochemicals, steel and textiles. The port of Singapore is one of the world's largest and Singapore is a major financial centre. Britain took over the island in 1824. It was part of Malaysia from 1963 but it became a separate republic in 1965.

Area: 581 km² (224 sq mi); **Population:** 2,476,000; **Capital:** Singapore; **Highest point:** 177 m (581 ft); **Official languages:** Malay, Chinese, Tamil, English; **Religions:** Buddhism, Confucianism and Taoism (among the Chinese), Islam (the Malays), Hinduism (Indians), Christianity; **Adult literacy rate:** 75 per cent; **Average life expectancy at birth:** 70 years; **Unit of currency:** Singapore dollar; **Main exports:** petroleum products, electronic products, rubber, machinery; **Per capita GNP:** US$3820.

SOLOMON ISLANDS, an island nation in the Commonwealth in the south-western Pacific. It lies to the east of New Guinea and Papua New Guinea includes the two most northern islands, Bougainville and Buka. The largest of the Solomon Islands is Guadalcanal which, like the other large islands in the group, is volcanic and mountainous. The climate is equatorial. Most people are Melanesians. Agriculture, forestry and fishing are the main activities: copra, timber and palm-oil are major exports. The Solomons became a British protectorate in 1893–99. Full independence was achieved in 1978. The British monarch, represented by a Governor-General, is the official Head of State.

Area: 28,446 km² (10,984 sq mi); **Population:** 242,000; **Capital:** Honiara on Guadalcanal (pop 15,000); **Unit of currency:** Solomon Islands dollar; **Per capita GNP:** US$430 (1978).

SOMALI REPUBLIC, in the Horn of Africa, faces the Gulf of Aden in the north and the Indian Ocean to the east. Behind the narrow northern coastal plain are highlands containing Somalia's highest peaks. The south consists of plateaux and plains. It contains the only permanent rivers: the Wabi Shebele and the Juba. Rainfall increases from the north, where less than 250 mm (10 in) falls per year, to the south. Mogadishu has 400 mm (16 in). Temperatures are high throughout the year. The main types of vegetation are semi-desert and savanna. Most people speak a Cushitic language, Somali, which is also used in parts of Djibouti, Ethiopia and Kenya. In 1978 agriculture employed 82 per cent of the people and accounted for 60 per cent of the GDP (industry contributed 11 per cent). Most people are nomadic pastoralists: there were 16 million goats, 10 million sheep, 5.4 million camels and 3.8 million cattle in 1979. Animals, meat and hides and skins account for about 70 per cent of the exports. The main arable areas are in the southern river valleys. The north became a British protectorate in 1884, while Italy took the south in 1905. The two territories merged and became an independent republic in 1960. The army took control in 1969 and, in 1977–78 it supported Somali-speaking secessionists in the Ethiopian Ogaden who wanted to join a Greater Somalia. Sporadic fighting continued in the Ogaden and hundreds of thousands of refugees flooded into Somalia. A People's Assembly was elected in 1979 but a state of emergency was declared in 1980.

Area: 637,657 km² (246,214 sq mi); **Population:** 4,125,000; **Capital:** Mogadishu (pop 400,000); **Highest point:** Erigavo, 2406 m (7894 ft); **Official language:** Somali; **Religion:** Islam; **Adult literacy rate:** 60 per cent; **Average life expectancy at birth:** 43 years; **Unit of currency:** Somali shilling; **Main exports:** live animals, fruit, hides and skins; **Per capita GNP:** US$130 (1978).

SOUTH AFRICA, a republic since 1961. The interior is a vast, saucer-shaped plateau, with an uptilted rim, the highest section being the Drakensberg range in the south-east. The Orange and Limpopo rivers drain much of the plateau. Around the plateau, the land descends in steps to the sea. In southern Cape province two such steps are the Great and Little Karoo; these are plateaux bounded by mountain ranges. Most of South Africa has a subtropical climate, modified by the altitude. About 90 per cent of the land has an average annual rainfall of less than 760 mm (30 in) and about 50 per cent is arid. The population includes black Africans (70.2 per cent), people of European origin (17.5 per cent), Coloureds of mixed descent (9.4 per cent) and Asians (2.9 per cent). The whites, who are mostly Afrikaans or English speakers, control the country. Since 1948 a policy of separate development has been pursued, whereby each ethnic group is supposed to develop separately. Hence, 10 African tribal Homelands have been set up for the main black groups, including the Zulu, Xhosa, Tswana, Sepedi (North Sotho) and Seshoeshoe (South Sotho). Agriculture employed 30 per cent of the workforce in 1978, industry 29 per cent and services 41 per cent. Their respective contributions to the GDP were 8 per cent, 45 per cent and 47 per cent. Manufacturing is especially important in the southern Transvaal and around the main ports: Cape Town, Durban and Port Elizabeth. South Africa produces most of the non-Communist world's gold and many other minerals, including asbestos, coal, diamonds, copper, iron ore, manganese, tin, uranium and zinc. Arable land covers 5 per cent of the country and pasture about 80 per cent: there were 13.2 million cattle and 31.5

PROVINCES OF SOUTH AFRICA

Province	Area sq km	Area sq mi	Population 1970	Seat of government
Cape of Good Hope	721,001	278,395	6,732,000	Cape Town
Natal	86,967	33,580	4,237,000	Pietermaritzburg
Transvaal	283,917	109,627	8,718,000	Pretoria
Orange Free State	129,152	49,869	1,716,000	Bloemfontein

million sheep in 1979. The chief food crop is maize, but a wide variety of cash crops is produced. Forestry, fishing and tourism are also important. The Portuguese Bartholomeu Dias rounded the Cape in 1488. The Dutch made the first settlement at the Cape in 1652. Gradually, European farmers spread inland where they clashed with Bantu-speaking peoples. In 1795–1803 and again in 1806, Britain occupied the Cape which became a British colony in 1814. The Dutch (called the Boers or Afrikaaners) resented British rule and many moved eastwards and north-eastwards to escape it. Anglo-Dutch rivalry finally led to wars in 1880–81 and 1899–1902. In 1910 the country was united in the Union of South Africa. In World War I, South Africa occupied Namibia (see Namibia). Since 1948 the racial policies involved in separate development have been increasingly criticized by the rest of the world. In 1961 South Africa became a republic and left the Commonwealth. In the 1970s and early 1980s four African Homelands (Transkei, Bophuthatswana, Venda and Ciskei) were declared independent, but the UN refused to accept that they had the status of independent sovereign states.

Area: 1,221,037 km² (471,471 sq mi); **Population:** 30,844,000; **Capitals:** Cape Town (seat of legislature, pop 1,097,000), Pretoria (seat of government, 562,000); **Other cities:** Johannesburg (1,433,000), Durban (843,000), Port Elizabeth (469,000); **Highest point:** Mont aux Sources, 3299 m (10,823 ft); **Official languages:** Afrikaans, English; **Religion:** mainly Christianity; **Average life expectancy at birth:** 60 years; **Unit of currency:** Rand; **Main exports:** minerals (including gold and diamonds), mineral products, metals and metal products, food, vegetable products, textiles, machinery, wool; **Per capita GNP:** US$1720.

HOMELANDS OF SOUTH AFRICA

The Homelands, with the main peoples in them, are as follows: Basotho-Qwaqwa (South Sotho); Bophuthatswana (Tswana, independent 1977); Ciskei (Xhosa, independent 1981); Gazankulu (Shangaan); Kwazulu (Zulu); Lebowa (Pedi); Ndebele (Ndebele); Swazi (Swazi); Transkei (Xhosa, independent 1976); Venda (Venda, independent 1979).

SPAIN, a kingdom in the Iberian peninsula. Most of Spain is a plateau, or *Meseta*, between 610 and 910 m (2001–2986 ft) which is broken by several mountain ranges, including the Sierra de Gredos and the Sierra de Guadarrama near the capital Madrid, which itself is about 655 m (2149 ft) above sea level. The fold ranges of the Pyrenees and the Cantabrian Mts are in the north, while the Sierra Nevada in the south contains Muhacen, Spain's highest peak. The coastal plains vary in width. Some, like those around Alicante and Valencia, are fertile. Four major rivers. the Duero, Tagus, Guadiana and Guadalquivir, rise in the Meseta and discharge into the Atlantic. The Ebro River rises in the Cantabrian Mts and flows into the Mediterranean. The Balearic Islands (notably Majorca, Minorca and Ibiza) form a province in the Mediterranean. The volcanic Canary Islands, about 100 km (62 mi) off southern Morocco, consists of 2 provinces: Las Palmas de Gran Canaria and Santa Cruz de Tenerife. The northern Atlantic coast region has mild wet winters and cool summers, with an average annual temperature range of 9°–21°C (48°–70°F), as compared with 5°–26°C (41°–79°F) on the Meseta and 10°–27°C (50–81°F) on the southern and eastern Mediterranean coasts. The average annual rainfall varies from 1230 mm (48 in) at Bilbao in the north to 440 mm (17 in) at Madrid and 600 mm (24 in) at Málaga in the south. The Spanish language is Castilian. Basque is spoken in the north in the provinces bordering the Bay of Biscay and also in south-western France. Catalan is spoken in the north-east and Galician in the north-west. Separatist movements have developed in these regions and, in 1980, regional governments were established for the Basques and Catalans. In 1981 a similar government was set up in Galicia. In 1980 74 per cent of Spain's people lived in urban areas, as compared with 57 per cent in 1960. This change reflected a fall in the relative importance of agriculture in the economy. In 1978 industry employed 43 per cent of the population, services 39 per cent and agriculture 18 per cent; their respective contributions to the GDP were 38 per cent, 53 per cent and 9 per cent. Important minerals include coal, iron ore, copper, lead and zinc. In 1978 hydro-electric and nuclear power stations supplied 43 per cent and 7 per cent respectively of Spain's electrical energy. The leading manufacturing centres are Madrid and the Mediterranean port of Barcelona. Textiles are the leading manufactures, but Spain has a wide range of light and heavy industry. In 1979 38.9 million tourists visited Spain; tourism is a major source of foreign exchange. Crops vary according to the climate; irrigation is practised in many arid areas. Barley, citrus fruits, grapes (for wine), olives, potatoes, wheat and vegetables are leading crops. Spain is Europe's 3rd largest wine producer. Spain had 4.65 million cattle (mostly in the wetter north), 14.5 million sheep, 2.3 million goats and 9.9 million pigs in 1979. The fishing fleet contained more than 17,000 vessels in 1978. The Phoenicians, Carthaginians and Romans colonized Spain in early times. From about AD 400, Germanic tribes, first Vandals and later Visigoths, occupied Spain. The Moorish invasion began in 711. A Christian revival was mounted in the 11th century and, by 1276, the

Cape of Good Hope extends south of Cape Town in South Africa. It was at Cape Town that the first European settlement in southern Africa was founded in 1652, as a provisioning centre for Dutch ships plying between Europe and Asia.

Moors had been driven back to the southern state of Granada, where the superb Alhambra testifies to their architectural genius. Granada finally fell to Christian armies in 1492. In the early 15th century, Castile had become the dominant kingdom in Spain and its union with Aragon in 1479 began the process that finally united the entire country. From the late 15th century, Spain became a world power, colonizing most of South America, parts of North America and Africa, and the Philippines in Asia. However, a gradual decline began in the late 16th century. The great Spanish Armada was destroyed in 1588 and Spanish sea power was finally crushed in the Battle of Trafalgar in 1805. France occupied Spain in 1808–13 and in the 1810s and 1820s most Spanish American colonies declared their independence. By the early 20th century, Spain was a poor agricultural nation. In 1931 Spain was declared a republic but a civil war in 1936–39 ended in defeat for the republicans. General Francisco Franco became dictator and Head of State, although Spain was technically a monarchy. When Franco died in 1975, Prince Don Juan Carlos de Borbón became king. Democracy was restored and a new Constitution was promulgated in 1978. An unsuccessful army coup took place in February 1981. Spain has a bicameral parliament, or *Cortes*, consisting of a 350-member Chamber of Deputies and a 248-member Senate.

Area: 504,782 km² (194,908 sq mi); **Population:** 38,671,000; **Capital:** Madrid (pop 3,146,000); **Other cities:** Barcelona (1,750,000), Valencia (648,000), Seville (546,000), Zaragoza (470,000); **Highest point:** Mulhacén, 3478 m (11,411 ft); **Official language:** Spanish; **Religion:** Roman Catholicism; **Average life expectancy at birth:** 73 years; **Unit of currency:** Peseta; **Main exports:** manufactures, textiles, chemical products, footwear and leather goods, food, wine, fruit, fish, olive oil, vegetables; **Per capita GNP:** US$4340.

SRI LANKA, called Ceylon until 1972, is a South Asian republic and member of the Commonwealth. It is mostly low-lying; the central highlands which cover less than 20 per cent of the land reach their highest peak in Pidurutalagala. The climate is tropical and the capital Colombo has an average annual temperature of 27°C (81°F) throughout the year. The average annual rainfall varies from 1000 mm (39 in) in the north and east to 2000 mm (79 in) or more in the south and west. In 1981 74 per cent of the people were Sinhalese, 18 per cent were Tamils and 7 per cent were Moors. There are Burgher (European) and Malay minorities. In 1978 agriculture employed 54 per cent of the people, industry 15 per cent and services 31 per cent. About 36 per cent of Sri Lanka is cultivated. Rice is the main food. Tea, rubber and coconuts are the main cash crops. There were 1.6 million cattle in 1979. Gemstones and graphite are mined and there is a variety of manufacturing industries. The Sinhalese, from northern India, conquered the island in the 6th century BC, pushing the Veddas into the interior. Tamils arrived in the 11th century AD and Arabs (Moors) in the 12th and 13th centuries. Portugal ruled the island in 1505–1655, being replaced by the Dutch. Britain took over in 1796. Full independence was achieved in 1948. In 1960 Mrs Sirimavo Bandaranaike became prime minister, the first woman ever to hold this rank. Sri Lanka became a republic in 1972 and in 1978 it adopted the title the Democratic Socialist Republic of Sri Lanka.

Area: 65,610 km² (25,334 sq mi); **Population:** 15,398,000; **Capital:** Colombo (pop 624,000); **Highest point:** Pidurutalagala, 2527 m (8291 ft); **Official language:** Sinhala; **Religions:** Buddhism (67 per cent), Hinduism (18 per cent), Christianity (8 per cent), Islam (7 per cent); **Adult literacy rate:** 78 per cent; **Average life expectancy at birth:** 69 years; **Unit of currency:** Rupee; **Main exports:** tea, rubber, industrial products, coconut products; **Per capita GNP:** US$230.

SUDAN, Africa's largest nation. The land is mostly flat. It includes much of the Upper Nile basin. Highlands border the Red Sea plains in the northeast, the Darfur highlands are in the west, but the highest peak, Kinyeti, is in the far south. The average annual temperature is about 21°C (70°F) but the central lowlands are hotter and the uplands cooler. The average annual rainfall varies from 50 mm (2 in) in the north to 1520 mm (60 in) in the far south. Much of Sudan is desert but large areas of *sudd* (masses of floating plants) occur in the Nile region south of latitude 10°N. In the north most people are Muslim Arabs, Hamites and Negroes. Negroid peoples predominate in the south: there is a cultural rift between the northerners and the animist and Christian southerners. In 1978 agriculture employed 79 per cent of the people, accounting for 43 per cent of the GDP, as opposed to industry 12 per cent and services 45 per cent. Cotton and cotton goods dominate the exports. Pastoral farming is also important: there were 17.3 million cattle, 17.2 million sheep and 12.2 million goats in 1979. Britain and Egypt ruled Sudan jointly as a condominium from 1899. Full independence was achieved in 1956. A North-South civil war (1964–72) ended when the government granted regional autonomy to the southern provinces but executive power is vested in the President and legislative power in the 304-member People's Assembly.

Area: 2,505,813 km² (967,553 sq mi); **Population:** 19,373,000; **Capital:** Khartoum (pop 1,000,000); **Other cities:** Omdurman (299,000); **Highest point:** Mt Kinyeti, 3187 m (10,456 ft); **Official language:** Arabic; **Religions:** Islam, traditional beliefs, Christianity; **Adult literacy rate:** 20 per cent; **Average life expectancy at birth:** 46 years; **Unit of currency:** Sudanese pound; **Main exports:** cotton, groundnuts, sesame, gum arabic; **Per capita GNP:** US$370.

SURINAME, a republic in north-eastern South America, formerly called Dutch Guiana. Behind the 25–80 km (16–50 mi) wide marshy coastal plain are savanna-covered hills that rise to forested highlands. The climate is tropical and the rainfall plentiful. About 35 per cent of the people are Creoles of mixed African and European origin, 35 per cent are Indians, 15 per cent are Javanese, 9 per cent are 'Bush Negroes' (descendants of runaway slaves), 2 per cent are Chinese and 2 per cent are pure Indians. Farming is confined to the coastal plain. Fruit, rice and sugar cane are major crops. Forestry is also important, but the most valuable resource is bauxite. Britain founded a colony in Suriname in 1650 but ceded the territory to the Dutch in 1667. The Dutch ruled it for most of the time until full independence was achieved in 1975.

Area: 163,265 km² (63,040 sq mi); **Population:** 404,000; **Capital:** Paramaribo (pop 152,000); **Official languages:** Dutch, English; **Religions:** Hinduism (29 per cent), Islam (19 per cent), Roman Catholicism (18 per cent), other Christians (14 per cent); **Unit of currency:** Guilder; **Main exports:** bauxite and aluminium, rice, citrus fruits; **Per capita GNP:** US$2360.

SWAZILAND, a landlocked kingdom in southern Africa between South Africa and Mozambique. There are 4 regions aligned north-south. The western High Veld, between 900 and 1830 m (2953–6004 ft), covers 30 per cent of Swaziland. The Middle Veld, mostly 400–850 m (1312–2789 ft) high, covers 28 per cent, and the Low Veld, 150–300 m (492–984 ft) above sea level, covers another 33 per cent. The fourth region, the Lebombo plateau in the east, reaches about 820 m (2690 ft). The average annual rainfall decreases from 1900 mm (75 in) in parts of the High Veld to 500 mm (20 in) in the east. Temperatures are modified by the altitude. Most Swazis live in rural areas. The main crops are citrus fruits, cotton, maize, pineapples, rice, sorghum, sugar cane and tobacco. In 1979 there were 650,000 cattle, 265,000 goats and 33,000 sheep. Asbestos and coal are mined and there are various factories in the towns. Tourism and remittances from Swazis working abroad are sources of foreign exchange. Swaziland came under the Transvaal Republic in 1894 but Britain ruled it after the Anglo-Boer War (1899–1902). Full independence in the Commonwealth was achieved in 1968. In 1973 the king (or Ngwenyama) took supreme power. Elections were held in 1978 but the king retained many powers.

Area: 17,363 km² (6704 sq mi); **Population:** 581,000; **Capital:** Mbabane (pop 22,000); **Official language:** English; **Religions:** Christianity (60 per cent), traditional beliefs (40 per cent); **Unit of currency:** Lilangeni; **Main exports:** sugar, wood pulp, asbestos, fruit; **Per capita GNP:** US$650.

SWEDEN, a Scandinavian monarchy. Norrland, north of latitude 61° North, contains vast coniferous forests and many streams and lakes in the glaciated valleys. Mountains run along the border with Norway; the highest peak Kebnekaise is in the north-west. But a plateau covers most of Norrland. In the far north of this thinly-populated region is part of Lapland, where some Lapps still follow their traditional nomadic way of life. South of Norrland, between Göteborg and Stockholm, is the Central Lake region, where lakes Vänern and Vättern are situated. This region has a milder climate than Norrland. South of the Lake region are the infertile southern uplands, but Scania in the far south is the most fertile region. Most of Sweden has long, cold winters and short, warm summers. Rainfall averages 500 mm (20 in) per year in the east and south-east. More than 2000 mm (79 in) falls on the western mountains. In 1980 87 per cent of the population lived in urban areas and Sweden is one of the world's most prosperous nations. In 1978 industry employed 37 per cent of the workforce, services 58 per cent and agriculture 5 per cent, their contributions to the GDP being 33 per cent, 63 per cent and 4 per cent. Sweden has little coal but hydro-electric and nuclear power stations produce 59 per cent and 22 per cent respectively of Sweden's electric energy. There are major reserves of metal ores, notably iron ore at Kiruna, Gällivare and Grängesberg. Steel and steel products are the chief manufactures. Forests cover 57 per cent of Sweden and timber and wood pulp are major exports. Only 8 per cent of the land is cultivated: cereals, potatoes, sugar beet and cattle fodder are grown. In 1979 Sweden had 1.9 million cattle and 2.7 million pigs. In the 9th–11th centuries. Swedish Vikings went eastwards and southwards, plundering, trading and colonizing. Sweden was united with Denmark and Norway in 1397. It broke away in 1523, becoming a major power in the 17th century. In 1809 Sweden lost Finland to Russia but, after Napoleon's defeat in 1814, it gained Norway, which became independent in 1905. Sweden was neutral in World Wars I and II. It is a constitutional monarchy, with a unicameral parliament (*Riksdag*) with 349 members elected to 3-year terms.

Area: 449,964 km² (173,742 sq mi); **Population:** 8,347,000; **Capital:** Stockholm (pop 654,000); **Other cities:** Göteborg (437,000), Malmö (237,000); **Highest point:** Mt Kebnekaise, 2117 m (6946 ft); **Official language:** Swedish; **Religion:** Evangelical Lutheran Church; **Adult literacy rate:** 99 per cent; **Average life expectancy at birth:** 75 years; **Unit of currency:** Krona; **Main exports:** machinery and transport equipment, metals and metal goods, timber and timber products; **Per capita GNP:** US$11,920.

Stockholm, Sweden's capital, is a pleasant, largely modern city. It is called the 'Venice of the North', because part of the city stands on a group of islands in the Baltic Sea.

SWITZERLAND, a landlocked federal republic. The Jura Mts run from the north-east to south-west along the border with France. These mountains are separated from the spectacularly scenic Alps, which make up 60 per cent of Switzerland, by the central plateau (*Mittelland*). This plateau contains 75 per cent of the population. It has many lakes between Lake Geneva in the south-west and Lake Constance in the north-east. Switzerland contains the headwaters of the Inn, Rhine, Rhône and Ticino rivers. The average annual temperature range on the plateau is 0°–19°C (32°–66°F). Basle has an average annual rainfall of 840 mm (33 in). The mountains are colder and wetter, although much of the precipitation falls as snow. Switzerland is a multilingual nation. In 1970 65 per cent of the population spoke German, 18 per cent French, 12 per cent Italian and 1 per cent Romansch (which is related to Latin). In 1978 agriculture employed 6 per cent of the workforce and industry and services 47 per cent each. Dairy farming is the main agricultural activity: there were 2 million cattle in 1979. Cereals, potatoes, sugar beet and fruits are grown and wine is produced. Switzerland is highly industrialized. Its superb precision instruments made it famous, but chemicals, processed foods, glassware, machinery, metal products and textiles are all important today. Tourism is a major source of foreign exchange. In 1291 the people of Schwyz, Unterwalden and Uri formed a league to win their independence from Hapsburg rule. This league gradually grew into a loose alliance of independent cantons, whose existence was recognized formally in 1648. France conquered the area in 1798 but, in 1815, the Congress of Vienna guaranteed Switzerland neutrality. In 1848 a new Constitution was adopted by the 22 cantons; it was revised in 1874 to give more power to the federal government. In 1979 a 23rd canton, Jura, was created. Each canton has its own government. There is a bicameral federal parliament, comprising a 46-member *Ständerat* (Council of States) and a 200-member *Nationalrat* (National Council).

Area: 41,288 km² (15,942 sq mi); **Population:** 6,350,000; **Capital:** Bern (pop with suburbs, 282,000); **Other cities:** Zürich (707,000), Basle (364,000); **Highest point:** Mt Rosa, 4634 m (15,203 ft); **Official languages:** French, German, Italian; **Religions:** Roman Catholicism (49 per cent), Protestantism (48 per cent); **Adult literacy rate:** 99 per cent; **Average life expectancy at birth:** 74 years: **Unit of currency:** Franc; **Main exports:** machinery, pharmaceutical goods, watches, processed foods; **Per capita GNP:** US$14,240.

The canton of Valais in southern Switzerland contains fertile valleys and pleasant villages, overlooked by Alpine mountains that rise in altitude towards the Italian border.

SYRIA, an Arab republic in south-western Asia. Behind the coastal plain, with its Mediterranean climate, is a low mountain range that overlooks the fertile River Orontes valley. The River Euphrates drains the inland plains in the north. The highest peaks are in the Anti-Lebanon range in the south-west. To the east, the land slopes down to the hot Syrian desert. The rainfall decreases from west to east: about 60 per cent of Syria has less than 250 mm (10 in) of rain a year. About 90 per cent of the people are Arabs, 6 per cent are Kurds and there is a Palestinian minority. In 1978 agriculture employed 49 per cent of the people, industry 22 per cent and services 29 per cent. But their respective contributions to the GDP were 20 per cent, 28 per cent and 52 per cent. Cotton is the leading crop. Oil is produced and manufacturing is increasing. Tourism is important in peaceful times. The Euphrates valley was the home of early civilizations and the Syrian coast was part of Phoenicia. But, for most of its history, Syria has been under foreign rule. Islam was introduced in AD 636. After World War I, France ruled the area, but Syria was fully independent by 1946. Syria has participated in the Arab-Israeli wars which have sapped its resources. Power is concentrated in the army, although the 1973 Constitution declares Syria to be 'a democratic, popular Socialist state'.

Area: 185,180 km² (71,502 sq mi); **Population:** 9,227,000; **Capital:** Damascus (pop 1,042,000); **Other cities:** Halab (1,523,000), Homs (629,000); **Highest point:** Jabal ash Sheikh (Mt Hermon), 2814 m (9232 ft); **Official language:** Arabic; **Religion:** Islam; **Adult literacy rate:** 53 per cent; **Average life expectancy at birth:** 57 years; **Unit of currency:** Syrian pound; **Main exports:** cotton, oil, cereals, live animals; **Per capita GNP:** US$1070.

TAIWAN, an island republic (formerly called Formosa) off the coast of China. It is largely mountainous, with fertile plains in the west. The climate is tropical. Nearly all the people are Chinese. Rice, sugar cane, sweet potatoes and tea are major crops, but agriculture accounts for only 10 per cent of the GDP as compared with industry 48 per cent. Taiwan produces coal, some oil and natural gas, and various metals. But manufactures dominate the exports. Taiwan became Chinese in the 1680s. Japan ruled it between 1895–1945. When the Communists took over China in 1949, their Nationalist opponents led by Gen Chiang Kai-shek, set up a government on Taiwan. The economy expanded rapidly with US aid. Taiwan represented China in the UN until 1971, when Communist China was admitted.

Area: 35,961 km² (13,885 sq mi); **Population:** 17,100,000 (1978); **Capital:** Taipei (pop 3,050,000); **Other cities:** Kaohsiung (1,115,000); **Highest point:** Yu Shan, 3997 m (13,114 ft); **Official language:** Chinese; **Religions:** Confucianism, Buddhism, Taoism, Christianity; **Adult literacy rate:** 82 per cent; **Average life expectancy at birth:** 72 years; **Unit of currency:** Dollar; **Main exports:** textiles, electrical machinery, food, other machinery, plastics; **Per capita GNP:** US$1400 (1978).

TANZANIA, a United Republic in East Africa, consisting of mainland Tanganyika and the coral islands of Zanzibar and Pemba. Most of Tanganyika is a plateau between 900 and 1500 m (2953–4921 ft) high. The plateau is broken by arms of the East African Rift Valley: the western arm encloses lakes Nyasa (Malawi) and Tanganyika; the eastern arm contains smaller salt lakes. Lake Victoria in the north-west occupies a shallow depression and is not in the Rift Valley. There are mountains in the north and south. Mt Kilimanjaro is Africa's highest peak. The climate is equatorial, but modified by the altitude. The rainfall around Lake Victoria averages 1100 mm (43 in) a year; the central plateau is drier and droughts are common. Savanna vegetation is the most common. The wildlife is rich and national parks cover 3 per cent of the land: tourism is expanding. The people are divided into 120 tribal groups. About 94 per cent of the people speak Bantu languages. Others speak Cushitic and Khoisan tongues. In 1978 agriculture employed 83 per cent of the people and accounted for 51 per cent of the GDP, as opposed to 13 per cent from industry. Major crops are coffee, cotton, cashew nuts and sisal. Diamonds are mined, but manufacturing is small-scale. In 1890 Tanganyika became a German territory, while Zanzibar (including Pemba) became a British protectorate. Britain occupied Tanganyika in World War I and ruled it until 1961 when it became an independent member of the Commonwealth. It became a republic in 1962. Zanzibar became independent in 1963 but, following a coup, it joined with Tanganyika in 1964, adopting the official title of the United Republic of Tanzania in October. But by 1981, Zanzibar was still not fully integrated into the union. Tanzania is a one-party state and it pursues socialist policies, concentrating on rural development.

Area: 945,087 km² (364,920 sq mi); **Population:** 19,388,000; **Capital:** Dar es Salaam (pop 757,000), but Dodoma is scheduled to become capital by the mid-1980s; **Highest point:** Mt Kilimanjaro, 5895 m (19,341 ft); **Official languages:** English, Swahili; **Religions:** Christianity (40 per cent), Islam (30 per cent), traditional beliefs (30 per cent); **Adult literacy rate:** 66 per cent; **Average life expectancy at birth:** 51 years; **Unit of currency:** Tanzanian shilling; **Main exports:** coffee, cloves, sisal, cotton, diamonds, cashew nuts; **Per capita GNP:** US$270.

THAILAND, a South-East Asian kingdom, called Siam until 1939. The fertile Chao Phraya river basin, the main farming region, is bordered by mountains in the east, west and north, where the highest peak, Inthanon, is situated. North-eastern Thailand, a plateau drained by the Mekong River, is infertile. The climate is tropical. Much of Thailand has an average annual rainfall of 1500 mm (59 in), but the north-eastern plateau has less than 250 mm (10 in). About 85 per cent of the people are Thais. There is a sizeable Chinese community, tribesmen in remote areas (Karen, Khmu, Mao and Yao), Malays and Indians. In 1978 agriculture employed 77 per cent of the people. It accounted for 27 per cent of the GDP, the same as industry. The main products are rice, rubber and tin. Manufacturing is increasing. The Thai state was founded in the 14th century. Its area was reduced in the 19th century but it remained independent. It was an absolute monarchy until 1932. In World War II it supported Japan. A military dictatorship ruled in 1947–51 and later it suffered from instability and frequent coups. Elections were held in 1979 under a new, democratic Constitution. A coup attempt was put down in 1981.

Area: 514,000 km² (198,467 sq mi); **Population:** 49,414,000; **Capital:** Bangkok (pop 4,871,000); **Highest point:** Inthanon Peak, 2595 m (8514 ft); **Official language:** Thai; **Religions:** Buddhism (94 per cent), Islam (4 per cent); **Adult literacy rate:** 84 per cent; **Average life expectancy at birth:** 61 years; **Unit of currency:** Baht; **Main exports:** rice, rubber, tapioca products, tin, maize; **Per capita GNP:** US$590.

TOGO, a West African republic. The Togo-Atacora Mts in the centre separate a low plateau in the north from the fertile southern plains. The climate is tropical, with an average temperature of 27°C (81°F) throughout the year. Lomé has an average annual rainfall of 740 mm (29 in). The rainfall increases inland to 1780 mm (70 in) in the mountains. There are about 30 tribal groups among the Negroid population. Farming is the main activity: cocoa and coffee are the leading crops. Phosphates made up 39 per cent of the exports in 1978, but manufacturing is small-scale. Togo was a German protectorate from 1884. It was invaded by British and French troops in World War I and partitioned between them. In 1957 the western (British) section joined Ghana. French Togo became a fully independent republic in 1960. Col Etienne Eyadéma took power in a coup in 1967. He was the sole candidate in an election in 1979 and remained the effective ruler of Togo.

Area: 56,000 km² (21,623 sq mi); **Population:** 2,693,000; **Capital:** Lomé (pop 229,000); **Highest point:** 1026 m (3366 ft); **Official language:** French; **Religions:** traditional beliefs (60 per cent), Christianity (25 per cent), Islam (7 per cent); **Adult literacy rate:** 18 per cent; **Average life expectancy at birth:** 46 years; **Unit of currency:** Franc CFA; **Main exports:** phosphates, cocoa, coffee; **Per capita GNP:** US$340.

TONGA, or the Friendly Islands, an island kingdom in the South Pacific. The 169 islands and islets are divided into 3 groups: Vava'u in the north; Ha'apai in the centre; and Tongatapu in the south, where Nuku'alofa is situated. There are both coral and volcanic islands. The climate is pleasant. Most people are Polynesians. Coconuts and bananas are leading products. Tonga was united under King George Tupou I in 1845. The islands were a British protectorate from 1900. Full independence within the Commonwealth was achieved in 1970.

Area: 699 km² (270 sq mi); **Population:** 99,000; **Capital:** Nuku'alofa (pop 18,000); **Unit of currency:** Pa'anga; **Per capita GNP:** US$460.

TRINIDAD AND TOBAGO, a West Indian republic close to South America. Trinidad covers 94 per cent of the country. Both islands are hilly and have a tropical climate. The people include Negroes (45 per cent), East Indians (35 per cent), people of mixed origin (17 per cent), Europeans (2 per cent) and Chinese (1 per cent). Oil is the main product. Citrus fruits, cocoa, coffee and sugar cane are grown. Columbus discovered the islands in 1498. They were both British by 1802. Full independence within the Commonwealth was achieved in 1962 and republican status was adopted in 1976.

Area: 5130 km² (1981 sq mi); **Population:** 1,193,000; **Capital:** Port-of-Spain (pop 63,000); **Official language:** English; **Unit of currency:** Dollar; **Main exports:** petroleum products, chemicals, food; **Per capita GNP:** US$3390.

TUNISIA, a North African republic. An extension of the Atlas Mts is in the north, surrounded by plains. A depression containing salt lakes, the Chott el-Djerid, is in the centre. Saharan plateaux are in the south. Tunis has an average annual temperature range of 10°–27°C (50°–81°F) and 460 mm (18 in) of rain a year. It becomes drier from north to south. Most people are Arabs or Berbers. In 1978 agriculture employed 45 per cent of the workforce, accounting for 18 per cent of the GDP as compared with 30 per cent from industry. Major crops are cereals, olives, grapes (for wine), fruit and vegetables. Fishing is important. Mining for oil, phosphates and metal ores has increased in recent years; manufacturing is also growing. Tourism is important: there were a million tourists in 1977. Carthage was founded (near present-day Tunis) in 814 BC, but Rome destroyed it in 146 BC. The Arabs conquered Tunisia in AD 647. France made Tunisia a protectorate in 1883. Full independence as a monarchy was achieved in 1956 and a republic was proclaimed in 1957. The first President, Habib Bourguiba, was elected President-for-life in 1974.

Area: 163,610 km² (63,174 sq mi); **Population:** 6,625,000; **Capital:** Tunis (pop 505,000); **Highest point:** Djebel Chambi, 1544 m (5066 ft); **Official language:** Arabic; **Religion:** Islam; **Adult literacy rate:** 55 per cent; **Average life expectancy at birth:** 57 years; **Unit of currency:** Dinar; **Main exports:** oil, olive oil, phosphates; **Per capita GNP:** US$1120.

TURKEY, a republic partly in Europe and partly in Asia. European Turkey, area 23,623 km² (9121 sq mi), lies west of the Dardanelles, the Sea of Marmara and the Bosporus. These waterways link the Mediterranean and Black seas. European Turkey is a fertile, low-lying region. Asian Turkey (Anatolia) has fertile coastal plains, with a Mediterranean climate. Central Anatolia, a mainly flat plateau, is arid with less than 250 mm (10 in) of rain per year. About 90 per cent of the people speak Turkish; Kurds make up 7 per cent of the population. In 1978 agriculture employed 60 per cent of the people and industry 14 per cent; their respective contributions to the GDP were 27 per cent and 28 per cent. Nearly 31 per cent of Turkey is cultivated. Major crops include barley, cotton, grapes (for wine), fruits, nuts, raisins, sugar beet and wheat. In 1979 Turkey had 14.9 million cattle, 43.9 million sheep (only the USSR, Australia, China and New Zealand had more), and 18.4 million goats. Turkey produces coal and lignite, chromium and some iron ore, copper and oil. Manufactures include iron and steel, petroleum products, paper, cement, chemicals, textiles and machinery. Tourism is important: there were more than 1.75 million tourists in 1978. From AD 330 Istanbul (then Constantinople) was capital of the Byzantine Empire. The Seljuk Turks invaded the area in the 11th century. The Ottoman Turks arrived in the late 13th century and, in 1453, they took Constantinople.

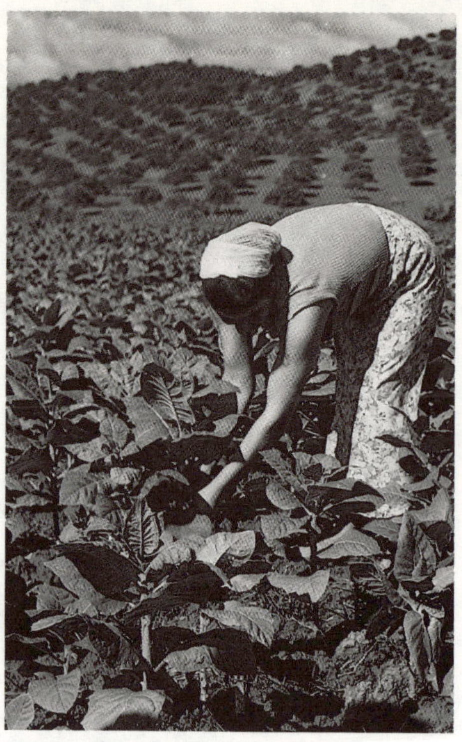

Right: Vast tracts of fertile land, particularly in the south-west, have made the USSR one of the world's great farming nations. This collective farm in the Caucasus region produces tobacco.

The Ottoman Empire gradually spread through south-eastern Europe, south-western Asia and northern Africa. It began its slow decline in the late 16th century and collapsed in World War I. In 1923 Mustafa Kemal (called Atatürk) made Turkey a republic and began to modernize it. Conflict with Greece continues and, in 1974, Turkey occupied northern Cyprus.

Area: 780,576 km² (301,399 sq mi); **Population:** 47,663,000; **Capital:** Ankara (pop 1,236,000); **Other cities:** Istanbul (2,132,000), Izmir (521,000); **Highest point:** Mt Ararat, 5165 m (16,946 ft); **Official language:** Turkish; **Religion:** Islam (98 per cent); **Adult literacy rate:** 60 per cent; **Average life expectancy at birth:** 61 years; **Unit of currency:** Turkish lira; **Main exports:** cotton, nuts, fruit, tobacco; **Per capita GNP:** US$1330.

TURKS AND CAICOS ISLANDS, a British colony in the south-eastern Bahamas. Only 6 of the 30 or so small islands are inhabited. The largest is Grand Caicos, but the seat of government is on Grand Turk. Most people are descendants of African slaves. Fishing is the main industry. The islands became British in 1670 and from 1848 to 1962 they were dependencies of Jamaica.

Area: 430 km² (166 sq mi); **Population:** 7200; **Seat of government:** Cockburn Town.

TUVALU, an independent member of the Commonwealth (formerly the Ellice Is) north of Fiji in the South Pacific. The islands are coral atolls. The people are Polynesians. Coconuts and copra are major products. The Gilbert and Ellice Is became a British protectorate in 1892. The Ellice Is broke away from the Micronesian Gilbert Is (now Kiribati) in 1975 to become Tuvalu. Full independence was achieved in 1978.

Area: 8 km² (3 sq mi); **Population:** 7349; **Capital:** Funafuti (pop 2000).

UGANDA, a landlocked republic in equatorial Africa. Part of Africa's largest lake, Victoria, is in the south-east; the marshy Lake Kyoga is in the centre; and lakes Edward and Mobutu Sese Seko are in the Rift Valley in the west. The high Ruwenzori borders the Rift Valley. Most of Uganda is a plateau between 1100–1400 m (3609–4593 ft). Temperatures in the south-east are around 21°–24°C (70°–75°F) throughout the year. The average annual rainfall is between 760 and 1520 mm (30–60 in). Uganda has about 40 tribal groups. Two-thirds of the people, including the largest single group, the Baganda, speak Bantu languages. Some Nilotic languages are also spoken. In 1978 agriculture employed 83 per cent of the workforce, accounting for 57 per cent of the GDP. Coffee, cotton, tea and hides and skins are important and copper is mined. Manufacturing is developing. Britain took over Uganda between 1894 and 1914. Full independence was achieved in 1962 and Uganda became a republic in 1967. Gen Idi Amin ruled as a military dictator in 1971–79. After his overthrow by Ugandan and Tanzanian forces, political conditions remained unstable despite elections being held in 1980.

Area: 236,036 km² (91,139 sq mi); **Population:** 13,983,000; **Capital:** Kampala (pop 332,000); **Highest point:** Ruwenzori range on Zaire border, 5119 m (16,795 ft); **Official language:** English; **Religions:** Roman Catholicism (33 per cent), Protestantism (30 per cent), Islam (6 per cent), traditional beliefs; **Average life expectancy at birth:** 53 years; **Unit of currency:** Ugandan shilling; **Main exports:** coffee, cotton, tea, copper; **Per capita GNP:** US$290.

UNION OF SOVIET SOCIALIST REPUBLICS, the USSR, is the world's largest nation. The European part, west of the Ural Mts, covers 5,571,000 km² (2,151,092 sq mi) – 25 per cent of the country – but it contains 75 per cent of the population. Much of the land is flat, including the fertile Ukraine, but there are many hilly areas. Major rivers are the Dnepr and Don which flow into the Black Sea, and the Volga which empties into the Caspian Sea. The Caspian Sea, at 438,695 km² (169,390 sq mi) is the world's largest lake, while the Volga, at 3690 km (2293 mi), is Europe's longest river. The highest point in the Urals is only 1894 m (6214 ft) but the Caucasus in the south contain Mt Elbruz, which, at 5633 m (18,481 ft), is Europe's highest. East of the Urals is the West Siberian Plain, drained by the

Top: The Trans-Siberian Railway links the USSR's capital Moscow to Vladivostok on the Pacific. Above: The Church of St Basil in Moscow.

REPUBLICS OF THE USSR

	Population 1980	Capital
Armenia	3,000,000	Yerevan
Azerbaijan	6,100,000	Baku
Belorussia	9,600,000	Minsk
Estonia	1,500,000	Tallinn
Georgia	5,000,000	Tbilisi
Kazakhstan	14,900,000	Alma-Ata
Kirgizia	3,600,000	Frunze
Latvia	2,500,000	Riga
Lithuania	3,400,000	Vilnius
Moldavia	4,000,000	Kishinev
Russian SFRS	138,400,000	Moscow
Tadzhikistan	3,900,000	Dushanbe
Turkmenistan	2,800,000	Ashkhabad
Ukraine	50,000,000	Kiev
Uzbekistan	15,800,000	Tashkent

River Ob. Between the Yenisey and Lena rivers is the Central Siberian plateau, which is mostly between 500 and 1500 m (1640–4921 ft). In the far east are a series of mountain ranges. The south-east, which is drained by the Amur River, contains Lake Baykal, the world's deepest lake. South of the West Siberian plain is the Kazakh plateau, several mountain ranges, including the Pamir, Altai and Tien Shan, and in the west the plains around the Aral Sea. The climate varies from the Arctic north to the warm Mediterranean climates along the Black and Caspian sea coasts. Inland areas have a continental climate. Moscow's average July temperature of 21°C (70°F) is nearly 30°C (54°F) higher than the average January temperature. The north-west and the Caucasus region are the wettest places. There are deserts east of the Caspian Sea (the Kara Kum and the Kyzyl Kum). About 60 languages are spoken in the USSR. In 1979 the largest groups were Russians (52.2 per cent), Ukrainians (16 per cent), Uzbeks (4.8 per cent), Belorussians (3.6 per cent), Kazakhs (2.5 per cent), Tatars (2.4 per cent), Azerbaijanians (2.1 per cent), Armenians (1.6 per cent), Georgians (1.4 per cent), Moldavians (1.1 per cent), Tadzhiks (1.1 per cent), Lithuanians (1.1 per cent) and Turkmenians (0.8 per cent). The USSR is divided into 15 republics. The largest, the Russian Soviet Federal Socialist Republic (RSFSR) covers 76 per cent of the country. In 1978 agriculture employed 17 per cent of the people, industry 47 per cent and services 36 per cent; their respective contributions to the GDP were 17 per cent, 62 per cent and 21 per cent. Arable land covers 10 per cent and pasture 17 per cent of the land. Crops vary with the climate. In 1979 the USSR led the world in producing apples, barley, coniferous wood, milk, mutton, lamb and goat's meat, oats, potatoes, rye, sugar beet and wheat. In 1980 there were 115 million cattle, 73.7 million pigs and 143 million sheep. Forests cover about one-third of the USSR. Most of the land and all industry are government-owned, but most farm workers have a private plot. The USSR has vast mineral resources. It leads the world in asbestos, coal, oil, iron ore, lead, manganese, mercury, nickel, potash and silver production. But manufacturing is the chief economic sector. The main industrial areas are: the Moscow region, the Ukraine; the Urals; Transcaucasia; and the area around Leningrad. Only the US produces more electrical energy than the USSR, and the USSR is the world's top steel producer. In the 10th–12th centuries, Kiev was the capital of the Russians but Kiev fell to Mongol invaders in the 13th century. Moscow then became the chief principality and by 1480 it had ended Mongol domination. In 1613 the Romanov dynasty was established. It lasted until 1917. Peter the Great westernized Russia in the early 18th century and extended its boundaries. By 1812, when Napoleon was defeated on Russian soil, Russia was a great European power. It was allied with Britain and France in World War I but Nicholas II, the last of the Romanovs, was forced to abdicate in 1917. The November 1917 Revolution led by Vladimir Lenin ousted a moderate government. The Bolsheviks

COUNTRIES OF THE WORLD

THE UNITED KINGDOM

	Area sq km	Area sq mi	Population (1981)	Capital	Population of capital
England	130,363	50,336	46,221,000	London	6,696,008
Wales	20,763	8,017	2,790,000	Cardiff	273,856
Scotland	78,772	30,416	5,116,000	Edinburgh	436,271
Northern Ireland	14,148	5,463	1,543,000[a]	Belfast	362,000[d]
Isle of Man	588	227	62,000[b]	Douglas	20,000
Channel Islands	195	75	131,000[c]	–	–

a 1979 est; b 1976 est; c estimates vary between islands; d 1971

took over and successfully overcame their enemies in 1918–22. From 1924, under Joseph Stalin, all opposition was ruthlessly suppressed. The economy was rebuilt with special emphasis on industrialization. The German invasion of 1941 caused much devastation and an estimated 20 million deaths. After the war, the USSR brought eastern Europe under its control and relations with the West deteriorated. Relations improved after Stalin's death in 1953, although relations with China then deteriorated. Soviet technology has made it one of the world's super-powers. It was the first, in 1961, to put a man into space.

Area: 22,402,200 km² (8,650,010 sq mi); **Population:** 270,376,000; **Capital:** Moscow (pop 8,099,000); **Other cities:** Leningrad (4,638,000), Kiev (2,192,000), Tashkent (1,816,000), Kharkhov (1,464,000), Gorki (1,358,000), Novosibirsk (1,328,000), Minsk (1,295,000), Kuibyshev (1,226,000), Sverdlovsk (1,225,000), Dnepropetrovsk (1,083,000), Tbilisi (1,080,000), Odessa (1,057,000), Chelyabinsk (1,042,000), Yerevan (1,036,000), Donetsk (1,032,000), Baku (1,030,000), Omsk (1,028,000), Perm (1,008,000), Kazan (1,002,000); **Highest point:** Communism Peak, 7495 m (24,590 ft); **Official language:** Russian; **Religions:** Christianity, Islam, Judaism, but all religions have been discouraged since 1917; **Adult literacy rate:** 99 per cent; **Average life expectancy at birth:** 70 years; **Unit of currency:** Rouble; **Main exports:** engineering products, transport equipment, oil and mineral ores, cotton, paper; **Per capita GNP:** US$4110.

UNITED ARAB EMIRATES, an oil-rich federation of 7 Emirates (formerly the Trucial States), with coastlines on the Persian Gulf and the Gulf of Oman. The Emirates are Abu Dhabi, Ajman, Dubai, Fujairah, Ras al Khaimah, Sharjah and Umm al Qaiwain. The main resource of this flat, hot, desert nation is oil. About 70 per cent of the people are Arabs. The rest are Iranians or other Asians. The states entered into treaties with Britain from 1820. Britain withdrew in 1971 and ended its responsibility for the states' defence and foreign relations. The states then joined in an independent federation. The 7 rulers form a Supreme Council, which appoints the Council of Ministers.

Area: 83,600 km² (32,280 sq mi); **Population:** 1,040,000; **Capital:** Abu Dhabi; **Unit of currency:** Dirham; **Main exports:** oil and natural gas; **Per capita GNP:** US$15,590.

UNITED KINGDOM OF GREAT BRITAIN AND NORTHERN IRELAND (Great Britain consists of England, Scotland and Wales.) The Channel Islands (Jersey, Guernsey and Guernsey's dependencies: Alderney, Brechou, Great Sark, Herm, Jethou, Lihou and Little Sark) and the Isle of Man in the Irish Sea are dependencies of the British Crown, but they are largely self-governing. *Scotland* has 3 main land regions. The highlands are divided by Glen More into the rugged north-western highlands and the Grampians, which include Ben Nevis. The main island groups are the Orkney and Shetland Islands to the north and the Hebrides to the west. The central lowlands are the most densely populated region, with coalfields, the leading cities and much farmland. Scotland's southern uplands are a mainly farming region. Northern *England* contains the Cumbrian Mts (or the Lake District), where England's highest peak, Scafell Pike, 978 m (3209 ft), is situated, and the Pennines which run north-south. Coalfields near the edge of the Pennines have stimulated the growth of major industrial regions. England's other highland region includes Exmoor and Dartmoor in the south-west. Lowland England contains many fertile plains crossed by ranges of low hills, such as the Cotswolds, Chilterns and the North and South Downs in the south-east. *Wales* is a mainly highland country, rising to Snowdon, 1085 m (3560 ft). South Wales contains a large coalfield on which a major industrial region has been built. *Northern Ireland* contains uplands and plains. In the east Lough Neagh, the UK's largest lake, covers 396 km² (153 sq mi). The UK's longest rivers are the Severn and the Thames, on which the capital London stands. The UK has a moist, temperate climate, moderated by the warm North Atlantic Drift (Gulf Stream). Average temperatures seldom exceed 18°C (64°F) in summer or fall below 3°C (37°F) in winter. The highlands are wet, with about 2030 mm (80 in) of rain a year in places. The rainfall decreases to the east, where it averages 760 mm (30 in) per year. The UK is highly urbanized: 91 per cent of the population lived in urban areas in 1980. In 1978 agriculture employed only 2 per cent of the population, industry 43 per cent and services 55 per cent; their respective contributions to the GDP were 2 per cent, 36 per cent and 62 per cent. Farming is highly efficient but food is imported. Generally, livestock farming is most important in the wetter west. In 1979 there were 13.5 million cattle, 29.9 million sheep and 7.8 million pigs. Arable farming is most important in the drier east. Major crops are cereals, potatoes, sugar beet and vegetables. Fishing is

This aerial view of London shows that this great city, the capital of the UK, is a mixture of the old and new. One of its principal landmarks is Big Ben which is part of the Houses of Parliament in Westminster. Winding through the city is the river Thames, London's outlet to the sea.

ENGLISH COUNTIES

Metropolitan counties	Population 1981 census	Administrative HQ
Greater London	6,696,008	–
Greater Manchester	2,594,778	–
Merseyside	1,513,070	Liverpool
South Yorkshire	1,301,813	Sheffield
Tyne and Wear	1,143,245	South Shields
West Midlands	2,644,634	Wolverhampton
West Yorkshire	2,037,510	Wakefield
Other counties		
Avon	909,408	Bristol
Bedfordshire	504,986	Bedford
Berkshire	675,153	Reading
Buckinghamshire	565,992	Aylesbury
Cambridgeshire	575,177	Cambridge
Cheshire	926,293	Chester
Cleveland	565,775	Middlesborough
Cornwall and the Isles of Scilly	430,506	Truro
Cumbria	483,427	Carlisle
Derbyshire	906,929	Matlock
Devon	952,000	Exeter
Dorset	591,990	Dorchester
Durham	604,728	Durham
East Sussex	652,568	Lewes
Essex	1,469,065	Chelmsford
Gloucestershire	499,351	Gloucester
Hampshire	1,456,367	Winchester
Hereford & Worcester	630,218	Worcester
Hertfordshire	954,535	Hertford
Humberside	847,666	Kingston upon Hull
Isle of Wight	118,192	Newport
Kent	1,463,055	Maidstone
Lancashire	1,372,118	Preston
Leicestershire	842,577	Leicester
Lincolnshire	547,560	Lincoln
Norfolk	693,490	Norwich
Northamptonshire	527,532	Northampton
Northumberland	299,905	Newcastle upon Tyne
North Yorkshire	666,610	Northallerton
Nottinghamshire	982,631	Nottingham
Oxfordshire	515,079	Oxford
Shropshire	375,610	Shrewsbury
Somerset	424,988	Taunton
Staffordshire	1,012,320	Stafford
Suffolk	596,354	Ipswich
Surrey	999,393	Kingston upon Thames
Warwickshire	473,620	Warwick
West Sussex	658,562	Chichester
Wiltshire	518,167	Trowbridge

WELSH COUNTIES

	Population 1981 census	Administrative HQ
Clwyd	390,173	Mold
Dyfed	329,977	Carmarthen
Gwent	439,684	Cwmbran
Gwynedd	230,468	Caernarvon
Mid-Glamorgan	537,866	Cardiff
Powys	110,467	Llandrindod
South Glamorgan	384,633	Cardiff
West Glamorgan	367,194	Swansea

SCOTTISH REGIONS

	Population 1981 census	Administrative HQ
Borders	99,248	Newton St Boswalls
Central	273,078	Stirling
Dumfries & Galloway	145,078	Dumfries
Fife	326,480	Glenrothes
Grampian	470,596	Aberdeen
Highland	200,030	Inverness
Lothian	735,892	Edinburgh
Strathclyde	2,397,827	Glasgow
Tayside	391,529	Dundee
Island Authorities		
Orkney	18,906	Kirkwall
Shetland	27,716	Lerwick
Western Isles	31,766	Stornaway

COUNTIES OF NORTHERN IRELAND

	Population 1971 census	Administrative HQ
Antrim	356,000	Belfast
Armagh	134,000	Armagh
Belfast CB	362,000	–
Down	312,000	Downpatrick
Fermanagh	50,000	Enniskillen
Londonderry	131,000	Londonderry
Londonderry CB	52,000	–
Tyrone	139,000	Omagh

important: there were nearly 7000 fishing vessels in 1979. The UK's industrial economy was originally based on its abundant coal and iron ore resources. Coal-mining, however, has declined, although the economy has recently been boosted by the discovery of oil and natural gas in the North Sea. Manufactures are extremely varied. Invisible earnings from banking, insurance, tourism and other services make a vital contribution to the economy. The UK's early history is one of successive invasions by various peoples, including Iberians, Celts, Romans, Angles, Saxons, Jutes, Norsemen, Danes and Normans (1066). Resistance to Norman rule continued in Wales, which was conquered in 1282 and united with England. In 1603 James VI of Scotland became James I of England. But the Act of Union giving England and Scotland a common parliament was not passed until 1707. In 1801 Ireland became part of the United Kingdom of Great Britain and Ireland. In the 18th century the UK began to build a great empire, although it lost its 13 American colonies in 1783. In the late 18th century, the UK was the first nation to change from an agricultural to an industrial society. Wealth from trade and industry made the UK one of the world's greatest nations in the 19th century. It played a major role in World War I, but this sapped its resources. After the war, southern Ireland broke away to become the Irish Free State (see Ireland). World War II proved an even greater drain on the UK's economy than World War I, and financial problems have marked its post-war history. However, the UK transformed its empire into the Commonwealth, which has given it a voice in world affairs. Many people from the non-white Commonwealth have settled in the UK, making up an estimated 3 per cent of the population in 1975. The UK joined the EEC in 1973, but it suffered from the world recession in the early 1980s. Its many problems included high inflation, increasing competition for its manufactures in world markets, and violent conflict in Northern Ireland.

Area: 244,046 km² (94,232 sq mi), not including the Isle of Man and the Channel Islands; **Population:** 55,670,000; **Capital:** London (pop 6,696,000); **Other cities** (prelim 1981 census): Birmingham (920,389), Glasgow (763,162), Liverpool (510,306), Sheffield (477,142), Manchester (449,168), Leeds (448,528), Edinburgh (436,271), Bristol (387,977), Belfast (362,000 in 1971), Coventry (314,124), Bradford (280,691), Leicester (279,791), Cardiff (273,856), Nottingham (271,080), Kingston upon Hull (268,302), Wolverhampton (252,447), Stoke-on-Trent (252,351); **Highest point:** Ben Nevis, 1347 m (4419 ft); **Official language:** English; **Religion:** mainly Christianity; **Adult literacy rate:** 99 per cent; **Average life expectancy at birth:** 73 years; **Unit of currency:** Pound sterling; **Main exports:** electrical and engineering products, transport equipment, textiles, chemicals and plastics, ceramics; **Per capita GNP:** US$6340 (Channel Is, US$5240 and Is of Man US$3890).

UNITED STATES OF AMERICA, a federal republic and the world's 4th largest nation. The bulk of the US lies between Canada and Mexico. The 49th state, Alaska, is in north-western North America, while the 50th state, Hawaii, is in the North Pacific Ocean, about 3870 km (2404 mi) south-west of San Francisco. (Both Alaska and Hawaii became states in 1959.) The main part of the US contains 5 land regions. The *eastern coastal plains* are broadest around the Gulf of Mexico. The Atlantic coastal plains are broadest in the south and narrowest in New England. The Atlantic coast is deeply indented and contains several natural harbours. West of the Atlantic seaboard are the *Appalachian Mts*. This complex region which runs roughly from Newfoundland (Canada) in the north-east to Alabama in the south-west contains many ridges, plateaux and deep valleys. The *central (interior) lowlands* stretch westwards from the Appalachians. In the north are the five Great Lakes: Lake Superior, which covers 82,409 km² (31,820 sq mi), is the world's largest freshwater lake. To the south, the central plains are drained by the Mississippi River and its tributaries, notably the Missouri and Ohio. To the west are the higher Great Plains, mostly between 450 and 1800 m (1476–5906 ft). Beyond these plains the land rises to the *western highlands*, which include the folded Rocky Mountains, the Sierra Nevada range and the Cascade range, which includes the volcano Mt St Helens which erupted in 1980. The Colorado

San Francisco, California's third largest city after Los Angeles and San Diego, is a largely modern city. It was rebuilt after it was devastated by the 1906 earthquake and the ensuing fires. A seaport with a fine harbour, San Francisco is a colourful, cosmopolitan city; its Chinatown district is the largest Chinese settlement outside Asia. California has a larger population than any other state in the United States and its thriving mixed economy is more substantial than those of many nations that are members of the United Nations.

U.S. STATES

State	Capital	Land Area sq km	Land Area sq mi	Population (1980)	State Bird/State Flower
Alabama	Montgomery	131,485	50,767	3,893,888	Yellowhammer/Camellia
Alaska	Juneau	1,478,451	570,833	401,851	Willow Ptarmigan/Forget-me-not
Arizona	Phoenix	293,984	113,508	2,718,425	Cactus Wren/Saguaro Cactus
Arkansas	Little Rock	134,881	52,079	2,286,435	Mockingbird/Apple Blossom
California	Sacramento	404,813	156,299	23,667,565	California Valley Quail/Golden Poppy
Colorado	Denver	268,310	103,595	2,889,735	Lark Bunting/Rocky Mountain Columbine
Connecticut	Hartford	12,618	4,871	3,107,576	Robin/Mountain Laurel
Delaware	Dover	5,004	1,932	594,317	Blue Hen Chicken/Peach Blossom
Florida	Tallahassee	140,256	54,153	9,746,342	Mockingbird/Orange Blossom
Georgia	Atlanta	150,364	58,056	5,463,105	Brown Thrasher/Cherokee Rose
Hawaii	Honolulu	16,641	6,425	964,691	Hawaiian Goose/Red Hibiscus
Idaho	Boise	213,449	82,412	944,038	Mountain Bluebird/Syringa
Illinois	Springfield	144,120	55,645	11,426,596	Cardinal/Violet
Indiana	Indianapolis	93,063	35,932	5,490,260	Cardinal/Peony
Iowa	Des Moines	144,949	55,965	2,913,808	Eastern Goldfinch/Wild Rose
Kansas	Topeka	211,812	81,778	2,364,236	Western Meadowlark/Sunflower
Kentucky	Frankfort	102,742	39,669	3,660,257	Kentucky Cardinal/Goldenrod
Louisiana	Baton Rouge	115,309	44,521	4,206,312	Pelican/Magnolia
Maine	Augusta	80,277	30,995	1,125,027	Chickadee/White Pine
Maryland	Annapolis	25,478	9,837	4,216,975	Baltimore Oriole/Black-eyed Susan
Massachusetts	Boston	20,264	7,824	5,737,037	Chickadee/Mayflower
Michigan	Lansing	147,510	56,954	9,262,078	Robin/Apple Blossom
Minnesota	St. Paul	206,028	79,548	4,075,970	Loon/Showy Lady's-slipper
Mississippi	Jackson	122,333	47,233	2,520,638	Mockingbird/Magnolia
Missouri	Jefferson City	178,567	68,945	4,916,759	Bluebird/Hawthorn
Montana	Helena	376,564	145,389	786,690	Western Meadowlark/Bitterroot
Nebraska	Lincoln	198,507	76,644	1,569,825	Western Meadowlark/Goldenrod
Nevada	Carson City	284,622	109,894	800,493	Mountain Bluebird/Shrub Sagebrush
New Hampshire	Concord	23,292	8,993	920,610	Purple Finch/Purple Lilac
New Jersey	Trenton	19,342	7,468	7,364,823	Eastern Goldfinch/Purple Violet
New Mexico	Santa Fe	314,256	121,336	1,302,981	Roadrunner/Yucca
New York	Albany	122,706	47,377	17,558,072	Bluebird/Rose
North Carolina	Raleigh	126,503	48,843	5,881,813	Cardinal/Dogwood
North Dakota	Bismarck	179,486	69,300	652,717	Western Meadowlark/Wild Prairie Rose
Ohio	Columbus	106,200	41,004	10,797,624	Cardinal/Scarlet Carnation
Oklahoma	Oklahoma City	177,816	68,655	3,025,290	Scissor-tailed Flycatcher/Mistletoe
Oregon	Salem	249,115	96,185	2,633,149	Western Meadowlark/Oregon Grape
Pennsylvania	Harrisburg	116,259	44,888	11,863,895	Ruffed Grouse/Mountain Laurel
Rhode Island	Providence	2,732	1,055	947,154	Rhode Island Red/Violet
South Carolina	Columbia	78,225	30,204	3,121,833	Carolina Wren/Carolina Jessamine
South Dakota	Pierre	196,715	75,952	690,768	Ringnecked Pheasant/Pasque
Tennessee	Nashville	106,591	41,155	4,591,120	Mockingbird/Iris
Texas	Austin	678,621	262,018	14,229,288	Mockingbird/Bluebonnet
Utah	Salt Lake City	212,568	82,073	1,461,037	Seagull/Sego Lily
Vermont	Montpelier	24,017	9,273	511,456	Hermit Thrush/Red Clover
Virginia	Richmond	102,830	39,704	5,346,818	Cardinal/Flowering Dogwood
Washington	Olympia	172,263	66,511	4,132,180	Willow Goldfinch/Rhododendron
West Virginia	Charleston	62,468	24,119	1,950,279	Cardinal/Rhododendron
Wisconsin	Madison	140,963	54,426	4,705,521	Robin/Violet
Wyoming	Cheyenne	251,200	96,990	469,557	Meadowlark/Indian Paint Brush

Much of Pennsylvania, a state in the north-eastern United States, lies in the Appalachian mountain region. The Appalachians, which extend from Newfoundland to Alabama, are a far older and more eroded range than the Rockies in the west. Hence, they have much gentler slopes and contain extensive farming regions. However, because of the slopes, soil erosion is always a danger in this moist region and contour ploughing is one of the ways of combatting this threat. Pennsylvania was one of the original 13 states of the USA.

River in the south-west has carved the Grand Canyon, which is more than 349 km (217 mi) long and 1675 m (5495 ft) deep in places. The *Pacific slope* contains fertile valleys and coastal ranges. One feature is the 960 km (597 mi) long San Andreas Fault in California. Movements along the fault cause earthquakes. Alaska also has much earthquake and volcanic activity and the Alaska range contains North America's highest peak, Mt McKinley. Hawaii consists of a string of volcanic and coral islands. The climate varies greatly from Arctic conditions in Alaska to deserts in the south-west, including Death Valley, the US's lowest point at 86 m (282 ft) below sea level, and a humid, subtropical climate in the south-east. California has a pleasant Mediterranean climate, but much of the interior has a continental climate, with hot summers, cold winters and a relatively low annual rainfall. The first inhabitants, American Indians, entered North America about 20,000 years ago. In 1970 they numbered 790,000. In 1980 about 83 per cent of the population was of European descent and 12 per cent were blacks, the descendants of slaves. Other races, including American Indians, Chinese, Japanese, Filipino and Mexican Americans, made up the other 5 per cent. Nearly 47 per cent of the land is farmed but only 2 per cent of the workforce was engaged in agriculture in 1978, as opposed to 33 per cent in industry and 65 per cent in services. Farming is highly efficient and the US is among the world's top producers of cotton, fruits, maize, oats, soya beans, sugar beet, tobacco, timber, wheat and livestock. In 1979 there were 110.9 million cattle, 59.9 million pigs and 12.2 million sheep. In 1979 agriculture accounted for 3 per cent of the GDP, industry 34 per cent and services 63 per cent. The US is one of the world's top producers of copper, iron ore, oil and natural gas, lead, phosphates, sulphur and uranium. The US is the world's most industrialized nation, accounting for about half of the world's industrial goods. Its technology was exemplified by its feat of landing men on the Moon in 1969. The first European to land in North America was probably Leif Ericson, a Viking, in about AD 986. The continent was rediscovered in 1497 by John Cabot. The first Europeans to settle in large numbers were the English, who founded a settlement in Virginia in 1607. By 1760 there were 13 colonies between Georgia and Massachusetts. The American War of Independence (1775–83) ended British rule. Under the 1787 Constitution, George Washington was elected the first President in 1789. In 1803 Louisiana was purchased from France and Florida was bought from Spain in 1809. The US-Mexican War of 1846–48 ended with the acquisition of much of the south-west: the US-Mexico border was fixed in 1853–54. The Civil War (1861–65) ended the threat of the secession of the South and slavery was abolished. Industrialization and the opening up of the West caused the economy to expand in the late 19th century. The US intervened in World War I in 1917. Between the wars there was a severe economic depression, but the New Deal policy of the 32nd President Franklin D Roosevelt helped it to recover. Roosevelt led the US into World War II in 1941 after the Japanese attack on Pearl Harbor in Hawaii. After World War II, the US accepted its role as a super-power, becoming involved in wars in Korea (1950–53) and Vietnam (1964–73) aimed at halting the spread of communism in Asia. Internally, the US has been troubled by ethnic conflict and assassinations of leading figures.

Spanish cultural influences are evident throughout Uruguay where more than 90 per cent of the people are of European descent. This Roman Catholic church is in Soriano, in south-western Uruguay.

Area: 9,529,104 km² (3,679,204 sq mi); **Population:** 226,547,346 (1980 census); **Capital:** Washington DC (pop 638,432); **Other cities:** New York (7,071,600), Chicago (3,005,100), Los Angeles (2,968,600), Philadelphia (1,688,200), Houston (1,595,100), Detroit (1,202,500), Dallas (904,100), San Diego (875,500), Phoenix (790,000), Baltimore (786,700), San Antonio (786,000), Indianapolis (700,800), San Francisco (679,000), Memphis (646,200), Milwaukee (636,300), San Jose (629,400), Cleveland (573,800), Columbus (565,000), Boston (563,000), New Orleans (557,900), Jacksonville (540,900), Seattle (493,800); **Highest Point:** Mt McKinley (Alaska), 6194 m (20,320 ft); **Official language:** English; **Religions:** in 1978, 54.7 per cent of church members were Protestants, 37.2 per cent were Roman Catholics, and 4.3 per cent were Jews; **Adult literacy rate:** 99 per cent; **Average life expectancy at birth:** 73 years; **Unit of currency:** Dollar; **Main exports:** machinery, vehicles, grains, aircraft and parts, chemicals, coal, soybeans, textiles, cotton, iron and steel goods; **Per capita GNP:** US$10,820.

UPPER VOLTA (name changed to **Burkina Faso**, 1984), a West African republic. Low plateaux cover most of the country. The east is in the River Niger basin; the centre and west are drained by the Black, Red and White Volta rivers. Upper Volta has a hot, tropical climate. The main rainy season is July-October and the average annual rainfall varies between 500 mm (20 in) in the north to 1140 mm (45 in) in the south-west. But droughts are common. Most people are Negroes: the Mossi (48 per cent) are the largest single group. In 1978 83 per cent of the population was engaged in agriculture, which accounted for 38 per cent of the GDP, with 20 per

Caracas, capital and by far the largest city of Venezuela, has grown rapidly in recent years, much of the development having been financed by revenue from the country's massive oil sales.

cent from industry and 42 per cent from services. Pastoralism is important: there were 2.7 million cattle, 1.8 million sheep and 2.7 million goats in 1979. Cotton and other cash crops are grown in the south and south-west. There are few minerals. Food, textiles and metal products are the main manufactures. Remittances from migrant workers and revenue from transit trade play a major part in the economy. France subdued the country by 1896. Full independence was achieved in 1960. Military coups occurred in 1966, 1974 and 1980, when power was vested in a Military Committee for National Recovery and Progress.

Area: 274,200 km² (105,875 sq mi); **Population:** 5,917,000; **Capital:** Ouagadougou (pop 173,000); **Official language:** French; **Religions:** traditional beliefs, Islam (30 per cent), Roman Catholicism (9 per cent); **Adult literacy rate:** 5 per cent; **Average life expectancy at birth:** 42 years; **Unit of currency:** Franc CFA; **Main exports:** cotton, livestock, karité nuts and oil, groundnuts; **Per capita GNP:** US$180.

URUGUAY, a South American republic facing the Atlantic Ocean. It is mostly low-lying, with hills in the north. The River Negro, a tributary of the Uruguay on the western border, drains the central region. The average annual temperature range is 10°–23°C (50°–73°F), while the annual rainfall averages 1000 mm (39 in) in the south and 1260 (50 in) in the north. More than 90 per cent of the population are of European descent. Most others are of mixed European and Indian descent. In 1979 agriculture employed 12 per cent of the workforce, industry 33 per cent and services 55 per cent. About 89 per cent of the land is farmed; 90 per cent of this is pasture. In 1979 Uruguay had 10 million cattle and 18.7 million sheep; livestock products are the chief exports. Crops include fruits, maize, rice, sugar and wheat. There are processing, oil refining, light engineering, transport, chemical and textile industries. Europeans first landed in Uruguay in 1515. Spain founded Montevideo in 1726 to stem Portugese influence in the area. The Portuguese were driven out in the late 18th century. Brazil annexed Uruguay in 1820, but Uruguay joined with Argentina in 1825 to fight Brazil. Uruguay finally became an independent nation in 1828. In 1903 José Batlle y Ordóñez became president and introduced many reforms, including extensive welfare services. Economic problems and the activities of the Tupamaros (an urban guerrilla movement) have caused political instability and army intervention in government in recent years.

Area: 176,215 km² (68,041 sq mi); **Population:** 2,934,000; **Capital:** Montevideo (pop 1,230,000); **Official language:** Spanish; **Religion:** Roman Catholicism; **Adult literacy rate:** 94 per cent; **Average life expectancy at birth:** 71 years; **Unit of currency:** Peso; **Main exports:** meat, wool, hides and skins; **Per capita GNP:** US$2090.

VANUATU, an island republic in the south-western Pacific Ocean, formerly called the New Hebrides. There are about 80 islands, which are mountainous and volcanic. The climate is tropical and the rainfall is generally abundant. Most people are Melanesians. Copra and fish are exported. Tourism is growing: there were 30,450 tourists in 1979. A Spanish explorer discovered the islands in 1606. Britain and France jointly ruled the islands as a condominium from 1906 until independence in 1980.

Area: 14,763 km² (5700 sq mi); **Population:** 113,000; **Capital:** Vila (pop 14,000); **Per capita GNP:** US$590.

VATICAN CITY STATE, the world's smallest independent state. It is in north-western Rome, on a hill on the right bank of the River Tiber. It contains the government of the Roman Catholic Church, headed by the Pope, and the magnificent St Peter's Basilica. It has been the residence of the Pope since the 5th century and was formerly centre of the Papal States in central Italy. In 1870 Victor Emmanuel II took Rome, making it capital of the newly united kingdom which included the Papal States. The Pope refused to recognize the new government. But, in 1929, the Italian government and Pope Pius IX signed the Lateran Treaty, which officially recognized the independence of the Vatican City State.

Area: 44 ha (108.7 acres); **Population:** 1000.

VENEZUELA, an oil-rich republic in northern South America. The hot Maracaibo lowlands surround Lake Maracaibo, a freshwater lake open to the sea, beneath which are large oil deposits. Overlooking the lowlands are the Venezuelan highlands, extensions of the Andes. The central plain is drained by the River Orinoco, one of the world's longest at 2560 km (1591 mi). This plain is covered by *llanos* (savanna). The south-eastern Guiana Highlands are thinly populated. They contain the world's highest waterfall, Angel Falls, with a drop of 979 m (3212 ft). The equatorial climate is modified by the altitude. About 70 per cent of the people are *mestizos* (of mixed white and Indian origin), 18 per cent are mulattos or blacks, 10 per cent are whites and 2 per cent are Indians. In 1978 agriculture employed 20 per cent of the people, industry 27 per cent and services 53 per cent. Their respective contributions to the GDP were 6 per cent, 46 per cent and 48 per cent. The chief resource is oil: Venezuela was the world's 5th largest producer in 1980. Other minerals, including bauxite, gold and iron ore, are now being exploited and manufacturing has been expanding quickly. Coffee, cocoa, maize and sugar cane are major crops; livestock are reared in the central plains. Spain ruled the area from the 16th century. Simón Bolívar liberated Venezuela from Spain in 1821, but it became part of Grand Colombia until 1830. Violence and dictatorships have marked much of its history. But democratic governments have ruled since 1958. The elected National Congress consists of a Senate and a Chamber of Deputies.

Area: 912,050 km² (352,164 sq mi); **Population:** 15,920,000; **Capital:** Caracas (pop 3,508,000); **Other cities:** Maracaibo (652,000); **Highest point:** Pico Bolívar, in Sierra Nevada de Mérida, 5007 m (16,427 ft); **Official language:** Spanish; **Religion:** Roman Catholicism; **Adult literacy rate:** 82 per cent; **Average life expectancy at birth:** 66 years; **Unit of currency:** Bolívar; **Main exports:** oil, iron ore, coffee, cocoa; **Per capita GNP:** US$3130.

VIETNAM, a Socialist Republic in South-East Asia. The northern Red River delta is ringed by hills and mountains, including Fan Si Pan, the nation's highest peak. In central Vietnam, a narrow coastal plain is backed by the Annamite range. In the far south is the huge delta of the Mekong River, one of the world's longest at 4184 km (2600 mi). Temperatures are around 26°C (79°F) throughout the year in the south, but temperatures average 17°C (63°F) in January–February in the north. The rainfall is generally abundant. About 84 per cent of the people are Vietnamese (Kinh). There are also Khmers, Thais and various remote tribal groups. In 1978 agriculture employed 73 per cent of the population, industry 8 per cent and services 19 per cent. Rice, maize, sugar cane, sweet potatoes and cotton are major crops. In 1979 there were 1.6 million cattle and 9.3 million pigs. Fishing is also important. The north is rich in minerals, including coal, lignite, bauxite, chromite, iron ore, manganese and titanium. Manufacturing has been steadily increasing. In the past the north was often under Chinese rule, while the south came under the Khmers. By 1802, Vietnam was united and independent. Between the 1860s and 1880s, France took over Vietnam which, with Laos and Cambodia (Kampuchea), became French Indochina. Japan occupied the area in World War II. In 1946 war began between the French and the nationalist Viet Minh. France withdrew in 1954 and Vietnam was partitioned into the Communist North and the non-Communist South. From 1959 Communist Viet Cong guerrillas fought against the government of South Vietnam, which was aided by the US. American forces withdrew in 1973 and South Vietnam fell to the North in 1975. Vietnam was united as a Socialist Republic with close relations with the USSR in 1976. Vietnamese troops attacked Kampuchea in December 1978 in support of a group friendly to the USSR. This group formed a government in 1979 although resistance to it continued into the 1980s. China attacked North Vietnam in 1979 but soon withdrew its forces.

Area: 329,556 km² (127,249 sq mi); **Population:** 51,742,000 (1978); **Capital:** Hanoi (pop 2,000,000); **Other cities:** Ho Chi Minh City (3,500,000); **Highest point:** Fan Si Pan, 3143 m (10,312 ft); **Official language:** Vietnamese; **Religions:** Buddhism, Taoism, Christianity; **Adult literacy rate:** 87 per cent; **Average life expectancy at birth:** 62 years; **Unit of currency:** Dong; **Main exports:** coal, farm produce, fish; **Per capita GNP:** US$170 (1978).

VIRGIN ISLANDS (British), a territory in the West Indies east of Puerto Rico. There are 36 main islands: 16 are inhabited. The climate is tropical. Most people are Negroes. The chief products are fish, fruit, livestock and vegetables, but tourism is the basis of the economy. British settlers became established on the islands in 1666.

Areas: 153 km² (59 sq mi); **Population:** 11,500; **Capital:** Road Town (pop 3500).

VIRGIN ISLANDS (US), an archipelago east of Puerto Rico. It includes 3 sizeable islands, St Thomas, St Croix and St John, and about 50 islets. The climate is tropical. About 90 per cent of the people are descendants of African slaves. Most others are Europeans. Tourism is the main industry: there were 1.2 million visitors in 1979. The US bought the islands from Denmark in 1917. The islanders were made US citizens in 1927, but the islands remain an 'unincorporated territory'.

Area: 344 km² (133 sq mi); **Population:** 119,000; **Capital:** Charlotte Amalie (pop 15,000); **Per capita GNP:** US$5580.

WALLIS AND FUTUNA ISLANDS, a French Overseas Territory in the south-western Pacific, about 400 km (249 mi) west of Samoa. The Wallis group contains Uvea on which the capital Mata-Utu is situated. The people are Polynesians. Bananas, copra, taro roots and yams are grown. The Wallis Islands became French in 1842 and the entire group became a French protectorate in 1887. The islands became an Overseas Territory of France in 1961.

Area: 200 km² (77 sq mi); **Population:** 9000; **Capital:** Mata-Utu (pop 6000).

WESTERN SAHARA, a North African territory facing the Atlantic Ocean. It was called Spanish Sahara until 1976. Behind the coastal plains are low plateaux dissected by watercourses formed when the region had a moist climate. Today, however, the climate is hot and arid, with generally less than 50 mm (2 in) of rain per year. There is little farming: most people are nomadic pastoralists. Fishing is important, but the chief resource is a huge deposit of phosphates at Bu Craa in the north, discovered in 1963. Spain ruled Western Sahara from 1884.

Beef Island and Guana Island are in the British Virgin Islands, the easternmost group in the Greater Antilles. Beef Island contains the chief airport. A bridge links Beef Island to Tortola, the largest of the islands where more than four-fifths of the territory's population lives.

In the 1970s the nationalist Popular Front for the Liberation of Saharan Territories (POLISARIO) demanded independence. In 1975, after consultation with community leaders and local chiefs, Spain agreed to withdraw and divide the territory between Morocco and Mauritania. In early 1976 Morocco took the northern two-thirds and Mauritania occupied the south. However, POLISARIO, with support from Algeria, proclaimed their country independent as the Sahrawi Arab Democratic Republic and launched a guerrilla war. Mauritania withdrew from the south in 1979 and Morocco moved in. In 1981 the Organization of African Unity sought to persuade Morocco to hold a referendum in Western Sahara on its future.

Area: 266,000 km² (102,709 sq mi); **Population:** 76,000 (1970); **Capital:** formerly El Aiun.

YEMEN ARAB REPUBLIC, in the south-western Arabian peninsula. The Red Sea coastal plain, called the *Tihama*, is 30–80 km (19–50 mi) wide. Behind it the land is mountainous, rising to 3760 m (12,336 ft), Arabia's highest point, west of San'a. The coastal plain is hot and arid, with an average annual rainfall of 130 mm (5 in). The highlands have around 510 mm (20 in) and contain Arabia's best farmland. Most people are Arabs; 90 per cent live in rural areas. In 1978 agriculture employed 76 per cent of the people, as compared with industry 11 per cent and services 13 per cent. Their respective contributions to the GDP were 35 per cent, 14 per cent and 51 per cent. Cereals, coffee, cotton, fruits and vegetables are grown and hides and skins are important products. In 1979 there were 7.8 million goats, 3.7 million sheep and nearly 1 million cattle. Some salt is mined and manufacturing is expanding, with aid from Arab and other nations. Yemen was part of the Ottoman Empire in 1849–1918. In 1962 the monarch (*Imam*) was overthrown and a republic proclaimed. A People's Constituent Assembly was established in 1978 as the legislative body, replacing the military Command Council.

Area: 195,000 km² (75,294 sq mi); **Population:** 6,142,000; **Capital:** San'a (pop 448,000); **Highest point:** Hadur Shu'ayb, 3760 m (12,336 ft); **Official language:** Arabic; **Religion:** Islam; **Adult literacy rate:** 13 per cent; **Average life expectancy at birth:** 39 years; **Unit of currency:** Riyal; **Main exports:** cotton, coffee, hides and skins; **Per capita GNP:** US$420.

YEMEN PEOPLE'S DEMOCRATIC REPUBLIC, in the southern Arabian peninsula, was formerly the Federation of South Arabia, including Aden. Behind the narrow coastal plain are mountains, a fertile valley (the Hadhramawt) and large deserts in the east. The average annual temperature range in Aden is 24°–32°C (75°–90°F) and the rainfall averages 130 mm (5 in) a year. But parts of the Hadhramawt have 760 mm (30 in). Most people are Arabs and 37 per cent live in urban areas. In 1978 agriculture employed 60 per cent of the people, industry 21 per cent and services 19 per cent. The chief crops are cereals; cotton is the main cash crop. In 1979 there were 1.3 million goats and nearly 1 million sheep. Fishing is also important. Aden has an oil refinery and oil products, made from imported oil, are exported. Transit trade is generally important. British influence in the area began in 1802 and Aden was annxed in 1839. It became a major strategic and trading centre after the opening of the Suez Canal in 1869. Nationalist unrest preceded independence in 1967. The rulers of the 17 Sultanates which made up the Federation of South Arabia were deposed by the Marxist National Liberation Front, which made the country a People's Republic.

Area: 332,968 km² (128,567 sq mi); **Population:** 1,905,000; **Capital:** Aden (pop 264,000); **Highest point:** 2469 m (8100 ft); **Official language:** Arabic; **Religion:** Islam; **Adult literacy rate:** 27 per cent; **Average life expectancy at birth:** 44 years; **Unit of currency:** Dinar; **Main exports:** cotton, fish, refined oil; **Per capita GNP:** US$500.

COUNTRIES OF THE WORLD

YUGOSLAVIA, a Socialist Federal Republic on the Adriatic Sea. Large areas are mountainous; the mountains are extensions of the Alpine system. They are narrowest in the north, but the entire south is mountainous. The limestone Dinaric Alps display typical karst scenery. The mountains on the coast have been submerged, such that former ridges now form long, narrow islands parallel to the coast and former valleys are harbours. To the north and east is hill country descending to the interior plains drained by the Danube river system. The coastal climate is typically Mediterranean, but the interior plains, the main farming region, have a continental climate. Belgrade has an average annual temperature range of −2°C to 22°C (28°–72°F). Its average annual rainfall is 610 mm (24 in). Most people are South Slavs: the Serbs and Croats are the two largest groups; the Slovenes live in the north; and the Montenegrins and Macedonians live in the south. Various non-Slav minorities live mainly in the east and south. The division of Yugoslavia into 6 republics reflects its cultural diversity. In 1978 agriculture employed 33 per cent of the workforce, industry 32 per cent and services 35 per cent. They contributed 16 per cent, 45 per cent and 39 per cent to the GDP respectively. Cereals, cotton, fruits, olives, sugar beet, sunflower seeds and tobacco are grown. In 1980 there were 7.3 million sheep, 7.5 million pigs and 5.4 million cattle. Forestry is important. Yugoslavia has many mineral resources and manufacturing has steadily expanded since 1945. Between 1459 and the mid-19th century, Turkey ruled most of the area, but before World War I, some parts, including Serbia, were independent, while other parts were in Austria-Hungary. The murder of Archduke Franz Ferdinand of Austria-Hungary by a Bosnian-Serb sparked off World War I. Yugoslavia was founded as a union of South Slavs in 1918, although the name Yugoslavia was not adopted until 1929. Germany invaded Yugoslavia in World War II. After the war, the monarchy was abolished and a socialist republic was established by the partisan leader Josip Broz (Tito). In 1948 Yugoslavia and the USSR severed relations. Yugoslavia then pursued an independent policy, After President Tito died in 1980, a collective presidency was established.

Area: 255,804 km² (98,772 sq mi); **Population:** 22,745,000; **Capital:** Belgrade (pop with suburbs, 1,209,000); **Other cities:** Zagreb (668,000); **Highest point:** Triglav, 2863 m (9393 ft); **Official languages:** Serbo-Croat, Slovene, Macedonian; **Religions** (1953): Orthodox (41 per cent), Roman Catholicism (32 per cent), Islam (12 per cent), Protestantism (1 per cent); **Adult literacy rate:** 85 per cent; **Average life expectancy at birth:** 69 years; **Unit of currency:** Dinar; **Main exports:** machinery, electrical goods and transport equipment, other manufactures, chemicals; **Per capita GNP:** US$2430.

ZAIRE, a republic in west-central Africa, is the continent's 2nd largest nation. Most of the country lies in the drainage basin of the River Zaire (formerly Congo), which is one of the world's longest at 4828 km (3000 mi). There are highlands and plateaux in the south and east along the Rift Valley where Zaire's border passes through lakes Tanganyika, Kivu, Edward and Mobutu Sese Seko (formerly Albert). The climate is equatorial with an average annual rainfall of 1250–2030 mm (49–80 in). There is rain forest in the centre and savanna in the north and south. About 200 language and ethnic groups live in Zaire. About two-thirds of the people speak Bantu languages: Hamitic, Nilotic, Sudanic and pygmy languages are also spoken. In 1978 agriculture employed 76 per cent of the people, accounting for 27 per cent of the GDP; 20 per cent came from industry and 53 per cent from services. The chief cash crops are coffee, cotton, palm products and rubber. Fishing is important but livestock can be reared only in areas free from the disease-carrying tsetse fly. Minerals made up 74 per cent of the exports in 1976–78. The main mining region is Shaba, where copper (the most valuable export), cobalt, manganese, silver, uranium and zinc are mined. Some oil is produced and diamonds are mined in the Kasai provinces. Hydroelectricity is being developed and manufacturing is growing especially around Kinshasa and Lubumbashi. The Portuguese reached the area in 1482 and slavery was practised along the coast. Henry Morton Stanley explored the Zaire River in 1874–77 and the country became the personal property of King Leopold of Belgium in 1884. Because of ill-treatment of local people by concessionaires, Belgium took over the country in 1908 as the Belgian Congo. Full independence in 1960 was followed by civil war, including a secessionist struggle in Shaba. In 1965 the army under Mobutu Sese Seko took power. Stability was restored although rebel forces had to be driven out of Shaba in 1977 and in 1978.

Area: 2,345,409 km² (905,617 sq mi); **Population:** 29,826,000; **Capital:** Kinshasa (pop 2,444,000); **Other cities:** Kananga (704,000), Lubumbashi (451,000); **Highest point:** Ruwenzori range on the Ugandan border, 5119 m (16,795 ft); **Official language:** French; **Religions:** traditional beliefs (59 per cent), Roman Catholicism (36 per cent), Protestantism (4 per cent), Islam (0.5 per cent); **Adult literacy rate:** 15 per cent; **Average life expectancy at birth:** 46 years; **Unit of currency:** Zaire; **Main exports:** copper, cobalt, coffee, diamonds, oil, cassiterite; **Per capita GNP:** US$260.

ZAMBIA, a landlocked republic in south-central Africa, called Northern Rhodesia until 1964. It consists mostly of a plateau, 900–1520 m (2953–

4987 ft). In the south and east, the Zambezi and Luangwa rivers occupy downfaulted troughs that are part of the East African Rift Valley system. The Zambezi has been dammed to form Lake Kariba, which Zambia shares with Zimbabwe. Kariba's hydro-electric plants have given Zambia an abundance of electrical energy. Parts of lakes Mweru and Tanganyika are in Zambia, as is the entire Lake Bangweulu. The main upland region is the Muchinga Mts in the north-east; they rise to more than 2100 m (6890 ft). The tropical climate is modified by the altitude. The rainfall varies between 1300 mm (51 in) in the north to 500 mm (20 in) in the south. Wildlife is abundant in the savanna, which covers most of Zambia. Six major Bantu languages and 66 dialects are spoken. In 1978 agriculture employed 68 per cent of the workforce (mostly at subsistence level), but it accounted for only 17 per cent of the GDP, compared with 39 per cent from industry and 44 per cent from services. The chief resource is copper, which accounts for 90 per cent of the exports. Cobalt, lead and zinc are also exported as are maize and tobacco, the main cash crop. There are processing and metal industries in the towns. The British South Africa Company entered the area in 1889 and, in 1911, it became the British protectorate of Northern Rhodesia. Full independence as the Republic of Zambia was achieved in 1964. Zambia became a one-party state in 1972.

Area: 752,614 km² (290,602 sq mi); **Population:** 5,992,000; **Capital:** Lusaka (pop 559,000); **Official language:** English; **Religions:** mostly Christianity; **Adult literacy rate:** 39 per cent; **Average life expectancy at birth:** 48 years; **Unit of currency:** Kwacha; **Main exports:** copper, zinc, cobalt, lead, tobacco; **Per capita GNP:** US$510.

ZIMBABWE, a landlocked republic in southern Africa, formerly called Rhodesia. The north is in a deep trough through which the River Zambezi flows. Lake Kariba, a man-made lake on the Zambezi, is shared with Zambia, as is the electricity produced at Kariba dam. Central Zimbabwe (the high veld) is between 1220 and 1530 m (4003–5020 ft), but the land rises to 2595 m (8514 ft) on the Mozambique border. The southern low veld is drained by the River Limpopo. These lowlands are less than 910 m (2986 ft) in height. The high veld has a pleasant climate with an average annual temperature of 20°C (68°F). The lowlands are much hotter. The high veld has an average annual rainfall of 700–900 mm (28–35 in), the eastern highlands getting 1520 mm (60 in). But the low veld is arid with 410 mm (16 in) per year. About 96 per cent of the people are black Africans who speak Bantu languages. The largest groups are the Ndebele in the south and the Shona in the north. Most other people are of European descent. There were 244,000 Europeans in mid-1979, but some emigration has occurred since then. Asians and Coloureds numbered 35,000 in 1979. In 1978 agriculture employed 60 per cent of the workforce. In 1977 it accounted for 20 per cent of the GDP, compared with 35 per cent from industry and 45 per cent from services. European farming is efficient but African farming is mostly at subsistence level. Tobacco, sugar cane, tea and fruits are the leading cash crops. In 1979 there were 5 million cattle. Asbestos, chrome, coal and gold are mined. Manufacturing is important in the towns. Political conditions have retarded the development of Zimbabwe's great tourist potential. Cecil Rhodes obtained mining rights in the area in the 1880s. Between 1898 and 1923, Southern Rhodesia (as Zimbabwe was then called) was ruled by a British High Commissioner based in South Africa. In 1923 it became a self-governing British colony. Its white government passed a law in 1930 reserving 47.6 per cent of the land for European settlement. This created long-term resentment among black Africans. In 1963 the white leaders asked for independence, which Britain did not grant because the whites were not prepared to give up their dominant status, a condition demanded by African nationalists. In 1965 Rhodesia declared its independence unilaterally. Britain declared this act illegal and imposed economic sanctions through the UN. A guerrilla war began in the early 1970s. Britain negotiated an independence Constitution in 1979 and independence, with a majority black government led by Prime Minister Robert Mugabe, was achieved in 1980.

Opposite: The Yugoslav market town of Mostar is on the river Neretva, which flows to the Adriatic Sea. It is the centre of a wine- and fruit-producing region. Its 16th-century Turkish bridge possibly stands on Roman foundations. Left: The man-made Lake Kariba is on the Zimbabwe-Zambia border. These countries share the electricity generated at the Kariba Dam.

Area: 390,580 km² (150,812 sq mi); **Population:** 7,878,000; **Capital:** Harare (pop 616,000); **Other cities:** Bulawayo (357,000); **Highest point:** Mt Inyangani, 2595 m (8514 ft); **Official language:** English; **Religions:** traditional beliefs, Christianity; **Average life expectancy at birth:** 54 years; **Unit of currency:** Dollar; **Main exports:** tobacco, asbestos, gold, cotton, steel, meat, ferrochrome, copper, maize; **Per capita GNP:** US$470.

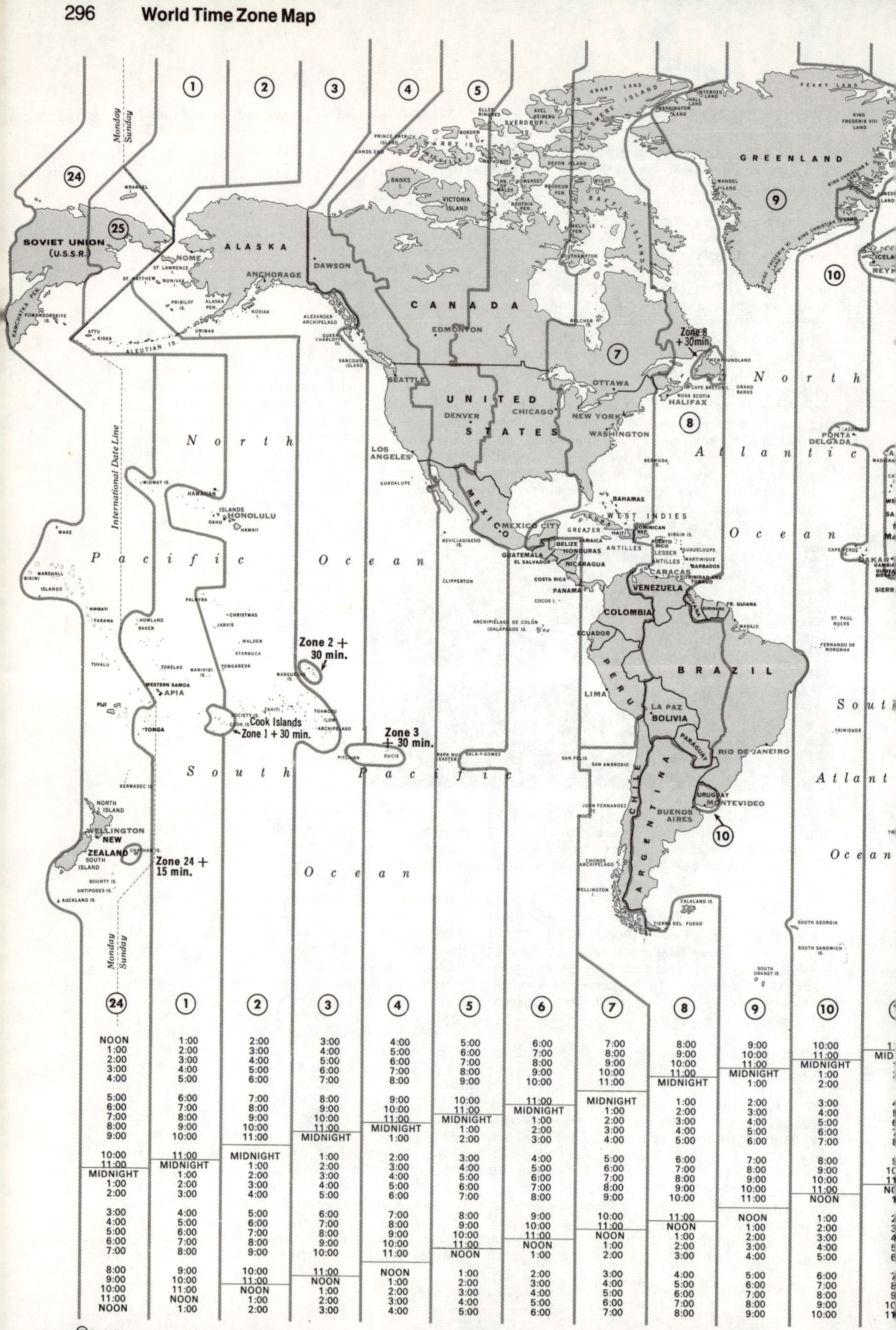

24	1	2	3	4	5	6	7	8	9	10
NOON	1:00	2:00	3:00	4:00	5:00	6:00	7:00	8:00	9:00	10:00
1:00	2:00	3:00	4:00	5:00	6:00	7:00	8:00	9:00	10:00	11:00
2:00	3:00	4:00	5:00	6:00	7:00	8:00	9:00	10:00	11:00	MIDNIGHT
3:00	4:00	5:00	6:00	7:00	8:00	9:00	10:00	11:00	MIDNIGHT	1:00
4:00	5:00	6:00	7:00	8:00	9:00	10:00	11:00	MIDNIGHT	1:00	2:00
5:00	6:00	7:00	8:00	9:00	10:00	11:00	MIDNIGHT	1:00	2:00	3:00
6:00	7:00	8:00	9:00	10:00	11:00	MIDNIGHT	1:00	2:00	3:00	4:00
7:00	8:00	9:00	10:00	11:00	MIDNIGHT	1:00	2:00	3:00	4:00	5:00
8:00	9:00	10:00	11:00	MIDNIGHT	1:00	2:00	3:00	4:00	5:00	6:00
9:00	10:00	11:00	MIDNIGHT	1:00	2:00	3:00	4:00	5:00	6:00	7:00
10:00	11:00	MIDNIGHT	1:00	2:00	3:00	4:00	5:00	6:00	7:00	8:00
11:00	MIDNIGHT	1:00	2:00	3:00	4:00	5:00	6:00	7:00	8:00	9:00
MIDNIGHT	1:00	2:00	3:00	4:00	5:00	6:00	7:00	8:00	9:00	10:00
1:00	2:00	3:00	4:00	5:00	6:00	7:00	8:00	9:00	10:00	11:00
2:00	3:00	4:00	5:00	6:00	7:00	8:00	9:00	10:00	11:00	NOON
3:00	4:00	5:00	6:00	7:00	8:00	9:00	10:00	11:00	NOON	1:00
4:00	5:00	6:00	7:00	8:00	9:00	10:00	11:00	NOON	1:00	2:00
5:00	6:00	7:00	8:00	9:00	10:00	11:00	NOON	1:00	2:00	3:00
6:00	7:00	8:00	9:00	10:00	11:00	NOON	1:00	2:00	3:00	4:00
7:00	8:00	9:00	10:00	11:00	NOON	1:00	2:00	3:00	4:00	5:00
8:00	9:00	10:00	11:00	NOON	1:00	2:00	3:00	4:00	5:00	6:00
9:00	10:00	11:00	NOON	1:00	2:00	3:00	4:00	5:00	6:00	7:00
10:00	11:00	NOON	1:00	2:00	3:00	4:00	5:00	6:00	7:00	8:00
11:00	NOON	1:00	2:00	3:00	4:00	5:00	6:00	7:00	8:00	9:00
NOON	1:00	2:00	3:00	4:00	5:00	6:00	7:00	8:00	9:00	10:00

2	13	14	15	16	17	18	19	20	21	22	23
NIGHT	1:00	2:00	3:00	4:00	5:00	6:00	7:00	8:00	9:00	10:00	11:00
:00	2:00	3:00	4:00	5:00	6:00	7:00	8:00	9:00	10:00	11:00	NOON
:00	3:00	4:00	5:00	6:00	7:00	8:00	9:00	10:00	11:00	NOON	1:00
:00	4:00	5:00	6:00	7:00	8:00	9:00	10:00	11:00	NOON	1:00	2:00
:00	5:00	6:00	7:00	8:00	9:00	10:00	11:00	NOON	1:00	2:00	3:00
:00	6:00	7:00	8:00	9:00	10:00	11:00	NOON	1:00	2:00	3:00	4:00
:00	7:00	8:00	9:00	10:00	11:00	NOON	1:00	2:00	3:00	4:00	5:00
:00	8:00	9:00	10:00	11:00	NOON	1:00	2:00	3:00	4:00	5:00	6:00
:00	9:00	10:00	11:00	NOON	1:00	2:00	3:00	4:00	5:00	6:00	7:00
:00	10:00	11:00	NOON	1:00	2:00	3:00	4:00	5:00	6:00	7:00	8:00
:00	11:00	NOON	1:00	2:00	3:00	4:00	5:00	6:00	7:00	8:00	9:00
:00	NOON	1:00	2:00	3:00	4:00	5:00	6:00	7:00	8:00	9:00	10:00
ON	1:00	2:00	3:00	4:00	5:00	6:00	7:00	8:00	9:00	10:00	11:00
:00	2:00	3:00	4:00	5:00	6:00	7:00	8:00	9:00	10:00	11:00	MIDNIGHT
:00	3:00	4:00	5:00	6:00	7:00	8:00	9:00	10:00	11:00	MIDNIGHT	1:00
:00	4:00	5:00	6:00	7:00	8:00	9:00	10:00	11:00	MIDNIGHT	1:00	2:00
:00	5:00	6:00	7:00	8:00	9:00	10:00	11:00	MIDNIGHT	1:00	2:00	3:00
:00	6:00	7:00	8:00	9:00	10:00	11:00	MIDNIGHT	1:00	2:00	3:00	4:00
:00	7:00	8:00	9:00	10:00	11:00	MIDNIGHT	1:00	2:00	3:00	4:00	5:00
:00	8:00	9:00	10:00	11:00	MIDNIGHT	1:00	2:00	3:00	4:00	5:00	6:00
:00	9:00	10:00	11:00	MIDNIGHT	1:00	2:00	3:00	4:00	5:00	6:00	7:00
:00	10:00	11:00	MIDNIGHT	1:00	2:00	3:00	4:00	5:00	6:00	7:00	8:00
:00	11:00	MIDNIGHT	1:00	2:00	3:00	4:00	5:00	6:00	7:00	8:00	9:00
:00	MIDNIGHT	1:00	2:00	3:00	4:00	5:00	6:00	7:00	8:00	9:00	10:00
IGHT	1:00	2:00	3:00	4:00	5:00	6:00	7:00	8:00	9:00	10:00	11:00

Guide to Major World Cities

This alphabetical guide shows geographical and travel information for major international cities. The list includes English publications, airport transportation, hotels, restaurants, banking hours, additional information sources, and other details.

Amsterdam, Netherlands

Altitude: 5 ft. (1.5m.) below sea level
Average Temp.: Jan., 35°F. (2°C.); July, 64°F. (18°C.)
English Language Publications:
This Week In Amsterdam, Holland Herald, Herald Tribune
Airport Transportation:
Eight miles to downtown Amsterdam. Taxicab and train service.
Selected Hotels:
Amstel, Amstel Riverside, Prof. Tulpplein 1
Amsterdam Hilton, 138 Apollolaan, on Noth Amstel Canal
Europe de'l, 2-4 Nieuwe Doelenstraat
Okura Amsterdam, 175 Ferd. Bolstraat
Selected Restaurants:
Het Begijntje, Bali, De Boerderij, Molen de Dikkert Amstelveen, De Prinsenkelder, Dikker en Thijs, D'Vijff Vlieghen, Excelsior, Sama Sebo, 't Swarte Schaep, De Gravenmolen
Banking: hours are 9 A.M. to 4 P.M. Monday through Friday.
Information Sources:
Amsterdam Tourist Office
5 Rokin
Amsterdam

Athens, Greece

Altitude: 230 ft. (70m.)
Average Temp.: Jan., 48°F. (9°C.); July, 80°F. (27°C.)
English Language Publication:
Athens News, Athens Daily Post
Airport Transportation:
Eight miles to downtown Athens. Taxicab and bus service.
Selected Hotels:
Acropole Palace, 51 Patission St.
Amalia, 10 Amalias Ave.
Athenaeum Intercontinental, 89-93 Syngrou Ave.
Athens Hilton, Vassilissis Sophias Ave.
Electra, 5 Hermou St.
Grande Bretagne, Constitution Sq.
King George, Constitution Sq.
Ledra Marriott, Syngrou Ave.
Meridien, Constitution Sq.
Park, 10 Alexandras Ave.
Selected Restaurants:
Athens Cellar, Blue Pine, Corfu, Dionyssos, Gerofinikas, Floca, L'Abreuvoir, Papakia, Prunier, Skorpios, Stagecoach, Ta Nissia, Tudor Hall, Zonars, Zafiris
Banking: hours are 8 A.M. to 1 P.M. Monday through Saturday.
Information Sources:
Greek National Tourist Office
2 Amerikis Street
Athens

Brussels, Belgium

Altitude: 53 ft. (16m.)
Average Temp.: Jan., 38°F. (3°C.); July, 66°F. (19°C.)
English Language Publications:
The Brussels News, The Bulletin
Airport Transportation:
Eight miles to downtown Brussels. Taxicab and train service.
Selected Hotels:
Amigo, 1-3 Rue de l'Amigo
Atlanta, 7 Blvd. Adolphe Max
Brussels Europa, 107 Rue de Loi
Brussels Hilton, 38 Blvd. de Waterloo
Hyatt Regency Brussels, 250 Rue Royale
Metropole, 31 Place de Brouckère
Palace, 22 Place Rogier
Royal Windsor, 5-7 Rue Duquesnoy
Sheraton Brussels, Manhattan Ctr., 3 Place Rogier
Selected Restaurants:
Bruneau, Chez Christopher, Comme Chez Soi, Dupont, En Plein Ciel, La Pomme Cannelle, L'Ecailler Du Palais Royal, L'Epaule de Mouton, Le Cygne, Le Filet De Boeuf, Les Provencaux, Savoy, Villa Lorraine
Banking: hours are normally 9 A.M. to 1 P.M. and 2:30 P.M. to 3:30 P.M. Tuesday through Thursday; 9 A.M. to 1 P.M. and 2:30 to 4:30 P.M. Monday and Friday.
Information Sources:
Tourist Information Brussels
Rue du Marché-aux-Herbes 61
Brussels

Buenos Aires, Argentina

Altitude: 65 ft. (20m.)
Average Temp.: Jan., 75°F. (24°C.); July, 51°F. (11°C.)
English Language Publications:
American News, Buenos Aires Herald
Airport Transportation:
Three miles from National airport to downtown; 28 miles from International to downtown.
Taxicab and bus service.
Selected Hotels:
Alvear Palace, Alvear Ave. 1891
Bauen Hotel, Callao 350
Elevage Hotel, Maipu 960
Libertador Hotel, Cordoba 680
Plaza, Plaza San Martín
Presidente, Cerrito 850, Avda. 9 de Julio
Selected Restaurants:
Alexandra, Au Bec Fin, Claridge Hotel Grill, Clark's, El Lagar del Virrey, El Repecho de Santelmo, La Cabaña, La Grotta di Bacco, La Posta de San Telmo, London Grill, Mesón Español, Plaza Grill
Banking: hours are 10 A.M. to 4 P.M. Monday through Friday.
Information Sources:
Embassy of the Argentine Republic
1600 New Hampshire Avenue NW
Washington, D.C. 20009

Cairo, Egypt

Altitude: 65 ft. (20m.)
Average Temp.: Jan., 57°F. (14°C.); July, 82°F. (28°C.)
English Language Publication:
Egyptian Gazette, Egyptian Mail
Airport Transportation:
About 8 miles to downtown Cairo. Taxicab and bus service.
Selected Hotels:
El Salam Hyatt, 61 Abdel-Hamid Badawy St, Heliopolis
Holiday Inn Pyramids, Alexandria Desert Rd.
Holiday Inn Sphinx, Alexandria Desert Rd.
Mena House, in front of Pyramids of Giza
Nile Hilton, Tahrir Square
Cairo Marriott, Saray El Guezira, Zamalek
Cairo Meridien, Roda Island
Radisson, Alexandria Desert Rd.
Cairo-Sheraton, Galae Square, Giza
Sheraton Heliopolis, Orouba St
Shephaerds, Corniche
El Nil, Garden City
Selected Restaurants:
Aladdin's, A l'Americaine, Cairo Tower, El Haty, Estoril, Groppi's, Kursaal, Le Grillon, Omar Khayyam, Sofar, Tamerina, Swiss Restaurant
Banking: hours are 8:30 A.M. to 1 P.M. Saturday through Thursday; 10 A.M. to noon on Sunday. Closed Friday.
Information Sources:
Egyptian Tourist Promotion Authority
Misr Travel Tower, Abbasiyya, Cairo

Calcutta, India

Altitude: 20 ft. (6m.)
Average Temp.: Jan., 68°F. (20°C.); July, 84°F. (29°C.)
English Language Publications:
Amrita Bazar Patrika, Hindustan Times, Indian Express, The Statesman, Times of India
Selected Hotels:
Airport Hotel, Dum Dum Airport
Great Eastern, Old Court House St.
Oberoi Grand, 117 J. Nehru Rd.

rk Hotel, Park St.
lected Restaurants:
nber, Blue Fox, Firpo's, Kwality, Maxims, Mocambo, Moulin Rouge, Prince's, Sky Room, Trinca's, Waldorf
nking: hours are 10 A.M. to 2 P.M. Monday through Friday; 10 A.M. to noon on Saturday.
formation Sources:
overnment of India Tourist Office
4 Shakespeare
Sarani
Calcutta

aracas, Venezuela

ltitude: 2,955 ft. (901m.)
verage Temp.: Jan., 67°F. (19°C.); July, 70°F. (21°C.)
nglish Language Publication:
aily Journal
irport Transportation:
welve miles to downtown Caracas.
axicab service.
elected Hotels:
vila, San Bernardino & Avenida Jorge Washington
aracas Hilton,
Avenida Libertador & Sur 25
neraton-Humboldt, Pico Del Avila
otel Tamanaco,
Apartado 467 Las Mercedes
elected Restaurants:
l Veccio Mulino, Aventino, Caruso, El Alamo, El Dragon Verde, El Porton, Henry IV, Franco, Il Padrino, Lee Hamilton, Rias Bajas, Hectors, Quince Letras, La Estancia.
anking: hours are 8 A.M. to 11:30 A.M. and 1 P.M. to 4 P.M. Monday through Friday.
formation Sources:
mbassy of Venezuela
2445 Massachusetts Avenue NW
Washington, D.C. 20008

openhagen, Denmark

ltitude: 20 ft. (6m.)
verage Temp.: Jan., 33°F. (1°C.); July, 63°F. (17°C.)
nglish Language Publications: None
irport Transportation:
ix miles to downtown Copenhagen.
axicab and bus service.
elected Hotels:
'Angleterre, 34 Kongens Nytorv
Falke, 9 Falkoner Allé
openhagen Admiral Hotel,
Tolbodgade 24
alace, 57 Radhuspladsen
he Plaza, 4 Bernstorffsgade
oyal, 1 Hammerichsgade
otel Scandinavia, Amager Blvd.
heraton-Copenhagen, 6 Vester Søgade
elected Restaurants:
oq d'Or, d'Angleterre Hotel Restaurant, Boef & Ost, De syv smaa Hjem, Fiskehuset, Den Gyldne Fortun, Langelinie Pavillonen terraces at Royal Yacht Club, Plaza Hotel Restaurant, Royal Hotel Restaurant
Banking: hours 9:30 A.M. to 4 P.M., Monday through Friday; close at 6 P.M. Thursday.
Information Sources:
Danish Tourist Board
75 Rockefeller Plaza
New York, New York 10019

Frankfurt am Main, Federal Republic of Germany

Altitude: 325 ft. (99m.)
Average Temp.: Jan., 34°F. (1°C.); July, 67°F. (19°C.)
English Language Publications: None
Airport Transportation:
About 6 miles to downtown Frankfurt.
Taxicab, limousine, train, and bus service.
Selected Hotels:
Frankfurter Hof, Kaiserplatz 17
Frankfurt Inter-Continental,
Wilhelm-Leuschner Str. 43
Hessische Hof,
Friedrich-Ebert Anlage 40
Parkhotel, Wiesenhüttenplatz 36
Schlosshotel Kronberg,
in Kronberg at Hain Str. 25
Sheraton Rhein-Main, Airport
Steigenberger Airport Hotel
Selected Restaurants:
Chez Henri, Da Franco, Taverne Royale, Weinhaus Brückenkeller, Hessische Hof Restaurants, Parkhotel Restaurants, Frankfurter Hof Grillroom, Kupferpfanne, Silhouette Supper Club in the Frankfurt Inter-Continental Hotel
Banking: hours 8:30 A.M. to 1 P.M. and 2:30 P.M. to 4 P.M., Monday through Friday; close at 5:30 P.M. Thursday.
Information Sources:
German National Tourist Board
Beethovenstrasse 69
6000 Frankfurt am Main

Hong Kong, Colony of

Altitude: 50 ft., (15m.)
Average Temp.: Jan., 59°F. (15°C.); July, 84°F. (29°C.)
English Language Publications:
South China Morning Post, Hong Kong Standard, Star, Wall Street Journal
Airport Transportation:
Four miles to downtown Kowloon.
Taxicab, airport coach, hire car and bus service from Hong Kong and Kowloon sides.
Selected Hotels:
Excelsior, Causeway Bay
Furma Hotel, 1 Connaught Rd.
Holiday Inn Golden Mile, 46-52 Nathan Rd., Kowloon
Holiday Inn Harbor View, 10 Ching Yee Rd., Kowloon
Hong Kong Hilton Hotel,
2-A Queen's Rd. Central
Hong Kong Hotel, 3 Canton Rd.
Hyatt Regency Hong Kong, 67 Nathan Rd., Kowloon
Lee Gardens, Hysan Ave.
Mandarin, 5 Connaught Rd.
Marco Polo, Harbor City Complex, Canton Rd., Kowloon
Miramar, 134 Nathan Rd., Kowloon
Peninsula, Salisbury Rd., Kowloon
Regal Meridian, Mody Rd., Kowloon
Regal Meridian Hong Kong Airport, Sa Po Rd.
Regent, Salisbury Rd., Kowloon
Royal Garden, East Tsimshatsui, Kowloon
Shangri-La, 4 Mody Rd., Kowloon
Sheraton Hong Kong, Nathan Rd. & Salisbury Ave., Kowloon
Selected Restaurants:
Chesa, Gaddi's, Harbour Room, Hilton's Eagle Nest, Hugo's, Jade Garden, Jimmy's Kitchen, Jumbo Floating Restaurant, Juno's Revolving Restaurant, Mandarin Grill, Peking Garden, Yung Kee
Banking: hours are 10 A.M. to 3 P.M. Monday through Friday; 9:30 A.M. to noon on Saturday.
Information Sources:
Hong Kong Tourist Association
421 Powell St. Suite 200
San Francisco, California
94102-1568
Connaught Centre, Hong Kong

Istanbul, Turkey

Altitude: 30 ft. (9m.)
Average Temp.: Jan., 42°F. (6°C.); July, 74°F. (23°C.)
English Language Publication:
Daily News, Outlook Magazine
Airport Transportation:
Fifteen miles to downtown Istanbul.
Taxicab and bus service.
Selected Hotels:
Büyük Tarabya, Tarabya
Carlton Hotel, Yenikoy
Cinar Hotel, Yesilköy
Divan Hotel, Harbiye
ETAP Hotel, Taksim
Istanbul Hilton, Harbiye
Etap Marmara Hotel
Macka Hotel, Emlak Caddesi
Park Hotel, Gümüssuyu Caddesi 6
Sheraton Hotel
Selected Restaurants:
Abdullah Restaurant, Divan Hotel Restaurant, Galata Tower, Etap Marmara Restaurant, Hotel Kalyon Restaurant, Konyali, Le Mangal (Sheraton Hotel), Liman (lunch), Park Hotel Restaurant, Roof Rotisserie, Sadirvan Supper Club at the Hilton Hotel, Topkapi Restaurant (lunch)
Banking: hours, 9 A.M. to noon and 1:30 P.M. to 5:30 P.M. Monday through Friday.

Information Sources:
Turkish Government Tourism and Information Office
821 United Nations Plaza
New York, New York 10017

Johannesburg, South Africa

Altitude: 5,750 ft. (1,753m.)
Average Temp.: Jan., 67°F. (19°C.); July, 51°F. (11°C.)
English Language Publications:
Rand Daily Mail, Star, Sunday Times, Sunday Express
Airport Transportation:
Fourteen miles to downtown Johannesburg.
Taxicab and bus service.
Selected Hotels:
Carlton, Main St.
Devonshire, Melle St.
Holiday Inn, Jan Smuts Airport
Landdrost, Twist St.
Millpark Holiday Inn, Empire Rd.
Rand International, 230 Bree St.
Rosebank, Turwhit Ave.
Sandton Sun Hotel, Sandton
Selected Restaurants:
Bougainvillia, Chez Zimmerli, De Fistermann, El Gaucho, Jorissen at Devonshire, Le Francais, Leo, L'Escargot, Lien Wah Chinese, Linger Longer, Pot Luck, Rugantino, Scratch Caniels, Three Ships, Zoo Lake
Banking: open at 9 A.M. and close at 3:30 P.M. except Wednesday, when closing hour is 1 P.M., and Saturday, when banks open at 8:30 A.M. and close at 11 A.M. On the last day of the month banks open at 8:30 A.M. and close at the normal hour for that day.
Information Sources:
Johannesburg Visitors' Bureau
Tower Mall, Upper Carlton Centre, Commercial St., Johannesburg

Lisbon, Portugal

Altitude: 150 ft. (46m.)
Average Temp.: Jan., 51°F. (11°C.); July, 72°F. (22°C.)
English Language Publication:
Portugal Welcomes You (quarterly)
Airport Transportation:
Six miles to downtown Lisbon.
Taxicab, bus.
Selected Hotels:
Alfa, Av. Columbano Bordalo Pinheiro
Altis, Rua Castilho II
Avenida Palace, Rua 1.° de Dezembro 123
Lisbon Plaza, Travessa do Salitre 7
Diplomatico, Rua Castilho 74
D. Manuel I, Avenida Duque de Avila 187
Fénix, Praca Marquês de Pombal 8
Flórida, Rua Duque de Palmela 32
Lisboa-Sheraton, Rua Latino Coelho 2
Lisbon Penta, Av. Dos Combatentes
Mundial, Rua D. Duarte 4
Principe Real, Rua da Alegria 53
Ritz, Rua Rodrigo da Fonseca 88-A
Tivoli, Av. da Liberdade 185
Tivoli Jardim, Rua Julio Cesar Machado 7
Selected Restaurants:
A Gôndola, Altis Hotel Grill Aviz, Bodegon (Fénix Hotel) Cozinha d'el Rey, Escorial, Gambrinus, Hong Kong, Macau, Pabe, Ritz Hotel Grill, Solmar, Tavares
Banking: hours, 8:30 A.M. to 11:45 A.M. and 1 to 2:45 P.M. Monday through Friday; closed Saturday.
Information Sources:
Portuguese National Tourist Office
548 Fifth Avenue
New York, New York 10036

London, England

Altitude: 20 ft. (6m.)
Average Temp.: Jan., 40°F. (4°C.); July, 64°F. (18°C.)
English Language Publication:
The Daily Telegraph, Financial Times, The Guardian, The Times, Daily Express, Daily Mail, Daily Mirror
Airport Transportation:
Fifteen miles to downtown London.
Taxicab, bus, subway, and train service.
Selected Hotels:
Berkeley, Wilton Pl., SW 1
Britannia, Grosvenor Sq., W1
Capital, Basil St., SW 3
Carlton Tower, Cadogan Place at Sloane St., SW 1
Churchill, 30 Portman Sq., W 1
Claridge's, Brook St., W 1
Connaught, Carlos Pl., W 1
Dorchester, Park Lane, W 1
Grosvenor House, Park Lane, W 1
Hilton, Park Lane, W 1
Ritz, Piccadilly, W 1
Savoy, Victoria Embankment, WC 2
Tower, St. Katherine's Way, E1
Waldorf, Aldwych, WC 2
Selected Restaurants:
Café Royal, Mirabelle, Quaglino's, Rules, Scott's Rotisserie Normande, Simpson's-in-the-Strand, Walton's
Banking: hours in England are 9:30 A.M. to 3:30 P.M. Monday through Friday.
Information Sources:
National Tourist Information Centre
Victoria Station Forecourt
London SW1
London Tourist Board
26 Grosvenor Gardens
London SW1W 0DU

Madrid, Spain

Altitude: 2,100 ft. (640m.)
Average Temp.: Jan., 41°F. (5°C.); July, 76°F. (24°C.)
English Language Publications:
Iberian Sun, Guidepost, Herald Tribune
Airport Transportation:
Eight miles to downtown Madrid.
Taxicab and bus service.
Selected Hotels:
Alameda, Av. Logrono 100
Barajas, Av. Logrono 305
Castellana, Paseo de la Castellana 57
Eurobuilding, Padre Damian 23
Luz Palacio, Castellana 67
Melia Madrid, Princesa 27
Miguel Angel, Miguel Angel 29
Mindanao, S. Francisco De Sales 15
Monte Real, Arroyo Fresno 17
Plaza, Plaza de España 8
Palace, Plaza de las Cortes 7
Princesa Plaza, Princesa 40
Melia Castilla, Capitan Haya Ritz, Plaza de la Lealtad 5
Villamagna, Castellana 22
Wellington, Velazquez 8
Selected Restaurants:
Club 31, Commodore, Cafe Chinitas, Jockey Club, Las Lanzas, Zalacain Sixt
Banking: hours are 9 A.M. to 2 P.M. Monday through Saturday.
Information Sources:
Spanish National Tourist Office
665 Fifth Avenue
New York, New York 10022

Manila, Philippines

Altitude: 10 ft. (3m.)
Average Temp.: Jan., 78°F. (26°C.); July, 82°F. (28°C.)
English Language Publications:
Bulletin Today, Daily Express, Times Journal
Airport Transportation:
Five miles to downtown Manila.
Taxicab, limousine, and bus service.
Selected Hotels:
Holiday Inn, 3001 Roxas Blvd.
Hotel Inter-Continental, Ayala Av.
Hyatt Regency Manila, 2702 Roxas Blvd.
Manila Garden, Fourth Quadrant, Makati Commercial Center
Manila Hilton, UN Av., Ermita
Manila Hotel, Rizal Park
Manila Mandarin Hotel, Makati Av., Makati
Manila Peninsula, Ayala and Makati Av.
Philippine Plaza, Cultural Center Complex
Regent of Manila, 2727 Roxas Blvd., Pasay
Silahis International, 1990 Roxas Blvd., Malate
Selected Restaurants:
Alta Vista, Aristocrat, Au Bon Vivant, Barrio Fiesta, Bay View House at the Bay View Hotel, Bulakeña, Champagne Room in Manila Hotel, Galing-Galing, Hilton Hotel Restaurant, Intercontinental Hotel Restaurant, Kamayan, Nayong

Filipino, Salamboo, Swiss Inn
anking: hours usually are 9:30 A.M. to 2:30 P.M. Monday through Friday.
formation Sources:
hilippine Department of Tourism
New York Field Office
556 Fifth Avenue
New York, New York 10036

lexico City, Mexico

ltitude: 7,300 ft. (2,225m.)
verage Temp.: Jan., 54°F. (12°C.); July, 64°F. (18°C.)
nglish Language Publications:
he News, Daily Bulletin, This Week, The Gazer
irport Transportation:
our miles to downtown Mexico City.
axicab and limousine service.
elected Hotels:
lameda, Avenida Juárez 50
ristos, Paseo de la Reforma 276
amino Real, Mariano Escobedo 700
el Prado, Avenida Juárez 70
Presidenté, Hamburg 135
Presidenté Chapultepec, Paseo de la Reforma and Chapultepec Park
iesta Palace, Paseo de la Reforma 80
iran Hotel,
No. 82 de Septiembre 16, Zocalo
oliday Inn Downtown
yatt, Paseo de la Reforma 166
laria Isabel-Sheraton,
Paseo de la Reforma 325
elected Restaurants:
mbassadeurs, Anderson's, Da Vinci, El Paseo, Focolare, Jena, Mirabel, Parador, Restaurant del Lago, Rivoli, San Angel Inn, Hacienda Los Morales, Fonda Santa Anita, Alex Cardini, Chalet Suizo, La Caua
anking: banks are open 9 A.M. to 1 P.M. Monday through Friday; 9 A.M. to 12:30 P.M. on Saturday.
formation Sources:
lexican National Tourist Council
Mariano Escobedo 726, 5, D.F.
linistry of Tourism
Av. Presidenté Masaryk 172, Mexico City

lilan, Italy

ltitude: 400 ft. (122m.)
verage Temp.: Jan., 34°F. (1°C.); July, 73°F. (23°C.)
nglish Language Publications: None
irport Transportation:
wenty-eight miles to downtown Milan.
axicab and limousine service.
elected Hotels:
avalieri, Piazza Missori 1
ontinental, Via Manzoni 7
uomo, Via S. Raffaele 1
xcelsior Gallia, Piazza Duca d'Aosta 9
irand Hotel et de Milan,
Via Manzoni 29
alace, Piazzale della Repubblica 20
Principe e Savoia,
Piazzale della Repubblica 17
Hilton, Via Galvani 12
Selected Restaurants:
Biffi Scala, Giannino, Gourmet, Savini, St. Andrew's
Banking: hours are 8:30 A.M. to 1:30 P.M. Monday through Friday.
Information Sources:
EPT—Ente Provinciale Turismo
AAST—Azienda Autonoma Soggiorno Turismo, Milan

Montréal, Canada

Altitude: 50 ft. (15m.)
Average Temp.: Jan., 16°F. (−9°C.); July, 71°F. (22°C.)
Telephone Area Number: 514
English Language Publications:
Montréal Gazette
Airport Transportation:
Fourteen miles from Dorval Airport to downtown Montréal, 34 miles from Mirabel Airport.
Taxicab and bus service.
Transit service between Dorval and Mirabel airports.
Selected Hotels:
Hotel Meridien-Montreal,
4 Complexe Desjardins
Le Chateau Champlain,
1050 Quest, Lagauchetiere W
Montréal Aeroport Hilton,
12505 Cote de Liesse Rd.
Mt. Royal, 1455 Peel St.
Queen Elizabeth,
900 Dorchester Blvd., W (2)
Ritz-Carlton,
1228 Sherbrooke, St. W
Ruby Foo's Motor Hotel,
7655 Decarie Blvd.
Westin Bonaventure,
1 Place Bonaventure
Selected Restaurants:
Beaver Club in the Queen Elizabeth Hotel, Café de Paris, Café Martin, Chez Bardet, Chez Bourgetel, Chez Fanny, Desjardins, Le Castillon in the Westin Bonaventure Hotel, Le Neufchatel, Le Vieux St. Gabriel, Les Filles du Roy, Les Halles, Ruby Foo's
Banking: hours are generally from 10 A.M. to 3 P.M. Monday through Thursday; 10 A.M. to 6 P.M. on Friday. If Friday is a holiday, Friday hours are observed on Thursday.
Information Sources:
City of Montréal,
Public Relations Department,
155 Notre Dame St. E
Montréal Convention &
Visitors Bureau,
Place Bonaventure, Mart F
49 Frontenac

Moscow, U.S.S.R.

Altitude: 395 ft. (120m.)
Average Temp.: Jan., 14°F. (−10°C.); July, 66°F. (19°C.)
English Language Publications:
Moscow News, Foreign Trade, New Times
Airport Transportation:
About 19 miles to downtown Moscow.
Taxicab and bus service.
Selected Hotels:
Berlin, 3 Zhdanov St.
Intourist, 3-5 Gorky St.
Metropole, 1 Marx Prospect Ave.
National, 14-1 Marx Prospect Ave.
Rossiya Hotel, 1 Moskvoretskaya St.
Ukraina, 10-9 Kutuzovsky Prospect Ave.
Selected Restaurants:
Aragvi, Ararat, Arbat, Baku, Budapest, Peking, Praga, Seventh Heaven, Sofia, Slavyansky Bazaar, Uzbekistan
Banking: banks are open from 9 A.M. to 1 P.M. Monday through Friday, except on days before holidays they close at noon.
Information Sources:
Intourist
630 Fifth Avenue
New York, New York 10111

Osaka, Japan

Altitude: 16 ft. (5m.)
Average Temp.: Jan., 40°F. (4°C.); July, 80°F. (27°C.)
English Language Publications:
Asahi Evening News, The Japan Times, The Daily Yomiuri, Mainichi Daily News
Airport Transportation:
Nine miles to downtown Osaka.
Taxicab, limousine, and bus service.
Selected Hotels:
Hotel Osaka Grand,
22, 2-chome, Nakanoshima, Kita-ku
International Hotel, 58 Hashizume-cho, Uchihommachi, Higashi-ku
Osaka Miyako Hotel, 110 Horikoshi-cho, Tennoji-ku
Osaka Royal Hotel,
1, 2-chome, Tamae-cho, Kita-ku
Plaza, 2 Minami
Oyodo, Oyodo-ku
Toyo Hotel, 1-21, Toyosaki Nishi-Dori, Oyodo-ku
Selected Restaurants:
Hommachi Suehiro, Kyomatsu, Hotel Shofukaku Restaurant, Suehiro-Asahi, Taiko-en
Banking: hours are 9 A.M. to 3 P.M. Monday through Friday, 9 A.M. to noon on Saturday.
Information Sources:
Japan National Tourist Organization
45 Rockefeller Plaza
New York, New York 10020

Paris, France

Altitude: 140 ft. (43m.)
Average Temp.: Jan., 38°F. (3°C.); July, 67°F. (19°C.)
English Language Publications:
International Herald Tribune, This Week in Paris
Airport Transportation:
About 11 miles from Orly Airport to downtown Paris; 16 miles from Charles De Gaulle Airport to Paris.
Taxicab, bus, and train service.
Selected Hotels:
Le Bristol, 112 Rue du Faubourg St., Honoré 8e
Crillon, 10 Place de la Concorde 8e
George V, 31 Ave. George V 8e
Inter-Continental Paris, 3 Rue de Castiglione, Paris 1e
Meridien Hotel, 81 Blvd. Gouvion-St. Cyr, Pte. Maillot, Paris 17e
Napoleon, 40 Ave. de Friedland 8e
Nova Park Elysées, 51 Rue Francois, 8e
Paris Hilton, 18 Ave. de Suffren, 15e
Plaza Athenée, 25 Ave. Montaigne 8e
P.L.M. St. Jacques, 17 Blvd. St. Jacques 14e
Prince de Galles, 33 Ave. George V 8e
Raphaël, 17 Ave. Kleber, Paris 16e, near Arc de Triomphe
Ritz, 15 Place Vendôme, overlooking Place Vendôme
Selected Restaurants:
Archestrate, Drouant, Grand Vefour, Lasserre, Ledoyen, Le Vivarois, Lucas-Carton, Maxim's, Taillevent, Tour d'Argent, La Marée, Pre Catelan
Banking: from 9 A.M. to 4:30 P.M. Monday through Friday; 9 A.M. to noon day before holidays.
Information Sources:
L'Office de Tourisme de Paris, 127 Champs-Elysées, Paris

Peking, P.R.C.

Altitude: 165 ft. (50m.)
Average Temp.: Jan., 23°F. (−5°C.); July, 79°F. (26°C.)
English Language Publication: China Daily and China News Agency daily bulletin
Airport Transportation: The China International Travel Service (Luxingshe), which makes all travel arrangements, also arranges for transportation from the airport.
Selected Hotels:
Although all travel arrangements are made by the China International Travel Service, here are the leading hotels and their telephone numbers for use by travelers while in Peking:
Peace Hotel, 55-5131
Chienmen Hotel, 33-8731
Hsinchiao Hotel, 55-7731
Nationalities Hotel, 66-8541
Peking Hotel, 55-2231
Selected Restaurants:
Peking Duck, Moslem Restaurant, Pei Hai Restaurant, Restaurants of the Summer Palace
Banking: hours vary from one branch to another of Bank of China—8:30 or 9 A.M. to 12 noon, 2 to 4 or 5 P.M.
Information Sources:
U.S.-China People's Friendship Association Tours (USCPFA)
110 Maryland Avenue NE
Washington, D.C. 20002

Rio de Janeiro, Brazil

Altitude: 30 ft. (9m.)
Average Temp.: Jan., 79°F. (26°C.); July, 69°F. (21°C.)
English Language Publications:
Brazil Herald, Latin American Post
Airport Transportation:
Fifteen miles to downtown Rio de Janeiro.
Taxicab and bus service.
Selected Hotels:
Ambassador, Rua Senador Dantas 25
Caesar Park, Ave. Vieria Souto 460
Copacabana Palace, Ave. Atlântica 1702
Everest Rio, R. Prudente de Morais 1117
Inter-Continental Hotel, Ave. Prefeito Mendes de Morais
Leme Palace, Ave. Atlântica 656
Marina Palace, R. Delfim Moreira 630
Meridien, Ave. Atlântica 1020
Miramar Palace, Ave. Atlântica 3668
Nacional, Ave. Niemeyer 769
Rio Othon Palace, Ave. Atlântica & Xavier da Silveira
Rio Palace, Ave. Atlantica & Francisco Otaviano
Sol Ipanema, Ave. Vieira Souto 320
Sheraton-Rio, Ave. Niemeyer 121
Selected Restaurants:
Maxim's, La Streghe, Florentino, Chalé, Churrascaria Recreio, Concorde, Ouro Verde Hotel, Esquilos, Las Brasas, Lisboa a Noite, Mario's, Michel, Museu Arte Moderna, Nino's, Open, Rio's, River Gauche, Saint Honoré
Banking: hours are 9 A.M. to 4 P.M. Monday through Friday.
Information Sources:
Embratur
60 East 42nd Street, Suite 1336
New York, New York 10165

Rome, Italy

Altitude: 80 ft. (24m.)
Average Temp.: Jan., 46°F. (8°C.); July, 75°F. (24°C.)
English Language Publication:
Daily American
Airport Transportation:
Twenty-two miles to downtown Rome.
Taxicab and bus service.
Selected Hotels:
Ambasciatori Palace, Via Veneto 70
Bernini Bristol, Piazza Barberini 23
Cavalieri Hilton, Via Cadlolo 101
Eden, Via Ludovisi 49
Excelsior, Via Vittorio Veneto 125
Flora, Via Vittorio Veneto 191
Grand, Via V.E. Orlando 3
Hassler Villa Medici, Trinità dei Monti 6
Mediterraneo, Via Cavour 15
Parco dei Principi, Via G. Frescobaldi 5
Quirinale, Via Nazionale 7
Sheraton Roma, Viale del Pattinaggic
Selected Restaurants:
Capriccio, Da Meo Patacca, George's, Hostaria dell'Orso, Passetto, Ranieri, San Souci, 31 al Vicaria, Taverna Flavia, Trilussa
Banking: from 8:30 A.M. to 1:30 P.M. Monday through Friday.
Information Sources:
EPT—Ente Provinciale Turismo, Rome

São Paulo, Brazil

Altitude: 2,375 ft. (724m.)
Average Temp.: Jan., 71°F. (22°C.); July, 58°F. (14°C.)
English Language Publications:
Brazil Herald, Latin American Post
Airport Transportation:
Sixty miles to downtown São Paulo from international airport at Viracopos. Eight miles from local airport at Congonhas to downtown
Taxicab, bus, bus/metro, and limousine service.
Selected Hotels:
Brasilton, Rua Martino Fontes 277
Caesar Park Hotel, Rua Augusta 1508
Eldorado, Ave. São Luis 234
Grande Hotel Ca D'Oro, Rua Avanhandava 308
Jaraguá, Viaduto Major Quedinho 40
Maksoud Plaza, Al. Campinas 150
Othon Pálace, Rua Libero Badaró 196
São Paulo Center, Lgo. Sta. Ifigenia 4
São Paulo Hilton, Ave. Ipiranga 165
Selected Restaurants:
Baiúca, Ao Franciscano, Cabeça Chata, Chalet Suisse, Don Fabrizio, Koebes, La Casserole, Le Tabarin, Os Vikings, Rodizio Rubayat, Terraço Italia Trastevere
Banking: hours are 8 A.M. to 6:30 P.M. Monday through Friday.
Information Sources:
Embratur
60 East 42nd Street, Suite 1336
New York, New York 10165

Seoul, Korea (South)

Altitude: 100 ft. (30m.)
Average Temp.: Jan., 24°F. (−4°C.); July, 78°F. (26°C.)
English Language Publications:
Korea Times, Korean Herald

rport Transportation:
n miles to downtown Seoul.
xicab service.
lected Hotels:
osun Hotel,
87 Sokong-Dong, Choong-ku
otel Lotte,
1 Sokong-Dong, Choong-ku
otel Shilla, 202, 2-Ga,
Jangchung-Dong,
Chung-Ku
yatt Regency Hotel,
747-7 Hannam-Dong, Yongsam-ku
jong Hotel,
61-3, 2-Ka Chung Moo Ro, Jung ku
oul Hilton International,
395, 5-Ka, Namdaemun-ro,
Chung-ku
oul Plaza Hotel,
Taipyung-Ro, Choong-ku
eraton Walker Hill Hotel,
21 Kwangjeng-Dong, Sung-Dong-ku
lected Restaurants:
ankuk Hwe Kwan, Hyang Won, Hanil Kwan, Korea House (Korean-style); Asti, Diplomatic Club (Western-style), Four Seasons
nking: hours are 10 A.M. to 4:30 P.M. Monday through Friday; 10:30 A.M. to 1:30 P.M. on Saturday.
formation Sources:
orea National Tourism Corp., 60-1, 3KA, Chungmu-Ro, Chung-ku, Seoul

ingapore, Singapore

titude: 35 ft. (11m.)
verage Temp.: Jan., 79°F. (26°C.); July, 81°F. (27°C.)
nglish Language Publications:
raits Times, Sunday Times, Monitor
irport Transportation:
even miles to downtown Singapore.
ini bus service between airport and major hotels. Limousine and taxicab service.
elected Hotels:
ynasty Singapore, 320 Orchard Rd.
oodwood Park, 22 Scotts Rd.
yatt Singapore, 10-12 Scotts Rd.
he Mandarin Singapore, 333 Orchard Rd.
he Marco Polo, Tanglin Circus
avilion Inter-Continental Singapore, 1 Cuscaden Rd.
hangri-La, 22 Orange Grove Rd.
ngapore Hilton, 581 Orchard Rd.
elected Restaurants:
athay, Celestial Room, Islamic, Jubilee, Mandarin Room, Omar Khayyam, Peking Shanghia, Troika
anking: hours are 10 A.M. to 3 P.M. Monday through Friday; 9:30 A.M. to 11:30 A.M. on Saturday.
formation Sources:
ngapore Tourist Promotion Board
251 Post Street, San Francisco, California 94108
ngapore Trade Development Board
745 Fifth Avenue, Suite 1601
New York, New York 10022
Embassy of the Republic of Singapore
1824 R Street NW,
Washington, D.C. 20009

Stockholm, Sweden

Altitude: 55 ft. (17m.)
Average Temp.: Jan., 27°F. (−3°C.); July, 64°F. (18°C.)
English Language Publications: None
Airport Transportation:
About 6 miles to downtown Stockholm.
Taxicab and bus service.
Selected Hotels:
Grand Hotel, Södra Blasieholmshamnen 8, opposite the Royal Palace
Strand, Nybrokajen 9
Diplomat, Strandvägen 7 C
Park, Karlavägen 43
Anglais, Humlegårdsgatan 23
Carlton, Kungsgatan 57 A
Sheraton Hotel, Tegelbacken 6
Selected Restaurants:
Den Glydene Freden, Fem Små Hus, Frati's Tre Remmare, Operakällaren, Rådhus Restauranten, Riche, Solliden at Skansen, Stallmästaregarden, Teatergrillen, Veranda of the Grand Hotel
Banking: hours from 9:30 A.M. to 3 P.M. on weekdays; some are open until 6 P.M.
Information Sources:
Tourist Information Offices, Hamngatan 27, Stockholm

Sydney, Australia

Altitude: 75 ft. (23m.)
Average Temp.: Jan., 71°F. (22°C.); July, 53°F. (12°C.)
English Language Publications:
The Australian, Daily Mirror, Daily Sun, Daily Telegraph, Financial Review, Morning Herald
Airport Transportation:
Six and one-half miles to downtown Sydney.
Taxicab and bus service.
Selected Hotels:
Boulevard Hotel, 90 William St.
Hyatt Kingsgate, Kings Cross
Menzies, 14-28 Carrington St.
Regent of Sydney, 199 George St.
Sheraton, 61-101 Phillip St.
Sydney Hilton, 259 Pitt St.
Town House, Elizabeth Bay Rd.
Selected Restaurants:
Argyle Tavern, Beppi's, Caprice at Rose Bay, Chelsea, The Coachmen, Doyle's at Rose & Watson's bays, French Tavern, Hunters Lodge at Double Bay, Le Trianon at King's Cross, Pruniers at Double Bay, Renzos at Rose Bay, Summit Restaurant (47th floor of Australia Square tower)
Banking: hours are 10 A.M. to 3 P.M. Monday through Thursday, 10 A.M. to 5 P.M. on Friday.
Information Sources:
New South Wales
Government Travel Centre,
16 Spring St., Sydney, N.S.W. 2000

Tel Aviv, Israel

Altitude: 35 ft. (11m.)
Average Temp.: Jan., 57°F. (14°C.); July, 77°F. (25°C.)
English Language Publications:
Jerusalem Post, This Week In Israel
Airport Transportation:
Twelve miles to downtown Tel Aviv.
Taxicab and bus service.
Selected Hotels:
Carlton Penta, Hayarkon St.
Dan, 99 Hayarkon St.
Diplomat, Hayarkon St.
Hilton, Independence Park
Plaza, Hayarkon St.
Ramada Continental, Hayarkon St.
Sheraton, Hayarkon St.
Selected Restaurants:
Apropos, Casba, Dolphin Bar, Patio, Zion Exclusive, Pundak Shaul (Shaul's Inn)
Banking: hours are 8:30 A.M. to 12:30 P.M.; banks that remain open in the afternoon have various closing hours. On Friday, on the eve of religious holidays, and during the week of Passover and of the Feast of Tabernacles, banking hours are 8:30 A.M. to noon only, and no banks are open in the afternoon. Banks are closed on Saturday and open on Sunday.
Information Sources:
Government Tourist Information Office,
7 Mendele St.,
Tel Aviv

Tokyo, Japan

Altitude: 20 ft. (6m.)
Average Temp.: Jan., 39°F. (4°C.); July, 77°F. (25°C.)
English Language Publications:
Asahi Evening News, The Japan Times, Mainichi News, The Yomiuri
Airport Transportation:
Thirty miles to downtown Tokyo.
Taxicab and bus service.
Selected Hotels:
Imperial Hotel, 1-chome, Uchisaiwaicho, Chiyoda-ku
Hotel New Otani, 4 Kioicho, Chiyoda-ku
Hotel Okura, 3 Aoicho Akasaka, Minato-ku
Keio Plaza Hotel, 2, 2-1, Nishi-Shinjuku, Shinju-ku
Palace Hotel, 1-1, 1-chome, Marunouchi, Chiyoda-ku
The Tokyo Hilton, 10-3, 2-chome, Nagatacho, Chiyoda-ku

Selected Restaurants:
Akassaka Misono, Asahi, Chinzan-So, Doh-Hana, Hilton Hotel Restaurant, Imperial Hotel Restaurant, Inagiku, Mansei, Misono, Okahan, Okura Hotel Restaurant, Palace Hotel Restaurant, Steak House Ginsen, Kico Plaza, Suehiro, Ten-ichi, Zakuro
Banking: hours from 9 A.M. to 3 P.M. Monday through Friday, 9 A.M. to noon on Saturday.
Information Sources:
Japan National Tourist Organization, 2-13, Yurakucho, Tokyo

Toronto, Canada

Altitude: 275 ft. (84m.)
Average Temp.: Jan., 23°F. (−5°C.); July, 69°F. (21°C.)
Telephone Area Number: 416
English Language Publications:
Toronto Daily Star, Toronto Globe and Mail, The Sun
Airport Transportation:
Eighteen miles to downtown Toronto.
Taxicab and bus service.
Selected Hotels:
Four Seasons Motor Hotel, 21 Avenue Rd.
Holiday Inn—Downtown, 89 Chestnut St.
Holiday Inn—Don Valley, 1250 Eglinton Ave.
Inn-on-the-Park, 1100 Eglinton Ave.
Loews Westbury, 475 Yonge St.
Park Plaza, 4 Avenue Rd.
Royal York, 100 Front St. W
Seaway Hotel, Ltd. 2000 Lakeshore Blvd. W
Sheraton Centre, 123 Queen St.
Sutton Place, 955 Bay St.
Selected Restaurants:
Chateauneuf, Ed's Warehouse, Fisherman's Wharf, Heritage Room in the Toronto Dominion Tower, Imperial Room, Julie's, Mr. Toni's, The Old Mill, Old Spaghetti Factory, Ports of Call, Loews Westbury
Banking: hours from 10 A.M. to 3 P.M. Monday through Thursday, 10 A.M. to 6 P.M. Friday. If Friday is a holiday, Friday hours are observed on Thursday.
Information Sources:
Metropolitan Toronto Convention & Tourist Bureau,
Toronto Eaton Centre,
220 Yonge St., Box 510, Toronto, Ontario M5B 2H1.

Vancouver, Canada

Altitude: 40 ft. (12m.)—sea level
Average Temp.: Jan., 36.5°F. (3°C.); July, 72°F. (22°C)
Telephone Area Number: 604
English Language Publications:
Vancouver Province, Vancouver Sun
Airport Transportation:
Eleven miles to downtown Vancouver.
Taxicab and bus service.
Selected Hotels:
Denman Place Inn, 1733 Comax St.
Hotel Georgia, 801 W. Georgia St.
Hotel Vancouver, 900 W. Georgia St.
Regency Hyatt House, Georgia & Burrand sts.
Rembrandt, 1160 Davie St.
Westin Bayshore, 1601 W. Georgia St.
Selected Restaurants:
The Attic, Cavalier Room in the Georgia Hotel, Geisha Gardens, Hy's Encore, Ming's, Ship of the Seven Seas, The Three Greenhorns
Banking: hours from 10 A.M. to 3 P.M. Monday through Thursday, 10 A.M. to 6 P.M. Friday.
Information Sources:
Greater Vancouver Convention & Visitors Bureau
Pacific Centre Mall, Box 10171
Vancouver, B.C. V7Y 1H5

West Berlin, Federal Republic of Germany

Altitude: 115 ft. (35m.)
Average Temp.: Jan., 31°F. (−1°C.); July, 66°F. (19°C.)
English Language Publications: None
Selected Hotels:
Ambassador, Bayreuther Str. 42-43
Berlin Hotel Intercontinental, Budapester Str. 2
Bristol Hotel Kempinski, Kurfürstendamm 27
Palace Hotel, Europa Center
Schweizerhof, Budapester Str. 21-29
Selected Restaurants:
Aben, Alexander, Bristol Kempinski Grill, Conti-Fischstuben, El Panorama, Hotel Berlin Restaurant, Kottler's, Maitre, Mampes Gute Stube, Ritz
Banking: hours are from 8:30 A.M. to 1 P.M. and 2:30 P.M. to 4 P.M. weekdays (Thursday to 5:30 P.M.). Closed Saturday and Sunday.
Information Sources:
German National Tourist Office
747 Third Avenue
New York, NY 10017

Vienna, Austria

Altitude: 560 ft. (171m.)
Average Temp.: Jan., 30°F. (−1°C.); July, 68°F. (20°C.)
English Language Publications:
Danube Weekly, Vienna Life
Airport Transportation:
Eleven miles to downtown Vienna.
Taxicab, train, and bus service.
Selected Hotels:
Ambassador, Neuer Markt 5, A-1010
Bristol, Kärntner Ring 1, A-1010 opposite Vienna Opera
Clima Villenhotel, Nussberggasse 2c, A-1190
Imperial, Kärntner Ring 16, A-1015
Parkhotel Schönbrunn, Hietzinger Haupstr. 12, A-1130
Sacher, Philharmonikerstr. 4, A-1015
Vienna Inter-Continental, Johannesgasse 28, A-1030
Wien Hilton, Am Stadtpark, A-1030
Selected Restaurants:
Am Franziskanerplatz, Ambassador Hotel Restaurant, Bristol Hotel Restaurant, Drei Husaren, Imperial Hotel Restaurant, Inter-Continental Hotel Restaurant, Le Palais, Palais Auersperg Restaurant, Priuz Euger Restaurant (Hilton), Sacher Hotel Restaurant, Wegenstein-Weisser Schwan, Wiener Stadtkrug
Banking: hours are 8:00 A.M. to 12:30 P.M. and 1:30 P.M. to 3:30 P.M. Monday, Tuesday, Wednesday, Friday, 8:00 A.M. to 12:30 P.M. and 1:30 P.M. to 5:30 P.M. Thursday.
Information Sources:
In Vienna, the Fremdenverkehrsverband (local tourist office).

Zürich, Switzerland

Altitude: 1,339 ft. (408m.)
Average Temp.: Jan., 31°F. (0°C.); July, 63°F. (17°C.)
English Language Publications: None
Airport Transportation:
Distance 7½ miles; travel time 10 minutes.
Railway service from airport to center of city; trains leave every 20 minutes from station under Terminal B.
Selected Hotels:
Atlantis Sheraton, Doeltschiweg 234
Baur au Lac, Talstrasse 1
Bellerive au Lac, Utoquai 47
Carlton-Elite, Bahnhofstrasse 41
Dolder Grand, Kurhausstr. 65
Eden au Lac, Utoquai 45
Savoy, Poststr. 12
Zum Storchen, Weinplatz 2
Zurich, Neumuhlequai 42
Selected Restaurants:
Ascot Hotel Restaurant, Haus zum Ruden, Kaiser's Reblaube, Kronenhalle, Tondury's Widder, Veltliner Keller, Zur Waage
Banking: hours 8:30 A.M. to 4:30 P.M. Monday through Friday; closed Saturday.
Information Sources:
Swiss National Tourist Office, Bellariastrasse 38, Zurich
Zurich Tourist Office Hauptbahnhof, Zurich

Air Distances Between World Cities

GIVEN IN STATUTE MILES

	Apia, Western Samoa	Azores Islands	Berlin, Germany	Bombay, India	Buenos Aires, Argentina	Calcutta, India	Cape Town, South Africa	Cape Verde Islands	Chicago, U. S. A.	Darwin, Australia	Denver, U. S. A.	Gibraltar	Hong Kong
Apia		9644	9743	8154	6931	7183	9064	10246	6557	3843	5653	10676	5591
Azores Islands	9644		2185	5967	5417	6549	5854	1499	3093	10209	3991	1249	7572
Berlin	9743	2185		3910	7376	4376	5977	3194	4402	8036	5077	1453	5500
Bombay	8154	5967	3910		9273	1041	5134	6297	8054	4503	8383	4814	2673
Buenos Aires	6931	5417	7376	9273		10242	4270	4208	5596	9127	5928	5963	11463
Calcutta	7183	6549	4376	1041	10242		6026	7148	7981	3744	8050	5521	1534
Cape Town	9064	5854	5977	5134	4270	6026		4509	8449	6947	9327	5076	7372
Cape Verde Islands	10246	1499	3194	6297	4208	7148	4509		4066	10664	4975	1762	8539
Chicago	6557	3093	4402	8054	5596	7981	8449	4066		9346	920	4258	7790
Darwin	3843	10209	8036	4503	9127	3744	6947	10664	9346		8557	9265	2642
Denver	5653	3991	5077	8383	5928	8050	9327	4975	920	8557		5122	7465
Gibraltar	10676	1249	1453	4814	5963	5521	5076	1762	4258	9265	5122		6828
Hong Kong	5591	7572	5500	2673	11463	1534	7372	8539	7790	2642	7465	6828	
Honolulu	2604	7180	7305	8020	7558	7037	11532	8311	4244	5355	3338	8075	5537
Istanbul	10175	2975	1078	2991	7568	3646	5219	3507	5476	7390	6154	1874	4980
Juneau	5415	4526	4560	6866	7759	6326	10330	5911	2305	7105	1831	5273	5634
London	9789	1527	574	4462	6918	4954	6005	2731	3950	8598	4688	1094	5981
Los Angeles	4828	4794	5782	8701	6118	8148	9969	5772	1745	7835	831	5936	7240
Manila	4993	8250	6128	3148	11042	2189	7525	9221	8128	1979	7661	7483	693
Melbourne	3113	12101	9919	6097	7234	5547	6412	10856	9668	1964	8759	10798	4607
Mexico City	5449	4385	6037	9722	4633	9495	8511	4857	1673	9081	1434	5629	8776
Moscow	9116	3165	996	3131	8375	3447	6294	3982	4984	7046	5485	2413	4439
New Orleans	6085	3524	5116	8865	4916	8803	8316	4194	833	9545	1082	4757	8480
New York	7242	2422	3961	7794	5297	7921	7801	3355	713	9959	1631	3627	8051
Nome	5438	4954	4342	5901	8848	5271	10107	6438	3314	6235	2925	5398	4547
Oslo	9247	2234	515	4130	7613	4459	6494	3444	4040	8022	4653	1791	5337
Panamá	6514	3778	5849	9742	3381	10114	7014	3734	2325	10352	2636	4926	10084
Paris	9990	1659	542	4359	6877	4889	5841	2666	4133	8575	4885	964	5956
Peking (Peiping)	5903	6565	4567	2964	11974	2024	8045	7763	6592	3728	6348	6009	1226
Port Said	10485	3391	1747	2659	7362	3506	4590	3672	6103	7159	6819	2179	4975
Quebec	7406	2240	3583	7371	5680	7481	7857	3355	878	9724	1752	3383	8650
Reykjavík	8678	1777	1479	5191	7099	5409	7111	3248	2954	8631	3596	2047	6031
Rio de Janeiro	8120	4428	6144	8257	1218	9376	3769	3040	5296	9960	5871	4775	10995
Rome	10475	2125	734	3843	6929	4496	5249	2772	4808	8190	5561	1034	5768
San Francisco	4786	4872	5657	8392	6474	7809	10241	5921	1858	7637	949	5936	6894
Seattle	5222	4501	5041	7741	6913	7224	10199	5714	1737	7619	1021	5462	6471
Shanghai	5399	7229	5215	3133	12197	2112	8059	8443	7053	3142	6698	6646	772
Singapore	5850	8326	6166	2429	9864	1791	6016	8700	9365	2075	9063	7231	1652
Tokyo	4656	7247	5538	4188	11400	3186	9071	8589	6303	3367	5795	6988	1796
Valparaíso	6267	5678	7795	10037	761	10993	4998	4649	5268	8961	5452	6408	11607
Washington, D. C.	7066	2667	4167	7988	5216	8088	7894	3486	597	9923	1494	3822	8148
Wellington	2062	11269	11265	7677	6260	7042	7019	10363	8349	3310	7516	12060	5853
Wien (Vienna)	10010	2291	328	3718	7368	4259	5671	3147	4694	7974	5383	1386	5429
Winnipeg	6283	3389	4286	7644	6297	7424	9054	4556	714	8684	798	4435	7096
Zanzibar	9892	5323	4309	2855	6421	3859	2346	4635	8358	6409	9221	4103	5414

Honolulu, Hawaii, U. S. A.	Istanbul (Constantinople), Turkey	Juneau, Alaska, U. S. A.	London, United Kingdom	Los Angeles, U.S.A.	Manila, Philippines	Melbourne, Australia	Mexico City, Mexico	Moscow, Soviet Union	New Orleans, U. S. A.	New York, U. S. A.	Nome, Alaska, U. S. A.	Oslo, Norway	Panamá, Panama	Paris, France	Peking, China	Port Said, Egypt
2604	10175	5415	9789	4828	4993	3113	5449	9116	6085	7242	5438	9247	6514	9990	5903	10485
7180	2975	4526	1527	4794	8250	12101	4385	3165	3524	2422	4954	2234	3778	1659	6565	3391
7305	1078	4560	574	5782	6128	9919	6037	996	5116	3961	4342	515	5849	542	4567	1747
8020	2991	6866	4462	8701	3148	6097	9722	3131	8865	7794	5901	4130	9742	4359	2964	2659
7558	7568	7759	6918	6118	11042	7234	4633	8375	4916	5297	8848	7613	3381	6877	11974	7362
7037	3646	6326	4954	8148	2189	5547	9495	3447	8803	7921	5271	4459	10114	4889	2024	3506
11532	5219	10330	6005	9969	7525	6412	8511	6294	8316	7801	10107	6494	7014	5841	8045	4590
8311	3507	5911	2731	5772	9221	10856	4857	3982	4194	3355	6438	3444	3734	2666	7763	3672
4244	5476	2305	3950	1745	8128	9668	1673	4984	833	713	3314	4040	2325	4133	6592	6103
5355	7390	7105	8598	7835	1979	1964	9081	7046	9545	9959	6235	8022	10352	8575	3728	7159
3338	6154	1831	4688	831	7661	8759	1434	5485	1082	1631	2925	4653	2636	4885	6348	6819
8075	1874	5273	1094	5936	7483	10798	5629	2413	4757	3627	5398	1791	4926	964	6009	2179
5537	4980	5634	5981	7240	693	4607	8776	4439	8480	8051	4547	5337	10084	5956	1226	4975
	8104	2815	7226	2557	5296	5513	3781	7033	4207	4959	3004	6784	5245	7434	5067	8738
8104		5498	1551	6843	5659	9088	7102	1088	6171	5009	5101	1518	6750	1401	4379	693
2815	5498		4418	1842	5869	8035	3219	4534	2905	2854	1094	4045	4460	4628	4522	6215
7226	1551	4418		5439	6667	10501	5541	1549	4627	3459	4381	714	5278	213	5054	2154
2557	6843	1842	5439		7269	7931	1542	6068	1673	2451	2876	5325	3001	5601	6250	7528
5296	5659	5869	6667	7269		3941	8829	5130	8724	8493	4817	6016	10283	6673	1770	5619
5513	9088	8035	10501	7931	3941		8422	8963	9275	10355	7558	9926	9022	10396	5667	8658
3781	7102	3219	5541	1542	8829	8422		6688	934	2085	4309	5706	1495	5706	7733	7671
7033	1088	4534	1549	6068	5130	8963	6688		5756	4662	4036	1016	6711	1541	3597	1710
4207	6171	2905	4627	1673	8724	9275	934	5756		1171	3937	4795	1603	4788	7314	6756
4959	5009	2854	3459	2451	8493	10355	2085	4662	1171		3769	3672	2231	3622	6823	5590
3004	5101	1094	4381	2876	4817	7558	4309	4036	3937	3769		3836	5541	4574	3428	5745
6784	1518	4045	714	5325	6016	9926	5706	1016	4795	3672	3836		5691	832	4360	2211
5245	6750	4460	5278	3001	10283	9022	1495	6711	1603	2231	5541	5691		5382	8906	7146
7434	1401	4628	213	5601	6673	10396	5706	1541	4788	3622	4574	832	5382		5101	1975
5067	4379	4522	5054	6250	1770	5667	7733	3597	7314	6823	3428	4360	8906	5101		4584
8738	693	6215	2154	7528	5619	8658	7671	1710	6756	5590	5745	2211	7146	1975	4584	
5000	4644	2660	3101	2579	8124	10497	2454	4242	1534	439	3489	3263	2659	3235	6423	5250
6084	2558	3268	1171	4306	6651	10544	4622	2056	3711	2576	3366	1083	4706	1380	4903	3227
8190	6395	7598	5772	6296	11254	8186	4770	7179	4796	4820	8586	6482	3294	5703	10768	6244
8022	854	5247	887	6326	6457	9934	6353	1474	5439	4273	5082	1243	5903	682	5047	1317
2392	6700	1525	5355	347	6963	7854	1885	5868	1926	2571	2547	5181	3322	5441	5902	7394
2678	6063	899	4782	959	6641	8186	2337	5199	2101	2408	1976	4591	3651	4993	5396	6759
4934	4959	4869	5710	6477	1152	5005	8039	4235	7720	7357	3784	5020	9324	5752	662	5132
6710	5373	7235	6744	8767	1479	3761	10307	5238	10082	9630	6148	6246	11687	6671	2774	5088
3850	5556	4011	5938	5470	1863	5089	7035	4650	6858	6735	2983	5221	8423	6033	1307	5842
6793	8172	7271	7263	5527	10930	6998	4053	8792	4514	5094	8360	7914	2943	7251	11774	8088
4829	5216	2834	3665	2300	8560	10173	1878	4883	966	205	3792	3870	2080	3828	6922	5796
4708	10663	7475	11682	6714	5162	1595	6899	10279	7794	8946	7383	10974	7433	11791	6698	10249
7626	783	4895	772	6108	6120	9792	6306	1044	5385	4224	4657	850	6026	644	4639	1429
3806	5361	1597	3918	1525	7414	9319	2097	4687	1418	1281	2599	3854	2998	4118	5907	6032
10869	3312	8795	4604	10021	5763	6802	9484	4270	8754	7698	8209	4803	8245	4396	5803	2729

Reykjavík, Iceland	Rio de Janeiro, Brazil	Rome, Italy	San Francisco, U. S. A.	Seattle, U. S. A.	Shanghai, China	Singapore, Singapore	Tokyo, Japan	Valparaíso, Chile	Washington, D. C., U. S. A.	Wellington, New Zealand	Wien (Vienna), Austria	Winnipeg, Canada	Zanzibar, Tanzania	
8678	8120	10475	4786	5222	5399	5850	4656	6267	7066	2062	10010	6283	9892	Apia
1777	4428	2125	4872	4501	7229	8326	7247	5678	2667	11269	2291	3389	5323	Azores Is.
1479	6114	734	5657	5041	5215	6166	5538	7795	4167	11265	328	4286	4309	Berlin
5191	8257	3843	8392	7741	3133	2429	4188	10037	7988	7677	3718	7644	2855	Bombay
7099	1218	6929	6474	6913	12197	9864	11400	761	5216	6260	7368	6297	6421	Buenos Aires
5409	9376	4496	7809	7224	2112	1791	3186	10993	8088	7042	4259	7424	3859	Calcutta
7111	3769	5249	10241	10199	8059	6016	9071	4998	7894	7019	5671	9054	2346	Cape Town
3248	3040	2772	5921	5714	8443	8700	8589	4649	3486	10363	3147	4556	4635	C. Verde Is.
2954	5296	4808	1858	1737	7053	9365	6303	5268	597	8349	4694	714	8358	Chicago
8631	9960	8190	7637	7619	3142	2075	3367	8961	9923	3310	7974	8684	6409	Darwin
3596	5871	5561	949	1021	6698	9063	5795	5452	1494	7516	5383	798	9221	Denver
2047	4775	1034	5936	5462	6646	7231	6988	6408	3822	12060	1386	4435	4103	Gibraltar
6031	10995	5768	6894	6471	772	1652	1796	11607	8148	5853	5429	7096	5414	Hong Kong
6084	8190	8022	2392	2678	4934	6710	3850	6793	4829	4708	7626	3806	10869	Honolulu
2558	6395	854	6700	6063	4959	5373	5556	8172	5216	10663	783	5361	3312	Istanbul
3268	7598	5247	1525	899	4869	7235	4011	7271	2834	7475	4895	1597	8795	Juneau
1171	5772	887	5355	4782	5710	6744	5938	7263	3665	11682	772	3918	4604	London
4306	6296	6326	347	959	6477	8767	5470	5527	2300	6714	6108	1525	10021	Los Angeles
6651	11254	6457	6963	6641	1152	1479	1863	10930	8560	5162	6120	7414	5763	Manila
10544	8186	9934	7854	8186	5005	3761	5089	6998	10173	1595	9792	9319	6802	Melbourne
4622	4770	6353	1885	2337	8039	10307	7035	4053	1878	6899	6306	2097	9484	Mexico City
2056	7179	1474	5868	5199	4235	5238	4650	8792	4883	10279	1044	4687	4270	Moscow
3711	4796	5439	1926	2101	7720	10082	6858	4514	966	7794	5385	1418	8754	New Orleans
2576	4820	4273	2571	2408	7357	9630	6735	5094	205	8946	4224	1281	7698	New York
3366	8586	5082	2547	1976	3784	6148	2983	8360	3792	7383	4657	2599	8209	Nome
1083	6482	1243	5181	4591	5020	6246	5221	7914	3870	10974	859	3854	4803	Oslo
4706	3294	5903	3322	3651	9324	11687	8423	2943	2080	7433	6026	2998	8245	Panamá
1380	5703	682	5441	4993	5752	6671	6033	7251	3828	11791	644	4118	4396	Paris
4903	10768	5047	5902	5396	662	2774	1307	11774	6922	6698	4639	5907	5803	Peking(Peiping)
3227	6244	1317	7394	6759	5132	5088	5842	8088	5796	10249	1429	6032	2729	Port Said
2189	5125	3943	2642	2353	6981	9097	6417	5504	610	9228	3858	1199	7443	Quebec
	6118	2044	4199	3614	5559	7160	5472	7225	2800	10724	1805	2804	5757	Reykjavík
6118		5684	6619	6891	11340	9774	11535	1855	4797	7349	6136	6010	5589	Rio de Jan.
2044	5684		6240	5659	5677	6232	6124	7420	4435	11524	463	4803	3712	Rome
4199	6619	6240		678	6132	8479	5131	5876	2442	6739	5988	1504	9958	San Francisco
3614	6891	5659	678		5703	8057	4777	6230	2329	7242	5376	1150	9359	Seattle
5559	11340	5677	6132	5703		2377	1094	11650	7442	6054	5270	6350	5971	Shanghai
7160	9774	6232	8479	8057	2377		3304	10226	9834	5292	6036	8685	4480	Singapore
5472	11535	6124	5131	4777	1094	3304		10635	6769	5760	5679	5575	7040	Tokyo
7225	1855	7420	5876	6230	11650	10226	10635		4977	5785	7783	5931	7184	Valparaíso
2800	4797	4435	2442	2329	7442	9834	6769	4977		8745	4429	1243	7884	Wash., D.C.
10724	7349	11524	6739	7242	6054	5292	5760	5785	8745		11278	8230	8122	Wellington
1805	6136	463	5988	5376	5270	6036	5679	7783	4429	11278		4604	3983	Wien
2804	6010	4803	1504	1150	6350	8685	5575	5931	1243	8230	4604		8416	Winnipeg
5757	5589	3712	9958	9359	5971	4480	7040	7184	7884	8122	3983	8416		Zanzibar

Largest Metropolitan Areas of the World, 1985

This table lists the major metropolitan areas of the world according to their estimated population on January 1, 1985. For convenience in reference, the areas are grouped by major region, and the number of areas in each region and size group is given.

There are 31 areas with more than 5 million population each; these are listed in rank order of estimated population, with the world rank given in parentheses following the name. For example, New York's 1985 rank is third. Below the 5 million level, the metropolitan areas are listed alphabetically within population classifications.

Altogether these 257 metropolitan areas have an estimated 1985 population of about 739 million, or 15.3 percent of the world total. The 31 metropolitan areas of 5 million or more account for about 308,450,000 population.

For ease of comparison, each metropolitan area has been defined by Rand McNally & Company according to consistent rules. A metropolitan area includes a central city, neighboring communities linked to it by continuous built-up areas, and more distant communities if the bulk of their population is supported by commuters to the central city. Some metropolitan areas have more than one central city, for example Tōkyō-Yokohama or San Francisco-Oakland-San Jose.

POPULATION CLASSIFICATION	UNITED STATES and CANADA	LATIN AMERICA	EUROPE (excl. U.S.S.R.)	U.S.S.R.	SOUTHWEST ASIA	EAST ASIA	AFRICA-OCEANIA
OVER–15,000,000 (4)	New York, U.S. (3)	Mexico City, Mex. (2)				Tōkyō-Yokohama, Jpn. (1) Ōsaka-Kōbe-Kyōto, Jpn. (4)	
10,000,000–15,000,000 (9)	Los Angeles, U.S. (12)	São Paulo, Braz. (5) Buenos Aires, Arg. (9)	London, Eng. (11)	Moscow (7)	Calcutta, India (8) Bombay, India (10)	Seoul, Kor. (6)	Cairo, Eg. (13)
5,000,000–10,000,000 (18)	Chicago, U.S. (20) Philadelphia-Trenton-Wilmington, U.S. (29)	Rio de Janeiro, Braz. (14) Bogotá, Col. (28) Lima, Peru (30)	Paris, Fr. (15)	Leningrad (25)	Delhi-New Delhi, India (17) Tehrān, Iran (22) Karāchi, Pak. (24) İstanbul, Tur. (27) Madras, India (31)	Shanghai, China (16) Jakarta, Indon. (18) Manila, Phil. (19) Bangkok, Thai. (21) Peking (Beijing), China (23) T'aipei, Taiwan (26)	
3,000,000–5,000,000 (33)	Boston, U.S. Dallas-Fort Worth, U.S. Detroit, U.S.-Windsor, Can. Houston, U.S. Miami-Fort Lauderdale, U.S. San Francisco-Oakland-San Jose, U.S. Toronto, Can. Washington, U.S.	Caracas, Ven. Santiago, Chile	Athens, Grc. Barcelona, Sp. Berlin, F.R.G. Essen-Dortmund-Duisburg (The Ruhr), F.R.G. Madrid, Sp. Milan, It. Rome, It.		Baghdād, Iraq Bangalore, India Dacca (Dhaka), Bngl. Hyderābād, India Lahore, Pak.	Ho Chi Minh City (Saigon), Viet. Nagoya, Jpn. Pusan, Kor. Rangoon, Bur. Shenyang (Mukden), China Tianjin (Tientsin), China Victoria, Hong Kong Wuhan, China	Alexandria, Eg. Johannesburg, S. Afr. Sydney, Austl.

2,000,000–3,000,000 (45)	Atlanta, U.S. Cleveland, U.S. Minneapolis-St. Paul, U.S. Montréal, Can. Pittsburgh, U.S. St. Louis, U.S. San Diego, U.S.-Tijuana, Mex. Seattle-Tacoma, U.S.	Belo Horizonte, Braz. Guadalajara, Mex. Havana, Cuba Medellín, Col. Monterrey, Mex. Porto Alegre, Braz. Recife, Braz. Salvador, Braz.	Birmingham, Eng. Brussels, Bel. Bucharest, Rom. Budapest, Hung. Hamburg, F.R.G. Katowice-Bytom-Gliwice, Pol. Lisbon, Port. Manchester, Eng. Naples, It. Warsaw, Pol.	Donetsk-Makeyevka Kiev Tashkent	Ahmadābād, India Ankara, Tur. Kānpur, India Pune (Poona), India	Canton (Guangzhou), China Chongqing (Chungking), China Harbin, China Singapore, Singapore Surabaya, Indon. Taegu, Kor.	Algiers, Alg. Cape Town, S. Afr. Casablanca, Mor. Kinshasa, Zaire Lagos, Nig. Melbourne, Austl.
1,500,000–2,000,000 (46)	Baltimore, U.S. Denver, U.S. Phoenix, U.S.	Brasilia, Braz. Cali, Col. Curitiba, Braz. Fortaleza, Braz. San Juan, P.R. Santo Domingo, Dom. Rep.	Amsterdam, Neth. Belgrade, Yugo. Cologne, F.R.G. Frankfurt am Main, F.R.G. Glasgow, Scot. Leeds-Bradford, Eng. Liverpool, Eng. Munich, F.R.G. Stuttgart, F.R.G. Turin, It. Vienna, Aus.	Baku Dnepropetrovsk Gorkiy Kharkov Minsk Novosibirsk Sverdlovsk	Beirut, Leb. Chittagong, Bngl. Colombo, Sri Lanka Damascus, Syr.	Bandung, Indon. Changchun (Hsinking), China Chengdu (Chengtu), China Fukuoka, Jpn. Hanoi, Viet. Hiroshima-Kure, Jpn. Kaohsiung, Taiwan Kitakyūshū-Shimonoseki, Jpn. Medan, Indon. P'yongyang, Kor. Nanjing (Nanking), China Sapporo, Jpn. Xi'an (Sian), China	Abidjan, I.C. Durban, S. Afr.
1,000,000–1,500,000 (102)	Buffalo-Niagara Falls, U.S.-Saint Catharines-Niagara Falls, Can. Cincinnati, U.S. El Paso, U.S.-Ciudad Juárez, Mex. Hartford-New Britain, U.S. Indianapolis, U.S. Kansas City, U.S. Milwaukee, U.S. New Orleans, U.S. Portland, U.S. San Antonio, U.S. Vancouver, Can.	Barranquilla, Col. Belém, Braz. Campinas, Braz. Córdoba, Arg. Guatemala, Guat. Guayaquil, Ec. Maracaibo, Ven. Montevideo, Ur. Port-au-Prince, Hai. Puebla, Mex. Rosario, Arg. Santos, Braz.	Antwerp, Bel. Copenhagen, Den. Dublin (Baile Átha Cliath), Ire. Düsseldorf, F.R.G. Hannover, F.R.G. Lille-Roubaix, Fr. Łódź, Pol. Lyon, Fr. Mannheim, F.R.G. Marseille, Fr. Newcastle-Sunderland, Eng. Nürnberg, F.R.G. Porto, Port. Prague, Czech. Rotterdam, Neth. Sofia, Bul. Stockholm, Swe. Valencia, Sp.	Alma-Ata Chelyabinsk Kazan Kuybyshev Odessa Omsk Perm Rostov-na-Donu Saratov Tbilisi Ufa Volgograd Yerevan	Aleppo (Ḥalab), Syr. 'Ammān, Jordan Asansol, India Coimbatore, India Eşfahān, Iran Faisalabad, Pak. İzmir, Tur. Jaipur, India Jiddah, Sau. Ar. Kābul, Afg. Kuwait, Kuw. Lucknow, India Madurai, India Mashhad, Iran Nāgpur, India Patna, India Rāwalpindi-Islāmābād, Pak. Riyadh, Sau. Ar. Surat, India Tel Aviv-Yafo, Isr. Vārānasi (Benares), India	Anshan, China Fushun, China Hangzhou (Hangchow), China Jinan (Tsinan), China Kuala Lumpur, Mala. Kunming, China Lanzhou (Lanchow), China Lüda (Dairen), China Qingdao (Tsingtao), China Qiqihar (Tsitsihar), China Semarang, Indon. Sendai, Jpn. Taiyuan, China Tangshan, China Zhengzhou (Chengchow), China	Accra, Ghana Addis Ababa, Eth. Brisbane, Austl. Dakar, Sen. Dar es Salaam, Tan. Harare, Zimb. Ibadan, Nig. Khartoum, Sud. Nairobi, Ken. Pretoria, S. Afr. Tripoli, Libya Tunis, Tun.
Total by Region (257)	**34**	**34**	**48**	**25**	**41**	**51**	**24**

Facts About the United States

GEOGRAPHICAL FACTS

ELEVATION

The highest elevation in the United States is Mount McKinley, Alaska, 20,320 feet.

The lowest elevation in the United States is in Death Valley, California, 282 feet below sea level.

The average elevation of the United States is 2,500 feet.

EXTREMITIES

Direction	Location	Latitude	Longitude
North	Point Barrow, Alaska	71°23′N.	156°29′W.
South	Ka Lae (point) Hawaii	18°56′N.	155°41′W.
East	West Quoddy Head, Maine	44°49′N.	66°57′W.
West	Cape Wrangell, Alaska	52°55′N.	172°27′E.

The two places in the United States separated by the greatest distance are Kure Island, Hawaii, and Mangrove Point, Florida. These points are 5,848 miles apart.

LENGTH OF BOUNDARIES

The total length of the Canadian boundary of the United States is 5,525 miles.

The total length of the Mexican boundary of the United States is 1,933 miles.

The total length of the Atlantic coastline of the United States is 2,069 miles.

The total length of the Pacific and Arctic coastline of the United States is 8,683 miles.

The total length of the Gulf of Mexico coastline of the United States is 1,631 miles.

The total length of all coastlines and land boundaries of the United States is 19,841 miles.

The total length of the tidal shoreline and land boundaries of the United States is 96,091 miles.

GEOGRAPHIC CENTERS

The geographic center of the United States (including Alaska and Hawaii) is in Butte County, South Dakota at 44°58′N., 103°46′W.

The geographic center of North America is in North Dakota, a few miles west of Devils Lake, at 48°10′N., 100°10′W.

EXTREMES OF TEMPERATURE

The highest temperature ever recorded in the United States was 134°F., at Greenland Ranch, Death Valley, California, on July 10, 1913.

The lowest temperature ever recorded in the United States was —76°F., at Tanana, Alaska, in January, 1886.

PRECIPITATION

The average annual precipitation for the United States is approximately 29 inches.

Hawaii is the wettest state, with an average annual rainfall of 82.48 inches. Nevada, with an average annual rainfall of 8.81 inches, is the driest state.

The greatest local average annual rainfall in the United States is at Mt. Waialeale, Kauai, Hawaii, 460 inches.

Greatest 24-hour rainfall in the United States, 23.22 inches at New Smyrna, Florida, October 10–11, 1924.

Extreme minimum rainfall records in the United States include a total fall of only 3.93 inches at Bagdad, California, for a period of 5 years, 1909–13, and an annual average of 1.78 inches at Death Valley, California.

Heavy snowfall records include 76 inches at Silver Lake, Colorado, in 1 day; 42 inches at Angola, New York, in 2 days; 87 inches at Giant Forest, California, in 3 days; and 108 inches at Tahoe, California, in 4 days.

Greatest seasonal snowfall, 1,000.3 inches, more than 83 feet, at Paradise Ranger Station, Washington, during the winter of 1955–56.

HISTORICAL FACTS

TERRITORIAL ACQUISITIONS

Accession	Date	Area (sq. mi.)	Cost in Dollars
Original territory of the Thirteen States	1790	888,685	....
Purchase of Louisiana Territory, from France	1803	827,192	$11,250,000.00
By treaty with Spain: Florida	1819	58,560	$ 5,000,000.00
Other areas	1819	13,443	
Annexation of Texas	1845	390,144	....
Oregon Territory, by treaty with Great Britain	1846	285,580	....
Mexican Cession	1848	529,017	$15,000,000.00
Gadsden Purchase, from Mexico	1853	29,640	$10,000,000.00
Purchase of Alaska, from Russia	1867	586,412	7,200,000.00
Annexation of Hawaiian Islands	1898	6,450	....
Puerto Rico, by treaty with Spain	1899	3,435	....
Guam, by treaty with Spain	1899	212	....
American Samoa, by treaty with Great Britain and Germany	1900	76	....
Virgin Islands, by purchase from Denmark	1917	133	$25,000,000.00
Total		3,618,979	$73,450,000.00

Note: The Philippines, ceded by Spain in 1898 for $20,000,000.00, were a territorial possession of the United States from 1898 to 1946. On July 4, 1946 they became the independent republic of the Philippines.

Note. The Canal Zone, ceded by Panama in 1903 for $10,000,000.00, was a territory of the United States from 1903 to 1979. As a result of treaties signed in 1977, sovereignty over the Canal Zone reverted to Panama in 1979.

WESTWARD MOVEMENT OF CENTER OF POPULATION

Year	U.S. Population Total at Census	Approximate Location
1790	3,929,214	23 miles east of Baltimore, Md.
1800	5,308,483	18 miles west of Baltimore, Md.
1810	7,239,881	40 miles northwest of Washington, D.C.
1820	9,638,453	16 miles east of Moorefield, W. Va.
1830	12,866,020	19 miles southwest of Moorefield, W. Va.
1840	17,069,453	16 miles south of Clarksburg, W. Va.
1850	23,191,876	23 miles southeast of Parkersburg, W. Va.
1860	31,443,321	20 miles southeast of Chillicothe, Ohio
1870	39,818,449	48 miles northeast of Cincinnati, Ohio
1880	50,155,783	8 miles southwest of Cincinnati, Ohio
1890	62,947,714	20 miles east of Columbus, Ind.
1900	75,994,575	6 miles southeast of Columbus, Ind.
1910	91,972,266	Bloomington, Ind.
1920	105,710,620	8 miles southeast of Spencer, Ind.
1930	122,775,046	3 miles northeast of Linton, Ind.
1940	131,669,275	2 miles southeast of Carlisle, Ind.
1950	150,697,361	8 miles northwest of Olney, Ill.
1960	179,323,175	6 miles northwest of Centralia, Ill.
1970	204,816,296	5 miles southeast of Mascoutah, Ill.
1980	226,504,825	Near DeSoto, Mo.

State	Land Area (square miles)	Water Area* (square miles)	Total Area (square miles)	Area Rank (land area)	1980 Resident Population	1980 Population (per square mile†)	1970 Population	1960 Population	1950 Population	Population Rank 1980	Population Rank 1970	Population Rank 1960
Alabama	50,767	938	51,705	28	3,893,888	77	3,444,165	3,266,740	3,061,743	22	21	19
Alaska	570,835	20,171	591,006	1	401,851	0.7	302,173	226,167	128,643	50	50	50
Arizona	113,509	491	114,000	6	2,718,425	24	1,772,482	1,302,161	749,587	29	33	35
Arkansas	52,079	1,108	53,187	27	2,286,435	44	1,923,295	1,786,272	1,909,511	33	32	31
California	156,299	2,407	158,706	3	23,667,565	151	19,953,134	15,717,204	10,586,223	1	1	2
Colorado	103,595	496	104,091	8	2,889,735	28	2,207,259	1,753,947	1,325,089	28	30	33
Connecticut	4,871	147	5,018	48	3,107,576	638	3,032,217	2,535,234	2,007,280	25	24	25
Delaware	1,932	112	2,044	49	594,317	308	548,104	446,292	318,085	47	46	46
District of Columbia	63	6	69	..	638,432	10,134	756,510	763,956	802,178	..	..	..
Florida	54,153	4,511	58,664	26	9,746,342	180	6,789,443	4,951,560	2,771,305	7	9	10
Georgia	58,056	854	58,910	21	5,463,105	94	4,589,575	3,943,116	3,444,578	13	15	16
Hawaii	6,425	46	6,471	47	964,691	150	769,913	632,772	499,794	39	40	43
Idaho	82,412	1,153	83,565	11	944,038	11	713,008	667,191	588,637	41	42	42
Illinois	55,645	2,226	57,871	23	11,426,596	205	11,113,976	10,081,158	8,712,176	5	5	4
Indiana	35,932	482	36,414	38	5,490,260	153	5,193,669	4,662,498	3,934,224	12	11	11
Iowa	55,965	311	56,276	24	2,913,808	52	2,825,041	2,757,537	2,621,073	27	25	24
Kansas	81,778	500	82,278	13	2,364,236	29	2,249,071	2,178,611	1,905,299	32	28	28
Kentucky	39,669	740	40,409	37	3,660,257	92	3,219,311	3,038,156	2,944,806	23	23	22
Louisiana	44,521	3,231	47,752	33	4,206,312	94	3,643,180	3,257,022	2,683,516	19	20	20
Maine	30,995	2,270	33,265	39	1,125,027	36	993,663	969,265	913,774	38	38	36
Maryland	9,837	623	10,460	42	4,216,975	429	3,922,399	3,100,689	2,343,001	18	18	21
Massachusetts	7,824	460	8,284	45	5,737,037	733	5,689,170	5,148,578	4,690,514	11	10	9
Michigan	56,954	40,148	97,102	22	9,262,078	163	8,875,083	7,823,194	6,371,766	8	7	7
Minnesota	79,548	7,066	86,614	14	4,075,970	51	3,805,069	3,413,864	2,982,483	21	19	18
Mississippi	47,233	457	47,690	31	2,520,638	53	2,216,912	2,178,141	2,178,914	31	29	29
Missouri	68,945	753	69,698	18	4,916,759	71	4,677,399	4,319,813	3,954,653	15	13	13
Montana	145,389	1,657	147,046	4	786,690	5.4	694,409	674,767	591,024	44	43	41
Nebraska	76,644	712	77,356	15	1,569,825	20	1,483,791	1,411,330	1,325,510	35	35	34
Nevada	109,894	667	110,561	7	800,493	7.3	488,738	285,278	160,083	43	47	49
New Hampshire	8,993	285	9,278	44	920,610	102	737,681	606,921	533,242	42	41	45
New Jersey	7,468	319	7,787	46	7,364,823	986	7,168,164	6,066,782	4,835,329	9	8	8
New Mexico	121,336	257	121,593	5	1,302,981	11	1,016,000	951,023	681,187	37	37	37
New York	47,377	5,358	52,735	30	17,558,072	371	18,241,266	16,782,304	14,830,192	2	2	1
North Carolina	48,843	3,826	52,669	29	5,881,813	120	5,082,059	4,556,155	4,061,929	10	12	12
North Dakota	69,300	1,403	70,703	17	652,717	9.4	617,761	632,446	619,636	46	45	44
Ohio	41,004	3,783	44,787	35	10,797,624	263	10,652,017	9,706,397	7,946,627	6	6	5
Oklahoma	68,655	1,301	69,956	19	3,025,290	44	2,559,253	2,328,284	2,233,351	26	27	27
Oregon	96,185	888	97,073	10	2,633,149	27	2,091,385	1,768,687	1,521,341	30	31	32
Pennsylvania	44,888	1,155	46,043	32	11,863,895	264	11,793,909	11,319,366	10,498,012	4	3	3
Rhode Island	1,055	157	1,212	50	947,154	898	949,723	859,488	791,896	40	39	39
South Carolina	30,204	909	31,113	40	3,121,833	103	2,590,516	2,382,594	2,117,027	24	26	26
South Dakota	75,952	1,164	77,116	16	690,768	9.1	666,257	680,514	652,740	45	44	40
Tennessee	41,155	989	42,144	34	4,591,120	112	3,924,164	3,567,089	3,291,718	17	17	17
Texas	262,018	4,790	266,808	2	14,229,288	54	11,196,730	9,579,677	7,711,194	3	4	6
Utah	82,073	2,827	84,900	12	1,461,037	18	1,059,273	890,627	688,862	36	36	38
Vermont	9,273	341	9,614	43	511,456	55	444,732	389,881	377,747	48	48	47
Virginia	39,704	1,063	40,767	36	5,346,818	135	4,648,494	3,966,949	3,318,680	14	14	14
Washington	66,511	1,628	68,139	20	4,132,180	62	3,409,169	2,853,214	2,378,963	20	22	23
West Virginia	24,119	112	24,231	41	1,950,279	81	1,744,237	1,860,421	2,005,552	34	34	30
Wisconsin	54,426	11,789	66,215	25	4,705,521	86	4,417,933	3,951,777	3,434,575	16	16	15
Wyoming	96,990	820	97,810	9	469,557	4.8	332,416	330,066	290,529	49	49	48
United States	3,539,297	139,907	3,679,204		226,547,346	64	203,235,298	179,323,175	151,325,798	..	..	..

*Includes the United States area of the Great Lakes. †Land area.

General Information About U.S. States

STATE	CAPITAL	LARGEST CITY	ENTERED UNION AS STATE		Greatest N-S Measurement (miles)	Greatest E-W Measurement (miles)
			Date of Entry	Rank of Entry		
Alabama	Montgomery	Birmingham	Dec. 14, 1819	22	330	200
Alaska	Juneau	Anchorage	Jan. 3, 1959	49	1,332	2,250
Arizona	Phoenix	Phoenix	Feb. 14, 1912	48	390	335
Arkansas	Little Rock	Little Rock	June 15, 1836	25	240	275
California	Sacramento	Los Angeles	Sept. 9, 1850	31	800	375
Colorado	Denver	Denver	Aug. 1, 1876	38	270	380
Connecticut*	Hartford	Hartford	Jan. 9, 1788	5	75	90
Delaware*	Dover	Wilmington	Dec. 7, 1787	1	95	35
District of Columbia	Washington	Washington	March 3, 1791	..	15	15
Florida	Tallahassee	Jacksonville	March 3, 1845	27	460	400
Georgia*	Atlanta	Atlanta	Jan. 2, 1788	4	315	250
Hawaii	Honolulu	Honolulu	Aug. 21, 1959	50	...	1,600
Idaho	Boise	Boise	July 3, 1890	43	480	305
Illinois	Springfield	Chicago	Dec. 3, 1818	21	380	205
Indiana	Indianapolis	Indianapolis	Dec. 11, 1816	19	265	160
Iowa	Des Moines	Des Moines	Dec. 28, 1846	29	205	310
Kansas	Topeka	Wichita	Jan. 29, 1861	34	205	410
Kentucky	Frankfort	Louisville	June 1, 1792	15	175	350
Louisiana	Baton Rouge	New Orleans	April 30, 1812	18	275	300
Maine	Augusta	Portland	March 15, 1820	23	310	210
Maryland*	Annapolis	Baltimore	April 28, 1788	7	120	200
Massachusetts*	Boston	Boston	Feb. 6, 1788	6	110	190
Michigan	Lansing	Detroit	Jan. 26, 1837	26	400	310
Minnesota	St. Paul	Minneapolis	May 11, 1858	32	400	350
Mississippi	Jackson	Jackson	Dec. 10, 1817	20	340	180
Missouri	Jefferson City	St. Louis	Aug. 10, 1821	24	280	300
Montana	Helena	Billings	Nov. 8, 1889	41	315	570
Nebraska	Lincoln	Omaha	March 1, 1867	37	210	415
Nevada	Carson City	Las Vegas	Oct. 31, 1864	36	485	315
New Hampshire*	Concord	Manchester	June 21, 1788	9	185	90
New Jersey*	Trenton	Newark	Dec. 18, 1787	3	166	70
New Mexico	Santa Fe	Albuquerque	Jan. 6, 1912	47	390	350
New York*	Albany	New York	July 26, 1788	11	310	330
North Carolina*	Raleigh	Charlotte	Nov. 21, 1789	12	200	520
North Dakota	Bismarck	Fargo	Nov. 2, 1889	39	210	360
Ohio	Columbus	Cleveland	March 1, 1803	17	230	205
Oklahoma	Oklahoma City	Oklahoma City	Nov. 16, 1907	46	210	460
Oregon	Salem	Portland	Feb. 14, 1859	33	290	375
Pennsylvania*	Harrisburg	Philadelphia	Dec. 12, 1787	2	180	310
Rhode Island*	Providence	Providence	May 29, 1790	13	50	35
South Carolina*	Columbia	Columbia	May 23, 1788	8	215	285
South Dakota	Pierre	Sioux Falls	Nov. 2, 1889	40	240	360
Tennessee	Nashville	Memphis	June 1, 1796	16	120	430
Texas	Austin	Houston	Dec. 29, 1845	28	710	760
Utah	Salt Lake City	Salt Lake City	Jan. 4, 1896	45	345	275
Vermont	Montpelier	Burlington	March 4, 1791	14	155	90
Virginia*	Richmond	Norfolk	June 25, 1788	10	205	425
Washington	Olympia	Seattle	Nov. 11, 1889	42	230	340
West Virginia	Charleston	Huntington	June 20, 1863	35	200	225
Wisconsin	Madison	Milwaukee	May 29, 1848	30	300	290
Wyoming	Cheyenne	Cheyenne	July 10, 1890	44	275	365
United States	Washington, D.C.	New York	....	..	...	...

*One of the Thirteen Original States.

HIGHEST POINT		STATE FLOWER	STATE BIRD	STATE NICKNAME
Location	Altitude (feet)			
Cheaha Mountain	2,407	Camellia	Yellowhammer	Yellowhammer
Mt. McKinley	20,320	Forget-me-not	Willow Ptarmigan	Last Frontier
Humphreys Peak	12,633	Saguaro Cactus	Cactus Wren	Grand Canyon
Magazine Mtn.	2,753	Apple Blossom	Mockingbird	Land of Opportunity
Mt. Whitney	14,494	Golden Poppy	California Valley Quail	Golden
Mt. Elbert	14,433	Rocky Mountain Columbine	Lark Bunting	Centennial
S. slope of Mt. Frissell	2,380	Mountain Laurel	Robin	Constitution
Ebright Road, New Castle Co.	442	Peach Blossom	Blue Hen Chicken	First
Tenleytown	410	American Beauty Rose	Wood Thrush	....
N. boundary, Walton Co.	345	Orange Blossom	Mockingbird	Sunshine
Brasstown Bald (mtn.)	4,784	Cherokee Rose	Brown Thrasher	Peach
Mauna Kea	13,796	Red Hibiscus	Nene (Hawaiian Goose)	Aloha
Borah Peak	12,662	Syringa	Mountain Bluebird	Gem
Charles Mound	1,235	Violet	Cardinal	Prairie
Near Spartanburg	1,257	Peony	Cardinal	Hoosier
N. W. corner Osceola Co.	1,670	Wild Rose	Eastern Goldfinch	Hawkeye
Mt. Sunflower	4,039	Sunflower	Western Meadowlark	Sunflower
Black Mountain	4,145	Goldenrod	Kentucky Cardinal	Bluegrass
Driskill Mountain	535	Magnolia	Pelican	Pelican
Mt. Katahdin	5,268	White Pine	Chickadee	Pine Tree
Backbone Mountain	3,360	Black-eyed Susan	Baltimore Oriole	Old Free
Mt. Greylock	3,491	Mayflower	Chickadee	Old Bay
Mt. Curwood	1,980	Apple Blossom	Robin	Wolverine
Eagle Mtn.	2,301	Showy Lady's-slipper	Loon	Gopher
Woodall Mountain	806	Magnolia	Mockingbird	Magnolia
Taum Sauk Mountain	1,772	Hawthorne	Bluebird	Show Me
Granite Peak	12,799	Bitterroot	Western Meadowlark	Big Sky
S.W. corner Kimball Co.	5,426	Goldenrod	Western Meadowlark	Cornhusker
Boundary Peak	13,143	Shrub Sagebrush	Mountain Bluebird	Silver
Mt. Washington	6,288	Purple Lilac	Purple Finch	Granite
High Point	1,803	Purple Violet	Eastern Goldfinch	Garden
Wheeler Peak	13,161	Yucca	Roadrunner	Land of Enchantment
Mt. Marcy	5,344	Rose	Bluebird	Empire
Mt. Mitchell	6,684	Dogwood	Cardinal	Tar Heel
White Butte	3,506	Wild Prairie Rose	Western Meadowlark	Flickertail
Campbell Hill	1,550	Scarlet Carnation	Cardinal	Buckeye
Black Mesa	4,973	Mistletoe	Scissor-tailed Flycatcher	Sooner
Mt. Hood	11,239	Oregon Grape	Western Meadowlark	Beaver
Mt. Davis	3,213	Mountain Laurel	Ruffed Grouse	Keystone
Jerimoth Hill	812	Violet	Rhode Island Red	Little Rhody
Sassafras Mountain	3,560	Carolina Jessamine	Carolina Wren	Palmetto
Harney Peak	7,242	Pasque	Ringnecked Pheasant	Coyote
Clingmans Dome	6,643	Iris	Mockingbird	Volunteer
Guadalupe Peak	8,751	Bluebonnet	Mockingbird	Lone Star
Kings Peak	13,528	Sego Lily	Seagull	Beehive
Mt. Mansfield	4,393	Red Clover	Hermit Thrush	Green Mountain
Mt. Rogers	5,729	Flowering Dogwood	Cardinal	Old Dominion
Mt. Rainier	14,410	Rhododendron	Willow Goldfinch	Evergreen
Spruce Knob	4,862	Rhododendron	Cardinal	Mountain
Timms Hill	1,952	Violet	Robin	Badger
Gannett Peak	13,804	Indian Paint Brush	Meadowlark	Equality
Mt. McKinley, Alaska	20,320	....	Bald Eagle	....

Populations of United States Colonies and States, 1650–1980

STATES	1650	1700	1750	1770	1790	1800	1820	1840
Alabama	......	......	......	......	......	......	127,901	590,75
Alaska	......	......	......	......	......	......	......	......
Arizona	......	......	......	......	......	......	......	......
Arkansas	......	......	......	......	......	......	14,273	97,57
California	......	......	......	......	......	......	......	......
Colorado	......	......	......	......	......	......	......	......
Connecticut	4,139	25,970	111,280	183,881	237,946	251,002	275,248	309,97
Delaware	185	2,470	28,704	35,496	59,096	64,273	72,749	78,08
District of Columbia	......	......	......	......	......	8,144	23,336	33,74
Florida	......	......	......	......	......	......	......	54,47
Georgia	......	......	5,200	23,375	82,548	162,686	340,989	691,39
Hawaii	......	......	......	......	......	......	......	......
Idaho	......	......	......	......	......	......	......	......
Illinois	......	......	......	......	......	......	55,211	476,18
Indiana	......	......	......	......	......	5,641	147,178	685,86
Iowa	......	......	......	......	......	......	......	43,11
Kansas	......	......	......	......	......	......	......	......
Kentucky	......	......	......	15,700	73,677	220,955	564,317	779,82
Louisiana	......	......	......	......	......	......	153,407	352,41
Maine[4]	......	......	......	31,257	96,540	151,719	298,335	501,79
Maryland	4,504	29,604	141,073	202,599	319,728	341,548	407,350	470,01
Massachusetts[4]	16,603	55,941	188,000	235,308	378,787	422,845	523,287	737,69
Michigan	......	......	......	......	......	......	8,896	212,267
Minnesota	......	......	......	......	......	......	......	......
Mississippi	......	......	......	......	......	8,850	75,448	375,651
Missouri	......	......	......	......	......	......	66,586	383,70
Montana	......	......	......	......	......	......	......	......
Nebraska	......	......	......	......	......	......	......	......
Nevada	......	......	......	......	......	......	......	......
New Hampshire	1,305	4,958	27,505	62,396	141,885	183,858	244,161	284,574
New Jersey	......	14,010	71,393	117,431	184,139	211,149	277,575	373,306
New Mexico	......	......	......	......	......	......	......	......
New York	4,116	19,107	76,696	162,920	340,120	589,051	1,372,812	2,428,921
North Carolina	......	10,720	72,984	197,200	393,751	478,103	638,829	753,419
North Dakota[3]	......	......	......	......	......	......	......	......
Ohio	......	......	......	......	......	45,365	581,434	1,519,467
Oklahoma[5]	......	......	......	......	......	......	......	......
Oregon	......	......	......	......	......	......	......	......
Pennsylvania	......	17,950	119,666	240,057	434,373	602,365	1,049,458	1,724,033
Rhode Island	785	5,894	33,226	58,196	68,825	69,122	83,059	108,830
South Carolina	......	5,704	64,000	124,244	249,073	345,591	502,741	594,398
South Dakota[3]	......	......	......	......	......	......	......	......
Tennessee	......	......	......	1,000	35,691	105,602	422,823	829,210
Texas	......	......	......	......	......	......	......	......
Utah	......	......	......	......	......	......	......	......
Vermont	......	......	......	10,000	85,425	154,465	235,981	291,948
Virginia[6]	18,731	58,560	231,033	447,016	691,737	807,557	938,261	1,025,227
Washington	......	......	......	......	......	......	......	......
West Virginia[6]	......	......	......	......	55,873	78,592	136,808	224,537
Wisconsin	......	......	......	......	......	......	......	30,945
Wyoming	......	......	......	......	......	......	......	......
Total[1]	50,368	250,888	1,170,760	2,148,076	3,929,214	5,308,483	9,638,453	17,069,453

[1] All figures prior to 1890 exclude uncivilized Indians. Figures for 1650 through 1770 include only the British coloni that later became the United States. No areas are included prior to their annexation to the United States. How ever, many of the figures refer to territories prior to their admission as States. U.S. total includes Alaska fro 1880 through 1970 and Hawaii from 1900 through 1970.

[2] U.S. total for 1840 includes 6,100 persons on public ships in service of the United States, not credited to any Stat

[3] South Dakota figure for 1860 represents entire Dakota Territory. North and South Dakota figures for 1880 a for the parts of Dakota Territory which later constituted the respective States.

1860	1880	1900	1920	1940	1950	1960	1970	1980
964,201	1,262,505	1,828,697	2,348,174	2,832,961	3,061,743	3,266,740	3,444,165	3,893,888
......	33,426	63,592	55,036	72,524	128,643	226,167	302,173	401,851
......	40,440	122,931	334,162	499,261	749,587	1,302,161	1,772,482	2,718,425
435,450	802,525	1,311,564	1,752,204	1,949,387	1,909,511	1,786,272	1,923,295	2,286,435
379,994	864,694	1,485,053	3,426,861	6,907,387	10,586,223	15,717,204	19,953,134	23,667,565
34,277	194,327	539,700	939,629	1,123,296	1,325,089	1,753,947	2,207,259	2,889,735
460,147	622,700	908,420	1,380,631	1,709,242	2,007,280	2,535,234	3,032,217	3,107,576
112,216	146,608	184,735	223,003	266,505	318,085	446,292	548,104	594,317
75,080	177,624	278,718	437,571	663,091	802,178	763,956	756,510	638,432
140,424	269,493	528,542	968,470	1,897,414	2,771,305	4,951,560	6,789,443	9,746,342
1,057,286	1,542,180	2,216,331	2,895,832	3,123,723	3,444,578	3,943,116	4,589,575	5,463,105
......	......	154,001	255,881	422,770	499,794	632,772	769,913	964,691
......	32,610	161,772	431,866	524,873	588,637	667,191	713,008	944,038
1,711,951	3,077,871	4,821,550	6,485,280	7,897,241	8,712,176	10,081,158	11,113,976	11,426,596
1,350,428	1,978,301	2,516,462	2,930,390	3,427,796	3,934,224	4,662,498	5,193,669	5,490,260
674,913	1,624,615	2,231,853	2,404,021	2,538,268	2,621,073	2,757,537	2,825,041	2,913,808
107,206	996,096	1,470,495	1,769,257	1,801,028	1,905,299	2,178,611	2,249,071	2,364,236
1,155,684	1,648,690	2,147,174	2,416,630	2,845,627	2,944,806	3,038,156	3,219,311	3,660,257
708,002	939,946	1,381,625	1,798,509	2,363,880	2,683,516	3,257,022	3,643,180	4,206,312
628,279	648,936	694,466	768,014	847,226	913,774	969,265	993,663	1,125,027
687,049	934,943	1,188,044	1,449,661	1,821,244	2,343,001	3,100,689	3,922,399	4,216,975
1,231,066	1,783,085	2,805,346	3,852,356	4,316,721	4,690,514	5,148,578	5,689,170	5,737,037
749,113	1,636,937	2,420,982	3,668,412	5,256,106	6,371,766	7,823,194	8,875,083	9,262,078
172,023	780,773	1,751,394	2,387,125	2,792,300	2,982,483	3,413,864	3,805,069	4,075,970
791,305	1,131,597	1,551,270	1,790,618	2,183,796	2,178,914	2,178,141	2,216,912	2,520,638
1,182,012	2,168,380	3,106,665	3,404,055	3,784,664	3,954,653	4,319,813	4,677,399	4,916,759
......	39,159	243,329	548,889	559,456	591,024	674,767	694,409	786,690
28,841	452,402	1,066,300	1,296,372	1,315,834	1,325,510	1,411,330	1,483,791	1,569,825
6,857	62,266	42,335	77,407	110,247	160,083	285,278	488,738	800,493
326,073	346,991	411,588	443,083	491,524	533,242	606,921	737,681	920,610
672,035	1,131,116	1,883,669	3,155,900	4,160,165	4,835,329	6,066,782	7,168,164	7,364,823
93,516	119,565	195,310	360,350	531,818	681,187	951,023	1,016,000	1,302,981
3,880,735	5,082,871	7,268,894	10,385,227	13,479,142	14,830,192	16,782,304	18,241,266	17,558,072
992,622	1,399,750	1,893,810	2,559,123	3,571,623	4,061,929	4,556,155	5,082,059	5,881,813
......	36,909	319,146	646,872	641,935	619,636	632,446	617,761	652,717
2,339,511	3,198,062	4,157,545	5,759,394	6,907,612	7,946,627	9,706,397	10,652,017	10,797,624
......	......	790,391	2,028,283	2,336,434	2,233,351	2,328,284	2,559,253	3,025,290
52,465	174,768	413,536	783,389	1,089,684	1,521,341	1,768,687	2,091,385	2,633,149
2,906,215	4,282,891	6,302,115	8,720,017	9,900,180	10,498,012	11,319,366	11,793,909	11,863,895
174,620	276,531	428,556	604,397	713,346	791,896	859,488	949,723	947,154
703,708	995,577	1,340,316	1,683,724	1,899,804	2,117,027	2,382,594	2,590,516	3,121,833
4,837	98,268	401,570	636,547	642,961	652,740	680,514	666,257	690,768
1,109,801	1,542,359	2,020,616	2,337,885	2,915,841	3,291,718	3,567,089	3,924,164	4,591,120
604,215	1,591,749	3,048,710	4,663,228	6,414,824	7,711,194	9,579,677	11,196,730	14,229,288
40,273	143,963	276,749	449,396	550,310	688,862	890,627	1,059,273	1,461,037
315,098	332,286	343,641	352,428	359,231	377,747	389,881	444,732	511,456
1,219,630	1,512,565	1,854,184	2,309,187	2,677,773	3,318,680	3,966,949	4,648,494	5,346,818
11,594	75,116	518,103	1,356,621	1,736,191	2,378,963	2,853,214	3,409,169	4,132,180
376,688	618,457	958,800	1,463,701	1,901,974	2,005,552	1,860,421	1,744,237	1,950,279
775,881	1,315,497	2,069,042	2,632,067	3,137,587	3,434,575	3,951,777	4,417,933	4,705,521
......	20,789	92,531	194,402	250,742	290,529	330,066	332,416	469,557
31,443,321	50,189,209	76,212,168	106,021,537	132,164,569	151,325,798	179,323,175	203,235,298	226,547,346

[4] Maine figures for 1770 through 1800 are for that area of Massachusetts which became the State of Maine in 1820. Massachusetts figures exclude Maine from 1770 through 1800, but include it from 1650 through 1750. Massachusetts figure for 1650 also includes population of Plymouth (1,566), a separate colony until 1691.

[5] Oklahoma figure for 1900 includes population of Indian Territory (392,060).

[6] West Virginia figures for 1790 through 1860 are for that area of Virginia which became West Virginia in 1863. These figures are excluded from the figures for Virginia from 1790 through 1860.

Largest Metropolitan Areas of the United States

This table ranks the largest cities of the United States according to metropolitan area population. The Ranally Metropolitan Area (RMA) populations reflect Rand McNally's exclusive definition of metropolitan areas. Each RMA includes one or more central cities, as well as socially and economically integrated surrounding areas. The table also indicates central city populations and compares the latest available data to the previous census. Populations are rounded totals. 1980 populations reflect final census data.

Rank 1980	Metropolitan Area	RMA Abbrev.	Metro Area Population Census 4/1/80	Metro Area Population Census 4/1/70	Metro Area Population %Change 1970-80	City Population Census 4/1/80	City Population %Change 1970-80
1	New York, NY-NJ-CT	N.Y.	16,573,600	17,326,300	−4.3	7,538,200	−10.5
	New York, NY					7,071,000	−10.4
	Newark, NJ					329,200	−13.8
	Paterson, NJ					138,000	−4.7
2	Los Angeles, CA	L.A.	9,840,200	8,716,600	12.9	2,966,800	5.5
3	Chicago, IL-IN-WI	CHI	7,803,800	7,676,200	1.7	3,005,100	−10.8
4	Philadelphia-, PA-NJ-DE-MD	PHIL-	5,153,900	5,285,400	−2.5	1,850,500	−13.3
	Philadelphia, PA					1,688,200	−13.4
	Trenton, NJ					92,100	−12.1
	Wilmington, DE					70,200	−12.7
5	San Francisco-Oakland-San Jose, CA	SF-O-	4,665,500	4,274,900	9.1	1,654,900	7.7
	San Francisco, CA					679,000	−5.1
	Oakland, CA					339,300	−6.2
	San Jose, CA					636,600	38.4
6	Detroit, MI-CAN.	DET	4,399,000	4,492,900	−2.1	1,310,600	−18.8
	Detroit, MI					1,203,300	−20.5
	Ann Arbor, MI					107,300	7.3
7	Boston, MA-NH	BOS	3,738,800	3,763,700	−.7	898,900	−8.1
	Boston, MA					563,000	−12.2
	Lowell, MA					92,400	−1.9
	Lawrence, MA					63,200	−5.5
	Haverhill, MA					46,900	1.7
	Brockton, MA					95,200	7.0
	Salem, MA					38,200	−5.9
8	Washington, DC-MD-VA	WASH	3,220,700	2,992,600	7.6	637,700	−15.7
9	Dallas-Fort Worth, TX	D-FW	2,811,800	2,263,200	24.2	1,289,200	4.1
	Dallas, TX					904,100	7.1
	Fort Worth, TX					385,100	−2.1
10	Houston, TX	HOU	2,689,200	1,871,100	43.7	1,594,100	29.2
11	Miami-Fort Lauderdale, FL	MIA-	2,689,100	1,914,400	40.5	500,200	5.4
	Miami, FL					346,900	3.6
	Fort Lauderdale, FL					153,300	9.8
12	Cleveland, OH	CLEV	2,218,300	2,360,600	−6.0	573,800	−23.6
13	St. Louis, MO-IL	ST. L	2,216,100	2,295,700	−3.5	453,100	−27.2
14	Pittsburgh, PA	PGH	2,165,100	2,302,600	−6.0	423,900	−18.5
15	Seattle-Tacoma, WA	SEAT-	2,077,100	1,823,500	13.9	706,700	−4.3
	Seattle, WA					493,800	−7.0
	Tacoma, WA					158,500	2.7
	Everett, WA					54,400	1.5
16	Minneapolis-St. Paul, MN-WI	MPLS-	1,978,000	1,869,100	5.8	641,300	−13.8
	Minneapolis, MN					371,000	−14.6
	St. Paul, MN					270,300	−12.8
17	Atlanta, GA	ATL	1,950,600	1,541,300	26.6	425,000	−14.1
18	Baltimore, MD	BAL	1,883,100	1,865,100	1.0	786,800	−13.1
19	San Diego, CA-MEX.	SDGO	1,597,000	1,206,800	32.3	875,500	25.5
20	Phoenix, AZ	PHOE	1,483,500	950,500	56.1	764,900	30.9
21	Cincinnati-, OH-KY-IN	CIN-	1,476,600	1,445,300	2.2	448,700	−13.9
	Cincinnati, OH					385,500	−15.0
	Hamilton, OH					63,200	−6.9

Rank 1980	Metropolitan Area	RMA Abbrev.	Metro Area Population Census 4/1/80	Metro Area Population Census 4/1/70	Metro Area Population %Change 1970-80	City Population Census 4/1/80	City Population %Change 1970-80
	Warren, OH					56,600	−10.9
60	Tuscon, AZ	TUC	495,200	324,800	52.5	330,500	25.7
61	Knoxville-, TN	KNOX-	490,000	419,400	16.8	228,300	5.4
	Knoxville, TN					183,100	4.9
	Maryville, TN					17,500	26.8
	Oak Ridge, TN					27,700	−2.1
62	Grand Rapids, MI	GDR	488,200	444,300	9.9	181,800	−8.0
63	Springfield-Holyoke, MA	SPRG-	485,800	498,300	−2.5	197,000	−7.9
	Springfield, MA					152,300	−7.1
	Holyoke, MA					44,700	−10.8
64	El Paso, TX-NM-MEX.	ELP	484,300	358,600	35.1	425,300	32.0
65	Charlotte, NC	CHRLT	479,200	416,800	15.0	314,400	30.2
66	Scranton Wilkes-Barre, PA	SCR-	467,400	478,300	−2.3	139,700	−13.6
	Scranton, PA					88,100	−14.2
	Wilkes-Barre, PA					51,600	−12.4
67	Albuquerque, NM	ALBU	445,400	327,400	36.0	331,800	35.7
68	Bridgeport, CT	BRDG	444,600	445,500	−.2	142,500	−8.9
69	Baton Rouge, LA	B.R.	441,800	337,400	30.9	219,500	32.3
70	Las Vegas, NV	LASV	441,600	261,900	68.6	164,700	30.9
71	South Bend-Elkhart, IN-MI	S.B.-	437,500	422,800	3.5	151,000	−10.5
	South Bend, IN					109,700	−12.7
	Elkhart, IN					41,300	−4.4
72	Austin, TX	AUS	422,700	292,800	44.4	345,500	36.3
73	Harrisburg, PA	HRBG	404,600	371,700	8.9	53,300	−21.7
74	West Palm Beach, FL	WPB	394,600	236,600	66.8	62,500	8.9
75	Little Rock, AR	L.R.	380,800	310,500	22.6	158,500	19.6
76	Fresno, CA	FRES	377,900	306,100	23.5	218,200	31.7
77	Greensboro-High Point, NC	GRNS-	371,100	334,100	11.1	219,700	6.0
	Greensboro, NC					155,600	8.0
	High Point, NC					64,100	1.4
78	Wichita, KS	WICH	367,400	350,400	4.9	279,300	1.0
79	Worcester, MA	WORC	361,200	358,100	.9	161,800	−8.4
80	Chattanooga, TN-GA	CHTN	360,000	317,300	13.5	169,600	41.5
81	Mobile, AL	MOB	353,500	305,900	15.6	200,500	5.5
82	Charleston, SC	CHAS	349,100	280,500	24.5	69,500	3.9
83	Columbia, SC	COL	345,000	286,000	20.6	99,300	−12.5
84	Beaumont-Port Arthur-Orange, TX	B-PA-O	339,400	315,600	7.5	202,900	1.8
	Beaumont, TX					118,100	.5
	Port Arthur, TX					61,200	6.6
	Orange, TX					23,600	−3.7
85	Greenville, SC	GRNV	329,400	266,900	23.4	58,200	−5.2
86	Lansing, MI	LANS	329,200	303,200	8.6	130,400	−.8
87	Davenport-Rock I.-Moline, IA-IL	D-RI-M	328,200	310,900	5.6	196,000	.6
	Davenport, IA					103,300	4.9
	Rock Island, IL					47,000	−6.4
	Moline, IL					45,700	−1.1
88	Des Moines, IA	DES	323,200	300,700	7.5	191,000	−5.2
89	Ventura-Oxnard, CA	V-OX	321,400	242,000	32.8	182,700	41.4
	Ventura, CA					74,500	28.4

24	Kansas City, MO-KS	K.C.	1,254,600	1,222,700	2.6	448,200	−9.8
25	Portland, OR-WA	POR	1,220,100	997,800	22.3	366,400	−3.6
26	New Orleans, LA	N.O.	1,175,800	1,042,000	12.8	557,500	−6.1
27	Buffalo-Niagara Falls, NY-CAN.	BUF-	1,154,600	1,265,200	−8.7	429,300	−21.7
	Buffalo, NY					357,900	−22.7
	Niagara Falls, NY					71,400	−16.6
28	Indianapolis, IN	IND	1,104,200	1,053,100	4.9	700,800	−6.2
29	Hartford-New Britain, CT	H-NB	1,055,700	1,039,100	1.6	210,200	−12.9
	Hartford, CT					136,400	−13.7
	New Britain, CT					73,800	−11.5
30	San Antonio, TX	SANT	1,012,300	846,600	19.6	785,400	20.1
31	Columbus, OH	COL	943,300	886,700	6.4	564,900	4.6
32	Dayton-Springfield, OH	DAY-	898,000	934,000	−3.9	276,200	−15.0
	Dayton, OH					203,600	−16.2
	Springfield, OH					72,600	−11.4
33	Providence-, RI-MA	PROV-	897,900	891,200	.8	273,900	−9.6
	Providence, RI					156,800	−12.5
	Pawtucket, RI					71,200	−7.5
	Woonsocket, RI					45,900	−1.9
34	Louisville, KY-IN	LOU	881,100	848,500	3.8	298,500	−17.5
35	Sacramento, CA	SAC	848,800	684,000	24.1	275,700	7.2
36	Memphis, TN-AR-MS	MEM	843,200	772,400	9.2	646,400	3.6
37	Rochester, NY	ROCH	809,500	805,400	.5	241,700	−18.1
38	Norfolk-Portsmouth, VA	NORF-	795,600	725,800	9.6	371,600	−11.3
	Norfolk, VA					267,000	−13.3
	Portsmouth, VA					104,600	−5.8
39	Honolulu, HI	HON	762,900	630,500	21.0	365,000	12.3
40	Oklahoma City, OK	O.C.	742,000	627,300	18.3	403,200	9.5
41	Albany-Schenectady-Troy, NY	A-S-T	740,300	727,000	1.8	226,300	−11.8
	Albany, NY					101,700	−12.2
	Schenectady, NY					68,000	−12.8
	Troy, NY					56,600	−10.0
42	San Bernardino-Riverside, CA	SBDO-	715,300	577,000	24.0	289,000	17.0
	San Bernardino, CA					118,100	10.5
	Riverside, CA					170,900	22.0
43	St. Petersburg-, FL	ST. PET-	699,800	509,300	37.4	322,400	20.2
	St. Petersburg, FL					236,900	9.6
	Clearwater, FL					85,500	64.1
44	Birmingham, AL	BIR	697,900	666,200	4.8	284,400	−5.5
45	Salt Lake City, UT	S.L.C.	686,200	503,700	36.2	163,000	−7.3
46	Jacksonville, FL	JAX	615,300	548,500	12.2	540,900	7.3
47	Akron, OH	AKR	614,100	635,300	−3.3	237,200	−13.9
48	Nashville, TN	NASH	608,400	520,100	17.0	455,700	7.0
49	Tampa, FL	TAM	573,100	442,700	29.5	271,500	−2.2
50	Toledo, OH-MI	TOL	571,200	566,600	.8	354,600	−7.4
51	Tulsa, OK	TUL	569,100	460,300	23.6	360,900	−9.2
52	Orlando, FL	ORL	568,300	367,400	54.7	128,400	29.7
53	Flint, MI	FLN	550,200	523,300	5.1	159,600	−17.4
54	Omaha-Council Bluffs, NE-IA	OMA-	548,400	525,500	4.4	368,100	−9.6
	Omaha, NE					311,700	−10.1
	Council Bluffs, IA					56,400	−6.5
55	Richmond, VA	RICH	548,100	494,500	10.8	219,200	−12.1
56	Syracuse, NY	SYR	546,200	546,900	−.1	170,100	−13.8
57	Allentown-Bethlehem-Easton, PA-NJ	AL-B-E	534,200	504,300	5.9	200,200	−5.6
	Allentown, PA					103,800	−5.6
	Bethlehem, PA					70,400	−3.2
	Easton, PA					26,000	−11.9
58	New Haven-Meriden, CT	N. HAV-	500,500	488,700	2.4	183,200	−5.4
	New Haven, CT					126,100	−8.4
	Meriden, CT					57,100	2.0
59	Youngstown-Warren, OH-PA	YNGS-	497,000	505,400	−1.7	172,000	−15.9
	Youngstown, OH					115,400	−18.1

91	Spokane, WA-ID	[illegible]	[illegible]	[illegible]	[illegible]	[illegible]	[illegible]
92	Newport News-Hampton, VA	NN-H	314,600	299,100	5.2	267,500	3.3
	Newport News, VA					144,900	4.8
	Hampton, VA					122,600	1.5
93	Canton-Massillon, OH	CAN-	311,200	311,100	.0	125,300	−12.1
	Canton, OH					94,700	−14.0
	Massillon, OH					30,600	−5.8
94	Fort Wayne, IN	FTWA	307,700	292,500	5.2	172,200	−3.4
95	Colorado Springs, CO	CSPG	303,500	230,600	31.6	215,200	58.8
96	Shreveport, LA-TX	SHRE	299,000	266,500	12.2	205,800	13.0
97	Jackson, MS	JAC	295,000	238,800	23.5	202,900	31.8
98	Stockton, CA	STOC	291,500	241,800	20.6	149,800	36.2
99	Madison, WI	MAD	287,300	259,600	10.7	170,600	−.7
100	Sarasota-Bradenton, FL	SAR-B	284,200	187,800	51.3	79,100	29.2
	Sarasota, FL					48,900	21.6
	Bradenton, FL					30,200	43.8
101	Raleigh, NC	RAL	282,800	216,900	30.4	149,800	22.0
102	Winston-Salem, NC	WNS	278,400	236,700	17.6	131,900	−1.3
103	Corpus Christi, TX	CRPX	277,100	243,800	13.7	232,000	13.4
104	Lexington, KY	LEX	262,900	217,900	20.7	204,200	88.9
105	Huntington-Ashland, WV-KY-OH	HNTG-	261,900	248,200	5.5	90,800	−12.3
	Huntington, WV					63,700	−14.3
	Ashland, KY					27,100	−7.2
106	Utica-Rome, NY	UT-R	259,900	281,800	−7.8	119,400	−15.6
	Utica, NY					75,600	−17.3
	Rome, NY					43,800	−12.6
107	Charleston, WV	CHAS	249,300	238,800	4.4	64,000	−10.5
108	Rockford, IL	RKFD	247,500	244,900	1.1	139,700	−5.2
109	New London-Norwich, CT-RI	N. LON-	244,600	237,600	2.9	66,900	−8.7
	New London, CT					28,800	−8.9
	Norwich, CT					38,100	−8.6
110	Binghamton, NY-PA	BING	240,500	248,600	−3.3	55,900	−12.8
111	Augusta, GA-SC	AUG	238,200	209,500	13.7	47,500	−20.7
112	Erie, PA	ERIE	237,300	228,100	4.0	119,100	−7.9
113	Fayetteville, NC	FAY	236,200	202,700	16.5	59,500	11.2
114	Macon-, GA	MAC-	235,900	209,700	12.5	156,800	.6
	Macon, GA					116,900	−4.5
	Warner Robins, GA					39,900	19.1
115	Columbus, GA-AL	COL	235,100	231,600	1.5	169,400	1.7
116	Bakersfield, CA	BAK	231,700	187,600	23.5	105,600	51.9
117	Poughkeepsie, NY	POK	231,200	205,300	12.6	29,800	−6.9
118	Evansville, IN-KY	EV	230,400	214,100	7.6	130,500	−6.0
119	Pensacola, FL	PENS	229,200	199,000	15.2	57,600	−3.2
120	Portland, ME	POR	225,200	203,500	10.7	61,600	−5.4
121	Kalamazoo, MI	KZOO	223,600	208,800	7.1	79,700	−6.9
122	Montgomery, AL	MTGY	223,600	183,400	21.9	178,200	33.6
123	Ogden, UT	OGD	221,700	175,500	26.3	64,400	−7.3
124	York, PA	YORK	220,000	199,100	10.5	44,600	−11.3
125	Eugene, OR	EUG	216,900	171,400	26.5	105,600	33.7
126	Provo, UT	PRVO	214,400	133,500	60.6	73,900	39.2
127	Oceanside-Vista, CA	OC-V	214,100	130,900	63.6	112,500	72.5
	Oceanside, CA					76,700	89.4
	Vista, CA					35,800	44.9
128	Waterbury, CT	WATB	213,900	204,100	4.8	103,300	−4.4
129	Reading, PA	READ	213,500	212,400	.5	78,700	−10.2
130	Roanoke, VA	ROAN	213,300	190,500	12.0	100,400	9.0
131	Savannah, GA	SAV	210,400	192,900	9.1	141,600	19.7
132	Lancaster, PA	LANC	209,700	189,200	10.8	54,700	−5.2
133	Huntsville, AL	HNTS	203,800	193,000	5.6	142,500	2.3
134	Durham-Chapel Hill, NC	DUR-	203,100	170,000	19.5	133,200	9.5
	Durham, NC					100,800	5.7
	Chapel Hill, NC					32,400	23.7

Guide to Major United States Cities

This alphabetical guide lists geographical and travel information for major United States cities. Included are area codes, time zones, hotels and restaurants, sources for additional information, and other details.

Atlanta, Georgia

Altitude: 1,050 feet
Average Temp.: Jan., 52°F.; July, 85°F.
Telephone Area Number: 404
Time & Weather: 936-8550
Time Zone: Eastern
Selected Hotels:
Atlanta American, 160 Spring St., 688-8600
Atlanta Hilton & Towers, Courtland & Harris sts., 659-2000
Atlanta Marriott Hotel, Courtland St. at International Blvd., 659-6500
Colony Square, 14th & Peachtree sts., 892-6000
Hilton Inn (Atlanta Airport), 1031 Virginia Ave., 767-0281
Holiday Inn—Airport, 1380 Virginia Ave., 762-8411
Howard Johnson's Airport, 1377 Virginia Ave., 762-5111
Hyatt Regency—Atlanta, 265 Peachtree Center, 577-1234
Marriott at Perimeter Center, 246 Perimeter Center Pkwy., 394-6500
Omni International/Atlanta Hotel, One Omni International, 659-0000
Sheraton-Atlanta Hotel, 590 W. Peachtree St., 881-6000
Stone Mountain Inn, U.S. 78, Stone Mountain Pk., 469-3311
Westin Peachtree Plaza Hotel, Peachtree St. at International Blvd., 659-1400
Selected Restaurants:
The Abbey, 163 Ponce de Leon Ave., 876-8532
Bugatti's, Omni International Hotel, 659-0000
Cafe de la Paix, 255 Courtland St., 659-2000
Coach And Six, 1776 Peachtree St. NW, 872-6666
Diplomat, 230 Spring St. NW, 525-6375
Garden Tree, 3405 Lenox Rd. NE, 261-9250
Hugo's, 265 Peachtree St. NE, 577-1234
La Grotta, 2637 Peachtree St. NE, 231-1368
The Midnight Sun, 225 Peachtree St. NE, 577-5050
Nikolai's Roof, 255 Courtland St., 659-2000
Pano's and Paul's, 1232 W. Paces Ferry Rd. NW, 261-3662
Airport Transportation:
Eight miles to downtown Atlanta.
Taxicab and limousine bus service.
Trade Exhibition Facilities:
Atlanta Civic Center, 395 Piedmont Ave. NE, 523-1879
Atlanta Market Center, 240 Peachtree St. NW, 688-8994
Georgia World Congress Center, 285 International Blvd., 656-4150
The Omni, 100 Techwood Dr. NW, 681-2161
Peachtree Center, 225 Peachtree St. NE, 659-0800
Information Sources:
Atlanta Convention & Visitors Bureau
Suite 200, 233 Peachtree St. NE
Atlanta, Georgia 30343
(404) 521-6600
Atlanta Chamber of Commerce
1300 N. Omni International
Atlanta, Georgia 30303
(404) 521-0845

Baltimore, Maryland

Altitude: Sea level to 489 feet
Average Temp.: Jan., 37°F.; July, 79°F.
Telephone Area Number: 301
Time: 844-1212 **Weather**: 936-1212
Time Zone: Eastern
Selected Hotels:
Baltimore Hilton Inn, 1726 Reisterstown Rd., Pikesville, 653-1100
Belvedere, 1 E. Chase St., 332-1000
Cross Keys Inn, 5100 Falls Rd., 532-6900
International Hotel, Airport, 859-3300
Hilton Baltimore, 101 W. Fayette St., 752-1100
Holiday Inn—Inner Harbor, Howard & Lombard sts., 685-3500
Hyatt Regency Baltimore, 300 Light St., 528-1234
Marriott's Hunt Valley Inn, Shawan Rd., Hunt Valley, 666-700
Ramada Hotel and Conference Center-Baltimore, Belmont Ave. at Security Blvd., 265-1100
Selected Restaurants:
Crossroads, in Cross Keys Inn Hotel, 532-6900
Danny's, 1201 N. Charles St., 539-13
Gordon's, 1017 Reisterstown Rd., Pikesville, 484-8343
Harvey House, 920 N. Charles St., 539-3110
Haussner's, 3244 Eastern Ave., 327-8365
John Eager Howard Room, 1 Chase St., 539-7110
The Prime Rib, 1101 N. Calvert St., 539-1804
Thompson's Sea Girt House, 5919 York Rd., 435-1800
Tio Pepe, 10 E. Franklin St., 539-4675
Airport Transportation:
Ten miles to downtown Baltimore.
Taxicab and limousine bus service.
Trade Exhibition Facilities:
Civic Center, 201 W. Baltimore St., 837-0903
Convention Center, One W. Pratt St., 659-7000
Information Sources:
Baltimore Office of Promotion and Tourism
110 W. Baltimore St.
Baltimore, Maryland 21201
(301) 752-8632 or 837-4636
Greater Baltimore Committee
Mercantile Building
Suite 900, 2 Hopkins Plaza
Baltimore, Maryland 21201
(301) 727-2820

Boston, Massachusetts

Altitude: Sea level to 330 feet
Average Temp: Jan., 29°F.; July, 72°F
Telephone Area Number: 617
Time: 637-1234 **Weather**: 936-1234
Time Zone: Eastern
Selected Hotels:
The Colonnade Hotel, 120 Huntington Ave., 424-7000
Copley Plaza Hotel, Copley Square, 267-5300
Logan Airport Hilton, Logan International Airport, 569-9300

Meridien, 250 Franklin St., 451-1900
Parker House, 60 School St., 227-8600
Ritz-Carlton Hotel, Arlington & Newbury sts., 536-5700
Selected Restaurants:
Anthony's Pier 4, 140 Northern Ave., 423-6363
Apley's Prudential Center, 236-2000
Cafe Budapest, 90 Exeter St., 734-3388
Cafe Plaza, 138 St. James Ave., 267-5300
Copley Plaza, 138 St. James Ave., 267-5300
Felicia's, 145A Richmond St., 523-9885
Genji, 327 Newbury St., 261-5656
Hermitage, 955 Boylston St., 267-3652
Julien, 250 Franklin St., 451-1900
Locke-Ober, 3 Winter Pl., 542-1340
Maison Robert, Old City Hall, 45 School St., 227-3370
Parker's, 60 School St., 227-8600
Ritz Carlton, Arlington & Newbury sts., 536-5700
Stella, 74 E. India Row, Harbor Tower Apartments, 227-3559
Airport Transportation:
Three miles to downtown Boston.
Taxicab and limousine bus service.
Trade Exhibition Facilities:
Bayside Exposition Center, 200 Mt. Vernon St., 265-5800
John B. Hynes Veterans Auditorium, 900 Boylston St., 262-8000
Northeast Trade Center, 100 Sylvan Rd., Woburn, 935-8090
Suffolk Downs, East Boston, 567-3900
Information Sources:
Greater Boston Convention & Tourist Bureau, Inc.
Prudential Plaza West, Box 490
Boston, Massachusetts 02199
(617) 536-4100
Greater Boston Chamber of Commerce
125 High St.
Boston, Massachusetts 02110
(617) 426-1250

Buffalo, New York

Altitude: 570 to 699 feet
Average Temp.: Jan., 26°F.; July, 71°F.
Telephone Area Number: 716
Time: 976-1616 **Weather:** 976-1212
Time Zone: Eastern
Selected Hotels:
Best Western Motor Inn, 510 Delaware Ave., 886-8333
Buffalo Hilton, Church and Terrace sts., 845-5100
Buffalo Marriott Inn, 1340 Millersport Hwy., Amherst, 689-6900
Holiday Inn-Intl Airport, 4600 Genesee St., Cheektowaga, 634-6969
Holiday Inn-Gateway, Rossler & Dingens sts., 896-2900
Holiday Inn Downtown, 620 Delaware Ave., 886-2121
Howard Johnson's, 6700 Transit Rd., Williamsville, 634-7500
Howard Johnson's Motor Lodge-Airport, 4217 Genesee St., Cheektowaga, 633-5500
Ramada Inn Buffalo, 6643 Transit Rd., Williamsville, 634-2700
Sheraton Inn-Buffalo East, 2040 Walden Ave., Cheektowaga, 681-2400
Williamsville Inn, 5447 Main St., Williamsville, 634-1111
Selected Restaurants:
Asa Ransom House, 10529 Main St., 759-2315
Cloister, 472 Delaware Ave., 886-0070
Daffodil's, 930 Maple Rd., 688-5413
Justine's, Church & Terrace sts., 845-5100
Old Red Mill Inn, 8326 Main St., Williamsville, 633-7878
Park Lane Manor House, 33 Gates Circle, 885-3250
Valentine's, 91 Niagara St., 856-8373
Airport Transportation:
Nine miles to downtown Buffalo.
Taxicab and limousine bus service.
Trade Exhibition Facilities:
Memorial Auditorium, 140 Main St., 855-5660
Buffalo Convention Center, Convention Center Plaza, 855-5514
Information Sources:
Buffalo Area Chamber of Commerce/ Convention and Visitors Bureau
107 Delaware Ave.
Buffalo, New York 14202
(716) 849-6677

Chicago, Illinois

Altitude: 579 to 672 feet
Average Temp.: Jan., 27°F.; July, 75°F.
Telephone Area Number: 312
Time: 976-1616 **Weather:** 976-1212
Time Zone: Central
Selected Hotels:
Ambassador East, 1301 N. State Pkwy., 787-7200
Ambassador West, 1300 N. State Pkwy., 787-7900
Barclay Chicago, 166 E. Superior, 787-6000
Chicago Marriott, 540 N. Michigan Ave., 836-0100
Drake Hotel, 140 E. Walton Place, 787-2200
Holiday Inn, 644 N. Lake Shore Dr., 943-9200; 350 N. Orleans St., 836-5000
Hyatt Regency Chicago, 151 E. Wacker Dr., 565-1234
Hyatt Regency O'Hare, River Rd. & Kennedy Expwy., 696-1234
Marriott O'Hare, 8535 W. Higgins Rd., 693-4444
Mayfair Regent, 181 E. Lakeshore Dr., 787-8500
Palmer House, 17 E. Monroe St., 726-7500
Park Hyatt, 800 N. Michigan Ave., 280-2222
Ritz-Carlton, 160 E. Pearson St., 266-1000
Tremont Hotel, 100 E. Chestnut St., 751-1900
The Westin, 909 N. Michigan Ave., 943-7200
Whitehall, 105 E. Delaware Pl., 944-6300
Selected Restaurants:
The Bakery, 2218 N. Lincoln Ave., 472-6942
Biggs, 1150 N. Dearborn Pkwy., 787-0900
Blackhawk, 139 N. Wabash Ave., 726-0100
Cape Cod Room, 140 E. Walton St., 787-2200
Cricket's, 100 E. Chestnut, 751-1900
Gordon, 512 N. Clark, 467-9780
La Tour, 800 N. Michigan Ave., 280-2222
Le Perroquet, 70 E. Walton Pl., 944-7990
Nick's Fishmarket, 1 First National Plaza, 621-0200
Ninety-Fifth, 172 E. Chestnut, 787-9596
Pump Room, 1300 N. State Pkwy., 266-0360
Truffles, 151 E. Wacker Dr., 565-1234
Airport Transportation:
Nineteen miles from O'Hare to downtown Chicago; 10 miles from Midway to downtown.
Taxicab and limousine bus service from both airports; also bus/rapid transit from O'Hare.
Trade Exhibition Facilities:
Apparel Center, 350 N. Orleans St., 527-4141
McCormick Place-on-the-Lake, lakefront at 23rd St., 791-7000
Navy Pier, lakefront at Grand Ave., 744-4000
O'Hare International Trade & Exposition Center, 9291 W. Bryn Mawr Ave., Rosemont, 692-2220
Arlington Park Convention-Exposition Center, Euclid Ave. & Rohlwing Rd., Arlington Heights, 394-2000
Information Sources:
Chicago Convention & Tourism Bureau
McCormick Place-on-the-Lake
Chicago, Illinois 60616
(312) 225-5000
Chicago Association of Commerce and Industry
130 S. Michigan Ave.
Chicago, Illinois 60603
(312) 786-0111

Cincinnati, Ohio

Altitude: 433 to 960 feet
Average Temp.: Jan., 35°F.; July, 78°F.
Telephone Area Number: 513
Time: 721-1700 **Weather**: 936-4850
Time Zone: Eastern
Selected Hotels:
Carrousel Inn, 8001 Reading Rd., 821-5110
Harley, 8020 Montgomery Rd., 793-4300
Hilton Inn, Sharonville, U.S. 42 & I-275, 563-8330
Howard Johnson's North, 11440 Chester Rd., 771-3400
Imperial House-West, 5510 Rybolt Rd., 574-6000
Marriott Inn, 11320 Chester Rd., 772-1720
Stouffer's Cincinnati Towers, 141 W. 6th St., 352-2100
Terrace Hilton, 15 W. 6th St., 381-4000
Vernon Manor, 400 Oak St., 281-3300
The Westin, Fountain Square, 5th & Vine, 621-7700
Selected Restaurants:
Celestial, 1071 Celestial St., 241-4455
Gourmet Room, Terrace Hilton, 15 W. 6th St., 381-4000
La Normandie Taverne & Chop House, 118 E. 6th St., 721-2761
Maisonette, 114 E. 6th St., 721-2260
Millcroft, 203 Mill St., Milford, 831-8654
Pigall's, 127 W. 4th St., 721-1345
Windjammer, 11330 Chester Rd., 771-3777
Airport Transportation:
Thirteen miles to downtown Cincinnati.
Taxicab and limousine bus service.
Trade Exhibition Facility:
Cincinnati Convention Exposition Center, 525 Elm St., 352-3750
Information Sources:
Greater Cincinnati Convention and Visitors Bureau
200 W. Fifth St.
Cincinnati, Ohio 45202
(513) 621-2142
Greater Cincinnati Chamber of Commerce
120 W. Fifth St.
Cincinnati, Ohio 45202
(513) 579-3100

Cleveland, Ohio

Altitude: 570 to 1,050 feet
Average Temp.: Jan., 29°F.; July, 74°F.
Telephone Area Number: 216
Time: 471-1212 **Weather**: 931-1212
Time Zone: Eastern
Selected Hotels:
Bond Court Hotel, E. 6th St. & St. Clair Ave., 771-7600
Harley Hotel East, 6041 SOM Center Rd., Willoughby, 944-4300
Harley Hotel West, 17000 Bagley Rd., 243-5200
Hilton Inn South, Int. 77 & Rockside Rd., 447-1300
Holiday Inn Lakeside City Center, Lakeside Ave. at E. 12th St., 241-5100
Hollenden House, E. 6th St. at Superior Ave., 621-0700
Marriott Inn Airport, Int. 71 & 150th St., 252-5333
Marriott Inn Cleveland East, Int. 271 & Chagrin Blvd., Beachwood, 464-5950
Sheraton Inn Airport, 5300 Riverside Dr., 267-1500
Stouffer's Inn on the Square, 24 Public Sq., 696-5600
Stouffer's Somerset Inn, 3550 Northfield Rd., Shaker Heights, 752-5600
Selected Restaurants:
Bit of Budapest, 6355 Pearl Rd., Parma Heights, 845-2660
Blue Fox, 11706 Clifton Blvd., 221-4388
Earth by April, 2151 Lee Rd., Cleveland Heights, 371-1438
French Connection, 24 Public Sq., 696-5600
Hollenden Tavern, E. 6th St. at Superior, 621-0700
Keg & Quarter, 1800 Euclid Ave., 861-5501
Samurai Japanese Steak House, 23611 Chagrin Blvd., Beachwood, 464-7575
That Place on Bellflower, 11401 Bellflower Rd., 231-4469
Airport Transportation:
Twelve miles from Hopkins to downtown Cleveland.
Taxicab, train, and limousine bus service.
Trade Exhibition Facility:
Cleveland Convention Center, 1220 E. 6th St., 523-2200
Information Sources:
Cleveland Convention and Visitors Bureau
1301 E. 6th St.
Cleveland, Ohio 44114
(216) 621-4110
Greater Cleveland Growth Association
690 Union Commerce Building
East 9th & Euclid sts.
Cleveland, Ohio 44115
(216) 621-3300

Columbus, Ohio

Altitude: 685 to 893 feet
Average Temp.: Jan., 31°F.; July, 76°F.
Telephone Area Number: 614
Time and Weather: 281-8211
Time Zone: Eastern
Selected Hotels:
The Christopher Inn, 300 E. Broad St., 228-3541
Harley Hotel, 1000 E. Granville Rd., 888-4300
Hilton Inn North, 7007 N. High St., 436-0700
Hilton Inn East, 4560 Hilton Lane, 868-1380
Holiday Inn Airport, 750 Stelzer Rd., 237-6360
Holiday Inn on the Lake, 328 W. Lane Ave., 294-4848
Hyatt Regency Columbus, 350 N. High St., 463-1234
Marriott Inn East, 2124 S. Hamilton Rd., 861-7220
Marriott Inn North, 6560 Doubletree Ave., 885-1885
Sheraton-Columbus Hotel, 50 N. 3rd St., 228-6060
Sheraton Inn Airport, 4300 E. 17th Ave., 237-2515
Sheraton Inn North, 888 E. Dublin-Granville Rd., 888-8230
University Hilton Inn, 3110 Olentangy River Rd., 267-7461
Selected Restaurants:
Casa Gallardo, 2600 S. Hamilton Rd., 866-0100
The Clarmont, 684 High St., 443-1125
Isabella's, 300 E. Broad St., 461-0768
Jai Lai, 1421 Olentangy River Rd., 421-7337
Kahiki, 3583 E. Broad St., 237-5425
L'Armagnac, 121 S. Sixth St., 221-4046
Oliver's Tavern, 3025 Olentangy River Rd., 267-0355
Ollie's Grandview Inn, 1127 Dublin Rd., 486-2419
One Nation, One Nationwide Plaza, 221-0001
Ziggy's, 3140 Riverside Dr., 488-0605
Airport Transportation:
Eight miles to downtown Columbus.
Taxicab and limousine bus service.
Trade Exhibition Facility:
Veterans Memorial Building, 300 W. Broad St., 463-9729, 224-7615
Information Sources:
Greater Columbus Convention & Visitors Bureau
50 W. Broad St.
Columbus, Ohio 43215
(614) 221-6623
Columbus Area Chamber of Commerce

0 W. Broad St.
Columbus, Ohio 43215
(614) 221-1321

Dallas, Texas

Altitude: 450 to 750 feet
Average Temp.: Jan., 44°F.; July, 86°F.
Telephone Area Number: 214
Time: 844-6611 **Weather**: 993-2626
Time Zone: Central
Selected Hotels:
Adolphus Hotel, 1321 Commerce St., 747-6411
AMFAC Hotel & Resort, Dallas-Ft. Worth Airport, 453-8400
Dallas Hilton Hotel, 1914 Commerce St., 747-2011
Fairmont Hotel, 1717 N. Akard St., Ross & Akard sts., 748-5454
Hilton Inn, 5600 N. Central Expwy., 827-4100
Howard Johnson's–Stemmons, 3111 Stemmons Frwy., 637-0060
Hyatt Regency Dallas, 300 Reunion Blvd., 651-1234
Ramada Hotel–Market Center, 1055 Regal Row, 634-8550
Loew's Anatole Dallas, 2201 Stemmons Frwy., 748-1200
Mandalay Four Seasons, 221 S. Colinas Blvd., Irving, 556-0800
Mansion on Turtle Creek, 2821 Turtle Creek Blvd., 559-2100
Marriott Market Center, 2101 Stemmons Frwy., 748-8551
Plaza of the Americas Hotel, 605 N. Pearl Blvd., 747-7222
Sheraton Park Central, 12580 Park Central Pl., 385-3000
Westin, 13340 Dallas Pkwy., 934-9494
Wyndham, 2222 Stemmons Frwy., 631-2222
Selected Restaurants:
Cafe Royale, Plaza of the Americas Hotel, 747-7222
Fausto's, Hyatt Regency, 300 Reunion Blvd., 651-1234
Il Sorrento, 8616 Turtle Creek Lane, 352-8759
L'Entrecote, 2201 Stemmons Frwy., 748-1200
Mr. Peppe, 5617 W. Lovers Lane, 352-5976
Old Warsaw, 2610 Maple Ave., 528-0032
Plum Blossom, 2201 Stemmons Frwy., 748-1200
Pyramid Room, Fairmont Hotel, 748-5454
Airport Transportation:
Seventeen miles from Dallas-Ft. Worth Airport to downtown Dallas.
Taxicab and limousine bus service.
Trade Exhibition Facilities:
Dallas Convention Center, 650 S. Griffin, 658-7000
State Fair Park, Dallas Fair Park, 565-9931
Dallas Market Center, 2100 Stemmons Frwy., 651-6100
Information Sources:
Dallas Convention & Visitors Bureau
1507 Pacific Ave.
Dallas, Texas 75201
(214) 954-1482
Dallas Visitor Information Center
400 S. Houston St., 747-2355
Dallas Chamber of Commerce
Information Department
1507 Pacific Ave.
Dallas, Texas 75201
(214) 954-1111

Denver, Colorado

Altitude: 5,130 to 5,470 feet
Average Temp.: Jan., 31°F.; July, 74°F.
Telephone Area Number: 303
Time: 639-1311 **Weather**: 639-1311
Time Zone: Mountain
Selected Hotels:
The Brown Palace Hotel, 321 17th St., 297-3111
Denver Hilton Hotel, 16th St. & Court Pl., 893-3333
Denver Marriott, 6363 E. Hampden Ave., 758-7000
Fairmont Hotel, 1750 Welton St., 571-1200
Hampshire House, 1000 Grant St., 837-1200
Holiday Inn Downtown, 1450 Glenarm Pl., 573-1450
Ramada Renaissance, 3200 S. Parker Rd., 695-1700
Stapleton Plaza, 3333 Quebec St., 525-1315
Stouffer's Denver Inn, 3203 Quebec St., 321-3333
Selected Restaurants:
Cafe Promenade, 1430 Larimer St., 893-2692
Churchills, 1730 S. Colorado Blvd., 756-8877
Dudley's, 1120 E. 6th Ave., 744-8634
Normandy French Restaurant, 1515 Madison St., 321-3311
Oak Room, at Stouffer's Denver Inn, 377-6122
Palace Arms, at the Brown Palace Hotel, 297-3111
San Marco Room, 321 17th St., 297-3111
Tante Louise, 4900 E. Colfax Ave., 355-4488
Airport Transportation:
Seven miles to downtown Denver.
Bus, taxicab, and limousine bus service.
Trade Exhibition Facilities:
Denver Convention Complex, 1323 Champa St., 575-2637
Denver Merchandise Mart, 451 E. 58th Ave., 292-6278
Information Sources:
Denver & Colorado Convention and Visitors Bureau
225 W. Colfax Ave.
Denver, Colorado 80202
(303) 892-1112
Denver Chamber of Commerce
1301 Welton St.
Denver, Colorado 80204
(303) 534-3211

Detroit, Michigan

Altitude: 573 to 672 feet
Average Temp.: Jan., 26°F.; July, 73°F.
Telephone Area Number: 313
Time: 472-1212 **Weather**: 976-1111
Time Zone: Eastern
Selected Hotels:
Book Cadillac Hotel
1114 Washington Blvd., 256-8000
Hilton Airport Inn, 31500 Wick Rd., Romulus, 292-3400
Holiday Inn Airport, 31200 Industrial Expwy., 728-2800
Hotel Pontchartrain, 2 Washington Blvd., 965-0200
Hotel St. Regis, 3071 W. Grand Blvd., 873-3000
Hyatt Regency Dearborn, Fairlane Town Center, Dearborn, 593-1234
Michigan Inn, 16400 J.L. Hudson Dr., Southfield, 559-6500
Northfield Hilton Inn, 5500 Crooks Rd. at Int. 75, Troy, 879-2100
Troy Hilton Inn, 1455 Stephenson Hwy., Troy, 583-9000
Westin, Renaissance Center, 568-8000
Selected Restaurants:
Anton's, 20930 Mack Ave., Grosse Point Woods, 886-6190
Carl's Chop House, 3024 Grand River Ave., 833-0700
Caucus Club, 150 W. Congress St., 965-4970
Charley's Crab, 5500 Crooks Rd., Troy, 879-2060
Golden Mushroom, 18100 W. 10 Mile Rd., Southfield, 559-4230
London Chop House, 155 W. Congress St., 962-0277
Top of the Pontch, in the Hotel Pontchartrain, 965-0200
Van Dyke Place, 649 Van Dyke St., 821-2620
Victoria Station, 28565 Northwestern Hwy., Southfield, 357-4424
Airport Transportation:
Nineteen miles from Metropolitan Airport to downtown Detroit.
Taxicab and limousine bus service.

Trade Exhibition Facilities:
Cobo Hall, 1 Washington Blvd., 224-1010
Detroit Light Guard Armory, 4400 E. 8 Mile Rd., 366-8900
Masonic Temple, 500 Temple St., 832-2232
State Fairgrounds, 1120 W. State Fair St., 368-1000
Information Sources:
Metropolitan Detroit Convention & Visitors Bureau
Suite 1950, 100 Renaissance Center
Detroit, Michigan 48243
(313) 259-4333
Detroit Visitor Information Center
2 E. Jefferson Ave., Civic Center
Detroit, Michigan 48226
(313) 567-1170
Greater Detroit Chamber of Commerce
150 Michigan Ave.
Detroit, Michigan 48226
(313) 964-4000

Hartford, Connecticut

Altitude: 10 to 290 feet
Average Temp.: Jan., 28°F.; July, 74°F.
Telephone Area Number: 203
Time Zone: Eastern **Time:** 524-8123
Selected Hotels:
Holiday Inn, Morgan & Market sts., 549-2400
Marriott-Farmington, 15 Farm Springs Rd., Farmington, 678-1000
Parkview Hilton, 1 Hilton Plaza, 249-5611
Ramada Hotel, 100 E. River Dr., E. Hartford, 528-9703
Sheraton-Hartford, Trumbull St. at Civic Center Plaza, 728-5151
Selected Restaurants:
Adajian's, 297 Asylum St., 524-5181
Blacksmith's Tavern, 2300 Main St., 659-0366
Carbone's Ristorante, 588 Franklin Ave., 249-9646
Cloister, Trumbull St. at Civic Center Plaza, 728-5151
Gaetano's, One Civic Center Plaza, 249-1629
Market, 3900 New London Tpke. Ext., Glastonbury, 633-3832
Parson's Daughter, 2 Hopewell Rd., S. Glastonbury, 633-8698
Airport Transportation:
Thirteen miles to downtown Hartford.
Taxicab and limousine bus service.
Trade Exhibition Facilities:
Hartford Armory, 130 Broad St., 566-4210
Hartford Civic Center, One Civic Center Plaza, 728-8080
West Hartford Armory, 836 Farmington Ave., 523-7246
Information Sources:
Greater Hartford Convention & Visitors Bureau, Inc.
One Civic Center Plaza
Hartford, Connecticut 06103
(203) 728-6789
Greater Hartford Chamber of Commerce
250 Constitution Plaza
Hartford, Connecticut 06103
(203) 525-4451

Honolulu, Hawaii

Altitude: Sea level to 4020 feet
Average Temp.: Jan., 72°F.; July, 80°F.
Telephone Area Number: 808
Time: 983-2311 **Weather:** 836-0234
Time Zone: Hawaiian (Two hours earlier than Pacific standard time)
Selected Hotels:
Halekulani, 2199 Kalia Rd., 923-2311
Hawaiian Regent, 2552 Kalakaua Ave., 922-6611
Hilton Hawaiian Village, 2005 Kalia Rd., 949-4321
Hyatt Regency Waikiki, 2424 Kalakaua Ave., 922-9292
Ilikai, 1777 Ala Moana Ave., 949-3811
Kahala Hilton, 5000 Kahala Ave., 734-2211
Moana Hotel, 2365 Kalakaua Ave., 923-3111
Outrigger, 2335 Kalakaua Ave., 923-0711
Princess Kaiulani, 120 Kaiulani Ave., 922-5811
Queen Kapiolani, 150 Kapahulu Ave., 922-1941
Royal Hawaiian, 2259 Kalakaua Ave., 923-7311
Surfrider, 2353 Kalakaua Ave., 922-3111
Selected Restaurants:
Canlis, 2100 Kalakaua Ave., 923-2324
Cavalier, 1630 Kapiolani Blvd., 949-4134
Chez Michel, 2126 B Kalakaua Ave., 923-0626
Furusato, 134 Kapahulu Ave., 923-8878; 2500 Kalakaua Ave., 922-5502
Golden Dragon Room (Chinese), 2005 Kalia Rd., 949-4321
Maile Room, 5000 Kahala Ave., 734-2211
Michel's, 2895 Kalakaua Ave., 923-6552
Prince Kuhio's, Ala Moana Center, 946-2102
The Third Floor, Hawaiian Regent Hotel, 2552 Kalakaua Ave., 922-6611
The Willows, 901 Hausten St., 946-4808
Airport Transportation:
Nine miles to Waikiki.
Taxicab and limousine bus service.
Trade Exhibition Facility:
Blaisdell Center, 777 Ward Ave., 536-7331
Information Sources:
Hawaii Visitors Bureau
Administrative Offices
P.O. Box 8527
Honolulu, Hawaii 96815
(808) 923-1811
Walk-in office: 2270 Kalakaua Ave.
Hawaii Chamber of Commerce
735 Bishop St.
Honolulu, Hawaii 96813
(808) 531-4111

Houston, Texas

Altitude: Sea level to 50 feet
Average Temp.: Jan., 59°F.; July, 82°F
Telephone Area Number: 713
Time: 844-7171 **Weather:** 529-4444
Time Zone: Central
Selected Hotels:
Four Seasons Hotel-Houston Center, 1300 Lamar, 650-1300
The Grand, 2525 W. Loop South, 961-3000
Guest Quarters Hotel, 2929 S. Post Oak Rd., 877-8100
Holiday Inn Downtown, 801 Calhoun St., 659-2222
Hyatt Regency Houston, 1200 Louisiana St., 654-1234
Inn on the Park, 4 Riverway Dr., 871-8181
Marriott at the Astrodome, 2100 S. Braeswood, 797-9000
Meridien, 400 Dallas St., 759-0202
Shamrock Hilton, Main St. at Holcombe Blvd., 668-9211
Sheraton Houston Hotel, 777 Polk Ave., 651-9041
Stouffer's Greenway Plaza Hotel, Southwest Frwy. at Edloe, 629-1200
The Warwick, 5701 Main St., 526-1991
Westin Galleria, 5060 W. Alabama St., 960-8100
Westin Oaks, 5011 Westheimer Rd., 623-4300
The Whitehall, 1700 Smith St., 659-5000
Selected Restaurants:
Brennan's, 3300 Smith St., Smith & Stuart sts., 522-9711
The Brownstone, 2736 Virginia St., 528-2844
Courtlandts, 3200 Louisiana St., 526-3247
The Great Caruso, 10001 Westheimer Rd., 780-4900
La Tour d'Argent, 2011 Ella Blvd., 864-9864

Maison de Ville, 1300 Lemar, 650-1300
Maxim's, 3755 Richmond, 877-8899
The Rivoli, 5636 Richmond Ave., 789-1900
Tony's, 1801 S. Post Oak Rd., 622-6778
Vargo's, 2401 Fondren Rd., 782-3888

Airport Transportation:
Twenty miles from Intercontinental Airport to downtown Houston; 10 miles from Hobby Airport to downtown.
Taxicab, limousine, coach bus, and helicopter service.

Trade Exhibition Facilities:
Albert Thomas Convention & Exhibit Center, 612 Smith St., 222-3561
Astrodomain, I-610 at Kirby Dr., 799-9555
Sam Houston Coliseum, Bagby St. at Walker Ave., 222-3561
The Summit, 10 E. Greenway Plaza, 627-9470

Information Sources:
Greater Houston Convention and Visitors Council
3300 Main St.
Houston, Texas 77002
(713) 523-5050
Houston Chamber of Commerce
1100 Milam Building
Houston, Texas 77002
(713) 651-1313

Indianapolis, Indiana

Altitude: 717 feet
Average Temp.: Jan., 29°F.; July, 76°F.
Telephone Area Number: 317
Time: 632-1511 **Weather:** 248-4040
Time Zone: Eastern

Selected Hotels:
Adam's Mark, 2544 Executive Drive, 248-2481
Hilton Inn Airport, 2500 S. High School Rd., 244-3361
Holiday Inn Airport, 2501 S. High School Rd., 244-6861
Holiday Inn North, 3850 De Pauw Blvd., 872-9790
Howard Johnson's Downtown, 501 W. Washington St., 635-4443
Hyatt Regency, Washington & Capital sts., 632-1234
Indianapolis Hilton, Meridian & Ohio sts., 635-2000
Indianapolis Motor Speedway, 4400 W. 16th St., 241-2500
Marriott, 7202 E. 21st St., 352-1231
Sheraton Meridian, 2820 N. Meridian St., 924-1241

Selected Restaurants:
Chanteclair Sur Le Toit, Holiday Inn Airport, 2501 S. High School Rd., 244-7378
Chez Jean, On IN67S, Camby, 831-0870
Harrison's, Hyatt Regency, Washington & Capital sts., 632-1234
J. Pierpont's, 148 E. Market, 634-2230
King Cole, 7 N. Meridian St., 638-5588
La Tour, One Indiana Square, 635-3535

Airport Transportation:
Eight miles to downtown Indianapolis.
Taxicab and limousine bus service.

Trade Exhibition Facilities:
Coliseum, Indiana State Fairgrounds, 923-3431
Expo Hall, Indiana State Fairgrounds, 923-3431
Indiana Convention Center, 100 S. Capitol Ave., 634-4321
Market Square Arena, 300 E. Market St., 639-6444

Information Sources:
Indianapolis Convention and Visitors Association
100 S. Capitol Ave.
Indianapolis, Indiana 46225
(317) 635-9567
Indianapolis Chamber of Commerce
320 N. Meridian St.
Indianapolis, Indiana 46204
(317) 267-2900

Kansas City, Missouri

Altitude: 722 to 1,105 feet
Average Temp.: Jan., 30°F.; July, 81°F.
Telephone Area Number: 816
Time: 844-1212 **Weather:** 471-4840
Time Zone: Central

Selected Hotels:
Adam's Mark, 9103 E. 39th St., 737-0200
Alameda Plaza Hotel, Wornall Rd. & Ward Pkwy., 756-1500
Hilton Airport Plaza Inn, 112th St. & Int. 29, 891-8900
Hilton Plaza Inn, 45th & Main sts., 753-7400
Holiday Inn City Center, 13th & Wyandotte sts., 221-8800
Inn at Executive Park, 1601 N. Universal Ave., 483-9900
Kansas City Marriott, K.C.I. Airport, 464-2200
Radisson Muehlebach, 12th St. & Baltimore Ave., 471-1400
Sheraton Inn-KCI, 7301 NW. Tiffany Springs Rd., 741-9500
The Westin Crown Center Hotel, 1 Pershing Rd., 474-4400

Selected Restaurants:
Alameda Roof, Wornall Rd. & Ward Pkwy., 756-1500
The American Restaurant, 25th & Grand sts., 471-8050
Carnegie's, 1215 Wyandotte, 471-1333
Jasper's, 405 W. 75th St., 363-3003
King's Wharf, K.C.I. Airport, 464-2200
Kona Kai, Galleria and El Patio, 45th & Main sts., 753-7400
La Bonne Auberge, 610 Washington St., 424-7025
La Mediterranee, 4742 Pennsylvania St., 561-2916
Plaza III, 4749 Pennsylvania Ave., 753-0000
Prospect of Westport, 4109 Pennsylvania Ave., 753-2227
Raphael, 325 Ward Pkwy., 756-3800
Stephenson's Apple Farm, U.S. 40 & Old Lee's Summit Rd., 373-5400
Trader Vic's, The Westin Crown Center Hotel, 1 Pershing Rd., 474-4894

Airport Transportation:
Eighteen miles to downtown Kansas City.
Taxicab and limousine bus service.

Trade Exhibition Facilities:
American Royal Center, 19th & Genessee sts., 421-6460
Kansas City Convention Center (Municipal Auditorium, H. Roe Bartle Exhibition Hall), 13th & Wyandotte sts., 421-8000

Information Sources:
Convention and Visitors Bureau of Greater Kansas City
City Center Square, 1100 Main St.
Suite 2550
Kansas City, Missouri 64105
(816) 221-5242
Chamber of Commerce of Greater Kansas City
920 Main St.
Kansas City, Missouri 64105
(816) 221-2424

Los Angeles, California

Altitude: Sea level to 5,074 feet
Average Temp.: Jan., 55°F.; July, 73°F.
Telephone Area Number: 213
Time: 853-1212 **Weather:** 554-1212
Time Zone: Pacific

Selected Hotels:
Ambassador Hotel, 3400 Wilshire Blvd., 387-7011
Bel-Air, 701 Stone Canyon Rd., 472-1211
Beverly Hills, 9641 Sunset Blvd., 276-2251
Biltmore Hotel, 515 S. Olive St., 624-1011
Century Plaza, 2025 Avenue of the Stars, 277-2000
Holiday Inn, 1755 N. Highland Ave., 462-7181
Hyatt House Hotel, 6225 W. Century Blvd., 670-9000
Hyatt Regency Los Angeles, 711 S. Hope St., 683-1234

L'Ermitage, 9291 Burton Way, 278-3344
Le Parc Hotel, 733 Knoll Dr., 855-8888
Los Angeles Hilton, 930 Wilshire Blvd., 629-4321
Los Angeles Marriott Hotel, 5855 W. Century Blvd., 641-5700
New Otani Hotel & Garden, 120 S. Los Angeles St., 629-1200
Sheraton-Universal, 30 Universal City Plaza, Universal City, 980-1212
Sheraton Town House, 2961 Wilshire Blvd., 382-7171
University Hilton, 3540 S. Figueroa St., 748-4141
The Westin Bonaventure, 5th & Figueroa sts., 624-1000

Selected Restaurants:
Alberto's, 8826 Melrose Ave., 278-2170
Bernard's, Biltmore Hotel, 612-1580
Francois, 555 S. Flower St., 680-2727
Lawry's Prime Rib, 55 N. La Cienega Blvd., 652-2827
L'Escoffier, 9876 Wilshire Blvd., 274-7777
Madame Wu's Garden, 2201 Wilshire Blvd., 828-5656
Perino's, 444 S. Flower St., 612-1300
Scandia, 9040 Sunset Strip, 278-3555
The Tower, 1150 S. Olive St., 746-1554
Yamato Restaurant, 2025 Ave. of the Stars, Century City, 277-1840

Airport Transportation:
Seventeen miles to downtown Los Angeles.
Taxicab, limousine bus and city bus service.

Trade Exhibition Facilities:
Los Angeles Convention Center, 1201 S. Figueroa St., 748-8531
Shrine Civic Auditorium, 649 W. Jefferson Blvd., 748-5116

Information Sources:
Greater Los Angeles Visitors & Convention Bureau
505 S. Flower St.
Los Angeles, California 90071
(213) 488-9100
Los Angeles Chamber of Commerce
404 S. Bixel St.
Los Angeles, California 90054
(213) 629-0711

Louisville, Kentucky

Altitude: 382 to 761 feet
Average Temp.: Jan., 35°F.; July, 78°F.
Telephone Area Number: 502
Time: 585-5961 **Weather:** 363-9655
Time Zone: Eastern

Selected Hotels:
Breckinridge Inn, 2800 Breckinridge Lane, 456-5050
Executive Inn, Watterson Expressway at Fairgrounds, 367-6161
Executive West, Freedom Way at Fairgrounds, 367-2251
Galt House, 4th St. & River Rd., 589-5200
Holiday Inn Southwest, 4110 Dixie Hwy., 448-2020
Howard Johnson's In-Towne, 100 E. Jefferson St., 582-2481
Hyatt Regency, 320 W. Jefferson St., 587-3434
Louisville Inn, 120 W. Broadway, 582-2241
Ramada Inn, 9700 Bluegrass Pkwy., 491-4830
Seelbach Hotel, 500 Fourth Ave., 585-3200

Selected Restaurants:
The Atrium at Hasenour's, 1028 Barrett Ave., 456-6789
Bill Boland's Dining Room, 3708 Bardstown Rd., 458-2666
Casa Grisanti, 1000 E. Liberty St., 584-4377
Embassy Supper Club, 4625 Shelbyville Rd., 893-2521
Lambs, 320 W. Jefferson St., 587-3434
Mama Grisanti, 3938 DuPont Circle, 893-0141
New Orleans House, 412 W. Chestnut St., 583-7231
Oak Room, 500 Fourth Ave., 585-3200
Old Stone Inn, Rte. 5, Simpsonville, 722-8882
Sixth Avenue, 600 W. Main, 587-6664

Airport Transportation:
Five miles to downtown Louisville.
Taxicab, limousine, and bus service.

Trade Exhibition Facilities:
Commonwealth Convention Center, 221 Rivercity Mall, 588-4381
Kentucky Exposition Center, Freedom Way, 366-9592
Louisville Gardens, 525 W. Muhammad Ali Blvd., 582-2601

Information Sources:
Louisville Convention & Visitors Bureau
226 W. Muhammad Ali Blvd.,
Louisville, Kentucky 40202
(502) 584-2121
Louisville Tourist Information
Founders Square
5th & Muhammad Ali Blvd.
Louisville, Kentucky 40202
(502) 582-3732
Louisville Area Chamber of Commerce
300 W. Liberty St.
Louisville, Kentucky 40202
(502) 582-2421

Memphis, Tennessee

Altitude: 195 to 335 feet
Average Temp.: Jan., 43°F.; July, 80°F.
Telephone Area Number: 901
Time: 526-5261 **Weather:** 345-6700
Time Zone: Central

Selected Hotels:
Best Western Winchester, 2201 Winchester, 345-6251
Hilton Inn Memphis Airport, 2240 Democrat Rd., 332-1130
Holiday Inn International Airport, 1441 Brooks Rd., 398-9211
Holiday Inn Overton Square, 1837 Union Ave., 278-4100
Holiday Inn Rivermont, 200 W. Georgia St., 525-0121
Hyatt Regency Memphis at Ridgeway, 939 Ridge Lake Blvd., 761-1234
The Peabody Hotel, 149 Union Ave., 529-4000
Quality Inn Airport, 1400 Springbrook, 332-8980
Sheraton Memphis, 300 N. Second St., 525-2511
Sheraton Inn Airport, 2411 Winchester Rd., 332-2370

Selected Restaurants:
Benihana of Tokyo, 912 Ridgelake, 683-7390
Bombay Bicycle Club, 2120 Madison, 726-6055
Boston Sea Party, 1575 East Brooks Rd., 345-1771
Four Flames, 1085 Poplar Ave., 526-3181
Grisanti's, 1489 Airways Blvd., 458-2648
J.P. Seafield's, 7730 Poplar, 754-0760
Justine's, 919 Coward Pl., 527-3815
Paulette's, 2110 Madison Ave., 726-5128
Sciara's Palazzino, 6155 Poplar Ave., 767-9541
Victoria Station, 2734 Mendenhall Rd., 365-7967

Airport Transportation:
Ten miles to downtown Memphis.
Taxicab and limousine bus service.

Trade Exhibition Facilities:
Cook Convention & Exhibition Center, 255 N. Main St., 523-2322
Holiday Hall, 200 W. Georgia Ave., 525-0121
Mid-South Coliseum, Fairgrounds, 274-3982

Information Sources:
Convention & Visitors Bureau of Memphis
12 S. Main St.
Memphis, Tennessee 38103
(901) 526-1919
Memphis Area Chamber of Commerce
P.O. Box 224
Memphis, Tennessee 38101
(901) 523-2322

liami, Florida

ltitude: Sea level to 30 feet
verage Temp.: Jan., 69°F.; July, 82°F.
elephone Area Number: 305
ime: 324-8811 **Weather**: 661-5065
ime Zone: Eastern
elected Hotels:
oconut Grove, 2649 S. Bayshore Dr., 858-2500
our Ambassadors, 801 S. Bayshore Dr., 377-1966
oliday Inn—Civic Center, 1170 NW. 11th St., 324-0800
larina Park, 340 Biscayne Blvd., 371-4400
larriott Miami Airport, 1201 NW. LeJeune Rd., 649-5000
liami Lakes Inn & Country Club, NW. 154th St., 821-1150
mni International, 1550 Biscayne Blvd., 374-0000
amada Inn Airport, 3941 NW. 22nd St., 871-1700
heraton River House, 3900 NW. 21st St., 871-3800
elected Restaurants:
afe Chauveron, 9561 E. Bay Harbor Dr., 866-8779
entro Vasco, 2235 SW. 8th St., 643-9606
ye's Rivergate, 444 Brickell Ave., 358-9100
our Ambassadors, 801 S. Bayshore Dr., 377-1966
a Belle Epoque, 1045 95th St., Bay Harbor Island, 865-6011
a Paloma, 10999 Biscayne Blvd., 891-0505
aimondo, 4612 SW. Le Jeune, 666-9355
iberio, 9700 Collins Ave., Bal Harbour, 861-6161
irport Transportation:
ive miles to downtown Miami.
axicab and limousine bus service.
rade Exhibition Facilities:
ayfront Park Auditorium, 499 Biscayne Blvd., 579-6335
Coconut Grove Exhibition Center, 3360 Pan American Dr., 579-3310
James L. Knight International Center, 400 SE. 2d Ave., 358-1234
Miami Beach Convention Center, 1901 Convention Center Dr., Miami Beach, 673-7311
nformation Sources:
Miami Office of Public Information
174 E. Flagler St.
Miami, Florida 33131
(305) 579-6325
Greater Miami Chamber of Commerce
1601 Biscayne Blvd.
Miami, Florida 33132
(305) 350-7700

Milwaukee, Wisconsin

Altitude: 579 to 799 feet
Average Temp.: Jan., 21°F.; July, 71°F.
Telephone Area Number: 414
Time: 844-1414 **Weather**: 936-1212
Time Zone: Central
Selected Hotels:
Hyatt Regency Milwaukee, 333 W. Kilbourn Ave., 276-1234
Marc Plaza, 509 W. Wisconsin Ave., 271-7250
Milwaukee River Hilton Inn, 4700 N. Port Washington Rd., 962-6040
Pfister Hotel & Tower, 424 E. Wisconsin Ave., 273-8222
Red Carpet Hotel Airport, 4747 S. Howell Ave., 481-8000
Sheraton Mayfair Motor Inn, 2303 N. Mayfair, Wauwatosa, 257-3400
Selected Restaurants:
English Room, Pfister Hotel & Tower, 424 E. Wisconsin Ave., 273-8222
Jean-Paul's Restaurant, 811 E. Wisconsin Ave., 271-5400
John Ernst Cafe, 600 E. Ogden Ave., 273-1878
Karl Ratzsch's, 320 E. Mason St., 276-2720
Le Bistro, 509 W. Wisconsin Ave., 271-7250
Mader's, 1037 N. 3rd St., 271-3377
Whitney's, 375 S. Moorland Rd., Brookfield, 786-1100
Airport Transportation:
Eight miles to downtown Milwaukee.
Taxicab, bus, and limousine bus service.
Trade Exhibition Facility:
MECCA (Milwaukee Exposition, Convention Center, Arena)
500 W. Kilbourn Ave., 271-4000
Information Sources:
Greater Milwaukee Convention & Visitors Bureau
756 N. Milwaukee St.
Milwaukee, Wisconsin 53202
(414) 273-7222
Metropolitan Milwaukee Association of Commerce
756 N. Milwaukee St.
Milwaukee, Wisconsin 53202
(414) 273-3000

Minneapolis-St. Paul, Minnesota

Altitude: 687 to 1,060 feet
Average Temp.: Jan., 15°F.; July, 74°F.
Telephone Area Number: 612
Time: 874-8700 **Weather**: 452-2323
Time Zone: Central
Selected Hotels: Minneapolis
Holiday Inn—Airport #2, 5401 Green Valley Dr., 831-8000
Hyatt Regency, 1300 Nicollet Mall, 370-1234
L'Hotel Sofitel, 5601 W. 78th St., 835-1900
Marquette Inn, 710 Marquette Ave., 332-2351
Marriott Hotel, 1919 E. 78th St., 854-7441
Northstar Inn, 618 2nd Ave. S, 338-2288
Radisson South, 7800 Normandale Blvd., 835-7800
Registry, 7901 24th Ave., 854-2244
Ramada Inn, 4200 W. 78th St., 831-4200
Sheraton Airport Inn, 2525 E. 78th St., 854-1771
Sheraton-Ritz, 315 Nicollet Mall, 332-4000
Selected Restaurants: Minneapolis
Anchorage, 1330 Industrial Blvd., 331-1900
Camelot, 5300 W. 78th St., 835-2455
Lord Fletcher's of the Lake, 3746 Sunset Dr., 471-8513
Willows Room, 1300 Nicollet Mall, 370-1234
Airport Transportation:
About 8 miles to downtown Minneapolis or St. Paul.
Taxicab, bus, and limousine bus service to Minneapolis and St. Paul.
Trade Exhibition Facilities: Minneapolis
Auditorium and Convention Center, 1403 Stevens Ave. S, 870-4436
Information Sources: Minneapolis
Minneapolis Convention & Visitor Commission
15 S. 5th St.
Minneapolis, Minnesota 55402
(612) 348-4330 (Tourism)
(612) 348-4313 (Conventions)
Greater Minneapolis Chamber of Commerce
15 S. 5th St.
Minneapolis, Minnesota 55402
(612) 348-4313
Selected Hotels: St. Paul
McGuire's Arden Hills, 1201 W. County Rd. E, 636-4123
Radisson Plaza St. Paul, 411 Minnesota St., 291-8800
Radisson St. Paul, 11 E. Kellogg Blvd., 292-1900
Ramada Inn, 1870 Old Hudson Rd., 735-2330
Selected Restaurants: St. Paul
Bali Hai, 2305 White Bear Ave., 777-5500
The Blue Horse, 1355 University Ave., 645-8101
Outrigger
11 E. Kellogg Blvd., 292-1900
Venetian Inn, 2814 Rice St., 484-7215
Trade Exhibition Facilities: St. Paul
National Guard Armory, 600 Cedar St., 296-6249
Prom Center, 1190 University Ave., 645-0596
St. Paul Civic Center & Auditorium, O'Shaughnessy Plaza, 224-7361

State Fairgrounds, 642-2200
Information Sources: St. Paul
Minnesota Tourism Division
240 Bremer Bldg.
St. Paul, Minnesota 55101
(612) 296-5029
St. Paul Area Chamber of Commerce
701 N. Central Tower
St. Paul, Minnesota 55101
(612) 222-5561
St. Paul Convention & Visitors Bureau
Landmark Center, B Level
St. Paul, Minnesota 55102
(612) 292-4360

New Orleans, Louisiana

Altitude: −5 to 25 feet
Average Temp.: Jan., 55°F.; July, 82°F.
Telephone Area Number: 504
Time: 529-6111 **Weather**: 525-8831
Time Zone: Central
Selected Hotels:
Fairmont, 123 Baronne St., 592-7111
Hyatt Regency, 500 Poydras Plaza, 561-1234
The Monteleone, 214 Royal St., 523-3341
New Orleans Hilton Riverside & Towers, Poydras S. at the Mississippi River, 561-0500
New Orleans Marriott, 555 Canal St., 581-1000
Pontchartrain, 2031 St. Charles Ave., 524-0581
Royal Orleans, 621 St. Louis St., 529-5333
Royal Sonesta, 300 Bourbon St., 586-0300
Selected Restaurants:
Broussard's, 819 Conti St., 581-3866
Caribbean Room, Pontchartrain Hotel, 2031 St. Charles Ave., 524-0581
Commander's Palace, 1403 Washington Ave., 899-8221
Corinne Dunbar's, 1617 St. Charles Ave., 525-2957
Galatoire's, 209 Bourbon St., 525-2021
Jonathan, 714 N. Rampart St., 586-1930
Louis XVI French Restaurant, 827 Toulouse St., 581-7000
Masson's Restaurant Français, 7200 Pontchartrain Blvd., 283-2525
Rib Room, Royal Orleans, 621 St. Louis St., 529-5333
Sazerac Restaurant, Fairmont Hotel, 123 Baronne St., 861-7551
Willy Coln's Chalet, 2505 Whitney Ave., Gretna, 361-3860
Winston's, New Orleans Hilton, Poydras St. at the Mississippi River, 561-0500
Airport Transportation:
Eleven miles to downtown New Orleans.
Taxicab and limousine bus service.
Trade Exhibition Facilities:
Louisiana Superdome, LaSalle & Poydras sts., 587-3663
Rivergate, 2 Canal St., 529-2861
Information Sources:
New Orleans Tourist & Convention Commission
334 Royal St.
New Orleans, Louisiana 70130
(504) 566-5011
Chamber of Commerce of the New Orleans Area
301 Camp St.
New Orleans, Louisiana 70130
(504) 527-6900

New York, New York

Altitude: Sea level to 410 feet
Average Temp.: Jan., 33°F.; July, 75°F.
Telephone Area Number: 212
Time: 976-1616 **Weather**: 976-1212
Time Zone: Eastern
Selected Hotels:
Carlyle, Madison Ave. at E. 76th St., 744-1600
Helmsley Palace, 455 Madison Ave., 888-7000
Marriott's Essex House, 160 Central Park S, 247-0300
New York Hilton at Rockefeller Center, 1335 Avenue of the Americas, 586-7000
Pierre, 5th Ave. at E. 61st St., 838-8000
Plaza, 5th Ave. at W. 59th St., 759-3000
Regency, 540 Park Ave., 759-4100
St. Regis-Sheraton, 5th Ave. at 55th St., 753-4500
Sherry-Netherland, 781 5th Ave., 355-2800
United Nations Plaza, 1 U.N. Plaza, 355-3400
Waldorf-Astoria, 301 Park Ave., 355-3000
Selected Restaurants:
Casa Brazil, 406 E. 85th St., 288-5284
Chez Pascal, 151 E. 82nd St., 249-1334
The Coach House, 110 Waverly Pl., 777-0303
The Four Seasons, 99 E. 52nd St., 754-9494
La Cote Basque, 5 E. 55th St., 688-6525
La Petite Marmite, 5 Mitchell Place, 826-1084
Le Chantilly, 106 E. 57th St., 751-2931
Le Perigord Park, 575 Park Ave., 752-0050
Lutèce, 249 E. 50th St., 752-2225
Mitsukoshi, 461 Park Ave., 935-6444
Quo Vadis, 26 E. 63rd St., 838-0590
"21" Club, 21 W. 52nd St., 582-7200
Airport Transportation:
Fifteen miles to Manhattan from JFK Airport; 8 miles from La Guardia Airport to Manhattan; 10 miles from Newark Airport to Manhattan.
Taxicab; limousine bus service to and from JFK, La Guardia, and Newark airports and East Side Airlines Terminal. Also JFK Express Subway/bus service from Manhattan to JFK Airport.
Trade Exhibition Facilities:
Coliseum Exhibition Corp., Columbus Circle, 757-5000
Madison Square Garden, bet. 7th & 8th aves. at 33rd St., 564-4400
Information Sources:
New York Convention and Visitors Bureau, Inc.
Two Columbus Circle
New York City, New York 10019
(212) 397-8222
New York Chamber of Commerce and Industry
200 Madison Ave.
New York City, New York 10016
(212) 561-2020

Oklahoma City, Oklahoma

Altitude: 1,050 to 1,334 feet
Average Temp: Jan., 37°F.; July, 82°F.
Telephone Area Number: 405
Time: 599-1234 **Weather**: 685-5577
Time Zone: Central
Selected Hotels:
Grand Continental Inn, 3850 S. Prospect, 672-4581
Hilton Inn Northwest, 2945 NW. Expwy., 848-4811
Hilton Inn West, 401 S. Meridian Ave., 947-7681
Holiday Inn East, 5701 W. Tinker Diagonal, Midwest City, 737-4481
Lincoln Plaza Inn, 4445 N. Lincoln Blvd., 528-2741
Ramada Inn Airport West, 800 S. Meridian Ave., 943-8551
Ramada Inn North, 2801 NW. 39th St., 946-0741
Red Carpet Inn, 2616 S. Int. 35, 677-0521
Sheraton-Century Center, One N. Broadway Ave., 235-2780
Sheraton Inn Airport, 6300 E. Terminal Dr., 681-7511
Skirvin Plaza, One Park Ave., 232-4411
Selected Restaurants:
Applewoods, 4400 W. Reno, 947-8484
Calla, 50 Penn Place Mezzanine, 843-0232
Chicago's, 5705 Mosteller Dr., 840-9912

Christopher's, 2920 NW. Grand Blvd., 943-8395
Eagle's Nest, 5900 Mosteller Dr., 840-5655
Eddy's Steak House, 4227 N. Meridian Ave., 787-2944
Glen's Hik'ry Inn, 2815 NW 10th St., 943-4445
Harry Bear's, 4540 NW. 23rd St., 946-1421
Hungry Peddler, 4500 W. Reno, 947-0779
Park Avenue Room, Skirvin Plaza, One Park Ave., 232-4411
R. L. Sullivan's, 4401 W. Reno Ave. 943-5740
Sheraton-Century Center, One N. Broadway, 235-2780
Sleepy Hollow, 1101 NE. 50th St., 424-1614
Texanna Red's, 4600 W. Reno Ave., 947-8665
Velvet Dove, 4301 SW. 3rd St., 946-5335

Airport Transportation:
Ten miles to downtown Oklahoma City.
Taxicab, limousine bus service.

Trade Exhibition Facilities:
Civic Center Music Hall, 201 N. Dewey Ave., 231-2584
Fairgrounds, N.W. 10th St. & N. May Ave., 942-5511
Myriad, One Myriad Gardens, 232-8871

Information Sources:
Oklahoma City Convention & Tourism Center
4 Santa Fe Plaza
Oklahoma City, Oklahoma 73102
(405) 232-2211
Oklahoma City Chamber of Commerce
One Santa Fe Plaza
Oklahoma City, Oklahoma 73102
(405) 232-6381

Philadelphia, Pennsylvania

Altitude: Sea level to 441 feet
Average Temp.: Jan., 35°F.; July, 78°F.
Telephone Area Number: 215
Time: 846-1212 **Weather:** 937-1212
Time Zone: Eastern

Selected Hotels:
Adam's Mark, City Line Ave. & Monument Rd., 581-5000
Barclay, 237 S. 18th St., 545-0300
Bellevue Stratford, Broad & Walnut sts., 893-1776
Franklin Plaza, 2 Franklin Plaza,17th & Race sts., 448-2000
Hilton Inn Northeast, 2400 Old Lincoln Hwy., Trevose, 638-8300
Hilton Hotel, 34th & Civic Center Blvd., 387-8333
Hotel Latham, 17th & Walnut sts., 563-7474
Marriott, City Line Ave. & Monument Rd. at Schuylkill Expwy., 667-0200
Marriott-Philadelphia Airport, 4509 Island Ave., 365-4150
Palace, Benjamin Franklin Pkwy. at 18th St., 963-2222
Philadelphia Centre, 1725 J.F. Kennedy Blvd., 568-3300
Warwick, 1701 Locust St., 735-6000

Selected Restaurants:
Bookbinders, 125 Walnut St., 925-7020
Deja Vu, 1609 Pine St., 546-1190
Deux Cheminees, 251 Camac St., 985-0367
Di Lullo, 7955 Oxford Ave., 725-6000
Hoffman House, 1214 Sansom St., 925-2772
Frog, 1524 Locust St., 735-8882
La Camargue, 1119 Walnut St., 922-3148
La Famaglia, 8 S. Front St., 922-2803
La Panatiere, 1602 Locust St., 546-5452
Lautrec, 408 S. Second St., 923-6660
Le Bec Fin, 1523 Walnut St., 567-1000
Monte Carlo Living Room, 2nd & South sts., 925-2220
20th St. Cafe, 261 S. 20th St., 546-6867
Wildflowers, 514 S. 5th St., 923-6708

Airport Transportation:
Eight miles to downtown Philadelphia.
Taxicab and limousine bus service.

Trade Exhibition Facility:
Philadelphia Civic Center, Civic Center Blvd. & 34th St., 686-1776

Information Sources:
Philadelphia Convention & Visitors Bureau
1525 John F. Kennedy Blvd.
Philadelphia, Pennsylvania 19102
(215) 568-6599
Greater Philadelphia Chamber of Commerce
Broad & Chestnut
Philadelphia, Pennsylvania 19102
(215) 568-4040

Phoenix, Arizona

Altitude: 1,086 to 1,160 feet
Average Temp.: Jan., 51°F.; July, 85.9°F.
Telephone Area Number: 602
Time: 976-1616 **Weather:** 957-8700
Time Zone: Mountain

Selected Hotels:
Arizona Biltmore, 24th St. & Missouri Ave., 955-6600
Doubletree Inn, 212 W. Osborn St., 248-0222
Granada Royale Hometel, 2333 E. Thomas Rd., 957-1910
Hyatt Regency, 122 N. 2nd St., 257-1234
Phoenix Hilton, Central & Adams sts., 257-1525
The Pointe, 7677 N. 16th St., 997-2626
Ramada Airport Resort, 3801 E. Van Buren St., 275-7878
Sheraton Airport Inn, 2901 E. Sky Harbor Blvd., 275-3634

Selected Restaurants:
Compass, 122 N. 2nd St., 257-1110
Different Pointe of View, 11111 N. 7th St., 866-7500
Golden Eagle, 201 N. Central Ave., 257-7700
Mancuso's, 4622 N. 7th Ave., 266-9594
Orangerie, 24th St. & Missourie Ave., 955-6600
Pointe of View, 7677 N. 16th St., 997-2626
Trumps, 10220 N. Metro Pkwy. E., 997-5900
Velvet Turtle, 3102 E. Camelback Rd., 957-7180
Willie & Guillermo's, 5600 N. Central, 266-1900

Airport Transportation:
Four miles to downtown Phoenix.
Taxicab, bus, and limousine bus service.

Trade Exhibition Facilities:
Arizona Veterans Memorial Coliseum & Exposition Center, 1826 W. McDowell Rd., 258-6711
Phoenix Civic Plaza, 225 E. Adams St., 262-7272

Information Sources:
Phoenix & Valley of the Sun Convention & Visitors Bureau
4455 E. Camelback Rd., Bldg. D
Phoenix, Arizona 85018
(602) 952-8687
Visitor Information Hotline, 840-4636

Pittsburgh, Pennsylvania

Altitude: 710 to 1,370 feet
Average Temp.: Jan., 33°F.; July, 75°F.
Telephone Area Number: 412
Time: 391-9500 **Weather:** 936-1212
Time Zone: Eastern

Selected Hotels:
Airport Hilton Inn, Cliff Mine Rd., 262-3800
Hilton, Gateway Center at Point State Park, 391-4600
Holiday Inn Airport, 1406 Beers School Rd., Coraopolis, 262-3600
Howard Johnson's, 5130 PA 8, Gibsonia, 443-5944
Hyatt Pittsburgh at Chatham Center, opp. Civic Arena, 391-5000
Marriott, 101 Marriott Dr.,

Greentree, 922-8400
Sheraton Inn, Station Square, 261-2000
Sheraton Inn-Airport, Thorn Run Rd. Extension, Coraopolis, 262-2400
William Penn, 530 William Penn Pl., 281-7100

Selected Restaurants:
Back Porch, 114 Speers St., Speers, 483-4500
Christopher's, 1411 Grandview Ave., Mt. Washington, 381-4500
Colony, Greentree & Cochran rds., 561-2060
Common Plea, 308 Ross St., 281-5140
D'Imperio's, 3412 Wm. Penn Hwy., Monroeville, 823-4800
Hugo's Rotisserie, Hyatt at Chatham Center, 288-9326
La Cité, 9999 Klummer St., Allison Park, 931-0661
La Normande, 5030 Center Ave., 621-0744
La Plume, William Penn Hotel, 530 William Penn Pl., 281-7100
Le Mont, 1114 Grandview Ave., Mt. Washington, 431-3100
Park Schenley, 3955 Dithridge St., 681-0800
Poli's, 2607 Murray Ave., 521-1222
Tambellini, W. of town on PA 51, 481-4429

Airport Transportation:
Seventeen miles to downtown Pittsburgh.
Taxicab and limousine bus service.

Trade Exhibition Facilities:
Civic Arena & Exhibit Hall, Washington Pl. & Bedford Ave., 642-1800
David L. Lawrence Convention Center, 1001 Penn Ave., 565-6000
Pittsburgh Expo Mart, 300 Monroeville Mall, Monroeville, 856-8100

Information Sources:
Pittsburgh Convention & Visitors Bureau, Inc.
4 Gateway Center
Pittsburgh, Pennsylvania 15222
(412) 281-7711
Greater Pittsburgh Chamber of Commerce
411 7th Ave.
Pittsburgh, Pennsylvania 15222
(412) 392-4500

Portland, Oregon

Altitude: Sea level to 1,073 feet
Average Temp.: Jan., 40°F.; July, 69°F.
Telephone Area Number: 503
Time: 229-1212 **Weather:** 255-6660
Time Zone: Pacific

Selected Hotels:
Best Western Flamingo, 9727 NE. Sandy Blvd., 255-1400
Cosmopolitan Airtel, 6221 NE. 82nd Ave., 255-6511
Holiday Inn Airport, 82nd Ave. & Columbia Blvd., 256-5000
Portland Hilton, SW. 6th Ave. at Salmon St., 226-1611
Portland Marriott, Front Ave. & Clay St., 226-7600
Portland Motor Hotel, 1414 SW. 6th Ave., 221-1611
Red Lion Motor Inn Jantzen Beach, 909 N. Hayden Island Dr., 283-4466
Red Lion Inn Portland Center, 310 SW. Lincoln Ave., 221-0450
Sheraton Inn Airport, 8235 N.E. Airport Way, 288-2500
Thunderbird Motor Inn Coliseum, 1225 Thunderbird Way, 235-8311
Thunderbird Motor Inn Jantzen Beach, 1401 N. Hayden Island Dr., 283-2111
The Westin Benson, SW. Broadway at Oak St., 228-9611

Selected Restaurants:
Couch Street Fish House, 3rd & Couch sts., 223-6173
Jade West, 122 SW. Harrison St., 226-1128
Jake's Famous Crawfish, 401 SW. 12th Ave., 226-1419
L'Omelette, 815 SW. Alder St., 248-9661
The London Grill, The Westin Benson, SW. Broadway at Oak St., 228-9611
Misty's, 1401 Hayden Island Dr., 283-2111
Panorama Room, atop Portland Hilton, SW 6th Ave. at Salmon St., 226-1611
Ringside, 2165 W. Burnside St., 223-1513
River Queen, 1300 NW. Front Ave., 228-8633
Sweet Tibbie Dunbar, 718 NE. 12th Ave., 232-1801
Top of the Cosmo, 1030 N.E. Union Ave., 235-8433
Tuck Ling, 140 NW. 4th Ave., 223-7475

Airport Transportation:
Nine miles to downtown Portland.
Taxicab, limousine bus service and public mass transit system.

Trade Exhibition Facilities:
Memorial Coliseum, 1401 N. Wheeler Ave., 239-4422
Multnomah County Exposition Center, 2060 N. Marine Dr., 285-7756

Information Source:
Greater Portland Convention & Visitors Association, Inc.
26 SW. Salmon St.
Portland, Oregon 97204
(503) 222-2223

St. Louis, Missouri

Altitude: 385 to 614 feet
Average Temp.: Jan., 32°F.; July, 79°F.
Telephone Area Number: 314
Time: 321-2522 **Weather:** 321-2222
Time Zone: Central

Selected Hotels:
Breckenridge Inn, 1335 S. Lindbergh Blvd., 933-1100
Chase Park Plaza, 212 N. Kingshighway Blvd., 361-2500
Cheshire Inn & Lodge, 6300 Clayton Rd., 647-7300
Marriott Hotel at the Airport, Int. 70 at Lambert Airport, 423-9700
Marriott's Pavilion, 1 S. Broadway, 421-1776
Sheraton Plaza, 900 Westport Plaza, 434-5010
Sheraton-West Port Inn, 191 West Port Plaza, 878-1500
Hilton Inn, 10330 Natural Bridge Rd., 426-5500
Stouffer's Riverfront Towers, 200 S. 4th St., 241-9500

Selected Restaurants:
Al Baker's, 8101 Clayton Rd., 863-8878
Anthony's, 10 S. Broadway, 231-2434
Catfish & Crystal, 409 N. 11th St., 231-7703
Cheshire Inn, 6301 Clayton Rd., 647-7300
Crest House, Broadway at Chestnut, 241-3700
Dominic's, 5101 Wilson Ave., 771-1632
Giovanni's, 5201 Shaw, 772-5958
Henry VIII, 4690 N. Lindbergh Blvd., 731-4888
Kemoll's, 4201 N. Grand Ave., 534-2705
Richard Perry, 3265 S. Jefferson Ave., 771-4100
Tenderloin Room, Chase Park Plaza, 212 N. Kingshighway Blvd., 361-2500
Tony's, 826 N. Broadway St., 231-7007
Top of the Sevens, 7777 Bonhomme Ave., Clayton, 725-7777
Wade's A Gathering Place, 611 N. Lindbergh Blvd., 997-5151

Airport Transportation:
Fifteen miles to downtown St. Louis.
Taxicab and limousine bus service.

Trade Exhibition Facilities:
Kiel Auditorium, 1400 Market St., 241-1010
Cervantes Convention & Exhibition Center, 801 Convention Plaza, 342-5000

Information Sources:
Convention & Visitors Bureau of Greater St. Louis
10 S. Broadway
St. Louis, Missouri 63102

(314) 421-1023, (800) 325-7962
St. Louis Regional Commerce & Growth Association
10 S. Broadway
St. Louis, Missouri 63102
(314) 231-5555

Salt Lake City, Utah

Altitude: 4,209 to 8,005 feet
Average Temp.: Jan., 27°F.; July, 77°F.
Telephone Area Number: 801
Weather: 524-5133 **Time:** 933-9122
Time Zone: Mountain
Selected Hotels:
Airport Hilton Inn, 5151 Wiley Post Way, 539-1515
Hilton, 150 W. 5th South St., 532-3344
Holiday Inn-Downtown, 230 W. 6th South St., 532-7000
Hotel Utah, South Temple & Main sts., 531-1000
Little America, 500 S. Main St., 363-6781
Marriott, 75 S. West Temple St., 531-0800
Selected Restaurants:
Benihana of Tokyo, 165 S. West Temple St., 322-2421
Cowboy Grub, 2350½ Foothill Blvd., 466-8334
The Heather, 6200 S. Holladay Blvd., 272-4468
La Caille, 9565 S. Wasatch Blvd., 942-1751
La Fleur de Lys, 165 S. West Temple St., 359-5753
Log Haven, 3800 S. Millcreek Canyon, 272-8255
Market Street Grill, 54 Post Office Pl., 322-4668
Mikado, 67 W. 100 South St., 328-0929
Ristorante Della Fontana, 366 S. 4th St. East, 328-4243
The Roof, South Temple & Main sts., 531-1000
Airport Transportation:
Six miles to downtown Salt Lake City.
Taxicab, bus, and limousine bus service.
Trade Exhibition Facilities:
ExpoMart, 230 W. 200 South, 531-6699
Hilton, 150 W. 5th St. South, 532-3344
Hotel Utah, South Temple & Main sts., 531-1000
Little America, 500 S. Main St., 363-6781
Salt Palace, bounded by W. Temple, 200 West, S. Temple & 200 South sts., 521-6060
Information Sources:
Salt Lake Valley Convention and Visitors Bureau
Suite 200, Salt Palace
100 S. West Temple St.
Salt Lake City, Utah 84101
(801) 521-2822
Salt Lake Area Chamber of Commerce
19 E. 2nd South
Salt Lake City, Utah 84111
(801) 364-3631

San Antonio, Texas

Altitude: 505 to 1,000 feet
Average Temp.: Jan., 51°F.; July, 84°F.
Telephone Area Number: 512
Time: 226-3232 **Weather:** 828-3384
Time Zone: Central
Selected Hotels:
Best Western Continental Inn, 9735 I-35 N., 655-3510
Four Seasons Plaza Nacional, 5555 S. Alamo St., 229-1000
Hilton Palacio del Rio, 200 S. Alamo St., 222-1400
Holiday Inn Northwest, 6023 NW. Expwy., 732-5141
Hyatt Regency San Antonio, 123 Losoya, 222-1234
La Mansion del Norte, 37 NE. Loop Expwy. (I-410), 341-3535
La Mansion del Rio, 112 College St., 225-2581
Marriott Hotel, 711 E. River Walk, 224-4555
Northwest San Antonio Granada Royale Hotemel, 7750 Briaridge, 340-5421
St. Anthony, 300 E. Travis St., 227-4392
Selected Restaurants:
Chez Ardid, 1919 San Pedro, 732-3203
Crystal Baking Company, 1039 NE. Loop Expwy. (I-410), 826-2371
Fig Tree, 515 Villita St., 224-1976
Grey Moss Inn, NW on Scenic Loop Rd., 695-8301
La Louisiane, 2632 Broadway, 225-7984
La Provence, 206 E. Locust, 225-0722
Las Canarias, La Mansion del Rio, 112 College St., 225-2581
Paesano's, 1715 McCullough Ave., 226-9541
San Angel, 37 NE. Loop Expwy. (I-410), 341-5897
Airport Transportation:
Eight miles to downtown San Antonio.
Taxicab and limousine bus service.
Trade Exhibition Facilities:
Convention Center, HemisFair Plaza, Market & S. Alamo sts., 299-8500
Villita Assembly Hall, Villita & Presa sts., 227-3211
Information Sources:
San Antonio Convention and Visitors Bureau
P.O. Box 2277
San Antonio, Texas 78298
(512) 299-8123, (800) 531-5700
Visitor Information Center
321 Alamo Plaza
San Antonio, Texas 78205
(512) 299-8155
San Antonio Chamber of Commerce
602 E. Commerce St.
San Antonio, Texas 78205
(512) 229-2100

San Diego, California

Altitude: Sea level to 823 feet
Average Temp.: Jan., 57°F.; July, 71°F.
Telephone Area Number: 619
Time: 853-1212 **Weather:** 289-1212
Time Zone: Pacific
Selected Hotels:
Executive Hotel, 1055 First Ave., 232-6141
Glorietta Bay Inn, 1630 Glorietta Blvd., 435-3101
Hanalei Hotel, 2270 Hotel Circle N, 297-1101
Holiday Inn Embarcadero, 1355 Harbor Dr., 232-3861
Hyatt Islandia, 1441 Quivira Rd., 224-3541
Mission Valley Inn, 875 Hotel Circle S, 298-8281
Rancho Bernardo Inn, 17550 Bernardo Oaks Dr., 487-1611
San Diego Hilton, 1775 E. Mission Bay Dr., 276-4010
Sheraton-Harbor Island East, 1380 Harbor Island Dr., 291-2900
Sheraton Inn-Airport, 1590 Harbor Island Dr., 291-6400
Westgate Plaza Hotel, 1055 2nd Ave., 238-1818
Selected Restaurants:
Anthony's Star of the Sea Room, 1360 Harbor Dr., 232-7408
El Bizcocho, 17550 Rancho Bernardo, 487-1611
Gourmet Room, 500 Hotel Circle North, 291-7131
La Maison des Pescadoux, 2265 Bacon St., 225-9579
Lubach's, 2101 N. Harbor Dr., 232-5129
Mister A's, 2550 5th Ave., 239-1377
Old Trieste, 2335 Morena Blvd., 276-1841
Thee Bungalow, 4996 W. Point Loma Blvd., 224-2884
Tom Ham's Lighthouse, 2150 Harbor Island Dr., 291-9110

Airport Transportation:
Three miles to downtown San Diego.
Taxicab and bus service.
Trade Exhibition Facilities:
Convention & Performing Arts Center, 202 C St., 236-6500
San Diego Sports Arena, 3500 Sports Arena Blvd., 226-8456
Town & Country Convention Center, 500 Hotel Circle N, 291-7131
Information Sources:
San Diego Convention and Visitors Bureau
1200 Third Ave., Suite 824
San Diego, California 92101
(714) 232-3101
San Diego Chamber of Commerce
110 West C Street, Suite 1600
San Diego, California 92101
(714) 232-0124

San Francisco, California

Altitude: Sea level to 934 feet
Average Temp.: Jan., 50°F.; July, 59°F.
Telephone Area Number: 415
Time: 767-8900 **Weather:** 936-1212
Time Zone: Pacific
Daily Events: 391-2000 (recorded)
Selected Hotels:
Fairmont Hotel & Tower, 950 Mason St., 772-5000
Four Seasons-Clift, 495 Geary St., 775-4700
Holiday Inn Union Square, 480 Sutter St., 398-8900
Huntington, 1075 California St., 474-5400
Hyatt Regency San Francisco, 5 Embarcardero Center, 788-1234
Hyatt on Union Square, 345 Stockton St., 398-1234
Mark Hopkins Intercontinental, 1 Nob Hill, 392-3434
Pacific Plaza, 501 Post St., 441-7100
Petite Auberge, 863 Bush St., 928-6000
The Queen Anne, 1590 Sutter St., 441-2828
San Francisco Hilton, 333 O'Farrell St., 771-1400
Sheraton Palace, 639 Market St., 392-8600
Stanford Court, 905 California St., 989-3500
Westin Miyako, 1625 Post St., 922-3200
Westin St. Francis, Union Square, 397-7000
Selected Restaurants:
Amelio's, 1630 Powell St., 397-4339
Blue Fox, 659 Merchant St., 981-1177
Doros, 714 Montgomery St., 397-6822
Empress of China, 838 Grant Ave., 434-1345
Ernie's, 847 Montgomery St., 397-5969
Fleur de Lys, 777 Sutter St., 673-7779
Fournou's Ovens, Stanford Court Hotel, California & Powell sts., 989-1910
La Bourgogne, 330 Mason St., 362-7352
La Mirabelle, 1326 Powell St., 421-3374
Le Club, 1250 Jones St., 771-5400
L'Etoile, 1075 California St., 771-1529
Airport Transportation:
Fifteen miles to downtown San Francisco.
Taxicab, bus, and limousine bus service.
Trade Exhibition Facilities:
Brooks Hall & Civic Auditorium, Grove betw. Polk & Larkin sts., 974-4000
Cow Palace, Geneva Ave. & Rio Verde St., 469-6000
George R. Moscone Convention Center, 747 Howard St., 974-4000
Masonic Temple Building, 1111 California St., 776-4702
Information Sources:
San Francisco Convention & Visitors Bureau
Convention Plaza, 201 Third Street
San Francisco, California 94103
(415) 974-6900
San Francisco Visitor Information Center
Swig Pavilion, Hallidie Plaza
Powell & Market sts.
San Francisco Chamber of Commerce
465 California Street
San Francisco, California 94104
(415) 392-4511

Seattle, Washington

Altitude: Sea level to 520 feet
Average Temp.: Jan., 41°F.; July, 66°F.
Telephone Area Number: 206
Time: 844-1111 **Weather:** 382-7246
Time Zone: Pacific
Selected Hotels:
Doubletree Inn, 205 Strander Blvd., 246-8220
Holiday Inn Airport, 17338 Pacific Hwy. S, 248-1000
Hyatt Seattle, 17001 Pacific Hwy. S, 244-6000
Marriott-Sea Tac, 3201 S. 176th St., 241-2000
Park Hilton, 6th Ave. and Seneca St., 464-1980
Red Lion Inn/Sea-Tac, 18740 Pacific Hwy. S, 246-8600
University Tower, 4507 Brooklyn Ave. NE, 634-2000
Westin Hotel Seattle, 5th Ave. at Westlake Ave., 624-7400
Selected Restaurants:
Alexis, 1007 1st Ave., 624-3646
Brasserie Pittsbourg, 602 1st Ave., 623-4167
Carvery, Seattle-Tacoma International Airport, 433-5622
Jonah & the Whale, 11211 Main St., Bellevue, 455-5240
Labuznik, 1924 1st Ave., 682-1624
Mirabeau, Sea-First Bank Building, 624-4550
Rosellinis' Four-10, 4th Ave. & Wall St., 624-5464
Rosellinis' Other Place, 319 Union St. 623-7340
Trader Vic's, 5th Avenue at Westlake, 624-7900
Airport Transportation:
Fourteen miles to downtown Seattle.
Taxicab, limousine bus, Metro Transit and Airporter service.
Trade Exhibition Facilities:
Kingdome, 201 S. King St., 628-3663
Seattle Center, 305 Harrison St., 625-4234
Seattle Trade Center, 2601 Elliot Ave., 624-5641
Westin Hotel Seattle, 5th Ave. at Westlake Ave., 624-7400
Information Sources:
Seattle/King County Convention & Visitors Bureau
1815 7th Ave. W.
Seattle, Washington 98119
(206) 447-7273
Seattle Chamber of Commerce
1201 Union Sq.
Seattle, Washington 98101
(206) 447-7273

Washington, D.C.

Altitude: 1 to 410 feet
Average Temp.: Jan., 36°F.; July, 79°F.
Telephone Area Number: 202
Time: 844-2525 **Weather:** 936-1212
Time Zone: Eastern
Selected Hotels:
The Capital Hilton, 16th & K sts. NW, 393-1000
Dolley Madison, 15th & M sts. NW, 862-1600
Four Seasons Hotel, 2800 Pennsylvania Ave. NW, 342-0444
Georgetown Inn, 1310 Wisconsin Ave. NW, 333-8900
Hay-Adams Hotel, 800 16th St. NW, 638-2260
Loew's L'Enfant Plaza, 480 L'Enfant Plaza, SW, 484-1000

e Washington Circle Hotel,
)ne Washington Circle NW,
72-1680
z-Carlton, 2100 Massachusetts Ave.
IW, 293-2100
eraton-Carlton,
23 16th St. NW, 638-2626
shington Hilton and Towers,
919 Connecticut Ave. NW,
83-3000
e Watergate Hotel,
650 Virginia Ave. NW, 965-2300
lected Restaurants:
x Beau Champs, Four Seasons
Hotel, 2800 Pennsylvania Ave. NW,
42-0444
ntina D'italia, 1214A 18th St. NW,
59-1830
ckey Club Restaurant, Ritz-Carlton,
2100 Massachusetts Ave. NW,
59-8000
Bagatelle, 2000 K St. NW, 872-8677
Le Lion D'or, 1150 Connecticut Ave. NW, 296-7972
Maison Blanche, 1725 F St. NW, 842-0070
Montpelier, 15th & M sts. NW, 862-1600
Trader Vic's, 16th & K sts. NW, 347-7100
Two Continents, 1420 F St. NW, 347-4499

Airport Transportation:
Three miles from Washington National Airport to downtown Washington; 26 miles from Dulles International Airport to downtown Washington; 37 miles from Baltimore-Washington International Airport to downtown Washington.
Taxicab, bus, and rapid service between National Airport and downtown Washington; taxicab and bus service to Dulles International Airport; taxicab, bus, and train service to Baltimore-Washington International Airport.

Trade Exhibition Facilities:
D. C. National Guard Armory, 2001 E. Capitol St., 433-5209
Washington Convention Center, 900 9th St. NW, 789-1600

Information Sources:
Washington Convention and Visitors Association
1575 Eye St. NW, Suite 250
Washington, D.C. 20005
(202) 789-7000
Greater Washington Board of Trade
1129 20th St. NW
Washington, D.C. 20036
(202) 857-5900

Railroad Distances Between United States Cities

	Albuquerque, N. Mex.	Amarillo, Tex.	Atlanta, Ga.	Baltimore, Md.	Billings, Mont.	Birmingham, Ala.	Boston, Mass.	Buffalo, N.Y.	Butte, Mont.	Cheyenne, Wyo.	Chicago, Ill.	Cincinnati, Ohio	Cleveland, Ohio	Columbia, S.C.	Dallas, Tex.	Denver, Colo.	Des Moines, Iowa	Detroit, Mich.	Duluth, Minn.	El Paso, Tex.	Fargo, N. Dak.
Albuquerque, N. Mex.		374	1554	2102	1133	1388	2356	1862	1369	583	1338	1528	1678	1801	723	477	1108	1610	1515	253	1605
Amarillo, Tex.	374		1181	1728	1121	1014	2028	1534	1357	571	1010	1154	1339	1434	370	465	780	1282	1191	444	1281
Atlanta, Ga.	1554	1181		676	1921	167	1091	934	2157	1532	734	490	750	254	825	1526	952	748	1202	1471	1372
Baltimore, Md.	2102	1728	676		2085	799	416	395	2305	1791	796	582	459	515	1448	1822	1154	624	1265	2095	1435
Billings, Mont.	1133	1121	1921	2085		1788	2296	1802	236	550	1278	1559	1618	2142	1491	656	1041	1550	899	1386	640
Birmingham, Ala.	1388	1014	167	799	1788		1215	925	2024	1399	651	481	741	420	658	1373	819	739	1119	1304	1289
Boston, Mass.	2356	2028	1091	416	2296	1215		494	2526	2013	1018	938	678	930	1864	2044	1376	746	1486	2414	1656
Buffalo, N.Y.	1862	1534	934	395	1802	925	494		2032	1519	524	444	184	910	1418	1550	882	252	992	1920	1162
Butte, Mont.	1369	1357	2157	2305	236	2024	2526	2032		786	1514	1795	1854	2378	1727	892	1377	1780	1135	1622	876
Cheyenne, Wyo.	583	571	1532	1791	550	1399	2013	1519	786		995	1259	1335	1753	941	106	652	1267	1007	836	1097
Chicago, Ill.	1338	1010	734	796	1278	651	1018	524	1514	995		281	340	867	968	1026	358	272	468	1396	638
Cincinnati, Ohio	1528	1154	490	582	1559	481	938	444	1795	1259	281		260	586	975	1252	639	258	749	1561	919
Cleveland, Ohio	1678	1339	750	459	1618	741	678	184	1854	1335	340	260		846	1234	1366	698	164	808	1736	978
Columbia, S.C.	1801	1434	254	515	2142	420	930	910	2378	1753	867	586	846		1078	1747	1173	844	1335	1724	1513
Dallas, Tex.	723	370	825	1448	1491	658	1864	1418	1727	941	968	975	1234	1078		835	738	1200	1149	646	1239
Denver, Colo.	477	465	1526	1822	656	1373	2044	1550	892	106	1026	1252	1366	1747	835		683	1298	1038	730	1128
Des Moines, Iowa	1108	780	952	1154	1041	819	1376	882	1377	652	358	639	698	1173	738	683		630	411	1166	501
Detroit, Mich.	1610	1282	748	624	1550	739	746	252	1780	1267	272	258	164	844	1200	1298	630		740	1668	910
Duluth, Minn.	1515	1191	1202	1265	899	1119	1486	992	1135	1007	468	749	808	1335	1149	1038	411	740		1577	259
El Paso, Tex.	253	444	1471	2095	1386	1304	2414	1920	1622	836	1396	1561	1736	1724	646	730	1166	1668	1577		1667
Fargo, N. Dak.	1605	1281	1372	1435	640	1289	1656	1162	876	1097	638	919	978	1513	1239	1128	501	910	259	1667	
Houston, Tex.	925	634	856	1517	1755	718	1933	1554	1991	1205	1205	1110	1370	1110	264	1099	1002	1368	1413	827	1503
Indianapolis, Ind.	1430	1056	585	691	1462	503	962	468	1692	1161	184	109	283	681	951	1154	542	303	652	1500	822
Jacksonville, Fla.	1819	1466	350	794	2226	438	1210	1190	2462	1877	1083	840	1100	280	1096	1811	1301	1098	1551	1764	1721
Kansas City, Mo.	887	559	890	1198	1051	737	1469	975	1287	702	451	616	791	1111	517	636	221	723	632	945	722
Knoxville, Tenn.	1556	1183	197	545	1849	254	961	737	2085	1460	574	296	553	293	903	1454	880	551	1042	1549	1212
Los Angeles, Calif.	889	1216	2285	2908	1452	2118	3244	2750	1216	1302	2227	2370	2555	2538	1460	1353	1954	2499	2309	814	2092
Louisville, Ky.	1463	1090	474	696	1583	392	1052	558	1809	1194	295	114	374	581	861	1188	614	372	763	1508	933
Memphis, Tenn.	1135	761	420	967	1535	253	1382	938	1771	1186	527	494	754	673	481	1120	645	752	1031	1128	1121
Miami, Fla.	2185	1832	716	1160	2592	804	1576	1556	2828	2243	1449	1206	1466	646	1462	2177	1667	1464	1917	2130	2087
Mobile, Ala.	1369	1016	353	1029	1958	266	1444	1191	2194	1569	917	747	1007	607	646	1481	988	1005	1374	1292	1464
Nashville, Tenn.	1374	1000	288	761	1634	205	1177	745	1870	1245	446	301	561	509	720	1238	664	559	914	1367	1084
New Orleans, La.	1229	876	493	1154	1924	355	1569	1280	2160	1447	921	836	1096	747	506	1341	1039	1094	1425	1152	1515
New York, N.Y.	2216	1866	862	187	2186	986	229	396	2416	1903	908	755	571	701	1635	1934	1266	648	1376	2310	1546
Oklahoma City, Okla.	648	274	907	1454	1394	740	1743	1249	1631	845	794	880	1065	1160	236	739	565	1031	976	718	1066
Omaha, Nebr.	1015	754	1025	1284	896	892	1506	1012	1132	507	488	752	828	1246	712	538	145	760	500	1140	590
Philadelphia, Pa.	2124	1775	771	95	2094	894	321	415	2330	1811	816	664	479	610	1543	1842	1174	644	1285	2190	1454
Pittsburgh, Pa.	1776	1427	806	328	1747	797	668	260	1983	1463	468	316	131	772	1291	1494	826	296	937	1834	1107
Portland, Oreg.	1849	1837	2798	3030	961	2665	3217	2723	725	1266	2199	2470	2539	3019	2227	1372	1918	2505	1820	2002	1601
Richmond, Va.	2038	1664	579	155	2140	735	570	550	2370	1840	862	581	544	360	1385	1833	1220	708	1330	2031	1500
St. Louis, Mo.	1190	816	612	920	1310	479	1202	708	1546	921	284	338	523	833	711	914	340	489	726	1223	816
St. Paul, Minn.	1363	1039	1130	1193	882	1047	1414	920	1112	855	396	677	736	1263	997	886	259	668	152	1425	242
Salt Lake City, Utah	985	973	2051	2310	669	1906	2532	2038	433	519	1514	1778	1854	2272	1343	570	1171	1786	1526	1238	1309
San Antonio, Tex.	870	617	1066	1720	1739	928	2125	1631	1975	1189	1208	1247	1447	1320	271	1083	1009	1413	1420	617	1510
San Francisco, Calif.	1209	1537	2718	3059	1418	2551	3281	2787	1182	1268	2263	2527	2603	2971	1930	1374	1920	2535	2275	1284	2058
Seattle, Wash.	2031	2019	2824	2937	903	2691	3159	2665	667	1448	2141	2422	2481	3045	2394	1554	1944	2413	1762	2184	1503
Spokane, Wash.	1726	1714	2514	2628	593	2381	2849	2355	357	1143	1831	2112	2171	2735	2084	1249	1634	2103	1452	1979	1193
Tucson, Ariz.	565	756	1783	2407	1698	1616	2726	2232	1718	1148	1708	1873	2048	2036	958	1042	1478	1980	1889	312	1979
Washington, D.C.	2047	1690	638	38	2043	761	454	434	2273	1759	764	544	427	476	1410	1790	1122	592	1233	2056	1403
Wichita, Kans.	721	347	986	1401	1236	819	1681	1187	1472	686	663	819	1003	1239	408	580	433	935	844	791	934

owing Travel Distances (Short Line) Between ailroad Centers of the United States in Statute Miles

ndianapolis, Ind.	Jacksonville, Fla.	Kansas City, Mo.	Knoxville, Tenn.	Los Angeles, Calif.	Louisville, Ky.	Memphis, Tenn.	Miami, Fla.	Mobile, Ala.	Nashville, Tenn.	New Orleans, La.	New York, N.Y.	Oklahoma City, Okla.	Omaha, Nebr.	Philadelphia, Pa.	Pittsburgh, Pa.	Portland, Oreg.	Richmond, Va.	St. Louis, Mo.	St. Paul, Minn.	Salt Lake City, Utah	San Antonio, Tex.	San Francisco, Calif.	Seattle, Wash.	Spokane, Wash.	Tucson, Ariz.	Washington, D.C.	Wichita, Kans.
30	1819	887	1556	889	1463	1135	2185	1369	1374	1229	2216	648	1015	2124	1776	1849	2038	1190	1363	985	870	1209	2031	1726	565	2047	721
56	1466	559	1183	1216	1090	761	1832	1016	1000	876	1866	274	754	1775	1427	1837	1664	816	1039	973	617	1537	2019	1714	756	1690	347
85	350	890	197	2285	474	420	716	353	288	493	862	907	1025	771	806	2798	579	612	1130	2051	1066	2718	2824	2514	1783	638	986
91	794	1198	545	2908	696	967	1160	1029	761	1154	187	1454	1284	95	328	3030	155	920	1193	2310	1720	3059	2937	2628	2407	38	1401
62	2226	1051	1849	1452	1583	1535	2592	1958	1634	1924	2186	1394	896	2094	1747	961	2140	1310	882	669	1739	1418	903	593	1698	2043	1236
03	438	737	254	2118	392	253	804	266	205	355	986	740	892	894	797	2665	735	479	1047	1906	928	2551	2691	2381	1616	761	819
62	1210	1469	961	3244	1052	1382	1576	1444	1177	1569	229	1743	1506	321	668	3217	570	1202	1414	2532	2125	3281	3159	2849	2726	454	1681
68	1190	975	737	2750	558	938	1556	1191	745	1280	396	1249	1012	415	260	2723	550	708	920	2038	1631	2787	2665	2355	2232	434	1187
92	2462	1287	2085	1216	1809	1771	2828	2194	1870	2160	2416	1631	1132	2330	1983	725	2370	1546	1112	433	1975	1182	667	357	1718	2273	1472
61	1877	702	1460	1302	1194	1186	2243	1569	1245	1447	1903	845	507	1811	1463	1266	1840	921	855	519	1189	1268	1448	1143	1148	1759	686
84	1083	451	574	2227	295	527	1449	917	446	921	908	794	488	816	468	2199	862	284	396	1514	1208	2263	2141	1831	1708	764	663
09	840	616	296	2370	114	494	1206	747	301	836	755	880	752	664	316	2470	581	338	677	1778	1247	2527	2422	2112	1873	544	819
83	1100	791	553	2555	374	754	1466	1007	561	1096	571	1065	828	479	131	2539	544	523	736	1854	1447	2603	2481	2171	2048	427	1003
81	280	1111	293	2538	581	673	646	607	509	747	701	1160	1246	610	772	3019	360	833	1263	2272	1320	2971	3045	2735	2036	476	1239
51	1096	517	903	1460	861	481	1462	646	720	506	1635	236	712	1543	1291	2227	1385	711	997	1343	271	1930	2394	2084	958	1410	408
54	1811	636	1454	1353	1188	1120	2177	1481	1238	1341	1934	739	538	1842	1494	1372	1833	914	886	570	1083	1374	1554	1249	1042	1790	580
42	1301	221	880	1954	614	645	1667	988	664	1039	1266	565	145	1174	826	1918	1220	340	259	1171	1009	1920	1944	1634	1478	1122	433
03	1098	723	551	2499	372	752	1464	1005	559	1094	648	1031	760	644	296	2505	708	489	668	1786	1413	2535	2413	2103	1980	592	935
52	1551	632	1042	2309	763	1031	1917	1374	914	1425	1376	976	500	1285	937	1820	1330	726	152	1526	1420	2275	1762	1452	1889	1233	844
00	1764	945	1549	814	1508	1128	2130	1292	1367	1152	2310	718	1140	2190	1834	2002	2031	1223	1425	1238	617	1284	2184	1979	312	2056	791
322	1721	722	1212	2092	933	1121	2087	1464	1084	1515	1546	1066	590	1454	1107	1601	1500	816	242	1309	1510	2058	1503	1193	1979	1403	934
107	975	781	972	1641	996	616	1341	503	855	363	1703	500	976	1612	1426	2491	1435	921	1261	1607	210	2111	2656	2348	1139	1478	672
	935	518	388	2272	111	491	1301	769	298	858	811	782	654	719	371	2427	690	240	580	1680	1164	2429	2325	2015	1775	653	721
35		1175	547	2578	824	691	366	472	637	612	981	1178	1330	890	1052	3148	640	917	1479	2344	1185	2989	3129	2819	2076	756	1257
518	1175		818	1776	552	484	1541	926	602	873	1329	343	195	1237	889	1968	1197	278	480	1206	788	1970	1954	1644	1257	1160	212
388	547	818		2363	277	422	913	520	216	609	732	909	953	640	609	2726	482	540	970	2001	1174	2720	2715	2405	1861	507	988
272	2578	1776	2363		2306	1942	2944	2106	2181	1966	3082	1490	1809	2991	2643	1188	2845	2032	2157	783	1431	470	1370	1556	502	2906	1563
111	824	552	277	2306		380	1190	658	187	747	869	867	687	778	430	2460	695	274	691	1713	1133	2462	2486	2176	1820	658	755
491	691	484	422	1942	380		1057	394	239	394	1153	487	679	1062	810	2496	903	305	879	1653	753	2298	2438	2128	1440	929	566
301	366	1541	913	2944	1190	1057		838	1003	978	1347	1544	1696	1256	1418	3514	1006	1283	1845	2710	1551	3355	3495	3185	2442	1122	1623
769	472	926	520	2106	658	394	838		471	140	1215	871	1062	1124	1063	2872	932	648	1222	1988	713	2553	2861	2551	1604	991	1053
298	637	602	216	2181	187	239	1003	471		560	948	726	738	856	617	2511	697	324	842	1892	992	2537	2537	2227	1679	723	805
858	612	873	609	1966	747	394	978	140	560		1355	742	1068	1264	1152	2732	1072	699	1273	1848	573	2436	2900	2590	1464	1115	913
811	981	1329	732	3082	869	1153	1347	1215	948	1355		1592	1396	91	439	3107	341	1051	1304	2422	1906	3171	3049	2739	2586	225	1532
782	1178	343	909	1490	867	487	1544	871	726	742	1592		538	1501	1153	2131	1390	542	824	1247	507	1811	2293	1987	1030	1424	172
654	1330	195	953	1809	687	679	1696	1062	738	1068	1396	538		1304	956	1773	1333	414	348	1026	983	1775	1799	1489	1452	1252	407
719	890	1237	640	2991	778	1062	1256	1124	856	1264	91	1501	1304		348	3015	250	959	1212	2330	1815	3079	2957	2647	2494	133	1440
371	1052	889	609	2643	430	810	1418	1063	617	1152	439	1153	956	348		2668	413	611	865	1982	1535	2731	2610	2300	2146	296	1092
427	3148	1968	2726	1188	2460	2496	3514	2872	2511	2732	3107	2131	1773	3015	2668		3095	2187	1803	884	2498	718	182	368	1690	3025	1971
690	640	1197	482	2845	695	903	1006	932	697	1072	341	1390	1333	250	413	3095		919	1258	2359	1645	3108	3003	2693	2343	117	1400
240	917	278	540	2032	274	305	1283	648	324	699	1051	542	414	959	611	2187	919		574	1440	924	2189	2213	1903	1572	882	481
580	1479	480	970	2157	691	879	1845	1222	842	1273	1304	824	348	1212	865	1803	1258	574		1374	1268	2123	1745	1435	1737	1161	692
680	2344	1206	2001	783	1713	1653	2710	1988	1892	1848	2422	1247	1026	2330	1982	884	2359	1440	1374		1614	821	1066	790	1285	2278	1087
164	1185	788	1174	1431	1133	753	1551	713	992	573	1906	507	983	1815	1535	2498	1645	924	1268	1614		1901	2666	2356	929	1681	679
429	2989	1970	2720	470	2462	2298	3355	2553	2537	2436	3171	1811	1775	3079	2731	718	3108	2189	2123	821	1901		900	1086	972	3028	1884
325	3129	1954	2715	1370	2486	2438	3495	2861	2537	2900	3049	2293	1799	2957	2610	182	3003	2213	1745	1066	2666	900		310	1872	2906	2139
015	2819	1644	2405	1556	2176	2128	3185	2551	2227	2590	2739	1987	1489	2647	2300	368	2693	1903	1435	790	2356	1086	310		2291	2596	1829
775	2076	1257	1861	502	1820	1440	2442	1604	1679	1464	2586	1030	1452	2494	2146	1690	2343	1572	1737	1285	929	972	1872	2291		2368	1103
653	756	1160	507	2906	658	929	1122	991	723	1115	225	1424	1252	133	296	3025	117	882	1161	2278	1681	3028	2906	2596	2368		1363
721	1257	212	988	1563	755	566	1623	1053	805	913	1532	172	407	1440	1092	1971	1400	481	692	1087	679	1884	2139	1829	1103	1363	

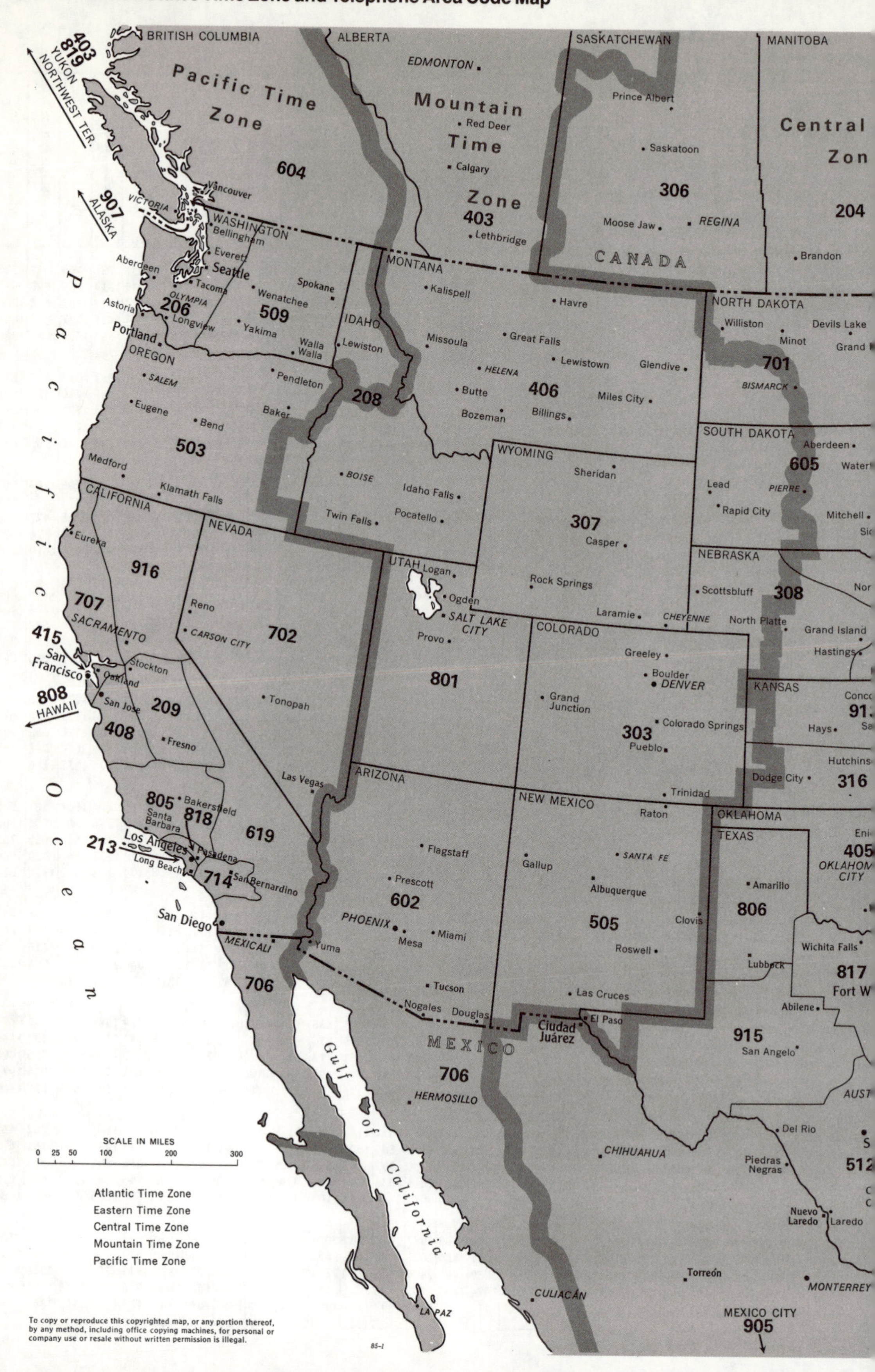
BRITISH COLUMBIA
ALBERTA
SASKATCHEWAN
MANITOBA
403
819
YUKON
NORTHWEST TER.
907
ALASKA
EDMONTON
Pacific Time Zone
Mountain Time Zone
Central Time Zon
Prince Albert
Red Deer
Saskatoon
604
Calgary
306
Vancouver
VICTORIA
403
Lethbridge
Moose Jaw
REGINA
204
Brandon
CANADA
WASHINGTON
Bellingham
Everett
Seattle
Aberdeen
Tacoma
OLYMPIA
206
Astoria
Longview
Spokane
Wenatchee
509
Yakima
Walla Walla
Portland
OREGON
SALEM
Pendleton
Eugene
Bend
Baker
503
Medford
Klamath Falls
IDAHO
Lewiston
208
BOISE
Idaho Falls
Pocatello
Twin Falls
MONTANA
Kalispell
Missoula
Great Falls
Havre
Lewistown
Glendive
HELENA
Butte
406
Miles City
Bozeman
Billings
NORTH DAKOTA
Williston
Minot
Devils Lake
Grand
701
BISMARCK
SOUTH DAKOTA
Aberdeen
605
Water
Lead
PIERRE
Rapid City
Mitchell
WYOMING
Sheridan
307
Casper
Rock Springs
Laramie
CHEYENNE
NEBRASKA
Scottsbluff
308
North Platte
Grand Island
Hastings
CALIFORNIA
Eureka
916
707
SACRAMENTO
415
San Francisco
Oakland
Stockton
808
HAWAII
San Jose
209
408
Fresno
NEVADA
Reno
CARSON CITY
702
Tonopah
Las Vegas
UTAH
Logan
Ogden
SALT LAKE CITY
Provo
801
COLORADO
Greeley
Boulder
DENVER
Grand Junction
303
Colorado Springs
Pueblo
Trinidad
KANSAS
Hays
Hutchins
Dodge City
316
805
Bakersfield
Santa Barbara
818
619
Los Angeles
Pasadena
213
Long Beach
714
San Bernardino
San Diego
MEXICALI
Yuma
706
ARIZONA
Flagstaff
Prescott
602
PHOENIX
Mesa
Miami
Tucson
Nogales
Douglas
NEW MEXICO
Raton
Gallup
SANTA FE
Albuquerque
505
Clovis
Roswell
Las Cruces
El Paso
Ciudad Juárez
OKLAHOMA
405
OKLAHOMA CITY
TEXAS
Amarillo
806
Lubbock
Wichita Falls
817
Fort W
Abilene
915
San Angelo
MEXICO
706
HERMOSILLO
Gulf of California
CHIHUAHUA
Del Rio
Piedras Negras
512
Nuevo Laredo
Laredo
Torreón
MONTERREY
CULIACÁN
LA PAZ
MEXICO CITY
905
Pacific Ocean
SCALE IN MILES
0 25 50 100 200 300
Atlantic Time Zone
Eastern Time Zone
Central Time Zone
Mountain Time Zone
Pacific Time Zone
85-I

ONTARIO
QUÉBEC
Atlantic Time Zone
709
NEWFOUNDLAND
418
NEW BRUNSWICK
506
MAINE
FREDERICTON
Saint John
807
Eastern Time Zone
819
QUÉBEC
705
Thunder Bay
207
Bangor
902
NOVA SCOTIA
PRINCE EDWARD I.
AUGUSTA
Lewiston
Portland
Hibbing
Hancock
Sault Ste. Marie
Montréal
514
VT.
802
Berlin
N.H.
218
Duluth
Superior
WISCONSIN
MICH.
906
Marquette
Escanaba
Iron Mountain
OTTAWA
CANADA
613
Burlington
MONTPELIER
Rutland
CONCORD
Manchester
715
Wausau
Eau Claire
Alpena
Traverse City
MICHIGAN
416
Watertown
NEW YORK
315
Utica
518
Schenectady
603
Lowell
BOSTON
617
612
Minneapolis
ST. PAUL
Green Bay
Appleton
Ludington
517
TORONTO
519
Hamilton
Niagara Falls
Rochester
Syracuse
607
ALBANY
Troy
MASS.
413
Springfield
PROVIDENCE
R.I.
401
Mankato
Rochester
La Crosse
Oshkosh
Fond du Lac
414
616
Bay City
Grand Rapids
Saginaw
Flint
313
Detroit
Buffalo
716
Elmira
Binghamton
914
HARTFORD
CONN.
203
Bridgeport
516
507
608
Milwaukee
Muskegon
Windsor
Erie
PENNSYLVANIA
717
Scranton
Paterson
New York
Mason City
319
Dubuque
MADISON
Beloit
Racine
Kenosha
Waukegan
LANSING
Kalamazoo
Jackson
Williamsport
Wilkes-Barre
Newark
N.J.
New York (City)
212 Bronx, Manhattan
718 Brooklyn, Queens, Staten Island
Ft. Dodge
Waterloo
Cedar Rapids
ILLINOIS
Elgin
Rockford
312
Chicago
IND.
OHIO
Toledo
216
Cleveland
Youngstown
814
Allentown
TRENTON
215
201
Camden
Reading
HARRISBURG
Philadelphia
Wilmington
Atlantic City
609
DES MOINES
515
Davenport
Moline
Aurora
Joliet
815
Gary
South Bend
419
Lima
Akron
Canton
Pittsburgh
412
Hagerstown
DOVER
Council Bluffs
Ottumwa
Rock Island
309
219
Ft. Wayne
Marion
Wheeling
Cumberland
Baltimore
301
ANNAPOLIS
DEL.
302
Burlington
Peoria
Bloomington
Kokomo
Muncie
513
Dayton
COLUMBUS
614
W. VA.
Fairmont
WASHINGTON
MD.
MISSOURI
Quincy
217
Decatur
Danville
317
INDIANAPOLIS
Cincinnati
Portsmouth
Clarksburg
VIRGINIA
Staunton
202 (Washington)
St. Joseph
816
Hannibal
SPRINGFIELD
Terre Haute
Covington
Huntington
CHARLESTON
RICHMOND
Newport News
Kansas City
Lawrence
Sedalia
St. Louis
Alton
E. St. Louis
618
812
Louisville
Ashland
304
703
Lynchburg
804
Petersburg
Norfolk
W. Frankfort
Evansville
FRANKFORT
Lexington
Bluefield
Roanoke
Portsmouth
JEFFERSON CITY
314
KENTUCKY
502
Hazard
606
Bowling Green
Middlesboro
Bristol
Danville
N. CAR.
Winston-Salem
Greensboro
Durham
Tarboro
417
Springfield
Cape Girardeau
Paducah
Cairo
Hopkinsville
Johnson City
704
High Point
RALEIGH
919
Fayetteville
Joplin
TENNESSEE
NASHVILLE
Knoxville
Asheville
Charlotte
Spartanburg
ARKANSAS
Jonesboro
901
Jackson
615
Chattanooga
S. CAR.
Greenville
Wilmington
Tulsa
Muskogee
918
Ft. Smith
Memphis
MISS.
Corinth
ALABAMA
Florence
Huntsville
GEORGIA
Gainesville
Rome
COLUMBIA
803
Florence
McAlester
LITTLE ROCK
Hot Springs
501
Gadsden
ATLANTA
404
Athens
Augusta
Orangeburg
Charleston
Greenville
Birmingham
205
Macon
El Dorado
601
Columbus
912
Savannah
Texarkana
LOUISIANA
Meridian
MONTGOMERY
Albany
Brunswick
Tyler
Shreveport
Monroe
Vicksburg
JACKSON
Waycross
Dothan
Alexandria
Hattiesburg
Jacksonville
409
318
BATON ROUGE
504
Biloxi
Mobile
Pensacola
FLORIDA
TALLAHASSEE
904
Gainesville
Beaumont
Lake Charles
New Orleans
Orlando
Port Arthur
Galveston
Tampa
St. Petersburg
813
W. Palm Beach
305
Ft. Lauderdale
Miami
809
BERMUDA
PUERTO RICO
VIRGIN ISLANDS
OTHER CARIBBEAN ISLANDS
Atlantic Ocean
Gulf of Mexico
The United States, Canada, Mexico, Puerto Rico, the Virgin Islands, and Bermuda have been divided into more than 125 telephone areas, each identified by a 3-digit Area Code number.
In no case does an area code number cross a state boundary.
City Population
• 500,000 and over
▪ 100,000 to 500,000
• under 100,000
State and province capitals are shown thus: TOPEKA
Copyright by RAND McNALLY & COMPANY Chicago

Telephone Area Codes

ALPHABETICAL LIST OF AREA CODES—STATE AND MAJOR CITY

The following is a complete list of area codes for the United States. Cities are not shown for states with only one area code.

Alabama 205
Alaska 907
Arizona 602
Arkansas 501
California
  Bakersfield 805
  Eureka 707
  Fresno 209
  Los Angeles 213
  Pasadena 818
  Riverside 714
  Sacramento 916
  San Diego 619
  San Francisco ... 415
  San Jose 408
Colorado 303
Connecticut 203
Delaware 302
District of Columbia . 202
Florida
  Jacksonville 904
  Miami 305
  St. Petersburg 813
  Tallahassee 904
Georgia
  Atlanta 404
  Savannah 912
Hawaii 808
Idaho 208
Illinois
  Chicago 312
  Peoria 309
  Rockford 815
  Springfield 217
  West Frankfort ... 618
Indiana
  Evansville 812
  Indianapolis 317
  South Bend 219
Iowa
  Council Bluffs 712
  Des Moines 515
  Dubuque 319
Kansas
  Topeka 913
  Wichita 316
Kentucky
  Covington 606
  Frankfort 606
  Louisville 502
Louisiana
  Baton Rouge 504
  New Orleans 504
  Shreveport 318
Maine 207
Maryland 301
Massachusetts
  Boston 617
  Springfield 413
Michigan
  Detroit 313
  Escanaba 906
  Grand Rapids 616
  Lansing 517
Minnesota
  Duluth 218
  Minneapolis 612
  Rochester 507
  Saint Paul 612
Mississippi 601
Missouri
  Jefferson City 314
  Kansas City 816
  Saint Louis 314
  Springfield 417
Montana 406
Nebraska
  Lincoln 402
  North Platte 308
  Omaha 402
Nevada 702
New Hampshire 603
New Jersey
  Newark 201
  Trenton 609
New Mexico 505
New York
  Albany 518
  Binghamton 607
  Buffalo 716
  Hempstead 516
  New York 212, 718
  Syracuse 315
  White Plains 914
North Carolina
  Charlotte 704
  Raleigh 919
North Dakota 701
Ohio
  Cincinnati 513
  Cleveland 216
  Columbus 614
  Toledo 419
Oklahoma
  Oklahoma City ... 405
  Tulsa 918
Oregon 503
Pennsylvania
  Erie 814
  Harrisburg 717
  Philadelphia 215
  Pittsburgh 412
Rhode Island 401
South Carolina 803
South Dakota 605
Tennessee
  Memphis 901
  Nashville 615
Texas
  Abilene 915
  Amarillo 806
  Austin 512
  Beaumont 409
  Dallas 214
  Fort Worth 817
  Houston 713
  San Antonio 512
Utah 801
Vermont 802
Virginia
  Richmond 804
  Roanoke 703
Washington
  Olympia 206
  Seattle 206
  Spokane 509
West Virginia 304
Wisconsin
  Eau Claire 715
  Madison 608
  Milwaukee 414
Wyoming 307

NUMERICAL LIST OF AREA CODES

The following list includes the United States, Canada, the Bahamas, Mexico, Puerto Rico, and the Virgin Islands.

201 New Jersey
202 District of Columbia*
203 Connecticut*
204 Manitoba*
205 Alabama*
206 Washington
207 Maine*
208 Idaho*
209 California
212 New York
213 California
214 Texas
215 Pennsylvania
216 Ohio
217 Illinois
218 Minnesota
219 Indiana
301 Maryland*
302 Delaware*
303 Colorado*
304 West Virginia*
305 Florida
306 Saskatchewan*
307 Wyoming*
308 Nebraska
309 Illinois
312 Illinois
313 Michigan
314 Missouri
315 New York
316 Kansas
317 Indiana
318 Louisiana
319 Iowa
401 Rhode Island*
402 Nebraska
403 Alberta*
403 Northwest Territories
403 Yukon*
404 Georgia
405 Oklahoma
406 Montana*
408 California
409 Texas
412 Pennsylvania
413 Massachusetts
414 Wisconsin
415 California
416 Ontario
417 Missouri
418 Quebec
419 Ohio
501 Arkansas*
502 Kentucky
503 Oregon*
504 Louisiana
505 New Mexico*
506 New Brunswick*
507 Minnesota
509 Washington
512 Texas
513 Ohio
514 Quebec
515 Iowa
516 New York
517 Michigan
518 New York
519 Ontario
601 Mississippi*
602 Arizona*
603 New Hampshire*
604 British Columbia*
605 South Dakota*
606 Kentucky
607 New York
608 Wisconsin
609 New Jersey
612 Minnesota
613 Ontario
614 Ohio
615 Tennessee
616 Michigan
617 Massachusetts
618 Illinois
619 California
701 North Dakota*
702 Nevada*
703 Virginia
704 North Carolina
705 Ontario
706 Mexico* (Northwest)
707 California
709 Newfoundland*
712 Iowa
713 Texas
714 California
715 Wisconsin
716 New York
717 Pennsylvania
718 New York
801 Utah*
802 Vermont*
803 South Carolina*
804 Virginia
805 California
806 Texas
807 Ontario
808 Hawaii*
809 Bahamas*
809 Puerto Rico*
809 Virgin Islands*
812 Indiana
813 Florida
814 Pennsylvania
815 Illinois
816 Missouri
817 Texas
818 California
819 Northwest Territories
819 Quebec
901 Tennessee
902 Nova Scotia*
902 Prince Edward I.*
904 Florida
905 Mexico (Mexico City*)
906 Michigan
907 Alaska*
912 Georgia
913 Kansas
914 New York
915 Texas
916 California
918 Oklahoma
919 North Carolina

*Area code for all locations in state, province, or country

For long distance information, dial the number 1, the area code, and 555-1212.

United States City and County Populations and ZIP Codes

The following alphabetical list shows populations for approximately 25,000 cities and counties and ZIP codes for cities. The state abbreviation following each name is that used by the United States Postal Service. A list of state abbreviations can be found on pages 423 to 424.

ZIP codes are listed for cities and towns after the state abbreviations. For each city with more than one ZIP code, the range of numbers assigned to the city is shown. For example, the ZIP code range for Chicago is 60601-99, and this indicates that the numbers between 60601 and 60699 are valid Chicago ZIP codes. ZIP code ranges are not listed for counties.

Populations for cities and towns appear as *italics* after the ZIP codes, and populations for counties appear after the state abbreviations. These populations are either 1980 census figures or, where census data are not available, estimates created by Rand McNally & Company. City populations are for central cities, not metropolitan areas. For New England, 1980 census populations are given for incorporated cities. Estimates are used for unincorporated places that are not treated separately by the census. "Town" (or "township") populations are not included unless the town is considered to be primarily urban and contains only one commonly used place-name.

□ **County**

A

Aaronsburg, PA 16820 • *500*
Abbeville, AL 36310 • *3,155*
Abbeville, GA 31001 • *985*
Abbeville, LA 70510 • *12,391*
Abbeville, MS 38601 • *448*
Abbeville, SC 29620 • *5,833*
Abbeville □, SC • *22,627*
Abbotsford, WI 54405 • *1,901*
Abbott Run Valley, RI 02864 • *1,300*
Abbottstown, PA 17301 • *689*
Abercrombie, ND 58001 • *260*
Aberdeen, ID 83210 • *1,528*
Aberdeen, MD 21001 • *11,533*
Aberdeen, MS 39730 • *7,184*
Aberdeen, NC 28315 • *1,945*
Aberdeen, OH 45101 • *1,566*
Aberdeen, SD 57401 • *25,851*
Aberdeen, WA 98520 • *18,739*
Abernant, AL 35440 • *250*
Abernathy, TX 79311 • *2,904*
Abilene, KS 67410 • *6,572*
Abilene, TX 79601-99 • *98,315*
Abingdon, IL 61410 • *4,210*
Abingdon, MD 21009 • *450*
Abingdon, VA 24210 • *4,318*
Abington, CT 06230 • *500*
Abington, MA 02351 • *13,517*
Abington, PA 19001 • *7,900*
Abita Springs, LA 70420 • *1,072*
Abrams, WI 54101 • *240*
Absarokee, MT 59001 • *750*
Absecon, NJ 08201 • *6,859*
Academia, OH 43050 • *1,447*
Acadia □, LA • *56,427*
Accident, MD 21520 • *246*
Accomac, VA 23301 • *522*
Accomack □, VA • *31,268*
Accord, NY 12404 • *500*
Accoville, WV 25606 • *500*
Ace, TX 77326 • *400*
Achille, OK 74720 • *480*
Ackerly, TX 79713 • *317*
Ackerman, MS 39735 • *1,598*
Ackley, IA 50601 • *1,900*
Acmar, AL 35004 • *250*
Acme, MI 49610 • *300*
Acme, WA 98220 • *250*
Acosta, PA 15520 • *500*
Acton, CA 93510 • *900*
Acton, MA 01720 • *2,500*
Acushnet, MA 02743 • *6,400*
Acworth, GA 30101 • *3,648*
Ada, LA 71080 • *325*
Ada, MN 56510 • *1,971*
Ada, OH 45810 • *5,669*
Ada, OK 74820 • *15,902*
Ada □, ID • *173,036*
Adair, IL 61411 • *250*
Adair, IA 50002 • *883*
Adair, OK 74330 • *508*
Adair □, IA • *9,509*
Adair □, KY • *15,233*
Adair □, MO • *24,870*
Adair □, OK • *18,575*
Adairsville, GA 30103 • *1,739*
Adairville, KY 42202 • *1,105*
Adams, IN 47240 • *300*
Adams, MA 01220 • *10,381*
Adams, MN 55909 • *797*
Adams, NE 68301 • *395*
Adams, ND 58210 • *303*
Adams, NY 13605 • *1,701*
Adams, OR 97810 • *240*
Adams, TN 37010 • *600*
Adams, WI 53910 • *1,744*
Adams □, CO • *245,944*
Adams □, ID • *3,347*
Adams □, IL • *71,622*
Adams □, IN • *29,619*
Adams □, IA • *5,731*
Adams □, MS • *38,035*
Adams □, NE • *30,656*
Adams □, ND • *3,584*
Adams □, OH • *24,328*
Adams □, PA • *68,292*
Adams □, WA • *13,267*
Adams □, WI • *13,457*
Adams Center, NY 13606 • *800*
Adams City, CO 80022 • *2,200*
Adams Run, SC 29426 • *600*
Adamston, NJ 08723 • *1,300*
Adamstown, MD 21710 • *300*
Adamstown, PA 19501 • *1,119*
Adamsville, AL 35005 • *2,498*
Adamsville, RI 02801 • *300*
Adamsville, TN 38310 • *1,453*
Addieville, IL 62214 • *286*
Addis, LA 70710 • *1,320*
Addison, AL 35540 • *746*
Addison, CT 06033 • *1,100*
Addison, IL 60101 • *29,826*
Addison, ME 04606 • *250*
Addison, NY 14801 • *2,028*
Addison, PA 15411 • *259*
Addison, TX 75001 • *5,553*
Addison □, VT • *29,406*
Addyston, OH 45001 • *1,195*
Adel, GA 31620 • *5,592*
Adel, IA 50003 • *2,846*
Adelanto, CA 92301 • *2,164*
Adell, WI 53001 • *545*
Adelphi, OH 43101 • *472*
Adena, OH 43901 • *1,062*
Adger, AL 35006 • *250*
Adin, CA 96006 • *575*
Adobe Acres, NM 87105 • *3,400*
Adolphus, KY 42120 • *250*
Adona, AR 72001 • *230*
Adrian, GA 31002 • *756*
Adrian, MI 49221 • *21,186*
Adrian, MN 56110 • *1,336*
Adrian, MO 64720 • *1,484*
Adrian, WV 26210 • *415*
Advance, IN 46102 • *559*
Advance, MO 63730 • *1,054*
Affton, MO 63123 • *23,181*
Afton, IA 50830 • *985*
Afton, MN 55001 • *2,550*
Afton, NY 13730 • *982*
Afton, OK 74331 • *1,174*
Afton, WY 83110 • *1,481*
Agate Beach, OR 97365 • *700*
Agawam, MA 01001 • *10,300*
Agency, IA 52530 • *657*
Agency, MO 64401 • *419*
Agoura, CA 91301 • *600*
Agra, KS 67621 • *321*
Agra, OK 74824 • *354*
Agua Fria, NM 87501 • *850*
Aguila, AZ 85320 • *600*
Aguilar, CO 81020 • *624*
Ahoskie, NC 27910 • *4,887*
Ahwahnee, CA 93601 • *900*
Aiea, HI 96701 • *15,200*
Aiken, SC 29801 • *14,978*
Aiken □, SC • *105,625*
Ailey, GA 30410 • *579*
Ainsworth, IA 52201 • *547*
Ainsworth, NE 69210 • *2,256*
Air Park West, NE 68524 • *3,100*
Aitkin, MN 56431 • *1,770*
Aitkin □, MN • *13,404*
Ajo, AZ 85321 • *5,189*
Akeley, MN 56433 • *486*
Akiachak, AK 99551 • *438*
Akron, AL 35441 • *604*
Akron, CO 80720 • *1,716*
Akron, IN 46910 • *1,045*
Akron, IA 51001 • *1,517*
Akron, MI 48701 • *538*
Akron, NY 14001 • *2,971*
Akron, OH 44301-99 • *237,177*
Akron, PA 17501 • *3,471*
Alabaster, AL 35007 • *7,079*
Alachua, FL 32615 • *3,561*
Alachua □, FL • *151,348*
Alakanuk, AK 99554 • *522*
Alamance, NC 27201 • *320*
Alamance □, NC • *99,319*
Alameda, CA 94501 • *63,852*
Alameda, NM 87114 • *7,800*
Alameda □, CA • *1,105,379*
Alamo, GA 30411 • *993*
Alamo, NV 89001 • *250*
Alamo, TN 38001 • *2,615*
Alamo, TX 78516 • *5,831*
Alamogordo, NM 88310 • *24,024*
Alamo Heights, TX 78209 • *6,252*
Alamosa, CO 81101 • *6,830*
Alamosa □, CO • *11,799*
Alamosa East, CO 81101 • *1,175*
Alanson, MI 49706 • *508*
Alapaha, GA 31622 • *771*
Alba, MI 49611 • *400*
Alba, MO 64830 • *474*
Alba, TX 75410 • *568*
Albany, CA 94706 • *15,130*
Albany, GA 31701-08 • *74,550*
Albany, IL 61230 • *1,014*
Albany, IN 47320 • *2,625*
Albany, KY 42602 • *2,083*
Albany, LA 70711 • *857*
Albany, MN 56307 • *1,569*
Albany, MO 64402 • *2,152*
Albany, NY 12201-99 • *101,727*
Albany, OH 45710 • *905*
Albany, OR 97321 • *26,678*
Albany, TX 76430 • *2,450*
Albany, WI 53502 • *1,051*
Albany □, NY • *285,909*
Albany □, WY • *29,062*
Albemarle, NC 28001 • *15,110*
Albemarle □, VA • *55,783*
Albert, KS 67511 • *236*
Alberta, VA 23821 • *394*
Albert City, IA 50510 • *818*
Albert Lea, MN 56007 • *19,200*
Alberton, MT 59820 • *368*
Albertson, NY 11507 • *11,200*
Albertville, AL 35950 • *12,039*
Albertville, MN 55301 • *564*
Albia, IA 52531 • *4,184*
Albion, CA 95410 • *400*
Albion, ID 83311 • *286*
Albion, IL 62806 • *2,285*
Albion, IN 46701 • *1,637*
Albion, IA 50005 • *739*
Albion, MI 49224 • *11,059*
Albion, NE 68620 • *1,997*
Albion, NY 14411 • *4,897*
Albion, PA 16401 • *1,818*
Albion, RI 02802 • *1,200*
Albion, WA 99102 • *631*
Albion, WI 53534 • *250*
Albuquerque, NM 87101-99 • *331,767*
Alburg, VT 05440 • *496*
Alburnett, IA 52202 • *411*
Alburtis, PA 18011 • *1,428*
Alcalde, NM 87511 • *800*
Alcester, SD 57001 • *885*
Alcoa, TN 37701 • *6,870*
Alcolu, SC 29001 • *600*
Alcona □, MI • *9,740*
Alcorn □, MS • *33,036*
Alda, NE 68810 • *601*
Alden, IA 50006 • *953*
Alden, MI 49612 • *300*
Alden, MN 56009 • *687*
Alden, NY 14004 • *2,488*
Alden, PA 18634 • *800*
Alderson, OK 74522 • *366*
Alderson, WV 24910 • *1,375*
Aldrich, AL 35115 • *600*
Aledo, IL 61231 • *3,881*
Aledo, TX 76008 • *1,027*
Alex, OK 73002 • *769*
Alexander, AR 72002 • *223*
Alexander, GA 30456 • *250*
Alexander, IL 62601 • *300*
Alexander, ND 58831 • *358*
Alexander, NY 14005 • *483*
Alexander □, IL • *12,264*
Alexander □, NC • *24,999*
Alexander City, AL 35010 • *13,807*
Alexander Mills, NC 28043 • *643*
Alexandria, AL 36250 • *300*
Alexandria, IN 46001 • *6,028*
Alexandria, KY 41001 • *4,735*
Alexandria, LA 71301-03 • *51,565*
Alexandria, MN 56308 • *7,608*
Alexandria, MO 63430 • *417*
Alexandria, NE 68303 • *255*
Alexandria, OH 43001 • *489*
Alexandria, PA 16611 • *435*
Alexandria, SD 57311 • *588*
Alexandria, TN 37012 • *689*
Alexandria, VA 22301-99 • *103,217*
Alexandria Bay, NY 13607 • *1,265*
Alexis, IL 61412 • *1,076*
Alfalfa □, OK • *7,077*
Alford, FL 32420 • *548*
Alfred, ME 04002 • *500*
Alfred, NY 14802 • *4,967*
Alger, OH 45812 • *992*
Alger □, MI • *9,225*
Algodones, NM 87001 • *250*
Algoma, WI 54201 • *3,656*
Algona, IA 50511 • *6,289*
Algona, WA 98002 • *1,467*
Algonac, MI 48001 • *4,412*
Algonquin, IL 60102 • *5,834*
Algood, TN 38501 • *2,406*
Alhambra, CA 91801-99 • *64,615*
Alhambra, IL 62001 • *643*
Alice, TX 78332 • *20,961*
Aliceville, AL 35442 • *3,207*
Alicia, AR 72410 • *246*
Aline, OK 73716 • *313*
Aliquippa, PA 15001 • *17,094*
Allamakee □, IA • *15,108*
Allardt, TN 38504 • *654*
Allegan, MI 49010 • *4,576*
Allegan □, MI • *81,555*
Allegany, NY 14706 • *2,078*
Allegany □, MD • *80,548*
Allegany □, NY • *51,742*

Alleghany □, NC • *9,587*
Alleghany □, VA • *14,333*
Allegheny □, PA • *1,450,085*
Alleman, IA 50007 • *307*
Allen, KY 41601 • *338*
Allen, NE 68710 • *390*
Allen, OK 74825 • *998*
Allen, PA 17007 • *350*
Allen, TX 75002 • *8,314*
Allen □, IN • *294,335*
Allen □, KS • *1,564*
Allen □, KY • *14,128*
Allen □, LA • *21,390*
Allen □, OH • *112,241*
Allendale, IL 62410 • *613*
Allendale, IN 47802 • *300*
Allendale, NJ 07401 • *5,901*
Allendale, SC 29810 • *4,400*
Allendale □, SC • *10,700*
Allenhurst, GA 31301 • *606*
Allenhurst, NJ 07711 • *912*
Allen Park, MI 48101 • *34,196*
Allensville, PA 17002 • *350*
Allenton, MO 63001 • *500*
Allenton, RI 02852 • *600*
Allenton, WI 53002 • *550*
Allentown, GA 31003 • *321*
Allentown, NJ 08501 • *1,962*
Allentown, NY 14707 • *400*
Allentown, PA 18101-99 • *103,758*
Allenwood, NJ 08720 • *500*
Allenwood, PA 17810 • *400*
Allerton, IL 61810 • *303*
Allerton, IA 50008 • *670*
Allgood, AL 35013 • *387*
Alliance, NE 69301 • *9,920*
Alliance, NC 28509 • *616*
Alliance, OH 44601 • *24,315*
Alligator, MS 38720 • *256*
Allison, IA 50602 • *1,132*
Allison, PA 15413 • *1,040*
Allison Park, PA 15101 • *5,600*
Allons, TN 38541 • *300*
Allouez, MI 49805 • *300*
Allouez, WI 54301 • *13,753*
Alloway, NJ 08001 • *1,370*
Allyn, WA 98524 • *900*
Alma, AR 72921 • *2,755*
Alma, GA 31510 • *3,819*
Alma, IL 62807 • *428*
Alma, KS 66401 • *925*
Alma, MI 48801 • *9,652*
Alma, MO 64001 • *445*
Alma, NE 68920 • *1,369*
Alma, WI 54610 • *876*
Alma Center, WI 54611 • *454*
Almena, KS 67622 • *517*
Almena, WI 54805 • *526*
Almira, WA 99103 • *330*
Almon, GA 30209 • *350*
Almond, NY 14804 • *568*
Almond, WI 54909 • *477*
Almont, MI 48003 • *1,857*
Almyra, AR 72003 • *294*
Almyville, CT 06354 • *400*
Aloha, OR 97007 • *10,000*
Alondra, CA 90249 • *12,096*
Alpaugh, CA 93201 • *900*
Alpena, AR 72611 • *344*
Alpena, MI 49707 • *12,214*
Alpena, SD 57312 • *288*
Alpena □, MI • *32,315*
Alpha, IL 61413 • *815*
Alpha, MI 49902 • *229*
Alpha, NJ 08865 • *2,644*
Alpharetta, GA 30201 • *3,128*
Alpine, AZ 85920 • *500*
Alpine, NJ 07620 • *1,549*
Alpine, TX 79830 • *5,465*
Alpine, UT 84003 • *2,649*
Alpine □, CA • *1,097*
Alsea, OR 97324 • *400*
Alsey, IL 62610 • *318*
Alsip, IL 60658 • *17,134*
Alstead, NH 03602 • *500*
Alta, IA 51002 • *1,720*
Alta, UT 84092 • *381*
Altadena, CA 91001 • *40,983*
Altamahaw, NC 27202 • *350*
Altamont, IL 62411 • *2,389*
Altamont, KS 67330 • *1,054*
Altamont, NY 12009 • *1,292*
Altamont, OR 97601 • *19,805*
Altamont, TN 37301 • *679*
Altamont, UT 84001 • *247*
Altamonte Springs, FL 32701 • *22,028*
Alta Vista, IA 50603 • *314*
Alta Vista, KS 66834 • *430*
Altavista, VA 24517 • *3,849*
Altenburg, MO 63732 • *280*
Altha, FL 32421 • *478*
Altheimer, AR 72004 • *1,231*
Altmar, NY 13302 • *347*
Alto, GA 30510 • *618*
Alto, MI 49302 • *250*
Alto, TX 75925 • *1,203*
Alton, IL 62002 • *34,171*
Alton, IA 51003 • *986*
Alton, LA 70458 • *300*
Alton, MO 65606 • *721*
Alton, NH 03809 • *900*
Alton, OH 43119 • *350*
Alton, RI 02894 • *300*
Altona, IL 61414 • *610*
Altona, IN 46738 • *263*
Altona, NY 12910 • *400*
Alton Bay, NH 03810 • *900*
Altoona, AL 35952 • *928*
Altoona, FL 32702 • *1,300*
Altoona, IA 50009 • *5,764*
Altoona, KS 66710 • *564*
Altoona, PA 16601-03 • *57,078*
Altoona, WI 54720 • *4,393*
Alto Pass, IL 62905 • *369*
Altro, KY 41306 • *300*
Altura, MN 55910 • *354*
Alturas, CA 96101 • *3,025*
Altus, AR 72821 • *441*
Altus, OK 73521 • *23,101*
Alum Bank, PA 15521 • *275*
Alum Creek, WV 25003 • *500*
Alum Rock, CA 95127 • *17,471*
Alva, FL 33920 • *1,200*
Alva, OK 73717 • *6,416*
Alvarado, MN 56710 • *385*
Alvarado, TX 76009 • *2,701*
Alverton, PA 15612 • *400*
Alvin, IL 61811 • *378*
Alvin, TX 77511 • *16,515*
Alvord, IA 51230 • *246*
Alvord, TX 76225 • *874*
Alvordton, OH 43501 • *362*
Ama, LA 70031 • *875*
Amador □, CA • *19,314*
Amagansett, NY 11930 • *1,800*
Amalga, UT 84335 • *323*
Amana, IA 52203 • *600*
Amanda, OH 43102 • *720*
Amarillo, TX 79101-99 • *149,230*
Amasa, MI 49903 • *600*
Amazonia, MO 64421 • *314*
Amber, OK 73004 • *416*
Amberg, WI 54102 • *350*
Ambia, IN 47917 • *274*
Ambler, PA 19002 • *6,628*
Amboy, IL 61310 • *2,377*
Amboy, IN 46911 • *450*
Amboy, MN 56010 • *606*
Amboy, WA 98601 • *300*
Ambridge, PA 15003 • *9,575*
Ambrose, GA 31512 • *360*
Ambrosia Lake, NM 87020 • *300*
Amelia, LA 70340 • *3,612*
Amelia, OH 45102 • *1,108*
Amelia □, VA • *8,405*
Amelia Court House, VA 23002 • *700*
Amenia, NY 12501 • *1,157*
American Falls, ID 83211 • *3,626*
American Fork, UT 84003 • *12,693*
Americus, GA 31709 • *16,120*
Americus, KS 66835 • *915*
Amery, WI 54001 • *2,404*
Ames, IA 50010 • *45,775*
Ames, OK 73718 • *314*
Amesbury, MA 01913 • *13,971*
Amherst, MA 01002 • *26,300*
Amherst, NE 68812 • *269*
Amherst, NH 03031 • *750*
Amherst, NY 14226 • *66,100*
Amherst, OH 44001 • *10,638*
Amherst, TX 79312 • *971*
Amherst, VA 24521 • *1,135*
Amherst, WI 54406 • *701*
Amherst □, VA • *29,122*
Amherstdale, WV 25607 • *800*
Amite, LA 70422 • *4,301*
Amite □, MS • *13,369*
Amity, AR 71921 • *859*
Amity, OR 97101 • *1,092*
Amityville, NY 11701 • *9,076*
Ammon, ID 83401 • *4,669*
Amo, IN 46103 • *444*
Amonate, VA 24601 • *400*
Amoret, MO 64722 • *238*
Amory, MS 38821 • *7,307*
Amsterdam, MO 64723 • *231*
Amsterdam, NY 12010 • *21,872*
Amsterdam, OH 43903 • *783*
Amston, CT 06231 • *300*
Anacoco, LA 71403 • *820*
Anaconda, MT 59711 • *12,518*
Anaconda, NM 87020 • *250*
Anacortes, WA 98221 • *9,013*
Anadarko, OK 73005 • *6,378*
Anaheim, CA 92801-99 • *219,494*
Anahola, HI 96703 • *915*
Anahuac, TX 77514 • *1,840*
Anamoose, ND 58710 • *355*
Anamosa, IA 52205 • *4,958*
Anandale, LA 71301 • *2,000*
Anawalt, WV 24808 • *652*
Anchorage, AK 99501-40 • *174,431*
Anchorage, KY 40223 • *1,726*
Anchor Point, AK 99556 • *226*
Anco, KY 41711 • *350*
Andale, KS 67001 • *538*
Andalusia, AL 36420 • *10,415*
Andalusia, IL 61232 • *1,238*
Anderson, AL 35610 • *405*
Anderson, AK 99704 • *517*
Anderson, CA 96007 • *7,381*
Anderson, IN 46011-18 • *64,695*
Anderson, MO 64831 • *1,237*
Anderson, SC 29621-24 • *27,965*
Anderson, TX 77830 • *600*
Anderson □, KS • *8,749*
Anderson □, KY • *12,567*
Anderson □, SC • *133,235*
Anderson □, TN • *67,346*
Anderson □, TX • *38,381*
Andersonville, GA 31711 • *267*
Andersonville, IN 47024 • *350*
Andes, NY 13731 • *372*
Andover, CT 06232 • *350*
Andover, IL 61233 • *612*
Andover, KS 67002 • *2,801*
Andover, ME 04216 • *470*
Andover, MA 01810 • *8,445*
Andover, MN 55303 • *9,387*
Andover, NH 03216 • *400*
Andover, NY 14806 • *1,120*
Andover, OH 44003 • *1,205*
Andrew, IA 52030 • *349*
Andrew □, MO • *13,980*
Andrews, IN 46702 • *1,243*
Andrews, NC 28901 • *1,621*
Andrews, SC 29510 • *3,129*
Andrews, TX 79714 • *11,061*
Andrews □, TX • *13,323*
Androscoggin □, ME • *99,657*
Aneta, ND 58212 • *341*
Angelica, NY 14709 • *982*
Angelina □, TX • *64,172*
Angels Camp, CA 95222 • *2,302*
Angie, LA 70426 • *311*
Angier, NC 27501 • *1,709*
Angleton, TX 77515 • *13,929*
Angola, IN 46703 • *5,486*
Angola, NY 14006 • *2,292*
Angoon, AK 99820 • *465*
Anguilla, MS 38721 • *950*
Aniak, AK 99557 • *341*
Anita, IA 50020 • *1,153*
Anita, PA 15711 • *600*
Aniwa, WI 54408 • *273*
Ankeny, IA 50021 • *15,429*
Anna, IL 62906 • *5,408*
Anna, OH 45302 • *1,038*
Annabella, UT 84711 • *463*
Annalee Heights, VA 22042 • *1,750*
Anna Maria, FL 33501 • *1,537*
Annandale, MN 55302 • *1,568*
Annandale, NJ 08801 • *1,040*
Annandale, VA 22003 • *35,300*
Annapolis, MD 21401-99 • *31,740*
Annapolis, MO 63620 • *370*
Annapolis Junction, MD 20701 • *600*
Ann Arbor, MI 48103-09 • *107,966*
Annawan, IL 61234 • *908*
Anne Arundel □, MD • *370,775*
Anniston, AL 36201-05 • *29,523*
Anniston, MO 63820 • *320*
Annville, KY 40402 • *240*
Annville, PA 17003 • *4,493*
Anoka, MN 55303 • *15,634*
Anoka □, MN • *195,998*
Ansley, NE 68814 • *644*
Anson, ME 04911 • *900*
Anson, TX 79501 • *2,831*
Anson □, NC • *25,649*
Ansonia, CT 06401 • *19,039*
Ansonia, OH 45303 • *1,267*
Ansonville, NC 28007 • *794*
Ansted, WV 25812 • *1,952*
Antelope, SD 57555 • *400*
Antelope □, NE • *8,675*
Antes Fort, PA 17720 • *300*
Anthon, IA 51004 • *687*
Anthony, FL 32617 • *1,200*
Anthony, KS 67003 • *2,661*
Anthony, NM 88021 • *3,285*
Anthony, RI 02816 • *4,500*
Antigo, WI 54409 • *8,653*
Antioch, CA 94509 • *42,683*
Antioch, IL 60002 • *4,419*
Antioch, IN 46041 • *300*
Antlers, OK 74523 • *2,989*
Anton, TX 79313 • *1,180*
Antonia, MO 63052 • *500*
Antonito, CO 81120 • *1,103*
Antrim, NH 03440 • *1,142*
Antrim, PA 16901 • *350*
Antrim □, MI • *16,194*
Antwerp, NY 13608 • *749*
Antwerp, OH 45813 • *1,765*
Apache, OK 73006 • *1,560*
Apache □, AZ • *52,108*
Apache Junction, AZ 85220 • *9,935*
Apalachicola, FL 32320 • *2,565*
Apalachin, NY 13732 • *1,233*
Apex, NC 27502 • *2,847*
Apison, TN 37302 • *450*
Aplington, IA 50604 • *1,027*
Apollo, PA 15613 • *2,212*
Apopka, FL 32703 • *6,019*
Appalachia, VA 24216 • *2,418*
Appanoose □, IA • *15,511*
Appleby, TX 75961 • *453*
Apple Creek, OH 44606 • *741*
Applegate, MI 48401 • *257*
Applegate, OR 97530 • *800*
Apple River, IL 61001 • *472*
Appleton, MN 56208 • *1,842*
Appleton, WI 54911-19 • *58,913*
Appleton City, MO 64724 • *1,257*
Apple Valley, CA 92307 • *14,305*
Apple Valley, MN 55124 • *21,818*
Apple Valley, ND 58558 • *250*
Applewood, CO 80401 • *7,200*
Appleyard, WA 98801 • *1,500*
Appling □, GA • *15,565*
Appomattox, VA 24522 • *1,345*
Appomattox □, VA • *11,971*
Aptos, CA 95003 • *7,039*
Aquebogue, NY 11931 • *1,300*
Arab, AL 35016 • *5,967*
Arabi, GA 31712 • *376*
Arabi, LA 70032 • *10,248*
Aragon, GA 30104 • *855*
Aransas □, TX • *14,260*
Aransas Pass, TX 78336 • *7,173*
Arapaho, OK 73620 • *851*
Arapahoe, NE 68922 • *1,107*
Arapahoe, NC 28510 • *467*
Arapahoe □, CO • *293,621*
Arbuckle, CA 95912 • *1,306*
Arbyrd, MO 63821 • *704*
Arcade, CA 95821 • *37,600*
Arcade, GA 30549 • *223*
Arcade, NY 14009 • *2,052*
Arcadia, CA 91006 • *45,994*
Arcadia, FL 33821 • *6,002*
Arcadia, IN 46030 • *1,801*
Arcadia, IA 51430 • *454*
Arcadia, KS 66711 • *460*
Arcadia, LA 71001 • *3,403*
Arcadia, MI 49613 • *350*
Arcadia, MO 63621 • *683*
Arcadia, NE 68815 • *412*
Arcadia, OH 44804 • *580*
Arcadia, OK 73007 • *400*
Arcadia, PA 15712 • *500*
Arcadia, SC 29320 • *2,088*
Arcadia, WI 54612 • *2,109*
Arcanum, OH 45304 • *2,002*
Arcata, CA 95521 • *12,850*
Archbald, PA 18403 • *6,295*
Archbold, OH 43502 • *3,318*
Archdale, NC 27263 • *5,326*
Archer, FL 32618 • *1,230*
Archer □, TX • *7,266*
Archer City, TX 76351 • *1,862*
Archie, MO 64725 • *753*
Archuleta □, CO • *3,664*
Arco, ID 83213 • *1,241*
Arcola, IL 61910 • *2,714*
Arcola, IN 46704 • *300*
Arcola, MS 38722 • *588*
Arden, NC 28704 • *500*
Arden Hills, MN 55112 • *8,012*
Ardmore, AL 35739 • *1,096*
Ardmore, IN 46628 • *3,400*
Ardmore, MD 20706 • *900*
Ardmore, OK 73401 • *23,689*
Ardmore, PA 19003 • *13,600*
Ardmore, TN 38449 • *835*
Ardsley, NY 10502 • *4,183*
Arena, WI 53503 • *451*

Arenac □, MI • *14,706*
Arenas Valley, NM 88022 • *500*
Arendtsville, PA 17303 • *600*
Arenzville, IL 62611 • *495*
Argenta, IL 62501 • *994*
Argonia, KS 67004 • *587*
Argonne, WI 54511 • *250*
Argos, IN 46501 • *1,547*
Argyle, MN 56713 • *741*
Argyle, NY 12809 • *320*
Argyle, WI 53504 • *720*
Arimo, ID 83214 • *338*
Aripeka, FL 33502 • *350*
Ariton, AL 36311 • *844*
Arizona Sunsites, AZ 85625 • *900*
Arjay, KY 40902 • *650*
Arkabutla, MS 38602 • *270*
Arkadelphia, AR 71923 • *10,005*
Arkansas □, AR • *24,175*
Arkansas City, AR 71630 • *668*
Arkansas City, KS 67005 • *13,201*
Arkoma, OK 74901 • *2,175*
Arkport, NY 14807 • *811*
Arkville, NY 12406 • *600*
Arkwright, RI 02816 • *1,500*
Arley, AL 35541 • *276*
Arlington, GA 31713 • *1,572*
Arlington, IL 61312 • *236*
Arlington, IN 46104 • *500*
Arlington, IA 50606 • *498*
Arlington, KS 67514 • *631*
Arlington, KY 42021 • *511*
Arlington, LA 70808 • *850*
Arlington, MA 02174 • *48,219*
Arlington, MN 55307 • *1,779*
Arlington, NE 68002 • *1,117*
Arlington, NC 28642 • *872*
Arlington, NY 12603 • *11,203*
Arlington, OH 45814 • *1,187*
Arlington, OR 97812 • *521*
Arlington, SC 29651 • *600*
Arlington, SD 57212 • *991*
Arlington, TN 38002 • *1,778*
Arlington, TX 76010-19 • *160,113*
Arlington, VT 05250 • *800*
Arlington, VA 22201-99 • *152,700*
Arlington, WA 98223 • *3,282*
Arlington, WI 53911 • *440*
Arlington □, VA • *152,599*
Arlington Heights, IL 60004-08 • *66,116*
Arma, KS 66712 • *1,676*
Armada, MI 48005 • *1,392*
Armijo, NM 87105 • *18,900*
Armington, IL 61721 • *297*
Armonk, NY 10504 • *5,900*
Armorel, AR 72310 • *300*
Armour, SD 57313 • *819*
Armstrong, IL 61812 • *275*
Armstrong, IA 50514 • *1,153*
Armstrong, MO 65230 • *360*
Armstrong □, PA • *77,768*
Armstrong □, TX • *1,994*
Armuchee, GA 30105 • *250*
Arnaudville, LA 70512 • *1,679*
Arnett, OK 73832 • *714*
Arnett, WV 25007 • *400*
Arnold, CA 95223 • *2,385*
Arnold, MN 55803 • *1,350*
Arnold, MO 63010 • *19,141*
Arnold, NE 69120 • *813*
Arnold, PA 15068 • *6,853*
Arnold Mills, RI 02864 • *600*
Arnolds Park, IA 51331 • *1,051*
Arnot, PA 16911 • *300*
Aroma Park, IL 60910 • *673*
Aroostook □, ME • *91,331*
Arp, TX 75750 • *939*
Arpin, WI 54410 • *361*
Arriba, CO 80804 • *236*
Arrowhead Village, NJ 08723 • *3,100*
Arrowsmith, IL 61722 • *292*
Arroyo Grande, CA 93420 • *11,290*
Arroyo Seco, NM 87514 • *500*
Artemus, KY 40903 • *500*
Artesia, CA 90701 • *14,301*
Artesia, MS 39736 • *526*
Artesia, NM 88210 • *10,385*
Artesian, SD 57314 • *227*
Arthur, IL 61911 • *2,122*
Arthur, IA 51431 • *288*
Arthur, ND 58006 • *445*
Arthur, TN 37707 • *350*
Arthur □, NE • *513*
Arundel Village, MD 21225 • *5,300*
Arvada, CO 80001-05 • *84,576*
Arvin, CA 93203 • *6,863*
Arvonia, VA 23004 • *700*
Asbury Park, NJ 07712 • *17,015*
Ascension □, LA • *50,068*
Ashaway, RI 02804 • *1,747*
Ashburn, GA 31714 • *4,766*
Ashburn, VA 22011 • *300*
Ashburnham, MA 01430 • *1,150*
Ashby, MA 01431 • *600*
Ashby, MN 56309 • *486*
Ashdown, AR 71822 • *4,218*
Ashe □, NC • *22,325*
Asheboro, NC 27203 • *15,252*
Asher, OK 74826 • *659*
Asherton, TX 78827 • *1,574*
Asheville, NC 28801-99 • *53,583*
Ashfield, MA 01330 • *600*
Ash Flat, AR 72513 • *524*
Ashford, AL 36312 • *2,165*
Ashford, WV 25009 • *280*
Ash Fork, AZ 86320 • *600*
Ash Grove, MO 65604 • *1,157*
Ashkum, IL 60911 • *735*
Ashland, AL 36251 • *2,052*
Ashland, CA 94541 • *13,893*
Ashland, IL 62612 • *1,351*
Ashland, KS 67831 • *1,096*
Ashland, KY 41101 • *27,064*
Ashland, LA 71002 • *307*
Ashland, ME 04732 • *800*
Ashland, MA 01721 • *9,165*
Ashland, MS 38603 • *532*
Ashland, MO 65010 • *1,021*
Ashland, NE 68003 • *2,274*
Ashland, NH 03217 • *1,479*
Ashland, OH 44805 • *20,326*
Ashland, OR 97520 • *14,943*
Ashland, PA 17921 • *4,235*
Ashland, VA 23005 • *4,640*
Ashland, WI 54806 • *9,115*
Ashland □, OH • *46,178*
Ashland □, WI • *16,783*
Ashland City, TN 37015 • *2,329*
Ashley, IL 62808 • *658*
Ashley, IN 46705 • *841*
Ashley, MI 48806 • *570*
Ashley, ND 58413 • *1,192*
Ashley, OH 43003 • *1,057*
Ashley, PA 18706 • *3,512*
Ashley □, AR • *26,538*
Ashley Falls, MA 01222 • *400*
Ashmore, IL 61912 • *883*
Ashokan, NY 12481 • *350*
Ashtabula, OH 44004 • *23,449*
Ashtabula □, OH • *104,215*
Ashton, ID 83420 • *1,219*
Ashton, IL 61006 • *1,140*
Ashton, IA 51232 • *441*
Ashton, MD 20861 • *1,010*
Ashton, NE 68817 • *273*
Ashton, RI 02864 • *875*
Ashuelot, NH 03441 • *350*
Ashville, AL 35953 • *1,489*
Ashville, OH 43103 • *2,046*
Ashwaubenon, WI 54304 • *14,486*
Ashwood, TN 38401 • *400*
Askov, MN 55704 • *350*
Asotin, WA 99402 • *943*
Asotin □, WA • *16,823*
Aspen, CO 81611 • *3,678*
Aspen Hill, MD 20906 • *9,800*
Aspermont, TX 79502 • *1,357*
Aspers, PA 17304 • *275*
Aspinwall, PA 15215 • *3,284*
Assaria, KS 67416 • *414*
Assinippi, MA 02339 • *1,400*
Assonet, MA 02702 • *900*
Assumption, IL 62510 • *1,283*
Assumption □, LA • *22,084*
Aston, PA 19014 • *6,900*
Astor, FL 32002 • *950*
Astoria, IL 61501 • *1,370*
Astoria, OR 97103 • *9,998*
Atalissa, IA 52720 • *360*
Atascadero, CA 93422 • *16,232*
Atascosa □, TX • *25,055*
Atchison, KS 66002 • *11,407*
Atchison □, KS • *18,397*
Atchison □, MO • *8,605*
Atco, NJ 08004 • *2,100*
Athalia, OH 45669 • *367*
Athena, OR 97813 • *965*
Athens, AL 35611 • *14,558*
Athens, GA 30601-13 • *42,549*
Athens, IL 62613 • *1,371*
Athens, LA 71003 • *419*
Athens, MI 49011 • *960*
Athens, NY 12015 • *1,738*
Athens, OH 45701 • *19,743*
Athens, PA 18810 • *3,622*
Athens, TN 37303 • *12,080*
Athens, TX 75751 • *10,197*
Athens, WV 24712 • *1,147*
Athens, WI 54411 • *988*
Athens □, OH • *56,399*
Atherton, CA 94025 • *7,797*
Athol, ID 83801 • *312*
Athol, MA 01331 • *10,634*
Atkins, AR 72823 • *3,002*
Atkins, VA 24311 • *500*
Atkinson, IL 61235 • *1,138*
Atkinson, NE 68713 • *1,521*
Atkinson, NH 03811 • *900*
Atkinson, NC 28421 • *298*
Atkinson □, GA • *6,141*
Atlanta, GA 30301-99 • *425,022*
Atlanta, IL 61723 • *1,807*
Atlanta, IN 46031 • *657*
Atlanta, KS 67008 • *256*
Atlanta, MI 49709 • *650*
Atlanta, MO 63530 • *441*
Atlanta, NY 14808 • *750*
Atlanta, TX 75551 • *6,272*
Atlantic, IA 50022 • *7,789*
Atlantic, NC 28511 • *900*
Atlantic □, NJ • *194,119*
Atlantic Beach, FL 32233 • *7,847*
Atlantic City, NJ 08401-99 • *40,199*
Atlantic Highlands, NJ 07716 • *4,950*
Atlantic Mine, MI 49905 • *400*
Atmore, AL 36502 • *8,789*
Atoka, OK 74525 • *3,409*
Atoka, TN 38004 • *691*
Atoka □, OK • *12,748*
Attala □, MS • *19,865*
Attalla, AL 35954 • *7,737*
Attapulgus, GA 31715 • *623*
Attawaugan, CT 06241 • *450*
Attica, IN 47918 • *3,841*
Attica, KS 67009 • *730*
Attica, MI 48412 • *350*
Attica, NY 14011 • *2,659*
Attica, OH 44807 • *865*
Attleboro, MA 02703 • *34,196*
Atwater, CA 95301 • *17,530*
Atwater, MN 56209 • *1,128*
Atwood, IL 61913 • *1,464*
Atwood, IN 46502 • *300*
Atwood, KS 67730 • *1,665*
Atwood, OK 74827 • *300*
Atwood, TN 38220 • *1,143*
Auberry, CA 93602 • *1,100*
Aubrey, AR 72311 • *267*
Auburn, AL 36830 • *28,471*
Auburn, CA 95603 • *7,540*
Auburn, GA 30203 • *692*
Auburn, IL 62615 • *3,616*
Auburn, IN 46706 • *8,122*
Auburn, IA 51433 • *320*
Auburn, KS 66402 • *890*
Auburn, KY 42206 • *1,467*
Auburn, ME 04210 • *23,128*
Auburn, MA 01501 • *14,845*
Auburn, MI 48611 • *1,921*
Auburn, NE 68305 • *3,482*
Auburn, NH 03032 • *400*
Auburn, NY 13021 • *32,548*
Auburn, PA 17922 • *999*
Auburn, WA 98002-03 • *26,417*
Auburndale, FL 33823 • *6,501*
Auburndale, WI 54412 • *641*
Auburn Heights, MI 48057 • *4,000*
Audrain □, MO • *26,458*
Audubon, IA 50025 • *2,841*
Audubon, MN 56511 • *383*
Audubon, NJ 08106 • *9,533*
Audubon □, IA • *8,559*
Auglaize □, OH • *42,554*
Au Gres, MI 48703 • *768*
Augusta, AR 72006 • *3,496*
Augusta, GA 30901-99 • *47,532*
Augusta, IL 62311 • *764*
Augusta, KS 67010 • *6,968*
Augusta, KY 41002 • *1,455*
Augusta, ME 04330 • *21,819*
Augusta, MI 49012 • *913*
Augusta, MO 63332 • *308*
Augusta, MT 59410 • *450*
Augusta, OH 44607 • *275*
Augusta, WI 54722 • *1,560*
Augusta □, VA • *53,732*
Augusta Springs, VA 24411 • *300*
Aulander, NC 27805 • *1,214*
Ault, CO 80610 • *1,056*
Aumsville, OR 97325 • *1,432*
Aurelia, IA 51005 • *1,143*
Aurora, CO 80010-17 • *158,588*
Aurora, IL 60504-07 • *81,293*
Aurora, IN 47001 • *3,816*
Aurora, IA 50607 • *248*
Aurora, MN 55705 • *2,670*
Aurora, MO 65605 • *6,437*
Aurora, NE 68818 • *3,717*
Aurora, NC 27806 • *698*
Aurora, NY 13026 • *926*
Aurora, OH 44202 • *8,177*
Aurora, OR 97002 • *523*
Aurora, SD 57002 • *507*
Aurora, UT 84620 • *874*
Aurora, WI 49801 • *400*
Aurora □, SD • *3,628*
Au Sable, MI 48750 • *1,240*
Au Sable Forks, NY 12912 • *2,100*
Austell, GA 30001 • *3,939*
Austin, AR 72007 • *269*
Austin, IN 47102 • *4,857*
Austin, MN 55912 • *23,020*
Austin, NV 89310 • *350*
Austin, PA 16720 • *740*
Austin, TX 78701-99 • *345,496*
Austin □, TX • *17,726*
Austinburg, OH 44010 • *600*
Austintown, OH 44512 • *33,636*
Austinville, VA 24312 • *800*
Austwell, TX 77950 • *280*
Autauga □, AL • *32,259*
Autaugaville, AL 36003 • *843*
Au Train, MI 49806 • *300*
Auxier, KY 41602 • *900*
Auxvasse, MO 65231 • *858*
Ava, IL 62907 • *811*
Ava, MO 65608 • *2,761*
Ava, OH 43711 • *250*
Avalon, CA 90704 • *2,022*
Avalon, NJ 08202 • *2,162*
Avalon, PA 15202 • *6,240*
Avant, OK 74001 • *461*
Avella, PA 15312 • *1,109*
Avenal, CA 93204 • *4,137*
Avenel, MD 20783 • *5,600*
Avenel, NJ 07001 • *11,500*
Avenue, MD 20609 • *300*
Avera, GA 30803 • *248*
Averill Park, NY 12018 • *1,500*
Avery, TX 75554 • *520*
Avery □, NC • *14,409*
Avery Island, LA 70513 • *575*
Avila Beach, CA 93424 • *600*
Avilla, IN 46710 • *1,272*
Avis, PA 17721 • *1,718*
Aviston, IL 62216 • *846*
Avoca, AR 72711 • *256*
Avoca, IN 47420 • *300*
Avoca, IA 51521 • *1,650*
Avoca, MI 48006 • *250*
Avoca, NE 68307 • *242*
Avoca, NY 14809 • *1,144*
Avoca, PA 18641 • *3,536*
Avoca, WI 53506 • *505*
Avocado Heights, CA 91746 • *11,721*
Avon, CT 06001 • *1,434*
Avon, IL 61415 • *1,019*
Avon, MA 02322 • *5,026*
Avon, MN 56310 • *804*
Avon, NC 27915 • *300*
Avon, NY 14414 • *3,006*
Avon, OH 44011 • *7,241*
Avon, SD 57315 • *576*
Avon by the Sea, NJ 07717 • *2,337*
Avondale, AZ 85323 • *8,168*
Avondale, CO 81022 • *800*
Avondale, LA 70094 • *6,699*
Avondale, MO 64117 • *612*
Avondale, OH 45404 • *5,000*
Avondale, PA 19311 • *891*
Avondale Estates, GA 30002 • *1,313*
Avon Lake, IA 50047 • *600*
Avon Lake, OH 44012 • *13,222*
Avonmore, PA 15618 • *1,234*
Avon Park, FL 33825 • *8,026*
Avoyelles □, LA • *41,393*
Axis, AL 36505 • *600*
Axtell, KS 66403 • *470*
Axtell, NE 68924 • *602*
Ayden, NC 28513 • *4,361*
Ayer, MA 01432-33 • *6,993*
Aynor, SC 29511 • *643*
Ayrshire, IA 50515 • *243*
Azalea Park, FL 32807 • *8,304*
Azle, TX 76020 • *5,822*
Aztec, NM 87410 • *5,512*
Azusa, CA 91702 • *29,380*

B

Babbie, AL 36420 • *553*
Babbitt, MN 55706 • *2,435*
Babbitt, NV 89416 • *1,800*
Babcock, WI 54413 • *250*
Baboosic Lake, NH 03031 • *400*
Babson Park, FL 33827 • *950*
Babylon, NY 11702-04 • *12,388*

Baca □, CO • 5,419
Backus, MN 56435 • 255
Bacobi, AZ 86030 • 300
Bacon □, GA • 9,379
Baconton, GA 31716 • 763
Bad Axe, MI 48413 • 3,184
Baden, PA 15005 • 5,318
Badger, IA 50516 • 653
Badger, MN 56714 • 320
Badin, NC 28009 • 1,514
Bagdad, AZ 86321 • 2,331
Bagdad, FL 32530 • 1,479
Bagdad, KY 40003 • 250
Baggs, WY 82321 • 433
Bagley, IA 50026 • 370
Bagley, MN 56621 • 1,321
Bagley, WI 53801 • 317
Bahama, NC 27503 • 400
Bailey, NC 27807 • 685
Bailey □, TX • 8,168
Bailey Island, ME 04003 • 650
Baileys Crossroads, VA 22041 • 4,600
Baileys Harbor, WI 54202 • 350
Baileyton, AL 35019 • 396
Baileyton, TN 37743 • 333
Bainbridge, GA 31717 • 10,553
Bainbridge, IN 46105 • 644
Bainbridge, NY 13733 • 1,603
Bainbridge, OH 45612 • 1,042
Bainville, MT 59212 • 245
Baird, TX 79504 • 1,696
Bairdford, PA 15006 • 950
Baker, CA 92309 • 650
Baker, FL 32531 • 600
Baker, LA 70714 • 12,865
Baker, MT 59313 • 2,354
Baker, OR 97814 • 9,471
Baker □, FL • 15,289
Baker □, GA • 3,808
Baker □, OR • 16,134
Baker Hill, AL 36004 • 250
Bakers, NC 28110 • 300
Bakersfield, CA 93301-99 • 105,735
Bakersfield, MO 65609 • 241
Bakersfield, VT 05441 • 350
Bakerstown, PA 15007 • 1,000
Bakersville, CT 06057 • 450
Bakersville, NC 28705 • 373
Bakerton, WV 25410 • 250
Bala-Cynwyd, PA 19004 • 8,600
Balaton, MN 56115 • 752
Balch Springs, TX 75180 • 13,746
Bald Knob, AR 72010 • 2,756
Baldwin, FL 32234 • 1,526
Baldwin, GA 30511 • 1,080
Baldwin, IL 62217 • 474
Baldwin, LA 70514 • 2,644
Baldwin, MI 49304 • 674
Baldwin, NY 11510 • 35,100
Baldwin, PA 15234 • 24,712
Baldwin, SC 29706 • 700
Baldwin, WI 54002 • 1,620
Baldwin □, AL • 78,556
Baldwin □, GA • 34,686
Baldwin City, KS 66006 • 2,829
Baldwin Park, CA 91706 • 50,554
Baldwinsville, NY 13027 • 6,446
Baldwinville, MA 01436 • 1,709
Baldwyn, MS 38824 • 3,427
Balfour, NC 28706 • 1,772
Ball, LA 71405 • 3,405
Ballard □, KY • 8,798
Ballardvale, MA 01810 • 1,300
Ball Ground, GA 30107 • 640
Ballinger, TX 76821 • 4,207
Ballouville, CT 06233 • 500
Ballston Spa, NY 12020 • 4,711
Ballwin, MO 63011 • 12,656
Bally, PA 19503 • 1,051
Balm, FL 33503 • 600
Balmorhea, TX 79718 • 568
Balmville, NY 12550 • 3,214
Balsam, NC 28707 • 350
Balsam Lake, WI 54810 • 749
Baltic, CT 06330 • 1,500
Baltic, OH 43804 • 563
Baltic, SD 57003 • 679
Baltimore, MD 21201-99 • 786,775
Baltimore, OH 43105 • 2,689
Baltimore □, MD • 655,615
Baltimore Highlands, MD 21227 • 6,750
Bamberg, SC 29003 • 3,672
Bamberg □, SC • 18,118
Bancroft, ID 83217 • 505
Bancroft, IA 50517 • 1,082
Bancroft, MI 48414 • 618
Bancroft, NE 68004 • 552
Bandana, KY 42022 • 250
Bandera, TX 78003 • 947
Bandera □, TX • 7,084
Bandon, OR 97411 • 2,311
Bangor, ME 04401 • 31,643
Bangor, MI 49013 • 2,001
Bangor, PA 18013 • 5,006
Bangor, WI 54614 • 1,012
Bangor Township, MI 48706 • 17,494
Bangs, TX 76823 • 1,716
Banks, OR 97106 • 489
Banks □, GA • 8,702
Banner □, NE • 918
Banner Elk, NC 28604 • 1,087
Banning, CA 92220 • 14,020
Bannock □, ID • 65,421
Bantam, CT 06750 • 860
Bapchule, AZ 85221 • 380
Baptistown, NJ 08803 • 350
Baraboo, WI 53913 • 8,081
Baraga, MI 49908 • 1,055
Baraga □, MI • 8,484
Barataria, LA 70036 • 1,123
Barber □, KS • 6,548
Barberton, OH 44203 • 29,751
Barberville, FL 32005 • 300
Barbour □, AL • 24,756
Barbour □, WV • 16,639
Barboursville, WV 25504 • 2,871
Barbourville, KY 40906 • 3,333
Bardolph, IL 61416 • 294
Bardstown, KY 40004 • 6,155
Bardwell, KY 42023 • 988
Bargersville, IN 46106 • 1,647
Bar Harbor, ME 04609 • 2,685
Barium Springs, NC 28010 • 250
Barker, NY 14012 • 535
Barker Heights, NC 28739 • 1,267
Barkeyville, PA 16038 • 266
Bark River, MI 49807 • 300
Barling, AR 72923 • 3,761
Barlow, KY 42024 • 746
Bar Mills, ME 04004 • 825
Barnard, MO 64423 • 234
Barnardsville, NC 28709 • 500
Barnegat, NJ 08005 • 1,012
Barnegat Light, NJ 08006 • 619
Barnegat Pines, NJ 08731 • 300
Barnes, KS 66933 • 257
Barnes □, ND • 13,960
Barnesboro, PA 15714 • 2,741
Barnes City, IA 50027 • 266
Barnesville, GA 30204 • 4,887
Barnesville, MN 56514 • 2,207
Barnesville, OH 43713 • 4,633
Barneveld, WI 53507 • 579
Barnhart, MO 63012 • 800
Barnhill, OH 44663 • 327
Barnsdall, OK 74002 • 1,501
Barnstable, MA 02630 • 2,033
Barnstable □, MA • 147,925
Barnstead, NH 03218 • 300
Barnum, MN 55707 • 464
Barnwell, SC 29812 • 5,572
Barnwell □, SC • 19,868
Baroda, MI 49101 • 627
Barrackville, WV 26559 • 1,815
Barre, MA 01005 • 1,136
Barre, VT 05641 • 9,824
Barrelville, MD 21545 • 350
Barren □, KY • 34,009
Barre Plains, MA 01005 • 550
Barrett, MN 56311 • 388
Barrett, WV 25013 • 800
Barrington, IL 60010 • 9,029
Barrington, NH 03825 • 300
Barrington, NJ 08007 • 7,418
Barrington, RI 02806 • 16,174
Barron, WI 54812 • 2,595
Barron □, WI • 38,730
Barron Lake, MI 49120 • 1,600
Barrow, AK 99723 • 2,207
Barrow □, GA • 21,354
Barrowsville, MA 02766 • 350
Barry, IL 62312 • 1,487
Barry □, MI • 45,781
Barry □, MO • 24,408
Barryton, MI 49305 • 422
Barryville, NY 12719 • 600
Barstow, CA 92311 • 17,690
Barstow, TX 79719 • 637
Bartelso, IL 62218 • 389
Barth, FL 32533 • 240
Bartholomew □, IN • 65,088
Bartlesville, OK 74003-06 • 34,568
Bartlett, IL 60103 • 13,254
Bartlett, NH 03812 • 700
Bartlett, TN 38134 • 17,170
Bartlett, TX 76511 • 1,567
Bartley, NE 69020 • 342
Barton, MD 21521 • 617
Barton, OH 43905 • 1,039
Barton, VT 05822 • 1,062
Barton □, KS • 31,343
Barton □, MO • 11,292
Bartonville, IL 61607 • 6,137
Bartow, FL 33830 • 14,780
Bartow, GA 30413 • 357
Bartow □, GA • 40,760
Barview, OR 97420 • 1,462
Barwick, GA 31720 • 413
Basalt, CO 81621 • 529
Basalt, ID 83218 • 414
Bascom, OH 44809 • 550
Basehor, KS 66007 • 1,483
Basile, LA 70515 • 2,635
Basin, WY 82410 • 1,349
Baskett, KY 42402 • 300
Baskin, FL 33540 • 800
Baskin, LA 71219 • 286
Basking Ridge, NJ 07920 • 4,800
Bassett, AR 72313 • 243
Bassett, NE 68714 • 1,009
Bassett, VA 24055 • 2,950
Bassett, WI 53101 • 250
Bassfield, MS 39421 • 325
Bass Harbor, ME 04653 • 400
Bass Lake, IN 46534 • 1,500
Bastian, VA 24314 • 400
Bastrop, LA 71220 • 15,527
Bastrop, TX 78602 • 3,789
Bastrop □, TX • 24,726
Batavia, IL 60510 • 12,574
Batavia, IA 52533 • 525
Batavia, NY 14020 • 16,703
Batavia, OH 45103 • 1,896
Batchtown, IL 62006 • 254
Bates □, MO • 15,873
Batesburg, SC 29006 • 4,023
Batesville, AR 72501 • 8,263
Batesville, IN 47006 • 4,152
Batesville, MS 38606 • 4,692
Batesville, TX 78829 • 800
Bath, IL 62617 • 475
Bath, ME 04530 • 10,246
Bath, MI 48808 • 600
Bath, NH 03740 • 300
Bath, NY 14810 • 6,042
Bath, PA 18014 • 1,953
Bath, SC 29816 • 2,242
Bath □, KY • 10,025
Bath □, VA • 5,860
Baton Rouge, LA 70801-99 • 219,419
Batson, TX 77519 • 650
Battery Park, VA 23304 • 300
Battleboro, NC 27809 • 632
Battle Creek, IA 51006 • 919
Battle Creek, MI 49014-17 • 35,724
Battle Creek, NE 68715 • 948
Battle Ground, IN 47920 • 812
Battle Ground, WA 98604 • 2,774
Battle Lake, MN 56515 • 708
Battle Mountain, NV 89820 • 2,755
Battles, MS 39362 • 300
Baudette, MN 56623 • 1,170
Bauxite, AR 72011 • 433
Bawcomville, LA 71291 • 2,500
Baxley, GA 31513 • 3,586
Baxter, IA 50028 • 951
Baxter, MN 56401 • 2,625
Baxter, TN 38544 • 1,411
Baxter, WV 26560 • 500
Baxter □, AR • 27,409
Baxter Springs, KS 66713 • 4,730
Bay, AR 72411 • 1,605
Bay □, FL • 97,740
Bay □, MI • 119,881
Bayard, IA 50029 • 637
Bayard, NE 69334 • 1,435
Bayard, NM 88023 • 3,036
Bayard, WV 26707 • 540
Bayberry, NY 13088 • 5,900
Bayboro, NC 28515 • 759
Bay Center, WA 98527 • 350
Bay City, MI 48706 • 41,593
Bay City, OR 97107 • 986
Bay City, TX 77414 • 17,837
Bay City, WI 54723 • 543
Bayfield, CO 81122 • 724
Bayfield, WI 54814 • 778
Bayfield □, WI • 13,822
Bay Head, NJ 08742 • 1,340
Baylis, IL 62314 • 299
Baylor □, TX • 4,919
Bay Minette, AL 36507 • 7,455
Bayonne, NJ 07002 • 65,047
Bayou George, FL 32401 • 1,500
Bayou Goula, LA 70716 • 800
Bayou La Batre, AL 36509 • 2,005
Bay Port, MI 48720 • 800
Bayport, MN 55003 • 2,932
Bayport, NY 11705 • 8,900
Bay Ridge, MD 21403 • 1,989
Bay Saint Louis, MS 39520 • 7,891
Bayshore, MI 49711 • 250
Bay Shore, NY 11706 • 31,200
Bayshore Gardens, FL 33507 • 14,945
Bayside, TX 78340 • 381
Bayside, WI 53217 • 4,724
Bay Springs, MS 39422 • 1,884
Baytown, TX 77520-22 • 56,923
Bayview, AL 35005 • 830
Bayview, ID 83803 • 320
Bay View, MI 49770 • 1,000
Bay Village, OH 44140 • 17,846
Bayville, NJ 08721 • 900
Bayville, NY 11709 • 7,034
Bazine, KS 67516 • 385
Beach, IL 60085 • 4,650
Beach, ND 58621 • 1,381
Beach City, OH 44608 • 1,083
Beach Haven, NJ 08008 • 1,714
Beach Haven, PA 18601 • 450
Beach Haven Terrace, NJ 08008 • 400
Beach Lake, PA 18405 • 240
Beachville, MD 20684 • 300
Beachwood, NJ 08722 • 7,687
Beachwood, OH 44122 • 9,983
Beacon, IA 52534 • 530
Beacon, NY 12508 • 12,937
Beacon Falls, CT 06403 • 1,500
Beadle □, SD • 19,195
Beallsville, OH 43716 • 601
Beals, ME 04611 • 430
Bean Lake, MO 64484 • 250
Bean Station, TN 37708 • 400
Bear, DE 19701 • 950
Bear Creek, AL 35543 • 353
Bear Creek, WI 54922 • 454
Bearden, AR 71720 • 1,191
Beards Fork, WV 25014 • 300
Beardsley, MN 56211 • 344
Beardstown, IL 62618 • 6,338
Bear Lake, MI 49614 • 388
Bear Lake, PA 16402 • 249
Bear Lake □, ID • 6,931
Bear River City, UT 84301 • 540
Bear Town, MS 39648 • 1,277
Beason, IL 62512 • 225
Beatrice, AL 36425 • 558
Beatrice, NE 68310 • 12,891
Beattie, KS 66406 • 316
Beatty, NV 89003 • 900
Beatty, OR 97621 • 250
Beattyville, KY 41311 • 1,068
Beaufort, NC 28516 • 3,826
Beaufort, SC 29902 • 8,634
Beaufort □, NC • 40,355
Beaufort □, SC • 65,364
Beaumont, CA 92223 • 6,818
Beaumont, MS 39423 • 1,112
Beaumont, TX 77701-99 • 118,102
Beauregard □, LA • 29,692
Beauty, KY 41203 • 450
Beaver, OH 45613 • 330
Beaver, OK 73932 • 1,939
Beaver, OR 97108 • 225
Beaver, PA 15009 • 5,441
Beaver, UT 84713 • 1,792
Beaver, WV 25813 • 1,400
Beaver □, OK • 6,806
Beaver □, PA • 204,441
Beaver □, UT • 4,378
Beaver Bay, MN 55601 • 283
Beaver City, NE 68926 • 775
Beaver Creek, MN 56116 • 260
Beavercreek, OH 45385 • 31,589
Beaver Crossing, NE 68313 • 458
Beaverdale, PA 15921 • 1,579
Beaver Dam, KY 42320 • 3,185
Beaverdam, OH 45808 • 492
Beaver Dam, WI 53916 • 14,149
Beaver Dams, NY 14812 • 300
Beaver Falls, NY 13305 • 400
Beaver Falls, PA 15010 • 12,525
Beaverhead □, MT • 8,186
Beaver Meadows, PA 18216 • 1,078
Beaver Springs, PA 17812 • 725
Beaverton, AL 35544 • 360
Beaverton, MI 48612 • 1,025
Beaverton, OR 97005-07 • 30,582
Beavertown, PA 17813 • 853
Beaverville, IL 60912 • 377
Beckemeyer, IL 62219 • 1,119
Becker, MN 55308 • 601
Becker □, MN • 29,336
Becket, MA 01223 • 500

Beckham □, OK • *19,243*
Beckley, WV 25801 • *20,492*
Beckville, TX 75631 • *945*
Bedford, IN 47421 • *14,410*
Bedford, IA 50833 • *1,692*
Bedford, KY 40006 • *835*
Bedford, MA 01730 • *13,067*
Bedford, NH 03102 • *1,300*
Bedford, OH 44146 • *15,056*
Bedford, PA 15522 • *3,326*
Bedford, TX 76021-22 • *20,821*
Bedford, VA 24523 • *5,991*
Bedford □, PA • *46,784*
Bedford □, TN • *27,916*
Bedford □, VA • *34,927*
Bedford Heights, OH 44146 • *13,214*
Bedford Hills, NY 10507 • *3,200*
Bedias, TX 77831 • *350*
Bedminster, NJ 07921 • *500*
Bee □, TX • *26,030*
Beebe, AR 72012 • *3,599*
Beebe Plain, VT 05823 • *300*
Beech Bottom, WV 26030 • *507*
Beech Creek, KY 42321 • *350*
Beech Creek, PA 16822 • *760*
Beecher, IL 60401 • *2,024*
Beecher, MI 48505 • *17,178*
Beecher City, IL 62414 • *492*
Beech Grove, IN 46107 • *13,196*
Beech Island, SC 29841 • *1,300*
Beechwood, MA 02025 • *400*
Beemer, NE 68716 • *853*
Bee Ridge, FL 33578 • *3,313*
Beersheba Springs, TN 37305 • *643*
Beesleys Point, NJ 08223 • *350*
Beeville, TX 78102 • *14,574*
Beggs, OK 74421 • *1,428*
Bel Air, MD 21014 • *7,814*
Bel Aire, KS 67220 • *2,650*
Bel Aire Estates, CT 06355 • *900*
Bel Alton, MD 20611 • *400*
Belcamp, MD 21017 • *650*
Belcher, LA 71004 • *436*
Belchertown, MA 01007 • *2,531*
Belcourt, ND 58316 • *1,803*
Belden, MS 38826 • *350*
Belding, MI 48809 • *5,634*
Belen, NM 87002 • *5,617*
Belfair, WA 98528 • *450*
Belfast, ME 04915 • *6,243*
Belfast, NC 27530 • *950*
Belfast, NY 14711 • *900*
Belfield, ND 58622 • *1,274*
Belford, NJ 07718 • *6,000*
Belfry, KY 41514 • *900*
Belfry, MT 59008 • *250*
Belgium, IL 61883 • *568*
Belgium, WI 53004 • *892*
Belgrade, MN 56312 • *805*
Belgrade, MO 63622 • *280*
Belgrade, MT 59714 • *2,336*
Belgrade Lakes, ME 04918 • *310*
Belhaven, NC 27810 • *2,430*
Belington, WV 26250 • *2,038*
Belknap □, NH • *42,884*
Bell, CA 90201 • *25,450*
Bell, FL 32619 • *227*
Bell □, KY • *34,330*
Bell □, TX • *157,820*
Bellair, FL 32073 • *5,200*
Bellaire, MI 49615 • *1,063*
Bellaire, OH 43906 • *8,241*
Bellaire, TX 77401 • *14,950*
Bellamy, AL 36901 • *750*
Bella Vista, AR 72712 • *2,589*
Bellbrook, OH 45305 • *5,174*
Bell Buckle, TN 37020 • *450*
Bell City, LA 70630 • *330*
Bell City, MO 63735 • *539*
Belle, MO 65013 • *1,233*
Belle, WV 25015 • *1,621*
Belleair, FL 33516 • *5,200*
Belle Center, OH 43310 • *930*
Belle Chasse, LA 70037 • *5,412*
Bellefontaine, MS 39737 • *250*
Bellefontaine, OH 43311 • *11,888*
Bellefontaine Neighbors, MO 63137 • *12,082*
Bellefonte, AR 72601 • *393*
Bellefonte, DE 19809 • *1,279*
Bellefonte, PA 16823 • *6,300*
Belle Fourche, SD 57717 • *4,692*
Belle Glade, FL 33430 • *16,535*
Belle Haven, VA 23306 • *589*
Belle Isle, FL 32809 • *2,848*
Belle Mead, NJ 08502 • *600*
Belle Meade, TN 37205 • *3,182*
Belle Mina, AL 35615 • *300*
Belleplain, NJ 08270 • *400*
Belle Plaine, IA 52208 • *2,903*
Belle Plaine, KS 67013 • *1,706*
Belle Plaine, MN 56011 • *2,754*
Belle Rive, IL 62810 • *401*
Belle Rose, LA 70341 • *700*
Belle Valley, OH 43717 • *329*
Belle Vernon, PA 15012 • *1,489*
Belleview, FL 32620 • *1,913*
Belleview, MO 63623 • *250*
Belle View, VA 22307 • *3,500*
Belleville, AR 72824 • *571*
Belleville, IL 62220-25 • *41,580*
Belleville, KS 66935 • *2,805*
Belleville, MI 48111 • *3,366*
Belleville, NJ 07109 • *35,367*
Belleville, NY 13611 • *400*
Belleville, PA 17004 • *1,817*
Belleville, WI 53508 • *1,302*
Bellevue, ID 83313 • *1,016*
Bellevue, IA 52031 • *2,450*
Bellevue, KY 41073 • *7,678*
Bellevue, MD 21662 • *300*
Bellevue, MI 49021 • *1,289*
Bellevue, NE 68005 • *21,813*
Bellevue, OH 44811 • *8,187*
Bellevue, PA 15202 • *10,128*
Bellevue, TX 76228 • *352*
Bellevue, WA 98004-09 • *73,903*
Bellflower, CA 90706 • *53,441*
Bellflower, IL 61724 • *421*
Bellflower, MO 63333 • *403*
Bell Gardens, CA 90201 • *34,117*
Bellingham, MA 02019 • *14,300*
Bellingham, MN 56212 • *290*
Bellingham, WA 98225-27 • *45,794*
Bellmawr, NJ 08031 • *13,721*
Bellmead, TX 76705 • *7,569*
Bellmont, IL 62811 • *307*
Bellmore, NY 11710 • *18,431*
Bellows Falls, VT 05101 • *3,456*
Bellport, NY 11713 • *2,809*
Bells, TN 38006 • *1,571*
Bellville, OH 44813 • *1,714*
Bellville, TX 77418 • *2,860*
Bellwood, AL 36313 • *275*
Bellwood, IL 60104 • *19,811*
Bellwood, NE 68624 • *407*
Bellwood, PA 16617 • *2,114*
Bellwood, VA 23234 • *600*
Belmar, NJ 07719 • *6,771*
Belmond, IA 50421 • *2,505*
Belmont, CA 94002 • *24,505*
Belmont, MA 02178 • *26,100*
Belmont, MS 38827 • *1,420*
Belmont, NH 03220 • *900*
Belmont, NC 28012 • *4,607*
Belmont, NY 14813 • *1,024*
Belmont, OH 43718 • *714*
Belmont, VT 05730 • *270*
Belmont, WV 26134 • *887*
Belmont, WI 53510 • *826*
Belmont □, OH • *82,569*
Belmont Heights, UT 84070 • *600*
Bel-Nor, MO 63133 • *2,047*
Beloit, KS 67420 • *4,367*
Beloit, OH 44609 • *1,093*
Beloit, WI 53511 • *35,207*
Beloit North, WI 53511 • *5,912*
Belpre, OH 45714 • *7,193*
Belspring, VA 24058 • *400*
Belt, MT 59412 • *825*
Belton, MO 64012 • *12,708*
Belton, SC 29627 • *5,312*
Belton, TX 76513 • *10,660*
Beltrami □, MN • *30,982*
Beltsville, MD 20705 • *12,760*
Belvedere, SC 29841 • *6,859*
Belvedere Park, GA 30032 • *17,766*
Belvidere, DE 19804 • *1,100*
Belvidere, IL 61008 • *15,176*
Belvidere, NJ 07823 • *2,475*
Belview, MN 56214 • *438*
Belzoni, MS 39038 • *2,982*
Bement, IL 61813 • *1,770*
Bemidji, MN 56601 • *10,949*
Bemis, TN 38314 • *1,883*
Bemiss, GA 31601 • *250*
Bemus Point, NY 14712 • *444*
Benavides, TX 78341 • *1,978*
Ben Bolt, TX 78342 • *240*
Benbrook, TX 76126 • *13,579*
Bend, OR 97701-09 • *17,263*
Bendersville, PA 17306 • *533*
Benedict, MD 20612 • *700*
Benedict, NE 68316 • *228*
Benewah □, ID • *8,292*
Benham, KY 40807 • *936*
Ben Hill □, GA • *16,000*
Benicia, CA 94510 • *15,376*
Benjamin, TX 79505 • *257*
Benkelman, NE 69021 • *1,235*
Benld, IL 62009 • *1,638*
Bennet, NE 68317 • *523*
Bennett, CO 80102 • *942*
Bennett, IA 52721 • *458*
Bennett, NC 27208 • *230*
Bennett □, SD • *3,044*
Bennettsville, SC 29512 • *8,774*
Bennington, KS 67422 • *579*
Bennington, NE 68007 • *631*
Bennington, NH 03442 • *500*
Bennington, OK 74723 • *302*
Bennington, VT 05201 • *9,349*
Bennington □, VT • *33,345*
Bennion, UT 84107 • *950*
Benoit, MS 38725 • *499*
Bensenville, IL 60106 • *16,124*
Bensley, VA 23234 • *3,300*
Benson, AZ 85602 • *4,190*
Benson, IL 61516 • *460*
Benson, MD 21018 • *400*
Benson, MN 56215 • *3,656*
Benson, NC 27504 • *2,792*
Benson □, ND • *7,944*
Bent □, CO • *5,945*
Bentley, KS 67016 • *311*
Bentleyville, PA 15314 • *2,525*
Benton, AR 72015 • *17,717*
Benton, IL 62812 • *7,778*
Benton, KS 67017 • *609*
Benton, KY 42025 • *3,700*
Benton, LA 71006 • *1,864*
Benton, MS 39039 • *250*
Benton, MO 63736 • *674*
Benton, PA 17814 • *981*
Benton, TN 37307 • *1,115*
Benton, WI 53803 • *983*
Benton □, AR • *78,115*
Benton □, IN • *10,218*
Benton □, IA • *23,649*
Benton □, MN • *25,187*
Benton □, MS • *8,153*
Benton □, MO • *12,183*
Benton □, OR • *68,211*
Benton □, TN • *14,901*
Benton □, WA • *109,444*
Benton City, WA 99320 • *1,980*
Benton Harbor, MI 49022 • *14,707*
Benton Heights, MI 49022 • *6,787*
Bentonia, MS 39040 • *518*
Benton Ridge, OH 45816 • *343*
Bentonville, AR 72712 • *8,756*
Bentonville, VA 22610 • *350*
Bentree, WV 25018 • *300*
Benwood, WV 26031 • *1,994*
Benzie □, MI • *11,205*
Benzonia, MI 49616 • *466*
Beowawe, NV 89821 • *250*
Berclair, TX 78107 • *250*
Berea, KY 40403 • *8,226*
Berea, OH 44017 • *19,567*
Berea, SC 29611 • *7,500*
Beresford, SD 57004 • *1,865*
Bergen, NY 14416 • *976*
Bergen □, NJ • *845,385*
Bergenfield, NJ 07621 • *25,568*
Bergholz, OH 43908 • *914*
Bergland, MI 49910 • *700*
Bergman, AR 72615 • *320*
Bergoo, WV 26298 • *300*
Berkeley, CA 94701-99 • *103,328*
Berkeley, IL 60162 • *5,467*
Berkeley, MO 63134 • *15,922*
Berkeley, RI 02864 • *930*
Berkeley □, SC • *94,727*
Berkeley □, WV • *46,775*
Berkeley Heights, NJ 07922 • *12,549*
Berkeley Springs, WV 25411 • *789*
Berkey, OH 43504 • *306*
Berkley, MI 48072 • *18,637*
Berks □, PA • *312,509*
Berkshire, MA 01224 • *500*
Berkshire, NY 13736 • *350*
Berkshire □, MA • *145,110*
Berlin, CT 06037 • *2,000*
Berlin, GA 31722 • *538*
Berlin, MD 21811 • *2,162*
Berlin, MA 01503 • *550*
Berlin, NH 03570 • *13,084*
Berlin, NJ 08009 • *5,786*
Berlin, NY 12022 • *850*
Berlin, OH 44610 • *800*
Berlin, PA 15530 • *1,999*
Berlin, WI 54923 • *5,478*
Berlin Corners, VT 05602 • *350*
Berlin Heights, OH 44814 • *756*
Bernalillo, NM 87004 • *3,012*
Bernalillo □, NM • *419,700*
Bernardston, MA 01337 • *700*
Bernardsville, NJ 07924 • *6,715*
Berne, IN 46711 • *3,300*
Bernice, LA 71222 • *1,956*
Bernice, OK 74331 • *318*
Bernie, MO 63822 • *1,975*
Bernville, PA 19506 • *798*
Berrien □, GA • *13,525*
Berrien □, MI • *171,276*
Berrien Springs, MI 49103 • *2,042*
Berry, AL 35546 • *916*
Berry, KY 41003 • *287*
Berry Hill, TN 37204 • *1,113*
Berryton, GA 30748 • *300*
Berryville, AR 72616 • *2,966*
Berryville, VA 22611 • *1,752*
Bertha, MN 56437 • *510*
Berthold, ND 58718 • *485*
Berthoud, CO 80513 • *2,362*
Bertie □, NC • *21,024*
Bertram, TX 78605 • *824*
Bertrand, MI 49120 • *5,000*
Bertrand, MO 63823 • *688*
Bertrand, NE 68927 • *775*
Berwick, IA 50032 • *400*
Berwick, LA 70342 • *4,466*
Berwick, ME 03901 • *2,378*
Berwick, PA 18603 • *11,850*
Berwind, WV 24815 • *600*
Berwyn, IL 60402 • *46,849*
Berwyn, PA 19312 • *9,300*
Bessemer, AL 35020-23 • *31,729*
Bessemer, MI 49911 • *2,553*
Bessemer, PA 16112 • *1,293*
Bessemer City, NC 28016 • *4,787*
Bessie, OK 73622 • *245*
Bethalto, IL 62010 • *8,630*
Bethany, CT 06525 • *890*
Bethany, IL 61914 • *1,550*
Bethany, MO 64424 • *3,095*
Bethany, OH 45042 • *300*
Bethany, OK 73008 • *22,130*
Bethany, WV 26032 • *1,336*
Bethany Beach, DE 19930 • *330*
Bethel, AK 99559 • *3,576*
Bethel, CT 06801 • *8,755*
Bethel, KY 40306 • *250*
Bethel, ME 04217 • *1,225*
Bethel, NC 27812 • *1,825*
Bethel, OH 45106 • *2,231*
Bethel, OK 74724 • *250*
Bethel, PA 19507 • *600*
Bethel, VT 05032 • *1,016*
Bethel Acres, OK 74801 • *747*
Bethel Park, PA 15102 • *34,755*
Bethel Springs, TN 38315 • *873*
Bethesda, MD 20814-17 • *63,022*
Bethesda, OH 43719 • *1,429*
Bethlehem, CT 06751 • *1,762*
Bethlehem, GA 30620 • *281*
Bethlehem, NH 03574 • *700*
Bethlehem, PA 18015-18 • *70,419*
Bethpage, NY 11714 • *29,900*
Bethpage, TN 37022 • *400*
Bethune, SC 29009 • *481*
Betsy Layne, KY 41605 • *900*
Bettendorf, IA 52722 • *27,381*
Betterton, MD 21610 • *356*
Bettsville, OH 44815 • *752*
Beulah, AL 36854 • *250*
Beulah, CO 81023 • *500*
Beulah, MI 49617 • *454*
Beulah, MS 38726 • *431*
Beulah, ND 58523 • *2,908*
Beulaville, NC 28518 • *1,060*
Beverly, MA 01915 • *37,655*
Beverly, NJ 08010 • *2,919*
Beverly, OH 45715 • *1,471*
Beverly, WV 26253 • *475*
Beverly Hills, CA 90210-13 • *32,367*
Beverly Hills, MI 48009 • *11,598*
Beverly Shores, IN 46301 • *864*
Bexar □, TX • *988,798*
Bexley, OH 43209 • *13,405*
Bibb □, AL • *15,723*
Bibb □, GA • *150,256*
Bibb City, GA 31904 • *667*
Bicknell, IN 47512 • *4,713*
Bicknell, UT 84715 • *296*
Biddeford, ME 04005 • *19,638*
Bidwell, OH 45614 • *350*
Bieber, CA 96009 • *600*
Bienville, LA 71008 • *249*
Bienville □, LA • *16,387*
Big Bay, MI 49808 • *350*
Big Bear City, CA 92314 • *3,500*
Big Bend, WI 53103 • *1,345*
Big Cabin, OK 74332 • *252*
Big Clifty, KY 42712 • *400*
Big Creek, CA 93605 • *700*
Big Creek, KY 40914 • *250*
Big Creek, WV 25505 • *250*
Big Delta, AK 99737 • *285*

Bigelow, AR 72016 • *373*
Bigelow, MN 56117 • *249*
Big Falls, MN 56627 • *490*
Big Flats, NY 14814 • *2,500*
Bigfork, MN 56628 • *457*
Bigfork, MT 59911 • *1,080*
Biggers, AR 72413 • *363*
Biggs, CA 95917 • *1,413*
Biggsville, IL 61418 • *411*
Big Horn, WY 82833 • *225*
Big Horn □, MT • *11,096*
Big Horn □, WY • *11,896*
Big Island, VA 24526 • *325*
Big Lake, MN 55309 • *2,210*
Big Lake, TX 76932 • *3,404*
Bigler, PA 16825 • *400*
Biglerville, PA 17307 • *991*
Big Pine, CA 93513 • *1,510*
Big Piney, WY 83113 • *530*
Bigpoint, MS 39567 • *900*
Big Prairie, OH 44611 • *250*
Big Rapids, MI 49307 • *14,361*
Big Rock, IL 60511 • *500*
Big Rock, TN 37023 • *250*
Big Run, PA 15715 • *822*
Big Sandy, MT 59520 • *835*
Big Sandy, TN 38221 • *650*
Big Sandy, TX 75755 • *1,258*
Big Spring, TX 79720 • *24,804*
Big Springs, NE 69122 • *505*
Big Stone □, MN • *7,716*
Big Stone City, SD 57216 • *672*
Big Stone Gap, VA 24219 • *4,748*
Big Sur, CA 93920 • *520*
Big Timber, MT 59011 • *1,690*
Big Wells, TX 78830 • *939*
Billerica, MA 01821 • *6,400*
Billings, MO 65610 • *911*
Billings, MT 59101-99 • *66,842*
Billings, OK 74630 • *632*
Billings □, ND • *1,138*
Billings Heights, MT 59105 • *8,480*
Biloxi, MS 39530-34 • *49,311*
Biltmore Forest, NC 28803 • *1,499*
Bim, WV 25021 • *350*
Binford, ND 58416 • *293*
Bingen, WA 98605 • *644*
Binger, OK 73009 • *791*
Bingham, ME 04920 • *1,074*
Bingham □, ID • *36,489*
Binghamton, NY 13901-99 • *55,860*
Biola, CA 93606 • *800*
Bippus, IN 46713 • *250*
Birch Run, MI 48415 • *1,196*
Birch Tree, MO 65438 • *622*
Birchwood, CT 06095 • *350*
Birchwood, TN 37308 • *400*
Birchwood, WI 54817 • *437*
Birchwood City, MD 20745 • *8,000*
Birchwood Park, DE 19711 • *1,500*
Bird City, KS 67731 • *546*
Bird Island, MN 55310 • *1,372*
Birdsboro, PA 19508 • *3,481*
Birdseye, IN 47513 • *533*
Birmingham, AL 35201-99 • *286,799*
Birmingham, IA 52535 • *410*
Birmingham, MI 48008-12 • *21,689*
Birmingham, MO 64161 • *240*
Birnamwood, WI 54414 • *688*
Biron, WI 54494 • *698*
Bisbee, AZ 85603 • *7,154*
Bisbee, ND 58317 • *257*
Biscayne Gardens, FL 33168 • *13,000*
Biscayne Park, FL 33161 • *3,088*
Biscoe, AR 72017 • *486*
Biscoe, NC 27209 • *1,334*
Bishop, CA 93514 • *3,333*
Bishop, TX 78343 • *3,706*
Bishops Head, MD 21611 • *300*
Bishopville, SC 29010 • *3,429*
Bismarck, IL 61814 • *750*
Bismarck, MO 63624 • *1,625*
Bismarck, ND 58501 • *44,485*
Bison, KS 67520 • *279*
Bison, SD 57620 • *457*
Bivalve, MD 21814 • *300*
Biwabik, MN 55708 • *1,428*
Bixby, OK 74008 • *6,969*
Blackburn, MO 65321 • *314*
Black Canyon City, AZ 85324 • *600*
Black Creek, NC 27813 • *523*
Black Creek, WI 54106 • *1,097*
Black Diamond, WA 98010 • *1,170*
Blackduck, MN 56630 • *653*
Black Eagle, MT 59414 • *1,100*
Black Earth, WI 53515 • *1,145*
Blackey, KY 41804 • *300*
Blackfoot, ID 83221 • *10,065*
Blackford □, IN • *15,570*
Black Forest, CO 80908 • *3,372*
Black Hawk, SD 57718 • *1,608*
Black Hawk □, IA • *137,961*
Black Jack, MO 63031 • *5,293*
Blacklick, OH 43004 • *300*
Black Lick, PA 15716 • *1,074*
Blacklick Estates, OH 43227 • *11,223*
Black Mountain, NC 28711 • *4,083*
Black Oak, AR 72414 • *309*
Black Oak, IN 46406 • *10,000*
Black Point Beach Club, CT 06357 • *500*
Black River, NY 13612 • *1,384*
Black River Falls, WI 54615 • *3,434*
Black Rock, AR 72415 • *848*
Black Rock, NM 87327 • *500*
Blacksburg, SC 29702 • *1,873*
Blacksburg, VA 24060 • *30,638*
Blackshear, GA 31516 • *3,222*
Blackstone, MA 01504 • *5,100*
Blackstone, VA 23824 • *3,624*
Blacksville, WV 26521 • *248*
Blackville, SC 29817 • *2,840*
Blackwater, MO 65322 • *290*
Blackwell, OK 74631 • *8,400*
Blackwell, TX 79506 • *286*
Blackwood, NJ 08012 • *5,219*
Bladen, NE 68928 • *298*
Bladen □, NC • *30,491*
Bladenboro, NC 28320 • *1,428*
Bladensburg, MD 20710 • *7,691*
Bladensburg, OH 43005 • *350*
Blades, DE 19973 • *664*
Blain, PA 17006 • *274*
Blaine, ME 04734 • *620*
Blaine, MN 55433 • *28,558*
Blaine, TN 37709 • *1,147*
Blaine, WA 98230 • *2,363*
Blaine □, ID • *9,841*
Blaine □, MT • *6,999*
Blaine □, NE • *867*
Blaine □, OK • *13,443*
Blair, NE 68008 • *6,418*
Blair, OK 73526 • *1,092*
Blair, WV 25022 • *600*
Blair, WI 54616 • *1,142*
Blair □, PA • *136,621*
Blairsburg, IA 50034 • *288*
Blairstown, IA 52209 • *695*
Blairsville, GA 30512 • *530*
Blairsville, PA 15717 • *4,166*
Blakely, GA 31723 • *5,880*
Blakely, PA 18447 • *7,438*
Blakesburg, IA 52536 • *404*
Blakeslee, PA 18610 • *225*
Blanca, CO 81123 • *252*
Blanchard, LA 71009 • *1,128*
Blanchard, MI 49310 • *400*
Blanchard, OK 73010 • *1,688*
Blanchard, PA 16826 • *750*
Blanchardville, WI 53516 • *803*
Blanchester, OH 45107 • *3,202*
Blanco, TX 78606 • *1,179*
Blanco □, TX • *4,681*
Bland, MO 65014 • *662*
Bland, VA 24315 • *450*
Bland □, VA • *6,349*
Blandburg, PA 16619 • *775*
Blandford, MA 01008 • *800*
Blanding, UT 84511 • *3,118*
Blandinsville, IL 61420 • *886*
Blanford, IN 47831 • *700*
Blanket, TX 76432 • *388*
Blasdell, NY 14219 • *3,288*
Blauvelt, NY 10913 • *5,426*
Blawenburg, NJ 08504 • *250*
Blawnox, PA 15238 • *1,653*
Bleckley □, GA • *10,767*
Bledsoe, TX 79314 • *250*
Bledsoe □, TN • *9,478*
Blencoe, IA 51523 • *247*
Blende, CO 81006 • *1,500*
Blennerhassett, WV 26101 • *2,200*
Blessing, TX 77419 • *950*
Blevins, AR 71825 • *314*
Bliss, NY 14024 • *300*
Blissfield, MI 49228 • *3,107*
Blocker, OK 74529 • *225*
Block Island, RI 02807 • *620*
Blockton, IA 50836 • *280*
Blodgett, MO 63824 • *255*
Bloomdale, OH 44817 • *744*
Bloomer, WI 54724 • *3,342*
Bloomfield, CT 06002 • *7,400*
Bloomfield, IN 47424 • *2,705*
Bloomfield, IA 52537 • *2,849*
Bloomfield, KY 40008 • *954*
Bloomfield, MO 63825 • *1,795*
Bloomfield, NE 68718 • *1,393*
Bloomfield, NJ 07003 • *47,792*
Bloomfield, NM 87413 • *4,881*
Bloomfield Hills, MI 48013 • *3,985*
Bloomingburg, OH 43106 • *869*
Bloomingdale, GA 31302 • *1,855*
Bloomingdale, IL 60108 • *12,659*
Bloomingdale, IN 47832 • *409*
Bloomingdale, MI 49026 • *537*
Bloomingdale, NJ 07403 • *7,867*
Bloomingdale, NY 12913 • *608*
Bloomingdale, TN 37660 • *9,000*
Blooming Grove, PA 18428 • *250*
Blooming Grove, TX 76626 • *823*
Blooming Prairie, MN 55917 • *1,969*
Bloomington, CA 92316 • *6,674*
Bloomington, IL 61701 • *44,189*
Bloomington, IN 47401 • *52,044*
Bloomington, MD 21523 • *400*
Bloomington, MN 55420 • *81,831*
Bloomington, TX 77951 • *1,750*
Bloomington, UT 84770 • *350*
Bloomington, WI 53804 • *743*
Bloomsburg, PA 17815 • *11,717*
Bloomsbury, NJ 08804 • *864*
Bloomsdale, MO 63627 • *397*
Bloomville, NY 13739 • *250*
Bloomville, OH 44818 • *1,019*
Blossburg, PA 16912 • *1,757*
Blossom, TX 75416 • *1,487*
Blount □, AL • *36,459*
Blount □, TN • *77,770*
Blountstown, FL 32424 • *2,632*
Blountsville, AL 35031 • *1,509*
Blountville, TN 37617 • *2,554*
Blowing Rock, NC 28605 • *1,337*
Bloxom, VA 23308 • *407*
Blue Anchor, NJ 08037 • *500*
Blue Ash, OH 45242 • *9,506*
Blue Creek, WV 25026 • *500*
Blue Diamond, NV 89004 • *300*
Blue Earth, MN 56013 • *4,132*
Blue Earth □, MN • *52,314*
Bluefield, VA 24605 • *5,946*
Bluefield, WV 24701 • *16,060*
Blue Grass, IA 52726 • *1,377*
Blue Hill, ME 04614 • *700*
Blue Hill, NE 68930 • *883*
Blue Hills, CT 06002 • *6,600*
Bluehole, KY 40917 • *230*
Blue Island, IL 60406 • *21,855*
Bluejacket, OK 74333 • *247*
Blue Lake, CA 95525 • *1,201*
Blue Mound, IL 62513 • *1,338*
Blue Mound, KS 66010 • *319*
Blue Mountain, AL 36201 • *284*
Blue Mountain, MS 38610 • *867*
Blue Mountain Lake, NY 12812 • *250*
Blue Point, ME 04074 • *400*
Blue Rapids, KS 66411 • *1,280*
Blue Ridge, GA 30513 • *1,376*
Blue Ridge, IN 46176 • *250*
Blue Ridge, VA 24064 • *1,200*
Blue Ridge Summit, PA 17214 • *800*
Blue River, OR 97413 • *300*
Blue River, WI 53518 • *412*
Blue Springs, MO 64015 • *25,927*
Blue Springs, NE 68318 • *521*
Bluewater, NM 87005 • *500*
Bluewell, WV 24701 • *1,000*
Bluff City, AR 71722 • *292*
Bluff City, IL 62471 • *300*
Bluff City, TN 37618 • *1,121*
Bluff Dale, TX 76433 • *300*
Bluffdale, UT 84065 • *1,300*
Bluff Park, AL 35226 • *12,000*
Bluffs, IL 62621 • *821*
Bluffton, IN 46714 • *8,705*
Bluffton, OH 45817 • *3,310*
Bluffton, SC 29910 • *541*
Bluford, IL 62814 • *728*
Blunt, SD 57522 • *424*
Bly, OR 97622 • *750*
Blythe, CA 92225 • *6,805*
Blythe, GA 30805 • *367*
Blytheville, AR 72315 • *23,844*
Boalsburg, PA 16827 • *950*
Boardman, OH 44512 • *39,161*
Boardman, OR 97818 • *1,261*
Boaz, AL 35957 • *7,151*
Bobtown, PA 15315 • *1,055*
Boca Grande, FL 33921 • *1,200*
Boca Raton, FL 33431-34 • *49,505*
Bode, IA 50519 • *406*
Boelus, NE 68820 • *228*
Boerne, TX 78006 • *3,229*
Bogalusa, LA 70427 • *16,976*
Bogard, MO 64622 • *285*
Bogart, GA 30622 • *819*
Bogata, TX 75417 • *1,508*
Boger City, NC 28092 • *2,252*
Boggstown, IN 46110 • *240*
Bogota, NJ 07603 • *8,344*
Bogota, TN 38007 • *300*
Bogue Chitto, MS 39629 • *600*
Bohemia, NY 11716 • *9,800*
Boiling Springs, NC 28017 • *2,381*
Boiling Springs, PA 17007 • *1,521*
Bois D'Arc, MO 65612 • *375*
Boise, ID 83701-99 • *102,160*
Boise □, ID • *2,999*
Boise City, OK 73933 • *1,761*
Bois Fort, MN 55772 • *385*
Boissevain, VA 24606 • *900*
Bokchito, OK 74726 • *628*
Bokeelia, FL 33922 • *900*
Bokoshe, OK 74930 • *556*
Bolckow, MO 64427 • *245*
Boles, NM 88310 • *300*
Boley, OK 74829 • *423*
Boling, TX 77420 • *1,000*
Bolingbrook, IL 60439 • *37,261*
Bolivar, MO 65613 • *5,919*
Bolivar, NY 14715 • *1,345*
Bolivar, OH 44612 • *989*
Bolivar, PA 15923 • *706*
Bolivar, TN 38008 • *6,597*
Bolivar, WV 25425 • *672*
Bolivar □, MS • *45,965*
Bolivia, NC 28422 • *252*
Bollinger □, MO • *10,301*
Bolton, MA 01740 • *500*
Bolton, MS 39041 • *664*
Bolton, NC 28423 • *563*
Bolton Landing, NY 12814 • *1,500*
Bon Air, VA 23235 • *13,000*
Bonaire, GA 31005 • *800*
Bonanza, AR 72901 • *553*
Bonanza, OR 97623 • *270*
Bonaparte, IA 52620 • *489*
Bond, KY 40407 • *400*
Bond, MS 39550 • *600*
Bond □, IL • *16,224*
Bondsville, MA 01009 • *1,906*
Bonduel, WI 54107 • *1,160*
Bondurant, IA 50035 • *1,283*
Bondville, IL 61815 • *442*
Bone Gap, IL 62815 • *350*
Bonesteel, SD 57317 • *358*
Bonfouca, LA 70458 • *480*
Bonham, TX 75418 • *7,338*
Bon Homme □, SD • *8,059*
Bonifay, FL 32425 • *2,534*
Bonita, LA 71223 • *503*
Bonita Springs, FL 33923 • *3,400*
Bonlee, NC 27213 • *245*
Bonneau, SC 29431 • *401*
Bonneauville, PA 17325 • *920*
Bonner □, ID • *24,163*
Bonners Ferry, ID 83805 • *1,906*
Bonner Springs, KS 66012 • *6,266*
Bonne Terre, MO 63628 • *3,797*
Bonneville □, ID • *65,980*
Bonney Lake, WA 98390 • *5,328*
Bonnie, IL 62816 • *452*
Bonnie Doone, NC 28303 • *5,950*
Bonnieville, KY 42713 • *372*
Bono, AR 72416 • *967*
Bon Secour, AL 36511 • *600*
Bon Wier, TX 75928 • *500*
Booker, TX 79005 • *1,219*
Boomer, WV 25031 • *1,100*
Boone, CO 81025 • *431*
Boone, IA 50036 • *12,602*
Boone, NC 28607 • *10,191*
Boone □, AR • *26,067*
Boone □, IL • *28,630*
Boone □, IN • *36,446*
Boone □, IA • *26,184*
Boone □, KY • *45,842*
Boone □, MO • *100,376*
Boone □, NE • *7,391*
Boone □, WV • *30,447*
Boones Mill, VA 24065 • *344*
Booneville, AR 72927 • *3,718*
Booneville, MS 38829 • *6,199*
Boonsboro, MD 21713 • *1,908*
Boonton, NJ 07005 • *8,620*
Boonville, CA 95415 • *1,000*
Boonville, IN 47601 • *6,300*
Boonville, MO 65233 • *6,959*
Boonville, NC 27011 • *1,028*
Boonville, NY 13309 • *2,344*
Boothbay, ME 04537 • *450*
Boothbay Harbor, ME 04538 • *2,207*
Boothville, LA 70038 • *600*
Boothwyn, PA 19061 • *7,100*
Bordelonville, LA 71320 • *400*
Borden, IN 47106 • *337*
Borden □, TX • *859*

Bordentown, NJ 08505 • *4,441*
Borderland, WV 25665 • *300*
Borger, TX 79007 • *15,837*
Boring, OR 97009 • *500*
Boron, CA 93516 • *2,040*
Borrego Springs, CA 92004 • *1,405*
Boscobel, WI 53805 • *2,662*
Bosque □, TX • *13,401*
Bossert Estates, NJ 08505 • *2,800*
Bossier □, LA • *80,721*
Bossier City, LA 71111-13 • *50,817*
Boston, GA 31626 • *1,424*
Boston, KY 40107 • *400*
Boston, MA 02101-99 • *562,994*
Boston Heights, OH 44236 • *781*
Bostwick, FL 32007 • *500*
Bostwick, GA 30623 • *357*
Boswell, IN 47921 • *810*
Boswell, OK 74727 • *702*
Boswell, PA 15531 • *1,480*
Bosworth, MO 64623 • *394*
Botetourt □, VA • *23,270*
Bothell, WA 98011-12 • *7,943*
Botkins, OH 45306 • *1,372*
Botsford, CT 06404 • *300*
Bottineau, ND 58318 • *2,829*
Bottineau □, ND • *9,239*
Boulder, CO 80301-99 • *76,685*
Boulder, MT 59632 • *1,441*
Boulder □, CO • *189,625*
Boulder City, NV 89005 • *9,590*
Boulder Hill, IL 60538 • *9,333*
Boulevard, CA 92005 • *245*
Boulevard Heights, MD 20743 • *1,700*
Boundary □, ID • *7,289*
Bound Brook, NJ 08805 • *9,710*
Bountiful, UT 84010 • *32,877*
Bourbon, IN 46504 • *1,522*
Bourbon, MO 65441 • *1,259*
Bourbon □, KS • *15,969*
Bourbon □, KY • *19,405*
Bourbonnais, IL 60914 • *13,280*
Bourg, LA 70343 • *2,073*
Bourne, MA 02532 • *800*
Bourneville, OH 45617 • *300*
Bouse, AZ 85325 • *450*
Boutte, LA 70039 • *1,200*
Bovey, MN 55709 • *813*
Bovill, ID 83806 • *289*
Bovina, TX 79009 • *1,499*
Bow, NH 03301 • *500*
Bow, WA 98232 • *400*
Bowbells, ND 58721 • *587*
Bowdens, NC 28322 • *300*
Bowdle, SD 57428 • *644*
Bowdoinham, ME 04008 • *350*
Bowdon, GA 30108 • *1,743*
Bowen, IL 62316 • *525*
Bowerston, OH 44695 • *487*
Bowersville, GA 30516 • *318*
Bowersville, OH 45307 • *329*
Bowie, AZ 85605 • *600*
Bowie, MD 20715-16 • *33,695*
Bowie, TX 76230 • *5,610*
Bowie □, TX • *75,301*
Bowlegs, OK 74830 • *522*
Bowler, WI 54416 • *339*
Bowling Green, FL 33834 • *2,310*
Bowling Green, KY 42101 • *40,450*
Bowling Green, MO 63334 • *3,022*
Bowling Green, OH 43402 • *25,728*
Bowling Green, SC 29703 • *850*
Bowling Green, VA 22427 • *665*
Bowlus, MN 56314 • *276*
Bowman, GA 30624 • *890*
Bowman, ND 58623 • *2,071*
Bowman, SC 29018 • *1,137*
Bowman □, ND • *4,229*
Bowmanstown, PA 18030 • *1,078*
Bow Mar, CO 80120 • *930*
Boxborough, MA 01719 • *500*
Box Butte □, NE • *13,696*
Box Elder, MT 59521 • *250*
Box Elder, SD 57719 • *3,186*
Box Elder □, UT • *33,222*
Boxford, MA 01921 • *1,841*
Boxholm, IA 50040 • *267*
Boyce, LA 71409 • *1,198*
Boyce, VA 22620 • *401*
Boyceville, WI 54725 • *862*
Boyd, MN 56218 • *329*
Boyd, TX 76023 • *889*
Boyd, WI 54726 • *660*
Boyd □, KY • *55,513*
Boyd □, NE • *3,331*
Boyden, IA 51234 • *708*
Boyds, MD 20841 • *300*
Boydton, VA 23917 • *486*
Boyers, PA 16020 • *300*
Boyertown, PA 19512 • *3,979*
Boykins, VA 23827 • *791*
Boyle, MS 38730 • *888*
Boyle □, KY • *25,066*
Boylston, MA 01505 • *950*
Boyne City, MI 49712 • *3,348*
Boyne Falls, MI 49713 • *378*
Boynton, OK 74422 • *518*
Boynton, PA 15532 • *330*
Boynton Beach, FL 33435-37 • *35,624*
Boys Ranch, TX 79010 • *650*
Boys Town, NE 68010 • *622*
Bozeman, MT 59715 • *21,645*
Bozman, MD 21612 • *300*
Braceville, IL 60407 • *721*
Bracken □, KY • *7,738*
Brackenridge, PA 15014 • *4,297*
Brackettville, TX 78832 • *1,676*
Braddock, PA 15104 • *5,634*
Braddock Heights, MD 21714 • *4,223*
Braden, TN 38010 • *293*
Bradenton, FL 33505-08 • *30,170*
Bradenville, PA 15620 • *1,200*
Bradford, AR 72020 • *950*
Bradford, IL 61421 • *924*
Bradford, NH 03221 • *450*
Bradford, OH 45308 • *2,166*
Bradford, PA 16701 • *11,211*
Bradford, RI 02808 • *1,354*
Bradford, TN 38316 • *1,146*
Bradford, VT 05033 • *831*
Bradford □, FL • *20,023*
Bradford □, PA • *62,919*
Bradfordsville, KY 40009 • *331*
Bradfordwoods, PA 15015 • *1,264*
Bradley, AR 71826 • *790*
Bradley, FL 33835 • *1,108*
Bradley, IL 60915 • *11,008*
Bradley, ME 04411 • *625*
Bradley, OK 73011 • *284*
Bradley, WV 25818 • *1,200*
Bradley □, AR • *13,803*
Bradley □, TN • *67,547*
Bradley Beach, NJ 07720 • *4,772*
Bradner, OH 43406 • *1,175*
Bradshaw, MD 21021 • *800*
Bradshaw, NE 68319 • *373*
Bradshaw, WV 24817 • *628*
Brady, MT 59416 • *225*
Brady, NE 69123 • *377*
Brady, TX 76825 • *5,969*
Braggadocio, MO 63826 • *450*
Braggs, OK 74423 • *351*
Braham, MN 55006 • *1,015*
Braidwood, IL 60408 • *3,429*
Brainard, NE 68626 • *275*
Brainerd, MN 56401 • *11,489*
Braintree, MA 02184 • *36,337*
Braman, OK 74632 • *355*
Bramwell, WV 24715 • *989*
Branch, AR 72928 • *353*
Branch □, MI • *40,188*
Branchland, WV 25506 • *400*
Branch Village, RI 02895 • *400*
Branchville, AL 35120 • *365*
Branchville, CT 06829 • *300*
Branchville, SC 29432 • *1,769*
Brandenburg, KY 40108 • *1,831*
Brandon, FL 33511 • *29,100*
Brandon, IA 52210 • *337*
Brandon, MN 56315 • *473*
Brandon, MS 39042 • *9,626*
Brandon, SC 29611 • *2,170*
Brandon, SD 57005 • *2,589*
Brandon, VT 05733 • *1,925*
Brandon, WI 53919 • *862*
Brandy Station, VA 22714 • *250*
Brandywine, MD 20613 • *1,319*
Branford, CT 06405 • *5,438*
Branford, FL 32008 • *622*
Branford Hills, CT 06405 • *2,200*
Branford Point, CT 06405 • *700*
Branson, MO 65616 • *2,550*
Brant Lake, NY 12815 • *700*
Brantley, AL 36009 • *1,151*
Brantley □, GA • *8,701*
Brant Rock, MA 02020 • *1,500*
Brashear, MO 63533 • *332*
Bratenahl, OH 44108 • *1,485*
Bratt, FL 32535 • *550*
Brattleboro, VT 05301 • *8,596*
Brave, PA 15316 • *390*
Brawley, CA 92227 • *14,946*
Braxton □, WV • *13,894*
Bray, OK 73012 • *591*
Braymer, MO 64624 • *986*
Brazil, IN 47834 • *7,852*
Brazil, TN 38382 • *300*
Brazoria, TX 77422 • *3,025*
Brazoria □, TX • *169,587*
Brazos □, TX • *93,588*
Brea, CA 92621 • *27,913*
Breathitt □, KY • *17,004*
Breaux Bridge, LA 70517 • *5,922*
Breckenridge, CO 80424 • *818*
Breckenridge, MI 48615 • *1,495*
Breckenridge, MN 56520 • *3,909*
Breckenridge, MO 64625 • *523*
Breckenridge, OK 73701 • *261*
Breckenridge, TX 76024 • *6,921*
Breckenridge Hills, MO 63114 • *5,666*
Breckinridge □, KY • *16,861*
Brecksville, OH 44141 • *10,132*
Breda, IA 51436 • *502*
Breese, IL 62230 • *3,516*
Breezy Point, MN 56472 • *384*
Bremen, GA 30110 • *3,966*
Bremen, IN 46506 • *3,565*
Bremen, OH 43107 • *1,432*
Bremer □, IA • *24,820*
Bremerton, WA 98310-15 • *36,208*
Bremond, TX 76629 • *1,025*
Brenham, TX 77833 • *10,966*
Brent, AL 35034 • *2,862*
Brent, FL 32503 • *4,100*
Brenton, WV 24818 • *800*
Brentwood, CA 94513 • *4,434*
Brentwood, MD 20722 • *2,988*
Brentwood, MO 63144 • *8,209*
Brentwood, NH 03042 • *350*
Brentwood, NY 11717 • *48,800*
Brentwood, OH 45231 • *5,508*
Brentwood, PA 15227 • *11,861*
Brentwood, SC 29405 • *2,000*
Brentwood, TN 37027 • *9,431*
Breton Woods, NJ 08723 • *1,300*
Brevard, NC 28712 • *5,323*
Brevard □, FL • *272,959*
Brewer, ME 04412 • *9,017*
Brewster, KS 67732 • *327*
Brewster, MA 02631 • *1,744*
Brewster, MN 56119 • *559*
Brewster, NY 10509 • *1,650*
Brewster, OH 44613 • *2,321*
Brewster, WA 98812 • *1,337*
Brewster □, TX • *7,573*
Brewton, AL 36426 • *6,680*
Briarcliff, PA 19036 • *9,300*
Briarcliff Manor, NY 10510 • *7,115*
Bricelyn, MN 56014 • *487*
Briceville, TN 37710 • *800*
Brick, NJ 08723-24 • *3,200*
Bridgeboro, GA 31705 • *230*
Bridge City, LA 70094 • *2,500*
Bridgehampton, NY 11932 • *950*
Bridgeport, AL 35740 • *2,974*
Bridgeport, CA 93517 • *900*
Bridgeport, CT 06601-99 • *142,546*
Bridgeport, IL 62417 • *2,281*
Bridgeport, MI 48722 • *3,500*
Bridgeport, NE 69336 • *1,668*
Bridgeport, NJ 08014 • *900*
Bridgeport, OH 43912 • *2,642*
Bridgeport, PA 19405 • *4,843*
Bridgeport, TX 76026 • *3,737*
Bridgeport, WA 98813 • *1,174*
Bridgeport, WV 26330 • *6,604*
Bridger, MT 59014 • *724*
Bridgeton, IN 47836 • *300*
Bridgeton, MO 63044 • *18,445*
Bridgeton, NJ 08302 • *18,795*
Bridgeton, NC 28519 • *461*
Bridgetown, OH 45211 • *11,460*
Bridgeview, IL 60455 • *14,155*
Bridgeville, DE 19933 • *1,238*
Bridgeville, PA 15017 • *6,154*
Bridgewater, CT 06752 • *400*
Bridgewater, IA 50837 • *233*
Bridgewater, ME 04735 • *325*
Bridgewater, MA 02324 • *6,781*
Bridgewater, NJ 08807 • *5,800*
Bridgewater, SD 57319 • *653*
Bridgewater, VT 05034 • *350*
Bridgewater, VA 22812 • *3,289*
Bridgman, MI 49106 • *2,235*
Bridgton, ME 04009 • *1,639*
Brielle, NJ 08730 • *4,068*
Brier Hill, NY 13614 • *350*
Brigantine, NJ 08203 • *8,318*
Briggs, TX 78608 • *230*
Briggsville, WI 53920 • *300*
Brigham City, UT 84302 • *15,596*
Brighton, AL 35020 • *5,308*
Brighton, CO 80601 • *12,773*
Brighton, IL 62012 • *2,364*
Brighton, IA 52540 • *804*
Brighton, MI 48116 • *4,268*
Brighton, NY 14610 • *35,776*
Brighton, TN 38011 • *976*
Brilliant, AL 35548 • *871*
Brilliant, OH 43913 • *1,751*
Brillion, WI 54110 • *2,907*
Brimfield, IL 61517 • *890*
Brimfield, MA 01010 • *500*
Brimley, MI 49715 • *500*
Brinkley, AR 72021 • *4,909*
Brinnon, WA 98320 • *600*
Brinson, GA 31725 • *274*
Briscoe □, TX • *2,579*
Bristol, CO 81028 • *250*
Bristol, CT 06010 • *57,370*
Bristol, FL 32321 • *1,044*
Bristol, IL 60512 • *400*
Bristol, IN 46507 • *1,203*
Bristol, ME 04539 • *225*
Bristol, NH 03222 • *1,258*
Bristol, PA 19007 • *10,867*
Bristol, RI 02809 • *20,128*
Bristol, SD 57219 • *445*
Bristol, TN 37620 • *23,986*
Bristol, VT 05443 • *1,793*
Bristol, VA 24201 • *19,042*
Bristol, WI 53104 • *500*
Bristol □, MA • *474,641*
Bristol □, RI • *46,942*
Bristolville, OH 44402 • *500*
Bristow, IA 50611 • *252*
Bristow, OK 74010 • *4,702*
Britt, IA 50423 • *2,185*
Britton, MI 49229 • *693*
Britton, SD 57430 • *1,590*
Broadalbin, NY 12025 • *1,415*
Broadbent, OR 97414 • *250*
Broad Brook, CT 06016 • *1,548*
Broaddus, TX 75929 • *225*
Broadlands, IL 61816 • *346*
Broadmoor, CO 80906 • *1,900*
Broad Top, PA 16621 • *340*
Broadus, MT 59317 • *712*
Broadview, IL 60153 • *8,618*
Broadview Heights, OH 44141 • *10,920*
Broadview Park, FL 33314 • *6,022*
Broadwater □, MT • *3,267*
Broadway, NJ 08808 • *450*
Broadway, NC 27505 • *908*
Broadway, OH 43007 • *350*
Broadway, VA 22815 • *1,234*
Brockport, NY 14420 • *9,776*
Brockport, PA 15823 • *450*
Brockton, MA 02401-99 • *95,172*
Brockton, MT 59213 • *374*
Brockway, PA 15824 • *2,376*
Brocton, IL 61917 • *393*
Brocton, NY 14716 • *1,416*
Broderick, CA 95605 • *9,900*
Brodhead, KY 40409 • *686*
Brodhead, WI 53520 • *3,153*
Brodheadsville, PA 18322 • *500*
Brodnax, VA 23920 • *492*
Brokaw, WI 54417 • *298*
Broken Arrow, OK 74012-14 • *35,761*
Broken Bow, NE 68822 • *3,979*
Broken Bow, OK 74728 • *3,965*
Bronson, FL 32621 • *853*
Bronson, IA 51007 • *289*
Bronson, KS 66716 • *414*
Bronson, MI 49028 • *2,271*
Bronson, TX 75930 • *254*
Bronte, TX 76933 • *983*
Bronwood, GA 31726 • *524*
Bronx □, NY • *1,168,972*
Bronxville, NY 10708 • *6,267*
Brook, IN 47922 • *926*
Brooke □, WV • *31,117*
Brooker, FL 32622 • *429*
Brookfield, CT 06804 • *1,000*
Brookfield, GA 31727 • *400*
Brookfield, IL 60513 • *19,395*
Brookfield, MA 01506 • *1,037*
Brookfield, MO 64628 • *5,555*
Brookfield, NY 13314 • *600*
Brookfield, VA 22021 • *2,500*
Brookfield, WI 53005 • *34,035*
Brookfield Center, CT 06805 • *900*
Brookford, NC 28601 • *467*
Brookhaven, MS 39601 • *10,800*
Brookhaven, PA 19015 • *7,912*
Brookhaven, WV 26505 • *1,200*
Brookings, OR 97415 • *3,384*
Brookings, SD 57006 • *14,951*
Brookings □, SD • *24,332*
Brookland, AR 72417 • *840*
Brooklandville, MD 21022 • *500*
Brooklawn, NJ 08030 • *2,133*
Brooklet, GA 30415 • *1,035*

Brookline, MA 02146 • 55,062
Brookline, NH 03033 • 400
Brooklyn, CT 06234 • 900
Brooklyn, IN 46111 • 889
Brooklyn, IA 52211 • 1,509
Brooklyn, MI 49230 • 1,110
Brooklyn, MS 39425 • 800
Brooklyn, OH 44144 • 12,342
Brooklyn, PA 18813 • 225
Brooklyn, SC 29720 • 1,800
Brooklyn, WI 53521 • 627
Brooklyn Center, MN 55429 • 31,230
Brooklyn Park, MD 21225 • 11,508
Brooklyn Park, MN 55443 • 43,332
Brookneal, VA 24528 • 1,454
Brook Park, OH 44142 • 26,195
Brookport, IL 62910 • 1,128
Brookridge, CO 80120 • 1,200
Brooks, KY 40109 • 1,344
Brooks, ME 04921 • 315
Brooks, OR 97305 • 400
Brooks □, GA • 15,255
Brooks □, TX • 8,428
Brookshire, TX 77423 • 2,175
Brookside, AL 35036 • 1,409
Brookside, DE 19713 • 15,255
Brooks Place, MA 02379 • 500
Brookston, IN 47923 • 1,701
Brooksville, FL 33512 • 5,582
Brooksville, KY 41004 • 680
Brooksville, MS 39739 • 1,038
Brooktondale, NY 14817 • 500
Brookville, IN 47012 • 2,874
Brookville, KS 67425 • 259
Brookville, MA 02343 • 950
Brookville, NY 11545 • 3,290
Brookville, OH 45309 • 4,322
Brookville, PA 15825 • 4,568
Brookwood, AL 35444 • 492
Brookwood, NJ 08527 • 4,000
Broomall, PA 19008 • 23,642
Broome □, NY • 213,648
Broomes Island, MD 20615 • 450
Broomfield, CO 80020 • 20,730
Brooten, MN 56316 • 647
Broughton, IL 62817 • 263
Broussard, LA 70518 • 2,923
Broward □, FL • 1,018,200
Browardale, FL 33311 • 7,571
Browerville, MN 56438 • 693
Brown □, IL • 5,411
Brown □, IN • 12,377
Brown □, KS • 11,955
Brown □, MN • 28,645
Brown □, NE • 4,377
Brown □, OH • 31,920
Brown □, SD • 36,962
Brown □, TX • 33,057
Brown □, WI • 175,280
Brown City, MI 48416 • 1,163
Brown Deer, WI 53209 • 12,921
Brownfield, TX 79316 • 10,387
Brownfields, LA 70811 • 1,800
Browning, IL 62624 • 246
Browning, MO 64630 • 368
Browning, MT 59417 • 1,226
Brownsburg, IN 46112 • 6,242
Brownsdale, MN 55918 • 691
Browns Mills, NJ 08015 • 10,568
Brownstown, IL 62418 • 708
Brownstown, IN 47220 • 2,704
Brownstown, PA 15906 • 800
Browns Valley, MN 56219 • 887
Brownsville, FL 33142 • 18,058
Brownsville, IN 47325 • 300
Brownsville, KY 42210 • 674
Brownsville, LA 71291 • 3,000
Brownsville, MN 55919 • 418
Brownsville, OR 97327 • 1,261
Brownsville, PA 15417 • 4,043
Brownsville, TN 38012 • 9,307
Brownsville, TX 78520-26 • 84,997
Brownton, MN 55312 • 697
Brownton, WV 26334 • 600
Browntown, WI 53522 • 284
Brownville, ME 04414 • 400
Brownville, NY 13615 • 1,099
Brownville Junction, ME 04415 • 775
Brownwood, MO 63738 • 250
Brownwood, TX 76801 • 19,396
Broxton, GA 31519 • 1,117
Broyhill Park, VA 22042 • 3,600
Bruce, FL 32455 • 250
Bruce, MS 38915 • 2,208
Bruce, SD 57220 • 254
Bruce, WI 54819 • 905
Bruce Crossing, MI 49912 • 300
Bruceton, TN 38317 • 1,579
Bruceton Mills, WV 26525 • 296
Bruceville, IN 47516 • 646
Brule, NE 69127 • 438
Brule, WI 54820 • 250
Brule □, SD • 5,245
Brundidge, AL 36010 • 3,213
Bruni, TX 78344 • 400
Bruning, NE 68322 • 330
Brunson, SC 29911 • 590
Brunswick, GA 31520 • 17,605
Brunswick, ME 04011 • 10,990
Brunswick, MD 21716 • 4,572
Brunswick, MO 65236 • 1,272
Brunswick, NC 28424 • 223
Brunswick, OH 44212 • 28,104
Brunswick □, NC • 35,777
Brunswick □, VA • 15,632
Brush, CO 80723 • 4,082
Brusly, LA 70719 • 1,762
Bryan, OH 43506 • 7,879
Bryan, TX 77801-06 • 44,337
Bryan □, GA • 10,175
Bryan □, OK • 30,535
Bryans Road, MD 20616 • 3,739
Bryant, AR 72022 • 2,682
Bryant, FL 33439 • 500
Bryant, IL 61519 • 333
Bryant, IN 47326 • 277
Bryant, SD 57221 • 388
Bryantown, MD 20617 • 300
Bryant Pond, ME 04219 • 350
Bryantville, MA 02327 • 1,500
Bryn Mawr, PA 19010 • 9,500
Bryn Mawr, WA 98178 • 2,100
Bryson, TX 76027 • 579
Bryson City, NC 28713 • 1,556
Buchanan, GA 30113 • 1,019
Buchanan, MI 49107 • 5,142
Buchanan, VA 24066 • 1,205
Buchanan □, IA • 22,900
Buchanan □, MO • 87,888
Buchanan □, VA • 37,989
Buchtel, OH 45716 • 585
Buckatunna, MS 39322 • 700
Buck Creek, IN 47924 • 300
Buckeye, AZ 85326 • 3,434
Buckeye Lake, OH 43008 • 2,521
Buckeystown, MD 21717 • 400
Buckfield, ME 04220 • 350
Buckhannon, WV 26201 • 6,820
Buck Hill Falls, PA 18323 • 400
Buckhorn, AZ 85205 • 4,000
Buckingham □, VA • 11,751
Buckland, OH 45819 • 271
Buckley, IL 60918 • 604
Buckley, MI 49620 • 357
Buckley, WA 98321 • 3,143
Bucklin, KS 67834 • 786
Bucklin, MO 64631 • 713
Bucknell Manor, VA 22307 • 2,350
Buckner, AR 71827 • 436
Buckner, IL 62819 • 520
Buckner, MO 64016 • 2,848
Bucks □, PA • 479,211
Bucksport, ME 04416 • 2,853
Bucksport, SC 29527 • 1,125
Bucoda, WA 98530 • 519
Bucyrus, OH 44820 • 13,433
Bud, WV 24716 • 400
Buda, IL 61314 • 668
Buda, TX 78610 • 597
Bude, MS 39630 • 1,092
Buechel, KY 40218 • 6,912
Buena, NJ 08310 • 3,642
Buena, WA 98921 • 800
Buena Park, CA 90620-24 • 64,165
Buena Vista, CO 81211 • 2,075
Buena Vista, FL 33589 • 3,000
Buena Vista, GA 31803 • 1,544
Buena Vista, VA 24416 • 6,717
Buena Vista □, IA • 20,774
Buffalo, IL 62515 • 514
Buffalo, IA 52728 • 1,569
Buffalo, KS 66717 • 386
Buffalo, MN 55313 • 4,560
Buffalo, MO 65622 • 2,217
Buffalo, ND 58011 • 226
Buffalo, NY 14201-99 • 357,870
Buffalo, OH 43722 • 800
Buffalo, OK 73834 • 1,381
Buffalo, SC 29321 • 1,641
Buffalo, SD 57720 • 453
Buffalo, TX 75831 • 1,507
Buffalo, WV 25033 • 1,034
Buffalo, WI 54622 • 894
Buffalo, WY 82834 • 3,799
Buffalo □, NE • 34,797
Buffalo □, SD • 1,795
Buffalo □, WI • 14,309
Buffalo Center, IA 50424 • 1,233
Buffalo Grove, IL 60090 • 22,230
Buffalo Lake, MN 55314 • 782
Buford, GA 30518 • 6,578
Buhl, ID 83316 • 3,629
Buhl, MN 55713 • 1,284
Buhler, KS 67522 • 1,188
Buies Creek, NC 27506 • 1,939
Buladean, NC 28705 • 250
Bulan, KY 41722 • 440
Bullhead, SD 57621 • 300
Bullhead City, AZ 86430 • 5,000
Bullitt □, KY • 43,346
Bulloch □, GA • 35,785
Bullock □, AL • 10,596
Bullock Creek, MI 48640 • 900
Bulls Gap, TN 37711 • 821
Bull Shoals, AR 72619 • 1,312
Bumpus Mills, TN 37028 • 250
Buna, TX 77612 • 1,900
Bunceton, MO 65237 • 419
Bunche Park, FL 33054 • 4,000
Buncombe, IL 62912 • 231
Buncombe □, NC • 160,934
Bunker, MO 63629 • 673
Bunker Hill, IL 62014 • 1,700
Bunker Hill, IN 46914 • 984
Bunker Hill, OR 97420 • 1,555
Bunker Hill, WV 25413 • 500
Bunker Hill, WV 25309 • 800
Bunkie, LA 71322 • 5,364
Bunn, NC 27508 • 505
Bunnell, FL 32010 • 1,816
Bunnlevel, NC 28323 • 500
Buras, LA 70041 • 2,600
Burbank, CA 91501-99 • 84,625
Burbank, IL 60459 • 28,462
Burbank, WA 99323 • 700
Burden, KS 67019 • 518
Burdett, KS 67523 • 275
Burdett, NY 14818 • 410
Burdette, AR 72321 • 328
Bureau, IL 61315 • 455
Bureau □, IL • 39,114
Burgaw, NC 28425 • 1,738
Burgettstown, PA 15021 • 1,867
Burgin, KY 40310 • 1,008
Burgoon, OH 43407 • 244
Burien, WA 98166 • 14,250
Burkburnett, TX 76354 • 10,668
Burke, NY 12917 • 226
Burke, SD 57523 • 859
Burke, VA 22015 • 1,500
Burke □, GA • 19,349
Burke □, NC • 72,504
Burke □, ND • 3,822
Burke City, MO 63135 • 2,600
Burkesville, KY 42717 • 2,051
Burket, IN 46508 • 260
Burkettsville, OH 45310 • 295
Burkeville, TX 75932 • 600
Burkeville, VA 23922 • 606
Burleigh, NJ 08210 • 600
Burleigh □, ND • 54,811
Burleson, TX 76028 • 11,734
Burleson □, TX • 12,313
Burley, ID 83318 • 8,761
Burley, WA 98322 • 300
Burlingame, CA 94010 • 26,173
Burlingame, KS 66413 • 1,239
Burlington, CO 80807 • 3,107
Burlington, CT 06013 • 400
Burlington, IL 60109 • 442
Burlington, IN 46915 • 680
Burlington, IA 52601 • 29,529
Burlington, KS 66839 • 2,901
Burlington, KY 41005 • 550
Burlington, MA 01803 • 23,486
Burlington, NJ 08016 • 10,246
Burlington, NC 27215 • 37,266
Burlington, ND 58722 • 762
Burlington, VT 05401 • 37,712
Burlington, WA 98233 • 3,894
Burlington, WI 53105 • 8,385
Burlington □, NJ • 362,542
Burlington Beach, IN 46383 • 900
Burlington Junction, MO 64428 • 657
Burnet, TX 78611 • 3,410
Burnet □, TX • 17,803
Burnett, IN 47805 • 325
Burnett □, WI • 12,340
Burnettown, SC 29834 • 359
Burnettsville, IN 47926 • 496
Burney, CA 96013 • 3,187
Burney, IN 47222 • 250
Burnham, PA 17009 • 2,457
Burns, KS 66840 • 224
Burns, OR 97720 • 3,579
Burns, TN 37029 • 777
Burns, WY 82053 • 268
Burns Flat, OK 73624 • 2,431
Burnside, KY 42519 • 775
Burnside, PA 15721 • 347
Burnsville, MN 55337 • 35,674
Burnsville, MS 38833 • 889
Burnsville, NC 28714 • 1,452
Burnsville, WV 26335 • 531
Burnt Hills, NY 12027 • 2,000
Burr Oak, KS 66936 • 366
Burr Oak, MI 49030 • 853
Burroughs, GA 31405 • 250
Burrows, IN 46916 • 300
Burrton, KS 67020 • 976
Burt, IA 50522 • 689
Burt □, NE • 8,813
Burton, MI 48509 • 29,976
Burton, OH 44021 • 1,401
Burton, TX 77835 • 325
Burwell, NE 68823 • 1,383
Busby, MT 59016 • 300
Bushkill, PA 18324 • 500
Bushnell, FL 33513 • 983
Bushnell, IL 61422 • 3,811
Bushton, KS 67427 • 388
Bussey, IA 50044 • 579
Butler, AL 36904 • 1,882
Butler, GA 31006 • 1,959
Butler, IL 62015 • 225
Butler, IN 46721 • 2,509
Butler, KY 41006 • 663
Butler, MO 64730 • 4,107
Butler, NJ 07405 • 7,616
Butler, OH 44822 • 991
Butler, OK 73625 • 388
Butler, PA 16001 • 17,026
Butler, TN 37640 • 400
Butler, WI 53007 • 2,059
Butler □, AL • 21,680
Butler □, IA • 17,668
Butler □, KS • 44,782
Butler □, KY • 11,064
Butler □, MO • 37,693
Butler □, NE • 9,330
Butler □, OH • 258,787
Butler □, PA • 147,912
Butlerville, IN 47223 • 350
Butner, NC 27509 • 4,240
Butte, MT 59701 • 37,205
Butte, NE 68722 • 529
Butte □, CA • 143,851
Butte □, ID • 3,342
Butte □, SD • 8,372
Butte Falls, OR 97522 • 428
Butterfield, MN 56120 • 634
Butterfield, MO 65623 • 234
Butternut, WI 54514 • 438
Butters, NC 28324 • 400
Buttonwillow, CA 93206 • 1,350
Butts □, GA • 13,665
Buxton, NC 27920 • 700
Buxton, ND 58218 • 336
Buzzards Bay, MA 02532 • 3,375
Byars, OK 74831 • 353
Bybee, TN 37713 • 300
Byers, CO 80103 • 1,100
Byesville, OH 43723 • 2,572
Byfield, MA 01922 • 950
Byhalia, MS 38611 • 757
Bylas, AZ 85530 • 1,175
Byng, OK 74820 • 833
Bynum, NC 27228 • 300
Byram, MS 39212 • 250
Byrdstown, TN 38549 • 884
Byromville, GA 31007 • 567
Byron, CA 94514 • 900
Byron, GA 31008 • 1,661
Byron, IL 61010 • 2,035
Byron, MN 55920 • 1,715
Byron, NY 14422 • 250
Byron, WY 82412 • 633

C

Cabarrus □, NC • 85,895
Cabell □, WV • 106,835
Cabery, IL 60919 • 327
Cabin Creek, WV 25035 • 900
Cabin John, MD 20818 • 1,500
Cable, WI 54821 • 227
Cabool, MO 65689 • 2,090
Cabot, AR 72023 • 4,806
Cabot, PA 16023 • 400
Cabot, VT 05647 • 259
Cache, OK 73527 • 1,661
Cache □, UT • 57,176
Caddo, OK 74729 • 923
Caddo □, LA • 252,358
Caddo □, OK • 30,905
Cade, LA 70519 • 400
Cades, SC 29518 • 300
Cadet, MO 63630 • 300

Cadillac, MI 49601 • 10,199
Cadiz, KY 42211 • 1,661
Cadiz, OH 43907 • 4,058
Cadogan, PA 16212 • 459
Cadott, WI 54727 • 1,247
Cadwell, GA 31009 • 353
Cahaba Heights, AL 35243 • 3,800
Cahokia, IL 62206 • 18,904
Cainsville, MO 64632 • 496
Cairnbrook, PA 15924 • 800
Cairo, GA 31728 • 8,777
Cairo, IL 62914 • 5,931
Cairo, MO 65239 • 315
Cairo, NE 68824 • 737
Cairo, NY 12413 • 725
Cairo, OH 45820 • 596
Cairo, WV 26337 • 428
Calabasas, CA 91302 • 900
Calais, ME 04619 • 4,262
Calamus, IA 52729 • 452
Calaveras □, CA • 20,710
Calavo Gardens, CA 92041 • 6,100
Calcasieu □, LA • 167,223
Calcutta, OH 43920 • 1,121
Caldwell, AR 72322 • 283
Caldwell, ID 83605 • 17,699
Caldwell, KS 67022 • 1,401
Caldwell, NJ 07006 • 7,624
Caldwell, OH 43724 • 1,935
Caldwell, TX 77836 • 2,953
Caldwell, WV 24925 • 300
Caldwell □, KY • 13,473
Caldwell □, LA • 10,761
Caldwell □, MO • 8,660
Caldwell □, NC • 67,746
Caldwell □, TX • 23,637
Caledonia, IL 61011 • 300
Caledonia, MI 49316 • 722
Caledonia, MN 55921 • 2,691
Caledonia, MS 39740 • 497
Caledonia, NY 14423 • 2,188
Caledonia, OH 43314 • 759
Caledonia □, VT • 25,808
Calera, AL 35040 • 2,035
Calera, OK 74730 • 1,390
Calexico, CA 92231 • 14,412
Calhan, CO 80808 • 541
Calhoun, GA 30701 • 5,563
Calhoun, IL 62419 • 267
Calhoun, KY 42327 • 1,080
Calhoun, LA 71225 • 425
Calhoun, MO 65323 • 427
Calhoun, TN 37309 • 590
Calhoun □, AL • 119,761
Calhoun □, AR • 6,079
Calhoun □, FL • 9,294
Calhoun □, GA • 5,717
Calhoun □, IL • 5,867
Calhoun □, IA • 13,542
Calhoun □, MI • 141,557
Calhoun □, MS • 15,664
Calhoun □, SC • 12,206
Calhoun □, TX • 19,574
Calhoun □, WV • 8,250
Calhoun City, MS 38916 • 2,033
Calhoun Falls, SC 29628 • 2,491
Calico Rock, AR 72519 • 1,046
Caliente, NV 89008 • 982
Califon, NJ 07830 • 1,023
California, MO 65018 • 3,381
California, PA 15419 • 5,703
Calion, AR 71724 • 638
Calipatria, CA 92233 • 2,636
Calistoga, CA 94515 • 3,879
Callahan, FL 32011 • 869
Callahan, KS 67209 • 900
Callahan □, TX • 10,992
Callao, MO 63534 • 326
Callao, VA 22435 • 450
Callaway, FL 32401 • 7,154
Callaway, MD 20620 • 300
Callaway, MN 56521 • 238
Callaway, NE 68825 • 579
Callaway □, MO • 32,252
Callender, IA 50523 • 446
Callensburg, PA 16213 • 248
Callery, PA 16024 • 415
Callicoon, NY 12723 • 500
Callicoon Center, NY 12724 • 300
Calloway □, KY • 30,031
Calmar, IA 52132 • 1,053
Calpella, CA 95418 • 300
Calumet, MI 49913 • 1,013
Calumet, MN 55716 • 469
Calumet □, WI • 30,867
Calumet City, IL 60409 • 39,697
Calumet Park, IL 60643 • 8,788
Calvert, AL 36513 • 500
Calvert, TX 77837 • 1,732
Calvert □, MD • 34,638
Calvert City, KY 42029 • 2,388
Calverton, MD 20705 • 7,649
Calverton, VA 22016 • 300
Calverton Park, MO 63136 • 1,717
Calvin, LA 71410 • 263
Calvin, OK 74531 • 315
Calwa, CA 93725 • 6,640
Calypso, NC 28325 • 689
Camak, GA 30807 • 283
Camanche, IA 52730 • 4,725
Camargo, IL 61919 • 428
Camargo, OK 73835 • 264
Camarillo, CA 93010 • 37,797
Camas, WA 98607 • 5,681
Camas □, ID • 818
Camas Valley, OR 97416 • 400
Cambria, CA 93428 • 3,061
Cambria, MI 49242 • 300
Cambria, WI 53923 • 680
Cambria □, PA • 183,263
Cambrian Park, CA 95124 • 4,000
Cambridge, ID 83610 • 428
Cambridge, IL 61238 • 2,217
Cambridge, IA 50046 • 732
Cambridge, MD 21613 • 11,703
Cambridge, MA 02138 • 95,322
Cambridge, MN 55008 • 3,287
Cambridge, NE 69022 • 1,206
Cambridge, NY 12816 • 1,820
Cambridge, OH 43725 • 13,573
Cambridge, WI 53523 • 844
Cambridge City, IN 47327 • 2,407
Cambridge Springs, PA 16403 • 2,102
Camden, AL 36726 • 2,406
Camden, AR 71701 • 15,356
Camden, DE 19934 • 1,757
Camden, IN 46917 • 618
Camden, ME 04843 • 3,743
Camden, MI 49232 • 420
Camden, NJ 08101-99 • 84,910
Camden, NC 27921 • 300
Camden, NY 13316 • 2,667
Camden, OH 45311 • 1,971
Camden, SC 29020 • 7,462
Camden, TN 38320 • 3,279
Camden □, GA • 13,371
Camden □, MO • 20,017
Camden □, NJ • 471,650
Camden □, NC • 5,829
Camden On Gauley, WV 26208 • 236
Camdenton, MO 65020 • 2,303
Cameron, AZ 86020 • 500
Cameron, IL 61423 • 300
Cameron, LA 70631 • 1,736
Cameron, MO 64429 • 4,519
Cameron, NC 28326 • 225
Cameron, OK 74932 • 365
Cameron, SC 29030 • 536
Cameron, TX 76520 • 5,721
Cameron, WV 26033 • 1,474
Cameron, WI 54822 • 1,115
Cameron □, LA • 9,336
Cameron □, PA • 6,674
Cameron □, TX • 209,727
Camilla, GA 31730 • 5,414
Camino, CA 95709 • 900
Cammack Village, AR 72207 • 920
Camp □, TX • 9,275
Campaign, TN 38550 • 500
Campbell, CA 95008 • 26,910
Campbell, FL 32741 • 2,941
Campbell, MN 56522 • 286
Campbell, MO 63933 • 2,134
Campbell, NE 68932 • 441
Campbell, NY 14821 • 300
Campbell, OH 44405 • 11,619
Campbell □, KY • 83,317
Campbell □, SD • 2,243
Campbell □, TN • 34,923
Campbell □, VA • 45,424
Campbell □, WY • 24,367
Campbell Hill, IL 62916 • 389
Campbellsburg, IN 47108 • 695
Campbellsburg, KY 40011 • 714
Campbellsport, WI 53010 • 1,740
Campbellsville, KY 42718 • 8,715
Campbellton, FL 32426 • 336
Camp Douglas, WI 54618 • 589
Camp Hill, AL 36850 • 1,628
Camp Hill, PA 17011 • 8,422
Campobello, SC 29322 • 472
Camp Point, IL 62320 • 1,285
Camp Springs, MD 20748 • 2,500
Campti, LA 71411 • 1,069
Campton, KY 41301 • 486
Campton, NH 03223 • 600
Campus, IL 60920 • 224
Camp Verde, AZ 86322 • 1,125
Camp Wood, TX 78833 • 728
Canaan, CT 06018 • 1,160
Canaan, ME 04924 • 360
Canaan, NH 03741 • 600
Canaan, VT 05903 • 350
Canada, KY 41519 • 400
Canadensis, PA 18325 • 800
Canadian, OK 74425 • 279
Canadian, TX 79014 • 3,491
Canadian □, OK • 56,452
Canajoharie, NY 13317 • 2,412
Canal Fulton, OH 44614 • 3,481
Canalou, MO 63828 • 369
Canal Point, FL 33438 • 950
Canal Winchester, OH 43110 • 2,749
Canandaigua, NY 14424 • 10,419
Canaseraga, NY 14822 • 700
Canastota, NY 13032 • 4,773
Canby, CA 96015 • 450
Canby, MN 56220 • 2,143
Canby, OR 97013 • 7,659
Candia, NH 03034 • 400
Candler, FL 32624 • 500
Candler □, GA • 7,518
Candlewood Isle, CT 06812 • 750
Candlewood Shores, CT 06804 • 1,950
Cando, ND 58324 • 1,496
Candor, NC 27229 • 868
Candor, NY 13743 • 917
Caney, KS 67333 • 2,284
Caneyville, KY 42721 • 642
Canfield, OH 44406 • 5,535
Canisteo, NY 14823 • 2,679
Canistota, SD 57012 • 626
Canjilon, NM 87515 • 300
Cannel City, KY 41408 • 250
Cannelton, IN 47520 • 2,373
Cannelton, WV 25036 • 750
Cannon □, TN • 10,234
Cannonball, ND 58528 • 400
Cannon Beach, OR 97110 • 1,187
Cannondale, CT 06897 • 1,300
Cannon Falls, MN 55009 • 2,653
Cannonsburg, KY 41101 • 600
Canon, GA 30520 • 704
Canon City, CO 81212 • 13,037
Canonsburg, PA 15317 • 10,459
Canterbury, DE 19943 • 500
Canterbury, NH 03224 • 250
Canton, CT 06019 • 1,680
Canton, GA 30114 • 3,601
Canton, IL 61520 • 14,626
Canton, KS 67428 • 926
Canton, ME 04221 • 500
Canton, MA 02021 • 18,182
Canton, MI 48187 • 5,000
Canton, MN 55922 • 386
Canton, MS 39046 • 11,116
Canton, MO 63435 • 2,435
Canton, NJ 08079 • 300
Canton, NC 28716 • 4,631
Canton, NY 13617 • 7,055
Canton, OH 44701-99 • 93,077
Canton, OK 73724 • 854
Canton, PA 17724 • 1,959
Canton, SD 57013 • 2,886
Canton, TX 75103 • 2,845
Canton Center, CT 06020 • 300
Cantonment, FL 32533 • 3,200
Cantril, IA 52542 • 299
Canute, OK 73626 • 676
Canutillo, TX 79835 • 2,000
Canyon, TX 79015 • 10,724
Canyon □, ID • 83,756
Canyon City, OR 97820 • 639
Canyon Lake, TX 78130 • 6,000
Canyonville, OR 97417 • 1,288
Capac, MI 48014 • 1,377
Cape Canaveral, FL 32920 • 5,733
Cape Charles, VA 23310 • 1,512
Cape Coral, FL 33904 • 32,103
Cape Elizabeth, ME 04107 • 7,838
Cape Girardeau, MO 63701 • 34,361
Cape Girardeau □, MO • 58,837
Capels, WV 24820 • 300
Cape May, NJ 08204 • 4,853
Cape May □, NJ • 82,266
Cape May Court House, NJ 08210 • 3,597
Cape May Point, NJ 08212 • 255
Cape Neddick, ME 03902 • 425
Cape Porpoise, ME 04014 • 500
Capeville, VA 23313 • 225
Cape Vincent, NY 13618 • 785
Capitan, NM 88316 • 762
Capitola, CA 95010 • 9,095
Capitol Heights, IA 50317 • 815
Capitol Heights, MD 20743 • 3,271
Capleville, TN 38118 • 500
Capron, IL 61012 • 678
Capron, VA 23829 • 238
Captain Cook, HI 96704 • 2,008
Captiva, FL 33924 • 1,200
Caraway, AR 72419 • 1,165
Carbon, IN 47837 • 307
Carbon □, MT • 8,099
Carbon □, PA • 53,285
Carbon □, UT • 22,179
Carbon □, WY • 21,896
Carbonado, WA 98323 • 456
Carbondale, CO 81623 • 2,084
Carbondale, IL 62901 • 26,414
Carbondale, KS 66414 • 1,518
Carbondale, PA 18407 • 11,255
Carbon Hill, AL 35549 • 2,452
Carbon Hill, IL 60416 • 406
Carbonville, UT 84501 • 500
Cardiff, MD 21024 • 450
Cardiff, NJ 08232 • 250
Cardiff-By-The-Sea, CA 92007 • 10,054
Cardington, OH 43315 • 1,665
Cardwell, MO 63829 • 831
Carencro, LA 70520 • 3,712
Caretta, WV 24821 • 950
Carey, ID 83320 • 600
Carey, OH 43316 • 3,674
Caribou, ME 04736 • 9,916
Caribou □, ID • 8,695
Carle Place, NY 11514 • 6,300
Carleton, MI 48117 • 2,786
Carlin, NV 89822 • 1,232
Carlinville, IL 62626 • 5,439
Carlisle, AR 72024 • 2,567
Carlisle, IN 47838 • 717
Carlisle, IA 50047 • 3,073
Carlisle, KY 40311 • 1,757
Carlisle, MA 01741 • 600
Carlisle, OH 45005 • 4,276
Carlisle, PA 17013 • 18,314
Carlisle, SC 29031 • 503
Carlisle □, KY • 5,487
Carl Junction, MO 64834 • 3,937
Carlock, IL 61725 • 410
Carlos, MN 56319 • 364
Carlotta, CA 95528 • 500
Carlsbad, CA 92008 • 35,490
Carlsbad, NM 88220 • 25,496
Carlsbad, TX 76934 • 500
Carlsborg, WA 98324 • 350
Carlstadt, NJ 07072 • 6,166
Carlton, GA 30627 • 291
Carlton, MN 55718 • 862
Carlton, OR 97111 • 1,302
Carlton, TX 76436 • 300
Carlton □, MN • 29,936
Carlyle, IL 62231 • 3,388
Carmel, CA 93923 • 4,707
Carmel, IN 46032 • 18,272
Carmel, ME 04419 • 370
Carmel, NJ 08332 • 500
Carmel, NY 10512 • 3,395
Carmen, OK 73726 • 516
Carmi, IL 62821 • 6,264
Carmichael, CA 95608 • 43,108
Carmichaels, PA 15320 • 630
Carmine, TX 78932 • 239
Carnation, WA 98014 • 913
Carnegie, OK 73015 • 2,016
Carnegie, PA 15106 • 10,099
Carnesville, GA 30521 • 465
Carney, OK 74832 • 622
Carneys Point, NJ 08069 • 7,574
Carnot, PA 15108 • 5,400
Caro, MI 48723 • 4,317
Carol City, FL 33055 • 47,349
Caroleen, NC 28019 • 1,000
Carolina, RI 02812 • 500
Carolina, WV 26563 • 650
Carolina Beach, NC 28428 • 2,000
Caroline, WI 54928 • 350
Caroline □, MD • 23,143
Caroline □, VA • 17,904
Carol Stream, IL 60187 • 15,472
Carpentersville, IL 60110 • 23,272
Carpinteria, CA 93013 • 10,835
Carpio, ND 58725 • 244
Carp Lake, MI 49718 • 300
Carrabelle, FL 32322 • 1,304
Carrboro, NC 27510 • 7,336
Carrier, OK 73727 • 259
Carriere, MS 39426 • 500
Carrier Mills, IL 62917 • 2,268
Carrington, ND 58421 • 2,641
Carrizo Springs, TX 78834 • 6,886
Carrizozo, NM 88301 • 1,222
Carroll, IA 51401 • 9,705
Carroll, NE 68723 • 246
Carroll, OH 43112 • 641

Carroll □, AR • 16,203
Carroll □, GA • 56,346
Carroll □, IL • 18,779
Carroll □, IN • 19,722
Carroll □, IA • 22,951
Carroll □, KY • 9,270
Carroll □, MD • 96,356
Carroll □, MS • 9,776
Carroll □, MO • 12,131
Carroll □, NH • 27,931
Carroll □, OH • 25,598
Carroll □, TN • 28,285
Carroll □, VA • 27,270
Carrolls, WA 98609 • 400
Carrollton, AL 35447 • 1,104
Carrollton, GA 30117 • 14,078
Carrollton, IL 62016 • 2,816
Carrollton, KY 41008 • 3,967
Carrollton, MI 48724 • 7,482
Carrollton, MS 38917 • 338
Carrollton, MO 64633 • 4,700
Carrollton, OH 44615 • 3,065
Carrollton, TX 75006-08 • 40,595
Carrolltown, PA 15722 • 1,395
Carrville, AL 36023 • 820
Carson, CA 90745 • 81,221
Carson, IA 51525 • 716
Carson, MS 39427 • 375
Carson, ND 58529 • 469
Carson, WA 98610 • 950
Carson □, TX • 6,672
Carson City, MI 48811 • 1,229
Carson City, NV 89701 • 32,022
Carson Spring, TN 37821 • 600
Carsonville, MI 48419 • 622
Carter, OK 73627 • 367
Carter, TN 37643 • 400
Carter □, KY • 25,060
Carter □, MO • 5,428
Carter □, MT • 1,799
Carter □, OK • 43,610
Carter □, TN • 50,205
Carteret, NJ 07008 • 20,598
Carteret □, NC • 41,092
Carter Lake, IA 51510 • 3,438
Cartersburg, IN 46114 • 400
Cartersville, GA 30120 • 9,247
Carterville, IL 62918 • 3,445
Carterville, MO 64835 • 1,973
Carthage, AR 71725 • 568
Carthage, IL 62321 • 2,978
Carthage, IN 46115 • 886
Carthage, MS 39051 • 3,453
Carthage, MO 64836 • 11,104
Carthage, NC 28327 • 925
Carthage, NY 13619 • 3,643
Carthage, SD 57323 • 274
Carthage, TN 37030 • 2,672
Carthage, TX 75633 • 6,447
Caruthersville, MO 63830 • 7,958
Carver, MA 02330 • 650
Carver, MN 55315 • 642
Carver □, MN • 37,046
Carver Ranch Estates, FL 33023 • 5,600
Carville, LA 70721 • 1,037
Cary, IL 60013 • 6,640
Cary, MS 39054 • 470
Cary, NC 27511 • 21,763
Caryville, FL 32427 • 633
Caryville, TN 37714 • 2,039
Casa Blanca, NM 87007 • 350
Casa Grande, AZ 85222 • 14,971
Casar, NC 28020 • 346
Casas Adobes, AZ 85704 • 5,300
Cascade, CO 80809 • 600
Cascade, ID 83611 • 945
Cascade, IA 52033 • 1,912
Cascade, MT 59421 • 773
Cascade, NH 03581 • 250
Cascade, WI 53011 • 615
Cascade □, MT • 80,696
Cascade Locks, OR 97014 • 838
Casco, ME 04015 • 370
Casco, WI 54205 • 484
Caseville, MI 48725 • 851
Casey, IL 62420 • 3,026
Casey, IA 50048 • 473
Casey □, KY • 14,818
Cash, AR 72421 • 285
Cashiers, NC 28717 • 533
Cashion, AZ 85329 • 3,014
Cashion, OK 73016 • 547
Cashmere, WA 98815 • 2,240
Cashton, WI 54619 • 827
Cashtown, PA 17310 • 250
Casmalia, CA 93429 • 300
Caspar, CA 95420 • 550
Casper, WY 82601-15 • 51,016
Caspian, MI 49915 • 1,038
Cass □, IL • 15,084
Cass □, IN • 40,936
Cass □, IA • 16,932
Cass □, MI • 49,499
Cass □, MN • 21,050
Cass □, MO • 51,029
Cass □, NE • 20,297
Cass □, ND • 88,247
Cass □, TX • 29,430
Cassadaga, NY 14718 • 821
Cass City, MI 48726 • 2,258
Casselberry, FL 32707-08 • 15,247
Casselton, ND 58012 • 1,661
Cassia □, ID • 19,427
Cass Lake, MN 56633 • 1,001
Cassopolis, MI 49031 • 1,933
Casstown, OH 45312 • 331
Cassville, GA 30123 • 300
Cassville, MO 65625 • 2,091
Cassville, WI 53806 • 1,270
Castalia, NC 27816 • 358
Castalia, OH 44824 • 973
Castana, IA 51010 • 228
Castanea, PA 17726 • 1,204
Castella, CA 96017 • 525
Castile, NY 14427 • 1,135
Castine, ME 04421 • 550
Castleberry, AL 36432 • 847
Castle Dale, UT 84513 • 1,910
Castle Hayne, NC 28429 • 1,087
Castle Hills, DE 19720 • 1,950
Castle Park, CA 92011 • 6,300
Castle Point, MO 63136 • 6,500
Castle Rock, CO 80104 • 3,921
Castle Rock, WA 98611 • 2,162
Castle Shannon, PA 15234 • 10,164
Castleton, VT 05735 • 600
Castleton on Hudson, NY 12033 • 1,627
Castlewood, SD 57223 • 557
Castlewood, VA 24224 • 400
Castorland, NY 13620 • 277
Castro □, TX • 10,556
Castro Valley, CA 94546 • 44,011
Castroville, CA 95012 • 4,396
Castroville, TX 78009 • 1,821
Caswell □, NC • 20,705
Catahoula □, LA • 12,287
Catalina Foothills, AZ 85718 • 1,500
Catasauqua, PA 18032 • 6,711
Cataula, GA 31804 • 500
Cataumet, MA 02534 • 800
Catawba, NC 28609 • 509
Catawba, SC 29704 • 300
Catawba □, NC • 105,208
Catawissa, PA 17820 • 1,568
Cateechee, SC 29629 • 500
Cathedral City, CA 92234 • 4,130
Cathlamet, WA 98612 • 635
Catlettsburg, KY 41129 • 3,005
Catlin, IL 61817 • 2,226
Cato, NY 13033 • 475
Catonsville, MD 21228 • 33,208
Catoosa, OK 74015 • 1,561
Catoosa □, GA • 36,991
Catron □, NM • 2,720
Catskill, NY 12414 • 4,718
Cattaraugus, NY 14719 • 1,200
Cattaraugus □, NY • 85,697
Cavalier, ND 58220 • 1,505
Cavalier □, ND • 7,636
Cave City, AR 72521 • 1,634
Cave City, KY 42127 • 2,098
Cave Creek, AZ 85331 • 1,589
Cave In Rock, IL 62919 • 468
Cave Junction, OR 97523 • 1,023
Cavendish, VT 05142 • 350
Cave Spring, GA 30124 • 883
Cave Spring, VA 24018 • 6,300
Cave Springs, AR 72718 • 429
Cavetown, MD 21720 • 1,533
Cawker City, KS 67430 • 640
Cawood, KY 40815 • 800
Cayce, SC 29033 • 11,701
Cayuga, IN 47928 • 1,258
Cayuga □, NY • 79,894
Cayuga Heights, NY 14850 • 3,170
Cazenovia, NY 13035 • 2,599
Cazenovia, WI 53924 • 259
Cecil, GA 31627 • 280
Cecil, OH 45821 • 267
Cecil, PA 15321 • 900
Cecil, WI 54111 • 445
Cecil □, MD • 60,430
Cecilia, KY 42724 • 500
Cecilton, MD 21913 • 508
Cedar □, IA • 18,635
Cedar □, MO • 11,894
Cedar □, NE • 11,375
Cedar Bluff, AL 35959 • 1,129
Cedar Bluff, TN 37722 • 1,200
Cedar Bluffs, NE 68015 • 632
Cedar Brook, NJ 08018 • 500
Cedarburg, WI 53012 • 9,005
Cedar City, MO 65022 • 427
Cedar City, UT 84720 • 10,972
Cedar Creek, NE 68016 • 311
Cedar Crest, NM 87008 • 900
Cedaredge, CO 81413 • 1,184
Cedar Falls, IA 50613 • 36,322
Cedar Grove, NJ 07009 • 12,600
Cedar Grove, WV 25039 • 1,479
Cedar Grove, WI 53013 • 1,420
Cedar Hill, MO 63016 • 1,512
Cedar Hill, TN 37032 • 420
Cedar Hill, TX 75104 • 6,849
Cedar Hills, OR 97225 • 8,000
Cedarhurst, NY 11516 • 6,162
Cedar Island, NC 28520 • 280
Cedar Key, FL 32625 • 700
Cedar Knolls, NJ 07927 • 3,000
Cedar Lake, IN 46303 • 8,754
Cedar Point, IL 61316 • 344
Cedar Rapids, IA 52401-99 • 110,243
Cedar Rapids, NE 68627 • 447
Cedar Run, NJ 08092 • 450
Cedar Springs, GA 31732 • 300
Cedar Springs, MI 49319 • 2,615
Cedartown, GA 30125 • 8,619
Cedar Vale, KS 67024 • 848
Cedar Valley, UT 84013 • 269
Cedarville, CA 96104 • 950
Cedarville, IL 61013 • 766
Cedarville, IN 46741 • 350
Cedarville, MA 02532 • 400
Cedarville, NJ 08311 • 990
Cedarville, NY 13357 • 250
Cedarville, OH 45314 • 2,799
Celina, OH 45822 • 9,137
Celina, TN 38551 • 1,580
Celina, TX 75009 • 1,520
Celoron, NY 14720 • 1,405
Celriver, SC 29730 • 300
Cement, OK 73017 • 884
Cement City, MI 49233 • 539
Cementon, PA 18052 • 1,200
Centenary, SC 29519 • 400
Center, CO 81125 • 1,630
Center, GA 30601 • 330
Center, MO 63436 • 669
Center, ND 58530 • 900
Center, TX 75935 • 5,827
Center Barnstead, NH 03225 • 300
Centerbrook, CT 06409 • 900
Centerburg, OH 43011 • 1,275
Center City, MN 55012 • 458
Center Conway, NH 03813 • 300
Center Creek, UT 84032 • 300
Centereach, NY 11720 • 34,600
Centerfield, UT 84622 • 653
Center Harbor, NH 03226 • 500
Center Hill, FL 33514 • 751
Center Line, MI 48015 • 9,293
Center Moriches, NY 11934 • 4,000
Center Ossipee, NH 03814 • 500
Center Point, AL 35215 • 23,317
Centerpoint, IN 47840 • 242
Center Point, IA 52213 • 1,591
Center Point, TX 78010 • 600
Center Rutland, VT 05736 • 475
Center Sandwich, NH 03227 • 400
Centerton, AR 72719 • 425
Centerton, IN 46116 • 300
Centertown, KY 42328 • 462
Centertown, MO 65023 • 304
Centertown, TN 37110 • 300
Center Tuftonboro, NH 03816 • 300
Centerview, MO 64019 • 223
Centerville, AR 72829 • 300
Centerville, DE 19807 • 300
Centerville, IN 47330 • 2,284
Centerville, IA 52544 • 6,558
Centerville, LA 70522 • 500
Centerville, MA 02632 • 3,640
Centerville, MO 63633 • 241
Centerville, OH 45459 • 18,886
Centerville, PA 16404 • 245
Centerville, PA 15417 • 4,207
Centerville, SD 57014 • 892
Centerville, TN 37033 • 2,824
Centerville, TX 75833 • 799
Centerville, UT 84014 • 8,069
Central, AZ 85531 • 250
Central, NM 88026 • 1,968
Central, SC 29630 • 1,914
Central Bridge, NY 12035 • 500
Central City, CO 80427 • 329
Central City, IL 62801 • 1,505
Central City, IA 52214 • 1,067
Central City, KY 42330 • 5,214
Central City, NE 68826 • 3,083
Central City, PA 15926 • 1,496
Central City, SD 57754 • 232
Central Falls, RI 02863 • 16,995
Centralhatchee, GA 30217 • 240
Central Heights, AZ 85501 • 1,500
Central Heights, IA 50401 • 400
Centralia, IL 62801 • 15,126
Centralia, KS 66415 • 486
Centralia, MO 65240 • 3,537
Centralia, WA 98531 • 11,555
Central Islip, NY 11722 • 26,000
Central Lake, MI 49622 • 895
Central Park, WA 98520 • 2,900
Central Point, OR 97502 • 6,357
Central Square, NY 13036 • 1,418
Central Valley, CA 96019 • 3,424
Central Valley, NY 10917 • 1,200
Central Village, CT 06332 • 1,200
Central Village, MA 02790 • 350
Centre, AL 35960 • 2,351
Centre □, PA • 112,760
Centre City, NJ 08051 • 2,500
Centre Hall, PA 16828 • 1,233
Centreville, AL 35042 • 2,504
Centreville, IL 62207 • 9,747
Centreville, MD 21617 • 2,018
Centreville, MI 49032 • 1,202
Centreville, MS 39631 • 1,844
Centreville, VA 22020 • 950
Centuria, WI 54824 • 711
Century, FL 32535 • 1,805
Century, WV 26214 • 250
Ceredo, WV 25507 • 2,255
Ceres, CA 95307 • 13,281
Ceres, NY 14721 • 400
Ceresco, NE 68017 • 836
Cerritos, CA 90701 • 53,020
Cerro, NM 87519 • 250
Cerro Gordo, IL 61818 • 1,553
Cerro Gordo, NC 28430 • 295
Cerro Gordo □, IA • 48,458
Cerulean, KY 42215 • 253
Ceylon, MN 56121 • 543
Chacon, NM 87713 • 300
Chadbourn, NC 28431 • 1,975
Chadds Ford, PA 19317 • 250
Chadron, NE 69337 • 5,933
Chadwick, IL 61014 • 631
Chadwicks, NY 13319 • 1,500
Chaffee, MO 63740 • 3,241
Chaffee □, CO • 13,227
Chaffin, MA 01520 • 3,700
Chagrin Falls, OH 44022 • 4,335
Chalfonte, DE 19810 • 2,200
Challis, ID 83226 • 758
Chalmers, IN 47929 • 554
Chalmette, LA 70043 • 33,847
Chama, CO 81126 • 250
Chama, NM 87520 • 1,090
Chamberlain, SD 57325 • 2,258
Chambers, AZ 86502 • 400
Chambers, NE 68725 • 390
Chambers □, AL • 39,191
Chambers □, TX • 18,538
Chambersburg, PA 17201 • 16,174
Chamblee, GA 30341 • 7,137
Chamisal, NM 87521 • 600
Chamois, MO 65024 • 546
Champaign, IL 61820-21 • 58,133
Champaign □, IL • 168,392
Champaign □, OH • 33,649
Champion, MI 49814 • 500
Champion, OH 44481 • 5,270
Champlain, NY 12919 • 1,410
Champlin, MN 55316 • 9,006
Chana, IL 61015 • 250
Chance, AL 36729 • 400
Chance, MD 21816 • 300
Chancellor, SD 57015 • 257
Chandler, AZ 85224 • 29,673
Chandler, IN 47610 • 3,043
Chandler, MN 56122 • 344
Chandler, OK 74834 • 2,926
Chandler, TX 75758 • 1,308
Chandler Heights, AZ 85227 • 750
Chandlerville, IL 62627 • 842
Changewater, NJ 07831 • 300
Chanhassen, MN 55317 • 6,359
Channahon, IL 60410 • 3,734
Channel Lake, IL 60002 • 1,613
Channelview, TX 77530 • 16,000
Channing, MI 49815 • 400
Channing, TX 79018 • 304
Chantilly, VA 22021 • 950
Chanute, KS 66720 • 10,506
Chapel Hill, NC 27514 • 32,421
Chapel Hill, TN 37034 • 861
Chapel Square, VA 22003 • 2,000

Chapin, IL 62628 • *648*
Chapin, SC 29036 • *311*
Chaplin, KY 40012 • *350*
Chapman, AL 36015 • *350*
Chapman, KS 67431 • *1,255*
Chapman, NE 68827 • *349*
Chapman Ranch, TX 78347 • *250*
Chapmanville, WV 25508 • *1,164*
Chappaqua, NY 10514 • *5,100*
Chappell, NE 69129 • *1,095*
Chardon, OH 44024 • *4,434*
Charenton, LA 70523 • *950*
Chariton, IA 50049 • *4,987*
Chariton □, MO • *10,489*
Charlemont, MA 01339 • *500*
Charleroi, PA 15022 • *5,717*
Charles □, MD • *72,751*
Charles City, IA 50616 • *8,778*
Charles City □, VA • *6,692*
Charles Mix □, SD • *9,680*
Charleston, AR 72933 • *1,748*
Charleston, IL 61920 • *19,355*
Charleston, MS 38921 • *2,878*
Charleston, MO 63834 • *5,230*
Charleston, OR 97420 • *700*
Charleston, SC 29401-25 • *69,510*
Charleston, TN 37310 • *756*
Charleston, UT 84032 • *320*
Charleston, WV 25301-99 • *63,968*
Charleston □, SC • *276,974*
Charlestown, IN 47111 • *5,596*
Charlestown, MD 21914 • *720*
Charlestown, NH 03603 • *1,294*
Charlestown, RI 02813 • *1,200*
Charles Town, WV 25414 • *2,857*
Charlevoix, MI 49720 • *3,296*
Charlevoix □, MI • *19,907*
Charlo, MT 59824 • *250*
Charlotte, IA 52731 • *442*
Charlotte, MI 48813 • *8,251*
Charlotte, NC 28201-99 • *314,447*
Charlotte, TN 37036 • *788*
Charlotte, TX 78011 • *1,443*
Charlotte, VT 05445 • *300*
Charlotte □, FL • *58,460*
Charlotte □, VA • *12,266*
Charlotte Court House, VA 23923 • *568*
Charlotte Hall, MD 20622 • *1,000*
Charlotte Harbor, FL 33950 • *2,084*
Charlottesville, IN 46117 • *380*
Charlottesville, VA 22901-10 • *39,916*
Charlton, MA 01507 • *300*
Charlton □, GA • *7,343*
Charlton City, MA 01508 • *1,100*
Charlton Depot, MA 01509 • *300*
Charlton Heights, WV 25040 • *600*
Charmco, WV 25958 • *800*
Charter Oak, IA 51439 • *615*
Chartley, MA 02712 • *600*
Chase, KS 67524 • *753*
Chase, MD 21027 • *700*
Chase □, KS • *3,309*
Chase □, NE • *4,758*
Chaseburg, WI 54621 • *279*
Chase City, VA 23924 • *2,749*
Chaska, MN 55318 • *8,346*
Chassell, MI 49916 • *700*
Chataignier, LA 70524 • *431*
Chateaugay, NY 12920 • *869*
Chatfield, MN 55923 • *2,055*
Chatfield, OH 44825 • *228*
Chatham, IL 62629 • *5,597*
Chatham, LA 71226 • *714*
Chatham, MA 02633 • *1,922*
Chatham, MI 49816 • *315*
Chatham, NJ 07928 • *8,537*
Chatham, NY 12037 • *2,001*
Chatham, VA 24531 • *1,390*
Chatham □, GA • *202,226*
Chatham □, NC • *33,415*
Chatom, AL 36518 • *1,122*
Chatsworth, GA 30705 • *2,493*
Chatsworth, IL 60921 • *1,187*
Chatsworth, NJ 08019 • *400*
Chattahoochee, FL 32324 • *5,332*
Chattahoochee □, GA • *21,732*
Chattanooga, OK 73528 • *403*
Chattanooga, TN 37401-99 • *169,558*
Chattaroy, WA 99003 • *400*
Chattaroy, WV 25667 • *1,200*
Chattooga □, GA • *21,856*
Chaumont, NY 13622 • *620*
Chauncey, GA 31011 • *350*
Chauncey, OH 45719 • *1,050*
Chautauqua, NY 14722 • *430*
Chautauqua □, KS • *5,016*
Chautauqua □, NY • *146,925*
Chauvin, LA 70344 • *3,338*
Chaves □, NM • *51,103*
Chazy, NY 12921 • *800*
Cheapside, VA 23310 • *250*
Cheatham □, TN • *21,616*
Chebanse, IL 60922 • *1,191*
Chebeague Island, ME 04017 • *300*
Cheboygan, MI 49721 • *5,106*
Cheboygan □, MI • *20,649*
Checotah, OK 74426 • *3,454*
Cheektowaga, NY 14225 • *100,400*
Chehalis, WA 98532 • *6,100*
Chelan, WA 98816 • *2,802*
Chelan □, WA • *45,061*
Chelan Falls, WA 98817 • *250*
Chelmsford, MA 01824 • *31,174*
Chelsea, AL 35043 • *600*
Chelsea, IA 52215 • *376*
Chelsea, MA 02150 • *25,431*
Chelsea, MI 48118 • *3,816*
Chelsea, OK 74016 • *1,754*
Chelsea, VT 05038 • *500*
Chelsea Estates, DE 19720 • *1,500*
Cheltenham, MD 20623 • *500*
Cheltenham, PA 19012 • *7,700*
Chelyan, WV 25035 • *800*
Chemult, OR 97731 • *425*
Chemung, IL 60033 • *250*
Chemung □, NY • *97,656*
Chenango □, NY • *49,344*
Chenango Bridge, NY 13745 • *2,600*
Chenango Forks, NY 13746 • *500*
Chenequa, WI 53029 • *532*
Cheney, KS 67025 • *1,404*
Cheney, WA 99004 • *7,630*
Cheneyville, LA 71325 • *865*
Chenoa, IL 61726 • *1,847*
Chenoweth, OR 97058 • *2,820*
Chepachet, RI 02814 • *900*
Cheraw, CO 81030 • *233*
Cheraw, SC 29520 • *5,654*
Cheriton, VA 23316 • *695*
Cherokee, AL 35616 • *1,589*
Cherokee, IA 51012 • *7,004*
Cherokee, KS 66724 • *775*
Cherokee, NC 28719 • *600*
Cherokee, OK 73728 • *2,105*
Cherokee, TX 76832 • *450*
Cherokee □, AL • *18,760*
Cherokee □, GA • *51,699*
Cherokee □, IA • *16,238*
Cherokee □, KS • *22,304*
Cherokee □, NC • *18,933*
Cherokee □, OK • *30,684*
Cherokee □, SC • *40,983*
Cherokee □, TX • *38,127*
Cherokee Falls, SC 29705 • *250*
Cherokee Village, AR 72525 • *3,200*
Cherry, IL 61317 • *541*
Cherry □, NE • *6,758*
Cherry Creek, NY 14723 • *677*
Cherry Creek, SD 57622 • *300*
Cherryfield, ME 04622 • *230*
Cherry Grove, OR 97119 • *300*
Cherry Hill, NJ 08002-03 • *68,785*
Cherry Hills Village, CO 80110 • *5,127*
Cherry Tree, PA 15724 • *520*
Cherryvale, KS 67335 • *2,769*
Cherry Valley, AR 72324 • *729*
Cherry Valley, IL 61016 • *946*
Cherry Valley, MA 01611 • *1,400*
Cherry Valley, NY 13320 • *684*
Cherryville, NC 28021 • *4,844*
Chesaning, MI 48616 • *2,656*
Chesapeake, OH 45619 • *1,370*
Chesapeake, VA 23320-25 • *114,486*
Chesapeake, WV 25315 • *2,364*
Chesapeake Beach, MD 20732 • *1,408*
Chesapeake City, MD 21915 • *899*
Cheshire, CT 06410 • *5,722*
Cheshire, MA 01225 • *1,100*
Cheshire, OH 45620 • *297*
Cheshire □, NH • *62,116*
Chesilhurst, NJ 08089 • *1,590*
Chesnee, SC 29323 • *1,069*
Chester, CA 96020 • *1,756*
Chester, CT 06412 • *1,388*
Chester, GA 31012 • *409*
Chester, ID 83421 • *420*
Chester, IL 62233 • *8,401*
Chester, MD 21619 • *600*
Chester, MA 01011 • *750*
Chester, MT 59522 • *963*
Chester, NE 68327 • *435*
Chester, NH 03036 • *500*
Chester, NJ 07930 • *1,433*
Chester, NY 10918 • *1,910*
Chester, OH 45720 • *250*
Chester, PA 19013-16 • *45,794*
Chester, SC 29706 • *6,820*
Chester, VT 05143 • *500*
Chester, VA 23831 • *7,000*
Chester, WV 26034 • *3,297*
Chester □, PA • *316,660*
Chester □, SC • *30,148*
Chester □, TN • *12,727*
Chester Depot, VT 05144 • *500*
Chesterfield, IL 62630 • *280*
Chesterfield, IN 46017 • *2,701*
Chesterfield, MA 01012 • *550*
Chesterfield, NH 03443 • *350*
Chesterfield, SC 29709 • *1,432*
Chesterfield, VA 23832 • *400*
Chesterfield □, SC • *38,161*
Chesterfield □, VA • *141,372*
Chesterhill, OH 43728 • *395*
Chesterton, IN 46304 • *8,531*
Chestertown, MD 21620 • *3,300*
Chestertown, NY 12817 • *750*
Chester Township, PA 19013 • *5,687*
Chesterville, OH 43317 • *242*
Chestnut, IL 62518 • *350*
Chestnut Hill Estates, DE 19713 • *2,000*
Cheswick, PA 15024 • *2,336*
Cheswold, DE 19936 • *269*
Chetek, WI 54728 • *1,931*
Chetopa, KS 67336 • *1,751*
Chevak, AK 99563 • *466*
Cheverly, MD 20785 • *5,751*
Cheviot, OH 45211 • *9,888*
Chevy Chase, MD 20815 • *12,232*
Chewelah, WA 99109 • *1,888*
Chewsville, MD 21721 • *350*
Chewton, PA 16157 • *600*
Cheyenne, OK 73628 • *1,207*
Cheyenne, WY 82001-09 • *47,283*
Cheyenne □, CO • *2,153*
Cheyenne □, KS • *3,678*
Cheyenne □, NE • *10,057*
Cheyenne Canon, CO 80907 • *1,100*
Cheyenne Wells, CO 80810 • *950*
Chicago, IL 60601-99 • *3,005,072*
Chicago Heights, IL 60411 • *37,026*
Chicago Ridge, IL 60415 • *13,473*
Chickamauga, GA 30707 • *2,232*
Chickasaw, AL 36611 • *7,402*
Chickasaw □, IA • *15,437*
Chickasaw □, MS • *17,853*
Chickasha, OK 73018 • *15,828*
Chico, CA 95926 • *26,603*
Chico, TX 76030 • *890*
Chico, WA 98310 • *750*
Chicopee, GA 30501 • *900*
Chicopee, KS 66762 • *250*
Chicopee, MA 01013-22 • *55,112*
Chicora, PA 16025 • *1,192*
Chicot □, AR • *17,793*
Chidester, AR 71726 • *342*
Chiefland, FL 32626 • *1,986*
Childersburg, AL 35044 • *5,084*
Childress, TX 79201 • *5,817*
Childress □, TX • *6,950*
Chilhowee, MO 64733 • *349*
Chilhowie, VA 24319 • *1,269*
Chili Center, NY 14624 • *5,300*
Chillicothe, IL 61523 • *6,176*
Chillicothe, MO 64601 • *9,089*
Chillicothe, OH 45601 • *23,420*
Chillicothe, TX 79225 • *1,052*
Chillum, MD 20783 • *14,900*
Chilmark, MA 02535 • *300*
Chilocco, OK 74647 • *500*
Chiloquin, OR 97624 • *778*
Chilton, TX 76632 • *500*
Chilton, WI 53014 • *2,965*
Chilton □, AL • *30,612*
Chimacum, WA 98325 • *600*
Chimayo, NM 87522 • *1,993*
China, ME 04926 • *350*
China Grove, NC 28023 • *2,081*
Chincoteague, VA 23336 • *1,607*
Chinle, AZ 86503 • *2,815*
Chino, CA 91710 • *40,165*
Chinook, MT 59523 • *1,660*
Chinook, WA 98614 • *650*
Chino Valley, AZ 86323 • *2,858*
Chinquapin, NC 28521 • *275*
Chipita Park, CO 80809 • *350*
Chipley, FL 32428 • *3,330*
Chippewa □, MI • *29,029*
Chippewa □, MN • *14,941*
Chippewa □, WI • *52,127*
Chippewa Falls, WI 54729 • *12,270*
Chireno, TX 75937 • *371*
Chisago □, MN • *25,717*
Chisago City, MN 55013 • *1,634*
Chisholm, ME 04239 • *1,796*
Chisholm, MN 55719 • *5,930*
Chittenango, NY 13037 • *4,290*
Chittenden, VT 05737 • *280*
Chittenden □, VT • *115,534*
Chloride, AZ 86431 • *300*
Chocorua, NH 03817 • *300*
Chocowinity, NC 27817 • *644*
Choctaw, OK 73020 • *7,520*
Choctaw □, AL • *16,839*
Choctaw □, MS • *8,996*
Choctaw □, OK • *17,203*
Chokio, MN 56221 • *559*
Chokoloskee, FL 33925 • *400*
Choteau, MT 59422 • *1,798*
Choudrant, LA 71227 • *809*
Chouteau, OK 74337 • *1,559*
Chouteau □, MT • *6,092*
Chowan □, NC • *12,558*
Chowchilla, CA 93610 • *5,122*
Chrisman, IL 61924 • *1,413*
Chrisney, IN 47611 • *537*
Christian □, IL • *36,446*
Christian □, KY • *66,878*
Christian □, MO • *22,402*
Christiana, DE 19702 • *500*
Christiana, PA 17509 • *1,183*
Christiana, TN 37037 • *300*
Christiansburg, OH 45389 • *593*
Christiansburg, VA 24073 • *10,345*
Christine, TX 78012 • *392*
Christmas, FL 32709 • *1,200*
Christopher, IL 62822 • *3,086*
Christoval, TX 76935 • *700*
Chubbuck, ID 83202 • *7,052*
Chuckey, TN 37641 • *300*
Chugwater, WY 82210 • *282*
Chuichu, AZ 85222 • *300*
Chula, MO 64635 • *244*
Chula Vista, CA 92010-12 • *83,927*
Chunchula, AL 36521 • *300*
Chunky, MS 39323 • *277*
Church Hill, MD 21623 • *319*
Church Hill, TN 37642 • *4,110*
Churchill, OH 44505 • *7,700*
Churchill □, NV • *13,917*
Church Point, LA 70525 • *4,599*
Church Rock, NM 87311 • *500*
Churchton, MD 20733 • *800*
Churchville, MD 21028 • *300*
Churchville, NY 14428 • *1,399*
Churchville, VA 24421 • *350*
Churdan, IA 50050 • *540*
Churubusco, IN 46723 • *1,638*
Cibecue, AZ 85911 • *950*
Cibola □, NM • *30,102*
Cicero, IL 60650 • *61,232*
Cicero, IN 46034 • *2,557*
Cimarron, KS 67835 • *1,491*
Cimarron, NM 87714 • *888*
Cimarron □, OK • *3,648*
Cincinnati, IA 52549 • *598*
Cincinnati, OH 45201-99 • *385,457*
Cincinnatus, NY 13040 • *500*
Cinnaminson, NJ 08077 • *16,072*
Circle, MT 59215 • *931*
Circle Pines, MN 55014 • *3,321*
Circleville, OH 43113 • *11,700*
Circleville, UT 84723 • *445*
Cisco, GA 30708 • *275*
Cisco, IL 61830 • *333*
Cisco, TX 76437 • *4,517*
Cisne, IL 62823 • *705*
Cissna Park, IL 60924 • *825*
Citra, FL 32627 • *1,500*
Citronelle, AL 36522 • *2,841*
Citrus □, FL • *54,703*
Citrus Heights, CA 95610 • *85,911*
City of Commerce, CA 90040 • *10,509*
City Point, FL 32922 • *400*
City View, SC 29611 • *1,662*
Clackamas, OR 97015 • *3,250*
Clackamas □, OR • *241,911*
Claflin, KS 67525 • *764*
Claiborne, LA 71291 • *2,000*
Claiborne □, LA • *17,095*
Claiborne □, MS • *12,279*
Claiborne □, TN • *24,595*
Clair-Mel City, FL 33619 • *7,000*
Clairton, PA 15025 • *12,188*
Clallam □, WA • *51,648*
Clallam Bay, WA 98326 • *600*
Clanton, AL 35045 • *5,832*
Clara, MS 39324 • *365*
Clara City, MN 56222 • *1,574*
Clare, IA 50524 • *229*
Clare, MI 48617 • *3,300*
Clare □, MI • *23,822*
Claremont, CA 91711 • *30,950*

Claremont, IL 62421 • 255
Claremont, MN 55924 • 591
Claremont, NH 03743 • 14,557
Claremont, NC 28610 • 880
Claremont, VA 23899 • 380
Claremore, OK 74017 • 12,085
Clarence, IA 52216 • 1,001
Clarence, LA 71414 • 612
Clarence, MO 63437 • 1,147
Clarence, PA 16829 • 600
Clarendon, AR 72029 • 2,361
Clarendon, PA 16313 • 776
Clarendon, TX 79226 • 2,220
Clarendon, VT 05759 • 300
Clarendon □, SC • 27,464
Clarendon Hills, IL 60514 • 6,870
Claridge, PA 15623 • 600
Clarinda, IA 51632 • 5,458
Clarington, OH 43915 • 558
Clarion, IA 50525 • 3,060
Clarion, PA 16214 • 6,198
Clarion □, PA • 43,362
Clarissa, MN 56440 • 663
Clark, MO 65243 • 304
Clark, NJ 07066 • 16,699
Clark, SD 57225 • 1,351
Clark □, AR • 23,326
Clark □, ID • 798
Clark □, IL • 16,913
Clark □, IN • 88,838
Clark □, KS • 2,599
Clark □, KY • 28,322
Clark □, MO • 8,493
Clark □, NV • 463,087
Clark □, OH • 150,236
Clark □, SD • 4,894
Clark □, WA • 192,227
Clark □, WI • 32,910
Clarkdale, AZ 86324 • 1,512
Clarkdale, GA 30020 • 550
Clarke □, AL • 27,702
Clarke □, GA • 74,498
Clarke □, IA • 8,612
Clarke □, MS • 16,945
Clarke □, VA • 9,965
Clarkesville, GA 30523 • 1,348
Clarkfield, MN 56223 • 1,171
Clark Fork, ID 83811 • 449
Clarks, LA 71415 • 931
Clarks, NE 68628 • 445
Clarksboro, NJ 08020 • 800
Clarksburg, IN 47225 • 300
Clarksburg, MD 20871 • 600
Clarksburg, MO 65025 • 352
Clarksburg, NJ 08510 • 400
Clarksburg, OH 43115 • 483
Clarksburg, TN 38324 • 400
Clarksburg, WV 26301 • 22,371
Clarksdale, MS 38614 • 21,137
Clarksdale, MO 64430 • 278
Clarks Grove, MN 56016 • 620
Clarks Hill, IN 47930 • 653
Clarkson, KY 42726 • 666
Clarkson, NE 68629 • 817
Clarks Summit, PA 18411 • 5,272
Clarkston, GA 30021 • 4,539
Clarkston, MI 48016 • 968
Clarkston, UT 84305 • 562
Clarkston, WA 99403 • 6,903
Clarksville, AR 72830 • 5,237
Clarksville, DE 19937 • 450
Clarksville, IN 47130 • 15,164
Clarksville, IA 50619 • 1,424
Clarksville, MD 21029 • 300
Clarksville, MI 48815 • 348
Clarksville, MO 63336 • 585
Clarksville, OH 45113 • 525
Clarksville, TN 37040-43 • 54,777
Clarksville, TX 75426 • 4,917
Clarksville, VA 23927 • 1,468
Clarkton, MO 63837 • 1,228
Clarkton, NC 28433 • 664
Clatonia, NE 68328 • 273
Clatskanie, OR 97016 • 1,648
Clatsop □, OR • 32,489
Claude, TX 79019 • 1,112
Clawson, MI 48017 • 15,103
Claxton, GA 30417 • 2,694
Clay, KY 42404 • 1,356
Clay, NY 13041 • 600
Clay, WV 25043 • 940
Clay □, AL • 13,703
Clay □, AR • 20,616
Clay □, FL • 67,052
Clay □, GA • 3,553
Clay □, IL • 15,283
Clay □, IN • 24,862
Clay □, IA • 19,576
Clay □, KS • 9,802
Clay □, KY • 22,752
Clay □, MN • 49,327
Clay □, MS • 21,082
Clay □, MO • 136,488
Clay □, NE • 8,106
Clay □, NC • 6,619
Clay □, SD • 13,689
Clay □, TN • 7,676
Clay □, TX • 9,582
Clay □, WV • 11,265
Clay Center, KS 67432 • 4,948
Clay Center, NE 68933 • 962
Clay Center, OH 43408 • 327
Clay City, IL 62824 • 1,038
Clay City, IN 47841 • 883
Clay City, KY 40312 • 1,276
Clayhatchee, AL 36322 • 560
Claymont, DE 19702 • 10,022
Claypool, AZ 85532 • 2,362
Claypool, IN 46510 • 464
Claysburg, PA 16625 • 1,516
Clay Springs, AZ 85923 • 275
Claysville, PA 15323 • 1,029
Clayton, AL 36016 • 1,589
Clayton, DE 19938 • 1,216
Clayton, GA 30525 • 1,838
Clayton, IL 62324 • 889
Clayton, IN 46118 • 703
Clayton, LA 71326 • 1,204
Clayton, MO 63105 • 14,273
Clayton, NJ 08312 • 6,013
Clayton, NM 88415 • 2,968
Clayton, NC 27520 • 4,091
Clayton, NY 13624 • 1,816
Clayton, OK 74536 • 833
Clayton, WI 54004 • 425
Clayton □, GA • 150,357
Clayton □, IA • 21,098
Clayville, RI 02815 • 300
Clearbrook, MN 56634 • 579
Clear Creek, IN 47426 • 250
Clear Creek, WV 25044 • 335
Clear Creek □, CO • 7,308
Clearfield, IA 50840 • 433
Clearfield, KY 40313 • 1,250
Clearfield, PA 16830 • 7,580
Clearfield, UT 84015 • 17,982
Clearfield □, PA • 83,578
Clearlake, CA 95422 • 13,300
Clear Lake, IA 50428 • 7,458
Clear Lake, MN 55319 • 266
Clear Lake, SD 57226 • 1,310
Clearlake, WA 98235 • 900
Clear Lake, WI 54005 • 899
Clear Lake City, TX 77062 • 8,700
Clear Lake Shores, TX 77565 • 755
Clearmont, MO 64431 • 261
Clear Spring, MD 21722 • 477
Clearview, OK 74835 • 300
Clearwater, FL 33515-20 • 85,528
Clearwater, KS 67026 • 1,684
Clearwater, MN 55320 • 379
Clearwater, NE 68726 • 409
Clearwater, SC 29822 • 3,967
Clearwater, WA 98331 • 250
Clearwater □, ID • 10,390
Clearwater □, MN • 8,761
Clearwater Lake, WI 54521 • 250
Cleaton, KY 42332 • 350
Cleburne, TX 76031 • 19,218
Cleburne □, AL • 12,595
Cleburne □, AR • 16,909
Cle Elum, WA 98922 • 1,773
Cleghorn, IA 51014 • 275
Cleland Heights, DE 19805 • 1,500
Clementon, NJ 08021 • 5,764
Clements, MN 56224 • 227
Clemmons, NC 27012 • 7,401
Clemson, SC 29631 • 8,118
Clendenin, WV 25045 • 1,373
Cleona, PA 17042 • 2,003
Cleo Springs, OK 73729 • 514
Clermont, FL 32711 • 5,461
Clermont, GA 30527 • 300
Clermont, IA 52135 • 602
Clermont □, OH • 128,483
Clermont Harbor, MS 39551 • 325
Cleveland, AL 35049 • 487
Cleveland, GA 30528 • 1,578
Cleveland, IL 61241 • 338
Cleveland, MN 56017 • 699
Cleveland, MS 38732 • 14,524
Cleveland, MO 64734 • 485
Cleveland, NM 87715 • 300
Cleveland, NC 27013 • 595
Cleveland, NY 13042 • 855
Cleveland, OH 44101-99 • 573,822
Cleveland, OK 74020 • 2,972
Cleveland, TN 37311 • 26,415
Cleveland, TX 77327 • 5,977
Cleveland, UT 84518 • 522
Cleveland, VA 24225 • 360
Cleveland, WI 53015 • 1,270
Cleveland □, AR • 7,868
Cleveland □, NC • 83,435
Cleveland □, OK • 133,173
Cleveland Heights, OH 44118 • 56,438
Clever, MO 65631 • 551
Cleves, OH 45002 • 2,094
Clewiston, FL 33440 • 5,219
Cliff, NM 88028 • 400
Clifford, IN 47226 • 310
Clifford, MI 48727 • 406
Clifford, PA 18413 • 350
Cliffside, NC 28024 • 600
Cliffside Park, NJ 07010 • 21,464
Cliffwood Beach, NJ 07735 • 6,300
Clifton, AZ 85533 • 4,245
Clifton, CO 81520 • 5,223
Clifton, IL 60927 • 1,390
Clifton, KS 66937 • 695
Clifton, NJ 07011-15 • 74,388
Clifton, SC 29324 • 800
Clifton, TN 38425 • 773
Clifton, TX 76634 • 3,063
Clifton Forge, VA 24422 • 5,046
Clifton Heights, PA 19018 • 7,320
Clifton Knolls, NY 12065 • 4,000
Clifton Springs, NY 14432 • 2,039
Climax, GA 31734 • 407
Climax, MI 49034 • 619
Climax, MN 56523 • 273
Clinch □, GA • 6,660
Clinchco, VA 24226 • 1,000
Clint, TX 79836 • 1,314
Clinton, AR 72031 • 1,284
Clinton, CT 06413 • 11,195
Clinton, IL 61727 • 8,014
Clinton, IN 47842 • 5,267
Clinton, IA 52732 • 32,828
Clinton, KY 42031 • 1,720
Clinton, LA 70722 • 1,919
Clinton, ME 04927 • 1,305
Clinton, MD 20735 • 16,438
Clinton, MA 01510 • 12,771
Clinton, MI 49236 • 2,342
Clinton, MN 56225 • 622
Clinton, MS 39056 • 14,660
Clinton, MO 64735 • 8,366
Clinton, NJ 08809 • 1,910
Clinton, NC 28328 • 7,552
Clinton, NY 13323 • 2,107
Clinton, OK 73601 • 8,796
Clinton, SC 29325 • 8,596
Clinton, TN 37716 • 5,245
Clinton, UT 84015 • 5,777
Clinton, WA 98236 • 2,000
Clinton, WI 53525 • 1,751
Clinton □, IL • 32,617
Clinton □, IN • 31,545
Clinton □, IA • 57,122
Clinton □, KY • 9,321
Clinton □, MI • 55,893
Clinton □, MO • 15,916
Clinton □, NY • 80,750
Clinton □, OH • 34,603
Clinton □, PA • 38,971
Clintonville, PA 16372 • 512
Clintonville, WI 54929 • 4,567
Clintwood, VA 24228 • 1,369
Clio, AL 36017 • 1,224
Clio, MI 48420 • 2,669
Clio, SC 29525 • 1,031
Clive, IA 50053 • 6,064
Cloquet, MN 55720 • 11,142
Closter, NJ 07624 • 8,164
Clothier, WV 25047 • 600
Cloud □, KS • 12,494
Cloudcroft, NM 88317 • 521
Clover, SC 29710 • 3,451
Cloverdale, AL 35617 • 500
Cloverdale, CA 95425 • 3,989
Cloverdale, IN 46120 • 1,357
Cloverdale, OR 97112 • 300
Cloverdale, VA 24077 • 850
Cloverleaf, TX 77015 • 11,800
Cloverport, KY 40111 • 1,585
Clovis, CA 93612 • 33,021
Clovis, NM 88101 • 31,194
Clune, PA 15727 • 350
Clute, TX 77531 • 9,577
Clutier, IA 52217 • 249
Clyattville, GA 31601 • 250
Clyde, KS 66938 • 909
Clyde, NC 28721 • 1,008
Clyde, NY 14433 • 2,491
Clyde, OH 43410 • 5,489
Clyde, TX 79510 • 2,562
Clyde Park, MT 59018 • 283
Clymer, NY 14724 • 500
Clymer, PA 15728 • 1,761
Clyo, GA 31303 • 350
Coachella, CA 92236 • 9,129
Coahoma, MS 38617 • 350
Coahoma, TX 79511 • 1,069
Coahoma □, MS • 36,918
Coal □, OK • 6,041
Coal City, IL 60416 • 3,028
Coal City, IN 47427 • 270
Coaldale, PA 18218 • 2,762
Coalfield, TN 37719 • 250
Coal Fork, WV 25306 • 900
Coalgate, OK 74538 • 2,001
Coalgood, KY 40818 • 400
Coal Grove, OH 45638 • 2,602
Coal Hill, AR 72832 • 859
Coaling, AL 35449 • 500
Coalinga, CA 93210 • 6,593
Coalmont, IN 47845 • 450
Coalmont, TN 37313 • 625
Coalport, PA 16627 • 739
Coalton, IL 62075 • 406
Coalton, OH 45621 • 639
Coalville, IA 50501 • 360
Coalville, UT 84017 • 1,031
Coalwood, WV 24824 • 1,100
Coatesville, IN 46121 • 474
Coatesville, PA 19320 • 10,698
Coats, NC 27521 • 1,385
Coatsburg, IL 62325 • 258
Cobalt, CT 06414 • 350
Cobalt, ID 83229 • 225
Cobb, WI 53526 • 409
Cobb □, GA • 297,718
Cobb Island, MD 20625 • 350
Cobbtown, GA 30420 • 494
Cobden, IL 62920 • 1,210
Cobleskill, NY 12043 • 5,272
Coburg, OR 97401 • 699
Coburn, PA 16832 • 300
Cochesett, MA 02379 • 300
Cochise □, AZ • 85,686
Cochiti, NM 87041 • 400
Cochituate, MA 01778 • 6,126
Cochran, GA 31014 • 5,121
Cochran □, TX • 4,825
Cochrane, WI 54622 • 512
Cochranton, PA 16314 • 1,240
Cochranville, PA 19330 • 600
Cocke □, TN • 28,792
Cockeysville, MD 21030 • 17,013
Cockrell Hill, TX 75211 • 3,262
Cocoa, FL 32922-27 • 16,096
Cocoa Beach, FL 32931 • 10,926
Cocoa West, FL 32922 • 6,432
Coconino □, AZ • 75,008
Coconut Creek, FL 33060 • 6,288
Coden, AL 36523 • 500
Codington □, SD • 20,885
Cody, WY 82414 • 6,790
Coeburn, VA 24230 • 2,625
Coeur d'Alene, ID 83814 • 20,054
Coffee □, AL • 38,533
Coffee □, GA • 26,894
Coffee □, TN • 38,311
Coffeen, IL 62017 • 842
Coffee Springs, AL 36318 • 339
Coffeeville, AL 36524 • 448
Coffeeville, MS 38922 • 1,129
Coffey □, KS • 9,370
Coffeyville, KS 67337 • 15,185
Cofield, NC 27922 • 465
Coggon, IA 52218 • 639
Cogswell, ND 58017 • 227
Cohasset, MA 02025 • 5,300
Cohasset, MN 55721 • 600
Cohocton, NY 14826 • 902
Cohoes, NY 12047 • 18,144
Cohutta, GA 30710 • 407
Coila, MS 38923 • 250
Coin, IA 51636 • 316
Coinjock, NC 27923 • 275
Cokato, MN 55321 • 2,056
Coke □, TX • 3,196
Coker, AL 35452 • 400
Cokesbury, SC 29653 • 275
Cokeville, WY 83114 • 515
Colbert, GA 30628 • 498
Colbert, OK 74733 • 1,122
Colbert □, AL • 54,519
Colbert Heights, AL 35674 • 500
Colburn, IN 47931 • 300
Colby, KS 67701 • 5,544
Colby, WI 54421 • 1,496
Colchester, CT 06415 • 3,190
Colchester, IL 62326 • 1,729
Colchester, VT 05446 • 400
Colcord, OK 74338 • 530
Cold Bay, AK 99571 • 228
Cold Spring, KY 41076 • 2,117

Cold Spring, MN 56320 • *2,294*
Cold Spring, NJ 08204 • *850*
Coldspring, TX 77331 • *569*
Cold Spring Harbor, NY 11724 • *5,490*
Coldwater, KS 67029 • *989*
Coldwater, MI 49036 • *9,461*
Coldwater, MS 38618 • *1,505*
Coldwater, OH 45828 • *4,220*
Cole, OK 73010 • *309*
Cole □, MO • *56,663*
Colebrook, CT 06021 • *300*
Colebrook, NH 03576 • *1,131*
Cole Camp, MO 65325 • *1,022*
Coleman, FL 33521 • *1,022*
Coleman, MI 48618 • *1,429*
Coleman, TX 76834 • *5,960*
Coleman, WI 54112 • *852*
Coleman □, TX • *10,439*
Colerain, NC 27924 • *284*
Coleraine, MN 55722 • *1,116*
Coleridge, NE 68727 • *673*
Coles □, IL • *52,260*
Colesburg, IA 52035 • *463*
Colfax, CA 95713 • *981*
Colfax, IL 61728 • *920*
Colfax, IN 46035 • *823*
Colfax, IA 50054 • *2,234*
Colfax, LA 71417 • *1,680*
Colfax, WA 99111 • *2,780*
Colfax, WI 54730 • *1,149*
Colfax □, NE • *9,890*
Colfax □, NM • *13,667*
Collbran, CO 81624 • *344*
College, AK 99701 • *800*
College City, AR 72476 • *432*
College Corner, OH 45003 • *364*
Collegedale, TN 37315 • *1,500*
College Grove, TN 37046 • *300*
College Park, GA 30337 • *24,632*
College Park, MD 20740 • *23,614*
College Place, WA 99324 • *5,771*
College Springs, IA 51637 • *307*
College Station, AR 72053 • *4,000*
College Station, TX 77840 • *37,272*
Collegeville, IN 47978 • *1,059*
Collegeville, PA 19426 • *3,406*
Colleton □, SC • *31,776*
Colleyville, TX 76034 • *6,700*
Collier □, FL • *85,971*
Colliers, WV 26035 • *600*
Collierville, TN 38017 • *7,839*
Collin □, TX • *144,576*
Collingdale, PA 19023 • *9,539*
Collingswood, NJ 08108 • *15,838*
Collingsworth □, TX • *4,648*
Collins, GA 30421 • *639*
Collins, IA 50055 • *451*
Collins, MS 39428 • *2,131*
Collins Park, DE 19720 • *2,850*
Collinston, LA 71229 • *439*
Collinsville, AL 35961 • *1,383*
Collinsville, CT 06022 • *2,555*
Collinsville, IL 62234 • *19,613*
Collinsville, MS 39325 • *300*
Collinsville, OK 74021 • *3,556*
Collinsville, VA 24078 • *7,400*
Collinwood, TN 38450 • *1,064*
Colman, SD 57017 • *501*
Colmar Manor, MD 20722 • *1,286*
Colmesneil, TX 75938 • *553*
Colo, IA 50056 • *808*
Cologne, MN 55322 • *545*
Cologne, NJ 08213 • *500*
Coloma, MI 49038 • *1,833*
Coloma, WI 54930 • *367*
Colome, SD 57528 • *361*
Colon, MI 49040 • *1,190*
Colonia, NJ 07067 • *20,900*
Colonial Beach, VA 22443 • *2,474*
Colonial Heights, TN 37663 • *6,744*
Colonial Heights, VA 23834 • *16,509*
Colonial Park, PA 17109 • *10,000*
Colonie, NY 12212 • *8,869*
Colony, KS 66015 • *474*
Colorado □, TX • *18,823*
Colorado City, AZ 86021 • *450*
Colorado City, CO 81019 • *950*
Colorado City, TX 79512 • *5,405*
Colorado Springs, CO 80901-99 • *214,821*
Colquitt, GA 31737 • *2,065*
Colquitt □, GA • *35,376*
Colstrip, MT 59323 • *1,476*
Colt, AR 72326 • *378*
Colter Bay, WY 83001 • *2,000*
Colton, CA 92324 • *15,201*
Colton, NY 13625 • *450*
Colton, OR 97017 • *300*
Colton, SD 57018 • *757*
Colton, WA 99113 • *307*
Coltons Point, MD 20626 • *500*
Colts Neck, NJ 07722 • *500*
Columbia, AL 36319 • *881*
Columbia, CA 95310 • *950*
Columbia, CT 06237 • *300*
Columbia, IL 62236 • *4,269*
Columbia, KY 42728 • *3,710*
Columbia, LA 71418 • *687*
Columbia, MD 21045-46 • *52,518*
Columbia, MS 39429 • *7,733*
Columbia, MO 65201-18 • *62,061*
Columbia, NC 27925 • *758*
Columbia, PA 17512 • *10,466*
Columbia, SC 29201-99 • *100,385*
Columbia, TN 38401 • *26,571*
Columbia □, AR • *26,644*
Columbia □, FL • *35,399*
Columbia □, GA • *40,118*
Columbia □, NY • *59,487*
Columbia □, OR • *35,646*
Columbia □, PA • *61,967*
Columbia □, WA • *4,057*
Columbia □, WI • *43,222*
Columbia City, IN 46725 • *5,091*
Columbia City, OR 97018 • *678*
Columbia Falls, MT 59912 • *3,112*
Columbia Heights, MN 55421 • *20,029*
Columbiana, AL 35051 • *2,655*
Columbiana, OH 44408 • *4,987*
Columbiana □, OH • *113,572*
Columbiaville, MI 48421 • *953*
Columbus, GA 31901-99 • *169,441*
Columbus, IN 47201-03 • *30,614*
Columbus, KS 66725 • *3,426*
Columbus, KY 42032 • *296*
Columbus, MS 39701-04 • *27,383*
Columbus, MT 59019 • *1,439*
Columbus, NE 68601 • *17,328*
Columbus, NJ 08022 • *700*
Columbus, NM 88029 • *414*
Columbus, NC 28722 • *727*
Columbus, ND 58727 • *325*
Columbus, OH 43201-99 • *565,032*
Columbus, PA 16405 • *500*
Columbus, TX 78934 • *3,923*
Columbus, WI 53925 • *4,049*
Columbus □, NC • *51,037*
Columbus City, IA 52737 • *367*
Columbus Grove, OH 45830 • *2,313*
Columbus Junction, IA 52738 • *1,429*
Colusa, CA 95932 • *4,075*
Colusa □, CA • *12,791*
Colver, PA 15927 • *1,175*
Colville, WA 99114 • *4,510*
Colwich, KS 67030 • *935*
Comal □, TX • *36,446*
Comanche, OK 73529 • *1,937*
Comanche, TX 76442 • *4,075*
Comanche □, KS • *2,554*
Comanche □, OK • *112,456*
Comanche □, TX • *12,617*
Combined Locks, WI 54113 • *2,573*
Combs, KY 41729 • *700*
Comer, GA 30629 • *930*
Comfort, TX 78013 • *950*
Comfort, WV 25049 • *250*
Comfrey, MN 56019 • *548*
Commack, NY 11725 • *24,300*
Commerce, GA 30529 • *4,092*
Commerce, OK 74339 • *2,556*
Commerce, TX 75428 • *8,136*
Commerce City, CO 80022 • *16,234*
Commercial Point, OH 43116 • *316*
Common Fence Point, RI 02871 • *850*
Como, MS 38619 • *1,378*
Compass Lake, FL 32448 • *250*
Comptche, CA 95427 • *555*
Compton, CA 90220-24 • *81,286*
Compton, IL 61318 • *376*
Comstock, MI 49041 • *5,310*
Conception Junction, MO 64434 • *252*
Conchas Dam, NM 88416 • *250*
Concho □, TX • *2,915*
Concord, AR 72523 • *234*
Concord, CA 94518-24 • *103,255*
Concord, GA 30206 • *317*
Concord, MA 01742 • *6,400*
Concord, MI 49237 • *900*
Concord, MO 63851 • *20,896*
Concord, NH 03301-06 • *30,400*
Concord, NC 28025 • *16,942*
Concord, TN 37922 • *400*
Concord, VT 05824 • *353*
Concord, VA 24538 • *400*
Concordia, KS 66901 • *6,847*
Concordia, MO 64020 • *2,129*
Concordia □, LA • *22,981*
Concrete, WA 98237 • *592*
Conde, SD 57434 • *259*
Condon, OR 97823 • *783*
Conecuh □, AL • *15,884*
Conejos □, CO • *7,794*
Conemaugh, PA 15909 • *2,128*
Conestee, SC 29636 • *540*
Conesville, IA 52739 • *301*
Conesville, OH 43811 • *451*
Coney Island 0Z, NY
Confluence, PA 15424 • *968*
Congers, NY 10920 • *5,000*
Congress, AZ 85332 • *450*
Conklin, MI 49403 • *275*
Conklin, NY 13748 • *1,900*
Conneaut, OH 44030 • *13,835*
Conneaut Lake, PA 16316 • *767*
Conneautville, PA 16406 • *971*
Connell, WA 99326 • *1,981*
Connellsville, PA 15425 • *10,319*
Connersville, IN 47331 • *17,023*
Conover, NC 28613 • *4,245*
Conowingo, MD 21918 • *300*
Conrad, IA 50621 • *1,133*
Conrad, MT 59425 • *3,074*
Conroe, TX 77301-05 • *18,034*
Conshohocken, PA 19428 • *8,475*
Constable, NY 12926 • *300*
Constableville, NY 13325 • *330*
Constance, KY 41009 • *230*
Constantia, NY 13044 • *900*
Constantine, MI 49042 • *1,680*
Continental, OH 45831 • *1,179*
Contoocook, NH 03229 • *1,499*
Contra Costa □, CA • *656,380*
Convent, LA 70723 • *400*
Converse, IN 46919 • *1,279*
Converse, LA 71419 • *449*
Converse, SC 29329 • *1,173*
Converse □, WY • *14,069*
Convoy, OH 45832 • *1,140*
Conway, AR 72032 • *20,375*
Conway, FL 32809 • *16,000*
Conway, MA 01341 • *600*
Conway, MO 65632 • *601*
Conway, NH 03818 • *1,781*
Conway, NC 27820 • *678*
Conway, PA 15027 • *2,747*
Conway, SC 29526 • *10,240*
Conway □, AR • *19,505*
Conway Springs, KS 67031 • *1,313*
Conyers, GA 30207-08 • *6,567*
Cook, MN 55723 • *800*
Cook, NE 68329 • *341*
Cook □, GA • *13,490*
Cook □, IL • *5,253,655*
Cook □, MN • *4,092*
Cooke □, TX • *27,656*
Cookeville, TN 38501 • *20,535*
Cooks Falls, NY 12728 • *300*
Cooks Mills, IL 61931 • *250*
Cookson, OK 74427 • *500*
Cookstown, NJ 08511 • *300*
Cooksville, IL 61730 • *259*
Cookville, TX 75558 • *450*
Cooleemee, NC 27014 • *1,448*
Coolidge, AZ 85228 • *6,851*
Coolidge, GA 31738 • *736*
Coolidge, TX 76635 • *810*
Coolin, ID 83821 • *300*
Cool Ridge, WV 25825 • *300*
Coolville, OH 45723 • *649*
Coon Rapids, IA 50058 • *1,448*
Coon Rapids, MN 55433 • *35,826*
Coon Valley, WI 54623 • *758*
Cooper, TX 75432 • *2,338*
Cooper □, MO • *14,643*
Cooper City, FL 33328 • *10,140*
Cooper Road, LA 71107 • *10,000*
Coopersburg, PA 18036 • *2,595*
Cooperstown, ND 58425 • *1,308*
Cooperstown, NY 13326 • *2,342*
Cooperstown, PA 16317 • *644*
Coopersville, MI 49404 • *2,889*
Coos □, NH • *35,147*
Coos □, OR • *64,047*
Coosa □, AL • *11,377*
Coosada, AL 36020 • *980*
Coosawhatchie, SC 29912 • *300*
Coos Bay, OR 97420 • *14,424*
Cooter, MO 63839 • *479*
Copake, NY 12516 • *700*
Copalis Beach, WA 98535 • *800*
Copan, OK 74022 • *960*
Copeland, FL 33926 • *700*
Copeland, KS 67837 • *323*
Copemish, MI 49625 • *287*
Copenhagen, NY 13626 • *656*
Copeville, TX 75018 • *300*
Copiague, NY 11726 • *21,000*
Copiah □, MS • *26,503*
Coplay, PA 18037 • *3,130*
Copperas Cove, TX 76522 • *19,469*
Copperhill, TN 37317 • *418*
Copperton, UT 84006 • *850*
Coquille, OR 97423 • *4,481*
Coral, PA 15731 • *700*
Coral Gables, FL 33134 • *43,241*
Coralville, IA 52241 • *7,687*
Coram, MT 59913 • *300*
Coram, NY 11727 • *5,400*
Coraopolis, PA 15108 • *7,308*
Corbin, KY 40701 • *8,075*
Corbin City, NJ 08270 • *254*
Corcoran, CA 93212 • *6,454*
Corcoran, MN 55340 • *4,252*
Cordaville, MA 01772 • *1,384*
Cordele, GA 31015 • *11,184*
Cordell, OK 73632 • *3,301*
Corder, MO 64021 • *483*
Cordova, AL 35550 • *3,123*
Cordova, AK 99574 • *1,879*
Cordova, IL 61242 • *697*
Cordova, MD 21625 • *350*
Cordova, NM 87523 • *600*
Cordova, NC 28330 • *1,200*
Cordova, TN 38018 • *300*
Corea, ME 04624 • *400*
Corfu, NY 14036 • *689*
Corinna, ME 04928 • *950*
Corinne, UT 84307 • *512*
Corinne, WV 25826 • *500*
Corinth, KY 41010 • *258*
Corinth, MS 38834 • *13,839*
Corinth, NY 12822 • *2,702*
Corn, OK 73024 • *542*
Cornelia, GA 30531 • *3,203*
Cornelius, NC 28031 • *1,460*
Cornelius, OR 97113 • *4,462*
Cornell, IL 61319 • *603*
Cornell, WI 54732 • *1,583*
Cornersville, TN 37047 • *722*
Corning, AR 72422 • *3,650*
Corning, CA 96021 • *4,745*
Corning, IA 50841 • *1,939*
Corning, NY 14830 • *12,953*
Corning, OH 43730 • *789*
Cornish, ME 04020 • *600*
Cornish Flat, NH 03746 • *300*
Cornville, AZ 86325 • *800*
Cornwall, PA 17016 • *2,653*
Cornwall On Hudson, NY 12520 • *3,164*
Cornwells Heights, PA 19020 • *8,700*
Corona, CA 91720 • *37,791*
Corona, NM 88318 • *236*
Coronado, CA 92118 • *18,790*
Corpus Christi, TX 78401-99 • *231,999*
Correctionville, IA 51016 • *935*
Corrigan, TX 75939 • *1,770*
Corriganville, MD 21524 • *1,020*
Corry, PA 16407 • *7,149*
Corsica, PA 15829 • *381*
Corsica, SD 57328 • *644*
Corsicana, TX 75110 • *21,712*
Corson □, SD • *5,196*
Corte Madera, CA 94925 • *8,074*
Cortez, CO 81321 • *7,095*
Cortez, FL 33522 • *1,450*
Cortland, IL 60112 • *1,019*
Cortland, NE 68331 • *403*
Cortland, NY 13045 • *20,138*
Cortland, OH 44410 • *5,011*
Cortland □, NY • *48,820*
Corunna, IN 46730 • *304*
Corunna, MI 48817 • *3,206*
Corvallis, MT 59828 • *400*
Corvallis, OR 97330-33 • *40,960*
Corwith, IA 50430 • *480*
Corydon, IN 47112 • *2,724*
Corydon, IA 50060 • *1,818*
Corydon, KY 42406 • *874*
Coryell □, TX • *56,767*
Coshocton, OH 43812 • *13,405*
Coshocton □, OH • *36,024*
Cosmopolis, WA 98537 • *1,575*
Cosmos, MN 56228 • *571*
Costa Mesa, CA 92626-27 • *82,562*
Costilla □, CO • *3,071*
Cottage Grove, MN 55016 • *18,994*
Cottage Grove, OR 97424 • *7,148*
Cottageville, SC 29435 • *371*
Cottageville, WV 25239 • *300*
Cotter, AR 72626 • *920*
Cottle □, TX • *2,947*
Cotton □, OK • *7,338*

Cotton Center, TX 79021 • 300
Cottondale, AL 35453 • 2,300
Cottondale, FL 32431 • 1,056
Cotton Plant, AR 72036 • 1,323
Cottonport, LA 71327 • 1,911
Cotton Valley, LA 71018 • 1,445
Cottonwood, AL 36320 • 1,352
Cottonwood, AZ 86326 • 4,550
Cottonwood, CA 96022 • 1,553
Cottonwood, ID 83522 • 941
Cottonwood, MN 56229 • 924
Cottonwood, UT 84121 • 11,554
Cottonwood □, MN • 14,854
Cottonwood Falls, KS 66845 • 954
Cottonwood Heights, UT 84121 • 18,000
Cotuit, MA 02635 • 1,300
Cotulla, TX 78014 • 3,912
Coudersport, PA 16915 • 2,791
Coulee City, WA 99115 • 510
Coulee Dam, WA 99116 • 1,412
Coulter, IA 50431 • 264
Coulterville, CA 95311 • 500
Coulterville, IL 62237 • 1,118
Counce, TN 38326 • 600
Council, ID 83612 • 917
Council Bluffs, IA 51501 • 56,449
Council Grove, KS 66846 • 2,381
Country Club Hills, IL 60477 • 14,676
Country Homes, WA 99218 • 3,850
Countryside, IL 60525 • 6,538
Countyline, OK 73025 • 500
Coupeville, WA 98239 • 1,006
Coupon, PA 16629 • 250
Courtland, AL 35618 • 456
Courtland, KS 66939 • 377
Courtland, MN 56021 • 399
Courtland, MS 38620 • 381
Courtland, VA 23837 • 976
Coushatta, LA 71019 • 2,084
Cove, AR 71937 • 391
Cove, OR 97824 • 451
Cove City, NC 28523 • 500
Covedale, OH 45238 • 6,530
Covelo, CA 95428 • 1,448
Coventry, CT 06238 • 3,769
Coventry, DE 19720 • 830
Coventry, RI 02816 • 8,000
Cove Point, MD 20657 • 330
Coverdales Crossroads, DE 19933 • 350
Covert, MI 49043 • 600
Covina, CA 91722-24 • 33,751
Covington, GA 30209 • 10,586
Covington, IN 47932 • 2,883
Covington, KY 41011-19 • 49,563
Covington, LA 70433 • 7,892
Covington, OH 45318 • 2,610
Covington, OK 73730 • 715
Covington, PA 16917 • 600
Covington, TN 38019 • 6,065
Covington, VA 24426 • 9,063
Covington, WA 98031 • 350
Covington □, AL • 36,850
Covington □, MS • 15,927
Cowan, IN 47302 • 350
Cowan, TN 37318 • 1,790
Cowansville, PA 16218 • 350
Coward, SC 29530 • 428
Cowarts, AL 36321 • 418
Cowden, IL 62422 • 623
Cowen, WV 26206 • 723
Coweta, OK 74429 • 4,554
Coweta □, GA • 39,268
Cowgill, MO 64637 • 267
Cowley, WY 82420 • 455
Cowley □, KS • 36,824
Cowlington, OK 74941 • 546
Cowlitz □, WA • 79,548
Cowpens, SC 29330 • 2,023
Coxsackie, NY 12051 • 2,786
Coy, AL 36435 • 400
Coyle, OK 73027 • 345
Cozad, NE 69130 • 4,453
Crab Orchard, KY 40419 • 843
Crab Orchard, TN 37723 • 1,065
Crab Orchard, WV 25827 • 1,900
Crabtree, OR 97335 • 300
Crabtree, PA 15624 • 1,021
Crafton, PA 15205 • 7,623
Craig, AK 99921 • 527
Craig, CO 81625 • 8,133
Craig, MO 64437 • 379
Craig, NE 68019 • 237
Craig □, OK • 15,014
Craig □, VA • 3,948
Craighead □, AR • 63,239
Craigmont, ID 83523 • 617
Craigsville, VA 24430 • 845
Craigsville, WV 26205 • 900
Cramerton, NC 28032 • 1,869
Cranberry, PA 16319 • 350
Cranberry Lake, NY 12927 • 300
Cranbury, NJ 08512 • 1,255
Crandall, TX 75114 • 831
Crandon, WI 54520 • 1,969
Crane, AZ 85364 • 2,400
Crane, IN 47522 • 297
Crane, MO 65633 • 1,185
Crane, TX 79731 • 3,622
Crane □, TX • 4,600
Crane Lake, MN 55725 • 300
Cranesville, PA 16410 • 703
Cranford, NJ 07016 • 24,573
Cranston, RI 02910 • 71,992
Craryville, NY 12521 • 300
Craven □, NC • 71,043
Crawford, CO 81415 • 268
Crawford, GA 30630 • 498
Crawford, MS 39743 • 495
Crawford, NE 69339 • 1,315
Crawford □, AR • 36,892
Crawford □, GA • 7,684
Crawford □, IL • 20,818
Crawford □, IN • 9,820
Crawford □, IA • 18,935
Crawford □, KS • 37,916
Crawford □, MI • 9,465
Crawford □, MO • 18,300
Crawford □, OH • 50,075
Crawford □, PA • 88,869
Crawford □, WI • 16,556
Crawfordsville, AR 72327 • 685
Crawfordsville, IN 47933 • 13,325
Crawfordsville, IA 52621 • 290
Crawfordville, FL 32327 • 1,110
Crawfordville, GA 30631 • 594
Creal Springs, IL 62922 • 845
Creede, CO 81130 • 610
Creedmoor, NC 27522 • 1,641
Creek □, OK • 59,016
Creekside, PA 15732 • 383
Creighton, MO 64739 • 301
Creighton, NE 68729 • 1,341
Creighton, PA 15030 • 1,658
Crellin, MD 21525 • 270
Crenshaw, MS 38621 • 1,019
Crenshaw, PA 15824 • 375
Crenshaw □, AL • 14,110
Creola, AL 36525 • 1,652
Cresaptown, MD 21502 • 4,645
Crescent, GA 31304 • 300
Crescent, IA 51526 • 547
Crescent, MO 63018 • 300
Crescent, OK 73028 • 1,651
Crescent, OR 97733 • 700
Crescent City, CA 95531 • 3,075
Crescent City, FL 32012 • 1,722
Crescent City, IL 60928 • 641
Crescent Mills, CA 95934 • 375
Crescent Springs, KY 41016 • 1,951
Cresco, IA 52136 • 3,860
Cresco, PA 18326 • 500
Cresskill, NJ 07626 • 7,609
Cresson, PA 16630 • 2,184
Cressona, PA 17929 • 1,810
Crested Butte, CO 81224 • 959
Cresthaven, FL 33064 • 2,400
Crest Hill, IL 60435 • 9,252
Crestline, OH 44827 • 5,406
Creston, IL 60113 • 527
Creston, IA 50801 • 8,429
Creston, OH 44217 • 1,828
Creston, WA 99117 • 309
Crestview, FL 32536 • 7,617
Crestview, HI 96797 • 1,000
Crestwood, IL 60445 • 10,852
Crestwood, KY 40014 • 531
Crestwood, MO 63126 • 12,815
Crestwood Village, NJ 08759 • 7,965
Creswell, NC 27928 • 426
Creswell, OR 97426 • 1,770
Crete, IL 60417 • 5,417
Crete, NE 68333 • 4,872
Creve Coeur, IL 61611 • 6,851
Creve Coeur, MO 63141 • 11,757
Crewe, VA 23930 • 2,325
Cricket, NC 28659 • 2,307
Cridersville, OH 45806 • 1,843
Cripple Creek, CO 80813 • 655
Crisfield, MD 21817 • 2,924
Crisp □, GA • 19,489
Crittenden, KY 41030 • 597
Crittenden □, AR • 49,499
Crittenden □, KY • 9,207
Crivitz, WI 54114 • 1,041
Crocker, MO 65452 • 979
Crockett, CA 94525 • 2,900
Crockett, TX 75835 • 7,405
Crockett □, TN • 14,941
Crockett □, TX • 4,608
Crofton, KY 42217 • 823
Crofton, MD 21114 • 12,009
Crofton, NE 68730 • 948
Croghan, NY 13327 • 703
Cromona, KY 41810 • 700
Cromwell, CT 06416 • 10,100
Cromwell, IN 46732 • 458
Cromwell, MN 55726 • 229
Cromwell, OK 74837 • 337
Crook □, OR • 13,091
Crook □, WY • 5,308
Crooks, SD 57020 • 594
Crookston, MN 56716 • 8,628
Crooksville, OH 43731 • 2,766
Cropper, KY 40057 • 250
Crosby, MN 56441 • 2,218
Crosby, MS 39633 • 349
Crosby, ND 58730 • 1,469
Crosby, PA 16724 • 400
Crosby, TX 77532 • 1,450
Crosby □, TX • 8,859
Crosbyton, TX 79322 • 2,289
Cross □, AR • 20,434
Cross Anchor, SC 29331 • 350
Cross City, FL 32628 • 2,154
Crossett, AR 71635 • 6,706
Cross Hill, SC 29332 • 604
Cross Keys, NJ 08080 • 400
Crosslake, MN 56442 • 1,064
Cross Lanes, WV 25313 • 3,500
Cross Mill, NC 28752 • 1,200
Cross Plains, TN 37049 • 655
Cross Plains, TX 76443 • 1,240
Cross Plains, WI 53528 • 2,156
Crossville, AL 35962 • 1,222
Crossville, IL 62827 • 944
Crossville, TN 38555 • 6,394
Crosswicks, NJ 08515 • 550
Croswell, MI 48422 • 2,073
Crothersville, IN 47229 • 1,747
Croton, OH 43013 • 455
Croton-on-Hudson, NY 10520 • 6,889
Crouse, NC 28033 • 900
Crow Agency, MT 59022 • 750
Crowder, MS 38622 • 789
Crowder, OK 74430 • 431
Crowell, TX 79227 • 1,509
Crowley, LA 70526 • 16,036
Crowley, TX 76036 • 5,852
Crowley □, CO • 2,988
Crown City, OH 45623 • 513
Crown Point, IN 46307 • 16,455
Crown Point, LA 70072 • 1,016
Crown Point, NE 68122 • 700
Crownpoint, NM 87313 • 1,134
Crown Point, NY 12928 • 900
Crow Wing □, MN • 41,722
Croydon, PA 19020 • 10,000
Crozet, VA 22932 • 1,433
Crucible, PA 15325 • 800
Cruger, MS 38924 • 540
Crum, WV 25669 • 300
Crumpton, MD 21628 • 350
Crumstown, IN 46554 • 300
Crystal, MI 48818 • 600
Crystal, MN 55428 • 25,543
Crystal, ND 58222 • 256
Crystal Bay, NV 89402 • 1,200
Crystal Beach, FL 33523 • 1,450
Crystal City, MO 63019 • 3,618
Crystal City, TX 78839 • 8,334
Crystal Falls, MI 49920 • 1,965
Crystal Lake, CT 06029 • 500
Crystal Lake, FL 33803 • 6,827
Crystal Lake, IL 60014 • 18,590
Crystal Lake, IA 50432 • 314
Crystal Lawns, IL 60435 • 2,800
Crystal Manor, IL 60014 • 750
Crystal River, FL 32629 • 2,778
Crystal Springs, FL 33524 • 800
Crystal Springs, MS 39059 • 4,902
Cuba, AL 36907 • 486
Cuba, IL 61427 • 1,648
Cuba, KS 66940 • 286
Cuba, MO 65453 • 2,120
Cuba, NM 87013 • 609
Cuba, NY 14727 • 1,739
Cuba City, WI 53807 • 2,129
Cubero, NM 87014 • 400
Cub Run, KY 42729 • 250
Cucamonga, CA 91730 • 55,250
Cudahy, CA 90201 • 17,984
Cudahy, WI 53110 • 19,547
Cuero, TX 77954 • 7,124
Culberson □, TX • 3,315
Culbertson, MT 59218 • 887
Culbertson, NE 69024 • 767
Culdesac, ID 83524 • 261
Cullen, LA 71021 • 1,869
Culleoka, TN 38451 • 300
Cullman, AL 35055 • 13,084
Cullman □, AL • 61,642
Culloden, GA 31016 • 281
Culloden, WV 25510 • 1,500
Cullom, IL 60929 • 608
Cullowhee, NC 28723 • 2,000
Culpeper, VA 22701 • 6,621
Culpeper □, VA • 22,620
Culver, IN 46511 • 1,601
Culver, OR 97734 • 514
Culver City, CA 90230-32 • 38,139
Cumberland, IA 50843 • 351
Cumberland, KY 40823 • 3,712
Cumberland, MD 21502 • 25,933
Cumberland, NC 28331 • 900
Cumberland, OH 43732 • 461
Cumberland, WI 54829 • 1,983
Cumberland □, IL • 11,062
Cumberland □, KY • 7,289
Cumberland □, ME • 215,789
Cumberland □, NJ • 132,866
Cumberland □, NC • 247,160
Cumberland □, PA • 178,541
Cumberland □, TN • 28,676
Cumberland □, VA • 7,881
Cumberland Center, ME 04021 • 2,015
Cumberland City, TN 37050 • 276
Cumberland Foreside, ME 04110 • 1,000
Cumberland Furnace, TN 37051 • 350
Cumberland Gap, TN 37724 • 263
Cumberland Hill, RI 02864 • 5,421
Cuming □, NE • 11,664
Cumming, GA 30130 • 2,094
Cumnock, NC 27237 • 250
Cunard, WV 25830 • 450
Cunningham, KS 67035 • 540
Cupertino, CA 95014 • 34,265
Currie, MN 56123 • 359
Currituck, NC 27929 • 350
Currituck □, NC • 11,089
Curry □, NM • 42,019
Curry □, OR • 16,992
Curryville, MO 63339 • 323
Curtice, OH 43412 • 800
Curtin, OR 97428 • 250
Curtis, MI 49820 • 500
Curtis, NE 69025 • 1,014
Curtisville, PA 15032 • 1,337
Curwensville, PA 16833 • 3,116
Cushing, IA 51018 • 270
Cushing, OK 74023 • 7,720
Cushing, TX 75760 • 518
Cushman, AR 72526 • 556
Cushman, MA 01002 • 350
Cusick, WA 99119 • 246
Cusseta, GA 31805 • 1,218
Custar, OH 43511 • 254
Custer, MI 49405 • 341
Custer, MT 59024 • 250
Custer, SD 57730 • 1,830
Custer, WA 98240 • 500
Custer □, CO • 1,528
Custer □, ID • 3,385
Custer □, MT • 13,109
Custer □, NE • 13,877
Custer □, OK • 25,995
Custer □, SD • 6,000
Custer City, OK 73639 • 530
Custer City, PA 16725 • 500
Cut Bank, MT 59427 • 3,688
Cutchogue, NY 11935 • 1,000
Cuthbert, GA 31740 • 4,340
Cutler, IL 62238 • 495
Cutler Ridge, FL 33157 • 20,886
Cutlerville, MI 49508 • 8,256
Cut Off, LA 70345 • 5,049
Cuyahoga □, OH • 1,498,400
Cuyahoga Falls, OH 44221-24 • 43,890
Cuylerville, NY 14481 • 300
Cyclone, PA 16726 • 500
Cygnet, OH 43413 • 646
Cynthiana, IN 47612 • 874
Cynthiana, KY 41031 • 5,881
Cypress, CA 90630 • 40,391
Cypress, FL 32432 • 300
Cypress, IL 62923 • 271
Cypress, TX 77429 • 700
Cypress Inn, TN 38452 • 300
Cypress Quarters, FL 33472 • 1,479
Cyril, OK 73029 • 1,220
Cyrus, MN 56323 • 334

D

Dacoma, OK 73731 • 226
Dacono, CO 80514 • 2,321
Dacula, GA 30211 • 1,577
Dade □, FL • 1,625,781
Dade □, GA • 12,318
Dade □, MO • 7,383
Dade City, FL 33525 • 4,923
Dadeville, AL 36853 • 3,263
Daggett, CA 92327 • 650
Daggett, MI 49821 • 274
Daggett □, UT • 769
Dagsboro, DE 19939 • 344
Dagus Mines, PA 15831 • 425
Dahlgren, IL 62828 • 508
Dahlgren, VA 22448 • 575
Dahlonega, GA 30533 • 2,844
Dailey, WV 26259 • 300
Daingerfield, TX 75638 • 3,030
Daisetta, TX 77533 • 1,177
Dakota, IL 61018 • 571
Dakota, MN 55925 • 350
Dakota □, MN • 194,279
Dakota □, NE • 16,573
Dakota City, IA 50529 • 1,072
Dakota City, NE 68731 • 1,440
Dale, IN 47523 • 1,693
Dale □, AL • 47,821
Dale City, VA 22193 • 23,000
Daleville, AL 36322 • 4,250
Daleville, IN 47334 • 2,000
Dalhart, TX 79022 • 6,854
Dallam □, TX • 6,531
Dallas, AL 35172 • 250
Dallas, GA 30132 • 2,508
Dallas, IA 50062 • 451
Dallas, NC 28034 • 3,340
Dallas, OR 97338 • 8,530
Dallas, PA 18612 • 2,679
Dallas, TX 75201-99 • 904,078
Dallas, WV 26036 • 300
Dallas, WI 54733 • 477
Dallas □, AL • 53,981
Dallas □, AR • 10,515
Dallas □, IA • 29,513
Dallas □, MO • 12,096
Dallas □, TX • 1,556,390
Dallas Center, IA 50063 • 1,360
Dallas City, IL 62330 • 1,408
Dallastown, PA 17313 • 3,949
Dalmatia, PA 17017 • 500
Dalton, GA 30720 • 20,939
Dalton, MA 01226 • 6,797
Dalton, MN 56324 • 248
Dalton, NE 69131 • 345
Dalton, NY 14836 • 500
Dalton, OH 44618 • 1,357
Dalton, PA 18414 • 1,383
Dalton, WI 53926 • 300
Dalton City, IL 61925 • 574
Dalton Gardens, ID 83814 • 1,795
Daly City, CA 94014-17 • 78,519
Dalzell, IL 61320 • 824
Dalzell, SC 29040 • 330
Damariscotta, ME 04543 • 950
Damascus, AR 72039 • 307
Damascus, GA 31741 • 403
Damascus, GA 30701 • 250
Damascus, MD 20872 • 4,129
Damascus, PA 18415 • 250
Damascus, VA 24236 • 1,330
Dames Quarter, MD 21820 • 300
Damon, TX 77430 • 700
Dana, IN 47847 • 803
Dana, NC 28724 • 500
Danbury, CT 06810-17 • 60,470
Danbury, IA 51019 • 492
Danbury, NH 03230 • 250
Danbury, TX 77534 • 1,357
Danbury, WI 54830 • 350
Danby, VT 05739 • 300
Dandridge, TN 37725 • 1,383
Dane, WI 53529 • 518
Dane □, WI • 323,545
Danforth, IL 60930 • 554
Danforth, ME 04424 • 500
Dania, FL 33004 • 11,811
Daniels □, MT • 2,835
Danielson, CT 06239 • 4,553
Danielsville, GA 30633 • 354
Dannebrog, NE 68831 • 356
Dannemora, NY 12929 • 3,770
Dansville, NY 14437 • 4,979
Dante, VA 24237 • 1,200
Danube, MN 56230 • 590
Danvers, IL 61732 • 921
Danvers, MA 01923 • 24,100
Danville, AR 72833 • 1,698
Danville, CA 94526 • 26,000
Danville, GA 31017 • 529
Danville, IL 61832-33 • 38,985
Danville, IN 46122 • 4,220
Danville, IA 52623 • 994
Danville, KY 40422 • 12,942
Danville, NH 03819 • 500
Danville, OH 43014 • 1,127
Danville, PA 17821 • 5,239
Danville, VT 05828 • 450
Danville, VA 24541-43 • 45,642
Danville, WV 25053 • 727
Daphne, AL 36526 • 3,406
Darby, MT 59829 • 581
Darby, PA 19023 • 11,513
Darbydale, OH 43123 • 825
Darbyville, OH 43136 • 282
Dardanelle, AR 72834 • 3,621
Dare □, NC • 13,377
Dargan, MD 25425 • 300
Darien, CT 06820 • 18,892
Darien, GA 31305 • 1,731
Darien, IL 60559 • 14,536
Darien, WI 53114 • 1,152
Darke □, OH • 55,096
Darkesville, WV 25428 • 250
Darley Woods, DE 19810 • 1,400
Darling, MS 38623 • 350
Darlington, IN 47940 • 811
Darlington, MD 21034 • 500
Darlington, SC 29532 • 7,989
Darlington, WI 53530 • 2,300
Darlington □, SC • 62,717
Darrington, WA 98241 • 1,064
Darrouzett, TX 79024 • 444
Darrow, LA 70725 • 425
Darwin, MN 55324 • 282
Dassel, MN 55325 • 1,066
Dauphin, PA 17018 • 901
Dauphin □, PA • 232,317
Dauphin Island, AL 36528 • 600
Davenport, CA 95017 • 300
Davenport, FL 33837 • 1,509
Davenport, IA 52801-99 • 103,264
Davenport, NE 68335 • 445
Davenport, NY 13750 • 260
Davenport, OK 74026 • 974
Davenport, WA 99122 • 1,559
David, KY 41616 • 250
David City, NE 68632 • 2,514
Davidson, NC 28036 • 3,241
Davidson, OK 73530 • 501
Davidson □, NC • 113,162
Davidson □, TN • 477,811
Davidsville, PA 15928 • 900
Davie, FL 33329 • 20,877
Davie □, NC • 24,599
Daviess □, IN • 27,836
Daviess □, KY • 85,949
Daviess □, MO • 8,905
Davis, CA 95616 • 36,640
Davis, IL 61019 • 560
Davis, NC 28524 • 500
Davis, OK 73030 • 2,782
Davis, WV 26260 • 979
Davis □, IA • 9,104
Davis □, UT • 146,540
Davisboro, GA 31018 • 433
Davis City, IA 50065 • 327
Davis Junction, IL 61020 • 289
Davison, MI 48423 • 6,087
Davison □, SD • 17,820
Daviston, AL 36256 • 334
Davisville, RI 02852 • 550
Davy, WV 24828 • 882
Dawes □, NE • 9,609
Dawson, GA 31742 • 5,699
Dawson, IA 50066 • 229
Dawson, MN 56232 • 1,901
Dawson, PA 15428 • 661
Dawson, TX 76639 • 747
Dawson □, GA • 4,774
Dawson □, MT • 11,805
Dawson □, NE • 22,304
Dawson □, TX • 16,184
Dawson Springs, KY 42408 • 3,275
Dawsonville, GA 30534 • 342
Day, FL 32013 • 250
Day □, SD • 8,133
Dayton, ID 83232 • 368
Dayton, IN 47941 • 781
Dayton, IA 50530 • 941
Dayton, KY 41074 • 6,979
Dayton, MD 21036 • 700
Dayton, MN 55327 • 4,070
Dayton, NV 89403 • 300
Dayton, NJ 08810 • 900
Dayton, NY 14041 • 480
14041 • 480
Dayton, OH 45401-99 • 193,444
Dayton, OR 97114 • 1,409
Dayton, PA 16222 • 648
Dayton, TN 37321 • 5,913
Dayton, TX 77535 • 4,908
Dayton, VA 22821 • 1,017
Dayton, WA 99328 • 2,565
Dayton, WY 82836 • 701
Daytona Beach, FL 32014-23 • 54,176
Dayville, CT 06241 • 1,100
Deadwood, SD 57732 • 2,035
Deaf Smith □, TX • 21,165
Deal, NJ 07723 • 1,952
Deale, MD 20751 • 3,008
Deal Island, MD 21821 • 500
Deans, NJ 08852 • 600
Dearborn, MI 48120-26 • 90,660
Dearborn, MO 64439 • 547
Dearborn □, IN • 34,291
Dearborn Heights, MI 48127 • 67,706
Dearing, GA 30808 • 539
Dearing, KS 67340 • 475
De Armanville, AL 36257 • 450
Deary, ID 83823 • 539
Deatsville, AL 36022 • 250
De Baca □, NM • 2,454
De Bary, FL 32713 • 4,980
De Beque, CO 81630 • 279
De Berry, TX 75639 • 420
Debolt, NE 68152 • 800
Decatur, AL 35601-03 • 42,002
Decatur, AR 72722 • 1,013
Decatur, GA 30030-38 • 18,404
Decatur, IL 62521-26 • 94,081
Decatur, IN 46733 • 8,649
Decatur, MI 49045 • 1,915
Decatur, MS 39327 • 1,148
Decatur, NE 68020 • 723
Decatur, TN 37322 • 1,069
Decatur, TX 76234 • 4,104
Decatur □, GA • 25,495
Decatur □, IN • 23,841
Decatur □, IA • 9,794
Decatur □, KS • 4,509
Decatur □, TN • 10,857
Decaturville, TN 38329 • 1,004
Decherd, TN 37324 • 2,233
Decker, IN 47524 • 256
Deckerville, MI 48427 • 887
Declo, ID 83323 • 276
Decorah, IA 52101 • 7,991
Decota, WV 25122 • 400
DeCoursey, KY 41015 • 300
Dedham, IA 51440 • 321
Dedham, MA 02026 • 25,298
Deep Gap, NC 28618 • 300
Deep River, CT 06417 • 2,495
Deep River, IA 52222 • 323
Deep Run, NC 28525 • 250
Deepwater, MO 64740 • 475
Deepwater, NJ 08023 • 650
Deep Water, WV 25057 • 500
Deer Creek, IL 61733 • 688
Deer Creek, MN 56527 • 392
Deerfield, IL 60015 • 17,430
Deerfield, KS 67838 • 538
Deerfield, MA 01342 • 550
Deerfield, MI 49238 • 957
Deerfield, NH 03037 • 350
Deerfield, OH 44411 • 450
Deerfield, WI 53531 • 1,466
Deerfield Beach, FL 33441 • 39,193
Deerfield Street, NJ 08313 • 400
Deer Isle, ME 04627 • 300
Deer Lodge, MT 59722 • 4,023
Deer Lodge □, MT • 12,518
Deer Park, MD 21550 • 486
Deer Park, NY 11729 • 33,400
Deer Park, OH 45236 • 6,745
Deer Park, TX 77536 • 22,648
Deer Park, WA 99006 • 2,140
Deer Park, WI 54007 • 232
Deer River, MN 56636 • 907
Deer Trail, CO 80105 • 463
Deerwood, MN 56444 • 580
Deferiet, NY 13628 • 326
Defiance, IA 51527 • 383
Defiance, OH 43512 • 16,810
Defiance □, OH • 39,987
De Forest, WI 53532 • 3,367
De Funiak Springs, FL 32433 • 5,563
De Graff, OH 43318 • 1,358
De Kalb, IL 60115 • 33,099
De Kalb, MS 39328 • 1,159
De Kalb, MO 64440 • 245
De Kalb, TX 75559 • 2,217
De Kalb □, AL • 53,658
De Kalb □, GA • 483,024
De Kalb □, IL • 74,624
De Kalb □, IN • 33,606
De Kalb □, MO • 8,222
De Kalb □, TN • 13,589
De Kalb Junction, NY 13630 • 375
Delacroix, LA 70085 • 400
Delafield, WI 53018 • 4,083
Del Aire, CA 90250 • 3,900
Delanco, NJ 08075 • 3,730
De Land, FL 32720-24 • 15,354
De Land, IL 61839 • 509
Delano, CA 93215 • 16,491
Delano, MN 55328 • 2,480
Delanson, NY 12053 • 448
Delavan, IL 61734 • 1,973
Delavan, MN 56023 • 262
Delavan, WI 53115 • 5,684
Delavan Lake, WI 53115 • 2,124
Delaware, OH 43015 • 18,780
Delaware, OK 74027 • 544
Delaware □, IN • 128,587
Delaware □, IA • 18,933
Delaware □, NY • 46,824
Delaware □, OH • 53,840
Delaware □, OK • 23,946
Delaware □, PA • 555,007
Delaware City, DE 19706 • 1,858
Delaware Water Gap, PA 18327 • 597
Delbarton, WV 25670 • 981
Delcambre, LA 70528 • 2,216
Del City, OK 73115 • 28,523
Delco, NC 28436 • 550
De Leon, TX 76444 • 2,478
De Leon Springs, FL 32028 • 1,669
Delevan, NY 14042 • 1,113
Delhi, IA 52223 • 511
Delhi, LA 71232 • 3,290
Delhi, NY 13753 • 3,374
Delhi Hills, OH 45238 • 7,650
Delight, AR 71940 • 431
De Lisle, MS 39571 • 600
Dell, AR 72426 • 310
Dell City, TX 79837 • 495
Dell Rapids, SD 57022 • 2,389
Dellroy, OH 44620 • 368
Dellslow, WV 26531 • 700
Dellwood, MO 63136 • 6,200
Del Mar, CA 92014 • 5,017
Delmar, DE 19940 • 948
Delmar, IA 52037 • 633
Delmar, MD 21875 • 1,232
Delmar, NY 12054 • 8,900
Delmont, NJ 08314 • 350
Delmont, SD 57330 • 290
Del Norte, CO 81132 • 1,709
Del Norte □, CA • 18,217
Deloit, IA 51441 • 345
Del Park Manor, DE 19808 • 1,700
Delphi, IN 46923 • 3,042
Delphos, KS 67436 • 570
Delphos, OH 45833 • 7,314
Delran, NJ 08075 • 10,065
Delray Beach, FL 33444-47 • 34,325
Del Rio, TX 78840 • 30,034
Delta, CO 81416 • 3,931
Delta, IA 52550 • 482
Delta, LA 71233 • 295
Delta, MO 63744 • 524
Delta, OH 43515 • 2,831
Delta, PA 17314 • 692
Delta, UT 84624 • 1,930
Delta □, CO • 21,225
Delta □, MI • 38,947
Delta □, TX • 4,839
Delta City, MS 39061 • 300
Delta Junction, AK 99737 • 945
Deltaville, VA 23043 • 600
Delton, MI 49046 • 350
Deltona, FL 32725 • 4,868
Demarest, NJ 07627 • 4,963
Deming, NM 88030 • 9,964
Deming, WA 98244 • 450
Demopolis, AL 36732 • 7,678
Demorest, GA 30535 • 1,130
Demotte, IN 46310 • 2,559
Dendron, VA 23839 • 307
Denham Springs, LA 70726 • 8,563
Denison, IA 51442 • 6,675
Denison, KS 66419 • 231
Denison, TX 75020 • 23,884
Denmark, IA 52624 • 400
Denmark, SC 29042 • 4,434
Denmark, WI 54208 • 1,475
Dennehotso, AZ 86535 • 500
Denning, AR 72821 • 238
Dennis, MA 02638 • 900
Dennison, OH 44621 • 3,398
Dennis Port, MA 02639 • 2,570
Dennisville, NJ 08214 • 400

Denny Terrace, SC 29203 • 1,885
Dent □, MO • 14,517
Denton, GA 31532 • 286
Denton, MD 21629 • 1,927
Denton, MT 59430 • 356
Denton, NC 27239 • 949
Denton, TX 76201-06 • 48,063
Denton □, TX • 143,126
Dentsville, SC 29204 • 5,000
Denver, CO 80201-99 • 492,365
Denver, IN 46926 • 589
Denver, IA 50622 • 1,647
Denver, NC 28037 • 350
Denver, PA 17517 • 2,018
Denver □, CO • 492,365
Denver City, TX 79323 • 4,704
Denville, NJ 07834 • 14,045
Depauville, NY 13632 • 275
De Pere, WI 54115 • 14,892
Depew, NY 14043 • 19,819
Depew, OK 74028 • 682
Depoe Bay, OR 97341 • 723
Deport, TX 75435 • 724
Deposit, NY 13754 • 1,897
Depue, IL 61322 • 1,873
Deputy, IN 47230 • 250
De Queen, AR 71832 • 4,594
De Quincy, LA 70633 • 3,966
Derby, CT 06418 • 12,346
Derby, KS 67037 • 9,786
Derby, MS 39470 • 300
Derby, NY 14047 • 1,200
Derby, OH 43117 • 400
Derby, VA 24216 • 300
Derby Line, VT 05830 • 874
De Ridder, LA 70634 • 11,057
Derma, MS 38839 • 793
Dermott, AR 71638 • 4,731
Derry, NH 03038 • 12,248
Derry, PA 15627 • 3,072
De Ruyter, NY 13052 • 542
Derwent, OH 43733 • 240
Derwood, MD 20855 • 550
Des Allemands, LA 70030 • 2,920
Des Arc, AR 72040 • 2,001
Des Arc, MO 63636 • 237
Deschutes □, OR • 62,142
Desert Hot Springs, CA 92240 • 5,941
Desha, AR 72527 • 750
Desha □, AR • 19,760
Deshler, NE 68340 • 997
Deshler, OH 43516 • 1,870
Desloge, MO 63601 • 2,934
De Smet, SD 57231 • 1,237
Des Moines, IA 50301-99 • 191,003
Des Moines, WA 98188 • 7,378
Des Moines □, IA • 46,203
De Soto, GA 31743 • 248
De Soto, IL 62924 • 1,589
De Soto, IA 50069 • 1,035
De Soto, KS 66018 • 2,061
De Soto, MO 63020 • 5,993
De Soto, TX 75115 • 15,538
De Soto, WI 54624 • 318
De Soto □, FL • 19,039
De Soto □, LA • 25,727
De Soto □, MS • 53,930
De Soto City, FL 33870 • 425
Despard, WV 26301 • 1,200
Des Peres, MO 63131 • 8,254
Des Plaines, IL 60016-18 • 53,568
Destin, FL 32541 • 3,672
Destrehan, LA 70047 • 2,382
De Tour Village, MI 49725 • 466
Detroit, AL 35552 • 326
Detroit, MI 48201-99 • 1,203,339
Detroit, OR 97342 • 367
Detroit, TX 75436 • 805
Detroit Lakes, MN 56501 • 7,106
Deuel □, NE • 2,462
Deuel □, SD • 5,289
De Valls Bluff, AR 72041 • 738
Devils Elbow, MO 65457 • 250
Devils Lake, ND 58301 • 7,442
Devine, TX 78016 • 3,756
Devola, OH 45750 • 2,708
Devon, PA 19333 • 6,700
Devonshire, DE 19810 • 1,800
Dewar, OK 74431 • 1,048
Dewey, AZ 86327 • 400
Dewey, OK 74029 • 3,545
Dewey □, OK • 5,922
Dewey □, SD • 5,366
Dewey Beach, DE 19971 • 1,500
Deweyville, TX 77614 • 950
Deweyville, UT 84309 • 311
De Witt, AR 72042 • 3,928
Dewitt, IL 61735 • 232
De Witt, IA 52742 • 4,512
De Witt, MI 48820 • 3,165
De Witt, NE 68341 • 642
De Witt, NY 13214 • 10,032
De Witt □, IL • 18,108
De Witt □, TX • 18,903
Dexter, GA 31019 • 527
Dexter, IA 50070 • 678
Dexter, KS 67038 • 366
Dexter, KY 42036 • 238
Dexter, ME 04930 • 3,118
Dexter, MI 48130 • 1,524
Dexter, MN 55926 • 279
Dexter, MO 63841 • 7,043
Dexter, NM 88230 • 882
Dexter, NY 13634 • 1,053
Dexter, OR 97431 • 300
D'Hanis, TX 78850 • 550
Diagonal, IA 50845 • 362
Diamond, WV 25015 • 500
Diamond Bar, CA 91765 • 28,045
Diamond Hill, RI 02864 • 1,150
Diamond Lake, IL 60060 • 1,503
Diamond Point, NY 12824 • 400
Diamond Springs, CA 95619 • 2,287
Diamondville, WY 83116 • 1,000
Diaz, AR 72043 • 1,192
Dibble, OK 73031 • 348
D'Iberville, MS 39532 • 9,000
Diboll, TX 75941 • 5,227
Dickens, IA 51333 • 289
Dickens, TX 79229 • 409
Dickens □, TX • 3,539
Dickenson □, VA • 19,806
Dickerson, MD 20842 • 300
Dickey □, ND • 7,207
Dickeyville, WI 53808 • 1,156
Dickinson, AL 36436 • 300
Dickinson, ND 58601 • 15,924
Dickinson, TX 77539 • 7,505
Dickinson □, IA • 15,629
Dickinson □, KS • 20,175
Dickinson □, MI • 25,341
Dickson, OK 73401 • 996
Dickson, TN 37055 • 7,040
Dickson □, TN • 30,037
Dickson City, PA 18519 • 6,699
Dierks, AR 71833 • 1,249
Dieterich, IL 62424 • 633
Dighton, KS 67839 • 1,390
Dighton, MA 02715 • 900
Dike, IA 50624 • 987
Dilkon, AZ 86047 • 250
Dillard, GA 30537 • 238
Dillard, OR 97432 • 1,000
Dill City, OK 73641 • 649
Dille, WV 26617 • 300
Diller, NE 68342 • 311
Dilley, TX 78017 • 2,579
Dilliner, PA 15327 • 300
Dillingham, AK 99576 • 914
Dillon, CO 80435 • 337
Dillon, MT 59725 • 3,976
Dillon, SC 29536 • 7,060
Dillon □, SC • 31,083
Dillonvale, OH 43917 • 912
Dillsboro, IN 47018 • 1,038
Dillsburg, PA 17019 • 1,733
Dillwyn, VA 23936 • 637
Dilworth, MN 56529 • 2,585
Dimmit □, TX • 11,367
Dimmitt, TX 79027 • 5,019
Dimondale, MI 48821 • 1,008
Dingle, ID 83233 • 230
Dingmans Ferry, PA 18328 • 300
Dinosaur, CO 81610 • 313
Dinuba, CA 93618 • 9,907
Dinwiddie, VA 23841 • 250
Dinwiddie □, VA • 22,602
Dishman, WA 99213 • 9,900
Disney, OK 74340 • 464
Disputanta, VA 23842 • 400
Distant, PA 16223 • 575
District Heights-Forestville, MD 20747 • 6,799
District of Columbia 0T • 638,432
Divernon, IL 62530 • 1,081
Divide □, ND • 3,494
Dividing Creek, NJ 08315 • 500
Dix, IL 62830 • 3,198
Dix, NE 69133 • 275
Dixfield, ME 04224 • 1,725
Dix Hills, NY 11746 • 10,500
Dixiana, AL 35059 • 600
35059 • 600
Dixie, GA 31629 • 259
Dixie, WV 25059 • 450
Dixie □, FL • 7,751
Dixon, CA 95620 • 7,541
Dixon, IL 61021 • 15,701
Dixon, IA 52745 • 312
Dixon, KY 42409 • 533
Dixon, MO 65459 • 1,402
Dixon, NM 87527 • 350
Dixon □, NE • 7,137
Dixonville, PA 15734 • 900
D'Lo, MS 39062 • 463
Dobbs Ferry, NY 10522 • 10,053
Dobson, NC 27017 • 1,222
Docena, AL 35060 • 1,140
Dock Junction, GA 31520 • 6,189
Dockton, WA 98070 • 300
Doctors Inlet, FL 32030 • 600
Doddridge □, WV • 7,433
Doddsville, MS 38736 • 232
Dodge, NE 68633 • 815
Dodge □, GA • 16,955
Dodge □, MN • 14,773
Dodge □, NE • 35,847
Dodge □, WI • 75,064
Dodge Center, MN 55927 • 1,816
Dodge City, KS 67801 • 18,001
Dodgeville, WI 53533 • 3,458
Dodson, LA 71422 • 469
Doerun, GA 31744 • 1,062
Doe Run, MO 63637 • 900
Doland, SD 57436 • 381
Dolgeville, NY 13329 • 2,602
Dollar Bay, MI 49922 • 900
Dolomite, AL 35061 • 2,400
Dolores, CO 81323 • 802
Dolores □, CO • 1,658
Dolton, IL 60419 • 24,766
Dona Ana, NM 88032 • 300
Dona Ana □, NM • 96,340
Donald, OR 97020 • 267
Donalds, SC 29638 • 366
Donaldson, AR 71941 • 300
Donaldson, PA 17981 • 465
Donaldsonville, LA 70346 • 7,901
Donalsonville, GA 31745 • 3,320
Doneraile, SC 29532 • 1,276
Dongola, IL 62926 • 886
Doniphan, MO 63935 • 1,921
Doniphan, NE 68832 • 696
Doniphan □, KS • 9,268
Donley □, TX • 4,075
Donna, TX 78537 • 9,952
Donnellson, IL 62019 • 256
Donnellson, IA 52625 • 972
Donnelly, MN 56235 • 317
Donner, LA 70352 • 400
Donora, PA 15033 • 7,524
Donovan, IL 60931 • 301
Doolittle, MO 65401 • 701
Dooly □, GA • 10,826
Doon, IA 51235 • 537
Door □, WI • 25,029
Dora, AL 35062 • 2,327
Doraville, GA 30340 • 7,414
Dorchester, NE 68343 • 611
Dorchester, NJ 08316 • 500
Dorchester, SC 29437 • 330
Dorchester, WI 54425 • 613
Dorchester □, MD • 30,623
Dorchester □, SC • 58,761
Dorchester Estates, SC 29483 • 350
Dorcyville, LA 70788 • 400
Dorena, OR 97434 • 250
Dormont, PA 15216 • 11,275
Dorothy, NJ 08317 • 600
Dorothy Pond, MA 01527 • 1,900
Dorr, MI 49323 • 500
Dorris, CA 96023 • 836
Dorris Heights, IL 62946 • 500
Dorset, VT 05251 • 550
Dorsey, MD 21227 • 1,186
Dorsey, MS 38843 • 260
Dorton, KY 41520 • 600
Dothan, AL 36301-03 • 48,750
Dothan, WV 25833 • 300
Doty, WA 98539 • 280
Double Beach, CT 06405 • 400
Double Springs, AL 35553 • 1,057
Doucette, TX 75942 • 600
Douds, IA 52551 • 275
Dougherty □, GA • 100,718
Douglas, AZ 85607 • 13,058
Douglas, GA 31533 • 10,980
Douglas, MA 01516 • 300
Douglas, MI 49406 • 948
Douglas, WY 82633 • 6,030
Douglas □, CO • 25,153
Douglas □, GA • 54,573
Douglas □, IL • 19,774
Douglas □, KS • 67,640
Douglas □, MN • 27,839
Douglas □, MO • 11,594
Douglas □, NE • 397,038
Douglas □, NV • 19,421
Douglas □, OR • 93,748
Douglas □, SD • 4,181
Douglas □, WA • 22,144
Douglas □, WI • 44,421
Douglass, KS 67039 • 1,450
Douglasville, GA 30133-35 • 7,641
Dousman, WI 53118 • 1,153
Dove Creek, CO 81324 • 826
Dover, AR 72837 • 948
Dover, DE 19901 • 23,507
Dover, FL 33527 • 2,354
Dover, KY 41034 • 305
Dover, MA 02030 • 2,051
Dover, MN 55929 • 312
Dover, NH 03820 • 22,377
Dover, NJ 07801 • 14,681
Dover, NC 28526 • 600
Dover, OH 44622 • 11,782
Dover, OK 73734 • 570
Dover, PA 17315 • 1,910
Dover, TN 37058 • 1,197
Dover-Foxcroft, ME 04426 • 2,974
Dover Plains, NY 12522 • 800
Dowagiac, MI 49047 • 6,307
Dow City, IA 51528 • 616
Dowell, IL 62927 • 480
Dowell, MD 20629 • 250
Dowelltown, TN 37059 • 341
Dowling Park, FL 32060 • 350
Downers Grove, IL 60515-17 • 42,572
Downey, CA 90240-42 • 82,602
Downey, ID 83234 • 645
Downieville, CA 95936 • 950
Downing, MO 63536 • 462
Downing, WI 54734 • 242
Downingtown, PA 19335 • 7,650
Downs, IL 61736 • 561
Downs, KS 67437 • 1,324
Downsville, NY 13755 • 950
Dows, IA 50071 • 771
Doyle, CA 96109 • 900
Doyle, TN 38559 • 344
Doylestown, OH 44230 • 2,493
Doylestown, PA 18901 • 8,717
Doyline, LA 71023 • 801
Dozier, AL 36028 • 494
Dracut, MA 01826 • 21,249
Drain, OR 97435 • 1,148
Drake, ND 58736 • 479
Drakesboro, KY 42337 • 798
Drakes Branch, VA 23937 • 617
Draper, UT 84020 • 5,521
Drayton, ND 58225 • 1,082
Drayton, SC 29333 • 1,443
Drayton Plains, MI 48020 • 18,000
Dreamland Villa, AZ 85205 • 3,200
Dresden, OH 43821 • 1,646
Dresden, TN 38225 • 2,256
Dresser, IN 47885 • 225
Dresser, WI 54009 • 670
Drew, MS 38737 • 2,528
Drew □, AR • 17,910
Drewryville, VA 23844 • 250
Drexel, MO 64742 • 908
Drexel, NC 28619 • 1,392
Drexel, OH 45427 • 2,250
Drexel Hill, PA 19026 • 29,600
Drift, KY 41619 • 600
Drifton, PA 18221 • 600
Driggs, ID 83422 • 727
Dripping Springs, TX 78620 • 606
Driscoll, TX 78351 • 648
Drummond, MT 59832 • 414
Drummond, OK 73735 • 482
Drummond, WI 54832 • 300
Drummond Island, MI 49726 • 500
Drumright, OK 74030 • 3,162
Dry Branch, GA 31020 • 400
Drybranch, WV 25061 • 700
Dryden, ME 04225 • 500
Dryden, MI 48428 • 650
Dryden, NY 13053 • 1,761
Dryden, WA 98821 • 400
Dry Mills, ME 04039 • 300
Dry Prong, LA 71423 • 526
Dry Ridge, KY 41035 • 1,250
Dry Run, PA 17220 • 250
Duarte, CA 91010 • 16,766
Dubach, LA 71235 • 1,161
Dubberly, LA 71024 • 421
Dublin, CA 94568 • 19,000
Dublin, GA 31021 • 16,083
Dublin, IN 47335 • 979
Dublin, MD 21034 • 500
Dublin, NH 03444 • 600
Dublin, NC 28332 • 477
Dublin, OH 43017 • 3,855
Dublin, PA 18917 • 1,565
Dublin, TX 76446 • 2,723
Dublin, VA 24084 • 2,368

Dubois, ID 83423 • *413*
Dubois, IL 62831 • *241*
Dubois, IN 47527 • *550*
Du Bois, PA 15801 • *9,290*
Dubois, WY 82513 • *1,067*
Dubois □, IN • *34,238*
Duboistown, PA 17701 • *1,218*
Dubuque, IA 52001 • *62,321*
Dubuque □, IA • *93,745*
Duchesne, UT 84021 • *1,677*
Duchesne □, UT • *12,565*
Duck Hill, MS 38925 • *706*
Ducktown, TN 37326 • *583*
Ducor, CA 93218 • *350*
Dudley, GA 31022 • *425*
Dudley, MA 01570 • *3,700*
Dudley, MO 63936 • *287*
Dudley, PA 16634 • *282*
Duenweg, MO 64841 • *703*
Due West, SC 29639 • *1,366*
Dufur, OR 97021 • *560*
Dugger, IN 47848 • *1,118*
Duke, OK 73532 • *484*
Duke Center, PA 16729 • *900*
Dukes □, MA • *8,942*
Dulac, LA 70353 • *400*
Dulce, NM 87528 • *1,648*
Duluth, GA 30136 • *2,956*
Duluth, MN 55801-99 • *92,811*
Dumas, AR 71639 • *6,091*
Dumas, MS 38625 • *312*
Dumas, TX 79029 • *12,194*
Dumfries, VA 22026 • *3,214*
Dumont, IA 50625 • *815*
Dumont, NJ 07628 • *18,334*
Dunaire, GA 30032 • *5,400*
Dunbar, PA 15431 • *1,369*
Dunbar, WV 25064 • *9,285*
Dunbridge, OH 43414 • *225*
Duncan, AZ 85534 • *603*
Duncan, MS 38740 • *501*
Duncan, NE 68634 • *410*
Duncan, OK 73533 • *22,517*
Duncan, SC 29334 • *1,259*
Duncan Falls, OH 43734 • *1,200*
Duncannon, PA 17020 • *1,645*
Duncansville, PA 16635 • *1,355*
Duncanville, TX 75116 • *27,781*
Duncombe, IA 50532 • *504*
Dundalk, MD 21222 • *71,293*
Dundas, MN 55019 • *422*
Dundee, FL 33838 • *2,227*
Dundee, IL 60118 • *3,551*
Dundee, MI 48131 • *2,575*
Dundee, NY 14837 • *1,556*
Dundee, OR 97115 • *1,223*
Dundy □, NE • *2,861*
Dunedin, FL 33528 • *30,203*
Duneland Beach, IN 46360 • *400*
Dunellen, NJ 08812 • *6,593*
Dunfermline, IL 61524 • *313*
Dungannon, VA 24245 • *339*
Dunkerton, IA 50626 • *718*
Dunkirk, IN 47336 • *3,180*
Dunkirk, NY 14048 • *15,310*
Dunkirk, OH 45836 • *954*
Dunklin □, MO • *36,324*
Dunlap, IL 61525 • *824*
Dunlap, IN 46514 • *2,500*
Dunlap, IA 51529 • *1,374*
Dunlap, TN 37327 • *3,681*
Dunleith, DE 19801 • *2,700*
Dunlo, PA 15930 • *950*
Dunmore, PA 18512 • *16,781*
Dunn, NC 28334 • *8,962*
Dunn □, ND • *4,627*
Dunn □, WI • *34,314*
Dunnellon, FL 32630 • *1,427*
Dunn Loring Woods, VA 22180 • *2,800*
Dunseith, ND 58329 • *625*
Dunsmuir, CA 96025 • *2,253*
Dunstable, MA 01827 • *900*
Dunwoody, GA 30338 • *5,100*
Du Page □, IL • *658,829*
Duplessis, LA 70728 • *250*
Duplin □, NC • *40,952*
Dupont, CO 80024 • *2,000*
Du Pont, GA 31630 • *267*
Dupont, IN 47231 • *392*
Dupont, OH 45837 • *308*
Dupont, PA 18641 • *3,460*
Du Pont, WA 98327 • *559*
Dupont City, WV 25015 • *900*
Dupont Manor, DE 19901 • *1,059*
Dupree, SD 57623 • *562*
Duquesne, PA 15110 • *10,094*
Du Quoin, IL 62832 • *6,594*
Durand, IL 61024 • *1,073*
Durand, MI 48429 • *4,241*
Durand, WI 54736 • *2,047*
Durango, CO 81301 • *11,649*
Durant, IA 52747 • *1,583*
Durant, MS 39063 • *2,889*
Durant, OK 74701 • *11,972*
Durbin, WV 26264 • *379*
Durham, CA 95938 • *950*
Durham, CT 06422 • *2,641*
Durham, NH 03824 • *8,448*
Durham, NC 27701-99 • *100,538*
Durham □, NC • *152,785*
Duryea, PA 18642 • *5,415*
Dushore, PA 18614 • *692*
Duson, LA 70529 • *1,253*
Dustin, OK 74839 • *498*
Dutchess □, NY • *245,055*
Dutch John, UT 84023 • *285*
Dutton, AL 35744 • *276*
Dutton, MT 59433 • *359*
Duval □, FL • *571,003*
Duval □, TX • *12,517*
Duxbury, MA 02332 • *1,685*
Dwight, IL 60420 • *4,146*
Dwight, KS 66849 • *320*
Dyckesville, WI 54217 • *350*
Dyer, AR 72935 • *608*
Dyer, IN 46311 • *9,555*
Dyer, TN 38330 • *2,419*
Dyer □, TN • *34,663*
Dyersburg, TN 38024 • *15,856*
Dyersville, IA 52040 • *3,825*
Dyess, AR 72330 • *446*
Dysart, IA 52224 • *1,355*

E

Eads, CO 81036 • *878*
Eads, TN 38028 • *250*
Eagan, MN 55121 • *20,700*
Eagar, AZ 85925 • *2,791*
Eagle, CO 81631 • *950*
Eagle, ID 83616 • *2,620*
Eagle, NE 68347 • *832*
Eagle, WI 53119 • *1,008*
Eagle □, CO • *13,320*
Eagle Bend, MN 56446 • *593*
Eagle Bridge, NY 12057 • *350*
Eagle Butte, SD 57625 • *435*
Eagle Grove, IA 50533 • *4,324*
Eagle Lake, ME 04739 • *600*
Eagle Lake, MN 56024 • *1,470*
Eagle Lake, TX 77434 • *3,921*
Eagle Lake, WI 53139 • *1,000*
Eagle Pass, TX 78852 • *21,407*
Eagle Point, OR 97524 • *2,764*
Eagle River, WI 54521 • *1,326*
Eagle Rock, VA 24085 • *300*
Eagle Springs, NC 27242 • *300*
Eagletown, OK 74734 • *500*
Eagleville, CT 06268 • *450*
Eagleville, MO 64442 • *364*
Eagleville, TN 37060 • *444*
Eakly, OK 73033 • *452*
Earle, AR 72331 • *3,517*
Earlham, IA 50072 • *1,140*
Earlimart, CA 93219 • *4,578*
Earling, IA 51530 • *520*
Earling, WV 25619 • *350*
Earlington, KY 42410 • *2,011*
Earl Park, IN 47942 • *469*
Earlsboro, OK 74840 • *266*
Earlville, IL 60518 • *1,382*
Earlville, IA 52041 • *844*
Earlville, NY 13332 • *985*
Early, IA 50535 • *670*
Early □, GA • *13,158*
Earth, TX 79031 • *1,512*
Easley, SC 29640 • *14,264*
Eastaboga, AL 36260 • *300*
East Acton, MA 01720 • *1,200*
East Alton, IL 62024 • *7,096*
East Andover, NH 03231 • *300*
East Arlington, VT 05252 • *600*
East Aurora, NY 14052 • *6,803*
East Baldwin, ME 04024 • *250*
East Bangor, PA 18013 • *955*
East Bank, WV 25067 • *1,155*
East Barre, VT 05649 • *900*
East Baton Rouge □, LA • *366,191*
East Bend, NC 27018 • *602*
East Berlin, CT 06023 • *900*
East Berlin, PA 17316 • *1,054*
East Bernard, TX 77435 • *1,700*
East Bernstadt, KY 40729 • *700*
East Bethel, MN 55005 • *6,626*
East Billerica, MA 01821 • *2,900*
East Bonne Terre, MO 63628 • *250*
East Boothbay, ME 04544 • *400*
Eastborough, KS 67206 • *854*
East Brady, PA 16028 • *1,153*
East Branch, NY 13756 • *300*
East Brewster, MA 02631 • *700*
East Brewton, AL 36426 • *3,012*
East Bridgewater, MA 02333 • *3,300*
East Brookfield, MA 01515 • *1,443*
East Brooklyn, CT 06239 • *1,251*
East Brunswick, NJ 08816 • *37,711*
East Butler, PA 16029 • *799*
East Canaan, CT 06024 • *800*
East Candia, NH 03040 • *250*
East Carbon, UT 84520 • *1,942*
East Carroll □, LA • *11,772*
East Chelmsford, MA 01824 • *2,900*
Eastchester, NY 10709 • *22,600*
East Chicago, IN 46312 • *39,786*
East Chicago Heights, IL 60411 • *5,347*
East Cleveland, OH 44112 • *36,957*
East Corinth, ME 04427 • *400*
East Dennis, MA 02641 • *800*
East Derry, NH 03041 • *600*
East Detroit, MI 48021 • *38,280*
East Dorset, VT 05253 • *300*
East Douglas, MA 01516 • *1,683*
East Dover, VT 05341 • *250*
East Dubuque, IL 61025 • *2,194*
East Eddington, ME 04428 • *250*
East Ellijay, GA 30539 • *469*
East Fairfield, VT 05448 • *300*
East Falmouth, MA 02536 • *5,181*
East Farmington Heights, CT 06032 • *370*
East Feliciana □, LA • *19,015*
East Flat Rock, NC 28726 • *3,365*
Eastford, CT 06242 • *500*
East Foxboro, MA 02035 • *500*
East Freetown, MA 02717 • *500*
East Fultonham, OH 43735 • *650*
East Gaffney, SC 29340 • *4,092*
East Galesburg, IL 61430 • *928*
Eastgate, WA 98004 • *5,300*
East Glacier Park, MT 59434 • *500*
East Glastonbury, CT 06025 • *400*
East Glenville, NY 12302 • *11,800*
East Granby, CT 06026 • *500*
East Grand Forks, MN 56721 • *8,537*
East Grand Rapids, MI 49506 • *10,914*
East Greenville, PA 18041 • *2,456*
East Greenwich, RI 02818 • *10,211*
East Haddam, CT 06423 • *600*
East Half Hollow Hills, NY 11746 • *9,691*
Eastham, MA 02642 • *1,100*
East Hampden, ME 04401 • *950*
East Hampstead, NH 03826 • *900*
East Hampton, CT 06424 • *2,152*
Easthampton, MA 01027 • *15,580*
East Hampton, NY 11937 • *1,886*
East Hanover, NJ 07936 • *9,319*
East Hartford, CT 06108 • *52,563*
East Haven, CT 06512 • *25,028*
East Helena, MT 59635 • *1,647*
East Hickory, PA 16321 • *250*
East Hills, NY 11576 • *7,160*
East Holden, ME 04429 • *570*
East Islip, NY 11730 • *13,700*
East Jordan, MI 49727 • *2,185*
East Kingston, NH 03827 • *250*
Eastlake, MI 49626 • *514*
Eastlake, OH 44094 • *22,104*
Eastland, TX 76448 • *3,747*
Eastland □, TX • *19,480*
East Lansing, MI 48823 • *51,392*
East Las Vegas, NV 89112 • *6,449*
East Laurinburg, NC 28352 • *536*
East Lebanon, ME 04027 • *250*
East Lempster, NH 03605 • *385*
East Liberty, OH 43319 • *480*
East Liverpool, OH 43920 • *16,687*
East Longmeadow, MA 01028 • *12,905*
East Los Angeles, CA 90022 • *110,017*
East Lyme, CT 06333 • *700*
East Lynn, WV 25512 • *250*
East Lynne, MO 64743 • *286*
East Machias, ME 04630 • *400*
East Madison, ME 04976 • *300*
Eastman, GA 31023 • *5,330*
Eastman, WI 54626 • *371*
East Mansfield, MA 02031 • *500*
East Marion, MA 02738 • *400*
East Marion, NY 11939 • *900*
East Meadow, NY 11554 • *47,300*
East Middlebury, VT 05740 • *550*
East Millbury, MA 01527 • *1,000*
East Millinocket, ME 04430 • *2,361*
East Moline, IL 61244 • *20,907*
East Montpelier, VT 05651 • *600*
East Naples, FL 33940 • *9,000*
East Newark, NJ 07029 • *1,923*
East New Market, MD 21631 • *230*
East Newnan, GA 30263 • *1,499*
East Norriton, PA 19401 • *12,711*
East Northport, NY 11731 • *22,200*
East Olympia, WA 98540 • *700*
Easton, CT 06612 • *400*
Easton, IL 62633 • *392*
Easton, KS 66020 • *460*
Easton, ME 04740 • *280*
Easton, MD 21601 • *7,536*
Easton, MA 02334 • *350*
Easton, MN 56025 • *283*
Easton, MO 64443 • *313*
Easton, PA 18042 • *26,027*
Easton, WA 98925 • *250*
Eastondale, MA 02375 • *900*
East Orange, NJ 07017-19 • *77,690*
East Orleans, MA 02643 • *1,200*
East Otto, NY 14729 • *300*
Eastover, SC 29044 • *899*
East Palatka, FL 32031 • *1,613*
East Palestine, OH 44413 • *5,306*
East Palo Alto, CA 94303 • *18,191*
East Patchogue, NY 11772 • *8,300*
East Pea Ridge, WV 25705 • *1,900*
East Peoria, IL 61611 • *22,385*
East Pepperell, MA 01437 • *2,212*
East Petersburg, PA 17520 • *3,600*
East Pittsburgh, PA 15112 • *2,493*
Eastpoint, FL 32328 • *1,246*
East Point, GA 30344 • *37,486*
Eastport, ME 04631 • *1,982*
Eastport, NY 11941 • *1,308*
East Poultney, VT 05741 • *450*
East Prairie, MO 63845 • *3,713*
East Princeton, MA 01517 • *350*
East Prospect, PA 17317 • *529*
East Providence, RI 02914 • *50,980*
East Quogue, NY 11942 • *1,200*
East Randolph, NY 14730 • *655*
East Ridge, TN 37412 • *21,236*
East River, CT 06443 • *1,800*
East Rochester, NY 14445 • *7,596*
East Rockaway, NY 11518 • *10,917*
East Rockingham, NC 28379 • *5,190*
East Rutherford, NJ 07073 • *7,849*
East Saint Louis, IL 62201-08 • *55,200*
East Sandwich, MA 02537 • *250*
East Sebago, ME 04029 • *300*
Eastside, OR 97420 • *1,601*
East Smithfield, PA 18817 • *350*
Eastsound, WA 98245 • *900*
East Sparta, OH 44626 • *868*
East Spencer, NC 28039 • *2,150*
East Stroudsburg, PA 18301 • *8,039*
East Sudbury, MA 01776 • *1,500*
East Sullivan, ME 04607 • *250*
East Sullivan, NH 03445 • *250*
East Swanzey, NH 03446 • *300*
East Tawas, MI 48730 • *2,584*
East Templeton, MA 01438 • *980*
East Thermopolis, WY 82443 • *359*
East Thompson, CT 06277 • *300*
East Troy, WI 53120 • *2,385*
East Tustin, CA 92705 • *10,000*
East Vestal, NY 13902 • *5,300*
East View, WV 26301 • *1,618*
Eastville, VA 23347 • *238*
East Wallingford, VT 05742 • *300*
East Walpole, MA 02032 • *4,900*
East Wareham, MA 02538 • *1,000*
East Washington, PA 15301 • *2,241*
East Waterboro, ME 04030 • *250*
East Wenatchee, WA 98801 • *1,640*
East Wilton, ME 04234 • *500*
East Windsor, NJ 08520 • *15,000*
East Windsor Hill, CT 06028 • *400*
Eastwood, KY 40018 • *300*
Eastwood, MI 49001 • *7,186*
Eastwood Hills, UT 84106 • *1,200*
East Woodstock, CT 06244 • *400*
East Worcester, NY 12064 • *400*
Eaton, CO 80615 • *1,932*
Eaton, IN 47338 • *1,804*
Eaton, NY 13334 • *450*
Eaton, OH 45320 • *6,839*
Eaton □, MI • *88,337*
Eaton Rapids, MI 48827 • *4,510*
Eatonton, GA 31024 • *4,833*
Eatontown, NJ 07724 • *12,703*
Eatonville, WA 98328 • *998*
Eau Claire, MI 49111 • *573*
Eau Claire, WI 54701-03 • *51,509*
Eau Claire □, WI • *78,805*
Eben Junction, MI 49825 • *450*

Ebensburg, PA 15931 • *4,096*
Ebro, FL 32437 • *233*
Eccles, WV 25836 • *1,100*
Echo, LA 71330 • *350*
Echo, MN 56237 • *334*
Echo, OR 97826 • *624*
Echols □, GA • *2,297*
Eckhart Mines, MD 21528 • *1,333*
Eckley, CO 80727 • *262*
Eckman, WV 24829 • *700*
Eclectic, AL 36024 • *1,124*
Economy, IN 47339 • *237*
Economy, PA 15005 • *9,538*
Ecorse, MI 48229 • *14,447*
Ecru, MS 38841 • *687*
Ector □, TX • *115,374*
Edcouch, TX 78538 • *3,092*
Eddy □, NM • *47,855*
Eddy □, ND • *3,554*
Eddystone, PA 19013 • *2,555*
Eddyville, IA 52553 • *1,116*
Eddyville, KY 42038 • *1,949*
Eden, GA 31307 • *450*
Eden, ID 83325 • *355*
Eden, MD 21822 • *250*
Eden, NC 27288 • *15,672*
Eden, NY 14057 • *3,000*
Eden, TX 76837 • *1,294*
Eden, UT 84310 • *225*
Eden, WI 53019 • *534*
Eden, WY 82926 • *250*
Edenborn, PA 15458 • *500*
Eden Prairie, MN 55344 • *16,263*
Edenton, NC 27932 • *5,357*
Eden Valley, MN 55329 • *763*
Edenville, MI 48620 • *350*
Edgar, NE 68935 • *705*
Edgar, WI 54426 • *1,194*
Edgar □, IL • *21,725*
Edgard, LA 70049 • *680*
Edgar Springs, MO 65462 • *271*
Edgartown, MA 02539 • *1,138*
Edgecombe □, NC • *55,988*
Edgefield, SC 29824 • *2,713*
Edgefield □, SC • *17,528*
Edgeley, ND 58433 • *843*
Edgemere, MD 21222 • *7,800*
Edgemont, SD 57735 • *1,468*
Edgemoor, DE 19802 • *7,397*
Edgemoor, SC 29712 • *300*
Edgerly, LA 70668 • *375*
Edgerton, KS 66021 • *1,214*
Edgerton, MN 56128 • *1,123*
Edgerton, MO 64444 • *584*
Edgerton, OH 43517 • *1,813*
Edgerton, WI 53534 • *4,335*
Edgerton, WY 82635 • *510*
Edgewater, AL 35224 • *1,400*
Edgewater, CO 80214 • *4,766*
Edgewater, FL 32032 • *6,726*
Edgewater, MD 21037 • *800*
Edgewater, NJ 07020 • *4,628*
Edgewater Park, NJ 08010 • *9,273*
Edgewood, IL 62426 • *574*
Edgewood, IN 46011 • *2,215*
Edgewood, IA 52042 • *900*
Edgewood, KY 41017 • *7,230*
Edgewood, MD 21040 • *19,455*
Edgewood, NM 87015 • *600*
Edgewood, OH 44004 • *3,099*
Edgewood, PA 15218 • *4,382*
Edgewood, WA 98371 • *1,800*
Edgeworth, PA 15143 • *1,738*
Edina, MN 55424 • *46,073*
Edina, MO 63537 • *1,520*
Edinboro, PA 16412 • *6,324*
Edinburg, IL 62531 • *1,231*
Edinburg, ND 58227 • *300*
Edinburg, NY 12134 • *250*
Edinburg, TX 78539 • *24,075*
Edinburg, VA 22824 • *752*
Edinburgh, IN 46124 • *4,856*
Edison, GA 31746 • *1,128*
Edison, NJ 08817-20 • *70,193*
Edison, OH 43320 • *504*
Edison, WA 98232 • *250*
Edmeston, NY 13335 • *600*
Edmond, OK 73034 • *34,637*
Edmonds, WA 98020 • *27,679*
Edmondson, AR 72332 • *344*
Edmondson Heights, MD 21207 • *5,000*
Edmonson □, KY • *9,962*
Edmonton, KY 42129 • *1,401*
Edmore, MI 48829 • *1,176*
Edmore, ND 58330 • *416*
Edmunds □, SD • *5,159*
Edna, KS 67342 • *537*
Edna, TX 77957 • *5,650*
Edon, OH 43518 • *947*
Edwards, IL 61528 • *350*
Edwards, MS 39066 • *1,515*
Edwards, NY 13635 • *561*
Edwards □, IL • *7,961*
Edwards □, KS • *4,271*
Edwards □, TX • *2,033*
Edwardsburg, MI 49112 • *1,135*
Edwardsport, IN 47528 • *459*
Edwardsville, IL 62025 • *12,480*
Edwardsville, KS 66113 • *3,364*
Edwardsville, PA 18704 • *5,729*
Eek, AK 99578 • *228*
Effingham, IL 62401 • *11,270*
Effingham, KS 66023 • *634*
Effingham, SC 29541 • *350*
Effingham □, GA • *18,327*
Effingham □, IL • *30,944*
Efland, NC 27243 • *600*
Egan, SD 57024 • *248*
Egg Harbor, WI 54209 • *238*
Egg Harbor City, NJ 08215 • *4,618*
Egypt, MA 02066 • *1,100*
Ehrenberg, AZ 85334 • *900*
Ehrenfeld, PA 15956 • *360*
Ehrhardt, SC 29081 • *353*
Eitzen, MN 55931 • *226*
Ekalaka, MT 59324 • *620*
Ekron, KY 40117 • *239*
Elaine, AR 72333 • *991*
Eland, WI 54427 • *230*
Elba, AL 36323 • *4,355*
Elba, NY 14058 • *750*
Elberfeld, IN 47613 • *640*
Elbert □, CO • *6,850*
Elbert □, GA • *18,758*
Elberta, AL 36530 • *491*
Elberta, GA 31093 • *500*
Elberta, MI 49628 • *556*
Elberton, GA 30635 • *5,686*
Elbow Lake, MN 56531 • *1,358*
Elburn, IL 60119 • *1,224*
El Cajon, CA 92020-22 • *73,892*
El Campo, TX 77437 • *10,462*
El Centro, CA 92243 • *23,996*
El Cerrito, CA 94530 • *22,731*
Elcho, WI 54428 • *450*
Elderton, PA 15736 • *420*
Eldon, IA 52554 • *1,255*
Eldon, MO 65026 • *4,342*
Eldora, IA 50627 • *3,063*
El Dorado, AR 71730 • *25,270*
Eldorado, GA 31794 • *1,000*
Eldorado, IL 62930 • *5,198*
El Dorado, KS 67042 • *10,510*
Eldorado, OH 45321 • *509*
Eldorado, OK 73537 • *688*
Eldorado, TX 76936 • *2,061*
El Dorado □, CA • *85,812*
Eldorado Springs, CO 80025 • *500*
El Dorado Springs, MO 64744 • *3,868*
Eldred, IL 62027 • *286*
Eldred, PA 16731 • *965*
Eldridge, AL 35554 • *230*
Eldridge, IA 52748 • *3,279*
Eleanor, WV 25070 • *1,282*
Electra, TX 76360 • *3,755*
Eleele, HI 96705 • *580*
El Encanto Heights, CA 93117 • *7,700*
Eleva, WI 54738 • *593*
Elfrida, AZ 85610 • *300*
Elgin, AL 35652 • *300*
Elgin, IL 60120 • *63,981*
Elgin, IA 52141 • *702*
Elgin, MN 55932 • *667*
Elgin, NE 68636 • *807*
Elgin, ND 58533 • *930*
Elgin, OK 73538 • *1,003*
Elgin, OR 97827 • *1,701*
Elgin, PA 16413 • *235*
Elgin, SC 29720 • *900*
Elgin, TX 78621 • *4,535*
Elida, OH 45807 • *1,349*
El Indio, TX 78860 • *250*
Eliot, ME 03903 • *2,450*
Elizabeth, CO 80107 • *789*
Elizabeth, GA 30060 • *1,700*
Elizabeth, IL 61028 • *772*
Elizabeth, LA 70638 • *454*
Elizabeth, NJ 07201-99 • *106,201*
Elizabeth, WV 26143 • *856*
Elizabeth City, NC 27909 • *13,784*
Elizabethton, TN 37643 • *12,431*
Elizabethtown, IL 62931 • *478*
Elizabethtown, IN 47232 • *603*
Elizabethtown, KY 42701 • *15,380*
Elizabethtown, NC 28337 • *3,551*
Elizabethtown, NY 12932 • *650*
Elizabethtown, PA 17022 • *8,233*
Elizabethville, PA 17023 • *1,531*
El Jebel, CO 81628 • *900*
Elk, CA 95432 • *300*
Elk □, KS • *3,918*
Elk □, PA • *38,338*
Elkader, IA 52043 • *1,688*
Elk City, ID 83525 • *670*
Elk City, KS 67344 • *404*
Elk City, OK 73644 • *9,579*
Elk Creek, CA 95939 • *350*
Elk Garden, WV 26717 • *291*
Elk Grove, CA 95624 • *10,059*
Elk Grove Village, IL 60007 • *28,907*
Elkhart, IL 62634 • *493*
Elkhart, IN 46514-17 • *41,305*
Elkhart, IA 50073 • *256*
Elkhart, KS 67950 • *2,243*
Elkhart, TX 75839 • *1,317*
Elkhart □, IN • *137,330*
Elkhart Lake, WI 53020 • *1,054*
Elk Horn, IA 51531 • *746*
Elkhorn, NE 68022 • *1,344*
Elkhorn, WV 24831 • *700*
Elkhorn, WI 53121 • *4,605*
Elkhorn City, KY 41522 • *1,446*
Elkin, NC 28621 • *2,858*
Elkins, AR 72727 • *579*
Elkins, WV 26241 • *8,536*
Elkins Park, PA 19117 • *14,000*
Elkland, PA 16920 • *1,974*
Elk Mills, MD 21920 • *300*
Elkmont, AL 35620 • *429*
Elk Mound, WI 54739 • *737*
Elk Mountain, WY 82324 • *338*
Elko, NV 89801 • *8,758*
Elko, SC 29826 • *329*
Elko □, NV • *17,269*
Elk Park, NC 28622 • *535*
Elk Point, SD 57025 • *1,661*
Elk Rapids, MI 49629 • *1,504*
Elkridge, MD 21227 • *2,100*
Elkridge, WV 25161 • *300*
Elk River, ID 83827 • *265*
Elk River, MN 55330 • *6,785*
Elkton, FL 32033 • *250*
Elkton, KY 42220 • *1,815*
Elkton, MD 21921 • *6,468*
Elkton, MI 48731 • *953*
Elkton, SD 57026 • *632*
Elkton, TN 38455 • *540*
Elkton, VA 22827 • *1,520*
Elk Valley, TN 37847 • *300*
Elkview, WV 25071 • *1,486*
Elkville, IL 62932 • *973*
Ellabell, GA 31308 • *350*
Ellaville, GA 31806 • *1,684*
Ellenboro, NC 28040 • *560*
Ellenboro, WV 26346 • *357*
Ellenburg Center, NY 12934 • *300*
Ellendale, DE 19941 • *361*
Ellendale, MN 56026 • *555*
Ellendale, ND 58436 • *1,967*
Ellensburg, WA 98926 • *11,752*
Ellenton, FL 33532 • *1,561*
Ellenton, GA 31747 • *277*
Ellenville, NY 12428 • *4,405*
Ellenwood, GA 30049 • *500*
Ellerbe, NC 28338 • *1,415*
Ellerslie, MD 21529 • *1,150*
Ellettsville, IN 47429 • *3,328*
Ellicott City, MD 21043 • *4,000*
Ellicottville, NY 14731 • *713*
Ellijay, GA 30540 • *1,507*
Ellington, CT 06029 • *1,000*
Ellington, MO 63638 • *1,215*
Ellinwood, KS 67526 • *2,508*
Elliott, IL 60933 • *370*
Elliott, IA 51532 • *493*
Elliott, MS 38926 • *1,200*
Elliott, SC 29046 • *500*
Elliott □, KY • *6,908*
Ellis, KS 67637 • *2,062*
Ellis □, KS • *26,098*
Ellis □, OK • *5,596*
Ellis □, TX • *59,743*
Ellisburg, NY 13636 • *307*
Ellis Grove, IL 62241 • *296*
Ellison Bay, WI 54210 • *250*
Ellis Pond, ME 04235 • *300*
Elliston, VA 24087 • *750*
Ellisville, MS 39437 • *4,652*
Ellisville, MO 63011 • *6,233*
Elloree, SC 29047 • *909*
Ellport, PA 16117 • *1,290*
Ellsinore, MO 63937 • *362*
Ellsworth, IL 61737 • *244*
Ellsworth, IA 50075 • *480*
Ellsworth, KS 67439 • *2,465*
Ellsworth, ME 04605 • *5,179*
Ellsworth, MI 49729 • *436*
Ellsworth, MN 56129 • *629*
Ellsworth, PA 15331 • *1,228*
Ellsworth, WI 54011 • *2,143*
Ellsworth □, KS • *6,640*
Ellwood City, PA 16117 • *9,998*
Elma, IA 50628 • *714*
Elma, WA 98541 • *2,720*
Elm City, NC 27822 • *1,561*
Elm Creek, NE 68836 • *862*
Elmendorf, TX 78112 • *492*
Elmer, NJ 08318 • *1,569*
Elm Grove, WI 53122 • *6,735*
Elmhurst, IL 60126 • *44,276*
Elmhurst, PA 18416 • *953*
Elmira, NY 14901-99 • *35,327*
Elmira, OR 97437 • *500*
El Mirage, AZ 85335 • *4,307*
Elmira Heights, NY 14903 • *4,279*
Elmo, UT 84521 • *300*
Elmont, NY 11003 • *30,000*
El Monte, CA 91731-35 • *79,494*
Elmora, PA 15737 • *950*
Elmore, AL 36025 • *350*
Elmore, MN 56027 • *882*
Elmore, OH 43416 • *1,271*
Elmore □, AL • *43,390*
Elmore □, ID • *21,565*
Elmore City, OK 73035 • *582*
Elm Springs, AR 72728 • *781*
Elmwood, IL 61529 • *2,117*
Elmwood, MA 02337 • *750*
Elmwood, NE 68349 • *598*
Elmwood, WI 54740 • *885*
Elmwood Park, IL 60635 • *24,016*
Elmwood Park, NJ 07407 • *18,377*
Elmwood Place, OH 45216 • *2,840*
Elnora, IN 47529 • *756*
Eloise, FL 33880 • *1,408*
Elon College, NC 27244 • *2,873*
Elora, TN 37328 • *350*
Eloy, AZ 85231 • *6,240*
El Paso, IL 61738 • *2,676*
El Paso, TX 79901-99 • *425,259*
El Paso □, CO • *309,424*
El Paso □, TX • *479,899*
El Portal, CA 95318 • *850*
El Portal, FL 33138 • *2,055*
El Prado, NM 87529 • *700*
Elrama, PA 15038 • *800*
El Reno, OK 73036 • *15,486*
El Rio, CA 93030 • *5,674*
Elrod, AL 35458 • *350*
Elroy, WI 53929 • *1,504*
Elsa, TX 78543 • *5,061*
Elsah, IL 62028 • *990*
Elsberry, MO 63343 • *1,272*
El Segundo, CA 90245 • *13,752*
Elsie, MI 48831 • *1,022*
Elsinore, UT 84724 • *612*
Elsmere, DE 19805 • *6,493*
Elsmere, KY 41018 • *7,203*
Elsmere, NY 12054 • *5,500*
El Sobrante, CA 94803 • *10,535*
Elton, LA 70532 • *1,450*
El Toro, CA 92630 • *38,153*
Elvaston, IL 62334 • *231*
Elverson, PA 19520 • *530*
Elvins, MO 63601 • *1,548*
Elwood, IN 46036 • *10,867*
Elwood, KS 66024 • *1,275*
Elwood, NE 68937 • *716*
Elwood, NJ 08217 • *900*
Elwood, NY 11731 • *15,400*
Elwood, UT 84337 • *481*
Elwood Park, FL 33505 • *500*
Ely, IA 52227 • *425*
Ely, MN 55731 • *4,820*
Ely, NV 89301 • *4,882*
Elyria, OH 44035-39 • *57,538*
Elysburg, PA 17824 • *1,337*
Elysian, MN 56028 • *454*
Emanuel □, GA • *20,795*
Embarrass, WI 54933 • *496*
Emden, IL 62635 • *527*
Emerado, ND 58228 • *596*
Emerson, AR 71740 • *444*
Emerson, GA 30137 • *1,110*
Emerson, IA 51533 • *502*
Emerson, NE 68733 • *874*
Emerson, NJ 07630 • *7,793*
Emery, SD 57332 • *399*
Emery, UT 84522 • *372*
Emery □, UT • *11,451*
Emily, MN 56447 • *588*
Eminence, KY 40019 • *2,260*
Eminence, MO 65466 • *614*
Emlenton, PA 16373 • *807*
Emlyn, KY 40730 • *300*
Emma, MO 65327 • *267*
Emmaus, PA 18049 • *11,001*

Emmet, AR 71835 • *475*
Emmet ☐, IA • *13,336*
Emmet ☐, MI • *22,992*
Emmetsburg, IA 50536 • *4,621*
Emmett, ID 83617 • *4,605*
Emmett, KS 66422 • *223*
Emmett, MI 48022 • *285*
Emmitsburg, MD 21727 • *1,552*
Emmonak, AK 99581 • *567*
Emmons, MN 56029 • *465*
Emmons ☐, ND • *5,877*
Emory, TX 75440 • *813*
Empire, AL 35063 • *250*
Empire, CO 80438 • *423*
Empire, GA 31026 • *250*
Empire, LA 70050 • *630*
Empire, MI 49630 • *340*
Empire, NV 89405 • *300*
Empire, OH 43926 • *484*
Emporia, KS 66801 • *25,287*
Emporia, VA 23847 • *4,840*
Emporium, PA 15834 • *2,837*
Emsworth, PA 15202 • *3,074*
Encampment, WY 82325 • *611*
Encinal, NM 87014 • *300*
Encinal, TX 78019 • *704*
Encinitas, CA 92024 • *10,796*
Encino, TX 78353 • *500*
Endeavor, PA 16322 • *300*
Endeavor, WI 53930 • *335*
Enderlin, ND 58027 • *1,151*
Endicott, NY 13760 • *14,457*
Endicott, WA 99125 • *290*
Endwell, NY 13760 • *15,999*
Enfield, CT 06082 • *8,151*
Enfield, IL 62835 • *890*
Enfield, ME 04433 • *250*
Enfield, NH 03748 • *1,581*
Enfield, NC 27823 • *2,995*
Engadine, MI 49827 • *500*
Engelhard, NC 27824 • *600*
England, AR 72046 • *3,081*
Engleside, VA 22309 • *21,400*
Englewood, CO 80110-12 • *30,021*
Englewood, FL 33533 • *10,242*
Englewood, NJ 07631-32 • *23,701*
Englewood, OH 45322 • *11,329*
Englewood, TN 37329 • *1,840*
Englewood Cliffs, NJ 07632 • *5,698*
English, IN 47118 • *633*
English Creek, NJ 08330 • *400*
Englishtown, NJ 07726 • *976*
Enid, OK 73701 • *50,363*
Enigma, GA 31749 • *574*
Enka, NC 28728 • *5,567*
Ennis, MT 59729 • *660*
Ennis, TX 75119 • *12,110*
Enoch, UT 84720 • *678*
Enola, PA 17025 • *3,600*
Enon, OH 45323 • *2,597*
Enoree, SC 29335 • *1,107*
Enosburg Falls, VT 05450 • *1,207*
Ensley, FL 32504 • *2,200*
Enterprise, AL 36330 • *18,033*
Enterprise, KS 67441 • *839*
Enterprise, MS 39330 • *607*
Enterprise, OR 97828 • *2,003*
Enterprise, UT 84725 • *905*
Enterprise, WV 26568 • *950*
Entiat, WA 98822 • *445*
Enumclaw, WA 98022 • *5,427*
Enville, TN 38332 • *287*
Eolia, MO 63344 • *401*
Epes, AL 35460 • *399*
Ephraim, UT 84627 • *2,810*
Ephraim, WI 54211 • *319*
Ephrata, PA 17522 • *11,095*
Ephrata, WA 98823 • *5,359*
Epping, NH 03042 • *1,384*
Epps, LA 71237 • *672*
Epworth, IA 52045 • *1,380*
Equality, IL 62934 • *831*
Erath, LA 70533 • *2,133*
Erath ☐, TX • *22,560*
Erdenheim, PA 19118 • *3,300*
Erial, NJ 08081 • *900*
Erick, OK 73645 • *1,375*
Erie, CO 80516 • *1,254*
Erie, IL 61250 • *1,725*
Erie, KS 66733 • *1,415*
Erie, MI 48133 • *700*
Erie, PA 16501-99 • *119,123*
Erie ☐, NY • *1,015,472*
Erie ☐, OH • *79,655*
Erie ☐, PA • *279,780*
Erin, TN 37061 • *1,614*
Erin Springs, OK 73052 • *225*
Erlanger, KY 41018 • *14,433*
Erma, NJ 08204 • *1,200*
Ernest, PA 15739 • *584*
Errol Heights, OR 97266 • *7,800*
Erskine, MN 56535 • *585*
Erving, MA 01344 • *400*
Erwin, NC 28339 • *2,828*
Erwin, TN 37650 • *4,739*
Erwinville, LA 70729 • *475*
Esbon, KS 66941 • *234*
Escalante, UT 84726 • *652*
Escalon, CA 95320 • *3,127*
Escambia ☐, AL • *38,440*
Escambia ☐, FL • *233,794*
Escanaba, MI 49829 • *14,355*
Escatawpa, MS 39552 • *5,367*
Escondido, CA 92025-27 • *64,355*
Eskdale, WV 25075 • *500*
Esko, MN 55733 • *500*
Eskridge, KS 66423 • *603*
Esmeralda ☐, NV • *777*
Esmond, ND 58332 • *337*
Esmond, RI 02917 • *3,500*
Espanola, FL 32010 • *400*
Espanola, NM 87532 • *6,803*
Esparto, CA 95627 • *1,303*
Espy, PA 17815 • *1,652*
Essex, CT 06426 • *2,501*
Essex, IL 60935 • *463*
Essex, IA 51638 • *1,001*
Essex, MD 21221 • *39,614*
Essex, MA 01929 • *1,490*
Essex, MO 63846 • *545*
Essex, NY 12936 • *300*
Essex, VT 05451 • *800*
Essex ☐, MA • *633,632*
Essex ☐, NJ • *851,116*
Essex ☐, NY • *36,176*
Essex ☐, VT • *6,313*
Essex ☐, VA • *8,864*
Essex Fells, NJ 07021 • *2,363*
Essex Junction, VT 05452 • *7,033*
Essexville, MI 48732 • *4,378*
Estacada, OR 97023 • *1,419*
Estancia, NM 87016 • *830*
Estelline, SD 57234 • *719*
Estelline, TX 79233 • *258*
Estell Manor, NJ 08319 • *848*
Estero, FL 33928 • *950*
Estes Park, CO 80517 • *2,703*
Estherville, IA 51334 • *7,518*
Estherwood, LA 70534 • *691*
Estill, SC 29918 • *2,308*
Estill ☐, KY • *14,495*
Estill Springs, TN 37330 • *1,324*
Esto, FL 32425 • *304*
Ethan, SD 57334 • *351*
Ethel, MS 39067 • *486*
Ethel, WV 25076 • *300*
Ether, NC 27247 • *300*
Ethridge, TN 38456 • *548*
Etna, CA 96027 • *754*
Etna, NH 03750 • *300*
Etna, NY 13062 • *500*
Etna, OH 43018 • *550*
Etna, PA 15223 • *4,534*
Etna, WY 83118 • *400*
Etna Green, IN 46524 • *522*
Eton, GA 30724 • *301*
Etowah, TN 37331 • *3,758*
Etowah ☐, AL • *103,057*
Etters, PA 17319 • *477*
Ettrick, VA 23803 • *4,000*
Ettrick, WI 54627 • *462*
Euclid, OH 44117 • *59,999*
Eudora, AR 71640 • *3,840*
Eudora, KS 66025 • *2,934*
Eufaula, AL 36027 • *12,097*
Eufaula, OK 74432 • *3,159*
Eugene, IN 47928 • *350*
Eugene, OR 97401-05 • *105,624*
Eulaton, AL 36201 • *1,869*
Euless, TX 76039-40 • *24,002*
Eulonia, GA 31331 • *350*
Eunice, LA 70535 • *12,479*
Eunice, NM 88231 • *2,970*
Eupora, MS 39744 • *2,048*
Eureka, CA 95501 • *24,153*
Eureka, IL 61530 • *4,306*
Eureka, KS 67045 • *3,425*
Eureka, MO 63025 • *3,862*
Eureka, MT 59917 • *1,119*
Eureka, NV 89316 • *500*
Eureka, NC 27830 • *303*
Eureka, SC 29706 • *1,627*
Eureka, SD 57437 • *1,360*
Eureka, UT 84628 • *670*
Eureka, WI 54934 • *300*
Eureka ☐, NV • *1,198*
Eureka Springs, AR 72632 • *1,989*
Eustis, FL 32726 • *9,453*
Eustis, NE 69028 • *460*
Eutaw, AL 35462 • *2,444*
Eutawville, SC 29048 • *615*
Evangeline, LA 70537 • *300*
Evangeline ☐, LA • *33,343*
Evans, CO 80620 • *5,063*
Evans, GA 30809 • *800*
Evans, WV 25241 • *300*
Evans ☐, GA • *8,428*
Evans City, PA 16033 • *2,299*
Evansdale, IA 50707 • *4,798*
Evans Mills, NY 13637 • *651*
Evansport, OH 43519 • *300*
Evanston, CO 80530 • *300*
Evanston, IL 60201-99 • *73,706*
Evanston, WY 82930 • *6,421*
Evansville, IL 62242 • *863*
Evansville, IN 47701-99 • *130,496*
Evansville, MN 56326 • *571*
Evansville, WI 53536 • *2,835*
Evansville, WY 82636 • *2,335*
Evant, TX 76525 • *425*
Evart, MI 49631 • *1,945*
Evarts, KY 40828 • *1,234*
Eveleth, MN 55734 • *5,042*
Evening Shade, AR 72532 • *397*
Everest, KS 66424 • *331*
Everett, GA 31520 • *300*
Everett, MA 02149 • *37,195*
Everett, PA 15537 • *1,828*
Everett, WA 98201-07 • *54,413*
Evergreen, AL 36401 • *4,171*
Evergreen, CO 80439 • *6,376*
Evergreen, LA 71333 • *272*
Evergreen, NC 28438 • *360*
Evergreen Park, IL 60642 • *22,260*
Everly, IA 51338 • *796*
Everman, TX 76140 • *5,387*
Everson, PA 15631 • *1,032*
Everson, WA 98247 • *898*
Everton, MO 65646 • *317*
Ewa, HI 96706 • *2,637*
Ewa Beach, HI 96706-07 • *14,369*
Ewell, MD 21824 • *350*
Ewen, MI 49925 • *500*
Ewing, IL 62836 • *321*
Ewing, MO 63440 • *400*
Ewing, NE 68735 • *520*
Ewing, VA 24248 • *500*
Ewing Township, NJ 08618 • *34,842*
Excel, AL 36439 • *385*
Excelsior Springs, MO 64024 • *10,424*
Exeter, CA 93221 • *5,606*
Exeter, MO 65647 • *588*
Exeter, NE 68351 • *807*
Exeter, NH 03833 • *8,947*
Exeter, PA 18643 • *5,493*
Exira, IA 50076 • *978*
Exmore, VA 23350 • *1,300*
23350 • *1,300*
Experiment, GA 30212 • *3,000*
Export, PA 15632 • *1,143*
Eyota, MN 55934 • *1,244*

F

Fabens, TX 79838 • *3,500*
Fabius, NY 13063 • *367*
Fabyan, CT 06245 • *250*
Fackler, AL 35746 • *300*
Factoryville, PA 18419 • *924*
Fairacres, NM 88033 • *600*
Fairbank, IA 50629 • *980*
Fairbanks, AK 99701 • *22,645*
Fairbanks, FL 32601 • *500*
Fairbanks, ME 04938 • *300*
Fair Bluff, NC 28439 • *1,095*
Fairborn, OH 45324 • *29,702*
Fairburn, GA 30213 • *3,466*
Fairbury, IL 61739 • *3,544*
Fairbury, NE 68352 • *5,265*
Fairchance, PA 15436 • *2,106*
Fairchild, WI 54741 • *577*
Fairdale, KY 40118 • *7,315*
Fairfax, AL 36854 • *3,776*
Fairfax, CA 94930 • *7,391*
Fairfax, DE 19803 • *2,850*
Fairfax, IA 52228 • *683*
Fairfax, MN 55332 • *1,405*
Fairfax, MO 64446 • *835*
Fairfax, OK 74637 • *1,949*
Fairfax, SC 29827 • *2,154*
Fairfax, SD 57335 • *225*
Fairfax, VT 05454 • *300*
Fairfax, VA 22030-39 • *19,390*
Fairfax ☐, VA • *596,901*
Fairfield, AL 35064 • *13,242*
Fairfield, CA 94533 • *58,099*
Fairfield, CT 06430 • *54,849*
Fairfield, ID 83327 • *404*
Fairfield, IL 62837 • *5,954*
Fairfield, IA 52556 • *9,428*
Fairfield, ME 04937 • *3,169*
Fairfield, MT 59436 • *650*
Fairfield, NE 68938 • *543*
Fairfield, NJ 07006 • *7,987*
Fairfield, NC 27826 • *400*
Fairfield, OH 45014 • *30,777*
Fairfield, PA 17320 • *591*
Fairfield, TX 75840 • *3,505*
Fairfield, WA 99012 • *582*
Fairfield ☐, CT • *807,143*
Fairfield ☐, OH • *93,678*
Fairfield ☐, SC • *20,700*
Fairfield Bay, AR 72088 • *1,000*
Fairgrove, MI 48733 • *691*
Fair Grove, MO 65648 • *863*
Fair Grove, NC 27360 • *1,500*
Fairhaven, MA 02719 • *15,759*
Fair Haven, MI 48023 • *900*
Fair Haven, NJ 07701 • *5,679*
Fair Haven, NY 13064 • *976*
Fair Haven, VT 05743 • *2,819*
Fairhope, AL 36532 • *7,286*
Fairland, IN 46126 • *900*
Fairland, OK 74343 • *1,073*
Fair Lawn, NJ 07410 • *32,229*
Fairlawn, OH 44313 • *6,100*
Fairlawn, VA 24141 • *2,000*
Fairlea, WV 24902 • *1,200*
Fairlee, VT 05045 • *400*
Fairless Hills, PA 19030 • *12,500*
Fairmont, IL 60441 • *2,600*
Fairmont, MN 56031 • *11,506*
Fairmont, NE 68354 • *767*
Fairmont, NC 28340 • *2,658*
Fairmont, OK 73736 • *419*
Fairmont, WV 26554 • *23,863*
Fairmount, GA 30139 • *842*
Fairmount, IL 61841 • *851*
Fairmount, IN 46928 • *3,286*
Fairmount, ND 58030 • *480*
Fairmount, NY 13219 • *8,700*
Fairmount Heights, MD 20743 • *1,616*
Fair Oaks, CA 95628 • *20,235*
Fair Oaks, GA 30060 • *8,486*
Fairoaks, PA 15003 • *1,854*
Fair Plain, MI 49022 • *8,289*
Fairplay, CO 80440 • *421*
Fair Play, MO 65649 • *384*
Fair Play, SC 29643 • *230*
Fairpoint, OH 43927 • *600*
Fairport, NY 14450 • *5,970*
Fairport Harbor, OH 44077 • *3,357*
Fairton, NJ 08320 • *1,107*
Fairview, IL 61432 • *594*
Fairview, KS 66425 • *258*
Fairview, KY 42221 • *250*
Fairview, MI 48621 • *500*
Fairview, MO 64842 • *282*
Fairview, MT 59221 • *1,366*
Fairview, NJ 07022 • *10,519*
Fairview, NY 12601 • *8,517*
Fairview, OH 43736 • *250*
Fairview, OK 73737 • *3,370*
Fairview, OR 97024 • *1,749*
Fairview, PA 16415 • *1,855*
Fairview, TN 37062 • *3,648*
Fairview, UT 84629 • *916*
Fairview, WV 26570 • *759*
Fairview Heights, IL 62208 • *12,414*
Fairview Park, IN 47842 • *1,545*
Fairview Park, OH 44126 • *19,311*
Fairview Shores, FL 32804 • *6,100*
Fair Water, WI 53931 • *310*
Fairway, KS 66205 • *4,619*
Faison, NC 28341 • *636*
Faith, NC 28041 • *552*
Faith, SD 57626 • *576*
Falcon, MS 38628 • *260*
Falcon, NC 28342 • *339*
Falconer, NY 14733 • *2,778*
Falcon Heights, MN 55113 • *5,291*
Falcon Heights, OR 97601 • *1,389*
Falfurrias, TX 78355 • *6,103*
Falkner, MS 38629 • *251*
Falkville, AL 35622 • *1,310*
Fall Branch, TN 37656 • *1,340*
Fallbrook, CA 92028 • *14,041*
Fall City, WA 98024 • *1,600*
Fall Creek, WI 54742 • *1,148*
Falling Water, TN 37343 • *450*
Falling Waters, WV 25419 • *300*
Fall Mountain Lake, CT 06786 • *730*
Fallon, MT 59326 • *265*
Fallon, NV 89406 • *4,262*
Fallon ☐, MT • *3,763*
Fall River, MA 02720-26 • *92,574*
Fall River, WI 53932 • *850*

Fall River □, SD • *8,439*
Fall River Mills, CA 96028 • *900*
Falls □, TX • *17,946*
Falls Church, VA 22040-48 • *9,515*
Falls City, NE 68355 • *5,374*
Falls City, OR 97344 • *804*
Falls Creek, PA 15840 • *1,208*
Fallston, MD 21047 • *5,572*
Fallston, NC 28042 • *614*
Falls Village, CT 06031 • *500*
Falmouth, KY 41040 • *2,482*
Falmouth, ME 04105 • *6,853*
Falmouth, MA 02540-41 • *4,200*
Falmouth, MI 49632 • *260*
Falmouth, VA 22403 • *970*
Fancy Farm, KY 42039 • *400*
Fannettsburg, PA 17221 • *300*
Fannin □, GA • *14,748*
Fannin □, TX • *24,285*
Fanwood, NJ 07023 • *7,767*
Farber, MO 63345 • *503*
Fargo, GA 31631 • *600*
Fargo, ND 58102-99 • *61,383*
Fargo, OK 73840 • *409*
Far Hills, NJ 07931 • *677*
Faribault, MN 55021 • *16,241*
Faribault □, MN • *19,714*
Farina, IL 62838 • *594*
Farley, IA 52046 • *1,287*
Farmer City, IL 61842 • *2,252*
Farmers Branch, TX 75234 • *24,863*
Farmersburg, IN 47850 • *1,240*
Farmersburg, IA 52047 • *276*
Farmersville, CA 93223 • *5,544*
Farmersville, IL 62533 • *686*
Farmersville, TX 75031 • *2,360*
Farmerville, LA 71241 • *3,768*
Farmingdale, ME 04345 • *2,014*
Farmingdale, NJ 07727 • *1,348*
Farmingdale, NY 11735 • *7,946*
Farmington, AR 72730 • *1,283*
Farmington, CT 06032 • *2,000*
Farmington, IL 61531 • *3,118*
Farmington, IA 52626 • *869*
Farmington, ME 04938 • *3,583*
Farmington, MI 48024 • *11,022*
Farmington, MN 55024 • *4,370*
Farmington, MO 63640 • *8,270*
Farmington, NH 03835 • *3,284*
Farmington, NM 87401 • *31,222*
Farmington, UT 84025 • *4,691*
Farmington, WV 26571 • *583*
Farmington Hills, MI 48018 • *58,056*
Farmingville, NY 11738 • *5,700*
Farmland, IN 47340 • *1,560*
Farmville, NC 27828 • *4,707*
Farmville, VA 23901 • *6,067*
Farnam, NE 69029 • *268*
Farnham, VA 22460 • *300*
Farnhamville, IA 50538 • *461*
Farragut, IA 51639 • *603*
Farrell, PA 16121 • *8,645*
Farwell, MI 48622 • *804*
Farwell, TX 79325 • *1,354*
Faulk □, SD • *3,327*
Faulkland Heights, DE 19808 • *1,650*
Faulkner □, AR • *46,192*
Faulkton, SD 57438 • *981*
Fauquier □, VA • *35,889*
Fayette, AL 35555 • *5,287*
Fayette, IA 52142 • *1,515*
Fayette, MS 39069 • *2,033*
Fayette, MO 65248 • *2,983*
Fayette, OH 43521 • *1,222*
Fayette □, AL • *18,809*
Fayette □, GA • *29,043*
Fayette □, IL • *22,167*
Fayette □, IN • *28,272*
Fayette □, IA • *25,488*
Fayette □, KY • *204,165*
Fayette □, OH • *27,467*
Fayette □, PA • *159,417*
Fayette □, TN • *25,305*
Fayette □, TX • *18,832*
Fayette □, WV • *57,863*
Fayetteville, AL 35150 • *300*
Fayetteville, AR 72701 • *36,608*
Fayetteville, GA 30214 • *2,715*
Fayetteville, NC 28301-08 • *59,507*
Fayetteville, OH 45118 • *478*
Fayetteville, PA 17222 • *2,449*
Fayetteville, TN 37334 • *7,559*
Fayetteville, WV 25840 • *2,366*
Fayville, MA 01745 • *1,000*
Feasterville, PA 19047 • *6,900*
Federal Heights, CO 80221 • *7,846*
Federalsburg, MD 21632 • *1,952*
Federal Way, WA 98003 • *17,850*
Fedscreek, KY 41524 • *400*
Feeding Hills, MA 01030 • *8,500*
Felch, MI 49831 • *250*
Felda, FL 33930 • *320*
Felicity, OH 45120 • *929*
Fellowship, NJ 08057 • *1,900*
Fellsmere, FL 32948 • *1,161*
Felton, CA 95018 • *4,000*
Felton, DE 19943 • *547*
Felton, MN 56536 • *264*
Felton, PA 17322 • *483*
Fennimore, WI 53809 • *2,212*
Fennville, MI 49408 • *934*
Fenton, IA 50539 • *394*
Fenton, LA 70640 • *491*
Fenton, MI 48430 • *8,098*
Fentress, TX 78622 • *300*
Fentress □, TN • *14,826*
Fenwick, WV 26202 • *400*
Ferdinand, IN 47532 • *2,192*
Fergus □, MT • *13,076*
Fergus Falls, MN 56537 • *12,519*
Ferguson, KY 42533 • *1,009*
Ferguson, MO 63135 • *24,740*
Fernandina Beach, FL 32034 • *7,224*
Fern Creek, KY 40291 • *16,866*
Ferndale, CA 95536 • *1,367*
Ferndale, MD 21061 • *2,600*
Ferndale, MI 48220 • *26,227*
Ferndale, PA 15905 • *2,204*
Ferndale, WA 98248 • *3,855*
Fernley, NV 89408 • *1,200*
Fernwood, ID 83830 • *680*
Fernwood, MS 39635 • *600*
Ferriday, LA 71334 • *4,472*
Ferris, TX 75125 • *2,228*
Ferron, UT 84523 • *1,718*
Ferrum, VA 24088 • *500*
Ferry □, WA • *5,811*
Ferry Farms, VA 22401 • *1,300*
Ferryville, WI 54628 • *227*
Fertile, IA 50434 • *372*
Fertile, MN 56540 • *869*
Fessenden, ND 58438 • *761*
Festus, MO 63028 • *7,574*
Fieldale, VA 24089 • *1,400*
Field Crest Estates, CT 06355 • *1,200*
Fielding, UT 84311 • *325*
Fieldon, IL 62031 • *299*
Fieldsboro, NJ 08505 • *597*
Fife Lake, MI 49633 • *402*
Fifield, WI 54524 • *300*
Fifty Lakes, MN 56448 • *263*
Fig Garden, CA 93704 • *9,000*
Filer, ID 83328 • *1,645*
Filer City, MI 49634 • *300*
Fillmore, CA 93015 • *9,602*
Fillmore, IL 62032 • *350*
Fillmore, IN 46128 • *550*
Fillmore, MO 64449 • *265*
Fillmore, NY 14735 • *563*
Fillmore, UT 84631 • *2,083*
Fillmore □, MN • *21,930*
Fillmore □, NE • *7,920*
Fincastle, VA 24090 • *282*
Findlay, IL 62534 • *868*
Findlay, OH 45840 • *35,594*
Fine, NY 13639 • *350*
Finger, TN 38334 • *245*
Fingerville, SC 29338 • *300*
Finland, MN 55603 • *300*
Finley, ND 58230 • *718*
Finley, TN 38030 • *1,014*
Finly, IN 46129 • *250*
Finney □, KS • *23,825*
Fircrest, WA 98466 • *5,477*
Firebaugh, CA 93622 • *3,740*
Firestone, CO 80520 • *1,204*
Firth, ID 83236 • *460*
Firth, NE 68358 • *384*
Fish Creek, WI 54212 • *250*
Fisher, AR 72429 • *302*
Fisher, IL 61843 • *1,572*
Fisher, LA 71426 • *325*
Fisher, MN 56723 • *453*
Fisher, PA 16225 • *250*
Fisher □, TX • *5,891*
Fishers, IN 46038 • *2,008*
Fishersville, VA 22939 • *700*
Fishertown, PA 15539 • *400*
Fishing Creek, MD 21634 • *650*
Fishkill, NY 12524 • *1,555*
Fisk, MO 63940 • *450*
Fiskdale, MA 01518 • *1,859*
Fitchburg, MA 01420 • *39,580*
Fitchville, CT 06334 • *600*
Fithian, IL 61844 • *540*
Fittstown, OK 74842 • *500*
Fitzgerald, GA 31750 • *10,187*
Fitzwilliam, NH 03447 • *600*
Fitzwilliam Depot, NH 03447 • *400*
Five Points, NM 87105 • *5,500*
Flagler, CO 80815 • *550*
Flagler □, FL • *10,913*
Flagler Beach, FL 32036 • *2,208*
Flagstaff, AZ 86001 • *34,743*
Flagtown, NJ 08821 • *800*
Flanagan, IL 61740 • *978*
Flanders, NJ 07836 • *6,000*
Flandreau, SD 57028 • *2,114*
Flasher, ND 58535 • *410*
Flathead □, MT • *51,966*
Flat Lick, KY 40935 • *700*
Flatonia, TX 78941 • *1,070*
Flat River, MO 63601 • *4,443*
Flat Rock, IL 62427 • *493*
Flat Rock, IN 47234 • *290*
Flat Rock, MI 48134 • *6,853*
Flat Rock, NC 28731 • *1,200*
Flat Rock, OH 44828 • *390*
Flatwood, AL 36110 • *300*
Flatwoods, KY 41139 • *8,354*
Flatwoods, TN 38458 • *350*
Flatwoods, WV 26621 • *405*
Fleetwood, PA 19522 • *3,422*
Fleischmanns, NY 12430 • *346*
Fleming, CO 80728 • *388*
Fleming, PA 16835 • *361*
Fleming □, KY • *12,323*
Fleming-Neon, KY 41816 • *1,195*
Flemingsburg, KY 41041 • *2,835*
Flemington, GA 31313 • *440*
Flemington, NJ 08822 • *4,132*
Flemington, PA 17745 • *1,416*
Flemington, WV 26347 • *452*
Flensburg, MN 56328 • *256*
Fletcher, NC 28732 • *700*
Fletcher, OH 45326 • *498*
Fletcher, OK 73541 • *1,074*
Flint, MI 48501-99 • *159,611*
Flint City, AL 35601 • *673*
Flint Hill, VA 22627 • *250*
Flintstone, MD 21530 • *250*
Flintville, TN 37335 • *300*
Flippin, AR 72634 • *1,072*
Flomaton, AL 36441 • *1,882*
Floodwood, MN 55736 • *648*
Flora, IL 62839 • *5,379*
Flora, IN 46929 • *2,303*
Flora, MS 39071 • *1,507*
Florahome, FL 32635 • *600*
Florala, AL 36442 • *2,165*
Floral City, FL 32636 • *1,181*
Floral Park, NY 11001-05 • *16,805*
Flora Vista, NM 87415 • *500*
Florence, AL 35630-33 • *37,029*
Florence, AZ 85232 • *3,391*
Florence, CA 90001 • *38,000*
Florence, CO 81226 • *2,987*
Florence, KS 66851 • *729*
Florence, KY 41042 • *15,586*
Florence, MS 39073 • *1,111*
Florence, NJ 08518 • *5,000*
Florence, OR 97439 • *4,411*
Florence, SC 29501-03 • *29,176*
Florence, TX 76527 • *744*
Florence, WI 54121 • *575*
Florence □, SC • *110,163*
Florence □, WI • *4,172*
Floresville, TX 78114 • *4,381*
Florham Park, NJ 07932 • *9,359*
Florida, NY 10921 • *1,947*
Florida, OH 43545 • *294*
Florida City, FL 33034 • *6,174*
Florien, LA 71429 • *964*
Florin, CA 95828 • *16,523*
Florissant, MO 63031-34 • *55,372*
Flossmoor, IL 60422 • *8,423*
Flourtown, PA 19031 • *5,200*
Flovilla, GA 30216 • *458*
Flower Hill, NY 11050 • *4,558*
Flowery Branch, GA 30542 • *755*
Flowood, MS 39208 • *943*
Floyd, IA 50435 • *408*
Floyd, VA 24091 • *411*
Floyd □, GA • *79,800*
Floyd □, IN • *61,205*
Floyd □, IA • *19,597*
Floyd □, KY • *48,764*
Floyd □, TX • *9,834*
Floyd □, VA • *11,563*
Floydada, TX 79235 • *4,193*
Floyds Knobs, IN 47119 • *500*
Flushing, MI 48433 • *8,624*
Flushing, OH 43977 • *1,266*
Fluvanna □, VA • *10,244*
Fly Creek, NY 13337 • *350*
Foard □, TX • *2,158*
Folcroft, PA 19032 • *8,231*
Foley, AL 36535 • *4,003*
Foley, MN 56329 • *1,606*
Folkston, GA 31537 • *2,243*
Follansbee, WV 26037 • *3,994*
Follett, TX 79034 • *547*
Folly Beach, SC 29439 • *1,478*
Folsom, CA 95630 • *11,003*
Folsom, LA 70437 • *319*
Folsom, NJ 08037 • *1,892*
Folsom, PA 19033 • *7,600*
Fonda, IA 50540 • *863*
Fonda, NY 12068 • *1,006*
Fond du Lac, WI 54935 • *35,863*
Fond du Lac □, WI • *88,964*
Fontana, CA 92335 • *37,107*
Fontana, WI 53125 • *1,764*
Fontanelle, IA 50846 • *805*
Fontanet, IN 47851 • *450*
Foothill Farms, CA 95841 • *13,700*
Footville, WI 53537 • *794*
Force, PA 15841 • *400*
Ford, KS 67842 • *272*
Ford, KY 40320 • *250*
Ford □, IL • *15,265*
Ford □, KS • *24,315*
Ford City, CA 93268 • *3,392*
Ford City, PA 16226 • *3,923*
Fordland, MO 65652 • *569*
Fordoche, LA 70732 • *676*
Fords, NJ 08863 • *12,600*
Fords Prairie, WA 98531 • *2,000*
Fordsville, KY 42343 • *561*
Fordville, ND 58231 • *326*
Fordyce, AR 71742 • *5,175*
Foreman, AR 71836 • *1,377*
Forest, IN 46039 • *350*
Forest, MS 39074 • *5,229*
Forest, OH 45843 • *1,633*
Forest □, PA • *5,072*
Forest □, WI • *9,044*
Forest Acres, SC 29206 • *6,071*
Forest City, IL 61532 • *298*
Forest City, IA 50436 • *4,270*
Forest City, MO 64451 • *387*
Forest City, NC 28043 • *7,688*
Forest City, PA 18421 • *1,924*
Forestdale, RI 02824 • *450*
Forest Dale, VT 05745 • *500*
Forest Glen, LA 70445 • *600*
Forest Grove, OR 97116 • *11,499*
Forest Hill, LA 71430 • *494*
Forest Hill, MD 21050 • *550*
Forest Hill, TX 76119 • *11,684*
Forest Hills, PA 15221 • *8,198*
Forest Knolls, CA 94933 • *2,000*
Forest Lake, MI 49862 • *460*
Forest Lake, MN 55025 • *4,596*
Foreston, MN 56330 • *283*
Forest Park, GA 30050 • *18,782*
Forest Park, IL 60130 • *15,177*
Forest Park, LA 71291 • *1,500*
Forest Park, OH 45240 • *18,675*
Forestport, NY 13338 • *500*
Forestville, MD 20747 • *16,401*
Forestville, NY 14062 • *804*
Forestville, PA 16035 • *300*
Forestville, WI 54213 • *455*
Forgan, OK 73938 • *611*
Forge Village, MA 01886 • *1,400*
Forked Island, LA 70510 • *250*
Forked River, NJ 08731 • *1,422*
Forkland, AL 36740 • *429*
Forks, WA 98331 • *3,060*
Fork Union, VA 23055 • *350*
Forman, ND 58032 • *629*
Forney, TX 75126 • *2,483*
Forrest, IL 61741 • *1,246*
Forrest □, MS • *66,018*
Forrest City, AR 72335 • *13,803*
Forreston, IL 61030 • *1,384*
Forsan, TX 79733 • *239*
Forsyth, GA 31029 • *4,624*
Forsyth, IL 62535 • *1,072*
Forsyth, MO 65653 • *1,010*
Forsyth, MT 59327 • *2,553*
Forsyth □, GA • *27,958*
Forsyth □, NC • *243,683*
Fort Ann, NY 12827 • *509*
Fort Apache, AZ 85926 • *350*
Fort Ashby, WV 26719 • *1,200*
Fort Atkinson, IA 52144 • *374*
Fort Atkinson, WI 53538 • *9,785*
Fort Barnwell, NC 28526 • *300*
Fort Belknap Agency, MT 59526 • *500*
Fort Bend □, TX • *130,846*
Fort Benton, MT 59442 • *1,693*
Fort Bidwell, CA 96112 • *230*
Fort Bragg, CA 95437 • *5,019*
Fort Branch, IN 47648 • *2,504*
Fort Calhoun, NE 68023 • *641*
Fort Cobb, OK 73038 • *760*

Fort Collins, CO 80521-26 • 65,092
Fort Covington, NY 12937 • 1,200
Fort Davis, AL 36031 • 300
Fort Davis, TX 79734 • 850
Fort Defiance, AZ 86504 • 3,431
Fort Deposit, AL 36032 • 1,519
Fort Dodge, IA 50501 • 29,423
Fort Dodge, KS 67843 • 300
Fort Edward, NY 12828 • 3,561
Fort Fairfield, ME 04742 • 2,282
Fort Gaines, GA 31751 • 1,260
Fort Garland, CO 81133 • 300
Fort Gay, WV 25514 • 886
Fort Gibson, OK 74434 • 2,477
Fort Hall, ID 83203 • 900
Fort Hancock, TX 79839 • 550
Fort Howard, MD 21052 • 1,050
Fort Jennings, OH 45844 • 538
Fort Jones, CA 96032 • 544
Fort Kent, ME 04743 • 2,375
Fort Laramie, WY 82212 • 356
Fort Lauderdale, FL 33301-99 • 153,279
Fort Lawn, SC 29714 • 471
Fort Lee, NJ 07024 • 32,449
Fort Loramie, OH 45845 • 977
Fort Loudon, PA 17224 • 900
Fort Lupton, CO 80621 • 4,251
Fort Madison, IA 52627 • 13,520
Fort McKinley, OH 45426 • 11,536
Fort Meade, FL 33841 • 5,546
Fort Mill, SC 29715 • 4,162
Fort Mitchell, AL 36856 • 600
Fort Mitchell, KY 41017 • 7,297
Fort Morgan, CO 80701 • 8,768
Fort Myers, FL 33901-14 • 36,638
Fort Myers Beach, FL 33931 • 5,753
Fort Ogden, FL 33842 • 900
Fort Oglethorpe, GA 30742 • 5,443
Fort Payne, AL 35967 • 11,485
Fort Peck, MT 59223 • 600
Fort Pierce, FL 33450-54 • 33,802
Fort Pierre, SD 57532 • 1,789
Fort Plain, NY 13339 • 2,555
Fort Recovery, OH 45846 • 1,370
Fort Scott, KS 66701 • 8,893
Fort Shawnee, OH 45806 • 4,541
Fort Smith, AR 72901-16 • 71,626
Fort Stanton, NM 88323 • 300
Fort Stockton, TX 79735 • 8,688
Fort Sumner, NM 88119 • 1,421
Fort Supply, OK 73841 • 559
Fort Thomas, KY 41075 • 16,012
Fort Thompson, SD 57339 • 300
Fort Totten, ND 58335 • 750
Fort Towson, OK 74735 • 789
Fortuna, CA 95540 • 7,591
Fortuna Ledge (Marshall), AK 99585 • 262
Fort Valley, GA 31030 • 9,000
Fortville, IN 46040 • 2,787
Fort Walton Beach, FL 32548 • 20,829
Fort Washakie, WY 82514 • 250
Fort Washington, PA 19034 • 4,500
Fort Washington Forest, MD 20744 • 1,800
Fort Wayne, IN 46801-99 • 172,028
Fort White, FL 32038 • 386
Fort Wingate, NM 87316 • 900
Fort Worth, TX 76101-99 • 385,164
Fort Wright, KY 41011 • 4,481
Fort Yates, ND 58538 • 771
Forty Fort, PA 18704 • 5,590
Fort Yukon, AK 99740 • 619
Fossil, OR 97830 • 535
Fosston, MN 56542 • 1,599
Foster, OR 97345 • 600
Foster □, ND • 4,611
Foster Brook, PA 16701 • 950
Foster City, CA 94404 • 23,287
Foster City, MI 49834 • 275
Foster Village, HI 96818 • 3,700
Fostoria, IA 51340 • 261
Fostoria, MI 48435 • 365
Fostoria, OH 44830 • 15,743
Fouke, AR 71837 • 614
Fountain, CO 80817 • 8,324
Fountain, FL 32438 • 500
Fountain, MN 55935 • 327
Fountain, NC 27829 • 424
Fountain □, IN • 19,033
Fountain City, IN 47341 • 839
Fountain City, WI 54629 • 963
Fountain Green, UT 84632 • 578
Fountain Hill, AR 71642 • 352
Fountain Hill, PA 18015 • 4,805
Fountain Inn, SC 29644 • 4,226
Fountain Lake, AR 71901 • 250
Fountain Place, LA 70811 • 9,200
Fountain Run, KY 42133 • 340
Fountain Valley, CA 92708 • 55,080
Four Corners, OR 97301 • 11,331
Four Lakes, WA 99014 • 350
Fourmile, KY 40939 • 500
Four Oaks, NC 27524 • 1,049
Fowler, CA 93625 • 2,496
Fowler, CO 81039 • 1,227
Fowler, IL 62338 • 300
Fowler, IN 47944 • 2,319
Fowler, KS 67844 • 592
Fowler, MI 48835 • 1,021
Fowlerton, IN 46930 • 300
Fowlerville, MI 48836 • 2,289
Fowlkes, TN 38033 • 300
Fowlstown, GA 31752 • 250
Fox, OK 73435 • 350
Foxboro, MA 02035 • 5,697
Fox Chapel, PA 15238 • 5,049
Fox Lake, IL 60020 • 6,831
Fox Lake, WI 53933 • 1,373
Fox Point, WI 53217 • 7,649
Fox River Grove, IL 60021 • 2,515
Foxvale, MA 02035 • 500
Foxville, VT 05654 • 300
Foxworth, MS 39483 • 1,000
Frackville, PA 17931 • 5,308
Framingham, MA 01701 • 65,113
Francesville, IN 47946 • 944
Francis, OK 74844 • 365
Francis, UT 84036 • 371
Francisco, IN 47649 • 612
Francis Creek, WI 54214 • 589
Franconia, NH 03580 • 600
Frankenmuth, MI 48734 • 3,753
Frankford, DE 19945 • 828
Frankford, MO 63441 • 443
Frankfort, IL 60423 • 4,357
Frankfort, IN 46041 • 15,168
Frankfort, KS 66427 • 1,038
Frankfort, KY 40601 • 25,973
Frankfort, MI 49635 • 1,603
Frankfort, NY 13340 • 2,995
Frankfort, OH 45628 • 1,008
Franklin, AR 72536 • 253
Franklin, GA 30217 • 711
Franklin, ID 83237 • 423
Franklin, IL 62638 • 645
Franklin, IN 46131 • 11,563
Franklin, KS 66735 • 400
Franklin, KY 42134 • 7,738
Franklin, LA 70538 • 9,584
Franklin, MA 02038 • 18,217
Franklin, MN 55333 • 512
Franklin, NE 68939 • 1,167
Franklin, NH 03235 • 7,901
Franklin, NJ 07416 • 4,486
Franklin, NC 28734 • 2,640
Franklin, NY 13775 • 440
Franklin, OH 45005 • 10,711
Franklin, PA 16323 • 8,146
Franklin, TN 37064 • 12,407
Franklin, TX 77856 • 1,349
Franklin, VA 23851 • 7,308
Franklin, WV 26807 • 780
Franklin, WI 53132 • 16,871
Franklin □, AL • 28,350
Franklin □, AR • 14,705
Franklin □, FL • 7,661
Franklin □, GA • 15,185
Franklin □, ID • 8,895
Franklin □, IL • 43,201
Franklin □, IN • 19,612
Franklin □, IA • 13,036
Franklin □, KS • 22,062
Franklin □, KY • 41,830
Franklin □, LA • 24,141
Franklin □, ME • 27,447
Franklin □, MA • 64,317
Franklin □, MS • 8,208
Franklin □, MO • 71,233
Franklin □, NE • 4,377
Franklin □, NC • 30,055
Franklin □, NY • 44,929
Franklin □, OH • 869,126
Franklin □, PA • 113,629
Franklin □, TN • 31,983
Franklin □, TX • 6,893
Franklin □, VT • 34,788
Franklin □, VA • 35,740
Franklin □, WA • 35,025
Franklin Grove, IL 61031 • 965
Franklin Lakes, NJ 07417 • 8,769
Franklin Mine, MI 49930 • 300
Franklin Park, IL 60131 • 17,507
Franklin Park, PA 15143 • 6,135
Franklin Square, NY 11010 • 32,800
Franklinton, LA 70438 • 4,119
Franklinton, NC 27525 • 1,394
Franklinville, NJ 08322 • 900
Franklinville, NC 27248 • 607
Franklinville, NY 14737 • 1,887
Frankston, TX 75763 • 1,255
Franksville, WI 53126 • 400
Frankton, IN 46044 • 2,080
Fraser, CO 80442 • 470
Fraser, MI 48026 • 14,560
Frazee, MN 56544 • 1,284
Frazer, MT 59225 • 300
Frazeysburg, OH 43822 • 1,025
Frazier Park, CA 93225 • 1,444
Frederic, MI 49733 • 500
Frederic, WI 54837 • 1,039
Frederica, DE 19946 • 864
Frederick, CO 80530 • 855
Frederick, MD 21701 • 28,086
Frederick, OK 73542 • 6,153
Frederick, SD 57441 • 307
Frederick □, MD • 114,792
Frederick □, VA • 34,150
Fredericksburg, IN 47120 • 233
Fredericksburg, IA 50630 • 1,075
Fredericksburg, OH 44627 • 511
Fredericksburg, PA 17026 • 750
Fredericksburg, TX 78624 • 6,412
Fredericksburg, VA 22401-05 • 15,322
Fredericktown, MO 63645 • 4,036
Fredericktown, OH 43019 • 2,299
Fredericktown, PA 15333 • 1,067
Frederika, IA 50631 • 223
Fredonia, AZ 86022 • 1,040
Fredonia, IA 52738 • 224
Fredonia, KS 66736 • 3,047
Fredonia, KY 42411 • 535
Fredonia, NY 14063 • 11,126
Fredonia, PA 16124 • 712
Fredonia, WI 53021 • 1,437
Freeborn, MN 56032 • 323
Freeborn □, MN • 36,329
Freeburg, IL 62243 • 2,989
Freeburg, MO 65035 • 554
Freeburg, PA 17827 • 643
Freedom, CA 95019 • 6,416
Freedom, NH 03836 • 300
Freedom, OK 73842 • 339
Freedom, PA 15042 • 2,272
Freedom, WI 54131 • 300
Freehold, NJ 07728 • 10,020
Freeland, MI 48623 • 1,364
Freeland, PA 18224 • 4,285
Freelandville, IN 47535 • 680
Freeman, MO 64746 • 485
Freeman, SD 57029 • 1,462
Freemansburg, PA 18017 • 1,879
Freemanville, AL 36502 • 300
Freeport, FL 32439 • 669
Freeport, IL 61032 • 26,266
Freeport, ME 04032 • 1,906
Freeport, MI 49325 • 479
Freeport, MN 56331 • 563
Freeport, NY 11520 • 38,272
Freeport, OH 43973 • 525
Freeport, PA 16229 • 2,381
Freeport, TX 77541 • 13,444
Freer, TX 78357 • 3,213
Freestone □, TX • 14,830
Freetown, IN 47235 • 600
Freeville, NY 13068 • 449
Fremont, CA 94536-39 • 131,945
Fremont, IN 46737 • 1,180
Fremont, IA 52561 • 730
Fremont, MI 49412 • 3,672
Fremont, NE 68025 • 23,979
Fremont, NH 03044 • 450
Fremont, NC 27830 • 1,736
Fremont, OH 43420 • 17,834
Fremont, WI 54940 • 510
Fremont □, CO • 28,676
Fremont □, ID • 10,813
Fremont □, IA • 9,401
Fremont □, WY • 38,992
Frenchburg, KY 40322 • 550
French Camp, MS 39745 • 306
French Gulch, CA 96033 • 600
French Island, WI 54601 • 3,000
French Lick, IN 47432 • 2,265
French River, MN 55804 • 400
French Settlement, LA 70733 • 761
Frenchtown, NJ 08825 • 1,573
Frenchville, ME 04745 • 615
Fresno, CA 93701-99 • 217,289
Fresno □, CA • 514,229
Frewsburg, NY 14738 • 2,000
Friant, CA 93626 • 500
Friars Point, MS 38631 • 1,400
Friday Harbor, WA 98250 • 1,200
Fridley, MN 55432 • 30,228
Friedens, PA 18080 • 900
Friend, NE 68359 • 1,079
Friendship, ME 04547 • 585
Friendship, NY 14739 • 1,285
Friendship, OH 45630 • 600
Friendship, TN 38034 • 763
Friendship, WI 53934 • 744
Friendsville, MD 21531 • 511
Friendsville, TN 37737 • 694
Friendswood, TX 77546 • 10,719
Fries, VA 24330 • 758
Friesland, WI 53935 • 267
Frio □, TX • 13,785
Friona, TX 79035 • 3,809
Frisco, CO 80443 • 1,221
Frisco, NC 27936 • 300
Frisco City, AL 36445 • 1,424
Fritch, TX 79036 • 2,299
Frohna, MO 63748 • 265
Froid, MT 59226 • 323
Fromberg, MT 59029 • 469
Frontenac, KS 66762 • 2,586
Frontier, WY 83121 • 250
Frontier □, NE • 3,647
Front Royal, VA 22630 • 11,126
Frost, MN 56033 • 293
Frost, TX 76641 • 564
Frostburg, MD 21532 • 7,715
Frostproof, FL 33843 • 2,995
Fruita, CO 81521 • 2,810
Fruitdale, AL 36539 • 400
Fruit Heights, UT 84037 • 2,728
Fruithurst, AL 36262 • 239
Fruitland, ID 83619 • 2,559
Fruitland, IA 52749 • 461
Fruitland, KS 67301 • 400
Fruitland, MD 21826 • 2,694
Fruitland, NM 87416 • 700
Fruitland Park, FL 32731 • 2,259
Fruitport, MI 49415 • 1,143
Fruitvale, CO 81504 • 400
Fruitvale, WA 98902 • 3,600
Fruitville, FL 33582 • 3,070
Fryburg, PA 16326 • 300
Fryeburg, ME 04037 • 1,644
Fulda, MN 56131 • 1,308
Fullerton, CA 92631-35 • 102,034
Fullerton, KY • 500
Fullerton, NE 68638 • 1,506
Fulshear, TX 77441 • 594
Fulton, AL 36446 • 606
Fulton, AR 71838 • 326
Fulton, IL 61252 • 3,936
Fulton, IN 46931 • 393
Fulton, KY 42041 • 3,137
Fulton, MD 20759 • 600
Fulton, MI 49052 • 750
Fulton, MI 49950 • 400
Fulton, MS 38843 • 3,238
Fulton, MO 65251 • 11,046
Fulton, NY 13069 • 13,312
Fulton, OH 43321 • 378
Fulton □, AR • 9,975
Fulton □, GA • 589,904
Fulton □, IL • 43,687
Fulton □, IN • 19,335
Fulton □, KY • 8,971
Fulton □, NY • 55,153
Fulton □, OH • 37,751
Fulton □, PA • 12,842
Fultondale, AL 35068 • 6,217
Funkstown, MD 21734 • 1,103
Fuquay-Varina, NC 27526 • 3,110
Furman, SC 29921 • 348
Furnas □, NE • 6,486
Future City, IL 62914 • 250
Fyffe, AL 35971 • 1,305

G

Gaastra, MI 49927 • 404
Gabbs, NV 89409 • 811
Gabriels, NY 12939 • 250
Gackle, ND 58442 • 456
Gadsden, AL 35901-05 • 47,565
Gadsden, AZ 85336 • 500
Gadsden, TN 38337 • 683
Gadsden □, FL • 41,565
Gaffney, SC 29340 • 13,453
Gage, OK 73843 • 667
Gage □, NE • 24,456
Gagetown, MI 48735 • 428
Gahanna, OH 43230 • 18,001
Gaines, MI 48436 • 440
Gaines □, TX • 13,150
Gainesboro, TN 38562 • 1,119
Gainesville, FL 32601-14 • 81,371
Gainesville, GA 30501-06 • 15,280
Gainesville, MO 65655 • 707
Gainesville, NY 14066 • 334
Gainesville, TX 76240 • 14,081

Gainesville, VA 22065 • *600*
Gaither, MD 21735 • *300*
Gaithersburg, MD 20877-79 • *26,424*
Galatia, IL 62935 • *1,042*
Galax, VA 24333 • *6,524*
Galena, AK 99741 • *765*
Galena, IL 61036 • *3,876*
Galena, KS 66739 • *3,587*
Galena, MD 21635 • *374*
Galena, MO 65656 • *423*
Galena, OH 43021 • *358*
Galena Park, TX 77547 • *9,879*
Galesburg, IL 61401 • *35,305*
Galesburg, MI 49053 • *1,822*
Gales Ferry, CT 06335 • *1,191*
Galesville, MD 20765 • *600*
Galesville, WI 54630 • *1,239*
Galeton, PA 16922 • *1,462*
Galeville, NY 13088 • *5,600*
Galien, MI 49113 • *692*
Galilee, RI 02882 • *300*
Galion, OH 44833 • *12,391*
Gallant, AL 35972 • *550*
Gallatin, MO 64640 • *2,063*
Gallatin, TN 37066 • *17,191*
Gallatin □, IL • *7,590*
Gallatin □, KY • *4,842*
Gallatin □, MT • *42,865*
Gallaway, TN 38036 • *804*
Gallia □, OH • *30,098*
Galliano, LA 70354 • *5,159*
Gallina, NM 87017 • *400*
Gallipolis, OH 45631 • *5,576*
Gallipolis Ferry, WV 25515 • *400*
Gallitzin, PA 16641 • *2,315*
Galloway, OH 43119 • *400*
Galloway, WV 26349 • *400*
Gallup, NM 87301 • *18,167*
Galt, CA 95632 • *5,514*
Galt, MO 64641 • *323*
Galva, IL 61434 • *3,185*
Galva, IA 51020 • *420*
Galva, KS 67443 • *651*
Galveston, IN 46932 • *1,822*
Galveston, TX 77550-53 • *61,902*
Galveston □, TX • *195,940*
Gamaliel, KY 42140 • *456*
Gambell, AK 99742 • *445*
Gambier, OH 43022 • *2,056*
Gambrills, MD 21054 • *650*
Gamerco, NM 87317 • *400*
Ganado, AZ 86505 • *1,200*
Ganado, TX 77962 • *1,770*
Gang Mills, NY 14870 • *1,258*
Gannon, MD 21562 • *360*
Gans, OK 74936 • *346*
Gansevoort, NY 12831 • *400*
Gantt, AL 36038 • *314*
Gantt, SC 29605 • *1,600*
Gap, PA 17527 • *1,022*
Gapland, MD 21736 • *225*
Garber, OK 73738 • *1,215*
Garberville, CA 95440 • *1,200*
Garciasville, TX 78547 • *400*
Garden, MI 49835 • *296*
Garden □, NE • *2,802*
Gardena, CA 90247-49 • *45,165*
Garden City, AL 35070 • *655*
Garden City, GA 31408 • *6,895*
Garden City, ID 83704 • *4,571*
Garden City, KS 67846 • *18,256*
Garden City, LA 70540 • *225*
Garden City, MI 48135 • *35,640*
Garden City, MN 56034 • *250*
Garden City, MO 64747 • *1,021*
Garden City, NY 11530 • *22,927*
Garden City, TX 79739 • *300*
Garden City, UT 84028 • *259*
Garden City Park, NY 11040 • *5,200*
Gardendale, AL 35071 • *7,928*
Garden Grove, CA 92640-45 • *123,307*
Garden Grove, IA 50103 • *297*
Garden Home, OR 97223 • *5,500*
Garden Plain, KS 67050 • *775*
Garden Prairie, IL 61038 • *350*
Garden Valley, ID 83622 • *320*
Gardiner, ME 04345 • *6,485*
Gardiner, MT 59030 • *600*
Gardiner, OR 97441 • *600*
Gardner, IL 60424 • *1,322*
Gardner, KS 66030 • *2,392*
Gardner, MA 01440 • *17,900*
Gardnerville, NV 89410 • *2,800*
Garfield, KS 67529 • *277*
Garfield, MN 56332 • *284*
Garfield, NJ 07026 • *26,803*
Garfield, NM 87936 • *300*
Garfield, WA 99130 • *599*
Garfield □, CO • *22,514*
Garfield □, MT • *1,656*
Garfield □, NE • *2,363*
Garfield □, OK • *62,820*
Garfield □, UT • *3,673*
Garfield □, WA • *2,468*
Garfield Heights, OH 44125 • *34,938*
Garfield Park, DE 19720 • *1,000*
Garibaldi, OR 97118 • *999*
Garland, AR 71839 • *660*
Garland, NE 68360 • *257*
Garland, NC 28441 • *885*
Garland, PA 16416 • *400*
Garland, TN 38019 • *301*
Garland, TX 75040-43 • *138,857*
Garland, UT 84312 • *1,405*
Garland □, AR • *70,531*
Garnavillo, IA 52049 • *723*
Garner, IA 50438 • *2,908*
Garner, KY 41817 • *400*
Garner, NC 27529 • *10,073*
Garnett, KS 66032 • *3,310*
Garrard □, KY • *10,853*
Garretson, SD 57030 • *963*
Garrett, IN 46738 • *4,751*
Garrett, KY 41630 • *300*
Garrett, PA 15542 • *563*
Garrett □, MD • *26,498*
Garrett Park, MD 20896 • *2,800*
Garrettsville, OH 44231 • *1,769*
Garrison, IA 52229 • *411*
Garrison, KY 41141 • *650*
Garrison, MD 21055 • *750*
Garrison, ND 58540 • *1,830*
Garrison, NY 10524 • *650*
Garrison, TX 75946 • *1,059*
Garvin □, OK • *27,856*
Garwin, IA 50632 • *626*
Garwood, NJ 07027 • *4,752*
Garwood, TX 77442 • *600*
Gary, IN 46401-99 • *151,953*
Gary, MN 56545 • *241*
Gary, SD 57237 • *354*
Gary, TX 75643 • *322*
Gary, WV 24836 • *2,233*
Garysburg, NC 27831 • *1,434*
Garyville, LA 70051 • *2,856*
Garza □, TX • *5,336*
Gas, KS 66742 • *543*
Gas City, IN 46933 • *6,370*
Gasconade, MO 65036 • *250*
Gasconade □, MO • *13,181*
Gasport, NY 14067 • *950*
Gassaway, WV 26624 • *1,225*
Gassville, AR 72635 • *859*
Gaston, IN 47342 • *1,150*
Gaston, NC 27832 • *883*
Gaston, OR 97119 • *471*
Gaston, SC 29053 • *960*
Gaston □, NC • *162,568*
Gastonia, NC 28052-54 • *47,333*
Gate City, VA 24251 • *2,494*
Gates, NC 27937 • *300*
Gates, NY 14624 • *29,756*
Gates, OR 97346 • *455*
Gates, TN 38037 • *729*
Gates □, NC • *8,875*
Gatesville, NC 27938 • *363*
Gatesville, TX 76528 • *6,260*
Gatlinburg, TN 37738 • *3,210*
Gauley Bridge, WV 25085 • *1,177*
Gause, TX 77857 • *500*
Gautier, MS 39553 • *8,917*
Gaylord, MI 49735 • *3,011*
Gaylord, MN 55334 • *1,933*
Gaylordsville, CT 06755 • *300*
Gays, IL 61928 • *290*
Gays Mills, WI 54631 • *627*
Gayville, SD 57031 • *407*
Gearhart, OR 97138 • *967*
Geary, OK 73040 • *1,700*
Geary □, KS • *29,852*
Geauga □, OH • *74,474*
Geddes, SD 57342 • *303*
Geff, IL 62842 • *340*
Geistown, PA 15904 • *3,304*
Gem □, ID • *11,972*
Genesee, ID 83832 • *791*
Genesee, MI 48437 • *950*
Genesee, PA 16923 • *300*
Genesee □, MI • *450,449*
Genesee □, NY • *59,400*
Genesee Depot, WI 53127 • *400*
Geneseo, IL 61254 • *6,373*
Geneseo, KS 67444 • *496*
Geneseo, NY 14454 • *6,746*
Geneva, AL 36340 • *4,866*
Geneva, GA 31810 • *232*
Geneva, IL 60134 • *9,881*
Geneva, IN 46740 • *1,430*
Geneva, NE 68361 • *2,400*
Geneva, NY 14456 • *15,133*
Geneva, OH 44041 • *6,655*
Geneva, PA 16316 • *260*
Geneva □, AL • *24,253*
Geneva-on-the-Lake, OH 44041 • *1,634*
Genoa, IL 60135 • *3,276*
Genoa, NE 68640 • *1,090*
Genoa, NY 13071 • *300*
Genoa, OH 43430 • *2,213*
Genoa, WI 54632 • *283*
Genoa City, WI 53128 • *1,202*
Genola, UT 84655 • *630*
Gentry, AR 72734 • *1,468*
Gentry □, MO • *7,887*
Gentryville, IN 47537 • *299*
George, IA 51237 • *1,241*
George, NC 27833 • *250*
George □, MS • *15,297*
Georgetown, CA 95634 • *2,000*
Georgetown, CO 80444 • *830*
Georgetown, CT 06829 • *1,834*
Georgetown, DE 19947 • *1,710*
Georgetown, FL 32039 • *400*
Georgetown, GA 31754 • *935*
Georgetown, ID 83239 • *544*
Georgetown, IL 61846 • *4,220*
Georgetown, IN 47122 • *1,494*
Georgetown, KY 40324 • *10,972*
Georgetown, LA 71432 • *381*
Georgetown, MA 01833 • *2,600*
Georgetown, MS 39078 • *343*
Georgetown, NY 13072 • *300*
Georgetown, OH 45121 • *3,467*
Georgetown, SC 29440 • *10,144*
Georgetown, TX 78626 • *9,468*
Georgetown □, SC • *42,461*
George West, TX 78022 • *2,627*
Georgiana, AL 36033 • *1,993*
Gerald, MO 63037 • *921*
Geraldine, AL 35974 • *911*
Geraldine, MT 59446 • *305*
Gerber, CA 96035 • *950*
Gering, NE 69341 • *7,760*
Germania, NJ 08215 • *300*
Germantown, IL 62245 • *1,191*
Germantown, KY 41044 • *347*
Germantown, MD 20874 • *9,721*
Germantown, OH 45327 • *5,015*
Germantown, TN 38138 • *21,482*
Germantown, WI 53022 • *10,729*
Germfask, MI 49836 • *250*
Geronimo, OK 73543 • *726*
Gerrardstown, WV 25420 • *250*
Gervais, OR 97026 • *799*
Gettysburg, OH 45328 • *545*
Gettysburg, PA 17325 • *7,194*
Gettysburg, SD 57442 • *1,623*
Geyserville, CA 95441 • *950*
Ghent, KY 41045 • *439*
Ghent, MN 56239 • *356*
Ghent, NY 12075 • *600*
Giants Neck, CT 06357 • *1,150*
Gibbon, MN 55335 • *787*
Gibbon, NE 68840 • *1,531*
Gibbstown, NJ 08027 • *5,676*
Gibsland, LA 71028 • *1,354*
Gibson, GA 30810 • *730*
Gibson, LA 70356 • *400*
Gibson, NC 28343 • *533*
Gibson, TN 38338 • *458*
Gibson □, IN • *33,156*
Gibson □, TN • *49,467*
Gibsonburg, OH 43431 • *2,479*
Gibson City, IL 60936 • *3,498*
Gibsonia, PA 15044 • *2,065*
Gibsonton, FL 33534 • *3,700*
Gibsonville, NC 27249 • *2,865*
Giddings, TX 78942 • *3,950*
Gideon, MO 63848 • *1,240*
Gifford, FL 32960 • *6,240*
Gifford, IL 61847 • *848*
Gifford, PA 16732 • *500*
Gig Harbor, WA 98335 • *2,429*
Gila, NM 88038 • *350*
Gila □, AZ • *37,080*
Gila Bend, AZ 85337 • *1,585*
Gilbert, AZ 85234 • *5,717*
Gilbert, IA 50105 • *805*
Gilbert, LA 71336 • *800*
Gilbert, MN 55741 • *2,721*
Gilbert, OR 97266 • *4,000*
Gilbert, WV 25621 • *757*
Gilbertsville, KY 42044 • *250*
Gilbertsville, NY 13776 • *455*
Gilbertsville, PA 19525 • *900*
Gilbertville, IA 50634 • *740*
Gilbertville, MA 01031 • *1,029*
Gilby, ND 58235 • *283*
Gilchrist, OR 97737 • *600*
Gilchrist □, FL • *5,767*
Gilcrest, CO 80623 • *1,025*
Gildford, MT 59525 • *300*
Giles □, TN • *24,625*
Giles □, VA • *17,810*
Gillespie, IL 62033 • *3,740*
Gillespie □, TX • *13,532*
Gillett, AR 72055 • *927*
Gillett, PA 16925 • *250*
Gillett, WI 54124 • *1,356*
Gillette, WY 82716 • *12,134*
Gillham, AR 71841 • *252*
Gilliam, LA 71029 • *244*
Gilliam, MO 65330 • *227*
Gilliam □, OR • *2,057*
Gilman, CO 81634 • *350*
Gilman, IL 60938 • *1,913*
Gilman, IA 50106 • *642*
Gilman, VT 05904 • *550*
Gilman, WI 54433 • *436*
Gilman City, MO 64642 • *414*
Gilmanton, NH 03237 • *600*
Gilmanton Iron Works, NH 03837 • *400*
Gilmer, TX 75644 • *5,167*
Gilmer □, GA • *11,110*
Gilmer □, WV • *8,334*
Gilmore, AR 72339 • *503*
Gilmore City, IA 50541 • *626*
Gilpin □, CO • *2,441*
Gilroy, CA 95020 • *21,641*
Gilson, IL 61436 • *235*
Gilsum, NH 03448 • *500*
Giltner, NE 68841 • *400*
Girard, GA 30426 • *225*
Girard, IL 62640 • *2,246*
Girard, KS 66743 • *2,888*
Girard, OH 44420 • *12,517*
Girard, PA 16417 • *2,615*
Girardville, PA 17935 • *2,268*
Girdletree, MD 21829 • *300*
Glacier □, MT • *10,628*
Gladbrook, IA 50635 • *970*
Glades □, FL • *5,992*
Glade Spring, VA 24340 • *1,722*
Gladewater, TX 75647 • *6,548*
Gladstone, IL 61437 • *354*
Gladstone, MI 49837 • *4,533*
Gladstone, MO 64118 • *24,990*
Gladstone, NJ 07934 • *2,038*
Gladstone, ND 58630 • *317*
Gladstone, OR 97027 • *9,500*
Gladwin, MI 48624 • *2,479*
Gladwin □, MI • *19,957*
Glandorf, OH 45848 • *746*
Glasco, KS 67445 • *710*
Glasco, NY 12432 • *1,169*
Glascock □, GA • *2,382*
Glasford, IL 61533 • *1,201*
Glasgow, KY 42141 • *12,958*
Glasgow, MO 65254 • *1,336*
Glasgow, MT 59230 • *4,455*
Glasgow, VA 24555 • *1,259*
Glasgow, WV 25086 • *1,031*
Glasgow Village, MO 63137 • *7,200*
Glassboro, NJ 08028 • *14,574*
Glasscock □, TX • *1,304*
Glassport, PA 15045 • *6,242*
Glastonbury, CT 06033 • *7,049*
Gleason, TN 38229 • *1,335*
Gleasondale, MA 01775 • *275*
Glen Allan, MS 38744 • *600*
Glen Allen, AL 35559 • *312*
Glen Allen, VA 23060 • *1,100*
Glen Alpine, NC 28628 • *645*
Glen Arbor, MI 49636 • *250*
Glen Avon, CA 92509 • *8,444*
Glenbeulah, WI 53023 • *423*
Glenbrook, NV 89413 • *300*
Glenburn, ND 58740 • *454*
Glen Burnie, MD 21061 • *30,000*
Glen Campbell, PA 15742 • *352*
Glen Carbon, IL 62034 • *5,197*
Glencoe, AL 35905 • *4,648*
Glencoe, IL 60022 • *9,200*
Glencoe, KY 41046 • *354*
Glencoe, MN 55336 • *4,396*
Glencoe, MO 63038 • *500*
Glencoe, OK 74032 • *490*
Glen Cove, NY 11542 • *24,618*
Glendale, AZ 85301-11 • *97,172*
Glendale, CA 91201-99 • *139,060*
Glendale, CO 80222 • *2,496*
Glendale, KY 42740 • *300*
Glendale, MA 01229 • *375*
Glendale, MS 39401 • *1,329*
Glendale, MO 63122 • *6,035*
Glendale, OH 45246 • *2,368*
Glendale, OR 97442 • *712*
Glendale, RI 02826 • *600*

Glendale, SC 29346 • *1,049*
Glendale, UT 84729 • *237*
Glen Dale, WV 26038 • *1,875*
Glendale, WI 53209 • *13,882*
Glendale Heights, IL 60139 • *23,163*
Glendale Heights, WV 26038 • *700*
Glendive, MT 59330 • *5,978*
Glendo, WY 82213 • *367*
Glendola, NJ 07719 • *2,300*
Glendora, CA 91740 • *38,500*
Glendora, NJ 08029 • *5,632*
Glen Echo, MD 20812 • *229*
Glen Elder, KS 67446 • *491*
Glen Ellyn, IL 60137 • *23,717*
Glen Ferris, WV 25090 • *250*
Glenfield, NY 13343 • *300*
Glen Flora, TX 77443 • *400*
Glen Gardner, NJ 08826 • *834*
Glenham, NY 12527 • *2,720*
Glen Head, NY 11545 • *6,800*
Glen Jean, WV 25846 • *500*
Glen Lyon, PA 18617 • *3,408*
Glenmont, OH 44628 • *270*
Glenmora, LA 71433 • *1,479*
Glenn □, CA • *21,350*
Glennallen, AK 99588 • *511*
Glenns Ferry, ID 83623 • *1,374*
Glennville, GA 30427 • *4,144*
Glenolden, PA 19036 • *7,633*
Glenoma, WA 98336 • *300*
Glenpool, OK 74033 • *2,706*
Glen Raven, NC 27215 • *2,755*
Glenridge, MA 02030 • *250*
Glen Ridge, NJ 07028 • *7,855*
Glen Rock, NJ 07452 • *11,497*
Glen Rock, PA 17327 • *1,662*
Glenrock, WY 82637 • *2,736*
Glen Rose, TX 76043 • *2,075*
Glen Saint Mary, FL 32040 • *462*
Glens Falls, NY 12801 • *15,897*
Glenshaw, PA 15116 • *14,000*
Glenside, PA 19038 • *17,400*
Glen Ullin, ND 58631 • *1,125*
Glenview, IL 60025 • *32,060*
Glenvil, NE 68941 • *363*
Glenville, MN 56036 • *851*
Glenville, NC 28736 • *500*
Glenville, WV 26351 • *2,155*
Glen White, WV 25849 • *500*
Glenwood, AL 36034 • *341*
Glenwood, AR 71943 • *1,402*
Glenwood, FL 32722 • *950*
Glenwood, GA 30428 • *824*
Glenwood, IL 60425 • *10,538*
Glenwood, IN 46133 • *370*
Glenwood, IA 51534 • *5,280*
Glenwood, MN 56334 • *2,523*
Glenwood, UT 84730 • *447*
Glenwood, VA 24541 • *1,000*
Glenwood, WA 98619 • *300*
Glenwood City, WI 54013 • *950*
Glenwood Farms, VA 23223 • *3,200*
Glenwood Springs, CO 81601 • *4,637*
Glidden, IA 51443 • *1,076*
Glidden, WI 54527 • *550*
Glide, OR 97443 • *900*
Globe, AZ 85501 • *6,886*
Globe, KY 41164 • *250*
Gloster, MS 39638 • *1,726*
Gloucester, MA 01930 • *27,768*
Gloucester, VA 23061 • *900*
Gloucester □, NJ • *199,917*
Gloucester □, VA • *20,107*
Gloucester City, NJ 08030 • *13,121*
Gloucester Point, VA 23062 • *850*
Glouster, OH 45732 • *2,211*
Glover, VT 05839 • *300*
Gloversville, NY 12078 • *17,836*
Gloverville, SC 29828 • *2,619*
Gluck, SC 29621 • *650*
Glyndon, MD 21071 • *1,100*
Glyndon, MN 56547 • *882*
Glynn □, GA • *54,981*
Gnadenhutten, OH 44629 • *1,320*
Gobles, MI 49055 • *816*
Goddard, KS 67052 • *1,427*
Godfrey, IL 62035 • *2,600*
Godley, TX 76044 • *614*
Godwin, NC 28344 • *233*
Goessel, KS 67053 • *421*
Goffstown, NH 03045 • *2,500*
Gogebic □, MI • *19,686*
Golconda, IL 62938 • *960*
Gold Bar, WA 98251 • *794*
Gold Beach, OR 97444 • *1,515*
Golden, CO 80401-19 • *12,237*
Golden, IL 62339 • *558*
Golden, MS 38847 • *292*
Golden Beach, FL 33160 • *612*
Golden City, MO 64748 • *900*
Goldendale, WA 98620 • *3,575*
Golden Meadow, LA 70357 • *2,282*
Golden Valley, MN 55427 • *22,775*
Goldenvalley, ND 58541 • *287*
Golden Valley □, MT • *1,026*
Golden Valley □, ND • *2,391*
Goldfield, IA 50542 • *789*
Goldfield, NV 89013 • *300*
Gold Hill, NC 28071 • *350*
Gold Hill, OR 97525 • *904*
Goldonna, LA 71031 • *526*
Goldsboro, NC 27530 • *31,871*
Goldsby, OK 73093 • *603*
Goldsmith, IN 46045 • *235*
Goldsmith, TX 79741 • *409*
Goldston, NC 27252 • *353*
Goldthwaite, TX 76844 • *1,783*
Goleta, CA 93117 • *28,100*
Golf Manor, OH 45237 • *4,317*
Goliad, TX 77963 • *1,990*
Goliad □, TX • *5,193*
Goltry, OK 73739 • *305*
Gonvick, MN 56644 • *362*
Gonzales, CA 93926 • *2,891*
Gonzales, LA 70737 • *7,287*
Gonzales, TX 78629 • *7,152*
Gonzales □, TX • *16,949*
Gonzalez, FL 32560 • *6,084*
Goochland, VA 23063 • *450*
Goochland □, VA • *11,761*
Goodfield, IL 61742 • *500*
Good Hope, IL 61438 • *457*
Good Hope, OH 43160 • *300*
Goodhue, MN 55027 • *657*
Goodhue □, MN • *38,749*
Gooding, ID 83330 • *2,949*
Gooding □, ID • *11,874*
Goodland, FL 33933 • *1,000*
Goodland, IN 47948 • *1,200*
Goodland, KS 67735 • *5,708*
Goodlettsville, TN 37072 • *8,327*
Goodman, MS 39079 • *1,285*
Goodman, MO 64843 • *1,030*
Goodman, WI 54125 • *600*
Good Pine, LA 71342 • *900*
Goodrich, ND 58444 • *288*
Goodrich, TX 77335 • *350*
Goodsprings, AL 35560 • *400*
Good Thunder, MN 56037 • *560*
Goodview, MN 55987 • *2,567*
Goodwater, AL 35072 • *1,895*
Goodwell, OK 73939 • *1,186*
Goodyear, AZ 85323 • *2,747*
Goose Creek, SC 29445 • *17,811*
Goose Lake, IA 52750 • *274*
Gordo, AL 35466 • *2,112*
Gordon, AL 36343 • *362*
Gordon, GA 31031 • *2,768*
Gordon, NE 69343 • *2,167*
Gordon, OH 45329 • *230*
Gordon, TX 76453 • *516*
Gordon, WI 54838 • *350*
Gordon □, GA • *30,070*
Gordonsville, TN 38563 • *893*
Gordonsville, VA 22942 • *1,421*
Gordonville, MO 63752 • *267*
Gore, OK 74435 • *445*
Goree, TX 76363 • *524*
Goreville, IL 62939 • *978*
Gorham, IL 62940 • *381*
Gorham, KS 67640 • *355*
Gorham, ME 04038 • *4,052*
Gorham, NH 03581 • *2,180*
Gorham, NY 14461 • *800*
Gorman, TX 76454 • *1,258*
Goshen, AL 36035 • *365*
Goshen, CT 06756 • *450*
Goshen, IN 46526 • *19,665*
Goshen, MA 01032 • *350*
Goshen, NH 03752 • *300*
Goshen, NJ 08218 • *400*
Goshen, NY 10924 • *4,874*
Goshen, OH 45122 • *1,400*
Goshen, UT 84633 • *582*
Goshen □, WY • *12,040*
Gosnell, AR 72319 • *3,215*
Gosper □, NE • *2,140*
Gosport, IN 47433 • *729*
Gotebo, OK 73041 • *457*
Gotham, WI 53540 • *250*
Gothenburg, NE 69138 • *3,479*
Gough, GA 30811 • *300*
Gould, AR 71643 • *1,671*
Gould, OK 73544 • *318*
Goulds, FL 33170 • *7,078*
Gouldsboro, ME 04607 • *300*
Gouldsboro, PA 18424 • *600*
Gouldtown, NJ 08302 • *250*
Gouverneur, NY 13642 • *4,285*
Gove □, KS • *3,726*
Government Camp, OR 97028 • *400*
Gowanda, NY 14070 • *2,713*
Gowen, MI 49326 • *350*
Gowen, OK 74545 • *350*
Gower, MO 64454 • *1,276*
Gowrie, IA 50543 • *1,089*
Grabill, IN 46741 • *658*
Grace, ID 83241 • *1,216*
Grace, MS 38745 • *240*
Gracemont, OK 73042 • *503*
Graceville, FL 32440 • *2,918*
Graceville, MN 56240 • *780*
Gracewood, GA 30812 • *500*
Grady, AR 71644 • *488*
Grady □, GA • *19,845*
Grady □, OK • *39,490*
Graettinger, IA 51342 • *923*
Graford, TX 76045 • *495*
Grafton, IL 62037 • *1,024*
Grafton, IA 50440 • *255*
Grafton, MA 01519 • *2,000*
Grafton, ND 58237 • *5,293*
Grafton, NY 12082 • *500*
Grafton, OH 44044 • *2,231*
Grafton, VT 05146 • *300*
Grafton, VA 23692 • *900*
Grafton, WV 26354 • *6,845*
Grafton, WI 53024 • *8,381*
Grafton □, NH • *65,806*
Graham, CA 90002 • *10,600*
Graham, KY 42344 • *400*
Graham, MO 64455 • *253*
Graham, NC 27253 • *8,674*
Graham, OK 73437 • *250*
Graham, TX 76046 • *9,170*
Graham □, AZ • *22,862*
Graham □, KS • *3,995*
Graham □, NC • *7,217*
Grahamsville, NY 12740 • *500*
Grahamville, SC 29936 • *260*
Grahn, KY 41142 • *500*
Grainfield, KS 67737 • *417*
Grainger □, TN • *16,751*
Grain Valley, MO 64029 • *1,327*
Grambling, LA 71245 • *4,226*
Gramercy, LA 70052 • *3,211*
Gramling, SC 29348 • *300*
Grammer, IN 47236 • *255*
Grampian, PA 16838 • *464*
Granada, CO 81041 • *557*
Granada, MN 56039 • *377*
Granbury, TX 76048 • *3,332*
Granby, CO 80446 • *963*
Granby, CT 06035 • *1,192*
Granby, MA 01033 • *1,302*
Granby, MO 64844 • *1,908*
Grand □, CO • *7,475*
Grand □, UT • *8,241*
Grand Bay, AL 36541 • *3,185*
Grand Blanc, MI 48439 • *6,848*
Grand Caillou, LA 70360 • *1,400*
Grand Cane, LA 71032 • *252*
Grand Canyon, AZ 86023 • *1,348*
Grand Chenier, LA 70643 • *300*
Grand Coteau, LA 70541 • *1,165*
Grand Coulee, WA 99133 • *1,180*
Grand Ecore, LA 71457 • *450*
Grandfalls, TX 79742 • *635*
Grandfield, OK 73546 • *1,445*
Grand Forks, ND 58201 • *43,765*
Grand Forks □, ND • *66,100*
Grand Gorge, NY 12434 • *800*
Grand Haven, MI 49417 • *11,763*
Grandin, MO 63943 • *265*
Grand Island, NE 68801 • *33,180*
Grand Isle, LA 70358 • *1,982*
Grand Isle, ME 04746 • *460*
Grand Isle □, VT • *4,613*
Grand Junction, CO 81501-05 • *27,956*
Grand Junction, IA 50107 • *970*
Grand Junction, MI 49056 • *250*
Grand Junction, TN 38039 • *360*
Grand Lake, CO 80447 • *382*
Grand Ledge, MI 48837 • *6,920*
Grand Marais, MI 49839 • *400*
Grand Marais, MN 55604 • *1,289*
Grand Meadow, MN 55936 • *965*
Grand Mound, IA 52751 • *674*
Grand Prairie, TX 75050-52 • *71,462*
Grand Rapids, MI 49501-99 • *181,843*
Grand Rapids, MN 55744 • *7,934*
Grand Rapids, OH 43522 • *962*
Grand Ridge, FL 32442 • *591*
Grand Ridge, IL 61325 • *684*
Grand Rivers, KY 42045 • *428*
Grand Ronde, OR 97347 • *550*
Grand Saline, TX 75140 • *2,709*
Grand Terrace, CA 92324 • *8,498*
Grand Tower, IL 62942 • *748*
Grand Traverse □, MI • *54,899*
Grand View, ID 83624 • *366*
Grandview, IN 47615 • *670*
Grandview, IA 52752 • *473*
Grandview, MO 64030 • *24,502*
Grandview, TN 37337 • *300*
Grandview, WA 98930 • *5,615*
Grand View, WI 54839 • *250*
Grandview Heights, OH 43212 • *7,420*
Grandville, MI 49418 • *12,412*
Grandy, NC 27939 • *600*
Granger, IN 46530 • *600*
Granger, IA 50109 • *619*
Granger, TX 76530 • *1,236*
Granger, WA 98932 • *1,812*
Grangeville, ID 83530 • *3,666*
Granite, OK 73547 • *1,617*
Granite, UT 84070 • *650*
Granite □, MT • *2,700*
Granite City, IL 62040 • *36,815*
Granite Falls, MN 56241 • *3,451*
Granite Falls, NC 28630 • *2,580*
Granite Falls, WA 98252 • *911*
Granite Park, UT 84106 • *5,554*
Granite Quarry, NC 28072 • *1,294*
Graniteville, MA 01886 • *1,000*
Graniteville, SC 29829 • *1,158*
Graniteville, VT 05654 • *1,800*
Grannis, AR 71944 • *349*
Grant, AL 35747 • *632*
Grant, FL 32949 • *900*
Grant, MI 49327 • *683*
Grant, NE 69140 • *1,270*
Grant, OK 74738 • *273*
Grant □, AR • *13,008*
Grant □, IN • *80,934*
Grant □, KS • *6,977*
Grant □, KY • *13,308*
Grant □, LA • *16,703*
Grant □, MN • *7,171*
Grant □, NE • *877*
Grant □, NM • *26,204*
Grant □, ND • *4,274*
Grant □, OK • *6,518*
Grant □, OR • *8,210*
Grant □, SD • *9,013*
Grant □, WA • *48,522*
Grant □, WV • *10,210*
Grant □, WI • *51,736*
Grant City, MO 64456 • *1,068*
Granton, WI 54436 • *399*
Grant Park, IL 60940 • *1,038*
Grants, NM 87020 • *11,439*
Grantsboro, NC 28529 • *550*
Grantsburg, WI 54840 • *1,153*
Grants Pass, OR 97526-27 • *15,032*
Grantsville, MD 21536 • *498*
Grantsville, UT 84029 • *4,419*
Grantsville, WV 26147 • *788*
Grant Town, WV 26574 • *987*
Grantville, GA 30220 • *1,110*
Grantville, PA 17028 • *300*
Granville, IL 61326 • *1,537*
Granville, IA 51022 • *336*
Granville, MA 01034 • *300*
Granville, ND 58741 • *281*
Granville, NY 12832 • *2,696*
Granville, OH 43023 • *3,851*
Granville, WV 26534 • *992*
Granville □, NC • *34,043*
Grapeland, TX 75844 • *1,634*
Grapeview, WA 98546 • *500*
Grapevine, KY 42431 • *900*
Grapevine, TX 76051 • *11,801*
Grasonville, MD 21638 • *1,910*
Grasselli, AL 35020 • *2,400*
Grassflat, PA 16839 • *750*
Grass Lake, IL 60002 • *2,191*
Grass Lake, MI 49240 • *962*
Grass Valley, CA 95945 • *6,697*
Gratiot, OH 43740 • *227*
Gratiot, WI 53541 • *280*
Gratiot □, MI • *40,448*
Gratis, OH 45330 • *809*
Gratz, PA 17030 • *678*
Graves □, KY • *34,049*
Gravette, AR 72736 • *1,218*
Gravity, IA 50848 • *245*
Gray, GA 31032 • *2,145*
Gray, KY 40734 • *750*
Gray, LA 70359 • *4,000*
Gray, ME 04039 • *900*
Gray, PA 15544 • *400*
Gray □, KS • *5,138*
Gray □, TX • *26,386*
Gray Court, SC 29645 • *988*
Gray Gables, MA 02532 • *500*

Grayland, WA 98547 • *600*
Grayling, MI 49738 • *1,792*
Graylyn Crest, DE 19810 • *5,000*
Grays Harbor □, WA • *66,314*
Grayslake, IL 60030 • *5,260*
Grayson, AL 35562 • *300*
Grayson, GA 30221 • *464*
Grayson, KY 41143 • *3,423*
Grayson, LA 71435 • *564*
Grayson □, KY • *20,854*
Grayson □, TX • *89,796*
Grayson □, VA • *16,579*
Grays River, WA 98621 • *300*
Gray Summit, MO 63039 • *500*
Graysville, AL 35073 • *2,642*
Graysville, TN 37338 • *1,380*
Grayville, IL 62844 • *2,313*
Greasewood, AZ 86505 • *450*
Great Barrington, MA 01230 • *3,150*
Great Bend, KS 67530 • *16,608*
Great Bend, PA 18821 • *740*
Great Cacapon, WV 25422 • *500*
Great Falls, MT 59401-06 • *56,725*
Great Falls, SC 29055 • *2,601*
Great Neck, NY 11020-24 • *5,604*
Great Neck Estates, NY 11021 • *2,936*
Greece, NY 14616 • *63,700*
Greeley, CO 80631-39 • *53,006*
Greeley, IA 52050 • *313*
Greeley, KS 66033 • *405*
Greeley, NE 68842 • *597*
Greeley, PA 18425 • *400*
Greeley □, KS • *1,845*
Greeley □, NE • *3,462*
Greeleyville, SC 29056 • *593*
Green, OR 97470 • *3,897*
Green □, KY • *11,043*
Green □, WI • *30,012*
Green Acres, DE 19803 • *1,200*
Greenacres, WA 99016 • *3,650*
Greenacres City, FL 33463 • *8,843*
Greenback, TN 37742 • *546*
Greenbackville, VA 23356 • *300*
Green Bay, WI 54301-99 • *87,899*
Greenbelt, MD 20770 • *17,332*
Greenbriar, VA 22033 • *6,000*
Greenbrier, AR 72058 • *1,423*
Green Brier, TN 37073 • *3,180*
Greenbrier □, WV • *37,665*
Green Brook, NJ 08812 • *4,500*
Greenbush, MN 56726 • *817*
Green Camp, OH 43322 • *475*
Greencastle, IN 46135 • *8,403*
Green Castle, MO 63544 • *285*
Greencastle, PA 17225 • *3,679*
Green City, MO 63545 • *719*
Green Cove Springs, FL 32043 • *4,154*
Green Creek, NJ 08219 • *500*
Greendale, IN 47025 • *3,795*
Greendale, WI 53129 • *16,928*
Greene, IA 50636 • *1,332*
Greene, ME 04236 • *300*
Greene, NY 13778 • *1,747*
Greene □, AL • *11,021*
Greene □, AR • *30,744*
Greene □, GA • *11,391*
Greene □, IL • *16,661*
Greene □, IN • *30,416*
Greene □, IA • *12,119*
Greene □, MS • *9,827*
Greene □, MO • *185,302*
Greene □, NC • *16,117*
Greene □, NY • *40,861*
Greene □, OH • *129,769*
Greene □, PA • *40,476*
Greene □, TN • *54,422*
Greene □, VA • *7,625*
Greeneville, TN 37743 • *14,097*
Greenfield, CA 93927 • *4,181*
Greenfield, IL 62044 • *1,090*
Greenfield, IN 46140 • *11,299*
Greenfield, IA 50849 • *2,243*
Greenfield, MA 01301 • *14,198*
Greenfield, MO 65661 • *1,394*
Greenfield, NH 03047 • *500*
Greenfield, OH 45123 • *5,150*
Greenfield, OK 73043 • *233*
Greenfield, TN 38230 • *2,109*
Greenfield, WI 53220 • *31,467*
Greenfield Plaza, IA 50315 • *2,100*
Green Forest, AR 72638 • *1,609*
Green Harbor, MA 02041 • *2,002*
Greenhill, AL 35630 • *550*
Greenhills, OH 45218 • *4,927*
Green Island, NY 12183 • *2,696*
Green Isle, MN 55338 • *357*
Green Lake, WI 54941 • *1,208*
Green Lake □, WI • *18,370*
Greenland, AR 72737 • *622*
Greenland, MI 49929 • *400*
Greenland, NH 03840 • *600*
Greenlawn, NY 11740 • *8,600*
Greenleaf, KS 66943 • *462*
Greenleaf, WI 54126 • *400*
Greenlee □, AZ • *11,406*
Green Manorville, CT 06082 • *3,250*
Green Mountain Falls, CO 80819 • *607*
Greenock, PA 15047 • *2,800*
Green Pond, AL 35074 • *500*
Greenport, NY 11944 • *2,273*
Green Ridge, MO 65332 • *488*
Green River, UT 84525 • *1,048*
Green River, WY 82935 • *12,807*
Green Rock, IL 61241 • *3,324*
Greensboro, AL 36744 • *3,248*
Greensboro, FL 32330 • *562*
Greensboro, GA 30642 • *2,985*
Greensboro, MD 21639 • *1,253*
Greensboro, NC 27401-99 • *155,642*
Greensboro, PA 15338 • *377*
Greensburg, IN 47240 • *9,254*
Greensburg, KS 67054 • *1,885*
Greensburg, KY 42743 • *2,377*
Greensburg, LA 70441 • *662*
Greensburg, PA 15601 • *17,558*
Greens Fork, IN 47345 • *426*
Green Spring, WV 26722 • *250*
Green Springs, OH 44836 • *1,568*
Greensville □, VA • *10,903*
Greentop, MO 63546 • *538*
Greentown, IN 46936 • *2,265*
Green Tree, PA 15220 • *5,722*
Greenup, IL 62428 • *1,655*
Greenup, KY 41144 • *1,386*
Greenup □, KY • *39,132*
Green Valley, AZ 85614 • *7,999*
Green Valley, IL 61534 • *768*
Greenview, IL 62642 • *830*
Greenville, AL 36037 • *7,807*
Greenville, CA 95947 • *1,537*
Greenville, DE 19807 • *500*
Greenville, FL 32331 • *1,096*
Greenville, GA 30222 • *1,213*
Greenville, IL 62246 • *5,271*
Greenville, IN 47124 • *537*
Greenville, KY 42345 • *4,631*
Greenville, ME 04441 • *1,640*
Greenville, MI 48838 • *8,019*
Greenville, MS 38701-03 • *40,613*
Greenville, NH 03048 • *1,447*
Greenville, NC 27834 • *35,740*
Greenville, NY 10583 • *5,500*
Greenville, OH 45331 • *12,999*
Greenville, PA 16125 • *7,730*
Greenville, RI 02828 • *7,576*
Greenville, SC 29601-16 • *58,242*
Greenville, TX 75401 • *22,161*
Greenville, VA 24440 • *350*
Greenville, WI 54942 • *225*
Greenville □, SC • *287,913*
Greenville Junction, ME 04442 • *600*
Greenwald, MN 56335 • *259*
Greenway, AR 72430 • *317*
Greenwich, CT 06830 • *59,578*
Greenwich, NJ 08323 • *400*
Greenwich, NY 12834 • *1,955*
Greenwich, OH 44837 • *1,458*
Greenwood, AR 72936 • *3,317*
Greenwood, DE 19950 • *578*
Greenwood, FL 32443 • *577*
Greenwood, IN 46142 • *19,327*
Greenwood, LA 71033 • *1,043*
Greenwood, MS 38930 • *20,115*
Greenwood, MO 64034 • *1,315*
Greenwood, NE 68366 • *587*
Greenwood, NY 14839 • *450*
Greenwood, PA 16601 • *1,700*
Greenwood, SC 29646 • *21,613*
Greenwood, WI 54437 • *1,124*
Greenwood □, KS • *8,764*
Greenwood □, SC • *57,847*
Greenwood Lake, NY 10925 • *2,809*
Greenwood Village, CO 80110 • *5,729*
Greer, SC 29651 • *10,525*
Greer □, OK • *7,028*
Gregg □, TX • *99,495*
Gregory, MI 48137 • *350*
Gregory, NC 27973 • *250*
Gregory, SD 57533 • *1,503*
Gregory □, SD • *6,015*
Greilickville, MI 49684 • *1,000*
Grenada, CA 96038 • *450*
Grenada, MS 38901 • *12,641*
Grenada □, MS • *21,043*
Grenola, KS 67346 • *335*
Grenora, ND 58845 • *362*
Gresham, NE 68367 • *320*
Gresham, OR 97030 • *33,005*
Gresham, WI 54128 • *534*
Gresham Park, GA 30316 • *6,232*
Gretna, FL 32332 • *1,448*
Gretna, LA 70053 • *20,615*
Gretna, NE 68028 • *1,609*
Gretna, VA 24557 • *1,255*
Greybull, WY 82426 • *2,277*
Grey Eagle, MN 56336 • *338*
Gridley, CA 95948 • *3,982*
Gridley, IL 61744 • *1,246*
Gridley, KS 66852 • *404*
Griffin, GA 30223 • *20,728*
Griffith, IN 46319 • *17,026*
Griffithsville, WV 25521 • *350*
Griffithville, AR 72060 • *254*
Grifton, NC 28530 • *2,179*
Griggs □, ND • *3,714*
Griggstown, NJ 08540 • *400*
Griggsville, IL 62340 • *1,301*
Grimes, AL 36301 • *298*
Grimes, IA 50111 • *1,973*
Grimes □, TX • *13,580*
Grimesland, NC 27837 • *453*
Grimsley, TN 38565 • *600*
Grindall Creek, VA 23234 • *1,900*
Grinnell, IA 50112 • *8,868*
Grinnell, KS 67738 • *410*
Griswold, IA 51535 • *1,176*
Griswoldville, MA 01340 • *300*
Groesbeck, OH 45239 • *9,594*
Groesbeck, TX 76642 • *3,373*
Groom, TX 79039 • *736*
Grosse Ile, MI 48138 • *9,320*
Grosse Pointe, MI 48236 • *5,901*
Grosse Pointe Park, MI 48236 • *13,639*
Grosse Pointe Woods, MI 48236 • *18,886*
Grosse Tete, LA 70740 • *749*
Grossmont, CA 92041 • *2,600*
Grosvenor Dale, CT 06246 • *700*
Groton, CT 06340 • *10,086*
Groton, MA 01450 • *1,264*
Groton, NY 13073 • *2,313*
Groton, SD 57445 • *1,230*
Groton, VT 05046 • *438*
Groton Long Point, CT 06340 • *800*
Grottoes, VA 24441 • *1,369*
Grove, OK 74344 • *3,378*
Grove City, FL 33533 • *2,587*
Grove City, MN 56243 • *596*
Grove City, OH 43123 • *16,816*
Grove City, PA 16127 • *8,162*
Grove Hill, AL 36451 • *1,912*
Groveland, CA 95321 • *350*
Groveland, FL 32736 • *1,992*
Groveland, MA 01834 • *4,300*
Groveland, NY 14462 • *350*
Groveport, OH 43125 • *3,286*
Grover, NC 28073 • *597*
Grover City, CA 93433 • *8,827*
Grover Hill, OH 45849 • *486*
Groves, TX 77619 • *17,090*
Groveton, NH 03582 • *1,389*
Groveton, TX 75845 • *1,262*
Groveton, VA 22306 • *6,800*
Groveton Gardens, VA 22303 • *2,800*
Grovetown, GA 30813 • *3,384*
Groveville, NJ 08620 • *1,200*
Grubbs, AR 72431 • *546*
Gruetli-Laager, TN 37339 • *2,000*
Grulla, TX 78548 • *1,442*
Grundy, VA 24614 • *1,699*
Grundy □, IL • *30,582*
Grundy □, IA • *14,366*
Grundy □, MO • *11,959*
Grundy □, TN • *13,787*
Grundy Center, IA 50638 • *2,880*
Gruver, TX 79040 • *1,216*
Gu Achi, AZ 85634 • *265*
Guadalupe, AZ 85283 • *4,506*
Guadalupe, CA 93434 • *3,629*
Guadalupe □, NM • *4,496*
Guadalupe □, TX • *46,708*
Guadalupita, NM 87722 • *250*
Gualala, CA 95445 • *700*
Guernsey, WY 82214 • *1,512*
Guernsey □, OH • *42,024*
Gueydan, LA 70542 • *1,695*
Guide Rock, NE 68942 • *344*
Guild, NH 03754 • *350*
Guilford, CT 06437 • *2,555*
Guilford, ME 04443 • *1,235*
Guilford, NY 13780 • *300*
Guilford □, NC • *317,154*
Guin, AL 35563 • *2,418*
Gulf, NC 27256 • *250*
Gulf □, FL • *10,658*
Gulf Breeze, FL 32561 • *5,478*
Gulf Gate Estates, FL 33581 • *9,428*
Gulf Hammock, FL 32639 • *400*
Gulfport, FL 33737 • *11,180*
Gulf Port, IL 52601 • *224*
Gulfport, MS 39501-03 • *39,676*
Gulf Shores, AL 36542 • *1,349*
Gum Springs, AR 71923 • *255*
Gunnison, CO 81230 • *5,785*
Gunnison, MS 38746 • *708*
Gunnison, UT 84634 • *1,255*
Gunnison □, CO • *10,689*
Guntersville, AL 35976 • *7,041*
Guntown, MS 38849 • *359*
Gurdon, AR 71743 • *2,707*
Gurley, AL 35748 • *735*
Gurnee, IL 60031 • *7,179*
Gustine, CA 95322 • *3,142*
Gustine, TX 76455 • *416*
Guthrie, KY 42234 • *1,361*
Guthrie, OK 73044 • *10,312*
Guthrie, TX 79236 • *250*
Guthrie, WV 25312 • *800*
Guthrie □, IA • *11,983*
Guthrie Center, IA 50115 • *1,713*
Guttenberg, IA 52052 • *2,428*
Guttenberg, NJ 07093 • *7,340*
Guymon, OK 73942 • *8,492*
Guys Mills, PA 16327 • *275*
Guyton, GA 31312 • *749*
Gwinhurst, DE 19809 • *1,400*
Gwinn, MI 49841 • *1,408*
Gwinner, ND 58040 • *725*
Gwinnett □, GA • *166,903*
Gwynneville, IN 46144 • *250*
Gypsum, CO 81637 • *743*
Gypsum, KS 67448 • *423*
Gypsum, OH 43433 • *250*

H

Haakon □, SD • *2,794*
Habersham □, GA • *25,020*
Hacienda Heights, CA 91745 • *49,422*
Hackberry, LA 70645 • *800*
Hackensack, MN 56452 • *285*
Hackensack, NJ 07601-08 • *36,039*
Hackett, AR 72937 • *505*
Hackettstown, NJ 07840 • *8,850*
Hackleburg, AL 35564 • *883*
Hadar, NE 68738 • *286*
Haddam, CT 06438 • *600*
Haddam, KS 66944 • *239*
Haddock, GA 31033 • *700*
Haddonfield, NJ 08033 • *12,337*
Haddon Heights, NJ 08035 • *8,361*
Hadley, MA 01035 • *890*
Hadley, NY 12835 • *500*
Hadlock, WA 98339 • *950*
Hadlyme, CT 06439 • *450*
Hagan, GA 30429 • *880*
Hagerman, ID 83332 • *602*
Hagerman, NM 88232 • *936*
Hagerstown, IN 47346 • *1,950*
Hagerstown, MD 21740 • *34,132*
Hague, NY 12836 • *600*
Hahira, GA 31632 • *1,534*
Hahnville, LA 70057 • *2,947*
Haigler, NE 69030 • *225*
Haiku, HI 96708 • *619*
Hailesboro, NY 13645 • *300*
Hailey, ID 83333 • *2,109*
Haileyville, OK 74546 • *832*
Haines, AK 99827 • *993*
Haines, OR 97833 • *341*
Haines City, FL 33844 • *10,799*
Haines Falls, NY 12436 • *700*
Hainesport, NJ 08036 • *900*
Hakalau, HI 96710 • *250*
Halaula, HI 96755 • *300*
Halawa Heights, HI 96701 • *7,000*
Halbur, IA 51444 • *229*
Haldeman, KY 40329 • *250*
Hale, MI 48739 • *350*
Hale, MO 64643 • *529*
Hale □, AL • *15,604*
Hale □, TX • *37,592*
Hale Center, TX 79041 • *2,297*
Haledon, NJ 07508 • *6,607*
Haleiwa, HI 96712 • *2,412*
Hales Corners, WI 53130 • *7,110*
Halethorpe, MD 21227 • *20,163*
Haleyville, AL 35565 • *5,306*
Half Hollow Hills, NY 11746 • *12,800*
Half Moon Bay, CA 94019 • *7,282*
Halfway, MD 21740 • *8,659*
Halfway, OR 97834 • *380*

Halifax, MA 02338 • *900*
Halifax, NC 27839 • *253*
Halifax, PA 17032 • *909*
Halifax, VA 24558 • *772*
Halifax □, NC • *55,286*
Halifax □, VA • *30,599*
Haliimaile, HI 96768 • *741*
Hall, NY 14463 • *300*
Hall □, GA • *75,649*
Hall □, NE • *47,690*
Hall □, TX • *5,594*
Hallam, NE 68368 • *290*
Hallandale, FL 33009 • *36,517*
Hallettsville, TX 77964 • *2,865*
Halliday, ND 58636 • *355*
Hallie, WI 54729 • *1,223*
Hallock, MN 56728 • *1,405*
Hallowell, ME 04347 • *2,502*
Halls, TN 38040 • *2,444*
Hallsboro, NC 28442 • *500*
Halls Crossroads, TN 37918 • *1,600*
Hallstead, PA 18822 • *1,280*
Hall Summit, LA 71034 • *276*
Hallsville, MO 65255 • *624*
Hallsville, TX 75650 • *1,556*
Hallwood, VA 23359 • *243*
Halsey, OR 97348 • *693*
Halstad, MN 56548 • *690*
Halstead, KS 67056 • *1,994*
Haltom City, TX 76117 • *29,014*
Hamblen □, TN • *49,300*
Hamburg, AR 71646 • *3,394*
Hamburg, IA 51640 • *1,597*
Hamburg, NJ 07419 • *1,832*
Hamburg, NY 14075 • *10,582*
Hamburg, PA 19526 • *4,011*
Hamburg, WI 54438 • *250*
Hamden, CT 06514 • *51,071*
Hamden, OH 45634 • *1,010*
Hamel, MN 55340 • *2,623*
Hamer, SC 29547 • *425*
Hamersville, OH 45130 • *688*
Hamilton, AL 35570 • *5,093*
Hamilton, GA 31811 • *506*
Hamilton, IL 62341 • *3,509*
Hamilton, IN 46742 • *587*
Hamilton, KS 66853 • *363*
Hamilton, MA 01936 • *1,000*
Hamilton, MI 49419 • *800*
Hamilton, MS 39746 • *500*
Hamilton, MO 64644 • *1,582*
Hamilton, MT 59840 • *2,661*
Hamilton, NC 27840 • *638*
Hamilton, NY 13346 • *3,725*
Hamilton, OH 45011-26 • *63,189*
Hamilton, TX 76531 • *3,189*
Hamilton, VA 22068 • *598*
Hamilton, WA 98255 • *268*
Hamilton □, FL • *8,761*
Hamilton □, IL • *9,172*
Hamilton □, IN • *82,027*
Hamilton □, IA • *17,862*
Hamilton □, KS • *2,514*
Hamilton □, NE • *9,301*
Hamilton □, NY • *5,034*
Hamilton □, OH • *873,224*
Hamilton □, TN • *287,740*
Hamilton □, TX • *8,297*
Hamilton City, CA 95951 • *800*
Hamilton Square, NJ 08690 • *10,000*
Ham Lake, MN 55303 • *7,832*
Hamler, OH 43524 • *625*
Hamlet, IN 46532 • *738*
Hamlet, NC 28345 • *4,720*
Hamlin, PA 18427 • *300*
Hamlin, TX 79520 • *3,248*
Hamlin, WV 25523 • *1,219*
Hamlin □, SD • *5,261*
Hammett, ID 83627 • *250*
Hammon, OK 73650 • *866*
Hammond, IL 61929 • *556*
Hammond, IN 46320-27 • *93,714*
Hammond, LA 70401 • *15,043*
Hammond, NY 13646 • *271*
Hammond, OR 97121 • *516*
Hammond, WI 54015 • *991*
Hammondsport, NY 14840 • *1,065*
Hammonton, NJ 08037 • *12,298*
Hampden, ME 04444 • *2,300*
Hampden, MA 01036 • *700*
Hampden □, MA • *443,018*
Hampden Highlands, ME 04444 • *1,540*
Hampshire, IL 60140 • *1,735*
Hampshire □, MA • *138,813*
Hampshire □, WV • *14,867*
Hampstead, MD 21074 • *1,293*
Hampstead, NH 03841 • *500*
Hampstead, NC 28443 • *700*
Hampton, AR 71744 • *1,627*
Hampton, CT 06247 • *320*
Hampton, FL 32044 • *466*
Hampton, GA 30228 • *2,059*
Hampton, IA 50441 • *4,630*
Hampton, MN 55031 • *299*
Hampton, NE 68843 • *419*
Hampton, NH 03842 • *6,779*
Hampton, NJ 08827 • *1,614*
Hampton, NY 12837 • *400*
Hampton, SC 29924 • *3,143*
Hampton, TN 37658 • *2,236*
Hampton, VA 23660-70 • *122,617*
Hampton □, SC • *18,159*
Hampton Bays, NY 11946 • *3,550*
Hampton Beach, NH 03842 • *900*
Hampton Falls, NH 03844 • *500*
Hamtramck, MI 48212 • *21,300*
Hana, HI 96713 • *643*
Hanahan, SC 29410 • *13,224*
Hanalei, HI 96714 • *483*
Hanamaulu, HI 96715 • *3,227*
Hanapepe, HI 96716 • *1,417*
Hanceville, AL 35077 • *2,220*
Hancock, IA 51536 • *254*
Hancock, ME 04640 • *400*
Hancock, MD 21750 • *1,887*
Hancock, MI 49930 • *5,122*
Hancock, MN 56244 • *877*
Hancock, NH 03449 • *400*
Hancock, NY 13783 • *1,526*
Hancock, WI 54943 • *419*
Hancock □, GA • *9,466*
Hancock □, IL • *23,877*
Hancock □, IN • *43,939*
Hancock □, IA • *13,833*
Hancock □, KY • *7,742*
Hancock □, ME • *41,781*
Hancock □, MS • *24,537*
Hancock □, OH • *64,581*
Hancock □, TN • *6,887*
Hancock □, WV • *41,053*
Hancocks Bridge, NJ 08038 • *600*
Hand □, SD • *4,948*
Handley, WV 25102 • *633*
Hanford, CA 93230 • *20,958*
Hanging Rock, OH 45635 • *353*
Hankinson, ND 58041 • *1,158*
Hanley Falls, MN 56245 • *265*
Hanna, IN 46340 • *500*
Hanna, WY 82327 • *2,288*
Hanna City, IL 61536 • *1,361*
Hannawa Falls, NY 13647 • *500*
Hannibal, MO 63401 • *18,811*
Hannibal, NY 13074 • *680*
Hannibal, OH 43931 • *650*
Hanover, CT 06350 • *300*
Hanover, IL 61041 • *1,069*
Hanover, IN 47243 • *4,054*
Hanover, KS 66945 • *802*
Hanover, MA 02339 • *2,500*
Hanover, MI 49241 • *490*
Hanover, MN 55341 • *647*
Hanover, NH 03755 • *6,861*
Hanover, NJ • *11,846*
Hanover, NM 88041 • *500*
Hanover, OH 43055 • *926*
Hanover, PA 17331 • *14,890*
Hanover, VA 23069 • *300*
Hanover □, VA • *50,398*
Hanover Center, MA 02339 • *1,000*
Hanover Park, IL 60103 • *28,850*
Hanoverton, OH 44423 • *490*
Hansen, ID 83334 • *1,078*
Hansford □, TX • *6,209*
Hanska, MN 56041 • *429*
Hanson, KY 42413 • *485*
Hanson, MA 02341 • *2,120*
Hanson □, SD • *3,415*
Hanston, KS 67849 • *257*
Hapeville, GA 30354 • *6,166*
Happy, TX 79042 • *674*
Happy Camp, CA 96039 • *1,110*
Happy Jack, AZ 86024 • *300*
Happy Valley, NM 88220 • *630*
Happy Valley, OR 97236 • *1,499*
Harahan, LA 70123 • *11,384*
Haralson □, GA • *18,422*
Harbeson, DE 19951 • *250*
Harbinger, NC 27941 • *250*
Harbor, OR 97415 • *2,856*
Harbor Beach, MI 48441 • *2,000*
Harborcreek, PA 16421 • *800*
Harbor Springs, MI 49740 • *1,567*
Harborton, VA 23389 • *250*
Harcourt, IA 50544 • *347*
Hardee □, FL • *19,379*
Hardeeville, SC 29927 • *1,250*
Hardeman □, TN • *23,873*
Hardeman □, TX • *6,368*
Hardesty, OK 73944 • *243*
Hardin, IL 62047 • *1,107*
Hardin, KY 42048 • *545*
Hardin, MO 64035 • *688*
Hardin, MT 59034 • *3,300*
Hardin □, IL • *5,383*
Hardin □, IA • *21,776*
Hardin □, KY • *88,917*
Hardin □, OH • *32,719*
Hardin □, TN • *22,280*
Hardin □, TX • *40,721*
Harding, MA 02052 • *950*
Harding □, NM • *1,090*
Harding □, SD • *1,700*
Hardinsburg, IN 47125 • *298*
Hardinsburg, KY 40143 • *2,211*
Hardshell, KY 41348 • *350*
Hardtner, KS 67057 • *336*
Hardwick, GA 31034 • *6,000*
Hardwick, MA 01037 • *500*
Hardwick, MN 56134 • *279*
Hardwick, VT 05843 • *1,476*
Hardy, AR 72542 • *643*
Hardy, NE 68943 • *232*
Hardy □, WV • *10,030*
Harford, PA 18823 • *240*
Harford □, MD • *145,930*
Hargill, TX 78549 • *800*
Harker Heights, TX 76543 • *7,345*
Harkers Island, NC 28531 • *1,901*
Harlan, IN 46743 • *1,000*
Harlan, IA 51537 • *5,357*
Harlan, KY 40831 • *3,024*
Harlan □, KY • *41,889*
Harlan □, NE • *4,292*
Harlem, FL 33440 • *2,669*
Harlem, GA 30814 • *1,485*
Harlem, MT 59526 • *1,023*
Harleton, TX 75651 • *250*
Harleyville, SC 29448 • *606*
Harlingen, TX 78550-52 • *43,543*
Harlowton, MT 59036 • *1,181*
Harman, VA 24618 • *500*
Harmans, MD 21077 • *600*
Harmon □, OK • *4,519*
Harmonsburg, PA 16422 • *250*
Harmony, IN 47853 • *613*
Harmony, ME 04942 • *250*
Harmony, MN 55939 • *1,133*
Harmony, NC 28634 • *470*
Harmony, PA 16037 • *1,334*
Harmony, RI 02829 • *800*
Harmony Hills, DE 19711 • *1,350*
Harned, KY 40144 • *250*
Harnett □, NC • *59,570*
Harney □, OR • *8,314*
Harold, FL 32563 • *225*
Harper, KS 67058 • *1,823*
Harper, TX 78631 • *400*
Harper, WA 98366 • *270*
Harper □, KS • *7,778*
Harper □, OK • *4,715*
Harpers Ferry, IA 52146 • *258*
Harpers Ferry, WV 25425 • *361*
Harpersville, AL 35078 • *934*
Harper Woods, MI 48225 • *16,361*
Harpster, OH 43323 • *239*
Harrah, OK 73045 • *2,897*
Harrah, WA 98933 • *343*
Harrell, AR 71745 • *302*
Harriman, TN 37748 • *8,303*
Harrington, DE 19952 • *2,405*
Harrington, ME 04643 • *300*
Harrington, WA 99134 • *507*
Harrington Park, NJ 07640 • *4,532*
Harris, IA 51345 • *228*
Harris, MN 55032 • *678*
Harris, RI 02816 • *1,000*
Harris □, GA • *15,464*
Harris □, TX • *2,409,547*
Harrisburg, AR 72432 • *1,921*
Harrisburg, IL 62946 • *10,410*
Harrisburg, MO 65256 • *283*
Harrisburg, OR 97446 • *1,881*
Harrisburg, PA 17101-99 • *53,264*
Harrisburg, SD 57032 • *558*
Harrison, AR 72601 • *9,567*
Harrison, GA 31035 • *456*
Harrison, ID 83833 • *260*
Harrison, IL 62966 • *450*
Harrison, ME 04040 • *465*
Harrison, MI 48625 • *1,700*
Harrison, NE 69346 • *361*
Harrison, NJ 07029 • *12,242*
Harrison, NY 10528 • *23,046*
Harrison, OH 45030 • *5,855*
Harrison, TN 37341 • *6,206*
Harrison □, IN • *27,276*
Harrison □, IA • *16,348*
Harrison □, KY • *15,166*
Harrison □, MS • *157,665*
Harrison □, MO • *9,890*
Harrison □, OH • *18,152*
Harrison □, TX • *52,265*
Harrison □, WV • *77,710*
Harrisonburg, LA 71340 • *610*
Harrisonburg, VA 22801 • *19,671*
Harrison Valley, PA 16927 • *225*
Harrisonville, MO 64701 • *6,372*
Harrisonville, NJ 08039 • *300*
Harriston, MS 39081 • *450*
Harristown, IL 62537 • *1,456*
Harrisville, MI 48740 • *559*
Harrisville, MS 39082 • *350*
Harrisville, NH 03450 • *400*
Harrisville, NY 13648 • *937*
Harrisville, PA 16038 • *1,033*
Harrisville, RI 02830 • *1,224*
Harrisville, UT 84404 • *1,371*
Harrisville, WV 26362 • *1,673*
Harrod, OH 45850 • *506*
Harrodsburg, IN 47434 • *325*
Harrodsburg, KY 40330 • *7,265*
Hart, MI 49420 • *1,888*
Hart, TX 79043 • *1,008*
Hart □, GA • *18,585*
Hart □, KY • *15,402*
Hartford, AL 36344 • *2,647*
Hartford, AR 72938 • *613*
Hartford, CT 06101-99 • *136,392*
Hartford, IL 62048 • *1,887*
Hartford, IA 50118 • *761*
Hartford, KS 66854 • *551*
Hartford, KY 42347 • *2,512*
Hartford, MI 49057 • *2,493*
Hartford, NJ 08057 • *300*
Hartford, SD 57033 • *1,207*
Hartford, VT 05047 • *600*
Hartford, WV 25247 • *556*
Hartford, WI 53027 • *7,046*
Hartford □, CT • *807,766*
Hartford City, IN 47348 • *7,622*
Hartington, NE 68739 • *1,730*
Hartland, ME 04943 • *1,041*
Hartland, MI 48029 • *450*
Hartland, MN 56042 • *322*
Hartland, VT 05048 • *500*
Hartland, WI 53029 • *5,559*
Hartley, IA 51346 • *1,700*
Hartley, TX 79044 • *280*
Hartley □, TX • *3,987*
Hartman, AR 72840 • *517*
Hartsburg, IL 62643 • *379*
Hartsdale, NY 10530 • *12,226*
Hartselle, AL 35640 • *8,858*
Hartshorne, OK 74547 • *2,380*
Hartsville, IN 47244 • *379*
Hartsville, SC 29550 • *7,631*
Hartsville, TN 37074 • *2,674*
Hartville, MO 65667 • *576*
Hartville, OH 44632 • *1,772*
Hartwell, GA 30643 • *4,855*
Hartwick, NY 13348 • *600*
Harvard, IL 60033 • *5,126*
Harvard, MA 01451 • *900*
Harvard, NE 68944 • *1,217*
Harvel, IL 62538 • *278*
Harvest, AL 35749 • *400*
Harvey, IL 60426 • *35,810*
Harvey, IA 50119 • *275*
Harvey, LA 70058 • *15,000*
Harvey, MI 49855 • *1,341*
Harvey, ND 58341 • *2,527*
Harvey, WV 25852 • *500*
Harvey □, KS • *30,531*
Harveysburg, OH 45032 • *425*
Harveyville, KS 66431 • *280*
Harviell, MO 63945 • *250*
Harwich, MA 02645 • *1,000*
Harwich Port, MA 02646 • *1,900*
Harwinton, CT 06791 • *3,293*
Harwood, MA 01460 • *900*
Harwood, ND 58042 • *326*
Harwood Heights, IL 60656 • *8,228*
Hasbrouck Heights, NJ 07604 • *12,166*
Haskell, AR 72015 • *1,074*
Haskell, OK 74436 • *1,953*
Haskell, TX 79521 • *3,782*
Haskell □, KS • *3,814*
Haskell □, OK • *11,010*
Haskell □, TX • *7,725*
Haskins, OH 43525 • *568*
Haslet, TX 76052 • *262*
Haslett, MI 48840 • *7,025*
Hastings, FL 32045 • *636*
Hastings, MI 49058 • *6,418*
Hastings, MN 55033 • *12,827*
Hastings, NE 68901 • *23,045*
Hastings, OK 73548 • *246*
Hastings, PA 16646 • *1,574*

Hastings-On-Hudson, NY 10706 • *8,573*
Hatboro, PA 19040 • *7,579*
Hatch, NM 87937 • *1,028*
Hatchechubbee, AL 36858 • *230*
Hatfield, AR 71945 • *410*
Hatfield, IN 47617 • *600*
Hatfield, MA 01038 • *1,251*
Hatfield, PA 19440 • *2,533*
Hatley, MS 38821 • *497*
Hatley, WI 54440 • *300*
Hatteras, NC 27943 • *700*
Hattiesburg, MS 39401 • *40,829*
Hatton, ND 58240 • *787*
Haubstadt, IN 47639 • *1,389*
Haugen, WI 54841 • *251*
Haughton, LA 71037 • *1,510*
Hauppauge, NY 11788 • *14,200*
Hauser, OR 97459 • *630*
Hauula, HI 96717 • *2,997*
Havana, AR 72842 • *352*
Havana, FL 32333 • *2,782*
Havana, IL 62644 • *4,277*
Havelock, IA 50546 • *279*
Havelock, NC 28532 • *17,718*
Haven, KS 67543 • *1,125*
Haverford, PA 19041 • *5,800*
Haverhill, MA 01830 • *46,865*
Haverhill, NH 03765 • *400*
Haverstraw, NY 10927 • *8,800*
Havertown, PA 19083 • *36,000*
Haviland, KS 67059 • *770*
Havre, MT 59501 • *10,891*
Havre de Grace, MD 21078 • *8,763*
Havre North, MT 59501 • *1,073*
Hawaii □, HI • *92,053*
Hawaiian Gardens, CA 90716 • *10,548*
Hawarden, IA 51023 • *2,722*
Hawesville, KY 42348 • *1,036*
Hawi, HI 96719 • *795*
Hawkeye, IA 52147 • *512*
Hawkins, WI 54530 • *407*
Hawkins □, TN • *43,751*
Hawkinsville, GA 31036 • *4,372*
Hawk Point, MO 63349 • *386*
Hawk Run, PA 16840 • *750*
Hawley, MN 56549 • *1,634*
Hawley, PA 18428 • *1,181*
Hawley, TX 79525 • *679*
Haworth, NJ 07641 • *3,509*
Haworth, OK 74740 • *341*
Haw River, NC 27258 • *1,858*
Hawthorn, PA 16230 • *547*
Hawthorne, CA 90250 • *56,447*
Hawthorne, FL 32640 • *1,303*
Hawthorne, NV 89415 • *3,741*
Hawthorne, NJ 07506 • *18,200*
Hawthorne, NY 10532 • *4,900*
Haxtun, CO 80731 • *1,014*
Hayden, AL 35079 • *268*
Hayden, AZ 85235 • *1,205*
Hayden, CO 81639 • *1,720*
Hayden, ID 83835 • *2,586*
Hayden, IN 47245 • *325*
Haydenville, MA 01039 • *900*
Haydenville, OH 43127 • *500*
Hayes, LA 70646 • *830*
Hayes □, NE • *1,356*
Hayes Center, NE 69032 • *231*
Hayesville, NC 28904 • *376*
Hayesville, OH 44838 • *518*
Hayesville, OR 97303 • *9,213*
Hayfield, MN 55940 • *1,243*
Hayfield, VA 22310 • *2,200*
Hayfork, CA 96041 • *1,788*
Haymarket, VA 22069 • *230*
Haynes, AR 72341 • *359*
Haynesville, LA 71038 • *3,454*
Hayneville, AL 36040 • *592*
Hays, KS 67601 • *16,301*
Hays, MT 59527 • *300*
Hays, NC 28635 • *900*
Hays □, TX • *40,594*
Haysi, VA 24256 • *371*
Hay Springs, NE 69347 • *794*
Haysville, IN 47546 • *350*
Haysville, KS 67060 • *8,006*
Hayti, MO 63851 • *3,964*
Hayti, SD 57241 • *371*
Hayti Heights, MO 63851 • *1,023*
Hayward, CA 94540-46 • *94,342*
Hayward, WI 54843 • *1,698*
Hayward Addition, SD 57106 • *725*
Haywood □, NC • *46,495*
Haywood □, TN • *20,318*
Hazard, KY 41701 • *5,371*
Hazardville, CT 06082 • *5,436*
Hazel, KY 42049 • *465*
Hazel Crest, IL 60429 • *13,973*
Hazel Dell, WA 98665 • *6,000*
Hazel Green, AL 35750 • *1,503*
Hazel Green, WI 53811 • *1,282*
Hazel Hurst, PA 16733 • *475*
Hazelhurst, WI 54531 • *400*
Hazel Park, MI 48030 • *20,914*
Hazelton, ID 83335 • *496*
Hazelton, ND 58544 • *266*
Hazelwood, MO 63042-45 • *12,935*
Hazelwood, NC 28738 • *1,811*
Hazen, AR 72064 • *1,636*
Hazen, ND 58545 • *2,365*
Hazlehurst, GA 31539 • *4,249*
Hazlehurst, MS 39083 • *4,437*
Hazlet, NJ 07730 • *28,013*
Hazleton, IN 47640 • *368*
Hazleton, IA 50641 • *877*
Hazleton, PA 18201 • *27,318*
Headland, AL 36345 • *3,327*
Head of Island, LA 70449 • *300*
Headquarters, ID 83534 • *250*
Headrick, OK 73549 • *223*
Healdsburg, CA 95448 • *7,217*
Healdton, OK 73438 • *3,769*
Healy, AK 99743 • *334*
Healy, KS 67850 • *250*
Heard □, GA • *6,520*
Hearne, TX 77859 • *5,418*
Heath, AL 36420 • *354*
Heath, OH 43055 • *6,969*
Heath Springs, SC 29058 • *979*
Heathsville, VA 22473 • *300*
Hebbronville, TX 78361 • *4,079*
Heber, AZ 85928 • *600*
Heber City, UT 84032 • *4,362*
Heber Springs, AR 72543 • *4,589*
Hebo, OR 97122 • *300*
Hebron, CT 06248 • *500*
Hebron, IL 60034 • *786*
Hebron, IN 46341 • *2,696*
Hebron, KY 41048 • *500*
Hebron, ME 04238 • *300*
Hebron, MD 21830 • *714*
Hebron, NE 68370 • *1,906*
Hebron, ND 58638 • *1,078*
Hebron, OH 43025 • *2,035*
Hebron, TX 75067 • *385*
Hecker, IL 62248 • *531*
Hecla, SD 57446 • *435*
Hector, AR 72843 • *449*
Hector, MN 55342 • *1,252*
Hedges, FL 32097 • *900*
Hedley, TX 79237 • *380*
Hedrick, IA 52563 • *847*
Heflin, AL 36264 • *3,014*
Heflin, LA 71039 • *279*
Hegins, PA 17938 • *900*
Heidelberg, MS 39439 • *1,098*
Heidrick, KY 40949 • *600*
Heilwood, PA 15745 • *700*
Heislerville, NJ 08324 • *600*
Helena, AL 35080 • *2,130*
Helena, AR 72342 • *9,598*
Helena, GA 31037 • *1,390*
Helena, MT 59601 • *23,938*
Helena, NY 13649 • *300*
Helena, OH 43435 • *307*
Helena, OK 73741 • *710*
Helena, SC 29108 • *250*
Helenwood, TN 37755 • *300*
Hellam, PA 17406 • *1,428*
Hellertown, PA 18055 • *6,025*
Helm, CA 93627 • *250*
Helmetta, NJ 08828 • *955*
Helotes, TX 78023 • *1,409*
Helper, UT 84526 • *2,724*
Heltonville, IN 47436 • *500*
Hematite, MO 63047 • *300*
Hemet, CA 92343-44 • *22,454*
Hemingford, NE 69348 • *1,023*
Hemingway, SC 29554 • *853*
Hemlock, MI 48626 • *1,362*
Hemlock, NY 14466 • *500*
Hemphill, TX 75948 • *1,353*
Hemphill □, TX • *5,304*
Hempstead, NY 11550-54 • *40,404*
Hempstead, TX 77445 • *3,456*
Hempstead □, AR • *23,635*
Henagar, AL 35978 • *1,188*
Henderson, IA 51541 • *236*
Henderson, KY 42420 • *24,834*
Henderson, LA 70517 • *1,560*
Henderson, MI 48841 • *280*
Henderson, MN 56044 • *739*
Henderson, NE 68371 • *1,072*
Henderson, NV 89015 • *24,363*
Henderson, NC 27536 • *13,522*
Henderson, NY 13650 • *300*
Henderson, TN 38340 • *4,449*
Henderson, TX 75652 • *11,473*
Henderson, WV 25106 • *604*
Henderson □, IL • *9,114*
Henderson □, KY • *40,849*
Henderson □, NC • *58,580*
Henderson □, TN • *21,390*
Henderson □, TX • *42,606*
Henderson's Point, MS 39571 • *1,114*
Hendersonville, NC 28739 • *6,862*
Hendersonville, TN 37075 • *26,561*
Hendricks, MN 56136 • *737*
Hendricks, WV 26271 • *390*
Hendricks □, IN • *69,804*
Hendrum, MN 56550 • *336*
Hendry □, FL • *18,599*
Henefer, UT 84033 • *547*
Henlawson, WV 25624 • *950*
Hennepin, IL 61327 • *716*
Hennepin, OK 73046 • *300*
Hennepin □, MN • *941,411*
Hennessey, OK 73742 • *2,287*
Henniker, NH 03242 • *1,538*
Henning, IL 61848 • *317*
Henning, MN 56551 • *832*
Henning, TN 38041 • *638*
Henrico □, VA • *180,735*
Henrietta, MO 64036 • *424*
Henrietta, NC 28076 • *1,412*
Henrietta, NY 14467 • *1,200*
Henrietta, TX 76365 • *3,149*
Henry, IL 61537 • *2,740*
Henry, TN 38231 • *295*
Henry, VA 24102 • *250*
Henry □, AL • *15,302*
Henry □, GA • *36,309*
Henry □, IL • *57,968*
Henry □, IN • *53,336*
Henry □, IA • *18,890*
Henry □, KY • *12,740*
Henry □, MO • *19,672*
Henry □, OH • *28,383*
Henry □, TN • *28,656*
Henry □, VA • *57,654*
Henryetta, OK 74437 • *6,432*
Henryville, IN 47126 • *1,132*
Hensley, AR 72065 • *450*
Hephzibah, GA 30815 • *1,452*
Heppner, OR 97836 • *1,498*
Herculaneum, MO 63048 • *2,293*
Hercules, CA 94547 • *5,963*
Hereford, MD 21111 • *600*
Hereford, TX 79045 • *15,853*
Herington, KS 67449 • *2,930*
Heritage Village, CT 06488 • *5,200*
Herkimer, NY 13350 • *8,383*
Herkimer □, NY • *66,714*
Herman, MN 56248 • *600*
Herman, NE 68029 • *340*
Hermann, MO 65041 • *2,695*
Hermansville, MI 49847 • *700*
Hermantown, MN 55811 • *6,759*
Hermanville, MS 39086 • *350*
Herminie, PA 15637 • *1,100*
Hermiston, OR 97838 • *9,408*
Hermitage, AR 71647 • *378*
Hermitage, MO 65668 • *384*
Hermitage, PA 16148 • *16,365*
Hermleigh, TX 79526 • *300*
Hermon, NY 13652 • *490*
Hermosa, SD 57744 • *251*
Hermosa Beach, CA 90254 • *18,070*
Hernando, FL 32642 • *1,653*
Hernando, MS 38632 • *2,969*
Hernando □, FL • *44,469*
Herndon, PA 17830 • *483*
Herndon, VA 22070-71 • *11,449*
Herndon, WV 24726 • *300*
Heron Bay, AL 36523 • *250*
Heron Lake, MN 56137 • *783*
Herreid, SD 57632 • *570*
Herrick, IL 62431 • *470*
Herriman, UT 84065 • *600*
Herrin, IL 62948 • *10,708*
Herscher, IL 60941 • *1,214*
Hersey, MI 49639 • *364*
Hershey, NE 69143 • *633*
Hershey, PA 17033 • *9,000*
Hertford, NC 27944 • *1,941*
Hertford □, NC • *23,368*
Hesperia, CA 92345 • *13,540*
Hesperia, MI 49421 • *876*
Hessel, MI 49745 • *250*
Hessmer, LA 71341 • *743*
Hesston, KS 67062 • *3,013*
Hettick, IL 62649 • *262*
Hettinger, ND 58639 • *1,739*
Hettinger □, ND • *4,275*
Heuvelton, NY 13654 • *777*
Hewitt, MN 56453 • *299*
Hewitt, NJ 07421 • *300*
Hewitt, TX 76643 • *5,247*
Hewitt, WI 54441 • *470*
Hewlett, NY 11557 • *6,880*
Heyburn, ID 83336 • *2,889*
Heyworth, IL 61745 • *1,598*
Hialeah, FL 33010-16 • *145,254*
Hiawassee, GA 30546 • *491*
Hiawatha, IA 52233 • *4,825*
Hiawatha, KS 66434 • *3,702*
Hiawatha, UT 84527 • *249*
Hibbing, MN 55746 • *21,193*
Hickman, KY 42050 • *2,894*
Hickman, NE 68372 • *687*
Hickman □, KY • *6,065*
Hickman □, TN • *15,151*
Hickory, MS 39332 • *670*
Hickory, NC 28601 • *20,757*
Hickory □, MO • *6,367*
Hickory Flat, MS 38633 • *458*
Hickory Grove, SC 29526 • *250*
Hickory Hills, IL 60457 • *13,778*
Hickory Ridge, AR 72347 • *478*
Hickory Valley, TN 38042 • *252*
Hicksville, NY 11801-99 • *50,000*
Hicksville, OH 43526 • *3,929*
Hico, TX 76457 • *1,375*
Hico, WV 25854 • *700*
Hidalgo, TX 78557 • *2,288*
Hidalgo □, NM • *6,049*
Hidalgo □, TX • *283,323*
Hiddenite, NC 28636 • *800*
Hideaway Park, CO 80482 • *450*
Higbee, MO 65257 • *817*
Higdon, AL 35979 • *300*
Higganum, CT 06441 • *1,660*
Higgins, TX 79046 • *702*
Higgins Lake, MI 48627 • *500*
Higginson, AR 72068 • *333*
Higginsport, OH 45131 • *343*
Higginsville, MO 64037 • *4,595*
High Bridge, KY 40390 • *250*
High Bridge, NJ 08829 • *3,435*
Highfalls, NC 27259 • *250*
Highfield, MD 21719 • *400*
Highgate Falls, VT 05459 • *250*
High Hill, MO 63350 • *254*
High Island, TX 77623 • *550*
Highland, CA 92346 • *10,400*
Highland, IL 62249 • *7,122*
Highland, IN 46322 • *25,935*
Highland, KS 66035 • *954*
Highland, MI 48031 • *1,000*
Highland, NY 12528 • *2,184*
Highland, OH 45132 • *284*
Highland, WI 53543 • *860*
Highland □, OH • *33,477*
Highland □, VA • *2,937*
Highland Falls, NY 10928 • *4,187*
Highland Heights, OH 44124 • *5,739*
Highland Home, AL 36041 • *250*
Highland Lakes, NJ 07422 • *2,888*
Highland Park, IL 60035 • *30,611*
Highland Park, MI 48203 • *27,909*
Highland Park, NJ 08904 • *13,396*
Highland Park, TX 75205 • *8,909*
Highlands, NJ 07732 • *5,187*
Highlands, NC 28741 • *653*
Highlands, TX 77562 • *4,450*
Highlands □, FL • *47,526*
Highland Springs, VA 23075 • *7,500*
Highmore, SD 57345 • *1,055*
High Point, NC 27260-64 • *63,808*
High Ridge, MO 63049 • *900*
High Rolls Mountain Park, NM 88325 • *650*
High Shoals, NC 28077 • *586*
High Spire, PA 17034 • *2,959*
High Springs, FL 32643 • *2,491*
Hightstown, NJ 08520 • *4,581*
Highview, KY 40228 • *13,286*
Highwood, IL 60040 • *5,452*
Hilbert, WI 54129 • *1,176*
Hilda, SC 29813 • *355*
Hildale, UT 86021 • *1,009*
Hildreth, NE 68947 • *394*
Hill, NH 03243 • *250*
Hill □, MT • *17,985*
Hill □, TX • *25,024*
Hill City, KS 67642 • *2,028*
Hill City, MN 55748 • *533*
Hill City, SD 57745 • *535*
Hillcrest, IL 61068 • *818*
Hillcrest, MI 49938 • *350*
Hillcrest, NY 10977 • *5,357*
Hillcrest Center, CA 93306 • *30,000*
Hillcrest Heights, MD 20748 • *17,021*
Hilliard, FL 32046 • *1,869*
Hilliard, OH 43026 • *8,008*
Hillman, MI 49746 • *373*

Hills, IA 52235 • 547
Hills, MN 56138 • 598
Hillsboro, AL 35643 • 278
Hillsboro, IL 62049 • 4,408
Hillsboro, IN 47949 • 561
Hillsboro, KS 67063 • 2,717
Hillsboro, MO 63050 • 1,508
Hillsboro, NH 03244 • 1,797
Hillsboro, ND 58045 • 1,600
Hillsboro, OH 45133 • 6,356
Hillsboro, OR 97123-24 • 27,664
Hillsboro, TX 76645 • 7,397
Hillsboro, WV 24946 • 276
Hillsboro, WI 54634 • 1,263
Hillsborough, CA 94010 • 10,372
Hillsborough, NC 27278 • 3,019
Hillsborough □, FL • 646,960
Hillsborough □, NH • 276,608
Hillsborough Upper Village, NH 03244 • 250
Hillsdale, IL 61257 • 731
Hillsdale, IN 47854 • 300
Hillsdale, KS 66036 • 250
Hillsdale, MI 49242 • 7,432
Hillsdale, NJ 07642 • 10,495
Hillsdale □, MI • 42,071
Hillside, IL 60162 • 8,279
Hillside, NJ 07205 • 21,440
Hillside Heights, DE 19711 • 800
Hillsville, PA 16132 • 915
Hillsville, VA 24343 • 2,123
Hilltonia, GA 30467 • 515
Hillview, IL 62050 • 328
Hillview, KY 40229 • 5,196
Hilo, HI 96720 • 35,269
Hilton, NY 14468 • 4,151
Hilton Head Island, SC 29928 • 11,344
Hiltons, VA 24258 • 250
Hima, KY 40951 • 700
Hinckley, IL 60520 • 1,447
Hinckley, MN 55037 • 963
Hinckley, OH 44233 • 500
Hinckley, UT 84635 • 464
Hindman, KY 41822 • 876
Hinds □, MS • 250,998
Hindsboro, IL 61930 • 407
Hines, OR 97738 • 1,632
Hinesburg, VT 05461 • 350
Hineston, LA 71438 • 500
Hinesville, GA 31313 • 11,309
Hingham, MA 02043 • 12,800
Hinkley, CA 92347 • 700
Hinsdale, IL 60521 • 16,726
Hinsdale, MA 01235 • 950
Hinsdale, NH 03451 • 1,546
Hinsdale, NY 14743 • 600
Hinsdale □, CO • 408
Hinton, IA 51024 • 659
Hinton, OK 73047 • 1,432
Hinton, WV 25951 • 4,622
Hiram, GA 30141 • 1,030
Hiram, ME 04041 • 270
Hiram, OH 44234 • 1,360
Hiseville, KY 42152 • 349
Hitchcock, TX 77563 • 6,655
Hitchcock □, NE • 4,079
Hitchcock Lake, CT 06716 • 1,600
Hitchins, KY 41146 • 700
Hitterdal, MN 56552 • 253
Hixton, WI 54635 • 364
Hoagland, IN 46745 • 650
Hobart, IN 46342 • 22,987
Hobart, NY 13788 • 473
Hobart, OK 73651 • 4,735
Hobbs, NM 88240 • 29,153
Hobe Sound, FL 33455 • 6,822
Hobgood, NC 27843 • 483
Hoboken, GA 31542 • 514
Hoboken, NJ 07030 • 42,460
Hobson, MT 59452 • 261
Hobucken, NC 28537 • 450
Hockessin, DE 19707 • 950
Hocking □, OH • 24,304
Hockingport, OH 45739 • 250
Hockley, TX 77447 • 500
Hockley □, TX • 23,230
Hodgdon, ME 04730 • 400
Hodge, LA 71247 • 708
Hodgeman □, KS • 2,269
Hodgenville, KY 42748 • 2,531
Hodges, AL 35571 • 250
Hoffman, MN 56339 • 631
Hoffman, NC 28347 • 389
Hoffman, OK 74439 • 407
Hoffman Estates, IL 60195 • 37,272
Hogansville, GA 30230 • 3,362
Hohenwald, TN 38462 • 3,922
Ho-Ho-Kus, NJ 07423 • 4,129
Hoisington, KS 67544 • 3,678
Hokah, MN 55941 • 686
Hoke □, NC • 20,383
Hokes Bluff, AL 35903 • 3,216
Holbrook, AZ 86025 • 5,785
Holbrook, MA 02343 • 11,140
Holbrook, NE 68948 • 297
Holbrook, NY 11741 • 12,800
Holcomb, KS 67851 • 816
Holcomb, MO 63852 • 632
Holden, LA 70744 • 250
Holden, MA 01520 • 3,900
Holden, MO 64040 • 2,195
Holden, UT 84636 • 364
Holden, WV 25625 • 1,600
Holden Heights, FL 32805 • 8,000
Holdenville, OK 74848 • 5,469
Holder, FL 32645 • 400
Holderness, NH 03245 • 300
Holdingford, MN 56340 • 635
Holdrege, NE 68949 • 5,624
Holgate, OH 43527 • 1,315
Holiday, FL 33590 • 15,400
Holladay, TN 38341 • 250
Holladay, UT 84117 • 22,189
Holland, IN 47541 • 683
Holland, IA 50642 • 278
Holland, MI 49423 • 26,281
Holland, MN 56139 • 234
Holland, MO 63853 • 295
Holland, NY 14080 • 1,000
Holland, OH 43528 • 1,048
Holland, TX 76534 • 863
Hollandale, MS 38748 • 4,336
Hollandale, WI 53544 • 271
Holland Patent, NY 13354 • 534
Hollansburg, OH 45332 • 339
Holley, NY 14470 • 1,882
Holliday, TX 76366 • 1,349
Hollidaysburg, PA 16648 • 5,892
Hollins, AL 35082 • 250
Hollins, VA 24019 • 11,000
Hollis, NH 03049 • 400
Hollis, OK 73550 • 2,958
Hollis Center, ME 04042 • 300
Hollister, CA 95023 • 11,488
Hollister, MO 65672 • 1,439
Hollister, NC 27844 • 400
Holliston, MA 01746 • 12,622
Holloway Terrace, DE 19720 • 1,000
Hollow Rock, TN 38342 • 955
Hollsopple, PA 15935 • 900
Holly, CO 81047 • 969
Holly, MI 48442 • 4,874
Holly Bluff, MS 39088 • 250
Holly Grove, AR 72069 • 754
Holly Hill, FL 32017 • 9,953
Holly Hill, SC 29059 • 1,785
Holly Pond, AL 35083 • 493
Holly Ridge, NC 28445 • 465
Holly Springs, GA 30142 • 687
Holly Springs, MS 38635 • 7,285
Holly Springs, NC 27540 • 688
Hollywood, AL 35752 • 1,110
Hollywood, FL 33020-29 • 121,323
Hollywood, MD 20636 • 300
Hollywood, SC 29449 • 729
Hollywood 0Z, CA
Holman, NM 87723 • 400
Holmdel, NJ 07733 • 800
Holmen, WI 54636 • 2,411
Holmes □, FL • 14,723
Holmes □, MS • 22,970
Holmes □, OH • 29,416
Holmesville, OH 44633 • 436
Holstein, IA 51025 • 1,477
Holstein, NE 68950 • 241
Holt, AL 35404 • 4,300
Holt, FL 32564 • 780
Holt, MI 48842 • 10,097
Holt, MO 64048 • 276
Holt □, MO • 6,882
Holt □, NE • 13,552
Holton, IN 47023 • 487
Holton, KS 66436 • 3,132
Holton, MI 49425 • 400
Holtville, AL 36022 • 300
Holtville, CA 92250 • 4,399
Holualoa, HI 96725 • 1,243
Holy Cross, AK 99602 • 241
Holy Cross, IA 52053 • 310
Holyoke, CO 80734 • 2,092
Holyoke, MA 01040 • 44,678
Holyrood, KS 67450 • 567
Home Corner, IN 46952 • 500
Homecroft, IN 46227 • 831
Homedale, ID 83628 • 2,078
Home Gardens, CA 91720 • 5,783
Homelake, CO 81135 • 250
Homeland, FL 33847 • 500
Homeland, GA 31537 • 683
Home Place, IN 46240 • 2,000
Homer, AK 99603 • 2,209
Homer, GA 30547 • 734
Homer, IL 61849 • 1,279
Homer, IN 46146 • 235
Homer, LA 71040 • 4,307
Homer, MI 49245 • 1,791
Homer, NE 68030 • 564
Homer, NY 13077 • 3,635
Homer City, PA 15748 • 2,248
Homerville, GA 31634 • 3,112
Homestead, FL 33030-35 • 20,668
Homestead, PA 15120 • 5,092
Hometown, IL 60456 • 5,324
Homewood, AL 35209 • 21,412
Homewood, CA 95718 • 500
Homewood, IL 60430 • 19,724
Homewood, OH 45015 • 2,550
Homeworth, OH 44634 • 300
Hominy, OK 74035 • 3,130
Homosassa, FL 32646 • 1,426
Honaker, VA 24260 • 1,475
Honaunau, HI 96726 • 600
Hondo, TX 78861 • 6,057
Honea Path, SC 29654 • 4,114
Honeoye Falls, NY 14472 • 2,410
Honesdale, PA 18431 • 5,128
Honey Brook, PA 19344 • 1,164
Honey Creek, WI 53138 • 300
Honey Grove, TX 75446 • 1,973
Honeypot Glen, CT 06410 • 900
Honeyville, UT 84314 • 915
Honokaa, HI 96727 • 1,936
Honokahua, HI 96761 • 309
Honolulu, HI 96801-99 • 365,048
Honolulu □, HI • 762,565
Honomu, HI 96728 • 559
Honor, MI 49640 • 281
Honouliuli, HI 96706 • 600
Hood □, TX • 17,714
Hood River, OR 97031 • 4,329
Hood River □, OR • 15,835
Hoodsport, WA 98548 • 900
Hooker, OK 73945 • 1,788
Hooker □, NE • 990
Hookerton, NC 28538 • 460
Hooksett, NH 03106 • 1,868
Hoolehua, HI 96729 • 250
Hoonah, AK 99829 • 680
Hooper, NE 68031 • 932
Hooper, UT 84315 • 400
Hooper Bay, AK 99604 • 627
Hoopersville, MD 21642 • 300
Hoopeston, IL 60942 • 6,411
Hoople, ND 58243 • 350
Hooppole, IL 61258 • 235
Hoosick Falls, NY 12090 • 3,609
Hoover, AL 35216 • 19,792
Hooverson Heights, WV 26037 • 1,500
Hooversville, PA 15936 • 863
Hopatcong, NJ 07843 • 15,531
Hop Bottom, PA 18824 • 405
Hope, AR 71801 • 10,290
Hope, IN 47246 • 2,185
Hope, KS 67451 • 468
Hope, ND 58046 • 406
Hope, RI 02831 • 490
Hopedale, IL 61747 • 913
Hopedale, LA 70085 • 300
Hopedale, MA 01747 • 3,905
Hopedale, OH 43976 • 857
Hopelawn, NJ 08861 • 12,600
Hope Mills, NC 28348 • 5,412
Hope Valley, RI 02832 • 1,414
Hopewell, NJ 08525 • 2,001
Hopewell, OH 43746 • 500
Hopewell, PA 16650 • 256
Hopewell, VA 23860 • 23,397
Hopewell Junction, NY 12533 • 2,055
Hopkins, MI 49328 • 536
Hopkins, MN 55343-45 • 15,336
Hopkins, MO 64461 • 634
Hopkins, SC 29061 • 1,600
Hopkins □, KY • 46,174
Hopkins □, TX • 25,247
Hopkinsville, KY 42240 • 27,318
Hopkinton, IA 52237 • 774
Hopkinton, MA 01748 • 2,542
Hopkinton, NH 03301 • 300
Hopland, CA 95449 • 900
Hopwood, PA 15445 • 2,190
Hoquiam, WA 98550 • 9,719
Horace, ND 58047 • 494
Horatio, AR 71842 • 989
Horatio, SC 29062 • 400
Horicon, WI 53032 • 3,584
Horine, MO 63070 • 850
Hornbeak, TN 38232 • 452
Hornbeck, LA 71439 • 470
Hornell, NY 14843 • 10,234
Hornerstown, NJ 08514 • 300
Hornersville, MO 63855 • 704
Hornick, IA 51026 • 239
Horn Lake, MS 38637 • 4,326
Hornsby, TN 38044 • 401
Hornsbyville, VA 23690 • 300
Horry □, SC • 101,419
Horse Branch, KY 42349 • 250
Horse Cave, KY 42749 • 2,045
Horseheads, NY 14845 • 7,348
Horseshoe Beach, FL 32648 • 304
Horseshoe Bend, ID 83629 • 700
Horsham, PA 19044 • 6,000
Hortense, GA 31543 • 300
Horton, KS 66439 • 2,130
Hortonville, WI 54944 • 2,016
Hoschton, GA 30548 • 490
Hosford, FL 32334 • 700
Hoskins, NE 68740 • 306
Hoskinston, KY 40844 • 300
Hosmer, SD 57448 • 385
Hospers, IA 51238 • 655
Hosston, LA 71043 • 480
Hotchkiss, CO 81419 • 849
Hotchkissville, CT 06798 • 300
Hotevilla, AZ 86030 • 700
Hot Spring □, AR • 26,819
Hot Springs, MT 59845 • 601
Hot Springs
→ Truth or Consequences, NM • 5,219
Hot Springs, NC 28743 • 678
Hot Springs, SD 57747 • 4,742
Hot Springs, VA 24445 • 300
Hot Springs □, WY • 5,710
Hot Springs National Park, AR 71901-13 • 35,781
Hot Sulphur Springs, CO 80451 • 405
Houck, AZ 86506 • 600
Houghton, MI 49931 • 7,512
Houghton, NY 14744 • 1,620
Houghton □, MI • 37,872
Houghton Lake, MI 48629 • 1,500
Houghton Lake Heights, MI 48630 • 2,449
Houghtonville, MA 01247 • 300
Houlka, MS 38850 • 710
Houlton, ME 04730 • 5,730
Houma, LA 70360-64 • 32,602
Housatonic, MA 01236 • 1,314
House Springs, MO 63051 • 400
Houston, DE 19954 • 357
Houston, MN 55943 • 1,057
Houston, MS 38851 • 3,747
Houston, MO 65483 • 2,157
Houston, PA 15342 • 1,568
Houston, TX 77001-99 • 1,595,138
Houston □, AL • 74,632
Houston □, GA • 77,605
Houston □, MN • 18,382
Houston □, TN • 6,871
Houston □, TX • 22,299
Houstonia, MO 65333 • 327
Houtzdale, PA 16651 • 1,222
Hoven, SD 57450 • 615
Howard, KS 67349 • 965
Howard, OH 43028 • 450
Howard, PA 16841 • 838
Howard, SD 57349 • 1,169
Howard, WI 54303 • 8,240
Howard □, AR • 13,459
Howard □, IN • 86,896
Howard □, IA • 11,114
Howard □, MD • 118,572
Howard □, MO • 10,008
Howard □, NE • 6,773
Howard □, TX • 33,142
Howard City, MI 49329 • 1,118
Howard Lake, MN 55349 • 1,240
Howards Grove-Millersville, WI 53081 • 1,838
Howardville, MO 63869 • 536
Howe, IN 46746 • 500
Howe, OK 74940 • 562
Howell, MI 48843 • 6,976
Howell □, MO • 28,807
Howells, NE 68641 • 677
Howland, ME 04448 • 1,602
Hoxie, AR 72433 • 2,961
Hoxie, KS 67740 • 1,462
Hoyleton, IL 62803 • 542
Hoyt, KS 66440 • 536
Hoyt Lakes, MN 55750 • 3,186
Hoytville, OH 43529 • 315
Huachuca City, AZ 85616 • 1,661
Hubbard, IA 50122 • 852
Hubbard, NE 68741 • 234

Hubbard, OH 44425 • 9,245
Hubbard, OR 97032 • 1,640
Hubbard, TX 76648 • 1,676
Hubbard □, MN • 14,098
Hubbardston, MA 01452 • 500
Hubbardston, MI 48845 • 421
Hubbell, MI 49934 • 1,278
Huber Heights, OH 45424 • 35,480
Huber South, OH 45439 • 4,800
Huckleberry Hill, CT 06001 • 700
Hudson, CO 80642 • 698
Hudson, FL 33567 • 5,799
Hudson, IL 61748 • 929
Hudson, IN 46747 • 447
Hudson, IA 50643 • 2,267
Hudson, MA 01749 • 9,714
Hudson, MI 49247 • 2,545
Hudson, NH 03051 • 6,248
Hudson, NC 28638 • 2,888
Hudson, NY 12534 • 7,986
Hudson, OH 44236 • 4,615
Hudson, SD 57034 • 388
Hudson, WI 54016 • 5,434
Hudson, WY 82515 • 514
Hudson □, NJ • 556,972
Hudson Falls, NY 12839 • 7,419
Hudson Lake, IN 46552 • 1,347
Hudsonville, MI 49426 • 4,844
Hudspeth □, TX • 2,728
Huerfano □, CO • 6,440
Hueytown, AL 35023 • 13,478
Hughes, AR 72348 • 1,919
Hughes □, OK • 14,338
Hughes □, SD • 14,220
Hughesville, MD 20637 • 1,208
Hughesville, PA 17737 • 2,174
Hugo, CO 80821 • 776
Hugo, MN 55038 • 3,771
Hugo, OK 74743 • 7,172
Hugoton, KS 67951 • 3,165
Huguley, AL 36854 • 2,947
Hulbert, MI 49748 • 275
Hulbert, OK 74441 • 633
Hulen, KY 40845 • 400
Hulett, WY 82720 • 291
Hull, IL 62343 • 529
Hull, IA 51239 • 1,714
Hull, MA 02045 • 9,714
Humansville, MO 65674 • 907
Humarock, MA 02047 • 300
Humbird, WI 54746 • 270
Humble, TX 77338-39 • 6,729
Humboldt, AZ 86329 • 400
Humboldt, IL 61931 • 499
Humboldt, IA 50548 • 4,794
Humboldt, KS 66748 • 2,230
Humboldt, NE 68376 • 1,176
Humboldt, SD 57035 • 487
Humboldt, TN 38343 • 10,209
Humboldt □, CA • 108,514
Humboldt □, IA • 12,246
Humboldt □, NV • 9,434
Hume, IL 61932 • 483
Hume, MO 64752 • 315
Hume, NY 14745 • 300
Humeston, IA 50123 • 671
Hummels Wharf, PA 17831 • 750
Humnoke, AR 72072 • 442
Humphrey, AR 72073 • 872
Humphrey, NE 68642 • 799
Humphreys □, MS • 13,931
Humphreys □, TN • 15,957
Humptulips, WA 98552 • 250
Hundred, WV 26575 • 485
Hungry Horse, MT 59919 • 900
Hunnewell, MO 63443 • 235
Hunt □, TX • 55,248
Hunter, ND 58048 • 369
Hunter, OK 74640 • 276
Hunterdon □, NJ • 87,361
Huntertown, IN 46748 • 1,265
Huntingburg, IN 47542 • 5,376
Huntingdon, PA 16652 • 7,042
Huntingdon, TN 38344 • 3,962
Huntingdon □, PA • 42,253
Huntingdon Valley, PA 19006 • 10,400
Huntington, AR 72940 • 662
Huntington, IN 46750 • 16,202
Huntington, MA 01050 • 950
Huntington, NJ 08865 • 700
Huntington, NY 11743 • 12,601
Huntington, OR 97907 • 539
Huntington, TX 75949 • 1,672
Huntington, UT 84528 • 2,316
Huntington, WV 25701-99 • 63,684
Huntington □, IN • 35,596
Huntington Bay, NY 11743 • 1,783
Huntington Beach, CA 92646-49 • 170,505
Huntington Park, CA 90255 • 46,223
Huntington Station, NY 11746 • 30,300
Huntington Woods, MI 48070 • 6,937
Huntingtown, MD 20639 • 250
Huntland, TN 37345 • 983
Huntley, IL 60142 • 1,646
Huntley, MT 59037 • 250
Huntsville, AL 35801-99 • 142,513
Huntsville, AR 72740 • 1,394
Huntsville, IN 46064 • 225
Huntsville, MO 65259 • 1,657
Huntsville, TN 37756 • 519
Huntsville, TX 77340 • 23,936
Huntsville, UT 84317 • 577
Hurdland, MO 63547 • 227
Hurley, MS 39555 • 600
Hurley, NM 88043 • 1,616
Hurley, NY 12443 • 4,081
Hurley, SD 57036 • 419
Hurley, VA 24620 • 400
Hurley, WI 54534 • 2,015
Hurleyville, NY 12747 • 500
Hurlock, MD 21643 • 1,690
Huron, IN 47437 • 300
Huron, OH 44839 • 7,123
Huron, SD 57350 • 13,000
Huron □, MI • 36,459
Huron □, OH • 54,608
Hurricane, UT 84737 • 2,361
Hurricane, WV 25526 • 3,751
Hurst, IL 62949 • 938
Hurst, TX 76053-54 • 31,420
Hurt, VA 24563 • 1,481
Hurtsboro, AL 36860 • 752
Hustisford, WI 53034 • 874
Hustonville, KY 40437 • 339
Hutchins, TX 75141 • 2,837
Hutchinson, KS 67501-05 • 40,284
Hutchinson, MN 55350 • 9,244
Hutchinson □, SD • 9,350
Hutchinson □, TX • 26,304
Hutsonville, IL 62433 • 705
Huttig, AR 71747 • 976
Hutto, TX 78634 • 659
Huttonsville, WV 26273 • 242
Huxley, IA 50124 • 1,884
Hyannis, MA 02601 • 8,000
Hyannis, NE 69350 • 336
Hyannis Port, MA 02647 • 1,150
Hyattsville, MD 20780-88 • 12,709
Hybla Valley, VA 22306 • 4,350
Hydaburg, AK 99922 • 298
Hyde, PA 16843 • 1,791
Hyde □, NC • 5,873
Hyde □, SD • 2,069
Hyden, KY 41749 • 488
Hyde Park, NY 12538 • 2,805
Hyde Park, UT 84318 • 1,495
Hyde Park, VT 05655 • 475
Hydetown, PA 16328 • 760
Hydeville, VT 05750 • 500
Hydro, OK 73048 • 938
Hygiene, CO 80533 • 350
Hymera, IN 47855 • 1,054
Hyndman, PA 15545 • 1,106
Hyrum, UT 84319 • 3,952
Hysham, MT 59038 • 449

I

Iaeger, WV 24844 • 833
Iberia, MO 65486 • 852
Iberia, OH 43325 • 350
Iberia □, LA • 63,752
Iberville, LA 70746 • 300
Iberville □, LA • 32,159
Ickesburg, PA 17037 • 250
Ida, LA 71044 • 306
Ida, MI 48140 • 1,000
Ida □, IA • 8,908
Ida Grove, IA 51445 • 2,285
Idaho □, ID • 14,769
Idaho City, ID 83631 • 300
Idaho Falls, ID 83401-15 • 39,590
Idaho Springs, CO 80452 • 2,077
Idalou, TX 79329 • 2,348
Idamay, WV 26576 • 600
Idanha, OR 97350 • 319
Idaville, IN 47950 • 625
Ideal, GA 31041 • 619
Ider, AL 35981 • 698
Idlewild, MI 49642 • 250
Idleyld Park, OR 97447 • 300
Ignacio, CO 81137 • 667
Ila, GA 30647 • 287
Ilchester, MD 21083 • 400
Ilion, NY 13357 • 9,450
Illiopolis, IL 62539 • 1,118
Illmo, MO 63754 • 1,368
Ilwaco, WA 98624 • 604
Imbler, OR 97841 • 292
Imboden, AR 72434 • 661
Imlay City, MI 48444 • 2,495
Imlaystown, NJ 08526 • 250
Immokalee, FL 33934 • 11,038
Imperial, CA 92251 • 3,451
Imperial, MO 63052 • 950
Imperial, NE 69033 • 1,941
Imperial, PA 15126 • 2,385
Imperial, TX 79743 • 750
Imperial □, CA • 92,110
Imperial Beach, CA 92032 • 22,689
Ina, IL 62846 • 460
Incline Village, NV 89450 • 4,500
Independence, CA 93526 • 1,000
Independence, IA 50644 • 6,392
Independence, KS 67301 • 10,598
Independence, KY 41051 • 7,998
Independence, LA 70443 • 1,684
Independence, MO 64050-58 • 111,806
Independence, OH 44131 • 6,607
Independence, OR 97351 • 4,024
Independence, VA 24348 • 1,112
Independence, WI 54747 • 1,180
Independence □, AR • 30,147
Indiahoma, OK 73552 • 364
Indiana, PA 15701 • 16,051
Indiana □, PA • 92,281
Indianapolis, IN 46201-99 • 700,807
Indian Cove, CT 06437 • 350
Indian Harbour Beach, FL 32937 • 5,967
Indian Head, MD 20640 • 1,381
Indian Heights, IN 46901 • 4,277
Indian Hills, CO 80454 • 900
Indian Lake, NY 12842 • 450
Indian Mound, TN 37079 • 300
Indian Mound Beach, MA 02532 • 800
Indian Neck, CT 06405 • 2,200
Indianola, IL 61850 • 370
Indianola, IA 50125 • 10,843
Indianola, MS 38751 • 8,221
Indianola, NE 69034 • 856
Indianola, OK 74442 • 254
Indian Ridge Estates, AZ 85715 • 2,300
Indian River, MI 49749 • 300
Indian River □, FL • 59,896
Indian Rocks Beach, FL 33535 • 3,717
Indian Springs, GA 30231 • 300
Indian Springs, NV 89018 • 900
Indiantown, FL 33456 • 3,383
Indian Trail, NC 28079 • 811
Indian Village, LA 70648 • 250
Indio, CA 92201 • 21,611
Indrio, FL 33450 • 400
Industry, IL 61440 • 600
Inez, KY 41224 • 413
Inez, TX 77968 • 900
Ingalls, IN 46048 • 909
Ingalls, KS 67853 • 274
Ingalls Park, IL 60431 • 3,500
Ingham □, MI • 275,520
Ingleside, TX 78362 • 5,436
Inglewood, CA 90301-99 • 94,245
Inglewood, NE 68025 • 257
Ingram, PA 15205 • 4,346
Inkom, ID 83245 • 830
Inkster, MI 48141 • 35,190
Inman, KS 67546 • 947
Inman, SC 29349 • 1,554
Inniswold, LA 70809 • 1,800
Inola, OK 74036 • 1,550
Inspiration, AZ 85532 • 300
Institute, WV 25112 • 1,500
Intercession City, FL 33848 • 950
Interlachen, FL 32048 • 848
Interlaken, MA 01266 • 300
Interlaken, NY 14847 • 685
International Falls, MN 56649 • 5,611
Intervale, NH 03845 • 300
Inver Grove Heights, MN 55075 • 17,171
Inverness, CA 94937 • 1,400
Inverness, FL 32650 • 4,095
Inverness, MS 38753 • 1,034
Inwood, FL 33880 • 6,668
Inwood, IA 51240 • 755
Inwood, NY 11696 • 8,200
Inwood, WV 25428 • 800
Inyo □, CA • 17,895
Inyokern, CA 93527 • 900
Iola, KS 66749 • 6,938
Iola, WI 54945 • 957
Iona, ID 83427 • 1,072
Iona, MN 56141 • 248
Ione, CA 95640 • 2,207
Ione, OR 97843 • 345
Ione, WA 99139 • 594
Ionia, IA 50645 • 350
Ionia, MI 48846 • 5,920
Ionia □, MI • 51,815
Iosco □, MI • 28,349
Iota, LA 70543 • 1,326
Iowa, LA 70647 • 2,437
Iowa □, IA • 15,429
Iowa □, WI • 19,802
Iowa City, IA 52240 • 50,508
Iowa Falls, IA 50126 • 6,174
Iowa Park, TX 76367 • 6,184
Ipava, IL 61441 • 661
Ipswich, MA 01938 • 4,548
Ipswich, SD 57451 • 1,153
Ira, TX 79527 • 350
Iraan, TX 79744 • 1,358
Iredell □, NC • 82,538
Ireland, IN 47545 • 450
Irene, SD 57037 • 523
Ireton, IA 51027 • 588
Irion □, TX • 1,386
Irmo, SC 29063 • 3,957
Iron □, MI • 13,635
Iron □, MO • 11,084
Iron □, UT • 17,349
Iron □, WI • 6,730
Iron Belt, WI 54536 • 520
Iron City, GA 31759 • 367
Iron City, TN 38463 • 482
Irondale, AL 35210 • 6,510
Irondale, MO 63648 • 349
Irondale, OH 43932 • 535
Irondequoit, NY 14617 • 57,648
Iron Gate, VA 24448 • 620
Ironia, NJ 07845 • 900
Iron Mountain, MI 49801 • 8,341
Iron Mountain, MO 63650 • 350
Iron Ridge, WI 53035 • 766
Iron River, MI 49935 • 2,426
Iron River, WI 54847 • 650
Ironton, MN 56455 • 537
Ironton, MO 63650 • 1,743
Ironton, OH 45638 • 14,290
Ironwood, MI 49938 • 7,741
Iroquois, IL 60945 • 227
Iroquois, SD 57353 • 348
Iroquois □, IL • 32,976
Irrigon, OR 97844 • 700
Irvine, CA 92714 • 62,134
Irvine, KY 40336 • 2,889
Irvine, PA 16329 • 350
Irving, IL 62051 • 612
Irving, TX 75060-63 • 109,943
Irvington, AL 36544 • 450
Irvington, IL 62848 • 789
Irvington, KY 40146 • 1,409
Irvington, NE 68134 • 500
Irvington, NJ 07111 • 61,493
Irvington, NY 10533 • 5,774
Irvington, VA 22480 • 567
Irvona, PA 16656 • 644
Irwin, IA 51446 • 427
Irwin, PA 15642 • 4,995
Irwin □, GA • 8,988
Irwinton, GA 31042 • 841
Isabel, SD 57633 • 332
Isabella, PA 15447 • 700
Isabella, TN 37346 • 300
Isabella □, MI • 54,110
Isanti, MN 55040 • 858
Isanti □, MN • 23,600
Iselin, NJ 08830 • 16,500
Iselin, PA 15681 • 400
Ishpeming, MI 49849 • 7,538
Islamorada, FL 33036 • 1,441
Island, KY 42350 • 532
Island □, WA • 44,048
Island City, OR 97850 • 477
Island Creek, MA 02332 • 450
Island Falls, ME 04747 • 650
Island Heights, NJ 08732 • 1,575
Island Park, NY 11558 • 4,847
Island Park, RI 02871 • 1,000
Island Pond, VT 05846 • 1,216
Isla Vista, CA 93117 • 16,700
Isle, MN 56342 • 573
Isle of Palms, SC 29451 • 3,421
Isle of Wight □, VA • 21,603
Isleta, NM 87022 • 1,246
Isleton, CA 95641 • 914
Islington, MA 02090 • 5,100
Islip, NY 11751 • 12,100
Islip Terrace, NY 11752 • 5,200
Isola, MS 38754 • 834

Issaquah, WA 98027 • 5,536
Issaquena □, MS • 2,513
Istachatta, FL 33536 • 335
Italy, TX 76651 • 1,306
Itasca, IL 60143 • 7,129
Itasca, TX 76055 • 1,600
Itasca □, MN • 43,069
Itawamba □, MS • 20,518
Ithaca, MI 48847 • 2,950
Ithaca, NY 14850 • 28,732
Itta Bena, MS 38941 • 2,904
Iuka, IL 62849 • 353
Iuka, KS 67066 • 235
Iuka, MS 38852 • 2,846
Iva, SC 29655 • 1,369
Ivanhoe, MN 56142 • 761
Ivanhoe, VA 24350 • 600
Ivesdale, IL 61851 • 339
Ivins, UT 84738 • 600
Ivor, VA 23866 • 403
Ivoryton, CT 06442 • 950
Ivydale, WV 25113 • 300
Ivywild, CO 80906 • 4,000
Izard □, AR • 10,768

J

Jacinto City, TX 77029 • 8,953
Jack □, TX • 7,408
Jackman, ME 04945 • 800
Jackpot, NV 89825 • 500
Jacksboro, TN 37757 • 1,722
Jacksboro, TX 76056 • 4,000
Jackson, AL 36545 • 6,073
Jackson, CA 95642 • 2,331
Jackson, GA 30233 • 4,133
Jackson, KY 41339 • 2,651
Jackson, LA 70748 • 3,133
Jackson, MI 49201-04 • 39,739
Jackson, MN 56143 • 3,797
Jackson, MS 39201-99 • 202,895
Jackson, MO 63755 • 7,827
Jackson, NE 68743 • 287
Jackson, NH 03846 • 300
Jackson, NJ 08527 • 600
Jackson, NC 27845 • 720
Jackson, OH 45640 • 6,675
Jackson, RI 02823 • 300
Jackson, SC 29831 • 1,771
Jackson, TN 38301-05 • 49,131
Jackson, WI 53037 • 1,817
Jackson, WY 83001 • 4,511
Jackson □, AL • 51,407
Jackson □, AR • 21,646
Jackson □, CO • 1,863
Jackson □, FL • 39,154
Jackson □, GA • 25,343
Jackson □, IL • 61,649
Jackson □, IN • 36,523
Jackson □, IA • 22,503
Jackson □, KS • 11,644
Jackson □, KY • 11,996
Jackson □, LA • 17,321
Jackson □, MI • 151,495
Jackson □, MN • 13,690
Jackson □, MS • 118,015
Jackson □, MO • 629,266
Jackson □, NC • 25,811
Jackson □, OH • 30,592
Jackson □, OK • 30,356
Jackson □, OR • 132,456
Jackson □, SD • 3,437
Jackson □, TN • 9,398
Jackson □, TX • 13,352
Jackson □, WV • 25,794
Jackson □, WI • 16,831
Jacksonboro, SC 29452 • 450
Jacksonburg, WV 26377 • 300
Jackson Center, OH 45334 • 1,310
Jackson Center, PA 16133 • 265
Jacksonport, AR 72075 • 288
Jacksons Gap, AL 36861 • 230
Jacksonville, AL 36265 • 9,735
Jacksonville, AR 72076 • 27,589
Jacksonville, FL 32201-99 • 540,920
Jacksonville, IL 62650 • 20,284
Jacksonville, NC 28540 • 18,237
Jacksonville, OH 45740 • 651
Jacksonville, OR 97530 • 2,030
Jacksonville, TX 75766 • 12,264
Jacksonville, VT 05342 • 252
Jacksonville Beach, FL 32250 • 15,462
Jacumba, CA 92034 • 600
Jaffrey, NH 03452 • 2,684
Jaffrey Center, NH 03454 • 240
Jakestown, TN 37130 • 500
Jal, NM 88252 • 2,675
Jamaica, IA 50128 • 275
Jamesburg, NJ 08831 • 4,114
James City, NC 28560 • 700
James City, PA 16734 • 450
James City □, VA • 22,763
James Island, SC 29412 • 24,124
Jamesport, MO 64648 • 651
Jamestown, CA 95327 • 2,206
Jamestown, CO 80455 • 223
Jamestown, IN 46147 • 924
Jamestown, KS 66948 • 440
Jamestown, KY 42629 • 1,441
Jamestown, MO 65046 • 317
Jamestown, NC 27282 • 2,148
Jamestown, ND 58401 • 16,280
Jamestown, NY 14701 • 35,775
Jamestown, OH 45335 • 1,702
Jamestown, PA 16134 • 854
Jamestown, RI 02835 • 4,040
Jamestown, TN 38556 • 2,364
James Town, WY 82935 • 275
Jamesville, NC 27846 • 604
Jamul, CA 92035 • 1,826
Jane Lew, WV 26378 • 406
Janesville, CA 96114 • 1,200
Janesville, IA 50647 • 840
Janesville, MN 56048 • 1,897
Janesville, WI 53545-47 • 51,071
Jansen, CO 81082 • 270
Jarales, NM 87023 • 350
Jarratt, VA 23867 • 614
Jarrettsville, MD 21084 • 1,485
Jarvisburg, NC 27947 • 300
Jasmine Estates, FL 33568 • 3,500
Jasonville, IN 47438 • 2,497
Jasper, AL 35501 • 11,894
Jasper, AR 72641 • 519
Jasper, FL 32052 • 2,093
Jasper, GA 30143 • 1,556
Jasper, IN 47546 • 9,097
Jasper, MN 56144 • 731
Jasper, MO 64755 • 1,012
Jasper, NY 14855 • 450
Jasper, OH 45642 • 250
Jasper, TN 37347 • 2,633
Jasper, TX 75951 • 6,959
Jasper □, GA • 7,553
Jasper □, IL • 11,318
Jasper □, IN • 26,138
Jasper □, IA • 36,425
Jasper □, MS • 17,265
Jasper □, MO • 86,958
Jasper □, SC • 14,504
Jasper □, TX • 30,781
Java, SD 57452 • 261
Jay, FL 32565 • 633
Jay, ME 04239 • 500
Jay, NY 12941 • 500
Jay, OK 74346 • 2,100
Jay □, IN • 23,239
Jayton, TX 79528 • 638
Jeanerette, LA 70544 • 6,511
Jeannette, PA 15644 • 13,106
Jeff Davis □, GA • 11,473
Jeff Davis □, TX • 1,647
Jeffers, MN 56145 • 437
Jefferson, AR 72079 • 250
Jefferson, GA 30549 • 1,820
Jefferson, IN 46041 • 270
Jefferson, IA 50129 • 4,854
Jefferson, LA 70121 • 15,550
Jefferson, ME 04348 • 250
Jefferson, MD 21755 • 300
Jefferson, MA 01522 • 800
Jefferson, NC 28640 • 1,086
Jefferson, OH 44047 • 2,952
Jefferson, OR 97352 • 1,702
Jefferson, PA 15025 • 8,643
Jefferson, SC 29718 • 651
Jefferson, SD 57038 • 592
Jefferson, TX 75657 • 2,643
Jefferson, WI 53549 • 5,647
Jefferson □, AL • 671,324
Jefferson □, AR • 90,718
Jefferson □, CO • 371,753
Jefferson □, FL • 10,703
Jefferson □, GA • 18,403
Jefferson □, ID • 15,304
Jefferson □, IL • 36,558
Jefferson □, IN • 30,419
Jefferson □, IA • 16,316
Jefferson □, KS • 15,207
Jefferson □, KY • 684,565
Jefferson □, LA • 454,592
Jefferson □, MS • 9,181
Jefferson □, MO • 146,183
Jefferson □, MT • 7,029
Jefferson □, NE • 9,817
Jefferson □, NY • 88,151
Jefferson □, OH • 91,564
Jefferson □, OK • 8,183
Jefferson □, OR • 11,599
Jefferson □, PA • 48,303
Jefferson □, TN • 31,284
Jefferson □, TX • 250,938
Jefferson □, WA • 15,965
Jefferson □, WV • 30,302
Jefferson □, WI • 66,152
Jefferson City, MO 65101 • 33,619
Jefferson City, TN 37760 • 5,612
Jefferson Davis □, LA • 32,168
Jefferson Davis □, MS • 13,846
Jefferson Farms, DE 19720 • 2,400
Jefferson Manor, VA 22303 • 2,550
Jeffersontown, KY 40299 • 15,795
Jefferson Village, VA 22042 • 2,800
Jeffersonville, GA 31044 • 1,473
Jeffersonville, IN 47130 • 21,220
Jeffersonville, KY 40337 • 1,528
Jeffersonville, NY 12748 • 554
Jeffersonville, OH 43128 • 1,252
Jeffersonville, VT 05464 • 491
Jeffrey, WV 25114 • 900
Jeffrey City, WY 82310 • 400
Jellico, TN 37762 • 2,798
Jemez Pueblo, NM 87024 • 1,503
Jemez Springs, NM 87025 • 316
Jemison, AL 35085 • 1,828
Jena, FL 32359 • 300
Jena, LA 71342 • 4,375
Jenera, OH 45841 • 302
Jenison, MI 49428 • 16,330
Jenkins, KY 41537 • 3,271
Jenkins □, GA • 8,841
Jenkinsburg, GA 30234 • 360
Jenkinsville, SC 29065 • 500
Jenkintown, PA 19046 • 4,942
Jenks, OK 74037 • 5,876
Jenners, PA 15546 • 800
Jennings, FL 32053 • 749
Jennings, LA 70546 • 12,401
Jennings, MO 63136 • 17,026
Jennings, OK 74038 • 395
Jennings □, IN • 22,854
Jennings Lodge, OR 97222 • 3,000
Jensen, UT 84035 • 400
Jensen Beach, FL 33457 • 6,639
Jerauld □, SD • 2,929
Jericho, NY 11753 • 14,200
Jericho, VT 05465 • 1,340
Jermyn, PA 18433 • 2,411
Jerome, AZ 86331 • 420
Jerome, FL 33926 • 675
Jerome, ID 83338 • 6,891
Jerome, PA 15937 • 1,158
Jerome □, ID • 14,840
Jeromesville, OH 44840 • 582
Jersey □, IL • 20,538
Jersey City, NJ 07301-99 • 223,532
Jersey Shore, PA 17740 • 4,631
Jerseyville, IL 62052 • 7,506
Jerusalem, OH 43747 • 237
Jessamine □, KY • 26,065
Jessup, MD 20794 • 4,288
Jessup, PA 18434 • 4,974
Jesup, GA 31545 • 9,418
Jesup, IA 50648 • 2,343
Jet, OK 73749 • 352
Jetmore, KS 67854 • 862
Jewell, IA 50130 • 1,145
Jewell, KS 66949 • 589
Jewell □, KS • 5,241
Jewell Ridge, VA 24622 • 600
Jewett, IL 62436 • 230
Jewett, OH 43986 • 972
Jewett, TX 75846 • 597
Jewett City, CT 06351 • 3,294
Jim Hogg □, TX • 5,168
Jim Thorpe, PA 18229 • 5,263
Jim Wells □, TX • 36,498
Joanna, SC 29351 • 1,839
Jobstown, NJ 08041 • 230
Jo Daviess □, IL • 23,520
Jodie, WV 26674 • 450
Johannesburg, CA 93528 • 300
Johannesburg, MI 49751 • 250
John Day, OR 97845 • 2,012
Johnsburg, IL 60050 • 900
Johnsburg, NY 12843 • 300
John Sevier, TN 37914 • 600
Johns Island, SC 29455 • 435
Johnson, AR 72741 • 519
Johnson, KS 67855 • 1,244
Johnson, NE 68378 • 341
Johnson, VT 05656 • 1,393
Johnson □, AR • 17,423
Johnson □, GA • 8,660
Johnson □, IL • 9,624
Johnson □, IN • 77,240
Johnson □, IA • 81,717
Johnson □, KS • 270,269
Johnson □, KY • 24,432
Johnson □, MO • 39,059
Johnson □, NE • 5,285
Johnson □, TN • 13,745
Johnson □, TX • 67,649
Johnson □, WY • 6,700
Johnsonburg, PA 15845 • 3,938
Johnson City, NY 13790 • 17,126
Johnson City, TN 37601 • 39,753
Johnson City, TX 78636 • 872
Johnson Creek, WI 53038 • 1,136
Johnsonville, SC 29555 • 1,421
Johnston, IA 50131 • 2,617
Johnston, RI 02919 • 24,907
Johnston, SC 29832 • 2,624
Johnston □, NC • 70,599
Johnston □, OK • 10,356
Johnston City, IL 62951 • 3,873
Johnstown, CO 80534 • 1,535
Johnstown, NY 12095 • 9,360
Johnstown, OH 43031 • 3,158
Johnstown, PA 15901-15 • 35,496
Joice, IA 50446 • 223
Joiner, AR 72350 • 725
Joliet, IL 60431-36 • 77,956
Joliet, MT 59041 • 580
Jones, OK 73049 • 2,270
Jones □, GA • 16,579
Jones □, IA • 20,401
Jones □, MS • 61,912
Jones □, NC • 9,705
Jones □, SD • 1,463
Jones □, TX • 17,268
Jonesboro, AR 72401 • 31,530
Jonesboro, GA 30236 • 4,132
Jonesboro, IL 62952 • 1,842
Jonesboro, IN 46938 • 2,279
Jonesboro, LA 71251 • 5,061
Jonesboro, TN 37659 • 2,829
Jonesburg, MO 63351 • 614
Jones Creek, TX 77541 • 2,634
Jones Mill, AR 72105 • 850
Jonesport, ME 04649 • 1,050
Jonestown, MS 38639 • 1,231
Jonestown, MS 39194 • 350
Jonestown, PA 17038 • 814
Jonesville, LA 71343 • 2,828
Jonesville, MI 49250 • 2,172
Jonesville, NC 28642 • 1,752
Jonesville, SC 29353 • 1,201
Jonesville, VT 05466 • 300
Jonesville, VA 24263 • 874
Joplin, MO 64801 • 39,023
Joppa, IL 62953 • 535
Joppa, MD 21085 • 11,348
Jordan, MN 55352 • 2,663
Jordan, MT 59337 • 485
Jordan, NY 13080 • 1,371
Jordan Valley, OR 97910 • 473
Joseph, OR 97846 • 999
Joseph City, AZ 86032 • 900
Josephine □, OR • 58,855
Joshua, TX 76058 • 1,470
Joshua Tree, CA 92252 • 2,083
Jourdanton, TX 78026 • 2,743
Joy, IL 61260 • 506
Joyce, LA 71440 • 900
Juab □, UT • 5,530
Juda, WI 53550 • 450
Judith Basin □, MT • 2,646
Judsonia, AR 72081 • 2,025
Julesburg, CO 80737 • 1,528
Juliaetta, ID 83535 • 522
Julian, CA 92036 • 1,320
Julian, WV 25529 • 700
Juliette, GA 31046 • 300
Juliustown, NJ 08042 • 400
Junction, TX 76849 • 2,593
Junction City, AR 71749 • 813
Junction City, GA 31812 • 254
Junction City, IL 62882 • 456
Junction City, KS 66441 • 19,305
Junction City, KY 40440 • 2,045
Junction City, LA 71749 • 727
Junction City, OH 43748 • 754
Junction City, OR 97448 • 3,320
Junction City, WI 54443 • 523
Juneau, AK 99801 • 19,528
Juneau, WI 53039 • 2,045
Juneau □, WI • 21,039
June Lake, CA 93529 • 900
Juniata, NE 68955 • 703
Juniata □, PA • 19,188
Juniata Terrace, PA 17044 • 631
Junior, WV 26275 • 591
Jupiter, FL 33458 • 9,868
Justice, IL 60458 • 10,552
Justin, TX 76247 • 920

K

Kaaawa, HI 96730 • 959
Kadoka, SD 57543 • 832
Kahaluu, HI 96725 • 380
Kahaluu, HI 96744 • 2,925
Kahoka, MO 63445 • 2,101
Kahuku, HI 96731 • 935
Kahului, HI 96732 • 12,978
Kaibito, AZ 86053 • 300
Kailua, HI 96734 • 35,812
Kailua Kona, HI 96740 • 4,751
Kainaliu, HI 96750 • 512
Kake, AK 99830 • 555
Kalaheo, HI 96741 • 2,500
Kalama, WA 98625 • 1,216
Kalamazoo, MI 49001-09 • 79,722
Kalamazoo □, MI • 212,378
Kalaoa Homesteads, HI 96725 • 275
Kalawao □, HI • 144
Kaleva, MI 49645 • 445
Kalispell, MT 59901 • 10,648
Kalkaska, MI 49646 • 1,654
Kalkaska □, MI • 10,952
Kalona, IA 52247 • 1,862
Kaltag, AK 99748 • 247
Kamas, UT 84036 • 1,064
Kamiah, ID 83536 • 1,478
Kamooloa, HI 96791 • 350
Kampsville, IL 62053 • 423
Kamrar, IA 50132 • 225
Kamuela (Waimea), HI 96743 • 1,179
Kanab, UT 84741 • 2,148
Kanabec □, MN • 12,161
Kanarraville, UT 84742 • 255
Kanauga, OH 45631 • 500
Kanawha, IA 50447 • 756
Kanawha □, WV • 231,414
Kandiyohi, MN 56251 • 447
Kandiyohi □, MN • 36,763
Kane, IL 62054 • 445
Kane, PA 16735 • 4,916
Kane □, IL • 278,405
Kane □, UT • 4,024
Kaneohe, HI 96744 • 29,919
Kangley, IL 61364 • 280
Kankakee, IL 60901 • 30,141
Kankakee □, IL • 102,926
Kannapolis, NC 28081 • 34,564
Kanopolis, KS 67454 • 729
Kanosh, UT 84637 • 435
Kansas, AL 35573 • 267
Kansas, IL 61933 • 791
Kansas, OH 44841 • 400
Kansas, OK 74347 • 491
Kansas City, KS 66101-99 • 161,148
Kansas City, MO 64101-99 • 448,159
Kansasville, WI 53139 • 250
Kapaa, HI 96746 • 4,467
Kapaau, HI 96755 • 237
Kaplan, LA 70548 • 5,016
Kapowsin, WA 98344 • 230
Karlstad, MN 56732 • 934
Karnak, IL 62956 • 646
Karnes □, TX • 13,593
Karnes City, TX 78118 • 3,296
Karns, TN 37921 • 1,173
Karns City, PA 16041 • 354
Karthaus, PA 16845 • 300
Kasota, MN 56050 • 739
Kasson, MN 55944 • 2,827
Kathleen, FL 33849 • 1,866
Katy, TX 77449-50 • 5,660
Kauai □, HI • 39,082
Kaufman, TX 75142 • 4,658
Kaufman □, TX • 39,029
Kaukauna, WI 54130 • 11,310
Kaumakani, HI 96747 • 888
Kaunakakai, HI 96748 • 2,231
Kawailoa Beach, HI 96712 • 400
Kaw City, OK 74641 • 283
Kay □, OK • 49,852
Kaycee, WY 82639 • 271
Kayenta, AZ 86033 • 3,343
Kayford, WV 25122 • 250
Kaysville, UT 84037 • 9,811
Keaau, HI 96749 • 775
Kealakekua, HI 96750 • 1,033
Kealia, HI 96751 • 700
Keams Canyon, AZ 86034 • 600
Keanae, HI 96708 • 250
Keansburg, NJ 07734 • 10,613
Kearney, MO 64060 • 1,433
Kearney, NE 68847 • 21,158
Kearney □, NE • 7,053
Kearneysville, WV 25430 • 500
Kearns, UT 84118 • 21,353
Kearny, AZ 85237 • 2,646
Kearny, NJ 07032 • 35,735
Kearny □, KS • 3,435
Kearsarge, MI 49942 • 285
Kearsarge, NH 03847 • 300
Keatchie, LA 71046 • 342
Keaton, KY 41226 • 250
Keddie, CA 95952 • 285
Keedysville, MD 21756 • 476
Keegan, ME 04785 • 300
Keego Harbor, MI 48033 • 3,083
Keene, CA 93531 • 250
Keene, KY 40339 • 250
Keene, NH 03431 • 21,449
Keene, NY 12942 • 450
Keene, TX 76059 • 3,013
Keenesburg, CO 80643 • 541
Keene Valley, NY 12943 • 400
Keensburg, IL 62852 • 244
Keeseville, NY 12944 • 2,025
Keewatin, MN 55753 • 1,443
Keezletown, VA 22832 • 250
Keiser, AR 72351 • 962
Keith □, NE • 9,364
Keithsburg, IL 61442 • 936
Keizer, OR 97303 • 18,592
Kekaha, HI 96752 • 3,260
Kelford, NC 27847 • 254
Kell, IL 62853 • 283
Keller, TX 76248 • 4,156
Keller, VA 23401 • 236
Kellerton, IA 50133 • 278
Kelley, IA 50134 • 237
Kelliher, MN 56650 • 324
Kellnersville, WI 54215 • 369
Kellogg, ID 83837 • 3,417
Kellogg, IA 50135 • 654
Kellogg, MN 55945 • 440
Kelly, LA 71441 • 250
Kelly Lake, MN 55754 • 900
Kellyton, AL 35089 • 300
Kellyville, NH 03743 • 350
Kellyville, OK 74039 • 960
Kelseyville, CA 95451 • 1,567
Kelso, MO 63758 • 455
Kelso, WA 98626 • 11,129
Kemmerer, WY 83101 • 3,273
Kemp, TX 75143 • 1,035
Kemper □, MS • 10,148
Kempner, TX 76539 • 280
Kempton, IL 60946 • 265
Kempton, IN 46049 • 410
Kenai, AK 99611 • 4,324
Kenansville, FL 32739 • 700
Kenansville, NC 28349 • 931
Kenbridge, VA 23944 • 1,352
Kendall, FL 33156 • 51,000
Kendall, NY 14476 • 375
Kendall, WI 54638 • 486
Kendall □, IL • 37,202
Kendall □, TX • 10,635
Kendall Park, NJ 08824 • 7,419
Kendallville, IN 46755 • 7,299
Kendrick, ID 83537 • 395
Kenduskeag, ME 04450 • 370
Kenedy, TX 78119 • 4,356
Kenedy □, TX • 543
Kenesaw, NE 68956 • 854
Kenilworth, IL 60043 • 2,708
Kenilworth, NJ 07033 • 8,221
Kenilworth, UT 84529 • 350
Kenly, NC 27542 • 1,433
Kenmare, ND 58746 • 1,456
Kenmawr, PA 15136 • 5,100
Kenmore, NY 14217 • 18,474
Kenmore, WA 98028 • 7,900
Kenna, WV 25248 • 300
Kennard, IN 47351 • 441
Kennard, NE 68034 • 372
Kennard, TX 75847 • 424
Kennebec, SD 57544 • 334
Kennebec □, ME • 109,889
Kennebunk, ME 04043 • 3,294
Kennebunkport, ME 04046 • 1,685
Kennedale, TX 76060 • 2,594
Kennedy, AL 35574 • 604
Kennedy, MN 56733 • 405
Kennedy, NY 14747 • 500
Kennedy Heights, LA 70094 • 2,000
Kenner, LA 70062-65 • 66,382
Kennesaw, GA 30144 • 5,095
Kennett, MO 63857 • 10,145
Kennett Square, PA 19348 • 4,715
Kennewick, WA 99336-37 • 34,397
Kenney, IL 61749 • 443
Kennydale, WA 98055 • 1,000
Keno, OR 97627 • 900
Kenosha, WI 53140-42 • 77,685
Kenosha □, WI • 123,137
Kenova, WV 25530 • 4,454
Ken Rock, IL 61109 • 5,945
Kensett, AR 72082 • 1,751
Kensett, IA 50448 • 360
Kensington, CA 94707 • 5,342
Kensington, CT 06037 • 7,502
Kensington, KS 66951 • 681
Kensington, MD 20895 • 1,822
Kensington, MN 56343 • 331
Kensington, OH 44427 • 300
Kent, AL 36045 • 500
Kent, CT 06757 • 500
Kent, OH 44240 • 26,164
Kent, WA 98031-32 • 23,152
Kent □, DE • 98,219
Kent □, MD • 16,695
Kent □, MI • 444,506
Kent □, RI • 154,163
Kent □, TX • 1,145
Kent City, MI 49330 • 860
Kentland, IN 47951 • 1,936
Kenton, DE 19955 • 243
Kenton, KY 41053 • 300
Kenton, MI 49943 • 250
Kenton, OH 43326 • 8,605
Kenton, TN 38233 • 1,551
Kenton □, KY • 137,058
Kentwood, LA 70444 • 2,667
Kentwood, MI 49508 • 30,438
Kenvil, NJ 07847 • 3,000
Kenvir, KY 40847 • 950
Kenwood, OH 45236 • 9,928
Kenyon, MN 55946 • 1,529
Kenyon, RI 02836 • 350
Keokea, HI 96790 • 900
Keokuk, IA 52632 • 13,536
Keokuk □, IA • 12,921
Keosauqua, IA 52565 • 1,003
Keota, IA 52248 • 1,034
Keota, OK 74941 • 661
Kerby, OR 97531 • 550
Kerens, TX 75144 • 1,582
Kerhonkson, NY 12446 • 1,243
Kerkhoven, MN 56252 • 761
Kermit, TX 79745 • 8,015
Kermit, WV 25674 • 705
Kern □, CA • 403,089
Kernersville, NC 27284 • 6,802
Kernville, CA 93238 • 1,660
Kerr □, TX • 28,780
Kerrville, TX 78028 • 15,276
Kersey, CO 80644 • 913
Kersey, PA 15846 • 600
Kershaw, SC 29067 • 1,993
Kershaw □, SC • 39,015
Keshena, WI 54135 • 500
Keswick, IA 50136 • 300
Ketchikan, AK 99901 • 7,198
Ketchum, ID 83340 • 2,200
Ketchum, OK 74349 • 326
Ketona, AL 35217 • 600
Kettering, OH 45429 • 61,186
Kettle Falls, WA 99141 • 1,087
Kettleman City, CA 93239 • 1,051
Kevil, KY 42053 • 382
Kewanee, IL 61443 • 14,508
Kewanna, IN 46939 • 711
Kewaskum, WI 53040 • 2,381
Kewaunee, WI 54216 • 2,801
Kewaunee □, WI • 19,539
Keweenaw □, MI • 1,963
Keya Paha □, NE • 1,301
Keyes, OK 73947 • 557
Keyesport, IL 62253 • 499
Key Largo, FL 33037 • 7,447
Keyport, NJ 07735 • 7,413
Keyser, WV 26726 • 6,569
Keystone, IA 52249 • 618
Keystone, SD 57751 • 295
Keystone, WV 24852 • 902
Keystone Heights, FL 32656 • 1,056
Keysville, GA 30816 • 300
Keysville, VA 23947 • 704
Keytesville, MO 65261 • 689
Key West, FL 33040 • 24,382
Key West, IA 52001 • 500
Kezar Falls, ME 04047 • 900
Kiana, AK 99749 • 345
Kidder, MO 64649 • 265
Kidder □, ND • 3,833
Kiefer, OK 74041 • 912
Kiel, WI 53042 • 3,083
Kiester, MN 56051 • 670
Kihei, HI 96753 • 5,644
Kilauea, HI 96754 • 895
Kilbourne, IL 62655 • 382
Kilbourne, LA 71253 • 286
Kilbourne, OH 43032 • 250
Kilgore, TX 75662 • 11,006
Killbuck, OH 44637 • 937
Killdeer, ND 58640 • 790
Killeen, TX 76541-46 • 46,296
Killen, AL 35645 • 747
Killian, LA 70462 • 611
Killona, LA 70066 • 600
Kilmarnock, VA 22482 • 945
Kilmichael, MS 39747 • 906
Kiln, MS 39556 • 650
Kimball, MN 55353 • 651
Kimball, NE 69145 • 3,120
Kimball, SD 57355 • 752
Kimball, WV 24853 • 871
Kimball □, NE • 4,882
Kimballton, IA 51543 • 362
Kimberlin Heights, TN 37920 • 600
Kimberly, AL 35091 • 1,043
Kimberly, ID 83341 • 2,307
Kimberly, WV 25118 • 800
Kimberly, WI 54136 • 5,881
Kimble □, TX • 4,063
Kimbolton, OH 43749 • 255
Kimbrough, NM 88240 • 250
Kimmell, IN 46760 • 290
Kincaid, IL 62540 • 1,591
Kincaid, WV 25119 • 700
Kinde, MI 48445 • 600
Kinder, LA 70648 • 2,603
Kinderhook, IL 62345 • 259
Kinderhook, NY 12106 • 1,377
Kindred, ND 58051 • 568
King, NC 27021 • 5,000
King, WI 54946 • 750
King □, TX • 425
King □, WA • 1,269,749
King and Queen □, VA • 5,968
King City, CA 93930 • 5,495
King City, MO 64463 • 1,063
King Cove, AK 99612 • 460
King Ferry, NY 13081 • 400
Kingfield, ME 04947 • 700
Kingfisher, OK 73750 • 4,245
Kingfisher □, OK • 14,187
King George □, VA • 10,543
King Lake, NE 68064 • 400
Kingman, AZ 86401 • 9,257
Kingman, IN 47952 • 566
Kingman, KS 67068 • 3,563
Kingman □, KS • 8,960
King of Prussia, PA 19406 • 18,200
Kings, MS 39180 • 1,165
Kings □, CA • 73,738
Kings □, NY • 2,230,936
King Salmon, AK 99613 • 545
Kingsburg, CA 93631 • 5,115
Kingsbury, IN 46345 • 329
Kingsbury □, SD • 6,679
Kings Corner, CT 06088 • 400
Kingsford, MI 49801 • 5,290
Kingsland, AR 71652 • 320
Kingsland, GA 31548 • 2,008
Kingsland, TX 78639 • 1,600
Kingsley, IA 51028 • 1,209
Kingsley, MI 49649 • 664
Kings Mills, OH 45034 • 500
Kings Mountain, NC 28086 • 9,080
Kings Park, VA 22151 • 4,450
Kings Park West, VA 22030 • 5,000
Kings Point, NY 11024 • 5,234
Kingsport, TN 37660-65 • 32,027
Kingston, GA 30145 • 733
Kingston, ID 83839 • 1,000
Kingston, IL 60145 • 618
Kingston, MA 02364 • 4,405
Kingston, MI 48741 • 417
Kingston, MO 64650 • 280
Kingston, NH 03848 • 900
Kingston, NJ 08528 • 900
Kingston, NY 12401 • 24,481
Kingston, OH 45644 • 1,208
Kingston, OK 73439 • 1,171
Kingston, PA 18704 • 15,681
Kingston, RI 02881 • 5,419
Kingston, TN 37763 • 4,441
Kingston, WI 53939 • 328
Kingston Springs, TN 37082 • 1,017
Kingstown, MD 21620 • 1,192
Kingstree, SC 29556 • 4,147
Kingsville, MD 21087 • 2,824
Kingsville, MO 64061 • 365
Kingsville, OH 44048 • 1,243
Kingsville, TX 78363 • 28,808
King William □, VA • 9,334
Kingwood, WV 26537 • 2,877
Kinloch, MO 63140 • 4,455
Kinmundy, IL 62854 • 945
Kinnelon, NJ 07405 • 7,770
Kinney □, TX • 2,279
Kinsale, VA 22488 • 250
Kinsey, AL 36301 • 1,239
Kinsley, KS 67547 • 2,074
Kinsman, OH 44428 • 800
Kinston, AL 36453 • 604

Kinston, NC 28501 • *25,234*
Kinta, OK 74552 • *303*
Kinzua, OR 97830 • *300*
Kiowa, KS 67070 • *1,409*
Kiowa, OK 74553 • *866*
Kiowa □, CO • *1,936*
Kiowa □, KS • *4,046*
Kiowa □, OK • *12,711*
Kipling, MI 49837 • *300*
Kipnuk, AK 99614 • *371*
Kipton, OH 44049 • *352*
Kirby, AR 71950 • *250*
Kirby, TX 78280 • *6,435*
Kirbyville, TX 75956 • *1,972*
Kirkersville, OH 43033 • *626*
Kirkland, IL 60146 • *1,155*
Kirkland, WA 98033-34 • *18,779*
Kirklin, IN 46050 • *662*
Kirksville, MO 63501 • *17,167*
Kirkwood, DE 19708 • *400*
Kirkwood, IL 61447 • *1,008*
Kirkwood, MO 63122 • *27,987*
Kiron, IA 51448 • *317*
Kirtland, NM 87417 • *2,358*
Kirtland, OH 44094 • *5,969*
Kirwin, KS 67644 • *249*
Kismet, KS 67859 • *368*
Kissimmee, FL 32741-43 • *15,487*
Kistler, WV 25628 • *750*
Kit Carson, CO 80825 • *278*
Kit Carson □, CO • *7,599*
Kite, GA 31049 • *328*
Kitsap □, WA • *147,152*
Kittanning, PA 16201 • *5,432*
Kittery, ME 03904 • *5,465*
Kittery Point, ME 03905 • *1,260*
Kittitas, WA 98934 • *782*
Kittitas □, WA • *24,877*
Kittrell, NC 27544 • *225*
Kitts, KY 40848 • *500*
Kittson □, MN • *6,672*
Kitty Hawk, NC 27949 • *600*
Kitzmiller, MD 21538 • *387*
Kivalina, AK 99750 • *241*
Klamath, CA 95548 • *850*
Klamath □, OR • *59,117*
Klamath Falls, OR 97601-03 • *16,661*
Klamath Glen, CA 95548 • *600*
Klawock, AK 99925 • *318*
Kleberg □, TX • *33,358*
Klein, TX 77379 • *9,000*
Klemme, IA 50449 • *620*
Klickitat, WA 98628 • *700*
Klickitat □, WA • *15,822*
Kline, SC 29814 • *315*
Klondike, IN 47906 • *300*
Klotzville, LA 70341 • *350*
Knapp, WI 54749 • *419*
Knife River, MN 55609 • *350*
Knightdale, NC 27545 • *985*
Knights Landing, CA 95645 • *1,000*
Knightstown, IN 46148 • *2,325*
Knightsville, IN 47857 • *763*
Knippa, TX 78870 • *400*
Knobel, AR 72435 • *503*
Knob Noster, MO 65336 • *2,040*
Knollwood, CT 06475 • *300*
Knollwood, WV 25302 • *700*
Knott □, KY • *17,940*
Knotts Island, NC 27950 • *400*
Knottsville, KY 42366 • *350*
Knox, IN 46534 • *3,674*
Knox, PA 16232 • *1,364*
Knox □, IL • *61,607*
Knox □, IN • *41,838*
Knox □, KY • *30,239*
Knox □, ME • *32,941*
Knox □, MO • *5,508*
Knox □, NE • *11,457*
Knox □, OH • *46,304*
Knox □, TN • *319,694*
Knox □, TX • *5,329*
Knox City, MO 63446 • *281*
Knox City, TX 79529 • *1,546*
Knox Dale, PA 15847 • *275*
Knoxville, AR 72845 • *264*
Knoxville, IL 61448 • *3,432*
Knoxville, IA 50138 • *8,143*
Knoxville, MD 21758 • *300*
Knoxville, PA 16928 • *650*
Knoxville, TN 37901-99 • *175,045*
Kodiak, AK 99615 • *4,756*
Kohler, WI 53044 • *1,651*
Kokomo, HI 96708 • *250*
Kokomo, IN 46901-02 • *47,808*
Koloa, HI 96756 • *1,457*
Komatke, AZ 85339 • *250*
Konawa, OK 74849 • *1,711*
Koochiching □, MN • *17,571*
Koontz Lake, IN 46574 • *1,436*
Kooskia, ID 83539 • *784*
Kootenai, ID 83840 • *280*
Kootenai □, ID • *59,770*
Koppel, PA 16136 • *1,146*
Kosciusko, MS 39090 • *7,415*
Kosciusko □, IN • *59,555*
Koshkonong, MO 65692 • *245*
Kosse, TX 76653 • *484*
Kossuth □, IA • *21,891*
Kotlik, AK 99620 • *293*
Kotzebue, AK 99752 • *2,054*
Kountze, TX 77625 • *2,716*
Kouts, IN 46347 • *1,619*
Kraemer, LA 70371 • *500*
Krebs, OK 74554 • *1,754*
Kremlin, OK 73753 • *301*
Kremmling, CO 80459 • *1,296*
Kresgeville, PA 18333 • *250*
Kress, TX 79052 • *783*
Krotz Springs, LA 70750 • *1,374*
Kualapuu, HI 96757 • *502*
Kukuihaele, HI 96727 • *332*
Kukuiula, HI 96756 • *280*
Kula, HI 96790 • *1,300*
Kulm, ND 58456 • *570*
Kulpmont, PA 17834 • *3,675*
Kuna, ID 83634 • *1,767*
Kunia, HI 96759 • *550*
Kurtistown, HI 96760 • *1,200*
Kuttawa, KY 42055 • *560*
Kutztown, PA 19530 • *4,040*
Kwethluk, AK 99621 • *454*
Kwigillingok, AK 99622 • *354*
Kyle, TX 78640 • *2,093*

L

Labadie, MO 63055 • *250*
Labadieville, LA 70372 • *2,138*
La Barge, WY 83123 • *302*
La Belle, FL 33935 • *2,287*
La Belle, MO 63447 • *845*
Labette □, KS • *25,682*
La Canada Flintridge, CA 91011 • *20,153*
Lac du Flambeau, WI 54538 • *900*
La Center, KY 42056 • *1,044*
Lacey, WA 98503 • *13,940*
Laceys Spring, AL 35754 • *400*
Laceyville, PA 18623 • *498*
Lackawanna, NY 14218 • *22,701*
Lackawanna □, PA • *227,908*
Lackawaxen, PA 18435 • *500*
Laclede, ID 83841 • *400*
Laclede, MO 64651 • *445*
Laclede □, MO • *24,323*
Lacombe, LA 70445 • *5,146*
Lacon, IL 61540 • *2,135*
Lacona, IA 50139 • *376*
Lacona, NY 13083 • *582*
Laconia, NH 03246 • *15,575*
La Conner, WA 98257 • *633*
Lacoochee, FL 33537 • *1,720*
Lac Qui Parle □, MN • *10,592*
La Crescent, MN 55947 • *3,674*
La Crescenta, CA 91214 • *12,500*
La Crosse, IN 46348 • *713*
La Crosse, KS 67548 • *1,618*
La Crosse, VA 23950 • *734*
Lacrosse, WA 99143 • *373*
La Crosse, WI 54601-03 • *48,347*
La Crosse □, WI • *91,056*
La Cygne, KS 66040 • *1,025*
Ladd, IL 61329 • *1,337*
Laddonia, MO 63352 • *726*
Ladera Heights, CA 90045 • *6,647*
Ladoga, IN 47954 • *1,151*
Ladonia, TX 75449 • *761*
Ladora, IA 52251 • *289*
Ladson, SC 29456 • *13,246*
Lady Lake, FL 32659 • *1,193*
Ladysmith, WI 54848 • *3,826*
La Farge, WI 54639 • *746*
LaFargeville, NY 13656 • *500*
Lafayette, AL 36862 • *3,647*
Lafayette, CA 94549 • *20,879*
Lafayette, CO 80026 • *8,985*
Lafayette, GA 30728 • *6,517*
La Fayette, IL 61449 • *281*
Lafayette, IN 47901-07 • *43,011*
Lafayette, LA 70501-09 • *81,961*
Lafayette, MN 56054 • *507*
Lafayette, NJ 07848 • *250*
Lafayette, NC 28304 • *4,100*
La Fayette, NY 13084 • *400*
Lafayette, OR 97127 • *1,215*
La Fayette, RI 02852 • *680*
Lafayette, TN 37083 • *3,808*
Lafayette □, AR • *10,213*
Lafayette □, FL • *4,035*
Lafayette □, LA • *150,017*
Lafayette □, MS • *31,030*
Lafayette □, MO • *29,925*
Lafayette □, WI • *17,412*
Lafayette Hill, PA 19444 • *6,600*
Lafayette Southwest, LA 70501 • *5,500*
La Feria, TX 78559 • *3,495*
Lafferty, OH 43951 • *600*
Lafitte, LA 70067 • *1,312*
La Follette, TN 37766 • *8,198*
La Fontaine, IN 46940 • *946*
Lafourche, LA 70301 • *600*
Lafourche □, LA • *82,483*
La France, SC 29656 • *800*
Lagonda, LA 70380 • *5,805*
La Grande, OR 97850 • *11,354*
La Grange, AR 72352 • *250*
Lagrange, FL 32780 • *460*
La Grange, GA 30240 • *24,204*
La Grange, IL 60525 • *15,445*
Lagrange, IN 46761 • *2,164*
La Grange, KY 40031 • *2,971*
La Grange, MO 63448 • *1,217*
La Grange, NC 28551 • *3,147*
Lagrange, OH 44050 • *1,258*
La Grange, TX 78945 • *3,768*
Lagrange, WY 82221 • *232*
Lagrange □, IN • *25,550*
La Grange Highlands, IL 60525 • *7,100*
La Grange Park, IL 60525 • *13,359*
Lagro, IN 46941 • *549*
Laguna, NM 87026 • *800*
Laguna Beach, CA 92651-53 • *17,901*
Laguna Hills, CA 92653 • *16,400*
La Habra, CA 90631 • *45,232*
Lahaina, HI 96761 • *6,095*
La Harpe, IL 61450 • *1,471*
La Harpe, KS 66751 • *687*
Lahoma, OK 73754 • *537*
Laie, HI 96762 • *4,643*
Laingsburg, MI 48848 • *1,145*
La Jara, CO 81140 • *858*
La Junta, CO 81050 • *8,338*
Lake, MI 48632 • *300*
Lake, MS 39092 • *524*
Lake □, CA • *36,366*
Lake □, CO • *8,830*
Lake □, FL • *104,870*
Lake □, IL • *440,372*
Lake □, IN • *522,965*
Lake □, MI • *7,711*
Lake □, MN • *13,043*
Lake □, MT • *19,056*
Lake □, OH • *212,801*
Lake □, OR • *7,532*
Lake □, SD • *10,724*
Lake □, TN • *7,455*
Lake Alfred, FL 33850 • *3,134*
Lake Andes, SD 57356 • *1,029*
Lake Ariel, PA 18436 • *450*
Lake Arrowhead, CA 92352 • *2,500*
Lake Arthur, LA 70549 • *3,615*
Lake Arthur, NM 88253 • *327*
Lake Barcroft, VA 22041 • *2,250*
Lake Benton, MN 56149 • *869*
Lake Beseck, CT 06455 • *500*
Lake Beulah, WI 53120 • *300*
Lake Bluff, IL 60044 • *4,434*
Lake Bronson, MN 56734 • *298*
Lake Butler, FL 32054 • *1,830*
Lake Butte Des Morts, WI • *1,111*
Lake Charles, LA 70601-11 • *75,226*
Lake City, AR 72437 • *1,842*
Lake City, FL 32055 • *9,257*
Lake City, IA 51449 • *2,006*
Lake City, MI 49651 • *843*
Lake City, MN 55041 • *4,505*
Lake City, PA 16423 • *2,384*
Lake City, SC 29560 • *6,731*
Lake City, TN 37769 • *2,335*
Lake Cormorant, MS 38641 • *350*
Lake Crystal, MN 56055 • *2,078*
Lake Delta, NY 13440 • *2,400*
Lake Delton, WI 53940 • *1,158*
Lake Elmo, MN 55042 • *5,296*
Lake Elsinore, CA 92330 • *5,982*
Lake Erie Beach, NY 14006 • *3,500*
Lakefield, MN 56150 • *1,845*
Lake Forest, FL 33023 • *5,400*
Lake Forest, IL 60045 • *15,245*
Lake Geneva, WI 53147 • *5,612*
Lake George, MI 48633 • *300*
Lake George, NY 12845 • *1,047*
Lake Grove, NY 11755 • *9,692*
Lake Hamilton, AR 71913 • *1,054*
Lake Havasu City, AZ 86403 • *15,909*
Lake Helen, FL 32744 • *2,047*
Lake Hiawatha, NJ 07034 • *14,000*
Lake Hubert, MN 56459 • *300*
Lake Hughes, CA 93532 • *800*
Lake Huntington, NY 12752 • *350*
Lakehurst, NJ 08733 • *2,908*
Lake in the Hills, IL 60102 • *5,651*
Lake Jackson, TX 77566 • *19,102*
Lake Katrine, NY 12449 • *1,092*
Lakeland, FL 33801-07 • *47,406*
Lakeland, GA 31635 • *2,647*
Lake Leelanau, MI 49653 • *300*
Lake Lillian, MN 56253 • *329*
Lake Linden, MI 49945 • *1,181*
Lake Luzerne, NY 12846 • *1,000*
Lake Magdalene, FL 33612 • *13,331*
Lake Mary, FL 32746 • *2,853*
Lake Mills, IA 50450 • *2,281*
Lake Mills, WI 53551 • *3,670*
Lakemont, PA 16602 • *1,500*
Lakemore, OH 44250 • *2,744*
Lake Nebagamon, WI 54849 • *780*
Lake Norden, SD 57248 • *417*
Lake Odessa, MI 48849 • *2,171*
Lake Of The Woods □, MN • *3,764*
Lake Orion, MI 48035 • *2,907*
Lake Oswego, OR 97034 • *22,527*
Lake Ozark, MO 65049 • *427*
Lake Park, FL 33403 • *6,909*
Lake Park, GA 31636 • *448*
Lake Park, IA 51347 • *1,123*
Lake Park, MN 56554 • *716*
Lake Placid, FL 33852 • *963*
Lake Placid, NY 12946 • *2,490*
Lake Pleasant, NY 12108 • *300*
Lakeport, CA 95453 • *3,675*
Lake Preston, SD 57249 • *789*
Lake Providence, LA 71254 • *6,361*
Lakeridge, NV 89448 • *400*
Lake Ridge, VA 22191 • *6,500*
Lake Ronkonkoma, NY 11779 • *9,600*
Lake Shore, MD 21122 • *2,100*
Lakeshore, MS 39558 • *800*
Lakeside, AZ 85929 • *1,333*
Lakeside, CA 92040 • *23,921*
Lakeside, CT 06758 • *400*
Lakeside, CT 06488 • *900*
Lakeside, IA 50588 • *589*
Lakeside, MT 59922 • *500*
Lakeside, NJ 07421 • *250*
Lakeside, OH 43440 • *950*
Lakeside, OR 97449 • *1,453*
Lakeside, VA 23228 • *29,400*
Lakeside Park, KY 41017 • *3,038*
Lake Station, IN 46405 • *14,294*
Lake Station, OK 74127 • *800*
Lake Stevens, WA 98258 • *1,660*
Lake Tansi, TN 38555 • *500*
Lake Telemark, NJ 07866 • *1,216*
Lake Tomahawk, WI 54539 • *600*
Laketon, IN 46943 • *500*
Laketown, UT 84038 • *271*
Lake Toxaway, NC 28747 • *300*
Lakeview, GA 30741 • *5,403*
Lake View, IA 51450 • *1,291*
Lakeview, MI 48850 • *1,139*
Lake View, NY 14085 • *4,600*
Lakeview, OH 43331 • *1,089*
Lakeview, OR 97630 • *2,770*
Lake View, SC 29563 • *939*
Lakeview, TX 79239 • *244*
Lake Villa, IL 60046 • *1,462*
Lake Village, AR 71653 • *3,088*
Lake Village, IN 46349 • *650*
Lakeville, CT 06039 • *1,200*
Lakeville, IN 46536 • *629*
Lakeville, MA 02346 • *1,948*
Lakeville, MN 55044 • *14,790*
Lakeville, NY 14480 • *950*
Lake Waccamaw, NC 28450 • *1,133*
Lake Wales, FL 33853 • *8,466*
Lake Wilson, MN 56151 • *380*
Lake Winola, PA 18625 • *350*
Lake Wissota, WI 54729 • *1,419*
Lakewood, CA 90712-16 • *74,654*
Lakewood, CO 80215 • *113,808*
Lakewood, IA 50211 • *900*
Lakewood, NJ 08701 • *22,863*
Lakewood, NY 14750 • *3,941*
Lakewood, OH 44107 • *61,963*
Lakewood, WA 98259 • *500*
Lakewood, WI 54138 • *250*
Lakewood Center, WA 98499 • *51,300*
Lake Worth, FL 33460-67 • *27,048*
Lake Zurich, IL 60047 • *8,225*
Lakin, KS 67860 • *1,823*

Lakota, IA 50451 • 330
Lakota, ND 58344 • 963
La Luz, NM 88337 • 1,194
Lamar, AR 72846 • 708
Lamar, CO 81052 • 7,713
Lamar, MO 64759 • 4,053
Lamar, PA 16848 • 650
Lamar, SC 29069 • 1,333
Lamar □, AL • 16,453
Lamar □, GA • 12,215
Lamar □, MS • 23,821
Lamar □, TX • 42,156
La Marque, TX 77568 • 15,372
Lamb □, TX • 18,669
Lambert, MS 38643 • 1,624
Lamberton, MN 56152 • 1,032
Lambertville, MI 48144 • 6,341
Lambertville, NJ 08530 • 4,044
Lame Deer, MT 59043 • 600
La Mesa, CA 92041 • 50,308
La Mesa, NM 88044 • 900
Lamesa, TX 79331 • 11,790
La Mirada, CA 90638 • 40,986
La Moille, IL 61330 • 734
Lamoille □, VT • 16,767
Lamoni, IA 50140 • 2,705
Lamont, CA 93241 • 9,616
Lamont, IA 50650 • 554
Lamont, OK 74643 • 571
La Monte, MO 65337 • 1,054
La Motte, IA 52054 • 322
La Moure, ND 58458 • 1,077
La Moure □, ND • 6,473
Lampasas, TX 76550 • 6,165
Lampasas □, TX • 12,005
Lanagan, MO 64847 • 440
Lanai City, HI 96763 • 2,092
Lanare, CA 93656 • 400
Lanark, IL 61046 • 1,483
Lanark, WV 25860 • 600
Lanark Village, FL 32323 • 650
Lancaster, CA 93534-39 • 48,027
Lancaster, KS 66041 • 274
Lancaster, KY 40444 • 3,365
Lancaster, MA 01523 • 900
Lancaster, MN 56735 • 368
Lancaster, MO 63548 • 855
Lancaster, NH 03584 • 2,134
Lancaster, NY 14086 • 13,056
Lancaster, OH 43130 • 34,953
Lancaster, PA 17601-99 • 54,725
Lancaster, SC 29720 • 9,703
Lancaster, TX 75146 • 14,807
Lancaster, WI 53813 • 4,076
Lancaster □, NE • 192,884
Lancaster □, PA • 362,346
Lancaster □, SC • 53,361
Lancaster □, VA • 10,129
Lancer, KY 41653 • 400
Lander, WY 82520 • 7,867
Lander □, NV • 4,076
Landis, NC 28088 • 2,092
Landisburg, PA 17040 • 227
Lando, SC 29724 • 850
Land O'lakes, WI 54540 • 500
Landrum, SC 29356 • 2,141
Lane, KS 66042 • 249
Lane, SC 29564 • 554
Lane □, KS • 2,472
Lane □, OR • 275,226
Lanesboro, MA 01237 • 950
Lanesboro, MN 55949 • 923
Lanesboro, PA 18827 • 465
Lanesville, IN 47136 • 570
Lanett, AL 36863 • 6,897
Langdale, AL 36854 • 2,034
Langdon, ND 58249 • 2,335
Langeloth, PA 15054 • 950
Langford, SD 57454 • 307
Langhorne, PA 19047 • 1,697
Langlade □, WI • 19,978
Langley, KY 41645 • 600
Langley, OK 74350 • 582
Langley, SC 29834 • 1,714
Langley, WA 98260 • 650
Langley Park, MD 20787 • 11,100
Langleyville, IL 62568 • 400
Langston, OK 73050 • 443
Lanham, MD 20706 • 7,300
Lanier □, GA • 5,654
Lannon, WI 53046 • 987
Lanoka Harbor, NJ 08734 • 700
Lansdale, PA 19446 • 16,526
Lansdowne, MD 21227 • 10,000
Lansdowne, PA 19050 • 11,891
L'Anse, MI 49946 • 2,500
Lansford, ND 58750 • 294
Lansford, PA 18232 • 4,466
Lansing, IL 60438 • 29,039
Lansing, IA 52151 • 1,181
Lansing, KS 66043 • 5,307
Lansing, MI 48901-99 • 130,414
Lansing, WV 25862 • 500
Lantana, FL 33462 • 8,048
Laona, WI 54541 • 700
Laotto, IN 46763 • 400
La Palma, CA 90623 • 15,399
Lapaz, IN 46537 • 651
La Paz □, AZ • 12,557
Lapeer, MI 48446 • 6,198
Lapeer □, MI • 70,038
Lapel, IN 46051 • 1,881
La Pine, OR 97739 • 900
La Place, IL 61936 • 400
La Place, LA 70068 • 16,112
La Plata, MD 20646 • 2,484
La Plata, MO 63549 • 1,423
La Plata □, CO • 27,195
La Platte, NE 68123 • 300
Lapoint, UT 84039 • 250
Laporte, CO 80535 • 900
La Porte, IN 46350 • 21,796
Laporte, PA 18626 • 230
La Porte, TX 77571 • 16,836
La Porte □, IN • 108,632
La Porte City, IA 50651 • 2,324
La Prairie, MN 55744 • 536
La Pryor, TX 78872 • 1,000
La Puente, CA 91744-49 • 30,882
La Push, WA 98350 • 600
Lapwai, ID 83540 • 1,043
Laramie, WY 82070 • 24,410
Laramie □, WY • 68,649
Larchmont, NY 10538 • 6,308
Larchmont North, NY 10538 • 11,500
Larchwood, IA 51241 • 701
Laredo, MO 64652 • 340
Laredo, TX 78040-44 • 91,449
Largo, FL 33540-43 • 58,977
Larimer □, CO • 149,184
Larimore, ND 58251 • 1,524
Lark, UT 84065 • 500
Larkspur, CA 94939 • 11,064
Larksville, PA 18704 • 4,410
Larned, KS 67550 • 4,811
Larose, LA 70373 • 5,234
La Rue, OH 43332 • 861
Larue □, KY • 11,922
Larwill, IN 46764 • 286
La Salle, CO 80645 • 1,929
La Salle, IL 61301 • 10,347
La Salle □, IL • 112,033
La Salle □, LA • 17,004
La Salle □, TX • 5,514
Las Animas, CO 81054 • 2,818
Las Animas □, CO • 14,897
Las Cruces, NM 88001-08 • 45,086
Lassen □, CA • 21,661
Las Vegas, NV 89101-99 • 164,674
Las Vegas, NM 87701 • 14,322
Latah □, ID • 28,749
Latexo, TX 75849 • 312
Latham, IL 62543 • 564
Latham, NY 12110 • 8,000
Lathrop, MO 64465 • 1,732
Lathrop Wells, NV 89020 • 250
Latimer, IA 50452 • 441
Latimer □, OK • 9,840
Laton, CA 93242 • 1,100
Latrobe, PA 15650 • 10,799
Latta, SC 29565 • 1,804
Lattimer Mines, PA 18234 • 650
Lattimore, NC 28089 • 237
Latty, OH 45855 • 261
Lauderdale, MS 39335 • 750
Lauderdale □, AL • 80,546
Lauderdale □, MS • 77,285
Lauderdale □, TN • 24,555
Lauderdale Lakes, FL 33313 • 25,426
Lauderhill, FL 33313 • 37,271
Laughlintown, PA 15655 • 750
Laupahoehoe, HI 96764 • 500
Laura, OH 45337 • 501
Laurel, DE 19956 • 3,052
Laurel, FL 33545 • 1,500
Laurel, IN 47024 • 819
Laurel, IA 50141 • 278
Laurel, MD 20707-08 • 12,103
Laurel, MS 39440 • 21,897
Laurel, MT 59044 • 5,481
Laurel, NE 68745 • 1,031
Laurel, VA 23060 • 1,500
Laurel □, KY • 38,982
Laurel Bay, SC 29902 • 5,238
Laureldale, NJ 08330 • 300
Laureldale, PA 19605 • 4,047
Laurel Hill, FL 32567 • 610
Laurel Hill, NC 28351 • 2,314
Laurel Run, PA 18702 • 725
Laurelton, PA 17835 • 250
Laurelville, OH 43135 • 591
Laurelwood Academy, OR 97119 • 400
Laurence Harbor, NJ 08879 • 5,000
Laurens, IA 50554 • 1,606
Laurens, SC 29360 • 10,587
Laurens □, GA • 36,990
Laurens □, SC • 52,214
Laurinburg, NC 28352 • 11,480
Laurium, MI 49913 • 2,678
Lavaca, AR 72941 • 1,092
Lavaca □, TX • 19,004
Lava Hot Springs, ID 83246 • 467
La Vale, MD 21502 • 5,500
La Valle, WI 53941 • 412
Lavallette, NJ 08735 • 2,072
Laveen, AZ 85339 • 600
La Vergne, TN 37086 • 5,495
La Verkin, UT 84745 • 1,174
La Verne, CA 91750 • 23,508
Laverne, OK 73848 • 1,563
La Vernia, TX 78121 • 632
La Veta, CO 81055 • 611
La Vista, GA 30329 • 5,200
La Vista, NE 68128 • 9,588
Lavonia, GA 30553 • 2,024
Lawai, HI 96765 • 950
Lawler, IA 52154 • 534
Lawn, TX 79530 • 390
Lawndale, CA 90260 • 23,460
Lawndale, NC 28090 • 469
Lawnside, NJ 08045 • 3,042
Lawrence, IN 46226 • 25,591
Lawrence, KS 66044-46 • 52,738
Lawrence, MA 01840-45 • 63,175
Lawrence, MI 49064 • 903
Lawrence, NE 68957 • 350
Lawrence, NY 11559 • 6,175
Lawrence, PA 15055 • 970
Lawrence □, AL • 30,170
Lawrence □, AR • 18,447
Lawrence □, IL • 17,807
Lawrence □, IN • 42,472
Lawrence □, KY • 14,121
Lawrence □, MS • 12,518
Lawrence □, MO • 28,973
Lawrence □, OH • 63,849
Lawrence □, PA • 107,150
Lawrence □, SD • 18,339
Lawrence □, TN • 34,110
Lawrenceburg, IN 47025 • 4,403
Lawrenceburg, KY 40342 • 5,167
Lawrenceburg, TN 38464 • 10,184
Lawrence Park, PA 16511 • 4,584
Lawrenceville, GA 30245 • 8,928
Lawrenceville, IL 62439 • 5,652
Lawrenceville, NJ 08648 • 1,800
Lawrenceville, PA 16929 • 327
Lawrenceville, VA 23868 • 1,484
Lawson, MO 64062 • 1,688
Lawsonia, MD 21817 • 1,687
Lawtell, LA 70550 • 1,014
Lawtey, FL 32058 • 692
Lawton, IA 51030 • 447
Lawton, KY 41153 • 300
Lawton, MI 49065 • 1,558
Lawton, OK 73501-05 • 80,054
Layland, WV 25864 • 350
Laysville, CT 06371 • 250
Layton, UT 84041 • 26,393
Laytonville, CA 95454 • 1,096
Lea □, NM • 55,993
Leachville, AR 72438 • 1,882
Lead, SD 57754 • 4,330
Lead Hill, AR 72644 • 247
Leadville, CO 80461 • 3,879
Leadwood, MO 63653 • 1,371
Leaf, MS 39450 • 270
Leaf River, IL 61047 • 637
League City, TX 77573 • 16,578
Leake □, MS • 18,790
Leakesville, MS 39451 • 1,120
Leakey, TX 78873 • 468
Lealman, FL 33717 • 19,875
Leary, GA 31762 • 783
Leasburg, MO 65535 • 304
Leatherwood, KY 41756 • 250
Leavenworth, IN 47137 • 356
Leavenworth, KS 66048 • 33,656
Leavenworth, WA 98826 • 1,522
Leavenworth □, KS • 54,809
Leavittsburg, OH 44430 • 2,220
Leawood, KS 66206 • 13,360
Lebam, WA 98554 • 240
Lebanon, CT 06249 • 300
Lebanon, IL 62254 • 3,245
Lebanon, IN 46052 • 11,456
Lebanon, KS 66952 • 440
Lebanon, KY 40033 • 6,590
Lebanon, MO 65536 • 9,507
Lebanon, NH 03766 • 11,134
Lebanon, NJ 08833 • 820
Lebanon, OH 45036 • 9,636
Lebanon, OK 73440 • 250
Lebanon, OR 97355 • 10,413
Lebanon, PA 17042 • 25,711
Lebanon, TN 37087 • 11,872
Lebanon, VA 24266 • 3,206
Lebanon □, PA • 108,582
Lebanon Junction, KY 40150 • 1,581
Lebec, CA 93243 • 900
Lebo, KS 66856 • 966
Le Center, MN 56057 • 1,967
Le Claire, IA 52753 • 2,899
Lecompte, LA 71346 • 1,661
Lecompton, KS 66050 • 576
Ledgewood, NJ 07852 • 1,100
Lee, FL 32059 • 297
Lee, IL 60530 • 304
Lee, MA 01238 • 2,140
Lee □, AL • 76,283
Lee □, AR • 15,539
Lee □, FL • 205,266
Lee □, GA • 11,684
Lee □, IL • 36,328
Lee □, IA • 43,106
Lee □, KY • 7,754
Lee □, MS • 57,061
Lee □, NC • 36,718
Lee □, SC • 18,929
Lee □, TX • 10,952
Lee □, VA • 25,956
Lee Center, IL 61331 • 250
Leechburg, PA 15656 • 2,682
Leedey, OK 73654 • 499
Leedom Estates, DE 19720 • 1,300
Leeds, AL 35094 • 8,638
Leeds, ND 58346 • 678
Leeds Point, NJ 08220 • 400
Leelanau □, MI • 14,007
Lee Park, PA 18702 • 3,900
Leeper, PA 16233 • 300
Leesburg, FL 32748-49 • 13,191
Leesburg, GA 31763 • 1,301
Leesburg, IN 46538 • 629
Leesburg, NJ 08327 • 700
Leesburg, OH 45135 • 1,019
Leesburg, VA 22075 • 8,357
Lees Summit, MO 64063 • 28,741
Leesville, LA 71446 • 9,054
Leesville, OH 44639 • 233
Leesville, SC 29070 • 2,296
Leeton, MO 64761 • 604
Leetonia, OH 44431 • 2,121
Leetsdale, PA 15056 • 1,604
Lee Vining, CA 93541 • 900
Leffingwell, CT 06360 • 450
Leflore, OK 74942 • 322
Leflore □, MS • 41,525
Le Flore □, OK • 40,698
Lefors, TX 79054 • 829
Leggett, CA 95455 • 700
Le Grand, CA 95333 • 1,500
Le Grand, IA 50142 • 921
Lehi, UT 84043 • 6,848
Lehigh, IA 50557 • 654
Lehigh, OK 74556 • 284
Lehigh □, PA • 272,349
Lehigh Acres, FL 33936 • 9,604
Lehighton, PA 18235 • 5,826
Lehman, PA 18627 • 250
Lehr, ND 58460 • 254
Leicester, MA 01524 • 3,400
Leicester, NY 14481 • 462
Leigh, NE 68643 • 509
Leighton, AL 35646 • 1,218
Leipers Fork, TN 37064 • 300
Leipsic, DE 19901 • 228
Leipsic, OH 45856 • 2,171
Leisure City, FL 33033 • 17,905
Leitchfield, KY 42754 • 4,533
Leitersburg, MD 21740 • 400
Leiters Ford, IN 46945 • 300
Lejunior, KY 40849 • 600
Leland, IL 60531 • 775
Leland, IA 50453 • 274
Leland, MI 49654 • 600
Leland, MS 38756 • 6,667
Le Mars, IA 51031 • 8,276
Lemasters, PA 17231 • 280
Lemay, MO 63125 • 35,424
Lemhi □, ID • 7,460
Lemitar, NM 87823 • 400
Lemmon, SD 57638 • 1,871
Lemmon Valley, NV 89501 • 2,000
Lemon Grove, CA 92045 • 20,780
Lemont, IL 60439 • 5,640
Lemont, PA 16851 • 2,613

Lemoore, CA 93245 • 8,832
Lemoyne, OH 43441 • 300
Lena, IL 61048 • 2,295
Lena, MS 39094 • 231
Lena, WI 54139 • 585
Lenapah, OK 74042 • 350
Lenawee □, MI • 89,948
Lenexa, KS 66215 • 18,639
Lennox, CA 90304 • 18,445
Lennox, SD 57039 • 1,827
Lenoir, NC 28645 • 13,748
Lenoir □, NC • 59,819
Lenoir City, TN 37771 • 5,446
Lenora, KS 67645 • 444
Lenox, GA 31637 • 965
Lenox, IA 50851 • 1,338
Lenox, MA 01240 • 2,668
Lenox, TN 38047 • 275
Lenox Dale, MA 01242 • 600
Leo, IN 46765 • 800
Leola, AR 72084 • 481
Leola, SD 57456 • 645
Leoma, TN 38468 • 300
Leominster, MA 01453 • 34,508
Leon, IA 50144 • 2,094
Leon, KS 67074 • 667
Leon, NY 14751 • 300
Leon, WV 25123 • 228
Leon □, FL • 148,655
Leon □, TX • 9,594
Leonard, MI 48038 • 423
Leonard, ND 58052 • 289
Leonard, TX 75452 • 1,421
Leonardo, NJ 07737 • 3,600
Leonardsville, NY 13364 • 500
Leonardtown, MD 20650 • 1,448
Leonardville, KS 66449 • 437
Leonia, NJ 07605 • 8,027
Leon Valley, TX 78280 • 9,088
Leonville, LA 70551 • 1,143
Leota, MN 56153 • 320
Leoti, KS 67861 • 1,869
Lepanto, AR 72354 • 1,964
Le Raysville, PA 18829 • 356
Lerna, IL 62440 • 386
Le Roy, IL 61752 • 2,870
Leroy, IN 46355 • 350
Le Roy, KS 66857 • 701
Le Roy, MI 49655 • 293
Le Roy, MN 55951 • 930
Le Roy, NY 14482 • 4,900
Leslie, AR 72645 • 501
Leslie, GA 31764 • 470
Leslie, MI 49251 • 2,110
Leslie, SC 29730 • 1,102
Leslie, WV 25972 • 400
Leslie □, KY • 14,882
Lester, IA 51242 • 274
Lester, WV 25865 • 626
Lester Prairie, MN 55354 • 1,229
Le Sueur, MN 56058 • 3,763
Le Sueur □, MN • 23,434
Letcher □, KY • 30,687
Leto, FL 33614 • 9,003
Letohatchee, AL 36047 • 250
Letona, AR 72085 • 231
Le Tourneau, MS 39180 • 400
Letts, IN 47240 • 250
Letts, IA 52754 • 473
Leucadia, CA 92024 • 9,478
Levan, UT 84639 • 453
Levelland, TX 79336-38 • 13,809
Levering, MI 49755 • 400
Levittown, NY 11756 • 65,400
Levittown, PA 19053-59 • 78,600
Levy □, FL • 19,870
Lewellen, NE 69147 • 368
Lewes, DE 19958 • 2,197
Lewis, IA 51544 • 497
Lewis, KS 67552 • 551
Lewis, NY 12950 • 500
Lewis □, ID • 4,118
Lewis □, KY • 14,545
Lewis □, MO • 10,901
Lewis □, NY • 25,035
Lewis □, TN • 9,700
Lewis □, WA • 56,025
Lewis □, WV • 18,813
Lewis And Clark □, MT • 43,039
Lewisberry, PA 17339 • 309
Lewisburg, KY 42256 • 972
Lewisburg, LA 70525 • 240
Lewisburg, OH 45338 • 1,450
Lewisburg, PA 17837 • 5,407
Lewisburg, TN 37091 • 8,760
Lewisburg, WV 24901 • 3,065
Lewis Center, OH 43035 • 250
Lewisport, KY 42351 • 1,832
Lewis Run, PA 16738 • 677
Lewiston, ID 83501 • 27,986
Lewiston, ME 04240 • 40,481
Lewiston, MI 49756 • 600
Lewiston, MN 55952 • 1,226
Lewiston, NY 14092 • 3,326
Lewiston, UT 84320 • 1,438
Lewiston Woodville, NC 27849 • 671
Lewistown, IL 61542 • 2,758
Lewistown, MD 21701 • 275
Lewistown, MO 63452 • 502
Lewistown, MT 59457 • 7,104
Lewistown, PA 17044 • 9,830
Lewisville, AR 71845 • 1,476
Lewisville, ID 83431 • 502
Lewisville, IN 47352 • 577
Lewisville, MN 56060 • 273
Lewisville, OH 43754 • 285
Lewisville, TX 75067 • 24,273
Lexa, AR 72355 • 500
Lexington, AL 35648 • 884
Lexington, GA 30648 • 278
Lexington, IL 61753 • 1,806
Lexington, KY 40501-99 • 204,165
Lexington, MA 02173 • 29,479
Lexington, MI 48450 • 765
Lexington, MS 39095 • 2,628
Lexington, MO 64067 • 5,063
Lexington, NE 68850 • 7,040
Lexington, NC 27292 • 15,711
Lexington, NY 12452 • 300
Lexington, OH 44904 • 3,823
Lexington, OK 73051 • 1,731
Lexington, OR 97839 • 307
Lexington, SC 29072 • 2,131
Lexington, TN 38351 • 5,934
Lexington, TX 78947 • 1,065
Lexington, VA 24450 • 7,292
Lexington, WA 98626 • 500
Lexington □, SC • 140,353
Lexington Park, MD 20653 • 10,361
Libby, MT 59923 • 2,748
Liberal, KS 67901 • 14,911
Liberal, MO 64762 • 701
Liberty, IL 62347 • 587
Liberty, IN 47353 • 1,844
Liberty, KY 42539 • 2,206
Liberty, MS 39645 • 669
Liberty, MO 64068 • 16,251
Liberty, NC 27298 • 1,997
Liberty, NY 12754 • 4,293
Liberty, SC 29657 • 3,167
Liberty, TN 37095 • 365
Liberty, TX 77575 • 7,945
Liberty □, FL • 4,260
Liberty □, GA • 37,583
Liberty □, MT • 2,329
Liberty □, TX • 47,088
Liberty Acres, CA 90250 • 4,600
Liberty Center, IN 46766 • 300
Liberty Center, OH 43532 • 1,111
Liberty Corner, NJ 07938 • 800
Liberty Lake, WA 99019 • 900
Libertytown, MD 21762 • 500
Libertyville, IL 60048 • 16,520
Libertyville, IA 52567 • 281
Libuse, LA 71348 • 700
Licking, MO 65542 • 1,272
Licking □, OH • 120,981
Lidgerwood, ND 58053 • 971
Liftwood, DE 19803 • 800
Lighthouse Point, FL 33064 • 11,488
Lignite, ND 58752 • 332
Ligonier, IN 46767 • 3,134
Ligonier, PA 15658 • 1,917
Lihue, HI 96766 • 4,000
Likely, CA 96116 • 265
Lilbourn, MO 63862 • 1,463
Lilburn, GA 30247 • 3,765
Lilesville, NC 28091 • 588
Lillian, AL 36549 • 600
Lillington, NC 27546 • 1,948
Lilly, PA 15938 • 1,462
Lilly Grove, WV 24740 • 1,700
Lily, KY 40740 • 400
Lima, MT 59739 • 272
Lima, NY 14485 • 2,025
Lima, OH 45801-09 • 47,381
Limerick, ME 04048 • 325
Lime Rock, CT 06039 • 300
Limerock, RI 02865 • 600
Lime Springs, IA 52155 • 476
Limestone, ME 04750 • 1,334
Limestone, NY 14753 • 466
Limestone, TN 37681 • 350
Limestone □, AL • 46,005
Limestone □, TX • 20,224
Limon, CO 80828 • 1,805
Linch, WY 82640 • 250
Lincoln, AL 35096 • 2,081
Lincoln, AR 72744 • 1,422
Lincoln, CA 95648 • 4,132
Lincoln, DE 19960 • 500
Lincoln, ID 83401 • 700
Lincoln, IL 62656 • 16,327
Lincoln, KS 67455 • 1,599
Lincoln, ME 04457 • 3,524
Lincoln, MA 01773 • 3,300
Lincoln, MI 48742 • 361
Lincoln, MO 65338 • 819
Lincoln, MT 59639 • 500
Lincoln, NE 68501-99 • 171,932
Lincoln, VA 22078 • 300
Lincoln □, AR • 13,369
Lincoln □, CO • 4,663
Lincoln □, GA • 6,716
Lincoln □, ID • 3,436
Lincoln □, KS • 4,145
Lincoln □, KY • 19,053
Lincoln □, LA • 39,763
Lincoln □, ME • 25,691
Lincoln □, MN • 8,207
Lincoln □, MS • 30,174
Lincoln □, MO • 22,193
Lincoln □, MT • 17,752
Lincoln □, NE • 36,455
Lincoln □, NV • 3,732
Lincoln □, NM • 10,997
Lincoln □, NC • 42,372
Lincoln □, OK • 26,601
Lincoln □, OR • 35,264
Lincoln □, SD • 13,942
Lincoln □, TN • 26,483
Lincoln □, WA • 9,604
Lincoln □, WV • 23,675
Lincoln □, WI • 26,555
Lincoln □, WY • 12,177
Lincoln Acres, CA 92047 • 1,800
Lincoln Center, ME 04458 • 300
Lincoln City, OR 97367 • 5,469
Lincoln Heights, OH 45215 • 5,259
Lincoln Park, CO 81212 • 3,426
Lincoln Park, GA 30286 • 1,755
Lincoln Park, MI 48146 • 45,105
Lincoln Park, NJ 07035 • 8,806
Lincolnshire, IL 60069 • 4,151
Lincolnton, GA 30817 • 1,406
Lincolnton, NC 28092 • 4,879
Lincoln Village, CA 95207 • 6,476
Lincoln Village, OH 43228 • 10,548
Lincolnville, KS 66858 • 235
Lincolnville, SC 29483 • 808
Lincolnwood, IL 60645 • 11,921
Lincroft, NJ 07738 • 4,100
Lind, WA 99341 • 567
Linda, CA 95901 • 10,225
Lindale, GA 30147 • 2,958
Lindale, TX 75771 • 2,180
Linden, AL 36748 • 2,773
Linden, IN 47955 • 700
Linden, IA 50146 • 264
Linden, MI 48451 • 2,174
Linden, NJ 07036 • 37,836
Linden, NC 28356 • 365
Linden, TN 37096 • 1,087
Linden, TX 75563 • 2,443
Linden, WI 53553 • 395
Lindenhurst, IL 60046 • 6,220
Lindenhurst, NY 11757 • 26,919
Lindenwold, NJ 08021 • 18,196
Lindon, UT 84062 • 2,796
Lindsay, CA 93247 • 6,924
Lindsay, NE 68644 • 383
Lindsay, OK 73052 • 3,454
Lindsborg, KS 67456 • 3,155
Lindsey, OH 43442 • 571
Lindstrom, MN 55045 • 1,972
Lineboro, MD 21088 • 225
Linesville, PA 16424 • 1,198
Lineville, AL 36266 • 2,257
Lineville, IA 50147 • 319
Lingle, WY 82223 • 475
Linglestown, PA 17112 • 3,000
Linn, KS 66953 • 483
Linn, MO 65051 • 1,211
Linn, TX 78563 • 260
Linn □, IA • 169,775
Linn □, KS • 8,234
Linn □, MO • 15,495
Linn □, OR • 89,495
Linn Creek, MO 65052 • 242
Linneus, ME 04730 • 300
Linneus, MO 64653 • 421
Lino Lakes, MN 55014 • 4,966
Linthicum Heights, MD 21090 • 7,457
Linton, IN 47441 • 6,315
Linton, ND 58552 • 1,561
Linville, NC 28646 • 500
Linwood, GA 30728 • 417
Linwood, KS 66052 • 343
Linwood, MA 01525 • 1,100
Linwood, MI 48634 • 400
Linwood, NJ 08221 • 6,144
Linworth, OH 43085 • 650
Lionville, PA 19353 • 500
Lipan, TX 76462 • 435
Lippitt Estate, RI 02864 • 400
Lipscomb, AL 35020 • 3,741
Lipscomb □, TX • 3,766
Lisbon, IL 60541 • 259
Lisbon, IA 52253 • 1,458
Lisbon, ME 04250 • 1,200
Lisbon, NH 03585 • 1,151
Lisbon, ND 58054 • 2,283
Lisbon, NY 13658 • 400
Lisbon, OH 44432 • 3,159
Lisbon Center, ME 04251 • 625
Lisbon Falls, ME 04252 • 4,370
Liscomb, IA 50148 • 296
Lisle, IL 60532 • 13,625
Lisman, AL 36912 • 638
Lismore, MN 56155 • 276
Listie, PA 15549 • 500
Litchfield, CA 96117 • 350
Litchfield, CT 06759 • 1,489
Litchfield, IL 62056 • 7,204
Litchfield, MI 49252 • 1,353
Litchfield, MN 55355 • 5,904
Litchfield, NE 68852 • 256
Litchfield □, CT • 156,769
Litchfield Park, AZ 85340 • 3,657
Litchville, ND 58461 • 251
Lithia Springs, GA 30057 • 9,145
Lithonia, GA 30058 • 2,637
Lititz, PA 17543 • 7,590
Little Acres, AZ 85501 • 600
Little Boars Head, NH 03862 • 500
Little Canada, MN 55110 • 7,102
Little Chute, WI 54140 • 7,907
Little Compton, RI 02837 • 300
Little Creek, DE 19961 • 230
Little Deer Isle, ME 04650 • 275
Little Eagle, SD 57639 • 300
Little Falls, MN 56345 • 7,250
Little Falls, NJ 07424 • 11,496
Little Falls, NY 13365 • 6,156
Little Ferry, NJ 07643 • 9,399
Littlefield, TX 79339 • 7,409
Littlefork, MN 56653 • 918
Little Hocking, OH 45742 • 800
Little Lake, MI 49833 • 900
Little Meadows, PA 18830 • 375
Little Mexico, TX 79735 • 600
Little Mountain, SC 29075 • 282
Little River, KS 67457 • 529
Little River, SC 29566 • 500
Little River □, AR • 13,952
Little Rock, AR 72201-99 • 158,461
Little Rock, IA 51243 • 490
Little Rock, SC 29567 • 450
Littlerock, WA 98556 • 300
Little Silver, NJ 07739 • 5,548
Little Sioux, IA 51545 • 251
Littlestown, PA 17340 • 2,870
Littleton, CO 80120-27 • 28,631
Littleton, ME 04730 • 600
Littleton, MA 01460 • 3,109
Littleton, NH 03561 • 4,480
Littleton, NC 27850 • 820
Littleton, WV 26581 • 335
Little Valley, NY 14755 • 1,203
Littleville, AL 35653 • 1,262
Little York, IL 61453 • 347
Live Oak, CA 95953 • 3,103
Live Oak, FL 32060 • 6,732
Live Oak, TX 78233 • 8,183
Live Oak □, TX • 9,606
Live Oak Manor, LA 70094 • 1,500
Livermore, CA 94550 • 48,349
Livermore, IA 50558 • 490
Livermore, KY 42352 • 1,672
Livermore Falls, ME 04254 • 2,441
Liverpool, PA 17045 • 809
Liverpool, TX 77577 • 602
Livingston, AL 35470 • 3,187
Livingston, CA 95334 • 5,326
Livingston, IL 62058 • 949
Livingston, KY 40445 • 334
Livingston, LA 70754 • 1,260
Livingston, MT 59047 • 6,994
Livingston, NJ 07039 • 28,040
Livingston, NY 12541 • 270
Livingston, TN 38570 • 3,372
Livingston, TX 77351 • 4,928
Livingston, WI 53554 • 642
Livingston □, IL • 41,381
Livingston □, KY • 9,219
Livingston □, LA • 58,806
Livingston □, MI • 100,289
Livingston □, MO • 15,739
Livingston □, NY • 57,006

Livingston Manor, NY 12758 • *1,522*
Livonia, LA 70755 • *980*
Livonia, MI 48150-54 • *104,814*
Livonia, NY 14487 • *1,238*
Lizella, GA 31052 • *600*
Lizton, IN 46149 • *456*
Llangollen Estates, DE 19720 • *870*
Llano, TX 78643 • *3,071*
Llano □, TX • *10,144*
Lloyd, FL 32337 • *300*
Lloyd, KY 41156 • *400*
Lloyd Harbor, NY 11743 • *3,405*
Loa, UT 84747 • *364*
Loachapoka, AL 36865 • *335*
Loami, IL 62661 • *770*
Lobelville, TN 37097 • *993*
Loch Lomond, VA 22110 • *2,300*
Loch Lynn Heights, MD 21550 • *503*
Lockbourne, OH 43137 • *373*
Locke, NY 13092 • *500*
Locke Mills, ME 04255 • *300*
Lockesburg, AR 71846 • *616*
Lockhart, AL 36455 • *547*
Lockhart, FL 32810 • *10,571*
Lockhart, TX 78644 • *7,953*
Lock Haven, PA 17745 • *9,617*
Lockland, OH 45215 • *4,292*
Lockney, TX 79241 • *2,334*
Lockport, IL 60441 • *9,170*
Lockport, LA 70374 • *2,424*
Lockport, NY 14094 • *24,844*
Lockridge, IA 52635 • *271*
Lockwood, MO 65682 • *971*
Lockwood, MT 59101 • *1,600*
Loco Hills, NM 88255 • *300*
Locust, NJ 07760 • *700*
Locust, NC 28097 • *1,590*
Locust Grove, GA 30248 • *1,479*
Locust Grove, MD 21779 • *250*
Locust Grove, NY 11791 • *11,648*
Locust Grove, OK 74352 • *1,179*
Loda, IL 60948 • *486*
Lodge Grass, MT 59050 • *771*
Lodgepole, NE 69149 • *413*
Lodi, CA 95240 • *35,221*
Lodi, NJ 07644 • *23,956*
Lodi, NY 14860 • *334*
Lodi, OH 44254 • *2,942*
Lodi, WI 53555 • *1,959*
Logan, IL 62856 • *328*
Logan, IA 51546 • *1,540*
Logan, KS 67646 • *720*
Logan, NM 88426 • *735*
Logan, OH 43138 • *6,557*
Logan, UT 84321 • *26,844*
Logan, WV 25601 • *3,029*
Logan □, AR • *20,144*
Logan □, CO • *19,800*
Logan □, IL • *31,802*
Logan □, KS • *3,478*
Logan □, KY • *24,138*
Logan □, NE • *983*
Logan □, ND • *3,493*
Logan □, OH • *39,155*
Logan □, OK • *26,881*
Logan □, WV • *50,679*
Logandale, NV 89021 • *375*
Logansport, IN 46947 • *17,731*
Logansport, LA 71049 • *1,565*
Loganton, PA 17747 • *474*
Loganville, GA 30249 • *1,841*
Loganville, PA 17342 • *1,020*
Loganville, WI 53943 • *239*
Log Lane Village, CO 80701 • *709*
Lohrville, IA 51453 • *521*
Lolo, MT 59847 • *2,418*
Loma Linda, CA 92354 • *10,694*
Lomax, IL 61454 • *601*
Lombard, IL 60148 • *36,897*
Lometa, TX 76853 • *666*
Lomira, WI 53048 • *1,446*
Lomita, CA 90717 • *18,807*
Lompoc, CA 93436 • *26,267*
Lonaconing, MD 21539 • *1,420*
London, AR 72847 • *859*
London, KY 40741 • *4,002*
London, OH 43140 • *6,958*
Londonderry, NH 03053 • *950*
Londonderry, OH 45647 • *350*
London Mills, IL 61544 • *587*
Londontowne, MD 21037 • *3,500*
Lone Grove, OK 73443 • *3,369*
Lone Jack, MO 64070 • *420*
Lone Oak, KY 42001 • *443*
Lone Oak, TX 75453 • *467*
Lone Pine, CA 93545 • *1,684*
Lone Rock, WI 53556 • *577*
Lone Tree, IA 52755 • *1,014*
Lone Wolf, OK 73655 • *613*
Long □, GA • *4,524*
Longacre, WV 25127 • *450*
Long Bar Harbor, MD 21009 • *700*
Long Beach, CA 90801-99 • *361,334*
Long Beach, IN 46360 • *2,262*
Long Beach, MD 20685 • *900*
Long Beach, MN 56334 • *263*
Long Beach, MS 39560 • *7,967*
Long Beach, NY 11561 • *34,073*
Long Beach, WA 98631 • *1,199*
Longboat Key, FL 33548 • *4,843*
Long Branch, NJ 07740 • *29,819*
Longbranch, WA 98351 • *900*
Long Creek, OR 97856 • *252*
Longdale, OK 73755 • *405*
Long Eddy, NY 12760 • *300*
Long Grove, IA 52756 • *596*
Long Hill, CT 06340 • *300*
Longisland, NC 28648 • *350*
Long Lake, IL 60041 • *2,201*
Long Lake, NY 12847 • *500*
Longleaf, LA 71448 • *400*
Longmeadow, MA 01106 • *16,301*
Longmont, CO 80501 • *42,942*
Long Pine, NE 69217 • *521*
Long Point, IL 61333 • *313*
Longport, NJ 08403 • *1,249*
Long Prairie, MN 56347 • *2,859*
Longstreet, LA 71050 • *281*
Longton, KS 67352 • *396*
Long Valley, NJ 07853 • *1,682*
Long View, KY 42701 • *650*
Longview, MS 39759 • *300*
Long View, NC 28601 • *3,587*
Longview, TX 75601-08 • *62,762*
Longview, WA 98632 • *31,052*
Longwood, FL 32750 • *10,029*
Longwood, NC 28452 • *250*
Lonoke, AR 72086 • *4,128*
Lonoke □, AR • *34,518*
Lonsdale, MN 55046 • *1,160*
Lonsdale, RI 02865 • *4,100*
Loogootee, IN 47553 • *3,100*
Lookout, CA 96054 • *350*
Lookout, KY 41542 • *550*
Lookout, WV 25868 • *400*
Lookout Mountain, TN 37350 • *1,886*
Loomis, NE 68958 • *447*
Loon Lake, WA 99148 • *650*
Loop, TX 79342 • *450*
Loose Creek, MO 65054 • *300*
Lopez, PA 18628 • *300*
Lorado, WV 25630 • *400*
Lorain, OH 44052-55 • *75,416*
Lorain □, OH • *274,909*
Loraine, IL 62349 • *382*
Loraine, TX 79532 • *929*
Lordsburg, NM 88045 • *3,195*
Lords Point, CT 06378 • *460*
Loreauville, LA 70552 • *860*
Lore City, OH 43755 • *443*
Lorenzo, TX 79343 • *1,394*
Loretto, KY 40037 • *954*
Loretto, MI 49852 • *350*
Loretto, PA 15940 • *1,395*
Loretto, TN 38469 • *1,612*
Lorida, FL 33857 • *620*
Lorimor, IA 50149 • *405*
Loris, SC 29569 • *2,193*
Lorman, MS 39096 • *650*
Los Alamitos, CA 90720 • *11,529*
Los Alamos, CA 93440 • *950*
Los Alamos, NM 87544 • *11,039*
Los Alamos □, NM • *17,599*
Los Altos, CA 94022 • *25,769*
Los Altos Hills, CA 94022 • *7,421*
Los Angeles, CA 90001-99 • *2,966,850*
Los Angeles □, CA • *7,477,503*
Losantville, IN 47354 • *306*
Los Banos, CA 93635 • *10,341*
Los Ebanos, TX 78565 • *400*
Los Fresnos, TX 78566 • *2,173*
Los Gatos, CA 95030 • *26,906*
Los Lunas, NM 87031 • *3,525*
Los Molinos, CA 96055 • *1,241*
Los Nietos, CA 90606 • *7,100*
Los Ojos, NM 87551 • *350*
Los Padillas, NM 87105 • *2,500*
Los Ranchos de Albuquerque, NM 87107 • *2,702*
Lostant, IL 61334 • *539*
Lost Creek, WV 26385 • *604*
Lost Hills, CA 93249 • *800*
Lostine, OR 97857 • *250*
Lost Nation, IA 52254 • *524*
Los Trujillos, NM 87002 • *500*
Lothair, KY 41701 • *600*
Lott, TX 76656 • *865*
Louann, AR 71751 • *282*
Loudon, TN 37774 • *3,943*
Loudon □, TN • *28,553*
Loudonville, NY 12211 • *9,000*
Loudonville, OH 44842 • *2,945*
Loudoun □, VA • *57,427*
Loughman, FL 33858 • *800*
Louin, MS 39338 • *338*
Louisa, KY 41230 • *1,832*
Louisa, VA 23093 • *932*
Louisa □, IA • *12,055*
Louisa □, VA • *17,825*
Louisburg, KS 66053 • *1,744*
Louisburg, NC 27549 • *3,238*
Louise, MS 39097 • *400*
Louise, TX 77455 • *900*
Louisiana, MO 63353 • *4,261*
Louisville, AL 36048 • *791*
Louisville, CO 80027 • *5,593*
Louisville, GA 30434 • *2,823*
Louisville, IL 62858 • *1,166*
Louisville, KY 40201-99 • *298,840*
Louisville, MS 39339 • *7,323*
Louisville, NE 68037 • *1,022*
Louisville, NY 13662 • *400*
Louisville, OH 44641 • *7,996*
Louisville, TN 37777 • *250*
Loup □, NE • *859*
Loup City, NE 68853 • *1,368*
Louvale, GA 31814 • *250*
Louviers, CO 80131 • *350*
Love □, OK • *7,469*
Lovelady, TX 75851 • *509*
Loveland, CO 80537 • *30,244*
Loveland, OH 45140 • *9,106*
Loveland Park, OH 45140 • *1,653*
Lovell, WY 82431 • *2,447*
Lovelock, NV 89419 • *1,680*
Lovely, KY 41231 • *700*
Loves Park, IL 61111 • *13,192*
Lovettsville, VA 22080 • *613*
Lovilia, IA 50150 • *637*
Loving, NM 88256 • *1,355*
Loving □, TX • *91*
Lovingston, VA 22949 • *550*
Lovington, IL 61937 • *1,313*
Lovington, IA 50322 • *850*
Lovington, NM 88260 • *9,727*
Lowden, IA 52255 • *717*
Lowell, AR 72745 • *1,078*
Lowell, IN 46356 • *5,827*
Lowell, MA 01850-54 • *92,418*
Lowell, MI 49331 • *3,707*
Lowell, NC 28098 • *2,917*
Lowell, OH 45744 • *729*
Lowell, OR 97452 • *661*
Lowell, WI 53557 • *326*
Lowellville, OH 44436 • *1,558*
Lower Brule, SD 57548 • *300*
Lower Burrell, PA 15068 • *13,200*
Lower Paia, HI 96779 • *1,500*
Lower Peach Tree, AL 36751 • *350*
Lower Village, VT 05672 • *300*
Lowgap, NC 27024 • *350*
Lowland, NC 28552 • *600*
Low Moor, IA 52757 • *346*
Lowmoor, VA 24457 • *700*
Lowndes □, AL • *13,253*
Lowndes □, GA • *67,972*
Lowndes □, MS • *57,304*
Lowry, MN 56349 • *283*
Lowry City, MO 64763 • *676*
Lowrys, SC 29706 • *225*
Lowville, NY 13367 • *3,364*
Loxley, AL 36551 • *804*
Loyal, WI 54446 • *1,252*
Loyall, KY 40854 • *1,210*
Loyalton, CA 96118 • *1,030*
Loysburg, PA 16659 • *250*
Loysville, PA 17047 • *500*
Luana, IA 52156 • *246*
Lubbock, TX 79401-99 • *173,979*
Lubbock □, TX • *211,651*
Lubec, ME 04652 • *990*
Lucama, NC 27851 • *1,070*
Lucan, MN 56255 • *262*
Lucas, IA 50151 • *292*
Lucas, KS 67648 • *524*
Lucas, OH 44843 • *753*
Lucas □, IA • *10,313*
Lucas □, OH • *471,741*
Lucasville, OH 45648 • *3,349*
Luce □, MI • *6,659*
Lucedale, MS 39452 • *2,429*
Lucerne, CA 95458 • *1,767*
Lucernemines, PA 15754 • *1,380*
Lucerne Valley, CA 92356 • *1,300*
Lucinda, PA 16235 • *250*
Luck, WI 54853 • *997*
Luckey, OH 43443 • *895*
Lucy, LA 70049 • *450*
Ludington, MI 49431 • *8,937*
Ludlow, IL 60949 • *397*
Ludlow, KY 41016 • *4,959*
Ludlow, MA 01056 • *18,150*
Ludlow, PA 16333 • *800*
Ludlow, VT 05149 • *1,352*
Ludlow Falls, OH 45339 • *248*
Ludowici, GA 31316 • *1,286*
Lueders, TX 79533 • *420*
Lufkin, TX 75901 • *28,562*
Lugoff, SC 29078 • *2,909*
Lukachukai, AZ 86507 • *1,049*
Luke, MD 21540 • *329*
Lula, GA 30554 • *857*
Lula, MS 38644 • *394*
Luling, LA 70070 • *4,006*
Luling, TX 78648 • *5,039*
Lumber City, GA 31549 • *1,426*
Lumberport, WV 26386 • *939*
Lumberton, MS 39455 • *2,217*
Lumberton, NJ 08048 • *700*
Lumberton, NC 28358 • *18,241*
Lumpkin, GA 31815 • *1,335*
Lumpkin □, GA • *10,762*
Luna, NM 87824 • *250*
Luna □, NM • *15,585*
Luna Pier, MI 48157 • *1,443*
Lund, NV 89317 • *300*
Lunenburg, MA 01462 • *1,789*
Lunenburg, VT 05906 • *270*
Lunenburg □, VA • *12,124*
Luray, KS 67649 • *295*
Luray, VA 22835 • *3,584*
Lusk, WY 82225 • *1,650*
Lutcher, LA 70071 • *4,730*
Lutesville, MO 63762 • *865*
Luther, MI 49656 • *414*
Luther, OK 73054 • *1,159*
Luthersville, GA 30251 • *597*
Lutherville-Timonium, MD 21093 • *17,854*
Lutsen, MN 55612 • *250*
Luttrell, TN 37779 • *962*
Lutz, FL 33549 • *5,555*
Luverne, AL 36049 • *2,639*
Lu Verne, IA 50560 • *418*
Luverne, MN 56156 • *4,568*
Luxemburg, IA 52056 • *271*
Luxemburg, WI 54217 • *1,040*
Luxora, AR 72358 • *1,739*
Luzerne, MI 48636 • *500*
Luzerne, PA 18709 • *3,703*
Luzerne □, PA • *343,079*
Lycoming, NY 13093 • *250*
Lycoming □, PA • *118,416*
Lyerly, GA 30730 • *482*
Lyford, IN 47874 • *360*
Lyford, TX 78569 • *1,618*
Lykens, PA 17048 • *2,181*
Lyle, MN 55953 • *576*
Lyle, WA 98635 • *700*
Lyles, TN 37098 • *240*
Lyman, MS 39503 • *350*
Lyman, NE 69352 • *551*
Lyman, SC 29365 • *1,067*
Lyman, WA 98263 • *285*
Lyman, WY 82937 • *2,284*
Lyman □, SD • *3,864*
Lyme, CT 06371 • *500*
Lyme, NH 03768 • *350*
Lynch, KY 40855 • *1,614*
Lynch, NE 68746 • *357*
Lynchburg, OH 45142 • *1,205*
Lynchburg, SC 29080 • *534*
Lynchburg, TN 37352 • *668*
Lynchburg, VA 24501-15 • *66,743*
Lynch Station, VA 24571 • *400*
Lynd, MN 56157 • *304*
Lynden, WA 98264 • *4,022*
Lyndhurst, NJ 07071 • *20,326*
Lyndhurst, OH 44124 • *18,092*
Lyndon, IL 61261 • *777*
Lyndon, KS 66451 • *1,132*
Lyndon, KY 40222 • *1,553*
Lyndon, VT 05849 • *425*
Lyndon Center, VT 05850 • *300*
Lyndon Station, WI 53944 • *375*
Lyndonville, NY 14098 • *916*
Lyndonville, VT 05851 • *1,401*
Lyndora, PA 16045 • *1,900*
Lynn, AL 35575 • *554*
Lynn, AR 72440 • *345*
Lynn, IN 47355 • *1,250*
Lynn, MA 01901-10 • *78,471*
Lynn □, TX • *8,605*
Lynne, FL 32688 • *500*
Lynne Acres, MD 21207 • *7,700*
Lynnfield, MA 01940 • *11,267*
Lynn Garden, TN 37665 • *7,213*
Lynn Haven, FL 32444 • *6,239*

Lynnville, IN 47619 • 566
Lynnville, IA 50153 • 406
Lynnville, TN 38472 • 383
Lynnwood, WA 98036-37 • 22,641
Lynwood, CA 90262 • 48,548
Lyon, MS 38645 • 428
Lyon □, IA • 12,896
Lyon □, KS • 35,108
Lyon □, KY • 6,490
Lyon □, MN • 25,207
Lyon □, NV • 13,594
Lyon Mountain, NY 12952 • 950
Lyons, CO 80540 • 1,137
Lyons, GA 30436 • 4,203
Lyons, IL 60534 • 9,925
Lyons, IN 47443 • 782
Lyons, KS 67554 • 4,134
Lyons, MI 48851 • 708
Lyons, NE 68038 • 1,214
Lyons, NY 14489 • 4,160
Lyons, OH 43533 • 596
Lyons, OR 97358 • 877
Lyons, TX 77863 • 360
Lyons, WI 53148 • 540
Lyons Falls, NY 13368 • 755
Lyons Plains, CT 06880 • 360
Lytle, OH 45068 • 300
Lytle, TX 78052 • 1,920
Lytton, IA 50561 • 377

M

Mabank, TX 75147 • 1,443
Mabel, MN 55954 • 861
Mabelvale, AR 72103 • 550
Maben, MS 39750 • 855
Mableton, GA 30059 • 20,200
Mabscott, WV 25871 • 1,668
Mabton, WA 98935 • 1,248
McAdams, MS 39107 • 250
McAdoo, PA 18237 • 2,940
McAlester, OK 74501 • 17,255
McAlisterville, PA 17049 • 650
McAllen, TX 78501-04 • 66,281
McAlmont, AR 72117 • 1,600
McAlpine, MD 21043 • 2,500
McAndrews, KY 41543 • 400
McArthur, OH 45651 • 1,912
McBain, MI 49657 • 519
McBee, SC 29101 • 774
McCall, ID 83638 • 2,188
McCalla, AL 35111 • 500
McCallsburg, IA 50154 • 304
McCamey, TX 79752 • 2,436
McCammon, ID 83250 • 770
McCandless, PA 15237 • 26,250
McCartys, NM 87049 • 400
McCaysville, GA 30555 • 1,219
McClain □, OK • 20,291
McCleary, WA 98557 • 1,419
McClellanville, SC 29458 • 436
MacClenny, FL 32063 • 3,851
MacClesfield, NC 27852 • 504
McCloud, CA 96057 • 1,656
McClure, IL 62957 • 700
McClure, OH 43534 • 694
McClure, PA 17841 • 1,024
McClure, VA 24269 • 400
McClusky, ND 58463 • 658
McColl, SC 29570 • 2,677
McComas, WV 24735 • 800
McComb, MS 39648 • 12,331
McComb, OH 45858 • 1,608
McCone □, MT • 2,702
McConnell, IL 61050 • 250
McConnellsburg, PA 17233 • 1,178
McConnellstown, PA 16660 • 300
McConnelsville, OH 43756 • 2,018
McCook, NE 69001 • 8,404
McCook □, SD • 6,444
McCook Lake, SD 57038 • 600
McCoole, MD 26726 • 300
McCool Junction, NE 68401 • 404
McCordsville, IN 46055 • 400
McCormick, SC 29835 • 1,725
McCormick □, SC • 7,797
McCracken, KS 67556 • 292
McCracken □, KY • 61,310
McCreary □, KY • 15,634
McCrory, AR 72101 • 1,942
McCulloch □, TX • 8,735
McCune, KS 66753 • 528
McCurtain, OK 74944 • 549
McCurtain □, OK • 36,151
McCutchenville, OH 44844 • 350
McDade, TX 78650 • 400
McDavid, FL 32568 • 300
McDermott, OH 45652 • 550
McDonald, KS 67745 • 239
MacDonald, WV 25880 • 250
McDonald □, MO • 14,917
McDonough, GA 30253 • 2,778
McDonough □, IL • 37,467
McDougal, AR 72441 • 239
McDowell, KY 41647 • 400
McDowell □, NC • 35,135
McDowell □, WV • 49,899
McDuffie □, GA • 18,546
Macedon, NY 14502 • 1,400
Macedonia, IA 51549 • 279
Macedonia, OH 44056 • 6,571
McElhattan, PA 17748 • 300
Maceo, KY 42355 • 400
McEwen, TN 37101 • 1,352
McFarland, CA 93250 • 5,151
McFarland, KS 66501 • 242
McFarland, WI 53558 • 3,783
McGaheysville, VA 22840 • 300
McGehee, AR 71654 • 5,671
McGill, NV 89318 • 1,419
McGrady, NC 28649 • 500
McGrath, AK 99627 • 355
McGraw, NY 13101 • 1,188
McGraws, WV 25875 • 300
McGregor, IA 52157 • 945
McGregor, MN 55760 • 447
McGregor, TX 76657 • 4,513
McGuffey, OH 45859 • 646
McHenry, IL 60050 • 11,949
McHenry, KY 42354 • 582
McHenry, MD 21541 • 375
McHenry, MS 39561 • 260
McHenry □, IL • 147,897
McHenry □, ND • 7,858
Machias, ME 04654 • 1,277
Machias, NY 14101 • 700
McIntosh, AL 36553 • 319
McIntosh, FL 32664 • 404
McIntosh, MN 56556 • 681
McIntosh, SD 57641 • 418
McIntosh □, GA • 8,046
McIntosh □, ND • 4,800
McIntosh □, OK • 15,562
McIntyre, GA 31054 • 386
McIntyre, PA 15756 • 335
Mackay, ID 83251 • 541
McKean, PA 16426 • 465
McKean □, PA • 50,635
McKee, KY 40447 • 759
McKee City, NJ 08232 • 600
McKeesport, PA 15130-35 • 31,012
McKees Rocks, PA 15136 • 8,742
McKenney, VA 23872 • 473
McKenzie, AL 36456 • 605
McKenzie, TN 38201 • 5,405
McKenzie □, ND • 7,132
Mackeyville, PA 17750 • 325
Mackinac □, MI • 10,178
Mackinac Island, MI 49757 • 479
Mackinaw, IL 61755 • 1,354
Mackinaw City, MI 49701 • 820
McKinley □, NM • 56,536
McKinleyville, CA 95521 • 7,772
McKinney, TX 75069 • 16,256
McKittrick, CA 93251 • 300
Macksburg, OH 45746 • 295
Macksville, KS 67557 • 546
Mackville, KY 40040 • 229
McLain, MS 39456 • 688
McLaughlin, SD 57642 • 754
McLaurin, MS 39401 • 400
McLean, IL 61754 • 836
McLean, TX 79057 • 1,160
McLean, VA 22101-03 • 22,000
McLean □, IL • 119,149
McLean □, KY • 10,090
McLean □, ND • 12,383
McLeansboro, IL 62859 • 2,960
McLemoresville, TN 38235 • 311
McLennan □, TX • 170,755
McLeod □, MN • 29,657
McLoud, OK 74851 • 4,061
McLouth, KS 66054 • 700
McMechen, WV 26040 • 2,402
McMinn □, TN • 41,878
McMinnville, OR 97128 • 14,080
McMinnville, TN 37110 • 10,683
McMullen □, TX • 789
McNabb, IL 61335 • 342
McNairy □, TN • 22,525
McNary, AZ 85930 • 1,320
McNary, LA 71433 • 240
McNeil, AR 71752 • 725
McNeill, MS 39457 • 500
McNulty, OR 97051 • 1,805
Macomb, IL 61455 • 19,863
Macomb □, MI • 694,600
Macon, GA 31201-99 • 116,896
Macon, IL 62544 • 1,300
Macon, MS 39341 • 2,396
Macon, MO 63552 • 5,680
Macon □, AL • 26,829
Macon □, GA • 14,003
Macon □, IL • 131,375
Macon □, MO • 16,313
Macon □, NC • 20,178
Macon □, TN • 15,700
Macoupin □, IL • 49,384
McPherson, KS 67460 • 11,753
McPherson □, KS • 26,855
McPherson □, NE • 593
McPherson □, SD • 4,027
McQueeney, TX 78123 • 950
McRae, AR 72102 • 641
McRae, GA 31055 • 3,409
McRoberts, KY 41835 • 1,106
McSherrystown, PA 17344 • 2,764
Macungie, PA 18062 • 1,899
McVeigh, KY 41546 • 800
McVeytown, PA 17051 • 447
McVille, ND 58254 • 626
McWilliams, AL 36753 • 300
Macy, IN 46951 • 282
Macy, NE 68039 • 500
Madawaska, ME 04756 • 4,165
Madden, MS 39109 • 250
Maddock, ND 58348 • 677
Madeira, OH 45243 • 9,341
Madelia, MN 56062 • 2,130
Madera, CA 93637-39 • 21,732
Madera, PA 16661 • 900
Madera □, CA • 63,116
Madill, OK 73446 • 3,173
Madison, AL 36110 • 500
Madison, AL 35758 • 4,057
Madison, AR 72359 • 1,238
Madison, CT 06443 • 2,069
Madison, FL 32340 • 3,487
Madison, GA 30650 • 2,954
Madison, IL 62060 • 5,915
Madison, IN 47250 • 12,472
Madison, KS 66860 • 1,099
Madison, ME 04950 • 2,788
Madison, MD 21648 • 300
Madison, MN 56256 • 2,212
Madison, MS 39110 • 2,241
Madison, MO 65263 • 656
Madison, NE 68748 • 1,950
Madison, NJ 07940 • 15,357
Madison, NC 27025 • 2,806
Madison, NY 13402 • 396
Madison, OH 44057 • 2,291
Madison, SD 57042 • 6,210
Madison, VA 22727 • 267
Madison, WV 25130 • 3,228
Madison, WI 53701-99 • 170,616
Madison □, AL • 196,966
Madison □, AR • 11,373
Madison □, FL • 14,894
Madison □, GA • 17,747
Madison □, ID • 19,480
Madison □, IL • 247,661
Madison □, IN • 139,336
Madison □, IA • 12,597
Madison □, KY • 53,352
Madison □, LA • 15,975
Madison □, MS • 41,613
Madison □, MO • 10,725
Madison □, MT • 5,448
Madison □, NE • 31,382
Madison □, NC • 16,827
Madison □, NY • 65,150
Madison □, OH • 33,004
Madison □, TN • 74,546
Madison □, TX • 10,649
Madison □, VA • 10,232
Madisonburg, PA 16852 • 250
Madison Heights, MI 48071 • 35,375
Madison Heights, VA 24572 • 3,500
Madison Lake, MN 56063 • 592
Madisonville, KY 42431 • 16,979
Madisonville, LA 70447 • 799
Madisonville, TN 37354 • 2,884
Madisonville, TX 77864 • 3,660
Madras, OR 97741 • 2,235
Madrid, IA 50156 • 2,281
Madrid, NE 69150 • 284
Madrid, NY 13660 • 800
Maeser, UT 84078 • 2,216
Magalia, CA 95954 • 950
Magazine, AR 72943 • 799
Magdalena, NM 87825 • 1,022
Magee, MS 39111 • 3,497
Magna, UT 84044 • 13,138
Magnet Cove, AR 72104 • 500
Magnetic Springs, OH 43036 • 314
Magnolia, AR 71753 • 11,909
Magnolia, IL 61336 • 308
Magnolia, KY 42757 • 450
Magnolia, MN 56158 • 234
Magnolia, MS 39652 • 2,461
Magnolia, NJ 08049 • 4,881
Magnolia, NC 28453 • 592
Magnolia, OH 44643 • 986
Magnolia, TX 77355 • 867
Magnolia Springs, AL 36555 • 400
Magoffin □, KY • 13,515
Mahaffey, PA 15757 • 513
Mahanoy City, PA 17948 • 6,167
Mahaska □, IA • 22,867
Mahnomen, MN 56557 • 1,283
Mahnomen □, MN • 5,535
Mahomet, IL 61853 • 1,986
Mahoning □, OH • 289,487
Mahopac, NY 10541 • 5,265
Mahwah, NJ 07430 • 7,500
Maiden, NC 28650 • 2,574
Maili, HI 96792 • 5,026
Maine, NY 13802 • 700
Maitland, FL 32751 • 8,763
Maitland, MO 64466 • 415
Maize, KS 67101 • 1,294
Majestic, KY 41547 • 400
Major □, OK • 8,772
Makaha, HI 96792 • 7,905
Makakilo City, HI 96706 • 7,691
Makanda, IL 62958 • 402
Makawao, HI 96788 • 1,066
Makaweli, HI 96769 • 700
Malabar, FL 32950 • 1,118
Malad City, ID 83252 • 1,915
Malaga, NJ 08328 • 950
Malakoff, TX 75148 • 2,082
Malcolm, NE 68402 • 355
Malcom, IA 50157 • 418
Malden, IL 61337 • 359
Malden, MA 02148 • 53,386
Malden, MO 63863 • 6,096
Malden, WV 25306 • 950
Malesus, TN 38301 • 225
Malheur □, OR • 26,896
Malibu, CA 90265 • 10,000
Malin, OR 97632 • 539
Malinta, OH 43535 • 327
Mallard, IA 50562 • 407
Mallet Creek, OH 44256 • 300
Malone, FL 32445 • 897
Malone, NY 12953 • 7,668
Malone, WA 98559 • 250
Malott, WA 98829 • 350
Malta, IL 60150 • 995
Malta, MT 59538 • 2,367
Malta, OH 43758 • 956
Malta Bend, MO 65339 • 292
Malvern, AL 36349 • 558
Malvern, AR 72104 • 10,163
Malvern, IA 51551 • 1,244
Malvern, OH 44644 • 1,032
Malvern, PA 19355 • 2,999
Malverne, NY 11565 • 9,262
Mamaroneck, NY 10543 • 17,616
Mamers, NC 27552 • 300
Mammoth, AZ 85618 • 1,906
Mammoth, WV 25132 • 750
Mammoth Lakes, CA 93546 • 3,000
Mammoth Spring, AR 72554 • 1,158
Mamou, LA 70554 • 3,194
Man, WV 25635 • 1,333
Manahawkin, NJ 08050 • 1,467
Manasquan, NJ 08736 • 5,354
Manassa, CO 81141 • 945
Manassas, VA 22110-11 • 15,438
Manassas Park, VA 22111 • 6,524
Manatee □, FL • 148,442
Manawa, WI 54949 • 1,205
Mancelona, MI 49659 • 1,432
Manchaug, MA 01526 • 1,000
Manchester, CT 06040 • 49,761
Manchester, GA 31816 • 4,796
Manchester, IL 62663 • 387
Manchester, IA 52057 • 4,942
Manchester, KY 40962 • 1,838
Manchester, ME 04351 • 600
Manchester, MD 21102 • 1,830
Manchester, MA 01944 • 5,424
Manchester, MI 48158 • 1,686
Manchester, MO 63011 • 6,191
Manchester, NH 03101-99 • 90,936
Manchester, NY 14504 • 1,698
Manchester, OH 45144 • 2,313
Manchester, PA 17345 • 2,027
Manchester, TN 37355 • 7,250
Manchester, VT 05254 • 563
Manchester Center, VT 05255 • 1,719
Mancos, CO 81328 • 870
Mandan, ND 58554 • 15,513
Mandaree, ND 58757 • 300
Mandeville, AR 75501 • 700

Mandeville, LA 70448 • *6,076*
Mangham, LA 71259 • *867*
Mangum, OK 73554 • *3,833*
Manhasset, NY 11030 • *8,530*
Manhattan, KS 66502 • *32,644*
Manhattan, MT 59741 • *988*
Manhattan Beach, CA 90266 • *31,542*
Manheim, PA 17545 • *5,015*
Manila, AR 72442 • *2,553*
Manila, UT 84046 • *272*
Manilla, IN 46150 • *350*
Manilla, IA 51454 • *1,020*
Manistee, MI 49660 • *7,566*
Manistee □, MI • *23,019*
Manistique, MI 49854 • *3,962*
Manito, IL 61546 • *1,869*
Manitou, OK 73555 • *322*
Manitou Beach, MI 49779 • *4,500*
Manitou Springs, CO 80829 • *4,475*
Manitowoc, WI 54220 • *32,547*
Manitowoc □, WI • *82,918*
Mankato, KS 66956 • *1,205*
Mankato, MN 56001 • *28,651*
Manlius, IL 61338 • *439*
Manlius, NY 13104 • *5,241*
Manly, IA 50456 • *1,496*
Mannford, OK 74044 • *1,610*
Manning, IA 51455 • *1,609*
Manning, SC 29102 • *4,746*
Mannington, WV 26582 • *3,036*
Manns Choice, PA 15550 • *286*
Manns Harbor, NC 27953 • *350*
Mannsville, NY 13661 • *431*
Mannsville, OK 73447 • *568*
Manokin, MD 21836 • *250*
Manokotak, AK 99628 • *294*
Manomet, MA 02345 • *950*
Manor, GA 31550 • *400*
Manor, TX 78653 • *1,044*
Manorhaven, NY 11050 • *5,384*
Manorville, PA 16238 • *409*
Mansfield, AR 72944 • *1,000*
Mansfield, GA 30255 • *435*
Mansfield, IL 61854 • *921*
Mansfield, LA 71052 • *6,485*
Mansfield, MA 02048 • *6,786*
Mansfield, MO 65704 • *1,423*
Mansfield, OH 44901-99 • *53,927*
Mansfield, PA 16933 • *3,322*
Mansfield, TX 76063 • *8,102*
Mansfield, WA 98830 • *315*
Mansfield Center, CT 06250 • *1,043*
Mansfield Four Corners, CT 06268 • *250*
Manson, IA 50563 • *1,924*
Manson, WA 98831 • *500*
Mansura, LA 71350 • *2,074*
Mantachie, MS 38855 • *732*
Manteca, CA 95336 • *24,925*
Manteno, IL 60950 • *3,155*
Manteo, NC 27954 • *902*
Manti, UT 84642 • *2,080*
Manton, MI 49663 • *1,212*
Mantorville, MN 55955 • *705*
Mantua, NJ 08051 • *1,900*
Mantua, OH 44255 • *1,041*
Mantua, UT 84302 • *484*
Mantua Hills, VA 22030 • *1,550*
Manvel, ND 58256 • *308*
Manvel, TX 77578 • *3,549*
Manville, NJ 08835 • *11,278*
Manville, RI 02838 • *3,100*
Many, LA 71449 • *3,988*
Many Farms, AZ 86538 • *1,364*
Manzanita, OR 97130 • *443*
Manzanola, CO 81058 • *459*
Mapaville, MO 63065 • *400*
Maple Bluff, WI 53704 • *1,351*
Maple Grove, MN 55369 • *20,525*
Maple Heights, OH 44137 • *29,735*
Maple Hill, KS 66507 • *381*
Maple Hill, NC 28454 • *550*
Maple Lake, MN 55358 • *1,132*
Maple Mount, KY 42356 • *500*
Maple Plain, MN 55359 • *1,421*
Maple Rapids, MI 48853 • *683*
Maple Shade, NJ 08052 • *20,525*
Maplesville, AL 36750 • *754*
Mapleton, IA 51034 • *1,495*
Mapleton, ME 04757 • *500*
Mapleton, MN 56065 • *1,516*
Mapleton, ND 58059 • *306*
Mapleton, OR 97453 • *900*
Mapleton, UT 84663 • *2,726*
Mapleton Depot, PA 17052 • *591*
Maple Valley, WA 98038 • *900*
Mapleville, RI 02839 • *900*
Maplewood, MN 55109 • *26,990*
Maplewood, MO 63143 • *10,960*
Maplewood, NJ 07040 • *22,950*
Maquoketa, IA 52060 • *6,313*
Maquon, IL 61458 • *350*
Marana, AZ 85238 • *1,674*
Marathon, FL 33050 • *7,508*
Marathon, IA 50565 • *442*
Marathon, NY 13803 • *1,046*
Marathon, TX 79842 • *750*
Marathon, WI 54448 • *1,552*
Marathon □, WI • *111,270*
Marble, MN 55764 • *757*
Marble, NC 28905 • *700*
Marble City, OK 74945 • *294*
Marble Cliff, OH 43212 • *630*
Marbledale, TN 37914 • *300*
Marble Falls, TX 78654 • *3,252*
Marblehead, MA 01945 • *20,126*
Marblehead, OH 43440 • *679*
Marblehill, GA 30148 • *300*
Marble Hill, MO 63764 • *601*
Marblemount, WA 98267 • *350*
Marble Rock, IA 50653 • *419*
Marbleton, WY 83113 • *537*
Marbury, AL 36051 • *300*
Marbury, MD 20658 • *1,189*
Marceline, MO 64658 • *2,938*
Marcellus, MI 49067 • *1,134*
Marco, FL 33937 • *4,679*
Marcola, OR 97454 • *500*
Marcus, IA 51035 • *1,206*
Marcus Hook, PA 19061 • *2,638*
Mardela Springs, MD 21837 • *320*
Marengo, IL 60152 • *4,361*
Marengo, IN 47140 • *892*
Marengo, IA 52301 • *2,308*
Marengo, OH 43334 • *329*
Marengo □, AL • *25,047*
Marenisco, MI 49947 • *600*
Marfa, TX 79843 • *2,466*
Margaret, AL 35112 • *757*
Margaretville, NY 12455 • *755*
Margate, FL 33063 • *35,900*
Margate, MD 21061 • *4,800*
Margate City, NJ 08402 • *9,179*
Mariah Hill, IN 47556 • *300*
Marianna, AR 72360 • *6,220*
Marianna, FL 32446 • *7,006*
Maria Stein, OH 45860 • *300*
Maribel, WI 54227 • *363*
Maricopa, AZ 85239 • *900*
Maricopa, CA 93252 • *946*
Maricopa □, AZ • *1,509,262*
Mariemont, OH 45227 • *3,295*
Marienville, PA 16239 • *900*
Maries □, MO • *7,551*
Marietta, GA 30060-69 • *30,829*
Marietta, IN 46176 • *285*
Marietta, MN 56257 • *279*
Marietta, MS 38856 • *298*
Marietta, OH 45750 • *16,467*
Marietta, OK 73448 • *2,494*
Marietta, SC 29661 • *900*
Marin □, CA • *222,592*
Marina, CA 93933 • *20,647*
Marina del Rey, CA 90292 • *8,065*
Marine, IL 62061 • *957*
Marine City, MI 48039 • *4,414*
Marine On St. Croix, MN 55047 • *543*
Marinette, WI 54143 • *11,965*
Marinette □, WI • *39,314*
Maringouin, LA 70757 • *1,291*
Marion, AL 36756 • *4,467*
Marion, AR 72364 • *2,996*
Marion, CT 06444 • *800*
Marion, IL 62959 • *14,031*
Marion, IN 46952-53 • *35,874*
Marion, IA 52302 • *19,474*
Marion, KS 66861 • *1,951*
Marion, KY 42064 • *3,392*
Marion, LA 71260 • *989*
Marion, MA 02738 • *1,438*
Marion, MI 49665 • *816*
Marion, MS 39342 • *771*
Marion, NC 28752 • *3,684*
Marion, NY 14505 • *950*
Marion, OH 43302 • *37,040*
Marion, PA 17235 • *900*
Marion, SC 29571 • *7,700*
Marion, SD 57043 • *830*
Marion, VA 24354 • *7,029*
Marion, WI 54950 • *1,348*
Marion □, AL • *30,041*
Marion □, AR • *11,334*
Marion □, FL • *122,488*
Marion □, GA • *5,297*
Marion □, IL • *43,523*
Marion □, IN • *765,233*
Marion □, IA • *29,669*
Marion □, KS • *13,522*
Marion □, KY • *17,910*
Marion □, MS • *25,708*
Marion □, MO • *28,638*
Marion □, OH • *67,974*
Marion □, OR • *204,692*
Marion □, SC • *34,179*
Marion □, TN • *24,416*
Marion □, TX • *10,360*
Marion □, WV • *65,789*
Marion Center, PA 15759 • *494*
Marion Heights, IN 47885 • *300*
Marion Junction, AL 36759 • *300*
Marion Station, MD 21838 • *500*
Marionville, MO 65705 • *1,920*
Mariposa, CA 95338 • *1,150*
Mariposa □, CA • *11,108*
Marissa, IL 62257 • *2,568*
Mark, IL 61340 • *424*
Mark Center, OH 43536 • *250*
Marked Tree, AR 72365 • *3,201*
Markesan, WI 53946 • *1,446*
Markham, IL 60426 • *15,172*
Markham, TX 77456 • *1,100*
Markle, IN 46770 • *975*
Markleville, IN 46056 • *427*
Markleysburg, PA 15459 • *356*
Marks, MS 38646 • *2,260*
Marksville, LA 71351 • *5,113*
Marland, OK 74644 • *340*
Marlboro, NJ 07746 • *5,700*
Marlboro, NY 12542 • *1,580*
Marlboro, VA 23224 • *950*
Marlboro □, SC • *31,634*
Marlborough, CT 06447 • *1,039*
Marlborough, MA 01752 • *30,617*
Marlborough, NH 03455 • *1,231*
Marlene Village, OR 97005 • *1,500*
Marlette, MI 48453 • *1,761*
Marley, MD 21061 • *4,800*
Marlin, TX 76661 • *7,099*
Marlinton, WV 24954 • *1,352*
Marlow, GA 31312 • *300*
Marlow, NH 03456 • *300*
Marlow, OK 73055 • *5,017*
Marlowe, WV 25419 • *700*
Marlton, NJ 08053 • *9,411*
Marmaduke, AR 72443 • *1,168*
Marmet, WV 25315 • *2,196*
Marmora, NJ 08223 • *500*
Marne, MI 49435 • *500*
Maroa, IL 61756 • *1,760*
Marquand, MO 63655 • *397*
Marquette, IA 52158 • *528*
Marquette, KS 67464 • *639*
Marquette, MI 49855 • *23,288*
Marquette, NE 68854 • *303*
Marquette □, MI • *74,101*
Marquette □, WI • *11,672*
Marquette Heights, IL 61554 • *3,386*
Marquez, TX 77865 • *231*
Marrero, LA 70072 • *36,548*
Marrtown, WV 26101 • *900*
Mars, PA 16046 • *1,803*
Marseilles, IL 61341 • *4,766*
Marshall, AR 72650 • *1,595*
Marshall, IL 62441 • *3,655*
Marshall, IN 47859 • *413*
Marshall, MI 49068 • *7,201*
Marshall, MN 56258 • *11,161*
Marshall, MO 65340 • *12,781*
Marshall, NC 28753 • *809*
Marshall, OK 73056 • *372*
Marshall, TX 75670 • *24,921*
Marshall, VA 22115 • *600*
Marshall, WI 53559 • *2,363*
Marshall □, AL • *65,622*
Marshall □, IL • *14,479*
Marshall □, IN • *39,155*
Marshall □, IA • *41,652*
Marshall □, KS • *12,787*
Marshall □, KY • *25,637*
Marshall □, MN • *13,027*
Marshall □, MS • *29,296*
Marshall □, OK • *10,550*
Marshall □, SD • *5,404*
Marshall □, TN • *19,698*
Marshall □, WV • *41,608*
Marshallberg, NC 28553 • *600*
Marshallton, DE 19808 • *3,950*
Marshalltown, IA 50158 • *26,938*
Marshallville, GA 31057 • *1,540*
Marshallville, OH 44645 • *788*
Marshes Siding, KY 42631 • *500*
Marshfield, MA 02050 • *4,421*
Marshfield, MO 65706 • *3,871*
Marshfield, VT 05658 • *301*
Marshfield, WI 54449 • *18,290*
Marshfield Hills, MA 02051 • *2,308*
Mars Hill, ME 04758 • *1,500*
Mars Hill, NC 28754 • *2,126*
Marshville, NC 28103 • *2,011*
Marsing, ID 83639 • *786*
Marsteller, PA 15760 • *250*
Marston, MO 63866 • *742*
Marston, NC 28363 • *250*
Marstons Mills, MA 02648 • *600*
Mart, TX 76664 • *2,324*
Martelle, IA 52305 • *316*
Martensdale, IA 50160 • *438*
Marthasville, MO 63357 • *543*
Marthaville, LA 71450 • *270*
Martin, GA 30557 • *305*
Martin, KY 41649 • *827*
Martin, LA 71019 • *584*
Martin, MI 49070 • *447*
Martin, OH 43445 • *250*
Martin, SD 57551 • *1,018*
Martin, TN 38237 • *8,898*
Martin □, FL • *64,014*
Martin □, IN • *11,001*
Martin □, KY • *13,925*
Martin □, MN • *24,687*
Martin □, NC • *25,948*
Martin □, TX • *4,684*
Martin City, MT 59926 • *500*
Martindale, TX 78655 • *500*
Martinez, CA 94553 • *22,582*
Martinez, GA 30907 • *16,472*
Martinsburg, MO 65264 • *309*
Martinsburg, NY 13404 • *300*
Martinsburg, OH 43037 • *240*
Martinsburg, PA 16662 • *2,231*
Martinsburg, WV 25401 • *13,063*
Martins Ferry, OH 43935 • *9,331*
Martinsville, IL 62442 • *1,298*
Martinsville, IN 46151 • *11,311*
Martinsville, OH 45146 • *539*
Martinsville, VA 24112 • *18,149*
Martinton, IL 60951 • *363*
Marvell, AR 72366 • *1,724*
Maryland City, MD 20707 • *6,250*
Maryland Heights, MO 63043 • *5,676*
Maryland Line, MD 21105 • *250*
Marysvale, UT 84750 • *359*
Marysville, CA 95901 • *9,898*
Marysville, ID 83420 • *250*
Marysville, KS 66508 • *3,670*
Marysville, MI 48040 • *7,345*
Marysville, OH 43040 • *7,414*
Marysville, PA 17053 • *2,452*
Marysville, WA 98270 • *5,080*
Maryville, KY 40229 • *6,000*
Maryville, MO 64468 • *9,558*
Maryville, TN 37801 • *17,480*
Masaryktown, FL 33512 • *800*
Mascot, TN 37806 • *2,203*
Mascoutah, IL 62258 • *4,962*
Mashpee, MA 02649 • *500*
Mason, IL 62443 • *480*
Mason, MI 48854 • *6,019*
Mason, OH 45040 • *8,692*
Mason, TN 38049 • *471*
Mason, TX 76856 • *2,153*
Mason, WV 25260 • *1,432*
Mason □, IL • *19,492*
Mason □, KY • *17,765*
Mason □, MI • *26,365*
Mason □, TX • *3,683*
Mason □, WA • *31,184*
Mason □, WV • *27,045*
Mason City, IL 62664 • *2,719*
Mason City, IA 50401 • *30,144*
Masontown, PA 15461 • *4,909*
Masontown, WV 26542 • *1,052*
Masonville, CO 80541 • *300*
Masonville, NY 13804 • *400*
Massac □, IL • *14,990*
Massapequa, NY 11758 • *27,500*
Massapequa Park, NY 11762 • *19,779*
Massena, IA 50853 • *518*
Massena, NY 13662 • *12,851*
Massillon, OH 44646 • *30,557*
Mastic, NY 11950 • *5,200*
Mastic Beach, NY 11951 • *5,200*
Masury, OH 44438 • *1,836*
Matador, TX 79244 • *1,052*
Matagorda, TX 77457 • *850*
Matagorda □, TX • *37,828*
Matamoras, PA 18336 • *2,111*
Matawan, NJ 07747 • *8,837*
Matewan, WV 25678 • *822*
Matfield, MA 02379 • *700*
Mather, PA 15346 • *860*
Matherville, IL 61263 • *793*
Mathews, LA 70375 • *900*
Mathews, VA 23109 • *650*
Mathews □, VA • *7,995*
Mathis, TX 78368 • *5,667*

Mathiston, MS 39752 • *632*
Matoaca, VA 23803 • *2,000*
Matoaka, WV 24736 • *613*
Mattapoisett, MA 02739 • *3,159*
Mattawamkeag, ME 04459 • *750*
Mattawana, PA 17054 • *250*
Matteson, IL 60443 • *10,223*
Matthews, IN 46957 • *745*
Matthews, MO 63867 • *547*
Matthews, NC 28105 • *1,648*
Mattituck, NY 11952 • *1,200*
Mattoon, IL 61938 • *19,055*
Mattoon, WI 54450 • *382*
Mattydale, NY 13211 • *8,292*
Matunuck, RI 02879 • *500*
Maud, OH 45069 • *600*
Maud, OK 74854 • *1,444*
Maugansville, MD 21767 • *1,707*
Maui □, HI • *70,847*
Mauldin, SC 29662 • *8,143*
Maumee, OH 43537 • *15,747*
Maunaloa, HI 96770 • *633*
Maunawili, HI 96734 • *2,200*
Maunie, IL 62861 • *225*
Maupin, OR 97037 • *495*
Maurice, IA 51036 • *288*
Maurice, LA 70555 • *478*
Mauricetown, NJ 08329 • *500*
Maury, NC 28554 • *450*
Maury □, TN • *51,095*
Maury City, TN 38050 • *989*
Mauston, WI 53948 • *3,284*
Maverick □, TX • *31,398*
Max, ND 58759 • *317*
Max Meadows, VA 24360 • *550*
Maxton, NC 28364 • *2,711*
Maxwell, CA 95955 • *800*
Maxwell, IN 46154 • *300*
Maxwell, IA 50161 • *783*
Maxwell, NE 69151 • *410*
Maxwell, NM 87728 • *316*
Maxwell Acres, WV 26041 • *1,000*
May, TX 76857 • *300*
Maybee, MI 48159 • *490*
Maybeury, WV 24861 • *700*
Mayer, AZ 86333 • *950*
Mayersville, MS 39113 • *378*
Mayes □, OK • *32,261*
Mayesville, SC 29104 • *663*
Mayetta, KS 66509 • *287*
Mayfield, KY 42066 • *10,705*
Mayfield, NY 12117 • *944*
Mayfield, PA 18433 • *1,812*
Mayfield, UT 84643 • *397*
Mayfield Heights, OH 44124 • *21,550*
Mayflower, AR 72106 • *1,381*
Mayland, TN 38555 • *300*
Maynard, AR 72444 • *381*
Maynard, IA 50655 • *561*
Maynard, MA 01754 • *9,590*
Maynard, MN 56260 • *428*
Maynardville, TN 37807 • *924*
Mayo, FL 32066 • *891*
Mayo, MD 21106 • *1,500*
Mayo, SC 29368 • *900*
Mayodan, NC 27027 • *2,627*
May Park, OR 97850 • *1,466*
Mays Landing, NJ 08330 • *2,054*
Mays Lick, KY 41055 • *400*
Maysville, GA 30558 • *619*
Maysville, KY 41056 • *7,983*
Maysville, MO 64469 • *1,187*
Maysville, NC 28555 • *877*
Maysville, OK 73057 • *1,396*
Mayview, MO 64071 • *291*
Mayville, MI 48744 • *958*
Mayville, ND 58257 • *2,255*
Mayville, NY 14757 • *1,626*
Mayville, WI 53050 • *4,333*
Maywood, CA 90270 • *21,810*
Maywood, IL 60153 • *27,998*
Maywood, NE 69038 • *332*
Maywood, NJ 07607 • *9,895*
Maywood Park, OR 97220 • *1,083*
Mazeppa, MN 55956 • *680*
Mazomanie, WI 53560 • *1,248*
Mazon, IL 60444 • *828*
Mead, CO 80542 • *356*
Mead, NE 68041 • *506*
Mead, WA 99021 • *1,400*
Meade, KS 67864 • *1,777*
Meade □, KS • *4,788*
Meade □, KY • *22,854*
Meade □, SD • *20,717*
Meadow, TX 79345 • *571*
Meadow, UT 84644 • *265*
Meadow Bridge, WV 25976 • *530*
Meadowbrook, WV 26404 • *500*
Meadow Grove, NE 68752 • *400*
Meadow Lands, PA 15347 • *1,200*
Meadowood, DE 19711 • *2,260*
Meadowview, VA 24361 • *600*
Meadville, MS 39653 • *575*
Meadville, MO 64659 • *416*
Meadville, PA 16335 • *15,544*
Meagher □, MT • *2,154*
Mears, MI 49436 • *350*
Mebane, NC 27302 • *2,782*
Mecca, CA 92254 • *1,698*
Mecca, IN 47860 • *482*
Mechanic Falls, ME 04256 • *2,616*
Mechanicsburg, OH 43044 • *1,792*
Mechanicsburg, PA 17055 • *9,487*
Mechanicsville, IA 52306 • *1,166*
Mechanicsville, MD 20659 • *300*
Mechanicsville, VA 23111 • *9,000*
Mechanicville, NY 12118 • *5,500*
Mecklenburg □, NC • *404,270*
Mecklenburg □, VA • *29,444*
Mecosta, MI 49332 • *428*
Mecosta □, MI • *36,961*
Medanales, NM 87548 • *250*
Medaryville, IN 47957 • *731*
Medfield, MA 02052 • *6,108*
Medford, MA 02155 • *58,076*
Medford, MN 55049 • *775*
Medford, NJ 08055 • *1,448*
Medford, NY 11763 • *5,000*
Medford, OK 73759 • *1,419*
Medford, OR 97501-04 • *39,603*
Medford, WI 54451 • *4,035*
Medford Lakes, NJ 08055 • *4,958*
Media, PA 19063-65 • *6,119*
Mediapolis, IA 52637 • *1,685*
Medical Lake, WA 99022 • *3,600*
Medicine Bow, WY 82329 • *953*
Medicine Lake, MT 59247 • *408*
Medicine Lodge, KS 67104 • *2,384*
Medicine Park, OK 73557 • *437*
Medina, ND 58467 • *521*
Medina, NY 14103 • *6,392*
Medina, OH 44256 • *15,268*
Medina, TN 38355 • *687*
Medina, TX 78055 • *400*
Medina, WA 98039 • *3,220*
Medina □, OH • *113,150*
Medina □, TX • *23,164*
Medora, IL 62063 • *532*
Medora, IN 47260 • *853*
Medway, ME 04460 • *525*
Medway, MA 02053 • *4,300*
Meeker, CO 81641 • *2,356*
Meeker, OK 74855 • *1,032*
Meeker □, MN • *20,594*
Meeteetse, WY 82433 • *512*
Megargel, TX 76370 • *381*
Meggett, SC 29460 • *249*
Mehlville, MO 63129 • *22,900*
Mehoopany, PA 18629 • *350*
Meigs, GA 31765 • *1,231*
Meigs □, OH • *23,641*
Meigs □, TN • *7,431*
Meiners Oaks, CA 93023 • *5,600*
Melba, ID 83641 • *276*
Melber, KY 42069 • *250*
Melbourne, AR 72556 • *1,619*
Melbourne, FL 32901-19 • *46,536*
Melbourne, IA 50162 • *732*
Melbourne, KY 41059 • *628*
Melbourne Beach, FL 32951 • *2,713*
Melcher, IA 50163 • *953*
Meldrim, GA 31318 • *400*
Mellen, WI 54546 • *1,046*
Mellette □, SD • *2,249*
Mellott, IN 47958 • *294*
Melmore, OH 44845 • *275*
Melrose, FL 32666 • *1,700*
Melrose, MA 02176 • *30,055*
Melrose, MN 56352 • *2,409*
Melrose, NM 88124 • *649*
Melrose, OH 45861 • *315*
Melrose, WI 54642 • *507*
Melrose Park, FL 33312 • *5,725*
Melrose Park, IL 60160-65 • *20,735*
Melstone, MT 59054 • *238*
Melvern, KS 66510 • *481*
Melville, LA 71353 • *1,764*
Melville, NY 11747 • *10,250*
Melvin, IL 60952 • *519*
Melvin, IA 51350 • *277*
Melvin, KY 41650 • *700*
Melvindale, MI 48122 • *12,322*
Melvin Village, NH 03850 • *350*
Memphis, FL 33561 • *5,501*
Memphis, IN 47143 • *500*
Memphis, MI 48041 • *1,171*
Memphis, MO 63555 • *2,105*
Memphis, TN 38101-99 • *646,174*
Memphis, TX 79245 • *3,352*
Mena, AR 71953 • *5,154*
Menahga, MN 56464 • *980*
Menan, ID 83434 • *605*
Menands, NY 12204 • *4,012*
Menard, TX 76859 • *1,697*
Menard □, IL • *11,700*
Menard □, TX • *2,346*
Menasha, WI 54952 • *14,728*
Mendenhall, MS 39114 • *2,533*
Mendham, NJ 07945 • *4,899*
Mendocino, CA 95460 • *1,008*
Mendocino □, CA • *66,738*
Mendon, IL 62351 • *979*
Mendon, MA 01756 • *900*
Mendon, MI 49072 • *951*
Mendon, MO 64660 • *252*
Mendon, OH 45862 • *749*
Mendon, UT 84325 • *663*
Mendota, CA 93640 • *5,038*
Mendota, IL 61342 • *7,134*
Mendota Heights, MN 55118 • *7,288*
Menifee, AR 72107 • *368*
Menifee □, KY • *5,117*
Menlo, GA 30731 • *611*
Menlo, IA 50164 • *410*
Menlo Park, CA 94025 • *26,369*
Menno, SD 57045 • *793*
Menominee, MI 49858 • *10,099*
Menominee □, MI • *26,201*
Menominee □, WI • *3,373*
Menomonee Falls, WI 53051 • *27,845*
Menomonie, WI 54751 • *12,769*
Mentone, AL 35984 • *476*
Mentone, IN 46539 • *973*
Mentor, OH 44060 • *42,065*
Mentor, TN 37777 • *400*
Mentor-on-the-Lake, OH 44060 • *7,919*
Mequon, WI 53092 • *16,193*
Meraux, LA 70075 • *4,100*
Merced, CA 95340 • *36,499*
Merced □, CA • *134,558*
Mercedes, TX 78570 • *11,851*
Mercer, MO 64661 • *442*
Mercer, PA 16137 • *2,532*
Mercer, TN 38392 • *400*
Mercer, WI 54547 • *1,250*
Mercer □, IL • *19,286*
Mercer □, KY • *19,011*
Mercer □, MO • *4,685*
Mercer □, NJ • *307,863*
Mercer □, ND • *9,404*
Mercer □, OH • *38,334*
Mercer □, PA • *128,299*
Mercer □, WV • *73,942*
Mercer Island, WA 98040 • *21,522*
Mercersburg, PA 17236 • *1,617*
Mercerville, NJ 08619 • *15,500*
Merchantville, NJ 08109 • *3,972*
Meredith, NH 03253 • *1,202*
Meredosia, IL 62665 • *1,272*
Meriden, CT 06450 • *57,118*
Meriden, IA 51037 • *233*
Meriden, KS 66512 • *707*
Meriden, NH 03770 • *400*
Meridian, ID 83642 • *6,658*
Meridian, MS 39301-05 • *46,577*
Meridian, NY 13113 • *344*
Meridian, PA 16001 • *2,400*
Meridian, TX 76665 • *1,330*
Meridian Hills, IN 46260 • *1,801*
Meridianville, AL 35759 • *1,403*
Merigold, MS 38759 • *574*
Merino, CO 80741 • *255*
Merion Station, PA 19066 • *7,400*
Meriwether □, GA • *21,229*
Merkel, TX 79536 • *2,493*
Merlin, OR 97532 • *500*
Mermentau, LA 70556 • *771*
Merna, NE 68856 • *389*
Merom, IN 47861 • *360*
Merriam, KS 66203 • *10,794*
Merrick, NY 11566 • *26,400*
Merrick □, NE • *8,945*
Merrifield, MN 56465 • *350*
Merrifield, VA 22116 • *2,100*
Merrill, IA 51038 • *737*
Merrill, MI 48637 • *851*
Merrill, OR 97633 • *809*
Merrill, WI 54452 • *9,578*
Merrillan, WI 54754 • *587*
Merrillville, IN 46410 • *27,677*
Merrimac, MA 01860 • *2,300*
Merrimac, WI 53561 • *365*
Merrimack, NH 03054 • *1,200*
Merrimack □, NH • *98,302*
Merrimacport, MA 01860 • *450*
Merritt Island, FL 32952-54 • *30,708*
Mer Rouge, LA 71261 • *802*
Merrow, CT 06251 • *250*
Merryville, LA 70653 • *1,286*
Merton, WI 53056 • *1,045*
Mertzon, TX 76941 • *687*
Mesa, AZ 85201-08 • *152,453*
Mesa □, CO • *81,530*
Mescalero, NM 88340 • *1,259*
Meservey, IA 50457 • *324*
Meshoppen, PA 18630 • *571*
Mesic, NC 28515 • *390*
Mesick, MI 49668 • *374*
Mesilla, NM 88046 • *2,029*
Mesita, NM 87026 • *300*
Mesquite, NV 89024 • *700*
Mesquite, NM 88048 • *400*
Mesquite, TX 75149-50 • *67,053*
Meta, MO 65058 • *336*
Metairie, LA 70001-11 • *164,160*
Metaline Falls, WA 99153 • *296*
Metamora, IL 61548 • *2,482*
Metamora, IN 47030 • *400*
Metamora, MI 48455 • *552*
Metamora, OH 43540 • *556*
Metcalf, IL 61940 • *278*
Metcalfe, MS 38760 • *952*
Metcalfe □, KY • *9,484*
Methuen, MA 01844 • *36,701*
Metlakatla, AK 99926 • *1,056*
Metolius, OR 97741 • *451*
Metropolis, IL 62960 • *7,171*
Metter, GA 30439 • *3,531*
Metuchen, NJ 08840 • *13,762*
Metzger, OR 97223 • *5,544*
Mexia, TX 76667 • *7,094*
Mexican Springs, NM 87320 • *500*
Mexico, IN 46958 • *850*
Mexico, ME 04257 • *3,207*
Mexico, MO 65265 • *12,276*
Mexico, NY 13114 • *1,621*
Mexico, PA 17056 • *450*
Meyersdale, PA 15552 • *2,581*
Miami, AZ 85539 • *2,716*
Miami, FL 33101-99 • *346,865*
Miami, IN 46959 • *400*
Miami, OK 74354 • *14,237*
Miami, TX 79059 • *813*
Miami, WV 25134 • *500*
Miami □, IN • *39,820*
Miami □, KS • *21,618*
Miami □, OH • *90,381*
Miami Beach, FL 33139 • *96,298*
Miamisburg, OH 45342 • *15,304*
Miami Shores, FL 33153 • *9,244*
Miami Springs, FL 33166 • *12,350*
Miamitown, OH 45041 • *650*
Micanopy, FL 32667 • *737*
Micco, FL 32958 • *3,585*
Michie, TN 38357 • *530*
Michigamme, MI 49861 • *300*
Michigan, ND 58259 • *502*
Michigan Center, MI 49254 • *5,244*
Michigan City, IN 46360 • *36,850*
Michigantown, IN 46057 • *453*
Micro, NC 27555 • *438*
Middle, IA 52307 • *400*
Middleboro, MA 02346 • *7,012*
Middlebourne, WV 26149 • *941*
Middlebranch, OH 44652 • *600*
Middlebrook, VA 24459 • *250*
Middleburg, FL 32068 • *2,500*
Middleburg, MD 21768 • *250*
Middleburg, NY 12122 • *1,358*
Middleburg, OH 43336 • *250*
Middleburg, PA 17842 • *1,357*
Middleburg, VA 22117 • *619*
Middleburgh, NY 12122 • *1,358*
Middleburg Heights, OH 44130 • *16,218*
Middlebury, CT 06762 • *3,900*
Middlebury, IN 46540 • *1,665*
Middlebury, VT 05753 • *5,591*
Middlefield, CT 06455 • *600*
Middlefield, OH 44062 • *1,997*
Middle Granville, NY 12849 • *600*
Middle Haddam, CT 06456 • *500*
Middle Point, OH 45863 • *709*
Middleport, NY 14105 • *1,995*
Middleport, OH 45760 • *2,971*
Middle River, MD 21220 • *26,756*
Middle River, MN 56737 • *349*
Middlesboro, KY 40965 • *12,251*
Middlesex, NJ 08846 • *13,480*
Middlesex, NC 27557 • *837*
Middlesex, NY 14507 • *350*
Middlesex □, CT • *129,017*
Middlesex □, MA • *1,367,034*
Middlesex □, NJ • *595,893*
Middlesex □, VA • *7,719*
Middleton, ID 83644 • *1,901*
Middleton, MA 01949 • *4,135*

Middleton, MI 48856 • *500*
Middleton, NH 03887 • *300*
Middleton, TN 38052 • *596*
Middleton, WI 53562 • *11,848*
Middletown, CA 95461 • *2,000*
Middletown, CT 06457 • *39,040*
Middletown, DE 19709 • *2,946*
Middletown, IL 62666 • *503*
Middletown, IN 47356 • *2,978*
Middletown, IA 52638 • *487*
Middletown, KY 40243 • *414*
Middletown, MD 21769 • *1,748*
Middletown, MO 63359 • *268*
Middletown, NJ 07748 • *61,615*
Middletown, NY 10940 • *21,454*
Middletown, OH 45042-43 • *43,719*
Middletown, PA 17057 • *10,122*
Middletown, RI 02840 • *3,350*
Middletown, VA 22645 • *841*
Middleville, MI 49333 • *1,797*
Middleville, NY 13406 • *647*
Midfield, AL 35228 • *6,203*
Midland, AR 72945 • *286*
Midland, IN 47445 • *250*
Midland, LA 70557 • *400*
Midland, MD 21542 • *601*
Midland, MI 48640 • *37,250*
Midland, NC 28107 • *600*
Midland, OH 45148 • *365*
Midland, PA 15059 • *4,310*
Midland, SD 57552 • *277*
Midland, TX 79701-11 • *70,525*
Midland □, MI • *73,578*
Midland □, TX • *82,636*
Midland City, AL 36350 • *1,903*
Midland Park, KS 67216 • *1,350*
Midland Park, NJ 07432 • *7,381*
Midland Park, SC 29405 • *1,300*
Midlothian, IL 60445 • *14,274*
Midlothian, MD 21543 • *250*
Midlothian, TX 76065 • *3,219*
Midlothian, VA 23113 • *1,000*
Midpines, CA 95345 • *390*
Midvale, OH 44653 • *654*
Midvale, UT 84047 • *10,146*
Midville, GA 30441 • *670*
Midway, AL 36053 • *593*
Midway, DE 19971 • *500*
Midway, FL 32343 • *450*
Midway, KY 40347 • *1,445*
Midway, OR 97233 • *19,000*
Midway, PA 15060 • *1,187*
Midway, TN 37809 • *350*
Midway, UT 84049 • *1,194*
Midwest, WY 82643 • *638*
Midwest City, OK 73110 • *49,559*
Mifflin, PA 17058 • *648*
Mifflin □, PA • *46,908*
Mifflinburg, PA 17844 • *3,151*
Mifflintown, PA 17059 • *783*
Mifflinville, PA 18631 • *1,074*
Mikana, WI 54857 • *250*
Milaca, MN 56353 • *2,104*
Milam □, TX • *22,732*
Milan, GA 31060 • *1,115*
Milan, IL 61264 • *6,264*
Milan, IN 47031 • *1,566*
Milan, MI 48160 • *4,182*
Milan, MN 56262 • *417*
Milan, MO 63556 • *1,947*
Milan, NM 87021 • *3,747*
Milan, OH 44846 • *1,569*
Milan, TN 38358 • *8,083*
Milano, TX 76556 • *468*
Milbank, SD 57252 • *4,120*
Milbridge, ME 04658 • *465*
Milburn, OK 73450 • *376*
Mildred, PA 18632 • *800*
Miles, IA 52064 • *398*
Miles, TX 76861 • *720*
Milesburg, PA 16853 • *1,309*
Miles City, MT 59301 • *9,602*
Milford, CT 06460 • *49,101*
Milford, IL 60953 • *1,716*
Milford, IN 46542 • *1,153*
Milford, IA 51351 • *2,076*
Milford, KS 66514 • *465*
Milford, ME 04461 • *1,688*
Milford, MA 01757 • *23,390*
Milford, MI 48042 • *5,041*
Milford, NE 68405 • *2,108*
Milford, NH 03055 • *6,289*
Milford, NJ 08848 • *1,368*
Milford, NY 13807 • *514*
Milford, OH 45150 • *5,232*
Milford, PA 18337 • *1,143*
Milford, UT 84751 • *1,293*
Milford, VA 22514 • *500*
Milford Center, OH 43045 • *764*
Mililani Town, HI 96789 • *20,351*
Milladore, WI 54454 • *250*
Millard □, UT • *8,970*
Millboro, VA 24460 • *300*
Millbrae, CA 94030 • *20,058*
Millbrook, AL 36054 • *3,101*
Millbrook, NY 12545 • *1,343*
Millburn, NJ 07041 • *19,543*
Millbury, MA 01527 • *5,700*
Millbury, OH 43447 • *955*
Mill City, OR 97360 • *1,565*
Mill City, PA 18414 • *300*
Mill Creek, OK 74856 • *431*
Mill Creek, PA 17060 • *367*
Millcreek, UT 84109 • *24,150*
Mill Creek, WV 26280 • *801*
Millcreek Township, PA 16505 • *44,303*
Milldale, CT 06467 • *1,100*
Milledgeville, GA 31061 • *12,176*
Milledgeville, IL 61051 • *1,209*
Milledgeville, TN 38359 • *392*
Mille Lacs □, MN • *18,430*
Millen, GA 30442 • *3,988*
Miller, SD 57362 • *1,931*
Miller □, AR • *37,766*
Miller □, GA • *7,038*
Miller □, MO • *18,532*
Millersburg, IN 46543 • *809*
Millersburg, KY 40348 • *987*
Millersburg, MI 49759 • *231*
Millersburg, OH 44654 • *3,247*
Millersburg, PA 17061 • *2,770*
Millers Falls, MA 01349 • *1,101*
Millersport, OH 43046 • *844*
Millerstown, PA 17062 • *550*
Millersville, PA 17551 • *7,668*
Millerton, NY 12546 • *1,013*
Millerton, OK 74750 • *262*
Millerton, PA 16936 • *350*
Mill Grove, MO 64673 • *850*
Mill Hall, PA 17751 • *1,744*
Millheim, PA 16854 • *800*
Milligan, FL 32537 • *500*
Milligan, NE 68406 • *332*
Milligan College, TN 37682 • *1,200*
Milliken, CO 80543 • *1,506*
Millington, MD 21651 • *546*
Millington, MI 48746 • *1,237*
Millington, OR 97420 • *300*
Millington, TN 38053 • *20,236*
Millinocket, ME 04462 • *7,567*
Millis, MA 02054 • *3,777*
Millport, AL 35576 • *1,287*
Mill River, MA 01244 • *300*
Mill Run, PA 15464 • *400*
Millry, AL 36558 • *956*
Mills, WY 82646 • *2,139*
Mills □, IA • *13,406*
Mills □, TX • *4,477*
Millsboro, DE 19966 • *1,233*
Millsboro, PA 15348 • *900*
Mill Shoals, IL 62862 • *333*
Mill Spring, MO 63952 • *257*
Millstadt, IL 62260 • *2,736*
Millstone, NJ 08876 • *530*
Milltown, IN 47145 • *1,006*
Milltown, MT 59851 • *300*
Milltown, NJ 08850 • *7,136*
Milltown, WI 54858 • *732*
Millvale, PA 15209 • *4,772*
Mill Valley, CA 94941 • *12,967*
Mill Village, PA 16427 • *427*
Millville, KY 40601 • *230*
Millville, MA 01529 • *1,764*
Millville, NJ 08332 • *24,815*
Millville, OH 45013 • *809*
Millville, PA 17846 • *975*
Millville, UT 84326 • *848*
Millville, WV 25432 • *400*
Millville Lake, NH • *600*
Millwood, VA 22646 • *400*
Millwood, WA 99212 • *1,717*
Milmay, NJ 08340 • *250*
Milner, GA 30257 • *320*
Milnor, ND 58060 • *716*
Milo, IA 50166 • *778*
Milo, ME 04463 • *2,255*
Milo, OR 97429 • *300*
Milpitas, CA 95035 • *37,820*
Milroy, IN 46156 • *900*
Milroy, MN 56263 • *242*
Milroy, PA 17063 • *1,575*
Milstead, GA 30207 • *1,157*
Milton, DE 19968 • *1,359*
Milton, FL 32570 • *7,206*
Milton, IL 62352 • *349*
Milton, IN 47357 • *729*
Milton, IA 52570 • *567*
Milton, KY 40045 • *718*
Milton, LA 70558 • *350*
Milton, MA 02186 • *25,860*
Milton, NH 03851 • *1,000*
Milton, NC 27305 • *235*
Milton, NY 12547 • *520*
Milton, PA 17847 • *6,730*
Milton, VT 05468 • *1,411*
Milton, WA 98354 • *3,162*
Milton, WV 25541 • *2,178*
Milton, WI 53563 • *4,092*
Milton-Freewater, OR 97862 • *5,086*
Milton Mills, NH 03852 • *350*
Miltonvale, KS 67466 • *588*
Milwaukee, NC 27854 • *300*
Milwaukee, WI 53201-99 • *636,236*
Milwaukee □, WI • *964,988*
Milwaukie, OR 97222 • *17,931*
Mimosa Park, LA 70070 • *3,737*
Mims, FL 32754 • *7,583*
Mina, NV 89422 • *425*
Minatare, NE 69356 • *969*
Minburn, IA 50167 • *390*
Minco, OK 73059 • *1,489*
Minden, IA 51553 • *419*
Minden, LA 71055 • *15,084*
Minden, NE 68959 • *2,939*
Minden, NV 89423 • *1,300*
Minden, WV 25879 • *800*
Minden City, MI 48456 • *284*
Mindenmines, MO 64769 • *318*
Mine Hill, NJ 07801 • *3,250*
Mineola, NY 11501 • *20,757*
Mineola, TX 75773 • *4,346*
Miner, MO 63801 • *1,182*
Miner □, SD • *3,739*
Mineral, CA 96063 • *320*
Mineral, IL 61344 • *325*
Mineral, VA 23117 • *399*
Mineral, WA 98355 • *500*
Mineral □, CO • *804*
Mineral □, MT • *3,675*
Mineral □, NV • *6,217*
Mineral □, WV • *27,234*
Mineral City, OH 44656 • *884*
Mineral Hills, MI 49935 • *257*
Mineral Point, MO 63660 • *358*
Mineral Point, WI 53565 • *2,259*
Mineral Springs, AR 71851 • *936*
Mineral Wells, MS 38648 • *250*
Mineral Wells, TX 76067 • *14,468*
Minersville, PA 17954 • *5,635*
Minersville, UT 84752 • *552*
Minerva, NY 12851 • *500*
Minerva, OH 44657 • *4,549*
Minetto, NY 13115 • *900*
Mineville, NY 12956 • *1,000*
Mingo, IA 50168 • *303*
Mingo □, WV • *37,336*
Mingo Junction, OH 43938 • *4,834*
Minidoka □, ID • *19,718*
Minier, IL 61759 • *1,261*
Minneapolis, KS 67467 • *2,075*
Minneapolis, MN 55401-99 • *370,951*
Minneapolis, NC 28652 • *300*
Minnehaha □, SD • *109,435*
Minneola, KS 67865 • *712*
Minneota, MN 56264 • *1,470*
Minnesota Lake, MN 56068 • *744*
Minnetonka, MN 55345 • *38,683*
Minnewaukan, ND 58351 • *461*
Minocqua, WI 54548 • *900*
Minong, WI 54859 • *557*
Minonk, IL 61760 • *2,039*
Minooka, IL 60447 • *1,565*
Minor Hill, TN 38473 • *564*
Minot, MA 02055 • *800*
Minot, ND 58701 • *32,843*
Minquadale, DE 19720 • *1,700*
Minster, OH 45865 • *2,557*
Mint Hill, NC 28212 • *7,915*
Minto, ND 58261 • *592*
Minturn, CO 81645 • *1,060*
Mio, MI 48647 • *1,500*
Mira Loma, CA 91752 • *8,707*
Miramar, FL 33023 • *32,813*
Mirando City, TX 78369 • *450*
Mirror Lake, NH 03853 • *250*
Misenheimer, NC 28109 • *1,250*
Mishawaka, IN 46544-45 • *40,201*
Mishicot, WI 54228 • *1,503*
Missaukee □, MI • *10,009*
Mission, KS 66222 • *8,643*
Mission, SD 57555 • *748*
Mission, TX 78572 • *22,653*
Mission Hills, KS 66205 • *3,904*
Mission Viejo, CA 92691 • *50,666*
Mississippi □, AR • *59,517*
Mississippi □, MO • *15,726*
Mississippi State, MS 39762 • *4,595*
Missoula, MT 59801-12 • *33,388*
Missoula □, MT • *76,016*
Missouri City, MO 64072 • *343*
Missouri City, TX 77459 • *24,533*
Missouri Valley, IA 51555 • *3,107*
Mitchell, IL 62040 • *1,500*
Mitchell, IN 47446 • *4,641*
Mitchell, NE 69357 • *1,956*
Mitchell, SD 57301 • *13,916*
Mitchell □, GA • *21,114*
Mitchell □, IA • *12,329*
Mitchell □, KS • *8,117*
Mitchell □, NC • *14,428*
Mitchell □, TX • *9,088*
Mitchellsburg, KY 40452 • *300*
Mitchellville, IA 50169 • *1,530*
Mize, MS 39116 • *363*
Mizpah, NJ 08342 • *600*
Moab, UT 84532 • *5,333*
Mobeetie, TX 79061 • *291*
Moberly, MO 65270 • *13,418*
Mobile, AL 36601-99 • *200,452*
Mobile □, AL • *364,980*
Mobridge, SD 57601 • *4,174*
Mocanaqua, PA 18655 • *990*
Mocksville, NC 27028 • *2,637*
Moclips, WA 98562 • *700*
Modale, IA 51556 • *373*
Modena, NY 12548 • *350*
Modesto, CA 95350-56 • *106,602*
Modesto, IL 62667 • *260*
Modoc, IN 47358 • *243*
Modoc □, CA • *8,610*
Moenkopi, AZ 86045 • *900*
Moffat □, CO • *13,133*
Moffett, OK 74946 • *269*
Mogadore, OH 44260 • *4,190*
Mohall, ND 58761 • *1,049*
Mohave □, AZ • *55,865*
Mohave Valley, AZ 86440 • *750*
Mohawk, MI 49950 • *950*
Mohawk, NY 13407 • *2,956*
Mohegan, CT 06382 • *400*
Mohegan, RI 02895 • *250*
Mohnton, PA 19540 • *2,156*
Moira, NY 12957 • *400*
Mojave, CA 93501 • *2,886*
Mokane, MO 65059 • *293*
Mokelumne Hill, CA 95245 • *950*
Mokena, IL 60448 • *4,578*
Molalla, OR 97038 • *2,992*
Molena, GA 30258 • *379*
Moline, IL 61265 • *46,278*
Moline, KS 67353 • *553*
Moline, MI 49335 • *800*
Moline, OH 43465 • *450*
Molino, FL 32577 • *1,456*
Momence, IL 60954 • *3,297*
Mona, UT 84645 • *536*
Monaca, PA 15061 • *7,661*
Monahans, TX 79756 • *8,397*
Monarch Mills, SC 29379 • *2,353*
Moncks Corner, SC 29461 • *3,699*
Moncure, NC 27559 • *600*
Mondamin, IA 51557 • *423*
Mondovi, WI 54755 • *2,545*
Monee, IL 60449 • *993*
Monessen, PA 15062 • *11,928*
Monett, MO 65708 • *6,148*
Monette, AR 72447 • *1,165*
Monfort Heights, OH 45239 • *9,745*
Mongo, IN 46771 • *225*
Monico, WI 54549 • *250*
Moniteau □, MO • *12,068*
Mon Louis, AL 36523 • *250*
Monmouth, IL 61462 • *10,706*
Monmouth, ME 04259 • *500*
Monmouth, OR 97361 • *5,594*
Monmouth □, NJ • *503,173*
Monmouth Beach, NJ 07750 • *3,318*
Monmouth Junction, NJ 08852 • *2,579*
Mono □, CA • *8,577*
Monon, IN 47959 • *1,540*
Monona, IA 52159 • *1,530*
Monona, WI 53716 • *8,809*
Monona □, IA • *11,692*
Monongah, WV 26554 • *1,132*
Monongahela, PA 15063 • *5,950*
Monongalia □, WV • *75,024*
Monponsett, MA 02350 • *600*
Monroe, CT 06468 • *760*
Monroe, GA 30655 • *8,854*
Monroe, IN 46772 • *739*
Monroe, IA 50170 • *1,875*
Monroe, LA 71201-12 • *57,597*
Monroe, MI 48161 • *23,531*
Monroe, NE 68647 • *294*
Monroe, NJ 07871 • *350*
Monroe, NC 28110 • *12,639*
Monroe, NY 10950 • *5,996*
Monroe, OH 45050 • *4,256*

Monroe, OK 74947 • 250
Monroe, OR 97456 • 412
Monroe, UT 84754 • 1,476
Monroe, VA 24574 • 400
Monroe, WA 98272 • 2,869
Monroe, WI 53566 • 10,027
Monroe □, AL • 22,651
Monroe □, AR • 14,052
Monroe □, FL • 63,188
Monroe □, GA • 14,610
Monroe □, IL • 20,117
Monroe □, IN • 98,785
Monroe □, IA • 9,209
Monroe □, KY • 12,353
Monroe □, MI • 134,659
Monroe □, MS • 36,404
Monroe □, MO • 9,716
Monroe □, NY • 702,238
Monroe □, OH • 17,382
Monroe □, PA • 69,409
Monroe □, TN • 28,700
Monroe □, WV • 12,873
Monroe □, WI • 35,074
Monroe Center, CT 06468 • 6,950
Monroe Center, IL 61052 • 380
Monroe City, IN 47557 • 569
Monroe City, MO 63456 • 2,557
Monroe Park, DE 19807 • 1,250
Monroeton, PA 18832 • 677
Monroeville, AL 36460 • 5,674
Monroeville, IN 46773 • 1,372
Monroeville, NJ 08343 • 300
Monroeville, OH 44847 • 1,329
Monroeville, PA 15146 • 30,977
Monrovia, CA 91016 • 30,531
Monrovia, IN 46157 • 450
Monsey, NY 10952 • 7,400
Monson, ME 04464 • 500
Monson, MA 01057 • 2,167
Montague, CA 96064 • 1,285
Montague, MA 01351 • 900
Montague, MI 49437 • 2,332
Montague, TX 76251 • 350
Montague □, TX • 17,410
Mont Alto, PA 17237 • 1,592
Montandon, PA 17850 • 650
Montauk, NY 11954 • 1,300
Mont Belvieu, TX 77580 • 1,730
Montcalm □, MI • 47,555
Montchanin, DE 19710 • 350
Montclair, CA 91763 • 22,628
Montclair, NJ 07042-44 • 38,321
Mont Clare, PA 19453 • 1,274
Montcoal, WV 25135 • 300
Monteagle, TN 37356 • 1,126
Montebello, CA 90640 • 52,929
Montecito, CA 93108 • 9,300
Montegut, LA 70377 • 800
Montello, WI 53949 • 1,273
Monterey, CA 93940 • 27,558
Monterey, IN 46960 • 236
Monterey, MA 01245 • 500
Monterey, TN 38574 • 2,610
Monterey, VA 24465 • 247
Monterey □, CA • 290,444
Monterey Park, CA 91754 • 54,338
Montesano, WA 98563 • 3,247
Montevallo, AL 35115 • 3,965
Montevideo, MN 56265 • 5,845
Monte Vista, CO 81144 • 3,902
Montezuma, GA 31063 • 4,830
Montezuma, IN 47862 • 1,352
Montezuma, IA 50171 • 1,485
Montezuma, KS 67867 • 730
Montezuma, NM 87731 • 250
Montezuma □, CO • 16,510
Montezuma Creek, UT 84534 • 300
Montfort, WI 53569 • 616
Montgomery, AL 36101-99 • 177,857
Montgomery, IL 60538 • 3,369
Montgomery, IN 47558 • 390
Montgomery, LA 71454 • 843
Montgomery, MA 01085 • 300
Montgomery, MI 49255 • 408
Montgomery, MN 56069 • 2,349
Montgomery, NY 12549 • 2,316
Montgomery, OH 45242 • 10,088
Montgomery, PA 17752 • 1,653
Montgomery, WV 25136 • 3,104
Montgomery □, AL • 197,038
Montgomery □, AR • 7,771
Montgomery □, GA • 7,011
Montgomery □, IL • 31,686
Montgomery □, IN • 35,501
Montgomery □, IA • 13,413
Montgomery □, KS • 42,281
Montgomery □, KY • 20,046
Montgomery □, MD • 579,053
Montgomery □, MS • 13,366
Montgomery □, MO • 11,537
Montgomery □, NC • 22,469
Montgomery □, NY • 53,439
Montgomery □, OH • 571,697
Montgomery □, PA • 643,621
Montgomery □, TN • 83,342
Montgomery □, TX • 128,487
Montgomery □, VA • 63,516
Montgomery Center, VT 05471 • 350
Montgomery City, MO 63361 • 2,101
Montgomery Creek, CA 96065 • 800
Montgomery Village, MD 20879 • 16,600
Monticello, AR 71655 • 8,259
Monticello, FL 32344 • 2,994
Monticello, GA 31064 • 2,382
Monticello, IL 61856 • 4,753
Monticello, IN 47960 • 5,162
Monticello, IA 52310 • 3,641
Monticello, KY 42633 • 5,677
Monticello, ME 04760 • 425
Monticello, MN 55362 • 2,830
Monticello, MS 39654 • 1,834
Monticello, NY 12701 • 6,306
Monticello, UT 84535 • 1,929
Monticello, WI 53570 • 1,021
Montmorenci, IN 47962 • 250
Montmorenci, SC 29839 • 900
Montmorency □, MI • 7,492
Montour, IA 50173 • 387
Montour □, PA • 16,675
Montour Falls, NY 14865 • 1,791
Montoursville, PA 17754 • 5,403
Montpelier, ID 83254 • 3,107
Montpelier, IN 47359 • 1,995
Montpelier, IA 52759 • 250
Montpelier, OH 43543 • 4,431
Montpelier, VT 05602 • 8,241
Montreal, WI 54550 • 887
Montreat, NC 28757 • 741
Montrose, AL 36559 • 1,200
Montrose, AR 71658 • 641
Montrose, CO 81401 • 8,722
Montrose, IL 62445 • 321
Montrose, IA 52639 • 1,038
Montrose, MI 48457 • 1,706
Montrose, MO 64770 • 498
Montrose, PA 18801 • 1,980
Montrose, SD 57048 • 396
Montrose, VA 23231 • 2,200
Montrose □, CO • 24,352
Montross, VA 22520 • 456
Montvale, NJ 07645 • 7,318
Montvale, VA 24122 • 450
Mont Vernon, NH 03057 • 300
Montville, CT 06353 • 1,711
Montville, NJ 07045 • 2,700
Montz, LA 70068 • 500
Monument, CO 80132 • 690
Monument Beach, MA 02553 • 1,500
Monument Heights, VA 23226 • 3,100
Moodus, CT 06469 • 1,179
Moody, ME 04054 • 515
Moody, TX 76557 • 1,385
Moody □, SD • 6,692
Moody Beach, ME 04054 • 3,000
Moonachie, NJ 07074 • 2,706
Moon Run, PA 15136 • 700
Moorcroft, WY 82721 • 1,014
Moore, MT 59464 • 229
Moore, OK 73160 • 35,063
Moore, TX 78057 • 330
Moore □, NC • 50,505
Moore □, TN • 4,510
Moore □, TX • 16,575
Moorefield, WV 26836 • 2,257
Moore Haven, FL 33471 • 1,250
Mooreland, IN 47360 • 479
Mooreland, OK 73852 • 1,383
Mooresburg, TN 37811 • 300
Moores Hill, IN 47032 • 566
Moorestown, NJ 08057 • 15,596
Mooresville, IN 46158 • 5,349
Mooresville, NC 28115 • 8,575
Moorhead, IA 51558 • 264
Moorhead, MN 56560 • 29,998
Moorhead, MS 38761 • 2,358
Mooringsport, LA 71060 • 911
Moorland, IA 50566 • 257
Mooseheart, IL 60539 • 600
Moose Lake, MN 55767 • 1,408
Moosic, PA 18507 • 6,068
Moosup, CT 06354 • 3,308
Mora, MN 55051 • 2,890
Mora, NM 87732 • 900
Mora □, NM • 4,205
Moraga, CA 94556 • 15,014
Moraine, OH 45439 • 5,325
Moran, KS 66755 • 643
Moran, TX 76464 • 344
Morann, PA 16663 • 500
Morattico, VA 22523 • 300
Moravia, IA 52571 • 706
Moravia, NY 13118 • 1,582
Moreauville, LA 71355 • 853
Morehead, KY 40351 • 7,789
Morehead City, NC 28557 • 4,359
Morehouse, MO 63868 • 1,220
Morehouse □, LA • 34,803
Moreland, GA 30259 • 358
Moreland, ID 83256 • 400
Moreland, KY 40437 • 300
Morenci, AZ 85540 • 1,200
Morenci, MI 49256 • 2,110
Morgan, GA 31766 • 364
Morgan, MN 56266 • 975
Morgan, TX 76671 • 485
Morgan, UT 84050 • 1,896
Morgan □, AL • 90,231
Morgan □, CO • 22,513
Morgan □, GA • 11,572
Morgan □, IL • 37,502
Morgan □, IN • 51,999
Morgan □, KY • 12,103
Morgan □, MO • 13,807
Morgan □, OH • 14,241
Morgan □, TN • 16,604
Morgan □, UT • 4,917
Morgan □, WV • 10,711
Morgan City, LA 70380 • 16,114
Morgan City, MS 38946 • 319
Morganfield, KY 42437 • 3,781
Morgan Hill, CA 95037 • 17,060
Morganton, GA 30560 • 263
Morganton, NC 28655 • 13,763
Morgantown, IN 46160 • 897
Morgantown, KY 42261 • 2,000
Morgantown, MS 39120 • 3,445
Morgantown, MS 39484 • 320
Morgantown, PA 19543 • 800
Morgantown, TN 37321 • 600
Morgantown, WV 26505 • 27,605
Morganville, KS 67468 • 261
Morganville, NJ 07751 • 900
Morganza, LA 70759 • 846
Moriah, NY 12960 • 500
Moriarty, NM 87035 • 1,276
Morland, KS 67650 • 223
Morley, MI 49336 • 507
Morley, MO 63767 • 745
Morningdale, MA 01530 • 1,150
Morning Sun, IA 52640 • 959
Moro, AR 72368 • 327
Moro, OR 97039 • 336
Morocco, IN 47963 • 1,348
Moroni, UT 84646 • 1,086
Morral, OH 43337 • 454
Morrill, KS 66515 • 336
Morrill, NE 69358 • 1,097
Morrill □, NE • 6,085
Morrilton, AR 72110 • 7,355
Morris, AL 35116 • 623
Morris, IL 60450 • 8,833
Morris, IN 47033 • 250
Morris, MN 56267 • 5,367
Morris, NY 13808 • 681
Morris, OK 74445 • 1,288
Morris □, KS • 6,419
Morris □, NJ • 407,630
Morris □, TX • 14,629
Morrisdale, PA 16858 • 600
Morrison, CO 80465 • 478
Morrison, IL 61270 • 4,605
Morrison, OK 73061 • 671
Morrison, TN 37357 • 587
Morrison □, MN • 29,311
Morrison City, TN 37660 • 2,032
Morrisonville, IL 62546 • 1,208
Morrisonville, NY 12962 • 1,500
Morris Plains, NJ 07950 • 5,305
Morris Run, PA 16939 • 425
Morriston, FL 32668 • 300
Morristown, IN 46161 • 989
Morristown, MN 55052 • 639
Morristown, NJ 07960 • 16,614
Morristown, NY 13664 • 461
Morristown, TN 37814 • 19,683
Morrisville, MO 65710 • 331
Morrisville, NY 13408 • 2,707
Morrisville, PA 19067 • 9,845
Morrisville, VT 05661 • 2,074
Morro Bay, CA 93442 • 9,064
Morrow, GA 30260 • 3,791
Morrow, LA 71356 • 460
Morrow, OH 45152 • 1,254
Morrow □, OH • 26,480
Morrow □, OR • 7,519
Morse, LA 70559 • 835
Morse, TX 79062 • 280
Morton, IL 61550 • 14,178
Morton, MN 56270 • 549
Morton, MS 39117 • 3,303
Morton, TX 79346 • 2,674
Morton, WA 98356 • 1,264
Morton □, KS • 3,454
Morton □, ND • 25,177
Morton Grove, IL 60053 • 23,747
Mortons Gap, KY 42440 • 1,201
Morven, GA 31638 • 471
Morven, NC 28119 • 765
Mosby, MO 64073 • 284
Moscow, ID 83843 • 16,513
Moscow, IA 52760 • 250
Moscow, KS 67952 • 228
Moscow, OH 45153 • 324
Moscow, PA 18444 • 1,536
Moscow, TN 38057 • 499
Moscow, VT 05662 • 350
Moscow Mills, MO 63362 • 484
Moselle, MS 39459 • 500
Moses Lake, WA 98837 • 10,629
Mosheim, TN 37818 • 1,539
Mosier, OR 97040 • 340
Mosinee, WI 54455 • 3,015
Moss Bluff, LA 70611 • 7,004
Moss Point, MS 39563 • 18,998
Mossyrock, WA 98564 • 463
Motley, MN 56466 • 444
Motley □, TX • 1,950
Mott, ND 58646 • 1,315
Moulton, AL 35650 • 3,197
Moulton, IA 52572 • 762
Moultrie, GA 31768 • 15,708
Moultrie □, IL • 14,546
Mound, MN 55364 • 9,280
Mound Bayou, MS 38762 • 2,917
Mound City, IL 62963 • 1,102
Mound City, KS 66056 • 755
Mound City, MO 64470 • 1,447
Moundridge, KS 67107 • 1,453
Mounds, IL 62964 • 1,669
Mounds, OK 74047 • 1,086
Mounds View, MN 55432 • 12,593
Moundsville, WV 26041 • 12,419
Mound Valley, KS 67354 • 381
Moundville, AL 35474 • 1,310
Mountainair, NM 87036 • 1,170
Mountainaire, AZ 86001 • 700
Mountainboro, AL 35957 • 266
Mountain Brook, AL 35223 • 19,718
Mountainburg, AR 72946 • 595
Mountain City, GA 30562 • 701
Mountain City, TN 37683 • 2,125
Mountain Dale, NY 12763 • 1,200
Mountain Grove, MO 65711 • 3,974
Mountain Home, AR 72653 • 8,066
Mountain Home, ID 83647 • 7,540
Mountainhome, PA 18342 • 600
Mountain Iron, MN 55768 • 4,134
Mountain Lake, MN 56159 • 2,277
Mountain Lake Park, MD 21550 • 1,597
Mountain Lakes, NJ 07046 • 4,153
Mountain Park, OK 73559 • 557
Mountain Pine, AR 71956 • 1,068
Mountain Point, AK 99901 • 396
Mountainside, NJ 07092 • 7,118
Mountain View, AR 72560 • 2,147
Mountain View, CA 94040-43 • 58,655
Mountain View, CO 80212 • 584
Mountain View, CO 80521 • 1,693
Mountainview, HI 96771 • 540
Mountain View, MO 65548 • 1,664
Mountain View, NM 87105 • 1,900
Mountain View, OK 73062 • 1,189
Mountain View, WY 82601 • 1,500
Mountain View, WY 82939 • 628
Mountain Village, AK 99632 • 583
Mount Airy, GA 30563 • 670
Mount Airy, MD 21771 • 2,450
Mount Airy, NC 27030 • 6,862
Mount Angel, OR 97362 • 2,876
Mount Arlington, NJ 07856 • 4,251
Mount Auburn, IL 62547 • 598
Mount Ayr, IA 50854 • 1,938
Mount Berry, GA 30149 • 500
Mount Blanchard, OH 45867 • 492
Mount Calvary, WI 53057 • 585
Mount Carmel, IL 62863 • 8,908
Mount Carmel, OH 45244 • 900
Mount Carmel, PA 17851 • 8,190
Mount Carroll, IL 61053 • 1,936
Mount Clare, WV 26408 • 900
Mount Clemens, MI 48043-46 • 18,806
Mount Cory, OH 45868 • 276
Mount Crawford, VA 22841 • 315
Mount Desert, ME 04660 • 400

Mount Dora, FL 32757 • *5,883*
Mount Eaton, OH 44659 • *289*
Mount Enterprise, TX 75681 • *485*
Mount Ephraim, NJ 08059 • *4,863*
Mount Freedom, NJ 07970 • *1,621*
Mount Gay, WV 25637 • *1,650*
Mount Gilead, NC 27306 • *1,423*
Mount Gilead, OH 43338 • *2,911*
Mount Healthy, OH 45231 • *7,562*
Mount Hermon, MA 01354 • *600*
Mount Holly, AR 71758 • *300*
Mount Holly, NJ 08060 • *10,818*
Mount Holly, NC 28120 • *4,530*
Mount Holly Springs, PA 17065 • *2,068*
Mount Hope, KS 67108 • *791*
Mount Hope, WV 25880 • *1,849*
Mount Horeb, WI 53572 • *3,251*
Mount Ida, AR 71957 • *1,023*
Mount Jackson, VA 22842 • *1,419*
Mount Jewett, PA 16740 • *1,053*
Mount Joy, IA 52804 • *300*
Mount Joy, PA 17552 • *5,680*
Mount Juliet, TN 37122 • *2,879*
Mount Kisco, NY 10549 • *8,025*
Mountlake Terrace, WA 98043 • *16,534*
Mount Lebanon, PA 15228 • *34,414*
Mount Lemmon, AZ 85619 • *300*
Mount Morris, IL 61054 • *2,989*
Mount Morris, MI 48458 • *3,246*
Mount Morris, NY 14510 • *3,039*
Mount Morris, PA 15349 • *600*
Mount Olive, AL 35117 • *1,900*
Mount Olive, IL 62069 • *2,357*
Mount Olive, MS 39119 • *993*
Mount Olive, NC 28365 • *4,876*
Mount Olive, TN 37920 • *600*
Mount Olivet, KY 41064 • *346*
Mount Orab, OH 45154 • *1,573*
Mount Penn, PA 19606 • *3,025*
Mount Pleasant, AR 72561 • *438*
Mount Pleasant, IA 52641 • *7,322*
Mount Pleasant, MI 48858 • *23,746*
Mount Pleasant, MS 38649 • *300*
Mount Pleasant, NC 28124 • *1,210*
Mount Pleasant, PA 15666 • *5,354*
Mount Pleasant, SC 29464 • *14,209*
Mount Pleasant, TN 38474 • *3,375*
Mount Pleasant, TX 75455 • *11,003*
Mount Pleasant, UT 84647 • *2,049*
Mount Pocono, PA 18344 • *1,237*
Mount Prospect, IL 60056 • *52,634*
Mount Pulaski, IL 62548 • *1,783*
Mountrail □, ND • *7,679*
Mount Rainier, MD 20712 • *7,361*
Mount Savage, MD 21545 • *1,640*
Mount Shasta, CA 96067 • *2,837*
Mount Sidney, VA 24467 • *550*
Mount Sterling, IL 62353 • *2,186*
Mount Sterling, KY 40353 • *5,820*
Mount Sterling, OH 43143 • *1,623*
Mount Storm, WV 26739 • *300*
Mount Summit, IN 47361 • *357*
Mount Sunapee, NH 03772 • *250*
Mount Union, PA 17066 • *3,101*
Mount Upton, NY 13809 • *500*
Mount Vernon, AL 36560 • *1,038*
Mount Vernon, GA 30445 • *1,737*
Mount Vernon, IL 62864 • *17,193*
Mount Vernon, IN 47620 • *7,656*
Mount Vernon, IA 52314 • *3,325*
Mount Vernon, KY 40456 • *2,334*
Mount Vernon, MD 21853 • *300*
Mount Vernon, MO 65712 • *3,341*
Mount Vernon, NY 10550-59 • *66,713*
Mount Vernon, OH 43050 • *14,323*
Mount Vernon, OR 97865 • *569*
Mount Vernon, SD 57363 • *402*
Mount Vernon, TX 75457 • *2,025*
Mount Vernon, WA 98273 • *13,009*
Mount Victory, OH 43340 • *667*
Mount View, RI 02852 • *560*
Mount Washington, KY 40047 • *3,997*
Mount Wolf, PA 17347 • *1,517*
Mount Zion, GA 30150 • *445*
Mount Zion, IL 62549 • *4,563*
Mousie, KY 41839 • *300*
Moville, IA 51039 • *1,273*
Moweaqua, IL 62550 • *1,922*
Mower □, MN • *40,390*
Mowrystown, OH 45155 • *475*
Moxahala, OH 43761 • *350*
Moxee City, WA 98936 • *687*
Moyie Springs, ID 83845 • *386*
Moyock, NC 27958 • *700*
Mozelle, KY 40858 • *250*
Mud Lake, ID 83450 • *243*
Muenster, TX 76252 • *1,408*
Muhlenberg □, KY • *32,238*
Muir, MI 48860 • *698*
Mukilteo, WA 98275 • *1,426*
Mukwonago, WI 53149 • *4,014*
Mulberry, AR 72947 • *1,444*
Mulberry, FL 33860 • *2,932*
Mulberry, IN 46058 • *1,225*
Mulberry, KS 66756 • *647*
Mulberry, NC 28659 • *1,210*
Mulberry, OH 45150 • *800*
Mulberry Grove, IL 62262 • *707*
Muldraugh, KY 40155 • *1,752*
Muldrow, OK 74948 • *2,538*
Muleshoe, TX 79347 • *4,842*
Mulga, AL 35118 • *405*
Mulhall, OK 73063 • *301*
Mulino, OR 97042 • *350*
Mullan, ID 83846 • *1,269*
Mullen, NE 69152 • *720*
Mullens, WV 25882 • *2,919*
Mullica Hill, NJ 08062 • *1,050*
Mulliken, MI 48861 • *550*
Mullins, SC 29574 • *6,068*
Mullinville, KS 67109 • *339*
Multnomah □, OR • *562,640*
Mulvane, KS 67110 • *4,254*
Muncie, IN 47302-06 • *77,216*
Muncy, PA 17756 • *2,700*
Munday, TX 76371 • *1,738*
Mundelein, IL 60060 • *17,053*
Munford, AL 36268 • *600*
Munford, TN 38058 • *2,336*
Munfordville, KY 42765 • *1,783*
Munger, MI 48747 • *250*
Munhall, PA 15120 • *14,535*
Munich, ND 58352 • *300*
Munising, MI 49862 • *3,083*
Munith, MI 49259 • *300*
Munjor, KS 67601 • *260*
Munnsville, NY 13409 • *499*
Munson, PA 16860 • *350*
Munsonville, NH 03457 • *300*
Munster, IN 46321 • *20,671*
Murdo, SD 57559 • *723*
Murdock, FL 33938 • *250*
Murdock, MN 56271 • *343*
Murdock, NE 68407 • *242*
Murfreesboro, AR 71958 • *1,883*
Murfreesboro, NC 27855 • *3,007*
Murfreesboro, TN 37130 • *32,845*
Murphy, MO 63026 • *8,121*
Murphy, NC 28906 • *2,070*
Murphy, OR 97533 • *300*
Murphys, CA 95247 • *950*
Murphysboro, IL 62966 • *9,866*
Murray, IA 50174 • *703*
Murray, KY 42071 • *14,248*
Murray, NE 68409 • *465*
Murray, UT 84107 • *25,750*
Murray □, GA • *19,685*
Murray □, MN • *11,507*
Murray □, OK • *12,147*
Murray City, OH 43144 • *579*
Murrayville, IL 62668 • *712*
Murrells Inlet, SC 29576 • *950*
Murrieta, CA 92362 • *350*
Murrysville, PA 15668 • *16,036*
Muscatine, IA 52761 • *23,467*
Muscatine □, IA • *40,436*
Muscle Shoals, AL 35662 • *8,911*
Muscoda, WI 53573 • *1,331*
Muscogee □, GA • *170,108*
Muscotah, KS 66058 • *248*
Muscoy, CA 92405 • *6,188*
Muse, PA 15350 • *1,358*
Muskego, WI 53150 • *15,277*
Muskegon, MI 49440-45 • *40,823*
Muskegon □, MI • *157,589*
Muskegon Heights, MI 49444 • *14,611*
Muskingum □, OH • *83,340*
Muskogee, OK 74401-03 • *40,011*
Muskogee □, OK • *66,939*
Musselshell □, MT • *4,428*
Mustang, OK 73064 • *7,496*
Myerstown, PA 17067 • *3,131*
Myersville, MD 21773 • *432*
Myrtle, MS 38650 • *402*
Myrtle Beach, SC 29577-79 • *18,446*
Myrtle Creek, OR 97457 • *3,365*
Myrtle Grove, FL 32506 • *14,238*
Myrtle Point, OR 97458 • *2,859*
Myrtlewood, AL 36763 • *252*
Mystic, CT 06355 • *2,333*
Mystic, GA 31769 • *300*
Mystic, IA 52574 • *665*
Myton, UT 84052 • *500*

N

Naalehu, HI 96772 • *1,168*
Nabb, IN 47147 • *250*
Nabnasset, MA 01886 • *4,800*
Naches, WA 98937 • *644*
Naco, AZ 85620 • *800*
Nacogdoches, TX 75961 • *27,149*
Nacogdoches □, TX • *46,786*
Nadeau, MI 49863 • *250*
Nags Head, NC 27959 • *1,020*
Nahant, MA 01908 • *3,947*
Nahma, MI 49864 • *250*
Nahunta, GA 31553 • *951*
Naknek, AK 99633 • *600*
Nampa, ID 83651 • *25,112*
Nanakuli, HI 96792 • *8,185*
Nance □, NE • *4,740*
Nankin, OH 44848 • *340*
Nanticoke, MD 21840 • *430*
Nanticoke, PA 18634 • *13,044*
Nantucket, MA 02554 • *3,229*
Nantucket □, MA • *5,087*
Nanty Glo, PA 15943 • *3,936*
Nanuet, NY 10954 • *8,300*
Naoma, WV 25140 • *600*
Napa, CA 94558-59 • *50,879*
Napa □, CA • *99,199*
Napakiak, AK 99634 • *262*
Napanoch, NY 12458 • *800*
Napavine, WA 98565 • *611*
Naperville, IL 60540 • *42,601*
Naplate, IL 61350 • *581*
Naples, FL 33940-42 • *17,581*
Naples, ME 04055 • *400*
Naples, NY 14512 • *1,225*
Naples, TX 75568 • *1,908*
Naples, UT 84078 • *250*
Napoleon, IN 47034 • *246*
Napoleon, MO 64074 • *271*
Napoleon, ND 58561 • *1,103*
Napoleon, OH 43545 • *8,614*
Napoleonville, LA 70390 • *829*
Nappanee, IN 46550 • *4,694*
Naranja, FL 33032 • *5,000*
Narberth, PA 19072 • *4,496*
Narragansett, RI 02882 • *3,342*
Narrows, VA 24124 • *2,516*
Narrowsburg, NY 12764 • *700*
Naruna, VA 24576 • *250*
Naselle, WA 98638 • *900*
Nash, OK 73761 • *301*
Nash, TX 75569 • *2,022*
Nash □, NC • *67,153*
Nashua, IA 50658 • *1,846*
Nashua, MT 59248 • *495*
Nashua, NH 03060-63 • *67,865*
Nashville, AR 71852 • *4,554*
Nashville, GA 31639 • *4,831*
Nashville, IL 62263 • *3,186*
Nashville, IN 47448 • *705*
Nashville, MI 49073 • *1,628*
Nashville, NC 27856 • *3,033*
Nashville, TN 37201-99 • *455,651*
Nashwauk, MN 55769 • *1,419*
Nason, IL 62866 • *272*
Nasonville, RI 02895 • *300*
Nassau, NY 12123 • *1,285*
Nassau □, FL • *32,894*
Nassau □, NY • *1,321,582*
Nassau Shores, NY 11758 • *5,500*
Nassawadox, VA 23413 • *630*
Natalbany, LA 70451 • *700*
Natalia, TX 78059 • *1,264*
Natchez, MS 39120 • *22,015*
Natchitoches, LA 71457 • *16,664*
Natchitoches □, LA • *39,863*
Natick, MA 01760 • *29,461*
National City, CA 92050 • *48,772*
National Gardens, FL 32074 • *300*
National Park, NJ 08063 • *3,552*
Natoma, KS 67651 • *515*
Natrona □, WY • *71,856*
Natrona Heights, PA 15065 • *13,252*
Natural Bridge, NY 13665 • *650*
Naturita, CO 81422 • *819*
Naugatuck, CT 06770 • *26,456*
Nautilus Park, CT 06340 • *6,500*
Nauvoo, AL 35578 • *259*
Nauvoo, IL 62354 • *1,133*
Navajo □, AZ • *67,629*
Navarre, OH 44662 • *1,343*
Navarro □, TX • *35,323*
Navasota, TX 77868 • *5,971*
Navassa, NC 28404 • *439*
Navesink, NJ 07752 • *1,500*
Naylor, GA 31641 • *228*
Naylor, MO 63953 • *602*
Nazareth, KY 40048 • *700*
Nazareth, PA 18064 • *5,443*
Nazareth, TX 79063 • *299*
Nazlini, AZ 86505 • *400*
Neah Bay, WA 98357 • *1,000*
Neavitt, MD 21652 • *250*
Nebo, IL 62355 • *487*
Nebo, KY 42441 • *269*
Nebraska City, NE 68410 • *7,127*
Necedah, WI 54646 • *773*
Neche, ND 58265 • *471*
Nederland, CO 80466 • *1,212*
Nederland, TX 77627 • *16,855*
Nedrow, NY 13120 • *3,000*
Needham, MA 02192 • *27,901*
Needles, CA 92363 • *4,120*
Needmore, IN 47421 • *600*
Needville, TX 77461 • *1,417*
Neelyville, MO 63954 • *474*
Neenah, WI 54956 • *22,432*
Neeses, SC 29107 • *557*
Neffs, OH 43940 • *1,106*
Neffsville, PA 17601 • *1,300*
Negaunee, MI 49866 • *5,189*
Negley, OH 44441 • *900*
Nehalem, OR 97131 • *258*
Nehawka, NE 68413 • *270*
Neillsville, WI 54456 • *2,780*
Nekoosa, WI 54457 • *2,519*
Neligh, NE 68756 • *1,893*
Nelson, GA 30151 • *562*
Nelson, MO 65347 • *248*
Nelson, NE 68961 • *733*
Nelson, PA 16940 • *400*
Nelson, WI 54756 • *389*
Nelson □, KY • *27,584*
Nelson □, ND • *5,233*
Nelson □, VA • *12,204*
Nelsonville, OH 45764 • *4,567*
Nemacolin, PA 15351 • *1,273*
Nemaha □, KS • *11,211*
Nemaha □, NE • *8,367*
Nenana, AK 99760 • *470*
Neodesha, KS 66757 • *3,414*
Neoga, IL 62447 • *1,736*
Neola, IA 51559 • *839*
Neola, UT 84053 • *550*
Neopit, WI 54150 • *1,122*
Neosho, MO 64850 • *9,493*
Neosho, WI 53059 • *575*
Neosho □, KS • *18,967*
Neosho Rapids, KS 66864 • *289*
Neotsu, OR 97364 • *300*
Nephi, UT 84648 • *3,285*
Neponset, IL 61345 • *575*
Neptune, NJ 07753 • *28,366*
Neptune Beach, FL 32233 • *5,248*
Neptune City, NJ 07753 • *5,276*
Nerstrand, MN 55053 • *255*
Nesco, NJ 08037 • *430*
Nesconset, NY 11767 • *8,300*
Nescopeck, PA 18635 • *1,768*
Neshanic Station, NJ 08853 • *400*
Neshkoro, WI 54960 • *386*
Neshoba □, MS • *23,789*
Nesika Beach, OR 97444 • *250*
Nespelem, WA 99155 • *284*
Nesquehoning, PA 18240 • *3,346*
Ness □, KS • *4,498*
Ness City, KS 67560 • *1,769*
Netcong, NJ 07857 • *3,557*
Nettie, WV 26681 • *600*
Nett Lake, MN 55772 • *300*
Nettleton, MS 38858 • *1,911*
Nevada, IA 50201 • *5,912*
Nevada, MO 64772 • *9,044*
Nevada, OH 44849 • *945*
Nevada □, AR • *11,097*
Nevada □, CA • *51,645*
Nevada City, CA 95959 • *2,431*
Nevis, MN 56467 • *332*
New Albany, IN 47150 • *37,103*
New Albany, MS 38652 • *7,072*
New Albany, OH 43054 • *409*
New Albany, PA 18833 • *336*
New Albin, IA 52160 • *609*
Newald, WI 54551 • *225*
Newark, AR 72562 • *1,128*
Newark, CA 94560 • *32,126*
Newark, DE 19711-13 • *25,247*
Newark, IL 60541 • *798*
Newark, NJ 07101-99 • *329,248*
Newark, NY 14513 • *10,017*
Newark, OH 43055 • *41,200*
Newark, TX 76071 • *466*
Newark Valley, NY 13811 • *1,190*
New Athens, IL 62264 • *1,937*
New Athens, OH 43981 • *440*
New Auburn, MN 55366 • *331*
New Auburn, WI 54757 • *466*
New Augusta, MS 39462 • *589*

Newaygo, MI 49337 • *1,271*
Newaygo □, MI • *34,917*
New Baden, IL 62265 • *2,476*
New Baltimore, MI 48047 • *5,439*
New Baltimore, NY 12124 • *700*
New Baltimore, OH 45030 • *250*
New Bedford, MA 02740-48 • *98,478*
New Bedford, PA 16140 • *900*
Newberg, OR 97132 • *10,394*
New Berlin, IL 62670 • *834*
New Berlin, NY 13411 • *1,392*
New Berlin, PA 17855 • *783*
New Berlin, TX 78121 • *253*
New Berlin, WI 53151 • *30,529*
Newbern, AL 36765 • *307*
New Bern, NC 28560 • *14,557*
Newbern, TN 38059 • *2,794*
Newberry, FL 32669 • *1,826*
Newberry, IN 47449 • *246*
Newberry, MI 49868 • *2,120*
Newberry, SC 29108 • *9,866*
Newberry □, SC • *31,242*
Newberry Springs, CA 92365 • *900*
New Bethlehem, PA 16242 • *1,441*
New Bloomfield, MO 65063 • *519*
New Bloomfield, PA 17068 • *1,109*
New Bloomington, OH 43341 • *303*
Newborn, GA 30262 • *391*
New Boston, IL 61272 • *731*
New Boston, MI 48164 • *1,200*
New Boston, NH 03070 • *400*
New Boston, OH 45662 • *3,188*
New Boston, TX 75570 • *4,628*
New Braintree, MA 01531 • *600*
New Braunfels, TX 78130 • *22,402*
New Bremen, OH 45869 • *2,393*
New Brighton, MN 55112 • *23,269*
New Brighton, PA 15066 • *7,364*
New Britain, CT 06050-53 • *73,840*
New Brockton, AL 36351 • *1,392*
New Brunswick, NJ 08901-99 • *41,442*
New Buffalo, MI 49117 • *2,821*
Newburg, MO 65550 • *743*
Newburg, PA 17240 • *303*
Newburg, WV 26410 • *418*
Newburg, WI 53060 • *783*
Newburgh, IN 47630 • *2,906*
Newburgh, NY 12550 • *23,438*
Newburgh Heights, OH 44105 • *2,678*
New Burnside, IL 62967 • *276*
Newbury, MA 01950 • *900*
Newbury, VT 05051 • *425*
Newburyport, MA 01950 • *15,900*
New Cambria, MO 63558 • *246*
New Canaan, CT 06840 • *17,931*
New Canton, IL 62356 • *420*
New Carlisle, IN 46552 • *1,439*
New Carlisle, OH 45344 • *6,498*
New Carrollton, MD 20784 • *12,632*
New Cassel, NY 11590 • *8,817*
New Castle, AL 35119 • *1,000*
New Castle, CO 81647 • *563*
New Castle, DE 19720 • *4,907*
New Castle, IN 47362 • *20,056*
New Castle, KY 40050 • *832*
Newcastle, ME 04553 • *490*
Newcastle, NE 68757 • *348*
New Castle, NH 03854 • *975*
Newcastle, OK 73065 • *3,076*
New Castle, PA 16101-08 • *33,621*
Newcastle, TX 76372 • *688*
Newcastle, WY 82701 • *3,596*
New Castle □, DE • *398,115*
New City, NY 10956 • *30,800*
New Columbia, PA 17856 • *475*
Newcomb, NY 12852 • *800*
Newcomb, TN 37819 • *300*
Newcomerstown, OH 43832 • *3,986*
New Concord, OH 43762 • *1,860*
New Cumberland, PA 17070 • *8,051*
New Cumberland, WV 26047 • *1,752*
Newdale, ID 83436 • *329*
New Durham, NH 03855 • *300*
New Effington, SD 57255 • *261*
New Egypt, NJ 08533 • *2,111*
Newell, IA 50568 • *913*
Newell, SD 57760 • *638*
Newell, WV 26050 • *1,900*
New Ellenton, SC 29809 • *2,628*
Newellton, LA 71357 • *1,726*
New England, ND 58647 • *825*
New Enterprise, PA 16664 • *275*
New Era, MI 49446 • *534*
New Fairfield, CT 06812 • *2,150*
Newfane, NY 14108 • *2,700*
Newfield, NJ 08344 • *1,563*
Newfields, NH 03856 • *700*
New Florence, MO 63363 • *731*
New Florence, PA 15944 • *855*
Newfolden, MN 56738 • *384*
Newfoundland, NJ 07435 • *900*
Newfoundland, PA 18445 • *450*
New Franklin, MO 65274 • *1,228*
New Freedom, PA 17349 • *2,205*
New Galilee, PA 16141 • *596*
New Glarus, WI 53574 • *1,763*
New Gloucester, ME 04260 • *225*
New Goshen, IN 47863 • *500*
New Gretna, NJ 08224 • *550*
Newhalem, WA 98283 • *300*
Newhall, CA 91321 • *12,029*
Newhall, IA 52315 • *899*
Newhall, WV 24866 • *300*
New Hampton, IA 50659 • *3,940*
New Hampton, MO 64471 • *358*
New Hampton, NH 03256 • *250*
New Hanover □, NC • *103,471*
New Harbor, ME 04554 • *450*
New Harmony, IN 47631 • *945*
New Hartford, CT 06057 • *1,310*
New Hartford, IA 50660 • *764*
New Haven, CT 06501-99 • *126,109*
New Haven, IL 62867 • *559*
New Haven, IN 46774 • *6,714*
New Haven, KY 40051 • *926*
New Haven, MI 48048 • *1,871*
New Haven, MO 63068 • *1,581*
New Haven, NY 13121 • *300*
New Haven, OH 44850 • *450*
New Haven, WV 25265 • *1,723*
New Haven □, CT • *761,337*
Newhebron, MS 39140 • *470*
New Hill, NC 27562 • *250*
New Holland, GA 30501 • *800*
New Holland, IL 62671 • *295*
New Holland, OH 43145 • *783*
New Holland, PA 17557 • *4,147*
New Holstein, WI 53061 • *3,412*
New Hope, AL 35760 • *1,546*
New Hope, MN 55428 • *23,087*
New Hope, PA 18938 • *1,473*
New Hudson, MI 48165 • *800*
New Hyde Park, NY 11040 • *9,801*
New Iberia, LA 70560 • *32,766*
Newington, CT 06111 • *28,841*
Newington, GA 30446 • *402*
Newington, VA 22122 • *400*
New Ipswich, NH 03071 • *500*
New Johnsonville, TN 37134 • *1,824*
New Kensington, PA 15068 • *17,660*
New Kent □, VA • *8,781*
Newkirk, OK 74647 • *2,413*
New Knoxville, OH 45871 • *760*
New Laguna, NM 87038 • *600*
Newland, NC 28657 • *722*
New Lebanon, NY 12125 • *800*
New Leipzig, ND 58562 • *352*
New Lenox, IL 60451 • *5,792*
New Lexington, OH 43764 • *5,179*
New Lima, OK 74884 • *300*
New Lisbon, IN 47366 • *270*
New Lisbon, NJ 08064 • *250*
New Lisbon, WI 53950 • *1,390*
Newllano, LA 71461 • *2,213*
New London, CT 06320 • *28,842*
New London, IA 52645 • *2,043*
New London, MN 56273 • *812*
New London, MO 63459 • *1,161*
New London, NH 03257 • *1,335*
New London, NC 28127 • *454*
New London, OH 44851 • *2,449*
New London, WI 54961 • *6,210*
New London □, CT • *238,409*
New Lothrop, MI 48460 • *646*
New Madison, OH 45346 • *1,008*
New Madrid, MO 63869 • *3,204*
New Madrid □, MO • *22,945*
Newman, CA 95360 • *2,785*
Newman, IL 61942 • *1,079*
New Manchester, WV 26056 • *600*
Newman Grove, NE 68758 • *930*
Newmanstown, PA 17073 • *1,532*
New Market, AL 35761 • *550*
New Market, IN 47965 • *608*
New Market, IA 51646 • *554*
New Market, MD 21774 • *306*
New Market, MN 55054 • *286*
Newmarket, NH 03857 • *3,749*
New Market, TN 37820 • *1,216*
New Market, VA 22844 • *1,118*
New Marshfield, OH 45766 • *400*
New Martinsville, WV 26155 • *7,109*
New Matamoras, OH 45767 • *1,172*
New Meadows, ID 83654 • *576*
New Miami, OH 45011 • *2,980*
New Milford, CT 06776 • *5,186*
New Milford, NJ 07646 • *16,876*
New Milford, PA 18834 • *1,040*
New Minden, IL 62263 • *223*
New Munich, MN 56356 • *302*
New Munster, WI 53152 • *280*
Newnan, GA 30263-65 • *11,449*
New Orleans, LA 70101-99 • *557,927*
New Oxford, PA 17350 • *1,921*
New Palestine, IN 46163 • *749*
New Paltz, NY 12561 • *4,938*
New Paris, IN 46553 • *1,062*
New Paris, OH 45347 • *1,709*
New Philadelphia, OH 44663 • *16,883*
New Philadelphia, PA 17959 • *1,341*
New Plymouth, ID 83655 • *1,186*
New Point, IN 47263 • *296*
Newport, AR 72112 • *8,339*
Newport, DE 19804 • *1,167*
Newport, FL 32327 • *250*
Newport, IN 47966 • *704*
Newport, KY 41071-76 • *21,587*
Newport, ME 04953 • *1,748*
Newport, MI 48166 • *900*
Newport, MN 55055 • *3,323*
Newport, NH 03773 • *4,388*
Newport, NJ 08345 • *400*
Newport, NC 28570 • *1,883*
Newport, NY 13416 • *746*
Newport, OH 45768 • *950*
Newport, OR 97365 • *7,519*
Newport, PA 17074 • *1,600*
Newport, RI 02840 • *29,259*
Newport, TN 37821 • *7,580*
Newport, VT 05855 • *4,756*
Newport, WA 99156 • *1,665*
Newport □, RI • *81,383*
Newport Beach, CA 92660-63 • *62,556*
Newport Hills, WA 98006 • *6,000*
Newport News, VA 23601-07 • *144,903*
New Port Richey, FL 33552-53 • *11,196*
New Prague, MN 56071 • *2,952*
New Preston, CT 06777 • *1,209*
New Providence, IA 50206 • *249*
New Providence, NJ 07974 • *12,426*
New Richland, MN 56072 • *1,263*
New Richmond, IN 47967 • *403*
New Richmond, OH 45157 • *2,769*
New Richmond, WI 54017 • *4,306*
New Riegel, OH 44853 • *329*
New River, AZ 85026 • *300*
New Roads, LA 70760 • *3,924*
New Rochelle, NY 10801-99 • *70,794*
New Rockford, ND 58356 • *1,791*
New Ross, IN 47968 • *306*
Newry, SC 29665 • *240*
New Salem, IN 46173 • *230*
New Salem, MA 01355 • *350*
New Salem, ND 58563 • *1,081*
New Salisbury, IN 47161 • *300*
New Sarpy, LA 70078 • *2,249*
New Sharon, IA 50207 • *1,225*
New Sharon, ME 04955 • *250*
New Site, AL 35010 • *340*
New Smyrna Beach, FL 32069 • *13,557*
Newsoms, VA 23874 • *368*
New Straitsville, OH 43766 • *937*
New Tazewell, TN 37825 • *1,677*
Newton, AL 36352 • *1,540*
Newton, GA 31770 • *711*
Newton, IL 62448 • *3,186*
Newton, IA 50208 • *15,292*
Newton, KS 67114 • *16,332*
Newton, MA 02158 • *83,622*
Newton, MS 39345 • *3,708*
Newton, NH 03858 • *450*
Newton, NJ 07860 • *7,748*
Newton, NC 28658 • *7,624*
Newton, TX 75966 • *1,620*
Newton, UT 84327 • *623*
Newton □, AR • *7,756*
Newton □, GA • *34,489*
Newton □, IN • *14,844*
Newton □, MS • *19,944*
Newton □, MO • *40,555*
Newton □, TX • *13,254*
Newton Falls, NY 13666 • *560*
Newton Falls, OH 44444 • *4,960*
Newton Grove, NC 28366 • *564*
Newton Hamilton, PA 17075 • *317*
Newton Junction, NH 03859 • *450*
Newtonsville, OH 45158 • *434*
Newtonville, NJ 08346 • *500*
Newtown, CT 06470 • *2,022*
Newtown, IN 47969 • *277*
New Town, ND 58763 • *1,335*
Newtown, OH 45244 • *1,817*
Newtown Square, PA 19073 • *11,775*
New Trenton, IN 47035 • *300*
New Ulm, MN 56073 • *13,755*
New Ulm, TX 78950 • *250*
New Underwood, SD 57761 • *517*
New Vienna, IA 52065 • *430*
New Vienna, OH 45159 • *1,133*
New Village, NJ 08886 • *400*
Newville, AL 36353 • *814*
Newville, PA 17241 • *1,370*
New Virginia, IA 50210 • *512*
New Washington, IN 47162 • *600*
New Washington, OH 44854 • *1,213*
New Washoe City, NV 89701 • *2,543*
New Waterford, OH 44445 • *1,314*
New Waverly, TX 77358 • *824*
New Whiteland, IN 46184 • *4,502*
New Wilmington, PA 16142 • *2,774*
New Windsor, IL 61465 • *863*
New Windsor, MD 21776 • *799*
New Windsor, NY 12550 • *8,803*
New Woodstock, NY 13122 • *450*
New York, NY 10001-99 • *7,071,639*
New York □, NY • *1,428,285*
New York Mills, MN 56567 • *972*
Ney, OH 43549 • *379*
Nezperce, ID 83543 • *517*
Nez Perce □, ID • *33,220*
Niagara, WI 54151 • *2,079*
Niagara □, NY • *227,354*
Niagara Falls, NY 14301-99 • *71,384*
Niangua, MO 65713 • *376*
Niantic, CT 06357 • *3,151*
Nibley, UT 84321 • *1,036*
Niceville, FL 32578 • *8,543*
Nicholas □, KY • *7,157*
Nicholas □, WV • *28,126*
Nicholasville, KY 40356 • *10,319*
Nicholls, GA 31554 • *1,114*
Nichols, IA 52766 • *375*
Nichols, NY 13812 • *613*
Nichols, SC 29581 • *606*
Nichols Hills, OK 73116 • *4,171*
Nicholson, MS 39463 • *400*
Nicholson, PA 18446 • *945*
Nicholville, NY 12965 • *300*
Nickelsville, VA 24271 • *464*
Nickerson, KS 67561 • *1,292*
Nickerson, NE 68044 • *254*
Nicollet, MN 56074 • *709*
Nicollet □, MN • *26,929*
Nicoma Park, OK 73066 • *2,588*
Nikishka, AK 99611 • *1,109*
Niland, CA 92257 • *1,042*
Niles, IL 60648 • *30,363*
Niles, MI 49120 • *13,115*
Niles, OH 44446 • *23,088*
Nilwood, IL 62672 • *278*
Nine Mile Falls, WA 99026 • *300*
Ninety Six, SC 29666 • *2,249*
Ninilchik, AK 99639 • *341*
Ninnekah, OK 73067 • *300*
Niobrara, NE 68760 • *419*
Niobrara □, WY • *2,924*
Niota, IL 62358 • *300*
Niota, TN 37826 • *765*
Nipomo, CA 93444 • *5,247*
Niskayuna, NY 12309 • *17,471*
Nisswa, MN 56468 • *1,407*
Nitro, WV 25143 • *8,074*
Niwot, CO 80544 • *500*
Nixa, MO 65714 • *2,662*
Nixon, TX 78140 • *2,008*
Noank, CT 06340 • *1,406*
Noatak, AK 99761 • *273*
Noble, IL 62868 • *832*
Noble, OK 73068 • *3,497*
Noble □, IN • *35,443*
Noble □, OH • *11,310*
Noble □, OK • *11,573*
Nobles □, MN • *21,840*
Noblesville, IN 46060 • *12,056*
Nobleton, FL 33554 • *240*
Nocatee, FL 33864 • *1,300*
Nocona, TX 76255 • *2,992*
Nodaway □, MO • *21,996*
Noel, MO 64854 • *1,161*
Nogales, AZ 85621 • *15,683*
Nokomis, FL 33555 • *3,108*
Nokomis, IL 62075 • *2,656*
Nolan, WV 25687 • *350*
Nolan □, TX • *17,359*
Nolensville, TN 37135 • *500*
Nome, AK 99762 • *2,301*
Nooksack, WA 98276 • *429*
Noonan, ND 58765 • *283*
Noorvik, AK 99763 • *492*
Nora Springs, IA 50458 • *1,572*

Norborne, MO 64668 • *931*
Norcatur, KS 67653 • *226*
Norco, CA 91760 • *21,126*
Norco, LA 70079 • *4,416*
Norcross, GA 30071 • *3,317*
Nordland, WA 98358 • *500*
Norfolk, CT 06058 • *1,500*
Norfolk, MA 02056 • *450*
Norfolk, NE 68701 • *19,449*
Norfolk, NY 13667 • *1,379*
Norfolk, VA 23501-99 • *266,979*
Norfolk □, MA • *606,587*
Norfork, AR 72658 • *399*
Norland, FL 33169 • *19,471*
Norlina, NC 27563 • *901*
Norma, NJ 08347 • *800*
Normal, AL 35762 • *5,000*
Normal, IL 61761 • *35,672*
Norman, AR 71960 • *539*
Norman, NC 28367 • *252*
Norman, OK 73069-71 • *68,020*
Norman □, MN • *9,379*
Normandy, MO 63121 • *5,174*
Normangee, TX 77871 • *636*
Norman Park, GA 31771 • *757*
Norphlet, AR 71759 • *756*
Norridge, IL 60656 • *16,483*
Norridgewock, ME 04957 • *1,318*
Norris, IL 61553 • *276*
Norris, SC 29667 • *903*
Norris, TN 37828 • *1,374*
Norris City, IL 62869 • *1,515*
Norristown, PA 19401-09 • *34,684*
North, SC 29112 • *1,304*
North Abington, MA 02351 • *165,630*
North Acton, MA 01720 • *900*
North Adams, MA 01247 • *18,063*
North Adams, MI 49262 • *565*
North Albany, OR 97321 • *4,499*
North Amherst, MA 01059 • *5,616*
North Amityville, NY 11701 • *11,936*
Northampton, MA 01060 • *29,286*
Northampton, PA 18067 • *8,240*
Northampton □, NC • *22,584*
Northampton □, PA • *225,418*
Northampton □, VA • *14,625*
North Andover, MA 01845 • *20,129*
North Andrews Gardens, FL 33308 • *8,967*
North Anson, ME 04958 • *600*
North Apollo, PA 15673 • *1,487*
North Arlington, NJ 07032 • *16,587*
North Atlanta, GA 30319 • *22,800*
North Attleboro, MA 02760-63 • *21,095*
North Augusta, SC 29841 • *13,593*
North Aurora, IL 60542 • *5,205*
North Babylon, NY 11703 • *23,000*
North Baltimore, OH 45872 • *3,127*
North Bangor, NY 12966 • *400*
North Beach, MD 20714 • *1,504*
North Bellmore, NY 11710 • *23,600*
North Belmont, NC 28012 • *5,000*
North Bend, NE 68649 • *1,368*
North Bend, OH 45052 • *546*
North Bend, OR 97459 • *9,779*
North Bend, PA 17760 • *700*
North Bend, WA 98045 • *1,701*
North Bennington, VT 05257 • *1,635*
North Bergen, NJ 07047 • *47,019*
North Berwick, ME 03906 • *1,436*
North Billerica, MA 01862 • *6,700*
North Bloomfield, OH 44450 • *500*
North Bonneville, WA 98639 • *394*
Northborough, MA 01532 • *5,670*
North Braddock, PA 15104 • *8,711*
North Branch, MI 48461 • *896*
North Branch, MN 55056 • *1,597*
North Branch, NH 03440 • *800*
North Branch, NJ 08876 • *2,500*
North Branford, CT 06471 • *5,200*
Northbridge, MA 01534 • *3,321*
North Bridgton, ME 04057 • *500*
Northbrook, IL 60062 • *30,778*
Northbrook, OH 45231 • *8,357*
North Brookfield, MA 01535 • *2,677*
North Brunswick, NJ 08902 • *22,220*
North Caldwell, NJ 07006 • *5,832*
North Canton, GA 30114 • *300*
North Canton, OH 44720 • *14,228*
North Cape May, NJ 08204 • *4,029*
North Carrollton, MS 38947 • *859*
North Carver, MA 02355 • *700*
North Cedar, IA 50613 • *1,950*
North Charleston, SC 29406 • *62,534*
North Chicago, IL 60064 • *38,774*
North Chichester, NH 03263 • *230*
North City, WA 98155 • *6,200*
North Clarendon, VT 05759 • *500*
North Cohasset, MA 02025 • *900*
North Cohocton, NY 14868 • *400*
North College Hill, OH 45239 • *11,114*
North Collins, NY 14111 • *1,496*
North Conway, NH 03860 • *2,184*
North Corbin, KY 40701 • *1,000*
North Creek, NY 12853 • *950*
North Crossett, AR 71635 • *3,513*
North Dartmouth, MA 02747 • *6,000*
North Decatur, GA 30033 • *11,830*
North Dighton, MA 02764 • *1,174*
North Druid Hills, GA 30033 • *8,700*
North Eagle Butte, SD 57625 • *1,354*
North East, MD 21901 • *1,469*
North East, PA 16428 • *4,568*
North Eastham, MA 02651 • *1,318*
Northeast Harbor, ME 04662 • *550*
Northeast Henrietta, NY 14534 • *12,000*
North Easton, MA 02356 • *6,100*
North Egremont, MA 01252 • *300*
North English, IA 52316 • *990*
North Enid, OK 73701 • *992*
North Fairfield, OH 44855 • *525*
North Fair Oaks, CA 94025 • *10,294*
North Falmouth, MA 02556 • *1,800*
Northfield, CT 06778 • *600*
Northfield, IL 60093 • *5,807*
Northfield, MA 01360 • *1,182*
Northfield, MN 55057 • *12,562*
Northfield, NH 03276 • *1,340*
Northfield, NJ 08225 • *7,795*
Northfield, OH 44067 • *3,913*
Northfield, VT 05663 • *2,033*
Northfield Falls, VT 05664 • *600*
North Fond du Lac, WI 54935 • *3,844*
Northford, CT 06472 • *2,800*
North Fork, CA 93643 • *950*
North Fork, ID 83466 • *250*
North Fort Myers, FL 33903 • *17,200*
North Freedom, WI 53951 • *616*
Northglenn, CO 80233 • *29,847*
North Grafton, MA 01536 • *3,400*
North Granby, CT 06060 • *300*
North Great River, NY 11722 • *12,400*
North Grosvenordale, CT 06255 • *1,856*
North Gulfport, MS 39501 • *6,660*
North Haledon, NJ 07508 • *8,177*
North Hampton, NH 03862 • *1,000*
North Hanover, MA 02339 • *900*
North Hartland, VT 05052 • *300*
North Hatfield, MA 01066 • *450*
North Haven, CT 06473 • *22,080*
North Haven, ME 04853 • *375*
North Haverhill, NH 03774 • *400*
North Henderson, IL 61466 • *234*
North Highlands, CA 95660 • *37,825*
North Hudson, WI 54016 • *2,218*
North Hyde Park, VT 05665 • *325*
North Industry, OH 44707 • *3,250*
North Judson, IN 46366 • *1,653*
North Kansas City, MO 64116 • *4,507*
North Kingstown, RI 02852 • *3,100*
North Kingsville, OH 44068 • *2,939*
North La Junta, CO 81050 • *1,076*
Northlake, IL 60164 • *12,166*
North Lake, MI 49849 • *500*
North Lake, WI 53064 • *600*
North Las Vegas, NV 89030 • *42,739*
North Lauderdale, FL 33068 • *18,653*
North Lawrence, NY 12967 • *300*
North Lewisburg, OH 43060 • *1,072*
North Liberty, IN 46554 • *1,211*
North Liberty, IA 52317 • *2,046*
North Lima, OH 44452 • *900*
North Lindenhurst, NY 11757 • *11,400*
North Little Rock, AR 72114-19 • *64,288*
North Logan, UT 84321 • *2,258*
North Loup, NE 68859 • *405*
North Manchester, IN 46962 • *5,998*
North Mankato, MN 56001 • *9,145*
North Marshfield, MA 02059 • *450*
North Massapequa, NY 11758 • *23,100*
North Merrick, NY 11566 • *13,650*
North Merrydale, LA 70812 • *3,500*
North Miami, FL 33161 • *36,553*
North Miami, OK 74358 • *544*
North Miami Beach, FL 33162 • *36,481*
North Middletown, KY 40357 • *637*
North Monmouth, ME 04265 • *350*
Northmoor, MO 64152 • *506*
North Muskegon, MI 49445 • *4,024*
North Myrtle Beach, SC 29582 • *3,960*
North Naples, FL 33940 • *7,950*
North New Hyde Park, NY 11040 • *16,100*
North New Portland, ME 04961 • *270*
North Norwich, NY 13814 • *500*
North Oaks, CA 91350 • *5,800*
North Ogden, UT 84404 • *9,309*
North Olmsted, OH 44070 • *36,486*
North Omaha, NE 68112 • *1,100*
Northome, MN 56661 • *312*
North Oxford, MA 01537 • *1,550*
North Palm Beach, FL 33408 • *11,344*
North Park, IL 61111 • *15,806*
North Patchogue, NY 11772 • *8,000*
North Pembroke, MA 02358 • *2,215*
North Plainfield, NJ 07060 • *19,108*
North Plains, OR 97133 • *715*
North Platte, NE 69101 • *24,509*
Northport, AL 35476 • *14,291*
North Port, FL 33596 • *6,205*
Northport, MI 49670 • *611*
Northport, NY 11768 • *7,651*
Northport, WA 99157 • *368*
North Powder, OR 97867 • *430*
North Pownal, VT 05260 • *300*
North Prairie, WI 53153 • *938*
North Providence, RI 02911 • *18,220*
North Reading, MA 01864 • *11,455*
North Richland Hills, TX 76118 • *30,592*
Northridge, OH 45502 • *5,559*
North Ridgeville, OH 44039 • *21,522*
North Riverside, IL 60546 • *6,764*
North Robinson, OH 44856 • *302*
Northrop, MN 56075 • *269*
North Rose, NY 14516 • *700*
North Royalton, OH 44133 • *17,671*
North Salem, IN 46165 • *581*
North Salem, NH 03073 • *600*
North Salt Lake, UT 84054 • *5,548*
North Sanbornton, NH 03269 • *250*
North Scituate, MA 02060 • *4,100*
North Scituate, RI 02857 • *325*
Northside, NC 27564 • *300*
North Sioux City, SD 57049 • *1,992*
North Springfield, VT 05150 • *750*
North Springfield, VA 22151 • *8,631*
North Star, DE 19711 • *650*
North Star, MI 48862 • *300*
North Star, OH 45350 • *254*
North Stonington, CT 06359 • *230*
North St. Paul, MN 55109 • *11,921*
North Stratford, NH 03590 • *650*
North Sudbury, MA 01776 • *1,700*
North Sutton, NH 03260 • *250*
North Swansea, MA 02777 • *950*
North Swanzey, NH 03431 • *950*
North Syracuse, NY 13212 • *7,970*
North Tarrytown, NY 10591 • *7,994*
North Terre Haute, IN 47805 • *1,500*
North Tewksbury, MA 01876 • *1,400*
North Tonawanda, NY 14120 • *35,760*
North Troy, VT 05859 • *717*
North Truro, MA 02652 • *700*
North Tunica, MS 38676 • *1,026*
Northumberland, PA 17857 • *3,636*
Northumberland □, PA • *100,381*
Northumberland □, VA • *9,828*
North Uxbridge, MA 01538 • *1,400*
Northvale, NJ 07647 • *5,046*
North Valley Stream, NY 11580 • *14,881*
North Vassalboro, ME 04962 • *850*
North Vernon, IN 47265 • *5,768*
North Versailles, PA 15137 • *13,294*
Northville, MI 48167 • *5,698*
Northville, NY 12134 • *1,304*
North Wales, PA 19454 • *3,391*
North Walpole, NH 03609 • *950*
North Wantagh, NY 11793 • *15,117*
North Warren, PA 16365 • *1,360*
North Webster, IN 46555 • *709*
North Westminster, VT 05101 • *310*
North Wildwood, NJ 08260 • *4,714*
North Wilkesboro, NC 28659 • *3,260*
North Wilmington, MA 01887 • *4,200*
North Windham, CT 06256 • *750*
North Windham, ME 04062 • *5,492*
Northwood, IA 50459 • *2,193*
Northwood, NH 03261 • *350*
Northwood, ND 58267 • *1,240*
Northwood, OH 43619 • *5,495*
Northwood Ridge, NH 03261 • *250*
Northwoods, MO 63121 • *5,831*
North Woodstock, CT 06244 • *400*
North Woodstock, NH 03262 • *600*
North York, PA 17404 • *1,755*
North Zulch, TX 77872 • *500*
Norton, KS 67654 • *3,400*
Norton, MA 02766 • *2,035*
Norton, OH 44203 • *12,242*
Norton, VA 24273 • *4,757*
Norton, WV 26285 • *400*
Norton □, KS • *6,689*
Norton Shores, MI 49441 • *22,025*
Nortonville, KS 66060 • *692*
Nortonville, KY 42442 • *1,336*
Norwalk, CA 90650 • *85,286*
Norwalk, CT 06850-57 • *77,767*
Norwalk, IA 50211 • *2,676*
Norwalk, OH 44857 • *14,358*
Norwalk, WI 54648 • *517*
Norway, IN 47960 • *500*
Norway, IA 52318 • *633*
Norway, ME 04268 • *2,653*
Norway, MI 49870 • *2,919*
Norway, SC 29113 • *518*
Norwell, MA 02061 • *800*
Norwich, CT 06360 • *38,074*
Norwich, KS 67118 • *476*
Norwich, NY 13815 • *8,082*
Norwich, VT 05055 • *1,000*
Norwood, CO 81423 • *478*
Norwood, GA 30821 • *306*
Norwood, LA 70761 • *421*
Norwood, MA 02062 • *29,711*
Norwood, MN 55368 • *1,219*
Norwood, MO 65717 • *391*
Norwood, NJ 07648 • *4,413*
Norwood, NC 28128 • *1,818*
Norwood, NY 13668 • *1,902*
Norwood, OH 45212 • *26,342*
Norwood, PA 19074 • *6,647*
Norwoodville, IA 50317 • *1,400*
Notasulga, AL 36866 • *876*
Nottoway □, VA • *14,666*
Notus, ID 83656 • *437*
Nova, OH 44859 • *300*
Novato, CA 94947 • *43,916*
Novi, MI 48050 • *22,525*
Novinger, MO 63559 • *626*
Nowata, OK 74048 • *4,270*
Nowata □, OK • *11,486*
Noxapater, MS 39346 • *516*
Noxen, PA 18636 • *800*
Noxon, MT 59853 • *250*
Noxubee □, MS • *13,212*
Nuckolls □, NE • *6,726*
Nucla, CO 81424 • *1,027*
Nueces □, TX • *268,215*
Nulato, AK 99765 • *350*
Nu Mine, PA 16244 • *475*
Nunda, NY 14517 • *1,169*
Nunica, MI 49448 • *350*
Nunn, CO 80648 • *295*
Nunnelly, TN 37137 • *250*
Nuremberg, PA 18241 • *800*
Nursery, TX 77976 • *250*
Nutley, NJ 07110 • *28,998*
Nutter Fort, WV 26301 • *2,078*
Nutting Lake, MA 01865 • *2,400*
Nyack, NY 10960 • *6,428*
Nye □, NV • *9,048*
Nyssa, OR 97913 • *2,862*

O

Oacoma, SD 57365 • *289*
Oak Bluffs, MA 02557 • *1,984*
Oakboro, NC 28129 • *587*
Oak Brook, IL 60521 • *6,641*
Oak City, NC 27857 • *475*
Oak City, UT 84649 • *389*
Oak Creek, CO 80467 • *929*
Oak Creek, WI 53154 • *16,932*
Oakdale, CA 95361 • *8,474*
Oakdale, CT 06370 • *400*
Oakdale, GA 30080 • *800*
Oakdale, LA 71463 • *7,155*
Oakdale, MA 01583 • *600*
Oakdale, MN 55119 • *12,123*
Oakdale, NE 68761 • *410*
Oakdale, NY 11769 • *7,800*
Oakdale, PA 15071 • *1,955*
Oakdale, TN 37829 • *323*
Oakdale Manor, CT 06488 • *300*
Oakes, ND 58474 • *2,112*
Oakesdale, WA 99158 • *444*

Oakfield, ME 04763 • *500*
Oakfield, NY 14125 • *1,791*
Oakfield, WI 53065 • *990*
Oakford, IL 62673 • *351*
Oakford, IN 46965 • *300*
Oak Forest, IL 60452 • *26,096*
Oak Grove, AR 72660 • *265*
Oak Grove, KY 42262 • *2,088*
Oak Grove, LA 71263 • *2,214*
Oak Grove, OR 97268 • *11,640*
Oakham, MA 01068 • *250*
Oak Harbor, OH 43449 • *2,678*
Oak Harbor, WA 98277 • *12,271*
Oak Hill, FL 32759 • *938*
Oak Hill, MI 49660 • *1,000*
Oak Hill, OH 45656 • *1,713*
Oak Hill, WV 25901 • *7,120*
Oakhurst, NJ 07755 • *4,600*
Oakhurst, OK 74050 • *2,000*
Oakland, CA 94601-99 • *339,337*
Oakland, FL 32760 • *658*
Oakland, IL 61943 • *1,035*
Oakland, IA 51560 • *1,552*
Oakland, KY 42159 • *264*
Oakland, ME 04963 • *3,387*
Oakland, MD 21550 • *1,994*
Oakland, MS 38948 • *540*
Oakland, NE 68045 • *1,393*
Oakland, NJ 07436 • *13,443*
Oakland, OK 73452 • *485*
Oakland, OR 97462 • *886*
Oakland, PA 18847 • *734*
Oakland, RI 02858 • *500*
Oakland, TN 38060 • *472*
Oakland □, MI • *1,011,793*
Oakland City, IN 47660 • *3,301*
Oakland Park, FL 33334 • *23,035*
Oak Lawn, IL 60453-59 • *60,590*
Oaklawn, KS 67216 • *4,200*
Oaklawn, LA 70445 • *400*
Oakley, ID 83346 • *663*
Oakley, KS 67748 • *2,343*
Oakley, MI 48649 • *412*
Oakley, MS 39154 • *250*
Oakley, UT 84055 • *470*
Oaklyn, NJ 08107 • *4,223*
Oakman, AL 35579 • *770*
Oakmont, PA 15139 • *7,039*
Oak Orchard, DE 19966 • *250*
Oak Park, GA 30401 • *256*
Oak Park, IL 60301-99 • *54,887*
Oak Park, MI 48237 • *31,537*
Oak Ridge, LA 71264 • *257*
Oak Ridge, MO 63769 • *252*
Oak Ridge, NC 27310 • *950*
Oakridge, OR 97463 • *3,729*
Oak Ridge, PA 16245 • *400*
Oak Ridge, TN 37830 • *27,662*
Oaks, OK 74359 • *591*
Oaks, PA 19456 • *700*
Oakton, VA 22124 • *900*
Oaktown, IN 47561 • *776*
Oak Valley, NJ 08090 • *7,000*
Oakville, CT 06779 • *8,737*
Oakville, IN 47367 • *250*
Oakville, IA 52646 • *470*
Oakville, MO 63129 • *1,100*
Oakville, WA 98568 • *537*
Oakwood, GA 30566 • *723*
Oakwood, IL 61858 • *1,627*
Oakwood, OH 45873 • *886*
Oakwood, OH 45419 • *3,786*
Oakwood, TX 75855 • *606*
Oakwood, VA 24631 • *325*
Oakwood Beach, NJ 08079 • *350*
Oberlin, KS 67749 • *2,387*
Oberlin, LA 70655 • *1,764*
Oberlin, OH 44074 • *8,660*
Obetz, OH 43207 • *3,095*
Obion, TN 38240 • *1,282*
Obion □, TN • *32,781*
Oblong, IL 62449 • *1,840*
O'Brien, FL 32071 • *250*
O'Brien, OR 97534 • *400*
O'Brien □, IA • *16,972*
Ocala, FL 32670-78 • *37,170*
Occoquan, VA 22125 • *241*
Ocean, NJ 07755 • *23,570*
Ocean □, NJ • *346,038*
Oceana, WV 24870 • *2,143*
Oceana □, MI • *22,002*
Ocean Bluff, MA 02065 • *2,500*
Ocean City, FL 32548 • *5,582*
Ocean City, MD 21842 • *4,946*
Ocean City, NJ 08226 • *13,949*
Ocean City, WA 98569 • *500*
Ocean Gate, NJ 08740 • *1,385*
Ocean Grove, MA 02777 • *4,000*
Ocean Grove, NJ 07756 • *4,200*
Ocean Heights, MA 02539 • *500*
Ocean Park, WA 98640 • *1,500*
Ocean Port, NJ 07757 • *5,888*
Oceanside, CA 92054-56 • *76,698*
Oceanside, NY 11572 • *36,400*
Ocean Springs, MS 39564 • *14,504*
Ocean View, DE 19970 • *495*
Ocean View, NJ 08230 • *400*
Oceanville, NJ 08231 • *600*
Ochelata, OK 74051 • *480*
Ocheyedan, IA 51354 • *599*
Ochiltree □, TX • *9,588*
Ochlocknee, GA 31773 • *627*
Ochopee, FL 33943 • *400*
Ocilla, GA 31774 • *3,436*
Ocoee, FL 32761 • *7,803*
Oconee, GA 31067 • *306*
Oconee, IL 62553 • *240*
Oconee □, GA • *12,427*
Oconee □, SC • *48,611*
Oconomowoc, WI 53066 • *9,909*
Oconto, WI 54153 • *4,505*
Oconto □, WI • *28,947*
Oconto Falls, WI 54154 • *2,500*
Ocotillo, AZ 85224 • *300*
Ocracoke, NC 27960 • *600*
Odd, WV 25902 • *550*
Odebolt, IA 51458 • *1,299*
Odell, IL 60460 • *1,083*
Odell, NE 68415 • *322*
Odell, OR 97044 • *600*
Odem, TX 78370 • *2,363*
Odenton, MD 21113 • *7,500*
Odenville, AL 35120 • *724*
Odessa, DE 19730 • *384*
Odessa, FL 33556 • *950*
Odessa, MO 64076 • *3,088*
Odessa, NY 14869 • *613*
Odessa, TX 79760-68 • *90,027*
Odessa, WA 99159 • *1,009*
Odin, IL 62870 • *1,285*
Odon, IN 47562 • *1,463*
O'Donnell, TX 79351 • *1,200*
Odum, GA 31555 • *401*
Oelwein, IA 50662 • *7,564*
Ofahoma, MS 39141 • *375*
O'Fallon, IL 62269 • *12,241*
O'Fallon, MO 63366 • *8,677*
Offerle, KS 67563 • *244*
Offerman, GA 31556 • *350*
Ogallala, NE 69153 • *5,638*
Ogden, AR 71853 • *334*
Ogden, IL 61859 • *818*
Ogden, IA 50212 • *1,953*
Ogden, KS 66517 • *1,804*
Ogden, UT 84401-99 • *64,407*
Ogdensburg, NJ 07439 • *2,737*
Ogdensburg, NY 13669 • *12,375*
Ogema, WI 54459 • *250*
Ogemaw □, MI • *16,436*
Ogilvie, MN 56358 • *423*
Ogle □, IL • *46,338*
Oglesby, IL 61348 • *3,979*
Oglethorpe, GA 31068 • *1,305*
Oglethorpe □, GA • *8,929*
Ogunquit, ME 03907 • *1,492*
Ohatchee, AL 36271 • *860*
Ohio, IL 61349 • *544*
Ohio □, IN • *5,114*
Ohio □, KY • *21,765*
Ohio □, WV • *61,389*
Ohio City, OH 45874 • *881*
Ohioville, PA 15059 • *4,217*
Oil Center, NM 88266 • *270*
Oil City, LA 71061 • *1,323*
Oil City, PA 16301 • *13,881*
Oildale, CA 93308 • *23,382*
Oilton, OK 74052 • *1,244*
Oilton, TX 78371 • *250*
Oil Trough, AR 72564 • *280*
Ojai, CA 93023 • *6,816*
Ojo Caliente, NM 87549 • *500*
Okabena, MN 56161 • *263*
Okaloosa □, FL • *109,920*
Okanogan, WA 98840 • *2,302*
Okanogan □, WA • *30,639*
Okarche, OK 73762 • *1,064*
Okauchee, WI 53069 • *1,800*
Okauchee Lake, WI 53058 • *1,400*
Okawville, IL 62271 • *1,337*
Okay, OK 74446 • *554*
O'Kean, AR 72449 • *291*
Okeechobee, FL 33472 • *4,225*
Okeechobee □, FL • *20,264*
Okeene, OK 73763 • *1,601*
Okemah, OK 74859 • *3,381*
Okemos, MI 48864 • *8,882*
Okfuskee □, OK • *11,125*
Oklahoma □, OK • *568,933*
Oklahoma City, OK 73101-99 • *403,136*
Oklawaha, FL 32679 • *1,200*
Oklee, MN 56742 • *536*
Okmulgee, OK 74447 • *16,263*
Okmulgee □, OK • *39,169*
Okoboji, IA 51355 • *559*
Okolona, KY 40219 • *20,039*
Okolona, MS 38860 • *3,409*
Oktaha, OK 74450 • *376*
Oktibbeha □, MS • *36,018*
Ola, AR 72853 • *1,121*
Olalla, WA 98359 • *450*
Olancha, CA 93549 • *450*
Olanta, SC 29114 • *699*
Olar, SC 29843 • *381*
Olathe, CO 81425 • *1,262*
Olathe, KS 66061-62 • *37,258*
Olberg, AZ 85247 • *250*
Olcott, NY 14126 • *1,650*
Olcott, WV 25314 • *300*
Old Bennington, VT 05201 • *353*
Old Bethpage, NY 11804 • *7,160*
Old Bridge, NJ 08857 • *12,500*
Olden, TX 76466 • *500*
Oldenburg, IN 47036 • *770*
Old Forge, NY 13420 • *950*
Old Forge, PA 18518 • *9,304*
Old Fort, NC 28762 • *752*
Oldham □, KY • *27,795*
Oldham □, TX • *2,283*
Oldham Village, MA 02359 • *900*
Old Harbor, AK 99643 • *340*
Old Lyme, CT 06371 • *400*
Old Monroe, MO 63369 • *272*
Old Mystic, CT 06372 • *500*
Old Northwood, NH 03261 • *350*
Old Orchard Beach, ME 04064 • *6,291*
Olds, IA 52647 • *225*
Old Saybrook, CT 06475 • *1,857*
Oldsmar, FL 33557 • *2,608*
Old Tappan, NJ 07675 • *4,168*
Old Town, FL 32680 • *550*
Old Town, ID 83822 • *257*
Old Town, ME 04468 • *8,422*
Oldtown, MD 21555 • *400*
Old Washington, OH 43768 • *279*
Oldwick, NJ 08858 • *450*
Olean, NY 14760 • *18,207*
Oley, PA 19547 • *700*
Olin, IA 52320 • *735*
Olive Branch, IL 62969 • *550*
Olive Branch, MS 38654 • *2,067*
Olive Hill, KY 41164 • *2,539*
Olivehurst, CA 95961 • *8,929*
Oliver, GA 30449 • *239*
Oliver, PA 15472 • *1,500*
Oliver, WI 54880 • *253*
Oliver □, ND • *2,495*
Oliver Springs, TN 37840 • *3,659*
Olivet, IL 61846 • *350*
Olivet, MD 20657 • *230*
Olivet, MI 49076 • *1,604*
Olivette, MO 63132 • *7,985*
Olivia, MN 56277 • *2,802*
Olivia, NC 28368 • *500*
Olla, LA 71465 • *1,603*
Ollie, IA 52576 • *232*
Olmito, TX 78575 • *1,500*
Olmos Park, TX 78212 • *2,069*
Olmsted, IL 62970 • *439*
Olmsted □, MN • *92,006*
Olmsted Falls, OH 44138 • *5,868*
Olmstedville, NY 12857 • *350*
Olney, IL 62450 • *9,026*
Olney, MD 20832 • *10,000*
Olney, TX 76374 • *4,060*
Olney Springs, CO 81062 • *253*
Olpe, KS 66865 • *477*
Olton, TX 79064 • *2,235*
Olustee, FL 32072 • *450*
Olustee, OK 73560 • *721*
Olympia, KY 40358 • *300*
Olympia, WA 98501-07 • *27,447*
Olympia Heights, FL 33165 • *33,112*
Olyphant, PA 18447 • *5,204*
Omaha, IL 62871 • *295*
Omaha, NE 68101-99 • *313,911*
Omak, WA 98841 • *4,007*
Omar, WV 25638 • *950*
Omega, GA 31775 • *996*
Omer, MI 48749 • *403*
Omro, WI 54963 • *2,763*
Onaga, KS 66521 • *752*
Onalaska, WA 98570 • *560*
Onalaska, WI 54650 • *9,249*
Onamia, MN 56359 • *691*
Onancock, VA 23417 • *1,461*
Onarga, IL 60955 • *1,269*
Onawa, IA 51040 • *3,283*
Onaway, ID 83855 • *254*
Onaway, MI 49765 • *1,084*
Oneco, CT 06373 • *500*
Oneco, FL 33558 • *6,417*
Oneida, IL 61467 • *765*
Oneida, KY 40972 • *600*
Oneida, NY 13421 • *10,810*
Oneida, OH 45042 • *1,650*
Oneida, TN 37841 • *3,717*
Oneida □, ID • *3,258*
Oneida □, NY • *253,466*
Oneida □, WI • *31,216*
O'Neill, NE 68763 • *4,049*
Onekama, MI 49675 • *582*
Oneonta, AL 35121 • *4,824*
Oneonta, NY 13820 • *14,933*
Onida, SD 57564 • *851*
Onley, VA 23418 • *526*
Onondaga, MI 49264 • *300*
Onondaga □, NY • *463,920*
Onset, MA 02558 • *1,493*
Onslow □, NC • *112,784*
Onsted, MI 49265 • *670*
Ontario, CA 91761-62 • *88,820*
Ontario, NY 14519 • *750*
Ontario, OH 44862 • *4,123*
Ontario, OR 97914 • *8,814*
Ontario, WI 54651 • *398*
Ontario □, NY • *88,909*
Ontonagon, MI 49953 • *2,182*
Ontonagon □, MI • *9,861*
Ookala, HI 96774 • *401*
Oolitic, IN 47451 • *1,495*
Oologah, OK 74053 • *798*
Ooltewah, TN 37363 • *900*
Oostburg, WI 53070 • *1,647*
Opal Cliffs, CA 95062 • *5,041*
Opa-Locka, FL 33054-56 • *14,460*
Opelika, AL 36801 • *21,896*
Opelousas, LA 70570 • *18,903*
Opp, AL 36467 • *7,204*
Oppelo, AR 72110 • *486*
Opportunity, WA 99214 • *17,600*
Oquawka, IL 61469 • *1,533*
Oracle, AZ 85623 • *2,484*
Oradell, NJ 07649 • *8,658*
Oraibi, AZ 86039 • *600*
Oran, MO 63771 • *1,266*
Orange, CA 92667-69 • *91,450*
Orange, CT 06477 • *13,237*
Orange, MA 01364 • *3,942*
Orange, NJ 07050-52 • *31,136*
Orange, TX 77630 • *23,628*
Orange, VA 22960 • *2,631*
Orange □, CA • *1,932,709*
Orange □, FL • *471,016*
Orange □, IN • *18,677*
Orange □, NC • *77,055*
Orange □, NY • *259,603*
Orange □, TX • *83,838*
Orange □, VT • *22,739*
Orange □, VA • *18,063*
Orange Beach, AL 36561 • *300*
Orangeburg, SC 29115 • *14,933*
Orangeburg □, SC • *82,276*
Orange City, FL 32763 • *2,795*
Orange City, IA 51041 • *4,588*
Orange Grove, MS 39501 • *2,700*
Orange Grove, TX 78372 • *1,212*
Orange Lake, FL 32681 • *950*
Orangevale, CA 95662 • *20,585*
Orangeville, IL 61060 • *598*
Orangeville, UT 84537 • *1,309*
Orbisonia, PA 17243 • *506*
Orchard, NE 68764 • *482*
Orchard City, CO 81410 • *1,914*
Orchard Homes, MT 59801 • *4,000*
Orchard Mesa, CO 81501 • *4,876*
Orchard Park, NY 14127 • *3,671*
Orchards, WA 98662 • *3,950*
Orchard Valley, WY 82001 • *800*
Orcutt, CA 93455 • *1,500*
Ord, NE 68862 • *2,658*
Orderville, UT 84758 • *423*
Ordway, CO 81063 • *1,135*
Oreana, IL 62554 • *999*
Ore City, TX 75683 • *1,050*
Oregon, IL 61061 • *3,559*
Oregon, MO 64473 • *901*
Oregon, OH 43616 • *18,675*
Oregon, WI 53575 • *3,876*
Oregon □, MO • *10,238*
Oregon City, OR 97045 • *14,673*
Oreland, PA 19075 • *9,000*
Orem, UT 84057-59 • *52,399*
Orestes, IN 46063 • *539*
Orford, NH 03777 • *350*
Orfordville, NH 03777 • *300*
Orfordville, WI 53576 • *1,143*
Organ, NM 88052 • *500*
Orick, CA 95555 • *600*

Orient, IL 62874 • *480*
Orient, IA 50858 • *416*
Orient, NY 11957 • *800*
Orient, OH 43146 • *283*
Oriental, NC 28571 • *536*
Orinda, CA 94563 • *16,825*
Orion, IL 61273 • *2,013*
Oriskany, NY 13424 • *1,680*
Oriskany Falls, NY 13425 • *802*
Orland, CA 95963 • *4,031*
Orland, IN 46776 • *424*
Orland, ME 04472 • *225*
Orlando, FL 32801-99 • *128,291*
Orland Park, IL 60462 • *23,045*
Orleans, CA 95556 • *900*
Orleans, IN 47452 • *2,161*
Orleans, IA 51360 • *546*
Orleans, MA 02653 • *1,811*
Orleans, NE 68966 • *527*
Orleans, VT 05860 • *983*
Orleans □, LA • *557,927*
Orleans □, NY • *38,496*
Orleans □, VT • *23,440*
Orlinda, TN 37141 • *382*
Ormond Beach, FL 32074 • *21,378*
Ormond By The Sea, FL 32074 • *7,665*
Orofino, ID 83544 • *3,711*
Oro Grande, CA 92368 • *900*
Orono, ME 04473 • *10,578*
Orono, MN 55323 • *6,845*
Oronoco, MN 55960 • *574*
Oronogo, MO 64855 • *525*
Oroville, CA 95965 • *8,683*
Oroville, WA 98844 • *1,483*
Orr, MN 55771 • *294*
Orrick, MO 64077 • *922*
Orrington, ME 04474 • *400*
Orrs Island, ME 04066 • *500*
Orrstown, PA 17244 • *247*
Orrville, AL 36767 • *349*
Orrville, OH 44667 • *7,511*
Orting, WA 98360 • *1,787*
Ortonville, MI 48462 • *1,190*
Ortonville, MN 56278 • *2,550*
Orviston, PA 16864 • *250*
Orwell, NY 13426 • *300*
Orwell, OH 44076 • *1,067*
Orwigsburg, PA 17961 • *2,700*
Osage, IA 50461 • *3,718*
Osage, MN 56570 • *250*
Osage, OK 74054 • *243*
Osage, WY 82723 • *350*
Osage □, KS • *15,319*
Osage □, MO • *12,014*
Osage □, OK • *39,327*
Osage Beach, MO 65065 • *1,992*
Osage City, KS 66523 • *2,667*
Osakis, MN 56360 • *1,355*
Osawatomie, KS 66064 • *4,459*
Osborn, MO 64474 • *381*
Osborne, KS 67473 • *2,120*
Osborne □, KS • *5,959*
Osbornsville, NJ 08723 • *800*
Osburn, ID 83849 • *2,220*
Oscar, LA 70762 • *250*
Osceola, AR 72370 • *8,881*
Osceola, IN 46561 • *1,990*
Osceola, IA 50213 • *3,750*
Osceola, MO 64776 • *841*
Osceola, NE 68651 • *975*
Osceola, PA 16942 • *500*
Osceola, WI 54020 • *1,581*
Osceola □, FL • *49,287*
Osceola □, IA • *8,371*
Osceola □, MI • *18,928*
Osceola Mills, PA 16666 • *1,466*
Oscoda, MI 48750 • *2,431*
Oscoda □, MI • *6,858*
Osgood, IN 47037 • *1,554*
Osgood, OH 45351 • *306*
Oshkosh, NE 69154 • *1,057*
Oshkosh, WI 54901 • *49,620*
Oskaloosa, IA 52577 • *10,989*
Oskaloosa, KS 66066 • *1,092*
Oslo, MN 56744 • *379*
Osmond, NE 68765 • *871*
Osprey, FL 33559 • *1,660*
Osseo, MN 55369 • *2,974*
Osseo, WI 54758 • *1,474*
Ossian, IN 46777 • *1,945*
Ossian, IA 52161 • *829*
Ossining, NY 10562 • *20,196*
Ossipee, NH 03864 • *300*
Osteen, FL 32764 • *900*
Osterville, MA 02655 • *1,799*
Ostrander, MN 55961 • *293*
Ostrander, OH 43061 • *397*
Oswegatchie, NY 13670 • *500*
Oswego, IL 60543 • *3,021*
Oswego, KS 67356 • *2,218*
Oswego, NY 13126 • *19,793*
Oswego □, NY • *113,901*
Osyka, MS 39657 • *581*
Otay, CA 92010 • *6,400*
Oteen, NC 28805 • *2,200*
Otego, NY 13825 • *1,089*
Otero □, CO • *22,567*
Otero □, NM • *44,665*
Othello, WA 99344 • *4,454*
Otho, IA 50569 • *692*
Otis, CO 80743 • *534*
Otis, IN 46367 • *300*
Otis, KS 67565 • *410*
Otis, MA 01253 • *500*
Otisco, IN 47163 • *350*
Otis Orchards, WA 99027 • *1,000*
Otisville, MI 48463 • *682*
Otoe □, NE • *15,183*
Otsego, MI 49078 • *3,802*
Otsego □, MI • *14,993*
Otsego □, NY • *59,075*
Ottawa, IL 61350 • *18,166*
Ottawa, KS 66067 • *11,016*
Ottawa, OH 45875 • *3,874*
Ottawa □, KS • *5,971*
Ottawa □, MI • *157,174*
Ottawa □, OH • *40,076*
Ottawa □, OK • *32,870*
Ottawa Hills, OH 43606 • *4,065*
Otterbein, IN 47970 • *1,118*
Otter Creek, ME 04665 • *250*
Otter Lake, MI 48464 • *456*
Otter River, MA 01436 • *600*
Ottertail, MN 56571 • *239*
Otter Tail □, MN • *51,937*
Otterville, MO 65348 • *472*
Ottoville, OH 45876 • *833*
Ottumwa, IA 52501 • *27,381*
Otwell, IN 47564 • *500*
Ouachita □, LA • *139,241*
Ouray, CO 81427 • *684*
Ouray □, CO • *1,925*
Outagamie □, WI • *128,730*
Outlook, WA 98938 • *300*
Overbrook, KS 66524 • *930*
Overgaard, AZ 85933 • *300*
Overland, MO 63114 • *19,620*
Overland Park, KS 66204 • *81,784*
Overlea, MD 21206 • *6,200*
Overton, NE 68863 • *633*
Overton, NV 89040 • *1,111*
Overton, TX 75684 • *2,430*
Overton □, TN • *17,575*
Ovett, MS 39464 • *400*
Ovid, CO 80744 • *439*
Ovid, MI 48866 • *1,712*
Ovid, NY 14521 • *666*
Owaneco, IL 62555 • *285*
Owasso, OK 74055 • *6,149*
Owatonna, MN 55060 • *18,632*
Owego, NY 13827 • *4,364*
Owen, WI 54460 • *998*
Owen □, IN • *15,841*
Owen □, KY • *8,924*
Owendale, MI 48754 • *308*
Owensboro, KY 42301 • *54,450*
Owensburg, IN 47453 • *300*
Owens Cross Roads, AL 35763 • *804*
Owensville, IN 47665 • *1,261*
Owensville, MO 65066 • *2,241*
Owensville, OH 45160 • *858*
Owenton, KY 40359 • *1,341*
Owings Mills, MD 21117 • *9,526*
Owingsville, KY 40360 • *1,419*
Owls Head, ME 04854 • *350*
Owosso, MI 48867 • *16,455*
Owsley □, KY • *5,709*
Owyhee, NV 89832 • *700*
Owyhee □, ID • *8,272*
Oxford, AL 36203 • *8,939*
Oxford, AR 72565 • *520*
Oxford, CT 06483 • *900*
Oxford, FL 32684 • *400*
Oxford, GA 30267 • *1,750*
Oxford, IN 47971 • *1,327*
Oxford, IA 52322 • *676*
Oxford, KS 67119 • *1,125*
Oxford, ME 04270 • *625*
Oxford, MD 21654 • *754*
Oxford, MA 01540 • *6,369*
Oxford, MI 48051 • *2,746*
Oxford, MS 38655 • *9,882*
Oxford, NE 68967 • *1,109*
Oxford, NJ 07863 • *1,587*
Oxford, NC 27565 • *7,603*
Oxford, NY 13830 • *1,765*
Oxford, OH 45056 • *17,655*
Oxford, PA 19363 • *3,633*
Oxford, WI 53952 • *432*
Oxford □, ME • *48,968*
Oxford Junction, IA 52323 • *600*
Oxly, MO 63955 • *250*
Oxnard, CA 93030-39 • *108,195*
Oxon Hill, MD 20745 • *8,100*
Oyster Bay, NY 11771 • *7,200*
Ozark, AL 36360 • *13,188*
Ozark, AR 72949 • *3,597*
Ozark, MO 65721 • *2,980*
Ozark □, MO • *7,961*
Ozaukee □, WI • *66,981*
Ozawkie, KS 66070 • *472*
Ozona, FL 33560 • *1,200*
Ozona, TX 76943 • *2,864*

P

Paauhau, HI 96775 • *380*
Paauilo, HI 96776 • *755*
96776 • *755*
Pace, FL 32570 • *5,006*
Pace, MS 38764 • *519*
Pachuta, MS 39347 • *256*
Pacific, MO 63069 • *4,410*
Pacific, WA 98047 • *2,261*
Pacific □, WA • *17,237*
Pacifica, CA 94044 • *36,866*
Pacific Beach, WA 98571 • *1,000*
Pacific City, OR 97135 • *1,500*
Pacific Grove, CA 93950 • *15,755*
Pacific Junction, IA 51561 • *511*
Pacific Palisades, HI 96782 • *9,500*
Packwaukee, WI 53953 • *260*
Packwood, WA 98361 • *1,150*
Pacolet, SC 29372 • *1,556*
Pacolet Mills, SC 29373 • *1,051*
Pactolus, NC 27834 • *250*
Paddock Lake, WI 53168 • *2,207*
Paden, OK 74860 • *448*
Paden City, WV 26159 • *3,671*
Paducah, KY 42001 • *29,315*
Paducah, TX 79248 • *2,216*
Page, AZ 86040 • *4,907*
Page, ND 58064 • *329*
Page, WV 25152 • *350*
Page □, IA • *19,063*
Page □, VA • *19,401*
Pageland, SC 29728 • *2,720*
Page Manor, OH 45431 • *9,300*
Pagosa Springs, CO 81147 • *1,331*
Paguate, NM 87040 • *400*
Pahala, HI 96777 • *1,619*
Pahoa, HI 96778 • *923*
Pahokee, FL 33476 • *6,346*
Pahrump, NV 89041 • *1,000*
Paia, HI 96779 • *1,000*
Paincourtville, LA 70391 • *2,004*
Painesdale, MI 49955 • *650*
Painesville, OH 44077 • *16,391*
Painted Post, NY 14870 • *2,196*
Painter, VA 23420 • *321*
Paint Lick, KY 40461 • *250*
Paint Rock, TX 76866 • *256*
Paintsville, KY 41240 • *3,815*
Paisley, FL 32767 • *600*
Paisley, OR 97636 • *343*
Pajarito, NM 87105 • *2,000*
Palacios, TX 77465 • *4,667*
Palatine, IL 60067 • *32,166*
Palatka, FL 32077 • *10,175*
Palco, KS 67657 • *329*
Palenville, NY 12463 • *300*
Palestine, AR 72372 • *976*
Palestine, IL 62451 • *1,718*
Palestine, TX 75801 • *15,948*
Palisade, CO 81526 • *1,551*
Palisade, NE 69040 • *401*
Palisades Park, NJ 07650 • *13,732*
Palm Bay, FL 32905 • *18,560*
Palm Beach, FL 33480 • *9,729*
Palm Beach □, FL • *576,863*
Palm Beach Gardens, FL 33410 • *6,102*
Palmdale, CA 93550 • *12,277*
Palmdale, FL 33944 • *300*
Palm Desert, CA 92260 • *11,801*
Palmer, AK 99645 • *2,141*
Palmer, IL 62556 • *278*
Palmer, IA 50571 • *288*
Palmer, MA 01069 • *3,854*
Palmer, MI 49871 • *900*
Palmer, MS 39401 • *2,765*
Palmer, NE 68864 • *487*
Palmer, TN 37365 • *1,027*
Palmer, TX 75152 • *1,187*
Palmer, WA 98048 • *250*
Palmer Lake, CO 80133 • *1,130*
Palmer Park, MD 20785 • *7,986*
Palmerton, PA 18071 • *5,455*
Palmetto, FL 33561 • *8,637*
Palmetto, GA 30268 • *2,086*
Palmetto, LA 71358 • *327*
Palm Harbor, FL 33563 • *5,215*
Palm Springs, CA 92262-64 • *32,366*
Palm Springs, FL 33460 • *8,166*
Palm Valley, FL 32082 • *400*
Palmyra, IL 62674 • *864*
Palmyra, IN 47164 • *692*
Palmyra, MO 63461 • *3,469*
Palmyra, NE 68418 • *512*
Palmyra, NJ 08065 • *7,085*
Palmyra, NY 14522 • *3,729*
Palmyra, PA 17078 • *7,228*
Palmyra, WI 53156 • *1,515*
Palo, IA 52324 • *529*
Palo, MI 48870 • *350*
Palo Alto, CA 94301-99 • *55,225*
Palo Alto □, IA • *12,721*
Palo Pinto, TX 76072 • *525*
Palo Pinto □, TX • *24,062*
Palos Heights, IL 60463 • *11,096*
Palos Hills, IL 60465 • *16,654*
Palos Park, IL 60464 • *3,150*
Palos Verdes Estates, CA 90274 • *14,376*
Palouse, WA 99161 • *1,005*
Palo Verde, CA 92266 • *600*
Pamlico □, NC • *10,398*
Pampa, TX 79065 • *21,396*
Pamplico, SC 29583 • *1,213*
Pamplin, VA 23958 • *273*
Pana, IL 62557 • *6,040*
Panaca, NV 89042 • *550*
Panacea, FL 32346 • *950*
Panama, IL 62077 • *637*
Panama, IA 51562 • *229*
Panama, NY 14767 • *511*
Panama, OK 74951 • *1,425*
Panama City, FL 32401-10 • *33,346*
Panama City Beach, FL 32407 • *2,148*
Pandora, OH 45877 • *977*
Pangburn, AR 72121 • *673*
Panguitch, UT 84759 • *1,343*
Panhandle, TX 79068 • *2,226*
Pankey, AR 72207 • *450*
Panola □, MS • *28,164*
Panola □, TX • *20,724*
Panora, IA 50216 • *1,211*
Panthersville, GA 30032 • *11,366*
Paola, KS 66071 • *4,557*
Paoli, IN 47454 • *3,637*
Paoli, OK 73074 • *573*
Paoli, PA 19301 • *6,100*
Paonia, CO 81428 • *1,425*
Papaaloa, HI 96780 • *350*
Papaikou, HI 96781 • *1,567*
Papillion, NE 68046 • *6,399*
Parachute, CO 81635 • *338*
Paradis, LA 70080 • *800*
Paradise, CA 95969 • *22,571*
Paradise, MI 49768 • *300*
Paradise, MT 59856 • *300*
Paradise, NV 89109 • *45,000*
Paradise, PA 17963 • *900*
Paradise, UT 84328 • *542*
Paradise Hills, NM 87114 • *5,096*
Paradise Valley, AZ 85253 • *11,085*
Paradise Valley, WY 82601 • *2,300*
Paragon, IN 46166 • *538*
Paragonah, UT 84760 • *310*
Paragould, AR 72450 • *15,248*
Paramount, CA 90723 • *36,407*
Paramount, MD 21740 • *1,878*
Paramus, NJ 07652 • *26,474*
Parchment, MI 49004 • *1,817*
Pardeeville, WI 53954 • *1,594*
Paris, AR 72855 • *3,991*
Paris, ID 83261 • *707*
Paris, IL 61944 • *9,885*
Paris, KY 40361 • *7,935*
Paris, ME 04271 • *300*
Paris, MO 65275 • *1,598*
Paris, TN 38242 • *10,728*
Paris, TX 75460 • *25,498*
Parish, NY 13131 • *535*
Parishville, NY 13672 • *550*
Park □, CO • *5,333*
Park □, MT • *12,869*
Park □, WY • *21,639*
Park City, KS 67219 • *3,778*
Park City, KY 42160 • *614*
Park City, MT 59063 • *300*
Park City, UT 84060 • *2,823*
Parkdale, AR 71661 • *471*
Parkdale, MI 49660 • *600*
Parkdale, OR 97041 • *250*
Parke □, IN • *16,372*

Parker, AZ 85344 • 2,542
Parker, FL 32401 • 4,298
Parker, ID 83438 • 262
Parker, KS 66072 • 270
Parker, PA 16049 • 808
Parker, SD 57053 • 999
Parker, WA 98939 • 550
Parker □, TX • 44,609
Parker City, IN 47368 • 1,414
Parker Dam, CA 92267 • 250
Parkersburg, IL 62452 • 268
Parkersburg, IA 50665 • 1,968
Parkersburg, WV 26101-05 • 39,967
Parkers Prairie, MN 56361 • 917
Parkertown, NJ 08087 • 500
Parkesburg, PA 19365 • 2,578
Park Falls, WI 54552 • 3,192
Park Forest, IL 60466 • 26,222
Park Forest South, IL 60466 • 6,245
Park Hall, MD 20667 • 400
Park Hills, KY 41015 • 3,500
Parkin, AR 72373 • 2,035
Parkland, WA 98444 • 22,300
Park Layne, OH 45431 • 5,372
Parkman, OH 44080 • 600
Park Place, OR 97045 • 280
Park Rapids, MN 56470 • 2,976
Park Ridge, IL 60068 • 38,704
Park Ridge, NJ 07656 • 8,515
Park River, ND 58270 • 1,844
Parkrose, OR 97220 • 21,103
Parks, LA 70582 • 545
Parksley, VA 23421 • 979
Parkston, SD 57366 • 1,545
Parksville, NY 12768 • 500
Parkton, NC 28371 • 564
Parkville, MD 21234 • 35,159
Parkville, MO 64152 • 1,997
Parkwater, WA 99211 • 4,850
Parkway, CA 95823 • 12,000
Parkwood, NC 27707 • 3,420
Parlier, CA 93648 • 2,902
Parma, ID 83660 • 1,820
Parma, MI 49269 • 873
Parma, MO 63870 • 1,081
Parma, OH 44129 • 92,548
Parma Heights, OH 44130 • 23,112
Parmele, NC 27861 • 484
Parmelee, SD 57566 • 400
Parmer □, TX • 11,038
Parnell, IA 52325 • 234
Parnell, MO 64475 • 223
Parowan, UT 84761 • 1,836
Parrish, AL 35580 • 1,583
Parrish, FL 33564 • 950
Parrott, VA 24132 • 525
Parshall, ND 58770 • 1,059
Parsippany, NJ 07054 • 8,000
Parsons, KS 67357 • 12,898
Parsons, TN 38363 • 2,422
Parsons, WV 26287 • 1,937
Parsonsburg, MD 21849 • 500
Partridge, KS 67566 • 268
Pasadena, CA 91101-99 • 118,072
Pasadena, MD 21122 • 3,900
Pasadena, TX 77501-07 • 112,560
Pascagoula, MS 39567 • 29,318
Pasco, WA 99301 • 18,425
Pasco □, FL • 193,661
Pascoag, RI 02859 • 3,807
Paso Robles, CA 93446 • 9,163
Pasquotank □, NC • 28,462
Passaic, NJ 07055 • 52,463
Passaic □, NJ • 447,585
Pass Christian, MS 39571 • 5,014
Patagonia, AZ 85624 • 980
Pataskala, OH 43062 • 2,284
Patchogue, NY 11772 • 11,291
Pateros, WA 98846 • 555
Paterson, NJ 07501-99 • 137,970
Pathfork, KY 40863 • 300
Patoka, IL 62875 • 662
Patoka, IN 47666 • 832
Paton, IA 50217 • 291
Patrick, SC 29584 • 375
Patrick □, VA • 17,647
Patricksburg, IN 47455 • 275
Patrick Springs, VA 24133 • 300
Patriot, IN 47038 • 265
Patten, ME 04765 • 1,057
Pattenburg, NJ 08802 • 270
Patterson, AR 72123 • 567
Patterson, GA 31557 • 763
Patterson, LA 70392 • 4,693
Patterson, NY 12563 • 950
Patterson, VA 24633 • 250
Pattison, MS 39144 • 280
Patton, PA 16668 • 2,441
Pattonsburg, MO 64670 • 502
Paul, ID 83347 • 940
Paulding, MS 39348 • 250
Paulding, OH 45879 • 2,754
Paulding □, GA • 26,110
Paulding □, OH • 21,302
Paulina, LA 70763 • 980
Pauline, SC 29374 • 400
Paullina, IA 51046 • 1,224
Paulsboro, NJ 08066 • 6,944
Paul Smiths, NY 12970 • 600
Pauls Valley, OK 73075 • 5,664
Paupack, PA 18451 • 400
Pauwela, HI 96708 • 468
Pavilion, NY 14525 • 550
Pavillion, WY 82523 • 287
Pavo, GA 31778 • 830
Pawcatuck, CT 06379 • 5,216
Paw Creek, NC 28130 • 1,700
Pawhuska, OK 74056 • 4,771
Pawleys Island, SC 29585 • 2,200
Pawling, NY 12564 • 1,996
Pawnee, IL 62558 • 2,577
Pawnee, OK 74058 • 1,688
Pawnee, TX 78145 • 300
Pawnee □, KS • 8,065
Pawnee □, NE • 3,937
Pawnee □, OK • 15,310
Pawnee City, NE 68420 • 1,156
Pawnee Rock, KS 67567 • 409
Pawpaw, IL 61353 • 839
Paw Paw, MI 49079 • 3,211
Paw Paw, WV 25434 • 644
Pawtucket, RI 02860-65 • 71,204
Pax, WV 25904 • 274
Paxton, FL 32538 • 659
Paxton, IL 60957 • 4,258
Paxton, IN 47865 • 300
Paxton, MA 01612 • 1,800
Paxton, NE 69155 • 568
Paxtonville, PA 17861 • 400
Paxville, SC 29102 • 244
Payette, ID 83661 • 5,448
Payette □, ID • 15,825
Payne, OH 45880 • 1,399
Payne □, OK • 62,435
Paynesville, MN 56362 • 2,140
Payson, AZ 85541 • 5,068
Payson, IL 62360 • 1,065
Payson, UT 84651 • 8,246
Peabody, KS 66866 • 1,474
Peabody, MA 01960 • 45,976
Peace Dale, RI 02883 • 3,100
Peach □, GA • 19,151
Peach Creek, WV 25639 • 600
Peachland, NC 28133 • 506
Peach Orchard, AR 72453 • 243
Peach Orchard, GA 30906 • 14,000
Peach Springs, AZ 86434 • 600
Peachtree City, GA 30269 • 6,429
Pea Ridge, AR 72751 • 1,488
Pearisburg, VA 24134 • 2,128
Pearl, IL 62361 • 322
Pearl, MS 39208 • 18,580
Pearland, TX 77581 • 13,248
Pearl City, HI 96782 • 33,000
Pearl City, IL 61062 • 661
Pearlington, MS 39572 • 600
Pearl River, LA 70452 • 1,693
Pearl River, NY 10965 • 17,146
Pearl River □, MS • 33,795
Pearsall, TX 78061 • 7,383
Pearson, GA 31642 • 1,827
Pecatonica, IL 61063 • 1,732
Peck, MI 48466 • 606
Pecos, NM 87552 • 885
Pecos, TX 79772 • 12,855
Pecos □, TX • 14,618
Peculiar, MO 64078 • 1,571
Pedricktown, NJ 08067 • 900
Peebles, OH 45660 • 1,790
Peekskill, NY 10566 • 18,236
Pe Ell, WA 98572 • 617
Peever, SD 57257 • 232
Pegram, TN 37143 • 1,081
Pekin, IL 61554 • 33,967
Pekin, IN 47165 • 1,125
Pelahatchie, MS 39145 • 1,445
Pelham, AL 35124 • 6,759
Pelham, GA 31779 • 4,306
Pelham, MA 01002 • 500
Pelham, NH 03076 • 500
Pelham, NC 27311 • 300
Pelham, NY 10803 • 6,848
Pelham, SC 29651 • 450
Pelham, TN 37366 • 300
Pelham Manor, NY 10803 • 6,130
Pelican Rapids, MN 56572 • 1,867
Pella, IA 50219 • 8,349
Pell City, AL 35125 • 6,616
Pell Lake, WI 53157 • 1,400
Pellston, MI 49769 • 565
Pemberton, NJ 08068 • 1,198
Pemberton, OH 45353 • 260
Pemberville, OH 43450 • 1,321
Pembina, ND 58271 • 673
Pembina □, ND • 10,399
Pembine, WI 54156 • 475
Pembroke, GA 31321 • 1,400
Pembroke, KY 42266 • 636
Pembroke, ME 04666 • 280
Pembroke, MA 02359 • 1,800
Pembroke, NC 28372 • 2,698
Pembroke, VA 24136 • 1,302
Pembroke Pines, FL 33024 • 35,776
Pemiscot □, MO • 24,987
Pena Blanca, NM 87041 • 375
Pen Argyl, PA 18072 • 3,388
Penasco, NM 87553 • 900
Penbrook, PA 17103 • 3,006
Pender, NE 68047 • 1,318
Pender □, NC • 22,262
Pendergrass, GA 30567 • 302
Pendleton, IN 46064 • 2,130
Pendleton, OR 97801 • 14,521
Pendleton, SC 29670 • 3,154
Pendleton □, KY • 10,989
Pendleton □, WV • 7,910
Pendley Hills, GA 30032 • 5,800
Pend Oreille □, WA • 8,580
Penfield, IL 61862 • 250
Penfield, NY 14526 • 9,600
Penfield, PA 15849 • 350
Peninsula, OH 44264 • 604
Penitas, TX 78576 • 450
Penn Acres, DE 19720 • 1,950
Penney Farms, FL 32079 • 630
Penn Hills, PA 15235 • 57,632
Pennington, AL 36916 • 355
Pennington, NJ 08534 • 2,109
Pennington □, MN • 15,258
Pennington □, SD • 70,361
Pennington Gap, VA 24277 • 1,716
Pennock, MN 56279 • 410
Pennsauken, NJ 08110 • 33,775
Pennsboro, WV 26415 • 1,652
Pennsburg, PA 18073 • 2,339
Penns Grove, NJ 08069 • 5,760
Pennsville, NJ 08070 • 12,467
Pennsville, OH 43770 • 250
Penn Valley, PA 19072 • 6,100
Pennville, IN 47369 • 805
Penn Yan, NY 14527 • 5,242
Penobscot □, ME • 137,015
Pensacola, FL 32501-23 • 57,619
Pentwater, MI 49449 • 1,165
Peoria, AZ 85345 • 12,307
Peoria, IL 61601-99 • 124,160
Peoria, OH 43067 • 250
Peoria □, IL • 200,466
Peoria Heights, IL 61613 • 7,453
Peotone, IL 60468 • 2,832
Pepeekeo, HI 96783 • 1,800
Pepin, WI 54759 • 890
Pepin □, WI • 7,477
Pepperell, MA 01463 • 2,076
Pepper Pike, OH 44124 • 6,177
Pequabuck, CT 06781 • 1,400
Pequannock, NJ 07440 • 13,776
Pequot Lakes, MN 56472 • 681
Peralta, NM 87042 • 325
Percy, IL 62272 • 1,053
Perdido, AL 36562 • 1,100
Perham, MN 56573 • 2,086
Peridot, AZ 85542 • 300
Perkasie, PA 18944 • 5,241
Perkins, MI 49872 • 350
Perkins, OK 74059 • 1,762
Perkins □, NE • 3,637
Perkins □, SD • 4,700
Perkinston, MS 39573 • 650
Perl-Mack, CO 80221 • 6,002
Perquimans □, NC • 9,486
Perrin, TX 76075 • 400
Perrine, FL 33157 • 16,129
Perrineville, NJ 08535 • 300
Perris, CA 92370 • 6,827
Perry, AR 72125 • 254
Perry, FL 32347 • 8,254
Perry, GA 31069 • 9,453
Perry, IL 62362 • 487
Perry, IA 50220 • 7,053
Perry, KS 66073 • 907
Perry, LA 70575 • 300
Perry, MI 48872 • 2,051
Perry, MO 63462 • 836
Perry, NY 14530 • 4,198
Perry, OH 44081 • 961
Perry, OK 73077 • 5,796
Perry, SC 29124 • 273
Perry, UT 84302 • 1,084
Perry □, AL • 15,012
Perry □, AR • 7,266
Perry □, IL • 21,714
Perry □, IN • 19,346
Perry □, KY • 33,763
Perry □, MS • 9,864
Perry □, MO • 16,784
Perry □, OH • 31,032
Perry □, PA • 35,718
Perry □, TN • 6,111
Perry Hall, MD 21128 • 13,455
Perry Heights, OH 44646 • 9,206
Perryman, MD 21130 • 1,819
Perry Point, MD 21902 • 500
Perrysburg, NY 14129 • 405
Perrysburg, OH 43551 • 10,215
Perrysburg Heights, OH 43551 • 650
Perrysville, IN 47974 • 532
Perrysville, OH 44864 • 836
Perrysville, PA 15237 • 5,300
Perryton, TX 79070 • 7,991
Perryville, AR 72126 • 1,058
Perryville, KY 40468 • 841
Perryville, MD 21903 • 2,018
Perryville, MO 63775 • 7,343
Perryville, TN 38363 • 250
Pershing, IN 47370 • 438
Pershing, IA 50221 • 350
Pershing □, NV • 3,408
Persia, IA 51563 • 355
Person □, NC • 29,164
Perth Amboy, NJ 08861-63 • 38,951
Peru, IL 61354 • 10,886
Peru, IN 46970 • 13,764
Peru, KS 67360 • 286
Peru, NE 68421 • 998
Peru, NY 12972 • 1,300
Pescadero, CA 94060 • 500
Peshastin, WA 98847 • 900
Peshtigo, WI 54157 • 2,807
Pesotum, IL 61863 • 651
Petal, MS 39465 • 8,476
Petaluma, CA 94952 • 33,834
Peterborough, NH 03458 • 2,100
Peter Dana Point, ME 04668 • 250
Peterman, AL 36471 • 500
Petersburg, AK 99833 • 2,821
Petersburg, IL 62675 • 2,419
Petersburg, IN 47567 • 2,987
Petersburg, KY 41080 • 430
Petersburg, MI 49270 • 1,222
Petersburg, NE 68652 • 381
Petersburg, NJ 08270 • 400
Petersburg, ND 58272 • 230
Petersburg, NY 12138 • 500
Petersburg, OH 44454 • 950
Petersburg, PA 16669 • 543
Petersburg, TN 37144 • 681
Petersburg, TX 79250 • 1,633
Petersburg, VA 23803-05 • 41,055
Petersburg, WV 26847 • 2,084
Petersham, MA 01366 • 550
Peterson, AL 35478 • 550
Peterson, IA 51047 • 470
Peterson, MN 55962 • 291
Peterstown, WV 24963 • 648
Petersville, AL 35633 • 2,000
Petoskey, MI 49770 • 6,097
Petroleum □, MT • 655
Petrolia, PA 16050 • 472
Petrolia, TX 76377 • 755
Petros, TN 37845 • 1,286
Pettaquamscutt Lake Shores, RI 02874 • 450
Pettis □, MO • 36,378
Pettisville, OH 43553 • 500
Pettus, TX 78146 • 600
Pevely, MO 63070 • 2,732
Pewamo, MI 48873 • 488
Pewaukee, WI 53072 • 4,637
Pewee Valley, KY 40056 • 982
Pharr, TX 78577 • 21,381
Pheba, MS 39755 • 300
Phelps, KY 41553 • 1,120
Phelps, NY 14532 • 2,004
Phelps, WI 54554 • 700
Phelps □, MO • 33,633
Phelps □, NE • 9,769
Phenix, VA 23959 • 250
Phenix City, AL 36867 • 26,928
Philadelphia, MS 39350 • 6,434
Philadelphia, NY 13673 • 855
Philadelphia, PA 19101-99 • 1,688,210
Philadelphia, TN 37846 • 507
Philadelphia □, PA • 1,688,210
Phil Campbell, AL 35581 • 1,549
Philip, SD 57567 • 1,088
Philipp, MS 38950 • 350
Philippi, WV 26416 • 3,194
Philipsburg, MT 59858 • 1,138

Philipsburg, PA 16866 • 3,533
Phillips, ME 04966 • 700
Phillips, NE 68865 • 405
Phillips, TX 79007 • 3,000
Phillips, WI 54555 • 1,522
Phillips □, AR • 34,772
Phillips □, CO • 4,542
Phillips □, KS • 7,406
Phillips □, MT • 5,367
Phillipsburg, KS 67661 • 3,229
Phillipsburg, NJ 08865 • 16,647
Philmont, NY 12565 • 1,539
Philo, IL 61864 • 973
Philo, OH 43771 • 799
Philomath, OR 97370 • 2,673
Phoenicia, NY 12464 • 700
Phoenix, AZ 85001-99 • 789,704
Phoenix, IL 60426 • 2,850
Phoenix, MD 21131 • 300
Phoenix, NY 13135 • 2,357
Phoenix, OR 97535 • 2,309
Phoenixville, PA 19460 • 14,165
Piatt □, IL • 16,581
Picacho, AZ 85241 • 550
Picayune, MS 39466 • 10,361
Picher, OK 74360 • 2,180
Pickaway □, OH • 43,662
Pickens, MS 39146 • 1,386
Pickens, SC 29671 • 3,199
Pickens, WV 26230 • 250
Pickens □, AL • 21,481
Pickens □, GA • 11,652
Pickens □, SC • 79,292
Pickerel, WI 54465 • 300
Pickerington, OH 43147 • 3,917
Pickett □, TN • 4,358
Pickford, MI 49774 • 500
Pickstown, SD 57367 • 260
Pico Rivera, CA 90660 • 53,387
Picture Rocks, PA 17762 • 615
Piedmont, AL 36272 • 5,544
Piedmont, CA 94611 • 10,498
Piedmont, MO 63957 • 2,359
Piedmont, OK 73078 • 2,016
Piedmont, SC 29673 • 2,992
Piedmont, SD 57769 • 300
Piedmont, WV 26750 • 1,491
Piedra, CA 93649 • 500
Pierce, CO 80650 • 878
Pierce, ID 83546 • 1,060
Pierce, NE 68767 • 1,535
Pierce □, GA • 11,897
Pierce □, NE • 8,481
Pierce □, ND • 6,166
Pierce □, WA • 485,667
Pierce □, WI • 31,149
Pierce City, MO 65723 • 1,391
Pierceton, IN 46562 • 1,086
Piercy, CA 95467 • 350
Pierpont, OH 44082 • 350
Pierre, SD 57501 • 11,973
Pierre Part, LA 70339 • 3,153
Pierron, IL 62273 • 577
Pierson, FL 32080 • 1,085
Pierson, IA 51048 • 408
Pierz, MN 56364 • 1,018
Pigeon, MI 48755 • 1,247
Pigeon Cove, MA 01966 • 1,700
Pigeon Falls, WI 54760 • 338
Pigeon Forge, TN 37863 • 1,822
Piggott, AR 72454 • 3,762
Pike, NY 14130 • 367
Pike □, AL • 28,050
Pike □, AR • 10,373
Pike □, GA • 8,937
Pike □, IL • 18,896
Pike □, IN • 13,465
Pike □, KY • 81,123
Pike □, MS • 36,173
Pike □, MO • 17,568
Pike □, OH • 22,802
Pike □, PA • 18,271
Pike Lake, MN 55811 • 1,004
Pikesville, MD 21208 • 20,000
Piketon, OH 45661 • 1,726
Pikeville, KY 41501 • 4,756
Pikeville, NC 27863 • 662
Pikeville, TN 37367 • 2,085
Pilger, NE 68768 • 400
Pilgrim, KY 41250 • 400
Pilgrim Gardens, PA 19026 • 8,400
Pillager, MN 56473 • 341
Pillow, PA 17080 • 359
Pilot Grove, MO 65276 • 745
Pilot Knob, MO 63663 • 722
Pilot Mound, IA 50223 • 223
Pilot Mountain, NC 27041 • 1,090
Pilot Point, TX 76258 • 2,211
Pilot Rock, OR 97868 • 1,630
Pilot Station, AK 99650 • 325
Pima, AZ 85543 • 1,599
Pima □, AZ • 531,443
Pimmit Hills, VA 22043 • 7,200
Pinal □, AZ • 90,918
Pinardville, NH 03045 • 4,500
Pinckard, AL 36371 • 771
Pinckney, MI 48169 • 1,390
Pinckneyville, IL 62274 • 3,319
Pinconning, MI 48650 • 1,430
Pine, AZ 85544 • 500
Pine, CO 80470 • 250
Pine □, MN • 19,871
Pine Apple, AL 36768 • 298
Pine Bluff, AR 71601-13 • 56,636
Pinebluff, NC 28373 • 935
Pine Bluffs, WY 82082 • 1,077
Pine Bridge, CT 06403 • 870
Pine Bush, NY 12566 • 1,200
Pine Castle, FL 32809 • 9,992
Pine City, MN 55063 • 2,489
Pinedale, WY 82941 • 1,066
Pine Grove, PA 17963 • 2,244
Pine Grove Mills, PA 16868 • 900
Pine Hall, NC 27042 • 500
Pine Hill, AL 36769 • 510
Pine Hill, NJ 08021 • 8,684
Pine Hills, FL 32808 • 26,000
Pinehurst, GA 31070 • 431
Pinehurst, MA 01866 • 6,588
Pinehurst, NJ 08201 • 1,500
Pinehurst, NC 28374 • 3,421
Pine Island, MN 55963 • 1,986
Pine Island, NY 10969 • 950
Pine Knot, KY 42635 • 1,389
Pine Lake, GA 30072 • 901
Pine Lake, MA 01776 • 800
Pine Lawn, MO 63120 • 6,662
Pine Level, NC 27568 • 953
Pinellas □, FL • 728,531
Pinellas Park, FL 33565 • 32,811
Pine Meadow, CT 06061 • 400
Pine Mountain, GA 31822 • 984
Pineora, GA 31312 • 387
Pine Orchard, CT 06405 • 1,500
Pine Park, GA 31728 • 330
Pine Plains, NY 12567 • 950
Pine Point, ME 04074 • 700
Pine Prairie, LA 70576 • 734
Pine Rest, MA 01776 • 900
Pine Ridge, KY 41360 • 350
Pine Ridge, SD 57770 • 3,059
Pine River, MN 56474 • 881
Pinesdale, MT 59841 • 300
Pinetop, AZ 85935 • 1,527
Pinetops, NC 27864 • 1,465
Pinetta, FL 32350 • 300
Pine Valley, CA 92062 • 950
Pineview, GA 31071 • 564
Pine Village, IN 47975 • 257
Pineville, KY 40977 • 2,599
Pineville, LA 71360 • 12,034
Pineville, MO 64856 • 504
Pineville, NC 28134 • 1,525
Pineville, WV 24874 • 1,140
Pinewald, NJ 08721 • 900
Pinewood, FL 33168 • 7,900
Pinewood, SC 29125 • 689
Piney Flats, TN 37686 • 300
Piney Fork, OH 43941 • 500
Piney Point, MD 20674 • 900
Piney View, WV 25906 • 800
Piney Woods, MS 39148 • 400
Pink Hill, NC 28572 • 644
Pinnacle, NC 27043 • 600
Pinole, CA 94564 • 14,253
Pinon, AZ 86510 • 400
Pinopolis, SC 29469 • 500
Pinson, AL 35126 • 1,600
Pinson, TN 38366 • 225
Pioche, NV 89043 • 700
Pioneer, OH 43554 • 1,133
Piper, KS 66109 • 730
Piper City, IL 60959 • 905
Pipestone, MN 56164 • 4,887
Pipestone □, MN • 11,690
Piqua, OH 45356 • 20,480
Pirtleville, AZ 85626 • 1,425
Piscataquis □, ME • 17,634
Piscataway, NJ 08854 • 42,223
Pisgah, AL 35765 • 699
Pisgah, IA 51564 • 307
Pisgah, OH 45069 • 1,000
Pisgah Forest, NC 28768 • 1,899
Pismo Beach, CA 93449 • 5,364
Pitcairn, PA 15140 • 4,175
Pitkin, LA 70656 • 750
Pitkin □, CO • 10,338
Pitman, NJ 08071 • 9,744
Pitsburg, OH 45358 • 460
Pitt □, NC • 90,146
Pittman Center, TN 37738 • 488
Pitts, GA 31072 • 384
Pittsboro, IN 46167 • 891
Pittsboro, MS 38951 • 269
Pittsboro, NC 27312 • 1,332
Pittsburg, CA 94565 • 33,034
Pittsburg, IL 62974 • 605
Pittsburg, KS 66762 • 18,770
Pittsburg, KY 40755 • 620
Pittsburg, OK 74560 • 305
Pittsburg, TX 75686 • 4,245
Pittsburg □, OK • 40,524
Pittsburgh, PA 15201-99 • 423,959
Pittsfield, IL 62363 • 4,170
Pittsfield, ME 04967 • 3,117
Pittsfield, MA 01201 • 51,974
Pittsfield, NH 03263 • 1,584
Pittsfield, PA 16340 • 300
Pittsford, MI 49271 • 500
Pittsford, VT 05763 • 666
Pittston, PA 18640-44 • 9,930
Pittsview, AL 36871 • 300
Pittsville, MD 21850 • 519
Pittsville, WI 54466 • 810
Pittsylvania □, VA • 66,147
Piute □, UT • 1,329
Pixley, CA 93256 • 2,488
Placentia, CA 92670 • 35,041
Placer □, CA • 117,247
Placerville, CA 95667 • 6,739
Placida, FL 33946 • 700
Placitas, NM 87043 • 450
Plain, WI 53577 • 676
Plain City, OH 43064 • 2,102
Plain City, UT 84404 • 2,379
Plain Dealing, LA 71064 • 1,213
Plainfield, CT 06374 • 2,799
Plainfield, IL 60544 • 3,767
Plainfield, IN 46168 • 9,191
Plainfield, IA 50666 • 469
Plainfield, NH 03781 • 300
Plainfield, NJ 07060-63 • 45,555
Plainfield, VT 05667 • 599
Plainfield, WI 54966 • 813
Plainfield Heights, MI 49505 • 5,000
Plains, GA 31780 • 651
Plains, KS 67869 • 1,044
Plains, MT 59859 • 1,116
Plains, PA 18705 • 6,606
Plains, TX 79355 • 1,457
Plainsboro, NJ 08536 • 800
Plainview, AR 72857 • 752
Plainview, MN 55964 • 2,416
Plainview, NE 68769 • 1,483
Plainview, NY 11803 • 32,300
Plainview, TX 79072 • 22,187
Plainville, CT 06062 • 16,401
Plainville, GA 30733 • 281
Plainville, IL 62365 • 289
Plainville, IN 47568 • 556
Plainville, KS 67663 • 2,458
Plainville, MA 02762 • 4,953
Plainwell, MI 49080 • 3,751
Plaistow, NH 03865 • 1,800
Plankinton, SD 57368 • 644
Plano, IL 60545 • 4,875
Plano, TX 75074-75 • 72,331
Plantation, FL 33317 • 48,653
Plant City, FL 33566 • 17,064
Plantersville, AL 36758 • 650
Plantersville, MS 38862 • 920
Plantsite, AZ 85540 • 1,500
Plantsville, CT 06479 • 5,700
Plaquemine, LA 70764 • 7,521
Plaquemines □, LA • 26,049
Platea, PA 16417 • 492
Platte, SD 57369 • 1,334
Platte □, MO • 46,341
Platte □, NE • 28,852
Platte □, WY • 11,975
Platte Center, NE 68653 • 367
Platte City, MO 64079 • 2,114
Plattenville, LA 70393 • 280
Platteville, CO 80651 • 1,662
Platteville, WI 53818 • 9,580
Plattsburg, MO 64477 • 2,095
Plattsburgh, NY 12901 • 21,057
Plattsmouth, NE 68048 • 6,295
Pleasant City, OH 43772 • 481
Pleasant Dale, NE 68423 • 259
Pleasant Gap, PA 16823 • 1,773
Pleasant Garden, NC 27313 • 1,991
Pleasant Grove, AL 35127 • 7,102
Pleasant Grove, UT 84062 • 10,833
Pleasant Hill, CA 94523 • 25,124
Pleasant Hill, IL 62366 • 1,112
Pleasant Hill, IA 50301 • 3,493
Pleasant Hill, LA 71065 • 776
Pleasant Hill, ME 04032 • 240
Pleasant Hill, MS 38651 • 350
Pleasant Hill, MO 64080 • 3,301
Pleasant Hill, OH 45359 • 1,051
Pleasant Hills, PA 15236 • 9,374
Pleasant Hope, MO 65725 • 354
Pleasant Lake, IN 46779 • 500
Pleasant Lake, MA 02645 • 300
Pleasant Mills, IN 46780 • 225
Pleasanton, CA 94566 • 35,160
Pleasanton, KS 66075 • 1,303
Pleasanton, NE 68866 • 349
Pleasanton, TX 78064 • 6,346
Pleasant Plains, AR 72568 • 267
Pleasant Plains, IL 62677 • 688
Pleasant Prairie, WI 53158 • 500
Pleasants □, WV • 8,236
Pleasant Valley, CT 06063 • 300
Pleasant Valley, IA 52767 • 750
Pleasant Valley, MO 64068 • 1,545
Pleasant Valley, NY 12569 • 1,372
Pleasant Valley, OH 45601 • 650
Pleasant View, CO 80401 • 4,500
Pleasant View, IN 46126 • 300
Pleasant View, KY 40769 • 330
Pleasant View, TN 37146 • 250
Pleasant View, UT 84404 • 3,983
Pleasant View, WI 54615 • 700
Pleasantville, IA 50225 • 1,531
Pleasantville, NJ 08232 • 13,435
Pleasantville, NY 10570 • 6,749
Pleasantville, OH 43148 • 780
Pleasantville, PA 16341 • 1,099
Pleasure Beach, CT 06385 • 1,356
Pleasure Ridge Park, KY 40258 • 27,332
Pleasureville, KY 40057 • 837
Pledger, TX 77468 • 350
Plentywood, MT 59254 • 2,476
Plover, WI 54467 • 5,310
Plum, PA 15239 • 25,390
Plumas □, CA • 17,340
Plum Beach, RI 02874 • 435
Plum City, WI 54761 • 505
Plumerville, AR 72127 • 785
Plummer, ID 83851 • 634
Plummer, MN 56748 • 353
Plum Point, RI 02874 • 265
Plumsteadville, PA 18949 • 250
Plymouth, CT 06782 • 1,000
Plymouth, FL 32768 • 2,700
Plymouth, IL 62367 • 649
Plymouth, IN 46563 • 7,693
Plymouth, IA 50464 • 463
Plymouth, ME 04969 • 300
Plymouth, MA 02360 • 7,232
Plymouth, MI 48170 • 9,986
Plymouth, MN 55441 • 31,615
Plymouth, NE 68424 • 506
Plymouth, NH 03264 • 3,628
Plymouth, NC 27962 • 4,571
Plymouth, OH 44865 • 1,939
Plymouth, PA 18651 • 7,605
Plymouth, UT 84330 • 238
Plymouth, WI 53073 • 6,027
Plymouth □, IA • 24,743
Plymouth □, MA • 405,437
Plymouth Meeting, PA 19462 • 6,000
Plymouth Valley, PA 19401 • 8,200
Plympton, MA 02367 • 300
Poca, WV 25159 • 1,142
Pocahontas, AR 72455 • 5,995
Pocahontas, IL 62275 • 866
Pocahontas, IA 50574 • 2,352
Pocahontas, VA 24635 • 708
Pocahontas □, IA • 11,369
Pocahontas □, WV • 9,919
Pocasset, MA 02559 • 2,000
Pocasset, OK 73079 • 240
Pocatalico, WV 25320 • 900
Pocatello, ID 83201-09 • 46,340
Pocola, OK 74902 • 3,268
Pocomoke City, MD 21851 • 3,558
Pocono Pines, PA 18350 • 500
Poinsett □, AR • 27,032
Point Arena, CA 95468 • 425
Point Clear, AL 36564 • 1,812
Pointe a la Hache, LA 70082 • 600
Pointe Coupee □, LA • 24,045
Pointers, NJ 08079 • 400
Point Hope, AK 99766 • 464
Point Independence, MA 02532 • 700
Point Lookout, MO 65726 • 900
Point Marion, PA 15474 • 1,642
Point Pleasant, NJ 08742 • 17,747
Point Pleasant, WV 25550 • 5,682
Point Pleasant Beach, NJ 08742 • 5,415
Point Roberts, WA 98281 • 750
Poipu, HI 96756 • 685
Pojoaque Valley, NM 87501 • 900

Polacca, AZ 86042 • *600*
Poland, ME 04273 • *250*
Poland, NY 13431 • *553*
Polk, NE 68654 • *440*
Polk, OH 44866 • *351*
Polk, PA 16342 • *1,884*
Polk □, AR • *17,007*
Polk □, FL • *321,652*
Polk □, GA • *32,386*
Polk □, IA • *303,170*
Polk □, MN • *34,844*
Polk □, MO • *18,822*
Polk □, NE • *6,320*
Polk □, NC • *12,984*
Polk □, OR • *45,203*
Polk □, TN • *13,602*
Polk □, TX • *24,407*
Polk □, WI • *32,351*
Polk City, FL 33868 • *576*
Polk City, IA 50226 • *1,658*
Polkton, NC 28135 • *762*
Pollard, AR 72456 • *298*
Pollock, LA 71467 • *399*
Pollock, SD 57648 • *355*
Pollocksville, NC 28573 • *318*
Polo, IL 61064 • *2,643*
Polo, MO 64671 • *583*
Polson, MT 59860 • *2,798*
Pomaria, SC 29126 • *271*
Pomeroy, IA 50575 • *895*
Pomeroy, OH 45769 • *2,728*
Pomeroy, WA 99347 • *1,716*
Pomfret, CT 06258 • *500*
Pomfret, MD 20675 • *300*
Pomfret Center, CT 06259 • *300*
Pomoho, HI 96786 • *340*
Pomona, CA 91766-69 • *92,742*
Pomona, KS 66076 • *868*
Pomona, MO 65789 • *250*
Pomona, NJ 08240 • *2,358*
Pomona Park, FL 32081 • *791*
Pompano Beach, FL 33060-68 • *52,618*
Pompano Beach Highlands, FL 33064 • *9,000*
Pompton Lakes, NJ 07442 • *10,660*
Ponca, NE 68770 • *1,057*
Ponca City, OK 74601-04 • *26,238*
Ponce de Leon, FL 32455 • *454*
Poncha Springs, CO 81242 • *321*
Ponchatoula, LA 70454 • *5,469*
Pond Creek, OK 73766 • *949*
Pondera □, MT • *6,731*
Ponderay, ID 83852 • *399*
Poneto, IN 46781 • *250*
Ponte Vedra Beach, FL 32082 • *1,700*
Pontiac, IL 61764 • *11,227*
Pontiac, MI 48053-59 • *76,715*
Pontotoc, MS 38863 • *4,723*
Pontotoc □, MS • *20,918*
Pontotoc □, OK • *32,598*
Poole, KY 42444 • *400*
Pooler, GA 31322 • *2,543*
Poolesville, MD 20837 • *3,428*
Pootatuck Park, CT 06482 • *350*
Pope □, AR • *39,021*
Pope □, IL • *4,404*
Pope □, MN • *11,657*
Poplar, MT 59255 • *995*
Poplar, NC 28740 • *350*
Poplar, WI 54864 • *569*
Poplar Bluff, MO 63901 • *17,139*
Poplar Branch, NC 27965 • *350*
Poplar Grove, AR 72374 • *400*
Poplar Grove, IL 61065 • *818*
Poplarville, MS 39470 • *2,562*
Poquonock, CT 06064 • *900*
Poquonock Bridge, CT 06340 • *2,549*
Poquoson, VA 23662 • *8,726*
Portage, IN 46368 • *27,409*
Portage, ME 04768 • *450*
Portage, MI 49081 • *38,157*
Portage, PA 15946 • *3,510*
Portage, WI 53901 • *7,896*
Portage □, OH • *135,856*
Portage □, WI • *57,420*
Portage Des Sioux, MO 63373 • *488*
Portage Lakes, OH 44319 • *11,310*
Portageville, MO 63873 • *3,470*
Portageville, NY 14536 • *300*
Portal, GA 30450 • *694*
Portal, ND 58772 • *238*
Portales, NM 88130 • *9,940*
Port Allegany, PA 16743 • *2,593*
Port Allen, LA 70767 • *6,114*
Port Amherst, WV 25306 • *400*
Port Angeles, WA 98362 • *17,311*
Port Aransas, TX 78373 • *1,968*
Port Arthur, TX 77640-43 • *61,251*
Port Austin, MI 48467 • *839*
Port Barre, LA 70577 • *2,625*
Port Birmingham, AL 35118 • *400*
Port Bolivar, TX 77650 • *1,600*
Port Byron, IL 61275 • *1,289*
Port Byron, NY 13140 • *1,400*
Port Carbon, PA 17965 • *2,576*
Port Charlotte, FL 33952 • *25,770*
Port Chester, NY 10573 • *23,565*
Port Clinton, OH 43452 • *7,223*
Port Clyde, ME 04855 • *500*
Port Colden, NJ 07882 • *250*
Port Deposit, MD 21904 • *664*
Port Dickinson, NY 13901 • *1,974*
Port Edwards, WI 54469 • *2,077*
Port Elizabeth, NJ 08348 • *500*
Porter, IN 46304 • *2,988*
Porter, OK 74454 • *642*
Porter, TX 77365 • *5,000*
Porter □, IN • *119,816*
Porter Corners, NY 12859 • *300*
Porterdale, GA 30270 • *1,451*
Portersville, PA 16051 • *320*
Porterville, CA 93257 • *19,707*
Port Ewen, NY 12466 • *2,600*
Port Gamble, WA 98364 • *300*
Port Gibson, MS 39150 • *2,371*
Port Henry, NY 12974 • *1,450*
Port Hope, MI 48468 • *369*
Port Hueneme, CA 93041 • *17,803*
Port Huron, MI 48060 • *33,981*
Portia, AR 72457 • *480*
Port Isabel, TX 78578 • *3,769*
Port Jefferson, NY 11777 • *6,731*
Port Jefferson, OH 45360 • *482*
Port Jefferson Station, NY 11776 • *7,500*
Port Jervis, NY 12771 • *8,699*
Portland, AR 71663 • *701*
Portland, CT 06480 • *8,383*
Portland, IN 47371 • *7,074*
Portland, ME 04101-99 • *61,572*
Portland, MI 48875 • *3,963*
Portland, ND 58274 • *627*
Portland, NY 14769 • *600*
Portland, OH 45770 • *250*
Portland, OR 97201-99 • *366,383*
Portland, PA 18351 • *540*
Portland, TN 37148 • *4,030*
Portland, TX 78374 • *12,023*
Port Lavaca, TX 77979 • *10,911*
Port Leyden, NY 13433 • *740*
Port Ludlow, WA 98365 • *500*
Port Matilda, PA 16870 • *647*
Port Monmouth, NJ 07758 • *3,600*
Port Morris, NJ 07850 • *600*
Port Murray, NJ 07865 • *400*
Port Neches, TX 77651 • *13,944*
Port Norris, NJ 08349 • *1,730*
Port O'Connor, TX 77982 • *1,500*
Portola, CA 96122 • *1,885*
Port Orange, FL 32019 • *18,756*
Port Orchard, WA 98366 • *4,787*
Port Orford, OR 97465 • *1,061*
Port Penn, DE 19731 • *300*
Port Reading, NJ 07064 • *4,300*
Port Republic, NJ 08241 • *837*
Port Richey, FL 33568 • *2,165*
Port Royal, KY 40058 • *250*
Port Royal, PA 17082 • *835*
Port Royal, SC 29935 • *2,977*
Port Royal, VA 22535 • *291*
Port Saint Joe, FL 32456 • *4,027*
Port Saint Lucie, FL 33450 • *14,690*
Port Salerno, FL 33492 • *4,511*
Port Sanilac, MI 48469 • *598*
Port Sewall, FL 33494 • *400*
Portsmouth, IA 51565 • *240*
Portsmouth, NH 03801 • *26,254*
Portsmouth, OH 45662 • *25,943*
Portsmouth, RI 02871 • *4,300*
Portsmouth, VA 23701-99 • *104,577*
Port Sulphur, LA 70083 • *3,318*
Port Townsend, WA 98368 • *6,067*
Portville, NY 14770 • *1,136*
Port Vincent, LA 70726 • *450*
Port Vue, PA 15133 • *5,316*
Port Washington, NY 11050 • *15,923*
Port Washington, OH 43837 • *622*
Port Washington, WI 53074 • *8,612*
Port Wentworth, GA 31407 • *3,947*
Port William, OH 45164 • *300*
Porum, OK 74455 • *668*
Posen, IL 60469 • *4,642*
Posen, MI 49776 • *270*
Posey □, IN • *26,414*
Poseyville, IN 47633 • *1,247*
Post, TX 79356 • *3,961*
Post Falls, ID 83854 • *5,736*
Post Mills, VT 05058 • *300*
Poston, SC 29588 • *250*
Postville, IA 52162 • *1,475*
Poteau, OK 74953 • *7,089*
Poteet, TX 78065 • *3,086*
Poth, TX 78147 • *1,461*
Potlatch, ID 83855 • *819*
Potomac, IL 61865 • *874*
Potomac, MD 20854 • *22,800*
Potomac Heights, MD 20640 • *2,456*
Potomac Park, MD 21502 • *1,250*
Potosi, MO 63664 • *2,528*
Potosi, WI 53820 • *736*
Potsdam, NY 13676 • *10,635*
Potsdam, OH 45361 • *289*
Pottawatomie □, KS • *14,782*
Pottawatomie □, OK • *55,239*
Pottawattamie □, IA • *86,561*
Potter, NE 69156 • *369*
Potter, WI 54160 • *275*
Potter □, PA • *17,726*
Potter □, SD • *3,674*
Potter □, TX • *98,637*
Potter Hill, RI 02891 • *285*
Pottersville, NJ 07979 • *350*
Pottersville, NY 12860 • *600*
Potter Valley, CA 95469 • *1,500*
Potts Camp, MS 38659 • *525*
Pottstown, PA 19464 • *22,729*
Pottsville, AR 72858 • *564*
Pottsville, PA 17901 • *18,195*
Potwin, KS 67123 • *563*
Poughkeepsie, NY 12601-99 • *29,757*
Poulan, GA 31781 • *818*
Poulsbo, WA 98370 • *3,453*
Poultney, VT 05764 • *1,554*
Pound, VA 24279 • *1,086*
Pound, WI 54161 • *407*
Poway, CA 92064 • *33,300*
Powder River □, MT • *2,520*
Powder Springs, GA 30073 • *3,381*
Powell, OH 43065 • *387*
Powell, WY 82435 • *5,310*
Powell □, KY • *11,101*
Powell □, MT • *6,958*
Powell Butte, OR 97753 • *600*
Powellhurst, OR 97236 • *9,000*
Powellsville, NC 27967 • *320*
Powellton, WV 25161 • *1,200*
Power □, ID • *6,844*
Powers, MI 49874 • *490*
Powers, OR 97466 • *819*
Powers Lake, ND 58773 • *466*
Poweshiek □, IA • *19,306*
Powhatan, LA 71066 • *279*
Powhatan, VA 23139 • *400*
Powhatan □, VA • *13,062*
Powhatan Point, OH 43942 • *2,181*
Pownal, VT 05261 • *300*
Pownal Center, VT 05261 • *300*
Poyen, AR 72128 • *329*
Poynette, WI 53955 • *1,447*
Poy Sippi, WI 54967 • *500*
Praco, AL 35129 • *400*
Prague, NE 68050 • *285*
Prague, OK 74864 • *2,208*
Prairie □, AR • *10,140*
Prairie □, MT • *1,836*
Prairie City, IL 61470 • *580*
Prairie City, IA 50228 • *1,278*
Prairie City, OR 97869 • *1,106*
Prairie du Chien, WI 53821 • *5,859*
Prairie Du Rocher, IL 62277 • *701*
Prairie du Sac, WI 53578 • *2,145*
Prairie Farm, WI 54762 • *387*
Prairie Grove, AR 72753 • *1,708*
Prairie Home, MO 65068 • *279*
Prairie View, TX 77446 • *3,993*
Prairie Village, KS 66208 • *24,657*
Prairieville, LA 70769 • *400*
Pratt, KS 67124 • *6,885*
Pratt, WV 25162 • *821*
Pratt □, KS • *10,275*
Prattsburg, NY 14873 • *750*
Prattsville, AR 72129 • *317*
Prattsville, NY 12468 • *500*
Prattville, AL 36067 • *18,647*
Preble □, OH • *38,223*
Premont, TX 78375 • *2,984*
Prenter, WV 25163 • *400*
Prentice, WI 54556 • *605*
Prentiss, MS 39474 • *1,465*
Prentiss □, MS • *24,025*
Prescott, AZ 86301 • *20,055*
Prescott, AR 71857 • *4,103*
Prescott, IA 50859 • *349*
Prescott, KS 66767 • *319*
Prescott, MI 48756 • *332*
Prescott, WA 99348 • *341*
Prescott, WI 54021 • *2,654*
Presho, SD 57568 • *760*
Presidio, TX 79845 • *1,100*
Presidio □, TX • *5,188*
Presque Isle, ME 04769 • *11,172*
Presque Isle □, MI • *14,267*
Preston, GA 31824 • *429*
Preston, ID 83263 • *3,759*
Preston, IA 52069 • *1,120*
Preston, KS 67569 • *227*
Preston, MD 21655 • *498*
Preston, MN 55965 • *1,478*
Preston, OK 74456 • *400*
Preston, WA 98050 • *500*
Preston □, WV • *30,460*
Prestonsburg, KY 41653 • *4,011*
Pretty Prairie, KS 67570 • *655*
Prewitt, NM 87045 • *400*
Price, TX 75687 • *650*
Price, UT 84501 • *9,086*
Price □, WI • *15,788*
Prichard, AL 36610 • *39,541*
Prichard, WV 25555 • *320*
Priest River, ID 83856 • *1,639*
Primghar, IA 51245 • *1,050*
Prince Edward □, VA • *16,456*
Prince Frederick, MD 20678 • *1,805*
Prince George □, VA • *25,733*
Prince Georges □, MD • *665,071*
Princes Lakes, IN 46164 • *937*
Princess Anne, MD 21853 • *1,499*
Princeton, CA 95970 • *540*
Princeton, FL 33032 • *5,300*
Princeton, IL 61356 • *7,342*
Princeton, IN 47670 • *8,976*
Princeton, IA 52768 • *965*
Princeton, KS 66078 • *244*
Princeton, KY 42445 • *7,073*
Princeton, ME 04668 • *800*
Princeton, MA 01541 • *600*
Princeton, MI 49875 • *400*
Princeton, MN 55371 • *3,146*
Princeton, MO 64673 • *1,264*
Princeton, NJ 08540 • *12,035*
Princeton, NC 27569 • *1,034*
Princeton, WV 24740 • *7,493*
Princeton, WI 54968 • *1,479*
Princeton Junction, NJ 08550 • *2,419*
Princeville, IL 61559 • *1,712*
Princeville, NC 27886 • *1,508*
Prince William □, VA • *144,703*
Prineville, OR 97754 • *5,276*
Prinsburg, MN 56281 • *557*
Prior Lake, MN 55372 • *7,284*
Proctor, MN 55810 • *3,180*
Proctor, VT 05765 • *1,998*
Proctorsville, VT 05153 • *481*
Proctorville, OH 45669 • *975*
Prophetstown, IL 61277 • *2,141*
Prospect, CT 06712 • *6,807*
Prospect, KY 40059 • *1,981*
Prospect, OH 43342 • *1,159*
Prospect, OR 97536 • *1,200*
Prospect, PA 16052 • *1,016*
Prospect, TN 38477 • *250*
Prospect, VA 23960 • *300*
Prospect Harbor, ME 04669 • *350*
Prospect Heights, IL 60070 • *11,808*
Prospect Park, NJ 07508 • *5,142*
Prospect Park, PA 19076 • *6,593*
Prosperity, SC 29127 • *803*
Prosperity, WV 25909 • *1,000*
Prosser, WA 99350 • *3,896*
Protection, KS 67127 • *684*
Protivin, IA 52163 • *368*
Provencal, LA 71468 • *695*
Providence, FL 32054 • *250*
Providence, KY 42450 • *4,434*
Providence, RI 02901-99 • *156,804*
Providence, UT 84332 • *2,675*
Providence □, RI • *571,349*
Provincetown, MA 02657 • *3,536*
Provo, UT 84601-04 • *74,108*
Prowers □, CO • *13,070*
Prudenville, MI 48651 • *1,000*
Prue, OK 74060 • *554*
Pryor, OK 74361 • *8,483*
Puckett, MS 39151 • *279*
Pueblo, CO 81001-19 • *101,686*
Pueblo □, CO • *125,972*
Puhi, HI 96766 • *991*
Pukalani, HI 96788 • *3,950*
Pukwana, SD 57370 • *234*
Pulaski, GA 30451 • *257*
Pulaski, IL 62976 • *477*
Pulaski, IA 52584 • *267*
Pulaski, NY 13142 • *2,415*
Pulaski, TN 38478 • *7,184*
Pulaski, VA 24301 • *10,106*

Pulaski, WI 54162 • *1,875*
Pulaski □, AR • *340,613*
Pulaski □, GA • *8,950*
Pulaski □, IL • *8,840*
Pulaski □, IN • *13,258*
Pulaski □, KY • *45,803*
Pulaski □, MO • *42,011*
Pulaski □, VA • *35,229*
Pullman, MI 49450 • *500*
Pullman, WA 99163 • *23,579*
Pumphrey, MD 21227 • *3,300*
Punta Gorda, FL 33950-55 • *6,797*
Punxsutawney, PA 15767 • *7,479*
Purcell, MO 64857 • *322*
Purcell, OK 73080 • *4,638*
Purcellville, VA 22132 • *1,567*
Purdin, MO 64674 • *243*
Purdy, MO 65734 • *928*
Pursglove, WV 26546 • *600*
Purvis, MS 39475 • *2,256*
Puryear, TN 38251 • *624*
Pushmataha □, OK • *11,773*
Putnam, CT 06260 • *6,855*
Putnam □, FL • *50,549*
Putnam □, GA • *10,295*
Putnam □, IL • *6,085*
Putnam □, IN • *29,163*
Putnam □, MO • *6,092*
Putnam □, NY • *77,193*
Putnam □, OH • *32,991*
Putnam □, TN • *47,690*
Putnam □, WV • *38,181*
Putney, GA 31782 • *650*
Putney, VT 05346 • *1,100*
Puunene, HI 96784 • *572*
Puxico, MO 63960 • *833*
Puyallup, WA 98371-73 • *18,251*
Pyote, TX 79777 • *382*

Q

Quaddick, CT 06277 • *300*
Quail Oaks, VA 23234 • *1,700*
Quaker City, OH 43773 • *698*
Quaker Hill, CT 06375 • *2,052*
Quakertown, PA 18951 • *8,867*
Quanah, TX 79252 • *3,890*
Quantico, VA 22134 • *621*
Quapaw, OK 74363 • *1,097*
Quarryville, CT 06040 • *300*
Quarryville, PA 17566 • *1,558*
Quartzsite, AZ 85346 • *600*
Quasqueton, IA 52326 • *599*
Quay □, NM • *10,577*
Quechee, VT 05059 • *500*
Quecreek, PA 15555 • *275*
Queen Anne, MD 21657 • *259*
Queen Annes □, MD • *25,508*
Queen City, MO 63561 • *783*
Queen City, TX 75572 • *1,748*
Queen Creek, AZ 85242 • *900*
Queens □, NY • *1,891,325*
Queenstown, MD 21658 • *491*
Queets, WA 98331 • *300*
Quemado, NM 87829 • *250*
Quemado, TX 78877 • *350*
Quenemo, KS 66528 • *413*
Questa, NM 87556 • *1,202*
Quidnessett, RI 02852 • *3,300*
Quidnick, RI 02816 • *2,300*
Quilcene, WA 98376 • *950*
Quimby, IA 51049 • *424*
Quinault, WA 98575 • *350*
Quincy, CA 95971 • *2,700*
Quincy, FL 32351 • *8,591*
Quincy, IL 62301 • *42,554*
Quincy, KY 41166 • *300*
Quincy, MA 02169 • *84,743*
Quincy, MI 49082 • *1,569*
Quincy, OH 43343 • *633*
Quincy, PA 17247 • *400*
Quincy, WA 98848 • *3,525*
Quinebaug, CT 06262 • *1,088*
Quinhagak, AK 99655 • *412*
Quinlan, TX 75474 • *1,002*
Quinnesec, MI 49876 • *900*
Quinnville, RI 02865 • *320*
Quinter, KS 67752 • *951*
Quinton, NJ 08072 • *500*
Quinton, OK 74561 • *1,228*
Quinwood, WV 25981 • *460*
Quitaque, TX 79255 • *696*
Quitman, AR 72131 • *556*
Quitman, GA 31643 • *5,188*
Quitman, LA 71268 • *231*
Quitman, MS 39355 • *2,632*
Quitman, TX 75783 • *1,893*
Quitman □, GA • *2,357*
Quitman □, MS • *12,636*
Qulin, MO 63961 • *545*
Quonochontaug, RI 02808 • *1,000*

R

Rabun □, GA • *10,466*
Raceland, KY 41169 • *1,970*
Raceland, LA 70394 • *6,302*
Racine, MN 55967 • *285*
Racine, MO 64858 • *275*
Racine, OH 45771 • *908*
Racine, WV 25165 • *650*
Racine, WI 53401-99 • *85,725*
Racine □, WI • *173,132*
Racket, MO 64735 • *250*
Radcliff, KY 40160 • *14,519*
Radcliffe, IA 50230 • *593*
Radford, VA 24141 • *13,225*
Radisson, WI 54867 • *280*
Radnor, OH 43066 • *350*
Raeford, NC 28376 • *3,630*
Ragland, AL 35131 • *1,860*
Rahway, NJ 07065-67 • *26,723*
Raiford, FL 32083 • *259*
Rainbow City, AL 35901 • *6,299*
Rainelle, WV 25962 • *1,983*
Rainier, OR 97048 • *1,655*
Rainier, WA 98576 • *891*
Rains □, TX • *4,839*
Rainsboro, OH 45165 • *250*
Rainsville, AL 35986 • *3,907*
Rake, IA 50465 • *283*
Raleigh, FL 32696 • *350*
Raleigh, IL 62977 • *352*
Raleigh, MS 39153 • *998*
Raleigh, NC 27601-99 • *150,255*
Raleigh, WV 25911 • *900*
Raleigh □, WV • *86,821*
Raleigh Hills, OR 97225 • *6,500*
Ralls, TX 79357 • *2,422*
Ralls □, MO • *8,984*
Ralston, NE 68127 • *5,143*
Ralston, OK 74650 • *495*
Ralston, PA 17763 • *375*
Ramah, NM 87321 • *600*
Rambleton Acres, DE 19720 • *1,500*
Ramblewood, NJ 08054 • *6,475*
Ramer, AL 36069 • *375*
Ramer, TN 38367 • *429*
Ramey, PA 16671 • *568*
Ramona, CA 92065 • *8,173*
Ramona, OK 74061 • *567*
Ramona, SD 57054 • *241*
Ramsay, MI 49959 • *1,068*
Ramseur, NC 27316 • *1,162*
Ramsey, IL 62080 • *1,058*
Ramsey, MN 55303 • *10,093*
Ramsey, NJ 07446 • *12,899*
Ramsey □, MN • *459,784*
Ramsey □, ND • *13,048*
Ranburne, AL 36273 • *417*
Ranchester, WY 82839 • *655*
Ranchito, NM 87571 • *300*
Rancho Cordova, CA 95670 • *42,881*
Rancho Mirage, CA 92270 • *6,281*
Rancho Palos Verdes, CA 90274 • *36,577*
Rancho Rinconado, CA 95014 • *5,100*
Rancho Santa Fe, CA 92067 • *4,014*
Ranchos de Taos, NM 87557 • *1,411*
Rancocas, NJ 08073 • *600*
Rancocas Woods, NJ 08060 • *1,400*
Rand, WV 25306 • *2,500*
Randall, MN 56475 • *527*
Randall □, TX • *75,062*
Randallstown, MD 21133 • *20,500*
Randle, WA 98377 • *600*
Randleman, NC 27317 • *2,156*
Randlett, OK 73562 • *461*
Randolph, AZ 85222 • *300*
Randolph, IA 51649 • *223*
Randolph, ME 04345 • *1,834*
Randolph, MA 02368 • *22,218*
Randolph, NE 68771 • *1,106*
Randolph, NY 14772 • *1,398*
Randolph, OH 44265 • *800*
Randolph, UT 84064 • *659*
Randolph, VT 05060 • *2,217*
Randolph, WI 53956 • *1,691*
Randolph □, AL • *20,075*
Randolph □, AR • *16,834*
Randolph □, GA • *9,599*
Randolph □, IL • *35,652*
Randolph □, IN • *29,997*
Randolph □, MO • *25,460*
Randolph □, NC • *91,728*
Randolph □, WV • *28,734*
Randolph Center, VT 05061 • *250*
Randolph Hills, MD 20852 • *500*
Random Lake, WI 53075 • *1,287*
Randsburg, CA 93554 • *280*
Rangeley, ME 04970 • *700*
Rangely, CO 81648 • *2,113*
Ranger, TX 76470 • *3,142*
Ranier, MN 56668 • *237*
Rankin, IL 60960 • *727*
Rankin, PA 15104 • *2,892*
Rankin, TX 79778 • *1,216*
Rankin □, MS • *69,427*
Ransom, IL 60470 • *456*
Ransom, KS 67572 • *448*
Ransom □, ND • *6,698*
Ransomville, NY 14131 • *1,500*
Ranson, WV 25438 • *2,471*
Rantoul, IL 61866 • *20,161*
Rantowles, SC 29460 • *400*
Raoul, GA 30510 • *1,400*
Rapid City, MI 49676 • *350*
Rapid City, SD 57701-08 • *46,492*
Rapides □, LA • *135,282*
Rapid River, MI 49878 • *700*
Rapids City, IL 61278 • *1,058*
Rappahannock □, VA • *6,093*
Raquette Lake, NY 13436 • *250*
Raritan, NJ 08869 • *6,128*
Rathdrum, ID 83858 • *1,369*
Raton, NM 87740 • *8,225*
Rattan, OK 74562 • *332*
Ravalli □, MT • *22,493*
Raven, VA 24639 • *1,880*
Ravena, NY 12143 • *3,091*
Ravenden, AR 72459 • *338*
Ravenden Springs, AR 72460 • *230*
Ravenel, SC 29470 • *1,655*
Ravenna, KY 40472 • *793*
Ravenna, MI 49451 • *951*
Ravenna, NE 68869 • *1,296*
Ravenna, OH 44266 • *11,987*
Ravensdale, WA 98051 • *500*
Ravenswood, IN 46240 • *424*
Ravenswood, WV 26164 • *4,126*
Ravenwood, MO 64479 • *436*
Ravia, OK 73455 • *487*
Rawlings, MD 21557 • *300*
Rawlins, WY 82301 • *11,547*
Rawlins □, KS • *4,105*
Rawson, OH 45881 • *477*
Ray, ND 58849 • *766*
Ray □, MO • *21,378*
Ray City, GA 31645 • *658*
Raymond, CA 93653 • *425*
Raymond, GA 30263 • *300*
Raymond, IL 62560 • *957*
Raymond, ME 04071 • *500*
Raymond, MN 56282 • *723*
Raymond, MS 39154 • *1,967*
Raymond, NH 03077 • *1,192*
Raymond, WA 98577 • *2,991*
Raymondville, MO 65555 • *388*
Raymondville, NY 13678 • *600*
Raymondville, TX 78580 • *9,493*
Raymore, MO 64083 • *3,154*
Rayne, LA 70578 • *9,066*
Raynham, MA 02767 • *2,124*
Raynham Center, MA 02768 • *3,776*
Raytown, MO 64133 • *31,759*
Rayville, LA 71269 • *4,610*
Reader, WV 26167 • *700*
Readfield, ME 04355 • *350*
Reading, KS 66868 • *244*
Reading, MA 01867 • *22,678*
Reading, MI 49274 • *1,203*
Reading, OH 45215 • *12,843*
Reading, PA 19601-99 • *78,686*
Readlyn, IA 50668 • *858*
Readsboro, VT 05350 • *402*
Readstown, WI 54652 • *396*
Reagan □, TX • *4,135*
Real □, TX • *2,469*
Realitos, TX 78376 • *250*
Reamstown, PA 17567 • *1,050*
Reardan, WA 99029 • *498*
Reasnor, IA 50232 • *277*
Reaville, NJ 08822 • *250*
Rebecca, GA 31783 • *272*
Rebersburg, PA 16872 • *500*
Rector, AR 72461 • *2,336*
Red Bank, NJ 07701 • *12,031*
Red Bank, SC 29072 • *300*
Red Bank, TN 37415 • *13,299*
Red Banks, MS 38661 • *350*
Red Bay, AL 35582 • *3,232*
Redbay, FL 32455 • *300*
Redbird, OH 44057 • *1,600*
Red Bluff, CA 96080 • *9,490*
Red Boiling Springs, TN 37150 • *1,173*
Red Bud, IL 62278 • *2,850*
Redby, MN 56670 • *400*
Redcliff, CO 81649 • *409*
Red Cloud, NE 68970 • *1,300*
Red Creek, NY 13143 • *645*
Reddell, LA 70580 • *550*
Reddick, FL 32686 • *657*
Reddick, IL 60961 • *243*
Redding, CA 96001-03 • *41,995*
Redding, CT • *800*
Redding Ridge, CT 06876 • *325*
Redfield, AR 72132 • *745*
Redfield, IA 50233 • *959*
Redfield, SD 57469 • *3,027*
Redford, MI 48239 • *58,441*
Redford, NY 12978 • *500*
Redford, TX 79846 • *250*
Redgranite, WI 54970 • *976*
Red Hook, NY 12571 • *1,692*
Red Jacket, WV 25692 • *1,000*
Redkey, IN 47373 • *1,537*
Redlake, MN 56671 • *600*
Red Lake □, MN • *5,471*
Red Lake Falls, MN 56750 • *1,732*
Redlands, CA 92373-74 • *43,619*
Red Level, AL 36474 • *504*
Red Lion, PA 17356 • *5,824*
Red Lodge, MT 59068 • *1,896*
Redmon, IL 61949 • *224*
Redmond, OR 97756 • *6,452*
Redmond, UT 84652 • *619*
Redmond, WA 98052-53 • *23,318*
Red Oak, GA 30272 • *1,200*
Red Oak, IA 51566 • *6,810*
Red Oak, NC 27868 • *314*
Red Oak, OK 74563 • *676*
Red Oak, TX 75154 • *1,882*
Red Oaks, LA 70815 • *2,000*
Redondo, WA 98054 • *600*
Redondo Beach, CA 90277-78 • *57,102*
Red River, NM 87558 • *332*
Red River □, LA • *10,433*
Red River □, TX • *16,101*
Red Rock, AZ 87420 • *300*
Red Rock, OK 74651 • *376*
Red Springs, NC 28377 • *3,607*
Red Willow □, NE • *12,615*
Red Wing, MN 55066 • *13,736*
Redwood, NY 13679 • *600*
Redwood, UT 84119 • *2,000*
Redwood □, MN • *19,341*
Redwood City, CA 94061-65 • *54,951*
Redwood Falls, MN 56283 • *5,210*
Redwood Valley, CA 95470 • *1,300*
Reece City, AL 35954 • *718*
Reed City, MI 49677 • *2,221*
Reeder, ND 58649 • *355*
Reedley, CA 93654 • *11,071*
Reedsburg, WI 53959 • *5,038*
Reedsport, OR 97467 • *4,984*
Reeds Spring, MO 65737 • *461*
Reedsville, OH 45772 • *329*
Reedsville, PA 17084 • *950*
Reedsville, WV 26547 • *564*
Reedsville, WI 54230 • *1,134*
Reedurban, OH 44710 • *6,650*
Reedville, VA 22539 • *500*
Reedy, WV 25270 • *338*
Reese, MI 48757 • *1,645*
Reese Station, OH 43207 • *500*
Reeseville, WI 53579 • *649*
Reesville, OH 45166 • *280*
Reeves □, TX • *15,801*
Reevesville, SC 29471 • *241*
Reform, AL 35481 • *2,245*
Refugio, TX 78377 • *3,898*
Refugio □, TX • *9,289*
Regent, ND 58650 • *297*
Register, GA 30452 • *300*
Rehoboth, MA 02769 • *300*
Rehoboth Beach, DE 19971 • *1,730*
Reidland, KY 42001 • *3,730*
Reidsville, GA 30453 • *2,296*
Reidsville, NC 27320 • *12,492*
Reidville, SC 29375 • *460*
Reinbeck, IA 50669 • *1,808*
Reisterstown, MD 21136 • *19,385*
Reliance, TN 37369 • *300*
Reliance, WY 82943 • *500*
Rembert, SC 29128 • *350*
Rembrandt, IA 50576 • *291*
Remer, MN 56672 • *396*
Remerton, GA 31601 • *443*
Remington, IN 47977 • *1,268*
Remington, VA 22734 • *425*
Remsen, IA 51050 • *1,592*

Remsen, NY 13438 • 621
Remus, MI 49340 • 450
Rena Lara, MS 38767 • 250
Renault, IL 62279 • 300
Renick, WV 24966 • 240
Reno, NV 89501-99 • 100,756
Reno, OH 45773 • 850
Reno □, KS • 64,983
Renovo, PA 17764 • 1,812
Rensselaer, IN 47978 • 4,944
Rensselaer, NY 12144 • 9,047
Rensselaer □, NY • 151,966
Rensselaer Falls, NY 13680 • 360
Rensselaerville, NY 12147 • 325
Renton, WA 98055-57 • 30,612
Rentz, GA 31075 • 337
Renville, MN 56284 • 1,493
Renville □, MN • 20,401
Renville □, ND • 3,608
Renwick, IA 50577 • 410
Repton, AL 36475 • 313
Republic, KS 66964 • 223
Republic, MI 49879 • 1,000
Republic, MO 65738 • 4,485
Republic, OH 44867 • 656
Republic, PA 15475 • 1,500
Republic, WA 99166 • 1,018
Republic □, KS • 7,569
Republican City, NE 68971 • 231
Rescue, VA 23424 • 325
Reserve, LA 70084 • 7,288
Reserve, NM 87830 • 439
Reston, VA 22090 • 32,000
Retsof, NY 14539 • 300
Revelo, KY 42638 • 550
Revere, MA 02151 • 42,423
Revloc, PA 15948 • 800
Rew, PA 16744 • 400
Rewey, WI 53580 • 233
Rex, GA 30273 • 700
Rexburg, ID 83440 • 11,559
Rexhame, MA 02050 • 550
Reydon, OK 73660 • 252
Reyno, AR 72462 • 521
Reynolds, GA 31076 • 1,298
Reynolds, IL 61279 • 701
Reynolds, IN 47980 • 632
Reynolds, ND 58275 • 309
Reynolds □, MO • 7,230
Reynoldsburg, OH 43068 • 20,661
Reynoldsville, PA 15851 • 3,016
Rhea □, TN • 24,235
Rhine, GA 31077 • 590
Rhinebeck, NY 12572 • 2,542
Rhinelander, WI 54501 • 7,873
Rhodell, WV 25915 • 472
Rhodes, IA 50234 • 367
Rhodhiss, NC 28667 • 727
Rhome, TX 76078 • 478
Rialto, CA 92376 • 37,474
Rib Lake, WI 54470 • 945
Rice, MN 56367 • 499
Rice □, KS • 11,900
Rice □, MN • 46,087
Rice Lake, WI 54868 • 7,691
Rices Landing, PA 15357 • 516
Riceville, IA 50466 • 919
Riceville, TN 37370 • 500
Rich □, UT • 2,100
Richards, TX 77873 • 300
Richardson, TX 75080-85 • 72,496
Richardson □, NE • 11,315
Richardton, ND 58652 • 699
Richburg, NY 14774 • 494
Richburg, SC 29729 • 269
Rich Creek, VA 24147 • 746
Richey, MT 59259 • 417
Richfield, ID 83349 • 357
Richfield, MN 55423 • 37,851
Richfield, NC 28137 • 373
Richfield, PA 17086 • 475
Richfield, UT 84701 • 5,482
Richfield, WI 53076 • 250
Richfield Springs, NY 13439 • 1,561
Richford, NY 13835 • 300
Richford, VT 05476 • 1,471
Rich Hill, MO 64779 • 1,471
Richland, GA 31825 • 1,802
Richland, IN 47634 • 550
Richland, IA 52585 • 600
Richland, MI 49083 • 486
Richland, MO 65556 • 1,922
Richland, NJ 08350 • 800
Richland, NY 13144 • 600
Richland, WA 99352 • 33,578
Richland □, IL • 17,587
Richland □, LA • 22,187
Richland □, MT • 12,243
Richland □, ND • 19,207
Richland □, OH • 131,205
Richland □, SC • 269,735
Richland □, WI • 17,476
Richland Center, WI 53581 • 4,997
Richlands, NC 28574 • 825
Richlands, VA 24641 • 5,796
Richland Springs, TX 76871 • 420
Richlandtown, PA 18955 • 1,180
Richmond, CA 94801-99 • 74,676
Richmond, IL 60071 • 1,068
Richmond, IN 47374 • 41,349
Richmond, KS 66080 • 510
Richmond, KY 40475 • 21,705
Richmond, ME 04357 • 1,578
Richmond, MI 48062 • 3,536
Richmond, MN 56368 • 867
Richmond, MO 64085 • 5,499
Richmond, TX 77469 • 9,692
Richmond, UT 84333 • 1,705
Richmond, VT 05477 • 865
Richmond, VA 23201-99 • 219,214
Richmond □, GA • 181,629
Richmond □, NC • 45,481
Richmond □, NY • 352,121
Richmond □, VA • 6,952
Richmond Beach, WA 98160 • 8,000
Richmond Dale, OH 45673 • 650
Richmond Heights, FL 33156 • 8,577
Richmond Heights, MO 63117 • 11,516
Richmond Heights, OH 44143 • 10,095
Richmond Highlands, WA 98133 • 20,300
Richmond Hill, GA 31324 • 1,177
Richmondville, NY 12149 • 792
Rich Square, NC 27869 • 1,057
Richton, MS 39476 • 1,205
Richton Park, IL 60471 • 9,403
Richview, IL 62877 • 299
Richville, MI 48758 • 400
Richville, NY 13681 • 336
Richwood, OH 43344 • 2,181
Richwood, WV 26261 • 3,568
Richwoods, MO 63071 • 300
Rickman, TN 38580 • 400
Riddle, OR 97469 • 1,265
Riddlesburg, PA 16672 • 300
Ridgecrest, CA 93555 • 15,929
Ridgecrest, NC 28770 • 500
Ridgecrest, WA 98155 • 7,000
Ridgedale, MO 65739 • 325
Ridge Farm, IL 61870 • 1,096
Ridgefield, CT 06877 • 6,066
Ridgefield, NJ 07657 • 10,294
Ridgefield, WA 98642 • 1,062
Ridgefield Park, NJ 07660 • 12,738
Ridgeland, MS 39157 • 5,461
Ridgeland, SC 29936 • 1,143
Ridgeland, WI 54763 • 300
Ridgeley, WV 26753 • 994
Ridgely, MD 21660 • 933
Ridgely, TN 38080 • 1,932
Ridgemont, NY 14626 • 8,500
Ridgeside, TN 37411 • 417
Ridge Spring, SC 29129 • 969
Ridgetop, TN 37152 • 1,225
Ridgeview, WV 25169 • 500
Ridgeville, IN 47380 • 933
Ridgeville, SC 29472 • 603
Ridgeville Corners, OH 43555 • 600
Ridgeway, IA 52165 • 308
Ridgeway, MO 64481 • 516
Ridgeway, OH 43345 • 388
Ridgeway, SC 29130 • 343
Ridgeway, VA 24148 • 858
Ridgeway, WI 53582 • 503
Ridgewood, NJ 07450-52 • 25,208
Ridgway, CO 81432 • 369
Ridgway, IL 62979 • 1,245
Ridgway, PA 15853 • 5,604
Ridley Park, PA 19078 • 7,889
Rienzi, MS 38865 • 423
Riesel, TX 76682 • 691
Rifle, CO 81650 • 3,215
Rigby, ID 83442 • 2,624
Riggins, ID 83549 • 527
Riley, IN 47871 • 269
Riley, KS 66531 • 779
Riley □, KS • 63,505
Rillito, AZ 85246 • 400
Rimersburg, PA 16248 • 1,096
Rincon, GA 31326 • 1,988
Rineyville, KY 40162 • 450
Ringgold, GA 30736 • 1,882
Ringgold, LA 71068 • 1,655
Ringgold, TX 76261 • 300
Ringgold □, IA • 6,112
Ringling, OK 73456 • 1,561
Ringoes, NJ 08551 • 650
Ringsted, IA 50578 • 557
Ringwood, NJ 07456 • 12,625
Ringwood, OK 73768 • 389
Rio, FL 33457 • 1,205
Rio, IL 61472 • 282
Rio, WI 53960 • 785
Rio Arriba □, NM • 29,282
Rio Blanco □, CO • 6,255
Rio Dell, CA 95562 • 2,687
Rio Grande, NJ 08242 • 2,016
Rio Grande, OH 45674 • 864
Rio Grande □, CO • 10,511
Rio Grande City, TX 78582 • 7,000
Rio Hondo, TX 78583 • 1,673
Rio Linda, CA 95673 • 7,359
Rio Rancho, NM 87124 • 12,000
Rio Vista, CA 94571 • 3,142
Ripley, CA 92272 • 500
Ripley, MS 38663 • 4,271
Ripley, NY 14775 • 1,000
Ripley, OH 45167 • 2,174
Ripley, OK 74062 • 451
Ripley, TN 38063 • 6,366
Ripley, WV 25271 • 3,464
Ripley □, IN • 24,398
Ripley □, MO • 12,458
Ripon, WI 54971 • 7,111
Rippey, IA 50235 • 304
Ririe, ID 83443 • 555
Risco, MO 63874 • 446
Rising City, NE 68658 • 392
Rising Star, TX 76471 • 1,204
Rising Sun, IN 47040 • 2,478
Rising Sun, MD 21911 • 1,160
Risingsun, OH 43457 • 698
Rison, AR 71665 • 1,325
Rison, MD 20658 • 300
Ritchie □, WV • 11,442
Rittman, OH 44270 • 6,063
Ritzville, WA 99169 • 1,800
Riverbank, CA 95367 • 5,695
Riverdale, CA 93656 • 1,866
Riverdale, GA 30274 • 7,121
Riverdale, IL 60627 • 13,233
Riverdale, IA 52722 • 462
Riverdale, MD 20737 • 4,748
Riverdale, NJ 07457 • 2,530
Riverdale, ND 58565 • 500
Riverdale, UT 84401 • 6,031
Riverdale, VA 24592 • 500
River Edge, NJ 07661 • 11,111
River Falls, AL 36476 • 669
River Falls, WI 54022 • 9,019
River Forest, IL 60305 • 12,392
River Grove, IL 60171 • 10,368
Riverhaven, IN 46802 • 700
Riverhead, NY 11901 • 7,400
River Heights, UT 84321 • 1,211
River Hills, WI 53217 • 1,642
River Oaks, TX 76114 • 6,890
River Pines, MA 01821 • 3,700
River Ridge, LA 70123 • 17,146
River Road, OR 97404 • 10,370
River Rouge, MI 48218 • 12,912
Riverside, AL 35135 • 849
Riverside, CA 92501-99 • 170,591
Riverside, IL 60546 • 9,236
Riverside, IA 52327 • 826
Riverside, MA 01376 • 300
Riverside, NJ 08075 • 7,941
Riverside, PA 17868 • 2,266
Riverside, UT 84334 • 240
Riverside, WA 98849 • 243
Riverside □, CA • 663,199
Riverton, CT 06065 • 400
Riverton, IL 62561 • 2,783
Riverton, IA 51650 • 342
Riverton, KS 66770 • 550
Riverton, NJ 08077 • 3,068
Riverton, UT 84065 • 7,293
Riverton, VT 05668 • 500
Riverton, VA 22651 • 350
Riverton, WY 82501 • 9,247
Riverton Heights, WA 98188 • 33,500
River Vale, NJ 07675 • 9,489
River View, AL 36854 • 1,314
Riverview, FL 33569 • 3,200
Riverview, MI 48192 • 14,569
Rives, TN 38253 • 386
Rives Junction, MI 49277 • 450
Rivesville, WV 26588 • 1,327
Riviera, AZ 86442 • 4,500
Riviera, TX 78379 • 600
Riviera Beach, FL 33404 • 26,489
Riviera Beach, MD 21122 • 5,600
Riviera Beach, NJ 08723 • 2,000
Rixford, PA 16745 • 475
Roachdale, IN 46172 • 958
Roane □, TN • 48,425
Roane □, WV • 15,952
Roan Mountain, TN 37687 • 1,108
Roann, IN 46974 • 548
Roanoke, AL 36274 • 5,896
Roanoke, IL 61561 • 2,001
Roanoke, IN 46783 • 891
Roanoke, LA 70581 • 600
Roanoke, TX 76262 • 910
Roanoke, VA 24001-50 • 100,220
Roanoke □, VA • 72,945
Roanoke Rapids, NC 27870 • 14,702
Roaring Branch, PA 17765 • 250
Roaring Spring, PA 16673 • 2,962
Roaring Springs, TX 79256 • 315
Robards, KY 42452 • 500
Robbins, IL 60472 • 8,853
Robbins, NC 27325 • 1,256
Robbins, TN 37852 • 450
Robbinsdale, MN 55422 • 14,422
Robbinsville, NJ 08691 • 550
Robbinsville, NC 28771 • 1,370
Robeline, LA 71469 • 238
Robersonville, NC 27871 • 1,981
Roberta, GA 31078 • 859
Roberta Mills, NC 28025 • 240
Robert Lee, TX 76945 • 1,202
Roberts, ID 83444 • 466
Roberts, IL 60962 • 422
Roberts, MT 59070 • 300
Roberts, WI 54023 • 833
Roberts □, SD • 10,911
Roberts □, TX • 1,187
Robertsdale, AL 36567 • 2,306
Robertsdale, PA 16674 • 550
Robertson □, KY • 2,265
Robertson □, TN • 37,021
Robertson □, TX • 14,653
Robeson □, NC • 101,610
Robins, IA 52328 • 726
Robinson, IL 62454 • 7,285
Robinson, KS 66532 • 324
Robinson, PA 15949 • 660
Robinson, TX 76706 • 6,074
Robinsonville, MS 38664 • 250
Robstown, TX 78380 • 12,100
Roby, TX 79543 • 814
Rochdale, MA 01542 • 1,105
Roche Harbor, WA 98250 • 250
Rochelle, GA 31079 • 1,626
Rochelle, IL 61068 • 8,982
Rochelle, TX 76872 • 310
Rochelle Park, NJ 07662 • 5,603
Rocheport, MO 65279 • 272
Rochester, IL 62563 • 2,488
Rochester, IN 46975 • 5,050
Rochester, KY 42273 • 250
Rochester, MA 02770 • 450
Rochester, MI 48063-64 • 7,203
Rochester, MN 55901-04 • 57,890
Rochester, NH 03867 • 21,560
Rochester, NY 14601-99 • 241,741
Rochester, PA 15074 • 4,759
Rochester, TX 79544 • 492
Rochester, VT 05767 • 500
Rochester, WA 98579 • 900
Rochester, WI 53167 • 746
Rock, MA 02346 • 500
Rock, MI 49880 • 475
Rock □, MN • 10,703
Rock □, NE • 2,383
Rock □, WI • 139,420
Rockaway, NJ 07866 • 6,852
Rockaway, OR 97136 • 906
Rockaway Beach, MO 65740 • 292
Rockbridge, IL 62081 • 258
Rockbridge, OH 43149 • 450
Rockbridge □, VA • 17,911
Rockcastle □, KY • 13,973
Rock Creek, MN 55067 • 890
Rock Creek, OH 44084 • 652
Rockdale, IL 60436 • 1,913
Rockdale, MD 21207 • 4,200
Rockdale, TX 76567 • 5,611
Rockdale □, GA • 36,747
Rockfall, CT 06481 • 500
Rock Falls, IL 61071 • 10,633
Rockfield, IN 46977 • 300
Rockford, AL 35136 • 494
Rockford, IL 61101-99 • 139,712
Rockford, IA 50468 • 1,012
Rockford, MI 49341 • 3,324
Rockford, MN 55373 • 2,408
Rockford, OH 45882 • 1,245
Rockford, TN 37853 • 567
Rockford, WA 99030 • 442
Rock Hall, MD 21661 • 1,511
Rock Hill, MO 63124 • 5,702
Rock Hill, SC 29730 • 35,344
Rockhill Furnace, PA 17249 • 472
Rockingham, NC 28379 • 8,300
Rockingham □, NH • 190,345

Rockingham □, NC • 83,426
Rockingham □, VA • 57,038
Rock Island, IL 61201 • 46,928
Rock Island, WA 98850 • 491
Rock Island □, IL • 165,968
Rocklake, ND 58365 • 287
Rockland, ID 83271 • 283
Rockland, ME 04841 • 7,919
Rockland, MA 02370 • 15,695
Rockland, MI 49960 • 330
Rockland, NY 12776 • 350
Rockland □, NY • 259,530
Rockledge, FL 32955 • 11,877
Rockledge, PA 19111 • 2,538
Rockledge, PA • 2,538
Rocklin, CA 95677 • 7,344
Rockmart, GA 30153 • 3,645
Rock Point, AZ 86503 • 400
Rock Point, MD 20682 • 300
Rockport, AR 72104 • 231
Rockport, IN 47635 • 2,590
Rockport, KY 42369 • 511
Rockport, ME 04856 • 1,000
Rockport, MA 01966 • 4,600
Rock Port, MO 64482 • 1,511
Rockport, TX 78382 • 3,686
Rock Rapids, IA 51246 • 2,693
Rock River, WY 82083 • 415
Rocksprings, TX 78880 • 1,317
Rock Springs, WI 53961 • 426
Rock Springs, WY 82901 • 19,458
Rockton, IL 61072 • 2,313
Rockvale, CO 81244 • 338
Rock Valley, IA 51247 • 2,706
Rockville, IN 47872 • 2,785
Rockville, MD 20850-58 • 43,811
Rockville, MA 02054 • 300
Rockville, MN 56369 • 597
Rockville, MO 64780 • 281
Rockville Centre, NY 11570 • 25,412
Rockwall, TX 75087 • 5,939
Rockwall □, TX • 14,528
Rockwell, IA 50469 • 1,039
Rockwell, NC 28138 • 1,339
Rockwell City, IA 50579 • 2,276
Rockwell Park, NC 28213 • 2,600
Rockwood, MI 48173 • 3,346
Rockwood, OR 97233 • 11,000
Rockwood, PA 15557 • 1,058
Rockwood, TN 37854 • 5,767
Rocky, OK 73661 • 242
Rocky Creek, FL 33615 • 7,800
Rocky Ford, CO 81067 • 4,804
Rocky Ford, GA 30455 • 223
Rocky Hill, CT 06067 • 14,559
Rocky Hill, NJ 08553 • 717
Rocky Mount, NC 27801 • 41,283
Rocky Mount, VA 24151 • 4,198
Rocky Point, NC 28457 • 600
Rocky Ripple, IN 46208 • 778
Rocky River, OH 44116 • 21,084
Rodeo, CA 94572 • 8,286
Roderfield, WV 24881 • 1,100
Rodessa, LA 71069 • 337
Rodney Village, DE 19901 • 1,100
Roebling, NJ 08554 • 3,600
Roebuck, SC 29376 • 1,088
Roeland Park, KS 66203 • 7,962
Roessleville, NY 12205 • 5,476
Roff, OK 74865 • 729
Roganville, TX 75956 • 240
Roger Mills □, OK • 4,799
Rogers, AR 72756 • 17,429
Rogers, CT 06263 • 500
Rogers, MN 55374 • 652
Rogers, OH 44455 • 298
Rogers, TX 76569 • 1,242
Rogers □, OK • 46,436
Rogers City, MI 49779 • 3,923
Rogersville, AL 35652 • 1,224
Rogersville, MO 65742 • 741
Rogersville, PA 15359 • 325
Rogersville, TN 37857 • 4,368
Rogue River, OR 97537 • 1,308
Rohnert Park, CA 94928 • 22,965
Roland, AR 72135 • 300
Roland, IA 50236 • 1,005
Roland, OK 74954 • 1,472
Rolesville, NC 27571 • 381
Rolette, ND 58366 • 667
Rolette □, ND • 12,177
Rolfe, IA 50581 • 796
Rolla, KS 67954 • 417
Rolla, MO 65401 • 13,303
Rolla, ND 58367 • 1,538
Rollingbay, WA 98061 • 700
Rolling Fork, MS 39159 • 2,590
Rolling Hills Estates, CA 90274 • 7,701
Rolling Meadows, IL 60008 • 20,167
Rollingstone, MN 55969 • 528
Rollinsford, NH 03869 • 1,173
Roma, TX 78584 • 3,384
Romayor, TX 77368 • 500
Rome, GA 30161 • 29,654
Rome, IL 61562 • 2,744
Rome, MS 38768 • 300
Rome, NY 13440 • 43,826
Rome, OH 45669 • 600
Rome, PA 18837 • 426
Rome City, IN 46784 • 1,319
Romeo, CO 81148 • 308
Romeo, MI 48065 • 3,509
Romeoville, IL 60441 • 15,519
Romney, IN 47981 • 300
Romney, WV 26757 • 2,094
Romulus, MI 48174 • 24,857
Romulus, NY 14541 • 350
Ronan, MT 59864 • 1,530
Ronceverte, WV 24970 • 2,312
Ronda, NC 28670 • 457
Rondo, AR 72355 • 330
Ronkonkoma, NY 11779 • 20,200
Roodhouse, IL 62082 • 2,364
Rooks □, KS • 7,006
Roopville, GA 30170 • 229
Roosevelt, NJ 08555 • 835
Roosevelt, NY 11575 • 15,000
Roosevelt, OK 73564 • 396
Roosevelt, UT 84066 • 3,842
Roosevelt □, MT • 10,467
Roosevelt □, NM • 15,695
Roosevelt Park, MI 49441 • 4,015
Rootstown, OH 44272 • 650
Roper, NC 27970 • 795
Ropesville, TX 79358 • 489
Rosalia, WA 99170 • 572
Rosalie, NE 68055 • 224
Rosamond, CA 93560 • 2,869
Roscoe, IL 61073 • 1,388
Roscoe, NY 12776 • 300
Roscoe, PA 15477 • 1,123
Roscoe, SD 57471 • 370
Roscoe, TX 79545 • 1,628
Roscommon, MI 48653 • 834
Roscommon □, MI • 16,374
Roseau, MN 56751 • 2,272
Roseau □, MN • 12,574
Roseboro, NC 28382 • 1,227
Rosebud, MO 63091 • 326
Rosebud, SD 57570 • 600
Rosebud, TX 76570 • 2,076
Rosebud □, MT • 9,899
Roseburg, OR 97470 • 16,644
Rosebush, MI 48878 • 336
Rose City, MI 48654 • 661
Rose Creek, MN 55970 • 371
Rosedale, IN 47874 • 744
Rosedale, MD 21237 • 19,956
Rosedale, MS 38769 • 2,793
Rosedale, WA 98335 • 300
Rose Hill, KS 67133 • 1,557
Rose Hill, NC 28458 • 1,508
Rose Hill, VA 24281 • 800
Roseland, CA 95407 • 7,915
Roseland, FL 32957 • 1,607
Roseland, IN 46635 • 832
Roseland, LA 70456 • 1,346
Roseland, NE 68973 • 254
Roseland, NJ 07068 • 5,330
Roseland, OH 44906 • 3,000
Roselawn, IN 46372 • 300
Roselle, IL 60172 • 16,948
Roselle, NJ 07203 • 20,641
Roselle Park, NJ 07204 • 13,377
Rosemead, CA 91770 • 42,604
Rosemont, WV 26424 • 300
Rosemount, MN 55068 • 5,083
Rosenberg, TX 77471 • 17,995
Rosendale, MO 64483 • 223
Rosendale, WI 54974 • 725
Rosenhayn, NJ 08352 • 750
Rosepine, LA 70659 • 953
Roseto, PA 18013 • 1,484
Roseville, CA 95678 • 24,347
Roseville, IL 61473 • 1,254
Roseville, MI 48066 • 54,311
Roseville, MN 55113 • 35,820
Roseville, OH 43777 • 1,915
Rosewood, OH 43070 • 300
Rosewood Heights, IL 62024 • 5,085
Rosharon, TX 77583 • 500
Rosholt, SD 57260 • 446
Rosholt, WI 54473 • 520
Rosiclare, IL 62982 • 1,441
Roslyn, PA 19001 • 13,400
Roslyn, SD 57261 • 261
Roslyn, WA 98941 • 938
Roslyn Heights, NY 11577 • 7,270
Rosman, NC 28772 • 512
Ross, OH 45061 • 2,767
Ross □, OH • 65,004
Rossburg, OH 45362 • 260
Rosser, TX 75157 • 350
Rossford, OH 43460 • 5,978
Rossiter, PA 15772 • 750
Rossmoor, CA 90720 • 10,457
Rosston, AR 71858 • 274
Rossville, GA 30741 • 3,851
Rossville, IL 60963 • 1,363
Rossville, IN 46065 • 1,148
Rossville, KS 66533 • 1,045
Rossville, TN 38066 • 379
Roswell, GA 30075-77 • 23,337
Roswell, NM 88201 • 39,676
Rotan, TX 79546 • 2,284
Rothbury, MI 49452 • 522
Rothsay, MN 56579 • 476
Rothschild, WI 54474 • 3,338
Rothsville, PA 17543 • 1,318
Rotterdam, NY 12303 • 24,800
Rougemont, NC 27572 • 500
Rougon, LA 70773 • 400
Roulette, PA 16746 • 1,100
Roundhead, OH 43346 • 300
Round Hill, VA 22141 • 510
Round Lake, IL 60073 • 2,644
Round Lake, MN 56167 • 480
Round Lake, NY 12151 • 791
Round Lake Beach, IL 60073 • 12,921
Round Oak, GA 31038 • 300
Round Pond, ME 04564 • 300
Round Rock, AZ 86503 • 300
Round Rock, TX 78664 • 12,740
Roundup, MT 59072 • 2,119
Rouses Point, NY 12979 • 2,266
Rouseville, PA 16344 • 734
Routt □, CO • 13,404
Rouzerville, PA 17250 • 1,371
Rowan, IA 50470 • 259
Rowan □, KY • 19,049
Rowan □, NC • 99,186
Rowena, TX 76875 • 465
Rowesville, SC 29133 • 388
Rowland, NC 28383 • 1,841
Rowland Heights, CA 91748 • 28,252
Rowlesburg, WV 26425 • 966
Rowlett, TX 75088 • 7,522
Rowletts, KY 42772 • 350
Rowley, IA 52329 • 275
Rowley, MA 01969 • 1,321
Roxabell, OH 45628 • 300
Roxana, DE 19945 • 250
Roxboro, NC 27573 • 7,532
Roxbury, CT 06783 • 300
Roxbury, NY 12474 • 700
Roxbury, VT 05669 • 300
Roxie, MS 39661 • 591
Roxobel, NC 27872 • 278
Roxton, TX 75477 • 735
Roy, NM 87743 • 381
Roy, UT 84067 • 19,694
Roy, WA 98580 • 417
Royal, AR 71968 • 300
Royal, IA 51357 • 522
Royal, TN 37160 • 300
Royal Center, IN 46978 • 908
Royal Oak, MD 21662 • 300
Royal Oak, MI 48067-73 • 70,893
Royal Pines, NC 28704 • 2,041
Royalston, MA 01368 • 300
Royalton, IL 62983 • 1,320
Royalton, KY 41464 • 270
Royalton, MN 56373 • 660
Royersford, PA 19468 • 4,243
Royerton, IN 47302 • 650
Royse City, TX 75089 • 1,566
Royston, GA 30662 • 2,404
Rubidoux, CA 92509 • 13,200
Rubonia, FL 33561 • 550
Ruby, SC 29741 • 256
Rudd, IA 50471 • 460
Rudolph, OH 43462 • 600
Rudyard, MI 49780 • 900
Rudyard, MT 59540 • 600
Ruffin, NC 27326 • 600
Ruffin, SC 29475 • 280
Rufus, OR 97050 • 352
Rugby, ND 58368 • 3,335
Ruidoso, NM 88345 • 4,260
Ruidoso Downs, NM 88346 • 949
Rule, TX 79547 • 1,015
Ruleville, MS 38771 • 3,332
Rulo, NE 68431 • 261
Ruma, IL 62278 • 254
Rumford, ME 04276 • 6,256
Rumney, NH 03266 • 300
Rumsey, KY 42371 • 300
Rumson, NJ 07760 • 7,623
Runge, TX 78151 • 1,244
Runnells, IA 50237 • 377
Runnels □, TX • 11,872
Runnemede, NJ 08078 • 9,461
Rupert, ID 83350 • 5,476
Rupert, WV 25984 • 1,276
Rural Hall, NC 27045 • 1,336
Rural Retreat, VA 24368 • 1,083
Rush, KY 41168 • 260
Rush □, IN • 19,604
Rush □, KS • 4,516
Rush City, MN 55069 • 1,198
Rushford, MN 55971 • 1,478
Rushford, NY 14777 • 500
Rushmore, MN 56168 • 387
Rush Springs, OK 73082 • 1,451
Rushsylvania, OH 43347 • 610
Rush Valley, UT 84069 • 356
Rushville, IL 62681 • 3,348
Rushville, IN 46173 • 6,113
Rushville, MO 64484 • 271
Rushville, NE 69360 • 1,217
Rushville, NY 14544 • 548
Rusk, TX 75785 • 4,681
Rusk □, TX • 41,382
Rusk □, WI • 15,589
Ruskin, FL 33570 • 5,117
Ruskin, NE 68974 • 224
Russell, AR 72139 • 232
Russell, FL 32043 • 300
Russell, IA 50238 • 593
Russell, KS 67665 • 5,427
Russell, KY 41169 • 3,824
Russell, MA 01071 • 650
Russell, MN 56169 • 412
Russell, NY 13684 • 300
Russell, PA 16345 • 800
Russell □, AL • 47,356
Russell □, KS • 8,868
Russell □, KY • 13,708
Russell □, VA • 31,761
Russell Springs, KY 42642 • 1,831
Russellville, AL 35653 • 8,195
Russellville, AR 72801 • 14,031
Russellville, IN 46175 • 376
Russellville, KY 42276 • 7,520
Russellville, MO 65074 • 667
Russellville, OH 45168 • 445
Russellville, OR 97216 • 6,500
Russellville, TN 37860 • 1,069
Russia, OH 45363 • 438
Russiaville, IN 46979 • 973
Rustburg, VA 24588 • 600
Ruston, LA 71270 • 20,585
Ruston, WA 98407 • 612
Ruth, MI 48470 • 300
Ruth, NV 89319 • 735
Ruth, NC 28139 • 381
Rutherford, NJ 07070-75 • 19,068
Rutherford, TN 38369 • 1,378
Rutherford □, NC • 53,787
Rutherford □, TN • 84,058
Rutherfordton, NC 28139 • 3,434
Ruthton, MN 56170 • 328
Ruthven, IA 51358 • 769
Rutland, IL 61358 • 487
Rutland, MA 01543 • 2,312
Rutland, ND 58067 • 250
Rutland, OH 45775 • 635
Rutland, VT 05701 • 18,436
Rutland □, VT • 58,347
Rutledge, AL 36071 • 496
Rutledge, GA 30663 • 694
Rutledge, TN 37861 • 1,058
Ryan, IA 52330 • 390
Ryan, OK 73565 • 1,083
Ryderwood, WA 98581 • 360
Rye, CO 81069 • 232
Rye, NH 03870 • 800
Rye, NY 10580 • 15,083
Rye Beach, NH 03871 • 600
Ryegate, MT 59074 • 273

S

Sabattus, ME 04280 • 1,234
Sabetha, KS 66534 • 2,286
Sabillasville, MD 21780 • 250
Sabin, MN 56580 • 446
Sabina, OH 45169 • 2,799
Sabinal, TX 78881 • 1,827
Sabine, WV 25916 • 300
Sabine □, LA • 25,280
Sabine □, TX • 8,702
Sabine Pass, TX 77655 • 900
Sabinsville, PA 16943 • 275
Sabula, IA 52070 • 824
Sac □, IA • 14,118

Sacaton, AZ 85247 • *1,951*
Sac City, IA 50583 • *3,000*
Sachem Head, CT 06437 • *390*
Sachse, TX 75040 • *1,640*
Sackets Harbor, NY 13685 • *1,017*
Saco, ME 04072 • *12,921*
Saco, MT 59261 • *252*
Sacramento, CA 95801-99 • *275,741*
Sacramento, KY 42372 • *538*
Sacramento □, CA • *783,381*
Sacred Heart, MN 56285 • *666*
Sacul, TX 75788 • *250*
Saddle Brook, NJ 07662 • *14,084*
Saddle River, NJ 07458 • *2,763*
Sadieville, KY 40370 • *253*
Sadorus, IL 61872 • *435*
Saegertown, PA 16433 • *942*
Safety Harbor, FL 33572 • *6,461*
Safford, AZ 85546 • *7,010*
Sagadahoc □, ME • *28,795*
Sagamore, MA 02561 • *1,152*
Sagamore, PA 16250 • *850*
Sagamore Beach, MA 02562 • *800*
Sagamore Hills, OH 44067 • *4,700*
Sag Harbor, NY 11963 • *2,581*
Saginaw, AL 35137 • *400*
Saginaw, MI 48601-08 • *77,508*
Saginaw, TX 76179 • *5,736*
Saginaw □, MI • *228,059*
Saguache, CO 81149 • *656*
Saguache □, CO • *3,935*
Sahuarita, AZ 85629 • *600*
Saint Agatha, ME 04772 • *425*
Saint Albans, VT 05478 • *7,308*
Saint Albans, WV 25177 • *12,402*
Saint Albans Bay, VT 05481 • *400*
Saint Andrews, SC 29210 • *20,245*
Saint Andrews, SC 29407 • *9,908*
Saint Andrews, TN 37372 • *240*
Saint Ann, MO 63074 • *15,523*
Saint Anne, IL 60964 • *1,421*
Saint Ansgar, IA 50472 • *1,100*
Saint Anthony, ID 83445 • *3,212*
Saint Anthony, IN 47575 • *350*
Saint Augustine, FL 32084-86 • *11,985*
Saint Bernard, AL 35055 • *600*
Saint Bernard, LA 70085 • *720*
Saint Bernard, OH 45217 • *5,396*
Saint Bernard □, LA • *64,097*
Saint Bernice, IN 47875 • *900*
Saint Bethlehem, TN 37155 • *350*
Saint Catharine, KY 40061 • *225*
Saint Charles, IL 60174 • *17,492*
Saint Charles, IA 50240 • *507*
Saint Charles, KY 42453 • *405*
Saint Charles, MI 48655 • *2,276*
Saint Charles, MN 55972 • *2,184*
Saint Charles, MO 63301-03 • *37,379*
Saint Charles, VA 24282 • *241*
Saint Charles □, LA • *37,259*
Saint Charles □, MO • *144,107*
Saint Clair, MI 48079 • *4,780*
Saint Clair, MN 56080 • *655*
Saint Clair, MO 63077 • *3,485*
Saint Clair, PA 17970 • *4,037*
Saint Clair □, AL • *41,205*
Saint Clair □, IL • *267,531*
Saint Clair □, MI • *138,802*
Saint Clair □, MO • *8,622*
Saint Clair Shores, MI 48080-82 • *76,210*
Saint Clairsville, OH 43950 • *5,452*
Saint Cloud, FL 32769 • *7,840*
Saint Cloud, MN 56301 • *42,566*
Saint Cloud, WI 53079 • *560*
Saint Croix □, WI • *43,262*
Saint Croix Falls, WI 54024 • *1,497*
Saint David, AZ 85630 • *950*
Saint David, IL 61563 • *786*
Saint Edward, NE 68660 • *891*
Saint Elizabeth, MO 65075 • *312*
Saint Elmo, AL 36568 • *450*
Saint Elmo, IL 62458 • *1,611*
Saint Florian, AL 35630 • *305*
Saint Francis, AR 72464 • *266*
Saint Francis, KS 67756 • *1,610*
Saint Francis, MN 55070 • *1,184*
Saint Francis, SD 57572 • *766*
Saint Francis, WI 53207 • *10,042*
Saint Francis □, AR • *30,858*
Saint Francisville, IL 62460 • *1,040*
Saint Francisville, LA 70775 • *1,471*
Saint Francois □, MO • *42,600*
Saint Gabriel, LA 70776 • *400*
Sainte Genevieve, MO 63670 • *4,481*
Sainte Genevieve □, MO • *15,180*
Saint George, GA 31646 • *300*
Saint George, KS 66535 • *309*
Saint George, ME 04857 • *250*
Saint George, SC 29477 • *2,134*
Saint George, UT 84770 • *11,350*
Saint Georges, DE 19733 • *500*
Saint Helena, CA 94574 • *4,898*
Saint Helena □, LA • *9,827*
Saint Helens, OR 97051 • *7,064*
Saint Henry, OH 45883 • *1,596*
Saint Hilaire, MN 56754 • *388*
Saint Ignace, MI 49781 • *2,632*
Saint Ignatius, MT 59865 • *877*
Saint Jacob, IL 62281 • *792*
Saint James, LA 70086 • *250*
Saint James, MN 56081 • *4,346*
Saint James, MO 65559 • *3,328*
Saint James, NY 11780 • *11,000*
Saint James □, LA • *21,495*
Saint James City, FL 33956 • *1,298*
Saint Jo, TX 76265 • *1,071*
Saint Joe, IN 46785 • *546*
Saint John, IN 46373 • *3,974*
Saint John, KS 67576 • *1,501*
Saint John, ND 58369 • *401*
Saint John, WA 99171 • *529*
Saint Johns, AZ 85936 • *3,368*
Saint Johns, IL 62832 • *284*
Saint Johns, MI 48879 • *7,376*
Saint Johns, MO 63114 • *7,854*
Saint Johns, OH 45884 • *250*
Saint Johns □, FL • *51,303*
Saint Johnsbury, VT 05819 • *7,150*
Saint Johnsbury Center, VT 05863 • *450*
Saint Johnsville, NY 13452 • *1,974*
Saint John the Baptist □, LA • *31,924*
Saint Joseph, IL 61873 • *1,900*
Saint Joseph, LA 71366 • *1,687*
Saint Joseph, MI 49085 • *9,622*
Saint Joseph, MN 56374 • *2,994*
Saint Joseph, MO 64501-08 • *76,691*
Saint Joseph, TN 38481 • *897*
Saint Joseph □, IN • *241,617*
Saint Joseph □, MI • *56,083*
Saint Landry, LA 71367 • *400*
Saint Landry □, LA • *84,128*
Saint Lawrence, SD 57373 • *223*
Saint Lawrence □, NY • *114,254*
Saint Leo, FL 33574 • *917*
Saint Leon, IN 47060 • *515*
Saint Libory, NE 68872 • *250*
Saint Louis, MI 48880 • *4,107*
Saint Louis, MO 63101-99 • *453,085*
Saint Louis □, MN • *222,229*
Saint Louis □, MO • *973,896*
Saint Louis Park, MN 55426 • *42,931*
Saint Louisville, OH 43071 • *375*
Saint Lucie, FL 33452 • *593*
Saint Lucie □, FL • *87,182*
Sainte Marie, IL 62459 • *312*
Saint Maries, ID 83861 • *2,794*
Saint Marks, FL 32355 • *286*
Saint Martin □, LA • *40,214*
Saint Martinville, LA 70582 • *7,965*
Saint Mary, KY 40063 • *300*
Saint Mary, MO 63673 • *565*
Saint Mary □, LA • *64,253*
Saint Mary-of-the-Woods, IN 47876 • *650*
Saint Marys, AK 99658 • *382*
Saint Marys, GA 31558 • *3,596*
Saint Marys, IN 46556 • *1,700*
Saint Marys, KS 66536 • *1,598*
Saint Marys, OH 45885 • *8,414*
Saint Marys, PA 15857 • *6,417*
Saint Marys, WV 26170 • *2,219*
Saint Marys □, MD • *59,895*
Saint Marys City, MD 20686 • *900*
Saint Matthews, KY 40207 • *13,519*
Saint Matthews, SC 29135 • *2,496*
Saint Meinrad, IN 47577 • *500*
Saint Michael, AK 99659 • *239*
Saint Michael, MN 55376 • *1,519*
Saint Michaels, MD 21663 • *1,301*
Saint Nazianz, WI 54232 • *738*
Saint Paris, OH 43072 • *1,742*
Saint Paul, AK 99660 • *551*
Saint Paul, IN 47272 • *976*
Saint Paul, KS 66771 • *746*
Saint Paul, MN 55101-99 • *270,230*
Saint Paul, MO 63366 • *607*
Saint Paul, NE 68873 • *2,094*
Saint Paul, OR 97137 • *312*
Saint Paul, VA 24283 • *973*
Saint Paul Park, MN 55071 • *4,864*
Saint Pauls, NC 28384 • *1,639*
Saint Peter, IL 62880 • *372*
Saint Peter, MN 56082 • *9,056*
Saint Peters, MO 63376 • *15,700*
Saint Petersburg, FL 33701-99 • *238,647*
Saint Petersburg, PA 16054 • *452*
Saint Petersburg Beach, FL 33736 • *9,354*
Saint Philip, IN 47620 • *300*
Saint Regis, MT 59866 • *600*
Saint Regis Falls, NY 12980 • *950*
Saint Rose, LA 70087 • *2,800*
Saint Simons Island, GA 31522 • *6,566*
Saint Stephen, SC 29479 • *1,850*
Saint Tammany □, LA • *110,869*
Saint Thomas, MO 65076 • *337*
Saint Thomas, ND 58276 • *528*
Saint Thomas, PA 17252 • *700*
Saint Wendells, IN 47712 • *500*
Salamanca, NY 14779 • *6,890*
Sale City, GA 31784 • *336*
Sale Creek, TN 37373 • *900*
Salem, AL 36874 • *300*
Salem, AR 72576 • *1,424*
Salem, FL 32356 • *300*
Salem, IL 62881 • *7,813*
Salem, IN 47167 • *5,290*
Salem, IA 52649 • *463*
Salem, KY 42078 • *833*
Salem, MA 01970 • *38,220*
Salem, MI 48175 • *300*
Salem, MO 65560 • *4,454*
Salem, NH 03079 • *11,500*
Salem, NJ 08079 • *6,959*
Salem, NY 12865 • *959*
Salem, OH 44460 • *12,869*
Salem, OR 97301-14 • *89,233*
Salem, SD 57058 • *1,486*
Salem, UT 84653 • *2,233*
Salem, VA 24153 • *23,958*
Salem, WV 26426 • *2,706*
Salem, WI 53168 • *1,000*
Salem □, NJ • *64,676*
Salemburg, NC 28385 • *742*
Salida, CO 81201 • *4,870*
Salina, KS 67401 • *41,843*
Salina, OK 74365 • *1,115*
Salina, UT 84654 • *1,992*
Salinas, CA 93901-15 • *80,479*
Saline, LA 71070 • *293*
Saline, MI 48176 • *6,483*
Saline □, AR • *53,161*
Saline □, IL • *28,448*
Saline □, KS • *48,905*
Saline □, MO • *24,919*
Saline □, NE • *13,131*
Salineno, TX 78585 • *450*
Salineville, OH 43945 • *1,629*
Salisbury, CT 06068 • *900*
Salisbury, MD 21801 • *16,429*
Salisbury, MA 01950 • *3,265*
Salisbury, MO 65281 • *1,975*
Salisbury, NH 03268 • *300*
Salisbury, NC 28144 • *22,677*
Salisbury, PA 15558 • *817*
Salisbury Center, NY 13454 • *300*
Salitpa, AL 36570 • *350*
Salix, IA 51052 • *429*
Salkum, WA 98582 • *300*
Salladasburg, PA 17740 • *273*
Salley, SC 29137 • *584*
Sallisaw, OK 74955 • *6,403*
Salmon, ID 83467 • *3,308*
Salmon Creek, WA 98665 • *1,950*
Salome, AZ 85348 • *600*
Salter Path, NC 28575 • *600*
Salters, SC 29590 • *300*
Saltillo, MS 38866 • *1,271*
Saltillo, PA 17253 • *373*
Saltillo, TN 38370 • *434*
Salt Lake □, UT • *619,066*
Salt Lake City, UT 84101-99 • *163,697*
Salt Lick, KY 40371 • *347*
Salt River, KY 40165 • *400*
Salt Rock, WV 25559 • *900*
Saltsburg, PA 15681 • *964*
Salt Springs, FL 32627 • *1,500*
Saltville, VA 24370 • *2,376*
Saluda, NC 28773 • *607*
Saluda, SC 29138 • *2,752*
Saluda, VA 23149 • *350*
Saluda □, SC • *16,150*
Salvisa, KY 40372 • *300*
Salyer, CA 95563 • *950*
Salyersville, KY 41465 • *1,352*
Samburg, TN 38254 • *465*
Samoa, CA 95564 • *850*
Samoset, FL 33508 • *5,747*
Sampson □, NC • *49,687*
Samson, AL 36477 • *2,402*
Samtown, LA 71301 • *4,125*
Samuels, ID 83862 • *650*
San Andreas, CA 95249 • *1,564*
San Angelo, TX 76901-09 • *73,240*
San Anselmo, CA 94960 • *12,067*
San Antonio, FL 33576 • *529*
San Antonio, TX 78201-99 • *786,023*
San Ardo, CA 93450 • *450*
Sanatorium, MS 39112 • *700*
San Augustine, TX 75972 • *2,930*
San Augustine □, TX • *8,785*
San Benito, TX 78586 • *17,988*
San Benito □, CA • *25,005*
San Bernardino, CA 92401-99 • *118,794*
San Bernardino □, CA • *895,016*
Sanborn, IA 51248 • *1,398*
Sanborn, MN 56083 • *518*
Sanborn, ND 58480 • *237*
Sanborn □, SD • *3,213*
Sanbornville, NH 03872 • *800*
San Bruno, CA 94066 • *35,417*
San Carlos, AZ 85550 • *2,668*
San Carlos, CA 94070 • *24,710*
San Clemente, CA 92672 • *27,325*
Sandborn, IN 47578 • *576*
Sand Coulee, MT 59472 • *250*
Sanders, AZ 86512 • *400*
Sanders, KY 41083 • *332*
Sanders □, MT • *8,675*
Sanderson, TX 79848 • *1,300*
Sandersville, GA 31082 • *6,137*
Sandersville, MS 39477 • *800*
Sandford, IN 47877 • *280*
Sand Fork, WV 26430 • *280*
Sand Hill, MA 02066 • *1,750*
Sandia, TX 78383 • *250*
Sandia Park, NM 87047 • *250*
San Diego, CA 92101-99 • *875,538*
San Diego, TX 78384 • *5,225*
San Diego □, CA • *1,861,846*
San Dimas, CA 91773 • *24,014*
Sand Lake, MI 48748 • *388*
Sandoval, IL 62882 • *1,734*
Sandoval □, NM • *34,799*
Sandown, NH 03873 • *250*
Sand Point, AK 99661 • *625*
Sandpoint, ID 83864 • *4,460*
Sand Springs, OK 74063 • *13,121*
Sandston, VA 23150 • *4,500*
Sandstone, MN 55072 • *1,594*
Sandstone, WV 25985 • *250*
Sandusky, MI 48471 • *2,071*
Sandusky, NY 14133 • *400*
Sandusky, OH 44870 • *31,360*
Sandusky □, OH • *63,267*
Sandwich, IL 60548 • *5,244*
Sandwich, MA 02563 • *1,784*
Sandy, OR 97055 • *2,905*
Sandy, UT 84070 • *52,210*
Sandy Creek, NY 13145 • *765*
Sandy Hook, CT 06482 • *950*
Sandy Hook, KY 41171 • *627*
Sandy Lake, PA 16145 • *779*
Sandy Ridge, AL 36047 • *250*
Sandy Ridge, NC 27046 • *250*
Sandy Ridge, PA 16677 • *500*
Sandy Springs, GA 30328 • *20,300*
Sandy Springs, SC 29677 • *1,100*
Sandyville, MD 21048 • *600*
Sandyville, WV 25275 • *300*
San Elizario, TX 79849 • *1,100*
San Felipe Pueblo, NM 87001 • *1,465*
San Fernando, CA 91340-46 • *17,731*
Sanford, CO 81151 • *687*
Sanford, FL 32771 • *23,176*
Sanford, ME 04073 • *10,268*
Sanford, MI 48657 • *864*
Sanford, NC 27330 • *14,773*
Sanford, TX 79078 • *249*
San Francisco, CA 94101-99 • *678,974*
San Francisco □, CA • *678,974*
San Gabriel, CA 91775-78 • *30,072*
Sangamon □, IL • *176,070*
Sanger, CA 93657 • *12,542*
Sanger, TX 76266 • *2,574*
Sangerville, ME 04479 • *550*
San Gregorio, CA 94074 • *240*
Sanibel, FL 33957 • *3,363*
Sanilac □, MI • *40,789*
San Isidro, TX 78588 • *700*
San Jacinto, CA 92383 • *7,098*
San Jacinto □, TX • *11,434*
San Joaquin □, CA • *347,342*
San Jon, NM 88434 • *341*
San Jose, AZ 85546 • *300*
San Jose, CA 95101-99 • *629,546*

San Jose, IL 62682 • *784*
San Juan, TX 78589 • *7,608*
San Juan □, CO • *833*
San Juan □, NM • *81,433*
San Juan □, UT • *12,253*
San Juan □, WA • *7,838*
San Juan Capistrano, CA 92675 • *18,959*
San Juan Pueblo, NM 87566 • *600*
San Leandro, CA 94577-79 • *63,952*
San Lorenzo, CA 94580 • *20,545*
San Lorenzo, NM 88041 • *230*
San Luis, CO 81152 • *842*
San Luis Obispo, CA 93401 • *34,252*
San Luis Obispo □, CA • *155,435*
San Manuel, AZ 85631 • *5,443*
San Marcos, CA 92069 • *17,479*
San Marcos, TX 78666 • *23,420*
San Marino, CA 91108 • *13,307*
San Mateo, CA 94401-99 • *77,640*
San Mateo, FL 32088 • *950*
San Mateo □, CA • *587,329*
San Miguel, CA 93451 • *800*
San Miguel □, CO • *3,192*
San Miguel □, NM • *22,751*
San Pablo, CA 94806 • *19,750*
San Patricio, NM 88348 • *300*
San Patricio □, TX • *58,013*
San Pedro, TX • *5,294*
Sanpete □, UT • *14,620*
San Pierre, IN 46374 • *300*
San Rafael, CA 94901-15 • *44,700*
San Rafael, NM 87051 • *560*
San Remo, NY 11754 • *8,700*
San Saba, TX 76877 • *2,847*
San Saba □, TX • *6,204*
San Simeon, CA 93452 • *260*
San Simon, AZ 85632 • *400*
Santa Ana, CA 92701-99 • *204,023*
Santa Anna, TX 76878 • *1,535*
Santa Barbara, CA 93101-99 • *74,414*
Santa Barbara □, CA • *298,694*
Santa Clara, CA 95050-55 • *87,700*
Santa Clara, OR 97401 • *11,288*
Santa Clara, UT 84765 • *1,091*
Santa Clara □, CA • *1,295,071*
Santa Clara Pueblo, NM 87532 • *450*
Santa Claus, IN 47579 • *514*
Santa Cruz, CA 95060-66 • *41,483*
Santa Cruz, NM 87567 • *600*
Santa Cruz □, AZ • *20,459*
Santa Cruz □, CA • *188,141*
Santa Fe, NM 87501-09 • *48,953*
Santa Fe, TX 77510 • *6,172*
Santa Fe □, NM • *75,360*
Santa Fe Springs, CA 90670 • *14,520*
Santa Margarita, CA 93453 • *1,200*
Santa Maria, CA 93454-56 • *39,685*
Santa Monica, CA 90401-99 • *88,314*
Santa Paula, CA 93060 • *20,552*
Santaquin, UT 84655 • *2,175*
Santa Rita Park, CA 93661 • *350*
Santa Rosa, CA 95401-07 • *83,320*
Santa Rosa, NM 88435 • *2,469*
Santa Rosa □, FL • *55,988*
Santa Rosa Beach, FL 32459 • *950*
Santa Ynez, CA 93460 • *3,335*
Santee, CA 92071 • *40,313*
Santee, NE 68760 • *388*
Santo, TX 76472 • *500*
Santo Domingo Pueblo, NM 87052 • *2,082*
Santuit, MA 02635 • *400*
San Ygnacio, TX 78067 • *900*
Sappington, MO 63126 • *11,388*
Sapulpa, OK 74066 • *15,853*
Saragosa, TX 79780 • *600*
Saraland, AL 36571 • *9,833*
Saranac, MI 48881 • *1,421*
Saranac, NY 12981 • *300*
Saranac Lake, NY 12983 • *5,578*
Sarasota, FL 33577-83 • *48,868*
Sarasota □, FL • *202,251*
Saratoga, CA 95070 • *29,261*
Saratoga, IN 47382 • *338*
Saratoga, NC 27873 • *381*
Saratoga, TX 77585 • *1,000*
Saratoga, WY 82331 • *2,410*
Saratoga □, NY • *153,759*
Saratoga Springs, NY 12866 • *23,906*
Sarcoxie, MO 64862 • *1,381*
Sardinia, OH 45171 • *826*
Sardis, AL 36775 • *300*
Sardis, GA 30456 • *1,180*
Sardis, MS 38666 • *2,278*
Sardis, OH 43946 • *500*
Sardis, OK 74536 • *253*
Sardis, TN 38371 • *301*
Sarepta, LA 71071 • *831*
Sargent, GA 30275 • *700*
Sargent, NE 68874 • *828*
Sargent □, ND • *5,512*
Sarita, TX 78385 • *250*
Sarpy □, NE • *86,015*
Sartell, MN 56377 • *3,427*
Sasakwa, OK 74867 • *335*
Saspamco, TX 78153 • *300*
Sasser, GA 31785 • *407*
Satanta, KS 67870 • *1,117*
Satellite Beach, FL 32937 • *9,163*
Satsop, WA 98583 • *300*
Satsuma, AL 36572 • *3,822*
Satsuma, FL 32089 • *950*
Saucier, MS 39574 • *250*
Saugatuck, MI 49453 • *1,079*
Saugerties, NY 12477 • *3,882*
Saugus, CA 91350 • *16,283*
Saugus, MA 01906 • *24,746*
Sauk □, WI • *43,469*
Sauk Centre, MN 56378 • *3,709*
Sauk City, WI 53583 • *2,703*
Sauk Rapids, MN 56379 • *5,793*
Sauk Village, IL 60411 • *10,906*
Saukville, WI 53080 • *3,494*
Saunders □, NE • *18,716*
Saunderstown, RI 02874 • *350*
Saunemin, IL 61769 • *463*
Sausalito, CA 94965 • *7,338*
Savage, MD 20763 • *2,928*
Savage, MT 59262 • *300*
Savanna, IL 61074 • *4,529*
Savanna, OK 74565 • *828*
Savannah, GA 31401-99 • *141,390*
Savannah, MO 64485 • *4,184*
Savannah, NY 13146 • *640*
Savannah, OH 44874 • *351*
Savannah, TN 38372 • *6,992*
Savona, NY 14879 • *932*
Savoonga, AK 99769 • *491*
Savoy, IL 61874 • *2,126*
Sawmill, AZ 86504 • *400*
Sawyer, MI 49125 • *550*
Sawyer, ND 58781 • *417*
Sawyer □, WI • *12,843*
Saxapahaw, NC 27340 • *500*
Saxis, VA 23427 • *415*
Saxon, SC • *1,200*
Saxon, WI 54559 • *225*
Saxonburg, PA 16056 • *1,336*
Saxton, PA 16678 • *814*
Saxtons River, VT 05154 • *593*
Saybrook, IL 61770 • *882*
Saybrook Manor, CT 06475 • *1,140*
Saydel, IA 50313 • *4,200*
Saylesville, RI 02865 • *3,200*
Saylorsburg, PA 18353 • *600*
Saylorville, IA 50313 • *780*
Sayner, WI 54560 • *400*
Sayre, AL 35139 • *350*
Sayre, OK 73662 • *3,177*
Sayre, PA 18840 • *6,951*
Sayreton, AL • *550*
Sayreville, NJ 08872 • *29,969*
Sayville, NY 11782 • *15,300*
Scales Mound, IL 61075 • *347*
Scalp Level, PA 15963 • *1,186*
Scaly Mountain, NC 28775 • *300*
Scammon, KS 66773 • *501*
Scammon Bay, AK 99662 • *250*
Scandia, KS 66966 • *480*
Scandinavia, WI 54977 • *292*
Scanlon, MN 55720 • *1,050*
Scantic, CT 06088 • *300*
Scappoose, OR 97056 • *3,213*
Scarborough, ME 04074 • *2,280*
Scarbro, WV 25917 • *400*
Scarsdale, NY 10583 • *17,650*
Schaefferstown, PA 17088 • *800*
Schaghticoke, NY 12154 • *677*
Schaller, IA 51053 • *832*
Schaumburg, IL 60194 • *53,305*
Schell City, MO 64783 • *327*
Schellsburg, PA 15559 • *325*
Schenectady, NY 12301-99 • *67,972*
Schenectady □, NY • *149,946*
Schenevus, NY 12155 • *625*
Schererville, IN 46375 • *13,209*
Schertz, TX 78154 • *7,262*
Schiller Park, IL 60176 • *11,458*
Schlater, MS 38952 • *429*
Schleicher □, TX • *2,820*
Schleswig, IA 51461 • *868*
Schley □, GA • *3,433*
Schneider, IN 46376 • *364*
Schofield, WI 54476 • *2,226*
Schoharie, NY 12157 • *1,016*
Schoharie □, NY • *29,710*
Schoolcraft, MI 49087 • *1,359*
Schoolcraft □, MI • *8,575*
Schram City, IL 62049 • *708*
Schriever, LA 70395 • *500*
Schroeder, MN 55613 • *400*
Schroon Lake, NY 12870 • *1,000*
Schulenburg, TX 78956 • *2,469*
Schulter, OK 74460 • *300*
Schurz, NV 89427 • *325*
Schuyler, NE 68661 • *4,151*
Schuyler, VA 22969 • *250*
Schuyler □, IL • *8,365*
Schuyler □, MO • *4,979*
Schuyler □, NY • *17,686*
Schuyler Lake, NY 13457 • *300*
Schuylerville, NY 12871 • *1,256*
Schuylkill □, PA • *160,630*
Schuylkill Haven, PA 17972 • *5,977*
Science Hill, KY 42553 • *655*
Scio, NY 14880 • *600*
Scio, OH 43988 • *1,003*
Scio, OR 97374 • *579*
Scioto □, OH • *84,545*
Scioto Furnace, OH 45677 • *400*
Scipio, UT 84656 • *257*
Scituate, MA 02066 • *5,351*
Scobey, MT 59263 • *1,382*
Scooba, MS 39358 • *511*
Scotch Plains, NJ 07076 • *20,774*
Scotia, CA 95565 • *1,200*
Scotia, NE 68875 • *349*
Scotia, NY 12302 • *7,280*
Scotland, PA 17254 • *600*
Scotland, SD 57059 • *1,022*
Scotland □, MO • *5,415*
Scotland □, NC • *32,273*
Scotland Neck, NC 27874 • *2,834*
Scotlandville, LA 70807 • *15,113*
Scotrun, PA 18355 • *225*
Scott, LA 70583 • *2,239*
Scott, MS 38772 • *320*
Scott, OH 45886 • *340*
Scott □, AR • *9,685*
Scott □, IL • *6,142*
Scott □, IN • *20,422*
Scott □, IA • *160,022*
Scott □, KS • *5,782*
Scott □, KY • *21,813*
Scott □, MN • *43,784*
Scott □, MS • *24,556*
Scott □, MO • *39,647*
Scott □, TN • *19,259*
Scott □, VA • *25,068*
Scott City, KS 67871 • *4,154*
Scott City, MO 63780 • *4,630*
Scottdale, GA 30079 • *8,777*
Scottdale, PA 15683 • *5,833*
Scotts, MI 49088 • *300*
Scottsbluff, NE 69361 • *14,156*
Scotts Bluff □, NE • *38,344*
Scottsboro, AL 35768 • *14,758*
Scottsburg, IN 47170 • *5,068*
Scottsburg, VA 24589 • *335*
Scottsdale, AZ 85251-69 • *88,622*
Scotts Hill, TN 38374 • *668*
Scotts Mills, OR 97375 • *249*
Scotts Valley, CA 95066 • *6,891*
Scottsville, KY 42164 • *4,278*
Scottsville, NY 14546 • *1,789*
Scottsville, VA 24590 • *250*
Scott Township, PA 15106 • *20,413*
Scottville, MI 49454 • *1,241*
Scow Bay, AK 99833 • *250*
Scranton, AR 72863 • *244*
Scranton, IA 51462 • *748*
Scranton, KS 66537 • *664*
Scranton, ND 58653 • *415*
Scranton, PA 18501-99 • *88,117*
Scranton, SC 29591 • *861*
Screven, GA 31560 • *872*
Screven □, GA • *14,043*
Scribner, NE 68057 • *1,011*
Scullville, NJ 08330 • *350*
Scurry □, TX • *18,192*
Seaboard, NC 27876 • *687*
Seabreeze, DE 19971 • *350*
Sea Bright, NJ 07760 • *1,812*
Seabrook, MD 20706 • *7,100*
Seabrook, NH 03874 • *700*
Seabrook, NJ 08302 • *1,411*
Seabrook, TX 77586 • *4,670*
Seabrook Beach, NH 03874 • *600*
Sea Cliff, NY 11579 • *5,364*
Seadrift, TX 77983 • *1,277*
Seaford, DE 19973 • *5,256*
Seaford, NY 11783 • *17,150*
Seaford, VA 23696 • *1,700*
Sea Girt, NJ 08750 • *2,650*
Seagoville, TX 75159 • *7,304*
Seagraves, TX 79359 • *2,596*
Seagrove, NC 27341 • *294*
Sea Isle City, NJ 08243 • *2,644*
Seal Beach, CA 90740 • *25,975*
Seale, AL 36875 • *350*
Seal Harbor, ME 04675 • *300*
Seal Rock, OR 97376 • *800*
Sealy, TX 77474 • *3,875*
Seaman, OH 45679 • *1,039*
Seanor, PA 15953 • *300*
Searchlight, NV 89046 • *300*
Searcy, AR 72143 • *13,612*
Searcy □, AR • *8,847*
Searsport, ME 04974 • *1,348*
Seaside, CA 93955 • *36,567*
Seaside, OR 97138 • *5,193*
Seaside Heights, NJ 08751 • *1,802*
Seaside Park, NJ 08752 • *1,795*
Seaton, IL 61476 • *255*
Seat Pleasant, MD 20743 • *5,217*
Seattle, WA 98101-99 • *493,846*
Seaview, WA 98644 • *500*
Seaville, NJ 08230 • *250*
Sebago Lake, ME 04075 • *600*
Sebastian, FL 32958 • *2,831*
Sebastian □, AR • *95,172*
Sebastopol, CA 95472 • *5,595*
Sebastopol, MS 39359 • *314*
Sebeka, MN 56477 • *774*
Sebewaing, MI 48759 • *2,046*
Sebree, KY 42455 • *1,516*
Sebring, FL 33870 • *8,736*
Sebring, OH 44672 • *5,078*
Secaucus, NJ 07094 • *13,719*
Secor, IL 61771 • *488*
Secretary, MD 21664 • *487*
Section, AL 35771 • *821*
Security, CO 80911 • *11,000*
Sedalia, CO 80135 • *250*
Sedalia, KY 42079 • *300*
Sedalia, MO 65301 • *20,927*
Sedalia, OH 43151 • *339*
Sedan, KS 67361 • *1,579*
Sedgwick, CO 80749 • *258*
Sedgwick, KS 67135 • *1,471*
Sedgwick □, CO • *3,266*
Sedgwick □, KS • *367,088*
Sedley, VA 23878 • *400*
Sedona, AZ 86336 • *5,368*
Sedro Woolley, WA 98284 • *6,110*
Seekonk, MA 02771 • *12,269*
Seeley, CA 92273 • *1,058*
Seeley Lake, MT 59868 • *800*
Seelyville, IN 47878 • *1,374*
Seelyville, PA 18431 • *400*
Seguin, TX 78155 • *17,854*
Seiling, OK 73663 • *1,103*
Sekiu, WA 98381 • *600*
Selah, WA 98942 • *4,500*
Selawik, AK 99770 • *361*
Selby, SD 57472 • *884*
Selbyville, DE 19975 • *1,251*
Selden, KS 67757 • *266*
Selden, NY 11784 • *24,100*
Seldovia, AK 99663 • *479*
Selfridge, ND 58568 • *273*
Seligman, AZ 86337 • *950*
Seligman, MO 65745 • *508*
Selinsgrove, PA 17870 • *5,227*
Sellers, SC 29592 • *388*
Sellersburg, IN 47172 • *3,211*
Sellersville, PA 18960 • *3,143*
Sells, AZ 85634 • *1,864*
Selma, AL 36701 • *26,684*
Selma, CA 93662 • *10,942*
Selma, IN 47383 • *1,056*
Selma, NC 27576 • *4,762*
Selmer, TN 38375 • *3,979*
Seminary, MS 39479 • *327*
Seminole, AL 36567 • *250*
Seminole, OK 74868 • *8,590*
Seminole, TX 79360 • *6,080*
Seminole □, FL • *179,752*
Seminole □, GA • *9,057*
Seminole □, OK • *27,473*
Seminole Park, FL 33540 • *8,000*
Semmes, AL 36575 • *1,200*
Senath, MO 63876 • *1,728*
Senatobia, MS 38668 • *5,013*
Seneca, IL 61360 • *2,098*
Seneca, KS 66538 • *2,389*
Seneca, MO 64865 • *1,853*
Seneca, OR 97873 • *285*
Seneca, PA 16346 • *980*
Seneca, SC 29678 • *7,436*
Seneca, WI 54654 • *225*
Seneca □, NY • *33,733*
Seneca □, OH • *61,901*
Seneca Falls, NY 13148 • *7,466*

Senecaville, OH 43780 • 458
Seney, MI 49883 • 230
Senoia, GA 30276 • 900
Sentinel, OK 73664 • 1,016
Sequatchie, TN 37374 • 400
Sequatchie □, TN • 8,605
Sequim, WA 98382 • 3,013
Sequoyah □, OK • 30,749
Sergeant Bluff, IA 51054 • 2,416
Sergeantsville, NJ 08557 • 240
Sesser, IL 62884 • 2,238
Seth, WV 25181 • 650
Seven Hills, OH 44131 • 13,650
Seven Mile, OH 45062 • 841
Severance, NH 03105 • 300
Severn, MD 21144 • 20,147
Severn, NC 27877 • 309
Severna Park, MD 21146 • 21,253
Severy, KS 67137 • 54,800
Sevier □, AR • 14,060
Sevier □, TN • 41,418
Sevier □, UT • 14,727
Sevierville, TN 37862 • 4,556
Seville, FL 32090 • 800
Seville, OH 44273 • 1,568
Sewanee, TN 37375 • 2,218
Seward, AK 99664 • 1,843
Seward, NE 68434 • 5,713
Seward, PA 15954 • 675
Seward □, KS • 17,071
Seward □, NE • 15,789
Sewaren, NJ 07077 • 2,300
Sewell, NJ 08080 • 1,900
Sewickley, PA 15143 • 4,778
Sextonville, WI 53584 • 250
Seymour, CT 06483 • 13,434
Seymour, IL 61875 • 450
Seymour, IN 47274 • 15,050
Seymour, IA 52590 • 1,036
Seymour, MO 65746 • 1,535
Seymour, TN 37865 • 250
Seymour, TX 76380 • 3,657
Seymour, WI 54165 • 2,530
Seymourville, LA 70764 • 2,891
Shabbona, IL 60550 • 851
Shackelford □, TX • 3,915
Shady Cove, OR 97539 • 1,097
Shady Grove, PA 17256 • 500
Shady Point, OK 74956 • 235
Shady Rest, CT 06482 • 250
Shady Side, MD 20764 • 2,877
Shadyside, OH 43947 • 4,315
Shady Spring, WV 25918 • 1,000
Shafter, CA 93263 • 7,010
Shaftsbury, VT 05262 • 700
Shaker Heights, OH 44122 • 32,487
Shakopee, MN 55379 • 9,941
Shallotte, NC 28459 • 680
Shallowater, TX 79363 • 1,932
Shamokin, PA 17872 • 10,357
Shamokin Dam, PA 17876 • 1,622
Shamrock, FL 32628 • 250
Shamrock, TX 79079 • 2,834
Shandaken, NY 12480 • 500
Shandon, CA 93461 • 800
Shannock, RI 02875 • 600
Shannon, GA 30172 • 2,040
Shannon, IL 61078 • 938
Shannon, MS 38868 • 680
Shannon □, MO • 7,885
Shannon □, SD • 11,323
Shannontown, SC 29150 • 7,900
Shapleigh, ME 04076 • 235
Sharkey □, MS • 7,964
Sharon, CT 06069 • 900
Sharon, KS 67138 • 283
Sharon, MA 02067 • 13,601
Sharon, PA 16146 • 19,057
Sharon, SC 29742 • 323
Sharon, TN 38255 • 1,134
Sharon, WV 25182 • 400
Sharon, WI 53585 • 1,280
Sharon Grove, KY 42280 • 250
Sharon Hill, PA 19079 • 6,221
Sharon Park, OH 45011 • 600
Sharon Springs, KS 67758 • 982
Sharon Springs, NY 13459 • 514
Sharonville, OH 45241 • 10,108
Sharp □, AR • 14,607
Sharpes, FL 32959 • 1,250
Sharples, WV 25183 • 500
Sharpley, DE 19803 • 1,700
Sharpsburg, KY 40374 • 339
Sharpsburg, MD 21782 • 721
Sharpsburg, NC 27878 • 997
Sharpsburg, PA 15215 • 4,351
Sharpsville, IN 46068 • 617
Sharpsville, PA 16150 • 5,375
Sharptown, MD 21861 • 654
Sharptown, NJ 08098 • 250

Shasta □, CA • 115,715
Shattuck, OK 73858 • 1,759
Shaw, MS 38773 • 2,461
Shawano, WI 54166 • 7,013
Shawano □, WI • 35,928
Shawboro, NC 27973 • 350
Shawmut, AL 36854 • 2,284
Shawnee, KS 66203 • 29,653
Shawnee, OH 43782 • 924
Shawnee, OK 74801 • 26,506
Shawnee □, KS • 154,916
Shawnee Hills, OH 43065 • 430
Shawneetown, IL 62984 • 1,841
Shawsville, VA 24162 • 400
Sheboygan, WI 53081 • 48,085
Sheboygan □, WI • 100,935
Sheboygan Falls, WI 53085 • 5,253
Sheffield, AL 35660-62 • 11,903
Sheffield, IL 61361 • 1,130
Sheffield, IA 50475 • 1,224
Sheffield, MA 01257 • 1,100
Sheffield, PA 16347 • 1,564
Sheffield, TX 79781 • 450
Sheffield Lake, OH 44054 • 10,484
Shelbiana, KY 41562 • 500
Shelbina, MO 63468 • 2,169
Shelburn, IN 47879 • 1,259
Shelburne, VT 05482 • 300
Shelburne Falls, MA 01370 • 2,046
Shelby, AL 35143 • 600
Shelby, IN 46377 • 700
Shelby, IA 51570 • 665
Shelby, MI 49455 • 1,624
Shelby, MS 38774 • 2,540
Shelby, MT 59474 • 3,142
Shelby, NE 68662 • 724
Shelby, NC 28150 • 15,310
Shelby, OH 44875 • 9,646
Shelby □, AL • 66,298
Shelby □, IL • 23,923
Shelby □, IN • 39,887
Shelby □, IA • 15,043
Shelby □, KY • 23,328
Shelby □, MO • 7,826
Shelby □, OH • 43,089
Shelby □, TN • 777,113
Shelby □, TX • 23,084
Shelby City, KY 40422 • 700
Shelbyville, IL 62565 • 5,259
Shelbyville, IN 46176 • 14,989
Shelbyville, KY 40065 • 5,329
Shelbyville, MO 63469 • 645
Shelbyville, TN 37160 • 13,530
Sheldahl, IA 50243 • 315
Sheldon, IL 60966 • 1,215
Sheldon, IA 51201 • 5,003
Sheldon, MO 64784 • 491
Sheldon, TX 77028 • 2,800
Sheldon, WI 54766 • 292
Sheldon Springs, VT 05485 • 300
Sheldonville, MA 02070 • 250
Shell Creek, TN 37687 • 400
Shelley, ID 83274 • 3,300
Shell Lake, WI 54871 • 1,135
Shellman, GA 31786 • 1,254
Shellman Bluff, GA 31331 • 250
Shell Rock, IA 50670 • 1,478
Shellsburg, IA 52332 • 771
Shelly, MN 56581 • 276
Shelter Island, NY 11964 • 1,000
Shelton, CT 06484 • 31,314
Shelton, NE 68876 • 1,046
Shelton, WA 98584 • 7,629
Shenandoah, IA 51601 • 6,274
Shenandoah, PA 17976 • 7,589
Shenandoah, VA 22849 • 1,861
Shenandoah □, VA • 27,559
Shepardsville, IN 47880 • 350
Shepherd, MI 48883 • 1,534
Shepherd, TX 77371 • 1,674
Shepherdstown, WV 25443 • 1,791
Shepherdsville, KY 40165 • 4,454
Sheppton, PA 18248 • 650
Sherborn, MA 01770 • 950
Sherburn, MN 56171 • 1,275
Sherburne, NY 13460 • 1,561
Sherburne □, MN • 29,908
Sheridan, AR 72150 • 3,042
Sheridan, CO 80110 • 5,377
Sheridan, IL 60551 • 719
Sheridan, IN 46069 • 2,200
Sheridan, MI 48884 • 664
Sheridan, MT 59749 • 646
Sheridan, OR 97378 • 2,249
Sheridan, WY 82801 • 15,146
Sheridan □, KS • 3,544
Sheridan □, MT • 5,414
Sheridan □, NE • 7,544
Sheridan □, ND • 2,819
Sheridan □, WY • 25,048

Sherman, MS 38869 • 499
Sherman, NY 14781 • 775
Sherman, TX 75090 • 30,413
Sherman □, KS • 7,759
Sherman □, NE • 4,226
Sherman □, OR • 2,172
Sherman □, TX • 3,174
Sherman Mills, ME 04776 • 450
Sherman Station, ME 04777 • 425
Sherrard, IL 61281 • 811
Sherrelwood, CO 80221 • 11,450
Sherrill, NY 13461 • 2,830
Sherrodsville, OH 44675 • 396
Sherwood, AR 72116 • 10,406
Sherwood, ND 58782 • 294
Sherwood, OH 43556 • 915
Sherwood, OR 97140 • 2,386
Sherwood, TN 37376 • 450
Sherwood, WI 54169 • 372
Sherwood Manor, CT 06082 • 6,303
Sherwood Park, DE 19808 • 2,300
Sheyenne, ND 58374 • 307
Shiawassee □, MI • 71,140
Shickley, NE 68436 • 413
Shickshinny, PA 18655 • 1,192
Shideler, IN 47338 • 250
Shidler, OK 74652 • 708
Shillington, PA 19607 • 5,601
Shiloh, GA 31826 • 392
Shiloh, NJ 08353 • 604
Shiloh, OH 44878 • 857
Shiner, TX 77984 • 2,213
Shinglehouse, PA 16748 • 1,310
Shingleton, MI 49884 • 300
Shinnston, WV 26431 • 3,059
Shiocton, WI 54170 • 805
Ship Bottom, NJ 08008 • 1,427
Shipman, IL 62685 • 581
Shippensburg, PA 17257 • 5,261
Shippenville, PA 16254 • 558
Shiprock, NM 87420 • 7,237
Shipshewana, IN 46565 • 466
Shirley, AR 72153 • 354
Shirley, IN 47384 • 919
Shirley, MA 01464 • 1,630
Shirley, NY 11967 • 8,200
Shirley Basin, WY 82615 • 450
Shishmaref, AK 99772 • 394
Shively, KY 40216 • 16,819
Shoals, IN 47581 • 967
Shoemakersville, PA 19555 • 1,391
Shongopovi, AZ 86043 • 300
Shonto, AZ 86054 • 600
Shore Acres, MA 02066 • 1,200
Shore Acres, NJ 08723 • 1,300
Shoreham, MI 49085 • 742
Shoreview, MN 55112 • 17,300
Shorewood, IL 60435 • 4,714
Shorewood, MN 55331 • 4,646
Shorewood, WI 53211 • 14,327
Shorewood Hills, WI 53705 • 1,837
Short Beach, CT 06405 • 1,200
Shorterville, AL 36373 • 275
Shortsville, NY 14548 • 1,669
Shoshone, CA 92384 • 250
Shoshone, ID 83352 • 1,242
Shoshone □, ID • 19,226
Shoshoni, WY 82649 • 879
Shouns, TN 37683 • 250
Showell, MD 21862 • 250
Show Low, AZ 85901 • 4,298
Shreve, OH 44676 • 1,608
Shreveport, LA 71101-10 • 205,820
Shrewsbury, MA 01545 • 22,674
Shrewsbury, MO 63119 • 5,077
Shrewsbury, NJ 07701 • 2,962
Shrewsbury, PA 17361 • 2,688
Shubert, NE 68437 • 267
Shubuta, MS 39360 • 626
Shulerville, SC 29480 • 300
Shullsburg, WI 53586 • 1,484
Shumway, IL 62461 • 278
Shuqualak, MS 39361 • 554
Shushan, NY 12873 • 300
Shutesbury, MA 01072 • 300
Siasconset, MA 02564 • 225
Sibert, KY 40962 • 300
Sibley, IL 61773 • 370
Sibley, IA 51249 • 3,051
Sibley, LA 71073 • 1,211
Sibley, MO 64088 • 382
Sibley □, MN • 15,448
Sichomovi, AZ 86042 • 350
Sicily Island, LA 71368 • 691
Sicklerville, NJ 08081 • 850
Sidell, IL 61876 • 625
Sidnaw, MI 49961 • 300
Sidney, AR 72577 • 270
Sidney, IL 61877 • 886
Sidney, IA 51652 • 1,308

Sidney, MT 59270 • 5,726
Sidney, NE 69162 • 6,010
Sidney, NY 13838 • 4,861
Sidney, OH 45365 • 17,657
Sidney Center, NY 13839 • 600
Sidon, MS 38954 • 450
Siegle, LA 71291 • 1,400
Sierra □, CA • 3,073
Sierra □, NM • 8,454
Sierra Blanca, TX 79851 • 900
Sierra City, CA 96125 • 800
Sierra Madre, CA 91024 • 10,837
Sierraville, CA 96126 • 390
Sierra Vista, AZ 85635 • 24,937
Sigel, IL 62462 • 360
Sigel, PA 15860 • 330
Signal Hill, CA 90806 • 5,734
Signal Mountain, TN 37377 • 5,818
Sigourney, IA 52591 • 2,330
Sigurd, UT 84657 • 386
Sikes, LA 71473 • 226
Sikeston, MO 63801 • 17,431
Silas, AL 36919 • 343
Siler City, NC 27344 • 4,446
Siletz, OR 97380 • 1,001
Silex, MO 63377 • 287
Siloam, GA 30665 • 446
Siloam Springs, AR 72761 • 7,940
Silsbee, TX 77656 • 7,684
Silt, CO 81652 • 923
Silver Bay, MN 55614 • 2,917
Silver Bell, AZ 85270 • 600
Silver Bow □, MT • 38,092
Silver City, IA 51571 • 291
Silver City, MS 39166 • 378
Silver City, NM 88061 • 9,887
Silver Cliff, CO 81249 • 280
Silver Creek, GA 30173 • 400
Silver Creek, MS 39663 • 272
Silver Creek, NE 68663 • 496
Silver Creek, NY 14136 • 3,088
Silverdale, WA 98383 • 1,500
Silver Grove, KY 41085 • 1,260
Silverhill, AL 36576 • 624
Silver Hill, MD 20746 • 2,400
Silver Lake, IN 46982 • 576
Silver Lake, KS 66539 • 1,350
Silver Lake, MA 01887 • 3,400
Silver Lake, MN 55381 • 698
Silver Lake, NH 03875 • 300
Silver Lake, WI 53170 • 1,598
Silver Spring, MD 20901-99 • 64,100
Silver Springs, FL 32688 • 1,082
Silver Springs, NV 89429 • 300
Silver Springs, NY 14550 • 801
Silverton, CO 81433 • 794
Silverton, ID 83867 • 750
Silverton, NJ 08753 • 7,236
Silverton, OH 45236 • 6,172
Silverton, OR 97381 • 5,168
Silverton, TX 79257 • 918
Silview, DE 19804 • 1,650
Silvis, IL 61282 • 7,130
Simi Valley, CA 93065 • 77,500
Simla, CO 80835 • 494
Simmesport, LA 71369 • 2,293
Simms, MT 59477 • 300
Simpson, LA 71474 • 534
Simpson, NC 27879 • 407
Simpson, PA 18407 • 2,200
Simpson, WV 26435 • 250
Simpson □, KY • 14,673
Simpson □, MS • 23,441
Simpsonville, KY 40067 • 642
Simpsonville, SC 29681 • 9,037
Sims, IL 62886 • 355
Sims, IN 46983 • 250
Simsboro, LA 71275 • 553
Simsbury, CT 06070 • 5,488
Sinclair, ME 04779 • 370
Sinclair, WY 82334 • 586
Sinclairville, NY 14782 • 772
Sinking Spring, OH 45172 • 239
Sinnamahoning, PA 15861 • 400
Sinton, TX 78387 • 6,044
Sioux □, IA • 30,813
Sioux □, NE • 1,845
Sioux □, ND • 3,620
Sioux Center, IA 51250 • 4,588
Sioux City, IA 51101-11 • 82,003
Sioux Falls, SD 57101-99 • 81,343
Sioux Rapids, IA 50585 • 897
Sipsey, AL 35584 • 678
Siren, WI 54872 • 896
Siskiyou □, CA • 39,732
Sisseton, SD 57262 • 2,789
Sissonville, WV 25320 • 500
Sister Bay, WI 54234 • 564
Sisters, OR 97759 • 696
Sistersville, WV 26175 • 2,367

Sitka, AK 99835 • *7,803*
Six Mile, SC 29682 • *470*
Skagit □, WA • *64,138*
Skagway, AK 99840 • *768*
Skamania □, WA • *7,919*
Skamokawa, WA 98647 • *250*
Skaneateles, NY 13152 • *2,789*
Skellytown, TX 79080 • *899*
Skene, MS 38775 • *300*
Skiatook, OK 74070 • *3,596*
Skidmore, MO 64487 • *437*
Skidmore, TX 78389 • *800*
Skokie, IL 60076-77 • *60,278*
Skowhegan, ME 04976 • *6,517*
Skull Valley, AZ 86338 • *300*
Skyland, NV 89448 • *500*
Skyland, NC 28776 • *2,200*
Skyway, CO 80906 • *3,600*
Skyway, WA 98178 • *12,500*
Slackwood, NJ 08638 • *8,100*
Slater, IA 50244 • *1,312*
Slater, MO 65349 • *2,492*
Slater, SC 29683 • *1,000*
Slatersville, RI 02876 • *2,000*
Slatington, PA 18080 • *4,277*
Slaton, TX 79364 • *6,804*
Slaughter, LA 70777 • *729*
Slaughters, KY 42456 • *269*
Slayton, MN 56172 • *2,420*
Sledge, MS 38670 • *699*
Sleepy Eye, MN 56085 • *3,581*
Slemp, KY 41763 • *250*
Slickville, PA 15684 • *1,066*
Slidell, LA 70458-61 • *26,718*
Sligo, PA 16255 • *798*
Slinger, WI 53086 • *1,612*
Slippery Rock, PA 16057 • *3,047*
Sloan, IA 51055 • *978*
Sloan, NY 14225 • *4,529*
Sloatsburg, NY 10974 • *3,154*
Slocomb, AL 36375 • *2,153*
Slope □, ND • *1,157*
Slovan, PA 15078 • *900*
Smackover, AR 71762 • *2,453*
Smartt, TN 37378 • *250*
Smelterville, ID 83868 • *776*
Smethport, PA 16749 • *1,797*
Smiley, TX 78159 • *439*
Smith □, KS • *5,947*
Smith □, MS • *15,077*
Smith □, TN • *14,935*
Smith □, TX • *128,366*
Smithboro, IL 62284 • *236*
Smith Center, KS 66967 • *2,240*
Smithers, WV 25186 • *1,482*
Smithfield, IL 61477 • *340*
Smithfield, NC 27577 • *7,288*
Smithfield, OH 43948 • *1,308*
Smithfield, PA 15478 • *1,084*
Smithfield, UT 84335 • *4,993*
Smithfield, VA 23430 • *3,718*
Smithfield, WV 26437 • *278*
Smithland, IA 51056 • *282*
Smithland, KY 42081 • *512*
Smithmill, PA 16680 • *600*
Smith Mills, KY 42457 • *420*
Smith River, CA 95567 • *1,000*
Smiths, AL 36877 • *900*
Smithsburg, MD 21783 • *833*
Smiths Grove, KY 42171 • *767*
Smithton, IL 62285 • *1,447*
Smithton, MO 65350 • *559*
Smith Town, KY 42647 • *250*
Smithtown, NY 11787 • *23,000*
Smithville, GA 31787 • *867*
Smithville, IN 47458 • *300*
Smithville, MS 38870 • *866*
Smithville, MO 64089 • *1,873*
Smithville, OH 44677 • *1,467*
Smithville, TN 37166 • *3,839*
Smithville, TX 78957 • *3,470*
Smithville Flats, NY 13841 • *350*
Smyrna, DE 19977 • *4,750*
Smyrna, GA 30080 • *20,312*
Smyrna, NY 13464 • *225*
Smyrna, TN 37167 • *8,839*
Smyrna Mills, ME 04780 • *250*
Smyth □, VA • *33,366*
Sneads, FL 32460 • *1,690*
Sneads Ferry, NC 28460 • *600*
Sneedville, TN 37869 • *1,110*
Snellville, GA 30278 • *8,514*
Snohomish, WA 98290 • *5,294*
Snohomish □, WA • *337,720*
Snoqualmie, WA 98065 • *1,370*
Snover, MI 48472 • *300*
Snowflake, AZ 85937 • *3,510*
Snow Hill, MD 21863 • *2,192*
Snow Hill, NC 28580 • *1,374*
Snow Shoe, PA 16874 • *852*
Snowville, UT 84336 • *237*
Snyder, NE 68664 • *387*
Snyder, OK 73566 • *1,848*
Snyder, TX 79549 • *12,705*
Snyder □, PA • *33,584*
Soap Lake, WA 98851 • *1,196*
Socastee, SC 29577 • *1,082*
Social Circle, GA 30279 • *2,591*
Society Hill, SC 29593 • *848*
Socorro, NM 87801 • *7,173*
Socorro □, NM • *12,566*
Soda Springs, ID 83276 • *4,051*
Soddy-Daisy, TN 37379 • *8,388*
Sodus, NY 14551 • *1,790*
Sodus Point, NY 14555 • *1,334*
Solana, FL 33950 • *1,408*
Solana Beach, CA 92075 • *13,047*
Solano □, CA • *235,203*
Soldier, IA 51572 • *257*
Soldier, KY 41173 • *240*
Soldiers Grove, WI 54655 • *622*
Soldotna, AK 99669 • *2,320*
Soledad, CA 93960 • *5,928*
Solomon, AZ 85551 • *350*
Solomon, KS 67480 • *1,018*
Solomons, MD 20688 • *500*
Solon, IA 52333 • *969*
Solon, ME 04979 • *350*
Solon, OH 44139 • *14,341*
Solon Springs, WI 54873 • *590*
Solvay, NY 13209 • *7,140*
Somerdale, NJ 08083 • *5,900*
Somers, CT 06071 • *1,643*
Somers, MT 59932 • *800*
Somers, WI 53171 • *400*
Somerset, IN 46984 • *300*
Somerset, KY 42501 • *10,649*
Somerset, MA 02725 • *18,813*
Somerset, NJ 08873 • *21,731*
Somerset, OH 43783 • *1,432*
Somerset, PA 15501 • *6,474*
Somerset, TX 78069 • *1,102*
Somerset, WI 54025 • *860*
Somerset □, ME • *45,046*
Somerset □, MD • *19,188*
Somerset □, NJ • *203,129*
Somerset □, PA • *81,243*
Somers Point, NJ 08244 • *10,330*
Somersville, CT 06072 • *750*
Somersworth, NH 03878 • *10,350*
Somerton, AZ 85350 • *5,761*
Somervell □, TX • *4,154*
Somerville, IN 47683 • *340*
Somerville, MA 02143 • *77,372*
Somerville, NJ 08876 • *11,973*
Somerville, OH 45064 • *357*
Somerville, TN 38068 • *2,264*
Somerville, TX 77879 • *1,814*
Somonauk, IL 60552 • *1,344*
Sondheimer, LA 71276 • *290*
Sonoma, CA 95476 • *6,054*
Sonoma □, CA • *299,681*
Sonora, CA 95370 • *3,247*
Sonora, KY 42776 • *416*
Sonora, TX 76950 • *3,856*
Sonyea, NY 14556 • *250*
Sopchoppy, FL 32358 • *444*
Soper, OK 74759 • *465*
Soperton, GA 30457 • *2,981*
Sophia, NC 27350 • *300*
Sophia, WV 25921 • *1,216*
Soquel, CA 95073 • *6,212*
Sorento, IL 62086 • *677*
Sorrento, FL 32776 • *950*
Sorrento, LA 70778 • *1,197*
Soso, MS 39480 • *434*
Soudan, MN 55782 • *950*
Souderton, PA 18964 • *6,657*
Sound Beach, NY 11789 • *5,400*
Sourlake, TX 77659 • *1,807*
South Acton, MA 01720 • *4,600*
South Amboy, NJ 08879 • *8,322*
South Amherst, MA 01002 • *4,861*
South Amherst, OH 44001 • *1,848*
Southampton, MA 01073 • *500*
Southampton, NY 11968 • *4,000*
Southampton, PA 18966 • *9,500*
Southampton □, VA • *18,731*
South Ashburnham, MA 01466 • *1,123*
Southaven, MS 38671 • *16,071*
South Barre, MA 01074 • *600*
South Barre, VT 05670 • *1,301*
South Bay, FL 33493 • *3,886*
Southbeach, OR 97366 • *300*
South Belmar, NJ 07719 • *1,566*
South Beloit, IL 61080 • *4,088*
South Bend, IN 46601-99 • *109,727*
South Bend, WA 98586 • *1,686*
South Berwick, ME 03908 • *2,120*
South Bethlehem, NY 12161 • *500*
South Bloomfield, OH 43103 • *934*
Southborough, MA 01772 • *1,600*
South Boston, VA 24592 • *7,093*
South Bound Brook, NJ 08880 • *4,331*
Southbridge, MA 01550 • *16,665*
South Bristol, ME 04568 • *600*
South Britain, CT 06487 • *350*
South Broadway, WA 98902 • *3,620*
South Burlington, VT 05401 • *10,679*
Southbury, CT 06488 • *900*
South Byron, NY 14557 • *300*
South Carver, MA 02366 • *600*
South Charleston, OH 45368 • *1,682*
South Charleston, WV 25303 • *15,968*
South Chatham, MA 02659 • *950*
South Chicago Heights, IL 60411 • *3,932*
South China, ME 04358 • *300*
South Cle Elum, WA 98943 • *449*
South Coffeyville, OK 74072 • *873*
South Colby, WA 98384 • *500*
South Colton, NY 13687 • *350*
South Congaree, SC 29169 • *2,113*
South Connellsville, PA 15425 • *2,296*
South Corning, NY 14830 • *1,195*
South Dartmouth, MA 02748 • *7,000*
South Dayton, NY 14138 • *661*
South Daytona, FL 32021 • *11,252*
South Decatur, GA 30037 • *28,100*
South Deerfield, MA 01373 • *1,926*
South Dennis, MA 02660 • *1,500*
South Dennis, NJ 08245 • *250*
South Dos Palos, CA 93665 • *850*
South Duxbury, MA 02332 • *2,985*
South Easton, MA 02375 • *1,400*
South Egremont, MA 01258 • *600*
South Elgin, IL 60177 • *5,970*
South El Monte, CA 91733 • *16,623*
Southern Pines, NC 28387 • *8,620*
South Euclid, OH 44121 • *25,713*
South Fallsburg, NY 12779 • *1,590*
South Farmingdale, NY 11735 • *20,500*
Southfield, MA 01259 • *250*
Southfield, MI 48034 • *75,568*
South Fork, CO 81154 • *250*
South Fork, PA 15956 • *1,401*
South Freeport, ME 04078 • *400*
South Fulton, TN 38257 • *2,735*
South Gastonia, NC 28052 • *2,000*
South Gate, CA 90280 • *66,784*
Southgate, KY 41071 • *2,833*
Southgate, MI 48195 • *32,058*
South Glastonbury, CT 06073 • *1,600*
Southglenn, CO 80122 • *3,800*
South Glens Falls, NY 12801 • *3,714*
South Grafton, MA 01560 • *3,000*
South Hackensack, NJ 07606 • *2,229*
South Hadley, MA 01075 • *8,900*
South Hadley Falls, MA 01075 • *5,600*
South Hamilton, MA 01982 • *2,900*
South Hanover, MA 02339 • *950*
South Harwich, MA 02661 • *900*
South Haven, IN 46383 • *6,679*
South Haven, KS 67140 • *439*
South Haven, MI 49090 • *5,943*
South Heart, ND 58655 • *294*
South Hero, VT 05486 • *300*
South Hill, VA 23970 • *4,347*
South Hingham, MA 02043 • *5,200*
South Holland, IL 60473 • *24,977*
South Hooksett, NH 03106 • *1,200*
South Hopkinton, RI 02808 • *500*
South Houston, TX 77587 • *13,293*
South Huntington, NY 11746 • *9,115*
South Hutchinson, KS 67505 • *2,226*
Southington, CT 06489 • *17,400*
South International Falls, MN 56679 • *2,806*
South Jacksonville, IL 62650 • *3,382*
South Jordan, UT 84065 • *7,492*
South Kenosha, WI 53140 • *875*
South Lake Tahoe, CA 95705 • *20,681*
South Lancaster, MA 01561 • *2,329*
South Laramie, WY 82070 • *1,500*
South Laurel, MD 20707 • *8,500*
South Lebanon, ME 04027 • *400*
South Lebanon, OH 45065 • *2,700*
South Lee, MA 01260 • *500*
South Londonderry, VT 05155 • *400*
South Lyme, CT 06376 • *350*
South Lyndeborough, NH 03082 • *250*
South Lyon, MI 48178 • *5,214*
South Mansfield, LA 71052 • *1,463*
South Medford, OR 97501 • *2,898*
South Miami, FL 33143 • *10,944*
South Miami Heights, FL 33157 • *18,000*
South Middleboro, MA 02346 • *400*
South Milford, IN 46786 • *500*
South Mills, NC 27976 • *800*
South Milwaukee, WI 53172 • *21,069*
South Modesto, CA 95350 • *12,492*
Southmont, NC 27351 • *700*
South Montrose, PA 18843 • *500*
South Mountain, PA 17261 • *400*
South New Berlin, NY 13843 • *450*
South Nyack, NY 10960 • *3,602*
South Ogden, UT 84403 • *11,366*
Southold, NY 11971 • *2,030*
South Orange, NJ 07079 • *15,864*
South Orrington, ME 04474 • *300*
South Otselic, NY 13155 • *450*
South Paris, ME 04281 • *2,128*
South Pasadena, CA 91030 • *22,681*
South Patrick Shores, FL 32937 • *9,816*
South Pekin, IL 61564 • *1,243*
South Pittsburg, TN 37380 • *3,636*
South Plainfield, NJ 07080 • *20,521*
Southport, FL 32409 • *1,992*
Southport, IN 46217 • *2,266*
Southport, NC 28461 • *2,824*
Southport, NY 14904 • *8,700*
South Portland, ME 04106 • *22,712*
South Portsmouth, KY 41174 • *550*
South Range, MI 49963 • *861*
South Renovo, PA 17764 • *663*
South River, NJ 08882 • *14,361*
South Royalston, MA 01331 • *370*
South Royalton, VT 05068 • *700*
South Ryegate, VT 05069 • *450*
South Salem, OH 45681 • *252*
South Salt Lake, UT 84115 • *9,884*
South San Francisco, CA 94080 • *49,393*
South San Gabriel, CA 91770 • *5,421*
South Seaville, NJ 08246 • *300*
South Shore, MO 63301 • *450*
South Shore, SD 57263 • *241*
Southside, AL 35901 • *5,141*
Southside Place, TX 77005 • *1,366*
South Sioux City, NE 68776 • *9,339*
South Solon, OH 43153 • *416*
South Stony Brook, NY 11790 • *15,329*
South St. Paul, MN 55075 • *21,235*
South Streator, IL 61364 • *2,334*
South Superior, WY 82945 • *586*
South Swansea, MA 02777 • *1,700*
South Toms River, NJ 08757 • *3,954*
South Torrington, WY 82240 • *300*
South Tucson, AZ 85725 • *6,554*
South Valley Stream, NY 11581 • *6,600*
South Van Buren, MO 63965 • *300*
South Venice, FL 33595 • *8,075*
South Vienna, OH 45369 • *464*
South Walpole, MA 02071 • *1,600*
South Waverly, PA 14892 • *1,176*
South Wayne, WI 53587 • *495*
South Webster, OH 45682 • *886*
South Wellfleet, MA 02663 • *600*
Southwest, PA 15685 • *700*
South Westbury, NY 11590 • *10,700*
South West City, MO 64863 • *516*
Southwest Harbor, ME 04679 • *1,052*
South Whitley, IN 46787 • *1,575*
South Whittier, CA 90605 • *43,815*
Southwick, MA 01077 • *1,400*
South Williamson, KY 41503 • *1,016*
South Williamsport, PA 17701 • *6,581*
South Willington, CT 06265 • *250*
South Wilmington, IL 60474 • *747*
South Windham, CT 06266 • *1,399*
South Windham, ME 04082 • *1,366*
South Windsor, CT 06074 • *10,200*
South Wolfeboro, NH 03894 • *300*
Southwood, CO 80120 • *2,600*
Southwood Acres, CT 06082 • *9,779*
South Woodstock, CT 06267 • *1,319*
South Yarmouth, MA 02664 • *7,525*
South Zanesville, OH 43701 • *1,739*
Spalding, NE 68665 • *645*
Spalding □, GA • *47,899*
Spanaway, WA 98387 • *5,940*

Spangle, WA 99031 • 276
Spangler, PA 15775 • 2,399
Spanishburg, WV 25922 • 250
Spanish Fork, UT 84660 • 9,825
Spanish Fort, AL 36527 • 3,415
Spanish Lake, MO 63138 • 20,632
Sparkman, AR 71763 • 622
Sparks, GA 31647 • 1,353
Sparks, NV 89431-33 • 40,780
Sparks, OK 74869 • 772
Sparland, IL 61565 • 624
Sparr, FL 32690 • 1,100
Sparta, GA 31087 • 1,745
Sparta, IL 62286 • 4,957
Sparta, MI 49345 • 3,373
Sparta, MO 65753 • 743
Sparta, NJ 07871 • 8,498
Sparta, NC 28675 • 1,687
Sparta, TN 38583 • 4,864
Sparta, WI 54656 • 6,934
Spartanburg, SC 29301-18 • 43,826
Spartanburg □, SC • 201,861
Spartansburg, PA 16434 • 403
Spavinaw, OK 74366 • 623
Spearfish, SD 57783 • 5,251
Spearman, TX 79081 • 3,413
Spearville, KS 67876 • 693
Speculator, NY 12164 • 408
Speed, IN 47172 • 650
Speedway, IN 46224 • 12,641
Speedwell, VA 24374 • 250
Speight, KY 41565 • 230
Spelter, WV 26438 • 450
Spenard 0Z, AK
Spencer, IN 47460 • 2,732
Spencer, IA 51301 • 11,726
Spencer, MA 01562 • 6,350
Spencer, NE 68777 • 596
Spencer, NC 28159 • 2,938
Spencer, NY 14883 • 863
Spencer, OH 44275 • 764
Spencer, SD 57374 • 380
Spencer, TN 38585 • 1,126
Spencer, WV 25276 • 2,799
Spencer, WI 54479 • 1,754
Spencer □, IN • 19,361
Spencer □, KY • 5,929
Spencerport, NY 14559 • 3,424
Spencerville, IN 46788 • 350
Spencerville, MD 20868 • 1,100
Spencerville, OH 45887 • 2,184
Sperry, OK 74073 • 1,276
Spiceland, IN 47385 • 940
Spicer, MN 56288 • 909
Spickard, MO 64679 • 389
Spillville, IA 52168 • 415
Spindale, NC 28160 • 4,246
Spink □, SD • 9,201
Spirit Lake, ID 83869 • 834
Spirit Lake, IA 51360 • 3,976
Spiro, OK 74959 • 2,221
Spofford, NH 03462 • 400
Spokane, WA 99201-99 • 171,300
Spokane □, WA • 341,835
Spooner, WI 54801 • 2,365
Spotswood, NJ 08884 • 7,840
Spotsylvania □, VA • 34,435
Spottsville, KY 42458 • 500
Sprague, WA 99032 • 473
Sprague, WV 25926 • 900
Sprague River, OR 97639 • 250
Spragueville, RI 02917 • 430
Spreckelsville, HI 96779 • 280
Spring, TX 77373 • 3,000
Springboro, OH 45066 • 4,962
Springboro, PA 16435 • 557
Spring City, PA 19475 • 3,389
Spring City, TN 37381 • 1,951
Spring City, UT 84662 • 671
Springdale, AR 72764 • 23,458
Springdale, OH 45246 • 10,111
Springdale, OR 97060 • 300
Springdale, PA 15144 • 4,418
Springdale, SC 29169 • 2,985
Springdale, UT 84767 • 258
Springdale, WA 99173 • 281
Spring Dale, WV 25986 • 250
Springer, NM 87747 • 1,657
Springer, OK 73458 • 679
Springerville, AZ 85938 • 1,452
Springfield, CO 81073 • 1,657
Springfield, FL 32401 • 7,220
Springfield, GA 31329 • 1,075
Springfield, IL 62701-99 • 100,054
Springfield, KY 40069 • 3,179
Springfield, LA 70462 • 424
Springfield, MA 01101-99 • 152,319
Springfield, MI 49015 • 5,917
Springfield, MN 56087 • 2,303
Springfield, MO 65801-99 • 133,116
Springfield, NE 68059 • 782
Springfield, NJ 07081 • 13,955
Springfield, OH 45501-99 • 72,563
Springfield, OR 97477-78 • 41,621
Springfield, PA 19064 • 25,326
Springfield, SC 29146 • 604
Springfield, SD 57062 • 1,377
Springfield, TN 37172 • 10,814
Springfield, VT 05156 • 5,603
Springfield, VA 22150-61 • 12,500
Springfield, WV 26763 • 350
Spring Glen, UT 84526 • 800
Spring Green, WI 53588 • 1,265
Spring Grove, IL 60081 • 571
Spring Grove, IN 47374 • 469
Spring Grove, MN 55974 • 1,275
Spring Grove, PA 17362 • 1,832
Spring Hill, FL 33526 • 6,468
Spring Hill, KS 66083 • 2,005
Springhill, LA 71075 • 6,516
Spring Hill, TN 37174 • 989
Spring Hope, NC 27882 • 1,254
Spring Lake, FL 33512 • 230
Spring Lake, MI 49456 • 2,731
Spring Lake, NJ 07762 • 4,215
Spring Lake, NC 28390 • 6,273
Spring Lake, UT 84651 • 300
Spring Lake Heights, NJ 07762 • 5,424
Spring Mills, PA 16875 • 600
Spring Place, GA 30705 • 246
Springport, MI 49284 • 675
Springvale, ME 04083 • 2,940
Spring Valley, CA 92077-78 • 40,191
Spring Valley, IL 61362 • 5,822
Spring Valley, MN 55975 • 2,616
Spring Valley, NY 10977 • 20,537
Spring Valley, OH 45370 • 541
Spring Valley, WI 54767 • 982
Springview, NE 68778 • 326
Springville, AL 35146 • 1,476
Springville, IN 47462 • 230
Springville, IA 52336 • 1,165
Springville, NY 14141 • 4,285
Springville, PA 18844 • 300
Springville, UT 84663 • 12,101
Springwater, NY 14560 • 500
Spruce Pine, AL 35585 • 600
Spruce Pine, NC 28777 • 2,282
Spur, TX 79370 • 1,690
Spurgeon, IN 47584 • 250
Squire, WV 24884 • 900
Staatsburg, NY 12580 • 950
Stacyville, IA 50476 • 538
Stafford, CT 06075 • 500
Stafford, KS 67578 • 1,425
Stafford, NY 14143 • 285
Stafford, VA 22554 • 650
Stafford □, KS • 5,694
Stafford □, VA • 40,470
Stafford Springs, CT 06076 • 3,392
Staffordsville, KY 41256 • 700
Staffordville, CT 06077 • 600
Stambaugh, MI 49964 • 1,442
Stamford, CT 06901-99 • 102,453
Stamford, NY 12167 • 1,240
Stamford, TX 79553 • 4,542
Stamford, VT 05352 • 500
Stamping Ground, KY 40379 • 562
Stamps, AR 71860 • 2,859
Stanaford, WV 25927 • 1,000
Stanardsville, VA 22973 • 284
Stanberry, MO 64489 • 1,387
Standard, IL 61363 • 277
Standish, ME 04084 • 400
Standish, MI 48658 • 1,264
Stanfield, AZ 85272 • 900
Stanfield, OR 97875 • 1,568
Stanford, CA 94305 • 11,045
Stanford, IL 61774 • 720
Stanford, KY 40484 • 2,764
Stanford, MT 59479 • 595
Stanhope, IA 50246 • 492
Stanhope, NJ 07874 • 3,638
Stanislaus □, CA • 265,900
Stanley, KY 42375 • 350
Stanley, NC 28164 • 2,341
Stanley, ND 58784 • 1,631
Stanley, VA 22851 • 1,204
Stanley, WI 54768 • 2,095
Stanley □, SD • 2,533
Stanleytown, VA 24168 • 650
Stanleyville, NC 27045 • 5,039
Stanly □, NC • 48,517
Stansbury Park, UT 84074 • 300
Stanton, AL 36790 • 280
Stanton, CA 90680 • 23,723
Stanton, IA 51573 • 747
Stanton, KY 40380 • 2,691
Stanton, MI 48888 • 1,315
Stanton, MO 63079 • 300
Stanton, NE 68779 • 1,603
Stanton, NJ 08885 • 300
Stanton, ND 58571 • 623
Stanton, TN 38069 • 540
Stanton, TX 79782 • 2,314
Stanton □, KS • 2,339
Stanton □, NE • 6,549
Stantonsburg, NC 27883 • 920
Stantonville, TN 38379 • 271
Stanwood, IA 52337 • 705
Stanwood, WA 98292 • 1,646
Staplehurst, NE 68439 • 306
Staples, MN 56479 • 2,887
Staples, TX 78670 • 300
Stapleton, AL 36578 • 900
Stapleton, GA 30823 • 388
Stapleton, NE 69163 • 340
Star, ID 83669 • 600
Star, MS 39167 • 500
Star, NC 27356 • 816
Starbuck, MN 56381 • 1,224
Star City, AR 71667 • 2,066
Star City, IN 46985 • 500
Star City, WV 26505 • 1,464
Starford, PA 15777 • 400
Stargo, AZ 85540 • 1,038
Stark □, IL • 7,389
Stark □, ND • 23,697
Stark □, OH • 378,823
Starke, FL 32091 • 5,306
Starke □, IN • 21,997
Starks, LA 70661 • 780
Starkville, MS 39759 • 15,169
Star Prairie, WI 54026 • 420
Starr, SC 29684 • 241
Starr □, TX • 27,266
Startex, SC 29377 • 1,006
Startup, WA 98293 • 450
State Center, IA 50247 • 1,292
State College, PA 16801-05 • 36,130
State Line, IN 47982 • 233
State Line, MS 39362 • 484
Stateline, NV 89449 • 1,500
State Line, PA 17263 • 700
Statenville, GA 31648 • 650
State Road, NC 28676 • 800
Statesboro, GA 30458 • 14,866
Statesville, NC 28677 • 18,622
Statham, GA 30666 • 1,101
Staunton, IL 62088 • 4,744
Staunton, IN 47881 • 607
Staunton, VA 24401 • 21,857
Stayton, OR 97383 • 4,396
Steamboat Canyon, AZ 86505 • 400
Steamboat Rock, IA 50672 • 387
Steamboat Springs, CO 80487 • 5,098
Stearns, KY 42647 • 1,557
Stearns □, MN • 108,161
Stebbins, AK 99671 • 331
Steele, AL 35987 • 795
Steele, MO 63877 • 2,419
Steele, ND 58482 • 796
Steele □, MN • 30,328
Steele □, ND • 3,106
Steeleville, IL 62288 • 2,240
Steelton, PA 17113 • 6,484
Steelville, MO 65565 • 1,470
Steep Falls, ME 04085 • 350
Steger, IL 60475 • 9,269
Steilacoom, WA 98388 • 4,886
Steinhatchee, FL 32359 • 800
Stella, MO 64867 • 230
Stella, NE 68442 • 289
Stephen, MN 56757 • 898
Stephens, AR 71764 • 1,366
Stephens □, GA • 21,763
Stephens □, OK • 43,419
Stephens □, TX • 9,926
Stephens City, VA 22655 • 1,179
Stephenson, MI 49887 • 967
Stephenson □, IL • 49,536
Stephenville, TX 76401 • 11,881
Sterling, AK 99672 • 919
Sterling, CO 80751 • 11,385
Sterling, CT 06377 • 400
Sterling, IL 61081 • 16,281
Sterling, KS 67579 • 2,312
Sterling, MA 01564 • 1,200
Sterling, MI 48659 • 457
Sterling, NE 68443 • 526
Sterling, OK 73567 • 702
Sterling, VA 22170 • 12,000
Sterling □, TX • 1,206
Sterling City, TX 76951 • 915
Sterling Heights, MI 48077 • 108,999
Sterlington, LA 71280 • 1,400
Sterrett, AL 35147 • 400
Stetsonville, WI 54480 • 487
Steuben □, IN • 24,694
Steuben □, NY • 99,217
Steubenville, OH 43952 • 26,400
Stevens, NJ 08016 • 300
Stevens □, KS • 4,736
Stevens □, MN • 11,322
Stevens □, WA • 28,979
Stevenson, AL 35772 • 2,568
Stevenson, CT 06491 • 450
Stevenson, WA 98648 • 1,172
Stevens Point, WI 54481 • 22,970
Stevensville, MD 21666 • 450
Stevensville, MI 49127 • 1,268
Stevensville, MT 59870 • 1,207
Steward, IL 60553 • 298
Stewardson, IL 62463 • 745
Stewart, MN 55385 • 616
Stewart, OH 45778 • 400
Stewart □, GA • 5,896
Stewart □, TN • 8,665
Stewartstown, PA 17363 • 1,072
Stewartsville, MO 64490 • 832
Stewartsville, NJ 08886 • 900
Stewartville, MN 55976 • 3,925
Stickney, IL 60402 • 5,893
Stickney, SD 57375 • 409
Stigler, OK 74462 • 2,630
Stilesville, IN 46180 • 350
Stillman Valley, IL 61084 • 961
Stillmore, GA 30464 • 527
Still Pond, MD 21667 • 300
Still River, MA 01467 • 280
Stillwater, MN 55082 • 12,290
Stillwater, NY 12170 • 1,572
Stillwater, OK 74074-78 • 38,268
Stillwater □, MT • 5,598
Stillwell, IN 46351 • 300
Stilwell, OK 74960 • 2,369
74960 • 2,369
Stinesville, IN 47464 • 227
Stinnett, TX 79083 • 2,222
Stirling, NJ 07980 • 2,000
Stirling City, CA 95978 • 300
Stirrat, WV 25645 • 350
Stites, ID 83552 • 253
Stockbridge, GA 30281 • 2,103
Stockbridge, MA 01262 • 1,109
Stockbridge, MI 49285 • 1,213
Stockbridge, WI 53088 • 567
Stockdale, OH 45683 • 250
Stockdale, TX 78160 • 1,265
Stockertown, PA 18083 • 661
Stockholm, ME 04783 • 235
Stockholm, NJ 07460 • 600
Stockport, IA 52651 • 272
Stockport, OH 43787 • 558
Stockton, CA 95201-12 • 149,779
Stockton, GA 31649 • 300
Stockton, IL 61085 • 1,872
Stockton, KS 67669 • 1,825
Stockton, MD 21864 • 400
Stockton, MO 65785 • 1,432
Stockton, NJ 08559 • 643
Stockton, NY 14784 • 300
Stockton, UT 84071 • 437
Stockton Springs, ME 04981 • 300
Stockwell, IN 47983 • 500
Stoddard, WI 54658 • 762
Stoddard □, MO • 29,009
Stokes, NC 27884 • 300
Stokes □, NC • 33,086
Stokesdale, NC 27357 • 1,070
Stollings, WV 25646 • 900
Stone, KY 41567 • 400
Stone □, AR • 9,022
Stone □, MS • 9,716
Stone □, MO • 15,587
Stoneboro, PA 16153 • 1,177
Stonefort, IL 62987 • 316
Stonega, VA 24285 • 450
Stoneham, MA 02180 • 21,424
Stone Harbor, NJ 08247 • 1,187
Stone Lake, WI 54876 • 250
Stone Mountain, GA 30086-88 • 4,867
Stoneville, NC 27048 • 1,054
Stonewall, LA 71078 • 1,175
Stonewall, MS 39363 • 1,345
Stonewall, OK 74871 • 672
Stonewall, TX 78671 • 300
Stonewall □, TX • 2,406
Stonewood, WV 26301 • 2,058
Stonington, CT 06378 • 1,228
Stonington, IL 62567 • 1,184
Stonington, ME 04681 • 700
Stony Brook, NY 11790 • 6,600
Stony Creek, CT 06405 • 700
Stony Creek, NY 12878 • 450
Stony Creek, VA 23882 • 329
Stonyford, CA 95979 • 250

Stony Point, NC 28678 • *1,150*
Stony Point, NY 10980 • *8,270*
Stony Ridge, OH 43463 • *450*
Storden, MN 56174 • *341*
Storey □, NV • *1,503*
Storm Lake, IA 50588 • *8,814*
Storrs, CT 06268 • *11,394*
Story, WY 82842 • *700*
Story □, IA • *72,326*
Story City, IA 50248 • *2,762*
Stotts City, MO 65756 • *232*
Stottville, NY 12172 • *1,300*
Stoughton, MA 02072 • *26,710*
Stoughton, WI 53589 • *7,589*
Stoutland, MO 65567 • *286*
Stoutsville, OH 43154 • *537*
Stovall, NC 27582 • *417*
Stover, MO 65078 • *1,041*
Stow, MA 01775 • *1,100*
Stow, OH 44224 • *25,303*
Stowe, PA 19464 • *4,038*
Stowe, VT 05672 • *531*
Stowe Township, PA 15136 • *10,119*
Stoystown, PA 15563 • *432*
Strabane, PA 15363 • *1,900*
Strafford, MO 65757 • *1,121*
Strafford, NH 03884 • *300*
Strafford □, NH • *85,408*
Strasburg, CO 80136 • *1,105*
Strasburg, IL 62465 • *488*
Strasburg, ND 58573 • *623*
Strasburg, OH 44680 • *2,091*
Strasburg, PA 17579 • *1,999*
Strasburg, VA 22657 • *2,311*
Stratford, CA 93266 • *850*
Stratford, CT 06497 • *50,541*
Stratford, IA 50249 • *806*
Stratford, NJ 08084 • *8,005*
Stratford, NY 13470 • *250*
Stratford, OK 74872 • *1,459*
Stratford, TX 79084 • *1,917*
Stratford, WI 54484 • *1,385*
Stratford Landing, VA 22308 • *2,650*
Stratham, NH 03885 • *500*
Strathmore, CA 93267 • *1,221*
Strathmore, NJ 07747 • *7,674*
Strattanville, PA 16258 • *555*
Stratton, CO 80836 • *705*
Stratton, ME 04982 • *400*
Stratton, NE 69043 • *499*
Stratton, OH 43961 • *356*
Stratton Meadows, CO 80906 • *6,223*
Straughn, IN 47387 • *331*
Strausstown, PA 19559 • *377*
Strawberry, AR 72469 • *280*
Strawberry Plains, TN 37871 • *400*
Strawberry Point, IA 52076 • *1,463*
Strawn, KS 66839 • *457*
Strawn, TX 76475 • *694*
Streamwood, IL 60103 • *23,456*
Streator, IL 61364 • *14,795*
Streeter, ND 58483 • *264*
Streetman, TX 75859 • *415*
Streetsboro, OH 44240 • *9,055*
Stringer, MS 39481 • *380*
Stringtown, KY 40342 • *350*
Stringtown, OK 74569 • *1,047*
Stroh, IN 46789 • *450*
Stromsburg, NE 68666 • *1,290*
Stronach, MI 49660 • *250*
Strong, AR 71765 • *785*
Strong, ME 04983 • *700*
Strong City, KS 66869 • *675*
Stronghurst, IL 61480 • *865*
Strongs, MI 49790 • *350*
Strongsville, OH 44136 • *28,577*
Stroud, OK 74079 • *3,148*
Stroudsburg, PA 18360 • *5,148*
Strum, WI 54770 • *944*
Struthers, OH 44471 • *13,624*
Stryker, OH 43557 • *1,423*
Strykersville, NY 14145 • *400*
Stuart, FL 33494-97 • *9,467*
Stuart, IA 50250 • *1,650*
Stuart, NE 68780 • *641*
Stuart, OK 74570 • *235*
Stuart, VA 24171 • *1,131*
Stuarts Draft, VA 24477 • *950*
Stump Creek, PA 15863 • *300*
Stumpy Point, NC 27978 • *300*
Sturbridge, MA 01566 • *1,891*
Sturgeon, MO 65284 • *901*
Sturgeon Bay, WI 54235 • *8,847*
Sturgis, KY 42459 • *2,293*
Sturgis, MI 49091 • *9,468*
Sturgis, MS 39769 • *269*
Sturgis, SD 57785 • *5,184*
Sturtevant, WI 53177 • *4,130*
Stutsman □, ND • *24,154*
Stuttgart, AR 72160 • *10,941*
Subiaco, AR 72865 • *744*
Sublette, IL 61367 • *442*
Sublette, KS 67877 • *1,293*
Sublette □, WY • *4,548*
Sublimity, OR 97385 • *1,077*
Succasunna, NJ 07876 • *9,000*
Success, AR 72470 • *223*
Sudan, TX 79371 • *1,091*
Sudbury, MA 01776 • *2,200*
Sudbury Center, MA 01776 • *2,900*
Sudlersville, MD 21668 • *443*
Suffern, NY 10901 • *10,794*
Suffield, CT 06078 • *1,122*
Suffolk, VA 23434-38 • *47,621*
Suffolk □, MA • *650,142*
Suffolk □, NY • *1,284,231*
Sugar City, CO 81076 • *306*
Sugar City, ID 83448 • *1,022*
Sugar Creek, MO 64054 • *4,305*
Sugarcreek, PA 16323 • *5,954*
Sugar Grove, NC 28679 • *300*
Sugar Grove, OH 43155 • *407*
Sugargrove, PA 16350 • *630*
Sugar Grove, VA 24375 • *500*
Sugar Hill, GA 30518 • *2,473*
Sugar Land, TX 77478-79 • *8,826*
Sugarland Run, VA 22170 • *4,500*
Sugar Loaf, VA 24018 • *6,000*
Sugar Notch, PA 18706 • *1,191*
Suisun City, CA 94585 • *11,087*
Suitland, MD 20746 • *24,800*
Sulligent, AL 35586 • *2,130*
Sullivan, IL 61951 • *4,526*
Sullivan, IN 47882 • *4,774*
Sullivan, KY 42460 • *300*
Sullivan, MO 63080 • *5,461*
Sullivan, OH 44880 • *300*
Sullivan, WI 53178 • *434*
Sullivan □, IN • *21,107*
Sullivan □, MO • *7,434*
Sullivan □, NH • *36,063*
Sullivan □, NY • *65,155*
Sullivan □, PA • *6,349*
Sullivan □, TN • *143,968*
Sullivans Island, SC 29482 • *1,867*
Sully, IA 50251 • *828*
Sully □, SD • *1,990*
Sulphur, KY 40070 • *250*
Sulphur, LA 70663 • *19,709*
Sulphur, OK 73086 • *5,516*
Sulphur Rock, AR 72579 • *316*
Sulphur Springs, AR 72768 • *496*
Sulphur Springs, IN 47388 • *345*
Sulphur Springs, OH 44881 • *350*
Sulphur Springs, TX 75482 • *12,804*
Sultan, WA 98294 • *1,578*
Sumas, WA 98295 • *712*
Sumatra, FL 32335 • *250*
Sumava Resorts, IN 46379 • *300*
Sumiton, AL 35148 • *2,815*
Summerdale, AL 36580 • *546*
Summerfield, FL 32691 • *550*
Summerfield, KS 66541 • *225*
Summerfield, NC 27358 • *1,680*
Summerfield, OH 43788 • *299*
Summerland Key, FL 33042 • *400*
Summers □, WV • *15,875*
Summer Shade, KY 42166 • *250*
Summersville, KY 42782 • *450*
Summersville, MO 65571 • *551*
Summersville, WV 26651 • *2,972*
Summerton, SC 29148 • *1,173*
Summerville, GA 30747 • *4,878*
Summerville, PA 15864 • *830*
Summerville, SC 29483 • *6,706*
Summit, AR 72677 • *506*
Summit, IL 60501 • *10,110*
Summit, MS 39666 • *1,753*
Summit, NJ 07901 • *21,071*
Summit, SD 57266 • *290*
Summit, TN 37363 • *1,500*
Summit □, CO • *8,848*
Summit □, OH • *524,472*
Summit □, UT • *10,198*
Summit Hill, PA 18250 • *3,418*
Summit Point, WV 25446 • *400*
Summit Station, OH 43073 • *500*
Summitville, IN 46070 • *1,085*
Summitville, TN 37382 • *600*
Sumner, IL 62466 • *1,238*
Sumner, IA 50674 • *2,335*
Sumner, MS 38957 • *452*
Sumner, NE 68878 • *254*
Sumner, WA 98390 • *4,936*
Sumner □, KS • *24,928*
Sumner □, TN • *85,790*
Sumrall, MS 39482 • *1,197*
Sumter, SC 29150-52 • *24,890*
Sumter □, AL • *16,908*
Sumter □, FL • *24,272*
Sumter □, GA • *29,360*
Sumter □, SC • *88,243*
Sun, LA 70463 • *404*
Sunapee, NH 03782 • *900*
Sunbright, TN 37872 • *500*
Sunburst, MT 59482 • *476*
Sunbury, NC 27979 • *500*
Sunbury, OH 43074 • *2,101*
Sunbury, PA 17801 • *12,292*
Sun City, AZ 85351 • *40,505*
Sun City, CA 92381 • *6,500*
Sun City, FL 33586 • *700*
Suncook, NH 03275 • *4,698*
Sundance, WY 82729 • *1,087*
Sunderland, MA 01375 • *600*
Sunderland, VT 05250 • *240*
Sundown, TX 79372 • *1,511*
Sunfield, MI 48890 • *591*
Sunflower, MS 38778 • *1,027*
Sunflower □, MS • *34,844*
Sunland Park, NM 88063 • *3,377*
Sunman, IN 47041 • *924*
Sunnyland, FL 33583 • *650*
Sunnymead, CA 92388 • *11,554*
Sunnyside, FL 32461 • *600*
Sunnyside, UT 84539 • *611*
Sunnyside, WA 98944 • *9,225*
Sunnyvale, CA 94086-88 • *106,618*
Sunol, CA 94586 • *750*
Sun Prairie, WI 53590 • *12,931*
Sunray, TX 79086 • *1,952*
Sunrise, FL 33313 • *39,681*
Sunrise Manor, NV 89110 • *44,155*
Sunset, LA 70584 • *2,300*
Sunset, TX 76270 • *500*
Sunset, UT 84015 • *5,733*
Sunset Beach, HI 96712 • *800*
Sunset Park, KS 67217 • *1,050*
Sun Valley, ID 83353 • *545*
Sun Valley, NV 89433 • *8,822*
Superior, AZ 85273 • *4,600*
Superior, MT 59872 • *1,054*
Superior, NE 68978 • *2,502*
Superior, WI 54880 • *29,571*
Supply, NC 28462 • *300*
Suquamish, WA 98392 • *1,500*
Surf City, NJ 08008 • *1,571*
Surfside, FL 33154 • *3,763*
Surfside Beach, SC 29577 • *2,522*
Surgoinsville, TN 37873 • *1,536*
Suring, WI 54174 • *581*
Surprise, AZ 85345 • *3,723*
Surrency, GA 31563 • *368*
Surrey, ND 58785 • *999*
Surry, ME 04684 • *225*
Surry, VA 23883 • *237*
Surry □, NC • *59,449*
Surry □, VA • *6,046*
Susanville, CA 96130 • *6,520*
Susquehanna, PA 18847 • *1,994*
Susquehanna □, PA • *37,876*
Sussex, NJ 07461 • *2,418*
Sussex, WI 53089 • *3,482*
Sussex □, DE • *97,983*
Sussex □, NJ • *116,119*
Sussex □, VA • *10,874*
Sutherland, IA 51058 • *897*
Sutherland, NE 69165 • *1,238*
Sutherland Springs, TX 78161 • *300*
Sutherlin, OR 97479 • *4,560*
Sutter □, CA • *52,246*
Sutter Creek, CA 95685 • *1,705*
Sutton, MA 01527 • *500*
Sutton, NE 68979 • *1,416*
Sutton, WV 26601 • *1,192*
Sutton □, TX • *5,130*
Sutton Park, NJ 07836 • *2,500*
Suttons Bay, MI 49682 • *504*
Suwanee, GA 30174 • *1,026*
Suwannee, FL 32692 • *350*
Suwannee □, FL • *22,287*
Svensen, OR 97103 • *650*
Swain □, NC • *10,283*
Swainsboro, GA 30401 • *7,602*
Swampscott, MA 01907 • *13,837*
Swan Lake, MS 38958 • *350*
Swannanoa, NC 28778 • *5,586*
Swanquarter, NC 27885 • *450*
Swansboro, NC 28584 • *976*
Swansea, IL 62221 • *5,347*
Swansea, MA 02777 • *750*
Swansea, SC 29160 • *888*
Swansea Center, MA 02777 • *300*
Swanton, OH 43558 • *3,424*
Swanton, VT 05488 • *2,520*
Swanville, MN 56382 • *295*
Swanwyck Estates, DE 19720 • *1,700*
Swanzey Center, NH 03431 • *700*
Swarthmore, PA 19081 • *5,950*
Swartswood, NJ 07877 • *400*
Swartz, LA 71281 • *450*
Swartz Creek, MI 48473 • *5,013*
Swayzee, IN 46986 • *1,127*
Swea City, IA 50590 • *813*
Swedesboro, NJ 08085 • *2,031*
Sweeny, TX 77480 • *3,538*
Sweet Briar, VA 24595 • *900*
Sweet Grass □, MT • *3,216*
Sweet Home, AR 72164 • *1,100*
Sweet Home, OR 97386 • *6,921*
Sweetser, IN 46987 • *944*
Sweet Springs, MO 65351 • *1,694*
Sweet Valley, PA 18656 • *300*
Sweet Water, AL 36782 • *253*
Sweetwater, TN 37874 • *4,725*
Sweetwater, TX 79556 • *12,242*
Sweetwater □, WY • *41,723*
Sweetwater Creek, FL 33614 • *18,000*
Swepsonville, NC 27359 • *900*
Swift □, MN • *12,920*
Swifton, AR 72471 • *859*
Swink, CO 81077 • *668*
Swisher, IA 52338 • *654*
Swisher □, TX • *9,723*
Swisshome, OR 97480 • *225*
Swissvale, PA 15218 • *11,345*
Switz City, IN 47465 • *300*
Switzer, WV 25647 • *1,000*
Switzerland, FL 32043 • *2,400*
Switzerland □, IN • *7,153*
Swoyerville, PA 18704 • *5,795*
Sycamore, AL 35149 • *900*
Sycamore, GA 31790 • *474*
Sycamore, IL 60178 • *9,219*
Sycamore, OH 44882 • *1,059*
Sycamore, SC 29846 • *261*
Sykesville, MD 21784 • *1,712*
Sykesville, PA 15865 • *1,537*
Sylacauga, AL 35150 • *12,708*
Sylva, NC 28779 • *1,699*
Sylvan Beach, NY 13157 • *1,243*
Sylvan Grove, KS 67481 • *376*
Sylvan Hills, AR 72116 • *2,900*
Sylvania, AL 35988 • *1,156*
Sylvania, GA 30467 • *3,352*
Sylvania, OH 43560 • *15,527*
Sylvania, PA 16945 • *236*
Sylvan Lake, MI 48053 • *1,949*
Sylvester, GA 31791 • *5,860*
Sylvester, TX 79560 • *250*
Sylvia, KS 67581 • *353*
Symsonia, KY 42082 • *550*
Syosset, NY 11791 • *10,200*
Syracuse, IN 46567 • *2,579*
Syracuse, KS 67878 • *1,654*
Syracuse, NE 68446 • *1,638*
Syracuse, NY 13201-99 • *170,105*
Syracuse, OH 45779 • *946*
Syracuse, UT 84041 • *3,702*

T

Table Grove, IL 61482 • *489*
Table Rock, NE 68447 • *393*
Tabor, IA 51653 • *1,088*
Tabor, SD 57063 • *460*
Tabor City, NC 28463 • *2,710*
Tacna, AZ 85352 • *500*
Tacoma, WA 98401-99 • *158,501*
Taconite, MN 55786 • *331*
Tad, WV 25201 • *500*
Taft, CA 93268 • *5,316*
Taft, OK 74463 • *489*
Taft, TX 78390 • *3,686*
Tahlequah, OK 74464 • *9,708*
Tahoe City, CA 95730 • *1,300*
Tahoka, TX 79373 • *3,262*
Taholah, WA 98587 • *800*
Tahoma, CA 95733 • *300*
Tahuya, WA 98588 • *300*
Takilma, OR 97523 • *250*
Takoma Park, MD 20912 • *16,231*
Talbot □, GA • *6,536*
Talbot □, MD • *25,604*
Talbotton, GA 31827 • *1,140*
Talco, TX 75487 • *751*
Talcott, WV 24981 • *450*
Talent, OR 97540 • *2,577*
Taliaferro □, GA • *2,032*
Talihina, OK 74571 • *1,387*
Talisheek, LA 70464 • *330*
Talkeetna, AK 99676 • *264*
Talladega, AL 35160 • *19,128*
Talladega □, AL • *73,826*
Tallahassee, FL 32301-17 • *81,548*
Tallahatchie □, MS • *17,157*

Tallapoosa, GA 30176 • 2,647
Tallapoosa □, AL • 38,676
Tallassee, AL 36078 • 4,763
Talleyville, DE 19803 • 6,880
Tallmadge, OH 44278 • 15,269
Tallula, IL 62688 • 681
Tallulah, LA 71282 • 11,634
Talmage, NE 68448 • 246
Taloga, OK 73667 • 446
Tama, IA 52339 • 2,968
Tama □, IA • 19,533
Tamaqua, PA 18252 • 8,843
Tamarac, FL 33321 • 29,376
Tamaroa, IL 62888 • 885
Tamina, TX 77302 • 900
Tamms, IL 62988 • 826
Tampa, FL 33601-99 • 271,523
Tampico, IL 61283 • 966
Tamworth, NH 03886 • 400
Tanana, AK 99777 • 388
Taney □, MO • 20,467
Taneytown, MD 21787 • 2,618
Taneyville, MO 65759 • 300
Tangent, OR 97389 • 478
Tangier, VA 23440 • 771
Tangipahoa, LA 70465 • 493
Tangipahoa □, LA • 80,698
Tanner, AL 35671 • 550
Tannersville, NY 12485 • 685
Tanque Verde, AZ • 400
Taos, MO 65101 • 759
Taos, NM 87571 • 3,369
Taos □, NM • 19,456
Taos Pueblo, NM 87571 • 1,030
Tapoco, NC 28780 • 250
Tappahannock, VA 22560 • 1,821
Tappan, NY 10983 • 6,100
Tappen, ND 58487 • 271
Tara Hills, CA 94564 • 6,000
Tarboro, GA 31568 • 250
Tarboro, NC 27886 • 8,634
Tarentum, PA 15084 • 6,419
Tariffville, CT 06081 • 1,324
Tarkiln, RI 02895 • 300
Tarkio, MO 64491 • 2,375
Tarlton, OH 43156 • 394
Tarpey, CA 93727 • 4,000
Tarpon Springs, FL 33589-90 • 13,251
Tarrant □, TX • 860,880
Tarrant City, AL 35217 • 8,148
Tarrytown, FL 33597 • 350
Tarrytown, NY 10591 • 10,648
Tate, GA 30177 • 900
Tate □, MS • 20,119
Tateville, KY 42558 • 725
Tattnall □, GA • 18,134
Tatum, NM 88267 • 896
Taunton, MA 02780 • 45,001
Taunton Lakes, NJ 08053 • 350
Tavares, FL 32778 • 4,103
Tavernier, FL 33070 • 1,834
Tawas City, MI 48763 • 1,967
Taycheedah, WI 53090 • 250
Taylor, AZ 85939 • 1,915
Taylor, AR 71861 • 657
Taylor, MI 48180 • 77,568
Taylor, MS 38673 • 301
Taylor, NE 68879 • 278
Taylor, ND 58656 • 239
Taylor, PA 18517 • 7,246
Taylor, TX 76574 • 10,619
Taylor, WI 54659 • 411
Taylor □, FL • 16,532
Taylor □, GA • 7,902
Taylor □, IA • 8,353
Taylor □, KY • 21,178
Taylor □, TX • 110,932
Taylor □, WV • 16,584
Taylor □, WI • 18,817
Taylor Mill, KY 41015 • 4,509
Taylors, SC 29687 • 12,100
Taylors Falls, MN 55084 • 623
Taylors Island, MD 21669 • 250
Taylor Springs, IL 62089 • 671
Taylorsville, GA 30178 • 266
Taylorsville, IN 47280 • 1,247
Taylorsville, KY 40071 • 801
Taylorsville, MS 39168 • 1,387
Taylorsville, NC 28681 • 1,103
Taylorsville, UT 84107 • 17,448
Taylorville, IL 62568 • 11,386
Tazewell, TN 37879 • 2,090
Tazewell, VA 24651 • 4,468
Tazewell □, IL • 132,078
Tazewell □, VA • 50,511
Tchula, MS 39169 • 1,931
Tea, SD 57064 • 729
Teachey, NC 28464 • 373
Teague, TX 75860 • 3,390
Teaneck, NJ 07666 • 39,007
Teaticket, MA 02536 • 2,000
Tecopa, CA 92389 • 250
Tecumseh, KS 66542 • 350
Tecumseh, MI 49286 • 7,320
Tecumseh, NE 68450 • 1,926
Tecumseh, OK 74873 • 5,123
Tedrow, OH 43567 • 225
Teec Nos Pos, AZ 86514 • 250
Tehachapi, CA 93561 • 4,126
Tehama □, CA • 38,888
Tekamah, NE 68061 • 1,886
Tekoa, WA 99033 • 854
Tekonsha, MI 49092 • 755
Telephone, TX 75488 • 250
Telfair □, GA • 11,445
Telford, PA 18969 • 3,507
Tell City, IN 47586 • 8,704
Teller □, CO • 8,034
Tellico Plains, TN 37385 • 698
Telluride, CO 81435 • 1,047
Telogia, FL 32360 • 300
Temecula, CA 92390 • 1,783
Tempe, AZ 85281-89 • 106,743
Temperance, MI 48182 • 3,500
Temperanceville, VA 23442 • 425
Temple, GA 30179 • 1,520
Temple, MI 48625 • 250
Temple, NH 03084 • 280
Temple, OK 73568 • 1,339
Temple, PA 19560 • 1,486
Temple, TX 76501-08 • 42,354
Temple City, CA 91780 • 28,972
Temple Terrace, FL 33617 • 11,097
Templeton, IA 51463 • 319
Templeton, MA 01468 • 900
Templeton, PA 16259 • 700
Tenafly, NJ 07670 • 13,552
Tenaha, TX 75974 • 1,005
Tenants Harbor, ME 04860 • 300
Tenino, WA 98589 • 1,280
Tennent, NJ 07763 • 300
Tennessee Ridge, TN 37178 • 1,325
Tennga, GA 30751 • 300
Tennille, GA 31089 • 1,709
Tennyson, IN 47637 • 331
Tensas □, LA • 8,525
Ten Sleep, WY 82442 • 407
Terra Alta, WV 26764 • 1,946
Terral, OK 73569 • 604
Terrebonne, OR 97760 • 900
Terrebonne □, LA • 94,393
Terre Haute, IN 47801-12 • 61,125
Terre Hill, PA 17581 • 1,217
Terrell, TX 75160 • 13,269
Terrell □, GA • 12,017
Terrell □, TX • 1,595
Terrell Hills, TX 78209 • 4,644
Terreton, ID 83450 • 400
Terril, IA 51364 • 420
Terry, MS 39170 • 655
Terry, MT 59349 • 929
Terry □, TX • 14,581
Terrytown, NE 69341 • 727
Terryville, CT 06786 • 5,234
Terryville, NY 11776 • 5,900
Tescott, KS 67484 • 331
Tesuque, NM 87574 • 1,014
Teton, ID 83451 • 559
Teton □, ID • 2,897
Teton □, MT • 6,491
Teton □, WY • 9,355
Teutopolis, IL 62467 • 1,414
Tewksbury, MA 01876 • 11,500
Texarkana, AR 75502 • 21,459
Texarkana, TX 75501-07 • 31,271
Texas □, MO • 21,070
Texas □, OK • 17,727
Texas City, TX 77590-91 • 41,403
Texhoma, OK 73949 • 785
Texhoma, TX 73949 • 358
Texico, NM 88135 • 958
Texline, TX 79087 • 477
Thackerville, OK 73459 • 431
Thatcher, AZ 85552 • 3,374
Thawville, IL 60968 • 275
Thaxton, MS 38871 • 404
Thayer, IL 62689 • 759
Thayer, IN 46381 • 300
Thayer, KS 66776 • 517
Thayer, MO 65791 • 2,211
Thayer □, NE • 7,582
Thayne, WY 83127 • 256
Thealka, KY 41259 • 500
Thebes, IL 62990 • 455
The Colony, TX 75056 • 11,586
The Dalles, OR 97058 • 10,820
Thedford, NE 69166 • 313
Theodore, AL 36582 • 6,392
The Plains, OH 45780 • 2,044
The Plains, VA 22171 • 382
Theresa, NY 13691 • 827
Theresa, WI 53091 • 766
Thermopolis, WY 82443 • 3,852
The Village, OK 73120 • 11,049
Thibodaux, LA 70301-02 • 15,810
Thief River Falls, MN 56701 • 9,105
Thiensville, WI 53092 • 3,341
Thomas, OK 73669 • 1,515
Thomas, WV 26292 • 747
Thomas □, GA • 38,098
Thomas □, KS • 8,451
Thomas □, NE • 973
Thomasboro, IL 61878 • 1,242
Thomaston, AL 36783 • 679
Thomaston, CT 06787 • 3,500
Thomaston, GA 30286 • 9,682
Thomaston, ME 04861 • 2,348
Thomaston, TX 77989 • 250
Thomastown, MS 39171 • 500
Thomasville, AL 36784 • 4,387
Thomasville, GA 31792 • 18,463
Thomasville, NC 27360 • 14,144
Thompson, CT 06277 • 500
Thompson, IA 50478 • 668
Thompson, ND 58278 • 785
Thompson, OH 44086 • 250
Thompson, PA 18465 • 303
Thompson Falls, MT 59873 • 1,478
Thompsons Station, TN 37179 • 350
Thompsontown, PA 17094 • 593
Thompsonville, IL 62890 • 610
Thompsonville, MI 49683 • 331
Thomson, GA 30824 • 7,001
Thomson, IL 61285 • 911
Thonotosassa, FL 33592 • 1,500
Thoreau, NM 87323 • 1,099
Thorndale, TX 76577 • 1,300
Thorndike, MA 01079 • 1,000
Thornton, AR 71766 • 711
Thornton, CO 80229 • 40,343
Thornton, IA 50479 • 442
Thornton, TX 76687 • 498
Thorntonville, TX 79756 • 717
Thorntown, IN 46071 • 1,468
Thornville, OH 43076 • 838
Thornwood, NY 10594 • 5,400
Thorofare, NJ 08086 • 1,400
Thorp, WA 98946 • 350
Thorp, WI 54771 • 1,635
Thorsby, AL 35171 • 1,422
Thousand Oaks, CA 91359-63 • 77,072
Three Bridges, NJ 08887 • 650
Three Forks, MT 59752 • 1,247
Three Lakes, WI 54562 • 600
Three Mile Bay, NY 13693 • 600
Three Oaks, MI 49128 • 1,774
Three Rivers, MA 01080 • 3,322
Three Rivers, MI 49093 • 7,015
Three Rivers, TX 78071 • 2,133
Three Springs, PA 17264 • 501
Throckmorton, TX 76083 • 1,174
Throckmorton □, TX • 2,053
Throop, PA 18512 • 4,166
Thunderbolt, GA 31404 • 2,165
Thurmont, MD 21788 • 2,934
Thurston, OH 43157 • 527
Thurston □, NE • 7,186
Thurston □, WA • 124,264
Tiawah, OK 74017 • 250
Tibbie, AL 36583 • 300
Tiburon, CA 94920 • 6,685
Tice, FL 33905 • 6,645
Tickfaw, LA 70466 • 571
Ticonderoga, NY 12883 • 2,938
Tidioute, PA 16351 • 844
Tie Plant, MS 38960 • 450
Tierra Amarilla, NM 87575 • 800
Tieton, WA 98947 • 528
Tiffin, IA 52340 • 413
Tiffin, OH 44883 • 19,549
Tift □, GA • 32,862
Tifton, GA 31794 • 13,749
Tigard, OR 97223 • 14,286
Tiger, GA 30576 • 299
Tigerton, WI 54486 • 865
Tignall, GA 30668 • 733
Tijeras, NM 87059 • 311
Tilden, IL 62292 • 1,025
Tilden, NE 68781 • 1,012
Tilden, TX 78072 • 450
Tilghman, MD 21671 • 900
Tillamook, OR 97141 • 3,981
Tillamook □, OR • 21,164
Tillar, AR 71670 • 280
Tillman, SC 29943 • 260
Tillman □, OK • 12,398
Tillmans Corner, AL 36619 • 5,000
Tillson, NY 12486 • 1,300
Tilton, IL 61833 • 2,405
Tilton, NH 03276 • 1,230
Tiltonsville, OH 43963 • 1,750
Timberlake, NC 27583 • 250
Timber Lake, SD 57656 • 660
Timberlake, VA 24502 • 2,700
Timberville, VA 22853 • 1,510
Timmonsville, SC 29161 • 2,112
Timpson, TX 75975 • 1,164
Tinley Park, IL 60477 • 26,171
Tinsley, MS 39173 • 300
Tinton Falls, NJ 07724 • 7,740
Tioga, LA 71477 • 1,200
Tioga, ND 58852 • 1,597
Tioga □, NY • 49,812
Tioga □, PA • 40,973
Tiona, PA 16352 • 400
Tionesta, PA 16353 • 659
Tippah □, MS • 18,739
Tipp City, OH 45371 • 5,595
Tippecanoe, IN 46570 • 360
Tippecanoe □, IN • 121,702
Tipton, CA 93272 • 1,185
Tipton, IN 46072 • 5,004
Tipton, IA 52772 • 3,055
Tipton, KS 67485 • 321
Tipton, MO 65081 • 2,155
Tipton, OK 73570 • 1,475
Tipton, TN 38071 • 265
Tipton □, IN • 16,819
Tipton □, TN • 32,930
Tiptonville, TN 38079 • 2,438
Tire Hill, PA 15959 • 750
Tiro, OH 44887 • 279
Tisch Mills, WI 54240 • 250
Tishomingo, MS 38873 • 387
Tishomingo, OK 73460 • 3,212
Tishomingo □, MS • 18,434
Tiskilwa, IL 61368 • 990
Titonka, IA 50480 • 607
Titus □, TX • 21,442
Titusville, FL 32780-83 • 31,910
Titusville, NJ 08560 • 900
Titusville, PA 16354 • 6,884
Tiverton, RI 02878 • 7,653
Tivoli, NY 12583 • 711
Tivoli, TX 77990 • 600
Toadlena, NM 87324 • 300
Toano, VA 23168 • 750
Toast, NC 27049 • 2,339
Tobyhanna, PA 18466 • 700
Toccoa, GA 30577 • 9,104
Toccoa Falls, GA 30598 • 400
Todd □, KY • 11,874
Todd □, MN • 24,991
Todd □, SD • 7,328
Todd Estates, DE 19713 • 2,050
Toddville, MD 21672 • 300
Tofte, MN 55615 • 250
Togiak, AK 99678 • 470
Tohatchi, NM 87325 • 1,011
Tok, AK 99780 • 589
Tokeland, WA 98590 • 400
Toledo, IL 62468 • 1,284
Toledo, IA 52342 • 2,445
Toledo, OH 43601-99 • 354,635
Toledo, OR 97391 • 3,151
Toledo, WA 98591 • 637
Toler, KY 41569 • 500
Tolland, CT 06084 • 500
Tolland □, CT • 114,823
Tollesboro, KY 41189 • 808
Tolleson, AZ 85353 • 4,433
Tollette, AR 71851 • 407
Tollhouse, CA 93667 • 300
Tolna, ND 58380 • 241
Tolono, IL 61880 • 2,434
Toluca, IL 61369 • 1,471
Tomah, WI 54660 • 7,204
Tomahawk, WI 54487 • 3,527
Tomball, TX 77375 • 3,996
Tombstone, AZ 85638 • 1,632
Tome, NM 87060 • 400
Tom Green □, TX • 84,784
Tomkins Cove, NY 10986 • 700
Tompkins □, NY • 87,085
Tompkinsville, KY 42167 • 4,366
Toms River, NJ 08753-59 • 7,465
Tonasket, WA 98855 • 985
Tonawanda, NY 14150 • 18,693
Toney, AL 35773 • 300
Tonganoxie, KS 66086 • 1,864
Tonica, IL 61370 • 695
Tonkawa, OK 74653 • 3,524
Tonopah, NV 89049 • 1,952
Tontitown, AR 72770 • 615
Tontogany, OH 43565 • 367
Tooele, UT 84074 • 14,335
Tooele □, UT • 26,033
Toole □, MT • 5,559

Toombs □, GA • *22,592*
Toomsboro, GA 31090 • *673*
Toomsuba, MS 39364 • *300*
Toone, TN 38381 • *355*
Topawa, AZ 85639 • *250*
Topaz, CA 96133 • *235*
Topeka, IN 46571 • *876*
Topeka, KS 66601-99 • *115,266*
Topinabee, MI 49791 • *300*
Topock, AZ 86436 • *300*
Toppenish, WA 98948 • *6,517*
Topsfield, MA 01983 • *2,647*
Topsham, ME 04086 • *4,657*
Topton, PA 19562 • *1,818*
Toquerville, UT 84774 • *277*
Tornillo, TX 79853 • *600*
Toronto, KS 66777 • *466*
Toronto, OH 43964 • *6,934*
Toronto, SD 57268 • *236*
Torrance, CA 90501-99 • *129,881*
Torrance □, NM • *7,491*
Torrington, CT 06790 • *30,987*
Torrington, WY 82240 • *5,441*
Totowa, NJ 07512 • *11,448*
Totz, KY 40870 • *350*
Touchet, WA 99360 • *400*
Touisset, MA 02777 • *1,300*
Toulon, IL 61483 • *1,390*
Tovey, IL 62570 • *598*
Tow, TX 78672 • *250*
Towaco, NJ 07082 • *1,400*
Towanda, IL 61776 • *630*
Towanda, KS 67144 • *1,332*
Towanda, PA 18848 • *3,526*
Towaoc, CO 81334 • *300*
Tower, MI 49792 • *500*
Tower, MN 55790 • *640*
Tower City, ND 58071 • *293*
Tower City, PA 17980 • *1,667*
Tower Hill, IL 62571 • *715*
Town and Country, WA 99210 • *7,100*
Town Creek, AL 35672 • *1,201*
Town Creek Manor, MD 20653 • *900*
Towner, ND 58788 • *867*
Towner □, ND • *4,052*
Townley, AL 35587 • *500*
Town of Tonawanda, NY 14223 • *78,100*
Towns □, GA • *5,638*
Townsend, DE 19734 • *386*
Townsend, GA 31331 • *300*
Townsend, MA 01469 • *1,266*
Townsend, MT 59644 • *1,587*
Townsend, TN 37882 • *351*
Townsend, VA 23443 • *300*
Townsville, NC 27584 • *300*
Townville, PA 16360 • *364*
Townville, SC 29689 • *240*
Towson, MD 21204 • *51,083*
Toxey, AL 36921 • *265*
Tracy, CA 95376 • *18,428*
Tracy, IA 50256 • *300*
Tracy, MN 56175 • *2,478*
Tracy, MO 64079 • *310*
Tracy City, TN 37387 • *1,356*
Tracyton, WA 98393 • *1,600*
Traer, IA 50675 • *1,703*
Trafalgar, IN 46181 • *466*
Trafford, PA 15085 • *3,662*
Trail, OR 97541 • *300*
Trail Creek, IN 46360 • *2,581*
Traill □, ND • *9,624*
Trammel, VA 24289 • *500*
Tranquillity, CA 93668 • *950*
Transfer, PA 16154 • *300*
Transylvania □, NC • *23,417*
Trappe, MD 21673 • *739*
Traskwood, AR 72167 • *459*
Travelers Rest, SC 29690 • *3,017*
Traverse □, MN • *5,542*
Traverse City, MI 49684 • *15,516*
Travis □, TX • *419,573*
Treasure □, MT • *981*
Treasure Island, FL 33740 • *6,316*
Trees, LA 71081 • *250*
Trego □, KS • *4,165*
Tremont, IL 61568 • *2,096*
Tremont, MS 38876 • *379*
Tremont, PA 17981 • *1,796*
Tremont City, OH 45372 • *374*
Tremonton, UT 84337 • *3,464*
Trempealeau, WI 54661 • *956*
Trempealeau □, WI • *26,158*
Trenary, MI 49891 • *250*
Trent, TX 79561 • *313*
Trenton, FL 32693 • *1,131*
Trenton, GA 30752 • *1,636*
Trenton, IL 62293 • *2,504*
Trenton, KY 42286 • *465*
Trenton, MI 48183 • *22,762*
Trenton, MO 64683 • *6,811*
Trenton, NE 69044 • *796*
Trenton, NJ 08601-99 • *92,124*
Trenton, NC 28585 • *407*
Trenton, OH 45067 • *6,401*
Trenton, SC 29847 • *404*
Trenton, TN 38382 • *4,601*
Trenton, TX 75490 • *691*
Trenton, UT 84338 • *447*
Tresckow, PA 18254 • *1,146*
Treutlen □, GA • *6,087*
Trevor, WI 53179 • *500*
Trevorton, PA 17881 • *2,196*
Trevose, PA 19047 • *7,000*
Treynor, IA 51575 • *981*
Trezevant, TN 38258 • *921*
Triadelphia, WV 26059 • *1,461*
Triangle, VA 22172 • *3,050*
Tribune, KS 67879 • *955*
Tri City, OR 97457 • *3,439*
Trigg □, KY • *9,384*
Tri Lakes, IN 46725 • *1,356*
Trilby, FL 33593 • *950*
Trilla, IL 62469 • *280*
Trimble, MO 64492 • *262*
Trimble, TN 38259 • *722*
Trimble □, KY • *6,253*
Trimont, MN 56176 • *805*
Trinidad, CO 81082 • *9,663*
Trinidad, TX 75163 • *1,130*
Trinity, AL 35673 • *1,328*
Trinity, TX 75862 • *2,620*
Trinity □, CA • *11,858*
Trinity □, TX • *9,450*
Trinity Center, CA 96091 • *650*
Trinway, OH 43842 • *500*
Trio, SC 29595 • *230*
Trion, GA 30753 • *1,732*
Tripoli, IA 50676 • *1,280*
Tripp, SD 57376 • *804*
Tripp □, SD • *7,268*
Triumph, LA 70041 • *1,600*
Trona, CA 93562 • *1,400*
Tropic, UT 84776 • *338*
Trotwood, OH 45426 • *7,802*
Troup, TX 75789 • *1,911*
Troup □, GA • *50,003*
Trousdale □, TN • *6,137*
Trout, LA 71371 • *500*
Trout Creek, MI 49967 • *250*
Troutdale, ME 04985 • *400*
Troutdale, OR 97060 • *5,908*
Trout Dale, VA 24378 • *248*
Trout Lake, MI 49793 • *300*
Trout Lake, WA 98650 • *550*
Troutman, NC 28166 • *1,360*
Trout Run, PA 17771 • *300*
Troutville, VA 24175 • *496*
Troy, AL 36081 • *12,945*
Troy, ID 83871 • *820*
Troy, IL 62294 • *3,772*
Troy, IN 47588 • *550*
Troy, KS 66087 • *1,240*
Troy, MI 48084 • *67,102*
Troy, MO 63379 • *2,624*
Troy, MT 59935 • *1,088*
Troy, NH 03465 • *1,318*
Troy, NC 27371 • *2,702*
Troy, NY 12180-83 • *56,638*
Troy, OH 45373 • *19,086*
Troy, PA 16947 • *1,381*
Troy, SC 29848 • *705*
Troy, TN 38260 • *1,093*
Troy, VT 05868 • *300*
Troy Grove, IL 61372 • *297*
Troy Mills, IA 52344 • *250*
Truchas, NM 87578 • *400*
Truckee, CA 95734 • *2,389*
Truman, MN 56088 • *1,392*
Trumann, AR 72472 • *6,405*
Trumansburg, NY 14886 • *1,722*
Trumbull, CT 06611 • *32,989*
Trumbull □, OH • *241,863*
Truro, IA 50257 • *407*
Truro, MA 02666 • *500*
Trussville, AL 35173 • *3,507*
Truth or Consequences (Hot Springs), NM 87901 • *5,219*
Truxton, NY 13158 • *400*
Tryon, NC 28782 • *1,796*
Tryon, OK 74875 • *435*
Tualatin, OR 97062 • *7,483*
Tuba City, AZ 86045 • *5,041*
Tuckahoe, NJ 08250 • *650*
Tuckahoe, NY 10707 • *6,076*
Tucker, AR 72168 • *350*
Tucker, GA 30084 • *18,200*
Tucker □, WV • *8,675*
Tuckerman, AR 72473 • *2,078*
Tuckerton, NJ 08087 • *2,472*
Tucson, AZ 85701-99 • *330,537*
Tucumcari, NM 88401 • *6,765*
Tukwila, WA 98188 • *3,578*
Tulare, CA 93274 • *22,526*
Tulare, SD 57476 • *238*
Tulare □, CA • *245,738*
Tularosa, NM 88352 • *2,536*
Tulelake, CA 96134 • *783*
Tuleta, TX 78162 • *300*
Tulia, TX 79088 • *5,033*
Tullahoma, TN 37388 • *15,800*
Tullos, LA 71479 • *776*
Tully, NY 13159 • *1,049*
Tulsa, OK 74101-99 • *360,919*
Tulsa □, OK • *470,593*
Tumacacori, AZ 85640 • *250*
Tumalo, OR 97701 • *500*
Tumtum, WA 99034 • *350*
Tumwater, WA 98502 • *6,705*
Tunica, MS 38676 • *1,361*
Tunica □, MS • *9,652*
Tunkhannock, PA 18657 • *2,144*
Tunnel Hill, GA 30755 • *936*
Tunnelton, WV 26444 • *510*
Tununak, AK 99681 • *298*
Tuolumne, CA 95379 • *1,708*
Tuolumne □, CA • *33,928*
Tupelo, AR 72169 • *248*
Tupelo, MS 38801 • *23,905*
Tupelo, OK 74572 • *542*
Tupman, CA 93276 • *280*
Tupper Lake, NY 12986 • *4,478*
Turbeville, SC 29162 • *549*
Turbotville, PA 17772 • *675*
Turin, GA 30289 • *260*
Turin, NY 13473 • *284*
Turkey, NC 28393 • *417*
Turkey, TX 79261 • *644*
Turkey Creek, LA 70585 • *366*
Turley, OK 74156 • *6,336*
Turlock, CA 95380 • *26,287*
Turner, ME 04282 • *400*
Turner, OR 97392 • *1,116*
Turner □, GA • *9,510*
Turner □, SD • *9,255*
Turners Falls, MA 01376 • *4,711*
Turney, MO 64493 • *379*
Turon, KS 67583 • *481*
Turpin, OK 73950 • *425*
Turrell, AR 72384 • *1,041*
Turtle Creek, PA 15145 • *6,959*
Turtle Lake, ND 58575 • *802*
Turtle Lake, WI 54889 • *762*
Tuscaloosa, AL 35401-06 • *75,211*
Tuscaloosa □, AL • *137,541*
Tuscarawas □, OH • *84,614*
Tuscola, IL 61953 • *3,839*
Tuscola, TX 79562 • *660*
Tuscola □, MI • *56,961*
Tuscumbia, AL 35674 • *9,137*
Tuscumbia, MO 65082 • *241*
Tushka, OK 74525 • *358*
Tuskegee, AL 36083 • *13,327*
Tustin, CA 92680 • *32,317*
Tustin, MI 49688 • *264*
Tuttle, OK 73089 • *3,051*
Tutwiler, MS 38963 • *1,174*
Tuxedo, NC 28784 • *950*
Tuxedo Park, DE 19804 • *1,700*
Twelve Mile, IN 46988 • *250*
Twentynine Palms, CA 92277 • *7,465*
Twiggs □, GA • *9,354*
Twin Bridges, MT 59754 • *437*
Twin City, GA 30471 • *1,402*
Twin Falls, ID 83301 • *26,209*
Twin Falls □, ID • *52,927*
Twin Knolls, AZ 85207 • *4,700*
Twin Lakes, GA 31636 • *800*
Twin Lakes, WI 53181 • *3,474*
Twin Mountain, NH 03595 • *400*
Twin Rivers, NJ 08520 • *7,742*
Twin Rocks, PA 15960 • *700*
Twinsburg, OH 44087 • *7,632*
Twin Valley, MN 56584 • *907*
Twisp, WA 98856 • *911*
Two Harbors, MN 55616 • *4,039*
Two Rivers, WI 54241 • *13,354*
Tyaskin, MD 21865 • *225*
Tybee Island, GA 31328 • *2,240*
Tygh Valley, OR 97063 • *500*
Tyler, MN 56178 • *1,353*
Tyler, TX 75701-12 • *70,508*
Tyler □, TX • *16,223*
Tyler □, WV • *11,320*
Tyler Heights, WV 25312 • *3,200*
Tylersburg, PA 16361 • *225*
Tylersville, PA 17773 • *225*
Tylertown, MS 39667 • *1,976*
Tyndall, SD 57066 • *1,253*
Tyner, IN 46572 • *225*
Tyner, NC 27980 • *250*
Tyonek, AK 99682 • *239*
Tyro, KS 67364 • *289*
Tyrone, NM 88065 • *950*
Tyrone, OK 73951 • *928*
Tyrone, PA 16686 • *6,346*
Tyronza, AR 72386 • *777*
Tyrrell □, NC • *3,975*
Ty Ty, GA 31795 • *618*

U

Ubly, MI 48475 • *862*
Ucon, ID 83454 • *833*
Udall, KS 67146 • *891*
Uehling, NE 68063 • *273*
Uhrichsville, OH 44683 • *6,130*
Uinta □, WY • *13,021*
Uintah, UT 84403 • *439*
Uintah □, UT • *20,506*
Ukiah, CA 95482 • *12,035*
Ukiah, OR 97880 • *249*
Ulen, MN 56585 • *514*
Uleta, FL 33164 • *10,000*
Ullin, IL 62992 • *550*
Ulm, MT 59485 • *350*
Ulster, PA 18850 • *400*
Ulster □, NY • *158,158*
Ulysses, KS 67880 • *4,653*
Ulysses, NE 68669 • *270*
Ulysses, PA 16948 • *654*
Umatilla, FL 32784 • *1,872*
Umatilla, OR 97882 • *3,199*
Umatilla □, OR • *58,861*
Unadilla, GA 31091 • *1,566*
Unadilla, NE 68454 • *291*
Unadilla, NY 13849 • *1,367*
Unalakleet, AK 99684 • *623*
Uncasville, CT 06382 • *1,597*
Underhill, VT 05489 • *325*
Underhill Center, VT 05490 • *340*
Underwood, AL 35630 • *750*
Underwood, IN 47177 • *500*
Underwood, IA 51576 • *448*
Underwood, MN 56586 • *332*
Underwood, ND 58576 • *1,329*
Underwood, WA 98651 • *400*
Unicoi, TN 37692 • *600*
Unicoi □, TN • *16,362*
Union, IL 60180 • *622*
Union, IA 50258 • *515*
Union, KY 41091 • *601*
Union, LA 70723 • *600*
Union, ME 04862 • *500*
Union, MS 39365 • *1,931*
Union, MO 63084 • *5,506*
Union, NE 68455 • *307*
Union, NH 03887 • *350*
Union, NJ 07083 • *50,184*
Union, NC 27910 • *300*
Union, OH 45322 • *5,219*
Union, OR 97883 • *2,062*
Union, SC 29379 • *10,523*
Union, UT 84047 • *3,100*
Union, WA 98592 • *600*
Union, WV 24983 • *743*
Union □, AR • *48,573*
Union □, FL • *10,166*
Union □, GA • *9,390*
Union □, IL • *17,765*
Union □, IN • *6,860*
Union □, IA • *13,858*
Union □, KY • *17,821*
Union □, LA • *21,167*
Union □, MS • *21,741*
Union □, NJ • *504,094*
Union □, NM • *4,725*
Union □, NC • *70,380*
Union □, OH • *29,536*
Union □, OR • *23,921*
Union □, PA • *32,870*
Union □, SC • *30,764*
Union □, SD • *10,938*
Union □, TN • *11,707*
Union Beach, NJ 07735 • *6,354*
Union Bridge, MD 21791 • *927*
Union City, CA 94587 • *39,406*
Union City, GA 30291 • *4,780*
Union City, IN 47390 • *3,908*
Union City, MI 49094 • *1,667*
Union City, NJ 07087 • *55,593*
Union City, OH 45390 • *1,716*
Union City, OK 73090 • *558*
Union City, PA 16438 • *3,623*
Union City, TN 38261 • *10,436*
Uniondale, IN 46791 • *303*

Uniondale, NY 11553 • 24,500
Union Dale, PA 18470 • 321
Union Furnace, OH 43158 • 350
Union Gap, WA 98903 • 3,184
Union Grove, WI 53182 • 3,517
Union Lake, MI 48085 • 12,000
Union Mill, HI 96719 • 400
Union Mills, IN 46382 • 550
Union Pier, MI 49129 • 1,039
Union Point, GA 30669 • 1,750
Union Springs, AL 36089 • 4,431
Union Springs, NY 13160 • 1,201
Union Star, MO 64494 • 423
Uniontown, AL 36786 • 2,112
Uniontown, KS 66779 • 371
Uniontown, KY 42461 • 1,169
Uniontown, MD 21157 • 250
Uniontown, OH 44685 • 1,450
Uniontown, PA 15401 • 14,510
Uniontown, WA 99179 • 286
Union Village, RI 02895 • 2,400
Unionville, CT 06085 • 4,900
Unionville, MI 48767 • 578
Unionville, MO 63565 • 2,178
Unionville, OH 44088 • 500
Unionville, VA 22567 • 250
Unionville Center, OH 43077 • 272
United, PA 15689 • 950
Unity, ME 04988 • 445
Universal, IN 47884 • 428
Universal City, TX 78148 • 10,720
University City, MO 63130 • 42,738
University Gardens, NY 11020 • 5,400
University Heights, IA 52240 • 1,069
University Heights, OH 44118 • 15,401
University Park, IA 52595 • 645
University Park, NM 88003 • 4,383
University Park, TX 75205 • 22,254
University Place, WA 98465 • 13,620
Upham, ND 58789 • 227
Upland, CA 91786 • 47,647
Upland, IN 46989 • 3,335
Upper Arlington, OH 43221 • 35,648
Upper Black Eddy, PA 18972 • 440
Upperco, MD 21155 • 300
Upper Darby, PA 19082-84 • 50,200
Upper Fairmount, MD 21867 • 300
Upper Frenchville, ME 04784 • 340
Upper Gloucester, ME 04260 • 300
Upper Graniteville, VT 05654 • 375
Upper Greenwood Lake, NJ 07421 • 2,734
Upper Jay, NY 12987 • 350
Upper Marlboro, MD 20772 • 828
Upper Saddle River, NJ 07458 • 7,958
Upper Saint Clair, PA 15241 • 19,023
Upper Sandusky, OH 43351 • 5,967
Upper Strasburg, PA 17265 • 300
Upperville, VA 22176 • 325
Upsala, MN 56384 • 400
Upshur □, TX • 28,595
Upshur □, WV • 23,427
Upson □, GA • 25,998
Upton, KY 42784 • 731
Upton, MA 01568 • 1,500
Upton, WY 82730 • 1,193
Upton □, TX • 4,619
Urania, LA 71480 • 849
Uravan, CO 81436 • 800
Urbana, AR 71768 • 250
Urbana, IL 61801 • 35,978
Urbana, IN 46990 • 400
Urbana, IA 52345 • 574
Urbana, MD 21701 • 250
Urbana, MO 65767 • 329
Urbana, OH 43078 • 10,762
Urbancrest, OH 43123 • 880
Urbandale, IA 50322 • 17,869
Urbanna, VA 23175 • 518
Uriah, AL 36480 • 400
Urich, MO 64788 • 509
Ursa, IL 62376 • 454
Ursina, PA 15485 • 311
Usquepaug, RI 02892 • 250
Utah □, UT • 218,106
Ute, IA 51060 • 479
Utica, IL 61373 • 1,067
Utica, IN 47130 • 644
Utica, KS 67584 • 275
Utica, KY 42376 • 300
Utica, MI 48077-78 • 5,282
Utica, MS 39175 • 865
Utica, MO 64686 • 375
Utica, NE 68456 • 689
Utica, NY 13501-99 • 75,632
Utica, OH 43080 • 2,238
Utica, PA 16362 • 255
Utopia, TX 78884 • 400
Uvalda, GA 30473 • 646
Uvalde, TX 78801 • 14,178
Uvalde □, TX • 22,441
Uxbridge, MA 01569 • 3,500

V

Vacaville, CA 95688 • 43,367
Vacherie, LA 70090 • 2,169
Vader, WA 98593 • 406
Vadnais Heights, MN 55110 • 5,111
Vaiden, MS 39176 • 924
Vail, CO 81657 • 2,261
Vail, IA 51465 • 490
Vail Homes, NJ 07724 • 900
Valatie, NY 12184 • 1,492
Valders, WI 54245 • 984
Valdese, NC 28690 • 3,364
Valdez, AK 99686 • 3,079
Valdosta, GA 31601-05 • 37,596
Vale, OR 97918 • 1,558
Valencia, AZ 85326 • 1,300
Valencia, PA 16059 • 340
Valencia □, NM • 31,013
Valencia Heights, SC 29205 • 5,328
Valentine, NE 69201 • 2,829
Valentine, TX 79854 • 328
Valhalla, NY 10595 • 6,600
Valhermoso Springs, AL 35775 • 550
Valier, IL 62891 • 729
Valier, MT 59486 • 640
Valier, PA 15780 • 300
Valinda, CA 91744 • 18,700
Vallejo, CA 94590-92 • 80,303
Valley, NE 68064 • 1,716
Valley □, ID • 5,604
Valley □, MT • 10,250
Valley □, NE • 5,633
Valley Bend, WV 26293 • 300
Valley Center, KS 67147 • 3,300
Valley City, ND 58072 • 7,774
Valley City, OH 44280 • 300
Valley Cottage, NY 10989 • 6,007
Valley Falls, KS 66088 • 1,189
Valley Falls, RI 02864 • 10,892
Valley Farms, AZ 85291 • 320
Valley Forge, PA 19481 • 950
Valley Grove, WV 26060 • 597
Valley Head, AL 35989 • 609
Valley Head, WV 26294 • 300
Valley Mills, TX 76689 • 1,236
Valley Park, MO 63088 • 3,232
Valley Springs, SD 57068 • 801
Valley Station, KY 40272 • 20,000
Valley Stream, NY 11580-83 • 35,769
Valley View, PA 17983 • 1,585
Valley View, TX 76272 • 514
Valliant, OK 74764 • 927
Vallonia, IN 47281 • 500
Vallscreek, WV 24890 • 900
Valmeyer, IL 62295 • 898
Valparaiso, FL 32580 • 6,142
Valparaiso, IN 46383 • 22,247
Valparaiso, NE 68065 • 484
Valsetz, OR 97393 • 345
Val Verda, UT 84010 • 6,422
Val Verde □, TX • 35,910
Van, TX 75790 • 1,881
Van, WV 25206 • 500
Van Alstyne, TX 75095 • 1,860
Van Buren, AR 72956 • 12,020
Van Buren, IN 46991 • 935
Van Buren, ME 04785 • 3,282
Van Buren, MO 63965 • 850
Van Buren, OH 45889 • 342
Van Buren □, AR • 13,357
Van Buren □, IA • 8,626
Van Buren □, MI • 66,814
Van Buren □, TN • 4,728
Vance □, NC • 36,748
Vanceboro, ME 04491 • 250
Vanceboro, NC 28586 • 833
Vanceburg, KY 41179 • 1,939
Vancleave, MS 39564 • 1,330
Vancouver, WA 98660-68 • 42,834
Vandalia, IL 62471 • 5,338
Vandalia, MO 63382 • 3,170
Vandalia, OH 45377 • 13,161
Vandemere, NC 28587 • 335
Vander, NC 28301 • 1,671
Vanderbilt, MI 49795 • 525
Vanderbilt, PA 15486 • 689
Vanderbilt, TX 77991 • 750
Vanderburgh □, IN • 167,515
Vandercook Lake, MI 49203 • 4,975
Vandergrift, PA 15690 • 6,823
Vanderwagen, NM 87326 • 300
Vandiver, AL 35176 • 300
Vandling, PA 18421 • 557
Vanduser, MO 63784 • 320
Vandyne, WI 54979 • 300
Van Etten, NY 14889 • 559
Van Horn, TX 79855 • 2,772
Van Horne, IA 52346 • 682
Van Lear, KY 41265 • 2,035
Vanleer, TN 37181 • 401
Vanlue, OH 45890 • 390
Van Meter, IA 50261 • 747
Vanndale, AR 72387 • 350
Vansant, VA 24656 • 600
Van Vleck, TX 77482 • 1,300
Van Vleet, MS 38877 • 270
Van Wert, GA 30153 • 303
Van Wert, IA 50262 • 245
Van Wert, OH 45891 • 11,035
Van Wert □, OH • 30,458
Van Wyck, SC 29744 • 325
Van Zandt □, TX • 31,426
Vardaman, MS 38878 • 1,009
Varina, VA 23231 • 2,000
Varna, IL 61375 • 441
Varnado, LA 70467 • 249
Varnville, SC 29944 • 1,948
Varysburg, NY 14167 • 300
Vashon, WA 98070 • 250
Vass, NC 28394 • 828
Vassar, MI 48768 • 2,727
Vaucluse, SC 29850 • 450
Vaughan, MS 39179 • 275
Vaughn, MT 59487 • 2,270
Vaughn, NM 88353 • 737
Vaughnsville, OH 45893 • 400
Veachland, KY • 700
Veazie, ME 04401 • 1,610
Veblen, SD 57270 • 368
Veedersburg, IN 47987 • 2,261
Vega, TX 79092 • 900
Velarde, NM 87582 • 400
Velda Rose Estates, AZ 85201 • 2,250
Velma, OK 73091 • 831
Velva, ND 58790 • 1,101
Venango, NE 69168 • 230
Venango, PA 16440 • 298
Venango □, PA • 64,444
Veneta, OR 97487 • 2,449
Venice, FL 33595-96 • 12,153
Venice, IL 62090 • 3,480
Venice, LA 70091 • 350
Ventnor City, NJ 08406 • 11,704
Ventura (San Buenaventura), CA 93001-09 • 74,393
Ventura, IA 50482 • 614
Ventura □, CA • 529,174
Venus, FL 33960 • 370
Venus, TX 76084 • 518
Verbena, AL 36091 • 400
Verda, KY 40828 • 1,132
Verden, OK 73092 • 625
Verdi, NV 89439 • 800
Verdigre, NE 68783 • 617
Verdigris, OK 74017 • 300
Verdon, NE 68457 • 278
Verdunville, WV 25649 • 950
Vergas, MN 56587 • 287
Vergennes, IL 62994 • 360
Vergennes, VT 05491 • 2,273
Vermilion, IL 61955 • 299
Vermilion, OH 44089 • 11,012
Vermilion □, IL • 95,222
Vermilion □, LA • 48,458
Vermillion, SD 57069 • 10,136
Vermillion □, IN • 18,229
Vermont, IL 61484 • 885
Vermontville, MI 49096 • 832
Vernal, UT 84078 • 6,600
Verndale, MN 56481 • 504
Vernon, AL 35592 • 2,609
Vernon, CT 06066 • 27,974
Vernon, FL 32462 • 885
Vernon, IN 47282 • 329
Vernon, TX 76384 • 12,695
Vernon, VT 05354 • 250
Vernon □, LA • 53,475
Vernon □, MO • 19,806
Vernon □, WI • 25,642
Vernon Center, MN 56090 • 365
Vernon Hills, IL 60061 • 9,827
Vernonia, OR 97064 • 1,785
Vero Beach, FL 32960-64 • 16,176
Verona, IL 60479 • 251
Verona, KY 41092 • 300
Verona, MS 38879 • 2,497
Verona, MO 65769 • 592
Verona, NJ 07044 • 14,166
Verona, NC 28540 • 600
Verona, OH 45378 • 571
Verona, PA 15147 • 3,179
Verona, WI 53593 • 3,336
Versailles, CT 06383 • 300
Versailles, IL 62378 • 513
Versailles, IN 47042 • 1,560
Versailles, KY 40383 • 6,427
Versailles, MO 65084 • 2,406
Versailles, OH 45380 • 2,384
Vesper, WI 54489 • 554
Vesta, MN 56292 • 360
Vestaburg, MI 48891 • 400
Vestal, NY 13850 • 6,000
Vestal Center, NY 13850 • 900
Vestavia Hills, AL 35216 • 15,722
Vevay, IN 47043 • 1,343
Vian, OK 74962 • 1,521
Viborg, SD 57070 • 812
Viburnum, MO 65566 • 836
Vicco, KY 41773 • 456
Vici, OK 73859 • 845
Vickery, OH 43464 • 230
Vicksburg, MI 49097 • 2,224
Vicksburg, MS 39180 • 25,434
Victor, CO 80860 • 265
Victor, ID 83455 • 323
Victor, IA 52347 • 1,046
Victor, MT 59875 • 450
Victor, NY 14564 • 2,370
Victoria, IL 61485 • 389
Victoria, KS 67671 • 1,328
Victoria, MS 38679 • 950
Victoria, TX 77901-04 • 50,695
Victoria, VA 23974 • 2,004
Victoria □, TX • 68,807
Victorville, CA 92392 • 14,220
Vidalia, GA 30474 • 10,393
Vidalia, LA 71373 • 5,936
Vidor, TX 77662 • 11,834
Vidor, TX 77662 • 12,117
Vienna, GA 31092 • 2,886
Vienna, IL 62995 • 1,420
Vienna, LA 71270 • 519
Vienna, MD 21869 • 300
Vienna, MO 65582 • 514
Vienna, VA 22180 • 15,469
Vienna, WV 26105 • 11,618
View Park, CA 90043 • 5,900
Vigo □, IN • 112,385
Vilas □, WI • 16,535
Villa Grove, IL 61956 • 2,707
Villanova, PA 19085 • 6,600
Villanueva, NM 87583 • 300
Villa Park, CA 92667 • 7,137
Villa Park, IL 60181 • 23,185
Villard, MN 56385 • 275
Villa Rica, GA 30180 • 3,420
Villa Ridge, IL 62996 • 450
Villas, NJ 08251 • 5,909
Ville Platte, LA 70586 • 9,201
Villisca, IA 50864 • 1,434
Vilonia, AR 72173 • 736
Vina, AL 35593 • 346
Vina, CA 96092 • 400
Vinalhaven, ME 04863 • 900
Vincennes, IN 47591 • 20,857
Vincent, AL 35178 • 1,652
Vincent, OH 45784 • 350
Vincentown, NJ 08088 • 800
Vine Grove, KY 40175 • 3,583
Vineland, NJ 08360 • 53,753
Vinemont, AL 35179 • 615
Vineyard Haven, MA 02568 • 1,704
Vinita, OK 74301 • 6,740
Vinton, IA 52349 • 5,040
Vinton, LA 70668 • 3,631
Vinton, OH 45686 • 375
Vinton, VA 24179 • 8,027
Vinton □, OH • 11,584
Vintondale, PA 15961 • 697
Viola, AR 72583 • 362
Viola, IL 61486 • 1,144
Viola, WI 54664 • 696
Violet, LA 70092 • 6,000
Virden, IL 62690 • 3,899
Virden, NM 85534 • 246
Virginia, AL 35020 • 700
Virginia, IL 62691 • 1,825
Virginia, MN 55792 • 11,056
Virginia Beach, VA 23450-65 • 262,199
Virginia City, NV 89440 • 600
Viroqua, WI 54665 • 3,716
Visalia, CA 93277-79 • 49,729
Vista, CA 92083 • 35,834
Vivian, LA 71082 • 4,146
Volcano, HI 96785 • 900
Volga, IA 52077 • 310
Volga, SD 57071 • 1,221

Voluntown, CT 06384 • 300
Volusia □, FL • 258,762
Vonore, TN 37885 • 528
Von Ormy, TX 78073 • 500
Votaw, TX 77376 • 280
Vredenburgh, AL 36481 • 433
Vulcan, MI 49892 • 600

W

Wabash, IN 46992 • 12,985
Wabash □, IL • 13,713
Wabash □, IN • 36,640
Wabasha, MN 55981 • 2,372
Wabasha □, MN • 19,335
Wabasso, FL 32970 • 2,157
Wabasso, MN 56293 • 745
Wabaunsee □, KS • 6,867
Wabbaseka, AR 72175 • 428
Wabeno, WI 54566 • 700
Wachapreague, VA 23480 • 404
Wacissa, FL 32361 • 300
Waco, GA 30182 • 471
Waco, NE 68460 • 225
Waco, NC 28169 • 322
Waco, TX 76701-99 • 101,261
Waconia, MN 55387 • 2,638
Waddington, NY 13694 • 980
Wade, NC 28395 • 474
Wadena, IA 52169 • 230
Wadena, MN 56482 • 4,699
Wadena □, MN • 14,192
Wadesboro, NC 28170 • 4,206
Wadesville, IN 47638 • 300
Wading River, NY 11792 • 2,500
Wadley, AL 36276 • 532
Wadley, GA 30477 • 2,438
Wadsworth, IL 60083 • 1,104
Wadsworth, NV 89442 • 350
Wadsworth, OH 44281 • 15,166
Waelder, TX 78959 • 942
Wagarville, AL 36585 • 300
Wagener, SC 29164 • 903
Waggoner, IL 62572 • 277
Wagner, SD 57380 • 1,453
Wagners Lake, NE 68601 • 400
Wagoner, OK 74467 • 6,191
Wagoner □, OK • 41,801
Wagon Mound, NM 87752 • 416
Wagram, NC 28396 • 617
Wahiawa, HI 96786 • 16,911
Wahkiakum □, WA • 3,832
Wahkon, MN 56386 • 271
Wahoo, NE 68066 • 3,555
Wahpeton, ND 58075 • 9,064
Waialua, HI 96791 • 4,051
Waianae, HI 96792 • 5,000
Waihee, HI 96793 • 413
Waikapu, HI 96793 • 698
Wailua, HI 96746 • 1,587
Wailuku, HI 96793 • 10,260
Waimanalo, HI 96795 • 3,562
Waimea, HI 96712 • 600
Waimea, HI 96796 • 1,569
Wainwright, AK 99782 • 405
Wainwright, OH 44686 • 350
Waipahu, HI 96797 • 29,139
Waipio Acres, HI 96786 • 4,091
Waite Park, MN 56387 • 3,496
Waitsburg, WA 99361 • 1,035
Waitsfield, VT 05673 • 300
Wakarusa, IN 46573 • 1,281
Wake □, NC • 301,327
Wa Keeney, KS 67672 • 2,388
Wakefield, KS 67487 • 803
Wakefield, MA 01880 • 24,895
Wakefield, MI 49968 • 2,591
Wakefield, NE 68784 • 1,125
Wakefield, OH 45687 • 250
Wakefield, RI 02879-83 • 3,400
Wakefield, VA 23888 • 1,355
Wake Forest, NC 27587 • 3,780
Wakeman, OH 44889 • 906
Wakita, OK 73771 • 526
Wakonda, SD 57073 • 383
Wakpala, SD 57658 • 250
Wakulla, FL 32327 • 250
Wakulla □, FL • 10,887
Walbridge, OH 43465 • 2,900
Walcott, IA 52773 • 1,425
Walden, CO 80480 • 947
Walden, NY 12586 • 5,659
Waldo, AR 71770 • 1,685
Waldo, FL 32694 • 993
Waldo, OH 43356 • 347
Waldo □, ME • 28,414
Waldoboro, ME 04572 • 1,195
Waldorf, MD 20601 • 9,782
Waldorf, MN 56091 • 249
Waldport, OR 97394 • 1,274
Waldron, AR 72958 • 2,642
Waldron, IN 46182 • 800
Waldron, MI 49288 • 570
Waldwick, NJ 07463 • 10,802
Wales, MA 01081 • 500
Waleska, GA 30183 • 450
Walhalla, MI 49458 • 400
Walhalla, ND 58282 • 1,429
Walhalla, SC 29691 • 3,977
Walker, IA 52352 • 733
Walker, LA 70785 • 2,957
Walker, MI 49504 • 15,088
Walker, MN 56484 • 970
Walker, MO 64790 • 325
Walker □, AL • 68,660
Walker □, GA • 56,470
Walker □, TX • 41,789
Walkersville, MD 21793 • 2,212
Walkerton, IN 46574 • 2,051
Walkertown, NC 27051 • 2,100
Walkerville, MI 49459 • 296
Walkerville, MT 59701 • 887
Wall, SD 57790 • 770
Wallace, ID 83873 • 1,736
Wallace, NE 69169 • 349
Wallace, NC 28466 • 2,903
Wallace, NY 14890 • 300
Wallace, WV 26448 • 900
Wallace □, KS • 2,045
Walland, TN 37886 • 400
Walla Walla, WA 99362 • 25,618
Walla Walla □, WA • 47,435
Walled Lake, MI 48088 • 4,748
Wallen, IN 46806 • 1,200
Waller, TX 77484 • 1,241
Waller □, TX • 19,798
Wallingford, CT 06492 • 37,274
Wallingford, IA 51365 • 256
Wallingford, VT 05773 • 1,141
Wallington, NJ 07057 • 10,741
Wallis, TX 77485 • 1,138
Wallkill, NY 12589 • 1,849
Wall Lake, IA 51466 • 892
Wallowa, OR 97885 • 847
Wallowa □, OR • 7,273
Walls, MS 38680 • 400
Wallsburg, UT 84082 • 239
Walnut, CA 91789 • 12,478
Walnut, IL 61376 • 1,513
Walnut, IA 51577 • 897
Walnut, KS 66780 • 308
Walnut, MS 38683 • 513
Walnut, NC 28753 • 550
Walnut Bottom, PA 17266 • 400
Walnut Cove, NC 27052 • 1,147
Walnut Creek, CA 94595-98 • 53,643
Walnut Grove, AL 35990 • 510
Walnut Grove, MN 56180 • 753
Walnut Grove, MS 39189 • 439
Walnut Grove, MO 65770 • 504
Walnut Hill, FL 32568 • 300
Walnut Hill, ME 04021 • 300
Walnut Park, CA 90255 • 11,811
Walnutport, PA 18088 • 2,007
Walnut Ridge, AR 72476 • 4,152
Walpole, MA 02081 • 5,274
Walpole, NH 03608 • 700
Walsenburg, CO 81089 • 3,945
Walsh, CO 81090 • 884
Walsh □, ND • 15,371
Walston, PA 15781 • 300
Walterboro, SC 29488 • 6,209
Walters, OK 73572 • 2,778
Waltersville, MS 39180 • 300
Walterville, OR 97489 • 250
Walthall □, MS • 13,761
Waltham, MA 02154 • 58,200
Walthill, NE 68067 • 847
Walthourville, GA 31333 • 905
Walton, FL 33457 • 300
Walton, IN 46994 • 1,202
Walton, KS 67151 • 269
Walton, KY 41094 • 1,651
Walton, NY 13856 • 3,329
Walton, WV 25286 • 250
Walton □, FL • 21,300
Walton □, GA • 31,211
Waltonville, IL 62894 • 414
Walworth, NY 14568 • 600
Walworth, WI 53184 • 1,607
Walworth □, SD • 7,011
Walworth □, WI • 71,507
Wamac, IL 62801 • 1,665
Wamego, KS 66547 • 3,159
Wamesit, MA 01876 • 2,700
Wampsville, NY 13163 • 569
Wampum, PA 16157 • 851
Wamsutter, WY 82336 • 681
Wanamie, PA 18634 • 600
Wanamingo, MN 55983 • 717
Wanaque, NJ 07465 • 10,025
Wanatah, IN 46390 • 879
Wanblee, SD 57577 • 350
Wanchese, NC 27981 • 1,105
Wando Woods, SC 29405 • 5,253
Wanette, OK 74878 • 473
Wantagh, NY 11793 • 22,300
Wapakoneta, OH 45895 • 8,402
Wapanucka, OK 73461 • 472
Wapato, WA 98951 • 3,307
Wapella, IL 61777 • 768
Wapello, IA 52653 • 2,011
Wapello □, IA • 40,241
Wappingers Falls, NY 12590 • 5,110
Waquoit, MA 02536 • 400
War, WV 24892 • 2,158
Ward, AR 72176 • 981
Ward □, ND • 58,392
Ward □, TX • 13,976
Wardell, MO 63879 • 299
Warden, WA 98857 • 1,479
Wardensville, WV 26851 • 241
Wardner, ID 83837 • 423
Ware, MA 01082 • 6,806
Ware □, GA • 37,180
Wareham, MA 02571 • 2,473
Warehouse Point, CT 06088 • 1,850
Waresboro, GA 31564 • 350
Ware Shoals, SC 29692 • 2,370
Waretown, NJ 08758 • 1,175
Warfield, KY 41267 • 350
Warm Beach, WA 98292 • 300
Warminster, PA 18974 • 35,543
Warm Springs, GA 31830 • 425
Warm Springs, OR 97761 • 500
Warm Springs, VA 24484 • 425
Warner, NH 03278 • 700
Warner, OK 74469 • 1,310
Warner, SD 57479 • 322
Warner Robins, GA 31093 • 39,893
Warr Acres, OK 73132 • 9,940
Warren, AR 71671 • 7,646
Warren, IL 61087 • 1,595
Warren, IN 46792 • 1,254
Warren, ME 04864 • 400
Warren, MA 01083 • 1,548
Warren, MI 48089-93 • 161,134
Warren, MN 56762 • 2,105
Warren, NH 03279 • 450
Warren, OH 44481-86 • 56,629
Warren, OR 97053 • 800
Warren, PA 16365 • 12,146
Warren, RI 02885 • 10,640
Warren, TX 77664 • 600
Warren, VT 05674 • 500
Warren □, GA • 6,583
Warren □, IL • 21,943
Warren □, IN • 8,976
Warren □, IA • 34,878
Warren □, KY • 71,828
Warren □, MS • 51,627
Warren □, MO • 14,900
Warren □, NJ • 84,429
Warren □, NC • 16,232
Warren □, NY • 54,854
Warren □, OH • 99,276
Warren □, PA • 47,449
Warren □, TN • 32,653
Warren □, VA • 21,200
Warrendale, PA 15086 • 800
Warren Park, IN 46219 • 1,803
Warrens, WI 54666 • 300
Warrensburg, IL 62573 • 1,372
Warrensburg, MO 64093 • 13,807
Warrensburg, NY 12885 • 2,743
Warrensville Heights, OH 44122 • 16,565
Warrenton, GA 30828 • 2,172
Warrenton, MO 63383 • 3,219
Warrenton, NC 27589 • 908
Warrenton, OR 97146 • 2,493
Warrenton, VA 22186 • 3,907
Warrenville, IL 60555 • 7,519
Warrenville, SC 29851 • 1,029
Warrick □, IN • 41,474
Warrington, FL 32507 • 15,792
Warrior, AL 35180 • 3,260
Warriors Mark, PA 16877 • 275
Warroad, MN 56763 • 1,216
Warsaw, IL 62379 • 1,842
Warsaw, IN 46580 • 10,647
Warsaw, KY 41095 • 1,328
Warsaw, MO 65355 • 1,494
Warsaw, NC 28398 • 2,910
Warsaw, NY 14569 • 3,619
Warsaw, OH 43844 • 765
Warsaw, VA 22572 • 771
Wartburg, TN 37887 • 761
Warthen, GA 31094 • 250
Wartrace, TN 37183 • 540
Warwick, GA 31796 • 488
Warwick, MD 21912 • 350
Warwick, NY 10990 • 4,320
Wasatch □, UT • 8,523
Wasco, CA 93280 • 9,613
Wasco, OR 97065 • 415
Wasco □, OR • 21,732
Waseca, MN 56093 • 8,219
Waseca □, MN • 18,448
Washakie □, WY • 9,496
Washburn, IL 61570 • 1,206
Washburn, IA 50706 • 1,400
Washburn, ME 04786 • 1,221
Washburn, MO 65772 • 289
Washburn, ND 58577 • 1,767
Washburn, WI 54891 • 2,080
Washburn □, WI • 13,174
Washington, AR 71862 • 265
Washington, CT 06793 • 600
Washington, DC 20001-99 • 638,432
Washington, GA 30673 • 4,662
Washington, IL 61571 • 10,364
Washington, IN 47501 • 11,325
Washington, IA 52353 • 6,584
Washington, KS 66968 • 1,488
Washington, KY 41096 • 624
Washington, LA 70589 • 1,266
Washington, MS 39190 • 900
Washington, MO 63090 • 9,251
Washington, NJ 07882 • 6,429
Washington, NC 27889 • 8,418
Washington, OK 73093 • 477
Washington, PA 15301 • 18,363
Washington, UT 84780 • 3,092
Washington, VT 05675 • 300
Washington, VA 22747 • 247
Washington, WV 26181 • 300
Washington □, AL • 16,821
Washington □, AR • 100,494
Washington □, CO • 5,304
Washington □, FL • 14,509
Washington □, GA • 18,842
Washington □, ID • 8,803
Washington □, IL • 15,472
Washington □, IN • 21,932
Washington □, IA • 20,141
Washington □, KS • 8,543
Washington □, KY • 10,764
Washington □, LA • 44,207
Washington □, ME • 34,963
Washington □, MD • 113,086
Washington □, MN • 113,571
Washington □, MS • 72,344
Washington □, MO • 17,983
Washington □, NE • 15,508
Washington □, NC • 14,801
Washington □, NY • 54,795
Washington □, OH • 64,266
Washington □, OK • 48,113
Washington □, OR • 245,860
Washington □, PA • 217,074
Washington □, RI • 93,317
Washington □, TN • 88,755
Washington □, TX • 21,998
Washington □, UT • 26,065
Washington □, VT • 52,393
Washington □, VA • 46,487
Washington □, WI • 84,848
Washington Court House, OH 43160 • 12,682
Washington Crossing, NJ 08560 • 500
Washington Depot, CT 06794 • 600
Washington Park, IL 62204 • 8,223
Washington Terrace, UT 84403 • 8,212
Washington Township, NJ 07675 • 9,550
Washita □, OK • 13,798
Washoe □, NV • 193,623
Washoe City, NV 89701 • 400
Washougal, WA 98671 • 3,834
Washta, IA 51061 • 320
Washtenaw □, MI • 264,748
Washtucna, WA 99371 • 266
Wasilla, AK 99687 • 1,559
Waskom, TX 75692 • 1,821
Wataga, IL 61488 • 996
Watauga, TN 37694 • 376
Watauga, TX 76148 • 10,284
Watauga □, NC • 31,666
Watch Hill, RI 02891 • 350
Watchung, NJ 07060 • 5,290
Waterboro, ME 04087 • 500
Waterbury, CT 06701-49 • 103,266
Waterbury, VT 05676 • 1,892
Waterbury Center, VT 05677 • 500
Waterflow, NM 87421 • 500
Waterford, CT 06385 • 2,736

Waterford, IN 46360 • *600*
Waterford, MI 48095 • *6,420*
Waterford, MS 38685 • *250*
Waterford, NY 12188 • *2,405*
Waterford, OH 45786 • *480*
Waterford, PA 16441 • *1,568*
Waterford, VA 22190 • *325*
Waterford, WI 53185 • *2,051*
Waterford Works, NJ 08089 • *600*
Waterloo, AL 35677 • *260*
Waterloo, IL 62298 • *4,646*
Waterloo, IN 46793 • *1,951*
Waterloo, IA 50701-99 • *75,985*
Waterloo, NE 68069 • *450*
Waterloo, NY 13165 • *5,303*
Waterloo, WI 53594 • *2,393*
Waterman, IL 60556 • *943*
Waterproof, LA 71375 • *1,339*
Watersmeet, MI 49969 • *700*
Watertown, CT 06795 • *6,000*
Watertown, FL 32055 • *600*
Watertown, MA 02172 • *34,384*
Watertown, NY 13601 • *27,861*
Watertown, SD 57201 • *15,649*
Watertown, TN 37184 • *1,300*
Watertown, WI 53094 • *18,113*
Water Valley, KY 42085 • *395*
Water Valley, MS 38965 • *4,147*
Water Valley, TX 76958 • *300*
Waterville, KS 66548 • *694*
Waterville, ME 04901 • *17,779*
Waterville, MA 01475 • *300*
Waterville, MN 56096 • *1,717*
Waterville, NY 13480 • *1,672*
Waterville, OH 43566 • *3,884*
Waterville, WA 98858 • *908*
Watervliet, MI 49098 • *1,867*
Watervliet, NY 12189 • *11,354*
Watford City, ND 58854 • *2,119*
Wathena, KS 66090 • *1,418*
Watkins, MN 55389 • *757*
Watkins Glen, NY 14891 • *2,440*
Watkinsville, GA 30677 • *1,240*
Watonga, OK 73772 • *4,139*
Watonwan □, MN • *12,361*
Watseka, IL 60970 • *5,543*
Watson, AR 71674 • *433*
Watson, IL 62473 • *551*
Watson, IN 47130 • *400*
Watson, MN 56295 • *238*
Watson Chapel, AR 71601 • *900*
Watsontown, PA 17777 • *2,366*
Watsonville, CA 95076 • *23,663*
Watts, OK 74964 • *316*
Watts 0Z, CA
Wattsburg, PA 16442 • *513*
Wattsville, SC 29360 • *1,324*
Waubay, SD 57273 • *675*
Waubun, MN 56589 • *390*
Wauchula, FL 33873 • *2,986*
Waucoma, IA 52171 • *308*
Wauconda, IL 60084 • *5,688*
Waukau, WI 54980 • *260*
Waukee, IA 50263 • *2,227*
Waukegan, IL 60085-87 • *67,653*
Waukesha, WI 53186 • *50,365*
Waukesha □, WI • *280,080*
Waukomis, OK 73773 • *1,551*
Waukon, IA 52172 • *3,983*
Wauna, WA 98395 • *300*
Waunakee, WI 53597 • *3,866*
Wauneta, NE 69045 • *746*
Waupaca, WI 54981 • *4,472*
Waupaca □, WI • *42,831*
Waupun, WI 53963 • *8,132*
Wauregan, CT 06387 • *900*
Waurika, OK 73573 • *2,258*
Wausa, NE 68786 • *647*
Wausau, FL 32463 • *347*
Wausau, WI 54401 • *32,426*
Wausaukee, WI 54177 • *648*
Wauseon, OH 43567 • *6,173*
Waushara □, WI • *18,526*
Wautoma, WI 54982 • *1,629*
Wauwatosa, WI 53213 • *51,308*
Wauzeka, WI 53826 • *580*
Waveland, IN 47989 • *559*
Waveland, MS 39576 • *4,186*
Waverly, AL 36879 • *228*
Waverly, GA 31565 • *250*
Waverly, IL 62692 • *1,537*
Waverly, IA 50677 • *8,444*
Waverly, KS 66871 • *671*
Waverly, KY 42462 • *434*
Waverly, MN 55390 • *470*
Waverly, MO 64096 • *941*
Waverly, NE 68462 • *1,726*
Waverly, NY 14892 • *4,738*
Waverly, OH 45690 • *4,603*
Waverly, TN 37185 • *4,405*
Waverly, VA 23890 • *2,284*
Waverly, WV 26184 • *400*
Waverly Hall, GA 31831 • *913*
Wawaka, IN 46794 • *250*
Waxahachie, TX 75165 • *14,624*
Waxhaw, NC 28173 • *1,208*
Waycross, GA 31501 • *19,371*
Wayland, IA 52654 • *720*
Wayland, KY 41666 • *601*
Wayland, MA 01778 • *5,500*
Wayland, MI 49348 • *2,023*
Wayland, MO 63472 • *498*
Wayland, NY 14572 • *1,846*
Waylyn, SC 29405 • *2,400*
Waymart, PA 18472 • *1,248*
Wayne, MI 48184 • *21,159*
Wayne, NE 68787 • *5,240*
Wayne, NJ 07470 • *46,474*
Wayne, NY 14893 • *450*
Wayne, OH 43466 • *894*
Wayne, OK 73095 • *621*
Wayne, PA 19087 • *8,900*
Wayne, WV 25570 • *1,495*
Wayne □, GA • *20,750*
Wayne □, IL • *18,059*
Wayne □, IN • *76,058*
Wayne □, IA • *8,199*
Wayne □, KY • *17,022*
Wayne □, MI • *2,337,891*
Wayne □, MS • *19,135*
Wayne □, MO • *11,277*
Wayne □, NE • *9,858*
Wayne □, NC • *97,054*
Wayne □, NY • *84,581*
Wayne □, OH • *97,408*
Wayne □, PA • *35,237*
Wayne □, TN • *13,946*
Wayne □, UT • *1,911*
Wayne □, WV • *46,021*
Wayne City, IL 62895 • *1,132*
Waynesboro, GA 30830 • *5,760*
Waynesboro, MS 39367 • *5,349*
Waynesboro, PA 17268 • *9,726*
Waynesboro, TN 38485 • *2,109*
Waynesboro, VA 22980 • *15,329*
Waynesburg, KY 40489 • *250*
Waynesburg, OH 44688 • *1,160*
Waynesburg, PA 15370 • *4,482*
Waynesville, GA 31566 • *300*
Waynesville, IL 61778 • *569*
Waynesville, MO 65583 • *2,879*
Waynesville, NC 28786 • *6,765*
Waynesville, OH 45068 • *1,796*
Waynetown, IN 47990 • *915*
Waynewood, VA 22308 • *4,500*
Waynoka, OK 73860 • *1,377*
Wayside, MS 38780 • *300*
Wayzata, MN 55391 • *3,621*
Weakley □, TN • *32,896*
Weare, NH 03281 • *250*
Weatherford, OK 73096 • *9,640*
Weatherford, TX 76086 • *12,049*
Weatherly, PA 18255 • *2,891*
Weatogue, CT 06089 • *2,249*
Weaubleau, MO 65774 • *464*
Weaver, AL 36277 • *2,765*
Weaverville, CA 96093 • *2,787*
Weaverville, NC 28787 • *1,495*
Webb, AL 36376 • *448*
Webb, MS 38966 • *782*
Webb □, TX • *99,258*
Webb City, MO 64870 • *7,309*
Webbers Falls, OK 74470 • *461*
Webberville, MI 48892 • *1,535*
Weber □, UT • *144,616*
Weber City, VA 24251 • *1,543*
Webster, FL 33597 • *856*
Webster, IN 47392 • *350*
Webster, MA 01570 • *14,480*
Webster, NY 14580 • *5,499*
Webster, PA 15087 • *800*
Webster, SD 57274 • *2,417*
Webster, TX 77598 • *2,405*
Webster, WI 54893 • *610*
Webster □, GA • *2,341*
Webster □, IA • *45,953*
Webster □, KY • *14,832*
Webster □, LA • *43,631*
Webster □, MS • *10,300*
Webster □, MO • *20,414*
Webster □, NE • *4,858*
Webster □, WV • *12,245*
Webster City, IA 50595 • *8,572*
Webster Groves, MO 63119 • *23,097*
Webster Springs, WV 26288 • *939*
Websterville, VT 05678 • *600*
Wedderburn, OR 97491 • *250*
Wedgewood, MO 63031 • *5,700*
Wedowee, AL 36278 • *908*
Wedron, IL 60557 • *300*
Weed, CA 96094 • *2,879*
Weed Heights, NV 89447 • *650*
Weedsport, NY 13166 • *1,952*
Weedville, PA 15868 • *600*
Weehawken, NJ 07087 • *13,168*
Weekapaug, RI 02891 • *275*
Weeksbury, KY 41667 • *700*
Weeksville, NC 27909 • *450*
Weems, VA 22576 • *250*
Weeping Water, NE 68463 • *1,109*
Weidman, MI 48893 • *450*
Weimar, TX 78962 • *2,128*
Weiner, AR 72479 • *750*
Weinert, TX 76388 • *253*
Weippe, ID 83553 • *828*
Weir, KS 66781 • *705*
Weir, MS 39772 • *553*
Weirsdale, FL 32695 • *1,500*
Weirton, WV 26062 • *25,371*
Weiser, ID 83672 • *4,771*
Welaka, FL 32093 • *492*
Welch, OK 74369 • *697*
Welch, TX 79377 • *400*
Welch, WV 24801 • *3,885*
Welches, OR 97067 • *500*
Welcome, LA 70086 • *450*
Welcome, MN 56181 • *855*
Welcome, SC 29611 • *6,922*
Weld □, CO • *123,438*
Weldon, IL 61882 • *531*
Weldon, NC 27890 • *1,844*
Weleetka, OK 74880 • *1,195*
Wellborn, FL 32094 • *400*
Wellersburg, PA 15564 • *265*
Wellesley, MA 02181 • *27,209*
Wellfleet, MA 02667 • *950*
Wellford, SC 29385 • *2,143*
Wellington, CO 80549 • *1,215*
Wellington, IL 60973 • *370*
Wellington, KS 67152 • *8,212*
Wellington, MO 64097 • *780*
Wellington, OH 44090 • *4,146*
Wellington, TX 79095 • *3,043*
Wellington, UT 84542 • *1,406*
Wellman, IA 52356 • *1,125*
Wellman, TX 79378 • *239*
Wellpinit, WA 99040 • *250*
Wells, ME 04090 • *850*
Wells, MI 49894 • *1,100*
Wells, MN 56097 • *2,777*
Wells, NV 89835 • *1,218*
Wells, NY 12190 • *570*
Wells, TX 75976 • *926*
Wells, VT 05774 • *400*
Wells □, IN • *25,401*
Wells □, ND • *6,979*
Wells Beach, ME 04090 • *300*
Wellsboro, PA 16901 • *3,805*
Wellsburg, IA 50680 • *761*
Wellsburg, NY 14894 • *647*
Wellsburg, WV 26070 • *3,963*
Wells River, VT 05081 • *396*
Wellston, MI 49689 • *250*
Wellston, OH 45692 • *6,016*
Wellston, OK 74881 • *802*
Wellsville, KS 66092 • *1,612*
Wellsville, MO 63384 • *1,546*
Wellsville, NY 14895 • *5,769*
Wellsville, OH 43968 • *5,095*
Wellsville, PA 17365 • *347*
Wellsville, UT 84339 • *1,952*
Wellton, AZ 85356 • *911*
Welsh, LA 70591 • *3,515*
Wemme, OR 97067 • *500*
Wenatchee, WA 98801 • *17,257*
Wendell, ID 83355 • *1,974*
Wendell, NC 27591 • *2,222*
Wenden, AZ 85357 • *300*
Wendover, UT 84083 • *1,099*
Wenham, MA 01984 • *3,897*
Wenona, IL 61377 • *1,025*
Wenona, MD 21870 • *320*
Wenonah, NJ 08090 • *2,303*
Wentworth, NH 03282 • *250*
Wentzville, MO 63385 • *3,193*
Weott, CA 95571 • *450*
Wequetequock, CT 02891 • *800*
Weskan, KS 67762 • *250*
Weslaco, TX 78596 • *19,331*
Wesley, IA 50483 • *598*
Wesleyville, PA 16510 • *3,998*
Wessington, SD 57381 • *327*
Wessington Springs, SD 57382 • *1,203*
Wesson, MS 39191 • *1,313*
West, MS 39192 • *253*
West, TX 76691 • *2,485*
West Abington, MA 02351 • *2,000*
West Acton, MA 01720 • *5,800*
West Alexander, PA 15376 • *286*
West Alexandria, OH 45381 • *1,313*
West Allis, WI 53214 • *63,982*
Westalton, MO 63386 • *500*
West Amityville, NY 11758 • *6,470*
West Andover, MA 01810 • *3,700*
West Athens, CA 90247 • *8,531*
West Babylon, NY 11704 • *32,500*
West Baden Springs, IN 47469 • *796*
West Barnstable, MA 02668 • *500*
West Barrington, RI 02806 • *3,700*
West Baton Rouge □, LA • *19,086*
West Bay, FL 32407 • *300*
West Bay Shore, NY 11706 • *8,900*
West Bend, IA 50597 • *941*
West Bend, WI 53095 • *21,484*
West Berlin, NJ 08091 • *3,300*
West Billerica, MA 01862 • *2,000*
West Blocton, AL 35184 • *1,147*
West Bloomfield, NY 14585 • *500*
Westborough, MA 01581 • *13,619*
West Bountiful, UT 84087 • *3,556*
West Boylston, MA 01583 • *3,500*
West Branch, IA 52358 • *1,867*
West Branch, MI 48661 • *1,785*
West Bridgewater, MA 02379 • *2,100*
Westbrook, CT 06498 • *2,035*
Westbrook, ME 04092 • *14,976*
Westbrook, MN 56183 • *978*
Westbrook, TX 79565 • *298*
West Brookfield, MA 01585 • *1,423*
Westbrook Park, PA 19018 • *5,700*
Westbrookville, NY 12785 • *300*
West Burke, VT 05871 • *338*
West Burlington, IA 52655 • *3,371*
Westbury, NY 11590 • *13,871*
West Buxton, ME 04093 • *400*
Westby, MT 59275 • *291*
Westby, WI 54667 • *1,797*
West Caldwell, NJ 07006 • *11,407*
West Cape May, NJ 08204 • *1,091*
West Carroll □, LA • *12,922*
West Carrollton, OH 45449 • *13,148*
West Carson, CA 90502 • *17,997*
West Carthage, NY 13619 • *1,824*
West Charleston, VT 05872 • *300*
West Chatham, MA 02669 • *1,398*
West Chazy, NY 12992 • *700*
Westchester, FL 33144 • *20,000*
Westchester, IL 60153 • *17,730*
West Chester, OH 45069 • *400*
West Chester, PA 19380-82 • *17,435*
Westchester □, NY • *866,599*
West Chesterfield, NH 03466 • *450*
West Chicago, IL 60185 • *12,550*
West City, IL 62812 • *886*
Westcliffe, CO 81252 • *324*
West College Corner, IN 45003 • *614*
West Columbia, SC 29169 • *10,409*
West Columbia, TX 77486 • *4,109*
West Concord, MA 01742 • *5,331*
West Concord, MN 55985 • *762*
West Concord, NC 28025 • *3,200*
West Cornwall, CT 06796 • *250*
West Covina, CA 91790-93 • *80,291*
West Creek, NJ 08092 • *500*
West Crossett, AR 71635 • *1,466*
West Cumberland, ME 04021 • *800*
Westdale, IL • *10,300*
West Decatur, PA 16878 • *600*
West Dennis, MA 02670 • *2,030*
West Des Moines, IA 50265 • *21,894*
West Dover, VT 05356 • *250*
West Dudley, MA 01550 • *350*
West Elkton, OH 45070 • *277*
West Elmira, NY 14905 • *5,901*
West Elwood, IN 46036 • *250*
West End, IL • *7,554*
West End, NC 27376 • *900*
West Enfield, ME 04493 • *440*
West Epping, NH 03042 • *300*
Westerly, RI 02891 • *14,093*
Western, NE 68464 • *336*
Western Grove, AR 72685 • *378*
Western Hills, CO 80221 • *6,000*
Westernport, MD 21562 • *2,706*
Western Springs, IL 60558 • *12,876*
Westerville, OH 43081 • *23,414*
West Fairview, PA 17025 • *1,426*
West Falmouth, MA 02574 • *1,200*
West Fargo, ND 58078 • *10,099*
West Farmington, ME 04992 • *350*
West Farmington, OH 44491 • *563*
West Feliciana □, LA • *12,186*
Westfield, IL 62474 • *733*
Westfield, IN 46074 • *2,783*
Westfield, ME 04787 • *245*

Westfield, MA 01085 • *36,465*
Westfield, NJ 07090-92 • *30,447*
Westfield, NC 27053 • *600*
Westfield, NY 14787 • *3,446*
Westfield, PA 16950 • *1,268*
Westfield, WI 53964 • *1,033*
Westfield Center, OH 44251 • *791*
Westfir, OR 97492 • *312*
Westford, MA 01886 • *1,000*
West Fork, AR 72774 • *1,526*
West Frankfort, IL 62896 • *9,437*
West Friendship, MD 21794 • *500*
Westgate, FL 33401 • *2,100*
Westgate, IA 50681 • *263*
West Glacier, MT 59936 • *250*
West Goshen, CT 06756 • *600*
West Granby, CT 06090 • *600*
West Groton, MA 01472 • *950*
West Grove, PA 19390 • *1,820*
Westham, VA 23229 • *3,600*
West Hamlin, WV 25571 • *643*
Westhampton, MA 01027 • *250*
West Hanover, MA 02339 • *1,600*
West Harrison, IN 47060 • *328*
West Hartford, CT 06107 • *61,306*
West Hartford, VT 05084 • *275*
West Hartland, CT 06091 • *300*
West Hatfield, MA 01088 • *400*
West Haven, CT 06516 • *53,184*
West Haven, OR 97225 • *3,400*
West Haverstraw, NY 10993 • *9,181*
West Hazleton, PA 18201 • *4,871*
West Helena, AR 72390 • *11,367*
West Hempstead, NY 11552 • *26,500*
West Hickory, PA 16370 • *380*
Westhoff, TX 77994 • *450*
West Hollywood, CA 90069 • *35,703*
Westhope, ND 58793 • *741*
West Huntington, NY 11743 • *6,170*
West Hyannisport, MA 02672 • *1,200*
West Islip, NY 11795 • *29,533*
West Jefferson, NC 28694 • *822*
West Jefferson, OH 43162 • *4,448*
West Jordan, UT 84084 • *27,192*
West Kennebunk, ME 04094 • *400*
West Kingston, RI 02892 • *700*
West Lafayette, IN 47906 • *21,247*
West Lafayette, OH 43845 • *2,225*
Westlake, LA 70669 • *5,246*
Westlake, OH 44145 • *19,483*
Westland, MI 48185 • *84,603*
West Laramie, WY 82070 • *2,000*
West Lawn, PA 19609 • *1,686*
West Lebanon, IN 47991 • *946*
West Lebanon, ME 04027 • *280*
West Leisenring, PA 15489 • *700*
West Leyden, NY 13489 • *250*
West Liberty, IA 52776 • *2,723*
West Liberty, KY 41472 • *1,381*
West Liberty, OH 43357 • *1,653*
West Liberty, WV 26074 • *744*
West Linn, OR 97068 • *12,956*
West Long Branch, NJ 07764 • *7,380*
West Manchester, OH 45382 • *448*
West Mansfield, MA 02048 • *500*
West Mansfield, OH 43358 • *716*
West Marion, NC 28752 • *1,596*
West Medway, MA 02053 • *2,269*
West Melbourne, FL 32901 • *5,078*
West Memphis, AR 72301 • *28,138*
Westmere, NY 12203 • *5,500*
West Miami, FL 33174 • *6,076*
West Middlesex, PA 16159 • *1,064*
West Middleton, IN 46995 • *360*
West Mifflin, PA 15122 • *26,552*
West Milford, NJ 07480 • *1,600*
West Milton, OH 45383 • *4,119*
West Milton, PA 17886 • *775*
West Milwaukee, WI 53214 • *3,535*
West Mineral, KS 66782 • *229*
Westminster, CA 92683 • *71,133*
Westminster, CO 80030 • *50,211*
Westminster, MD 21157 • *8,808*
Westminster, MA 01473 • *950*
Westminster, SC 29693 • *3,114*
Westminster, VT 05158 • *319*
West Modesto, CA 95351 • *6,135*
West Monroe, LA 71291 • *14,993*
Westmont, CA 90044 • *27,916*
Westmont, IL 60559 • *16,718*
Westmont, NJ 08108 • *5,700*
Westmont, PA 15905 • *6,113*
Westmoreland, KS 66549 • *598*
Westmoreland, TN 37186 • *1,754*
Westmoreland □, PA • *392,294*
Westmoreland □, VA • *14,041*
Westmorland, CA 92281 • *1,590*

West Muncie, IN 47396 • *300*
West Mystic, CT 06388 • *3,364*
West Newbury, MA 01985 • *950*
West Newton, PA 15089 • *3,387*
West New York, NJ 07093 • *39,194*
West Norriton, PA 19401 • *14,034*
Weston, CT 06883 • *1,200*
Weston, ID 83286 • *310*
Weston, MA 02193 • *11,169*
Weston, MO 64098 • *1,440*
Weston, NE 68070 • *286*
Weston, OH 43569 • *1,708*
Weston, OR 97886 • *719*
Weston, VT 05161 • *300*
Weston, WV 26452 • *6,250*
Weston, WI 54476 • *3,400*
Weston □, WY • *7,106*
West Orange, NJ 07052 • *39,400*
West Ossipee, NH 03890 • *250*
Westover, MD 21871 • *525*
Westover, PA 16692 • *517*
Westover, TN 38301 • *500*
Westover, WV 26505 • *4,884*
West Palm Beach, FL 33401-16 • *63,305*
West Paris, ME 04289 • *500*
West Park, NY 12493 • *700*
West Paterson, NJ 07424 • *11,293*
West Pawlet, VT 05775 • *500*
West Pelham, MA 01002 • *450*
West Pelzer, SC 29669 • *944*
West Pensacola, FL 32505 • *24,571*
West Peoria, IL 61604 • *5,219*
West Peru, ME 04290 • *435*
West Peterborough, NH 03468 • *500*
Westphalia, MI 48894 • *896*
Westphalia, MO 65085 • *285*
West Pittsburg, CA 94565 • *6,000*
West Pittsburg, PA 16160 • *950*
West Pittston, PA 18643 • *5,980*
West Plains, MO 65775 • *7,741*
West Point, AL 35055 • *248*
West Point, AR 72178 • *226*
West Point, CA 95255 • *1,500*
West Point, GA 31833 • *4,294*
West Point, IL 62380 • *223*
Westpoint, IN 47992 • *500*
West Point, IA 52656 • *1,133*
West Point, KY 40177 • *1,339*
West Point, MS 39773 • *8,811*
West Point, NE 68788 • *3,609*
West Point, NY 10996 • *8,000*
Westpoint, TN 38486 • *350*
West Point, UT 84015 • *2,170*
West Point, VA 23181 • *2,726*
Westport, CT 06880 • *25,290*
Westport, IN 47283 • *1,450*
47283 • *1,450*
Westport, MA 02790 • *1,850*
Westport, NH 03470 • *450*
Westport, NY 12993 • *613*
Westport, OR 97016 • *500*
Westport, WA 98595 • *1,954*
Westport Point, MA 02791 • *450*
West Portsmouth, OH 45662 • *4,095*
West Puente Valley, CA 91744 • *20,445*
West Reading, PA 19611 • *4,507*
West Redding, CT 06896 • *250*
West Ridge, AR 72391 • *350*
West Rupert, VT 05776 • *300*
West Rutland, VT 05777 • *2,351*
West Sacramento, CA 95691 • *10,875*
West Saint Paul, MN 55118 • *18,527*
West Salem, IL 62476 • *1,145*
West Salem, OH 44287 • *1,357*
West Salem, WI 54669 • *3,276*
West Sayville, NY 11796 • *5,000*
West Scarborough, ME 04074 • *700*
West Seneca, NY 14224 • *51,210*
Westside, IA 51467 • *387*
West Simsbury, CT 06092 • *2,140*
West Slope, OR 97225 • *5,364*
West Springfield, MA 01089 • *27,042*
West Springfield, VA 22152 • *16,000*
West Stafford, CT 06076 • *450*
West Stockbridge, MA 01266 • *800*
West Suffield, CT 06093 • *500*
West Sunbury, PA 16061 • *300*
West Swanzey, NH 03469 • *1,022*
West Terre Haute, IN 47885 • *2,806*
West Tisbury, MA 02575 • *250*
West Townsend, MA 01474 • *700*
West Union, IL 62477 • *350*
West Union, IA 52175 • *2,783*
West Union, OH 45693 • *2,791*
West Union, SC 29696 • *300*
West Union, WV 26456 • *1,090*

West Unity, OH 43570 • *1,639*
West University Place, TX 77005 • *12,010*
West Upton, MA 01587 • *1,000*
Westvale, NY 13219 • *7,300*
West Valley, NY 14171 • *350*
West Valley City, UT 84120 • *72,511*
West Van Lear, KY 41268 • *900*
West View, PA 15229 • *7,648*
Westville, FL 32464 • *343*
Westville, IL 61883 • *3,573*
Westville, IN 46391 • *2,887*
Westville, NH 03865 • *700*
Westville, NJ 08093 • *4,786*
Westville, OK 74965 • *1,049*
West Wareham, MA 02576 • *1,837*
West Warren, MA 01092 • *1,200*
West Warwick, RI 02893 • *27,026*
West Webster, NY 14580 • *10,600*
Westwego, LA 70094 • *12,663*
West Whittier, CA 90606 • *13,800*
West Willington, CT 06279 • *250*
West Wilton, NH 03086 • *250*
West Winfield, NY 13491 • *979*
Westwood, CA 96137 • *2,081*
Westwood, KS 66205 • *1,783*
Westwood, KY 41101 • *5,973*
Westwood, MA 02090 • *6,500*
Westwood, MI 49007 • *8,519*
Westwood, NJ 07675 • *10,714*
Westwood Lakes, FL 33165 • *11,478*
West Wyoming, PA 18644 • *3,288*
West Yarmouth, MA 02673 • *3,882*
West Yellowstone, MT 59758 • *735*
West York, IL 62478 • *250*
West York, PA 17404 • *4,526*
Wethersfield, CT 06109 • *26,013*
Wetmore, KS 66550 • *376*
Wetmore, MI 49895 • *300*
Wetumka, OK 74883 • *1,725*
Wetumpka, AL 36092 • *4,341*
Wetzel □, WV • *21,874*
Wewahitchka, FL 32465 • *1,742*
Wewoka, OK 74884 • *5,480*
Wexford □, MI • *25,102*
Weyauwega, WI 54983 • *1,549*
Weyerhaeuser, WI 54895 • *313*
Weyers Cave, VA 24486 • *300*
Weymouth, MA 02188 • *55,601*
Weymouth, NJ 08330 • *250*
Whaleysville, MD 21872 • *300*
Whalom, MA 01420 • *1,400*
Wharton, NJ 07885 • *5,485*
Wharton, OH 43359 • *432*
Wharton, TX 77488 • *9,033*
Wharton □, TX • *40,242*
What Cheer, IA 50268 • *803*
Whatcom □, WA • *106,701*
Whately, MA 01093 • *450*
Whatley, AL 36482 • *450*
Wheatcroft, KY 42463 • *325*
Wheatfield, IN 46392 • *755*
Wheatland, CA 95692 • *1,474*
Wheatland, IN 47597 • *532*
Wheatland, IA 52777 • *840*
Wheatland, MO 65779 • *364*
Wheatland, PA 16161 • *1,132*
Wheatland, WY 82201 • *5,816*
Wheatland □, MT • *2,359*
Wheatley, AR 72392 • *523*
Wheaton, IL 60187-89 • *43,043*
Wheaton, MD 20902 • *48,600*
Wheaton, MN 56296 • *1,969*
Wheaton, MO 64874 • *548*
Wheat Ridge, CO 80033 • *30,293*
Wheeler, IN 46393 • *600*
Wheeler, MS 38880 • *600*
Wheeler, OR 97147 • *319*
Wheeler, TX 79096 • *1,584*
Wheeler, WI 54772 • *231*
Wheeler □, GA • *5,155*
Wheeler □, NE • *1,060*
Wheeler □, OR • *1,513*
Wheeler □, TX • *7,137*
Wheelersburg, OH 45694 • *4,796*
Wheeling, IL 60090 • *23,266*
Wheeling, MO 64688 • *379*
Wheeling, WV 26003 • *43,070*
Wheelockville, MA 01569 • *400*
Wheelwright, KY 41669 • *865*
Wheelwright, MA 01094 • *300*
Whigham, GA 31797 • *507*
Whigville, CT 06010 • *290*
Whipple, WV 25917 • *250*
Whitacres, CT 06082 • *2,500*
Whitakers, NC 27891 • *924*
White, GA 30184 • *501*
White, SD 57276 • *474*
White □, AR • *50,835*

White □, GA • *10,120*
White □, IL • *17,864*
White □, IN • *23,867*
White □, TN • *19,567*
White Bear Lake, MN 55110 • *22,538*
White Bluff, TN 37187 • *2,055*
White Castle, LA 70788 • *2,160*
White Center, WA 98126 • *19,700*
White City, FL 32465 • *725*
White City, KS 66872 • *534*
White City, OR 97503 • *5,445*
White City, UT 84070 • *1,180*
White Cloud, KS 66094 • *234*
White Cloud, MI 49349 • *1,101*
White Deer, PA 17887 • *300*
White Deer, TX 79097 • *1,210*
White Earth, MN 56591 • *250*
Whiteface, TX 79379 • *463*
Whitefield, NH 03598 • *1,005*
Whitefield, OK 74472 • *240*
Whitefish, MT 59937 • *3,703*
Whitefish Bay, WI 53217 • *14,930*
Whiteford, MD 21160 • *400*
White Hall, AR 71602 • *2,214*
White Hall, IL 62092 • *2,935*
Whitehall, MI 49461 • *2,856*
Whitehall, MT 59759 • *1,030*
Whitehall, NY 12887 • *3,241*
Whitehall, OH 43213 • *21,299*
Whitehall, PA 15227 • *15,143*
Whitehall, WI 54773 • *1,530*
White Haven, PA 18661 • *1,921*
White Heath, IL 61884 • *400*
White Horse, NJ 08610 • *10,098*
White Horse Beach, MA 02381 • *800*
Whitehouse, OH 43571 • *2,137*
White House, TN 37188 • *2,225*
White House Station, NJ 08889 • *1,019*
White Island Shores, MA 02538 • *950*
White Lake, SD 57383 • *414*
White Lake, WI 54491 • *309*
Whitelaw, WI 54247 • *649*
White Meadow Lake, NJ 07866 • *8,429*
White Mills, PA 18473 • *600*
White Oak, OH 45239 • *4,900*
White Oak, PA 15131 • *9,480*
White Pigeon, MI 49099 • *1,478*
White Pine, MI 49971 • *1,400*
White Pine, TN 37890 • *1,900*
White Pine □, NV • *8,167*
White Plains, GA 30678 • *231*
White Plains, KY 42464 • *859*
White Plains, MD 20695 • *5,167*
White Plains, NC 27031 • *300*
White Plains, NY 10601-99 • *46,999*
Whiteriver, AZ 85941 • *1,400*
White River, SD 57579 • *561*
White River Junction, VT 05001 • *2,582*
White Rock, RI 02891 • *300*
White Rock, SC 29177 • *400*
White Salmon, WA 98672 • *1,853*
Whitesboro, NJ 08252 • *900*
Whitesboro, NY 13492 • *4,460*
Whitesboro, OK 74577 • *400*
Whitesboro, TX 76273 • *3,197*
Whitesburg, GA 30185 • *775*
Whitesburg, KY 41858 • *1,525*
White Settlement, TX 76108 • *13,508*
Whiteside, TN 37396 • *400*
Whiteside □, IL • *65,970*
White Springs, FL 32096 • *781*
Whitestone, GA 30186 • *400*
White Stone, VA 22578 • *409*
Whitestown, IN 46075 • *497*
White Sulphur Springs, MT 59645 • *1,302*
White Sulphur Springs, WV 24986 • *3,371*
Whitesville, KY 42378 • *788*
Whitesville, NY 14897 • *600*
Whitesville, WV 25209 • *689*
White Swan, WA 98952 • *600*
Whiteville, NC 28472 • *5,565*
Whiteville, TN 38075 • *1,270*
Whitewater, KS 67154 • *751*
Whitewater, WI 53190 • *11,520*
Whitewood, SD 57793 • *821*
Whitewright, TX 75491 • *1,760*
Whitfield □, GA • *65,789*
Whitfield Estates, FL 33580 • *3,000*
Whiting, IN 46394 • *5,630*
Whiting, IA 51063 • *734*
Whiting, KS 66552 • *270*
Whiting, NJ 08759 • *700*

Whiting, WI 54481 • 2,050
Whitingham, VT 05361 • 300
Whitinsville, MA 01588 • 5,379
Whitley □, IN • 26,215
Whitley □, KY • 33,396
Whitley City, KY 42653 • 1,683
Whitman, MA 02382 • 13,534
Whitman, WV 25652 • 950
Whitman □, WA • 40,103
Whitman Square, NJ 08012 • 2,600
Whitmer, WV 26296 • 375
Whitmire, SC 29178 • 2,038
Whitmore Lake, MI 48189 • 2,920
Whitmore Village, HI 96786 • 2,318
Whitney, PA 15693 • 500
Whitney, SC 29303 • 1,800
Whitney, TX 76692 • 1,631
Whitney Point, NY 13862 • 1,093
Whitsett, NC 27377 • 500
Whittemore, IA 50598 • 647
Whittemore, MI 48770 • 438
Whittier, CA 90601-12 • 69,717
Whittier, NC 28789 • 500
Whitwell, TN 37397 • 1,783
Wibaux, MT 59353 • 782
Wibaux □, MT • 1,476
Wichita, KS 67201-99 • 279,835
Wichita □, KS • 3,041
Wichita □, TX • 121,082
Wichita Falls, TX 76301-11 • 94,201
Wickatunk, NJ 07765 • 400
Wickenburg, AZ 85358 • 3,535
Wickes, AR 71973 • 464
Wickett, TX 79788 • 689
Wickliffe, KY 42087 • 1,034
Wickliffe, OH 44515 • 8,800
Wicomico □, MD • 64,540
Wiconisco, PA 17097 • 1,236
Widefield, CO 80911 • 7,500
Widen, WV 25211 • 250
Widener, AR 72394 • 316
Wiergate, TX 75977 • 310
Wiggins, CO 80654 • 531
Wiggins, MS 39577 • 3,205
Wikieup, AZ 85360 • 250
Wilbarger □, TX • 15,931
Wilber, NE 68465 • 1,624
Wilberforce, OH 45384 • 2,512
Wilbraham, MA 01095 • 3,379
Wilbur, OR 97494 • 350
Wilbur, WA 99185 • 1,122
Wilburton, OK 74578 • 2,996
Wilcox, NE 68982 • 379
Wilcox, PA 15870 • 900
Wilcox □, AL • 14,755
Wilcox □, GA • 7,682
Wilder, ID 83676 • 1,260
Wilder, VT 05088 • 1,461
Wildersville, TN 38388 • 300
Wilderville, OR 97543 • 300
Wild Rose, WI 54984 • 741
Wildsville, LA 71377 • 350
Wildwood, FL 32785 • 2,665
Wildwood, IL 60081 • 400
Wildwood, NJ 08260 • 4,913
Wildwood Crest, NJ 08260 • 4,149
Wiley, CO 81092 • 425
Wilhoit, AZ 86332 • 250
Wilkes □, GA • 10,951
Wilkes □, NC • 58,657
Wilkes-Barre, PA 18701-99 • 51,551
Wilkesboro, NC 28697 • 2,335
Wilkeson, WA 98396 • 321
Wilkin □, MN • 8,454
Wilkinsburg, PA 15221 • 23,669
Wilkinson, IN 46186 • 493
Wilkinson, WV 25653 • 700
Wilkinson □, GA • 10,368
Wilkinson □, MS • 10,021
Will □, IL • 324,460
Willacoochee, GA 31650 • 1,166
Willacy □, TX • 17,495
Willamina, OR 97396 • 1,749
Willapa, WA 98577 • 300
Willard, MO 65781 • 1,799
Willard, NC 28478 • 400
Willard, NY 14588 • 700
Willard, OH 44890 • 5,720
Willard, UT 84340 • 1,241
Willards, MD 21874 • 540
Willcox, AZ 85643 • 3,243
Willet, NY 13863 • 250
Williams, AZ 86046 • 2,266
Williams, CA 95987 • 1,655
Williams, IN 47470 • 300
Williams, IA 50271 • 410
Williams □, ND • 22,237
Williams □, OH • 36,369
Williams Bay, WI 53191 • 1,763
Williamsburg, IN 47393 • 425
Williamsburg, IA 52361 • 2,033
Williamsburg, KS 66095 • 362
Williamsburg, KY 40769 • 5,560
Williamsburg, MA 01096 • 950
Williamsburg, NM 87942 • 433
Williamsburg, OH 45176 • 1,952
Williamsburg, PA 16693 • 1,400
Williamsburg, VA 23185 • 9,870
Williamsburg □, SC • 38,226
Williamsfield, IL 61489 • 585
Williamson, GA 30292 • 250
Williamson, NY 14589 • 1,991
Williamson, WV 25661 • 5,219
Williamson □, IL • 56,538
Williamson □, TN • 58,108
Williamson □, TX • 76,507
Williamsport, IN 47993 • 1,747
Williamsport, MD 21795 • 2,153
Williamsport, OH 43164 • 792
Williamsport, PA 17701 • 33,401
Williamston, MI 48895 • 2,981
Williamston, NC 27892 • 6,159
Williamston, SC 29697 • 4,310
Williamstown, KY 41097 • 2,502
Williamstown, MA 01267 • 4,798
Williamstown, NJ 08094 • 5,768
Williamstown, NY 13493 • 400
Williamstown, PA 17098 • 1,664
Williamstown, VT 05679 • 650
Williamstown, WV 26187 • 3,095
Williamsville, IL 62693 • 996
Williamsville, MS 39090 • 400
Williamsville, MO 63967 • 418
Williamsville, NY 14221 • 6,017
Willimantic, CT 06226 • 14,652
Willingboro, NJ 08046 • 39,912
Willis, MI 48191 • 300
Willis, TX 77378 • 1,674
Willisburg, KY 40078 • 235
Williston, FL 32696 • 2,240
Williston, NC 28589 • 350
Williston, ND 58801 • 13,336
Williston, SC 29853 • 3,173
Williston, TN 38076 • 395
Williston, VT 05495 • 400
Williston Park, NY 11596 • 8,216
Willisville, IL 62997 • 628
Willis Wharf, VA 23486 • 400
Willits, CA 95490 • 4,008
Willmar, MN 56201 • 15,895
Willoughby, OH 44094 • 19,329
Willoughby Hills, OH 44092 • 8,612
Willow Brook, CA 90222 • 30,845
Willow City, ND 58384 • 329
Willow Glen, LA 71301 • 500
Willow Grove, PA 19090 • 21,300
Willow Hill, IL 62480 • 292
Willowick, OH 44094 • 17,834
Willow Lake, SD 57278 • 375
Willow River, MN 55795 • 303
Willow Run, DE 19805 • 1,950
Willow Run, MI 48197 • 6,400
Willows, CA 95988 • 4,777
Willow Springs, IL 60480 • 4,147
Willow Springs, MO 65793 • 2,215
Willsboro, NY 12996 • 950
Willshire, OH 45898 • 564
Willston, VA 22044 • 2,500
Wilmar, AR 71675 • 747
Wilmer, AL 36587 • 581
Wilmer, TX 75172 • 2,367
Wilmerding, PA 15148 • 2,421
Wilmette, IL 60091 • 28,229
Wilmington, DE 19801-99 • 70,195
Wilmington, IL 60481 • 4,424
Wilmington, MA 01887 • 17,471
Wilmington, NC 28401-06 • 44,000
Wilmington, NY 12997 • 500
Wilmington, OH 45177 • 10,431
Wilmington, VT 05363 • 545
Wilmington Manor, DE 19720 • 2,000
Wilmington Manor Gardens, DE 19720 • 1,600
Wilmont, MN 56185 • 380
Wilmore, KY 40390 • 3,787
Wilmot, AR 71676 • 1,227
Wilmot, OH 44689 • 329
Wilmot, SD 57279 • 507
Wilmot Flat, NH 03287 • 300
Wilson, AR 72395 • 1,115
Wilson, KS 67490 • 978
Wilson, LA 70789 • 656
Wilson, NC 27893 • 34,424
Wilson, NY 14172 • 1,259
Wilson, OK 73463 • 1,585
Wilson, PA 18042 • 7,564
Wilson, TX 79381 • 578
Wilson, UT 84401 • 350
Wilson, WY 83014 • 300
Wilson □, KS • 12,128
Wilson □, NC • 63,132
Wilson □, TN • 56,064
Wilson □, TX • 16,756
Wilsons Mills, NC 27593 • 580
Wilsonville, AL 35186 • 914
Wilsonville, CT 06255 • 250
Wilsonville, IL 62093 • 608
Wilsonville, OR 97070 • 2,920
Wilton, AL 35187 • 642
Wilton, AR 71865 • 495
Wilton, CT 06897 • 6,500
Wilton, IA 52778 • 2,502
Wilton, ME 04294 • 2,262
Wilton, NH 03086 • 1,310
Wilton, ND 58579 • 950
Wilton, WI 54670 • 465
Wilton Manors, FL 33334 • 12,742
Wimauma, FL 33598 • 1,477
Wimbledon, ND 58492 • 330
Winamac, IN 46996 • 2,370
Winburne, PA 16879 • 650
Winchendon, MA 01475 • 4,030
Winchendon Springs, MA 01477 • 420
Winchester, AR 71677 • 279
Winchester, ID 83555 • 343
Winchester, IL 62694 • 1,716
Winchester, IN 47394 • 5,659
Winchester, KS 66097 • 570
Winchester, KY 40391 • 15,216
Winchester, MA 01890 • 20,701
Winchester, NV 89101 • 19,728
Winchester, NH 03470 • 1,732
Winchester, OH 45697 • 1,080
Winchester, TN 37398 • 5,821
Winchester, VA 22601 • 20,217
Winchester Bay, OR 97467 • 900
Windber, PA 15963 • 5,585
Windcrest, TX 78239 • 5,332
Winder, GA 30680 • 6,705
Windfall, IN 46076 • 911
Windgap, PA 18091 • 2,651
Windham, CT 06280 • 700
Windham, NY 12496 • 450
Windham, OH 44288 • 3,721
Windham □, CT • 92,312
Windham □, VT • 36,933
Windham Center, ME 04082 • 500
Wind Lake, WI 53185 • 2,400
Windom, MN 56101 • 4,666
Window Rock, AZ 86515 • 2,230
Wind Point, WI 53402 • 1,695
Windsor, CO 80550 • 4,277
Windsor, CT 06095 • 17,517
Windsor, IL 61957 • 1,228
Windsor, MO 65360 • 3,058
Windsor, NJ 08561 • 400
Windsor, NC 27983 • 2,126
Windsor, PA 17366 • 1,205
Windsor, VT 05089 • 4,084
Windsor, VA 23487 • 985
Windsor □, VT • 51,030
Windsor Forest, GA 31406 • 7,288
Windsor Heights, IA 50311 • 5,474
Windsor Hills, CA 90052 • 6,200
Windsor Locks, CT 06096 • 12,190
Windsorville, CT 06016 • 300
Windthorst, TX 76389 • 409
Windy Hill, SC 29501 • 1,605
Windy Hills, DE 19711 • 1,300
Winfall, NC 27985 • 634
Winfield, AL 35594 • 3,781
Winfield, IA 52659 • 1,042
Winfield, KS 67156 • 10,736
Winfield, MO 63389 • 592
Winfield, NJ 07036 • 1,785
Winfield, WV 25213 • 329
Wingate, IN 47994 • 373
Wingate, MD 21675 • 250
Wingate, NC 28174 • 2,615
Wingo, KY 42088 • 606
Winifrede, WV 25214 • 800
Wink, TX 79789 • 1,182
Winkelman, AZ 85292 • 1,060
Winkler □, TX • 9,944
Winlock, WA 98596 • 1,052
Winn, ME 04495 • 300
Winn, MI 48896 • 450
Winn □, LA • 17,253
Winnebago, IL 61088 • 1,644
Winnebago, MN 56098 • 1,869
Winnebago, NE 68071 • 902
Winnebago, WI 54985 • 300
Winnebago □, IL • 250,884
Winnebago □, IA • 13,010
Winnebago □, WI • 131,772
Winneconne, WI 54986 • 1,935
Winnemucca, NV 89445 • 4,140
Winner, SD 57580 • 3,472
Winneshiek □, IA • 21,876
Winnetka, IL 60093 • 12,772
Winnfield, LA 71483 • 7,311
Winnisquam, NH 03289 • 600
Winnsboro, LA 71295 • 5,921
Winnsboro, SC 29180 • 2,919
Winnsboro, TX 75494 • 3,458
Winnsboro Mills, SC 29180 • 1,890
Winona, KS 67764 • 258
Winona, MN 55987 • 25,075
Winona, MS 38967 • 6,177
Winona, MO 65588 • 1,050
Winona, WV 25942 • 250
Winona □, MN • 46,256
Winona Lake, IN 46590 • 2,827
Winooski, VT 05404 • 6,318
Winside, NE 68790 • 439
Winslow, AZ 86047 • 7,921
Winslow, AR 72959 • 247
Winslow, IL 61089 • 361
Winslow, IN 47598 • 1,017
Winslow, ME 04901 • 5,903
Winslow, NJ 08095 • 500
Winslow, WA 98110 • 2,196
Winsted, CT 06098 • 8,092
Winsted, MN 55395 • 1,522
Winston, FL 33803 • 5,500
Winston, MO 64689 • 246
Winston, OR 97496 • 3,359
Winston □, AL • 21,953
Winston □, MS • 19,474
Winston-Salem, NC 27101-99 • 131,885
Winstonville, MS 38781 • 486
Winter, WI 54896 • 376
Winter Beach, FL 32971 • 700
Winter Garden, FL 32787 • 6,789
Winter Harbor, ME 04693 • 900
Winter Haven, FL 33880-88 • 21,119
Winter Park, CO 80482 • 480
Winter Park, FL 32789-93 • 22,339
Winter Park, NC 28401 • 4,504
Winterport, ME 04496 • 1,126
Winters, CA 95694 • 2,652
Winters, TX 79567 • 3,061
Winterset, IA 50273 • 4,021
Winter Springs, FL 32708 • 10,475
Wintersville, OH 43952 • 4,724
Winterville, GA 30683 • 621
Winterville, NC 28590 • 2,052
Winthrop, AR 71866 • 238
Winthrop, CT 06417 • 400
Winthrop, IA 50682 • 767
Winthrop, ME 04364 • 3,264
Winthrop, MA 02152 • 19,294
Winthrop, MN 55396 • 1,376
Winthrop, NY 13697 • 500
Winthrop, WA 98862 • 413
Winthrop Harbor, IL 60096 • 5,431
Winton, MN 55796 • 276
Winton, NC 27986 • 825
Wirt □, WV • 4,922
Wiscasset, ME 04578 • 1,350
Wisconsin Dells, WI 53965 • 2,521
Wisconsin Rapids, WI 54494 • 17,995
Wise, NC 27594 • 500
Wise, VA 24293 • 3,894
Wise □, TX • 26,575
Wise □, VA • 43,863
Wishek, ND 58495 • 1,345
Wishram, WA 98673 • 675
Wisner, LA 71378 • 1,424
Wisner, NE 68791 • 1,335
Withamsville, OH 45245 • 3,650
Withee, WI 54498 • 509
Witherbee, NY 12998 • 1,000
Witt, IL 62094 • 1,205
Witt, TN 37814 • 250
Wittenberg, WI 54499 • 997
Wittman, MD 21676 • 400
Wittmann, AZ 85361 • 700
Wixom, MI 48096 • 6,705
Woburn, MA 01801 • 36,626
Woden, IA 50484 • 287
Wolbach, NE 68882 • 301
Wolcott, CT 06716 • 5,500
Wolcott, IN 47995 • 923
Wolcott, NY 14590 • 1,496
Wolcottville, IN 46795 • 890
Wolf Creek, OR 97497 • 600
Wolfe □, KY • 6,698
Wolfeboro, NH 03894 • 1,800
Wolfeboro Falls, NH 03896 • 500
Wolfe City, TX 75496 • 1,594
Wolf Lake, IL 62998 • 275
Wolflake, IN 46796 • 450
Wolf Lake, MI 49442 • 3,876
Wolf Point, MT 59201 • 3,074
Wolsey, SD 57384 • 437

Wolverine, MI 49799 • *364*
Womelsdorf, PA 19567 • *1,827*
Wonder Lake, IL 60097 • *752*
Wonderland, CA 96003 • *250*
Wonewoc, WI 53968 • *842*
Wood, PA 16694 • *500*
Wood □, OH • *107,372*
Wood □, TX • *24,697*
Wood □, WV • *93,648*
Wood □, WI • *72,799*
Woodbine, GA 31569 • *910*
Woodbine, IA 51579 • *1,463*
Woodbine, KY 40771 • *500*
Woodbine, NJ 08270 • *2,809*
Woodbourne, NY 12788 • *1,155*
Woodbridge, CT 06525 • *7,600*
Woodbridge, NJ 07095 • *16,400*
Woodbridge, VA 22191-99 • *35,000*
Woodburn, IN 46797 • *1,002*
Woodburn, KY 42170 • *330*
Woodburn, OR 97071 • *11,196*
Woodbury, CT 06798 • *1,290*
Woodbury, GA 30293 • *1,738*
Woodbury, MN 55119 • *10,297*
Woodbury, NJ 08096 • *10,353*
Woodbury, PA 16695 • *267*
Woodbury, TN 37190 • *2,160*
Woodbury □, IA • *100,884*
Woodcliff Lake, NJ 07675 • *5,644*
Wood Dale, IL 60191 • *11,251*
Woodfield, SC 29206 • *9,588*
Woodford □, IL • *33,320*
Woodford □, KY • *17,778*
Woodfords, CA 96120 • *300*
Woodhaven, MI 48183 • *10,902*
Woodhull, IL 61490 • *901*
Woodhull, NY 14898 • *315*
Woodlake, CA 93286 • *4,343*
Wood Lake, MN 56297 • *420*
Woodlake, TX 75865 • *300*
Woodland, CA 95695 • *30,235*
Woodland, GA 31836 • *664*
Woodland, IL 60974 • *333*
Woodland, ME 04694 • *1,363*
Woodland, MI 48897 • *431*
Woodland, NC 27897 • *861*
Woodland, PA 16881 • *600*
Woodland, WA 98674 • *2,341*
Woodland Acres, CO 81069 • *800*
Woodland Mills, TN 38271 • *526*
Woodland Park, CO 80863 • *2,634*
Woodlawn, IL 62898 • *471*
Woodlawn, KY 42001 • *1,200*
Woodlawn, MD 21207 • *8,000*
Woodlawn, OH 45215 • *2,715*
Woodleaf, NC 27054 • *350*
Woodlyn, PA 19094 • *6,000*
Woodlynne, NJ 08107 • *2,578*
Woodmere, NY 11598 • *19,700*
Woodmont, CT 06460 • *1,797*
Woodmoor, MD 21207 • *7,600*
Woodport, NJ 07885 • *500*
Woodridge, IL 60517 • *22,561*
Wood-Ridge, NJ 07075 • *7,929*
Wood River, IL 62095 • *12,446*
Wood River, NE 68883 • *1,334*
Wood River Junction, RI 02894 • *250*
Woodruff, AZ 85942 • *250*
Woodruff, SC 29388 • *5,171*
Woodruff, WI 54568 • *900*
Woodruff □, AR • *11,222*
Woods □, OK • *10,923*
Woodsboro, MD 21798 • *506*
Woodsboro, TX 78393 • *1,974*
Woods Cross, UT 84087 • *4,263*
Woodsfield, OH 43793 • *3,145*
Woods Hole, MA 02543 • *1,080*
Woodside, CA 94062 • *5,291*
Woodside, DE 19980 • *248*
Woodson, AR 72180 • *600*
Woodson, IL 62695 • *503*
Woodson, TX 76091 • *291*
Woodson □, KS • *4,600*
Woodstock, AL 35188 • *250*
Woodstock, CT 06281 • *300*
Woodstock, GA 30188 • *2,699*
Woodstock, IL 60098 • *11,725*
Woodstock, MD 21163 • *700*
Woodstock, NY 12498 • *1,073*
Woodstock, OH 43084 • *292*
Woodstock, VT 05091 • *1,178*
Woodstock, VA 22664 • *2,627*
Woodstown, NJ 08098 • *3,250*
Woodsville, NH 03785 • *1,195*
Woodville, FL 32362 • *1,768*
Woodville, GA 30669 • *455*
Woodville, MA 01784 • *350*
Woodville, MS 39669 • *1,512*
Woodville, OH 43469 • *2,050*
Woodville, TX 75979 • *2,821*
Woodville, WI 54028 • *725*
Woodward, IA 50276 • *1,212*
Woodward, OK 73801 • *13,610*
Woodward □, OK • *21,172*
Woodway, TX 76710 • *7,091*
Woodworth, LA 71485 • *412*
Woolford, MD 21677 • *300*
Woolmarket, MS 39532 • *670*
Woolrich, PA 17779 • *700*
Woolstock, IA 50599 • *235*
Woolwich, ME 04579 • *500*
Woonsocket, RI 02895 • *45,914*
Woonsocket, SD 57385 • *799*
Wooster, AR 72181 • *398*
Wooster, OH 44691 • *19,289*
Worcester, MA 01601-99 • *161,799*
Worcester, NY 12197 • *950*
Worcester, VT 05682 • *250*
Worcester □, MD • *30,889*
Worcester □, MA • *646,352*
Worden, IL 62097 • *953*
Worden, MT 59088 • *300*
Worland, WY 82401 • *6,391*
Woronoco, MA 01097 • *300*
Worth, IL 60482 • *11,592*
Worth □, GA • *18,064*
Worth □, IA • *9,075*
Worth □, MO • *3,008*
Wortham, TX 76693 • *1,187*
Worthing, SD 57077 • *388*
Worthington, IN 47471 • *1,574*
Worthington, IA 52078 • *432*
Worthington, KY 41183 • *1,948*
Worthington, MN 56187 • *10,243*
Worthington, OH 43085 • *15,016*
Worthington, PA 16262 • *760*
Worthington, WV 26591 • *329*
Worthville, KY 41098 • *272*
Worthville, NC 27317 • *240*
Worton, MD 21678 • *225*
Wounded Knee, SD 57794 • *250*
Wrangell, AK 99929 • *2,184*
Wray, CO 80758 • *2,131*
Wren, OH 45899 • *282*
Wrens, GA 30833 • *2,415*
Wrenshall, MN 55797 • *333*
Wrentham, MA 02093 • *1,400*
Wright □, IA • *16,319*
Wright □, MN • *58,681*
Wright □, MO • *16,188*
Wright City, MO 63390 • *1,179*
Wright City, OK 74766 • *1,168*
Wrightstown, NJ 08562 • *3,031*
Wrightstown, WI 54180 • *1,169*
Wrightsville, AR 72183 • *1,100*
Wrightsville, GA 31096 • *2,526*
Wrightsville, PA 17368 • *2,365*
Wrightsville Beach, NC 28480 • *2,910*
Wrightwood, CA 92397 • *2,511*
Wrigley, TN 37098 • *400*
Wurtsboro, NY 12790 • *1,128*
Wyaconda, MO 63474 • *359*
Wyalusing, PA 18853 • *716*
Wyandanch, NY 11798 • *17,900*
Wyandot □, OH • *22,651*
Wyandotte, MI 48192 • *34,006*
Wyandotte, OK 74370 • *336*
Wyandotte □, KS • *172,335*
Wyanet, IL 61379 • *1,069*
Wyatt, IN 46595 • *320*
Wyatt, MO 63882 • *441*
Wyckoff, NJ 07481 • *15,500*
Wykoff, MN 55990 • *482*
Wylliesburg, VA 23976 • *250*
Wymore, NE 68466 • *1,841*
Wyncote, PA 19095 • *5,300*
Wyndmere, ND 58081 • *550*
Wyndmoor, PA 19118 • *5,800*
Wynnburg, TN 38077 • *250*
Wynne, AR 72396 • *7,805*
Wynnewood, OK 73098 • *2,615*
Wynnewood, PA 19096 • *7,700*
Wynona, OK 74084 • *780*
Wyocena, WI 53969 • *548*
Wyoming, DE 19934 • *960*
Wyoming, IL 61491 • *1,614*
Wyoming, IA 52362 • *702*
Wyoming, MI 49509 • *59,616*
Wyoming, MN 55092 • *1,559*
Wyoming, NY 14591 • *507*
Wyoming, OH 45215 • *8,282*
Wyoming, PA 18644 • *3,655*
Wyoming, RI 02898 • *600*
Wyoming □, NY • *39,895*
Wyoming □, PA • *26,433*
Wyoming □, WV • *35,993*
Wyomissing, PA 19610 • *6,551*
Wythe □, VA • *25,522*
Wytheville, VA 24382 • *7,135*

X

Xenia, IL 62899 • *475*
Xenia, OH 45385 • *24,653*

Y

Yachats, OR 97498 • *482*
Yacolt, WA 98675 • *544*
Yadkin □, NC • *28,439*
Yadkinville, NC 27055 • *2,216*
Yakima, WA 98901-09 • *49,826*
Yakima □, WA • *172,508*
Yakutat, AK 99689 • *449*
Yalaha, FL 32797 • *950*
Yale, IA 50277 • *299*
Yale, MI 48097 • *1,814*
Yale, OK 74085 • *1,652*
Yalobusha □, MS • *13,139*
Yamhill, OR 97148 • *690*
Yamhill □, OR • *55,332*
Yampa, CO 80483 • *472*
Yancey □, NC • *14,934*
Yanceyville, NC 27379 • *1,511*
Yankeetown, FL 32698 • *600*
Yankeetown, IN 47630 • *250*
Yankton, SD 57078 • *12,011*
Yankton □, SD • *18,952*
Yardley, PA 19067 • *2,533*
Yardville, NJ 08620 • *8,400*
Yarmouth, ME 04096 • *2,421*
Yarmouth, MA 02675 • *900*
Yarmouth Port, MA 02675 • *2,490*
Yarnell, AZ 85362 • *950*
Yates □, NY • *21,459*
Yatesboro, PA 16263 • *700*
Yates Center, KS 66783 • *1,998*
Yates City, IL 61572 • *860*
Yatesville, GA 31097 • *390*
Yavapai □, AZ • *68,145*
Yazoo □, MS • *27,349*
Yazoo City, MS 39194 • *12,092*
Yeadon, PA 19050 • *11,727*
Yeagertown, PA 17099 • *1,363*
Yell □, AR • *17,026*
Yellow Medicine □, MN • *13,653*
Yellow Springs, OH 45387 • *4,077*
Yellowstone □, MT • *108,035*
Yellowstone National Park, WY 82190 • *350*
Yellowstone National Park □, MT • *275*
Yellville, AR 72687 • *1,044*
Yelm, WA 98597 • *1,294*
Yemassee, SC 29945 • *789*
Yerington, NV 89447 • *2,021*
Yermo, CA 92398 • *1,092*
Yoakum, TX 77995 • *6,148*
Yoakum □, TX • *8,299*
Yoder, IN 46798 • *250*
Yolo □, CA • *113,374*
Yoncalla, OR 97499 • *805*
Yonkers, NY 10701-99 • *195,351*
Yorba Linda, CA 92686 • *28,254*
York, AL 36925 • *3,392*
York, ME 03909 • *3,130*
York, NE 68467 • *7,723*
York, PA 17401-99 • *44,619*
York, SC 29745 • *6,412*
York □, ME • *139,666*
York □, NE • *14,798*
York □, PA • *312,963*
York □, SC • *106,720*
York □, VA • *35,463*
York Beach, ME 03910 • *860*
York Harbor, ME 03911 • *1,400*
York Haven, PA 17370 • *746*
Yorklyn, DE 19736 • *600*
Yorkshire, NY 14173 • *850*
York Springs, PA 17372 • *556*
Yorktown, IN 47396 • *3,945*
Yorktown, NY 10598 • *5,400*
Yorktown, TX 78164 • *2,498*
Yorktown, VA 23690 • *390*
Yorktown Heights, NY 10598 • *5,900*
Yorktown Manor, RI 02852 • *1,300*
Yorkville, IL 60560 • *3,422*
Yorkville, NY 13495 • *3,115*
Yorkville, OH 43971 • *1,447*
Yorkville, TN 38389 • *272*
Yosemite National Park, CA 95389 • *1,073*
Young, AZ 85554 • *300*
Young □, TX • *19,083*
Young America, IN 46998 • *300*
Young Harris, GA 30582 • *687*
Youngstown, FL 32466 • *355*
Youngstown, NY 14174 • *2,191*
Youngstown, OH 44501-99 • *115,436*
Youngsville, LA 70592 • *1,053*
Youngsville, NC 27596 • *486*
Youngsville, PA 16371 • *2,006*
Youngtown, AZ 85363 • *2,254*
Youngwood, PA 15697 • *3,749*
Ypsilanti, MI 48197 • *24,031*
Yreka, CA 96097 • *5,916*
Yuba □, CA • *49,733*
Yuba City, CA 95991 • *18,736*
Yucaipa, CA 92399 • *20,000*
Yukon, OK 73099 • *17,112*
Yukon, WV 24899 • *500*
Yulee, FL 32097 • *3,168*
Yuma, AZ 85364-69 • *42,481*
Yuma, CO 80759 • *2,824*
Yuma □, AZ • *78,054*
Yuma □, CO • *9,682*
Yutan, NE 68073 • *631*

Z

Zachary, LA 70791 • *7,297*
Zaleski, OH 45698 • *347*
Zanesville, IN 46799 • *550*
Zanesville, OH 43701 • *28,655*
Zap, ND 58580 • *511*
Zapata, TX 78076 • *2,500*
Zapata □, TX • *6,628*
Zavala □, TX • *11,666*
Zavalla, TX 75980 • *762*
Zearing, IA 50278 • *630*
Zebulon, GA 30295 • *995*
Zebulon, KY 41501 • *400*
Zebulon, NC 27597 • *2,055*
Zeeland, MI 49464 • *4,764*
Zeeland, ND 58581 • *253*
Zeigler, IL 62999 • *1,858*
Zelienople, PA 16063 • *3,502*
Zenith, WA 98188 • *300*
Zephyr, TX 76890 • *350*
Zephyr Cove, NV 89448 • *1,300*
Zephyrhills, FL 33599 • *5,742*
Zia Pueblo, NM 87053 • *400*
Ziebach □, SD • *2,308*
Zillah, WA 98953 • *1,599*
Zilwaukee, MI 48604 • *2,201*
Zimmerman, MN 55398 • *1,074*
Zion, IL 60099 • *17,861*
Zionsville, IN 46077 • *3,948*
Zolfo Springs, FL 33890 • *1,495*
Zumbrota, MN 55992 • *2,129*
Zuni, NM 87327 • *5,551*
Zuni, VA 23898 • *225*
Zwolle, LA 71486 • *2,602*

Colleges and Universities of the United States

NOTE: This list includes accredited four-year colleges and universities with 100 or more students. The colleges and universities are arranged in alphabetical order, by state. The city or town in which the college or university is located, or is associated with, appears in italic type. The student enrollment for each school is the last item in each entry. These figures are based on Fall 1982 enrollment.

ALABAMA

Alabama Agricultural and Mechanical University, *Normal* . 4,100
Alabama State University, *Montgomery* 4,000
Athens State College, *Athens* 1,000
Auburn University, *Auburn* 18,400
Auburn University at Montgomery, *Montgomery* 5,000
Birmingham Southern College, *Birmingham* 1,600
Huntingdon College, *Montgomery* 700
International Bible College, *Florence* 130
Jacksonville State University, *Jacksonville* 6,300
Judson College, *Marion* 400
Livingston University, *Livingston* 1,500
Miles College, *Fairfield* 750
Mobile College, *Mobile* 950
Oakwood College, *Huntsville* 1,400
Samford University, *Homewood* 4,200
Selma University, *Selma* 350
Southeastern Bible College, *Birmingham* 170
Spring Hill College, *Mobile* 1,100
Stillman College, *Tuscaloosa* 500
Talladega College, *Talladega* 550
Troy State University at Dothan-Fort Rucker, *Dothan* 1,600
Troy State University at Montgomery, *Montgomery* 2,100
Troy State University Main Campus, *Troy* 6,900
Tuskegee Institute, *Tuskegee* 3,400
University of Alabama, *Tuscaloosa* 16,000
University of Alabama in Birmingham, *Birmingham* 13,900
University of Alabama in Huntsville, *Huntsville* 6,000
University of Montevallo, *Montevallo* 2,600
University of North Alabama, *Florence* 5,300
University of South Alabama, *Mobile* 9,400

ALASKA

Alaska Pacific University, *Anchorage* 780
Sheldon Jackson College, *Sitka* 220
University of Alaska Anchorage, *Anchorage* 3,500
University of Alaska Fairbanks, *Fairbanks* 4,500
University of Alaska Juneau, *Juneau* 1,800

ARIZONA

American Graduate School of International Management, *Glendale* 1,000
Arizona College of the Bible, *Phoenix* 140
Arizona State University, *Tempe* 39,300
Devry Institute of Technology, *Phoenix* 4,800
Grand Canyon College, *Phoenix* 1,300
Northern Arizona University, *Flagstaff* 11,900
Prescott College, *Prescott* 130
Southwestern Baptist Bible College, *Phoenix* 210
University of Arizona, *Tucson* 30,700
University of Phoenix, *Phoenix* 2,000
Western International University, *Phoenix* 260

ARKANSAS

Arkansas Baptist College, *Little Rock* 170
Arkansas College, *Batesville* 550
Arkansas State University, *Jonesboro* 7,800
Arkansas Tech University, *Russellville* 3,300
Central Baptist College, *Conway* 240
College of the Ozarks, *Clarksville* 700
Harding University Main Campus, *Searcy* 3,000
Henderson State University, *Arkadelphia* 3,000
Hendrix College, *Conway* 1,000
John Brown University, *Siloam Springs* 800
Ouachita Baptist University, *Arkadelphia* 1,700
Philander Smith College, *Little Rock* 500
Southern Arkansas University, *Magnolia* 2,100
University of Arkansas, *Fayetteville* 16,100
University of Arkansas at Little Rock, *Little Rock* 9,600
University of Arkansas at Monticello, *Monticello* 1,900
University of Arkansas at Pine Bluff, *Pine Bluff* 2,700
University of Arkansas for Medical Sciences, *Little Rock* 1,400
University of Central Arkansas, *Conway* 5,900

CALIFORNIA

American Film Institute-Center for Advance Film Studies, *Los Angeles* 100
Armstrong College, *Berkeley* 380
Art Center College of Design, *Pasadena* 1,500
Azusa Pacific College, *Azusa* 2,500
Bethany Bible College, *Scotts Valley* 500
Biola University, *La Mirada* 3,100
Brooks Institute, *Santa Barbara* 800
California Baptist College, *Riverside* 650
California College of Arts and Crafts, *Oakland* 1,000
California College of Podiatric Medicine, *San Francisco* 400
California Institute of Integral Studies, *San Francisco* 190
California Institute of Technology, *Pasadena* 1,800
California Institute of the Arts, *Valencia* 850
California Lutheran College, *Thousand Oaks* 2,500
California Maritime Academy, *Vallejo* 500
California Polytechic State University-San Luis Obispo, *San Luis Obispo* 15,800
California School of Professional Psychology at Berkeley, *Berkeley* 350
California School of Professional Psychology at Fresno, *Fresno* 190
California School of Professional Psychology at Los Angeles, *Los Angeles* 300
California School of Professional Psychology at San Diego, *San Diego* 320
California State College-Bakersfield, *Bakersfield* 3,600
California State College-San Bernardino, *San Bernardino* . 5,200
California State College-Stanislaus, *Turlock* 4,600
California State Polytechnic University-Pomona, *Pomona* 17,100
California State University-Chico, *Chico* 14,300
California State University Dominguez Hills, *Carson* 10,400
California State University-Fresno, *Fresno* 16,400
California State University-Fullerton, *Fullerton* 24,400
California State University-Hayward, *Hayward* 12,400
California State University-Long Beach, *Long Beach* 36,400
California State University-Los Angeles, *Los Angeles* 22,700
California State University-Northridge, *Los Angeles* 28,100
California State University-Sacramento, *Sacramento* 21,700
California Western School of Law, *San Diego* 800
Chapman College, *Orange* 5,600
Christ College Irvine, *Irvine* 270
Christian Heritage College, *El Cajon* 350
Church Divinity School of the Pacific, *Berkeley* 100
Claremont Graduate School, *Claremont* 1,600
Claremont McKenna College, *Claremont* 850
Cleveland Chiropractic College, *Los Angeles* 600
Cogswell College, *San Francisco* 450
Coleman College, *La Mesa* 850

College of Law-University of San Fernando Valley, *Los Angeles* 250
College of Notre Dame, *Belmont* 1,400
College of Osteopathic Medicine of the Pacific, *Pomona* 290
Columbia College-Hollywood, *Los Angeles* 360
Consortium of California State University, *Long Beach* 1,500
Dominican College of San Rafael, *San Rafael* 600
Fielding Institute, *Santa Barbara* 400
Franciscan School of Theology, *Berkeley* 150
Fresno Pacific College, *Fresno* 800
Fuller Theological Seminary, *Pasadena* 2,700
Golden Gate Baptist Theological Seminary, *Strawberry Point* 550
Golden Gate University, *San Francisco* 11,000
Graduate Theological Union, *Berkeley* 400
Harvey Mudd College, *Claremont* 500
Heald Institute of Technology-San Francisco, *San Francisco* 1,100
Holy Names College, *Oakland* 650
Humboldt State University, *Arcata* 7,300
International College, *Los Angeles* 700
Jesuit School of Theology, *Berkeley* 160
John F. Kennedy University, *Orinda* 1,700
L. I. F. E. Bible College, *Los Angeles* 450
Life Chiropractic College-West, *San Lorenzo* 400
Lincoln University, *San Francisco* 600
Loma Linda University, *Loma Linda* 5,200
Los Angeles Baptist College, *Newhall* 300
Los Angeles College of Chiropractic, *Whittier* 700
Loyola Marymount University, *Los Angeles* 6,400
Menlo College, *Menlo Park* 650
Mennonite Brethren Biblical Seminary, *Fresno* 130
Mills College, *Oakland* 900
Monterey Institute of International Studies, *Monterey* 400
Mount Saint Mary's College, *Los Angeles* 1,100
National University, *San Diego* 6,800
Naval Postgraduate School, *Monterey* 1,500
New College of California, *San Francisco* 600
Northrop University, *Inglewood* 1,400
Occidental College, *Los Angeles* 1,600
Otis Art Institute of Parsons School of Design, *Los Angeles* 650
Pacific Christian College, *Fullerton* 500
Pacific Lutheran Theological Seminary, *Berkeley* 170
Pacific Oaks College, *Pasadena* 250
Pacific School of Religion, *Berkeley* 240
Pacific Union College, *Angwin* 1,600
Palmer College of Chiropractic-West, *Sunnyvale* 530
Pasadena College of Chiropractic, *Pasadena* 180
Patten College, *Oakland* 140
Pepperdine University, *Malibu* 6,500
Pitzer College, *Claremont* 750
Point Loma Nazarine College, *San Diego* 1,900
Pomona College, *Claremont* 1,400
Saint John's College, *Camarillo* 200
Saint Joseph's College, *Mountain View* 100
Saint Mary's College of California, *Moraga* 3,000
San Diego State University, *San Diego* 33,900
San Francisco Art Institute, *San Francisco* 650
San Francisco Conservatory of Music, *San Francisco* 220
San Francisco State University, *San Francisco* 26,200
San Francisco Theological Seminary, *San Anselmo* 970
San Jose Bible College, *San Jose* 190
San Jose State University, *San Jose* 26,300
Saybrook Institute, *San Francisco* 150
School of Theology at Claremont, *Claremont* 250
Scripps College, *Claremont* 580
Simpson College, *San Francisco* 300
Sonoma State University, *Rohnert Park* 6,700
Southern California College, *Costa Mesa* 740
Southern California College of Optometry, *Fullerton* 400
Southern California Institute of Architecture, *Santa Monica* 400
Southwestern University School of Law, *Los Angeles* 1,500
Stanford University, *Stanford* 13,800
United States International University, *San Diego* 2,200
University of California-Berkeley, *Berkeley* 29,300
University of California-Davis, *Davis* 19,300
University of California Hastings College of Law, *San Francisco* 1,500
University of California-Irvine, *Irvine* 11,300
University of California-Los Angeles, *Los Angeles* 34,600
University of California-Riverside, *Riverside* 4,800
University of California-San Diego, *San Diego* 13,100
University of California-San Francisco, *San Francisco* 3,800
University of California-Santa Barbara, *Isla Vista* 16,200
University of California-Santa Cruz, *Santa Cruz* 6,800
University of Judaism, *Los Angeles* 200
University of La Verne, *La Verne* 4,000
University of Redlands, *Redlands* 2,600
University of San Diego, *San Diego* 5,000
University of San Francisco, *San Francisco* 6,300
University of Santa Clara, *Santa Clara* 7,200
University of Southern California, *Los Angeles* 29,400
University of the Pacific, *Stockton* 6,000
University of West Los Angeles, *Culver City* 700
West Coast Christian College, *Fresno* 280
West Coast University, *Los Angeles* 900
West Coast University Orange County Center, *Orange* 500
Western State University College of Law of Orange County, *Fullerton* 1,300
Western State University College of Law of San Diego, *San Diego* 800
Westmont College, *Santa Barbara* 1,000
Whittier College, *Whittier* 1,500
Woodbury University, *Los Angeles* 1,100
Wright Institute, *Berkeley* 160

COLORADO

Adams State College, *Alamosa* 1,900
Colorado College, *Colorado Springs* 2,000
Colorado School of Mines, *Golden* 2,900
Colorado State University, *Fort Collins* 18,900
Colorado Technical College, *Colorado Springs* 600
Denver Conservative Baptist Seminary, *Englewood* 500
Fort Lewis College, *Durango* 3,500
Iliff School of Theology, *Denver* 300
Loretto Heights College, *Denver* 800
Mesa College, *Grand Junction* 4,600
Metropolitan State College, *Denver* 14,400
Naropa Institute, *Boulder* 130
Regis College, *Denver* 3,400
Rockmont College, *Lakewood* 300
Saint Thomas Seminary, *Denver* 130
United States Air Force Academy, *USAF Academy* 4,500
University of Colorado at Boulder, *Boulder* 22,200
University of Colorado at Colorado Springs, *Colorado Springs* 5,300
University of Colorado at Denver, *Denver* 10,700
University of Colorado Health Sciences Center, *Denver* 1,400
University of Denver, *Denver* 8,200
University of Northern Colorado, *Greeley* 9,700
University of Southern Colorado, *Pueblo* 5,400
Western Bible College, *Morrison* 200
Western State College of Colorado, *Gunnison* 2,900

CONNECTICUT

Albertus Magnus College, *New Haven* 500
Bridgeport Engineering Institute, *Bridgeport* 900
Central Connecticut State College, *New Britain* 12,500
Charter Oak College, *Hartford* 1,100
Connecticut College, *New London* 1,900
Eastern Connecticut State College, *Willimantic* 3,400
Fairfield University, *Fairfield* 5,000
Hartford Graduate Center, *Hartford* 1,900
Hartford Seminary, *Hartford* 100
Holy Apostles College, *Cromwell* 150
Paier College of Art Incorporated, *Hamden* 450
Post College, *Waterbury* 1,500
Quinnipiac College, *Hamden* 3,600
Sacred Heart University, *Bridgeport* 5,000
Saint Joseph College, *West Hartford* 1,200
Southern Connecticut State College, *New Haven* 10,500
Trinity College, *Hartford* 2,000

United States Coast Guard Academy, *New London* 950
University of Bridgeport, *Bridgeport* 6,300
University of Connecticut, *Storrs* 22,800
University of Connecticut Health Center, *Farmington* 500
University of Hartford, *West Hartford* 8,600
University of New Haven, *West Haven* 7,300
Wesleyan University, *Middletown* 3,000
Western Connecticut State College, *Danbury* 6,000
Yale University, *New Haven* 10,300

DELAWARE

Delaware Law School of Widener University, *Wilmington* 850
Delaware State College, *Dover* 2,200
Goldey Beacom College, *Sherwood Park* 2,100
University of Delaware, *Newark* 18,600
Wesley College, *Dover* 1,200
Wilmington College, *New Castle* 900

DISTRICT OF COLUMBIA

American University, *Washington* 11,200
Beacon College, *Washington* 110
Benjamin Franklin University, *Washington* 400
Catholic University of America, *Washington* 7,100
Corcoran School of Art, *Washington* 500
Defense Intelligence College, *Washington* 500
Gallaudet College, *Washington* 1,200
Georgetown University, *Washington* 12,000
George Washington University, *Washington* 19,200
Howard University, *Washington* 11,400
Mount Vernon College, *Washington* 500
Southeastern University, *Washington* 1,600
Strayer College, *Washington* 1,800
Trinity College, *Washington* 700
University of the District of Columbia, *Washington* 14,100
Wesley Theological Seminary, *Washington* 330

FLORIDA

Baptist Bible Institute, *Graceville* 400
Barry College, *Miami Shores* 3,000
Bethune Cookman College, *Daytona Beach* 1,600
Biscayne College, *Opa-Locka* 3,300
Central Florida Bible College, *Orlando* 130
Clearwater Christian College, *Clearwater* 220
College of Boca Raton, *Boca Raton* 500
Eckerd College, *St. Petersburg* 1,100
Edward Waters College, *Jacksonville* 850
Embry-Riddle Aeronautical University, *Bunnell* 8,100
Flagler College, *St. Augustine* 1,000
Florida Agricultural and Mechanical University, *Tallahassee* 4,800
Florida Atlantic University, *Boca Raton* 9,100
Florida Institute of Technology, *Melbourne* 7,000
Florida International University, *Sweetwater* 13,600
Florida Memorial College, *Opa-Locka* 900
Florida Southern College, *Lakeland* 3,300
Florida State University, *Tallahassee* 22,000
Fort Lauderdale College, *Fort Lauderdale* 950
Hobe Sound Bible College, *Hobe Sound* 230
Jacksonville University, *Jacksonville* 2,400
Jones College Jacksonville, *Jacksonville* 1,600
Miami Christian College, *Miami* 320
Nova University, *Davie* 5,600
Orlando College, *Kingswood Manor* 1,100
Palm Beach Atlantic College, *West Palm Beach* 650
Regional Seminary of Saint Vincent De Paul in Florida, Inc., *Boynton Beach* 100
Ringling School of Art and Design, *Sarasota* 450
Rollins College, *Winter Park* 3,400
Saint Leo College, *St. Leo* 4,700
Southeastern College of Osteopathic Medicine, *North Miami Beach* 100
Southeastern College of the Assemblies of God, *Lakeland* 1,100
Stetson University, *De Land* 2,900
Tampa College, *Tampa* 1,800
University of Central Florida, *Orlando* 14,200
University of Florida, *Gainesville* 34,300
University of Miami, *Coral Gables* 14,700
University of North Florida, *Jacksonville* 5,400
University of Sarasota, *Sarasota* 170
University of South Florida, *Tampa* 25,700
University of Tampa, *Tampa* 2,000
University of West Florida, *Pensacola* 5,300
Warner Southern College, *Lake Wales* 300
Webber College, *Babson Park* 300

GEORGIA

Agnes Scott College, *Decatur* 550
Albany State College, *Albany* 1,900
Armstrong State College, *Savannah* 3,000
Atlanta Christian College, *East Point* 180
Atlanta College of Art, *Atlanta* 270
Atlanta University, *Atlanta* 1,200
Augusta College, *Augusta* 4,100
Berry College, *Mount Berry* 1,500
Brenau College, *Gainesville* 1,600
Clark College, *Atlanta* 2,000
Columbia Theological Seminary, *Decatur* 450
Columbus College, *Columbus* 4,200
Covenant College, *Lookout Mountain* 520
Devry Institute of Technology, *Atlanta* 2,600
Emory University, *Atlanta* 8,200
Fort Valley State College, *Fort Valley* 1,700
Georgia College, *Milledgeville* 3,500
Georgia Institute of Technology, *Atlanta* 11,400
Georgia Southern College, *Statesboro* 6,800
Georgia Southwestern College, *Americus* 2,300
Georgia State University, *Atlanta* 21,300
Interdenominational Theological Center, *Atlanta* 300
Kennesaw College, *Marietta* 4,800
La Grange College, *La Grange* 950
Life Chiropractic College, *Marietta* 1,600
Medical College of Georgia, *Augusta* 2,000
Mercer University in Atlanta, *Atlanta* 1,800
Mercer University Main Campus, *Macon* 3,000
Mercer University Southern School of Pharmacy, *Atlanta* ... 320
Morehouse College, *Atlanta* 1,900
Morris Brown College, *Atlanta* 1,300
North Georgia College, *Dahlonega* 2,000
Oglethorpe University, *North Atlanta* 1,200
Paine College, *Augusta* 820
Piedmont College, *Demorest* 400
Savannah College of Art and Design, *Savannah* 450
Savannah State College, *State College* 2,100
Shorter College, *Rome* 800
Southern Technical Institute, *Marietta* 3,200
Spelman College, *Atlanta* 1,500
Tift College, *Forsyth* 610
Toccoa Falls College, *Toccoa Falls* 650
University of Georgia, *Athens* 25,900
Valdosta State College, *Valdosta* 5,500
Wesleyan College, *Macon* 340
West Georgia College, *Carrollton* 6,000

HAWAII

Brigham Young University Hawaii Campus, *Laie* 1,600
Chaminade University of Honolulu, *Honolulu* 1,900
Hawaii Loa College, *Kaneohe* 390
Hawaii Pacific College, *Honolulu* 2,300
University of Hawaii at Hilo, *Hilo* 3,700
University of Hawaii at Manoa, *Honolulu* 20,900
University of Hawaii West Oahu College, *Aiea* 400

IDAHO

Boise State University, *Boise* 11,100
College of Idaho, *Caldwell* 700
Idaho State University, *Pocatello* 7,100
Lewis-Clark State College, *Lewiston* 2,000
Northwest Nazarene College, *Nampa* 1,200
University of Idaho, *Moscow* 9,200

ILLINOIS

Alfred Adler Institute of Chicago, *Chicago* 130
American Conservatory of Music, *Chicago* 340
Augustana College, *Rock Island* 2,400
Aurora College, *Aurora* 1,300
Barat College, *Lake Forest* 640
Bethany Theological Seminary, *Oak Brook* 120
Blackburn College, *Carlinville* 430
Bradley University, *Peoria* 5,600
Catholic Theological Union, *Chicago* 330
Chicago College of Osteopathic Medicine, *Chicago* 400
Chicago State University, *Chicago* 7,400
Chicago Theological Seminary, *Chicago* 140
Christ Seminary-Seminex, *Chicago* 230
College of Saint Francis, *Joliet* 3,600
Columbia College, *Chicago* 4,200
Concordia College, *River Forest* 1,300
De Lourdes College, *Des Plaines* 280
De Paul University, *Chicago* 12,900
Devry Institute of Technology, *Chicago* 6,600
Dr. William M. Scholl College of Podiatric Medicine, *Chicago* 570
Eastern Illinois University, *Charleston* 10,400
Elmhurst College, *Elmhurst* 3,500
Eureka College, *Eureka* 540
Forest Institute of Professional Psychology, *Des Plaines* 130
Garrett-Evangelical Theological Seminary, *Evanston* 360
George Williams College, *Downers Grove* 1,200
Governors State University, *Park Forest South* 4,900
Greenville College, *Greenville* 760
Harrington Institute of Interior Design, *Chicago* 390
Hebrew Theological College, *Skokie* 170
Illinois Benedictine College, *Lisle* 2,400
Illinois College, *Jacksonville* 770
Illinois College of Optometry, *Chicago* 550
Illinois Institute of Technology, *Chicago* 6,900
Illinois School of Professional Psychology, *Chicago* 300
Illinois State University, *Normal* 20,600
Illinois Wesleyan University, *Bloomington* 1,700
John Marshall Law School, *Chicago* 1,700
Judson College, *Elgin* 410
Keller Graduate School of Management, *Chicago* 1,200
Kendall College, *Evanston* 410
Knox College, *Galesburg* 940
Lake Forest College, *Lake Forest* 1,100
Lake Forest School of Management, *Lake Forest* 380
Lewis University, *Romeoville* 2,700
Lincoln Christian College, *Lincoln* 480
Loyola University of Chicago, *Chicago* 14,500
Lutheran School of Theology at Chicago, *Chicago* 310
McCormick Theological Seminary, *Chicago* 600
McKendree College, *Lebanon* 750
MacMurray College, *Jacksonville* 630
Mallinckrodt College, *Wilmette* 290
Midwest College of Engineering, *Lombard* 260
Millikin University, *Decatur* 1,500
Monmouth College; *Monmouth* 650
Moody Bible Institute, *Chicago* 1,300
Mundelein College, *Chicago* 1,300
National College of Chiropractic, *Lombard* 1,000
National College of Education, *Evanston* 3,200
North Central College, *Naperville* 1,400
Northeastern Illinois University, *Chicago* 10,300
Northern Baptist Theological Seminary, *Lombard* 220
Northern Illinois University, *De Kalb* 25,700
North Park College and Theological Seminary, *Chicago* 1,300
Northwestern University, *Evanston* 15,700
Olivet Nazarene College, *Bourbonnais* 1,900
Principia College, *Elsah* 800
Quincy College, *Quincy* 950
Rockford College, *Rockford* 1,500
Roosevelt University, *Chicago* 6,700
Rosary College, *River Forest* 1,600
Rush University, *Chicago* 1,100
Saint Louis University-Parks College, *Cahokia* 1,000
Saint Mary of the Lake Seminary, *Mundelein* 180
Saint Xavier College, *Chicago* 2,300
Sangamon State University, *Springfield* 3,300
School of the Art Institute of Chicago, *Chicago* 1,400
Southern Illinois University at Carbondale, *Carbondale* 23,700
Southern Illinois University at Edwardsville, *Edwardsville* 11,100
Spertus College of Judaica, *Chicago* 350
Trinity Christian College, *Palos Heights* 440
Trinity College, *Bannockburn* 550
Trinity Evangelical Divinity School, *Bannockburn* 900
University of Chicago, *Chicago* 9,000
University of Health Sciences-Chicago Medical School, *Chicago* 850
University of Illinois at Chicago, *Chicago* 26,300
University of Illinois Urbana Campus, *Urbana* 34,900
Vandercook College of Music, *Chicago* 170
Western Illinois University, *Macomb* 12,400
Wheaton College, *Wheaton* 2,500

INDIANA

Anderson College, *Anderson* 2,000
Ball State University, *Muncie* 18,200
Bethel College, *Mishawaka* 400
Butler University, *Indianapolis* 4,000
Calumet College, *Whiting* 1,300
Christian Theological Seminary, *Indianapolis* 300
Concordia Theological Seminary, *Fort Wayne* 550
De Pauw University, *Greencastle* 2,400
Earlham College, *Richmond* 1,100
Fort Wayne Bible College, *Fort Wayne* 450
Franklin College of Indiana, *Franklin* 550
Goshen College, *Goshen* 1,100
Grace College, *Winona Lake* 900
Grace Theological Seminary, *Winona Lake* 400
Hanover College, *Hanover* 1,000
Huntington College, *Huntington* 450
Indiana Central University, *Indianapolis* 3,300
Indiana Institute of Technology, *Fort Wayne* 550
Indiana State University, *Terre Haute* 11,900
Indiana State University Evansville Campus, *Evansville* 3,700
Indiana University at Kokomo, *Kokomo* 2,800
Indiana University at South Bend, *South Bend* 5,900
Indiana University Bloomington, *Bloomington* 32,700
Indiana University Northwest, *Gary* 4,900
Indiana University-Purdue University at Fort Wayne, *Fort Wayne* 10,100
Indiana University-Purdue University at Indianapolis, *Indianapolis* 23,300
Indiana University Southeast, *New Albany* 4,600
Manchester College, *North Manchester* 1,000
Marian College, *Indianapolis* 950
Marion College, *Marion* 1,100
Martin Center College, *Indianapolis* 130
Oakland City College, *Oakland City* 550
Purdue University, *West Lafayette* 32,600
Purdue University Calumet, *Hammond* 7,700
Purdue University North Central Campus, *Westville* 2,500
Rose-Hulman Institute of Technology, *Terre Haute* 1,300
Saint Francis College, *Fort Wayne* 1,300
Saint Joseph's College, *Collegeville* 950
Saint Mary-of-the-Woods College, *St. Mary-of-the-Woods* 650
Saint Mary's College, *St. Marys* 1,800
Saint Meinrad College, *St. Meinrad* 180
Saint Meinrad School of Theology, *St. Meinrad* 150
Taylor University, *Upland* 1,500
Tri-State University, *Angola* 1,200
University of Evansville, *Evansville* 4,800
University of Notre Dame, *Notre Dame* 10,000
Valparaiso University, *Valparaiso* 4,300
Wabash College, *Crawfordsville* 750

IOWA

Briar Cliff College, *Sioux City* 1,300
Buena Vista College, *Storm Lake* 1,400
Central University of Iowa, *Pella* 1,500
Clarke College, *Dubuque* 900
Coe College, *Cedar Rapids* 1,500
Cornell College, *Mount Vernon* 850

Divine Word College, *Epworth* 100
Dordt College, *Sioux Center* 1,100
Drake University, *Des Moines* 6,500
Faith Baptist Bible College, *Ankeny* 420
Graceland College, *Lamoni* 1,100
Grand View College, *Des Moines* 1,200
Grinnell College, *Grinnell* 1,200
Iowa State University of Science and Technology, *Ames* .. 25,300
Iowa Wesleyan College, *Mount Pleasant* 720
Loras College, *Dubuque* 1,800
Luther College, *Decorah* 2,100
Maharishi International University, *Fairfield* 750
Marycrest College, *Davenport* 1,400
Morningside College, *Sioux City* 1,300
Mount Mercy College, *Cedar Rapids* 1,200
Mount Saint Clare College, *Clinton* 350
Northwestern College, *Orange City* 900
Open Bible College, *Des Moines* 100
Palmer College of Chiropractic, *Davenport* 1,925
Saint Ambrose College, *Davenport* 2,100
Simpson College, *Indianola* 1,100
University of Dubuque, *Dubuque* 1,300
University of Iowa, *Iowa City* 28,900
University of Northern Iowa, *Cedar Falls* 11,200
University of Osteopathic Medicine and Health Sciences, *Des Moines* 750
Upper Iowa University, *Fayette* 1,600
Vennard College, *University Park* 200
Wartburg College, *Waverly* 1,100
Wartburg Theological Seminary, *Dubuque* 260
Westmar College, *Le Mars* 510
William Penn College, *Oskaloosa* 450

KANSAS

Baker University, *Baldwin City* 850
Benedictine College, *Atchison* 1,000
Bethany College, *Lindsborg* 800
Bethel College, *North Newton* 650
Central Baptist Theological Seminary, *Kansas City* 150
Emporia State University, *Emporia* 5,800
Fort Hays State University, *Hays* 5,500
Friends Bible College, *Haviland* 150
Friends University, *Wichita* 800
Kansas Newman College, *Wichita* 750
Kansas State University of Agriculture and Applied Science, *Manhattan* 19,500
Kansas Wesleyan, *Salina* 600
McPherson College, *Mc Pherson* 500
Manhattan Christian College, *Manhattan* 240
Marymount College of Kansas, *Salina* 700
Mid-America Nazarene College, *Olathe* 1,200
Ottawa University, *Ottawa* 2,100
Pittsburg State University, *Pittsburg* 5,100
Saint John's College, *Winfield* 250
Saint Mary College, *Leavenworth* 800
Saint Mary of the Plains College, *Dodge City* 600
Southwestern College, *Winfield* 600
Sterling College, *Sterling* 400
Tabor College, *Hillsboro* 400
United States Army Command and General Staff College, *Fort Leavenworth* 950
University of Kansas Main Campus, *Lawrence* 24,400
University of Kansas Medical Center, *Kansas City* 1,800
Washburn University, *Topeka* 6,500
Wichita State University, *Wichita* 16,600

KENTUCKY

Alice Lloyd College, *Pippa Passes* 500
Asbury College, *Wilmore* 1,200
Asbury Theological Seminary, *Wilmore* 700
Bellarmine College, *Louisville* 2,700
Berea College, *Berea* 1,500
Brescia College, *Owensboro* 900
Campbellsville College, *Campbellsville* 700
Centre College, *Danville* 700
Cumberland College, *Williamsburg* 1,700
Eastern Kentucky University, *Richmond* 13,000
Georgetown College, *Georgetown* 1,200
Kentucky Christian College, *Grayson* 450
Kentucky State University, *Frankfort* 2,200
Kentucky Wesleyan College, *Owensboro* 900
Lexington Theological Seminary, *Lexington* 120
Louisville Presbyterian Theological Seminary, *Louisville* 210
Morehead State University, *Morehead* 6,300
Murray State University, *Murray* 7,500
Northern Kentucky University, *Highland Heights* 9,000
Pikeville College, *Pikeville* 600
Southern Baptist Theological Seminary, *Louisville* 2,100
Spalding College, *Louisville* 950
Thomas More College, *Crestview Hills* 1,200
Transylvania University, *Lexington* 700
Union College, *Barbourville* 800
University of Kentucky, *Lexington* 23,000
University of Louisville, *Louisville* 19,700
Western Kentucky University, *Bowling Green* 12,800

LOUISIANA

Centenary College of Louisiana, *Shreveport* 1,400
Dillard University, *New Orleans* 1,100
Grambling State University, *Grambling* 4,000
Louisiana College, *Pineville* 1,100
Louisiana State University and Agricultural and Mechanical College Bato, *Baton Rouge* 31,100
Louisiana State University in Shreveport, *Shreveport* 4,300
Louisiana State University Medical Center, *New Orleans* .. 2,600
Louisiana Tech University, *Ruston* 11,100
Loyola University in New Orleans, *New Orleans* 3,900
McNeese State University, *Lake Charles* 7,300
New Orleans Baptist Theological Seminary, *New Orleans* .. 1,500
Nicholls State University, *Thibodaux* 7,200
Northeast Louisiana University, *Monroe* 11,100
Northwestern State University of Louisiana, *Natchitoches* . 6,400
Our Lady of Holy Cross College, *New Orleans* 750
Saint Joseph Seminary College, *St. Benedict* 120
Saint Mary's Dominican College, *New Orleans* 750
Southeastern Louisiana University, *Hammond* 9,500
Southern University Agricultural and Mechanical College Main Campus, *Scotlandville* 9,100
Southern University in New Orleans, *New Orleans* 2,600
Tulane University of Louisiana, *New Orleans* 10,500
University of New Orleans, *New Orleans* 15,900
University of Southwestern Louisiana, *Lafayette* 15,700
Xavier University of Louisiana, *New Orleans* 2,000

MAINE

Bates College, *Lewiston* 1,500
Bowdoin College, *Brunswick* 1,400
Colby College, *Waterville* 1,700
College of the Atlantic, *Bar Harbor* 160
Husson College, *Bangor* 1,500
Maine Maritime Academy, *Castine* 650
Portland School of Art, *Portland* 270
Saint Joseph's College, *North Windham* 3,800
Thomas College, *Waterville* 950
Unity College, *Unity* 330
University of Maine at Augusta, *Augusta* 3,400
University of Maine at Farmington, *Farmington* 1,900
University of Maine at Fort Kent, *Fort Kent* 700
University of Maine at Machias, *Machias* 800
University of Maine at Orono, *Orono* 11,700
University of Maine at Presque Isle, *Presque Isle* 1,200
University of New England, *Biddeford* 750
University of Southern Maine, *Portland* 8,200
Westbrook College, *Portland* 1,000

MARYLAND

Baltimore Hebrew College, *Baltimore* 250
Bowie State College, *Bowie* 2,200
Capitol Institute of Technology, *Kensington* 800
College of Notre Dame of Maryland, *Baltimore* 1,700
Columbia Union College, *Takoma Park* 500

Coppin State College, *Baltimore* ... 2,300
Frostburg State College, *Frostburg* ... 3,700
Goucher College, *Towson* ... 1,000
Hood College, *Frederick* ... 1,700
Johns Hopkins University, *Baltimore* ... 10,000
Loyola College, *Baltimore* ... 6,200
Maryland Institute College of Art, *Baltimore* ... 1,500
Morgan State University, *Baltimore* ... 4,700
Mount Saint Mary's College, *Emmitsburg* ... 1,700
Ner Israel Rabbinical College, *Baltimore* ... 350
Peabody Institute of Johns Hopkins University, *Baltimore* ... 400
Saint John's College, *Annapolis* ... 400
Saint Mary's College of Maryland, *St. Marys City* ... 1,300
Saint Mary's Seminary and University, *Baltimore* ... 300
Salisbury State College, *Salisbury* ... 4,300
Sojourner-Douglas College, *Baltimore* ... 450
Towson State University, *Towson* ... 14,900
Uniformed Services University of the Health Sciences, *Bethesda* ... 650
United States Naval Academy, *Annapolis* ... 4,600
University of Baltimore, *Baltimore* ... 5,400
University of Maryland Baltimore County Campus, *Catonsville* ... 7,400
University of Maryland Baltimore Professional Schools, *Baltimore* ... 4,800
University of Maryland College Park Campus, *College Park* ... 37,000
University of Maryland-Eastern Shore, *Princess Anne* ... 1,200
University of Maryland University College, *College Park* ... 11,300
Washington Bible College / Capital Bible Seminary, *Lanham* ... 550
Washington College, *Chestertown* ... 800
Washington Theological Union, *Silver Spring* ... 180
Western Maryland College, *Westminster* ... 1,800

MASSACHUSETTS

American International College, *Springfield* ... 2,100
Amherst College, *Amherst* ... 1,500
Andover Newton Theological School, *Newton* ... 450
Anna Maria College, *Paxton* ... 1,700
Assumption College, *Worcester* ... 2,800
Atlantic Union College, *South Lancaster* ... 600
Babson College, *Wellesley* ... 3,200
Bentley College, *Waltham* ... 3,200
Berklee College of Music, *Boston* ... 2,500
Berkshire Christian College, *Lenox* ... 130
Boston Architectural Center, *Boston* ... 600
Boston College, *Newton* ... 14,000
Boston Conservatory, *Boston* ... 400
Boston University, *Boston* ... 28,200
Bradford College, *Haverhill* ... 400
Brandeis University, *Waltham* ... 3,600
Bridgewater State College, *Bridgewater* ... 7,400
Cambridge College Institute of Open Education, *Cambridge* ... 400
Central New England College of Technology, *Worcester* ... 300
Clark University, *Worcester* ... 3,200
College of Our Lady of the Elms, *Chicopee* ... 800
College of the Holy Cross, *Worcester* ... 2,500
Curry College, *Milton* ... 1,300
Eastern Nazarene College, *Quincy* ... 850
Emerson College, *Boston* ... 2,200
Emmanuel College, *Boston* ... 1,000
Episcopal Divinity School, *Cambridge* ... 140
Fitchburg State College, *Fitchburg* ... 6,600
Framingham State College, *Framingham* ... 5,900
Gordon College, *Wenham* ... 1,100
Gordon-Cornwell Theological Seminary, *South Hamilton* ... 750
Hampshire College, *Amherst* ... 1,200
Harvard University, *Cambridge* ... 13,200
Hebrew College, *Brookline* ... 200
Hellenic College-Holy Cross Greek Orthodox School of Theology, *Brookline* ... 240
Lesley College, *Cambridge* ... 2,100
Massachusetts College of Art, *Boston* ... 2,000
Massachusetts College of Pharmacy and Allied Health Sciences, *Boston* ... 1,000
Massachusetts Institute of Technology, *Cambridge* ... 9,600
Massachusetts Maritime Academy, *Buzzards Bay* ... 850
Massachusetts School of Professional Psychology, *Newton* ... 140
Merrimack College, *North Andover* ... 3,800
Mount Holyoke College, *South Hadley* ... 2,000
Mount Ida College, *Newton* ... 800
New England College of Optometry, *Boston* ... 350
New England Conservatory of Music, *Boston* ... 700
New England School of Law, *Boston* ... 1,000
Nichols College, *Dudley Hill* ... 1,000
North Adams State College, *North Adams* ... 2,700
Northeastern University, *Boston* ... 38,900
Pine Manor College, *Brookline* ... 600
Radcliffe College, *Cambridge* ... 2,500
Regis College, *Weston* ... 1,100
Saint John's Seminary, *Boston* ... 200
Salem State College, *Salem* ... 8,600
School of the Museum of Fine Arts-Boston, *Boston* ... 800
Simmons College, *Boston* ... 2,800
Simon's Rock of Bard College, *Great Barrington* ... 300
Smith College, *Northampton* ... 3,000
Southeastern Massachusetts University, *North Dartmouth* ... 6,800
Springfield College, *Springfield* ... 2,300
Stonehill College, *North Easton* ... 2,700
Suffolk University, *Boston* ... 6,300
Swain School of Design, *New Bedford* ... 160
Tufts University, *Medford* ... 7,000
University of Lowell, *Lowell* ... 15,500
University of Massachusetts Amherst Campus, *Amherst* ... 26,500
University of Massachusetts Boston Campus, *Boston* ... 11,400
University of Massachusetts Medical School at Worcester, *Worcester* ... 450
Wellesley College, *Wellesley* ... 2,300
Wentworth Institute of Technology, *Boston* ... 3,700
Western New England College, *Springfield* ... 5,400
Westfield State College, *Westfield* ... 4,500
Weston School of Theology, *Cambridge* ... 200
Wheaton College, *Norton* ... 1,300
Wheelock College, *Boston* ... 1,100
Williams College, *Williamstown* ... 2,000
Worcester Polytechnic Institute, *Worcester* ... 3,600
Worcester State College, *Worcester* ... 6,200

MICHIGAN

Adrian College, *Adrian* ... 1,200
Albion College, *Albion* ... 1,700
Alma College, *Alma* ... 1,100
Andrews University, *Andrews* ... 2,900
Aquinas College, *Grand Rapids* ... 2,700
Calvin College, *Grand Rapids* ... 3,800
Calvin Theological Seminary, *Grand Rapids* ... 210
Center for Creative Studies - College of Art and Design, *Detroit* ... 1,100
Central Michigan University, *Mount Pleasant* ... 17,100
Cleary College, *Ypsilanti* ... 1,000
Concordia College, *Ann Arbor* ... 550
Cranbrook Academy of Art, *Bloomfield Hills* ... 140
Detroit College of Business, *Dearborn* ... 3,000
Detroit College of Law, *Detroit* ... 900
Eastern Michigan University, *Ypsilanti* ... 18,100
Ferris State College, *Big Rapids* ... 11,000
GMI Engineering and Management Institute, *Flint* ... 2,400
Grace Bible College, *Grand Rapids* ... 170
Grand Rapids Baptist College and Seminary, *Grand Rapids* ... 1,100
Grand Valley State Colleges, *Allendale* ... 6,400
Great Lakes Bible College, *Lansing* ... 180
Hillsdale College, *Hillsdale* ... 1,000
Hope College, *Holland* ... 2,500
Jordan College, *Cedar Springs* ... 1,000
Kalamazoo College, *Kalamazoo* ... 1,200
Kendall School of Design, *Grand Rapids* ... 600
Lake Superior State College, *Sault Ste. Marie* ... 2,500
Lawrence Institute of Technology, *Southfield* ... 5,900
Madonna College, *Livonia* ... 3,400
Marygrove College, *Detroit* ... 1,200
Mercy College of Detroit, *Detroit* ... 2,100
Michigan Christian College, *Rochester Hills* ... 350

Michigan State University, *East Lansing* 42,700
Michigan Technological University, *Houghton* 7,600
Nazareth College, *Kalamazoo* 550
Northern Michigan University, *Marquette* 8,400
Northwood Institute, *Midland* 2,100
Oakland University, *Rochester Hills* 11,700
Olivet College, *Olivet* 550
Reformed Bible College, *Grand Rapids* 220
Sacred Heart Seminary College, *Detroit* 200
Saginaw Valley State College, *Bay City* 4,400
Saint John's Provincial Seminary, *Plymouth* 190
Saint Mary's College, *Orchard Lake Village* 200
Shaw College at Detroit, *Detroit* 450
Siena Heights College, *Adrian* 1,400
Spring Arbor College, *Spring Arbor* 1,000
Thomas M. Cooley Law School, *Lansing* 1,100
University of Detroit, *Detroit* 6,000
University of Michigan-Ann Arbor, *Ann Arbor* 35,100
University of Michigan-Dearborn, *Dearborn* 6,400
University of Michigan-Flint, *Flint* 5,000
Walsh College of Accountancy and Business Administration, *Troy* 1,800
Wayne State University, *Detroit* 29,800
Western Michigan University, *Kalamazoo* 20,600
Western Theological Seminary, *Holland* 120
William Tyndale College, *Farmington Hills* 300

MINNESOTA

Augsburg College, *Minneapolis* 1,500
Bemidji State University, *Bemidji* 4,900
Bethel College, *St. Paul* 2,100
Bethel Theological Seminary, *St. Paul* 500
Carleton College, *Northfield* 1,900
College of Saint Benedict, *St. Joseph* 2,300
College of Saint Catherine, *St. Paul* 2,300
College of Saint Scholastica, *Duluth* 1,200
College of Saint Teresa, *Winona* 550
College of Saint Thomas, *St. Paul* 5,900
Concordia College at Moorhead, *Moorhead* 2,600
Concordia College-Saint Paul, *St. Paul* 700
Dr. Martin Luther College, *New Ulm* 750
Gustavus Adolphus College, *St. Peter* 2,300
Hamline University, *St. Paul* 1,900
Luther Northwestern Theological Seminary, *St. Paul* 850
Macalester College, *St. Paul* 1,700
Mankato State University, *Mankato* 14,100
Mayo Graduate School of Medicine, *Rochester* 950
Mayo Medical School, *Rochester* 160
Metropolitan State University, *St. Paul* 3,400
Minneapolis College of Art Design, *Minneapolis* 500
Moorhead State University, *Moorhead* 7,100
North Central Bible College, *Minneapolis* 900
Northwestern College, *Roseville* 900
Northwestern College of Chiropractic, *St. Paul* 450
Saint Cloud State University, *St. Cloud* 11,600
Saint John's University, *Collegeville* 2,000
Saint Mary's College, *Winona* 1,400
Saint Olaf College, *Northfield* 3,100
Saint Paul Bible College, *St. Bonifacius* 600
School of the Associated Arts, *St. Paul* 100
Southwest State University, *Marshall* 2,100
United Theological Seminary, *New Brighton* 250
University of Minnesota at Duluth, *Duluth* 10,900
University of Minnesota at Morris, *Morris* 1,700
University of Minnesota of Minneapolis Saint Paul, *Minneapolis* 64,500
William Mitchell College of Law, *St. Paul* 1,200
Winona State University, *Winona* 5,300

MISSISSIPPI

Alcorn State University, *Lorman* 2,400
Belhaven College, *Jackson* 950
Blue Mountain College, *Blue Mountain* 350
Delta State University, *Cleveland* 3,500
Jackson State University, *Jackson* 6,500
Millsaps College, *Jackson* 1,200
Mississippi College, *Clinton* 2,800
Mississippi State University, *Mississippi State* 13,400
Mississippi University for Women, *Columbus* 1,900
Mississippi Valley State University, *Itta Bena* 2,200
Reformed Theological Seminary, *Jackson* 220
Rust College, *Holly Springs* 850
Tougaloo College, *Tougaloo* 800
University of Mississippi, *Oxford* 9,400
University of Mississippi Medical Center, *Jackson* 1,700
University of Southern Mississippi, *Hattiesburg* 13,000
William Carey College, *Hattiesburg* 1,500

MISSOURI

Assemblies of God Graduate School, *Springfield* 210
Avila College, *Kansas City* 1,900
Baptist Bible College, *Springfield* 1,500
Calvary Bible College, *Kansas City* 500
Central Bible College, *Springfield* 900
Central Christian College of the Bible, *Moberly* 120
Central Methodist College, *Fayette* 550
Central Missouri State University, *Warrensburg* 9,500
Cleveland Chiropractic College, *Kansas City* 400
Columbia College, *Columbia* 2,400
Concordia Seminary, *Clayton* 750
Covenant Theological Seminary, *Creve Coeur* 150
Culver-Stockton College, *Canton* 600
Devry Institute of Technology, *Kansas City* 2,400
Drury College, *Springfield* 2,500
Eden Theological Seminary, *Webster Groves* 200
Evangel College, *Springfield* 1,800
Fontbonne College, *Clayton* 900
Hannibal-La Grange College, *Hannibal* 500
Harris-Stowe State College, *St. Louis* 1,000
Kansas City Art Institute, *Kansas City* 450
Kirksville College of Osteopathic Medicine, *Kirksville* 550
Lincoln University, *Jefferson City* 2,800
Logan College of Chiropractic, *Chesterfield* 700
Maryville College-Saint Louis, *Creve Coeur* 1,900
Midwestern Baptist Theological Seminary, *Kansas City* 500
Missouri Baptist College, *Creve Coeur* 400
Missouri Southern State College, *Joplin* 4,500
Missouri Valley College, *Marshall* 500
Missouri Western State College, *St. Joseph* 4,300
Nazarene Theological Seminary, *Kansas City* 450
Northeast Missouri State University, *Kirksville* 7,200
Northwest Missouri State University, *Maryville* 5,100
Ozark Bible College, *Joplin* 650
Park College, *Parkville* 3,200
Rockhurst College, *Kansas City* 3,200
Saint Louis Christian College, *Florissant* 160
Saint Louis College of Pharmacy, *St. Louis* 650
Saint Louis Conservatory of Music, *St. Louis* 100
Saint Louis University, *St. Louis* 8,700
Saint Paul School of Theology, *Kansas City* 200
School of the Ozarks, *Point Lookout* 1,300
Southeast Missouri State University, *Cape Girardeau* 9,100
Southwest Baptist University, *Bolivar* 1,400
Southwest Missouri State University, *Springfield* 15,000
Stephens College, *Columbia* 1,300
Tarkio College, *Tarkio* 600
The Lindenwood College, *St. Charles* 1,900
University of Health Sciences, *Kansas City* 600
University of Missouri-Columbia, *Columbia* 24,800
University of Missouri-Kansas City, *Kansas City* 11,400
University of Missouri-Rolla, *Rolla* 7,800
University of Missouri-Saint Louis, *Bellerive* 12,000
Washington University, *University City* 10,700
Webster University, *Webster Groves* 5,000
Westminster College, *Fulton* 700
William Jewell College, *Liberty* 1,600
William Woods College, *Fulton* 800

MONTANA

Carroll College, *Helena* 1,300
College of Great Falls, *Great Falls* 1,300
Eastern Montana College, *Billings* 4,200

Montana College of Mineral Science and Technology, *Butte* 2,200
Montana State University, *Bozeman* 11,200
Northern Montana College, *Havre* 1,700
Rocky Mountain College, *Billings* 400
University of Montana, *Missoula* 9,100
Western Montana College, *Dillon* 1,000

NEBRASKA

Bellevue College, *Bellevue* 2,700
Chadron State College, *Chadron* 1,900
College of Saint Mary, *Omaha* 1,100
Concordia Teachers College, *Seward* 1,100
Creighton University, *Omaha* 5,700
Dana College, *Blair* 550
Doane College, *Crete* 700
Grace College of the Bible, *Omaha* 300
Hastings College, *Hastings* 800
Kearney State College, *Kearney* 7,300
Midland Lutheran College, *Fremont* 900
Nebraska Christian College, *Norfolk* 200
Nebraska Wesleyan University, *Lincoln* 1,200
Peru State College, *Peru* 900
Union College, *Lincoln* 1,000
University of Nebraska at Omaha, *Omaha* 14,000
University of Nebraska-Lincoln, *Lincoln* 25,100
University of Nebraska Medical Center, *Omaha* 2,600
Wayne State College, *Wayne* 2,300

NEVADA

Old College, *Reno* 150
Sierra Nevada College, *Incline Village* 210
University of Nevada-Las Vegas, *Paradise* 11,500
University of Nevada-Reno, *Reno* 9,600

NEW HAMPSHIRE

Colby-Sawyer College, *New London* 550
Daniel Webster College, *Nashua* 1,100
Dartmouth College, *Hanover* 4,500
Franklin Pierce College, *Rindge* 1,800
Franklin Pierce Law Center, *Concord* 350
Hawthorne College, *North Branch* 700
New England College, *Henniker* 1,300
New Hampshire College, *Manchester* 6,800
Notre Dame College, *Manchester* 700
Rivier College, *Nashua* 2,200
Saint Anselm College, *Pinardville* 1,800
University of New Hampshire, *Durham* 12,400
University of New Hampshire Keene State College, *Keene* . 3,700
University of New Hampshire Plymouth State College, *Plymouth* 3,500

NEW JERSEY

Beth Medrash Govoha, *Lakewood* 900
Bloomfield College, *Bloomfield* 1,800
Caldwell College, *Caldwell* 750
Centenary College, *Hackettstown* 1,300
College of Saint Elizabeth, *Convent Station* 900
Drew University, *Madison* 2,300
Fairleigh Dickinson University Florhan-Madison Campus, *Madison* 5,000
Fairleigh Dickinson University Rutherford Campus, *Rutherford* 4,200
Fairleigh Dickinson University Teaneck Campus, *Teaneck* . 8,000
Felician College, *Lodi* 650
Georgian Court College, *Lakewood* 1,500
Glassboro State College, *Glassboro* 9,800
Immaculate Conception Seminary, *Ramsey* 180
Jersey City State College, *Jersey City* 9,000
Kean College of New Jersey, *Union* 13,000
Monmouth College, *West Long Branch* 4,100
Montclair State College, *Montclair* 14,800
New Brunswick Theological Seminary, *New Brunswick* 110
New Jersey Institute of Technology, *Newark* 6,900
Northeastern Bible College, *Essex Fells* 300
Princeton Theological Seminary, *Princeton* 900
Princeton University, *Princeton* 6,200
Rabbinical College of America, *Morristown* 230
Ramapo College of New Jersey, *Mahwah* 4,500
Rider College, *Lawrenceville* 5,500
Rutgers the State University of New Jersey Camden Campus, *Camden* 5,000
Rutgers the State University of New Jersey Newark Campus, *Newark* 9,500
Rutgers the State University of New Jersey New Brunswick Campus, *New Brunswick* 32,800
Saint Peter's College, *Jersey City* 4,200
Seton Hall University, *South Orange* 10,300
Stevens Institute of Technology, *Hoboken* 3,100
Stockton State College, *Pomona* 5,100
Thomas A. Edison College, *Trenton* 3,600
Trenton State College, *Ewing Township* 9,900
University of Medicine and Dentistry of New Jersey, *Newark* 1,900
Upsala College, *East Orange* 1,500
Westminster Choir College, *Princeton* 400
William Paterson College, *Wayne* 12,100

NEW MEXICO

Artesia Christian College, *Artesia* 110
College of Santa Fe, *Santa Fe* 1,000
College of the Southwest, *Hobbs* 200
Eastern New Mexico University, *Portales* 5,600
New Mexico Highlands University, *Las Vegas* 2,300
New Mexico Institute of Mining and Technology, *Socorro* . 1,400
New Mexico State University, *University Park* 13,400
Saint John's College at Santa Fe New Mexico, *Santa Fe* 350
University of Albuquerque, *Albuquerque* 1,800
University of New Mexico, *Albuquerque* 24,100
Western New Mexico University, *Silver City* 1,600

NEW YORK

Adelphi University, *Garden City* 11,200
Albany College of Pharmacy, *Albany* 600
Albany Law School, *Albany* 700
Albany Medical College of Union University, *Albany* 600
Alfred University, *Alfred* 1,600
Associated Beth Rivkah Schools, *New York* 350
Bank Street College of Education, *New York* 600
Bard College, *Annandale-on-Hudson* 750
Barnard College, *New York* 2,400
Belzer Yeshiva-Machzikei Torah Seminary, *New York* 240
Beth Jacob Hebrew Teachers College, *New York* 600
Boricua College, *New York* 1,100
Brooklyn Law School, *New York* 1,300
Canisius College, *Buffalo* 4,400
Cathedral College of the Immaculate Conception, *New York* 100
Central Yeshiva Tomchei Tmimin Lubavitz of the U.S.A., *New York* 400
Christ the King Seminary, *East Aurora* 130
City University of New York Bernard Baruch College, *New York* 15,200
City University of New York Brooklyn College, *New York* 15,600
City University of New York City College, *New York* 13,500
City University of New York City Technical College, *New York* 12,300
City University of New York College of Staten Island, *New York* 11,100
City University of New York Graduate School and University Center, *New York* 3,000
City University of New York Hunter College, *New York* 17,400
City University of New York John Jay College of Criminal Justice, *New York* 5,900
City University of New York Lehman College, *New York* 9,600
City University of New York Medgar Evers College, *New York* 2,600
City University of New York Queens College, *New York* 17,300
City University of New York York College, *New York* 4,100
Clarkson College of Technology, *Potsdam* 4,000

Colgate Rochester Divinity School-Bexley Hall-Crozer Theological Semina, *Rochester* 220
Colgate University, *Hamilton* 2,700
College for Human Services, *New York* 550
College of Insurance, *New York* 1,600
College of Mount Saint Vincent, *New York* 1,100
College of New Rochelle, *New Rochelle* 5,700
College of Saint Rose, *Albany* 2,700
Columbia University Main Division, *New York* 16,100
Columbia University Teachers College, *New York* 4,200
Concordia College, *Bronxville* 450
Cooper Union, *New York* 1,000
Cornell University Endcwed Colleges, *Ithaca* 10,600
Cornell University Medical Center, *New York* 550
Cornell University Statutory Colleges, *Ithaca* 7,600
Daemen College, *Amherst* 1,700
Dominican College of Blauvelt, *Orangeburg* 1,700
Dowling College, *Oakdale* 2,200
D'youville College, *Buffalo* 1,300
Elmira College, *Elmira* 2,500
Fashion Institute of Technology, *New York* 9,700
Fordham University, *New York* 13,100
Friends World College, *Lloyd Harbor* 160
General Theological Seminary, *New York* 180
Gruss Girls Seminary, *Spring Valley* 230
Hadar Hatorah Rabbinical Seminary, *New York* 260
Hamilton College, *Clinton* 1,600
Hartwick College, *Oneonta* 1,400
Hebrew Union College New York Branch, *New York* 110
Hobart-William Smith Colleges, *Geneva* 1,900
Hofstra University, *Hempstead* 10,800
Houghton College, *Houghton* 1,200
Institute for Advance Studies in the Humanities, *New York* 290
Iona College, *New Rochelle* 6,200
Ithaca College, *Ithaca* 5,000
Jewish Theological Seminary of America, *New York* 130
Kehilath Yakov Rabbinical Seminary, *New York* 210
Keuka College, *Keuka Park* 500
King's College, *Briarcliff Manor* 800
Laboratory Institute of Merchandising, *New York* 230
Le Moyne College, *De Witt* 2,100
Long Island University Brooklyn Center, *New York* 6,900
Long Island University C W Post Center, *Brookville* 12,400
Long Island University Southampton Center, *Southampton* 1,200
Manhattan College, *New York* 4,800
Manhattan School of Music, *New York* 700
Manhattanville College, *Harrison* 1,300
Mannes College of Music, *New York* 450
Marist College, *Fairview* 3,200
Maryknoll School of Theology, *Maryknoll* 170
Marymount College, *Tarrytown* 1,300
Marymount Manhattan College, *New York* 2,200
Medaille College, *Buffalo* 800
Mercy College, *Dobbs Ferry* 9,400
Mesivta Torah Vodaath Seminary, *New York* 500
Mesivtha Tifereth Jerusalem of America, *New York* 110
Mirrer Yeshiva Central Institute, *New York* 350
Molloy College, *Rockville Centre* 1,600
Mount Saint Mary College, *Newburgh* 1,000
Mount Sinai School of Medicine of City University of New York, *New York* 500
Nazareth College of Rochester, *Pittsford* 2,400
New School for Social Research, *New York* 4,400
New York Chiropractic College, *Old Brookville* 800
New York College of Podiatric Medicine, *New York* 500
New York Institute of Technology Main Campus, *Old Westbury* 8,100
New York Institute of Technology New York City Campus, *New York* 3,500
New York Law School, *New York* 1,500
New York Medical College, *Valhalla* 1,200
New York School of Interior Design, *New York* 800
New York State College of Ceramics at Alfred University, *Alfred* 750
New York Theological Seminary, *New York* 240
New York University, *New York* 32,500
Niagara University, *Niagara University* 3,800
Nyack College, *South Nyack* 760
Pace University New York Campus, *New York* 14,300
Pace University Pleasantville-Briarcliff Campus, *Pleasantville* 4,400
Pace University-White Plains Campus, *White Plains* 4,500
Parsons School of Design, *New York* 2,700
Polytechnic Institute of New York, *New York* 4,900
Pratt Institute, *New York* 4,100
Rabbi Isaac Elchanan Theological Seminary, *New York* 230
Rabbinical Academy Mesivta Rabbi Chaim Berlin, *New York* 450
Rabbinical College Bobover Yeshiva B'nei Zion, *New York* 280
Rabbinical College Ch'san Sofer of New York, *New York* 120
Rabbinical Seminary Adas Yereim, *New York* 110
Rabbinical Seminary of America, *New York* 180
Rabbinical Seminary of Munkacs, *New York* 500
Rensselaer Polytechnic Institute, *Troy* 6,700
Rika Breuer Teachers Seminary, *New York* 130
Roberts Wesleyan College, *North Chili* 600
Rochester Institute of Technology, *Rochester* 16,100
Russell Sage College Main Campus, *Troy* 3,100
Saint Bonaventure University, *St. Bonaventure* 2,800
Saint Francis College, *New York* 2,800
Saint John Fisher College, *East Rochester* 2,300
Saint John's University, *New York* 19,000
Saint Joseph's College, *New York* 1,000
Saint Joseph's College Suffolk Campus, *Brentwood* 1,300
Saint Joseph's Seminary and College, *Yonkers* 180
Saint Lawrence University, *Canton* 2,400
Saint Thomas Aquinas College, *Sparkill* 2,000
Sarah Lawrence College, *Yonkers* 1,000
School of Visual Arts, *New York* 4,800
Seminary of the Immaculate Conception, *Lloyd Harbor* 190
Sh'or Yoshuv Rabbinical College, *New York* 120
Siena College, *Loudonville* 3,400
Skidmore College, *Saratoga Springs* 2,500
State University of New York at Albany, *Albany* 15,700
State University of New York at Binghamton, *Binghamton* 11,700
State University of New York at Buffalo Main Campus, *Buffalo* 23,500
State University of New York at Stony Brook, *South Stony Brook* 14,700
State University of New York College at Brockport, *Brockport* 7,400
State University of New York College at Buffalo, *Buffalo* 11,400
State University of New York College at Cortland, *Cortland* 6,000
State University of New York College at Fredonia, *Fredonia* 5,200
State University of New York College at Geneseo, *Geneseo* 5,200
State University of New York College at New Paltz, *New Paltz* 7,400
State University of New York College at Old Westbury, *Old Westbury* 3,800
State University of New York College at Oneonta, *Oneonta* 6,200
State University of New York College at Oswego, *Oswego* 7,800
State University of New York College at Plattsburgh, *Plattsburgh* 6,000
State University of New York College at Potsdam, *Potsdam* 4,900
State University of New York College at Purchase, *Harrison* 3,700
State University of New York College of Environmental Science and For, *Syracuse* 1,600
State University of New York College of Optometry, *New York* 250
State University of New York College of Technology at Utica-Rome, *Utica* 3,100
State University of New York Downstate Medical Center, *New York* 1,400
State University of New York Empire State College, *Saratoga Springs* 5,200
State University of New York Health Sciences Center at Buffalo, *Buffalo* 3,400
State University of New York Health Sciences Center at Stony Brook, *South Stony Brook* 1,400
State University of New York Maritime College, *New York* 1,100

State University of New York Upstate Medical Center, *Syracuse* 900
Syracuse University, *Syracuse* 21,100
Talmudical Seminary Oholei Torah, *New York* 120
The Juilliard School, *New York* 1,200
Touro College, *New York* 2,200
Union College, *Schenectady* 3,400
Union Theological Seminary, *New York* 300
United States Merchant Marine Academy, *Kings Point* 1,100
United States Military Academy, *West Point* 4,500
United Talmudical Academy, *New York* 670
University of Rochester, *Rochester* 8,600
University of the State of New York Regents External Degree Program, *Albany* 18,700
Utica College of Syracuse University, *Utica* 2,300
Vassar College, *Arlington* 2,400
Wagner College, *New York* 2,300
Wells College, *Aurora* 500
Yeshiva of Nitra Rabbinical College, *New York* 120
Yeshivath Zichron Moshe, *South Fallsburg* 120
Yeshiva University, *New York* 4,400

NORTH CAROLINA

Appalachian State University, *Boone* 10,400
Atlantic Christian College, *Wilson* 1,500
Barber-Scotia College, *Concord* 350
Belmont Abbey College, *Belmont* 800
Bennett College, *Greensboro* 550
Campbell University, *Buies Creek* 3,100
Catawba College, *Salisbury* 1,000
Davidson College, *Davidson* 1,400
Duke University, *Durham* 9,800
East Carolina University, *Greenville* 14,500
East Coast Bible College, *Charlotte* 220
Elizabeth City State University, *Elizabeth City* 1,500
Elon College, *Elon College* 2,600
Fayetteville State University, *Fayetteville* 2,400
Gardner-Webb College, *Boiling Springs* 1,700
Greensboro College, *Greensboro* 600
Guilford College, *Greensboro* 1,600
High Point College, *High Point* 1,400
Johnson C. Smith University, *Charlotte* 1,200
Lenoir-Rhyne College, *Hickory* 1,400
Livingstone College, *Salisbury* 600
Mars Hill College, *Mars Hill* 1,500
Meredith College, *Raleigh* 1,600
Methodist College, *Fayetteville* 800
North Carolina Agricultural and Technical State University, *Greensboro* 5,200
North Carolina Central University, *Durham* 5,000
North Carolina School of the Arts, *Winston-Salem* 550
North Carolina State University at Raleigh, *Raleigh* 22,700
North Carolina Wesleyan College, *Rocky Mount* 950
Pembroke State University, *Pembroke* 2,200
Pfeiffer College, *Misenheimer* 800
Piedmont Bible College, *Winston-Salem* 400
Queens College, *Charlotte* 1,100
Roanoke Bible College, *Elizabeth City* 150
Sacred Heart College, *Belmont* 400
Saint Andrew's Presbyterian College, *Laurinburg* 750
Saint Augustine's College, *Raleigh* 1,600
Salem College, *Winston-Salem* 600
Shaw University, *Raleigh* 1,800
Southeastern Baptist Theological Seminary, *Wake Forest* 1,100
University of North Carolina at Asheville, *Asheville* 2,500
University of North Carolina at Chapel Hill, *Chapel Hill* 22,100
University of North Carolina at Charlotte, *Charlotte* 10,300
University of North Carolina at Greensboro, *Greensboro* 10,300
University of North Carolina at Wilmington, *Wilmington* 5,800
Wake Forest University, *Winston-Salem* 4,800
Warren Wilson College, *Swannanoa* 550
Western Carolina University, *Cullowhee* 6,400
Wingate College, *Wingate* 1,500
Winston-Salem State University, *Winston-Salem* 2,300

NORTH DAKOTA

Dickinson State College, *Dickinson* 1,200
Jamestown College, *Jamestown* 600
Mary College, *Bismarck* 1,100
Mayville State College, *Mayville* 700
Minot State College, *Minot* 2,700
North Dakota State University, *Fargo* 9,500
Northwest Bible College, *Minot* 110
Trinity Bible Institute, *Ellendale* 300
University of North Dakota, *Grand Forks* 10,900
Valley City State College, *Valley City* 1,100

OHIO

Air Force Institute of Technology, *Wright-Patterson Air Force Base* 1,000
Antioch University, *Yellow Springs* 3,200
Art Academy of Cincinnati, *Cincinnati* 240
Ashland College, *Ashland* 2,900
Athenaeum of Ohio, *Cincinnati* 170
Baldwin-Wallace College, *Berea* 3,800
Bluffton College, *Bluffton* 600
Borromeo College of Ohio, *Wickliffe* 110
Bowling Green State University, *Bowling Green* 17,200
Capital University, *Bexley* 2,600
Case Western Reserve University, *Cleveland* 8,500
Cedarville College, *Cedarville* 1,700
Central State University, *Wilberforce* 2,400
Cincinnati Bible Seminary, *Cincinnati* 800
Circleville Bible College, *Circleville* 230
Cleveland Institute of Art, *Cleveland* 600
Cleveland Institute of Music, *Cleveland* 270
Cleveland State University, *Cleveland* 18,900
College of Mount Saint Joseph-on-the-Ohio, *Mount St. Joseph* 1,700
College of Wooster, *Wooster* 1,800
Columbus College of Art and Design, *Columbus* 1,200
Defiance College, *Defiance* 800
Denison University, *Granville* 2,200
Devry Institute of Technology, *Columbus* 4,300
Dyke College, *Cleveland* 1,400
Findlay College, *Findlay* 1,200
Franklin University, *Columbus* 5,000
God's Bible School and College, *Cincinnati* 300
Hebrew Union College, *Cincinnati* 150
Heidelberg College, *Tiffin* 850
Hiram College, *Hiram* 1,200
John Carroll University, *University Heights* 3,800
Kent State University, *Kent* 19,900
Kenyon College, *Gambier* 1,400
Lake Erie College, *Painesville* 1,000
Lourdes College, *Sylvania* 750
Malone College, *Canton* 850
Marietta College, *Marietta* 1,400
Medical College of Ohio at Toledo, *Toledo* 550
Methodist Theological School of Ohio, *Delaware* 240
Miami University Oxford Campus, *Oxford* 14,900
Mount Union College, *Alliance* 1,000
Mount Vernon Nazarene College, *Mount Vernon* 1,000
Muskingum College, *New Concord* 1,000
Northeastern Ohio Universities of Medicine, *Rootstown* 350
Notre Dame College, *South Euclid* 650
Oberlin College, *Oberlin* 2,800
Ohio College of Podiatric Medicine, *Cleveland* 600
Ohio Dominican College, *Columbus* 1,000
Ohio Institute of Technology, *Columbus* 3,000
Ohio Northern University, *Ada* 2,600
Ohio State University, *Columbus* 53,400
Ohio State University Lima Branch, *Lima* 900
Ohio State University Mansfield Branch, *Mansfield* 1,100
Ohio State University Marion Branch, *Marion* 750
Ohio State University Newark Branch, *Newark* 900
Ohio University, *Athens* 15,700
Ohio Wesleyan University, *Delaware* 2,000
Otterbein College, *Westerville* 1,600
Pontifical College Josephinum, *Columbus* 210
Rabbinical College of Telshe, *Wickliffe* 160

Rio Grande College, *Rio Grande* 1,400
Tiffin University, *Tiffin* 500
Trinity Lutheran Seminary, *Columbus* 300
Union for Experimenting Colleges and Universities, *Cincinnati* 550
United Theological Seminary, *Dayton* 280
University of Akron Main Campus, *Akron* 24,600
University of Cincinnati, *Cincinnati* 32,900
University of Dayton, *Dayton* 11,000
University of Steubenville, *Steubenville* 900
University of Toledo, *Toledo* 21,400
Urbana College, *Urbana* 550
Ursuline College, *Cleveland Heights* 1,300
Walsh College, *Canton* 1,200
Wilberforce University, *Wilberforce* 1,000
Wilmington College, *Wilmington* 1,300
Wittenberg University, *Springfield* 2,200
Wright State University, *Fairborn* 13,900
Xavier University, *Cincinnati* 7,000
Youngstown State University, *Youngstown* 15,600

OKLAHOMA

Bartlesville Wesleyan College, *Bartlesville* 800
Bethany Nazarene College, *Bethany* 1,400
Cameron University, *Lawton* 5,500
Central State University, *Edmond* 12,300
East Central Oklahoma State University, *Ada* 3,800
Flaming Rainbow University, *Tahlequah* 210
Hillsdale Free Will Baptist College, *Moore* 170
Langston University, *Langston* 1,900
Midwest Christian College, *Oklahoma City* 110
Northeastern Oklahoma State University, *Tahlequah* 6,500
Northwestern Oklahoma State University, *Alva* 1,700
Oklahoma Baptist University, *Shawnee* 1,400
Oklahoma Christian College, *Oklahoma City* 1,600
Oklahoma City University, *Oklahoma City* 3,200
Oklahoma College of Osteopathic Medicine and Surgery, *Tulsa* 260
Oklahoma Panhandle State University, *Goodwell* 1,300
Oklahoma State University Main Campus, *Stillwater* 23,400
Oral Roberts University, *Tulsa* 4,000
Phillips University, *Enid* 1,100
Southeastern Oklahoma State University, *Durant* 4,200
Southwestern Oklahoma State University, *Weatherford* 4,600
University of Oklahoma Health Sciences Center, *Oklahoma City* 2,400
University of Oklahoma Norman Campus, *Norman* 21,800
University of Science and Arts of Oklahoma, *Chickasha* 1,400
University of Tulsa, *Tulsa* 5,900

OREGON

Bassist College, *Portland* 210
Columbia Christian College, *Portland* 220
Concordia College, *Portland* 300
Eastern Oregon State College, *La Grande* 1,900
Eugene Bible College, *Eugene* 130
George Fox College, *Newberg* 750
Judson Baptist College, *The Dalles* 250
Lewis and Clark College, *Portland* 3,100
Linfield College, *McMinnville* 1,500
Marylhurst College for Lifelong Learning, *Marylhurst* 700
Mount Angel Seminary, *St. Helens* 120
Multnomah School of the Bible, *Portland* 700
Northwest Christian College, *Eugene* 230
Oregon Health Sciences University, *Portland* 1,400
Oregon Institute of Technology, *Klamath Falls* 2,700
Oregon State University, *Corvallis* 16,800
Pacific Northwest College of Art, *Portland* 200
Pacific University, *Forest Grove* 1,100
Portland State University, *Portland* 15,000
Reed College, *Portland* 1,100
Southern Oregon State College, *Ashland* 4,300
University of Oregon, *Eugene* 15,400
University of Portland, *Portland* 2,900
Warner Pacific College, *Portland* 400
Western Baptist College, *Salem* 280
Western Conservative Baptist Seminary, *Portland* 500
Western Evangelical Seminary, *Gladstone* 200
Western Oregon State College, *Monmouth* 2,500
Western States Chiropractic College, *Portland* 450
Willamette University, *Salem* 1,900

PENNSYLVANIA

Academy of the New Church, *Bryn Athyn* 160
Albright College, *Reading* 2,100
Allegheny College, *Meadville* 1,900
Allentown College of Saint Francis de Sales, *Center Valley* 1,100
Alliance College, *Cambridge Springs* 290
Alvernia College, *Reading* 800
American College, *Bryn Mawr* 700
Baptist Bible College and School of Theology, *Clarks Summit* 800
Beaver College, *Glenside* 2,000
Bloomsburg University of Pennsylvania, *Bloomsburg* 6,200
Bryn Mawr College, *Bryn Mawr* 1,800
Bucknell University, *Lewisburg* 3,300
Cabrini College, *Radnor Township* 800
California University of Pennsylvania, *California* 4,500
Carlow College, *Pittsburgh* 1,000
Carnegie-Mellon University, *Pittsburgh* 6,000
Cedar Crest College, *Allentown* 1,000
Chatham College, *Pittsburgh* 700
Chestnut Hill College, *Philadelphia* 1,100
Cheyney University of Pennsylvania, *Cheyney* 1,900
Clarion University of Pennsylvania Main Campus, *Clarion* 5,000
College Misericordia, *Dallas* 1,300
Curtis Institute of Music, *Philadelphia* 140
Delaware Valley College of Science and Agriculture, *New Britain* 1,700
Dickinson College, *Carlisle* 1,800
Dickinson School of Law, *Carlisle* 500
Drexel University, *Philadelphia* 12,300
Duquesne University, *Pittsburgh* 6,300
Eastern Baptist Theological Seminary, *Philadelphia* 350
Eastern College, *St. Davids* 850
East Stroudsburg University of Pennsylvania, *East Stroudsburg* 4,100
Edinboro University of Pennsylvania, *Edinboro* 5,600
Elizabethtown College, *Elizabethtown* 1,800
Franklin and Marshall College, *Lancaster* 2,900
Gannon University, *Erie* 4,100
Geneva College, *Beaver Falls* 1,300
Gettysburg College, *Gettysburg* 1,900
Gratz College, *Philadelphia* 260
Grove City College, *Grove City* 2,200
Gwynedd-Mercy College, *Gwynedd Valley* 2,200
Hahnemann University, *Philadelphia* 2,000
Haverford College, *Haverford* 1,000
Holy Family College, *Philadelphia* 1,300
Immaculata College, *Immaculata* 1,700
Indiana University of Pennsylvania, *Indiana* 12,500
Juniata College, *Huntingdon* 1,300
King's College, *Wilkes-Barre* 2,300
Kutztown University of Pennsylvania, *Kutztown* 5,900
Lafayette College, *Easton* 2,400
Lancaster Bible College, *Lancaster* 350
Lancaster Theological Seminary, *Lancaster* 240
La Roche College, *McCandless* 1,600
La Salle College, *Philadelphia* 7,100
Lebanon Valley College, *Annville* 1,200
Lehigh University, *Bethlehem* 6,300
Lincoln University, *Lincoln University* 1,200
Lock Haven University of Pennsylvania, *Lock Haven* 2,600
Lutheran Theological Seminary at Gettysburg, *Gettysburg* 280
Lutheran Theological Seminary at Philadelphia, *Philadelphia* 230
Lycoming College, *Williamsport* 1,200
Mansfield University of Pennsylvania, *Mansfield* 2,700
Marywood College, *Scranton* 3,000
Medical College of Pennsylvania, *Philadelphia* 550
Mercyhurst College, *Erie* 1,600
Messiah College, *Grantham* 1,500
Millersville University of Pennsylvania, *Millersville* 6,400

Moore College of Art, *Philadelphia* 600
Moravian College, *Bethlehem* 1,800
Muhlenberg College, *Allentown* 2,400
Neumann College, *Aston* 850
Pennsylvania College of Optometry, *Philadelphia* 600
Pennsylvania College of Podiatric Medicine, *Philadelphia* 500
Pennsylvania State University Behrend College, *Erie* 1,900
Pennsylvania State University Capitol Campus, *Middletown* 2,700
Pennsylvania State University Hershey Medical Center, *Hershey* 500
Pennsylvania State University King of Prussia Center for Grad. Studies, *Upper Merion Township* 450
Pennsylvania State University Main Campus, *State College* 36,200
Philadelphia College of Art, *Philadelphia* 1,600
Philadelphia College of Osteopatic Medicine, *Philadelphia* 850
Philadelphia College of Pharmacy and Science, *Philadelphia* 1,100
Philadelphia College of Textiles and Science, *Philadelphia* 3,100
Philadelphia College of the Bible, *Langhorne Manor* 550
Philadelphia College of the Performing Arts, *Philadelphia* 350
Pittsburgh Theological Seminary, *Pittsburgh* 350
Point Park College, *Pittsburgh* 2,700
Robert Morris College, *Coraopolis* 5,700
Rosemont College, *Rosemont* 600
Saint Charles Borromeo Seminary, *Philadelphia* 550
Saint Francis College, *Loretto* 1,600
Saint Joseph's University, *Philadelphia* 6,100
Saint Vincent College and Seminary, *Latrobe* 1,100
Seton Hill College, *Greensburg* 950
Shippensburg University of Pennsylvania, *Shippensburg* 5,900
Slippery Rock University of Pennsylvania, *Slippery Rock* 5,800
Spring Garden College, *Philadelphia* 1,400
Susquehanna University, *Selinsgrove* 1,700
Swarthmore College, *Swarthmore* 1,300
Temple University, *Philadelphia* 29,600
Thiel College, *Greenville* 800
Thomas Jefferson University, *Philadelphia* 1,900
United Wesleyan College, *Allentown* 190
University of Pennsylvania, *Philadelphia* 22,300
University of Pittsburgh, *Pittsburgh* 29,400
University of Pittsburgh Bradford Campus, *Bradford* 1,000
University of Pittsburgh Johnstown Campus, *Scalp Level* 3,200
University of Scranton, *Scranton* 4,600
Ursinus College, *Collegeville* 2,100
Valley Forge Christian College, *Phoenixville* 450
Villa Maria College, *Erie* 600
Villanova University, *Villanova* 11,700
Washington and Jefferson College, *Washington* 1,300
Waynesburg College, *Waynesburg* 700
West Chester University of Pennsylvania, *West Chester* 9,700
Westminster College, *New Wilmington* 1,600
Westminster Theological Seminary, *Philadelphia* 400
Widener University Pennsylvania Campus, *Chester* 5,700
Wilkes College, *Wilkes-Barre* 3,000
Wilson College, *Chambersburg* 250
York College of Pennsylvania, *York* 4,400

RHODE ISLAND

Barrington College, *Barrington* 450
Brown University, *Providence* 6,900
Byrant College of Business Administration, *Providence* 6,600
Johnson and Wales College, *Providence* 4,700
Providence College, *Providence* 5,900
Rhode Island College, *Providence* 8,500
Rhode Island School of Design, *Providence* 1,700
Roger Williams College Main Campus, *Bristol* 2,500
Roger Williams College Providence Branch, *Providence* 1,500
Salve Regina-The Newport College, *Newport* 2,000
University of Rhode Island, *Kingston* 14,100

SOUTH CAROLINA

Allen University, *Columbia* 240
Baptist College at Charleston, *Goose Creek* 2,200
Benedict College, *Columbia* 1,400
Bob Jones University, *Greenville* 4,800
Central Wesleyan College, *Central* 400
Citadel Military College of South Carolina, *Charleston* 3,300
Claflin College, *Orangeburg* 650
Clemson University, *Clemson* 12,100
Coker College, *Hartsville* 300
College of Charleston, *Charleston* 5,400
Columbia Bible College, *Columbia* 900
Columbia College, *Columbia* 1,200
Converse College, *Spartanburg* 950
Erskine College and Seminary, *Due West* 650
Francis Marion College, *Florence* 2,900
Furman University, *Greenville* 3,100
Lander College, *Greenwood* 2,000
Limestone College, *Gaffney* 1,500
Lutheran Theological Southern Seminary, *Columbia* 170
Medical University of South Carolina, *Charleston* 1,900
Morris College, *Sumter* 650
Newberry College, *Newberry* 700
Presbyterian College, *Clinton* 900
Sherman College of Straight Chiropractic, *Spartanburg* 400
South Carolina State College, *Orangeburg* 3,900
University of South Carolina at Aiken, *Aiken* 1,800
University of South Carolina at Coastal Carolina, *Conway* 2,500
University of South Carolina at Columbia, *Columbia* 24,700
University of South Carolina at Spartanburg, *Spartanburg* 2,600
Voorhees College, *Denmark* 650
Winthrop College, *Rock Hill* 4,900
Wofford College, *Spartanburg* 1,100

SOUTH DAKOTA

Augustana College, *Sioux Falls* 2,000
Black Hills State College, *Spearfish* 1,900
Dakota State College, *Madison* 1,200
Dakota Wesleyan University, *Mitchell* 500
Huron College, *Huron* 350
Mount Marty College, *Yankton* 600
National College, *Rapid City* 3,000
North American Baptist Seminary, *Sioux Falls* 150
Northern State College, *Aberdeen* 2,700
Qgala Lakota College, *Kyle* 650
Sinte Gleska College, *Rosebud* 250
Sioux Falls College, *Sioux Falls* 850
South Dakota School of Mines and Technology, *Rapid City* 2,800
South Dakota State University, *Brookings* 8,000
University of South Dakota at Springfield, *Springfield* 800
University of South Dakota Main Campus, *Vermillion* 8,300
Yankton College, *Yankton* 280

TENNESSEE

American Baptist College of A. B. T. Seminary, *Nashville* 180
Austin Peay State University, *Clarksville* 3,900
Belmont College, *Nashville* 1,900
Bethel College, *McKenzie* 450
Bristol College, *Bristol* 450
Bryan College, *Dayton* 550
Carson-Newman College, *Jefferson City* 1,700
Christian Brothers College, *Memphis* 1,500
Church of God School of Theology, *Cleveland* 270
David Lipscomb College, *Nashville* 2,300
East Tennessee State University, *Johnson City* 9,600
Emmanuel School of Religion, *Johnson City* 150
Fisk University, *Nashville* 750
Freed-Hardeman College, *Henderson* 1,200
Free Will Baptist Bible College, *Nashville* 500
Harding Graduate School of Religion, *Memphis* 270
Johnson Bible College, *Knoxville* 350
King College, *Bristol* 450
Knoxville College, *Knoxville* 500
Lambuth College, *Jackson* 700
Lane College, *Jackson* 750
Lee College, *Cleveland* 1,100
Le Moyne-Owen College, *Memphis* 1,100
Lincoln Memorial University, *Harrogate* 1,400
Maryville College, *Maryville* 600

Meharry Medical College, *Nashville* 750
Memphis Academy of the Arts, *Memphis* 210
Memphis State University, *Memphis* 20,600
Memphis Theological Seminary, *Memphis* 160
Mid-America Baptist Theological Seminary, *Memphis* 300
Middle Tennessee State University, *Murfreesboro* 10,900
Mid-South Bible College, *Memphis* 130
Milligan College, *Milligan College* 650
O'More College of Design, *Franklin* 120
Rhodes College, *Memphis* 1,000
Southern College of Optometry, *Memphis* 550
Southern College of Seventh-Day Adventists, *Collegedale* 1,800
Tennessee State University, *Nashville* 8,000
Tennessee Technological University, *Cookeville* 7,900
Tennessee Temple University, *Chattanooga* 3,200
Tennessee Wesleyan College, *Athens* 300
Trevecca Nazarene College, *Nashville* 1,000
Tusculum College, *Tusculum College* 350
Union University, *Jackson* 1,400
University of Tennessee at Chattanooga, *Chattanooga* 7,500
University of Tennessee at Knoxville, *Knoxville* 27,000
University of Tennessee at Martin, *Martin* 5,500
University of Tennessee Center for the Health Sciences, *Memphis* 2,000
University of the South, *Sewanee* 1,100
Vanderbilt University, *Nashville* 8,700

TEXAS

Abilene Christian University, *Abilene* 4,500
Amber University, *Garland* 1,100
American Technological University, *Killeen* 450
Angelo State University, *San Angelo* 5,800
Arlington Baptist College, *Arlington* 400
Austin College, *Sherman* 1,200
Austin Presbyterian Theological Seminary, *Austin* 180
Baylor College of Dentistry, *Dallas* 650
Baylor College of Medicine, *Houston* 900
Baylor University, *Waco* 10,500
Bishop College, *Dallas* 1,200
Concordia Lutheran College, *Austin* 450
Corpus Christi State University, *Corpus Christi* 3,300
Criswell Center for Biblical Studies, *Dallas* 350
Dallas Baptist College, *Dallas* 1,300
Dallas Bible College, *Dallas* 200
Dallas Christian College, *Farmers Branch* 150
Dallas Theological Seminary, *Dallas* 1,200
Devry Institute of Technology, *Irving* 2,100
East Texas Baptist College, *Marshall* 900
East Texas State University, *Commerce* 7,800
East Texas State University at Texarkana, *Texarkana* 1,100
Gulf Coast Bible College, *Houston* 350
Hardin-Simmons University, *Abilene* 1,900
Houston Baptist University, *Houston* 2,700
Howard Payne University, *Brownwood* 1,100
Huston-Tillotson College, *Austin* 600
Incarnate Word College, *San Antonio* 1,400
Jarvis Christian College, *Hawkins* 550
Lamar University, *Beaumont* 14,600
Laredo State University, *Laredo* 900
Le Tourneau College, *Longview* 1,000
Lubbock Christian College, *Lubbock* 1,000
McMurry College, *Abilene* 1,300
Midwestern State University, *Wichita Falls* 4,800
North Texas State University, *Denton* 18,800
Our Lady of the Lake University of San Antonio, *San Antonio* 1,600
Pan American University, *Edinburg* 8,300
Paul Quinn College, *Waco* 450
Prairie View A & M University, *Prairie View* 4,500
Rice University, *Houston* 3,900
Saint Edward's University, *Austin* 2,600
Saint Mary's University of San Antonio, *San Antonio* 3,300
Sam Houston State University, *Huntsville* 10,500
Schreiner College, *Kerrville* 500
Southern Bible College, *Houston* 130
Southern Methodist University, *University Park* 9,200
South Texas College of Law, *Houston* 1,200
Southwestern Adventist College, *Keene* 700
Southwestern Assemblies of God College, *Waxahachie* 600
Southwestern Baptist Theological Seminary, *Fort Worth* 3,400
Southwestern University, *Georgetown* 1,000
Southwest Texas State University, *San Marcos* 16,400
Stephen F. Austin State University, *Nacogdoches* 11,900
Sul Ross State University, *Alpine* 2,300
Tarleton State University, *Stephenville* 4,200
Texas A & I University, *Kingsville* 5,200
Texas A & M University at Galveston, *Galveston* 600
Texas A & M University Main Campus, *College Station* 36,100
Texas Chiropractic College, *Pasadena* 500
Texas Christian University, *Fort Worth* 6,900
Texas College, *Tyler* 600
Texas College of Osteopathic Medicine, *Fort Worth* 350
Texas Lutheran College, *Seguin* 1,200
Texas Southern University, *Houston* 8,300
Texas Tech University, *Lubbock* 22,900
Texas Tech University Health Science Center, *Lubbock* 500
Texas Wesleyan College, *Fort Worth* 1,600
Texas Woman's University, *Denton* 7,800
Trinity University, *San Antonio* 3,100
University of Dallas, *Irving* 2,700
University of Houston - Clear Lake, *Houston* 6,600
University of Houston Downtown, *Houston* 6,400
University of Houston - University Park, *Houston* 30,500
University of Houston Victoria, *Victoria* 800
University of Mary Hardin-Baylor, *Belton* 1,200
University of Saint Thomas, *Houston* 2,000
University of Texas at Arlington, *Arlington* 22,200
University of Texas at Austin, *Austin* 48,000
University of Texas at Dallas, *Richardson* 7,400
University of Texas at El Paso, *El Paso* 15,100
University of Texas at San Antonio, *San Antonio* 11,100
University of Texas at Tyler, *Tyler* 2,600
University of Texas Health Science Center at Dallas, *Dallas* 1,300
University of Texas Health Science Center at Houston, *Houston* 2,700
University of Texas Health Science Center at San Antonio, *San Antonio* 2,300
University of Texas Medical Branch at Galveston, *Galveston* 1,700
University of Texas of the Permian Basin, *Odessa* 1,800
Wayland Baptist College, *Plainview* 1,500
West Texas State University, *Canyon* 6,800
Wiley College, *Marshall* 550

UTAH

Brigham Young University, *Provo* 29,700
Southern Utah State College, *Cedar City* 2,400
University of Utah, *Salt Lake City* 24,400
Utah State University, *Logan* 11,100
Weber State College, *Ogden* 10,400
Westminster College of Salt Lake City, *Salt Lake City* 1,200

VERMONT

Bennington College, *North Bennington* 650
Burlington College, *Burlington* 130
Castleton State College, *Castleton* 2,000
College of Saint Joseph the Provider, *Rutland* 350
Goddard College, *Plainfield* 150
Green Mountain College, *Poultney* 350
Johnson State College, *Johnson* 1,200
Lyndon State College, *Lyndonville* 1,100
Marlboro College, *Marlboro* 200
Middlebury College, *Middlebury* 2,000
Norwich University/Military College of Vermont, *Northfield* 1,500
Saint Michael's College, *Winooski* 2,000
School for International Training, *Brattleboro* 750
Southern Vermont College, *Bennington* 450
Trinity College, *Burlington* 900
University of Vermont and State Agricultural College, *Burlington* 11,100
Vermont College, *Montpelier* 1,000

Vermont Law School, *South Royalton* 400

VIRGINIA

Averett College, *Danville* 900
Bluefield College, *Bluefield* 400
Bridgewater College, *Bridgewater* 900
CBN University, *Virginia Beach* 210
Christopher Newport College, *Newport News* 4,200
College of William and Mary, *Williamsburg* 6,500
Eastern Mennonite College and Seminary, *Parkview* 1,000
Eastern Virginia Med. School of the Eastern Virginia Medical Authority, *Norfolk* 350
Emory and Henry College, *Emory* 750
Ferrum College, *Ferrum* 1,600
George Mason University, *Fairfax* 14,900
Hampden-Sydney College, *Hampden Sydney* 800
Hampton Institute, *Hampton* 3,800
Hollins College, *Hollins* 950
James Madison University, *Harrisonburg* 9,800
Liberty Baptist College, *Lynchburg* 3,400
Longwood College, *Farmville* 2,600
Lynchburg College, *Lynchburg* 2,400
Mary Baldwin College, *Staunton* 850
Marymount College of Virginia, *Arlington* 1,700
Mary Washington College, *Fredericksburg* 2,900
Norfolk State College, *Norfolk* 7,300
Old Dominion University, *Norfolk* 15,800
Protestant Episcopal Theological Seminary in Virginia, *Alexandria* 220
Radford College, *Radford* 5,900
Randolph-Macon College, *Ashland* 950
Randolph-Macon Woman's College, *Lynchburg* 750
Roanoke College, *Salem* 1,400
Saint Paul's College, *Lawrenceville* 700
Shenandoah College and Conservatory of Music, *Winchester* 900
Sweet Briar College, *Sweet Briar* 750
Union Theological Seminary in Virginia, *Richmond* 250
University of Richmond, *Richmond* 4,400
University of Virginia Clinch Valley College, *Wise* 1,200
University of Virginia Main Campus, *Charlottesville* 17,100
Virginia Commonwealth University, *Richmond* 20,000
Virginia Intermont College, *Bristol* 600
Virginia Military Institute, *Lexington* 1,300
Virginia Polytechnic Institute and State University, *Blacksburg* 22,900
Virginia State College, *Ettrick* 4,500
Virginia Union University, *Richmond* 1,300
Virginia Wesleyan College, *Norfolk* 850
Washington and Lee University, *Lexington* 1,700

WASHINGTON

Central Washington University, *Ellensburg* 7,000
City College, *Seattle* 2,200
Cornish Institute, *Seattle* 500
Eastern Washington University, *Cheney* 8,200
Evergreen State College, *Olympia* 2,600
Gonzaga University, *Spokane* 3,500
Griffin College, *Seattle* 1,900
Heritage College, *Toppenish* 290
Lutheran Bible Institute of Seattle, *Issaquah* 220
Northwest College of the Assemblies of God, *Kirkland* 700
Pacific Lutheran University, *Parkland* 3,600
Puget Sound College of the Bible, *Edmonds* 150
Saint Martin's College, *Lacey* 500
Seattle Pacific University, *Seattle* 2,700
Seattle University, *Seattle* 4,500
University of Puget Sound, *Tacoma* 4,200
University of Washington, *Seattle* 34,500
Walla Walla College, *College Place* 1,700
Washington State University, *Pullman* 16,700
Western Washington University, *Bellingham* 9,400
Whitman College, *Walla Walla* 1,200
Whitworth College, *Country Homes* 1,800

WEST VIRGINIA

Alderson Broaddus College, *Broaddus* 850
Appalachian Bible College, *Bradley* 200
Bethany College, *Bethany* 800
Bluefield State College, *Bluefield* 2,800
Concord College, *Athens* 2,300
Davis and Elkins College, *Elkins* 1,000
Fairmont State College, *Fairmont* 5,200
Glenville State College, *Glenville* 1,800
Marshall University, *Huntington* 11,700
Ohio Valley College, *Parkersburg* 280
Salem College Main Campus, *Salem* 800
Shepherd College, *Shepherdstown* 3,100
University of Charleston, *Charleston* 2,200
West Liberty State College, *West Liberty* 2,500
West Virginia College of Graduate Studies, *Institute* 3,000
West Virginia Institute of Technology, *Montgomery* 3,400
West Virginia School of Osteopathic Medicine, *Lewisburg* 230
West Virginia State College, *Institute* 4,400
West Virginia University, *Morgantown* 21,300
West Virginia Wesleyan College, *Buckhannon* 1,600
Wheeling College, *Wheeling* 1,000

WISCONSIN

Alverno College, *Milwaukee* 1,400
Beloit College, *Beloit* 1,100
Cardinal Stritch College, *Glendale* 1,300
Carroll College, *Waukesha* 1,400
Carthage College, *Kenosha* 1,400
Concordia College Wisconsin, *Mequon* 650
Edgewood College, *Madison* 750
Institute of Paper Chemistry, *Appleton* 100
Lakeland College, *Howards Grove-Millersville* 800
Lawrence University, *Appleton* 1,100
Marian College of Fond du Lac, *Fond du Lac* 550
Marquette University, *Milwaukee* 11,700
Medical College of Wisconsin, *Milwaukee* 900
Milwaukee School of Art and Design, *Milwaukee* 300
Milwaukee School of Engineering, *Milwaukee* 2,500
Mount Mary College, *Milwaukee* 1,100
Mount Senario College, *Ladysmith* 500
Northland College, *Ashland* 700
Northwestern College, *Watertown* 270
Ripon College, *Ripon* 900
Saint Norbert College, *De Pere* 1,700
Silver Lake College, *Manitowoc* 400
University of Wisconsin-Eau Claire, *Eau Claire* 10,900
University of Wisconsin-Green Bay, *Green Bay* 4,700
University of Wisconsin-La Crosse, *La Crosse* 8,700
University of Wisconsin-Madison, *Madison* 42,200
University of Wisconsin-Milwaukee, *Milwaukee* 26,100
University of Wisconsin-Oshkosh, *Oshkosh* 10,700
University of Wisconsin-Parkside, *Kenosha* 5,900
University of Wisconsin-Platteville, *Platteville* 5,300
University of Wisconsin-River Falls, *River Falls* 5,300
University of Wisconsin-Stevens Point, *Stevens Point* 9,000
University of Wisconsin-Stout, *Menomonie* 7,600
University of Wisconsin-Superior, *Superior* 2,200
University of Wisconsin-Whitewater, *Whitewater* 10,300
Viterbo College, *La Crosse* 1,200
Wisconsin Conservatory of Music, *Milwaukee* 120

WYOMING

University of Wyoming, *Laramie* 10,200

Major Military Installations of the United States

Abbreviations:

A.F.B.	Air Force Base
A.F.S.	Air Force Station
C.G.A.S.	Coast Guard Air Station
C.G.B.	Coast Guard Base
Ft.	Fort
M.C.A.S.	Marine Corps Air Station
M.C.B.	Marine Corps Base
N.A.S.	Naval Air Station
N.A.T.C.	Naval Air Test Center
N.B.	Naval Base
N.S.	Naval Station
N.T.C.	Naval Training Center

ALABAMA

Anniston Army Depot	Anniston
Ft. McClellan	Anniston
Ft. Rucker	Ozark
Gunter A.F.S.	Montgomery
Marshall Space Flight Center	Huntsville
Maxwell A.F.B.	Montgomery
Mobile C.G.B.	Mobile
Redstone Arsenal	Huntsville

ALASKA

Adak N.S.	Adak
Eielson A.F.B.	Fairbanks
Elmendorf A.F.B.	Anchorage
Ft. Greely	Big Delta
Ft. Jonathan Wainwright	Fairbanks
Ft. Richardson	Anchorage
Ketchikan C.G.B.	Ketchikan
Kodiak C.G.A.S.	Kodiak
Shemya A.F.B.	Anchorage
Sitka C.G.A.S.	Sitka

ARIZONA

Davis-Monthan A.F.B.	Tucson
Ft. Huachuca	Douglas
Luke A.F.B.	Glendale
Williams A.F.B.	Chandler
Yuma M.C.A.S.	Yuma
Yuma Proving Ground	Yuma

ARKANSAS

Blytheville A.F.B.	Blytheville
Ft. Chaffee	Fort Smith
Little Rock A.F.B.	Jacksonville
Pine Bluff Arsenal	Pine Bluff

CALIFORNIA

Alameda N.A.S.	Alameda
Beale A.F.B.	Marysville
Camp Pendleton M.C.B.	Oceanside
Castle A.F.B.	Merced
China Lake Naval Weapons Center	Ridgecrest
Concord Naval Weapons Station	Concord
Coronado Naval Amphibious Base	Coronado
Dryden Flight Research Center	Edwards
Edwards A.F.B.	Edwards
El Toro M.C.A.S.	Santa Ana
Ft. Hunter Liggett	Jolon
Ft. Ord	Monterey
George A.F.B.	Victorville
Humboldt Bay C.G.A.S.	McKinleyville
Lemoore N.A.S.	Lemoore
Long Beach Naval Shipyard	Long Beach
Los Angeles A.F.S.	El Segundo
McClellan A.F.B.	Sacramento
March A.F.B.	Riverside
Mare Island Naval Shipyard	Vallejo
Mather A.F.B.	Sacramento
Miramar N.A.S.	San Diego
Moffett Field N.A.S.	Mountain View
Naval Construction Battalion Center	Port Hueneme
North Island N.A.S.	San Diego
Norton A.F.B.	San Bernardino
Oakland Army Base	Oakland
Pacific Missile Test Center–Point Mugu	Oxnard
Presidio of Monterey	Monterey
Presidio of San Francisco	San Francisco
Sacramento Army Depot	Sacramento
San Diego N.S.	San Diego
San Francisco C.G.A.S.	San Francisco
Seal Beach Naval Weapons Station	Seal Beach
Sharpe Army Depot	Stockton
Sierra Army Depot	Reno, NV
Stockton Naval Communication Station	Stockton
Terminal Island C.G.B.	San Pedro
Travis A.F.B.	Fairfield
Twentynine Palms M.C.B.	Twentynine Palms
Vandenberg A.F.B.	Lompoc

COLORADO

Fitzsimmons Army Medical Center	Aurora
Ft. Carson	Colorado Springs
Lowry A.F.B.	Denver
Peterson A.F.B.	Colorado Springs
Rocky Mountain Arsenal	Denver
U.S. Air Force Academy	Colorado Springs

CONNECTICUT

New London Submarine Base	Groton
U.S. Coast Guard Academy	New London

DELAWARE

Dover A.F.B.	Dover

DISTRICT OF COLUMBIA

Bolling A.F.B.	Washington, D.C.
Ft. McNair	Washington, D.C.
Washington Navy Yard	Washington, D.C.

FLORIDA

Cecil Field N.A.S.	Jacksonville
Clearwater C.G.A.S.	Clearwater
Coastal Systems Laboratory	Panama City
Corry Station N.T.C.	Pensacola
Eglin A.F.B.	Valparaiso
Homestead A.F.B.	Homestead
Jacksonville N.A.S.	Orange Park
J. F. Kennedy Space Center	Orlando
Key West N.A.S.	Key West
MacDill A.F.B.	Tampa
Mayport N.S.	Mayport
Miami C.G.A.S.	Opa Locka
Miami Beach C.G.B.	Miami Beach
Orlando N.T.C.	Orlando
Patrick A.F.B.	Cocoa
Pensacola N.A.S.	Pensacola
Tyndall A.F.B.	Springfield
Whiting Field N.A.S.	Milton

GEORGIA

Atlanta N.A.S.	Marietta
Dobbins A.F.B.	Marietta
Ft. Benning	Columbus
Ft. Gordon	Augusta
Ft. McPherson	Atlanta
Ft. Stewart	Hinesville
Hunter Army Airfield	Savannah
Marine Corps Supply Center	Albany
Moody A.F.B.	Valdosta
Robins A.F.B.	Warner Robins

HAWAII

Barbers Point N.A.S.	Ewa Beach
Camp H. M. Smith M.C.B.	Halawa Heights
Ft. Shafter	Honolulu
Hickam A.F.B.	Honolulu
Kaneohe Bay M.C.A.S.	Kailua
Pearl Harbor Nav. Res.	Honolulu
Schofield Barracks	Wahiawa
Wheeler A.F.B.	Wahiawa

IDAHO

Mountain Home A.F.B.	Mountain Home

ILLINOIS

Chanute A.F.B.	Rantoul
Ft. Sheridan	Highwood
Glenview N.A.S.	Glenview
Great Lakes Naval Training Center	North Chicago
Joliet Army Ammunition Plant	Joliet
Rock Island Arsenal	Rock Island
Scott A.F.B.	Belleville

INDIANA

Crane Naval Weapons Support Center	Crane
Ft. Benjamin Harrison	Indianapolis
Grissom A.F.B.	Peru
Jefferson Proving Ground	Madison
Naval Avionics Center	Indianapolis

KANSAS

Ft. Leavenworth	Leavenworth
Ft. Riley	Junction City
McConnell A.F.B.	Wichita

KENTUCKY

Ft. Campbell	Clarksville, Tenn.
Ft. Knox	Louisville
Lexington-Bluegrass Army Depot	Lexington
Navy Ordnance Station	Louisville

LOUISIANA

Barksdale A.F.B.	Shreveport
England A.F.B.	Alexandria
Ft. Polk	Leesville
New Orleans C.G.B.	New Orleans
New Orleans N.A.S.	New Orleans

New Orleans Naval Support Activity . . . . New Orleans

MAINE

Brunswick N.A.S. . . . . Brunswick
Loring A.F.B. . . . . Limestone
Portsmouth Naval Shipyard . . . . Portsmouth, N.H.
South Portland C.G.B. . . . . . Portland
Southwest Harbor C.G.B. . . . . Southwest Harbor

MARYLAND

Aberdeen Proving Ground . . . . Aberdeen
Andrews A.F.B. . . . . . . Camp Springs
Ft. Detrick . . . . Frederick
Ft. Meade . . . . Odenton
Ft. Ritchie . . . . Cascade
Indian Head Naval Ordnance Station . . . . Indian Head
N.A.T.C. Patuxent River . . . . Patuxent River
U.S. Naval Academy . . . . . Annapolis

MASSACHUSETTS

Ft. Devens . . . . Ayer
Hanscom A.F.B. . . . . Bedford
Natick Laboratories . . . . Natick
Otis A.F.B. . . . . Falmouth
South Weymouth N.A.S. . . . . South Weymouth
Westover A.F.B. . . . . Chicopee
Woods Hole C.G.B. . . . . Woods Hole

MICHIGAN

Detroit Arsenal . . . . Warren
Detroit C.G.B. . . . . Detroit
K. I. Sawyer A.F.B. . . . . Gwynn
Michigan Army Missile Plant . . Detroit
Sault Ste. Marie C.G.B. . . . . Sault Ste. Marie
Traverse City C.G.A.S. . . . . Traverse City
Wurtsmith A.F.B. . . . . Oscoda

MISSISSIPPI

Columbus A.F.B. . . . . Columbus
Keesler A.F.B. . . . . Biloxi
Meridian N.A.S. . . . . Meridian
Naval Construction Battalion Center . . . . Gulfport

MISSOURI

Ft. Leonard Wood . . . . . . Waynesville
Richards-Gebaur A.F.B. . . Grandview
St. Louis C.G.B. . . . . St. Louis
Whiteman A.F.B. . . . . Knobnoster

MONTANA

Malmstrom A.F.B. . . . . . . Great Falls

NEBRASKA

Offutt A.F.B. . . . . Omaha

NEVADA

Nellis A.F.B. . . . . Las Vegas
Fallon N.A.S. . . . . Reno

NEW HAMPSHIRE

Pease A.F.B. . . . . Portsmouth

NEW JERSEY

Bayonne Military Ocean Terminal . . . . Bayonne
Cape May C.G.A.S. . . . . . Cape May
Ft. Dix . . . . Wrightstown
Ft. Monmouth . . . . Oceanport
McGuire A.F.B. . . . . Wrightstown
Picatinny Arsenal . . . . Dover

NEW MEXICO

Cannon A.F.B. . . . . Clovis
Holloman A.F.B. . . . . Alamogordo
Kirtland A.F.B. . . . . Albuquerque
Sandia Base . . . . Albuquerque
White Sands Missile Range . . . . Las Cruces

NEW YORK

Buffalo C.G.B. . . . . Buffalo
Ft. Drum . . . . Watertown
Ft. Hamilton . . . . New York
Griffiss A.F.B. . . . . Rome
Plattsburgh A.F.B. . . . . . . Plattsburgh
Seneca Army Depot . . . . . . Romulus
U.S. Military Academy . . . West Point
Watervliet Arsenal . . . . Watervliet

NORTH CAROLINA

Camp Lejeune M.C.B. . . Jacksonville
Cherry Point M.C.A.S. . . . . . Havelock
Elizabeth City C.G.A.S. . . . . Elizabeth City
Ft. Bragg . . . . Fayetteville
Ft. Macon C.G.B. . . . . Atlantic Beach
New River M.C.A.S. . . . . Jacksonville
Pope A.F.B. . . . . Springlake
Seymour Johnson A.F.B. . . Goldsboro

NORTH DAKOTA

Grand Forks A.F.B. . . . . Grand Forks
Minot A.F.B. . . . . Minot

OHIO

Newark A.F.S. . . . . Heath
Rickenbacker A.F.B. . . . . . Columbus
Wright-Patterson A.F.B. . . . . . Dayton

OKLAHOMA

Altus A.F.B. . . . . Altus
Ft. Sill . . . . Lawton
McAlester Army Ammunition Plant . . . . McAlester
Tinker A.F.B. . . . . Oklahoma City
Vance A.F.B. . . . . Enid

OREGON

Astoria C.G.B. . . . . Astoria
North Bend C.G.A.S. . . . . North Bend

PENNSYLVANIA

Carlisle Barracks . . . . Carlisle
Frankford Arsenal . . . . . . Philadelphia
Ft. Indiantown Gap . . . . Annville
Letterkenny Army Depot . . . . Chambersburg
New Cumberland Army Depot . . . . New Cumberland
Philadelphia Naval Shipyard . . . . Philadelphia
Tobyhanna Army Depot . . . . Scranton
Warminster Naval Air Development Center . . . . Warminster
Willow Grove N.A.S. . . . . Willow Grove

SOUTH CAROLINA

Beaufort M.C.A.S. . . . . Beaufort
Charleston A.F.B. . . . . Charleston
Charleston C.G.B. . . . . . . Charleston
Charleston Naval Shipyard . . . . Charleston
Charleston Naval Weapons Station . . . . Charleston
Ft. Jackson . . . . Columbia
Myrtle Beach A.F.B. . . . Myrtle Beach
Parris Island Marine Corps Recruit Depot . . . . Beaufort
Shaw A.F.B. . . . . Sumter

SOUTH DAKOTA

Ellsworth A.F.B. . . . . Box Elders

TENNESSEE

Memphis N.A.S. . . . . Millington

TEXAS

Bergstrom A.F.B. . . . . Austin
Brooks A.F.B. . . . . San Antonio
Carswell A.F.B. . . . . Fort Worth
Chase Field N.A.S. . . . . Beeville
Corpus Christi C.G.A.S. . . . . Corpus Christi
Corpus Christi N.A.S. . . . . Corpus Christi
Dallas N.A.S. . . . . Dallas
Dyess A.F.B. . . . . Abilene
Ft. Bliss . . . . El Paso
Ft. Hood . . . . Killeen
Ft. Sam Houston . . . . . . San Antonio
Galveston C.G.B. . . . . Galveston
Goodfellow A.F.B. . . . . . . San Angelo
Houston C.G.A.S. . . . . Houston
Kelly A.F.B. . . . . San Antonio
Kingsville N.A.S. . . . . Kingsville
Lackland A.F.B. . . . . San Antonio
Laughlin A.F.B. . . . . Del Rio
Lyndon B. Johnson Space Center . . . . Houston
Randolph A.F.B. . . . . Universal City
Red River Army Depot . . . Texarkana
Reese A.F.B. . . . . Lubbock
San Antonio A.F.S. . . . . San Antonio
Sheppard A.F.B. . . . . . Wichita Falls

UTAH

Dugway Proving Ground . . . . Dugway
Hill A.F.B. . . . . Ogden
Tooele Army Depot . . . . Tooele

VIRGINIA

Ft. Belvoir . . . . Alexandria
Ft. Eustis . . . . Newport News
Ft. Lee . . . . Petersburg
Ft. Monroe . . . . Hampton
Ft. Myer . . . . Arlington
Langley A.F.B. . . . . Hampton
Little Creek Naval Amphibious Base . . . . Norfolk
Norfolk N.A.S. . . . . Norfolk
Norfolk Naval Shipyard . . Portsmouth
Norfolk N.S. . . . . Norfolk
Oceana N.A.S. . . . . . . Virginia Beach
Quantico M.C.A.S. . . . . Quantico
Yorktown Naval Weapons Station . . . . Yorktown

WASHINGTON

Bangor Naval Submarine Base . . . . Bremerton
Fairchild A.F.B. . . . . Spokane
Ft. Lewis . . . . Tacoma
McChord A.F.B. . . . . Tacoma
Port Angeles C.G.A.S. . . Port Angeles
Puget Sound Naval Shipyard . . . . Bremerton
Seattle Naval Support Activity . . . . Seattle
Whidbey Island N.A.S. . . . Oak Harbor

WISCONSIN

Ft. McCoy . . . . Sparta
Milwaukee C.G.B. . . . . Milwaukee

WYOMING

Francis E. Warren A.F.B. . . Cheyenne

Glossary of Map Terminology

A

Altitude. The height of an object or elevation above a given level.

Antarctic Circle. The geographic parallel of 66°33′ S., enclosing the area within which the sun is continuously above the horizon on December 22, and below the horizon on June 21.

Antipodes. Two places on the surface of the globe diametrically opposite to each other, i.e., North Pole and South Pole; England and the Antipodes Is.

Archipelago. A group of islands more or less adjacent to each other and arranged in groups covering portions of the sea.

Arctic Circle. The geographic parallel of 66°33′ N., enclosing the area within which the sun is continuously above the horizon on June 21, and below the horizon on December 22.

Atlas. A bound collection of maps. First used in this sense by Mercator in the 16th century.

Atmosphere. Ocean of air surrounding the earth.

Atoll. A coral island in the form of a ring, more or less continuous, around an interior lagoon.

Autumnal Equinox. The time when the overhead sun crosses the Equator on its apparent migration from north to south, or about September 23, and the length of day and night is approximately the same in all latitudes.

Axis. The straight line passing through the center of the earth, about which the earth rotates.

Azimuth. A great circle direction, or the angle measured clockwise between any meridian and an intersecting great circle.

Azimuthal Projection. A map projection on which the directions of all lines radiating from a central point or pole are the same as the directions of the corresponding lines on the sphere. When centered on one of the poles, sometimes called a "polar projection."

B

Bank. An elevation of the ocean bottom above which the water is relatively shallow but sufficient for navigation.

Basin. Area drained by a river and its tributaries.

Bay. A penetration of the sea into the coast. A bay is usually very much wider in the middle than at the entrance.

Bayou. A sluggish watercourse, usually the outlet of a lake or of a river through its delta.

Butte. A conspicuous, isolated hill or mountain.

C

Calms, Belt of. A zone on either side of the Trade Winds where calms of long duration prevail.

Canal. An artificial watercourse.

Canyon. A deep gorge or ravine through which a river flows.

Cape. A point of land projecting into a body of water.

Cartography. The art or science of making maps.

Central Meridian. The vertical meridian of a map projection around which the map is centered.

Climate. The aggregate weather conditions of a given region over a long period of time.

Co-Latitude. The difference between the latitude of a place and 90°, or its distance in degrees from one of the poles of the earth.

Conformal Projection. A map projection on which all small or elementary figures upon the surface of the earth retain true shape, the meridians and parallels being at right angles to one another.

Conic Projection. A map projection which can be imagined as drawn on the surface of a cone. The meridians appear as straight lines along which the parallels, as concentric circles, may be spaced in such a way as to give some desired quality, such as conformality or equal area.

Continent. One of the main continuous bodies of land on the earth's surface. The number of continents considered to exist varies with usage from five to seven, i.e., America (North and South); Eurasia (Europe and Asia); Africa; Antarctica; and Australia.

Continental Divide. The height of land which separates the streams flowing into one ocean from those flowing into another.

Continental Shelf. The zone of the continental margin extending from the shore line to the depth, usually about 100 fathoms or 200 meters, where there is a marked or rather steep descent toward the ocean depth.

Contour Line. A line drawn on a map to indicate points of the same height or depth.

Coordinates, Geographical. The intersecting lines of latitude and longitude which determine the geographical position of any given place.

Cultural Feature. Any man-made feature of the earth's surface shown on a map.

Cylindrical Projection. A map projection produced by projecting the geographic meridians and parallels onto a cylinder which is tangent to the surface of a sphere, and then developing the cylinder into a plane.

D

Degree. A unit of measurement equal to 1/360 of a circle. A degree of latitude on the earth's surface is roughly equivalent to 69 statute miles. A degree of longitude varies in length but is always equivalent to about 4 minutes of time.

Delta. The tract of land formed by the deposit of silt at the mouth of a river.

Doldrums. The equatorial belt of calms and variable winds.

Downs. Certain hilly districts in southern England underlain by chalk and hence unforested.

E

Eastern Hemisphere. Usually considered in cartography to be half of the earth extending from pole to pole between 20° W. and 160° E., including continents of Eurasia, Africa, and Australia.

Elevation. The vertical distance of a point above or below a reference surface, usually mean sea level.

Equal Area Projection. A map projection on which a constant ratio of areas is preserved; that is, any given part of the map bears the same relation to the area on the sphere which it represents, as the whole map bears to the entire area represented.

Equator. The great circle around the earth equidistant from the poles.

Equatorial Current. Westward drift of surface water on either side of Equator in Trade Wind belts.

Estuary. The coastal section of a river which is to a greater or lesser extent invaded by the sea and subject to tidal influence.

F

Fathom. A unit of measurement used for soundings, equal to 1.83 meters or 6 feet.

Firth. A long arm of the sea, partially landlocked.

Fjord. A narrow arm of the sea between high lands.

G

Geodesy. Investigation of scientific questions connected with the shape and dimensions of the earth.

Geographic Center. That point on which any area would balance if it were a plate of uniform thickness. The geographic center of the conterminous United States is at latitude 39° 50′ longitude 98°35′, in the eastern part of Smith County, Kansas.

Geography. The scientific description and explanation of the earth's regions.

Glacier. A field or body of land-formed ice moving slowly down a mountainside or valley.

Globe. A spherical map of the earth or heavens.

Gnomonic Projection. A perspective map projection on a plane tangent to the surface of a sphere, having the point of projection at the center of the sphere. It is the only map projection on which all great circles represented are straight lines.

Great Circle. The line of intersection of the surface of a sphere and any plane which passes through the center of the sphere.

Great Circle Direction. The great circle direction of point A from point B is the angle, measured clockwise from true North, formed by the meridian of point B and the great circle passing through points A and B. See Azimuth.

Great Circle Distance. The distance between any two points, measured either in degrees or miles, along the great circle connecting them.

Greenwich Civil Time. Mean solar time for the Greenwich Meridian, counted from midnight.

Gulf Stream. The warm current which flows out of the Gulf of Mexico through the Straits of Florida and northward through the Atlantic Ocean until it merges with the West Wind Drift.

H

Hachures. Lines used in shading elevations on a map to outline them and to indicate slope.

Hemisphere. Any half of the earth's surface. See Northern, Southern, Eastern, Western, Land, and Water Hemisphere.

Horizon. The line at which the earth and sky appear to meet.

Horse Latitudes. Zones of high atmospheric pressure with calms and variable breezes, which border the polar edges of the Trade Wind areas.

Hydrography. The science of measuring and studying oceans, seas, rivers, and other waters, with their marginal land areas, especially for the purpose of aiding navigation. As a map feature, the pattern of rivers, oceans, etc. shown on a map.

I

Ice Cap. An ice sheet of vast extent covering the topographic features of a continental land mass.

Inclination of the Earth. The tilt of the earth's axis in relation to the plane of the earth's orbit. The angle of inclination is 23½° from vertical.

International Date Line. The line extending from pole to pole along the 180th meridian, with local variations, where each new calendar day begins with the passing of the midnight hour. Travelers crossing the line going west must advance their calendar one day, while those going east must retard the calendar one day.

Interrupted Map Projection. A projection in which the pattern of meridians and parallels is interrupted or broken so that certain areas may be centered upon different central meridians.

Isthmus. A narrow strip of land with water on both sides connecting two larger bodies of land.

K

Kilometer. A unit of length; 1,000 meters; 3,280.84 feet; approximately ⅝ of a mile.

L

Land Hemisphere. That half of the earth, centered near Nantes, France, which includes the greatest possible land area.

Latitude. The angular distance in degrees of a point on the earth north or south of the Equator.

Longitude. The angular distance (degrees) of a place east or west of the Prime Meridian.

M

Magnetic Declination. From any given place, the angle of magnetic North from true North.

Magnetic Poles. The two locations representing the poles of unlike magnetism belonging to the earth as a magnetized body. The **North Magnetic Pole** is currently located at approximately 73°N. Lat. and 100°W. Long. on Prince of Wales Island. The **South Magnetic Pole** is currently located at approximately 71°S. Lat. and 149°E. Long. in Antarctica.

Map. A graphic representation, on a plane, of certain selected features of a part or the whole of the earth's surface.

Map Grid. The framework of parallels and meridians by means of which map features are located.

Map Projection. A network of lines representing parallels of latitude and meridians of longitude, derived by geometrical construction or mathematical analysis.

Map Scale. The relationship which exists between a distance on a map and the corresponding distance on the earth. It may be expressed as an equivalence, one inch equals 16 statute miles; as a fraction or ratio, 1:1,000,000; or as a bar graph subdivided to show the distance which each of its parts represents on the earth.

Mean Solar Time. Also called Mean Time. Time measured by the daily motion of a fictitious body called the "mean sun." Since the apparent sun travels in the ecliptic with a variable motion, it cannot be used to measure time, and the "mean sun," supposedly moving uniformly in the Celestial Equator, is used.

Mercator Projection. A conformal projection on which the meridians and parallels are shown as parallel straight lines at right angles to one another, the divisions of latitude being expanded north and south of the Equator in the same proportion as the divisions of longitude have been lengthened by projection. On this projection a line of constant bearing, or rhumb line, is represented by a straight line.

Meridian. A great circle on the earth's surface which passes through the terrestrial poles.

Mesa. A flat-topped mountain or hill, usually bounded on at least one side by a steep cliff.

Meter. A unit of length equivalent in the United States to exactly 39.37 inches.

Monsoon. A periodic, seasonal movement of air from land to water and vice versa.

Moraine. A mound or ridge of unstratified rock material deposited by a glacier.

N

Nadir. Point in the heavens diametrically opposite to the Zenith, or point directly under observer.

Nautical Mile. A unit commonly used for measuring distances at sea; the length of a minute of latitude; 1,853 meters or 6,080 feet.

Northern Hemisphere. That half of the earth north of the Equator.

North Pole. The end or pole of the earth's axis pointing toward the star Polaris.

O

Ocean. A vast expanse of salt water bordered by the continents. The oceans are usually considered to be four in number: Pacific, Atlantic, Indian, and Arctic.

Ocean Current. A specific portion of any ocean moving in a definite direction. It may also be called a stream or drift.

Oceanography. The science of the oceans, their forms, physical features, and phenomena.

Orbit of the Earth. Curve which earth describes in the heavens as it revolves around the sun.

P

Parallels. Small circles on earth's surface, or lines on a map, perpendicular to axis of the earth, marking latitude north or south of Equator.

Physical Map. A map in which natural regions and physical features are emphasized by the use of different colors.

Planet. A celestial body revolving around the sun in a nearly circular orbit, such as the earth.

Plateau. Elevated area of relatively level land.

Polar Ice Pack. The entire area of thick and closely packed polar ice, more than one year old.

Polar Projection. One in which the meridians appear as straight lines radiating from the pole and the parallels of latitude as concentric circles with the pole as center.

Political Map. A map in which political divisions and boundaries are emphasized through use of color.

Prime Meridian. The meridian on the earth's surface from which longitude is measured, generally the meridian of Greenwich, England.

Projection. Any method of delineating on a plane surface the whole or a part of the surface of the earth, including parallels of latitude and meridians of longitude. See Azimuthal, Conformal, Conic, Cylindrical, Equal Area, Gnomonic, Mercator, and Polar Projections.

R

Reef. A rocky or coral elevation in the ocean bottom, which may show above water at times.

Revolution. The movement of the earth around the sun. One complete revolution of the earth requires 365 days, 5 hours, 48 minutes, 46 seconds.

Rhumb Line. A line which makes equal angles with all the meridians it crosses.

Roaring Forties. A term used by sailors to describe the stormy regions between 40° and 50° from Equator in northern and southern oceans.

Rotation. Movement of the earth around its axis. One complete rotation determines length of one day.

S

Savanna. Originally, an extensive treeless plain, but now more frequently used to mean a tropical landscape of scattered trees and extensive grasslands.

Sea. A mass of salt water more or less confined by portions of the continent or by chains of islands, and forming a basin distinct from the oceans.

Sea Level. The level of the surface of the sea considered at any moment at a given place.

Small Circle. Any circle on a sphere smaller than a great circle. Thus, all parallels on a globe or map except the Equator.

Solar System. The sun and all celestial bodies revolving around it, together with their satellites.

Solar Time. Also called true solar time. Time measured by the apparent daily motion of the sun.

Solstice. The time at which the overhead sun is at its greatest distance from the Equator. In the Northern Hemisphere the summer solstice occurs about June 21, and the winter solstice about December 22.

Southern Hemisphere. That half of the earth south of the Equator.

South Pole. The opposite end of the earth's axis from the North Pole.

Standard Parallel. A parallel of latitude which is used as a control line in the computation of a map projection, and is, therefore, true to scale.

Statute Mile. A unit of distance generally used in measurements on land, and equal to 5,280 feet.

Steppe. The grassy plains of Russia.

Strait. A relatively narrow waterway between two larger bodies of water.

T

Temperate Zones. The two belts or zones of the earth lying between Tropics and Polar Circles.

Time. The measurable aspect of duration based upon the happening of periodic events, such as: the rotation of the earth (day), the revolution of the moon around the earth (month), and the revolution of the earth around the sun (year). See Greenwich Civil Time, Mean Solar Time, Solar Time.

Time Zone. A belt or zone, extending from north to south across a country, which is given a designated time by law. The United States has four standard time zones, namely: Eastern, Central, Mountain, and Pacific.

Topography. The features of the actual surface of the earth, considered collectively as to form. A single feature, such as a mountain or valley, is called a topographic feature.

Torrid Zone. A term formerly used to describe the belt or zone of the earth's surface bounded by Tropic of Cancer and Tropic of Capricorn. Better geographical form today is "Tropical Zone."

Trade Winds. The regular easterly winds which prevail over the oceans on either side of the Equator to about 30° north and south latitudes.

Transverse Projection. A map projection which is turned 90° from its usual orientation, and consequently is centered upon some great circle other than a meridian.

Tropic. A line on a map or globe, usually broken or dotted, marking the limit reached by the overhead or vertical sun in its apparent annual migration. The northern line is called the **Tropic of Cancer,** and the southern line the **Tropic of Capricorn.** Both are about 23½° from the Equator.

Tundra. The marshy, treeless plains of northern Asia and northern North America.

Twilight. The periods of partial daylight after sunset and before sunrise, when light from the sun is reflected from the atmosphere overhead.

Typhoon. A violent, destructive storm similar to a hurricane, that occurs in the western Pacific Ocean.

V

Vernal Equinox. The date when the overhead sun crosses the Equator on its apparent migration from south to north, or about March 21, and the length of day and night is approximately the same in all latitudes.

Volcano. A more or less conical hill or mountain from which, when active, steam, gases, ashes, or molten rocks are ejected.

W

Water Hemisphere. That half of the earth centered near New Zealand which includes the greatest possible water area.

Westerlies. The prevailing winds of the middle latitudes, that is, between 30° and 60° in north and south latitudes.

Western Hemisphere. Usually considered in cartography to be that half of the earth extending from pole to pole between 160° E. and 20° W., thus including the Americas and Greenland.

West Wind Drift. A general term applied to the eastward movement of oceanic water under the influence of the westerly winds.

Z

Zenith. The point in the celestial sphere directly over a given point on the earth.

Metric Conversion Chart

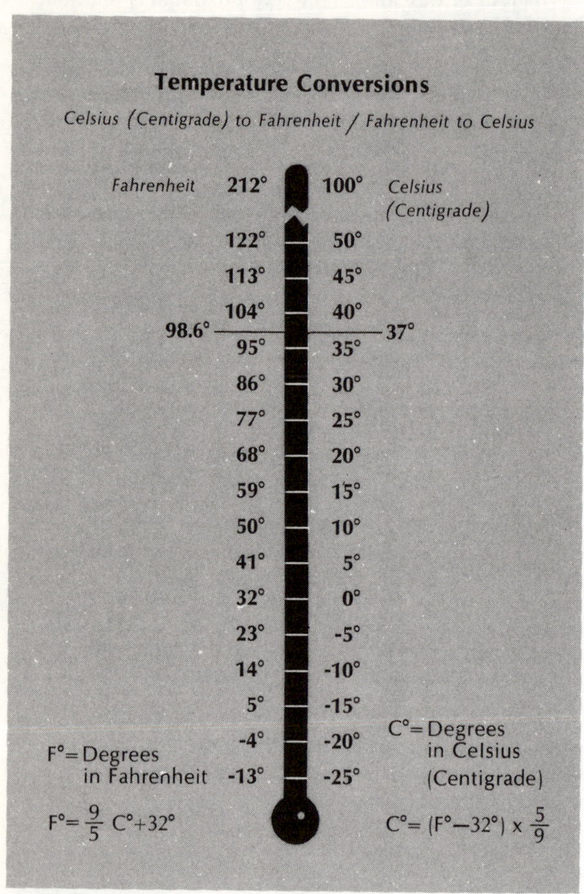

Length

1 inch	=	2.54 centimeters
1 foot	=	.305 meter
1 yard	=	.914 meter
1 mile	=	1.609 kilometers
1 nautical mile	=	1.151 statute miles
1 nautical mile	=	1.852 kilometers
1 meter	=	1.094 yards
1 kilometer	=	.621 mile

Volume

1 cubic inch	=	16.387 cubic centime[ters]
1 cubic foot	=	.028 cubic meter
1 cubic yard	=	.765 cubic meter
1 cubic meter	=	1.308 cubic yards

Weight

1 ounce	=	28.35 grams
1 pound	=	.454 kilogram
1 long ton	=	1.016 metric tons
1 gram	=	.035 ounce
1 kilogram	=	2.2 pounds

Area

1 square inch	=	6.452 square centimeters
1 square foot	=	.093 square meter
1 square yard	=	.836 square meter
1 acre	=	.405 hectare
1 square mile	=	2.59 square kilometers
1 square kilometer	=	.386 square mile
1 hectare	=	2.471 acres
1 square meter	=	1.196 square yards

Capacity

1 U.S. fluid ounce	=	2.957 centiliters
1 U.S. liquid pint	=	.473 liter
1 U.S. liquid quart	=	.946 liter
1 U.S. gallon	=	3.785 liters
1 U.S. gallon	=	.833 British gallon
1 liter	=	1.057 U.S. liquid quarts

Mathematical Formulae

Diameter of Circle: Circumference divided by 3.1416

Circumference of Circle: Diameter multiplied by 3.14

Area of Circle: Square of the radius multiplied by 3.1 or square of the diameter multiplied by .7854

Area of Triangle: Multiply base by .5 altitude

Area of Parallelogram: (including rectangle) Base multiplied by altitude

Surface Area of Sphere: Square of the diameter multiplied by 3.1416

Volume of Sphere: Cube of the diameter multiplied by .5236

Volume of Prism or Cylinder: Area of base multiplied by altitude

Volume of Pyramid or Cone: Area of base multiplied by ⅓ of the altitude

Amount of Simple Interest

Principal multiplied by rate (of interest) multiplied by time (in terms of years or fractions thereof)

Abbreviations

admin.	administered
Afg.	Afghanistan
Afr.	Africa
AK	Alaska
AL	Alabama
Alb.	Albania
Alg.	Algeria
Alta.	Alberta
Am.	American
Am. Sam.	American Samoa
And.	Andorra
Ang.	Angola
Ant.	Antarctica
AR	Arkansas
Arc.	Arctic
arch.	archipelago
Arg.	Argentina
Atl. O.	Atlantic Ocean
Aus.	Austria
Austl.	Australia, Australian
auton.	autonomous
AZ	Arizona
Az. Is.	Azores Islands
Ba.	Bahamas
Barb.	Barbados
B. C.	British Columbia
Bel.	Belgium, Belgian
Bhu.	Bhutan
Bis. Arch.	Bismarck Archipelago
Bngl.	Bangladesh
Bol.	Bolivia
Bots.	Botswana
Br.	British
Braz.	Brazil
Bru.	Brunei
Bul.	Bulgaria
Bur.	Burma
CA	California
Cam.	Cameroon
Can.	Canada
Can. Is.	Canary Islands
Cen. Afr. Rep.	Central African Republic
Cen. Am.	Central America
CO	Colorado
co.	county
Col.	Colombia
Con.	Congo
cont.	continent
C. R.	Costa Rica
CT	Connecticut
C. V.	Cape Verde
Cyp.	Cyprus
Czech.	Czechoslovakia
DC	District of Columbia
DE	Delaware
Den.	Denmark
dep.	dependency, dependencies
dept.	department
dist.	district
div.	division
Dji.	Djibouti
Dom. Rep.	Dominican Republic
Ec.	Ecuador
Eg.	Egypt
Eng.	England
Equat. Gui.	Equatorial Guinea
Eth.	Ethiopia
Eur.	Europe
Falk. Is.	Falkland Islands
Fed.	Federation
Fin.	Finland
FL	Florida
Fr.	France, French
Fr. Gu.	French Guiana
GA	Georgia
Gam.	Gambia
Ger., Fed. Rep. of	Federal Republic of Germany
Ger. Dem. Rep.	German Democratic Republic
Gib.	Gibraltar
Grc.	Greece
Grnld.	Greenland
Guad.	Guadeloupe
Gaut.	Guatemala
Guy.	Guyana
Hai.	Haiti
HI	Hawaii
Hond.	Honduras
Hung.	Hungary
i.	Island
IA	Iowa
I.C.	Ivory Coast
Ice.	Iceland
ID	Idaho
IL	Illinois
IN	Indiana
incl.	includes, including
Indian res.	Indian reservation
Indon.	Indonesia
I. of Man.	Isle of Man
Ire.	Ireland
is.	islands
isl.	island
Isr.	Israel
It.	Italy
Jam.	Jamaica
Jpn.	Japan
Kam.	Kampuchea
Ken.	Kenya
Kor.	Korea
KS	Kansas
Kuw.	Kuwait
KY	Kentucky
LA	Louisiana
Leb.	Lebanon
Le. Is.	Leeward Islands
Leso.	Lesotho
Lib.	Liberia
Liech.	Liechtenstein
Lux.	Luxembourg
MA	Massachusetts
Mad.	Madagascar
Mad. Is.	Madeira Islands
Mala.	Malaysia
Man.	Manitoba
Mart.	Martinique
Maur.	Mauritania
MD	Maryland
ME	Maine
Medit.	Mediterranean
Mex.	Mexico
MI	Michigan
MN	Minnesota
MO	Missouri
Mong.	Mongolia
Mor.	Morocco
Moz.	Mozambique
MS	Mississippi
MT	Montana
mt.	mount
mtn.	mountain
mts.	mountains
mun.	municipality
N.A.	North America
nat. mon.	national monument
nat. park	national park
N.B.	New Brunswick
NC	North Carolina
N. Cal.	New Caledonia
ND	North Dakota
NE	Nebraska
Nep.	Nepal
Neth.	Netherlands
Newf.	Newfoundland
NH	New Hampshire
Nic.	Nicaragua
Nig.	Nigeria
N. Ire.	Northern Ireland

NJ . . . . New Jersey
NM . . . . New Mexico
Nor. . . . . Norway, Norwegian
N.S. . . . . Nova Scotia
NV . . . . Nevada
N.W. Ter. . . . . Northwest Territories
NY . . . . New York
N.Z. . . . . New Zealand
occ.. . . . . occupied area
OH . . . . Ohio
OK . . . . Oklahoma
Om. . . . . Oman
Ont. . . . . Ontario
OR . . . . Oregon
PA . . . . Pennsylvania
Pac. O. . . . . Pacific Ocean
Pak. . . . . Pakistan
Pan. . . . . Panama
Pap. N. Gui. . . . . Papua New Guinea
Par.. . . . . Paraguay
par.. . . . . parish
P.D.R. of Yem.. . . Yemen, People's Democratic Republic of
P.E.I.. . . . . Prince Edward Island
pen. . . . . peninsula
Phil. . . . . Philippines
Pol.. . . . . Poland
pol. dist. . . . . political district
pop. . . . . population
Port.. . . . . Portugal, Portuguese
poss.. . . . . possession
P.R. . . . . Puerto Rico
pref. . . . . prefecture
prot. . . . . protectorate
prov.. . . . . province, provincial
pt.. . . . . point
Que. . . . . Quebec
reg.. . . . . region
rep.. . . . . republic
res.. . . . . reservation, reservoir
RI . . . . Rhode Island
riv. . . . . river
Rom.. . . . . Romania
S. A.. . . . . South America
S. Afr.. . . . . South Africa
Sal.. . . . . El Salvador
Sask. . . . . Saskatchewan
Sau. Ar.. . . . . Saudi Arabia
SC . . . . South Carolina
Scot.. . . . . Scotland
SD . . . . South Dakota
Sen. . . . . Senegal
S.L.. . . . . Sierra Leone
Sol. Is. . . . . Solomon Islands
Som.. . . . . Somalia
Sov. Un. . . . . Soviet Union
Sp. . . . . Spain, Spanish
St., Ste.. . . . . Saint, Sainte
Sud. . . . . Sudan
Sur.. . . . . Suriname
Swaz. . . . . Swaziland
Swe.. . . . . Sweden
Switz. . . . . Switzerland
Syr.. . . . . Syria
Tan. . . . . Tanzania
ter. . . . . territories, territory
Thai.. . . . . Thailand
TN . . . . Tennessee
Trin. . . . . Trinidad & Tobago
trust.. . . . . trusteeship
Tun. . . . . Tunisia
Tur.. . . . . Turkey
TX . . . . Texas
U.A.E.. . . . . United Arab Emirates
Ug.. . . . . Uganda
U.K. . . . . United Kingdom
Ur. . . . . Uruguay
U.S. . . . . United States
UT . . . . Utah
VA . . . . Virginia
Ven. . . . . Venezuela
Viet. . . . . Vietnam
Vir. Is.. . . . . Virgin Islands
vol.. . . . . volcano
VT . . . . Vermont
WA . . . . Washington
WI . . . . Wisconsin
W.I. . . . . West Indies
Win. Is.. . . . . Windward Islands
W. Sah.. . . . . Western Sahara
W. Sam. . . . . Western Samoa
WV . . . . West Virginia
WY . . . . Wyoming
Yugo. . . . . Yugoslavia
Zimb. . . . . Zimbabwe

Reference Map Index

This universal index includes in a single alphabetical list all important names that appear on the reference maps. Each place name is followed by its location; the map index key; and the page number of the map.

State locations are given for all places in the United States. Province and country locations are given for all places in Canada. All other place name entries show only country locations.

The index reference key, always a letter and figure combination, and the map page number are the last items in each entry. Because some places are shown on both a main map and an inset map, more than one index key may be given for a single map page number. Reference also may be made to more than a single map. In each case, however, the index key *letter and figure* precede the map page number to which reference is made. A lower case key letter indicates reference to an inset map which has been keyed separately.

All major and minor political divisions are followed by both a descriptive term (co., dist., region, prov., dept., state, etc), indicating political status, and by the country in which they are located. U.S. counties are listed with state locations; all others are given with country references.

The more important physical names that are shown on the maps are listed in the index. Each entry is followed by a descriptive term (bay, hill, range, riv., mtn.,isl., etc), to indicate its nature.

Country locations are given for all names, except for features entirely within States of the United States or provinces of Canada, in which case these divisions are also given.

Some names are included in the index that were omitted from the maps because of scale size or lack of space. These entries are identified by an asterisk (*) and reference is given to the approximate location on the map.

A long name may appear on the map in a shortened form, with the full name given in the index. The part of the name not on the map then appears in italics, thus: St. Gabriel *-de-Brandon.*

The system of alphabetizing used in the index is standard. When more than one name with the same spelling is shown, place names are listed *first* and political divisions *second.*

A

B

C

D

E

F

G

H

I

J

K

L

M

N

O

P

Q

R

S

T

U

V

W

X

Y

Z

Photo Credits: p.7,Dr. Georg Gerster/John Hillelson; p. 20, United States Geological Survey; p. 38, National Aeronautics and Space Administration; p.58, Colour Library International; p. 92, Tony Duffy/All Sport; p. 98, Ray Atkeson; p. 204, Robert Frerck/Odyssey.

Acknowledgment: "Gazetteer of the World" reprinted, with permission from The Webster's Desk Encyclopedia, published by Outlet Book Co., Inc., New York.